PRESENTED WITH

THE COMPLIMENTS OF

ROCHE LABORATORIES

DIVISION OF

HOFFMANN - LA ROCHE INC.

NUTLEY, N. J.

The Schizophrenic Syndrome

"The use of the term 'schizophrenia' has helped to perpetuate a tendency to think of this syndrome as a discrete, single, unitary disease. In research, it has led to looking for *one* etiologic or pathogenic factor even by investigators who themselves believe in a multiple factor nature of the disorder. In clinical practice, the pseudo-unity has helped obscure differential diagnosis, prognosis, and treatment; it also confounds and often sadly misleads the general public.

For all these reasons, a change to the term 'Schizophrenic Syndrome' is suggested, and its adoption in the Official Nomenclature and the Diagnostic Manual urged. It is hoped that such official designation will help clarify the multiple aspects of the disorder even though for the sake of brevity the term 'schizophrenia' will probably often continue to be used in general parlance as well as in this volume."

L. B.

The Schizophrenic Syndrome

LEOPOLD BELLAK, M.D. and LAURENCE LOEB, M.D.

Editors

GRUNE & STRATTON • NEW YORK • LONDON

First printing March 1969

Second printing January 1971

© 1969 by Grune & Stratton, Inc. All rights reserved. No part of this publication may be reproduced or transmitted in any form or by any means, electronic or mechanical, including photocopy, recording, or any information storage and retrieval system, without permission in writing from the publisher. Grune & Stratton, Inc., 757 Third Avenue, New York, New York 10017.

Library of Congress Catalog Card Number 68-21504
International Standard Book Number 0-8089-0048-X

Printed in the United States of America (K-A)

Contents

Acknowledgment

We are greatly indebted to Mrs. Ann Noll and Mrs. Eleanore Haas who have assisted in the preparation of the various phases of this volume.

We are also very grateful to the A. A. Brill Library of the New York Psychoanalytic Institute and its Librarian, Miss Liselotte Bendix, who has unfailingly supplied (LB) references to schizophrenia over many years, and the New York Hospital-Cornell Medical Center, Westchester Division, and its Librarian, Miss Lillian Wahrow, who has been equally helpful (to LL).

All the contributors were most cooperative with our editorial attempts to produce a well organized, high level volume on time. We are very grateful to them for the considerable forebearance involved in such an endeavor.

November 15, 1968   L. B.
                                                                 L. L.

1

Introduction, Personal Reflections and a Brief Review

LEOPOLD BELLAK, M.D.

Doctor Bellak studied medicine and psychoanalysis first in Vienna and then in New York, engaged in the graduate study of psychology at Boston University and Harvard University, and acquired his psychiatric training at Saint Elizabeth's Hospital in Washington, D.C. He graduated from New York Psychoanalytic Institute.

He has held a variety of teaching appointments, both in psychiatry and psychology, at New York University, New York Medical College, The New School for Social Research, City University of New York, and others. Chief Consulting Psychiatrist to Altro Health and Rehabilitation Services from 1947 to 1957, he concerned himself with the rehabilitation of tuberculous, cardiac, and psychiatric patients.

Doctor Bellak was Director of Psychiatry at City Hospital at Elmhurst, New York City (1958-64) and there he developed the (24-hour) Trouble Shooting Clinic and other community mental health services.

He has divided his interests among projective techniques, rehabilitation, research in psychoanalysis and in drug therapy, community psychiatry, and above all, schizophrenia.

Aside from being a Fellow and member of numerous professional organizations, he is a past president of the Westchester Psychoanalytic Society and a past president of the Society for Projective Techniques and Rorschach Institute, and a recipient of the Annual Merit Award of the New York Society of Clinical Psychologists in 1964. He has also served as Special Consultant to the National Institute of Mental Health.

Doctor Bellak has written and/or edited over a dozen books, is the originator of The Children's Apperception Test, and has written about 100 papers.

Currently, Doctor Bellak is Visiting Clinical Professor of Psychiatry at New York University, Visiting Professor of Education and Psychology at Columbia University, Consultant to the Westchester Mental Health Association and Psychiatric Consultant to the United States Military Academy at West Point, and principal investigator of a research project in schizophrenia supported by a NIMH grant.

In 1948 I published my first review of the field of schizophrenia, covering the decade 1936-1946.[3] Roughly ten years later, I edited and contributed to the next volume, covering the intervening period; and now the third volume, covering a third decade. An overview of thirty years almost inevitably generates some perspective and reflections.

The first volume, still called *Dementia Praecox,* was written when I was a

1

resident at St. Elizabeths' Hospital in Washington, D.C. It grew out of notes and abstracts I had made while on night duty, with the hospital library as headquarters.

Though then only a resident, I had been in almost continuous contact with psychiatry during the preceding decade. Instead of attending some other lectures, I spent time at the Wagner-Jauregg-Pötzl Psychiatric Clinic as a first-year medical student in Vienna from 1935 on. Later, in the United States, I learned considerably more about psychiatric patients, especially schizophrenics, as a male psychiatric nurse, psychologist, and laboratory technician in various institutions. I would not be surprised if I had learned most, clinically, about schizophrenics in the almost two years I spent as a male psychiatric nurse. Feeding catatonic schizophrenics, attending to all their other bodily needs, as well as in one institution, living in the same small cottage with them was most instructive. Some were recently admitted and acutely ill, and some had been there for many years. The foibles, symptoms, and details of their everyday lives could fill a volume and added much to my curiosity about the disorder. For instance, there were catatonics who were afraid to walk through any door and would cling to the door frame with desperation. There was a chronic schizophrenic who had refused for years to eat unless he was fed but automatically opened his mouth as a fork or spoon approached it; such automatism was also shown by a young schizophrenic who would continue to play pingpong as long as the ball kept coming to him but would freeze into a catatonic stance as soon as the ball was out of reach. There were also incredible rituals involved in eating and elimination for many schizophrenics. One hebephrenic woman had continued for many years to make boxlike objects into which she put smaller boxes, like a Chinese puzzle, within which she would then place a tiny dolllike figure. She repeated the same with pocketbook within pocketbook and a variety of other ways and sometimes verbally expressed bizarre notions about being pregnant, at times saying she was carrying Jesus.

It happens then that I can look back on camisoles and wet sheet restraints, physiotherapy, insulin and metrazol treatment, ECT, and assisting at a few lobotomies. I have seen the acute illnesses of wartime, as well as chronic patients with thirty years in hospitals. I had a chance to be engaged in the rehabilitation of state hospital-discharged chronic patients. I had the opportunity as well of treating ambulatory schizophrenics psychoanalytically in clinics and in private practice; and while in charge of a large psychiatry department in a general hospital, I learned something about schizophrenics in that setting.

I should like to ask the reader's indulgence for this personal account. Appropriately or not, I should like to "lay the foundation," as lawyers are wont to say, for some of my subsequent statements. It will become quite clear that I am somewhat impatient with the state of knowledge concerning schizophrenia and with much of the work reported widely as research in or treatment of schizophrenia.

The problem is indeed a serious one: Psychiatric patients still fill half of all hospital beds in the nation at any given time, and schizophrenics, one half of those again, or *one quarter of all beds.** Schizophrenia strikes early in life and can have a crippling effect. Estimates vary as to whether two, or five, or ten times as many schizophrenics as are in hospitals live in the community, presenting severe problems for themselves and often for society, ranging from inadequate functioning to endangering the community in the form of political lunacy or individual transgressions. From the standpoint of the number of hospital beds as well as cost to the economy (direct and indirect), and last but not least, personal suffering, schizophrenia can well be considered the number one public health problem of this country and, by all accounts therefore, most likely of any other country. As it strikes mostly in the second and third decade of life, it could be said to have a greater crippling effect than do heart disease or malignancies: the median age of all first admissions for schizophrenia is 33 years, as compared to 51 years for all other psychiatric admissions, and the older age group affected by circulatory disease and malignancies.

Nevertheless, there has been progress, but there has also been much "running just to stand still." Psychoanalysis applied to schizophrenics, by different schools of thought, was one ingredient of change: classical psychoanalysts such as Federn, Bychowski, Eissler on the one hand, and John Rosen's direct psychoanalysis on the other hand, caused much encouragement and progress. Sullivan and his school, especially Frieda Fromm-Reichman, filled the postwar years with students of psychotherapeutic enthusiasm. The British school of psychoanalysis—(Melanie Klein's) especially Rosenfeld, and others—added their enlightenments.

Chlorpromazine, reserpine, and, later, the other psychotropic drugs were the next major development, starting in the middle fifties. Almost simultaneously, new concepts of community psychiatry, closely intertwined with the developments in psychodynamics and psychopharmacological therapy, rounded out the development of today's picture: open wards, patient government, therapeutic milieu, and psychiatry in small units of general hospitals. Similarly, modern psychiatric rehabilitation is possible only with the help of the drugs and dynamic understanding of patients.

These changes reflect themselves in daily clinical life as well as in statistical data on lengths of hospitalization, discharge rates within the first year of hospitalization, and other figures. (See Chapter 3)

Yet, nobody claims that psychotropic drugs effect cures, or that community psychiatry measures are a definitive answer. Ideas on etiology have at best at-

---

*See also Epilogue.

tained some refinement, rather than offering some basic change or positive corroboration.

Fundamentally, the number of etiological or pathogenic factors which I listed in 1948 (then uncorroborated) are still being claimed by various investigators with almost as much certainty and no more confirmation. Hardly a month goes by without the daily press carrying stories of newly found biochemical claims for the cause of schizophrenia, or of some pathophysiological, psychological, sociological, or genogenic pathogeneses.

Much indeed remains to be desired in the field of schizophrenia research. This is due to the fact that many workers in the field have often had rather one-sided experience with schizophrenics—if any worth mentioning at all.

As a matter of fact, in reading the literature on pathogenesis and etiology of schizophrenia, one could obtain the definite impression that the farther away some investigators are from clinical contact with schizophrenia, the more certain they are of its basic nature. The number of distinguished scientists with perforce minimal, if any, actual clinical experience with schizophrenia includes Aldous Huxley,[44] Linus Pauling,[61a,61c] and many others. Internists often innocently jump into the fray and account for some of the spurious factors reported, being frequently unaware of the need for controls for the complexities of the schizophrenic way of life. No less a publication than the Journal of the American Medical Association happily hailed in an editorial some poorly controlled study suggestive of unique physiological factors operant in schizophrenia[46] and editorially pruned my critical reply.[13] In fact, psychiatrists themselves seem to feel at times that nonpsychiatrists might be the best ones to supply the answer to schizophrenia. Becoming aware of some aspect of schizophrenia, be it a sociological one, or a biochemical, or psychological one, often leads to an overgeneralization of the importance of that feature, especially if the investigator is not acquainted with the full clinical picture. In our culture of "instant expertise" authorities are quickly created.

This particular aspect of the problem of research into schizophrenia is one which is not unique for the field of schizophrenia. It is a battle for the sole possession of the truth, in this case between the clinicians (or applied scientists) and the "pure" scientists (or basic scientists). Rather than a scientific problem, it is a problem of personality and character not far removed from Spengler's somewhat murky Apollonian and Dionysian types, or even the psychoanalytic obsessive and hysterical types, or orthodoxy and serendipity.

In past decades such research as existed was usually totally uncontrolled, statistically unsophisticated. While it may be unfair to single out one example from many, let me point out that in 1946 the American Journal of Psychiatry found it possible to publish an article which without much ado proclaimed that schizophrenia could be diagnosed by the quality of the radial pulse.[55]

The swing to the extreme opposite side of the pendulum was probably attained in the decade from 1950 to 1960 when the main impetus for research in schizophrenia came from grants administered by the Research Branch of the National Institute of Mental Health. Administration and review committees were then under the heavy influence of nonclinicians, and one had the impression that relevance of a project was virtually unimportant in comparison to its statistical niceties. Luckily, the situation has changed there much to the better within the last few years.

Periodically, the pendulum swings from pure science or basic science, to clinical science, and back. Unless I am greatly mistaken, the pure and basic scientists are more beset with the feeling of being the true apostles: the concept of purity in "pure" and basic science lends itself more to the proposition of being anointed.

The fact is, of course, that it takes both clinical knowledge and scientific design, deductive and inductive reasoning, hunches and rigor, successively and simultaneously, to attain progress. Reasonable eclecticism is hard to maintain and the price for not aligning oneself with one group or another a heavy one. However, we seem on the way to more felicitous combinations of clinical and methodological competence. NIMH Careerfellowships and a change in NIMH organization (1966) has lately produced many changes to the better.

A balanced review of the foibles and follies in the psychodynamic as well as the toxicological and genetic search for etiology on the international scene is offered by Graham. An Australian, he has the long-range view from "Down Under" to see the various European, American, and Asian propositions in terms of their cultural setting.[33]

"It has been a truism for at least fifty years that strong, clear-cut views on the aetiology of schizophrenia reveal more about authors than about schizophrenia. To some extent, doubtless, convictions about schizophrenia reflect their country of origin—its values, medical orientations, and national characteristics."

Another generally excellent review of the field of research in schizophrenia was offered in a Mental Health Monograph of the National Institute of Mental Health,[61] giving a broad balanced view of the biological, psychological, social, and other factors. Editorial bias such as the following, however, slipped in: "It cannot be too often emphasized that significant contributions to an understanding of a clinical disorder such as schizophrenia will in the last analysis depend upon a vast armamentarium of basic information about the workings of the nervous system and of behavior." Maybe so, but I know of no evidence that this statement would hold more true for schizophrenia than it would for the learning of a foreign language, or obesity, and it is therefore much too broad a statement to be useful. If it is meant in a narrower sense, one would have to say that there is no evidence, so far, that the understanding of the nervous system has contributed anything to the understanding of schizophrenia today. The same can be said about another statement in the Monograph (p. 4): "Among the more cogent reasons for expanded interest in the biological factors in schizophrenia is the evidence for a familial or genetic tendency in the disorder and data suggesting a relationship between endocrine disorder and psychopathology.". . . Relationships such as stated in the latter part of this paragraph do indeed exist, e.g., for pituitary disorders, thyroid dysfunction, and the like. Such a statement, however, cannot be supported by any specific evidence of any relationship between endocrine disorder and schizophrenia to date. There is a tremendous amount of literature illustrating failures to demonstrate such a relationship, including work by M. Bleuler,[19] who has evidenced a great deal of interest in this area. (See also below)

Familial or genetic tendencies for schizophrenia on the other hand, have been claimed for well over fifty years, and all data suggesting this evidence have so far been followed by work discrediting it. Tienari's[80] work convincingly criticized the defective methodology of many of the classical studies in the field and failed to find evidence for specific inheritance of schizophrenia. If anything, his findings in the more easily studied Finnish environment suggest some nonspecific familial trends toward some kind of psychopathology.

At the present moment, work by Rosenthal[70] is the most suggestive of *some* role of genetic factors in *some* schizophrenics. This investigator's cautious and qualified claims may well be substantiated in the future, but, unless they are, they can only be considered another in the long series of attempts to comprehend schizophrenia.

Rosenthal's earlier intensive study of the interaction of environment and heredity in the Genain Quadruplets[71] was followed by a study by Rosenthal, Kety, and Wender.[72] They searched the records of 5,500 children in Denmark whose parents had been schizophrenic, and who had been adopted within the first year of life. Of 39 children found, one-third turned out to suffer from schizophrenia or a disorder closely related to it, or resembling it. Comparing these children with the adopted offspring of normal parents, the investigators found that the incidence of schizophrenia was three times as high in the first group as in the second. They concluded that heredity must be involved to account for these findings. A thorough study, surely, yet it must nevertheless be remembered that Spitz' work on infants' severe psychiatric disorders[78] gave pictorial evidence of depression, hospitalism, marasmus, and suggestion of other severe emotional disturbance in infants in relation to lack of appropriate maternal attention *within the first year of life.*

To be sure, a second phase of Rosenthal's study showed that the incidence of mental disturbance in real and adoptive families of schizophrenic and nonschizophrenic children was higher in the biological families of the children. A third phase showed that if the parents of schizophrenic children, the adoptive parents of schizophrenic children, and the adoptive parents of normal children were compared, the incidence of mental disturbance was greatest in the first group, less in the second, and least in the third. Details of the selection of children by parents were not as yet made available: if the children were freely chosen by parents it might be possible that disturbed adoptive parents recognize and choose disturbed infants. Otherwise, these data suggest that either the influence of adoptive parents produces schizophrenic children or that we deal with some statistical artifact. The claims of the investigators were moderate, saying that although their data prove that heredity plays a role in schizophrenia, "it is not schizophrenia as such that is inherited but rather the genes involved may lead to a variety of abnormalities." Many years ago I suggested a familial ego weakness as a common denominator for the greater incidence of schizophrenia as well as other disorders in some families (1958).

A Norwegian twin study by Kringlen, involving 50,000 twins in Norway was reported:[56] "The broad range of pathology which we have encountered in human beings with the same genotype shows the significance of environmental factors in the etiology of mental illness." The author also felt that a solution to schizophrenia is not likely to come from a biochemical breakthrough, not only because of the apparently primary importance of relevant environmental factors in his extensive study, but also because of the apparently polygenic nature of the hereditary predisposition to the disorder. A polygenic inheritance, he felt, could best explain the gliding transition from normalcy to severe mental illness found in twin partners (including monozygotic ones), siblings, and parents. (See my Diagnostic Continuum, p. 56, in the previous Schizophrenia volume.[7] See also Origin of Schizophrenia edited by John Romano.[68a])

Congenital and intrauterine differences were considered etiologic for the onset of schizophrenia in one of a pair of identical twins by Pollin and Stabenau.[62,62a] They report that in twelve pair of twins, the twin who in later life became schizophrenic had weighed up to a pound less than his mate at birth. In the first several weeks following birth, the later schizophrenic twin had greater difficulties in breathing, sleeping, and adjusting to feeding patterns.

Family attitudes toward the weaker twin tend to lead to psychological maladjustment. The authors are quoted as saying that the twin study data "suggest possible mechanisms where, in the absence of a genetic variable, we can understand the presence of schizophrenia in one twin and not in the other. We have noted nongenetic biological factors from the child's prenatal life that play a part in initiating a whole sequence of events related to the presence or the absence of the disease."

It appears from these latest extensive and methodologically most careful genetic investigations that a primary role of specific genetic transmission of schizophrenia for more than a fraction of patients is most unlikely.

It is difficult to avoid "unitary cause" thinking and to keep wishful thinking from superseding the facts. Endocrine or genetic or other factors may well play a role in *some* schizophrenics, but there is no evidence that they do in "schizophrenia" nor, as we shall attempt to illustrate further on, is it likely or logically plausible.

A review of the concept of schizophrenia within the last fifty years by Manfred Bleuler concludes:[19]

"For half a century, the principal aim of students of schizophrenia was assured: they sought to discover the single cause of a disease whose symptomatology and course seemed to suggest one single entity. These studies, however, were not successful. They did not lead one step nearer to the discovery of a specific cause of the hypothetical disease entity, schizophrenia. Today we have to ask ourselves why a specific cause of schizophrenia has not been found. The reason may be simple: perhaps none exists! There may be many different pathogenic factors responsible for the outbreak of the disease."

This, of course, has been the position of the present author since 1949.

In 1965, in testimony before a subcommittee of the Committee on Appropriations, House of Representatives, eighty-ninth Congress of the United States,[14] I again suggested the need for a centralized search for the multiple factors likely to be implicated in the schizophrenic syndrome. I strongly urged the establishment of a Schizophrenia Research Center at the National Institute of Mental Health because it seemed that enough money was being spent on research on schizophrenia ($54,000,000 by NIMH alone between 1948 and 1963), but the research was not well enough integrated to take advantage of all we already know:

Among other things I suggested that:

"1. I would say there are two basic misconceptions which confound the majority of all work on schizophrenia: one is that schizophrenia is investigated as if it were one single disease rather than a shared common path of a variety of etiological factors. Therefore, research is being done on "schizophrenics," hoping to find a common denominator for all of them, when there is reason to look for specific different causative factors in different groups.

"2. The second misconception most generally involved is related to the first one: namely, that often some physiological factor is isolated, which is claimed to be etiologic, but indeed, on controlled study, turns out to be secondary to the schizophrenic way of life: emotional stress, hospitalization, and others.

"3. Furthermore, there is a great lack of integration of studies. Many investigators do not seem to take into account the work of others. There is great fragmentation and no centrally directed attack on the problem."

I went on to say:

"I, therefore, feel that there might be a great advantage to a Schizophrenia Research Institute, maybe like one of the independent units of the Department of Health, for which Representative Fogarty has recently proposed legislation. I see such an Institute as having a multiple role: 1) a clearinghouse for information; 2) an advisory body, which would be able to bring significant areas in need of investigation to the attention of the psychiatric community, perhaps with financial support emanating from it, especially for projects deemed necessary to round out the picture, or to permit the simultaneous investigation of different facets. With the help of such an institute, difficult, controlled, long-range studies could be performed, which so far have been impossible and therefore have permitted a large variety of artifacts to be reported; 3) as a research institute, it would perform some basic work itself and serve as a control on significant work reported elsewhere. Just to be sure, I do not see such an institute as a source of dictated or overly controlled research which could stifle the necessary individual creativity.

"I firmly believe that we do already have the hypotheses, empirically speaking; even the knowledge to answer most of the questions concerning the etiology, and, to a certain extent, the prevention and treatment of schizophrenia. The current lack of integration simply stands in the way of solid demonstration of these facts experimentally. It seems, therefore, especially regrettable that such a serious and widespread disorder should not be successfully attacked, simply for the lack of appropriate organization and integration of research efforts."

Happily, new administrative enlightenment at NIMH actually led to the establishment of a Center for the Study of Schizophrenia as part of the Clinical Research Branch of NIMH in 1966.

At a conference of an Ad Hoc Advisory Committee to this new Center, in October, 1966, I submitted the following memorandum:

"1) The main defect of all etiological or pathogenic studies of schizophrenia is still that one factor is being looked for in *all* of the patients: be it serum factors, cognitive defects, or family interaction types.

Yet, most reviews of schizophrenia end with the statement that it most likely is not a disease of unitary etiology.

In this basic aspect current studies are not more sophisticated than the ones I have been reviewing from 1936 on.

"2) The cause of the above is fairly clear: no one group of investigators can very well study a large enough sample for a variety of possible operant factors simultaneously.

We need the type of research that would permit the search for several factors in a large sample simultaneously: serum factors, the contribution of "minimal brain disorder" in childhood towards perception and individuation, family constellation, etc.

The method of *repetitive sifting* of one large sample is called for, by several teams of investigators working on them simultaneously, and/or successively. Factor analysis will eventually be advisable.

"3) Any of the findings above will probably need *predictive studies* to establish not only which are the *necessary* but also which are *sufficient* factors for the development of schizophrenia: a study beginning in childhood, which at the same time could be a study of the effectiveness of therapeutic intervention, in part of the sample. It might well turn out that the interaction of several factors is necessary to produce schizophrenia, and that none alone virtually ever is significant, though different clusters might combine into the necessary condition.

"4) It appears mandatory that the Center formulate hunches concerning the currently thought-to-be most likely contributory factors and help initiate such studies.

"5) These studies should regularly, say, every half year, be reviewed and discussed by the Center and a regularly meeting advisory group.

"6) Therefore, fostering of *teams* of specifically trained schizophrenia researchers as well as the formation of an *advisory group* seems essential.

"7) Different problems will have to be studied in various "contract institutions," much as the Psychopharmacology Branch of NIMH arranged to have different drugs (and sometimes the same, for control purposes) studied in different hospitals. Synchronized, interlocking research and methodologically, centrally supervised, is essential at this stage of our knowledge of schizophrenia.

"8) A publication, similar to Psychopharmacology News, is advisable, to decrease the *publication lag.*"

The social importance of schizophrenia alone makes such a Center a very important institution and demands that it be enabled to play a major role in the primary, secondary, and tertiary prevention of schizophrenia.

These suggestions are of course entirely consistent with my previously stated *multiple-factor psychosomatic theory* of schizophrenia and its later elaborations in terms of a unified egopsychological theory of the schizophrenic syndrome.*

Black and white thinking is the easiest to sustain in any area. Among other things, black and white thinking—and its semantic expression—enjoys an economy, albeit spuriously, which more complex conceptions do not enjoy.

In accordance with that statement, I therefore believe we should stop using the term "schizophrenia" altogether and make the official term, for the official nomenclature, *"The Schizophrenic Syndrome."* Nevertheless, for (false) economy's sake, I myself will undoubtedly often continue to refer to "schizophrenia" as if there were such a unitary phenomenon.

I urge the American Psychiatric Association to revise its official nomenclature to speak of the "schizophrenic syndrome." I hope that this change will more often remind investigators of the complex nature of the disorder and possibly facilitate a more sophisticated approach.

I have given only the briefest overview of research in schizophrenia (and some of my thoughts about it) because etiological and pathogenic theories and studies will be more suitable reviewed in great detail in subsequent chapters on general, biological, biochemical, neurophysiological, psychological, and sociocultural aspects of schizophrenia. This seemed a better solution than having one chapter devoted exclusively to diverse studies of such possible causative variables.

This makes it also possible for me now to turn to my own attempts to study the schizophrenic syndrome and give a report on progress in this work since the last volume.

---

*For some reason—possibly because I insist that *all* factors must be taken into consideration, and am frequently critical of the particularly bald claims for various biological factors (to which the public press takes with special alacrity), I am often wrongly considered—or assumed to be—a champion of a purely psychological conception of the schizophrenic syndrome.

2

Research on Ego Function Patterns: A Progress Report

LEOPOLD BELLAK, M.D.

In my chapter on the schizophrenic syndrome in the 1958 volume, I outlined in some more detail than in previous writings an egopsychological view of the schizophrenic syndrome. The kernel of the multiple-factor psychosomatic theory of schizophrenia[3,4,6,7,10,12] had been the proposition that schizophrenia is not a circumscribed disease entity but rather a syndrome constituting the final common path of many different etiologies (singly, or, more often, in combination) manifested in severe disturbances of various ego functions.

I am quite well aware of the fact that I was far from the first one to suggest that schizophrenia was not a disease entity. Most outstandingly, of course, Eugen Bleuler had said so. Adolph Meyer had spoken of schizophrenic reaction patterns. I am also aware that other psychoanalysts have spoken of the affliction of the ego in schizophrenia, from Freud and Federn on to some formulations of Hartmann's and Beres' on which I elaborated in the 1958 volume. *However, the specific formulation of schizophrenia as the final common path of ego defects due to various etiologies and pathogenic factors, from sociopsychological to biological ones, stated in an experimentally verifiable form, I consider my own.*

In the 1958 volume, as well as in the volume on Manic Depressive Psychosis, and some papers,[14] I have stated what research needs to be done to investigate, confirm, modify, or reject my hypothesis. A grant by NIMH,* herewith gratefully acknowledged, finally enabled me, with the help of my associates† to put some of these hypotheses to the test.

---

*This account is part of a study "Ego Function Patterns in Schizophrenia" supported by NIMH Grant 5ROI-MH11662 and 14260, Leopold Bellak, M.D., Principal Investigator, carried out at first under the auspices of the Department of Psychology, Teachers College, Columbia University, and later under the sponsorship of the Postdoctoral Program, Department of Psychology, New York University. I wish to acknowledge with appreciation the cooperation of the Psychiatry Department, The Roosevelt Hospital, New York City; Gracie Square Hospital, New York City, in making their clinical facilities available for this subject.

†Especially Marvin Hurvich, Ph.D., and also Robert Beck, Ph.D., Jacob Cohen, Ph.D., Patricia Crawford, B.A., Helen Gediman, Ph.D., Stanley Grand, Ph.D., Nancy

11

In previous publications[9,10,12,43a] I have already discussed different pathological pictures involving different involvement of various ego functions and stated some hypotheses concerning possible etiological factors on the one hand and differential treatment on the other. There seem to be schizophrenics in whom object relations seem relatively good, but their thought processes very poor, and vice versa. There are those in whom virtually all ego functions are poorly established, and others who seem quite well off except for a relatively isolated disturbance, say, of the thought processes. Psychoanalysts have noted this fact in regard to treatment, as for instance Katan,[50] who spoke of a (different) intact residue in (different) schizophrenics which must be utilized in treatment.

The current project is specifically dedicated to the attempt to see if different ego function patterns can be established among schizophrenics. If fairly clear-cut patterns can be demonstrated, it is hoped that they will lend themselves to heuristic hunches about differential pathogenesis and etiology. If, for example, the object relations are primarily affected, it seems more likely that this particular person is primarily affected by experiential (sociopsychological) disturbances than one in whom the synthetic function and the autonomous functions are particularly poor. A genetic proposition may be more reasonable to investigate in such a patient, though severe early experiences could also possibly account for severe disturbances of the synthetic and autonomous function: it is merely *probable* that in such a group the hereditary factors will play a larger role than in those where object relations are primarily affected. A low stimulus barrier as the outstanding feature of the schizophrenic psychogram may be suggestive of neurophysiological factors especially, and a search for such in this particular group might be more rewarding than such a search in nonselected schizophrenics has been to date.

In other words, the study of ego function patterns in this project serves the purpose primarily of differentiating the large group of those afflicted with the

Israel, Ph.D., David Jacobs, Ph.D., Milton Kapit, Ph.D., Rose Kent, Ph.D., Frances Lippman, Ph.D., Milton Malev, M.D., Joan Nissenberg, M.A., Jean Schimek, Ph.D., Howard Schlossman, M.D., Mark Silvan, Ph.D., Steve Silverman, M.A., Leonard Small, Ph.D., Donald Spence, Ph.D., and Paul Wachtel, Ph.D.

Material in this chapter relies heavily on material from previous presentations: "A Systematic Study of Ego Functions" by L. Bellak, M.D. and Marvin Hurvich, Ph.D., presented at the Annual Meeting of the American Psychoanalytic Association in Detroit, May, 1967, (J. Nerv. Ment. Dis., in press) "Toward an Ego Psychological Appraisal of Drug Effects" by L. Bellak, M.D., Marvin Hurvich, Ph.D., Mark Silvan, Ph.D., Dave Jacobs, Ph.D., presented at the June, 1967 Meeting of the Early Clinical Drug Evaluation Unit in Montreal, upon invitation of the Psychopharmacology Research Branch, NIMH, (Am. J. Psychiatry, Vol. 125, No. 5, Nov., 1968), and a paper prepared by Mark Silvan, Ph.D., Dave Jacobs, Ph.D., Patricia Crawford, B.S., and L. Bellak, M.D.: "An Experimental Study of Ego Functions" (American Psychoanalytic Association, December, 1967).

schizophrenic syndrome and provides some rational basis for more intensive investigation of some etiologic or pathogenic propositions. The claim is not, therefore, that the schizophrenic syndrome is entirely a psychological one, due to ego function disturbances, but rather that it is due to a large variety of factors, often in interaction; that these factors manifest themselves in affecting the ego generally, but in some specific ego functions especially (and different ones in different patients), and that the study of these ego function patterns may lead back to causative factors.

Beyond the etiologic, the patterns of ego functions will, of course, be helpful in formulating therapy, of whatever kind it may be, and eventually prevention.

To attain this goal, we devised the following study: a group of schizophrenics, neurotics, and normals are studied by clinical interview, by standard psychological tests, and by a series of laboratory experiments with regard to their ego functions. Independent groups of raters evaluate the material from each source, and we attempt to see if there is statistical agreement within each group of raters on the status of twelve ego functions, rated on a thirteen-point scale, and then whether there is agreement among the results of the three approaches; whether clear-cut patterns emerged within the schizophrenic group, and whether the schizophrenic group is significantly delimited from the neurotic and the normal groups, and finally, whether clear-cut patterns emerge within the schizophrenic group.

All this was, of course, much easier said than done, as we needed, among other things, operational definitions of ego functions, statements in scale form for the different modalities, and raters appropriately trained in the clinical as well as the experimental field.

In a previous study[15] concerned with the appraisal of antidepressant drug effects, the *Global Ego Strength Scale* had been evolved.

Subsequent research concerned with ego function patterns in schizophrenia, permitted us the opportunity to revise, expand, and refine the scale. On the basis of an extensive literature review and a number of tryouts and revisions, we defined twelve ego functions and constructed rating scales for assessing these functions from clinical interviews, clinical psychological tests, and experimental procedures from the psychological laboratory. Examples from the three sources will be given to provide a picture of the techniques.*

In approaching the research, the following questions were raised:

1. Which ego functions merit inclusion?

---

*A future monograph "Ego function patterns in schizophrenics, neurotics and normals" will give a more detailed account of the procedural and conceptual aspects of of this study.

2. What are the characteristics of these ego functions, and how can they be measured?

3. In what ways are the various ego functions interrelated, i.e., to what extent do they overlap or correlate with each other? And, in what ways do various ego functions interfere with each other in the process of adaptation?

In formulating these questions, as well as a number of others, it was realized that the present state of knowledge about the ego and its relationships with the environment would allow only partial, tentative answers. Nevertheless, it was felt that the very attempt to examine these questions now would tend to clarify the issues and provide the basis for further amplifications, refinements, and the testing of their limits.

As to the question of which ego functions to include: in 1950 Hartmann[38] wrote that no complete list of ego functions had ever been attempted. Rapaport[67] in his historical survey commented that the history of ego psychology would be relatively simple to outline if a precise definition of the ego and a full listing of its functions were available.

Lists of ego functions have been provided (chronologically) by Hartmann[36,38] Bellak[4,5,6,7] Rapaport,[66] Beres,[17] Arlow and Brenner,[2] Rangell,[64] by Kanzer[48] as mentioned above, and by other authors. The ego functions enumerated by these analysts are similar in many of the items listed, and in turn, follow Freud's description of the characteristics of the ego in the *Outline of Psychoanalysis.*[27]

Reports of other attempts to rate or measure ego functions have been published by Bibring et al.,[18] Karush et al.,[49] Prelinger and Zimet,[63] Bolland and Sandler,[20] and others.

Recognizing that a degree of choice is always exercised when categories or functions are delineated for the purpose of ordering observable phenomena, we included as many separate psychoanalytic constructs as we believed to be *necessary* and *sufficient* to encompass the major currently recognized manifestations of ego functioning.

Starting with a list of seven ego functions enumerated by Beres[17] and elaborated by Bellak,[7] and based on further literature search, discussion, and the rating of clinical material, we revised and expanded the number to twelve. These are as follows: (See Appendix)

1) Reality Testing
2) Judgment
3) Sense of Reality
4) Regulation and Control of Drives
5) Object Relations
6) Thought Processes
7) Adaptive Regression in the Service of the Ego
8) Defensive Functions

9) Stimulus Barrier
10) Autonomous Functioning
11) Synthetic Functions
12) Mastery-Competence

CHARACTERISTICS OF THE EGO FUNCTIONS

Instead of offering detailed verbal definitions at this point of each ego function, we found it pragmatically more useful to state the *components* of each ego function and to utilize these as a basis for constructing operational definitions for a seven-point rating scale for each of the ego functions.

A review of the literature revealed that each of the ego functions we chose for study includes several subfunctions or component factors.* Our formulation of these component factors for each of the ten ego functions is as follows:

1) For *Reality Testing*, the major factors are:
   A:
   a) the distinction between inner and outer stimuli
   b) accuracy of perception (includes orientation to time and place, and interpretation of external events)
   c) accuracy of "inner reality testing" (psychologic mindedness and awareness of inner states).

2) Judgment†
   a) awareness of likely consequences of intended behavior (anticipating probable dangers, legal culpabilities and social censure, disapproval or inappropriateness)
   b) extent to which manifest behavior reflects the awareness of these likely consequences

3) For *Sense of Reality of the World and of the Self*, the component factors are:
   a) the extent to which external events are experienced as real and as being embedded in a familiar context
   b) the extent to which the body (or parts of it) and its functioning, and one's behavior are experienced as familiar and unobtrusive and as belonging to (or emanating from) the individual
   c) the degree to which the person has developed individuality, uniqueness, and a sense of self and self esteem

---

*I am grateful to Leonard Small, Ph.D. for pointing out this fact to me and contributing some of the essential ideas.

†Although we consider Judgment to be an aspect of Reality Testing, Judgment has been further extrapolated for the purposes of these ratings.

    d) the degree to which the person's self representations are separated from his object representations

4) Under *Regulation and Control of Drives, Affects and Impulses:*

    a) the directness of impulse expression (ranging from primitive acting out through neurotic acting out to relatively indirect forms of behavioral expression)

    b) the effectiveness of delay and control, the degree of frustration tolerance, and the extent to which drive derivatives are channeled through ideation, affective expression and manifest behavior.

5) For *Object (or Interpersonal) Relations,* the components are:

    a) the degree and kind of relatedness to others (taking account of withdrawal trends, narcissistic self concern, narcissistic object choice or mutuality)

    b) the extent to which present relationships are adaptively or maladaptively influenced by or patterned upon older ones and serve present, mature aims rather than past immature ones

    c) the degree to which he perceives others as separate entities rather than extensions of himself

    d) the extent to which he can maintain "object constancy"

6) For *Thought Processes,* the components are:

    a) the adequacy of processes which adaptively guide and sustain thought (e.g., attention, concentration, anticipation, concept formation, memory, language)

    b) the degree to which thinking is organized and oriented in accordance with reality consideration, as reflected in the relative primary-secondary process influences on thought (e.g., extent to which thinking is delusional, or autistic; degree of looseness of or intrusions upon associational processes)

7) For *Adaptive Regression in the Service of the Ego* (ARISE):

    a) first phase of the oscillating process; relaxation of perceptual and conceptual acuity (and other ego controls) with a concomitant increase in awareness of previously preconscious and unconscious contents

    b) second phase of the oscillating process; the induction of new configurations which increase adaptive potentials as a result of creative integrations.

8) For *Defensive Functioning:*

    a) degree to which defensive components adaptively or maladaptively affect ideation and behavior.

    b) extent to which these defenses have succeeded or failed (e.g., degree of emergence of anxiety, depression and/or other dysphoric affects, indicating inefficiency of defensive operations.

9) The component factors for *Stimulus Barrier* are:
   a) threshold for, sensitivity to, or awareness of stimuli impinging upon various sensory modalities (externally, primarily, but including pain)
   b) nature of response to various levels of sensory stimulation in terms of the extent of disorganization, avoidance, withdrawal or active coping mechanisms employed to deal with them.

10) For *Autonomous Functioning,* the components are:
   a) degree of freedom from or lack of freedom from impairment of apparatuses of primary autonomy (functional disturbances of sight, hearing, intention, language, memory, learning or motor function.
   b) degree of, or freedom from impairment of secondary autonomy (e.g., disturbances in habit patterns, learned complex skills, work routines, hobbies and interests)

11) For *Synthetic-Integrative Functioning,* we have included:
   a) degree of reconciliation or integration of *discrepant* or potentially incongruent (contradictory) attitudes, values, affects, behavior, and self representations (e.g., role conflicts)
   b) degree of *active* relating together (i.e., integrating) of psychic and behavioral events, whether contradictory or not

12) Finally, under *Mastery-Competence* the components are:
   a) competence: the person's performance in relation to his existing capacity to interact with and master his environment
   b) sense of competence: the person's expectation of success, or the subjective side of performance

As was true for the selection of the ego functions to be included, some choice was exercised in the formulation and grouping of the various component factors. One consideration which affected these formulations was the degree of overlap among the ego functions.

With regard to the component factors, we avoided the inclusion of any particular component factor under more than one ego function heading, although we assumed that the ego functions are interrelated and to some extent overlapping. It was recognized that a behavioral manifestation such as auditory hallucinations would merit a low (i.e., pathological) score on *Reality Testing, Thought Processes, Defensive, Autonomous and Synthetic Functioning.* But that for this particular manifestation, the above-mentioned ego functions would not all be affected to the same extent. Additional consideration will be given to the issue of overlap in a later section.

GUIDE FOR RATING EGO FUNCTIONS FROM CLINICAL INTERVIEWS

Definitions and component factors were worked out in detail for all twelve ego functions as just illustrated. On the basis of this material, we then developed a guide for Rating Ego Functions from Clinical Interviews. In constructing the Guide, which provides definitions and a thirteen-point rating scale for each ego function, the degree of adaptiveness of various forms of behavior reflecting the particular ego function provided the basis for the patients' score.

For example, in assessing *Reality Testing,* the presence of hallucinations and delusions (indicating an inability to differentiate images or ideations from perceptions) resulted in a low score for the patient, while the presence of periodic, fleeting illusions or excessive déjà vu or déjà reconnu experiences (in the absence of hallucinations and delusions) would define a somewhat more adaptive reality testing function of the ego and thus would merit a higher rating. Indications of accurate perception, even under difficult circumstances, result in a still higher score.

We encountered some problems in attempting to provide examples for each of the ego functions at progressive levels of adaptive success and failure: while the presence of hallucinations indicates a serious disturbance in *Reality Testing,* the strength of the *Reality Testing* function can only be assessed accurately if we know how much environmental pressure was present at the original onset and subsequently. If the hallucinations occur following catastrophic life conditions, (loss of a love object, severe financial reverses, armed combat, social isolation, an approaching surgical procedure, etc.) then the scales should somehow differentiate such a state of affairs from instances where hallucinations occur in the absence of objectively stressful circumstances.

Hartmann approached this difficulty through his conception of the "average expectable environment." He asked: "What makes a person succeed or fail in a given situation? The degree of adaptiveness can only be determined with reference to environmental situations (average expectable—i.e., typical situations, or on the average not expectable—i.e., atypical situations)."[36] Hartmann was well aware of the complexity of the adaptation concept. Also in the 1939 monograph, we find the following: "In judging the degree of a person's adaptation—which is the implied basis of our concept of health—many factors must be taken into account, the concrete forms of which we are in many cases not yet familiar with." (p. 32).

A related concept is psychological stress.* We are in agreement here with

---

*Levin[59] specified loss, attack, restraint, and threats of these as exernal factors which can induce psychological stress.

the formulation of Janis:[47] ". . . changes in the environment which in the average person induces a high degree of emotional tension and interferes with normal patterns of response." (p. 13)*

The ways in which various ego functions hold up differentially under environmental change have been elucidated in studies on sensory deprivation[77] and others, such as those of I. Kohler on visual distortion of the perceptual field[54] and G. Klein on the effects of reduced auditory feedback on behavior.[51] Much remains to be done in detailing the dimensions of various "average expectable environments."† Recent publications which include aspects of the problem are those of Heider,[42] Cumming and Cumming,[22] G. Klein,[51] and H. Weiner.[81]

We dealt with the problem of average expectable environment and deviations therefrom (and psychological stress) by instructing raters to score one scale point up when the given ego function deficit was found in the context of relatively difficult and stressful external circumstances, and to score one point down when the manifestation was found without evidence for stressful external conditions. We consider this problem, viz., how to evaluate adaptive functioning of the ego in conjunction with different environmental demands and requirements to be a major source of difficulty for ego psychology.[45] An ego function rating scale for clinical interview material was developed in the following way: after a preliminary manual was constructed, a group of psychoanalytic psychologists and psychiatrists independently rated the same clinical interview material on the ten ego functions, and then discussed their disagreements in a group setting. The manual was revised and refined, after which each participant was given new clinical interview material to rate, and another discussion conference was held. This process was repeated many times.

The point scale for the ego function *Thought Processes* will provide an illustration of what the full guide is like. The Guide descriptions for scores 1, 5, 9 and 13 will be presented. Instructions to the raters for this ego function are as follows:

Thought Processes, as considered in this scale, refer to: 1) structuralized constraints upon thinking, i.e., processes which adaptively guide and sustain thought by selectively making available traces of past experience (e.g., attention, concentration, memory and language), and 2) the degree to which thinking is organized and oriented in accordance with reality considerations as reflected in the characteristic primary-secondary process balances. Thus, thought is viewed formally in terms of orientation to reality. Both dimensions of thought are scaled from (1) extreme disruption, through (7) optimal func-

---

*The difficulties in scaling the degree of threat from the environment have recently been discussed by Lazarus.[58]

†Many studies from the anthropological and sociological literature are relevant here.

tioning, and raters should consider both aspects in making their judgments. Most likely, when one is rating pathology at the extremes of this scale both of these dimensions will be frequently observed together: i.e., extreme disruption of control processes will be accompanied by extreme disruption of reality orientation, while optimal functioning of control processes will be accompanied by optimal reality orientation. However, when rating pathology at the middle stops of this scale raters may find that only one of the dimensions will be represented in the interview material. In such a case ratings should be based upon the dimension represented.

Ratings will be based to a great extent on formal questioning, but the subject's overall style of response and communication in the interview in general will also be determining factors in evaluating this function.

Samples from the Seven-Point Scale for Thought Processes

1. A. *Extreme Disruption of Control Processes:* Attention severely distracted by irrelevancies. Minimal capacity to respond to questions due to complete loss of sustained concentration. Severe impairment of both recent and remote memory. Extreme loss of abstracting ability—can think only in most concrete or absurdly syncretistic (over-inclusive) modes. Minimal ability to communicate verbally due to either mutism, word salad productions, flood of barely related sounds, words, and phrases, word play including neologisms and clang associations.

B. *Extreme Breakdown of Reality Orientation and Organization:* Thought predominantly bizarre and delusional with loose and fluid associations, autistic logic, fragmentation, symbolization, condensation, and contradictions.

3. A. *Episodic Failures of Control Processes:* Frequent but circumscribed disruption in communication because of diverted attention and difficulty in sustaining trend of thought. Considerable impairment in remote memory seen either in inability to supply information on such events as job history and schooling, or in gross inaccuracies and inconsistancies. Relies heavily on concrete mode, but some ability to see relationships between events. Categorization is over-inclusive, hence crucial differences between events are missed. Thus, difficulty in discriminating between degrees leads to "all-or-none" type thinking. Unable to entertain more than one possibility. Rigidity of thought.

B. *Limited Failure of Reality Orientation and Organization:* Some doubt expressed about very circumscribed delusions indicating rudimentary forms of an adaptive, self-critical function in thinking. Other areas of functioning are free of distortion. At times thoughts are disorganized and difficult to follow. Questionable logic. Some peculiar or queer ideas. Intolerance for ambiguity.

5. A. *Minor Failures of Control Processes under Stress:* Some distractibility under stress but is able to recover and respond appropriately. Occasional inability to stick to trend of thought because of pressure from intruding associations (i.e., tangentially related by irrelevant thoughts or events). Some evidence of vagueness in remote memory or occasional and minor inconsistencies which are then corrected. Tendency toward concreteness or over-generality, but can correct when asked to expand or delimit concepts. Occasional vagueness or unclarity under stress and overly precise forms of expression (obsessional forms under stress).

B. *Minor Failures of Reality Orientation and Organization under Stress:* Possible reality distortion recognized and either questioned or corrected. Occasional peculiar thought or expression. Occasional vagueness or unclarity in some areas under stress. Rigidity, or inability to go beyond the objective facts.

7. A. *Optimal Functioning of Control Process:* Acute attention and unimpaired ability to concentrate (should be differentiated from paranoid and obsessional acuity to detail and error). No disruption from pressure of internal associations. Associations meaningfully integrated into communication. Memory acute and accurate. Flexible and appropriate use of functional, abstract, concrete, or symbolic frames of reference. Unusual clarity, coherence, and flexibility of expression, with no signs of disruption in the verbal flow.

B. *Optimal Reality Orientation and Organization:* Thinking is unusually well organized and logical, consistent with above average level of intellectual functioning. No peculiarities of expression. Flexibility expressed in ability to entertain contradictory thoughts and to shift levels of discourse.

In order to increase the flexibility of the procedure, the raters are asked to utilize all material relevant to the given ego function in making the rating, including the precipitating stress.

We experimented with a number of interview approaches, from a quite structured form to an entirely free one, and finally settled on a combination. There is now heavy emphasis on questions relating to ego functions, present and past, with the remainder of the two hour interview time being taken up with current complaints and life history, all embodied in an Interview Guide for the Assessment of Ego Functions.

ASSESSMENT OF EGO FUNCTIONS FROM PSYCHOLOGICAL TESTS*

The standard clinical psychologic tests (Rorschach, Bender-Gestalt, Wechsler Intelligence Scale, Figure Drawings, and Thematic Apperception Test) provide the second major basis for gauging ego functions. The value of these procedures for the assessment of ego functions was spelled out twenty years ago by Rapaport, Gill and Schafer.[65] More recently, specific scales for measuring ego functions from psychologic tests have appeared in the literature.[29,53,63] Based on this previous work, and guided by our own ego function definitions, rating scales were developed for assessing each of the ten ego functions from the clinical psychologic test findings. *Reality Testing* is evaluated from the accuracy of form perception on the Rorschach and from distortions of perceptual characteristics of the TAT cards. *Sense of Reality* is gauged from the extent of vagueness, fluidity, transparency and penetratedness characterizing Rorschach responses (this is related to ego boundaries), and responses reflecting concern with body integrity. From the TAT, we look for indicators of estrangement, flatness and a quality of unreality in the description of the story setting. In the Figure Drawings, the indicators of disturbances in the *Sense of Reality* are the presence of broken body contours, and distor-

---

*The aforementioned future monograph will reproduce details of this assessment.

tion of body parts. *Synthetic-Integrative* functioning is assessed from the overall consistency of responses to the various tests, and from the amount and kind of organizing effort reflected in the Rorschach responses, TAT stories, etc. *Object Relations* are scored on the basis of the kinds of interactions among story characters in TAT protocols, from the quality and quantity of the human responses (and especially the movement responses) on the Rorschach, and from the position, posture and various body features of the Draw a Person Figures.

ASSESSMENT OF EGO FUNCTIONS FROM PSYCHOLOGICAL LABORATORY PROCEDURES

The third basis for assessing ego functions is from experimental laboratory procedures. One purpose of employing laboratory techniques has been to evaluate ego functions under controlled conditions with the tools of general experimental psychology, and to compare these findings with results from the interviews and from the clinical psychological tests. The relevance of psychological laboratory procedures for psychoanalytic theory has been amply demonstrated in recent years by George Klein,[52] Gardner,[30] Goldberger and Holt,[32] Holzman,[43] Shevrin and Luborsky,[76] and Schlesinger[73] to mention a few and is all part of a growing trend to explore some of the traditional sub-fields of psychology—perception, memory, thinking, etc.—from the vantage of contemporary psychoanalytic ego psychology.*

Also encouraging is the recent endeavor to explore some of the conceptions and observations of ego psychology, utilizing the methodology of traditional experimental psychology. Thus, experimental psychology is both pacing and, at times, being paced by the best in psychoanalytic thinking.

> *Reality Testing*
>   1) Cattell Test of Auditory Hallucinations
> *Judgment*
>   1) Level of Aspiration
>   2) Time Estimation
> *Sense of Reality*
>   1) Finger Apposition
>   2) Draw A Frame
>   3) Rod and Frame
> *Regulation and Control of Drives*
>   1) Delayed Writing
>   2) Cognitive Inhibition
> *Object Relations*
>   1) Tomkin's Faces
>   2) Remembrance of Friends and Acquaintances

---

*See my reference to them in *Dementia Praecox*[2] p. 447, *Manic Depressive Psychoses*, etc.[5]

Thought Processes
    1) Benjamin Proverbs
    2) Pattern Perception
Adaptive Regression in the Service of the Ego
    (ARISE) Free Association
Defensive Functioning
    1) Tachistoscopic Presentation of Neutral and Drive-related Words
    2) Drive-related section of Stroop Color Word
Stimulus Barrier
    1) Reaction Time Study with Interfering Stimulus Conditions
Autonomous Functioning
    1) Hurvich Sorting
    2) Delayed Auditory Feedback
    3) Pursuit Rotor
Synthetic-Integrative Functioning
    1) Mooney Closure Figures
    2) Witkin Embedded Figures

The task at hand was to find laboratory procedures which could tap the ten ego functions without undue oversimplification or reductionism. The emphasis here has to be on "undue" since there is no doubt that in applying the experimental method to psychodynamic problems a compromise has to be struck under the very best circumstances between the highly complex clinical reality on the one hand (with its total lack of controls) and the relative artificiality of the experimental situation with its possibilities for public demonstration and repeatability as basic criteria of science on the other. We are painfully aware of the fact that a compromise was involved in every instance and tried to minimize the sacrifice of clinical validity and complexity for the sake of methodological requirements. At the least, we have attempted to construct a microcosmic reproduction of part of the vicissitudes of ego functions within the laboratory situation.

The present procedure is a time-consuming one, often cumbersome and yet to be proved valid, reliable, or optimally useful. It is hoped that further use of the method will lead not only to an improvement of its conceptual relevance, but also to an increasing degree of efficiency. In the long run one hopes that the application of an experimental ego function study may take no longer than an hour and, therefore, be available and useful for large-scale studies of subjects. Such an approach could be used for a variety of purposes, diagnostic and otherwise; in relation to schizophrenia and other chemical problems, or for studies of acting out, evaluation of psychotropic drugs,[16] evaluation of suitability for psychotherapy,[12] or generally a systematic prescription for any kind of therapy.

It is obvious that research of this type poses problems that are not capable of easy resolution. The relationship between interview and psychological tests is a relatively simple matter since they both evolve from a common set of concepts in psychoanalytic theory. The problems of developing a set of laboratory tasks for the evaluation of ego functions however, is much more difficult, and the reasons for this illuminate the nature of the problem.

The translation of psychoanalytic concepts into laboratory analogues has always been difficult and subject to criticism. Sears,[75] in his survey of experimental analysis of psychoanalytic concepts through 1940, concluded that experimental psychology had not yet made a major contribution to specific psychoanalytic hypotheses. Literally hundreds of experimental studies in this area have been carried out in the 25 subsequent years. But the question still remains whether it is presently possible to develop a set of laboratory tasks which will assess accurately concepts from psychoanalytic ego psychology.

A working approximation to the goal can be reached if two conditions are fulfilled: first and perhaps foremost, ego psychologists must make clear what they mean by their concepts in terms of behavior that is directly observable. Where that is not possible, and often it is not, it must be made clear what kinds of behavior ought to follow from their inferred processes. This will permit the experimental psychologists to get a sense of the range and kinds of behavior he will try to explore. Second, the experimental psychologists must loosen up on their definitions of behavior to include larger units. Discrete response analysis must give way to such methods as the analysis of patterns of responses over time and evaluations of the adequacy of such response in an "average expectable environment."[36] The end point of such attempts on the part of those separate groups should be the development of a common language with agreed upon definitions and criteria. Once this condition is met it is possible to begin work on the experimental evaluation of ego theory.

We believe that the major difficulty in earlier attempts at the experimental evaluation of psychoanalytic propositions was that they were too simplistic, reductionistic, and unidimensional. Most of the notions derived from psychoanalytic ego psychology have multiple aspects. Experimental procedures on the other hand, are typically concerned with single dimensions which at best can only be partially relevant to reality. In what follows we will describe a set of experimental tests selected or designed to evaluate and assess ego functions. We hold no brief that at this stage in our experimentation we have succeeded where others have failed in bridging the gap. As will become clear in subsequent remarks we have frequently been forced to compromise between the complexity of the ego function and the simplicity of the experimental task. We have no doubt that future research will reveal the inadequacies of this attempt, and look forward to more competent formulations. However, the significance of these laboratory tasks in relation to ego functioning should be understood not in terms of their separate adequacies, but rather in the light of their potentiality for revealing patterns of ego functions.

We will proceed to give a brief description of each of the ego functions, an analysis of the requirements for an adequate experimental task, a description of the tasks used and an evaluation of its adequacies. 1. *Reality Testing* is concerned with the capacity of the organism to distinguish between ideas and percepts, and to make appropriate judgments based upon the accuracy of the perception.

An experimental task which distinguishes between ideas and percepts is one which would provide stimulation where the subject can either respond accurately to external stimulation or to his own distortion of it.

a) The test we have chosen for Reality Testing is an "Auditory Hallucination" test developed by Cattell. From an audio tape the subject is presented a series of words, some actual English and some nonsense words. By using various techniques (cutting out certain frequency bands, using a different play back speed than the recording speed, etc.) the intelligibility of the words is decreased considerably. Before the subject is asked to identify these words, he is asked to read a scrap book containing aggressive headlines and pictures from a sensational newspaper. We would predict that subjects with poor reality testing will attempt to identify more of the nonsense syllables and will have more aggressive words in their misidentifications.

An evaluation of these tasks of reality testing leads to some interesting problems concerning the nature of this ego function. It was our experience that reality testing proved to be one of the most intractable ego functions with respect to experimental tests. In our initial work on this ego function, we attempted to develop procedures which would permit us to evaluate directly the quality and intensity of our subject's images. This is an essential part of an experimental evaluation of reality testing. But we have failed to develop procedures which would permit us to evaluate directly the quality and intensity of our subject's images. The work of Perky on the distinction between images and percepts is clearly relevant, but has proved to be a cumbersome and unreliable technique. In addition, no one has ever developed a test for how well subjects translate their judgments into behavior in a normal ecological environment. The best we can say is that we believe our tests to be relevant to reality testing, but incomplete.

2. a) With respect to judgment, the task requirement involves assessing the capacity of the subject to determine what kind of behavior is appropriate given an accurate perception of the situation. Two tests for this judgmental process have been selected. The first test is Cattell's "Responsiveness to Reality" test which taps the capacity of the subject to judge what he is capable of doing in a given situation. The subject performs a coding task five different times for a minute each time. After each performance, the subject is asked to estimate how many he will be able to do the next time, knowing how many he was able to accomplish previously. Inability to adjust his level of aspiration to actual performance would indicate defective judgment.

b) The second task of judgmental adequacies is a time estimation task. This is concerned with the capacity of the subject to judge duration of intervals under varying stimulus conditions.

3. A third major ego function is the *Sense of Reality,* which is briefly defined as the capacity of the organism to accurately perceive himself as a separate entity in the environment.

The requirements for tests of this ego function are that the test provides an opportunity for the subject to distinguish himself from the external environment as opposed to confusing the two and to maintain this distinction over time and stress.

Perhaps the most basic process involved in this ego function is the ability of the person to use inner cues in establishing ego boundaries. In Witkin's classical rod and frame test, the subject is seated in a darkened room, facing an illuminated rod and frame, each capable of independent movement. The subject is required to estimate deviations of the rod from the true upright under conditions of varying positions of the frame. To the extent to which the subject is capable of responding to his inner bodily cues in this situation he has a better sense of the nature of the real object. Accurate estimation of the verticality of the rod requires: a) that the subject attend selectively to bodily cues (his only source of information concerning the true vertical) and to respond to these cues effectively; and b) that he not attend to or in some way actively resist responding to the misleading frame.

a) Another technique we are using is the Draw A Frame test developed by Bernard Landis, Ph.D. The subject is asked to "draw a frame around a picture as though it were a real picture to be hung in their living room." The score obtained has been highly correlated to other body image scores (notably on the Rorschach) and indicates the presence of disturbed ego boundaries.

b) Another test of sense of reality is the Delayed Auditory Feedback. It consists of a circuit which briefly delays the sending of an auditory signal, typically the subject's own voice, into the auditory modality. This frequently produces not only a disruption of the ongoing speech pattern but such symptoms as anxiety, nausea, dizziness, etc. The effect of this stressful situation on a person's ability to maintain adequate functioning is assessed by a series of questions which elicit feelings of depersonalization and disturbances in sense of self.

c) Another approach to the study of the sense of self is one developed by Laurence Epstein and partially replicated here. Epstein employed the *Finger Apposition Test* in which the subject is shown pictures of pairs of hands in various positions with fingers touching. The subject's task is to reproduce with his own hands the finger positions shown in the pictures. Ability to maneuver the hands vicariously in order to achieve a particular relationship between them would appear to require a relatively well developed conception of his own sense of himself.

4. The third ego function is *Regulation and Control of Drives.* This is concerned with the capacity of the subject to appropriately control the expression

of drive derivatives and a measure of the degree to which aroused drives affect on-going behavior. Two tests of this ego function have been selected.

a) *The Cognitive Inhibition Task* consists of a two phase paired associate learning problem. In the first phase the subject is asked to respond with a word of his own choosing to a list of stimulus words composed of aggressive, sexual and "superego" words presented to him. In the second phase he is given the same list of stimulus words, but is asked to respond with different response words. The capacity to inhibit repetition of the first response in the second phase after it has been thoroughly learned in the first phase and the amount of time required to inhibit the learned response is an indication of drive control.

b) *The Delayed Writing Task* is one in which the subject is asked to write a neutral sentence as slowly as possible. The subject is thus required to inhibit what is normally a rapid motor response and to our surprise a number of our subjects appear unable to slow down their writing at all.

The critical problem with respect to the first of these tasks concerns the degree to which relevant drive states have in fact been aroused. The complex defense mechanisms ordinarily used to insure that such drive states remain muted undoubtedly function here as well. Present evaluation procedures simply do not permit us to measure the degree to which drive arousal has been accomplished. We have some question as to whether the simple process of presenting symbols having reference to these drive states is sufficient to achieve the desired effect.

5. The next ego function is *Object Relations*. Object Relations refers to the capacity of the organism to relate to all others, and particularly to significant others, with an accurate understanding of that person as he is today. Tests of this ego function would require the subject to evaluate stimuli representative of significant others in terms of their relations to him. Two such tests have been selected.

a) Using a variation of Sylvan Tomkins' *Recognition of Affects Test,* our subjects are asked to respond to a series of faces and to describe both the affect displayed and their own affective response to the different facial expressions. Not only will this permit a record of the accuracy of the perception of the emotions of another person, clearly a prime requisite for satisfactory object relations, but it will also give us some measure of the ways in which a person affectively responds to a human environment.

b) The second test is Cattell's *Friends and Acquaintances Test.* This task requires the subject, upon being given appropriate definitions of these terms, to list the names of his friends and his acquaintances. This provides an estimate of the extent of which the subject believes he is able to maintain some kind of a relationship with other people.

By its very nature, this ego function does not readily lend itself to laboratory tests. The processes involved in the development and maintenance of distortion-free relationships with others are long term and complex. They do not readily appear in short term, discreet laboratory tasks. We have little hope of developing really adequate tests of this ego function.

6. The sixth ego function is *Thought Processes* which is comprised of the sub-functions of memory, concept formation, attention, concentration, and anticipation.

Two tests have been chosen. a) The first is the *Test of Pattern Perception* in which the letters A and B are presented sequentially to the subjects in a consistent pattern which he must recognize. The capacity to remember previous events to concentrate on the sequence, and to maintain attention to the demands of the task provide an indication of the adequacy of these aspects of the subject's thought processes.

b) The second test is the *Benjamin Proverbs* which is a set of common sayings that the subject is required to interpret. His capacity to do this reflects the capacity to abstract in a relevant manner.

We believe that these two tests of thought processes are substantially relevant and adequate and that they tap rather directly the component factors involved in thought processes.

7. The seventh ego function is *Adaptive Regression in the Service of the Ego*. This reflects the capacity of the organism to relinquish well formed secondary processes to allow for the creative utilization of more primitive modes of thinking. Logical requirements of the test involve a task which is not capable of solution for the subject by ordinarily logical processes but which can be solved by creatively changing the mode of attack with the help of the primary process.[8]

Rather to our surprise we have found it quite difficult to find an objective procedure for this ego function: surprise, because the current literature abounds with volumes on creativity, some of them dealing with experimental studies. However, in reviewing them, we found they correlate too highly with intelligence for us to be able to make use of them. We are, nevertheless, attempting to measure flexibility vs. constriction which may be considered an important component factor of ARISE. A technique developed by Hartvig Dahl demands that the subject generate letters from the alphabet in a free associational way close to the clinical situation. Ability to do so indicates flexibility; the constricted subject will either repeat the alphabet from A-Z or will spell words. This experiment then has the advantage of resembling closely the adaptive regression necessary in the clinical process of free association.[11]

8. The next ego function is *Defensive Functioning* which is concerned with the capacity of the organism to control the emergence of anxiety or other dysphoric affect arousing content which may also conflict with superego or reality demands.

The logical requirements of the test involve the arousal of anxiety and conflicts and an evaluation of the degree to which that arousal affects ongoing behavior.

The test of defensive functioning is a threshold study of sexual, aggressive, and neutral verbal stimuli. These stimuli are presented tachistoscopically and the subject's thresholds for recognition of the verbal stimuli are recorded.

A second test which we are using is a variation of the *Stroop Color Word* test. The subject's task is to read off different colors that words are printed in, while ignoring the word itself, and he must do this for a series of neutral and drive-related words. The capacity to neutralize the meaning of the drive-related words so that they will not interfere with the demands of the task indicates the subject's ability to use defenses adaptively. At the completion of the test the subject is asked to recall as many words as possible from the list. His relative ability to do so is an indication of the degree of excessive repression.

9. The ninth ego function is *Stimulus Barrier* which is defined as the organism's capacity to integrate external sources of stimulation which are irrelevant to ongoing behavior in such a fashion that the behavior remains adaptive. The logical requirement of the task is that behavior which is substantially continuous in character be monitored under conditions of varying levels of irrelevant stimulation.

Our test for this is a disjunctive reaction time task. Our subjects are asked to perform this task under conditions of varying intensity levels of auditory stimulation. The auditory stimuli consist of a broad band of white noise delivered through the tape recorder to a set of earphones. The disjunctive time task is one which requires the subject to make rapid choices between alternatives. Increasing levels of stimulation should have differential effects on subjects depending upon their capacity to ignore or to adapt to stimulation from the environment.

We believe that this test while relevant is not totally adequate. It provides a measure of the effect of external stimulation. There is the possibility that different subjects might be more sensitive to stimulation in different modalities which our test does not tap.

10. The tenth ego function is *Autonomous Functioning*. The major focus here is on neutralization, defined by Hartmann[40] as a change of both libidinal and aggressive energy away from the instinctual and toward a noninstinctual mode. The experimental methods should be able to elicit behavior which indicates the degree of resistance of secondary autonomous structures to deneutralization. More specifically, tasks have been developed in which attempts are made to disrupt ongoing behavior with libidinal and aggressive material. Where resistance to deneutralization is high, performance will not be impeded. Where the resistance is minimal, invasions of the drive related material will become apparent.

a) Two tests have been selected for this purpose. The first is performance on a pursuit rotor under neutral and anger-provoking conditions. The pursuit rotor is a device containing a light source which travels in a continuous circular pattern. The subject's task is to maintain contact with this moving source by use of a pointer which tracks the light. Under the neutral condition our subjects are scored for performance in terms of number of errors per trial. Then the task is made extremely difficult by increasing the speed of the moving light to a point at which errors are continuous and then criticizing the subject for the poor performance. Difference in the score obtained under the neutral and drive related condition reflects the capacity of the subject to neutralize aggressive energy into autonomous functions.

b) The second test is a *Sorting Test* developed by Marvin Hurvich, Ph.D. (with the collaboration of Seymour Feshbach, Ph.D.) in which the subject is given twelve pictures, six of which are of an aggressive character, six are benign. These are cross categorized human, animal, and implement. Sorting behavior can occur on either category or any variation thereof. The degree to which the subject is capable of neutralizing the aggressive aspect is an index of this aspect of autonomous functioning.

The tests in this section are felt to be adequate as measures of one major component of autonomous functioning, i.e., the degree of resistance of both primary and secondary autonomous structures to deneutralization. They do not however, deal with the central problem of neutralization at the primary level. As we have previously indicated, processes such as these are not readily amenable to experimental tests.

11. The eleventh ego function is *The Synthetic-Integrative Functioning* which is defined as the capacity of the organism to reconcile or to integrate discrepancies in attitudes, values, affects, behavior and self representations. The requirements for testing of this ego function involve tasks in which there are disparate elements which must be combined to produce a coherent whole. Three tests for this ego function have been selected.

a) The first of them is the *Mooney-Gestalt Completion Test* which requires that the subject complete a figure when information is missing or misleading. The capacity of the subject to effectively select elements from the picture and from his own past experience provide a measure for synthetic functioning.

b) The second test is the *Witkin Embedded Figure Test* which provides an estimate of the capacity of the subject to resist distracting organizational influences in tracing a form in context. The test provides a measure of the extent to which perceptual organization is influenced by irrelevant stimulation.

c) The third test is the *Stroop Color Word Test,* a variation of which was previously described under defensive functioning. An index of synthetic functioning is derived from the capacity of the subject to analyze out the distracting attributes and to integrate the relevant attributes by correctly responding to the color name rather than to the color word.

Our tests for this ego function provide a classic example of a unidimensional testing of a multidimensional concept. Our tests deal almost exclusively with the problem of perceptual integration and fail to deal with the integration of conflict produced by discrepant attitudes, values and emotional states. This failure reflects a lack of adequate tools to provide measures in these crucial areas.*

As we have indicated, the tests often do not provide ideal measures of the complex processes involved. There are a variety of practical considerations which impose limitations on our performance. The first of these is the state of the art in experimental psychology. Until recently complex behavior was often ignored or oversimplified by laboratory workers. While this situation has changed to some extent, particularly in the area of cognitive behavior, it still remains substantially true. Without appropriate measurement instruments it is virtually impossible to make significant advances in our understanding of ego functioning via this approach. We hope that one of the by-products of this research will be to further the development of such instruments.

A second limitation is that we are frequently forced to decide against the use of certain tasks because they are too time-consuming and cumbersome, or because it is felt that our schizophrenic subject would simply not be able to perform them. As it stands now, our subjects are given a four hour battery in addition to the interview and testing procedures. These demands in terms of time and effort often seem excessive to our subjects and affect their motivation and subsequent performance.

Perhaps most important of all the difficulties is the relevance of laboratory bound experimental tasks to normal ego functioning. Ego functions as they are understood by the clinician concern processes occurring over time and in a normal ecological environment. One must continue to strive to attain batteries which adequately parallel real life situations.

Until our final data can be reported, we can only state that our current work seems to offer supportive evidence for our hypotheses in spite of all the limitations mentioned.

SOME FURTHER ASPECTS OF EGO FUNCTIONING

The Relationship of Id and Superego to Ego Functions

Traditionally the ego's task has been described as one of mediating between drives, superego, and reality interaction. While electronic computers can handle many signals simultaneously, it is one of the problems of verbal communication that one often has to extrapolate and isolate one particular thought, to the seeming neglect of other thoughts; let us hasten to say that while the previous discussion of ego functions made hardly any explicit reference to their interrelationship with superego and id, we have by no means forgotten it or in any way meant to minimize it.

---

*Maserty-Competence was not included in our list when the laboratory tests were selected.

Some aspects of superego activity are obviously relevant to ego functioning and to environmental adaptation, such as the transmission of values and traditions through identifications and ego ideal components,[26,36] and the functions of self observation and self evaluation.[38,79] Other facets of ego-superego relationships could also be mentioned.[37,60,67]

In addition to these interrelationships among ego and superego functions, recent systematic appraisals of psychoanalytic constructs have underscored the overlapping of ego and id functions, and that a hard and fast dichotomy among the structural constructs of id, ego, and superego is not an optimally fruitful approach to conceptualization.[31,37,74] Our definitions of the ego functions reflect this overlap at some points.

In attempting to gauge the interaction of the superego with the ego and its functions in our present experiment, we kept two avenues in mind: 1) a consideration of the role of the superego with regard to each individual ego function and 2) an independent assessment of certain aspects of the superego. For the first instance, we included considerations for the rater's appraisal in the manual on ego function ratings. For the appraisal of certain superego aspects, per se, we developed independent scales.

For instance, in the manual we discussed for reality testing the influence which strong latent hostility in conjunction with an adequate or excessive superego might have in distorting reality; for instance, by projection or denial of the hostility. Similarly, judgment can obviously be interfered with by the same mechanism. To remain with the same example, the sense of reality could be interfered with by guilt over hostility to the point of producing feelings of depersonalization and estrangement. By the same token, projection of superego attitudes such as blaming, fault-finding, vitally affect object relations. A weak superego permitting irresponsibility and other asocial tendencies would obviously affect vital object relations: secondary withdrawal could, to a large extent, be effected by superego aspects. With regard to the thought processes, obsessive mechanisms may be the result of superego prohibitions of aggressive and/or sexual drive derivatives. Adaptive regression in the service of the ego may be totally interfered with by a rigid superego which does not permit the necessary tolerance for ambiguity, and the necessary regression to primary process modes. It hardly deserves reminding one that a severe superego will be associated with excessive defensive functioning to the point of seriously crippling all coping mechanisms. That the stimulus barrier, for instance, towards visual stimuli may be greatly lowered by strong voyeuristic trends when disapproved by the superego has been discussed by Greenacre in her discussion of "Vision, Headache and Halo."[35] Perceptual vigilance and sensitization to sound stimuli is very often seen in depressed patients who are highly sensitive to noise, and both sensitivities may be seen in those suffering from insomnia, often as the direct result of projected aggression. Autonomous functions may be directly interfered with by the superego if sexualization of these functions is disapproved of by the superego: writer's cramp, reading disabilities, speech disturbances belong here classically. The synthetic function, also, is affected if deneutralized drives come to be registered by the superego; classically, dissociated states, fugues, and amnesias belong here especially.

In recent literature, Jacobson makes especially vivid how the superego or its forestages approve or disapprove, guide or threaten object images.[45] She discusses in detail the interrelationship of ego development at the end of the oedipal phase with superego formation. As she points out, the selective internalization of such conceptualized standards regarding desirable human behavior have a direct effect on reality testing and the sense of self.

Stein[79] elaborates specifically on this aspect pointing out that self observation is an essential element in the process of reality testing and that self observation and self evaluation are inextricably linked and intimately involved with superego functions. It follows quite logically, from these propositions, that superego functions play an essential role in reality testing and, in fact, in all reality adaptation.

Aside from attempting to include the functions of the superego in our rating of each of the ego functions, we also provided a seven-point scale in attempts to gauge: 1) overall superego intensity, 2) the consistency of the superego and 3) an overall judgment of the extent to which the superego interferes specifically with adaptive functioning. That the superego may be selectively severe with regard to one drive representation and excessively lenient with regard to others is a clinically well-known fact. A relative consistency of superego severity, or acuity, becomes then a particularly important variable.

The interrelationship between ego and superego on the one hand and ego and id on the other hand is also extensively considered by Anna Freud in *Normality and Pathology of Childhood*[25] and also by Anna Freud et al. in the "Metapsychological Assessment of the Adult Personality";[24] in the assessment, libidinal factors with regard to the distribution (cathexis of self, of objects), aggression and the degree to which it is under control, in the service of work or sublimated and neutralized in some other way, is examined there.

For our purposes we were first particularly interested in assessing some component aspects of the id: Namely, we want to take into consideration congenital endowment to the extent in which it could be inferred, as well as environmental stimulation of various drives and the contribution of the current life situation to drive manifestations. Following, for instance, Fries' and Woolf's work,[28] one has reason to believe that different infants may be born with varying congenital endowment, certainly with regard to activity patterns and, most likely, with regard to all drive aspects. Aside from the congenital endowment given, we know that sexual and aggressive overstimulation may have a marked effect on the personality in general and ego functioning specifically. Excessive aggressivisation or sexualization of any of the ego functions may directly interfere with the performance. Aggressively or sexually stimulating life situations definitely affect ego performance.

Aside from the contributions of these components to drive functioning, we wanted to gauge again in scale form *drive intensity,* keeping in mind the various pregenital drives as well as the phallic and genital drives in terms of the libidinal timetable and with regard to drive aim and drive impetus.

To merely assess the origin of the drive and its intensity would not be sufficient: In order to complete the assessment of id interrelationship with the ego, an appraisal of the degree to which the drives are neutralized or sublimated, is necessary. We therefore ask our raters to rate *neutralization and sublimation* on a separate scale.

Interrelationships Among the Ego Functions

With regard to the interrelationships among ego functions, Hartmann has expressed himself in the following way: "No definition of ego strength would I consider complete which does not refer to the intrasystemic structures, that is, which does not take into account the relative preponderance of certain ego functions over others; for instance, whether or not the autonomous functions are interfered with by the defensive functions, and also the extent to which the energies the various ego functions use are neutralized."[39]

All of a given individual's ego functions are likely to be interrelated to some degree. Thus, someone who has good *Reality Testing* usually tends to have a sound *Sense of Reality,* good *Synthetic Functioning,* etc. And, likewise, a person who has quite poor *Reality Testing* tends to have a poor *Sense of Reality,* etc. However, we also find clinically that considerable variation among the ego functions can exist within one person. An individual may have relatively poor *Object Relations* while major aspects of his *Thought Processes* and *Autonomous Functioning* operate at a much higher level.

It is likely that some ego functions vary more independently than others: for example, *Adaptive Regression in the Service of the Ego* and *Stimulus Barrier* appear to relate less closely to the other eight ego functions in our schema than does the *Synthetic Function.*

A number of propositions concerning the interrelationships among various ego functions can be found in the literature; for example, that defensive activity (denial, repression, projection) can interfere with learning, and with accurate reality testing; and, that rigid reality testing may interfere with *Adaptive Regression in the Service of the Ego.* The interference of defensive maneuvers with *Object Relations* has been detailed by Arlow and Brenner[2] in their book, and other examples from the literature could be cited. It is nevertheless true that no one has studied systematically the various possible forms of variation or of interference of one ego function with another.

The problem of the interrelationship of ego functions can probably be advantageously examined in the light of the history of the concept of intelligence. As with intelligence, the total adaptive ability, ego strength, tends to be seen as a unitary phenomenon. Primarily, those engaged in work with schizophrenics and others suffering from extremes of ego disturbance have been struck by the variant afflictions of different ego functions. Katan[50] has spoken of an "intact residue" of ego functions with the implication of different residues which one needs address oneself to in the treatment of schizophrenics. Eissler,[23] Bellak[7] and others have similarly spoken of the variable strengths and weaknesses of ego function within the same patient.

In the history of intelligence testing, there were those like William Stern who felt that intelligence was a unitary phenomenon (G). There were others like Thurston who felt that intelligence was the manifestation of many entirely separate and specific (s) functions such as a mathematical one, a verbal, special, social, and others (s_1, s_2, s_3, etc.). Then there was Spearman who suggested that intelligence could indeed best be understood as the manifestation of a general factor which interrated with a variety of specific factors (G + s_1, s_2, s_3, etc.).

It is the Spearman conception more than any other that underlies the internationally most widely used intelligence test, the Bellevue-Wechsler Intelligence Scales. It consists of ten subtests which correlate highly though in varying degree with each other and the total I.Q. For instance, there were the vocabulary subtests which tend to be more highly correlated with the overall I.Q. while rote memory and arithmetic relate least so. (There are, incidentally, those investigators like Cohen[21] who have questioned whether indeed ten independent variables are at work rather than only a cluster of three or four major factors.) Our conception of ego functions and our attempts to measure them follow the Spearman model logically and experimentally. We believe that there are only moderately arbitrarily ten major ego functions which correlate highly but in independently varying ways with each other and with total ego strength.

The question before us is just how much correlation and how much variation in correlations can be accepted and/or can be demonstrated. If indeed our ten ego functions correlate very highly with each other in everybody, there would be hardly any use for speaking of separate ego functions instead of simply ego strength. On the other hand, if they vary so much as to show only chance correlation, there would be hardly any basis for speaking of ego strength at all, or, for that matter, of such unitary concept as the ego itself.

To start with, we engaged in an armchair analysis of the likely degrees of independent variation of different ego functions. We drew up a list of the ego functions in relation to each other and asked ourselves on the basis of our interview data and other clinical experience just how high one ego function—say reality testing—can be if the sense of reality defenses, etc., are low. Conversely, we asked just how low reality testing could be if any of the other ego functions were optimal.

The result appeared to be a kind of cluster: if one ego function was as high as seven on our seven-point scale, it appeared unlikely that any except ARISE or Stimulus Barrier would have to be rated below four. In turn, if any ego function had to be rated as low as one—say extremely poor reality testing—the likelihood of any other ego functions being rated higher than four was small. Of course, even ex cathedra, this cannot be the whole answer. What if several ego functions were to merit a rating of three or four, could others deserve a six or seven? If so, what clusters are likely? So far we have not dealt with the possibility of an ego psychologic equivalent to an idiot savant who might be a mathematical genius but an idiot otherwise. There are probably quite a few people we all know who exceed in one ego function especially—an autonomous one while all other functions are on a low level. The only two functions which we found to vary rather independently quite often were ARISE (Adaptive Regression in the Service of the Ego) and Stimulus Barrier—a matter for further discussion.

It is not likely that knowledge about the interrelationship among the various ego functions will be rapidly increased when the source of the information is from individual analysis, or even the pooled experience of different analysts. This is because no standard operational definitions are available. Our study represents a first attempt along these lines. The component factors and scale definitions, while rough and preliminary, nevertheless, provide a specific focus for efforts at further clarification and refinement of functions. The need for clarifying definitions and the usage of terms in psychoanalysis, I believe, is rather generally recognized.

To find better than speculative, clinical, or empirical data, we have to try to identify the variances and interrelationships of the ten ego functions by statistical analysis of our whole sample. To date, we only demonstrate some patterns in form of a psychogram, showing individual variations rather than large-scale lawful ones.

There are other important considerations with which we have been concerned with which we can only deal briefly now. For one, there is the problem of individual differences in drive endowment,[28] and its influences on the development of various ego functions, as Alpert, Neubauer and Weil[1] have shown.

Another consideration is the question of the stability and changeability of each ego function throughout life, and the conditions under which these occur, both in childhood and after the personality has been formed.

Also, the question of congenital ego variations needs additional exploration: particularly, the relationship of phase-specific ego function deficits to various forms of psychopathology. Here, for instance, belong such statements as Greenacre's that disturbances in speech development at age two and a half may result in a predisposition to act out.[34] And, Anna Freud's discussion of the many relationships among drive and ego progressions, and the disharmonies in the rate of progress along different developmental lines.[25]

Some Preliminary Results on a Pilot Sample of Rated Interviews*

A preliminary analysis of the first 16 subjects (five schizophrenics, five neurotics, and six normals) was carried out to sample how our procedures were working. Specifically, we wanted to be sure that trained raters independently judging interview material would agree to an appreciable extent on the ego function level for subjects from all these diagnostic groups. As you very likely know, studies have shown that the degree of agreement in judging clinical material tends to be less than judges *assume* it to be when agreement is reached by the "conference" method, i.e., in a free-wheeling discussion. To insure against any bias due to our understandable wish for a high degree of agreement, the following procedures were utilized: each interview was tape recorded, and a complete typescript was given to each judge† who in turn recorded his ratings without any collaborative discussion about the case or the ratings with the other judges. For the ratings based on interviews, correlations for eight of the ego functions ranged from .89 to .80 for two judges. This reflects a substantial degree of agreement in rating the strength of ego functions from interview material, satisfying statistical expectations, and compares quite favorably with the amount of concurrence achieved by other workers in the personality field dealing with similar type material.

The next question was whether the ego function scales were distinguishing among the schizophrenic, neurotic, and normal subjects. That is, were the schizophrenic subjects receiving the lowest ego function scores, the neurotics next, and the normals the highest scores, and what was the likelihood that the obtained differences could have occurred by chance? Results, again for the interview ratings (based on an analysis of variance) showed that all ego function scores were in the predicted direction (i.e., schizophrenics lowest, neurotics next, and normals highest), and all were highly significant statistically, suggesting it is quite unlikely that the findings occurred by chance. These analyses of a preliminary sample of subjects, then, have shown that in rating ego function adequacy from interview material, trained judges can attain relatively high levels of agreement when using the ego function manual, and that subjects from three groups which would be expected to differ in the adequacy of ego functioning differ in the predicted direction on all the ego functions.

The important question of the degree of overlap or correlation of the various ego functions with each other cannot be accurately assessed from this relatively small sample. It was also not possible to determine the number and kind of ego function patterns within the schizophrenic, neurotic, and normal

---

*These data have been published elsewhere (Hurvich, M. and Bellak, L.: Ego function patterns in schizophrenia, Psychological Reports, 22, 1968).

†Later rating was done directly from the taperecording.

groups. Both these issues can be explored in detail when a larger sample of cases has been accumulated and a factor analysis performed.*

A monograph with the complete results of the study as well as all the conceptual and procedural details will be ready for publication in 1969.

FUTURE PROBLEMS

Other and Further Search Needed

The current project, even if it confirms the hypotheses, is not enough. Ambitious, or overambitious, as it has seemed at times, it is in fact not ambitious enough. To begin with, our relatively small sample of a hundred subjects may be enough for some reasonably acceptable inferences, but not more. Even were the data very convincing, the project would be worthless unless it

1) is replicated by several other teams elsewhere,

2) is supported by projects involving larger numbers of patients and controls than in the present project,

3) allows for application of more extensive measures, particularly in our laboratory study, as discussed there and,

4) if the methods described will be applied not only to acutely ill patients but also to subacute and chronic patients and preferably more than one time to each patient to gauge variability.

The Study of the Ego Functions by Physiological Tests is also desirable in the future. It was not excluded from the present study by an oversight or design. To the contrary, physiological tests have been part of my hypothesis of examining ego functions in schizophrenia since the first publication, Dementia Praecox, and mentioned in every subsequent publication. They were also part of the present research design, but problems of space, experimental population, and of financial support forced us to exclude it. To be sure, the conceptual aspects of relating physiological functions to ego functions are especially difficult. In a research outline submitted to NIMH we had to stress that presumably physiological indices would be more likely to furnish overall ego strength data rather than data specifically correlateable to a particular ego function. Stimulus barrier and drive control might be exceptions to this statement.

Pioneering efforts in this area have been made by Roessler, Greenfield and Alexander,[69] Lacey,[57] and Zahn and Rosenthal[82] but have not as yet been implemented. Measures of heart rate, respiratory patterns, finger blood volume, and galvanic skin response were considered, and were to be assessed while subjects were involved in tasks and situations with different degrees of struc-

---

*The paper by Bellak and Hurvich (J. Nerv. Ment. Dis., in press) includes a preliminary factor analysis on 65 subjects, in which four interrelated factors were tentatively identified.

ture, both before and after the introduction of high decibel sounds photostimuli, etc.

If the physiological measurements were recorded while subjects were performing the psychological laboratory tasks (each of the latter having been developed to assess a specific ego function), it is possible that response patterns would emerge which would be more meaningful than results from either of the two data sources alone. Thus, the operation of defenses, thought processes, stimulus barrier, synthetic and autonomous functioning all might be understood more meaningfully if physiological response measures were to accompany indices of behavioral performance.

Such laboratory procedures, well anchored in dynamic psychoanalytic hypotheses, might be especially desirable for evaluation, if fairly large numbers of subjects are involved. The actual testing and scoring could be performed by technicians, leaving clinically and psychodynamically trained professionals available for interview techniques and other intensive procedures with small subsamples.

If eventually subgroups of schizophrenics, isolated by their ego function patterns, are indeed followed up for etiological hunches, and if such subgrouping then leads to the isolation of several groups belonging to the schizophrenic syndrome who have a rather clear primary etiology and pathogenesis, and can therefore be treated more rationally, in the long run, such clearer recognition of the various etiologies should go a long way towards the real goal of all medical endeavor: the prevention of at least most manifest schizophrenic disorders.

EGOPSYCHOLOGICAL CONSIDERATIONS OF THERAPY OF THE SCHIZOPHRENIA SYNDROME

The egopsychological approach to schizophrenia does not presuppose a purely psychological etiology or pathogenesis of schizophrenia. It merely implies that whatever the causative factor or factors, they manifest themselves in various patterns of ego function disturbances. Similarly, the therapy of schizophrenia within an egopsychological framework does not necessarily mean a psychoanalytic or other psychotherapeutic intervention; it merely proposes that *whatever* therapy is designed should be predicated upon a careful appraisal of what intact functions can be utilized and what defective functions need to be improved *by one means or another*.

My conception of any form of therapy is one of careful diagnosis leading to carefully planned interventions, derived from specific theoretical propositions. That leaves no tolerance for vague pseudophilosophical, nonrational, or nonconceptualized approaches. Therefore, I have no sympathy for the ideas of existial therapy (unless a consideration of disturbances of the self so vividly described by existentialists becomes part of a larger clearly stated set of hypotheses), or for the idea that the personality of the therapist matters more than the therapy (unless equally incompetent therapists differ significantly in warmth, empathy, etc.). Of course, I do not believe that establishing rapport is enough nor is making the patient feel accepted or loved enough: these may be necessary preconditions, like general bed rest in internal medicine, but not a whole therapeutic program. Nor do I believe that any single therapeutic approach, from classical psychoanalysis to drug therapy can be the method of choice for *all* schizophrenics. To the contrary, I believe that almost any therapeutic approach *may* be useful under given circumstances with a given patient. The therapy of schizophrenics must be tailor-made, specifically designed for each individual patient, depending upon the nature of his or her specific disturbances.

In previous volumes[7,77a] I had occasion to describe in some detail the nature of ego functions, their development, and their disturbances, with some brief remarks about some therapeutic aspects. The ideas were further developed especially in two publications, "The Treatment of Schizophrenia and Psychoanalytic Theory,"[10] and "Methodology and Research in the Psychotherapy of Psychoses."[12] A specific consideration of the role of rehabilitation workshop in the restoration of some ego functions is also discussed in "Rehabilitation of the Mentally Ill through Controlled Transitional Employment" and "The Rehabilitation of Psychotics in the Community."* In the present chapter I will limit myself to a relatively brief schematic overview in terms of tables and brief discussion, leaving a very extensive consideration for another volume in preparation (*Schizophrenia and Ego Functions: A Systematic Study of Ego Functions in Normals, Neurotics, and Schizophrenics*).

1. REALITY TESTING

FUNCTION	DISTURBANCE

For *Reality Testing* the major component factors are:
 	
A) *the distinction between inner and outer stimuli*
 	
    1) accuracy of perception (includes orientation to time and place, and accuracy of perception and interpretation of external events)
 	
    2) accuracy of inner reality testing (i.e., psychological mindedness and awareness of inner states)
	Perceptual distortions, projections, delusions, hallucinations, disorientation in time, place, and person, déjà vu, déjà reconnu, perceptual vigilance, low awareness of inner psychological reactions.

---

*and in *Emergency Psychotherapy and Brief Psychotherapy*, with Leonard Small.[14a]

B) *Judgment*

a) awareness of likely consequences of intended behavior (e.g., anticipating probable dangers, legal culpabilities and social censure, disapproval or inappropriateness)

b) extent to which manifest behavior reflects the awareness of these likely consequences

Oblivious to severe dangers to life and limb, unrealistic appraisal of consequences of actions, fails to learn from previous experiences

TREATMENT

If the disturbance of *reality testing* is severe (e.g., the patient lives primarily in a world of delusions and hallucinations), a number of preliminary steps are necessary: entering into the patient's world, establishing contact on a primary process level, gaining the patient's confidence. Letting the patient know that he is being understood decreases his secondary terror (about his strange world) and makes some bridging of the psychotic world and reality possible.

Interpretation of some of the distortions are then possible. These may be cathartic interpretations of feared drive impulses, as best exemplified by John Rosen's technique,[69a] or interpretations of defenses, or of the superego, *in a judiciously paced way.*

Whatever the severity of the disturbance of reality testing, the therapist's role is to a certain extent that of an *auxiliary ego.*

Part of the therapeutic intervention may have to be to *sensitize* the patient to the perception of *internal reality,* such as of anger or anxiety: to be aware of them before they are being translated into projections of major or minor degree. Prediction of possible distortion of emerging events will have a major role in avoiding them and helping the patient recognize traumatic situations. This statement holds true particularly for defects in judgment, as seen in acting out of various degrees of severity.

Education may play a role if some of the defects in reality testing are facilitated by inadequate information (e.g., a fear of becoming pregnant from a kiss).

Drugs may play a major role in controlling the excess drives which are responsible for the distortion of reality. In that sense, psychotropic drugs can improve reality testing indirectly. It is also possible that the phenothiazines may have an effect on the synthetic function and by this means improve the quality of thinking and in turn improve reality testing.

Group psychotherapy, like a rehabilitation workshop setting, may have a reality testing feedback: if the patient behaves or talks unrealistically, the group or workshop personnel lets him know. Inasmuch as faulty reality testing in these settings does not lead to dire consequences, but to therapeutic intervention I tend to think of them as *"settings of self-correcting reality."*

Id and *superego* are actively involved in reality testing: concrete examples might be self-harming masochistic behavior predicated upon unrealistic guilt feelings. Excessive sexual push, e.g., in involutional disorders, may lead specifically to delusions and hallucinations of gross sexual nature. In that case, the whole therapeutic armamentarium from interpretations to achieve insight to drug therapy is appropriate in the service of improved reality testing.

2. SENSE OF REALITY

FUNCTION	DISTURBANCE
For *Sense of Reality of the World and of the Self,* the component factors are: a) the extent to which external events are experienced as real and as being embedded in a familiar context b) the extent to which the body (or parts of it) and its functioning and one's behavior are experienced as familiar and unobtrusive and as belonging to (or emanating from) the individual c) the degree to which the person has developed individuality, uniqueness, and a sense of self and self esteem d) the degree to which the person's self representations are separated from his object representations	Alienation, hypnagogic and hypnapompic stage fright, emotional isolation as a result of obsessive defenses, déjà vu Depersonalization, derealization, dreamlike states, trances, fugues, major dissociations, world destruction fantasies, identity diffusion

TREATMENT

A large variety of factors may cause disturbances of the *sense of self,* and therefore treatment also varies a great deal.

In some it may never have developed well because of autistic, or symbiotic, relations with the maternal figure, poor, inconsistent introjects, and for other reasons. A conflict between one part of the self and another, with an increase in the self observing function of the ego resulting from it is a crucial factor. Withdrawal of libidinal energy from outside subjects may play a role. On the other hand, hysterical focusing at the distance when looking at near objects may also produce it. So may hyperventilation with subsequent changes in proprioception and dizziness. Perceptual isolation, fatigue, and drug effects (a paradoxical, anxiety arousing effect of sedatives, for instance) may cause it. More than ordinary awareness of usually automatic functions, such as walking (on a stage for instance) may lead to what Simon[76a] speaks of as the de-automatizing effect of consciousness and of special effort.

Aside from interpretation of relevant dynamic aspects, depersonalization may be decreased or abated by drugs, if panic is responsible for the pathogenesis, and if depersonalization is due to overbreathing or nuchal rigidity.

In severe psychotic disturbances of the sense of self, Federn's and Sechehaye's work,[75a] and the discussion by Freeman et al.[23a] need referring to. While Sechehaye painstakingly restored a sense of self and self boundaries in individual patients by body contact and interpretation, the Body Ego Technique of Goertzel et al. permits patients via rhythmical movements, proprioception, etc. to relearn. Gindler's technique of muscle reeducation is also very useful, for minor disturbances of body image especially.[12]

The more disturbed the patient the more active the therapist has to be in helping the patient build self esteem (or rebuild it) and help him structure his life at least temporarily in such a way as to avoid self-esteem destroying experiences: do not let him take on more of a task than he is likely to be able to manage. Specific self concepts need analyzing: concretization of the self as something dirty, dangerous, loathsome are frequent and need great attention.

A few conjoint consultations of the patient with significant figures in his life may be very helpful if there are specific disturbances of role perception, especially in relation to one or more specific figures.

3. DRIVE REGULATION AND CONTROL

FUNCTION	DISTURBANCE
Drive Regulation and Control a) the directness of impulse expression (ranging from primitive acting out through neurotic acting out to relatively indirect forms of behavioral expression) b) the effectiveness of delay and control, the degree of frustration tolerance, and the extent to which drive derivatives are channeled through ideation, affective expression and manifest behavior	Temper outbursts, habit and conduct disorders, lack of frustration tolerance, acting out. Tendencies toward murder or suicide, impulsivity. Drive-dominated behavior, chronic irritability and rage, low frustration tolerance, catatonic excitement and rigidity, manic excitement, depressive psychomotor slow-up, accident proneness, parapraxes, lack of sphincter control, nailbiting, tics, excessive control of impulse.

TREATMENT

The traditional forms of dealing with disturbances of *drive regulation and control* of a severe type had been restraining sheets, wet packs, and a vast assortment of other hydrotherapeutic procedures, camisoles and locked doors. In dealing with psychotic disturbances of control, these means have been almost entirely replaced by the chemical restraints, the psychotropic drugs, supplemented by reform of hospital wards into therapeutic communities with patient government, nurses out of uniform, and open doors. Among the latest psychotropic drugs, lithium carbonate as specific treatment of manic excitement is particularly relevant with regard to the control of excessive drive.

The drugs play a crucial role not only generally but for psychotherapy and for the classical analysis of a patient who has an extreme disturbance in drive regulation and control: in Ostow's[61b] hands psychoanalysis of schizophrenics is made possible by a sort of "drug sandwich:" drugs of the phenothiazine variety are used to put a ceiling on the patient's drives, while stimulants, energizers, antidepressants are used to establish a bottom; something akin to titration establishes the most useful level between excessive control and lack of control within which to operate the analytic process.

The strictly psychotherapeutic intervention of lack in drive regulation and control still has a large role to play even without drugs. The cathartic interpretation as practiced especially by John Rosen[69a] may be very useful in diminishing uncontrolled behavior or interfering with (catatonic or depressed) excessive control. Aside from decrease of the drives by interpretation, a strengthening of the superego is often an important strategy. Typically, the superego of the very disturbed is inconsistent: in part too severe and another part too lenient; the appropriate psychotherapeutic operations strive toward greater consistency by strengthening some parts and weakening others. In acting out of all grades of severity, it is important to establish continuity where discontinuity exists for the patient by his use of denial, magic thinking, and other distortions. In addition, repeated prediction of consequences of acting out and inappropriate acting out is a useful therapeutic strategy.[12a] Excessive aggressive behavior may of course be the result of fear of passivity which he has to deny by aggressivity. Recent studies suggest that if delusions of grandeur as a means of inflating self esteem are interfered with, violent actions, including homicide, are particularly easily precipitated.

Very often a lack of adult regulation and control is due to the lack of their acquisition in childhood, as well as excessive overstimulation of aggressive and sexual drives. In such a case the building of controls and the decrease of overstimulation necessitates a long, drawn-out, therapeutic effort which to a large extent has to resemble an educational one. Interpretation of apperceptive distortions (which incite excessive response on the part of the patient) is a traditional helpful means of intervention. If it is difficult to modify an inconsistent superego, it is even more difficult psychotherapeutically to produce a drive progression from pre genital to a genital orientation and to produce neutralization and sublimation. Where strictly psychotherapeutic means do not suffice, active changes of the environment may be necessary: a patient who is excessively stimulated to aggression in a butcher shop or excessively aroused homosexually in a barber shop needs to be helped to change to another occupation.

Above all, the patient needs to be helped to develop a better signal function of the ego, both with regard to awareness of a dangerous build up of drive push and the lack of appropriate drive response (before it becomes excess).

Very general measures for tension reduction and drive reduction such as vigorous exercise (especially in the presence of an excessive aggressive drive) may play a temporarily very useful role.

4. OBJECT RELATIONS

FUNCTION

DISTURBANCE

For *Object Relations,* the components are:

a) the degree and kind of relatedness to others (taking account of withdrawal trends, narcissistic self-concern, narcissistic object choice or mutuality)

b) the extent to which present relationships are adaptively or unadaptively influenced by or patterned upon older ones and serve present mature aims rather than past immature ones

c) the degree to which he perceives others as separate entities rather than as extensions of himself

d) the extent to which he can maintain "object constancy" (i.e., sustain relationships over long periods of time and tolerate both the physical absence of the object, and frustration, anxiety and hostility related to the object)

Withdrawal, detachment, narcissistic overinvestment of self, cannibalistic symbiotic-dependent attachments.

TREATMENT

The disturbance in *object relations* is probably the one which will indisputably remain in the area of psychodynamic treatment (via transference) regardless of what future developments there might be in drugs or in terms of the etiology and pathogenesis of severe disturbances of object relations. Drugs may help bear object relations for those in whom they are too conflict-ridden and too tension-arousing, but they cannot help a person *develop* object relationships if they were never there.

Sechehaye's[75a] accounts of detailed painstaking development of object relations via the transference relationship are especially dramatic. Rosenfeld,[69b] as well as Searles,[74a] is particularly concerned with the fear of being destroyed or of destroying the object in schizophrenics.

Group therapy settings and those in rehabilitation workshops like Altro[9] attempt to help the patient learn object relationships in group settings and permit corrections in object relationships without great penalty, such as total rejection. The workshop especially may help someone develop an optimal distance or closeness to other people, as well as learn to tolerate what is for him an optimal number of object relationships. Except by the sociometrists, rather little attention has been paid so far to proximity and distance, as well as number of relationships and tolerance for them in different people.

5. THOUGHT PROCESSES

FUNCTION

For *Thought Processes,* the components are:
a) the adequacy of processes which adaptively guide and sustain thought (attention, concentration, anticipation, concept formation, memory, language)
b) the relative primary-secondary process influences on thought (extent to which thinking is unrealistic, illogical, and/or loose)

DISTURBANCE

Magical thinking, autistic logic, condensations, attention lapses, inability to concentrate, memory disturbances, concreteness, primary process manifestations and primitive thought processes as described by Freud, Piaget and others.

TREATMENT

Disturbances of *thought processes* can often be largely affected indirectly. By dealing with the drives and impulses which are causing a disturbance of the thought processes, the latter may be improved. This may be done either by drugs and/or by psychotherapy. A study by Bellak and Chassan[13a] suggested that Librium and psychotherapy were able to reduce primary process type thinking, and the phenothiazines are especially well able to produce this change in the severely disturbed. Such changes can be attained relatively easily if good secondary type thinking had ever been attained by the patient. Constant review of events for the patient may decrease dissociation and show him logical relationships between one mood and another.

The problem becomes much more difficult if a patient had never acquired very much secondary process type thinking. Then it becomes a matter of training the patient virtually in syllogisms, in the logical hierarchy of socially acceptable thought. Concrete thinking may become a particular problem: one often has to enter the extremely disturbed schizophrenic's world by thinking in "schizophrenese", for instance, in the case of a woman who feels she is able to understand and talk to birds, it is necessary to be able to understand the ellipses in the thinking and to enter in a meaningful way so as to establish communication with her. In patients suffering from somatic delusions, some interpretations, as practiced especially by John Rosen,[69a] are necessary. (For instance, with regard to some more or less disguised notion that something live interferes with the function of the intestine and needs to be taken out). The use of syllogistic interpretations is almost entirely without effect in such patients until they have very much improved. The paranoid delusions and thought disorders can be extremely tightly organized, as they represent an attempt at a solution of extremely painful conflicts that may show a great resistance to change. It is under such circumstances that the use of LSD for the production of a disorganization of a too well formed paranoid system may possibly be useful: after disorganization, it may be possible to help the patient attain better compromise formations than the paranoid one.

6. ADAPTIVE REGRESSION IN THE SERVICE OF THE EGO (ARISE)

FUNCTION	DISTURBANCE
a) first phase of an oscillating process: relaxation of perceptual and conceptual acuity (and other ego controls) with a concomitant increase in awareness of previous preconscious and unconscious contents	Extreme rigidity in character structure and thinking where fantasy and play are difficult or impossible; unevenness in shifting from passivity to activity; regression of any ego function produces anxiety and disruption of functioning, lack of creativity, stereotyped thinking, intolerance of ambiguity; prejudice and sterility. If first phase predominates, overideational thinking, pseudo-intellectuality, pseudo-artistic tendencies, eccentricity.
b) second phase of the oscillating process: the induction of new configurations which increase adaptive potentials as a result of creative integrations	
ARISE refers to the ability of the ego to initiate a partial, temporary and controlled lowering of its own functions (keep in mind here the component factors of the other ten ego functions) in the furtherance of its interests (i.e., promoting adaptation). Such regressions result from a relatively free but controlled play of the primary process and are called regressions in the service of the ego.	

TREATMENT

Disturbances of the *adaptive regression in the service of the ego* may involve a lack of tolerance of ambiguity, so that the syllogisms which are the basis for all dynamic interpretation are impossible for the patient to engage in. In the extreme we again see concrete thinking. It is the type of patient who even if not psychotic cannot possibly tell a story about the Thematic Apperception Test other than merest description. In those patients there is a disturbance of the first phase of the oscillating process. No decrease in perceptual acuity is permitted at all. In the workaday world there are many at best borderline psychotics who function by virtue of doing the same thing in the same way every day of their lives, and any attempt to have them react adaptively to a change in the circumstances is the despair of all those in contact with them.

A psychotherapeutic attempt to change this rigidity can be predicated sometimes on illustrating to them that other people see different things, and have different stories to tell to the TAT pictures, for instance. Long ago I suggested that barbiturates (sometimes mixed with stimulants) may help produce the first phase in the psychotherapeutic session and provide an avenue for further work.[4a] Interpretation of extremely rigid defenses may be helpful. Decreasing the equation of a thought with an act in the most concrete thinking people will also decrease anxiety and produce more adaptive ability.

Most often the extreme disturbance of the first phase of the oscillating process necessary for the adaptive regression in the service of the ego is seen in people whom one would best diagnose as psychotic characters, when it is present, more so than one encounters in obsessive character.

An extreme ability to regress in the first phase with insufficient ability to return to adaptive structural functioning in the second phase characterizes psychotic productivity in artistic media as well as other activities. These people often appear to be gifted not only as artists, but also as inventors, as politicians, and in every other walk of life, but structurally or educationally do not have enough of an adaptive potential to lead to any fruition. Psychotherapy strengthening their reality testing and drive control is necessary. There are probably exceptional people in whom a disturbance in the second phase of ARISE occurs in the presence of either congenital ability or acquired secondary characteristics of structural and adaptive nature which make it possible that though psychotic for all other purposes, the production may still be artistic in the sense of communicating powerfully (rather than having only private meaning). Some strengthening of the adaptive functions by psychotherapy, training (for instance, learning the craft aspects), and drugs is indicated in such instances.

7. DEFENSIVE FUNCTIONS

FUNCTION	DISTURBANCE
a) degree to which defensive components adaptively or maladaptively affect ideation and behavior b) extent to which these defenses have succeeded or failed (degree of emergence of anxiety, depression, and other dysphoric affects) Different defenses are important at different stages of development. The earlier the origin of a defense, the more pathological, e.g., projection and denial which affect relationship to reality.	Parallel to loss of synthetic function, e.g., repression fails and leads to primary process emergence and patient fails to "hold together"—secondary inability to concentrate, memory impaired, efficiency impaired. Probably because too much energy used at barrier function and not enough left for adaptation, e.g., with failure of defense have overstimulation by stimuli and mood lability. Failure of repression may lead to déjà vu, parapraxes, lack of control of drives. An overcontrol of affect, ideation and use

Assessment needs to be not only of type of defense but also of lability or stability, (e.g., obsessive isolation or phobic withdrawal may lead to depersonalization and projection).

of motor functions may be a last attempt to prevent breakthrough of drives.

With decompensation (and compensation) one can have the same content but change of defense in handling conflictual content: character trait, can, with decompensation, become neurotic symptom, then, with further decompensation, psychotic symptom, and the process be reversed with compensation. Weakening of repression possible at times when ego normally weakened, e.g., hypnagogic state, physical illness/fatigue, object loss, toxicity.

TREATMENT

The treatment of the disturbance of the *defensive functions* involves of course insight psychotherapy, par excellence, of the primary impulses, the apperceptive distortions, and the inappropriate defenses. It parallels in part treatment for loss of drive control—e.g., by manipulation of the environment to decrease stimulus, changes in vocation, living place, habits. Drugs are useful. The therapist must assess dynamics quickly and insist, in psychosis, without hesitation even upon drastic changes rather than be aloof from decisions which involve reality, if the disturbance is severe.

8. STIMULUS BARRIER

FUNCTION

The component factors for *Stimulus Barrier* are:

a) upper and lower threshold for, sensitivity to, or awareness of stimuli impinging upon various sensory modalities (externally, primarily, but including pain)

b) nature of response to various levels of sensory stimulation in terms of the extent of disorganization, avoidance, withdrawal, or active coping mechanisms employed to deal with them

Both thresholds and response to stimuli contribute to adaptation by the organism's potential for responding to high, average or low sensory input so that optimal homeostasis (as well as adaptation) is maintained: in the average expectable environment; as well as under conditions of unusual

DISTURBANCE

Easily upset by bright lights, loud sounds, temperature extremes, pain, resulting in withdrawal, physical symptoms or irritability. Or, thresholds overly high, where person is oblivious to nuances underresponsive to environmental stimuli, impoverishment of aesthetic sensibilities.

stress. Stimulus barrier determines, in part, how resilient a person is, or how he readapts after the stress and impingements are no longer present. Thresholds, as described for component a) refer not only to reaction to external stimuli, but also to internal stimuli which provide proprioceptive cues, or those originating within the body but eventually impinging on sensory organs. Light, sound, temperature, pain, pressure, drugs, and intoxicants are the stimuli to be considered relevant to assessing thresholds.

Responses, other than threshold variables, referred to in component b) include motor responses, coping mechanisms, effects on sleep, and certain aspects of psychosomatic illness.

Together, the two components represent a way of scaling the degree to which the ego effectively and adaptively organizes and integrates sensory experience.

TREATMENT

Stimulus barrier has not usually been treated as an ego function. At times the argument against doing so has been based on the idea that the stimulus barrier is congenital, rather than developmental: so are of course a variety of autonomous ego functions.

It is apparently likely that some children are born with a relatively low stimulus barrier and others with a relatively high stimulus barrier. If this is early enough diagnosed, it would appear rational to attempt to decrease the amount of perceptual input for children with a low stimulus barrier. If this is not done, difficulty in synthesis and integration in the first place and disorganization once it has been at all established in the second place is extremely likely. It is entirely possible that a low stimulus barrier and extreme overloading may be responsible for the development of some schizophrenic conditions. Such children are likely to overreact to physiological phenomena, such as teething, fatigue, and the auditory and visual and tactile stimulations of everyday life. On the other hand, some autistic-appearing children may primarily suffer from a high stimulus barrier, and in such a case greater efforts to communicate with them must be made. Systematic attempts to stimulate their sensory capacities may be appropriate and necessary for optimal maturation, (similar both to the Montessori methods and the ones used in Luria's Institute of Defectology in Moscow).

It is conceivable that a low stimulus barrier may be coexistent with evidence of a disturbed electroencephalogram *in some,* in which case it may be feasible that drugs correcting the electrical functioning of the brain may be useful.

Some physiological states such as premenstrual water retention and changes in the electrolyte balance lower the stimulus barrier and are probably primarily responsible for many marital conflicts. In turn, dehydrating drugs frequently upset the electrolyte balance which, in turn, may seriously affect the normal stimulus barrier.

Last, but not least, certain social conditions, such as the sharing of one room day and night by a large number of people in impoverished settings may produce such a tremendous overstimulation by aggressive, sexual, and other stimuli as to lead to a lack and loss of control and certainly interfere with optimal development. Only socioeconomic changes are likely to be an answer to those problems.

9. AUTONOMOUS FUNCTIONING

FUNCTION	DISTURBANCE
For *Autonomous Functioning* the components are: a) degree of freedom from (or lack of freedom from) impairment of "apparatuses" of primary autonomy (e.g., functional disturbances of sight, hearing, intention, language, memory, learning, or motor function, intelligence) b) degree of, or freedom from, impairment of secondary autonomy (e.g., disturbances in habit patterns, learned complex skills, work routines, hobbies and interests)	Functional blindness or deafness, catatonic postures, inability to feed, dress, or care for oneself, disturbances of will skills, habits and automatized behavior are readily interfered with by drive-related stimuli; greater effort must be expended to carry out routine tasks.

TREATMENT

Disturbances of *autonomous functioning* can be t r e a t e d psychotherapeutically if the autonomous functions have been secondarily libidinized; for instance a reading disorder predicated upon a voyeuristic interpretation of reading or passive-aggressive implications of arguing with the writer. In more severe disturbances of the autonomous functions, as in psychotics, the most general formula is to use the intact functions for improvement or reconstruction of the disturbance. Psychotherapy, workshops may be settings in which this can be accomplished. Any procedure which helps neutralize and sublimate drives would indirectly strengthen the various autonomous functions. Outright training, habit training, may be necessary in some. Drugs will be useful.

10. SYNTHETIC FUNCTIONS

FUNCTION

For *Synthetic-Integrative Functioning,* we have the following components:

a) the degree of reconciliation or integration of *discrepant* or potentially incongruent (contradictory) attitudes, values, affects, behavior, and self representations (e.g., role conflicts)

b) the degree of *active* relating together (i.e., integrating) of psychic and behavioral events, whether contradictory or not

DISTURBANCE

Disorganized behavior, incongruity between thoughts, feelings and actions; absence of consistent life goal; poor planning, little effort to relate different areas of experience together.

Fluctuating emotional states without appropriate awareness of the change, as in hysterics. Minor and major forms of dissociation, from parapraxes to amnesia, fugues and multiple personalities.

Many other ego functions are called into play, sometimes very pathologically as in psychotic defenses because of the basic feature of the integrative function.

TREATMENT

The treatment of disturbed *synthetic functions* may proceed by strengthening of other ego functions and dealing with drive disturbances impairing synthetic functions. Drugs again may be useful. If necessary, the patient must be advised to decrease burdens at least temporarily. In such a case the decreased demands serve like a splinting of a broken limb and permit the synthetic function to improve again almost spontaneously. In patients with a particular difficulty in synthesizing affect and thought and who suffer from continuously fluctuating emotional states accompanied by changing attitudes, a constant review of what seem to them the only truth the day before and establishing continuity where they experience discontinuity is essential.

It is very likely that perceptual-motor disturbances which are being increasingly paid attention to in relation to dyslexias and other learning difficulties may relate to some problems in synthetic functioning on a maturational, neurological basis and need educational help. In some of these children, for reasons of a primary lack of synthesis or possibly due to secondary continued frustration over their inability to perform routine motor and perceptual tasks, emotional explosiveness may also be part of a failure of the synthetic function.

Inconsistent upbringing is certainly likely to impede the maturation of synthetic functioning and prevention of disturbances will have to be the ultimate treatment.

THE EGO FUNCTION PROFILE*

The schematic presentation of egopsychological aspects of diagnosis and

---

*Material based on these profiles can be found in Bellak, L., Hurvich, M., and Crawford, P.: Psychotic egos, Psychoanalytic Review, in press.

treatment could easily lead to an impression of a mechanistic and excessively oversimplified approach. To be sure, neither would be appropriate. A scheme is a frame of reference, a guideline within which to operate with as much flexibility and individual variation and awareness of complexity as is possible and necessary. Drives and superego must be taken into consideration as well as the immediate family environment and the general social and cultural setting of the patient. Furthermore, the patient cannot be really understood unless his personal history is fully understood and closely related to all aspects of func-

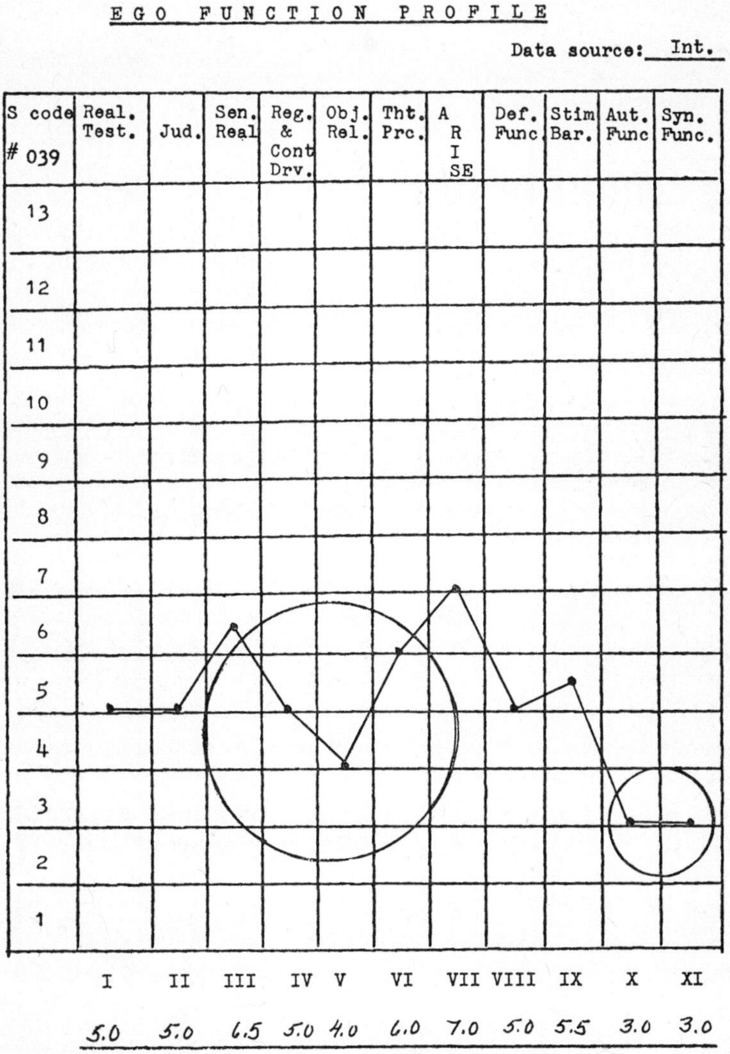

EGO FUNCTION PROFILE

Data source:__Int.__

FIG. 1.—See text.

tioning and malfunctioning at present. History is the present status of the past! All ahistoric attempts to understand personality are shortsighted, to say the least. In the case of each ego function, it is important to understand how it got that way, what function became structure and what malfunction is the cause of what failure to develop structure or what congenital lack might account for the absence of structure.

With these caveats in mind we find the presentation of ego functions in form of a profile very useful. Some schizophrenics may show overall poor ego

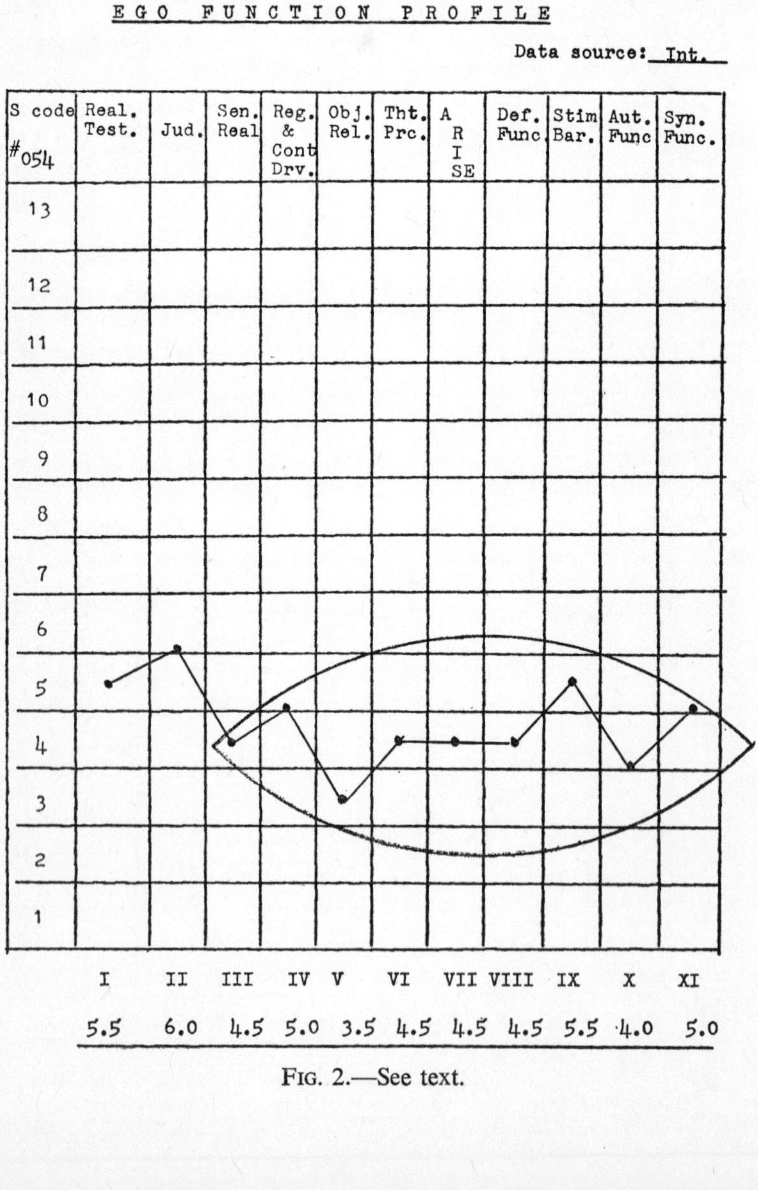

E G O   F U N C T I O N   P R O F I L E

Data source: Int.

S code #054	Real. Test.	Jud.	Sen. Real	Reg. & Cont Drv.	Obj. Rel.	Tht. Prc.	A R I SE	Def. Func.	Stim Bar.	Aut. Func	Syn. Func.
13											
12											
11											
10											
9											
8											
7											
6											
5											
4											
3											
2											
1											
	I	II	III	IV	V	VI	VII	VIII	IX	X	XI
	5.5	6.0	4.5	5.0	3.5	4.5	4.5	4.5	5.5	4.0	5.0

FIG. 2.—See text.

functioning (Fig. 1). Really severe damage due to psychogenic factors could in such a case be responsible as well as genetic, constitutional, or experiential somatic factors (infectious or traumatic). The clinical history is likely to offer further etiologic clues. In this particular patient not only was the life history, family relations, etc. very traumatic psychogenically speaking, but a control experiment was almost built in; only a sister brought up from early days in another home grew up well adjusted. The patient and another sibling fared very poorly.

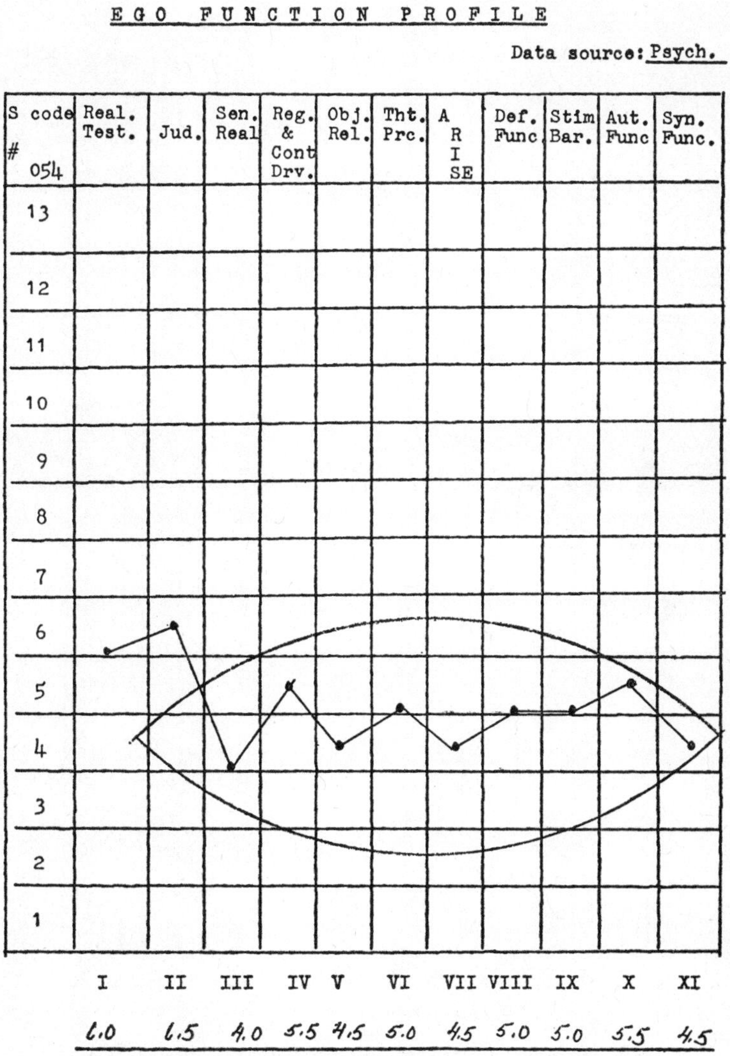

EGO FUNCTION PROFILE

Data source: Psych.

S code # 054	Real. Test.	Jud.	Sen. Real	Reg. & Cont Drv.	Obj. Rel.	Tht. Prc.	A R I SE	Def. Func.	Stim Bar.	Aut. Func	Syn. Func.
13											
12											
11											
10											
9											
8											
7											
6											
5											
4											
3											
2											
1											
	I	II	III	IV V		VI	VII VIII	IX		X	XI
	6.0	6.5	4.0	5.5 4.5		5.0	4.5 5.0	5.0		5.5	4.5

FIG. 3.—See text.

In such a patient, chances are that we deal less with *regressive* functioning and rather that we deal with *lack of progression* of nearly all ego functions. If at all possible, treatment would have to provide a virtual repetition of everything a normal upbringing should provide, in terms of object relations, thinking, habit training, acquisition of detour behavior and delayed drive gratification. Her poor object relations practically preclude ordinary psychoanalytic psychotherapy and the low autonomous and synthetic function generally bespeak poor therapeutic potential and a poor prognosis: Fairly good

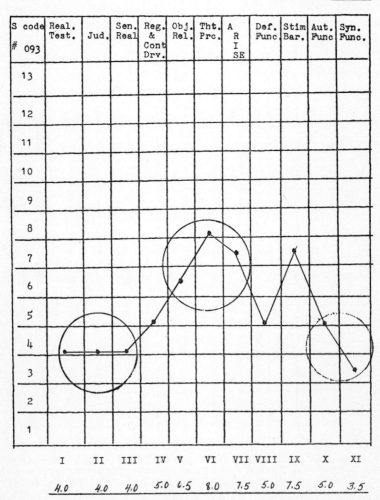

FIG. 4.—See text.

object relations are necessary for any kind of ordinary psychotherapeutic relationship (outside an institution). Unless thought processes are fairly good, the syllogistic thinking necessary for utilizing interpretations is impossible. Without a fairly good memory (as one autonomous function) and without some ability to synthesize affect and thought, ordinary psychotherapy cannot be expected to be successful or have any lasting binding effect.

On the other hand, her record still offers more than the one of a young man in his twenties (Fig. 2) whose functions nearly all fall around or below three. The most ominous predictor is probably the fact that his ratings on the psychological test performance (Fig. 3) and on interview performance are almost identical: ordinarily, the ratings on interview are considerably higher, reflecting the manifest clinical status while the tests show the full pathological potential. The most likely interpretation of the close similarity between the two levels in the case of this patient is that his clinical picture has leveled off at the lowest denominator and that chronicity has set in. At best, absolutely heroic, long drawn out individual therapeutic attention à la Sechehaye might offer some hope.

Then again, a patient with fairly good object relations and fairly good thought processes (Fig. 4) seemed a good prospect for psychotherapy, with a mixture of phenothiazine and amytryptilline providing control of drives and mood, and a rehabilitation workshop providing the general setting for a rebuilding of the defective structures (a low self esteem poorly compensated by grandiose goals within an oedipal setting among them).

While the cluster of high ratings for object relations, thought processes and ARISE indicate a psychotherapeutic method of intervention for this patient and constitute a basis for therapeutic optimism, the poor ratings on regulation and control of drives and the poor defenses are liabilities (acting out!) and the low autonomous function and synthetic function are reason for concern with regard to the ultimate stability of improvement.

The low score for reality testing and judgment reflect the fact of the acute disturbance, in the form of hallucinations and delusions. They constitute the *area* for intervention, i.e., for exploration of the dynamics of the apperceptive distortions. In this young man's prepsychotic state, his disturbance manifested itself primarily in unrealistic fantasies of achievement and the mechanism of denial, which were responsible sometimes for elation and sometimes even for not inconsiderable actual achievement, over a short pull.

A patient with a very low ARISE, by profession an accountant, also showed poor, rigid defenses and rather concrete thinking (Fig. 5). Psychotherapy seemed to have poor prospects under these circumstances and careful counseling with regard to a setting that would permit him to function within his defenses, consistent with his profession, seemed the most realistic, albeit very limited goal. The cluster of relatively good ratings on judgment, sense of self, regulation and control of drives and object relations suggest that in the proper limited setting he would indeed have some assets to count on. The cluster of low functioning of thought processes, ARISE, and defensive functions suggest the brittle nature of his adjustment.

A writer of some very modest success seems to have too poor a thought process to be very promising professionally despite a rather good ARISE (Fig. 6). This patient was a rather typically overideational and extremely anxious person who needed a great deal of tranquilizers to be able to function

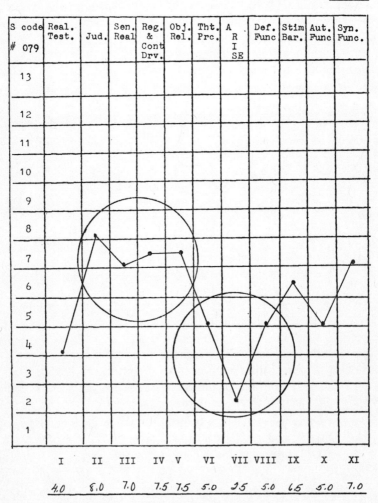

E G O   F U N C T I O N   P R O F I L E

Data source: Int.

S code # 079	Real. Test.	Jud.	Sen. Real	Reg. & Cont Drv.	Obj. Rel.	Tht. Prc.	A R I SE	Def. Func	Stim Bar.	Aut. Func	Syn. Func.

I   II   III   IV   V   VI   VII VIII   IX   X   XI

4.0   8.0   7.0   7.5 7.5   5.0   3.5   5.0   6.5   5.0   7.0

FIG. 5.—See text.

at all. Only very extensive psychotherapy of apperceptive distortions of his secondary processes by overwhelming anxiety (apparently primarily induced by an extremely anxious and probably psychotic mother) holds out any hope. In his case, the fairly good ability for creativity (ARISE) is offset by his poor thought processes and poor defensive functioning. His success at writing was very much of the extreme fringe variety, and chances are that he belongs to those pseudo-artists who have the ability to have access to the unconscious in the first phases of regression in the service of the ego but barely

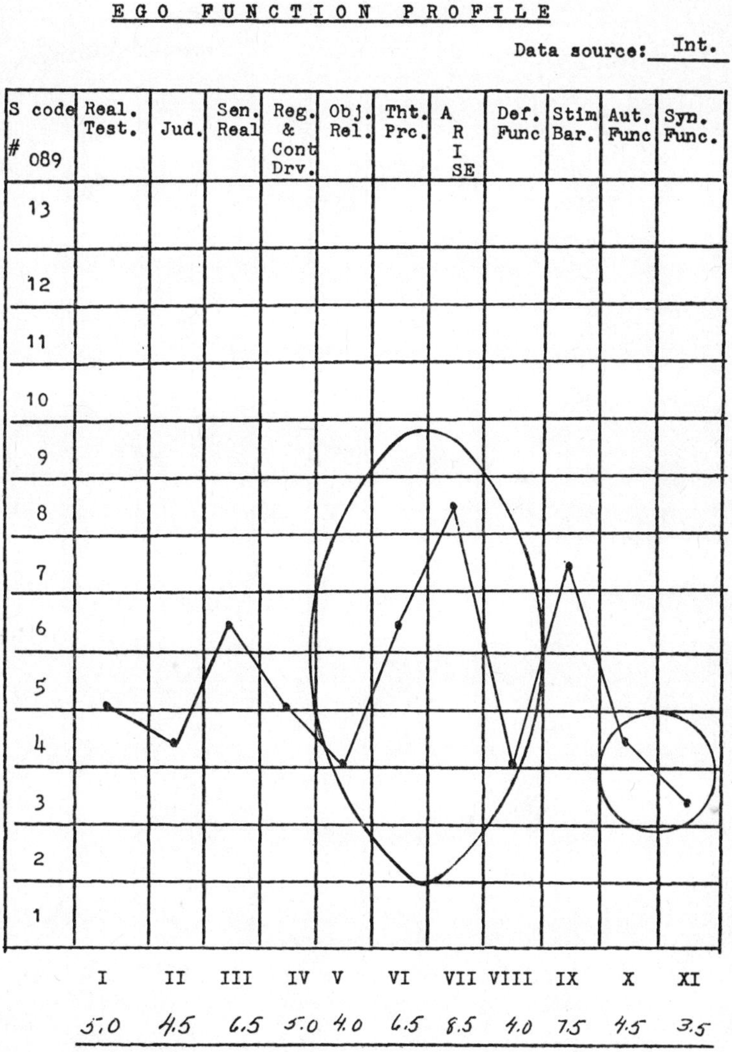

E G O   F U N C T I O N   P R O F I L E

Data source: Int.

I	II	III	IV	V	VI	VII	VIII	IX	X	XI
5.0	4.5	6.5	5.0	4.0	6.5	8.5	4.0	7.5	4.5	3.5

FIG. 6.—See text.

any adaptive-synthetic ability in the second phase of the oscillation and thus hardly communicates adaptively. His poor object relationships leave little hope for psychotherapy and the low autonomous and synthetic functions are a generally poor prognostic sign.

In the case of a commercial artist (Fig. 7), on the other hand, there is a whole cluster of relatively good functions and the relatively high autonomous and synthetic function suggests a good prognosis. The low score on defensive functioning suggests that this be the area of intervention, by reinforcing the

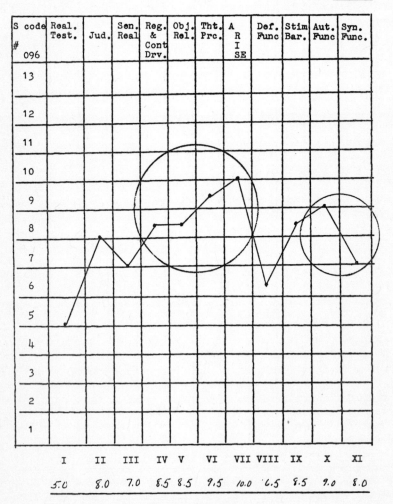

E G O   F U N C T I O N   P R O F I L E

Data source: Int.

S code # 096	Real. Test.	Jud.	Sen. Real	Reg. & Cont Drv.	Obj. Rel.	Tht. Prc.	A R I SE	Def. Func	Stim Bar.	Aut. Func	Syn. Func.
13											
12											
11											
10											
9											
8											
7											
6											
5											
4											
3											
2											
1											

	I	II	III	IV	V	VI	VII	VIII	IX	X	XI
	5.0	8.0	7.0	8.5	8.5	9.5	10.0	6.5	8.5	9.0	8.0

FIG. 7.—See text.

defenses by interpretations or drugs. The poor reality testing in her case seemed directly related to her being flooded with sexual and aggressive fantasies: it appeared likely that she would respond favorably to a fairly standard psychoanalytic psychotherapeutic approach.

The ego function patterns in the profiles depicted give a quick overall view which needs to be supported by details. It lends itself however to making comparisons for differential diagnoses and planning of therapy, and for charting therapeutic progress. Eventually we hope to find also some clearcut syndromes which will permit inferences toward differing etiology and pathogenesis within the large group called schizophrenics. Once isolated, early recognition of the various etiologies and pathogenic factors should lead to primary prevention and a significant decrease of the vast social problem psychoses present.

BIBLIOGRAPHY

1. Alpert, A., Neubauer, P., and Weil, A.: Unusual variations in drive endowment. In The Psychoanalytic Study of the Child. New York, International Universities Press, 1956. 2: 125-163.

2. Arlow, J., and Brenner, C.: Psychoanalytic Concepts and the Structural Theory. New York, International Universities Press, 1964.

3. Bellak, L.: Dementia Praecox. New York, Grune & Stratton, 1948.

4. Bellak, L.: A multiple-factor psychosomatic theory of schizophrenia. Psychiat. Quart. 23: 738-755, 1949.

4a. Bellak, L.: The use of oral barbiturates in psychotherapy. Am. J. Psychiat. 105: 849-850, 1949.

5. Bellak, L.: Manic-Depressive Psychosis and Allied Disorders. New York, Grune & Stratton, 1952, 306 pp.

6. Bellak, L.: Toward a unified concept of schizophrenia. J. Nerv. Ment. Dis. 121: 60-66, 1955.

7. Bellak, L., Ed.: Schizophrenia: A Review of the Syndrome. New York, Logos Press, 1958. 1,010 pp. now distributed by Grune & Stratton.

8. Bellak, L.: Creativity: some random notes to a systematic consideration. J. Proj. Tech. 22: 363-380, 1958.

9. Bellak, L., and Black, B.: The rehabilitation of psychotics in the community. Amer. J. Orthopsychiat. 30: 346-355, 1960.

10. Bellak, L.: The treatment of schizophrenia and psychoanalytic theory. J. Nerv. Ment. Dis. 131: 39-46, 1960.

11. Bellak, L.: Free association: conceptual and clinical aspects. Int. J. Psycho-Anal. 42: 9-20, 1961.

12. Bellak, L.: Methodology and research in the psychotherapy of psychoses. American Psychiatric Association Research Report No. 17, 1963.

12a. Bellak, L.: Acting Out: Some Conceptual and Therapeutic Considerations, Am. J. Psychother. 17: 375-389, 1963.

13. Bellak, L.: Physiological findings in schizophrenia, JAMA, 187: 871, March 14, 1964.

13a. Bellak, L., and Chassan, J.: An Approach to the Evaluation of Drug Effect during Psychotherapy; A Double Blind Study of a Single Case, J. Nerv. Ment. Dis., 139: 20-30, 1964.

14. Bellak, L.: Testimony before a Subcommittee of the Committee on Appropriations, House of Representatives, 89th Congress, 1965, p. 618-621.

14a. Bellak, L. and Small, L.: Emergency Psychotherapy and Brief Psychotherapy. New York, Grune & Stratton, 253 pp., 1965.

15. Bellak, L.: Effects of antidepressant

drugs on psychodynamics. Psychosom. 7, 1966.

16. Bellak, L., and Hurvich, M.: Toward an ego psychological appraisal of drug effects, presented upon invitation of the Psychopharmacology Research Branch, NIMH, for the meeting of the Early Clinical Drug Evaluation Unit in Montreal, June, 1967, Am. J. Psychiat. To be published Oct., 1968.

17. Beres, D.: Ego deviation and the concept of schizophrenia. In The Psychoanalytic Study of the Child, New York, International Universities Press, 1956. 2: 164-235.

18. Bibring, G., Dwyer, T., Huntington, D., and Valenstein, A.: A study of the psychological processes in pregnancy and of the earliest mother-child relationship. In The Psychoanalytic Study of the Child, New York, International Universities Press, 1956, 16: 9-72.

19. Bleuler, M.: Conception of schizophrenia within the last fifty years and today. The International Science Press, 1966, 7-19.

20. Bolland, J., and Sandler, J., et al.: The Hampstead Psychoanalytic Index: A study of the psychoanalytic case material of a two-year old child. In The Psychoanalytic Study of the Child, New York, International Universities Press, 1965, Monograph 1.

21. Cohen, J., A factor-analytically based rationale for the WAIS, J. Consult. Psychol. 21: 451-457, 1957.

22. Cumming, J., and Cumming, E., Ego and Milieu: The Theory and Practice of Environmental Therapy. New York, Atherton Press, 1962.

23. Eissler, K., Notes upon defects of ego structure in schizophrenia, Int. J. Psychoanal. 35: 41, 1954.

23a. Freeman, T., with Cameron, J., and McGhie, A., The state of the ego in chronic schizophrenia, Brit. J. Med. Psychol., 30, 9-18, 1957.

24. Freud, A., Nagera, H., and Freud, E., A metapsychological assessment of the adult personality: the adult profile. In The Psychoanalytic Study of the Child, New York, International Universities Press, 1965, 22.

25. Freud, A., Normality and Pathology in Childhood. New York, International Universities Press, 1965.

26. Freud, S., New Introductory Lectures on Psychoanalysis. New York, Norton, 1933.

27. Freud, S., An Outline of Psychoanalysis. New York, Norton, 1949.

28. Fries, M., and Woolf, P. Some hypotheses on the role of the congenital activity type in personality development. In The Psychoanalytic Study of the Child. New York, International Universities Press, 1953. 8.

29. Fromm, E., Hartman, L., and Marschak, M. A contribution to a dynamic theory of intelligence testing of children. J. Clin. Exper. Psychopath. 15: 73-95, 1954.

30. Gardner, R., Control, defense and centration effects: a study of scanning behavior, Brit. J. Psychol. 53: 129-140, 1962.

31. Gill, M. Topography and systems in psychoanalytic theory. In Psychological Issues, Monograph 10, New York, International Universities Press, 1963.

31a. Goertzel, V. et al.: Body-ego technique: an approach to the schizophrenic patient. J. Nerv. Ment. Dis. 141: 1, 1965.

32. Goldberger, L., and Holt, R., Experimental interference with reality contact: individual differences. In Solomon, P. et al. (eds.) Sensory Deprivation. Cambridge, Harvard University Press, 1961.

33. Graham, F., The aetiology of schizophrenia, The Med. J. Australia, May 8, 691, 1965.

34. Greenacre, P. General problems of acting out. Psychoanal. Quart. 19: 455-467, 1950.

35. Greenacre, P. Vision, headache, and the halo. In Trauma, Growth, and Personality, New York, Norton, 132-148, 1952.

36. Hartmann, H. Ego Psychology and the Problem of Adaptation. New York, International Universities Press, 1958.

37. Hartmann, H., Kris, E., and Loewenstein, R. Comments on the formation of psychic structure. In The Psychoanalytic

Study of the Child, New York, International Universities Press, 2: 11-38, 1946.

38. Hartmann, H. Comments on the psychoanalytic theory of the ego. *In* The Psychoanalytic Study of the Child, New York, International Universities Press, 5: 74-96, 1950.

39. Hartmann, H. Technical implications of ego psychology. *In* Essays on Ego Psychology. New York, International Universities Press, 12: 142-154, 1964.

40. Hartmann, H. Notes on the theory of sublimation. *In* Essays on Ego Psychology, New York, International Universities Press, 12: 215-240, 1964.

41. Hartmann, H. The development of the ego concept in Freud's work. *In* Essays on Ego Psychology, New York, International Universities Press, 14: 268-296, 1964.

42. Heider, F. On perception and event structures and the psychological environment. *In* Psychological Issues, Monograph 3, New York, International Universities Press, 1959.

43. Holzman, P. Repression and cognitive style. *In* Peatman, J., and Hartley, E., (Eds.) Festschrift for Gardner Murphy. New York, Harper, 1960.

43a. Hurvich, M., and Bellak, L.: Ego function patterns in schizophrenics. Psychological Reports, Feb., 1968.

44. Huxley, A., Osmond H., and Hoffer, A. Nature 204: 220, October 17, 1964.

45. Jacobson, E. The Self and the Object World. New York, International Universities Press, 1964.

46. Psychosis, biological or psychological? JAMA, 186: 510, November 2, 1963.

47. Janis, I. Psychological Stress. New York, John Wiley, 1958.

48. Kanzer, M. The functions of the ego: Freud's writing, Part I, paper delivered at Fall Meeting, American Psychoanalytic Association, New York, December, 1966.

49. Karush, A., Eassner, B., Cooper, A., and Swerdloff, B. The evaluation of ego strength. *In* A profile of adaptive balance, J. Nerv. Ment. Dis. 139: 332-349, 1964.

50. Katan, M. Schreber's pre-psychotic phase, Int. J. Psycho-Anal. 34: 43-51, 1953.

51. Klein, G. On hearing one's own voice: an aspect of cognitive control in spoken thought. *In* Schur, M. (Ed.) Drives, Affects, Behavior: Vol. 2. New York, International Universities Press, 87-117, 1965.

52. Klein, G. The several grades of memory. *In* Loewenstein R., Neuman, L., Schur, M., and Solnit, A. (Eds.) Psychoanalysis—A General Psychology: Essays in Honor of Heinz Hartmann. New York, International Universities Press, p. 377-389, 1966.

53. Klopfer, B., Crumpton, E., and Grayson, H. Rating Scales for Ego Functioning Applicable to Diagnostic Testing. Los Angeles, University of California, 1958.

54. Kohler, I. The formation and transformation of the perceptual world, tr. Fiss, H. *In* Psychological Issues, Monograph 12. New York, International Universities Press, 1964.

55. Klingman, T. Physical signs in schizophrenia, Am. J. Psychiat., 103: 69-71, July, 1946.

56. Kringlen, E. Norway twin study links schizophrenia to milieu, Medical Tribune, 8: 43, April 17, 1967.

57. Lacey, J. The evaluation of autonomic responses: toward a general solution. Ann. N.Y. Acad. Sci. 1967, 123-164, 1956.

58. Lazarus, R. Psychological Stress and the Coping Process. New York, McGraw-Hill, 1966.

59. Levin, S. Toward a classification of external factors capable of inducing psychological stress. Int. J. Psycho-Anal. 47: 546-551, 1966.

60. Nass, M. The superego and moral development in the theories of Freud and Piaget. *In* The Psychoanalytic Study of the Child, New York, International University Press, 21: 51-68, 1966.

61. NIMH Mental Health Monograph 4, Research in schizophrenia, April, 1964.

61a. Oken, D.: Vietnam therapy: treatment for the mentally ill. Letter to the editor, Science, Vol. 160, June 14, 1968.

61b. Ostow, M. Drugs in Psychoanalysis, New York, Basic Books, Inc., 1962.

61c. Pauling, L.: Orthomolecular psychiatry. Science, April 19, 1968.

62. Pollin, W., and Stabenau, J. Monitoring Childbirth, Newsweek, February 6, 1967, p. 84.

62a. Pollin, W., and Stabenau, J. Early Characteristics of Monozygotic Twins Discordant for Schizophrenia, Arch. Gen. Psychiat. Vol. 17, December, 1967, pp. 723-732.

63. Prelinger, E., and Zimet, C. An Ego Psychological Approach to Character Assessment. London, The Free Press of Glencoe, 1964.

64. Rangell, L. Some comments on psychoanalytic nosology: with recommendations for improvement. In Schur, M., (Ed.) Drives, Affects, Behavior: Vol. 2. New York, International Universities Press, 1965, pp. 128-160.

65. Rapaport, D., Gill, M., and Schafer, R. (Eds.) Diagnostic Psychological Testing, Vol. 1 and 2. Chicago, Year Book, 1946.

66. Rapaport, D. The Development and the Concepts of Psychoanalytic Ego Psychology. Twelve seminars given at the Western New England Institute for Psychoanalysis. Miller, S. (Ed.) Mimeographed ms., 1955.

67. Rapaport, D. An historical survey of psychoanalytic ego psychology. In Identity and the Life Cycle: Selected Papers, E. Erickson. Psychological Issues, Monograph 1. New York, International Universities Press, 1959.

68. Rapaport, D. A theoretical analysis of the superego concept. In Gill, M., (Ed.) The Collected Papers of David Rapaport, New York, Basic Books, 1967.

68a. Roman, J. (Ed.): Origin of Schizophrenia. Proceedings of the First Rochester International Conference on Schizophrenia, March 29-31, 1967. International Congress Series #151, New York, Excerpta Medica Foundation.

69. Roessler, R., Greenfield, M., Alexander, A. Ego strength and response stereotypy: Psychophysiology, 1: 142-150, 1964.

69a. Rosen, John, Direct Psychoanalytic Psychiatry, New York, Grune & Stratton, 1962.

69b. Rosenfeld, H. Notes on the psychopathology and psychoanalytic treatment of schizophrenia. In Azima, H., Glueck, M., Jr., (Eds.) Psychotherapy of schizophrenic and manic depressive states, Psychiat. Research Reports #17: 1963, American Psychiat. Assoc.

70. Rosenthal, D. In Heredity and Schizophrenia, Crosscurrents of Psychiatric Thought, Roche Laboratories, 1967.

71. Rosenthal, D. (Ed.) The Genain Quadruplets. New York, Basic Books, 1963.

72. Rosenthal, D., Kety, S., and Wender, P. Studies link adoptees' heredity, prenatal life to schizophrenia, Psychiat. News, August, 1967, p. 23.

73. Schlesinger, H. Cognitive attitudes in relation to susceptibility to interference. J. Personality, 22: 354-374, 1954.

74. Schur, M. The Id and the Regulatory Principles of Mental Functioning, New York, International Universities Press, 1966.

74a. Searles, H. Collected Papers on Schizophrenia and Related Subjects, New York, International Universities Press, 1965.

75. Sears, R. A survey of objective studies of psychoanalytic concepts. A report prepared for the Committee on Social Adjustment, New York, Social Science Research Council, 1943.

75a. Sechehaye, M. Principles and methods of symbolic realization, In Azima, H., and Glueck, B., Jr. (Eds.), Psychotherapy of schizophrenic and manic depressive states, Psychiat. Research Reports #17, 1963, American Psychiat. Assoc.

76. Shevrin, H., and Luborsky, L. The measurement of preconscious perception in dreams and images: an investigation of the Poetzl Phenomenon. J. Abnor. Social Psychol. 56: 285-294, 1958.

76a. Simon, J. The paradoxical effect of

effort, Brit. J. Med. Psychol. 40: 375, 1967.

77. Solomon, P., Kubzansky, P., Leiderman, P., Mendelson, J., Trumbull, R., and Wexler, D. (Eds.) Sensory Deprivation. Cambridge, Harvard University Press, 1961.

77a. Spence, D. (Ed.) The Broad Scope of Psychoanalysis: Selected Papers of Leopold Bellak, New York, Grune & Stratton, 1967.

78. Spitz, R. Anaclitic depression, an inquiry into the genesis of psychiatric conditions in early childhood. In The Psychoanalytic Study of the Child, New York, International Universities Press, 2: 1946.

79. Stein, M. Self observation, reality, and the superego. In Loewenstein, R., Neuman, L., Schur, M., and Solnit, A. (Ed.) Psychoanalysis—A General Psychology: Essays in Honor of Heinz Hartmann. New York, International Universities Press, pp. 275-297, 1966.

80. Tienari, P. Psychiatric Illnesses in Identical Twins. Acta Psychiat. Scand. Supp. 171, Vol. 39, Munksgaard, 1963.

81. Weiner, H. Some thoughts on the concept of primary autonomous ego functions. In Loewenstein, R., Neuman, L., Schur, M., and Solnit, A. (Eds.) Psychoanalysis—A General Psychology: Essays in Honor of Heinz Hartmann. New York, International Universities Press, pp. 583-600, 1966.

82. Zahn, T., and Rosenthal, D. Preparatory set in acute schizophrenia, J. Nerv. Ment. Dis., 141: pp. 352-358, 1965.

3

Vital Statistics

STANLEY F. YOLLES, M.D. and MORTON KRAMER, Sc.D

Doctor Yolles is Director of the National Institute of Mental Health and its far-flung activities. NIMH is the single largest of all the Institutes of Health. This was recently recognized when the NIMH was made an independent and separate bureau.

Dr. Yolles received his M.D. degree from New York University, an M.A. degree from Harvard University and an M.P.H. degree from the Johns Hopkins University. First entering the medical profession as a parasitologist in tropical medicine, Dr. Yolles later turned to psychiatry as a medical specialty. He was commissioned in the U.S. Public Health Service in 1950 and appointed Director of the NIMH in 1964.

He is a Fellow of the American Psychiatric Association, the American Public Health Association and the American College of Psychiatrists, and is a member of many professional organizations. He is also a Clinical Professor of Psychiatry at George Washington University, and a member of the National Advisory Committee in Neurology and Psychiatry to the V.A.

Dr. Kramer is Chief of the Office of Biometry of the National Institute of Mental Health.

He received an A.B. degree from the Johns Hopkins University College of Arts and Sciences in 1934 and a Doctor of Science in Hygiene (Biostatistics) from the Johns Hopkins School of Hygiene and Public Health in 1939.

Dr. Kramer has served as Statistician in the New York State Department of Health, in the Department of Health of Puerto Rico and in the Office of the Controller of Tuberculosis of Cuyahoga County, Ohio. He joined the staff of the National Institute of Mental Health in 1948. He has been a member of the Expert Panel on Health Statistics of the World Health Organization since 1959 and serves as a Consultant to the Mental Health Unit of the World Health Organization.

Dr. Kramer has written extensively on the application of biostatistical and epidemiologic methods to research on the prevention and control of mental disorders.

The vital statistics of a mental disorder—or to use a more appropriate phrase, its descriptive epidemiology—should provide systematic data on variations in its incidence, duration and prevalence from time to time and place to place by such factors as age, sex, race, marital status, occupation, residence, and a variety of other demographic, social and economic variables. Such an ideal state of affairs does not exist for schizophrenia, or, for that matter, for any of the mental disorders. The major impediments to achieving it have been the absence of a standard case finding technic that can be used in a uniform

66

and consistent fashion to detect persons in the general population with mental disorder and differential diagnostic technics to make it possible to assign each case to a specific diagnostic category with a high degree of reliability. As Frost stated in a classic paper on epidemiology published in 1927:[40]

". . . since the description of the distribution of any disease in a population obviously requires that the disease must be recognized when it occurs, the development of epidemiology must follow and be limited by that of clinical diagnosis and of the rather complex machinery required for the systematic collection of morbidity and morality statistics."

As a result, no health agency has as yet developed a mechanism for the systematic collection of morbidity data on the mental disorders which can be used to provide reliable current estimates of the total incidence and prevalence of these disorders in the population of a state, city, county or other geographic subdivision. However, data derived from a limited number of community surveys in different countries and from records of patients admitted to psychiatric facilities throughout the world, have established the serious nature of schizophrenia as a public health problem. Indeed, the systematic data derived from the records of patients admitted to mental hospitals in the United States and other countries with large mental hospital systems provide a first approximation to a descriptive epidemiology of schizophrenia.

This chapter summarizes some of the essential features of prevalence and incidence studies of schizophrenia carried out to date and the problems that must be solved in order to provide comparable morbidity data on this major mental disorder within and among countries. It will also provide salient facts concerning patterns of usage of mental hospitals and other psychiatric facilities by schizophrenics, both in the United States and elsewhere, specific for age, sex, and other demographic factors and the implications of these facts for clinical and field research and for current efforts to improve programs of care, treatment and rehabilitation for psychotics. A brief review of the morbidity rates used in the analysis of survey and institutional data may clarify the meanings of the various rates and highlight the differences between true morbidity data and medical care data.

COMMUNITY SURVEYS

Morbidity Rates

Two basic morbidity indices are used in epidemiologic studies of disease—the prevalence rate and the incidence rate.[66,86,117] *Prevalence* is defined as the total number of cases of a disease present in a defined population group as of a specific moment in time (point prevalence). Thus, the point prevalence rate is the ratio of a number of cases of a disease in a defined population as of a given date to the number of people in that population. Another measure of prevalence is the number of cases present in a population during a specific interval of time, that is the number of cases at the beginning of the interval of observation plus the number of new ones added during it (interval prevalence). *Incidence* is defined as the number of new cases of disease occurring in a specific population during a given interval of time (e.g., one year). The incidence rate is the ratio of the number of "new" cases of the disease occurring in the time interval to the population exposed to the risk of developing the disease. Prevalence and incidence rates may be made specific for such variables as age, sex, geographic area, socioeconomic status, and marital status.

In establishing either incidence or prevalence rates, the definition of what is to be counted as a case is of crucial importance. Thus, in determining the point prevalence of a disease, it is important to specify whether persons to be counted as cases are only those who are ill as of the survey date (active cases), or whether the count should include persons who have ever had a history of an illness (i.e., the cases currently ill plus those who were ill, recovered and are still alive). In determining incidence, the crucial issues are the definition of "new" (as, for example, the first or initial attack of a disease during an individual's lifetime) and the ability to establish the date of onset with sufficient accuracy so that a determination can be made as to whether the onset occurred during the interval being studied or earlier.

Prevalence is a function of the incidence of disease and its duration. Thus, a disease may have a low incidence, but, because of a long duration, a high prevalence. On the other hand, a disease may have a high incidence, but, because of a short duration, a low prevalence. Two diseases may have quite different incidence rates, but their prevalence may be identical because of the differences in duration, or the incidence of the same disease in two separate population groups may be identical but its prevalence quite different because of differences between the populations in the interaction of various biologic, therapeutic, health, socioeconomic, attitudinal and cultural factors that determine whether the duration of a disease is long or short.

Patient data generated by reporting programs on characteristics of patients admitted to psychiatric facilities, particularly to mental hospitals, have been used extensively for administrative and planning purposes and also for various epidemiologic, statistical and sociologic studies dealing with the more serious mental disorders.[4] The rates and ratios used to analyze the population dynamics of these institutions embody epidemiologic concepts. Thus, the number and rate of new (or first) admissions to a facility and the number and rate of patients in an institution as of a given day are modeled after the incidence and prevalence rates previously described. A disorder with a low admission rate but long duration of stay may account for a higher proportion of the resident population as of a given day than a disorder with a high admission rate but short duration of stay. Data describing patient flow have been analyzed by life table methods to determine retention, release and mortality rates.[70] However, such data derived from psychiatric facilities are medical care data, and, as such, provide information only on that portion of the universe of persons with mental disorders who come in contact with the defined set of facilities. In this regard, they have considerable limitations in providing estimates of true incidence and prevalence of mental disorders.

Prevalence Surveys:

A number of surveys of mental disorders carried out in Europe,[9,11,18,19,35,57,61,92,123,127] in Asia,[1,79,131,136,145] and in the United States[22,31,52,77,120] have reported a variety of prevalence rates for schizophrenics. Many problems arise in comparing the results shown in Table 1. These occur not only from lack of comparability in diagnostic and classification criteria and methods mentioned earlier, but from the varying definitions of a case and differences in case finding methods.[37] Other sources of difficulty arise from the selection of the population used in the computation of rates, differences in the composition of the study population by age and other demographic characteristics and the types of rates computed.[30,78,80,111]

A review of the details of the above studies emphasizes the different meanings of the reported rates (Table 1). For example, the European studies and those in Japan and Formosa usually determined the proportion of a population alive as of a given date that had ever had an attack of schizophrenia (i.e., active plus inactive cases). The case finding in these studies involved intensive investigation of whole populations. For example, case finding in Formosa was carried out through review of written records obtained from institutions and agencies, reports from various key informants in the community, psychiatric interviews by members of the survey teams with the entire population of each of three areas that were studied, and a confirmatory evaluation of all suspected cases by the principal investigator.[79] The Baltimore studies of 1933 and 1936 described the proportion of a population known to have active disease during the survey year on the books of institutions and agencies (medical, public health, social, welfare, correctional, legal and educational) that dealt with various types of mental health problems.[22,77] Even in these surveys the universe of agencies was not identical. The New Haven survey determined the proportion of the population of New Haven known to be under treatment with a psychiatrist, psychiatric hospital or clinic during a six month period.[52] The Baltimore and New Haven surveys thus involved studies of reports of patients and their case records, but no actual examination of patients by the survey team. In addition, the New Haven study included cases in treatment with private psychiatrists while the Baltimore surveys did not.

Dunham's comments underscore the basic difficulties encountered in comparing results:[30]

". . . The determination as to whether one country or area has a prevalence rate for total psychoses or for schizophrenia which differs significantly from similar rates in another section is, generally speaking, impossible. Some epi-

Table 1.—Prevalence Rates for All Psychoses and Schizophrenia Reported in Selected North American, European and Asiatic Surveys

Country	Investigator(s)	Date of Investigation	Size of Population Studied	Case Finding Method*	Type of Prevalence Measure†	Prevalence Rate per 1000 Total Population All Psychoses	Schizophrenia
EUROPE							
Germany							
Thuringia	Brugger[19]	1929	37,561	1, 2, 3, 4, 6	lifetime	3.8	1.9
Bavaria	Brugger[18]	1930-31	8,628	5	lifetime	5.6	2.5
Denmark							
Bornholm	Strömgren[127]	1935	45,930	1, 2, 3, 4, 6	lifetime	10.9	3.3
Finland							
S.F.B.	Kaila[61]	1936	418,472	1, 2, 6	lifetime	6.0	4.2
Norway							
West Coast Village	Bremer[11]	1939-1944	1,325	1, 2, 5	lifetime	14.3	4.5
Sweden							
A:bo	Sjogren[123]	1944	8,736	1, 2, 6	lifetime	9.8	4.6
North Sweden	Böök[9]	1946-49	8,981	1, 2, 4	lifetime	11.8	9.5
Rural Sweden	Essen-Möller[35]	1947	2,550	5	lifetime	23.5	6.7
Czechoslovakia							
Prague 8	Ivanys, Drdkova, Vana[57]	1960	66,165‖	1, 2, 6	period¶	6.1‖	1.7‖
Scotland	Mayer-Gross[92]	1948	56,000	1, 2, 4	lifetime	16.0	4.2
ASIA							
Japan							
Hashijo	Uchimura et al.[136]	1940	8,330	1, 2, 6	lifetime	6.2	3.8
Komoro	Akimoto et al.[1]	1941	5,207	1, 2, 5	lifetime	8.5	2.1
Tokyo	Tsuwaga[131]	1941	2,712	1, 2, 5	lifetime	9.2	2.2

Table 1.—Prevalence Rates for All Psychoses and Schizophrenia Reported in Selected North American, European and Asiatic Surveys

Country	Investigator(s)	Date of Investigation	Size of Population Studied	Case Finding Method*	Type of Prevalence Measure†	Prevalence Rate per 1000 Total Population	
						All Psychoses	Schizophrenia
Formosa	Lin[79]	1946-48	19,931	1, 2, 5, 6	lifetime	3.8	2.1
Korea	Yoo[145]	1956-60	11,974	1, 2, 5, 6	lifetime	7.8	3.8
NORTH AMERICA							
Baltimore	Cohen and Fairbank[22]	1933	56,044	1, 2	period‡	6.0	2.3
Baltimore	Lemkau et al.[77]	1936	57,002	1, 2	period‡	6.5	2.9
Tennessee, rural	Roth and Luton[120]	1938-40	24,804	1, 2, 3, 4, 6	lifetime	6.4	1.9
New Haven	Hollingshead and Redlich[52]	1950	236,940	1, 2, 3	period§	6.1	3.6
Canada, North and South Dakota	Eaton and Weil[31]	1951	8,542	4, 5	lifetime	6.2	1.0

‡ One year period
§ Six month period
‖ Per 1000 population aged 15 and over
¶ Five year period
*Method of case finding
1—Hospital records
2—Outpatient clinic and/or other agency records
3—Private psychiatrist and/or physician records
4—Population survey through informants
5—Population survey through household interviews
6—Verification through review by a psychiatrist of all or a sample of suspected cases

†Type of Prevalence Measure
Lifetime: The number of active and inactive cases discovered through the specified case finding methods alive as of the survey date per 1000 population

Period: The number of active cases discovered through the specified case finding methods that were active on the books of the specified agencies at some time during the study interval per 1000 population

demiological investigators have contended that a carefully worked out prevalence rate will be the best measure of mental illness that we can secure at this time because it is practically impossible to determine when a given disease began and this information is essential for the computation of an incidence rate. In other words, while an investigator cannot determine when, say, the schizophrenic illness began, he can determine if the person is sick at a given time. This argument is frequently heard more often in the United States than in Europe because there the investigators often assume that there can be no full and complete recovery from a functional psychosis. Consequently, in their surveys they tend to count all cases that have ever been sick with the disease, even though the person may be free of symptoms at the time of the survey. This method of counting is an added difficulty in the attempt to make any comparison between prevalence rates in Europe with those reported for the United States."

Dunham points out that the variability among reported prevalence rates for schizophrenia is much less than among rates for total psychosis.[30] On the basis of this, he argues that "there is much greater agreement among investigators in defining schizophrenia and less agreement among them when attempting to count all cases of mental disorder." Greater agreement in prevalence rates does not necessarily mean that there is greater agreement in diagnostic criteria. It is possible for a disease to show wide variation in prevalence rates even when there is a good prior agreement on diagnostic criteria. Since prevalence is a function of incidence and duration, variation in prevalence rates can be the result of differences in incidence and duration. As mentioned earlier, differences between countries in methods of treatment and care, health status of a population, socioeconomic, attitudinal and cultural factors may account for differential duration of a disease. For example, differences in survivorship rates for persons with psychosis is a factor that must be considered. Differences between countries in the mortality rates for psychotics and the rest of the population, as well as differences in rates of change in these rates over the period of time when these studies were carried out (1929-60 in Europe, 1940-60 in Asia, and 1933-51 in the United States), can also account for differences in the prevalence rates for psychosis and schizophrenia reported in these studies. For example, the mortality rates from tuberculosis, once the primary cause of death among schizophrenics, showed considerable worldwide variation during the period of time over which the various surveys were done.[62,89,129]

Despite the problems that make precise comparisons of the prevalence rates of schizophrenia impossible, the data in Table 1 underscore its worldwide seriousness as a public health problem. The European and Asian studies uniformly demonstrate that a sizeable proportion of a population alive as of a given moment in time has had an attack of a disorder which competent research workers in each country have called schizophrenia. The proportion ranges from 1.7 per 1,000 to 9.5 per 1,000, depending on the intensity of the case finding method and other characteristics of the population studied. The studies from North America emphasize that schizophrenia presents a major problem to mental hospitals, other psychiatric services and social agencies. And in every location where prevalence studies have been done, regardless of method, the cases designated as schizophrenia constitute a sizeable proportion of all psychoses. In the 20 studies reviewed, the reported schizophrenia rate accounted for more than 40 per cent of the rate for all psychoses in ten studies, between 25 and 40 per cent in seven, and less than 25 per cent in only three.

Further progress in research on the epidemiology and other aspects of schizophrenia is dependent upon improvement in diagnostic practice. As stated by a World Health Organization Study Group on Schizophrenia:[144]

"Some psychiatrists, preoccupied for clinical reasons with the dynamic interpretation of the schizophrenic illness, consider diagnosis of little consequence. We do not share this view, holding that for clinical and especially therapeutic purposes, and still more for the purpose of further study and fuller knowledge, sound classification is as essential as in other medical and scientific fields."

Several recent reviews emphasize the multiplicity of interpretations and theories regarding the etiology of schizophrenia. As stated by Knox and Tierney:[64]

". . . The many theories regarding this disorder range from the exclusively psychodynamic to the metabolic-genetic with vigorous adherents of both viewpoints."

Mishler and Scotch also underscore this problem.[94] They state:

"Each year innumerable research reports, reviews, and conceptual analyses appear. They represent a variety of points of view and present diverse types of data, reflecting a wide range of authors that includes psychiatrists, epidemiologists, psychologists, sociologists, anthropologists, and biological scientists. Despite this intensive effort and an increasing amount of interest in recent years, schizophrenia remains an illness about which there is little definite or reliable knowledge."

It is not the purpose of this chapter to deal with the details of the diagnostic and etiologic issues, and the reader is referred to the previously mentioned reviews and to the other chapters in this book that deal with these subjects. They are mentioned here because the disagreement and confusion with respect to theories of etiology carry over into clinical practice. As a result of adherence to different points of view, clinicians are not consistent in the way they use the diagnosis "schizophrenia" to characterize patients seen in their patient populations.[5,72,107] This, in turn, leads to difficulties in interpreting and comparing findings in epidemiologic studies and in statistical series describing trends in admission rates to psychiatric facilities as well as in attempts to evaluate the effect of specific therapies and therapeutic programs on the course of the disorder.

The World Health Organization is undertaking a long term research program which, hopefully, will lead to eventual resolution of some of these problems. Its Mental Health Unit is undertaking a pilot study of schizophrenia designed to devise standard instruments and procedures for case finding of schizophrenics in eight selected countries. If these efforts prove successful, it may eventually be possible to design and implement a series of studies to provide comparable prevalence data within and between countries.[142]

Incidence Surveys:

Attempts have also been made to determine the incidence of schizophrenia. All of the problems of case finding and differential diagnosis already mentioned also plague these studies. In addition, incidence studies require the investigator to determine date of onset of the disease. Thus, the psychiatrist faces the difficult task of evaluating data made available to him by the patient, members of his family and the significant others in the patient's life to establish this date.

Ideally, prospective studies of defined population groups are needed to establish incidence figures. But such studies are expensive and time-consuming. They require periodic examination of members of the study population, with standard methods for systematic and uniform clinical examinations and collection and evaluation of data on the person's life history, family relationships, marital adjustment, occupational history, participation in community activities, and related areas so as to gather the facts needed to determine date of onset with reasonable accuracy.

An approximation to this method of study was used by Fremming[38] in a survey of the incidence of mental disorders on the island of Bornholm. He established a register of 5,697 persons born on that island during the years 1883-1887 and traced every person (with the exception of 40 who migrated to Sweden or the United States) through personal visits to their homes, physicians, hospitals, relatives, friends, etc. In this way, he gathered the data necessary to establish the presence or absence of mental disorder and the specific diagnosis. Of the 4,130 such persons who survived to ten years of age, 34 were determined to have developed schizophrenia before reaching the age of 60 (.82 per cent). Fremming states that the major disadvantage of the method is that:

> "The results do not mirror strictly contemporary events; they express not so much the hazards of today as those of the past half century. The child born in 1950 will probably live longer and in a different cultural climate from his grandfather born in 1885, 65 years ago."

A more commonly used method for determining incidence is to determine the proportion of a population that has first contact with any one of a defined set of psychiatric facilities in a community. This is an extension of the notion of a first admission to a mental hospital to a broadened universe of psychiatric services, e.g., public and private mental hospitals, Veterans Administration hospitals, outpatient clinics, psychiatric services in a general hospital, private psychiatrist. This concept contains several underlying notions. Although it is impossible to establish with certainty the date of onset of a mental disorder (e.g., schizophrenia), it is possible to establish accurately the date of first contact with a facility. Also, the larger the network of facilities, the greater is the probability of a patient coming in contact with a psychiatric service, particularly when the patient has a serious illness. The major problems surrounding these concepts are variations in the number and types of psychiatric services available to the residents of an area, the extent to which all cases of a disorder will be admitted to a psychiatric service, and the time lag between actual date of onset and date of first contact.

It is difficult, if not impossible, in our present state of knowledge to determine precisely what proportion of schizophrenics are never admitted to a psychiatric service. Dunham[30] voices the opinion that in western society:

". . . while persons in some diagnostic groups may succeed in avoiding treatment, we think that this is much less likely with respect to the schizophrenic disorder and would hold that much of the evidence inferentially supports this position."

He further contends that every schizophrenic is admitted to a hospital eventually. His evidence is derived from a thorough check of all patients who were residents of two communities of contrasting social structure in Detroit, and were admitted to all public and private mental hospitals, general hospitals, outpatient clinics, diagnostic centers or private psychiatrists in the period 1956-1968. This procedure involved screening 500,000 psychiatric records of 45 hospitals and clinics and 131 private psychiatrists and standard psychiatric examinations of all cases that could be located. It yielded 3,086 individual patients, residents of the two study areas, of whom 490 were diagnosed schizophrenic. About 87 per cent of the schizophrenics were picked up in hospitals, as compared to about 55 per cent of the other cases. Of the schizophrenic cases, 76 per cent of the cases reported by private psychiatrists had already been in one of the hospitals, while the corresponding proportion for nonschizophrenics was only 22 per cent.

The time gap between appearance of first symptoms and entrance into a state hospital remains a problem. Dunham found that the median time gap was 20 months. The gap tended to increase with advancing age and was higher for males than females. For approximations of incidence in broad age groups, a time gap of this order is not too serious. However, the assumption that all schizophrenics are eventually admitted to a hospital does require further testing to determine whether this would be true in all types of population groups, rural as well as urban and varying levels of socioeconomic status. Studies are required that combine case finding in the general population and follow-up studies to determine the various treatment pathways experienced by patients. Other studies are needed to assess the effect of the extensive

Table 2.—Incidence Rates for Schizophrenia in Selected Surveys in the United States

Investigator	Date	Place	Population*	Definition of Incidence	Rate per 1,000 Population All Ages	15+	15-64
Faris and Dunham[36]	1922-34	Chicago	2,424,331	Average annual number of first admissions to public and private mental hospitals	X	X	.33
Cohen and Fairbank[22]	1933	Baltimore	40,565	Annual, as above	X	.47	X
Lemkau, et al.[77]	1933-39	Baltimore	42,216	Average annual, as above	X	.36	X
Malzberg[88]	1949-1951	New York State	14,830,192‡	Average annual, as above	.38	.48	.53
Clausen and Kohn[21]	1940-1952	Hagerstown	50,596	Average annual, as above	X	X	.19
Hollingshead and Redlich[62]	1950	New Haven	174,300	Annual† number of persons first admitted to a state, private, VA hospital, other public or private psychiatric service or private psychiatrist	X	.30	X
Dunham[30]	1958	Detroit Cass (high rate area)	37,512	Annual, as above	X	1.20	X
		Conner-Burbank (low rate area)	53,506	Annual, as above	X	.45	X

Table 2.—Incidence Rates for Schizophrenia in Selected Surveys in the United States

Investigator	Date	Place	Population*	Definition of Incidence	Rate per 1,000 Population		
					All Ages	15+	15-64
Jaco[88]	1951-1952	Texas	5,464,418	Average annual number of persons who sought treatment for first time from private psychiatrist, state, city, county, VA hospital, or teaching hospital	X	.35	X
Pollack et al.[113]	1960	Maryland	3,100,689‡	Annual number of persons first admitted to state or private mental hospital, VA hospital, psychiatric service of general hospital or outpatient psychiatric clinic	.48	.63	.70
	1960	Louisiana	3,257,022‡	Annual, as above	.43	.57	.63
Locke and Duvall[88]	1960	Ohio	5,730,734	Average annual, as above	X	X	.52
Warthen et al.[139]	1963	Maryland	3,227,000	Annual number of new cases reported to psychiatric register during its third year of operation (mental hospital, psychiatric service in general hospitals and outpatient clinics)	.50	X	X

*Population figures correspond to the age groups for which rates are shown unless otherwise noted
†Annual number of persons admitted was estimated by doubling the number observed over a six month interval in The Hollingshead and Redlich study. In the Dunham and Jaco studies, the actual number of first admissions for a year was observed.
‡Population of all ages.

networks of community care that are currently developing and of psychiatric insurance programs on patterns of use of psychiatric services.

Table 2 presents a summary of 12 incidence studies of schizophrenia that have been done in the United States covering the period 1924 to 1963 and using definitions of new cases that include more than patients first admitted to a state mental hospital.[21,22,30,36,52,58,77,83,88,113,139] The cases included are first admissions with a diagnosis of schizophrenia to a universe of psychiatric facilities consisting of state hospitals *plus* one or more of the following: VA neuropsychiatric hospitals, private mental hospitals, psychiatric service in a general hospital, outpatient psychiatric clinic or private psychiatrist.

An estimate of a minimum incidence rate for schizophrenia of 50 per 100,000 population has appeared frequently in the literature.[76] Although these data would tend to support an estimate of this level, the actual rate that would be found in any population is determined by the level of the age specific rates and the age distribution of the population as well as the level of the rates in various socioeconomic subgroups and the relative proportion of such groups in the total population. The reported data are primarily institutional and weighted with cases in the age group 15-64 years. The very intensive screening in a high risk area in Detroit revealed a rate of 120 per 100,000 15 years and over as compared to 45 per 100,000 in a low risk area. The maximum rate in the high risk area was 256 per 100,000 in the age group 30-39 years and, in the low risk area, 121. Data from studies done in Maryland,[113] Louisiana[113] and Ohio[83] using comparable methods of case finding for all public and private mental hospitals, general hospitals and outpatient clinics, also demonstrate considerable variation in the incidence rate not only by age, but also by race and place of residence. The highest rates reported were in the nonwhite population. Rates in excess of 100 per 100,000 were reported for nonwhite females in the age groups 15-24 years (185.0, Maryland; 108.7, Louisiana, 119.3, Ohio) and in the age groups 25-34 years (157.9, Maryland; 115.6, Louisiana; 218.3, Ohio). Rates of that level were reported for nonwhite males in the age groups 15-24 (101.2, Maryland; 148.5 Ohio), 25-34 years (157.3, Maryland; 153.2 Ohio) and 35-44 (198.4, Maryland). Thus, allowing for under-enumeration, it is possible to have rates in some age-sex-population groups that would exceed 300 per 100,000.

The implications of incidence rates of the order that have been reported in the Detroit studies and in those from Louisiana, Maryland and Ohio are considerable. If the age specific rates from the high risk area in Detroit applied to a cohort of births subjected throughout their lifetime to the mortality rates that existed in the United States during 1960, approximately six per cent of all such children who would reach the age of 15 years would develop schizophrenia during their subsequent lifetime. If the rates from the low risk area applied, the corresponding probability would be two per cent. In a population subjected to an estimated minimum incidence rate of 50 per

100,000 in all age groups and to the 1960 U.S. mortality rates, about *three per cent of the children reaching age 15 years would develop schizophrenia during their subsequent lifetime.*

PATTERNS OF USE OF PSYCHIATRIC FACILITIES

There is considerable variation in the completeness of reporting and the types of data available from the various categories of psychiatric facilities in the United States. At the national level reporting from the public mental hospitals has been relatively complete over the years and adequate time series are available on the patterns of use by age, sex and diagnosis. The National Institute of Mental Health has worked closely with the state mental hospital systems to develop standard definitions of patient movement categories and specifications for minimum tabulations.[65,97] It has also carried out special studies to provide additional data by various socioeconomic variables for first admission and resident patient rates and for measures of patient flow. The NIMH has also worked closely with the state mental health authorities over the years to develop clinic reporting and as a result all states now have such programs for their outpatient clinics. Although data on patient movement in outpatient clinics have been reasonably complete, the same was not true for diagnostic data by age and sex. The situation has now improved and it is possible to obtain reasonably complete data on the patient population by age, sex and diagnosis. The major types of psychiatric facilities for which it has been difficult to obtain satisfactory coverage are the private mental hospitals,

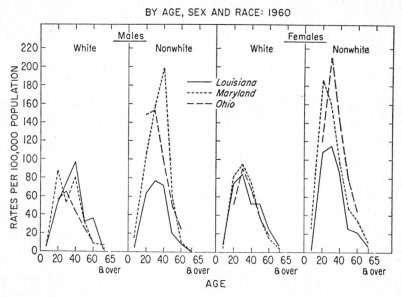

Fig. 1.—Schizophrenic first admission rates per 100,000 population to psychiatric facilities in Louisiana, Maryland, and Ohio, by age, sex, and race: 1960

psychiatric services in general hospitals and private psychiatrists. However, special studies have been carried out in several localities in relation to these facilities.[42,44]

In addition to the above, extensive psychiatric case registers have been developed in two areas[7,43] These provide systematic reporting on an individual patient basis from a broad universe of psychiatric facilities. These registers link reports of individuals over all episodes of care in the various reporting facilities, and thus make it possible to develop a longitudinal record for each individual patient, a procedure that is impractical at the national level.

Consistency of Diagnosis and Classification of Mental Disorders

As already indicated, a major problem in developing a descriptive epidemiology of mental disorders is that related to consistent use of diagnostic criteria and clinical terminology over time by psychiatrists within and between countries.[126] In an attempt to bring greater uniformity into the use of diagnostic criteria and terminology in the United States, the American Psychiatric Association issued its Diagnostic and Statistical Manual in 1952.[2] The diagnostic classification in this manual is used widely in mental hospitals, outpatient clinics and other psychiatric facilities in the United States in recording diagnostic data in patients' records, in statistical reporting and in presentations of statistical tabulations on diagnosis in official published reports. The APA Classification of Mental Disorders also constitutes the Psychobiologic Unit of the Standard Nomenclature of Diseases,[110] which is used in all general hospitals in the United States for recording diagnostic data. Thus, the definitions in the APA Manual also provided basic criteria and guidelines for use in the general hospital psychiatric departments.

Many investigators have emphasized that the setting in which a psychiatric diagnosis is made, the orientation of the psychiatrist toward diagnosis and treatment of mental disorders and their social consequences, the prior psychiatric treatment experience, are major factors in the classification procedure.

An early study (1925-26) revealed that 70 per cent of 323 patients given a diagnosis of dementia praecox in the Boston Psychopathic Hospital also received the same diagnosis in other state hospitals.[32] Norris, using data collected in London between 1947-49, reported that 68 per cent of 1704 patients given a diagnosis of schizophrenia in the observation ward also received the same diagnosis when transferred to a mental hospital.[100]

Babigian et al. carried out a study in Monroe County, New York, which provides some indication of the consistency with which specified diagnostic terms are applied to patients by psychiatrists in the multiple agencies which report to the psychiatric case register.[5] The study population was derived from the 3,491 patients reported to the register during 1961 by private psychiatrists, an inpatient observation unit and the emergency unit of an out-patient department of a university hospital. Of these patients, 35 per cent had one or more episodes of psychiatric services subsequent to their initial one. In 79 per cent of these cases the diagnosis on second and subsequent contacts remained the same as that on the first contact. Chronic brain syndrome was the diagnostic category for which diagnostic consistency was the highest (92 per cent). For schizophrenia the corresponding figure was 70 per cent, and for affective psychosis, 40 per cent. The time interval between consecutive contacts did not affect materially these measures of consistency.

Sandifer et al. carried out a study in which ten diagnosticians, selected from three geographically separate mental hospitals in North Carolina, were asked to diagnose each of 91 first admissions to mental hospitals in the age group 15-59 years.[121] A psychiatric resident or staff physician presented to the diagnosticians a digest of the patient's present, past, and family history, pertinent physical and laboratory findings, mental status and hospital course. Following the presentation, the patient was interviewed by one of the diagnosticians, and the others were given an opportunity to question the patient. The time of presentation and interview ranged from 15 to 30 minutes. Immediately after each patient was seen, the observers privately and individually recorded a diagnosis. The data were analyzed to answer the following question: "If one diagnostician selects a category for a particular case, what is the likelihood that a second diagnostician will select the same diagnostic category?" For all categories combined, there was a 57 per cent chance that the second diagnostician would render the same diagnosis. For schizophrenia the corresponding proportion was 74 per cent and for mental deficiency, 73 per cent. These were the two most reliable categories.

Although the level of consistency reported in the above studies leaves much to be desired, no practical method exists for making adjustments in diagnostic data reported to a public health agency engaged in collection of diagnostic data from the variety of governmental and nongovernmental facilities that provide psychiatric services. The increased interest in evaluative, epidemiologic and biostatistical research on the mental disorders throughout the world has led to an upsurge of interest in development of diagnostic criteria and methods for the mental disorders capable of uniform application within and between countries.[56,141,142,143] As a result of the research and program efforts now under way, it is hoped that practical solutions to this complex problem will result in the not too distant future.[125,142,143]

The Over-all Picture

Schizophrenia constitutes a major problem of psychiatric care. In the United States schizophrenics accounted for one half, or 289,055 of the total patients resident in the State and County mental hospitals[133] and VA neuropsychiatric hospitals at the end of 1964,[137] and 32 per cent, or 13,044 of the total admissions to these hospitals during that year.[137] They also constitute almost 20 per cent of the annual admissions to private mental hospitals, and about the same per cent of those to the general hospitals with psychiatric services.[133] Currently about 15 per cent of all annual admissions to the 2,000 outpatient psychiatric clinics in the United States are schizophrenics.[135]

As a result of under-reporting and incomplete diagnostic data from general hospitals with psychiatric services and private mental hospitals, and multiple admissions of many schizophrenics to more than one type of facility per year, it is not possible to present a reliable national picture of comparative admission rates to various types of facilities for schizophrenia and other psychiatric disorders. However, it is possible to illustrate the relative levels of such rates, specific for diagnosis and type of facility, for the state of Maryland, where, through the use of a psychiatric case register, it has been possible to link reports of patients obtained from each of 120 psychiatric facilities that provide services to residents of that state. These include state, county and private mental hospitals, VA hospitals, general hospitals with psychiatric services and outpatient clinics (Table 3).

The total admission rate for schizophrenia in Maryland during fiscal 1963, based on an unduplicated count of patients, was 117 per 100,000 population. This rate was six and one-half times that for affective disorders (18.2), three and one-half times that for diseases of the senium (33.6), twice that for psychoneurotic depressive reactions (59.2), and 1.7 times that for alcoholic disorders (67.2).

Schizophrenia ranks first as the admission diagnosis to the state and county mental hospitals, and it is the primary psychotic admission diagnosis for the private mental hospitals and the general hospitals. The schizophrenia admission rate to the state hospitals (70 per 100,000) is 3.2 times that to the private hospitals (21.8) and 1.2 times that to the outpatient facilities (57.4). A high proportion of schizophrenics have episodes of care in more than one type of facility during a year. Of the 3,937 persons admitted to a Maryland facility during 1962, at least 1,083, or 28 per cent, were admitted to more than one type.

In terms of patients under care on a given day, the one day prevalence rate for schizophrenics was 227 per 100,000, as compared to 372 for all other diagnoses. Schizophrenics accounted for 38 per cent of all patients under care in all the reporting facilities, 47 per cent of those in the state and county mental hospitals, 66 per cent of those in the VA hospitals, 31 per cent of those in the private and general hospitals, and 23 per cent of those in the outpatient clinics. They also accounted for 40 per cent of all patients on long-term leave from the state hospitals not under care of any facility.

Detailed data such as above can also be obtained from a case register in operation in Monroe County, New York,[93] but are not available for every state because of the complexity of the machinery required to develop and

Table 3.—Age Adjusted Rates* per 100,000 Population of Patients Admitted to Care in Psychiatric Facilities July 1, 1962-June 30, 1963 and of Patients Under Care in Psychiatric Facilities on July 1, 1963 by Type of Facility and Selected Diagnoses: Maryland

Diagnosis	Total†	Type of Facility				
		State and County Mental Hospitals‡	Private Mental Hospitals, General Hospitals	Veterans Administration Hospital	Outpatient Psychiatric Clinics	Long Term Leave not under Clinic Care
ADMISSIONS JULY 1, 1962-JUNE 30, 1963						
All patients	546.0	228.4	92.0	9.7	296.5	
Schizophrenic reactions	116.8	69.7	17.1	4.8	57.4	
Affective disorders	18.2	8.7	6.4	.5	4.6	
Psychoneurotic depressive reaction	59.2	12.6	26.3	.9	25.2	
Diseases of the senium	33.6	29.0	3.7	.2	4.1	
Alcoholic disorders	67.2	53.2	9.2	.4	15.3	
All other diagnoses	201.3	48.9	17.6	2.7	155.7	
Undiagnosed	49.7	6.3	11.7	.2	34.2	
ONE-DAY PREVALENCE JULY 1, 1963						
All patients	599.2	279.9	26.6	25.6	202.1	65.0
Schizophrenic reactions	226.7	129.5	8.2	17.0	46.9	25.1
Affective disorders	24.2	13.1	2.0	.9	4.1	4.1
Psychoneurotic depressive reaction	21.2	5.1	2.8	.9	8.8	3.6
Diseases of the senium	53.3	40.8	4.3	.4	1.7	6.1
Alcoholic disorders	35.7	17.5	1.2	.5	6.5	10.0
All other diagnoses	174.9	71.6	6.4	5.4	76.0	15.5
Undiagnosed	63.2	2.3	1.7	.5	58.1	.6

*Adjusted to 1960 U.S. civilian population total age distribution.
†Total admission rate does not equal the sum of admission to all facilities because patients may be admitted to more than one facility.
‡Including returns from long term leave.

maintain a reporting system that includes all of the psychiatric services of a state. Although patterns of use and the availability of different types of services vary throughout the United States, the Maryland data serve to illustrate the seriousness of schizophrenia as a public health problem and the burden it places on our psychiatric facilities.

Use of Public Mental Hospitals

It is now generally accepted that first admission and resident patient rates for mental hospitals are of limited usefulness as measures of incidence and prevalence of mental disorders.[30,71] These rates are the resultant not only of the incidence of the mental disorders, but also a series of factors that determine the number of persons that are eventually admitted to public mental hospitals. Thus, in interpreting variations in admission rates to mental hospitals between and within areas, it is important to know how these hospitals are used by the various medical, social, and welfare agencies and by the private psychiatrists and general practitioners in the communities within the catchment area of these hospitals, the relationships that exist between the mental hospitals, psychiatric services in general hospitals, outpatient clinics, and other medical and social services; and the prevailing attitudes toward the mentally ill and the mental hospitals among the inhabitants of the communities which these hospitals serve.

Despite such limitations, first admission and resident patient rates are useful in defining major problems of disability associated with mental disorders and can provide much useful data for planning and developing community programs for their control.[4] They delineate population groups in which high rates of disability exist and pinpoint groups which should be singled out for special attention in the planning of community services. They also suggest important variables to be considered in searches for causes and effects of mental disorders *per se*,[3,23,28,46,49,85,90] as well as of institutionalization.[4,10,54] One of their most important uses at this time is to provide indicators of the impact of the expanding programs of community services on flow of patients into and out of the large state mental hospitals and on the age, sex, socioeconomic, and diagnostic composition of their patient populations.[68]

FIRST ADMISSIONS

Total Rate

The rate of first admissions to state and county mental hospitals (age adjusted) has remained at a fairly stable level during the last 16 years (Fig. 2). Between 1950 and 1961 the total rate showed only minor fluctuations around an average of 19.5 per 100,000. The average rate for males was 18.9 and that for females 20.1. As a result of a change in definition for first admissions in 1962, the rate has been lower since that date, but it still remains stable around a level of 16 per 100,000 for both males and females. The change in definition lowers the rate because it uniformly excludes persons with prior psychiatric experience in an inpatient unit of a general hospital from the universe of first admissions to state and county mental hospitals. Prior to this date state systems were not consistent in the way they classified the admission status of patients with prior episodes of care in psychiatric service of general hospitals.

There is also considerable variation among the states in the current level of the rate. Thus, in 1964 it varied from a high of 31.1 per 100,000 to a low of 3.7 with a median of 15.3.

Although the first admission rate has remained relatively stable, the proportion of schizophrenics among the first admissions has tended to decrease from about 23 per cent in 1950 and 1955 to 19 per cent in 1964. The lower

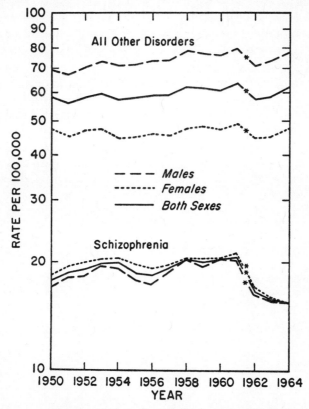

*Starting with 1962, the definition of first admissions was changed to admissions with no prior admission to any inpatient psychiatric facility.

Fig. 2.—Age adjusted first admission rates per 100,000 population to state and county mental hospitals for schizophrenia and all other disorders: United States: 1950-1964

Table 4.—Annual First Admissions and Resident Patients at End of Year by Selected Diagnoses: Number, Per Cent Distribution and Age Adjusted Rates, United States 1950, 1955 and 1964

DIAGNOSIS	First Admissions*			Resident Patients		
	1950	1955	1964	1950	1955	1964
	NUMBER					
All Mental Disorders	114,054	122,284	138,932	512,501	558,922	490,449
	PER CENT					
Brain Syndromes	38.7	32.5	23.2	26.3	24.8	22.8
Diseases of the Senium	25.9	24.2	17.1	12.4	13.2	12.5
Syphilitic	3.4	1.3	0.2	6.5	5.2	3.0
Other (excl. Alcoholism)	9.4	7.0	5.9	7.4	6.4	7.3
Functional Psychoses	34.4	32.3	26.3	58.2	59.6	58.8
Schizophrenic Reaction	23.3	23.3	19.0	45.3	47.9	50.1
Affective and Involutional	10.1	7.9	6.5	10.4	9.1	7.2
Other	1.0	1.1	0.8	2.5	2.6	1.5
Disorders Assoc. with						
Alcoholism	12.1	14.3	15.3	3.2	3.1	4.2
Brain Syndromes	4.5	5.2	4.5	2.2	2.2	3.0
Addiction	7.6	9.1	10.8	1.0	0.9	1.2
Psychoneurosis	5.0	5.4	11.3	1.1	1.0	1.6
Personality Disorders						
(excl. Alcohol.)	3.0	7.1	15.8	0.9	1.7	3.0
Mental Deficiency	3.6	3.1	2.9	9.4	8.5	8.4
All Other	3.2	5.3	5.2	0.9	1.3	1.2
	AGE ADJUSTED RATES†					
All Mental Disorders	76.0	76.8	77.3	341.2	344.3	262.1
Brain Syndromes	29.4	23.7	15.7	89.8	83.3	55.9
Diseases of the Senium	19.7	17.3	11.1	42.4	43.2	28.5
Syphilitic	2.6	1.0	0.1	22.2	17.8	7.7
Other (excl. Alcoholism)	7.1	5.4	4.5	25.2	22.3	19.7
Functional Psychoses	26.1	25.5	21.2	198.6	206.5	156.3
Schizophrenic Reaction	17.7	18.6	15.6	154.5	166.7	134.8
Affective and Involutional	7.6	6.0	5.0	35.5	30.8	17.9
Other	0.8	0.9	0.6	8.6	9.0	3.7
Disorders Assoc. with						
Alcoholism	9.2	11.0	12.3	10.9	10.6	10.9
Brain Syndromes	3.4	4.0	3.6	7.4	7.4	7.6
Addiction	5.8	7.0	8.7	3.5	3.2	3.2
Psychoneurosis	3.7	4.2	9.2	3.8	3.4	4.4
Personality Disorders						
(excl. Alcohol.)	2.3	5.8	12.6	3.0	6.2	8.2
Mental Deficiency	2.8	2.5	2.3	32.1	30.0	23.2
All Other	2.5	4.1	4.0	3.0	4.3	3.2

Source: *Patients in Mental Institutions,* Part II, 1950, 1955, 1964
State & County Mental Hospitals. U.S. DHEW, PHS, NIMH.
†U.S. 1950 civilian population was used as a standard.
*Beginning with 1962, the category of First Admissions was changed to Admissions with no prior psychiatric inpatient experience.

proportion reflects the increased numbers of patients with psychoneurosis and personality disorders admitted during this interval of time.

Rates by Age & Sex

The variations in the first admission rate for schizophrenics by age emphasize the high rate of disability this disorder causes in the productive middle years of life. Of the total first admissions during 1964, 53 per cent were between the ages of 25-44 years, while 27 per cent were less than 25 years of age, and 20 per cent were 45 years and older. The age specific rate rises from about one per 100,000 under 15 years to a maximum of 34 in the age group 25-34 years and declines steadily to 1.9 in the age group 65 years and over.

Both the shape of the age specific curve, and the magnitude of the rates have been remarkably stable over time. There have been no major changes in the rates within the various age groups, except for that under 15 years where between 1950 and 1964 the rate has at least doubled. This is most likely a reflection of the increased demand for inpatient psychiatric services for severely disturbed children and inadequate community facilities to meet the needs of these children. Figure 3 shows the relationship of the age specific first admission rates for schizophrenia to those for other types of disorders during 1964.

The total age adjusted rate for females is higher than that for males. In the

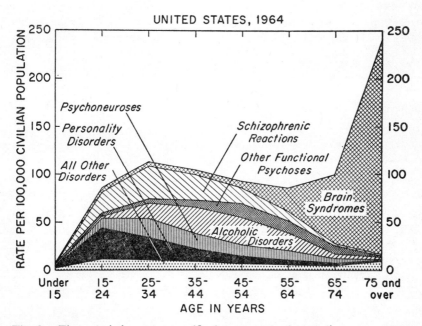

Fig. 3.—First admission rates specific for age and selected diagnoses, state and county mental hospitals, United States: 1964

individual age groups the male rates are the higher under 35 years of age. Above 35 years the female rates are the higher.

Rates by Other Factors

First admission rates by race, residence and marital status factors are not available for the entire United States. However, a collaborative study carried out by the NIMH in 1960 with 13 States* provided appropriate first admission data that could be used with the population data provided by the 1960 census for rate computation.[68]

Race: The age adjusted first admissions rate for schizophrenia for nonwhite males (40.0) and nonwhite females (47.7) were 2.6 times the corresponding white rates (15.5 for males and 18.1 for females). Excess nonwhite rates were found for all age groups except for that 65 years and over. This excess is in part a reflection of the lower socioeconomic status of nonwhites as compared to whites which in turn leads to higher rate of usage of public facilities by the nonwhites.

Place of Residence:

A comparison of schizophrenic admission rates for metropolitan counties (counties within the standard metropolitan statistical area)† with rates for nonmetropolitan counties in the 13 selected states previously mentioned demonstrated only moderately higher rates in metropolitan areas, and only below the age of 40. However, evaluation of the contribution of the person's place of residence to the risk of hospitalization for schizophrenia is dependent in part on the method of analysis.

Standard metropolitan areas are heterogeneous and comprise both the central city and outlying counties, including suburban and in some cases rural districts. A more useful ecologic comparison is the large central city with the suburban or rural areas. Hospital admission rates for schizophrenia derived from the Maryland psychiatric case register for Baltimore City by race and sex are generally about twice those of other parts of the State.[6] Rural county rates are slightly lower than the suburban rates but differences between these two areas were inconsistent. Nonwhite male rates showed the greatest dif-

---

*These States include Arkansas, California, Illinois, Kentucky, Louisiana, Michigan, Minnesota, New York, North Carolina, Ohio, Pennsylvania, Tennessee and Wisconsin.

†A standard metropolitan statistical area is defined by the U.S. Bureau of the Budget as county or group of contiguous counties containing at least one city of 50,000 inhabitants or more or twin cities with a combined population of at least 50,000. In addition to the county or counties containing such a city or cities, contiguous counties are included in a standard metropolitan statistical area if, according to certain criteria, they are essentially metropolitan in character and are socially and economically integrated with the central city.

ferentiation by residence with rates for rural counties considerably lower than those for the suburban.

The higher total schizophrenia admission rates for nonwhites as compared to whites referred to earlier is in part a reflection of the different geographic distribution of whites and nonwhites which is also related to socioeconomic status. Within the central city, the nonwhite rates are about the same or only slightly higher than the white. However, a much greater proportion of nonwhites than of whites live in the large central city where, as indicated, the hospital admission rates tend to be higher for both whites and nonwhites than in the more rural areas.

Studies by Census Tract within the large central cities focus still more precisely on place of residence and hospitalization rate. Recent ecologic studies of Baltimore[63] and Rochester[8] based on case registers have compared schizophrenic rates with the socioeconomic characteristic of the tract as well as with other indices of social disorganization and morbidity (tuberculosis and syphilis). In both cities, there is a relatively high association between overcrowding, poverty, ghetto living, crime and other aspects of the central city syndrome with high rates of schizophrenic admissions. As had been found earlier by Faris and Dunham in Chicago[36] the high level of association of schizophrenia and social pathology is not found for certain other disorders, such as affective disorders and psychoneuroses.

Possible factors that might account for both high schizophrenic rates and high social pathology in the central city include selective outmigration to the suburbs of the upper socioeconomic groups who tend to use private psychiatric facilities, immigration to the large city of persons from the rural south with subsequent dislocation, and immigration or retention in the city—particularly in the transient, boarding house, or slum areas—of persons whose social mobility is downward. Several major sociologic and epidemiologic investigations have been carried out to test various hypotheses that have been formulated concerning the relationship to the differential incidence of schizophrenia of such factors as a community's social organization,[30] its size,[21] social class structure,[30,5] social class mobility or "drift,"[30,45,96] and spatial mobility.[128] These studies will be considered in the chapter [Ch. 7] on the sociocultural aspects of schizophrenia.

Migration

A variety of studies have been carried out which show that migrant populations generally have higher hospital admission rates for schizophrenia than do nonmigrant populations.[30,58,75,82,84,91,102] This applies to migrants to the United States from abroad as well as to persons born in the United States who may move within a city or State or move from State of birth to another. Although data on migration status are not available for admissions to all mental hospitals throughout the United States, a series of studies have been done recently based on first admission rates to all mental hospitals in New York State and to state hospitals only in Ohio and California during 1950. These results demonstrate that foreign born whites show higher schizophrenia rates than do native born whites. However, rates for native nonwhites are considerably in excess of either of the preceding. A more recent study in Ohio for 1960 demonstrated the same differentials as found in 1950.[82] It also revealed that, among the native born, the schizophrenia rates were higher for those born out of the state for both the white and nonwhites than for those born in the state. On the other hand, Jaco's study in Texas in 1951-52 reported no systematic differences between native born and non-native born.[58] Various factors may account for differences in his findings, such as differences in coverage between the various studies, in migration patterns to Texas and the other states studied and in the attitude towards seeking care among members of different population groups.

Various reasons have been given for the higher rate of hospitalization among the migrants as compared to the nonmigrants. One is that individuals in a preschizoid stage may be migratory generally. The other is that the stress involved in moving and adjusting to a new culture and environment precipitates a schizophrenic attack. Probably both reasons operate under various circumstances. Regardless of cause, the high rate of mobility among the U.S. population, the major shifts from rural areas to the highly urbanized central cities and the population shifts from the large cities to the suburban areas, have created problems that must be taken into account by those responsible for the planning of community psychiatric services.

Marital Status

A consistent finding in all studies dealing with the hospitalized mentally ill is that the married have considerably lower first admission schizophrenia rates than do the never-married, separated, divorced and widowed.[13,67,68,90,100,103,104,116] Data from the 13 state study illustrate these findings.[68] Among males, the age adjusted rate for the single is 6 times; for the divorced and separated 8 times; and for the widowed, 5 times that for married males. Among the females, the corresponding rates are 3, 5 and 3 times those of married females. The total rate for the never married males is higher than that for the never married females, but in each of the other categories female rates tend to exceed male rates.

The most common explanation given for differences such as those illustrated here are social factors associated with the availability of a family and a home for the married and the lack of such firm supports for the other groups. However, the possibility should not be excluded that these differences may be due to other factors; for example, some underlying differences in the severity and malignancy of the disorders found in the never-married as compared to the married. Whatever the reasons may be, the data demonstrate convincingly that the never married, separated and divorced are high risk groups with respect to utilization of mental hospitals. Other studies have shown the higher rate of utilization of outpatient clinics by the never married, separated, divorced and widowed.[119] Thus, the significant characteristics of these groups, particularly their living arrangements and family relationships,[67,68] must certainly be taken into account in developing community and home care programs. They also emphasize the need for more intensive research on factors associated with bachelorhood, divorce and widowhood and their relationship to the incidence and prevalence of mental disorders and their prognosis.

Differences between Countries in First Admission Rates

Several countries provide data on first admission rates to mental hospitals by age, sex and diagnosis. Table 5 presents the age adjusted first admission rates for schizophrenia to the mental hospitals in the United States,[133] England and Wales,[34] Czechoslovakia,[24] Denmark,[26] Victoria (Australia),[138] New Zealand,[99] Canada[20] and Norway.[101] These rates vary from a low of 5 per 100,000 in Denmark to 27 per 100,000 in Canada. The median rate for these countries is about 16 per 100,000. Differences in these rates are the result not only of possible differences in the incidence of schizophrenia, but also of differences in the availability of mental hospital beds and of other types of psychiatric facilities, definitions of a first admission and a variety of cultural and social factors that determine differential patterns of admission to various types of psychiatric facilities. They are also the result of the differences among psychiatrists of the various countries in their diagnostic practice and the use of diagnostic terms.[9,143] This problem is illustrated by a comment of Jules-Nielsen and Stromgren on the low rate of schizophrenics for the mental hospitals in Denmark:[60]

It should be stressed that in Denmark the concept of schizophrenia is used in a considerably narrower sense, and the concept of manic-depressive psychosis in a wider sense, than in most other countries. "Psychogenic psychosis" is a diagnosis which is widely used in Denmark; it comprises psychoses which arise in close association with a mental stress, and their symptomatology and course is in most cases clearly influenced by the mental trauma. In Anglo-Saxon psychiatry, many of these cases are usually labelled as schizophrenias, others as neuroses.

If the cases of psychogenic psychosis are added to those for schizophrenia, the first admission rate to the mental hospitals in Denmark for these two disorders combined is 24 per 100,000 as opposed to 5 per 100,000 for schizophrenia only. A change of this magnitude emphasizes the persistent difficulties of making meaningful comparisons of psychiatric diagnostic data among countries.

Although the levels of the first admission rates among countries are quite different, there is a striking similarity in their age patterns. This is shown in

Table 5.—Relative Rates* of First Admissions for Schizophrenia to Mental Hospitals by Age: United States, 1964, England and Wales, 1960, Czechoslovakia, 1963, Denmark, 1961, Victoria (Australia), 1962, New Zealand, 1960, Canada, 1963, and Norway, 1960

Age (In Years)	United States	England & Wales	Czecho-slovakia	Denmark	Victoria, Australia	Age (In Years)	New Zealand	Canada	Age (In Years)	Norway
<15	8	3	7	2	3	<10	1	1	<15	0
15-24	148	171	156	137	108	10-19	66	57	15-24	130
25-34	217	216	189	208	187	20-29	215	220	25-34	202
35-44	171	152	180	137	193	30-39	193	201	35-34	178
45-54	103	91	102	112	126	40-49	118	126	45-59	105
55-64	55	61	60	104	67	50-59	94	75	60 and over	53
65 and over	12	34	28	67	73	60-69	32	30		
						70 and over	11	10		
Total†	100	100	100	100	100		100	100		100
Age Adjusted Rates‡	15.7	17.4	10.7	5.1	26.0		20.6	27.3		12.0

*Relative rate=age-specific rate expressed as a percentage of age-adjusted rate for both sexes.

†Age adjusted Total relative rate=100

‡Adjusted rate (All ages) based on 1950 U.S. Population as standard.

Table 5 which presents the relative age specific rates for schizophrenia obtained by determining the ratio of the rate in each age group to the total age adjusted rate for the country in question. The curve for each country is in the shape of an inverted "V" with the maximum usually occurring in the age group 25-34.

CHANCES OF RELEASE AND READMISSION

Probabilities of release from mental hospitals provide one of the few general measures of prognosis for schizophrenics. Within recent years a series of studies in the United States and Europe have documented time changes that have occurred in the release rates for first admissions with schizophrenia. Studies of the Warren State Hospital[70] demonstrated that the proportion of schizophrenics achieving a first significant release within one year following admission increased from 35 per cent in 1916-25 to 59 per cent in 1946-50. The median duration of continuous hospitalization decreased from 24 months to 9 months.

Further gains have occurred. A cohort study of 11 state mental hospital systems in 1954[112] showed that in four states the proportion of patients released in one year was 60 to 69 per cent; in five states 70 to 79 per cent, and in two states 80 per cent or above. More recently a comparison was made between the release rates of schizophrenic patients from several large state mental hospital systems as determined in 1954 with comparable data for these same states obtained during 1960.[55] This demonstrated further increases in proportion of patients released within the first year—from 61 per cent to 77 per cent in New York, 65 to 79 per cent in Illinois, 67 per cent to 74 per cent in Minnesota, 72 to 86 per cent in California and 74 to 93 per cent in Louisiana. Although differences exist between state systems in severity of illness of patients at intake, size of hospital, hospital organization and policies affecting release, demographic characteristics of communities served by the hospitals and the volume of other community psychiatric resources available to the population, it is significant that each of these states has shown a considerable increase in proportions of patients released within the first year. This means there is a substantial reduction in the proportion of patients who are experiencing more than 12 months of continuous hospitalization.

Much has been written about the effect of the tranquilizing drugs in producing the reported changes in release rates. The preceding findings and those from other countries have shown that a whole series of events in the period prior to 1955, including the introduction of insulin, E.C.T., total push and other intensive treatment, changing attitudes on the part of the hospital and community, increasing use of general hospitals ond outpatient clinics, had led to continuous increases in the rates of release of patients during their first year of hospitalization.[105,106,118,130,140]

Although increases in these rates would in all likelihood have continued, the introduction of the tranquilizers and their subsequent widespread use since 1955 undoubtedly accelerated this trend. The ability of these drugs to control agitated and excited behavior led to remarkable reductions in the numbers of patients placed in restraint and seclusion and provided increased opportunities for using additional treatment and rehabilitation procedures both in the hospital and in the community.[12,98,124] The resulting changes in hospital milieu led to modifications in hospital policies, administration and programs which, in turn, led to further gains in the overall treatment and rehabilitation of patients. These changes provided much of the impetus for accelerating the pace of development of improved methods of care, treatment and rehabilitation and led to the current national effort for development of comprehensive community mental health programs.[53,114,115]

Studies of hospital stay of schizophrenics as well as of other diagnostic groups have shown that the chances of first release fall off markedly after the first year of continuous hospitalization and become quite low after two years.[13,15,16,25,29,39,41,47,51,70,87,100,122] For example, the Warren State Hospital studies showed that the chances of release in the second and third years of hospitalization were about two-fifths and one-seventh, respectively, of those in the first year.[70] Brown has shown that the consistency of this finding in all studies of hospital stay has justified a commonly used *definition of a chronic schizophrenic, namely, one hospitalized continually for at least two years.*[15] Various factors are responsible for this phenomenon, such as severity of illness in patients, lack of adequate treatment and rehabilitation programs, insufficient staff, administrative problems relating to organizational structure and size of hospital, insufficient community resources to assist patients in bridging the gap between hospital and community and attitudes that result in decreased interest in patients on the parts of their families, relatives and the community at large.[16,95]

In addition, age, social class, occupation, education, marital status, and various other factors are related to the proportion of patients becoming chronic.[109] Thus, the chances of retention for schizophrenics over 45 years are greater than for those below that age. Patients from the lower socioeconomic classes have higher rates of retention than do those from the upper classes.[14] Among the various marital status groups, the married have the lowest retention rates and the never married usually the highest, while the rates for the separated, divorced and widowed fall somewhere in between.[13,59,68,81]

Comparative data are not available on changes that may have occurred since the 1950's in the chances of release for patients hospitalized for two years or more.[50] Although studies on patient movement by length of stay show that the net rate of return to the community for persons hospitalized continuously for *more* than one year is still considerably lower than for those hospitalized for *less* than one year, the fact that a relatively small proportion of first admissions now reach those long stay groups points to the considerable progress being made in the prevention of chronicity.

Patients also have differential experiences with respect to readmission to the state hospital. The 13 states cohort study found that, in 1960, nine per cent of schizophrenics released with less than 3 months of hospitalization were rehospitalized within three months following release and 15 per cent within six months. For those released after 3 to 5 months of hospitalization, the corresponding proportions rehospitalized were 7 and 14 per cent, respectively. Marital status also affects these rates with the married having slightly lower rates than those in the other categories.[68]

Brown and Carstairs have demonstrated an important relationship between probability of readmission to a mental hospital and the social group to which chronic schizophrenics return.[17] In a study of chronic male schizophrenics, discharged after more than two years stay in London mental hospitals, successful outcome depended not only on the patient's clinical state at the time of discharge and subsequent employment, but on the social group to which he returned. Thus patients staying with siblings or in lodging houses had appreciably lower rates of readmission to the hospital within their first year following release than did those staying with parents, with wife, or in large hostels.

Systematic time series are not available to show changes that may have taken place since 1955 in probabilities of readmission to mental hospitals for schizophrenics and other types of mental patients specific for length of hospitalization before release, age, sex and marital status. Although the proportion of all admissions to mental hospitals that are readmissions has increased, this does not necessarily mean that the probability of readmission has increased. It may simply be a reflection of the fact that there are now more previously hospitalized patients who are potential candidates for readmission. More adequate data on probability of readmission to state mental hospitals are needed to provide additional indexes of population changes taking place in these institutions as a result of changes in hospital treatment programs, early release of patients and increasing opportunities for community care. Such data are particularly important in view of the findings of a series of well designed studies which have demonstrated that drug therapies, in conjunction with services provided by public health nurses, day care centers, outpatient clinics and other community resources, can effect an appreciable reduction in the proportion of schizophrenics and other psychotics who must be readmitted to psychiatric hospitals.[27,33,48,73,74,108]

RESIDENT PATIENT POPULATION

Dynamics of growth and decline

The differential rates of first admission, release and readmission to mental hospitals previously described have operated over the years to produce the very heterogeneous patient population found in mental hospitals on any one day. This population, referred to as the resident patient population, consists of the survivors of groups of patients admitted over long periods of time. The

Table 6.—Number and Per Cent Distribution of Patients Resident in State and County Mental Hospitals at the End of Year by Length of Stay for Selected Mental Disorders: 23 Selected States: 1962

Length of Stay (In Years)	All Disorders	Schizophrenia	Mental Diseases of the Senium	All Other Disorders
		NUMBER		
Total	359,654	184,449	46,890	128,315
<1	66,302	24,923	13,499	27,880
1-4	79,012	31,162	20,337	27,513
5-9	52,514	24,711	8,251	19,552
10-19	73,451	41,431	3,855	28,165
20+	88,375	62,222	948	25,205
Median Length of Stay	8.4	12.8	3.0	8.3
Median Age (Years)	55.6	51.1	75+	54.4
		PER CENT OF TOTAL		
Total	100.0	100.0	100.0	100.0
<1	18.4	13.5	28.8	21.7
1-4	22.0	16.9	43.4	21.5
5-9	14.6	13.4	17.6	15.2
10-19	20.4	22.5	8.2	22.0
20+	24.6	33.7	2.0	19.6
	PER CENT OF LENGTH OF STAY CATEGORY			
Total	100.0	51.3	13.0	35.7
<1	100.0	37.6	20.4	42.0
1-4	100.0	39.4	25.7	34.9
5-9	100.0	47.1	15.7	37.2
10-19	100.0	56.4	5.2	38.4
20+	100.0	70.4	1.1	28.5

number in each residual group on a given date is a function of the initial size of the group of admissions and its subsequent rate of depletion.

Thus, an initial group of a given size, characterized by a low retention rate, makes a smaller contribution to the size of the resident population than another group of the same size with a higher retention rate. Under certain conditions a small initial group with a high retention rate can make a larger contribution to the resident population than a larger initial group with a very low retention rate. For example, patients with diseases of the senium have a very low retention rate because of the very high mortality rate which characterizes

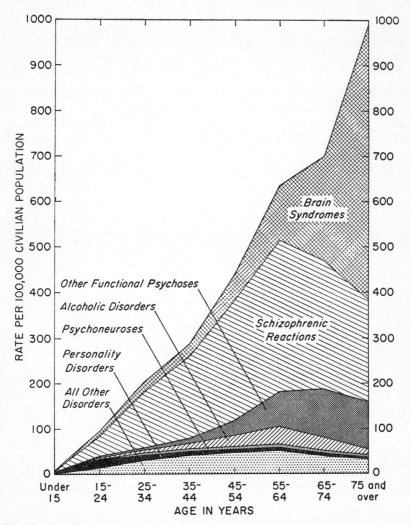

Fig. 4.—Resident patient rates, specific for age and selected diagnoses, state and county mental hospitals, United States: 1964

this group of aged patients. These patients constitute, therefore, a much smaller proportion of resident patients than they do of first admissions. The median duration of hospitalization for resident patients in this category is only three years. On the other hand, the schizophrenics have had a much higher retention and readmission rate and a relatively low mortality rate. This has resulted in the accumulation of large numbers of schizophrenics so that they constitute a considerably higher proportion of resident patients than they do of first admissions. *The median duration of stay for the resident schizophrenics is about 13 years.* These differences are illustrated in Table 6 which show the distributions of resident patients at end of 1962 by length of time on books during the current episode of hospitalization.[134]

Figure 4 shows the age specific resident patient rates for schizophrenics in relation to the other disorders for patients in state and county mental hospitals as of the end of 1964.

Trends

Studies of changes in the absolute number of resident patients and their ratios to the general population (resident patient rates) illustrate the impact that various intrahospital and community programs, devised to prevent the continuing buildup of long-term populations, are having on the size and composition of the populations of these institutions. Of particular importance is the steady reduction in the size of the resident patient population of the state and county mental hospitals of the nation since 1955. During the ten year period 1946-55 the year end resident patient population of these hospitals increased at an average rate of 1.9 per cent per year, reaching a high of 558,922 patients at the end of 1955. From that point on, the population decreased steadily by 1.3 per cent per year. This reduction in population occurred despite the fact that, during this same period of time, admissions were increasing steadily at an average rate of 6.8 per cent per year. Deaths increased only slightly. Thus, the population decrease has been achieved essentially by an increase in net releases rather than by a reduction in admissions or an excessive increase in deaths.[68,132]

Figure 5 shows the trend in the age adjusted resident patient rates for schizophrenics. Since 1955, the rate for males has been decreasing at an annual rate of 1.5 per cent and for females at an annual rate of 2.9 per cent. Prior to 1960 the rates for females exceeded those for males. Since that date the male rate has been consistently higher. There is still considerable geographic variation throughout the United States in these rates. Thus, at the end of 1964 the rate varied from a high of 254 per 100,000 to a low of 27.4. The median rate was 108.

The annual per cent rate of decrease in the total number of schizophrenics (.8 per cent) has been slower than that for the total number of patients with all other disorders combined (1.9 per cent). There are striking age variations in the patterns of change (Table 7). Schizophrenics are decreasing more rapidly than patients with other disorders in the age groups 25-34 years and 35-44 years. In each of these groups the annual relative rate of decrease is in excess of three per cent, compared to only two per cent for the other disorders combined. In the age group 45-54 years, the annual rate of decrease in the number of schizophrenics (1.3 per cent) is slower than that for all other disorders (3.5 per cent). On the other hand, schizophrenics are increasing in the age groups under 15 years, 15-24 years, 55-64 years, and 65 years and over by 16.2 per cent, 5.6 per cent, 1.3 per cent and 1.1 per cent per year, respectively.

Changes in the annual resident patient rate by age are also of importance since they take into account the corresponding shifts in the size of the same age groups in the general population. The striking increase in the rate for children under 15 years emphasizes that factors other than the increase in general population in this age group account for this change. The decrease in resident patient rates in the age groups 55-64 and 65 years and over, despite increases in the numbers of patients in these groups, indicates that the numbers of such patients are increasing more slowly than the general population in these age groups.

The direction and size of the change in numbers and rates in the various age groups thus provide indicators of problems as well as of progress. The continuing increase in the resident patient population of schizophrenics under 15 years, when related to the large expected increase in the general population under 15 years in the next decade (from 59 million in 1964 to 67 million in 1974), underscores the seriousness of the problem. The rapid decreases in numbers of patients as well as in rates in age groups 25-34, 35-44, and 45-54

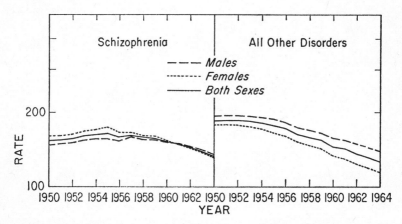

Fig. 5.—Age adjusted rates per 100,000 population of patients resident in state and county mental hospitals for schizophrenia and all other mental disorders: United States: 1950-1964

Table 7.—Numbers and Rates per 100,000 Population of Patients Resident in State and County Mental Hospitals at the End of the Years 1955 and 1964 and Average Per Cent Change During 1955 to 1964 by Age and Selected Mental Disorders: United States

Age (In Years)	All Mental Disorders		Schizophrenia		All Other Mental Disorders		Average Annual Per Cent Change†		
	1955	1964	1955	1964	1955	1964	All Disorders	Schizophrenia	All Other Mental Disorders
NUMBER									
Total	558,922	490,449	267,995	245,823	290,927	244,626	−1.3	−0.8	−1.9
<15	2,301	5,118	374	1,603	1,927	3,515	9.5	16.2	7.5
15-24	17,276	26,369	8,156	12,406	9,120	13,963	5.3	5.6	5.1
25-34	57,634	43,521	36,819	26,771	20,815	16,750	−2.8	−3.1	−2.1
35-44	96,304	70,098	63,269	44,058	33,035	26,040	−3.3	−3.8	−2.4
45-54	117,500	95,360	65,895	58,162	51,605	37,198	−2.2	−1.3	−3.5
55-64	109,622	106,150	50,302	55,894	59,320	50,256	−0.3	1.3	−1.7
65 and over	158,285	143,833	43,180	46,929	115,105	96,904	−1.1	1.1	−2.0
RATES PER 100,000									
Total*	344.3	262.1	166.7	134.8	177.6	127.3	−2.9	−2.2	−3.6
<15	4.7	8.6	0.8	2.7	3.9	5.9	7.2	13.1	5.3
15-24	86.1	94.5	40.7	44.4	45.4	50.1	1.5	1.7	1.3
25-34	246.0	201.3	157.1	123.9	88.9	77.4	−1.8	−2.2	−1.1
35-44	427.2	289.4	280.6	181.9	146.6	107.5	−4.2	−4.6	−3.3
45-54	622.8	439.4	349.3	268.0	273.5	171.4	−3.6	−2.7	−4.9
55-64	753.7	636.1	345.8	334.9	407.9	301.2	−1.8	−0.3	−3.2
65 and over	1125.1	805.3	306.9	262.7	818.2	542.6	−3.9	−1.8	−4.8

*Age adjusted rate based on 1950 U.S. population as standard.

†Average annual per cent change=100(B-1), computed by fitting a curve of the form $Y = AB^x$ to the figures for the 10 year interval for each age group 1955-1964.

years reflect the major impact of intensive hospital treatment programs, psychotropic drugs, open hospital wards and increased availability and usage of psychiatric services in general hospitals, outpatient facilities and various transitional facilities for patients in this age group. For example, in the age group 35-44 years, where the decrease in schizophrenics and other categories of hospital patients has been very marked, the patients under care in the outpatient psychiatric facilities have doubled in the six year period 1959-64 (from 367 per 100,000 to 737). This age group of outpatients is heavily weighted with functional psychotics. On the other hand, the increase in the hospitalized schizophrenic population 55 years and over emphasizes that additional effort is needed to develop hospital and community programs to prevent the further buildup of a long-term population. The schizophrenic patients in this age group still constitute 42 per cent of the entire schizophrenic resident patient population and 21 per cent of the entire hospital population.

The number of resident schizophrenics has also increased because of the marked reduction in death rates that has occurred in mental hospitals over the years. Although the death rates in the mental hospitals are still higher than those in the general population, there has been considerable improvement over the years in the mortality rates in every age group under 65 years. This reflects an overall improvement in the health situation in the hospitals. It was achieved by the application of advances in public health practice that resulted in better levels of environmental sanitation, control of tuberculosis and other infectious diseases, improved diet, and of the various advances in clinical medicine, such as the more effective treatment of pneumonia and acute infections by use of sulfonamides and antibiotics.[129] While a reduction has occurred in the mortality rates for schizophrenics in the age group 65 years and over, an increase has occurred in the mortality rates in this age group for all other disorders combined. This is a reflection of the fact that the aged schizophrenics consist almost entirely of patients who have grown old in the hospital, while the other group is heavily weighted with newly admitted patients with mental disorders of the senium whose mortality rates are excessively high both because of their poor physical condition and their very high average age at admission. In effect, the mental hospital has had to deal with two types of aging problems: one presented by the aging of the general population with a resultant increase of aged admissions with a high risk of mortality; the other resulting from the benefits of improved medical, psychiatric and public health practices within the hospital which have led to longer survivorship for the chronic schizophrenics and other types of long-term patients. The general changes in the mortality rates are illustrated by the experience of the New York state hospital system during 1930[89] and 1962[134] for all types of disorders and schizophrenia with corresponding mortality rates for the general population (Table 8).

Table 8.—Death Rates, by Age, Among all Patients and Schizophrenics in New York State Mental Hospitals for the Years 1930 and 1962 and for the General Population of New York State in 1930 and 1962 with Corresponding Per Cent Changes in the Death Rates

Age (In Years)	New York Mental Hospitals												New York State Population					
	All Disorders						Schizophrenia											
	Both Sexes		Male		Female		Both Sexes		Male		Female		Both Sexes		Male		Female	
	1930	1962	1930	1962	1930	1962	1930	1962	1930	1962	1930	1962	1930	1962	1930	1962	1930	1962
	Deaths per 1,000 Average Annual Resident Patients												Deaths per 1,000 Population					
Total, 15 and over																		
Adjusted*	78.4	51.4	87.0	57.3	72.3	47.4	35.4	22.3	37.4	24.7	33.8	20.6	20.0	13.4	21.7	16.2	18.3	11.0
Crude	87.0	99.8	93.2	97.3	81.3	102.2	32.4	29.9	31.3	29.6	33.4	30.1	13.5	13.7	14.5	16.0	12.4	11.6
15-24	51.2	4.7	48.6	3.5	55.0	1.3	32.2	5.1	35.9	4.1	29.9	7.0	2.8	0.9	2.9	1.3	2.6	0.6
25-34	41.3	8.0	37.5	9.0	45.6	8.0	24.8	6.5	22.8	7.8	27.5	4.7	4.1	1.4	4.4	1.8	3.7	1.1
35-44	45.7	13.9	48.2	12.9	43.3	15.0	19.5	9.7	18.2	9.3	20.7	10.1	6.6	3.0	7.7	3.7	5.6	2.3
45-54	58.6	26.2	65.9	28.6	52.0	23.9	21.1	15.7	19.6	17.0	22.3	14.4	13.7	7.6	16.0	9.8	11.3	5.6
55-64	92.8	58.9	106.6	70.4	78.6	48.2	39.5	31.9	43.9	36.7	36.6	27.7	28.5	17.4	32.2	23.2	24.9	12.1
65 and over	215.3	241.0	254.5	271.2	187.6	221.0	89.6	79.4	101.2	90.3	82.9	72.7	79.2	61.7	83.0	71.4	75.9	54.2
	Per cent Change (1930-1962)												Per cent Change (1930-1962)					
Total, 15 and over																		
(Adjusted)	—34.4		—34.1		—34.4		—37.0		—34.0		—39.1		—33.0		—25.3		—39.9	
15-24	—90.8		—92.8		—86.7		—84.2		—88.6		—71.9		—67.9		—55.2		—76.9	
25-34	—80.6		—78.7		—82.5		—73.8		—65.8		—82.9		—65.9		—59.1		—70.3	
35-44	—61.6		—73.2		—65.4		—50.3		—48.9		—51.2		—54.5		—51.9		—58.9	
45-54	—55.3		—56.6		—54.0		—25.6		—13.3		—35.4		—44.5		—38.8		—50.4	
55-64	—36.5		—36.3		—38.7		—19.2		—16.4		—24.3		—38.9		—28.0		—51.4	
65 and over	+11.9		+ 6.6		+17.8		—11.4		—10.8		—12.3		—22.1		—14.0		—28.6	

*1960 Population of New York State used as standard for age adjusted rates.

Implications of reduction of the resident patient population

The decreases occurring in the absolute numbers of patients in mental hospitals and their ratio to the general population have major implications for the planning of future services for the care, treatment and rehabilitation of the mentally ill.

Reductions in the size of the resident patient population have been documented rather fully for England and Wales and Canada. On the basis of trends in England and Wales, Tooth and Brooke have estimated that future needs for mental hospital beds in England will be reduced to 1.8 per 1,000 in the next two decades, one-half the rate of 3.6 that existed in 1954.[130] Richmond and Kennedy have shown that a similar rate of decrease is occurring in the resident patient rate in the Canadian mental hospitals, so that a 50 per cent reduction can be expected in their bed requirements within the next two decades.[118]

The trends shown in Table 7 indicate that a 50 per cent reduction in the resident patient rate per 100,000 population can also be achieved in the United States in the next two decades. The current annual per cent decrease in the resident patient rate for all disorders other than schizophrenia (3.6 per cent) is such that, if this rate is maintained, a 50 per cent reduction will certainly occur in this segment of the hospital population. The annual rate of decrease in the schizophrenic rate will have to be increased to achieve a 50 per cent reduction in the rate for this population of patients within two decades. An annual rate of decrease of 3.4 per cent between 1955-1964 would have been necessary to have achieved this, as opposed to the 2.2 per cent rate that existed. Table 7 shows the age variations in the current rates of change and emphasizes the dimensions of the problem in the various age groups. This varies from reversing the increasing rates for the population under 25 years to accelerating by considerable amounts the rates of decrease in the age groups 25-34, 45-54 and 55 years and over. The annual rate of decline in the age group 35-44 years (4.6 per cent per year) is such that a 50 per cent reduction should certainly occur well before 20 years, provided the current rate of decline for that age group can be maintained.

The trends in the resident patient rates that have been reported characterized the period before the passage of the major national legislation that has stimulated the intensive development of comprehensive mental health programs throughout the nation.[114,115] These programs will provide a basic framework within which persons in charge of hospital programs and those in charge of community programs can collaborate closely in the planning of integrated and coordinated programs to provide continuity of care and free flow of patients between facilities. Efforts must be made to prevent patients from slipping into the long-term groups by intensive treatment, frequent evaluations of their condition to determine who can best be served by the services within the hospital and who can best be served by other medical, nursing and rehabilitation services in the community. It is particularly important for the persons in charge of hospital programs and those in charge of the community programs to collaborate closely in the planning of community facilities and associated services which will meet effectively changing needs of patients. Such combined efforts should lead to effective application of the knowledge gained in the past decade and also provide a basis for acquiring and applying new knowledge necessary to make further gains in the prevention and control of disability associated with schizophrenia and other mental disorders.

SUMMARY

The development of an adequate vital statistics or descriptive epidemiology of schizophrenia has been impeded by the absence of standard case finding techniques for the mental disorders that can be used in consistent and uniform fashion from time to time and place to place to detect persons in the general population with mental disorders, and of differential diagnostic techniques that make it possible to assign each case to a specific diagnostic category with a high degree of reliability. However, data derived from a limited number of community surveys in different countries and from records of patients admitted to psychiatric facilities throughout the world have established the serious nature of schizophrenia as a public health problem. Precise comparisons of the level of the prevalence rates in these studies are impossible not only because of the lack of comparability in case finding, diagnostic and classification methods, but also because of differences in the composition of the populations studied with respect to age and other demographic characteristics. Nevertheless, these studies show that at least 1.0 person per 1,000 total population was found to provide evidence of an attack of a mental disorder which the investigators called schizophrenia. The reported figures ranged from 1.0 per 1,000 to 9.5 per 1,000 depending on the intensity of the case finding method and other characteristics of the populations studied. On the basis of data derived from incidence studies done in the United States, which determined the number of persons diagnosed as schizophrenic who have had a first contact with one of a broad network of psychiatric facilities per year, it is estimated that at a *minimum two per cent of the persons born in 1960 would have an attack of schizophrenia some time during their subsequent lifetime.* Under certain conditions *the maximum could be as high as six per cent.* The precise figure depends on the levels of the age specific incidence rates, the demographic and social structure of the community and other related factors.

Schizophrenia constitutes a major problem of psychiatric care. In the United States as of the end of 1964, schizophrenics accounted for one-half of the resident patients in the state and county mental hospitals and Veterans Administration neuropsychiatric hospitals on any one day and 32 per cent of the admissions to these hospitals. They also constituted almost 20 per cent of the admissions to private mental hospitals, and about the same per cent of admissions to the general hospitals with psychiatric services. Currently about 15 per cent of all admissions to the 2,000 outpatient psychiatric clinics in the United States are schizophrenics.

The systematic data derived from the records of patients admitted to mental hospitals in the United States and other countries provide a first approximation to a descriptive epidemiology of schizophrenia. The most extensive data on disability associated with mental disorders in the United States are derived from the state and county mental hospitals. Studies of first admission rates to these hospitals have demonstrated that the age adjusted rates for schizophrenia have been remarkably stable over the period 1955-1964. The variations in these rates by age, sex, marital status, migration and related factors demonstrate quite clearly the high toll this disease takes in the lower socioeconomic groups, nonwhites, as compared to the whites; the highly urbanized areas as compared to the more rural; the nonmarried, separated, divorced and widowed, as compared to the married. These data are quite useful in the planning of community mental health services as well as in suggesting various hypotheses concerning the possible role of biological, social, economic and cultural factors in the etiology of schizophrenia and in the fate of persons attacked by the disease.

Major changes have taken place in the length of stay of new admissions with schizophrenia to mental hospitals. Currently only about ten per cent of these admissions are retained continuously for more than one year, as compared to a range of 20-40 per cent in 1954. The decreases in length of stay in new cases and more rapid turnover of all patients in the age groups under 55 years have led to an overall reduction between 1955 and 1964 in the number of schizophrenics in the resident patient population of the state hospitals. The decreases have been most marked in the age groups between 25 and 55 years.

The increased rates of release of patients have been particularly marked since 1955 and reflect the results of efforts made to improve patient care by pharmacotherapy, more intensive rehabilitation programs and the development of extensive programs of community care and related services. All of these activities are contributing to the prevention of long term hospitalization and its resultant problems of chronicity.

During the period 1955-64 the total number of patients in the year and resident patient population in the state and county mental hospitals of the United States decreased at the average annual rate of 1.3 per cent. However, the total annual rate of decrease for the schizophrenics was somewhat slower than for the remainder of the hospital population. The age variations in rates of decline are striking, with the decline being in excess of three per cent per year schizophrenics in the age groups 25-34 and 35-44 years, as compared to only two per cent for the other disorders. Marked increases have been occurring in the number of hospitalized schizophrenics in the adolescent and young adult population, both as a result of the large increases in numbers of such persons in the general population and inadequate community facilities for this age group of patients. Other increases have occurred in the hospitalized schizophrenic population 55 years and over as a result of the aging of chronic cases and lack of adequate community placement opportunities for this age group of patients.

These changes occurred on the basis of programs that were carried out during the period before the passage of major national legislation that has stimulated the intensive development of comprehensive mental health programs throughout the nation. The coordinated and integrated programs that should result from these efforts should make it possible to apply more effectively existing knowledge on the treatment and rehabilitation of schizophrenics and to acquire additional knowledge that will lead to further gains in the care, treatment and rehabilitation of schizophrenics and other mental disorders.

BIBLIOGRAPHY

1. Akimoto, H. et al.: Demographische und Psychiatrische Untersuchung der Abgegrenzten Kleinstadtbevolkerung. Psychiat. Neurol. Jap., 1942, 47: 351.

2. American Psychiatric Association. Diagnostic and Statistical Manual—Mental Disorders. Washington, D.C.: American Psychiatric Association, 1952.

3. American Psychopathological Association. Trends in Mental Disease. New York: King's Crown Press, Columbia University Press, 1945.

4. American Public Health Association, Program Area Committee on Mental Health. Mental Disorders: A Guide to Control Methods. New York: 1962.

5. Babigian, H. M., Gardner, E. A., Miles, H. C., and Romano, J.: Diagnostic Consistency and Change in a Follow-up Study of 1215 Patients. American Journal of Psychiatry, 121: 895-901, 1965.

6. Bahn, A. K., Gardner, E. A., Alltop, L., Knatterud, G. L., and Solomon, H.: Admission and Prevalence for Psychiatric Facilities in Four Register Areas. To be published in American Journal of Public Health, 1966.

7. Bahn, A. K., Gorwitz, K., and Kramer, M.: A Cross-Sectional Picture of Psychiatric Care in an Entire State. American Psychiatric Association, Psychiatric Studies & Projects, 1964, 2: 1-8.

8. Bodian, C., Gardner, E.A., Willis, E. M., and Bahn, A. K.: Socioeconomic Indicators from Census Tract Date Related to Rates of Mental Illness. Paper presented at Census Tract Conference, September, 1963. U.S. Department of Commerce, Bureau of the Census.

9. Book, A. J.: A. Genetic and Neuropsychiatric Investigation of a North-Swedish Population with Special Regard to Schizophrenia and Mental Deficiency. Acta Genetica et Statistica Medica. 1953, 4: 1-100.

10. Brandon, S., and Gruenberg, E. M.: Measurement of the Incidence of Chronic Severe Social Breakdown Syndrome. Milbank Memorial Fund Quarterly, Evaluating the Effectiveness of Mental Health Services. New York: 1966, 44: Part 2, 129-149.

11. Bremer, J.: A Social Psychiatric Investigation of a Small Community in Northern Norway. Acta Psychiatrica et Neurologica, 1951, Suppl. 62.

12. Brill, H., and Patton, R. E.: Analysis of 1955-1956 Population Fall in New York

State Mental Hospitals in First Year of Large-Scale Use of Tranquilizing Drugs. American Journal of Psychiatry, 1957, 114: 509-517.

13. Brooke, E. M.: A Cohort Study of Patients First Admitted to Mental Hospitals in 1954 and 1955. General Register Office, Studies on Medical and Population Subjects, No. 18. London, Eng.: Her Majesty's Stationery Office, 1963.

14. Brooke, E. M.: A National Study of Schizophrenic Patients in Relation to Occupation. Second International Congress for Psychiatry. Zurich: 1957, Vol. 3.

15. Brown, G. W.: Length of Hospital Stay and Schizophrenia: A Review of Statistical Studies. Acta Psychiatrica et Neurologica Scandinavica, 1960, 35: 414-430.

16. Brown, G. W.: Social Factors Influencing Length of Hospital Stay of Schizophrenic Patients. British Medical Journal, 1959, 2: 1300-1302.

17. Brown, G. W., Carstairs, G. M., and Topping, G.: Post-Hospital Adjustment of Chronic Mental Patients. Lancet, 1958, 2: 685-689.

18. Brugger, C.: Psychiatrische Ergebnisse einer Medizinischen, Anthropologischen und Soziologischen Revolkerungsuntersuchung. Z. Neurol. Psychiat., 1933, 146: 489.

19. Brugger, C.: Versuch einer Geisteskrankenzahlung in Thuringen. Z. Neurol. Psychiat., 1931, 133: 352.

20. Canada: Dominion Bureau of Statistics. Mental Health Statistics. Institutional Admissions and Separations, 1963. Ottawa, Can.: Queen's Printer and Controller of Stationery, 1964, Vol. 1.

21. Clausen, J. A., and Kohn, M. L.: Relation of Schizophrenia to the Social Structure of a Small City. In Epidemiology of Mental Disorders, Washington, D.C.: American Association for the Advancement of Science, 1959. Pp. 69-94. Publication 0. 60.

22. Cohen, B., and Fairbank, R.: Statistical Contributions from the Mental Hygiene Study of the Eastern Health District of Baltimore. American Journal of Psychiatry, 1938, 94: 1153-1161 & 1377-1395.

23. Crocetti, G. M., Kulcar, Z., Kesic, B., and Lemkau, P.: Differential Rates of Schizophrenia in Croatia, Yugoslavia. American Journal of Public Health, 1964, 54: 196-206.

24. Czechoslovakia: Ministertvo Zdravotnictvi. Zdravotnicka Statistika CSSR. Psychiatricka Pece V Roce, 1963.

25. Danziger, L.: Prognosis in Some Mental Disorders. Diseases of the Nervous System, 1946, 7: 229.

26. Denmark: National Health Service of Denmark. Medicinal Beretning II. Finansaret 1961/62. Beretzing om Sygehuse og Andre Helbredelsesinstitutioner. Danmark, Kobenhavn, 1965.

27. Dinitz, S., Scarpitti, F. R., Albini, J. L., Fefton, M., and Pasamanick, B.: An Experimental Study in the Prevention of Hospitalization of Schizophrenics. Thirty Months of Experience. American Journal of Orthopsychiatry. 1965, 35: 1-9.

28. Dorn, H.: The Incidence and Future Expectancy of Mental Disease. Public Health Reports, 1938, 53: 1991-2004.

29. Drasgow, J.: A Criterion for Chronicity in Schizophrenia. Psychiatric Quarterly, 1957, 31: 454.

30. Dunham, H. W.: Community and Schizophrenia—An Epidemiological Analysis. Lafayette Clinic Monographs in Psychiatry. Detroit, Mich.: Wayne State University Press, 1965.

31. Eaton, J. W., and Weil, R. J.: Culture and Mental Disorders. Glencoe, Ill.: Free Press, 1955.

32. Elkind, H. B., and Doering, C. G.: Epidemiology of Mental Disease: Further Studies I. Variation in Diagnosis and II. Seasonal Incidence, Reprint No. 5 in Schizophrenia. Statistical Studies from the Boston Psychopathic Hospital, 1925-1934. Abstract of Paper read at 84th Annual Meeting of the American Psychiatric Association, Minneapolis, 1928.

33. Engelhardt, D. M., and Freedman, N: An Approach to the Evaluation of Long-Term Pharmacological Therapy of Schizophrenia Outpatients: Mental Patients in Transition. Springfield, Ill.: Charles C. Thomas, 1961. Pp. 322-335.

108   THE SCHIZOPHRENIC SYNDROME

34. England & Wales: General Register Office. Registrar General's Statistical Review of England and Wales for the Year 1960. Supplement on Mental Health. London, Eng.: Her Majesty's Stationery Office, 1964.

35. Essen-Moller, E.: Individual Traits and Morbidity in a Swedish Rural Population. Acta Psychiatrica et Neurologica Scandinavica, 1956, Supplement 100.

36. Faris, R. E. L., and Dunham, H. W.: Mental Disorders in Urban Areas: An Ecological Study of Schizophrenia and Other Psychoses. Chicago: University of Chicago Press, 1939.

37. Felix, R. H., and Kramer, M.: Extent of the Problem of Mental Disorders. Annals of the American Academy of Political and Social Science, March 1953, 5-14.

38. Fremming, K. H.: Expectation of Mental Infirmity in a Sample of the Danish Population. Eugenics Society and Cassell & Co., Ltd. London: 1951.

39. Freyhan, F. A.: Eugen Bleuler's Concept of the Group of Schizophrenics at Mid-Century. American Journal of Psychiatry, 1958, 114: 769-779.

40. Frost, W. H.: Epidemiology. Nelson Looseleaf System. Public Health Preventive Medicine Vol. 2, Chap. 7: 163-190. New York: Thos. Nelson & Sons, 1927. Reprinted in papers of Wade Hampton Frost. A Contribution to Epidemiologic Method. Edited by Maxcy, K. F., Commonwealth Fund, 1941. Pp. 493-542.

41. Fuller, R. G.: Expectation of Hospital Life and Outcome for Mental Patients on First Admission. Psychiatric Quarterly, 1930, 4: 295.

42. Gardner, E. A., Bahn, A. K., and Miles, H. C.: Patient Experience in Psychiatric Units of General and State Mental Hospitals. Public Health Reports, 1964, 79: 755-767.

43. Gardner, E. A., Miles, H. C., Bahn, A. K., and Romano, J.: All Psychiatric Experience in a Community. A Cumulative Survey: Report of the First Year's Experience. Archives of General Psychiatry, 1963, 9: 369-378.

44. Giesler, R., Hurley, P. L., and Person, P. H., Jr.: Survey of General Hospitals Admitting Psychiatric Patients. PHS Publication No. 1462. Washington, D.C.: Government Printing Office, 1966.

45. Goldberg, E. M., and Morrison, S. L.: Schizophrenia and Social Class. British Journal of Psychiatry, 1963, 109: 785-802.

46. Goldhamer, H., and Marshall, A.: Psychosis and Civilization. Two Studies in the Frequency of Mental Disease. Glencoe, Ill.: Free Press, 1953.

47. Gorwitz, K., Bahn, A. K., Klee, G., and Solomon, M.: A Psychiatric Case Register Study of Release and Return Rates for State Mental Hospital Patients. To be published in Public Health Reports.

48. Gross, M., and Reeves, W. P.: Relapses after Withdrawal of Ataractic Drugs: An Interim Report. In Mental Patients in Transition. Springfield, Ill.: Charles C. Thomas, 1961. Pp. 313-321.

49. Group for the Advancement of Psychiatry, Committee on Preventive Psychiatry. Problems of Estimating Changes in Frequency of Mental Disorders. New York: Group for the Advancement of Psychiatry, 1961. Report No. 50.

50. Gurel, L.: Release and Community Stay in Chronic Schizophrenia. American Journal of Psychiatry, 1966, 122: 892-899.

51. Harris, A., and Norris, V.: Expectation of Life and Liberty in Patients Suffering from Functional Psychosis. Psychiat. Quart. 1955, 29: 33.

52. Hollingshead, A. B., and Redlich, F. C.: Social Class and Mental Illness: A Community Study. New York: John Wiley & Sons, Inc., 1958.

53. House of Representatives, Document No. 58. 88th Congress, 1st Session, February 5, 1963. Message from the President of the United States Relative to Mental Illness and Mental Retardation.

54. Hunt, R. C.: Ingredients of a Rehabilitation Program. In Approach to the Prevention of Disability from Chronic Psychoses. Milbank Memorial Fund, 1958. Pp. 9-28.

55. Hurley, P. L., and Conwell, M.: Release Rates from Public Mental Hospitals

1954 and 1960. A Report of Five States, National Institute of Mental Health, Office of Biometry. Public Health Reports. (In Press)

56. International Conference for the Eighth Revision of the International Classification of Diseases. Geneva 6-12 July 1965. Report WHO/HS/8 Rev. Conf/ 11.65.

57. Ivanys, E., Drdkova, S., and Vana, J.: Prevalence of Psychoses Recorded among Psychiatric Patients in a Part of the Urban Population. Ceskoslovenska Psychiatrie, 1964, 60: 152-163.

58. Jaco, E. G.: Social Epidemiology of Mental Disorders. A Psychiatric Survey of Texas. New York: Russell Sage Foundation, 1960.

59. Jenkins, R. L., and Gurel, L.: Predictive Factors in Early Release. Mental Hospitals, November 1959, 11-14.

60. Juel-Nielsen, N., and Stromgren, E.: Five Years Later. A Comparison between Census Studies of Patients in Psychiatric Institutions in Denmark in 1957 and 1962. Acta Jutlandica, 1936, 35: No. 1.

61. Kaila, M.: Uber die Durchschnittshäufigkeit der Geisterkrankheiten und des Schwachsinns in Finland. Acta Psychiat. Neurol. (Kbh.), 1942, 17: 47.

62. Katz, J., Kunofsky, S., and Locke, B. Z.: Tuberculosis Morbidity and Mortality Among Mental Patients as Compared with the General Population. American Review of Tuberculosis, 1954, 70: No. 1.

63. Klee, G. D., Spiro, E. S., Bahn, A. K., and Gorwitz, K.: An Ecological Analysis of Diagnosed Mental Illness in Baltimore. Paper read at American Psychiatric Association Regional Research Conference, Baltimore, April 21-22, 1966. (In Press)

64. Knox, R. S., and Tourney, G.: Conceptions of Schizophrenia and Methods of Study. Chapter IV in Dunham, H. Warren, Community and Schizophrenia—An Epidemiological Analysis. Detroit: Wayne State University Press, 1965. Pp. 39-63.

65. Kramer, M.: Collection and Utilization of Statistical Data from Psychiatric Facilities in the United States of America.

Bulletin of the World Health Organization, 1963, 29: 491-510.

66. Kramer, M.: Discussion of the Concepts of Incidence and Prevalence as Related to Epidemiologic Studies of Mental Disorders. American Journal of Public Health, 1957, 47: 826-840.

67. Kramer, M.: Epidemiology, Biostatistics and Mental Health Planning. Paper read at American Psychiatric Association Regional Research Conference, Baltimore, April 21-22, 1966. (In Press)

68. Kramer, M.: Some Implications of Trends in the Usage of Psychiatric Facilities for Community Mental Health Programs and Related Research. PHS Publication No. 1434, 1966. (In Press)

69. Kramer, M.: Some Problems for International Research Suggested by Observations on Differences in First Admission Rates to the Mental Hospitals of England and Wales and of the United States. Proceedings of the Third World Congress of Psychiatry, Montreal, Canada. June 1961, 153-160.

70. Kramer, M., Goldstein, H., Israel, R. H., and Johnson, N. A.: Application of Life Table Methodology to the Study of Mental Hospital Populations. Psychiatric Research Reports, 1956, 5: 49-76.

71. Kramer, M., Pollack, E. S., and Redick, R. W.: Studies of Incidence and Prevalence of Hospitalized Mental Disorders in the United States: Current Status and Future Goals. In Comparative Epidemiology of the Mental Disorders, P. H. Hoch and J. Zubin, Eds. New York: Grune & Stratton, Inc., 1961. Pp 56-100.

72. Kreitman, N.: Reliability of Psychiatric Diagnosis. Journal of Mental Science, 1961, 107: 876-886.

73. Kris, E. B.: Day Hospital Treatment versus Intramural Treatment of Mental Patients. Internat. J. Soc. Psychiatry, 1964, Congress Issue.

74. Kris, E. B.: Prevention of Rehospitalization through Relapse Control in a Day Hospital. Mental Patients in Transition. Springfield, Ill.: Charles C. Thomas, 1961. Pp. 155-162.

75. Lazarus, J., Locke, B. Z., and Thom-

as, D. S.: Migration Differentials in Mental Disease. Milbank Memorial Fund Quarterly, 1963, 41: 25-42.

76. Lemkau, P. V., and Crocetti, G. M.: Vital Statistics of Schizophrenia. In Schizophrenia, a Review of the Syndrome, Leopold Bellak, Ed. New York: Logos Press, 1958, and Grune & Stratton, 1967. Pp. 64-81.

77. Lemkau, P. V., Tietze, C., and Cooper, M.: Mental Hygiene Problems in an Urban District: I. Description of the Study, Mental Hygiene, 1941, 25: 624-646. II. Psychotics. The Neurotics. Mental Hygiene, 1942, 26: 100-119.

78. Lemkau, P. V., Tietze, C., and Cooper, M.: A Survey of Statistical Studies on the Prevalence and Incidence of Mental Disorder in Sample Populations. Public Health Reports, 1943, 58: 1909-1927.

79. Lin, Tsung-yi.: A Study of the Incidence of Mental Disorder in Chinese and Other Cultures. Psychiatry, 1953, 16: 313-336.

80. Lin, Tsung-yi, and Standley, C. C.: The Scope of Epidemiology in Psychiatry. World Health Organization, 1962, Public Health Papers No. 16.

81. Locke, B. Z.: Outcome of First Hospitalization of Patients with Schizophrenia. Public Health Reports, 1962, 77: 801-806.

82. Locke, B. Z., and Duvall, H. J.: Migration and Mental Illness. Eugenics Quarterly, 1964, 11: 216-221.

83. Locke, B. Z., and Duvall, H. J.: Patterns of Schizophrenic Admissions to the Ohio Public Mental Hospitals. Mental Hygiene, 1965, 49: 220-229.

84. Locke, B. Z., Kramer, M., and Pasamanick, B.: Immigration and Insanity. Public Health Reports, 1960, 75: 301-306.

85. Locke, B. Z., Kramer, M., Timberlake, C. E., Pasamanick, B., and Smeltzer, D.: Problems in Interpretation of Patterns of First Admissions to Ohio State Public Mental Hospitals for Patients with Schizophrenic Reactions. Psychiatric Research Reports, 1958, 10: 172-196.

86. MacMahon, B., Pugh, T. F., and Ipsen, J.: Epidemiologic Methods. Boston: Little, Brown & Co., 1960.

87. Malzberg, B.: Cohort Studies of Mental Disease in New York State, 1943-49. New York: National Association for Mental Health, 1958.

88. Malzberg, B.: Distribution of Mental Disease in New York State, 1949-51. Psychiatric Quarterly, 1955, Part 2 (Supplement).

89. Malzberg, B.: Mortality among Patients with Mental Disease. Utica, N. Y.: State Hospitals Press, 1934.

90. Malzberg, B.: Social and Biological Aspects of Mental Disease. Utica, N.Y.: State Hospitals Press, 1940.

91. Malzberg, B., and Lee, E. S.: Migration and Mental Disease. New York: Social Science Research Council, 1956.

92. Mayer-Gross, W.: Mental Health Survey in a Rural Area. Eugenics Quarterly, 1948, 40: 140-147.

93. Miles, H. C., and Gardner, E. A.: A Psychiatric Case Register. Use of a Psychiatric Case Register in Planning Community Mental Health Services. Archives of General Psychiatry, 1966, 14: 571-580.

94. Mishler, E. G., and Scotch, N. A.: Sociocultural Factors in the Epidemiology of Schizophrenia. Psychiatry, 1963, 26: 315-351.

95. Morgan, N. C., and Johnson, N. A.: Failures in Psychiatry: Chronic Hospital Patient. American Journal of Psychiatry, 1957, 113: 824-830.

96. Morris, J. N.: Uses of Epidemiology. Baltimore, Md.: Williams & Wilkins Co., 1964.

97. National Institute of Mental Health. Model Reporting Area for Mental Hospital Statistics—Development, Purpose and Program. PHS Publication No. 699. Washington, D.C. Government Printing Office, 1963.

98. National Institute of Mental Health. Psychopharmacology Service Center Collaborative Study Group. Phenothiazine Treatment in Acute Schizophrenia. Archives of General Psychiatry, 1964, 10: 246-261.

99. New Zealand: New Zealand Department of Health. Annual Report of the

Medical Statistician on the Mental Health Statistics of New Zealand for the Year 1960. Wellington, New Zealand.

100. Norris, V.: Mental Illness in London. Maudsley Monograph No. 6. London: Chapman & Hall, Ltd., 1959.

101. Norway: Central Bureau of Statistics. Norges Offisielle Statistikk XII 99. Sinnssykehusenes Virksombet 1960. Oslo: 1963.

102. Odegaard, Ornulv: Emigration and Insanity. Acta Psychiat. et Neurol., 1932, Supplement 4.

103. Odegaard, Ornulv: Marriage and Mental Disease. A Study in Social Psychopathology. Journal of Mental Science, 1946, 92: 35-59.

104. Odegaard, Ornulv: New Data on Marriage and Mental Disease. Incidence of Psychoses in Widowed and Divorced. Journal of Mental Science, 1953, 99: 778-785.

105. Odegaard, Ornulv: Pattern of Discharge and Readmission in Psychiatric Hospitals in Norway, 1926-1955. Mental Hygiene, 1961, 45: 185-193.

106. Odegaard, Ornulv: Pattern of Discharge from Norwegian Psychiatric Hospitals Before and After the Introduction of the Psychotropic Drugs. American Journal of Psychiatry, 1964, 120: 772-778.

107. Pasamanick, B., Dinitz, S., and Lefton, M.: Psychiatric Orientation and Its Relation to Diagnosis and Treatment in a Mental Hospital. American Journal of Psychiatry, 1959, 116: 127-132.

108. Pasamanick, B., Scarpitti, F. R., Lefton, M., Dinitz, S., Wernert, J. J., and McPheeters, H.: Home vs. Hospital Care for Schizophrenics. Journal of the American Medical Association, 1964, 187: 177-181.

109. Person, P. H., Jr.: Relationship Between Selected Social and Demographic Characteristics of Hospitalized Mental Patients and the Outcome of Hospitalization. Washington, D.C.: Government Printing Office, 1964.

110. Plunkett, R. J., and Haydon, A. B.: (Eds.) Standard Nomenclature of Diseases and Operations (4th Ed.). New York: Blakiston Div., 1952.

111. Pollack, E. S.: Uses of Census Matching for Study of Psychiatric Admission Rates. Proceedings of the Social Statistics Section, American Statistical Association, Washington, D.C., 1965.

112. Pollack, E. S., Person, P. H., Jr., Kramer, M., and Goldstein, H.: Patterns of Retention, Release and Death of First Admissions to State Mental Hospitals. PHS Publication No. 672, Public Health Monograph No. 58. Washington, D.C.: Government Printing Office, 1959.

113. Pollack, E. S., Redick, R. W., Norman, V. B., Wurster, C. R., and Gorwitz, K.: Socioeconomic and Family Characteristics of Patients Admitted to Psychiatric Services. American Journal of Public Health, 1964, 54: 506-518.

114. Public Law 88-164, Senate 1576, 88th Congress, October 31, 1963: Mental Retardation Facilities and Community Mental Health Centers Construction Act of 1963.

115. Public Law 89-105, H.R. 2985, 89th Congress, August 4, 1965: Mental Retardation Facilities and Community Mental Health Centers Construction Act Amendments of 1965.

116. Pugh, T. F., and MacMahon, B.: Epidemiologic Findings in United States Mental Hospital Data. Boston: Little, Brown & Co., 1962.

117. Reid, D. D.: Epidemiological Methods to the Study of Mental Disorders. World Health Organization, 1960. Public Health Papers No. 2.

118. Richman, A., and Kennedy, P.: Estimating Longitudinal Changes in the Number of Patients Hospitalized in Canadian Psychiatric Institutions. Acta Psychiatrica Scandinavica, 1965, 41: 177-203.

119. Rosen, B. M., Bahn, A. K., and Kramer, M.: Demographic and Diagnostic Characteristics of Psychiatric Clinic Outpatients in the U.S.A., 1961. American Journal of Orthopsychiatry, 1964, 34: 455-468.

120. Roth, W. F., and Luton, F. H.: Mental Health Program in Tennessee.

American Journal of Psychiatry, 1943: 99: 662-675.

121. Sandifer, M. G., Pettus, C., and Quade, D.: A Study of Psychiatric Diagnosis. Journal of Nervous and Mental Diseases, 1964, 139: 350-356.

122. Shepherd, M.: A Study of the Major Psychoses in an English County. Maudsley Monograph No. 3. London: Chapman & Hall, Ltd., 1957.

123. Sjogren, T.: Genetic-Statistical and Psychiatric Investigations of a West Swedish Population. Acta Psychiat., Neurol., 1948, Supplement 52.

124. Smith, T. C., Bower, W. H., and Wignall, C. M.: Influence of Policy and Drugs on Colorado State Hospital Population. Archives of General Psychiatry, 1965, 12: 352-362.

125. Spitzer, R. L., Fleiss, J., Kernohan, W., Lee, J. C., and Baldwin, I. T.: Mental Status Schedule—Comparing Kentucky and New York Schizophrenics. Archives of General Psychiatry, 1965, 21: 448-455.

126. Stengel, E.: Classification of Mental Disorders. Bulletin of the World Health Organization, 1960, 21: 601-663.

127. Stromgren, E.: Beiträge zur Psychischen Erblehre. Acta Psychiat. Neurol. (Kbh), 1938, Supplement 19.

128. Tietze, C., Lemkau, P., and Cooper, M.: Personality Disorder and Spatial Mobility. American Journal of Sociology, 1942, 48: 29-39.

129. Tokuhata, G. K., and Stehman, V. A.: Mortality in State Mental Hospitals of Michigan, 1950-54. Public Health Reports, 1958, 73: 750-761.

130. Tooth, G. C., and Brooks, E. M.: Trends in the Mental Population and Their Effect on Future Planning. Lancet, 1961, 1: 710-713.

131. Tsuwaga, T.: Uber die Psychiatrische Zensusuntersuchung in einem Stadtbezirk von Tokyo. Psychiat. Neurol. Jap., 1942, 46: 204.

132. U.S. Dept. of Health, Education and Welfare, Public Health Service, National Institutes of Health. National Institute of Mental Health. Mental Health Statistics—Current Reports. Series MHB-I-10, MHB-H-10, January 1966.

133. U.S. Dept. of Health, Education and Welfare, Public Health Service, National Institutes of Health, National Institute of Mental Health: Patients in Mental Institutions, 1964: Part II. State and County Mental Hospitals. Part III. Private Mental Hospitals and General Hospitals with Psychiatric Facilities. Part IV. Private Institutions for the Mentally Retarded. PHS Publication No. 1452.

134. U.S. Dept. of Health, Education and Welfare, Public Health Service, National Institutes of Health, National Institute of Mental Health. Patient Movement Data—State and County Mental Hospitals: 1960—PHS Publication No. 1144. 1961—PHS Publication No. 1189. 1962—PHS Publication No. 1282.

135. U.S. Dept. of Health, Education and Welfare, Public Health Service, National Institutes of Health, National Institute of Mental Health: Outpatient Psychiatric Clinics, 1964 (Annual Stat. Report, Data on Patients).

136. Uchimura, Y. et al.: Uber die Vergleichend-Psychiatrische und Erbpathologische Untersuchung auf Einer Japanischen Insel. Psychiat. Neurol. Jap., 1940, 44: 745.

137. Veterans Administration: Administrator of Veterans Affairs. Annual Report. Washington, D.C.: Government Printing Office, 1964.

138. Victoria, Australia: Mental Health Research Institute. Statistical Bulletin No. 3. Admissions, Discharges and Deaths, 1962. Melbourne, Australia, 1964.

139. Warthen, F. J., Klee, G. D., Bahn, A. K., and Gorwitz, K.: Diagnosed Schizophrenia in Maryland. Paper read at American Psychiatric Association Regional Research Conference on Psychiatric Epidemiology and Mental Health Planning, Baltimore, April 21-22, 1966. (In Press)

140. Wing, J. K., Denham, J., and Monro, A. B.: Duration of Stay in Hospital of Patients Suffering from Schizophrenia. Brit. J. Prev. & Soc. Med., 1959, 13: 145-148.

141. World Health Organization International Classification of Diseases, 8th Revision, Appendix 2. July 1965.

142. World Health Organization International Pilot Study of Schizophrenia. Planning for WHO International Pilot Study of Schizophrenia. Working Paper No. 2. Geneva, 5-12 July 1966. MENT/WP/66.2.

143. World Health Organization Report of First WHO Seminar on Psychiatric Diagnosis, Classification and Statistics, London, 11-15 October 1965.

144. World Health Organization Study Group on Schizophrenia (Report): American Journal of Psychiatry, 1959, 115: 865-872.

145. Yoo, P. S.: Mental Disorders in the Korean Rural Communities. Proceedings of the Third World Congress of Psychiatry, Montreal, Canada. June 1961, 1305-1309.

4

General Biological Studies

NORMAN Q. BRILL, M.D.

Dr. Norman Q. Brill, formerly Medical Director of the UCLA Neuropsychiatric Institute, is now Professor of Psychiatry at the UCLA School of Medicine. He is consultant in Psychiatry to the Brentwood Veteran's Administration Hospital, Los Angeles, and the Los Angeles County Harbor General Hospital.

Educated in New York, Dr. Brill received his M.D. degree from New York University Medical School in 1934. He served in the U.S. Army (1941-1946), the last two years in the Office of the Surgeon General as Chief of Psychiatry Branch, N.P. Consultants Division.

In the past, Dr. Brill has been Chief of the Research Section of the N.P. Division of the Department of Medicine and Surgery, VA, Washington, D.C., and Professor of Neurology and Head of the department at Georgetown University School of Medicine, Washington, D.C. He is a National consultant in psychiatry to both the Surgeon Generals of the U.S. Air Force and U.S. Army, and to the U.S. Navy Medical Neuropsychiatric Research Unit, San Diego, Calif.

In addition to many other articles he is co-author of "A Followup Study of War Neuroses" (a VA medical monograph), "The Treatment of Psychiatric Outpatients," and is editor of "Psychiatry in Medicine" (Univ. of Calif. Press).

Dr. Brill is a member of the American and International Psychoanalytical Associations, a former member of Council of the American Psychiatric Association, and a Fellow of the American College of Psychiatrists.

In studies of the relation between mental illness and early background factors, no pattern of environmental and traumatic factors has ever been found which would inevitably lead to mental abnormality. Landis and Bolles[148] found patterns which would *probably* lead to psychologic deviation in adult life, but none which would *surely* do so. This is obvious, since mental illness is a result of the interaction of at least two variables: 1) *the stress* to which the individual is exposed, and 2) the unique way he *reacts to it*. Since the individual's reaction to stress is a function of his temperament, and since temperamental differences in individuals are observed to be present from birth, and, since they must have a *biologic* or *somatic base* or *counterpart,* it is important to investigate biologic determinants of mental illness as well as psychologic.

Mr. Raymond Weinstein assisted greatly in the *review* of the literature. He is a doctoral candidate in the Department of Sociology, UCLA, and a research assistant at The Neuropsychiatric Institute. He received his B.B.A. degree in 1963 from the College of the City of New York and his M.A. degree in 1966 at UCLA.

Nurses working with newborn infants will report that some infants are more active than others, some more passive. Some cry a lot, some rarely cry, some cannot wait to be fed, others are almost indifferent. These differences exist even when such variables as medication that the mother has received, type of labor, birth weight, and developmental age are controlled. This is another way of saying that personality differences existing between individuals are to some extent, present at birth. Parents will testify to differences they have seen in the temperament of their children literally from the time they were born.

We are just beginning to learn how a variety of physical, physiologic and metabolic factors may influence the development of the fetus, but it would be no more reasonable to attribute all temperamental difference to such factors than it would be to attribute differences in fingerprints to them. There are undoubtedly inherited genetic determinants of temperament and personality in humans—as breeders of animals will insist there are in animals.

Growth and development of each infant assumes a distinctive pattern. These patterns were studied in Gesell's laboratory by taking moving pictures of the daily major activities of five infants.[147] Similar records of the same children were made at age five. Fifteen behavioral traits, such as social responsiveness, reaction to success, and energy output were rated at age one and again at age five in rank order for the children by an expert who had never seen the children. The agreement between the rankings at the two age periods clearly indicated that there were persisting traits in the makeup of each individual.

Washburn[241] observed individual differences in temperament in infants during the first year of life by examining such things as attentiveness to people and differences in the amount of laughing and crying. Although there are no extensive follow-up studies showing that these early infantile and childhood patterns continue as characteristics into adult life, it has been found that there is individual consistency over a period of years.

Shirley[210] found certain consistencies with regard to adaptability, timidity, and agressiveness based on observation for a two year period beginning at birth. She wrote personality sketches on 19 children, based on her two year acquaintance with them and their parents. Fifteen years later Neilon[170] did a follow-up study on these same children (with full data on sixteen of them and partial data on all). Adolescent personality sketches were prepared and matched with childhood sketches by impartial judges. The findings permitted the conclusion that identifiable personality similarities persist during the first 15 years of life. Some individuals were more readily identified at the end of 15 years, presumably due to greater uniqueness of personality.

Margaret Fries[74] has emphasized the point that infants of different temperaments will react to the same stress differently, everything else being equal, and that these differences may be related to the type of illness an individual develops (if one does develop).

We are inclined to think of the timing of stress in the life of an individual in psychologic terms, in terms of ego development, and not in biologic terms. In this connection, Dr. Jonas Salk's speculations are of interest. Commenting that an experimental overdose of an antigen can result in immunologic paralysis, that is, no antibody formation (in contrast to normal defensive antibody production from manageable doses of antigen,) he suggests that children exposed to excessive stress, for their stage of ego development, may fail to develop defenses against such stresses—a phenomenon that is as biologic as it is psychologic.

Turning now to specific problems of schizophrenia, most work done in the search for biologic factors has involved the anatomic, physiologic, biochemical, and endocrinologic status of schizophrenics, and comparing them to nonschizophrenics. Many people have found many things, and apart from the unreliability of some of the work, the question constantly arises in connection with that which seems reliable—how much is cause and how much effect—of schizophrenia itself? In this chapter biochemical and neurophysiologic aspects will not be reviewed as they will be considered in subsequent chapters.

IMPAIRMENT OF REACTIVITY

A great deal of research has suggested that somatic withdrawal accompanies psychic withdrawal in schizophrenic disorders, particularly in those which have existed for some time. Repeatedly clinical observation has been made that many withdrawn, regressed schizophrenic patients have grossly impaired reactions to painful stimuli. In several cases, patients have been observed to burn their fingers with lighted cigarettes without experiencing pain, very much as observed in patients with syringomyelia. Reactions to many drugs are often impaired. Catatonic schizophrenic patients will sit up and talk coherently after an injection of 7½ grains of sodium amytal or sodium pentothal, whereas the administration of this amount to a normal individual would put him to sleep. As a group, schizophrenics are able to tolerate much larger doses of phenothiazine and other tranquilizers than normals or patients with organic illnesses. Reactions to the intracutaneous injection of histamine have been described as impaired, as have similar decreased responses to injections of pitressin. Schizophrenics have been described as capable of tolerating large doses of thyroid medication with little effect, much larger doses of insulin than normals, and as demonstrating impaired adrenocortical response to experimental stress (with no similar impairment of response to the administration of ACTH). Impaired vestibular reactions in adult schizophrenics have been described by Angyal and Blockman.[5] Colbert et al. found depressed, variable or absent responses to caloric and rotational tests in children with schizophrenic disorders.[34] Differential responses to administration of adrenalin and mecholyl were described by Funkenstein et al.[76]

Decreased reaction to dinitrophenol and foreign protein administration has been reported, and it has been suggested that, in general, temperature regulation is impaired in many schizophrenics. They have been described as having lower skin temperatures, decreased heat production, lack of thermoregulatory adaptability, especially to cold; and decreased difference between oral and rectal temperature. Pupillary reactions have been described as sluggish; psychogalvanic responses as impaired, responses to the cold pressor test reduced; skin reactions to injections of foreign protein as impaired; and antibody response to pertussis vaccine decreased, especially in catatonics and hebephrenics. Abnormal responses to repeated injections of adrenalin were reported as were different blood count responses to high humidity and temperature.[186]

While some investigators have postulated some inherent defect in responsiveness, most clinicians are now of the opinion that the impaired reactivity which has been so commonly observed in schizophrenics is a concomitant of the disease, rather than a reflection of the etiology of the disease.

PATHOLOGY

Brain Studies

As modern techniques in neuropathology developed in the latter part of the nineteenth century, careful searches were made for the brain lesions which were believed to be causing schizophrenia. It is not surprising that Kraepelin in 1907 would say, "The fact is decisive that the morbid anatomy of dementia praecox (as it was called then) has disclosed not simple inadequacy of the nervous constitution, but destructive morbid processes as the background of the clinical picture."

According to Dastur, who wrote an outstanding historical survey of the pathology of schizophrenia,[39] Alzheimer, the great neuropathologist, "had by then reported severe changes in the cerebral cortex, with disorganization of the ganglion cells, and extensive glial reactions. He described not only swollen nuclei and shrunken neurons, with a frequent falling out of groups of cells, but also proliferative fibrous gliosis and pigmentary changes." In 1913, he reviewed the pathologic anatomy of 55 cases of dementia praecox and localized the major changes to layers II and III of the cerebral cortex. E. Bleuler,[22] too, believed there was some underlying toxic or organic basis in schizophrenic disorders. Southard, in 1919,[222] went to the extent of correlating the psychologic disturbances of schizophrenia with neuronal and glial lesions of the upper cortical layers or supracortex and then proceeded to correlate lesions of the "infracortex" of the temporal and parietal lobes with auditory hallucinosis and catatonia. Dastur reported, "The first word of caution regarding the interpretation of these diverse neuropathological observations came from Adolph Meyer."[165] In 1923 Josephy,[124] while himself reporting pathologic findings in the brain, criticized previous reports which had failed to take into consideration the patient's age and terminal illness (which, remarkably, had been ignored by renowned pathologists).

Dunlap in 1923[47] undertook the first carefully controlled study. He examined the brains of schizophrenics where the diagnosis was unquestioned, where the patient was under 40 years of age at the time of death, where death was due to an acute process, such as accident or suicide, and where autopsy was done immediately after death. Only eight cases fulfilled these criteria. In addition, he studied five brains from control cases, i.e., nonschizophrenic. His report, more than any other, laid to rest the ghost of swollen or shrunken nerve cells, gliosis, etc., which so many others had described. He found no significant difference between schizophrenics and the controls, and he concluded his study with the statement that there was not "even a suspicion of a consistent organic brain disease as a basis for the psychosis of schizophrenia."

Many others studied the brains of schizophrenics.* Their findings added to the controversy over whether schizophrenia was or was not an organic disease.

As recently as 1951, Papez and Batemen[178,179] claimed to have shown intracytoplasmic inclusions in the neurons in a large number of brain biopsy specimens from schizophrenics, which they believed might be the causal factor behind the many changes in neurons and glia they reported. (The long sought schizococcus!)

At about this time changes in the basal ganglia were being described by some as explaining catatonia, while others were examining the hypothalamus for an organic explanation for schizophrenia. Bäumer[9] investigated the nucleus medialis and lateralis of the thalamus of 14 schizophrenic patients and of 30 brains of control cases. She found various changes in the neurons in the schizophrenic brains, but not in the controls. The anteroventral thalamic nucleus of 18 schizophrenics was examined by Fünfgeld,[75] who also found cellular changes in all instances, but not in normal controls. Von Buttlar-Brentano[238] also reported pathologic changes in schizophrenics.

Changes in hypothalamic nuclei in eight cases of catatonic schizophrenia and two cases of paranoid schizophrenia, by means of Nissl- and Feulgenstained sections, were examined by Wahren.[239] Unlike Fünfgeld, he did not find destruction of nerve cells, or changes in the glia. Rather, he described changes which he attributed to aging or to "nerve diseases other than schizophrenia." According to Hopf[112] there was atrophy of cells and a distinct increase of lipofuscine and tigrolysis in the pallidum and striatum of catatonic schizophrenics, not seen in normals, hebephrenics, and paranoids. Extensive

---

*35, 50, 60, 157, 223, 245, 246, 249.

cellular changes were also observed in catatonics by Scharenberg and Brown.[202]

Ferraro[61] referred to the divergent viewpoints considering schizophrenia a functional disorder on the one hand and an organic disease on the other. His experience led him to conclude that, "typical clinical cases of the schizophrenic syndrome are compatible with both the presence or absence of cerebral structural histopathologic changes." He warned against the automatic categorization of schizophrenia as an organic disease even when these changes are present. Instead, Ferraro indicated three other possibilities that could explain the histopathological changes. They may be an expression of: a) a complicating secondary organic process; b) a primary organic brain disease which may precipitate a schizophrenic symptom complex; or c) the psychosomatic interaction which results from the interdependence of soma and psyche.

After a comprehensive review of the literature, Wolf and Cowen[250] concluded that there is nothing in the schizophrenic brain that cannot be duplicated in any nonschizophrenic state. They attributed the reported microscopic abnormalities to "misjudgments of the limits of normal variation, misinterpretation of artifacts, or the uncritical attribution of special significance to casual, coincidental findings." They further claimed that "there may be an organic basis for schizophrenia and other psychoses of unknown origin but if there be, there is at present, no reliable histologic evidence for it." In 1954 Weinstein[242] also felt that the voluminous literature dealing with neuropathology was "marked by inconclusiveness and contradiction." He exhorted investigators to look into "the metabolic activity of the brain in schizophrenia as the most reasonable and promising approach to the problem of dynamics and etiology of this disease."

Reports of a wide variety of brain pathology in schizophrenics and especially in catatonics continued to appear.[114,211,233,240] In 1956 another controlled study was published by Peters[184] who examined the brains of eight executed criminals and 14 schizophrenics and could find no histologic difference between them.

For some time because of the reported findings of abnormalities in the cardiovascular system, it was thought that there might be reduced blood flow and oxygen consumption in the brain, but the critical work of Kety[138] effectively dismissed this possibility.

Dastur,[39] after his thorough review of the literature (1959), says: "Looking back on this total historical picture of histopathology of schizophrenia, the conclusion seems inescapable that no specific change in any tissue or system of the body has been demonstrated that can account for the clinical syndrome of schizophrenia." He concludes with the thought derived from the lesson of the past and the fact that history repeats itself, that "one need not be shocked if the current notion of there being a distorted molecule behind a distorted thought is as difficult to demonstrate as the older belief of a defective neuron behind a defective thought."

Fingerprint Studies

Schlegel[204] reviewed the literature and discussed his own findings concerning constitutional and biologic observations of the hands of schizophrenics and of patients with other types of psychoses. He concluded that there is a relationship between schizophrenia and the patterns of the dermal ridges of fingertips.

The fingerprints of 100 very carefully selected male schizophrenics were studied by Raphael and Raphael.[190] Complicating factors such as convulsive disorder, left-handedness, patent homosexuality, difficult pregnancy or birth, congenital heart disease, etc., were excluded by careful screening. They noted an increased frequency of whorls and arches, fewer ulnar loops, and a high incidence of pattern dissociation. They believed these findings to be indicative of a constitutional deficit and that there is the "possibility (of) a general, basic genetic insufficiency or biologic lack, mirrored in various abnormalities and disorders, of which finger patterns seem to be an included manifestation." The *American Medical Association Journal*[4] commented that Raphael and Raphael's article "is both timely and topical." They felt that fingerprints are of constitutional or genotypic importance and certainly significant for the study of schizophrenia.

Cardiovascular Studies

In 1923, Nolan D. C. Lewis[152] found, with remarkable consistency, in autopsy studies of a large number of patients with dementia praecox an aplastic circulatory system, and disorders of the thyroid, adrenals, and gonads. The hypoplasia was described as extending throughout the entire cardiovascular system and associated with hyperplasia of the lymphatic system. He confirmed the observations of Mott regarding degenerative and atrophic changes in the testes. Olkon[174] in 1939, mindful of Lewis' concept of an aplastic cardiovascular system, studied the capillary structure of the finger webs of over 1000 schizophrenics and compared them to normals. He found a reduction in capillary density and very wide variability in size of capillaries in schizophrenics. There were many more bizarre shaped capillaries and an irregular rate of blood flow. He concluded that "schizophrenia was associated with a defect in capillaries and that the defect was directly related to the severity of the disease."[39]

The capillary structure in each of 75 schizophrenic patients was examined by Hauptmann and Myerson.[93] Their principal finding was that schizophrenics had an immature formation of the capillaries, similar to that observed in normal children before the end state of capillary development. Hauptmann and Myerson stressed that "the abnormal capillary picture in schizophrenics did not change during the course of the disease," and, while not claiming that the capillary picture should decide the clinical diagnosis, they stated, "that in some cases the capillary picture corresponded better to the course of the psychosis than the clinical diagnosis made at the beginning of the illness."

Doust[46] examined drawings and photomicrographs of the capillary structure of the nailfold skin of the ring fingers of both hands in schizophrenic patients, other psychiatric patients, and controls. He claimed that specific patterns of nailfold capillary structure were found to characterize the healthy subjects and patients of each of seven varieties of psychiatric disturbance. He concluded that "the nailfold capillary morphology is indicative of personality structure, liability to psychiatric breakdown and that it represents an index of constitutional maturation." Wertheimer and Wertheimer[243] reported on the capillary structure of schizophrenic patients, and designed their study to hold somatotype constant. They found that paranoid schizophrenics differed significantly on various capillary measures (particularly on plexus ratings) from a combined group of catatonic, hebephrenic, and simple schizophrenics. Both schizophrenic groups also differed from the normal group.

Capillary pattern in the nailfold of 50 familial schizophrenic patients, 42 nonfamilial, and 60 normals was studied by Maricq.[160] She reported that familial schizophrenics differed from nonfamilial in that they had "a distinctive capillary pattern in the nailfold," and "a more uniform picture of selected psychiatric traits." She also found that a high plexus rating was not related to age, sex, or duration of illness, and that "the incidence of hebephrenic type is greater in patients with high plexus ratings." Maricq claimed that these capillary findings agreed with earlier studies by Hauptmann and Myerson, Doust, and Wertheimer and Wertheimer. She concluded that "familial schizophrenic patients are different from the other schizophrenics in terms of both physical and psychiatric characteristics." In another paper Maricq[161] examined the capillary morphology of 285 schizophrenics selected at random plus a follow-up on the 92 schizophrenic patients previously reported. She found that the majority of patients with a high plexus rating and a positive family history were still hospitalized, while many patients with a negative family history and low rating had left the hospital. She also reported several cases where a significant change in the plexus appeared to parallel a marked change in the patient's clinical condition. Maricq concluded that "a high plexus score represents a useful criterion to assist in selecting a much more homogeneous group of schizophrenics than our present classification permits."

Endocrine Factors

Thyroid indices in a group of chronic schizophrenic patients were studied by Simpson et al.[213] None of the patients had suffered from hypothyroidism or debiliating diseases (which might lead to thyroid exhaustion), nor were they on any drugs (which might cause artificial lowering of the I_{131} uptake). They found: clinical manifestations of hypothyroidism in only 28 per cent of the cases, but decreased 24-hour I_{131} uptake in 93 per cent of the cases. Cerebrospinal fluid protein was elevated in 38 per cent of the patients, half of whom had an abnormal colloidal gold curve. They concluded that, "the lack of correlation between the various indices cannot be explained at this (time), but may be related to the small size of the sample or to biological inconsistencies in a schizophrenic population." They further tested[214] and confirmed their finding of "functional hypothyroidism," rather than clinical hypothyroidism, by administering triiodothyronine (T_3) to a series of patients. Four improved somewhat, eighteen showed no improvement, and six were judged to be worse. They also investigated the "rebound" effect following T_3 withdrawal to determine if the reduced thyroid activity was caused by an abnormality of the pituitary-thyroid "feedback," but found no abnormality. The possibility of the functional hypothyroidism being a result of prolonged institutionalization was investigated[212] with negative findings. It was observed to be present in many newly admitted patients.

Elsässer and Siebke[49] found ovarian insufficiency in 24 per cent of schizophrenic patients and in 21 per cent of nonschizophrenic mental patients. Cavé[32] investigated the role of endocrine factors in a case of schizophrenia with hyperfolliculinism and concluded that this disorder played little part in the schizophrenic reaction. The possible endocrinologic basis for schizophrenia was discussed by Co Tui.[33]

The relationship of menstrual disturbance to psychiatric illness was examined by Gregory[86] in a group of 22 schizophrenic patients "suffering from prolonged and severe psychoses, with a record of frequent outbursts of violence and resistive behavior." He found that 56 per cent of such disturbances occurred during a time of normal cycle, and that the remaining 44 per cent occurred during periods of amenorrhoea or prolonged cycle. Gregory concluded that disturbed behavior occurs in psychotics only slightly more often during periods of regular cycles than during periods of amenorrhoea, and that "prolongation of cycle and amenorrhoea is a very common event following the development of acute psychotic disturbance." Dalton[37] concluded that the onset of acute psychiatric disorders was related to the menstrual cycle. She found that 46 per cent of 276 psychiatric admissions and 47 per cent of schizophrenic admissions occurred during menstruation or the premenstruum.

The prevalence of common menstrual disorders in psychiatric patients and controls (matched for age and parity) was investigated by Coppen.[36] Neurotic patients were found to have experienced the greatest amount of symptoms including menstrual pain, irritability, headaches, swelling, and irregularity. Those with affective disorders had a normal prevalence, and schizophrenics experienced the least amount of such disorders. Schizophrenic patients showed less dysmenorrhoea and premenstrual symptoms than their normal controls, and Coppen speculated that this is so ". . . because these patients are less sensitive than normal, or because they have certain endocrinological or other physiological characteristics that provoke fewer of these menstrual symptoms." However, nearly 40 per cent of schizophrenics had menstrual irregularity, and it was claimed that this suggests ". . . there may be some underlying hormonal abnormality in these patients."

In 1919 Mott[168] examined microscopically the testes of schizophrenics and described poor nuclear staining, fewer spermatocytes, and more degenerated spermatozoa in some, and almost total fibrotic atrophy in others. Some years later Hemphill and Reiss[97] also studied histopathologic changes in the testis in schizophrenia. They maintained that their biopsy material "consistently showed an abnormal histological picture in schizophrenia in early life." Abnormalities noted were "gross disorder of spermatogenic elements, with destruction of many tubules, hyalinization of basement membrane, and infertility." Hemphill[96] concluded that it appeared likely that the testis atrophy was due to abnormal hypothalamic or anterior pituitary activity, and that there was an endogenous factor causing schizophrenia. In contrast, Blair et al.[21] examined testicular biopsies on 25 schizophrenic patients (in whom there was no question about diagnosis) who were under 40 and free of organic disease and reported that "there was not a single biopsy that could be regarded as pathological." They suggested that some other factor (such as the wartime diet or a higher frequency of mumps orchitis) may have influenced previously reported results.

Tourney et al.[232] evaluated the testicular morphology in biopsies from 23 patients with typical schizophrenia. Pathologic change was most often observed in the catatonics, suggesting that chronicity of illness and nutritional deficiency were contributing to, or responsible for, what testicular atrophy was observed. They hypothesized that "the longer the duration of illness, the greater the chance for subclinical nutritive failure to occur, particularly in patients with catatonia," and concluded that "specific abnormalities of testicular structure and function do not characterize schizophrenia." Nuremberg and Brambilla[173] reported a marked gonadotropin hyposecretion, reduced gonadal function, and androgen hypersecretion in female, but not male, schizophrenics. No other hormonal abnormality was found.

It was postulated by Krøll[145] that the endocrine changes around puberty may constitute a "psychosis-predisposing factor." He believed that schizophrenic reactions may be caused by hepatic dysfunction based on a congenital (or acquired) portocaval collateral circulation. Krøll maintained that, "since steroid hormones are inactivated mainly in the liver, there must be a possibility that hepatic dysfunction entails disturbances of the endocrine balance and, secondarily, changes of carbohydrate, protein, and electrolyte metabolism."

Minsker[166] studied the reactivity of certain links of the endocrine system in various forms of the course of schizophrenia, and Ischel[120] reported on the endocrine disorders in 8 cases of hebephrenia.

Many reports have indicated that schizophrenic patients exhibit increased adrenocortical activity,[3] decreased activity,[99] or normal activity.[23] The discrepancy in findings appeared to be related to the use of different indices of adrenocortical activity, and, at the present time consensus of opinion is that there is no significant relationship between adrenocortical activity and schizophrenia or the severity of a schizophrenic disorder.[79] Greater variability of adrenocortical activity has been repeatedly observed among schizophrenic patients (as compared with normals), but this greater variability has also been described for many other biologic functions.

Visceral Studies

Rupp and Wilson[201] did postmortem examinations on a group of 37 patients clinically diagnosed as having a so-called "functional psychosis." They reported the presence of extensive visceral and brain abnormalities which they did not consider coincidental nor secondary to the mental illness. They claimed their findings should warn all those who consider mental illness as having a purely psychogenic etiology against such a conclusion.

Extraneural pathology in schizophrenia was described by Buscaino.[30] His studies indicated that schizophrenics manifest abnormalities in liver function associated with digestive tract and reticuloendothelial system changes. He felt that schizophrenia was a generalized disease resulting in changes in the central nervous system, due to a hepato-enteric toxin which probably caused lesions within the brain. Scheidegger[203] attributed liver changes at autopsy to be the result of age and terminal illness rather than of schizophrenia.

Horwitt[113] emphasized that "many reports showing differences between patients with schizophrenia and normal individuals are based on environmental artifacts that are not related to the basic disorder." He claimed that studies of urinary excretion or blood constituents are performed without regard to nutritional controls, and studies of liver function make no attempt to determine whether the changes indicated are related to diet, inactivity, physiologic hibernation, infection, or other factors.

Hematologic Studies

Hoffer[106] studied erythrocytes in schizophrenia and found them slightly different from those found in normals. Hemoglobin derived from schizophrenic blood seemed optically more dense than that obtained from nonschizophrenic blood, and the schizophrenic erythrocytes were more fragile to hyptonic saline solutions. He concluded that this "may be related to the adrenochrome hypothesis" and "it may be that adrenochrome also plays a role within erythrocyte metabolism." Differences in cell fragility in erythrocytes were also studied by Hoare[100] but, unlike Hoffer, he designed his experiment to control for variables such as age, sex, race, length of hospitalization, and drug treatment. No differences were found between schizophrenic patients and controls.

More recently Lideman and Iryanov[153] found reduced resistance of erythrocytes to hemolytic agents in schizophrenic patients (as compared to normals and patients with other psychoses). This resistance was observed to increase with chlorpromazine medication. Turner and Chipps[234] found difrences in hemolysin in the blood of schizophrenics as compared to others, including normal controls, which appeared to be unrelated to diet, intestinal flora, duration of hospitalization, and many other variables.

The nucleus of the lymphocyte in 40 normal subjects and 60 chronic schizophrenics was examined by Vanderkamp.[236] He postulated that if a genetic difference exists between schizophrenics and normals, there may be a difference in protein structure and composition as well. Using Masson's trichrome stain, the nucleus of the lymphocyte stained a homogeneous blue in normals and black to dark purple in schizophrenics. Vanderkamp concluded that "the abnormalities that were demonstrated could indicate an abnormality in cellular metabolism and function in the schizophrenics." Fessel and Hirata-Hibi[64] confirmed the presence of abnormalities in circulating leukocytes of schizophrenic patients, but were unable to explain their significance. Pennington[183] also verified the finding of nuclear differences in the staining reactions of white blood cells from schizophrenic patients and excluded the possibility that the changes were the result of medication.

Gershon and Lonigro,[81] too, found a difference in the lymphocytic staining properties between hospitalized schizophrenic patients and normal controls. However, they found no difference between the staining properties of the lymphocyte of the same schizophrenic patients and hospitalized nonschizophrenic controls and concluded that the differences were caused by hospitalization. Bucci and Johnson[28] also attempted to duplicate Vanderkamp's study. They selected 20 schizophrenic patients and 5 controls, and samples of blood were examined by the Masson method. Their results showed no difference in staining properties of the lymphocytes between the schizophrenics and controls. They pointed out that Vanderkamp's patients had been hospitalized for many years, while their patients had been hospitalized for a relatively short duration. Like Gershon and Lonigro, they considered the possibility that changes reported by others were in some way related to hospitalization.

The morphology of white blood cells was also investigated by Erban[51,52] in 13 schizophrenic patients and 13 normal controls. He observed "atypical" cells more frequently in the schizophrenic group and considered his findings as evidence of a genetic etiology of mental diseases.

Hirata-Hibi and Fessel[98] examined the bone marrow of 7 chronic schizophrenic patients, and found "morphological abnormalities of lymphocytes and increased numbers of reticulum cells." They were uncertain as to the significance of these abnormalities, and postulated that it "may be related to the abnormal blood proteins seen in schizophrenic patients."

Fieve et al.[66] performed a controlled study "to determine the effect of phenothiazines on the frequency of occurrence of atypical lymphocytes. They found a significant difference "in the number of abnormal peripheral lymphocytes seen in those subjects, schizophrenic or not, on phenothiazine medication and in those not receiving the drug." They believed that the atypical lymphocytes were similar to those described by Fessel and Hirata-Hibi[64] and, contrary to Pennington,[183] they concluded that "these atypical lymphocytes are probably a phenothiazine drug effect, and not a function of the schizophrenic process."

The hypothesis that genetic or mental stress factors determine the morphology of abnormal lymphocytes in schizophrenia was examined by Fessel, et al.[65] Their results showed more abnormal lymphocytes in the family members of "process" schizophrenic patients than in the family members of "reactive" schizophrenic patients or normal families. They purported that these results "cannot be ascribed to technical artifact or to the hospitalization or treatment of the schizophrenic patients," as there was a nonrandom distribution of abnormal lymphocytes within the process schizophrenic families and a random distribution of (normal) variant lymphocytes in these same families. Thus, they concluded that the "genetic hypothesis is more strongly supported by the findings than is the stress hypothesis" and that "a genetic influence plays a major role and emotional stress a minor but important one in determining the appearance of abnormal lymphocytes."

Hollister,[110,111] after careful studies, was unable to find the differences in lymphocytes described by others.

Irvine and Miyashita[119] studied blood types in relation to schizophrenia and other psychoses. They found that blood groups A and A_1 occurred more often in schizophrenics than in nonschizophrenics. They concluded that "although these results are preliminary and generally fail to achieve conventionally acceptable levels of statistical significance, the fact that all the predicted directional trends were observed is encouraging, and suggests that the recent reports linking blood groups to certain mental illnesses may indicate important pervasive relationships."

Dietary and Metabolic

Believing that psychologic and sociologic explanations for the etiology of schizophrenia were inadequate, Cade[31] postulated that physical differences in environment, such as "the existence of a protective factor in diet present in foods of relatively limited production and distribution, in the semiluxury or at least the nonstaple category," can better explain the epidemiologic distribution of schizophrenia. An analysis of Australian country towns revealed that those towns with the lowest incidence of schizophrenia were noted for "the abundance of fruit trees in home gardens." Cade concluded that "when consumption of protective foods falls below a certain minimum level those with a constitutional predisposition develop frank schizophrenia."

Hoch,[101] in an address before the American Public Health Association, maintained that epidemiologic studies "have concentrated too much on severe cases only; we need to know more about the epidemiology of the less obvious cases." He indicated that "recent studies have shown that the older view that schizophrenia is basically an autistic disorder with associative impairments should be replaced by a recognition that schizophrenia consists of an impairment of capacity to integrate inner and outer stimuli in a repetitive way, probably due to damaged subcortical functioning, as a consequence of metabolic disturbances, psychogenic forces or both."

Prematurity

Terris et al.[229] studied the relationship between prematurity and childhood schizophrenia. In a series of 463 childhood schizophrenics and matched controls no association was found. However, they did observe that childhood schizophrenia was significantly associated with previous maternal fetal loss, but warned that, in view of the current uncertainty and disagreement concerning the nosology and diagnosis of childhood schizophrenia, the interpretation of this finding must be made with caution.

INFECTIONS, INTOXICATIONS AND TOXEMIAS

Infections

Because so many hospitalized schizophrenics were found to have tuberculosis, many psychiatrists entertained the possibility of some causal relationship. They wondered about schizophrenia being the result of tuberculous infection. Although the incidence of tuberculosis kept dropping and the frequency of its occurrence diminished, some continued to investigate the possibility of an etiologic relationship.

After noting, in 1945, that between 60 and 70 per cent of schizophrenics die of tuberculosis, Lowenstein[155] investigated the spinal fluid of 48 schizophrenic cases "free from tuberculosis symptoms by all clinical methods," and found that 21 spinal fluids, or 45 per cent, were positive. He disagreed with those who believed that tuberculosis was acquired during hospitalization (because other psychoses "do not show such a high mortality from tuberculosis in spite of long hospitalization") and implied a causal relationship between tuberculosis and schizophrenia, failing, however, to specify the nature of that relationship. Johnson and Johnson[123] responded to Lowenstein's claim that tuberculosis was linked to schizophrenia. Forty schizophrenic patients with long periods of hospitalization were selected, and their spinal fluids were examined by smears, culture, and guinea pig innoculation. Every effort was exerted to confirm the results of previous investigations, but they were unable to verify any etiologic relationship between tuberculosis and schizophrenia. Darke[38] likewise tried to confirm Lowenstein's findings. He examined the cerebrospinal fluids of 20 psychotic, nontuberculous patients and found no evidence of tubercle bacilli. Darke concluded that "there are not sufficient data in the present study alone to enable one to form a conclusion as to the relation of tubercle bacilli to schizophrenia." Nevertheless, he stated that his data "tend further to confirm the findings of those who feel there is no etiologic relationship between the tubercle bacilli and schizophrenia."

Nielsen[171] studied 123 psychotic patients who were treated for pulmonary tuberculosis and believed that the tuberculosis had precipitated the psychosis in 27 per cent of the cases, while the remainder had been psychotic prior to their infection.

Extended bacteriologic and immunologic studies on the etiology of schizophrenia and related mental disorders were conducted by Rosenow.[193-197] He reported that "these conditions are due to a specific type of nonhemolytic, neurotropic streptococcal infection or intoxication." He claimed that the streptococcus of schizophrenia has a low, general virulence but is highly neurotropic, localizing in the brain of persons stricken, and of animals following intravenous injection. He concluded that, despite current psychiatric tenets, which run contrary to the belief that schizophrenia is caused by an infectious process, his investigations indicated this to be the case. In refutation, Fleischhacker[70] pointed out that no inflammatory or allergic reactions have been observed in the brains of idiopathic schizophrenics, nor had the presence of any infections or toxic agents been demonstrated.

Illyine and Dzubenko[118] reported on "the problem of conditionally pathogenic organisms" in the blood or urine of schizophrenics. They concluded that these organisms played no role in the etiology of schizophrenia.

Malis[159] believed schizophrenia to be a somatic disease, following a chronic course, caused by a virus and leading to a specific toxic lesion of the brain. He examined the blood from chronic schizophrenic patients and discovered that "the blood of schizophrenic patients contains an unknown specific antigen of virus nature, and antibodies against it." He concluded that "the virus agent causing schizophrenia is present in the body for a long time in a latent state (like the herpes virus and many other viruses), and that only when conditions are especially suitable does it acquire pathogenic properties, enabling it to cause at first the development of a physical toxinfectious disease, with a very sluggish course, and later, as the result of specific toxic action on the central nervous system—neuropsychic disturbances in the form of the schizophrenic psychosis." Haddad and Rabe[91] claimed the results of their investigation supported Malis' contention of an abnormal antigen in the serum of chronic schizophrenic patients. However, they pointed out that "further experiments are needed to determine whether the antigenic abnormality is unique to, or characteristic of, schizophrenia." The studies of both Malis and Haddad and Rabe were duplicated by Faurbye et al.[58] They were unable to demonstrate the presence of this antigen, and speculated that the causes for this disagreement were due to differences in experimental technic and diagnosis.

Intoxications and Toxemias

Many drug intoxications have been reported capable of triggering a schizophrenic reaction. Despite many claims to the contrary, a possible causal relationship between intoxication and schizophrenia has not yet been established. It is likely that latent schizophrenic tendencies may become manifest as a result of some drug intoxication, and that some of the so-called schizophrenic reactions that occur with some intoxications are in effect organic psychoses. Levin[151] reported transitory schizophrenic reactions that were produced by bromide intoxication. He concluded that while bromide intoxication, like other intoxications and toxemias, is capable of triggering a schizophrenic episode, it may again become latent when favorable conditions have been restored.

Forty-three cases of psychosis associated with the administration of atabrine were studied by Greiber.[88] The cases were divided into two categories; a primary group of individuals whose histories indicated they were well balanced, and a "trigger" group of individuals whose histories reflected a predisposition to mental disease. Greiber concluded that "the primary group displayed a true sensitivity to the drug, whereas in the trigger group a predisposed personality as well as emotional conflicts or acute illnesses were as great a factor as the atabrine itself."

A case of "schizophreniform psychosis" associated with pernicious anemia was reported by Friedlander and Dagradi.[73] The patient's condition dramatically improved after specific anti-anemia therapy. Friedlander and Dagradi indicated that a psychosis may occur as a direct result of pernicious anemia, and there was evidence that suggested the symptom complex of schizophrenia may be the outward sign of pernicious anemia. From this they inferred that schizophrenia "is merely a syndrome, the result of some organic brain process of varying etiologies."

Osmond and Hoffer[176] claimed to have shown that "when the enormously powerful LSD-25 is given to normal subjects, if psychologic changes occur, there is usually a dramatic and coincident rise in the levels of adrenochrome in the blood, and that adrenochrome injected intravenously is destroyed much less rapidly." They concluded from this that "schizophrenic people seem less able to remove adrenochrome from blood than normals."

Several reports have been concerned with the presence of a toxic factor in the blood serum and urine of schizophrenics, which can be demonstrated by using tadpoles as test organisms. Malis[158] found that tadpoles injected with serum from schizophrenics exhibited a lag in their tempo of morphogenesis, in comparison with a control group with serum from normals and a control group without serum. He also reported the rapid death of tadpoles injected with serum from acutely disturbed catatonic patients.

Fischer[67,68] similarly obtained evidence for a toxic factor in the blood serum of schizophrenics, and believed that the toxicity to tadpoles of serum was positively correlated with the degree of stress that the patient experienced. He also found that the urine from schizophrenics caused a higher tadpole mortality than urine from normals. However, Georgi et al.[80] criticized Fischer's experimental technics and disagreed with his conclusions. They said that "despite considerable differences in some individual experiments, the results as a whole are *not significant*." In a rebuttal,[69] Fischer maintained that tadpoles are, in fact, reliable test animals and that the presence of a toxic factor has been demonstrated.

Earlier works on a toxic factor (Malis, Fischer, and others) were reviewed by Edisen.[48] He duplicated these experiments and reported that "a toxic factor in the blood serum of schizophrenics was not demonstrated" and that inconclusive results were obtained when the urine was tested for toxicity.

Serum from catatonic patients was administered to the spider Zilla-x notata by Bercel.[18] In approximately two-thirds of the experiments, a rudimentary web was obtained after which the spider showed withdrawal. This response also occurred occasionally with serum from paranoid, cyclothymic, and normals. Bercel claimed this "suggests the presence of a catatonic potential in a number of psychotic states, and in some normal subjects, too." Experiments with serum from other than catatonic forms of schizophrenia indicated no difference from normal controls.

It was reported by Winter and Flataker[247] that the injection of blood serum from schizophrenic patients impaired the ability of trained rats to climb ropes, an effect which they did not observe in control experiments. Ghent and Freedman[82] duplicated this experiment and were unable to confirm the presence of any "psychotoxic" substance in the blood of schizophrenics.

Bishop[20] found that rats injected with schizophrenic plasma showed significant impairment of learning as compared with animals injected with normal plasma or saline. Heath[94] reported that the injection of the taraxein fraction into monkeys produced changes in brain wave recordings similar to those he had obtained from psychotic schizophrenic patients and also caused the monkeys to become dazed and catatonic.

The role of acidosis in the pathogenesis of schizophrenia was studied by Iazgur,[117] while Giovannelli and Borghesi[83] did research on the amylolytic power in the blood and cerebrospinal fluid in schizophrenics.

ANTHROPOMETRIC

Ernst Kretschmer[141] was one of the first psychiatrists to suggest the existence of a relationship between an individual's physical makeup and his way of reacting emotionally. He was impressed with the correlation of introversion and the leptosomic (or asthenic) body type which was characterized by an angular, narrow, flat-chested frame. Later, he concluded that schizophrenia occurred more often in leptosomic individuals than in those with other body types. Sheldon,[209] too, studied the relationship of physical structure to temperament and reported that *endomorphic* body build tended to be associated with relaxed, sociable and comfort-loving personalities; *mesomorphic* with assertiveness and activity; and *ectomorphic* with sensitivity, postural and emotional restraint, love of privacy, self-consciousness, introversion and hypersensitivity. Schizophrenic disorders appeared to be more often associated with the ectomorphic (or cerebrotonic) body type.

Anthropometric data on 100 mental patients, gathered by Moore and Hsü,[167] suggested that "paranoids probably form an entirely different category of mental illness and perhaps should not be confused with the other schizophrenics," since the paranoid's physique was found to be different from the schizophrenic's. A possible relationship between psychiatric illness and birth weight was postulated by Barry[6] in view of the fact that premature infants are susceptible to intracranial hemorrhage or anoxia during parturition, and that abnormally large babies are likely to have difficult deliveries. He studied the birth weights of a series of psychiatric patients for whom data were obtainable and discovered that 20 per cent of these patients had abnormally large birth weights (9 pounds or over). However, Barry concluded that due to the many possibilities of inaccuracy or error in reporting birth weights, "the results must be considered as tentative until they can be confirmed by checking the informant's statements against hospital records or by obtaining other objective information."

In their study of the relationship between physical constitution and schizophrenia, Bellak and Holt[16] were not able to confirm Sheldon's findings. They found no significant differences in somatotype distribution between patients with schizophrenia and those with general paresis. They concluded that "the mere adoption of the technic of somatotyping opens up no royal road to the relationship between physique and psychosis."

Kline and Tenney[139] similarly employed the Sheldon method to somatotype 455 newly hospitalized schizophrenic patients. They found "a significantly positive correlation between mesomorphy and good prognosis and a suggestively poor one with high endomorphy." Another important finding was that "mesomorphs tended to be paranoid and not hebephrenic, whereas, ectomorphs tended to be hebephrenic and not paranoid." The correlation between somatotype and prognosis proved to be independent of the correlations between somatotype and diagnosis. However, Kline and Tenney emphasized that they "do not feel that somatotype is the final determining factor in the type or prognosis of schizophrenia." Instead, they advocated the introduction of somatotyping as an "organizing principle" or "frame of reference" for further research.

Other contributions in this field were made by Doust[45] and by Parnell.[180]

Gregory[87] very properly commented on the tendency for some investigators to lose sight of the fact that body structure may be modified by patterns of behavior which were established early in childhood—rather than vice-versa.

HALLUCINOGENIC DRUGS AND THE "MODEL PSYCHOSIS"

In recent years there have been an increasing number of experiments utilizing hallucinogenic drugs such as LSD, mescaline, and bufotenine. These drugs are capable of producing a "model psychosis," with hallucinations (mainly visual), perceptual disorders, and paranoid responses without disorientation. Some writers have speculated that schizophrenia results from an abnormal metabolism which produces a compound similar to these hallucinogenic drugs. Foremost among these are Hoffer and Osmond[107] who hypothesized that there are two basic conditions for the creation of schizophrenia; an increase in the concentration and activity of acetylcholine centrally and an abnormal diversion of adrenalin into some quinone indole. They anticipated that "any compound that will block acetylcholine esterase and which will cause an increased production of adrenalin, which is converted to an indole (or which itself is an indole), meets these two conditions and ought to be a very powerful hallucinogenic agent." In their experimental work with compounds, especially adrenochrome, they reported being able to produce perceptual disturbances, disorders of judgment, withdrawal of interest, severe depression, and other changes characteristic of schizophrenia. They also found that these compounds produced marked EEG abnormalities in normal subjects and aggravated EEG abnormalities in schizophrenic patients.

Hoffer, Osmond, and Smythies[109,177] had previously suggested that schizophrenia is the result of faulty adrenalin metabolism, which produces a mescaline-like compound or compounds, referred to as an "M substance." They claimed that schizophrenic disturbances in sensation, feeling, and thought depend upon such factors as age, the rate M substance is produced, previous personality, and the cultural setting in which the illness occurs.

The relationship between adrenochrome and adrenolutin, two oxidized derivatives of epinephrine, was also studied by Hoffer[103,104] and Hoffer and Osmond.[108] When administered to normal volunteers, these drugs instituted thought and mood changes, with or without perceptual changes. These symptoms, they believed, closely resembled those found in early schizophrenia, and the hypothesis was advanced that "in schizophrenia both branches of the autonomic nervous system are overly active as a result of an overproduction of both acetylcholine and epinephrine." Hoffer[105] found adrenochrome in the plasma of normal individuals, and a marked increase in adrenochrome levels in plasma after the administration of LSD-25. Szára et al.[227] investigated the presence of adrenochrome in the blood of normal and schizophrenic subjects, but were unable to find any in either. In a similar study, Feldstein[59] concluded that "the presence of adrenochrome in plasma of normal subjects and schizophrenic patients has not been proved."

The position of Hoffer et al.[109] that schizophrenia is caused by adrenochrome was accepted by Lea[149] who hypothesized that "a population of schizophrenics should contain an excess of deeply pigmented types and a deficiency of persons with allergy." Both of these findings were observed in his studies, except that the first was limited to the 15-19 age group. Lea believed that the excess of adrenochrome was due to both hereditary and acquired hepatic dysfunction. Fabing[55] likewise thought that schizophrenia was due to a metabolic error. He claimed "the known hallucinogens which produce a schizophrenic or pseudoschizophrenic state in man and in experimental animals are indoles or potential indoles," and that four etiologic possibilities exist: a) the formation of tryptamine in the body; b) the metabolism of serotonin to bufotenine; c) adrenalin oxidation to adrenochrome; and d) abnormal porphyrin metabolism. Rinkel et al.[191] alleged to have brought into focus "a new chemical concept in psychosis" by presenting evidence for a "natural error in the adrenalin cycle" as an important, though not the only, etiologic factor.

Tolerance to hallucinogenic drugs and the "model psychosis" was explored by Abramson[1] who held that "the establishment of tolerance and the rapid loss of tolerance are part of a unified mechanism which also involves the psychic actions of the drug." Turner et al.[235] did not agree that these hallucinogenic drugs were capable of producing a hallucinatory and schizophrenic state. Rather, they claimed the drugs are causes of disorientation and delirium. Considerable evidence was cited attesting to the fact that the results of experiments with these drugs (hashish, harmine, ibogaine, adrenochrome, bufotenine) do not support the view that schizophrenia is related to faulty indole metabolism.

Fabing[54,56] also studied the effects of Meratran (pipradrol) and Frenquel (azacyclonal) as blocking agents against model psychoses produced by LSD-25. He reported beneficial effects in patients suffering from schizophrenia, or from alcoholic or postoperative psychoses. The drugs' actions have not been consistent, but, according to Fabing, they have dramatically cleared up hallucinated, deluded, and dissociated patients. Also, observations on subjects in which mescaline sulphate was used, rather than LSD-25, suggested to him that "this type of model psychosis can be blocked in the same fashion." The effects of bufotenine on volunteers were reported by Fabing et al.[57] Visual disturbances, color hallucinations, and mental confusion were noted and when the injections ceased, there was a slow return to mental awareness, followed by a euphoric state lasting for several hours.

The psychotic effects of DMT (N,N-dimethyltryptamine) and T-9 (N,Ndiethyltryptamine) were compared with the effects of mescaline and LSD-25 by Szára.[226] In the DMT model psychosis, there was a rapid onset and short duration of symptoms, and Szára speculated that "DMT affects directly those brain structures that are affected indirectly by LSD and mescaline." He also claimed that the psychotic effects of tryptamine derivatives strengthen the indole theory of schizophrenia.

Experimental psychotic states were explored by MacDonald and Galvin.[156] They accepted the hypothesis that "an error in adrenalin metabolism may be an etiological factor in some naturally occurring psychoses." However, they claimed that experimental psychoses have a similarity to delirium and to a lesser extent schizophrenia, but are not identical to either. Unlike Hoffer and Osmond,[108] MacDonald and Galvin maintained that the use of lysergic acid for therapeutic purposes was not warranted. Terrill[228] concluded that LSD seems to overcome resistance to psychotherapy and speeds up its movement, but that it did not show promise as a diagnostic aide. "When therapeutic changes did occur they were often of a qualitatively different order than those which occur in traditional psychotherapy." Jackson,[122] like MacDonald and Galvin, also thought model psychoses to be distinctly different from schizophrenic states. He asserted that unless the LSD experience is reinforced by social experiences and additional therapy it diminishes and gradually fades away—the LSD experience "becomes a memory not a personality change."

The possibility that amphetamine psychosis was due to abnormal adrenaline metabolism, as theorized by Hoffer and Osmond,[108] was put forth by Beamish and Kiloh.[11] Since, in this theory, schizophrenia is activated by a metabolic disturbance, they saw the inordinate consumption of amphetamine as a likely catalyst. Bell and Trethowan[13] reported on fourteen patients addicted to amphetamine who were hospitalized with psychotic episodes. The patients all manifested personality instabilities, as do addicts using other drugs. Later on Bell was impressed with the similarity of amphetamine psychosis and paranoid schizophrenia.[12] Auditory and visual hallucinations, delusions of persecution, and disturbed behavior were present in all cases. Bell claimed that prolonged intoxication with this drug can cause schizophrenia; a gradually reversible change in the activity of the brain occurs that may be regarded as a physiologic reaction rather than as a latent psychologic process. He stressed that amphetamine "produces a 'model psychosis' that has a closer resemblance to schizophrenia than that produced by any other known hallucinogenic drug." Lemere[150] claimed that excessive amphetamine consumption may cause brain damage, which could very well produce serious psychiatric complications. He believed that amphetamine-produced psychoses usually mimic paranoid schizophrenia.

GENETICS

Genetic factors in schizophrenia have received increasing attention in recent years as genetics has advanced. These studies have usually focused on the incidence of schizophrenia in the general population and the expectancy rates in families of schizophrenics, often utilizing the "twin" approach. One of the first such investigations was conducted by Rosanoff et al.[192] who found a "marked contrast between monozygotic and dizygotic twins with respect to the proportion of cases of both twins of the pair affected." In 68.3 per cent of the monozygotic twins and 14.9 per cent of the dizygotic both were affected by schizophrenic psychoses. Rosanoff concluded that although genetic factors seem to play an important role "they are not alone sufficient to cause the disease."

The most prominent proponent of the genetic basis of schizophrenia had been Kallmann, whose extensive and painstaking studies appear rather convincing.[126-136] He presented statistical evidence to support the thesis that the disease occurs much more frequently in families with a known case of schizophrenia than in the general population. Children born to one schizophrenic parent have a 16.4 per cent probability of developing the psychosis, about nineteen times the average expectancy, while children of two schizophrenic parents have a 68.1 per cent probability, about eight times that found in the population at large. He also found that among dizygotic twins, one of whom is schizophrenic, there is a 16.4 per cent probability of the other twin developing schizophrenia; among monozygotic twins there is an 86.2 per cent probability. Kallmann's morbidity rates led him to conclude that "the chance of developing a schizophrenic psychosis increases in direct proportion to the degree of blood relationship to a schizophrenic index case—a rather convincing proof of the operation of heredity." He claimed that the predisposition to schizophrenia depends on the presence of a mutant, recessive gene which could cause a specific type of enzyme deficiency. Acute differences in the expression and severity of the disease "appear to be controlled by a *constitutional defence mechanism,* which is probably nonspecific genetically, and certainly multi-factorial in that portion which is determined by heredity." Nevertheless, Kallmann oftentimes underscored the fact that the genetic theory of schizophrenia did not invalidate existing psychologic theories of causation and did not preclude the use of psychotherapy for the prevention and treatment of schizophrenia. Indeed, he repeatedly maintained that the true nature of the disease is the result of the combined forces of both hereditary and environmental factors. Similarly, McColl[162] hypothesized that recessive genetic propensities are latent in many individuals, but it is environmental abnormalities which give rise to schizophrenia.

Kallmann's methodology was severely criticized by Pastore,[182] who raised many questions concerning his diagnostic procedures, statistical treatment of data, sampling procedure, and uncontrolled variables. Pastore did not minimize genetic influences in the etiology of schizophrenia but protested that Kallmann's studies offered no reliable information for assessing a genetic basis. In a reply to Pastore, Hurst[115] pointed out that Pastore had analyzed minutiae and neglected the general effect of the vast body of Kallmann's data. Hurst attributed considerable credence to Kallmann's work, as did Garrison.[78] The genetic theory of schizophrenia was reinforced by Strömgren[225] but, unlike Kallmann, he believed a dominant gene was the cause. Conversely, Semerari[208] adhered to the position that a recessive gene was responsible for the disease.

A study by Williams et al.[244] revealed that a number of metabolic traits found in patients were either absent or rare in the well population. They considered this to be "irresistable evidence" that schizophrenia has genetically determined physiologic concomitants. The development of similar schizophrenic reactions in monozygotic twins was traced by Gardner and Stephens[77] who concluded that some "hereditary mechanism" was strongly suggested.

Slater[218] performed a statistical analysis of schizophrenic brothers and sisters (using data previously reported by Zehnder) and found family resemblances in age of onset, course, outcome, and symptoms among the siblings too great to be accounted for by chance. He suggested that "individual differences of these kinds, though not determined by the presence or absence of the specific schizophrenic gene, are genetically caused and are to be attributed to the action of modifying genes." Böök[24] examined female schizophrenic patients and found that 4.6 per cent of the parents and 8.6 per cent of the siblings were likewise affected by the disease. These morbidity rates are not quite as high as those found by Kallmann,[127] but nevertheless, are many times that experienced by the general population.

A typical Swedish coastal population was studied by Sjögren[216] who found the occurrence of psychoses among siblings of psychotic patients to be significantly higher than for the general population. Similarly, Wittermans and Schultz[248] found that the parents and siblings of "cured schizophrenics" had a lower incidence of schizophrenia than had parents and siblings of schizophrenics chosen at random.

The biologic unity in schizophrenia was questioned by Rosenthal[198] who claimed his investigation of monozygotic twins furnishes evidence for the hypothesis of biologic heterogeneity. Schizophrenia was virtually absent in the families of the discordant twin pairs, but occurred in approximately 60 per cent of families of concordant twin pairs. Thus, he concluded that "at least two broad groups of schizophrenics can be differentiated—one in which the genetic factor is absent or minimal and the other in which it is apparently substantial." Rosenthal's study was reexamined by Kringlen[143] who claimed that his data clearly do not support Rosenthal's conclusions. Kringlen purports that there were errors in Rosenthal's classification of discordant twins. Meissner[164] also critically evaluated Rosenthal's study and postulated that the concordance-discordance method is applicable only if "average intrapair differences for all environmental factors which could possibly have etiologic relevance are substantially the same for both types of twins." His findings led him to conclude that "the occurrence of schizophrenia regardless of intrapair concordance or discordance is a function of premorbid adjustment." He believed genetic studies to suggest that schizophrenia is merely the result of a "transgenerational process" within the family. A failure to achieve a sense of identity leads to decreasing self differentiation from generation to generation and terminates in schizophrenia. In another report by Kringlen,[142] the general conclusion was that "genetic factors do not seem to play as great a role as has been assumed for the etiology of schizophrenia." He claimed his data suggest that childhood neurotic symptoms are caused by the environment and result in a predisposition to schizophrenia, and that it is not the disease *per se* which is inherited but rather a "vulnerable personality structure."

Benjamin[17] maintained that pedigree studies have supported the view that genetic factors play some sort of role in the pathogenesis and etiology of some schizophrenias, but have "failed in one of their major goals: that is the demonstration of *modes* of genetic transmission." Likewise, Böök[26] admitted that family and twin data furnish a sound basis for the genetic theory but "it does not imply that genetics is the complete answer to this illness." Jackson[121] also expressed doubt that genetics is the complete answer, as he opines that, although "hereditary factors do play a part in at least some of the schizophrenias, it remains to be established in what forms, how vital is a hereditary 'vulnerability', and what the phenotypical expression is of the genotypical defect."

Previous studies on the genetics of schizophrenia (Rosanoff et al., Kallmann, Slater) have invariably found rather high concordance rates for identical twins and substantially lower rates for fraternal twins. However, the results of Tienari's investigation[230] are at variance with these. In none of his sixteen cases of schizophrenia was the other twin suffering from the disease. He ascribed this discrepancy to the fact that his twin data were taken from birth records, while records of hospitalized patients were the source of the other studies. In like manner, Rosenthal[199] has indicated possible biases in these other studies. His main conclusion was that "drawing one's index cases from a resident population favors the inclusion of chronically ill patients in the sample and the exclusion of patients with a more favorable course of illness." On the other hand, the *British Medical Journal*[27] indicated that some of Tienari's schizophrenics might be cases of exogenous organic psychosis and his "borderline" twin-partners concordant. No fewer than twelve of the sixteen partners were considered possible diagnostic errors.

Essen-Möller[53] reviewed the literature on twin research and concluded that the concordance figures may not be entirely reliable. He saw two possible sources of error: a sampling bias due to the heterogeneity of elements, and a diagnostic bias due to the common divergencies in diagnostic technics. The problems of sampling and diagnosis were more fully discussed by Rosenthal.[200] Ferreira[62] claimed that Jackson's critique of the literature[121] revealed several weaknesses in Kallmann's method, conclusions, and statistics.

The problem of the type of genetic deficiency operant in schizophrenia was investigated by Böök[25] who ventured that "the type of schizophrenia prevalent in the investigation area is primarily due to a major simple dominant gene with a heterozygous penetrance of about 20 per cent and a homozygous penetrance of about 100 per cent." Huxley et al.[116] similarly proposed that schizophrenia was caused by "a single partially dominant gene with low penetrance," and hypothesized that it involved a genetic morphism. The schizophrenic rate in all countries examined was at least one per cent. They claimed this was much too high to be accounted for by mutation alone and surmised that the major dominant gene must be in morphic balance. In an editorial comment in *Lancet*,[146] it was suggested that the presence of such a gene confers in schizophrenics some compensatory advantage, like greater resistance to trauma or surgical shock, allergies, pharmacologically active materials, or infections. However, the *Medical Journal of Australia*[163] was opposed to the propositions advanced by Huxley et al.[116] They questioned the fact that the major dominant gene has certain advantages with respect to fertility and viability, and believed that "clear-cut views on the aetiology of schizophrenia reveal more about authors than about schizophrenia."

Denber and Teller[44] presented various hypotheses for the etiology of schizophrenia reflecting one or more types of genetic defects: primary chromosomal failure, alteration in nucleotide sequences in both DNA and RNA through inversion, and semilethal, stress vulnerable enzymatic deficiencies. Mukherjee et al.[169] found heredity to be associated with 11.6 per cent of schizophrenia, 6.0 per cent in direct inheritance, and concluded that "the genes appear to be dominant in character but with low penetrance." In consideration of the factors such as the age at appearance of the disease, susceptibility to environmental stresses, and response to treatment, they claimed that the genes did not in themselves seem strong enough to produce the disease in all individuals with heredity backgrounds.

In a comprehensive investigation of the incidence of schizophrenia in twins, via birth registers, Kringlen[144] found 28 per cent concordance for monozygotic twins and 7 per cent concordance for dizygotic. When a rather liberal view of concordance was applied, the figures were 38 per cent and 14 per cent respectively. He indicated that these morbidity rates for monozygotic twins are considerably lower than those found in previous studies, while the rates for dizygotics are similar. Kringlen concluded that "the earlier studies probably contained many sources of error, the most important of which resided in the sampling technics that gave results in which the genetic factor was overestimated." He also claimed that *"the more accurate and careful the samplings, the lower the concordance figures."* His general conclusion was that his figures supported a genetic factor in the etiology of schizophrenia, but that this factor was much weaker than previously thought.

In discordant identical twin studies, Pollin et al.[187,188] discovered that the twin who became schizophrenic: a) weighed less at birth, b) was perceived by his parents as vulnerable, c) was the recipient of more concern and attention, d) was somewhat slower in earlier development, and e) was less successful and was viewed as less competent than the co-twin. Their finding that the schizophrenic index twin was the smaller at birth was consistent with Kallmann[131] but inconsistent with Slater[219] and Tienari.[230]

Lidz et al.[154] focused their attention on the pathogenic influence the family exerts upon the schizophrenic child, and its effect on the siblings. A definite "gender-linkage" (not genetic) was found: the brothers of the male schizophrenics were more disturbed than the sisters, and the sisters of female schizophrenics were more ill than the brothers. There was a dearth of brothers of female patients, thus limiting the latter finding. Also, the patient in half of the families was raised under different conditions than the siblings. In a report on an ongoing study of schizophrenic twins, Gottesman[85] admitted that his sample was not *truly* representative of the domain of schizophrenia, and neither were any of the other samples. He found 79 per cent of the co-twins of monozygotic schizophrenics to be abnormal (abnormality ranging from transient anxiety to conditions requiring hospitalization) while 45 per cent of the dizygotics were so affected. His data seemed to support a diathesis-stress theory of schizophrenia, involving a predisposition to developing schizophrenia. The diathesis takes the form of a polygenic system and lowers the individual's threshold for coping with stress. Gottesman maintained that, with this theory most instances of schizophrenia, mild or severe, could be regarded as biologically based.

Judd and Brandkamp[125] provided evidence to support the indication that abnormalities in the sex chromosomes tend to be associated with general emotional instability, but chromosomal abnormalities of this type cannot be directly implicated in the etiology of schizophrenia. In general, their data "failed to demonstrate any significant or constant chromosomal abnormalities" in a series of 40 adult schizophrenics, one-half of whom had family histories of schizophrenia. (A control group of 10 normal subjects was used in this study.) Nor was there any consistent difference in the chromosome patterns of the schizophrenics who had a family history of schizophrenia and those who did not. They concluded that "if genetic factors are present in the etiology of schizophrenia they exist below that which can be elicited by current cytogenetic methods."

Etiologic aspects of schizophrenia were examined by Burch[29] who employed age- and sex-specific first admission-rates to hospitals plus familial evidence. He concluded that schizophrenia was restricted to a carrier population that is homozygous for sa_1 and sb_1 chromosomes at the two, nonlinked autosomal loci sa and sb. Burch claimed that its phenotypic initiation was dependent upon autosomal somatic mutations, and suggested that "the somatic mutations may yield (in carriers) a forbidden-clone (or clones) of immunologically competent cells, carrying cell-bound auto-antibody." Biesele et al.[19] described a chromosomal abnormality in two mentally retarded, highly schizoid twin girls; both had 47 chromosomes, with the extra one being short and acrocentric. They claimed that chromosomal findings in adult schizophrenics "do not suggest that this extra chromosome is of general significance in schizophrenia." However, subgroups with different etiologies might exist among atypical and borderline cases, according to Biesele et al. and one subgroup might be the chromosomal abnormality which would be characterized by "an unusually early manifestation of schizoid traits." They then investigated this possibility among ten children with clinical schizophrenic symptoms but failed to identify a chromosomal abnormality in any of the children. They suggested that an examination of noninstitutionalized cases might prove their hypothesis.

Heath[95] hypothesized that schizophrenia is a biologic irregularity with an inherited predisposition. He argued that "a biochemical abnormality, existing as a consequence of the inherited error, influences cellular function in precise regions of the brain and produces a physiologic abnormality which underlies the behavioral disorder." His extensive research suggested that "the brain dysrhythmia which can be induced in higher primates and man through administration of a serological fraction from schizophrenic patients may result from an interference with acetylcholine activity within the brain." However, Heath maintained that the exact nature of the schizophrenic irregularity is still unknown.

The hypothesis advanced by Böök[25] that schizophrenia was due to a single partially dominant gene was explored by Slater.[220] Data obtained from other populations of schizophrenics and their relatives by Kallmann[131] and Slater[219] were analyzed, and it was concluded that the incidence of schizophrenia "could be adequately explained by the hypothesis of a single partially dominant gene, such as Böök proposed for the special circumstances of a North Swedish isolate."

An isolated Swiss community of about 400 persons was studied by Hanhart.[92] This fertile population was highly inbred and the occurrence of schizophrenia was at least 1.75 per cent. There were 14 cases of "sure or most probable" schizophrenia who did not exhibit a monomeric recessive inheritance. However, Hanhart maintained that "the undifferentiated oligophrenia of all degrees most probably depends on one specific simple recessive gene." Schizophrenia was probably inherited in this community in the same fashion, according to Hanhart, "provided there is a considerably reduced manifestation of a muted autosomal gene."

Other significant research in schizophrenia was Bautsch's study of uniovular twins,[10] and Saličková's investigation of genetic aspects of endogenous psychoses.[217] The genetic question was also explored by Alanen,[2] Fonseca,[71] Tienari,[231] and Haberlandt.[90]

DATE OF BIRTH AND POSITION IN FAMILY

Month or Season of Birth

The leading proponent of the date of birth theory was De Sauvage Nolting,[40-42] who found a higher incidence in the birth rate of schizophrenics during the winter months. The month of June contained the lowest incidence and there was a significant difference between March and June. In another investigation in 1952[43] he reported "a curious negative correlation" between the distribution of births and the vitamin C content of the blood of pregnant and suckling women. He hypothesized that a deficiency of vitamin C in the maternal blood would cause an impairment in the cerebral oxidative processess of the infants, from which a later manifest psychosis would result.

Pile[185] endeavored to verify De Sauvage Nolting's findings by collective statistics on patients resident in all four of Virginia's state hospitals. He discovered that schizophrenic births were evenly distributed throughout the winter and summer months. No difference was found between Negroes and whites, and the subdivisions of schizophrenia were evenly distributed as well. He therefore concluded that "the incidence of dementia praecox bears no relation to the individual birth dates of the patients nor to the seasons of the year in which the (schizophrenic) patients are born." However, Barry and Barry[7] reanalyzed Pile's data and found a "statistically significant difference between the number of patients born in winter vs. summer and the number to be expected from the control figures."

Monthly birth rates for Canadian normals and schizophrenics were compared by Norris and Chowning.[172] Their data revealed that: a) the birth rate for normals may vary significantly over time, b) birth rates between provinces can differ significantly, and c) schizophrenic birth rates differ from that of normals according to the years chosen for comparison. In the related field of mental retardation, Knobloch and Pasamanick[140] studied the admissions of mentally defective children and found a significantly higher percentage of them had been born during the winter months. They claimed that, if the third month of pregnancy, when the cerebral cortex of the fetus is developing, occurs during hot summer months, pregnant women might reduce their consumption of food. The resulting protein deficiency in the diet of pregnant women could cause brain damage. They hypothesized that more mental defectives would be born in winters following hot summers than cool ones, and went on to substantiate their hypothesis. However, Sterling[224] disagreed with their claims and pointed out several errors in their methodology. In a later publication[181] Pasamanick and Knobloch replied to Sterling's criticism and maintained their initial position.

Orme[175] investigated the association between season of birth and psychosis and found no significant relationship. He suggested that "the claimed relationship might be an artifact of the more substantiated relationship between intelligence and season of birth." In another study Barry and Barry[8] reported on the months of birth of schizophrenics admitted to private hospitals. They found little variation in the seasonal distribution of births, and suggested that previous investigations reporting differences probably c o n t a i n e d schizophrenics from the lowest socioeconomic class. It seemed to them that the middle and upper classes were protected from this adverse seasonal effect.

Position in Family

The connection between birth order and the incidence of schizophrenia was examined by Schooler.[205] He found a rather strong relationship between last-born siblings and the occurrence of the disease as compared to first-born, and a somewhat weaker relationship among last-half vs. first-half siblings. Schooler speculated that the mother's "increasing age or large numbers of previous children may affect the intrauterine environment in such a way as to leave the child with a physiologic predisposition to the disease." Another possible explanation was that first-born or first-half children have greater access to their parents and are thus more successful in alleviating their anxieties. Conversely, Rao[189] discovered that, in India, there was a preponderance of schizophrenic patients in the first and second sibling positions. There, the first- and second-born must fulfill traditional family obligations and Rao claims that sociocultural stresses such as these may precipitate a schizophrenic breakdown.

Smith and McIntyre[221] examined family size, birth order, and ordinal position in three groups of patients: schizophrenics, nonschizophrenic psychiatric patients, and medical controls. They found no significant difference in mean family size, and no significant excesses in any one birth rank or ordinal position. They concluded that their data "do not support the hypothesis that ordinal position or birth rank play an important role in determining vulnerability to psychiatric illness." Sibling patterns for groups of normals and psychiatric patients were compared by Vogel and Lauterbach.[237] They found that there were seven times as many "only" children in the latter group. Both groups were controlled for age, sex, and education (an index of socioeconomic status), mean number of siblings, and presence of both natural parents in the home. They claimed this "suggests that legitimate differences between normal and psychiatric populations have been obscured by failure to control for social class," and that "the only child is subjected to stresses to which children who have siblings are not subjected."

MULTIPLE-FACTOR THEORIES AND GENERAL STATEMENTS

The concept of a "multiple factor" theory for the etiology of schizophrenia was introduced by Bellak.[14] He believed schizophrenia, as it was diagnosed clinically, to be "the final common path from a number of widely differing etiologic factors," rather than a disease entity. Both somatic and psychogenic factors operate, but the delineating feature in all cases is a syndrome of severe ego disturbance. In another paper,[15] Bellak conceived of schizophrenia as lying at one end of a continuum of ego strength. The opposite end is "normality," and the neuroses and manic-depressive psychosis lie between. Since the severity of schizophrenia is manifested in varying degrees, the illness is represented by "a range on this continuum, not a point."

Grünthal[89] claimed that, with the schizophrenic illness "we have to think, not of a progressive destructive brain-process, but of a disturbance of function, reversible in both the physical and the mental field, such as a disturbance of circuits of communication." According to Schulman[206] the conflict between "heredity and environment, between the organic and the functional, between the biophysical and the psychosocial," is not likely to be reconciled in the near future. He maintained that "schizophrenia consists of a number of phenomena, defined on a cultural level, and understandable only by concepts unique to the interpersonal level of organization." Schulman hypothesized that "schizophrenia is primarily an interpersonal process, although involving biological, chemical, and physical processes operating on lower levels of organization." Rejecting a multiple-factor theory, Schulman develops a psychosocial theory of schizophrenia—whereby variables such as acculturation, role-taking, and interpersonal relations are seen as the prime etiologic agents—and attempts to demonstrate that this theory is not imcompatible with biologic and genetic evidence.

A different idea was proposed by Freedman[72] who believed that "schizophrenia is not a disease entity in the sense that it has a unique etiology, pathogenesis, etc., but that it represents the evocation of a final common path in the same sense as do headache, epilepsy, sore throat, or indeed any other symptom complex." He suggests that the concept of schizophrenia has outlived its usefullness as a clinical term.

Sclare[207] contended that the current knowledge on the pathogenesis of schizophrenia suggests that "no single school of thought is capable of producing a complete answer to the problem—in spite of many naive and wild assertions to this effect. "It would appear that a modern, global concept of schizophrenia depends upon accepting the principle of 'multiple causality'." He claims that the etiology can best be understood on the basis of an interaction of various factors, the most promising of which are psychoanalytic, genetic, and biochemical.

A multifactorial approach was also supported by Hoff[102] who urged that *all* of the various findings of psychiatric research be taken into account if one is to arrive at a satisfactory understanding of individual cases of psychopathology. Fessel,[63] too, strongly supported an approach that recognizes the multiple causation of schizophrenia. He claimed that "enough is known about the disease to make it abundantly clear that no factor, whether biologic, psychologic, or sociocultural, is singly or uniquely at the root of the illness. The failure to appreciate this multicausal aspect has discredited many findings because of claims for their etiological significance."

A difficulty emphasized by Kaplan[137] is that patients have been classified according to their symptoms instead of the disorders underlying the symptoms. He claimed that the "disagreement among psychiatrists regarding schizophrenic diagnoses minimizes the value of hypotheses designed to explain the general etiology of schizophrenia" and that the "value of *any* simple theory on the etiology of schizophrenia remains questionable as long as the concepts and diagnoses of 'schizophrenia' remain inconsistent and heterogeneous."

The concept of "organization" in order to reconcile the apparently conflicting theories of schizophrenia was introduced by Singer.[215] Organization is a theoretical concept referring to the relationships between the parts of a functional system. Singer presents the leading genetic, physiologic, psychologic, and sociocultural viewpoints on schizophrenia, and then offers an integrated viewpoint in terms of this conceptual framework. He defined schizophrenia as "an inability to keep the psychologic field organized, manifested as inability to pay attention to task requirements and an inability to coordinate messages from various internal systems so that predictable adaptive behavior may result."

Goldfarb,[84] in discussing childhood schizophrenia, advanced the hypothesis that multiple causes or varying combinations of multiple contributing factors are responsible for the schizophrenic child's impairment in ego functioning. He views these combinations in the form of a continuum. At one end are the organic disorders, while at the other the main etiologic factor is a pernicious psychosocial family atmosphere. "Thus, at one pole, would be found the brain-damaged child from a normal, well-functioning family. At the other pole, would be the child who is entirely free of somatic defects but who has been reared in an extremely disturbed family unit."

Without taking a position himself, Ferreira[62] rejected the eclectic position and left the problem of etiology up in the air.

SUMMARY AND CONCLUSION

No pattern of environmental and traumatic factors has ever been found which would inevitably lead to the development of schizophrenia. Numerous physiologic abnormalities have been observed in schizophrenics but these are generally believed to be concomitants of the disease rather than a reflection of the cause of the disease. Controlled studies of the histopathology of schizophrenia have led to the conclusion that no specific change in any tissue or body system has been demonstrated which can account for the clinical syndrome of schizophrenia. Some fingerprint, capillary and blood cell studies have suggested the existence of some constitutional factor but findings are inconsistent.

Endocrine activity has been extensively investigated with contradictory findings. Greater variability of adrenocortical activity that has been found in schizophrenics (as compared with normals) has also been described for many other biologic functions. Visceral changes reported to be found at autopsy are generally believed to be based on environmental artifacts that are not related to the basic disorder. The presence of a toxic factor in blood which was reported by some investigators, was not found by others. 'Model Psychoses' that have been produced by drugs like LSD are believed by most investigators to be distinctly different from schizophrenic states.

Although chromosomal differences have not been demonstrated by current cytogenetic technics, there is rather strong evidence that hereditary factors play some role—but by no means are the complete answer to this illness.

There is an increasing tendency to regard schizophrenia as a symptom complex resulting from combinations of a variety of etiologic factors.

BIBLIOGRAPHY

1. Abramson, H. A.: Tolerance to LSD-25 and a theory of psychoses. In Abramson, H. A. (Ed.) Neuropharmacology, Transactions of the Second Conference. New York, Josiah Macy Jr. Foundation, 259-300, 1955.

2. Alanen, Y. O., and Tahka, V.: On somatic and genetic studies in schizophrenia. Duodecim. 76: 95-112, 1960.

3. Altschule, M. D.: Biology of Mental Health and Disease. New York, Paul B. Hoeber, Inc. (Medical Book Dept. of Harper & Bros.), 449, 1952.

4. Amer. Med. Assn. J.: Dermatoglyphics, schizophrenia, and genetics. 180: 239-40, 1962.

5. Angyal, A., and Blockman, N.: Vestibular reactivity in schizophrenia. Arch. Neurol. and Psychiat., 44: 611, 1940.

6. Barry, H.: Abnormally large birth weights of psychiatric patients. Arch. Neurol. Psychiat. 57: 98-101, 1947.

7. Barry, H. III, and Barry, H. Jr.: Season of birth. Arch. Gen. Psychiat. 5: 100-08, 1961.

8. Barry, H. III, and Barry, H. Jr.:

Season of birth in schizophrenics. Arch. Gen. Psychiat. 11: 385-91, 1964.

9. Bäumer, H.: Investigations on the nucleus medialis and lateralis of the thalamus in schizophrenia. Intern. Cong. Neuropath. (Rome). 3: 636-47, 1952.

10. Batusch, A., et al.: A case of schizophrenia in uniovular twins. Neurol. Neurochir. Psychiat. Pol. 13: 715-9, 1963.

11. Beamish, P. and Kiloh, L. G.: Psychosis due to amphetamine consumption. J. Ment. Sci. 106: 337-43, 1960.

12. Bell, D. S.: Comparison of amphetamine psychosis and schizophrenia. Brit. J. Psychiat. 111: 701-7, 1965.

13. Bell, D. S., and Trethowan, W. H.: Amphetamine addiction. J. Nerv. Ment. Dis. 133: 489-96, 1961.

14. Bellak, L.: A multiple-factor psychosomatic theory of schizophrenia. Psychiat. Quart. 23: 738-55, 1949.

15. Bellak, L.: Toward a unified concept of schizophrenia. J. Nerv. Ment. Dis. 121: 60-6, 1955.

16. Bellak, L., and Holt, R. R.: Somato-

types in relation to dementia praecox. Amer. J. Psychiat. 104: 713-24, 1948.

17. Benjamin, J. D.: Some considerations in biological research in schizophrenia. Psychosom. Med. 20: 427-45, 1958.

18. Bercel, N. A.: A study of the influence of schizophrenic serum on the behavior of the spider Zilla-x-notata. Arch. Gen. Psychiat. 2: 189-209, 1960.

19. Biesele, J. J., Schmid, W., and Lawlis, M. G.: Mentally retarded schizoid twin girls with 47 chromosomes. Lancet. 1: 403-5, 1962.

20. Bishop, M. P.: Effect of schizophrenic plasma upon original learning in the rat. Dis. Nerv. Syst. 21: 1, 1960.

21. Blair, J. H., et al.: Question of histopathologic changes in testes. J. Ment. Sci. 98: 464-5, 1952.

22. Bleuler, E.: Physisch und psychisch in der pathologie. Ztschr. Ges. Neurol. Psychiat. 30: 426, 1916.

23. Bliss, E. L., Migeon, C. J., Hardin Branch, C. H., and Samuels, L. T.: Adrenocortical function in schizophrenia. Amer. J. Psychiat. 112: 358, 1955.

24. Böök, J. A.: Heredity, information acquired from history of patients. Nord. Med. 33: 785-87, 1947.

25. Böök, J. A.: A genetic and neuropsychiatric investigation of a North-Swedish population. Acta Genet. (Basel), 4: 1-100, 1953.

26. Böök, J. A.: Genetical aspects of schizophrenic psychoses. *In* Jackson, D. D. (Ed.). The Etiology of Schizophrenia. New York, Basic Books, Inc., 1960, pp. 23-36.

27. Brit. Med. J.: Schizophrenia in twins, 2: 647-48, 1964.

28. Bucci, L., and Johnson, E. E.: Lymphocytes and schizophrenia. Dis. Nerv. Syst. 25: 107-09, 1964.

29. Burch, P. R. J.: Schizophrenia: some new aetiological considerations. Brit. J. Psychiat. 110: 818-24, 1964.

30. Buscaino, V. M.: Extraneural pathology in schizophrenia. Acta Neurol. (Naples). 8: 1-60, 1953.

31. Cade, J. F. J.: The aetiology of schizophrenia. Med. J. Austral. 2: 135-9, 1956.

32. Cavé, M.: The role of endocrine factors in a case of schizophrenia with hyperfolliculinism. Ann. Med.-Psychol. 2: 171-4, 1948.

33. Co Tui: Endocrinologic orientation to psychiatric disorders. Part IV. Somatologic perspectives in psychiatric research. J. Clin. Exp. Psychopath. 12: 35, 1951.

34. Colbert, E. G., et al.: Vestibular dysfunction in childhood schizophrenia. Arch. Gen. Psychiat. 1: 600, 1959.

35. Conn, J. H.: An examination of the clinico-pathological evidence offered for the concept of dementia praecox as a specific disease entity. Amer. J. Psychiat. 90: 1039, 1934.

36. Coppen, A.: The prevalence of menstrual disorders in psychiatric patients. Brit. J. Psychiat. 111: 155-67, 1965.

37. Dalton, K.: Menstruation and acute psychiatric illnesses. Brit. Med. J. 1: 148-9, 1959.

38. Darke, R. A.: Tubercle bacilli in cerebrospinal fluid of dementia praecox. J. Nerv. Ment. Dis. 106: 686-93, 1947.

39. Dastur, D. K.: The pathology of schizophrenia. A.M.A. Arch. Neurol. Psychiat. 81: 601-14, 1959.

40. De Sauvage Nolting, W. J. J.: Correlation between dementia praecox and month of birth. Nederl. Tikdschr. Geneesk. 78: 528-30, 1934.

41. De Sauvage Nolting, W. J. J.: Further studies on correlation between schizophrenia and month of birth. Nederl. Tijdschr. Geneesk. 83: 3219-22, 1939.

42. De Sauvage Nolting, W. J. J.: Etiology and pathogenesis, correlation between month of birth, schizophrenia and manic-depressive disorders. Nederl. Tijdschr. Geneesk. 95: 3855-64, 1951.

43. De Sauvage Nolting, W. J. J.: A curious relation between schizophrenia and the vitamin-C content of blood during pre- and postnatal periods. Folia psychiat. Neurol. Neurochir. Neerl. 55: 388-402, 1952.

44. Denber, H. C. B., and Teller, D. N.: A biochemical genetic theory concerning

the nature of schizophrenia. Dis. Nerv. Syst. 24: 2, 106-14, 1963.

45. Doust, J. W. L.: Dysplastic growth differentials in patients with psychiatric disorders. Studies on the morphology of maturity. Brit. J. Soc. Med. 6: 169-77, 1952.

46. Doust, J. W. L.: The capillary system in patients with psychiatric disorder: the ontogenetic structural determination of the nailfold capillaries as observed by photomicroscopy. J. Nerv. Ment. Dis. 121: 516-26, 1955.

47. Dunlap, C. B.: Dementia praecox—some preliminary observations on brains from carefully selected cases and a consideration of certain sources of errors. Amer. J. Psychiat. 80: 403, 1924.

48. Edisen, C. B.: Studies of the toxicity of schizophrenic blood serum. Dis. Nerv. Syst. 17: 77-80, 1956.

49. Elsässer, G., and Siebke, H.: Ovarialfunktion und korperbau bei anstaltspatientinen unter besondere berücksichtigung der schizophrenie. Archiv. Psychiat. Z. Neurol. 188: 218-25, 1952.

50. Elvidge, A. R., and Reed, G. E.: Biopsy studies of cerebral pathologic changes in schizophrenia and manic depressive psychosis. Arch. Neurol. Psychiat. 40: 227, 1938.

51. Erban, E.: Changes in morphological properties of the leukocytes in patients with schizophrenia. Preliminary report. Cesk. Psychiat. 60: 145-51, 1964.

52. Erban, L.: Variability changes of white blood cells in patients with schizophrenic reaction. J. Psychiat. Res. 3: 73-7, 1965.

53. Essen-Möller, E.: Twin research and psychiatry. Acta Psychiat. Scand. 39: 65-77, 1963.

54. Fabing, H. D.: Frenquel: a blocking agent against experimental LSD-25 and mescaline psychosis. Neurol. 5: 319-28, 1955.

55. Fabing, H. D.: The dimensions of neurology. Neurol. 5: 603-11, 1955.

56. Fabing, H. D.: New blocking agent against the development of LSD-25 psychosis. Science. 121: 208-10, 1955.

57. Fabing, H. D., Kropa, E. L., Hawkins, J. R., and Leake, C. D.: Bufotenine effects in humans. Fed. Proc. 15: 421, 1956.

58. Faurbye, A., Lundberg, L., and Jensen, K. A.: Studies on the antigen demonstrated by Malis in serum from schizophrenic patients. Acta Path. Microbiol. Scand. 61: 633-51, 1964.

59. Feldstein, A.: On the relationship of adrenaline and its oxidation products to schizophrenia. Amer. J. Psychiat. 116: 454-6, 1959.

60. Ferraro, A.: Histopathological findings in 2 cases clinically diagnosed dementia praecox. Amer. J. Psychiat. 90: 883, 1934.

61. Ferraro, A.: Interpretation of cerebral histopathologic changes in cases of schizophrenia. J. Neuropath. Exp. Neurol. 10: 104-5, 1951.

62. Ferreira, A. J.: The etiology of schizophrenia: A review. Calif. Med. 94: 369-77, 1961.

63. Fessel, W. J.: Interaction of multiple determinants of schizophrenia. Arch. Gen. Psychiat. 11: 1-18, 1964.

64. Fessel, W. J., and Hirata-Hibi, M.: Abnormal leukocytes in schizophrenia. Arch. Gen. Psychiat. 9: 601-13, 1963.

65. Fessel, W. J., Hirata-Hibi, M., and Shapiro, I. M.: Genetic and stress factors affecting the abnormal lymphocyte in schizophrenia. J. Psychiat. Res. 3: 275-83, 1965.

66. Fieve, R. R., Blumenthal, B., and Little, B.: The relationship of atypical lymphocytes, phenothiazines, and schizophrenia. Arch. Gen. Psychiat. 15: 529-34, 1966.

67. Fischer, R.: Toxicity of schizophrenic serum and urine. Abstr. 19th Intern. Physiol. Cong., Montreal. 350, 1953.

68. Fischer, R.: Stress and the toxicity of schizophrenic serum. Science. 118: 409-410, 1953.

69. Fischer, R.: Communications. Science. 120: 505-06, 1954.

70. Fleischhacker, H.: Toxic-infectious

factors in schizophrenia. Conf. Neurol. 18: 217-22, 1958.

71. Fonseca, A. F. da.: Heredity in schizophrenia. J. Med. (Porto). 56: 461-8, 1965.

72. Freedman, D. A.: Various etiologies of the schizophrenic syndrome. Dis. Nerv. Syst. 19: 108-12, 1958.

73. Friedlander, J. H., and Dagradi, A. E.: Schizophreniform psychosis with pernicious anemia—A case report. Psychiat. Quart. 23: 444-56, 1949.

74. Fries, Margaret E.: Some hypotheses on the role of the congenital activity type in personality development. The Internl. J. Psychoanalysis. 35: 206, 1954.

75. Fünfgeld, E. W.: Pathogenic anatomic investigations on the anterior thalamic nucleus in schizophrenia. Intern. Cong. Neuropath. (Rome). 3: 648-59, 1952.

76. Funkenstein, D. H., Greenblatt, M., and Solomon, H. C.: An autonomic nervous system test of prognostic significance in relation to electroshock treatment. Psychosom. Med. 14: 347-62, 1952.

77. Gardner, E. J., and Stephens, F. E.: Schizophrenia in monozygotic twins. J. Hered. 40: 165-7, 1949.

78. Garrison, M. Jr.: The genetics of schizophrenia. J. Abnorm. Soc. Psychol. 42: 122-24, 1947.

79. Geller, E., Brill, N. Q., Crumpton, E., Eiduson, S., Liston, E., and Mazrahi, L.: Adrenocortical activity in relation to the severity of schizophrenia. Arch. Gen. Psychiat. 6: 384-7, 1962.

80. Georgi, F., Rieder, H. P., and Weber, R.: Remarks on Fischer's article, "Stress and toxicity of schizophrenic serum." Science. 120: 504-05, 1954.

81. Gershon, S., and Lonigro, A.: A study of lymphocytes stained with Masson's Trichrome Stain in psychiatric patients. J. Nerv. Ment. Dis. 139: 569-74, 1964.

82. Ghent, L., and Freedman, A. M.: Comparison of effects of normal and schizophrenic serum on motor performance in rats. Amer. J. Psychiat. 115: 465-6, 1958.

83. Giovannelli, G., and Borghesi, R.: Research on amylolytic power in the blood and cerebrospinal fluid in a group of schizophrenics. Rass. Stud. Psichiat. 53: 319-22, 1964.

84. Goldfarb, W.: Childhood schizophrenia. Inter. Psychiat. Clinics. 1: 821-45, 1964.

85. Gottesman, I. I.: Schizophrenia in twins: Unique 16-Year Study. Roche Report: Frontiers of Hospital Psychiatry, 3, 1, 1966.

86. Gregory, B. A. J. C.: The menstrual cycle and its disorders in psychiatric patients—II. J. Psychosom. Res. 2: 199-224, 1957.

87. Gregory, I.: Psychiatry: Biological and social. Philadelphia, Saunders, 1961, p. 209.

88. Greiber, M. F.: Psychoses associated with the administration of atabrine. Amer. J. Psychiat. 104: 306-14, 1947.

89. Grünthal, E.: On the problem of the schizophrenic illness. Monatsschr. Psychiat. Neurol. 124: 258-63, 1952.

90. Haberlandt, W. F.: On the genetic question in schizophrenia. Folia Clin. Int. (Barc). 13: 66-72, 1963.

91. Haddad, R. K., and Rabe, A.: An anaphylactic test for abnormal antigen(s) in schizophrenic serum. Proc. Third World Congress of Psychiatry, Montreal, 1: 658-61, 1961.

92. Hanhart, E.: Genetics problems of schizophrenia. Preliminary report on an isolated Swiss community. Acta Genet. Med. (Roma). 14: 13-40, 1965.

93. Hauptmann, A., and Myerson, A.: Studies of finger capillaries in schizophrenia and manic-depressive psychoses. J. Nerv. Ment. Dis. 108: 91-108, 1948.

94. Heath, R. G.: Studies toward correlating behavior with brain activity. Ann. N.Y. Acad. Sci. 92: 1106, 1961.

95. Heath, R. G.: Factors altering brain function and behavior in schizophrenia. Psychiat. Res. Rept. 19: 178-91, 1964.

96. Hemphill, R. E.: The significance of atrophy of the testis in schizophrenia. J. Ment. Sci. 90: 696, 1944.

97. Hemphill, R. E., and Reiss, M.: Experimental investigations in the endo-

crinology of schizophrenia. Proc. Roy. Soc. Med. 41: 533-40, 1948.

98. Hirata-Hibi, M., and Fessel, W. J.: The bone marrow in schizophrenia. Arch. Gen Psychiat. 10: 414-19, 1964.

99. Hoagland, H.: Study of adrenocortical physiology in normal and schizophrenic men. A.M.A. Arch. Neurol. Psychiat. 69: 470, 1953.

100. Hoare, R.: The cell fragility of erythrocytes from schizophrenic patients. Canad. Med. Ass. J. 84: 1201-3, 1961.

101. Hoch, P. H.: The etiology and epidemiology of schizophrenia. Amer. J. Publ. Health. 47: 1071-6, 1957.

102. Hoff, H.: The multifactorial approach in psychiatry. J. Neuropsychiat. 1: 173-81, 1960.

103. Hoffer, A.: Adrenochrome and adrenolutin and their relationship to mental disease. In Garattini, S. and Ghetti, V. (Eds.) Psychotropic Drugs. New York, Elsevier Pub. Co. 1957, pp. 10-20.

104. Hoffer, A.: Epinephrine derivatives as potential schizophrenic factors. J. Clin. Exp. Psychopath. 18: 27-60, 1957.

105. Hoffer, A.: Adrenochrome in blood plasma. Amer. J. Psychiat. 114: 752-3, 1958.

106. Hoffer, A.: Erythrocytes from schizophrenic patients. Dis. Nerv. Syst. 20: 87-89, 1959.

107. Hoffer, A., and Osmond, H.: Schizophrenia—an autonomic disease. J. Nerv. Ment. Dis. 122: 448-52, 1955.

108. Hoffer, A., and Osmond, H.: The adrenochrome model and schizophrenia. J. Nerv. Ment. Dis. 128: 18-35, 1959.

109. Hoffer, A., Osmond, H., and Smythies, J.: Schizophrenia: a new approach, II. Results of a year's research. J. Ment. Sci. 100: 29-45, 1954.

110. Hollister, L. E.: Research programs in the major mental illnesses: II. Hosp. Community Psychiat. 17: 233-38, 1966.

111. Hollister, L. E., and Kosek, J. C.: Abnormal lymphocytes in schizophrenia. Int. J. Neuropsychiat. 1: 559-60, 1965.

112. Hopf., A.: On the histopathological changes in the pallidum and striatum in

schizophrenia. Intern Cong. Neuropath. (Rome). 3: 627-35, 1952.

113. Horwitt, M. K.: Fact and artifact in the biology of schizophrenia. Science. 124: 429-30, 1956.

114. Howie, D. L.: Some pathological findings in schizophrenics. Amer. J. Psychiat. 117: 59-62, 1960.

115. Hurst, L. A.: Genetics of schizophrenia: Reply to Pastore. Psychol. Bull. 48: 402-12, 1951.

116. Huxley, J., Mayr, E., Osmond, H., and Hoffer, A.: Schizophrenia as a genetic morphism. Nature. 204: 220-21, 1964.

117. Iazgur, Ia. I.: Role of acidosis in the pathogenesis of schizophrenia. Vop. Psikhiat. Nevropat. 8: 332-40, 1962.

118. Ilyine, I. I., and Dzubenko, M. S.: Contribution to the problem of the role of conditionally pathogenic organisms in the etiology of schizophrenia. Zh. Nevropat. Psikhiat. (Moskova). 57: 1091-97, 1957.

119. Irvine, D. G., and Miyashita, H.: Blood types in relation to depressions and schizophrenia: a preliminary report. Canad. Med. Ass. J. 92: 551-4, 1965.

120. Ischel, M., et al.: Endocrine disorders in 8 cases of hebephrenia. Dapim. Refuiim. 23: 98-104, 1964.

121. Jackson, D. D.: A critique of the literature on the genetics of schizophrenia. In Jackson, D. D. (Ed.) The Etiology of Schizophrenia. New York, Basic Books, Inc., 1960, pp. 37-87.

122. Jackson, D. D.: LSD and the new beginning. J. Nerv. Ment. Dis. 135: 435-39, 1962.

123. Johnson, E. C., Jr., and Johnson, G. L. A.: Cerebrospinal fluid studies in advanced dementia praecox. Amer. J. Psychiat. 104: 778-80, 1948.

124. Josephy, H.: Beitrage zur histopathologie der dementia praecox. Ztschr. Ges. Neurol. Psychiat. 86: 391, 1923.

125. Judd., L. L., and Brandkamp, W. W.: Chromosome analyses in adult schizophrenics. Unpublished paper, Dept. of Psychiatry, U. California at Los Angeles, 1966.

126. Kallmann, F. J.: The genetics of

schizophrenia. New York, J. J. Augustin, 1938.

127. Kallmann, F. J.: The genetic theory of schizophrenia. Amer. J. Psychiat. 103: 309-22, 1946.

128. Kallmann, F. J.: Modern concepts of genetics in relation to mental health and abnormal personality development. Psychiat. Quart. 21: 535-53, 1947.

129. Kallmann, F. J.: Genetics in relation to mental disorders. J. Ment. Sci. 94: 250-7, 1948.

130. Kallmann, F. J.: The genetics of psychoses. Amer. J. Hum. Genet. 2: 385-90, 1950.

131. Kallmann, F. J.: Heredity in health and mental disorders. New York, W. W. Norton Co. 1953, pp. 143-181.

132. Kallmann, F. J.: Genetics of psychotic behavior patterns. In Hooker, D. and Hare, C. C. (Eds.) Genetics and the inheritance of integrated neurological and psychiatric patterns. Baltimore, Williams & Wilkins, 1954, pp. 357-66.

133. Kallmann, F. J., Falek, A., Hurzeler, M., and Erlenmeyer-Kimling, L.: The developmental aspects of children with two schizophrenic parents. Psychiat. Research Reports, 19: 136-45, 1964.

134. Kallmann, F. J., and Mickey, J. S.: Genetic concepts and folie à deux: a reexamination of "Induced Insanity" in family units. J. Hered. 37: 298-306, 1946.

135. Kallmann, F. J., and Rainer, J. D.: The genetic approach to schizophrenia: clinical, demographic, and family guidance problems. Int. Psychiat. Clinics. 1: 799-820, 1964.

136. Kallmann, F. J., and Roth, B.: Genetic aspects of preadolescent schizophrenia. Amer. J. Psychiat. 112: 599-606, 1956.

137. Kaplan, A. R.: On the genetics of schizophrenia. Eugenics. Quart. 12: 132-6, 1965.

138. Kety, S. S. et al.: Cerebral blood flow and metabolism in schizophrenia. Amer. J. Psychiat. 104: 765, 1948.

139. Kline, N. S., and Tenney, A. M.: Constitutional factors in the prognosis of schizophrenia. Amer. J. Psychiat. 107: 434-41, 1950.

140. Knobloch, H., and Pasamanick, B.: Seasonal variation in the births of the mentally deficient. Amer. J. Pub. Health, 48: 1201-08, 1958.

141. Kretschmer, E.: Physique and character. London, Paul, Trench, Trukner & Co., 1925.

142. Kringlen, E.: Schizophrenia in male monozygotic twins. Acta. Psychiat. Scand. 40: 1-76, Suppl. 178, 1964.

143. Kringlen, E.: Discordance with respect to schizophrenia in monozygotic male twins: some genetic aspects. J. Nerv. Ment. Dis. 138: 26-31, 1964.

144. Kringlen, E.: Schizophrenia in twins. Psychiat. 29: 172-84, 1966.

145. Krøll, J.: Liver dysfunction and schizophrenia. Lancet. 1: 763-64, 1965.

146. Lancet: Inheritance of schizophrenia. 1: 98, 1965.

147. Landis, C. et al.: Sex in development. New York, Paul C. Hoeber, 1940.

148. Landis, C., and Bolles, M. M.: Textbook in abnormal psychology. New York, Macmillan, 1950, pp. 344-45.

149. Lea, A. J.: Adrenochrome as the cause of schizophrenia: investigation of some deductions from this hypothesis. J. Ment. Sci. 101: 538-47, 1955.

150. Lemere, F.: Amphetamine psychoses may mimic schizophrenia. Roche Report: Frontiers of Hospital Psychiat. 3: 11, 1966.

151. Levin, M.: Transitory schizophrenias produced by bromide intoxication. Amer. J. Psychiat. 103: 229-37, 1946.

152. Lewis, N. D. C.: The constitutional factors in dementia praecox. Nerv. Ment. Dis. Mono. Ser. 35, Washington, D. C. Nerv. Ment. Dis. Pub. Co. 1923.

153. Lideman, R. R., and Iryanov, Y. I.: Hemolytic stability of erythrocytes in schizophrenia. Zh. Nevropat. Psikhiat. Korsakov. 65: 1201-4, 1966.

154. Lidz, T., Alanen, Y. Ö., Fleck, S., and Cornelison, A.: Schizophrenic patients and their siblings. Psychiat. 26: 1-18, 1963.

155. Lowenstein, E.: Tubercle bacilli in

the spinal fluid of dementia praecox. J. Nerv. Ment. Dis. 101: 576-82, 1945.

156. MacDonald, J. M., and Galvin, J. A. V.: Experimental psychotic states. Amer. J. Psychiat. 112: 970-6, 1956.

157. Malamud, N., and Boyd, D. A. Jr.: Sudden "brain death" in schizophrenia with extensive lesions in cerebral cortex. Arch. Neurol. Psychiat. 41: 352, 1939.

158. Malis, G.: The influence of the blood of mental patients on the development of larva rana temporara. Nevropat. Psikhiat. 16: 66-68, 1947.

159. Malis, G. Yu.: Research on the etiology of schizophrenia. Authorized translation from the Russian. New York, Consultants Bureau, 1961.

160. Maricq, H. R.: Familial schizophrenia as defined by nailfold capillary pattern and selected psychiatric traits. J. Nerv. Ment. Dis. 136: 216-26, 1963.

161. Maricq, H. R.: Capillary morphology and the course of illness in schizophrenia patients. J. Nerv. Ment. Dis. 142: 63-71, 1966.

162. McColl, M. G.: Influence of heredity on mental disease. Med. Press. 224: 529-33, 1950.

163. Med. J. Austral.: The aetiology of schizophrenia. 1: 691-93, 1965.

164. Meissner, W. W.: Schizophrenic concordance and discordance in monozygotic twins in the light of family dynamics. J. Nerv. Ment. Dis. 140: 464-67, 1965.

165. Meyer, A.: Constructive formulation of schizophrenia. Amer. J. Psychiat. 78: 355, 1922.

166. Minsker, E. K.: Reactivity of certain links of the endocrine system in various forms of the course of schizophrenia. Zh. Nevropat. Psikhiat. Korsakov. 63: 1388-97, 1963.

167. Moore, T. V., and Hsü, E. H.: Factorial analysis of anthropological measurement of psychotic patients. Hum. Biol. 18: 133-57, 1946.

168. Mott, F. W.: Normal and morbid conditions of the testis from youth to old age in 100 asylum and hospital cases. Brit. Med. J. 2: 737, 1919.

169. Mukherjee, A. N., Niyogi, A. K., and Shah, V. V.: Heredity as an epidemiological factor in schizophrenia and manic depressive psychoses. Indian J. Med. Sci. 18: 150-55, 1964.

170. Neilon, P.: Shirley's babies after fifteen years: a personality study. J. Genet. Psychol. 73: 175-86, 1948.

171. Nielsen, C. K.: Lung tuberculosis precipitating reactive psychoses. Acta Psychiat. Neurol. Scand. 26: 49-59, 1951.

172. Norris, A. S., and Chowning, J. R.: Season of birth and mental illness. Arch. Gen. Psychiat. 7: 206-12, 1962.

173. Nuremberg, T., and Brambilla, F.: Endocrine aspects of schizophrenia. Folia Endocr. (Roma). 17: 312-37, 1964.

174. Olkon, D. M.: Capillary structure in patients with schizophrenia. Arch. Neurol. Psychiat. 42: 652, 1939.

175. Orme, J. E.: Season of birth, psychosis and intelligence. Dis. Nerv. Syst. 24: 489-90, 1963.

176. Osmond, H., and Hoffer, A.: A small research in schizophrenia. Canad. Med. Assn. J. 80: 91-4, 1959.

177. Osmond, H., and Smythies, J.: Schizophrenia: a new approach. J. Ment. Sci. 98: 309-15, 1952.

178. Papez, J. W., and Bateman, J. F.: Cytological changes in nerve cells in dementia praecox. J. Nerv. Ment. Dis. 110: 425-37, 1949.

179. Papez, J. W., and Bateman, J. F.: Changes in nervous tissues and study of living organisms in mental disease. J. Nerv. Ment. Dis. 114: 400-12, 1951.

180. Parnell, R. W.: Behavior and physique: an introduction to practical and applied somatometry. London, Arnold, 1958.

181. Pasamanick, B., and Knobloch, H.: Seasonal variation in the births of the mentally deficient—a reply. Amer. J. Pub. Hlth. 50: 1737-42, 1960.

182. Pastore, N.: The genetics of schizophrenia. Psychol. Bull. 46: 285-302, 1949.

183. Pennington, V. M.: A study to determine possible differences in the formed blood elements of normal and schizo-

phrenic subjects. J. Neuropsychiat. 5: 21-7, 1963.

184. Peters, G.: Dementia praecox. *In* Lubarsch, O., Henke, F., and Rössle, R. (Eds.). Erkrankungen des Zentralen Nervensystem, Handbuch der Speziellen Pathologischen Anatomie und Histologie. Berlin, Springer-Verlag, 1956.

185. Pile, W. J.: A study on the correlation between dementia praecox and the month of birth. Virginia Med. Mono. 78: 438-40, 1951.

186. Pincus, G., and Elmadjian, F.: The lymphocytic response to heat stress on normal and psychotic subjects. J. Clin. Endocrin. 6: 295, 1946.

187. Pollin, W., Stabenau, J. R., Mosher, L., and Tupin, J.: Life history differences in identical twins discordant for schizophrenia. Amer. J. Orthopsychiat. 36: 492-509, 1966.

188. Pollin, W., Stabenau, J. R., and Tupin, J.: Family studies with identical twins discordant for schizophrenia. Psychiat. 28: 60-78, 1965.

189. Rao, S.: Birth order and schizophrenia. J. Nerv. Ment. Dis. 138: 87-9, 1964.

190. Raphael, T., and Raphael, L. G.: Fingerprints in schizophrenia. Amer. Med. Assn. J. 180: 215-9, 1962.

191. Rinkel, M., Hyde, R. W., and Solomon, H. C.: Experimental psychiatry. III: a chemical concept of psychosis. Dis. Nerv. Syst. 15: 259-64, 1954.

192. Rosanoff, A. J., Handy, L. M., Plesset, I. R., and Brush, S. The etiology of so-called schizophrenic psychoses. Amer. J. Psychiat. 91: 247-86, 1934.

193. Rosenow, E. C.: Bacteriologic, etiologic and serologic studies in epilepsy and schizophrenia. I. Postgrad. Med. 2: 346-57, 1947.

194. Rosenow, E. C.: Bacteriologic, etiologic and serologic studies in epilepsy and schizophrenia. II. Effects in animals following inoculation of alpha streptococci. Postgrad. Med. 3: 124-36, 1948.

195. Rosenow, E.·C.: Bacteriologic, etiologic and serologic studies in epilepsy and schizophrenia. III. Cutaneous reactions to intradermal injection of streptococcal antibody and antigen. Postgrad. Med. 3: 367-76, 1948.

196. Rosenow, E. C.: Bacteriological studies in idiopathic epilepsy and schizophrenia. So. Dak. J. Med. 5: 243-48, 1952.

197. Rosenow, E. C.: Bacterial studies on the etiology and chlorpromazine treatment of schizophrenia and related disorders. J. Nerv. Ment. Dis. 122: 321-31, 1955.

198. Rosenthal, D.: Some factors associated with concordance and discordance with respect to schizophrenia in monozygotic twins. J. Nerv. Ment. Dis. 129: 1-10, 1959.

199. Rosenthal, D.: Sex distribution and the severity of illness among samples of schizophrenic twins. J. Psychiat. Res. 1: 26-36, 1961.

200. Rosenthal, D.: Problems of sampling and diagnosis in the major twin studies of schizophrenia. J. Psychiat. Res. 1: 116-34, 1961.

201. Rupp, C., and Wilson, G.: General pathologic findings associated with cases of so-called functional psychoses. J. Nerv. Ment. Dis. 110: 419-24, 1949.

202. Scharenberg, K., and Brown, E. O. Jr.: Histopathology of catatonic states. J. Neuropath. Exp. Neurol. 13: 592-600, 1954.

203. Scheidegger, S.: Liver-tissue changes in schizophrenia. J. Neuropath. Exp. Neurol. 12: 397-99, 1953.

204. Schlegel, L.: Constitutional-biological observations on the hands of physically abnormal personalities with special regard to hand-furrows. Schweiz. Arch. Neurol. Psychiat. 62: 305-51, 1948.

205. Schooler, C.: Birth order and schizophrenia. Arch. Gen. Psychiat. 4: 91-97, 1961.

206. Schulman, A. J.: The etiology of schizophrenia. Psychiat. Quart. 24: 515-31, 1950.

207. Sclare, A. B.: The problem of schizophrenia. Med. Illust. 10: 532-36, 1956.

208. Semerari, A.: Recent views on the

inheritance of schizophrenia. Rass. Neuropsychiat. 4: 513, 1950.

209. Sheldon, W. H.: Constitutional factors in personality. In J. McV. Hunt (Ed.). Personality and the behavior disorders. New York, Ronald. I. 1944, pp. 526-49.

210. Shirley, M.: The first two years of life. Minneapolis, U. Minnesota Press. Vol. I, 1931, Vols. II and III, 1933.

211. Silveria, A.: Characterization of cerebral pathology, psychopathology and psychiatric heredobiology in Kleist's doctrine. Arq. Neuropsiquiat. (S. Paulo). 17: 102-42, 1959.

212. Simpson, G. M., and Cooper, T. B.: Thyroid indices in chronic schizophrenia: III. J. Nerv. Ment. Dis. 142: 58-62, 1966.

213. Simpson, G. M., Cranswick, E. H., and Blair, J. H.: Thyroid indices in chronic schizophrenia: I. J. Nerv. Ment. Dis. 137: 582-90, 1963.

214. Simpson, G. M., Cranswick, E. H., and Blair, J. H.: Thyroid indices in chronic schizophrenia: II. J. Nerv. Ment. Dis. 138: 581-85, 1964.

215. Singer, R. D.: Organization as a unifying concept in schizophrenia. A.M.A. Arch. Gen. Psychiat. 2: 61-74, 1960.

216. Sjögren, T.: Genetic-statistical and psychiatric investigations of a West-Swedish population. Acta Psychiat. Neurol. Suppl. 52, 1948.

217. Skaličková, O.: Genetic aspects of edogenous psychoses, especially schizophrenia. Cesk. Psychiat. 62: 12-17, 1966.

218. Slater, E.: Genetical causes of schizophrenia symptoms. Monatschr. Psychiat. Neurol. 113: 50-58, 1947.

219. Slater, E.: Psychotic and neurotic illnesses in twins. London, Stationery Office, 1953.

220. Slater, E.: The monogenic theory of schizophrenia. Acta Genet. (Basel). 8: 50-56, 1958.

221. Smith, C. M., and McIntyre, S.: Family size, birth rank, and ordinal position in psychiatric illness. Canad. Psychiat. Assn. J. 8: 244-48, 1963.

222. Southard, E. E.: On the focality of microscopic brain lesions found in dementia praecox. Arch. Neurol. Psychiat. 1: 172, 1919.

223. Spielmeyer, W.: The problem of the anatomy of schizophrenia. J. Nerv. Ment. Dis. 72: 241, 1930.

224. Sterling, T. D.: Seasonal variations in the births of the mentally deficient? Amer. J. Pub. Hlth. 50: 955-65, 1960.

225. Strömgren, E.: Psychiatric researches in heredity during recent years in the northern countries. Schweiz. Arch. Neurol. Psychiat. 62: 378-93, 1948.

226. Szára, S.: The comparison of the psychotic effect of tryptamine derivatives with the effects of mescaline and LSD-25 in self-experiments. In Garattini, S., and Ghetti, V. (Eds.) Psychotropic drugs. New York, Elsevier Pub. Co., 1957, pp. 460-67.

227. Szára, S., Axelrod, J., and Perlin, S.: Is adrenochrome present in the blood? Amer. J. Psychiat. 115: 162-63, 1958.

228. Terrill, J.: The nature of the LSD experience. J. Nerv. Ment. Dis. 135: 425-29, 1962.

229. Terris, M., Lapouse, R., and Monk, M. A.: The relation of prematurity and previous fetal loss to childhood schizophrenia. Amer. J. Psychiat. 121: 476-81, 1964.

230. Tienari, P.: Psychiatric illnesses in identical twins. Acta Psychiat. Scand. 39: 171, 1-195, 1963.

231. Tienari, P.: The genetic aspects of schizophrenia. Duodecim. 81: 273-75, 1965.

232. Tourney, G., Nelson, W. O., and Gottlieb, J. A.: Morphology of the testes in schizophrenia. Arch. Neurol. Psychiat. 70: 240-53, 1953.

233. Tsivilko, V. S.: On features of the pathology of nerve cells in the cerebral cortex in schizophrenia. Zh. Nevropat. Psikhiat. Korsakov. 62: 1712-22, 1962.

234. Turner, W. J., and Chipps, H. I.: A heterophil hemolysin in human blood. Arch. Gen. Psychiat. 15: 373-77, 1966.

235. Turner, W. J., Merlis, S., and Carl, A.: Concerning theories of indoles in schizophrenigenesis. Amer. J. Psychiat. 112: 466-67, 1955.

236. Vanderkamp, H.: Nuclear changes in the white blood cells of patients with schizophrenic reaction. J. Neuropsychiat. 4: 1-3, 1962.

237. Vogel, W., and Lauterbach, C. G.: Sibling patterns and social adjustment among normal and psychiatrically disturbed soldiers. J. Consult. Psychol. 27: 236-42, 1963.

238. Von Buttlar-Brentano, K.: Cellular pathology of the nucleus basalis in schizophrenia. J. Nerv. Ment. Dis. 116: 646-53, 1952.

239. Wahren, W.: The changes of hypothalamic nuclei in schizophrenia. Internl. Cong. Neuropath. (Rome). 3: 660-73, 1952.

240. Walker, R. G.: Schizophrenia and cortical involvement. J. Nerv. Ment. Dis. 125: 226-28, 1957.

241. Washburn, R. W.: A study of the smiling and laughing of infants in the first year of life. Genet. Psychol. Mono. 6: 397-537, 1929.

242. Weinstein, M. R.: Histopathological changes in the brain in schizophrenia. Arch. Neurol. Psychiat. 71: 539-53, 1954.

243. Wertheimer, N., and Wertheimer, M.: Capillary structure: its relation to psychiatric diagnosis and morphology. J. Nerv. Ment. Dis. 122: 14-27, 1955.

244. Williams, R. J., Berry, L. J., and Beerstecher, E. Jr.: Individual metabolic patterns, alcoholism, genetotrophic diseases. Proc. Nat. Acad. Sci. 35: 265-71, 1949.

245. Winkelman, N. W.: Importance of small blood vessels of brain in psychiatric problems. Amer. J. Psychiat. 89: 775, 1933.

246. Winkelman, N. W., and Book, M. H.: Observations on the histopathology of schizophrenia. I: The cortex. Amer. J. Psychiat. 105: 889-96, 1949.

247. Winter, C. A., and Flataker, L.: Effects of biological fluids from psychotic patients and normal subjects on the performance of trained rats. In M. Rinkel (Ed.) Chemical Concepts of Psychosis. New York, McDowell, Obolensky, Inc., 1958, p. 238.

248. Wittermans, A. W., and Schultz, B.: Genealogic contribution to the problem of cured schizophrenia. Arch. Psychiat. Nervenkr. 185: 211-32, 1950.

249. Wohlfahrt, S.: Die Histopathologie der Schizophrenie. Acta. Psychiat. Neurol. 11: 687, 1936.

250. Wolf, A., and Cowen, D.: Histopathology of schizophrenia and other psychoses of unknown origin. In The Biology of Mental Health and Disease. New York, Paul S. Hoeber, 1952, pp. 469-86.

5

Biochemical Hypotheses and Studies

SEYMOUR S. KETY, M.D.

Dr. Seymour S. Kety, Professor of Psychiatry at Harvard Medical School and Director of the Psychiatric Research Laboratories of the Massachusetts General Hospital, was born in Philadelphia in 1915. After receiving his baccalaureate and medical degrees from the University of Pennsylvania and a National Research Council fellowship at the Massachusetts General Hospital, he returned to the University of Pennsylvania and spent eight years there in the Department of Pharmacology and Physiology of the Undergraduate and Graduate Medical Schools. In 1951 he was appointed the first Scientific Director of the National Institutes of Mental Health and of Neurological Diseases in Bethesda, and established the intramural research programs of these Institutes. He directed the Laboratory of Clinical Science of the National Institute of Mental Health from 1956 to 1967 when he assumed his present position.

He has been a student and investigator of the role of biological mechanisms in psychiatric illness and, with his collaborators, has contributed significantly to genetic-environmental interactions in the transmission of schizophrenia and the possible role of catecholamines in the affective psychoses.

He is a member of the National Academy of Sciences, the American Academy of Arts and Sciences, a trustee of the Association for Research in Nervous and Mental Disease, and a member of the American Physiologic and Pharmacologic Societies. Because of his conviction that research is of crucial importance to the development of psychiatry, he was instrumental in organizing the Psychiatric Research Society and establishing the Journal of Psychiatric Research of which he is the editor.

Biochemistry, which has had notable success in elucidating etiologic factors in many areas of medicine, has also been brought to bear on the problem of schizophrenia. Although these efforts have not to date been successful in demonstrating a biochemical "lesion," a number of arguments can be made to support the viewpoint that chemical factors operate significantly and specifically in schizophrenia.

Perhaps the strongest of these arguments is the good evidence for the operation of genetic factors in the transmission of schizophrenia,[92] consisting of a higher concordance rate for the disorder in the monozygotic twins of afflicted individuals[43,57,59,67,99] and in the biologic families of schizophrenics where early adoption or removal from their natural parents has served to disentangle the operation of genetic and environmental factors in its transmission.[50,64,93]

Another argument which has been used is the ability of a number of exogenous chemical substances (iodides, mescaline, LSD, amphetamine, iproniazid, psilocybin) or some endogenous biochemical disturbances

155

porphyria, thyroid disorders) to produce psychoses resembling schizophrenia in some or many of its features.

Biochemical hypotheses and findings related to schizophrenia have been the subject of several exhaustive and critical reviews of which only a few are cited for further reference.[22,61,63,109] In spite of the large number of abnormal chemical findings which have been reported in schizophrenia, few have been independently confirmed and on none is there general agreement with regard to its significance. This may be attributed to the operation of an inordinate number of variables, difficult to control, which are associated with the clinical studies of schizophrenia.

Despite the phenomenologic similarities which permitted the concept of schizophrenia to emerge, there is little evidence that all of its forms have a common etiology or pathogenesis. Errors involved in the study of relatively small samples from heterogeneous populations may help to explain the frequency with which findings of one group fail to be confirmed by another.

Most biochemical research in schizophrenia has been carried out in patients with a long history of hospitalization in institutions where overcrowding is difficult to avoid and hygienic standards cannot always be maintained. It is easy to imagine the spread of chronic infections such as infectious hepatitis among such patients, and one wonders how often this may account for findings attributable to disturbed hepatic function or elevated plasma titres of antibody globulins. Even in the absence of previous or current infection, the development of a characteristic pattern of intestinal flora in a group of patients living together for long periods of time may occasionally contribute to the finding of what appear to be deviant metabolic pathways.

The variety and quality of the diet of the institutionalized schizophrenic is rarely comparable to that of the nonhospitalized normal control. In the case of the acute schizophrenic, the weeks of continual turmoil which precede recognition of the disorder are hardly conducive to a normal dietary intake. It is not surprising that a dietary vitamin deficiency has been found to account for at least one biochemical abnormality which had been attributed to schizophrenia.[77] Horwitt[55] found signs of liver dysfunction during long periods of borderline protein ingestion.

Emotional stress is known to cause profound changes in man, in adrenocortical and thyroid function, in excretion of water, electrolytes, creatinine, epinephrine and norepinephrine, to mention only a few recently reported findings. On the other hand, physical inactivity would be expected to produce changes in a number of body functions. Schizophrenic illness is often characterized by indolence and lack of exercise or by marked emotional disturbance in the basal state and frequently exaggerated anxiety in response to routine and research procedures. The disturbances in behavior and activity which mark the schizophrenic process would also be expected to cause deviations from the normal in many biochemical and metabolic measures: in urinary volume and concentration, in energy and nitrogen metabolism, in the state and activity of numerous organ systems and metabolic pathways. The biochemical changes which are secondary to the psychologic and behavioral state of the patient are often of interest in themselves; it is important, however, not to attribute to them etiologic roles.

Another incidental feature of the schizophrenic patient which differentiates him from the normal control and from many other types of patient is the long list of therapies to which he may have been exposed. The ataractic drugs which are often used over extended periods of time are particularly prone to produce metabolites which appear in the urine and interfere with a number of chemical determinations long after the drug has been withdrawn.

With this combination of many variables and the subjective judgments necessary for diagnosis and the evaluation of clinical course, it is not unexpected that subjective bias would from time to time affect the results of research in schizophrenia and make even more necessary in that field than in many others the employment of rigorous research design.

ENERGY METABOLISM

A decrease in basal metabolism was found in schizophrenia by earlier workers, although more recent work has not confirmed this,[89] and hypotheses attributing the disease to disturbances in the fundamental mechanisms of energy supply or conversion in the brain have been formulated but on the basis of rather inadequate evidence. Kelsey and co-workers[60] found a decreased B.M.R. in their series of schizophrenics to be associated with an increased uptake of ^{131}I by the thyroid, correctible by the addition of iodine to the diet, and attributed it to a lack of that element in the institutional diet. Periodic catatonia and some other schizophreniform psychoses seem to be associated with disturbances in thyroxine or thyrotropic hormone regulation,[21,40] but little evidence exists to suggest that such disturbances are characteristic of schizophrenia generally.

The oxygen consumption and blood flow of the brain as a whole have been found to lie within the normal range in a variety of forms of schizophrenia,[65] and although localized changes in these functions have sometimes been postulated, there is no evidence to support this supposition. The clear consciousness usually present in schizophrenia does not suggest the manifestation of cerebral anoxia.

Richter[89] has pointed out the uncontrolled factors in earlier work which implicated a defect in carbohydrate metabolism as a characteristic of the schizophrenic process. The finding in schizophrenia of an abnormal glucose tolerance in conjunction with other evidence of hepatic dysfunction, or evidence of a retarded metabolism of lactate by the schizophrenic,[2] does not completely exclude incidental hepatic disease, nutritional deficiencies or the psychophysiologic influences on carbohydrate metabolism as possible sources of error. Horwitt and associates[56] were able to demonstrate and correct similar abnormalities by altering the dietary intake of the B group of vitamins.

A deficiency of glucose-6-phosphate dehydrogenase, known to occur in 10-20 per cent of American Negroes, has been found to show an incidence significantly different from normal in Negro catatonic and paranoid schizophrenics,[19] an observation which has received partial confirmation by an independent group.[29] Findings that schizophrenia is associated with cellular changes in oxidative phosphorylation or in the uptake[44] or metabolism of glucose[35] require further confirmation.[17]

It is difficult to believe that a generalized defect in energy metabolism, a process fundamental to every cell in the body, could be responsible for the highly specialized features of schizophrenia. For this reason, perhaps, interest has developed in other aspects of metabolism, the substrates or products of which appear to have some special role in the brain.

PROTEIN

Although Gjessing[40] found definite alterations in bodily nitrogen balance correlated with and sometimes preceding the changes in mental state of periodic catatonics, there has been no evidence to indicate a major change in protein metabolism for schizophrenia generally. On the other hand, some interest has been focused recently on more specific protein constituents or the metabolism of particular amino acids or their amines.

Interest in the possible presence of an abnormal protein constituent of blood of schizophrenics was stimulated by a report, in 1958, that a serum fraction obtained from schizophrenic patients was capable of causing some of the symptoms of that disorder when injected into nonschizophrenic volunteers.[49] This material, which was given the name "taraxein," appeared to have some relationship to ceruloplasmin, the copper-containing globulin of normal plasma which the same group had found to be elevated in schizophrenia[71] and, upon its intravenous injection, to produce rapid clinical improvement.[48] Very recently, Martens, in a thorough examination of the relationships between ceruloplasmin and schizophrenia,[76] has reported an equivalent elevation of serum copper in that disorder and in delirium tremens. In a controlled, double blind series he was unable to confirm the earlier report of clinical improvement following intravenous injections of ceruloplasmin. One attempt to replicate the production of psychotic symptoms in volunteers by means of taraxein was not successful,[91] and to date the original findings have not been confirmed in a significant and well controlled series.

A number of groups, however, have reported evidence compatible with the thesis that an abnormal protein is present to a greater extent in the blood of some schizophrenics than in normals and that this substance is capable of producing certain behavioral, metabolic, or cellular changes in lower animals. Haddad and Rabe,[45] replicating and extending an earlier report by Malis,[78] found some evidence for an antigenic abnormality in the pooled serum of chronically ill schizophrenic patients. More recent studies by this group using different immunologic methods have yielded negative results which they do not regard as conclusive. Faurbye, Lundberg and Jensen[23] were unable to confirm Malis' results. Using another approach, Vartanyan[108] has found evidence for an immunologic abnormality in schizophrenia. Heath and co-workers[47] have advanced an auto-immune concept as the biologic basis of schizophrenia. The studies with fluorescent antibodies, electrophysiologic, immunologic and behavioral observations, on which the concept is based, await independent confirmation. Precipitin reactions have yielded positive[79] and negative[58,84,90] results with respect to the occurrence of specific proteins in the serum of schizophrenics.

Fessel and co-workers[26,28] have reported increases in 4S and 19S macroglobulins in a considerable proportion of schizophrenic patients and the ability to differentiate schizophrenic from manic depressive patients on this basis. Mental stress in nonpsychotic individuals was found to elevate the same macroglobulins.[27] Certain of these findings have been confirmed by two independent groups.[66,97] Gammack and Hector,[37] while failing to confirm Fessel's findings, observed a highly significant increase in the α-globulin fraction and the haptoglobin component in the serum of schizophrenics. They also questioned the specificity of such findings which occur frequently in many types of chronic disease. Others have not confirmed this increase in haptoglobins.[72] It seems fair to conclude that to the present time no abnormal protein characteristic of schizophrenia has been characterized by physicochemical technics.

Some special properties of the plasma of schizophrenics have been reported by workers using various biologic assays. Bishop[11] has reported evidence for the effect of plasma from schizophrenic patients upon learning and retention of learning in the rat. Other investigators[8,112] found a slowing of rope climbing activity in rats injected with whole serum or certain fractions from schizophrenic patients as compared with normal fractions. The specificity of this response for schizophrenia has not been demonstrated and later findings were not confirmatory.[96] German[38] reported an effect of serum of schizophrenics on cortical evoked responses in rats which in later, more rigorously controlled studies he and his associates were unable to confirm.[39] In well controlled studies of the effects of plasma from psychotic patients on behavior, Ferguson and Fisher[25] have reported observations using a precision timing task in cebus monkeys in which a highly significant delay in responsiveness was produced by the injection of plasma from some newly admitted catatonic patients. It is of interest that in their studies plasma from normal individuals under preoperative stress produced a similar but not as marked slowing of response.

Frohman and his associates[34] have reported increases in the ratio of lactate-to-pyruvate in the medium after chicken erythrocytes are incubated with plasma or plasma fractions of some schizophrenic patients as compared to normal controls. Mangoni and associates[74] have been unable to confirm this. In a subsequent paper, Frohman and associates[36] were able to demonstrate this difference in the lactate: pyruvate ratio only when the subjects had engaged in moderate exercise before the blood samples were drawn; no appreciable difference was found when the subjects were at complete rest, in normal activity, or exercising vigorously. This, plus the fact that exercise affected the lactate:pyruvate ratio in the incubation mixture more than did the presence or absence of schizophrenia, suggests the need for better definition of what may be a large number of variables involved in this reaction.

Recently, Ryan, Brown and Durell[94] have succeeded in clarifying some of the fundamental processes involved in the ability of human plasma to affect the lactate production of chicken erythrocytes, which appears to be the determining variable of the lactate:pyruvate ratio. In their test system, lactate production by aerobic glycolysis did not occur in completely intact erythrocytes but was contingent upon and correlated with hemolysis. This, in turn, was caused by a complement-requiring antibody present in variable titre in all human plasma tested. The plasma of schizophrenics could not be reliably distinguished from that of nonschizophrenic patients from the same hospital.[95] Turner and Chipps[107] found a higher heterophile hemolysin titre in the blood of schizophrenics than of nonschizophrenics. Chronic alcoholics, however, also showed a higher titre of the hemolysin. Although Frohman and his associates have consistently found this phenomenon with higher frequency among schizophrenics, a possibility which remains to be ruled out is that the titre of this antibody is more closely related to a history of chronic hospitalization and greater exposure to a variety of antigens than to the presence of schizophrenia. An interesting further possibility is the significantly greater antibody responsiveness of schizophrenic patients than normal or depressed individuals to a standard antigen challenge.[33a]

The evidence with regard to the biologic or behavioral effects of the plasma of schizophrenics is far from conclusive at the present time. Most of the effects reported have failed of confirmation and none have been shown to be properties of plasma which are characteristic of schizophrenia.

Further work is necessary to determine to what extent the abnormalities in plasma found by physico-chemical analysis, when they are confirmed, are characteristic of schizophrenia or a reflection of the stress, exposure to chronic endemic infections, dietary or other adventitious factors which accompany the disorder and are associated with chronic institutionalization.[61]

AMINO ACIDS AND AMINES

Although an earlier report indicated abnormalities in amino acid excretion in schizophrenia,[114] this has not been further confirmed. Much interest, on the other hand, has been attached to the possibility that abnormal metabolism of one or another amine could be of etiologic importance in schizophrenia.[51] The great sensitivity and relative nonspecificity of chromatographic methods and the ease with which findings may be affected by exogenous factors such as diet or drugs increase the likelihood of false positives in this area, and great caution must be exercized in identifying the particular metabolite which appears to be involved or interpreting the significance which should be attached to it.[42,75]

The significance of an unidentified Ehrlich positive substance ("the mauve spot") attributed to a new form of schizophrenia by Hoffer and Osmond[52] has been brought into question by O'Reilly and his associates[80,81] who found it with high frequency in the urines of patients with affective psychosis, alcoholism, psychoneurosis, personality disorders and cancer.

TRANSMETHYLATION

In 1952, Osmond and Smythies[82] pointed out some similarities between mescaline psychosis and schizophrenia and between that drug and epinephrine. They included a biochemical note by Harley-Mason which stated, in part:

> "It is extremely probable that the final stage in the biogenesis of adrenaline is a transmethylation of noradrenaline, the methyl group arising from methionine or choline. It is just possible that a pathological disordering of its transmethylation mechanism might lead to methylation of one or both of its phenolic hydroxyl groups instead of its amino group. . . . Methylation of phenolic hydroxyl groups in the animal body is of rare occurrence but a significant case has been reported recently. . . . It is particularly interesting to note that out of a series of phenylethylamine derivations tested by Noteboom, 3,4-dimethoxyphenylethylamine was the most potent in producing catatonia in animals."

Since that time the transmethylation of norepinephrine to epinephrine has been established,[12] while Axelrod, Senoh and Witkop[5] have demonstrated the O-methylation of both catecholamines as an important step in their normal metabolism.

The suggestion that pathologic transmethylation may occur in schizophrenia was further strengthened by the recognition that a number of psychotomimetic agents, in addition to mescaline, were methylated congeners of normal body metabolites. On this basis, Hoffer and associates[53] used niacin and niacinamide, methyl accepters, in an effort to inhibit competitively the possible abnormal process. They reported beneficial results which have not been independently confirmed. In 1961, Pollin, Cardon and Kety[86] tested this hypothesis by administering large doses of L-methionine to chronic schizophrenic patients in conjunction with a monoamine oxidase inhibitor to permit the accumulation of any monoamines formed. This substance is an essential precursor of S-adenosylmethionine, the active substance which was shown by Cantoni[18] to transfer its methyl group to accepter compounds in the process of transmethylation. In some of the patients during the administration of the L-methionine there was a brief intensification of psychosis which involved an exacerbation of some of the schizophrenic symptoms. No other amino acids tested (glycine, tyrosine, phenylalanine, tryptophan, histidine, glutamine) were associated with this phenomenon. The intensification of psychosis in schizophrenics with methionine has since, in essence, been confirmed by four other groups[1,15,46,83] and, in addition, Brune and Himwich[16] found that betaine, another methyl donor, was equally effective in accentuating psychotic symptoms in schizophrenics. Baldessarini and Kopin[6] found that feeding L-methionine to rats produced a significant increase in S-adenosylmethionine concentration in the liver and brain. Axelrod[4] demonstrated the presence in normal mammalian tissue of an enzyme capable of methylating normal metabolites, i.e., tryptamine and serotonin to their dimethyl derivatives for which psychotomimetic properties have been reported.

DIMETHOXYPHENYLETHYLAMINE

In 1962, Friedhoff and Van Winkle[32] examined the urine of patients with early schizophrenia and reported the occurrence of 3,4-dimethoxyphenylethylamine (DMPEA), to which Harley-Mason had alluded as a possible abnormally methylated metabolite. This compound is a dimethylated derivative of dopamine and closely related to mescaline, which represents a trimethylated congener of this biogenic amine.

Since 1962 a number of groups have attempted to confirm the excretion of DMPEA in schizophrenia and further to define the variables which affect it. Friedhoff and Van Winkle[32] had found it in the urine of 15 of 19 schizophrenics and in none of 14 normal urines. Kuehl and associates[68] confirmed its presence in 7 of 22 schizophrenics and in none of 10 normals. Takesada and associates[105] found it in 70 of 78 (90 per cent) schizophrenics but also in 35 of 67, or 52 per cent, of normals. Faurbye and Pind,[24] who modified the method to increase its sensitivity and to avoid interference by phenothiazine metabolites, were unable to detect DMPEA in the urine of 15 schizophrenics and 10 normals. Perry, Hansen and Macintyre[85] were unable to find the compound in 10 schizophrenics on a diet free of fruits and vegetables. After finding DMPEA in the urine of 4 out of 6 schizophrenics and 2 of 3 controls, Studnitz and Nyman[104] demonstrated its disappearance when the same individuals were placed on a pure carbohydrate regimen.

In an extensive series in which biochemical determinations and psychiatric diagnoses were made independently, Bourdillon and his associates[14] reported the presence of a "pink spot" having some of the characteristics of DMPEA in the urines of 46 of 84 (55 per cent) schizophrenics, while it was absent in all of 17 nonschizophrenic patients and 149 normal controls. A second experiment with less striking results showed a low incidence (3 per cent) of the spot in the urine of paranoid patients and a 29 per cent incidence in non-paranoid schizophrenics. Drug administration which was not controlled could have been different in type of drug or dosage for different diagnostic categories. Drugs or their metabolites are known to interfere with DMPEA determinations, and at least one group[24] has observed a phenothiazine metabolite with Rf value and color reactions similar to DMPEA which persisted in the urine for as long as 25 days after withdrawal of the drug. Williams[110] has examined the technic used by Bourdillon and found it relatively insensitive to DMPEA. Further studies by his group[111] and by others using more specific technics[7,13] have indicated that Bourdillon's "pink spot" was not, in fact, DMPEA and that DMPEA is not excreted in abnormal amounts by schizophrenics. Friedhoff,[33] on the other hand, on the basis of its behavior in six solvent systems, a number of color reactions, thin layer and gas chromatography and melting point determinations, has concluded that the material he has found in the urine of schizophrenics is identical to DMPEA. Although this substance, when administered to schizophrenics is rapidly converted to 3, 4-dimethoxyphenyl-acetic acid,[31] Kuehl and associates[69] could not detect a significant difference in the excretion of that acid between normal subjects and schizophrenics.

These findings—the intensification of psychosis in schizophrenics by methionine or betaine, the increase in S-adenosylmethionine in the brain and liver of rats by methionine feeding, the existence of at least one enzyme capable of transmethylating normal metabolites to psychoto-mimetic compounds, the evidence obtained by some workers for the excretion of DMPEA in a substantial number of schizophrenics—are compatible with the hypothesis that the process of biologic transmethylation is somehow disturbed in schizophrenia with the production or persistence of excessive amounts of methylated derivatives of normal metabolites capable of inducing some of the symptoms of schizophrenia. That hypothesis, however, is far from having been validated. Although methionine and betaine are the only ones of a large number of amino acids which have been shown capable of briefly exacerbating psychosis in some schizophrenics, it has not been established that the clinical changes resulted from any specific methylated derivatives, and the possibility that this was a nonspecific toxic psychosis or a peculiarly schizophrenic response to nonspecific toxic changes has not been ruled out. Haydu, et al.,[46] who confirm the ability of methionine to exacerbate schizophrenic symptomatology, found an ameliorating effect from hydroxychloroquine and suggest that the clinical effects of these agents result from their activation or suppression of thiol groups. A special sensitivity of schizophrenics to methionine has not been established although a similar regimen of methionine without iproniazid in a small number of normal volunteers produced no hint of a psychotic reaction.[62] The accumulated evidence for the excretion of dimethoxyphenylethylamine in association with some forms of schizophrenia is as yet inconclusive. Several groups have been unable to confirm it and the possibility that it is an artifact of drug therapy has not been completely ruled out. There is evidence that some dietary factors are necessary for its appearance although the same is true for phenylketonuria and does not argue against its significance or relevance to schizophrenia. On parenteral administration to man, DMPEA has not been shown to produce perceptible mental effects,[31] but this does not preclude an effect from higher concentrations locally within the brain. The transmethylation hypothesis appears to require and merit further examination and development.

INDOLEAMINES

Although Woolley[113] was impressed with indirect evidence for the possibility of a disorder in serotonin metabolism in schizophrenia, significant differences between schizophrenic and normal populations with respect to this amine or its metabolites have not been established.[61] Earlier findings of indolic compounds (indole acetamide and 6-hydroxyskatole) with abnormal frequency in the urine of schizophrenics[78,101] have more recently been found to a similar extent in the urine of other types of mental patient and are probably to be attributed to exogenous or nondisease-related factors.[20,100,115]

Tryptamine excretion may have some significance in schizophrenia since an increase has been found to occur in such patients before a period of exacerbation.[9] An increase in urinary tryptophan metabolites has also been observed following the administration of methionine,[10,102,103] and it has been suggested that the conversion of tryptamine to its hallucinogenic methylated derivative may occur. Aside from one positive report,[30] the search for dimethyltryptamine or dimethylserotonin in the urine of schizophrenics has yielded negative results.[98,102,106]

EPINEPHRINE

The hypothesis that adrenochrome or other abnormal metabolites of circulating epinephrine were formed in schizophrenia and accounted for many of the symptoms[54] has received careful scrutiny made possible by the recently acquired knowledge of the normal metabolism of this hormone.[3] No evidence was found for the abnormal metabolism of labeled epinephrine infused into schizophrenic patients,[88] and in one study which accounted almost entirely for the excreted label in terms of unchanged epinephrine and four metabolites (3-methoxy-4-hydroxymandelic acid, metanephrine, 3,4-dihydroxymandelic acid, and 3-methoxy-4-hydroxyphenylglycol), no qualitative or quantitative differences were found in this pattern between chronic schizophrenics and normal volunteers.[70] The infusion of epinephrine into schizophrenics was not found to intensify the psychosis[87] which would have been expected if the psychosis were associated with abnormal metabolites of circulating epinephrine.

SUMMARY AND CONCLUSIONS

Although it would be difficult to demonstrate that a definitive increase in our knowledge of biochemical mechanisms in the schizophrenic psychoses has occurred in the past decade, substantial progress has nonetheless been made. There is an increasing awareness of the complexity of the problem and of the sophistication of research design necessary to cope with it. Most important, there has been a burgeoning of fundamental knowledge in biochemistry and neurochemistry and their interaction with behavior on which depend meaningful hypotheses relating to schizophrenia and from which may eventually come an understanding of whatever biochemical mechanisms operate significantly in its etiology, pathogenesis, or therapy.

Before the etiology of any syndrome has been established, it is idle to regard it as a single disease, and, in the case of schizophrenia, the striking resemblance which certain temporal lobe epilepsies or chronic intoxications (bromidism, iodism, amphetamine psychosis, porphyria) bear to it makes tenable the possibility that the syndrome may emerge from different etiologic pathways. Recognition of such a possibility aids in the interpretation of genetic and biologic findings and would facilitate the characterization of more specific subgroups.

Those interested in exploring the biologic aspects of schizophrenic disorders cannot with impunity ignore the psychologic, social, and other environmental factors which operate significantly at various stages of their development. Leaving aside etiologic considerations, it is clear that exogenous factors may precipitate, intensify, or ameliorate the symptoms and confound the biologic picture. To what extent the classical psychologic features of chronic schizophrenia are created by prolonged isolation and hospitalization will become apparent with the increasing adoption of community-oriented treatment. Examples are readily found in which uncontrolled nutritional, infectious, or pharmacologic variables may have accounted for specific biochemical abnormalities in populations of chronic schizophrenics. These secondary variables are so manifold that it is hard to imagine a design which could anticipate and control them all, and successive studies concentrating on particularly relevant controls will probably continue to be called for. There is, in addition, much to be said for broadening the scope of the typical sample from chronic hospitalized schizophrenia to the early, more acute, remitting, episodic, or periodic forms[21,41] in which it may not only be possible to obviate some of the difficulties imposed by chronic hospitalization and drug administration but, by study of the same patient in psychotic and nonpsychotic states, to avoid the effects of interindividual variance.

An unavoidable difficulty at the present time is the fact that the crucial processes of diagnosis and evaluation of change are based almost entirely on subjective estimates. It is not insensitivity which diminishes the reliability of such measures as much as their vulnerability to bias; failure to recognize and guard against this source of error probably accounts for much of the inconsistency in the study of schizophrenia not only from biologic but also from sociologic and psychologic points of view.

The single-gene-single-enzyme concept of the biologic disorder in schizophrenia was encouraged by the very high concordance rate found in monozygotic twins in earlier studies. More recent twin studies in which selective bias in sampling has been more effectively controlled have yielded a concordance rate of 40 per cent or less. Studies with adopted schizophrenics[64,93] where environmental factors can be more successfully controlled have still reinforced the importance of genetic factors but have emphasized the genetic transmission of a vulnerability to schizophrenia or to a variety of personality or character disorders. This suggests that personality or intelligence may be more appropriate models for schizophrenia than phenylketonuria. A polygenic inadequacy interacting with particular life situations seems more compatible with all of the evidence.[92] The biologic component of the schizophreniform illnesses may lie in the mechanisms which underlie arousal, inhibition, perception, cognition, affect, or the complex relationships among them, all of which appear to be involved at one time or another. Although a single chemical substance such as mescaline or lysergic acid diethylamide may produce disturbances in all of these areas, it would be well to keep in mind the possibility that more complex neurochemical, neurophysiologic and psychologic interactions may form the biologic substrate of schizophrenia.

BIBLIOGRAPHY

1. Alexander, F., Curtis, G. C., Sprince, H., and Crosley, A. P.: L-Methionine and L-tryptophan feedings in nonpsychotic and schizophrenic patients with and without tranylcypromine. J. Nerv. Ment. Dis. 137: 135-142, 1963.

2. Altschule, M. D., Henneman, D. H., Holliday, P., and Goncz, R.-M.: Carbohydrate metabolism in brain disease. VI. Lactate metabolism after infusion of sodium d-lactate in manic-depressive and schizophrenic psychoses. AMA Arch. Intern. Med. 98: 35-38, 1956.

3. Axelrod, J.: Metabolism of epinephrine and other sympathomimetic amines. Physiol. Rev. 39: 751-776, 1959.

4. Axelrod, J.: Enzymatic formation of psychotomimetic metabolites from normally occurring compounds. Science 134: 343, 1961.

5. Axelrod, J., Senoh, S., and Witkop, B.: O-Methylation of catecholamines in vivo. J. Biol. Chem. 233: 697-701, 1958.

6. Baldessarini, R. J., and Kopin, I. J.: Assay of tissue levels of S-adenosylmethionine. Anal. Biochem. 6: 289-292, 1963.

7. Bell, C. E., and Somerville, A. R.: Identity of the "pink spot." Nature 211: 1405-1406, 1966.

8. Bergen, J. F., Pennell, R. B., Saravis, C. A., and Hoagland, H.: Further experiments with plasma proteins from schizophrenics. In Heath, R. G. (Ed.) Serological Fractions in Schizophrenia. New York, Harper & Row, 1963, pp. 67-76.

9. Berlet, H. H., Bull, C., Himwich, H. E., Kohl, H., Matsumoto, K., Pscheidt, G. R., Spaide, J., Tourlentes, T. T., and Valverde, J. M.: Endogenous metabolic factor in schizophrenic behavior. Science 144: 311-313, 1964.

10. Berlet, H. H., Matsumoto, K.,

Pscheidt, G. R., Spaide, J., Bull, C., and Himwich, H. E.: Biochemical correlates of behavior in schizophrenic patients. Arch. Gen. Psychiat. 13: 521-531, 1965.

11. Bishop, M. P.: Effects of plasma from schizophrenia subjects upon learning and retention in the rat. In Heath, R. G. (Ed.) Serological Fractions in Schizophrenia. New York, Harper & Row, 1963, pp. 77-91.

12. Blaschko, H.: The development of current concepts of catecholamine formation. Pharmacol. Rev. 11: 307-316, 1959.

13. Boulton, A. A., and Felton, C. A.: The "pink spot" and schizophrenia. Nature 211: 1404-1405, 1966.

14. Bourdillon, R. E., Clarke, C. A., Ridges, A. P., Sheppard, P. M., Harper, P., and Leslie, S. A.: "Pink spot" in the urine of schizophrenics. Nature 208: 453-455, 1965.

15. Brune, G. G., and Himwich, H. E.: Effects of methionine loading on the behavior of schizophrenic patients. J. Nerv. Ment. Dis. 134: 447-450, 1962.

16. Brune, G. G., and Himwich, H. E.: Biogenic amines and behavior in schizophrenic patients. In Recent Advances in Biological Psychiatry, Vol. 5. New York, Plenum Press, 1963, pp. 144-160.

17. Buhler, D. R., and Ihler, G. S.: Effect of plasma from normal and schizophrenic subjects on the oxidation of labeled glucose by chicken erythrocytes. J. Lab. Clin. Med. 62: 306-318, 1963.

18. Cantoni, G. L.: S-Adenosylmethinine: a new intermediate formed enzymatically from L-methionine and adenosine-triphosphate. J. Biol. Chem. 204: 403-416, 1953.

19. Dern, R. J., Glynn, M. F., and Brewer, G. J.: Studies on the influence of hereditary G-6-PD deficiency in the expression of schizophrenic patterns. Clin. Res. 10: 80, 1962.

20. Dohan, F. C., Ewing, J., Graff, H., and Sprince, H.: Schizophrenia: 6-hydroxyskatole and environment. Arch. Gen. Psychiat. 10: 420-422, 1964.

21. Durell, J., Lidow, L. S., Kellam, S. F., and Shader, R. I.: Interrelationships between regulation of thyroid gland function and psychosis. Res. Publ. Ass. Res. Nerv. Ment. Dis. 43: 387-399, 1966.

22. Durell, J., and Schildkraut, J. J.: Biochemical studies of the schizophrenic and affective disorders. In Arieti, S. (Ed.) American Handbook of Psychiatry, Vol. III. New York, Basic Books, 1966, pp. 423-457.

23. Faurbye, A., Lundberg, L., and Jensen, K. A.: Studies on the antigen demonstrated by Malis in serum from schizophenic patients. Acta Path. Microbiol. Scand. 61: 633-651, 1964.

24. Faurbye, A., and Pind, K.: Investigation on the occurrence of the dopamine metabolite 3,4-dimethoxyphenylethylamine in the urine of schizophrenics. Acta Psychiat. Scand. 40: 240-243, 1964.

25. Ferguson, D. C., and Fisher, A. E.: Behavior disruption in cebus monkeys as a function of injected substances. Science 139: 1281-1282, 1963.

26. Fessel, W. J.: Macroglobulin elevations in functional mental illness. Nature 193: 1005, 1962.

27. Fessel, W. J.: Mental stress, blood proteins and the hypothalamus: experimental results showing effect of mental stress upon 4S and 19S proteins. Arch. Gen. Psychiat. 7: 427-435, 1962.

28. Fessel, W. J., and Grunbaum, B. W.: Electrophoretic and analytical ultracentrifuge studies in sera of psychotic patients: elevation of gamma globulins and macroglobulins, and splitting of alpha$_2$ globulins. Ann. Intern. Med. 54: 1134-1145, 1961.

29. Fieve, R. R., Brauninger, G., Fleiss, J., and Cohen, G.: Glucose-6-phosphate dehydrogenase deficiency and schizophrenic behavior. J. Psychiat. Res. 3: 255-262, 1965.

30. Fischer, E., Fernández Lagravere, T. A., Vázquez, A. J., and Di Stefano, A. O.: A bufotenin-like substance in the urine of schizophrenics. J. Nerv. Ment. Dis. 133: 441-444, 1961.

31. Friedhoff, A. J., and Hollister, L. E.: Comparison of the metabolism of 3,4-dimethoxyphenylethylamine and mescaline in humans. Biochem. Pharmacol. 15: 269-273, 1966.

32. Friedhoff, A. J., and Van Winkle, E.: The characteristics of an amine found in the urine of schizophrenic patients. J. Nerv. Ment. Dis. 135: 550-555, 1962.

33. Friedhoff, A. J., and Van Winkle, E.: New developments in the investigation of the relationship of 3,4-dimethoxyphenylethylamine to schizophrenia. In Himwich, H. E., Kety, S. S., and Smythies, J. R. (Eds.) Amines and Schizophrenia. Oxford, Pergamon Press, 1967, pp. 19-21.

33a. Friedman, S. B., Cohen, J., and Iker, H.: Antibody response to cholera vaccine. Differences between depressed, schizophrenic, and normal subjects. Arch. Gen. Psychiat. 16: 312-315, 1967.

34. Frohman, C. E., Czajkowski, N. P., Luby, E. D., Gottlieb, J. S., and Senf, R.: Further evidence of a plasma factor in schizophrenia. Arch. Gen. Psychiat. 2: 263-267, 1960.

35. Frohman, C. E., Latham, L. K., Beckett, P. G. S., and Gottlieb, J. S.: Evidence of a plasma factor in schizophrenia. Arch. Gen. Psychiat. 2: 255-262, 1960.

36. Frohman, C. E., Latham, L. K., Warner, K. A., Brosius, C. O., Beckett, P. G. S., and Gottlieb, J. S.: Motor activity in schizophrenia; effect on plasma factor. Arch. Gen. Psychiat. 9: 83-88, 1963.

37. Gammack, D. B., and Hector, R. I.: A study of serum proteins in acute schizophrenia. Clin. Sci. 28: 469-475, 1965.

38. German, G. A.: Effects of serum from schizophrenics on evoked cortical potentials in the rat. Brit. J. Psychiat. 109: 616-623, 1963.

39. German, G. A., Antebi, R. N., Dear, E. M. A., and McCance, C.: A further study of the effects of serum from schizophrenics on evoked cortical potentials in the rat. Brit. J. Psychiat. 111: 345-347, 1965.

40. Gjessing, R.: Disturbances of somatic functions in catatonia with a periodic course, and their compensation. J. Ment. Sci. 84: 608-621, 1938.

41. Gjessing, L. R.: Studies of periodic catatonia. II. The urinary excretion of phenolic amines and acids with and without loads of different drugs. J. Psychiat. Res. 2: 149-162, 1964.

42. Goldenberg, H., Fishman, V., Whittier, J., and Brinitzer, W.: Urinary aromatic excretion patterns in schizophrenia. Arch. Gen. Psychiat. 2: 221-230, 1960.

43. Gottesman, I. I., and Shields, J.: Schizophrenia in twins: sixteen years' consecutive admissions to a psychiatric clinic. Dis. Nerv. Syst. 27 (Suppl.): 11-19, 1966.

44. Haavaldsen, R., Lingjaerde, O., and Walaas, O.: Disturbances of carbohydrate metabolism in schizophrenics: effect of serum fractions from schizophrenics on glucose uptake of rat diaphragm in vitro. Confin. Neurol. 18: 270, 1958.

45. Haddad, R. K., and Rabe, A.: An antigenic abnormality in the serum of chronically ill schizophrenic patients. In Heath, R. G. (Ed.) Serological Fractions in Schizophrenia. New York, Harper & Row, 1963, pp. 151-157.

46. Haydu, G. G., Dhrymiotis, A., Korenyi, C., and Goldschmidt, L.: Effects of methionine and hydroxychloroquine in schizophrenia. Amer. J. Psychiat. 122: 560-564, 1965.

47. Heath, R. G., and Krupp, I. M.: The biologic basis of schizophrenia: an autoimmune concept. In Walaas, O. (Ed.) Molecular Basis of Some Aspects of Mental Activity, Vol. 2. London, Academic Press, 1967, pp. 313-344.

48. Heath, R. G., Leach, B. E., Byers, L. W., Martens, S., and Feigley, C. A.: Pharmacological and biological psychotherapy. Amer. J. Psychiat. 114: 683-689, 1958.

49. Heath, R. G., Martens, S., Leach, B. E., Cohen, M., and Feigley, C. A.: Behavioral changes in nonpsychotic volunteers following the administration of taraxein, the substance obtained from serum of schizophrenic patients. Amer. J. Psychiat. 114: 917-920, 1958.

50. Heston, L. L.: Psychiatric disorders in foster home reared children of schizophrenic mothers. Brit. J. Psychiat. 112: 819-825, 1966.

51. Himwich, H. E., Kety, S. S., and Smythies, J. R. (Eds.): Amines and Schizophrenia. Oxford, Pergamon Press, 1967.

52. Hoffer, A., and Osmond, H.: Malvaria: A new psychiatric disease. Acta Psychiat. Scand. 39: 335-366, 1963.

53. Hoffer, A., Osmond, H., Callbeck, M. J, and Kahan, I.: Treatment of schizophrenia with nicotinic acid and nicotinamide. J. Clin. Exp. Psychopathol. 18: 131-158, 1957.

54. Hoffer, A., Osmond, H., and Smythies, J.: Schizophrenia: A new approach. II. Result of a year's research. J. Ment. Sci. 100: 29-45, 1954.

55. Horwitt, M. K.: Report of Elgin Project No. 3 with emphasis on liver dysfunction. In Nutrition Symposium Series No. 7. New York, National Vitamin Foundation, 1953, pp. 67-83.

56. Horwitt, M. K., Liebert, E., Kreisler, O., and Wittman, P.: Investigations of human requirements for B-complex vitamins. In National Research Council Bulletin No. 116. Washington, D.C., National Academy of Sciences, 1948.

57. Inouye, E.: Similarity and dissimilarity of schizophrenia in twins. In Proceedings of the Third World Congress of Psychiatry, Vol. I, Montreal, 1961, pp. 524-530.

58. Jensen, K., Clausen, J., and Osterman, E.: Serum and cerebrospinal fluid proteins in schizophrenia. Acta Psychiat. Scand. 40: 280-286, 1964.

59. Kallmann, F. J.: The genetic theory of schizophrenia. An analysis of 691 schizophrenic twin index families. Amer. J. Psychiat. 103: 309-322, 1946.

60. Kelsey, F. O., Gullock, A. H., and Kelsey, F. E.: Thyroid activity in hospitalized psychiatric patients. AMA Arch. Neurol. Psychiat. 77: 543-548, 1957.

61. Kety, S. S.: Biochemical theories of schizophrenia. Science 129: 1528-1532, 1590-1596, 1959.

62. Kety, S. S.: Possible relation of central amines to behavior in schizophrenic patients. Fed. Proc. 20: 894-896, 1961.

63. Kety, S. S.: Current biochemical approaches to schizophrenia. New Eng. J. Med. 276: 325-331, 1967.

64. Kety, S. S., Rosenthal, D., Wender, P. H., and Schulsinger, F.: The types and prevalence of mental illness in the bio-logical and adoptive families of adopted schizophrenics. J. Psychiat. Res. 6: Suppl., 1968 (in press).

65. Kety, S. S., Woodford, R. B., Harmel, M. H., Freyhan, F. A., Appel, K. E., and Schmidt, C. F.: Cerebral blood flow and metabolism in schizophrenia. The effects of barbiturate semi-narcosis, insulin coma and electroshock. Amer. J. Psychiat. 104: 765-770, 1948.

66. Kopeloff, L. M., and Fischel, E.: Serum levels of bactericidin and globulin in schizophrenia. Arch. Gen. Psychiat. 9: 524-528, 1963.

67. Kringlen, E.: Schizophrenia in twins: An epidemiological-clinical study. Psychiatry 29: 172-184, 1966.

68. Kuehl, F. A., Jr., Hichens, M., Ormond, R. E., Meisinger, M. A. P., Gale, P. H., Cirillo, V. J., and Brink, N. G.: Para-O-methylation of dopamine in schizophrenic and normal individuals. Nature 203: 154-155, 1964.

69. Kuehl, F. A., Jr., Ormond, R. E., and Vandenheuvel, W. J. A.: Occurrence of 3,4-dimethoxyphenylacetic acid in urines of normal and schizophrenic individuals. Nature 211: 606-608, 1966.

70. LaBrosse, E. H., Mann, J. D., and Kety, S. S.: The physiological and psychological effects of intravenously administered epinephrine and its metabolism in normal and schizophrenic men. III. Metabolism of 7-H³-epinephrine as determined in studies on blood and urine. J. Psychiat. Res. 1: 68-75, 1961.

71. Leach, B. E., Cohen, M., Heath, R. G., and Martens, S.: Studies of the role of ceruloplasmin and albumin in adrenaline metabolism. AMA Arch. Neurol. Psychiat. 76: 635-642, 1956.

72. Lovegrove, T. D., and Nicholls, D. M.: Haptoglobin subtypes in a schizophrenic and control population. J. Nerv. Ment. Dis. 141: 195-196, 1965.

73. Malis, C. Y.: K Etiologii Schizofrenii. Medgiz, Moscow, 1959.

74. Mangoni, A., Balazs, R., and Coppen, A. J.: The effect of plasma from schizophrenic patients on the chicken erythrocyte system. Brit. J. Psychiat. 109: 231-234, 1963.

75. Mann, J. D., and LaBrosse, E. H.: Urinary excretion of phenolic acids by normal and schizophrenic male patients. Arch. Gen. Psychiat. 1: 547-551, 1959.

76. Martens, S.: Effects of exogenous human ceruloplasmin in the schizophrenia syndrome. Stockholm, Tryckeri Balder AB, 1966.

77. McDonald, R. K., Weise, V. K., Evans, F. T., and Patrick, R. W.: Studies on plasma ascorbic acid and ceruloplasmin levels in schizophrenia. In Folch-Pi, J. (Ed.) Chemical Pathology of the Nervous System. Oxford, Pergamon Press, 1961, pp. 404-412.

78. Nakao, A., and Ball, M.: The appearance of a skatole derivative in the urine of schizophrenics. J. Nerv. Ment. Dis. 130: 417-419, 1960.

79. Noval, J. J., and Mao, T. S. S.: Abnormal immunological reaction of schizophrenic serum. Fed. Proc. 25: 560, 1966.

80. O'Reilly, P. O., Ernest, M., and Hughes, G.: The incidence of malvaria. Brit. J. Psychiat. 111: 741-744, 1965.

81. O'Reilly, P. O., Hughes, G., Russell, S., and Ernest, M.: The mauve factor: An evaluation. Dis. Nerv. Syst. 26: 562-568, 1965.

82. Osmond, H., and Smythies, J.: Schizophrenia: A new approach. J. Ment. Sci. 98: 309-315, 1952.

83. Park, L., Baldessarini, R. J., and Kety, S. S.: Methionine effects on chronic schizophrenics. Arch. Gen. Psychiat. 12: 346-351, 1965.

84. Pennell, R. B., Pawlus, C., Saravis, C. A., and Scrimshaw, G.: Further characterization of a human plasma component which influences animal behavior. Trans. NY Acad. Sci. 28: 47-58, 1965.

85. Perry, T. L., Hansen, S., and Macintyre, L.: Failure to detect 3,4-dimethoxyphenylethylamine in the urine of schizophrenics. Nature 202: 519-520, 1964.

86. Pollin, W., Cardon, P. V., and Kety, S. S.: Effects of amino acid feedings in schizophrenic patients treated with iproniazid. Science 133: 104-105, 1961.

87. Pollin, W., and Goldin, S.: The physiological and psychological effects of intravenously administered epinephrine and its metabolism in normal and schizophrenic men. II. Psychiatric observations. J. Psychiat. Res. 1: 50-67, 1961.

88. Resnick, O., and Elmadjian, F.: Excretion and metabolism of dl-epinephrine-7-C14-d-bitartrate infused into schizophrenic patients. Amer. J. Physiol. 187: 626, 1956.

89. Richter, D.: Biochemical aspects of schizophrenia. In Richter, D. (Ed.) Schizophrenia: Somatic Aspects. London, Pergamon Press, 1957, pp. 53-75.

90. Rieder, H. P., Ritzel, G., Spiegelberg, H., and Gnirss, F.: Serologische Versuche zum Nachweis von "Taraxein." Experientia 16: 561-562, 1960.

91. Robins, E., Smith, K., and Lowe, I. P.: Discussion of clinical studies with taraxein. In Abramson, H. A. (Ed.) Neuropharmacology: Transactions of the Fourth Conference. New York, Josiah Macy Jr. Foundation, 1957, pp. 123-135.

92. Rosenthal, D., and Kety, S. S. (Eds.): The Transmission of Schizophrenia. J. Psychiat. Res. 6: Suppl., 1968 (in press).

93. Rosenthal, D., Wender, P. H., Kety, S. S., Schulsinger, F., Welner, J., and Østergaard, L.: Schizophrenics' offspring reared in adoptive homes. J. Psychiat. Res. 6: Suppl., 1968 (in press).

94. Ryan, J. W., Brown, J. D., and Durell, J.: Antibodies affecting metabolism of chicken erythrocytes: examination of schizophrenic and other subjects. Science 151: 1408-1410, 1966.

95. Ryan, J. W., Steinberg, H. R., Green, R., Brown, J. D., and Durell, J.: Controlled study of effects of plasma of schizophrenic and non-schizophrenic psychiatric patients on chicken erythrocytes. J. Psychiat. Res. 6: 33-44, 1968.

96. Sanders, B. E., Small, S. M., Ayers, W. J., Oh, Y. H., and Axelrod, S.: Additional studies on plasma proteins obtained from schizophrenics and controls. Trans. NY Acad. Sci. 28: 22-39, 1965.

97. Sapira, J. D.: Immunoelectrophoresis of the serum of psychotic patients. Arch. Gen. Psychiat. 10: 196-198, 1964.

98. Siegel, M.: A sensitive method for the detection of N,N-dimethylserotonin (bufotenin) in urine; failure to demonstrate its presence in the urine of schizophrenic and normal subjects. J. Psychiat. Res. 3: 205-211, 1965.

99. Slater, E.: Psychotic and Neurotic Illnesses in Twins. London, H. M. Stationery Office, 1953.

100. Sohler, A., Noval, J. J., and Renz, R. H.: 6-Hydroxyskatole sulfate excretion in schizophrenia. J. Nerv. Ment. Dis. 137: 591-596, 1963.

101. Sprince, H., Houser, E., Jameson, D., and Dohan, F. C: Differential extraction of indoles from the urine of schizophrenic and normal subjects. Arch. Gen. Psychiat. 2: 268-270, 1960.

102. Sprince, H., Parker, C. M., Jameson, D., and Alexander, F.: Urinary indoles in schizophrenic and psychoneurotic patients after administration of tranylcypromine (parnate) and methionine or tryptophan. J. Nerv. Ment. Dis. 137: 246-251, 1963.

103. Sprince, H., Parker, C. M., Jameson, D., and Josephs, J. A.: Effect of methionine on nicotinic acid and indoleacetic acid pathways of tryptophan metabolism in vivo. Proc. Soc. Exp. Biol. Med. 119: 942-946, 1965.

104. Studnitz, W. v., and Nyman, G. E.: Excretion of 3,4-dimethoxyphenylethylamine in schizophrenia. Acta Psychiat. Scand. 41: 117-121, 1965.

105. Takesada, M., Kakimoto, Y., Sano, I., and Kaneko, Z.: 3,4-Dimethoxyphenylethylamine and other amines in the urine of schizophrenic patients. Nature 199: 203-204, 1963.

106. Takesada, M., Miyamoto, E., Kakimoto, Y., Sano, I., and Kaneko, Z.: Phenolic and indole amines in the urine of schizophrenics. Nature 207: 1199-1200, 1965.

107. Turner, W. J., and Chipps, H. I.: A heterophil hemolysin in human blood. I. Distribution in schizophrenics and nonschizophrenics. Arch. Gen. Psychiat. 15: 373-377, 1966.

108. Vartanyan, M. E.: Immunological investigation of schizophrenia. Zh. Nevropat. Psikhiat. Korsakov 63: 3-12, 1963.

109. Weil-Malherbe, H.: The biochemistry of the functional psychoses. In Advances in Enzymology, Vol. XXIX. New York, Interscience Publishers, 1967, pp. 479-553.

110. Williams, C. H.: The pink spot. Lancet 1: 599-600, 1966.

111. Williams, C. H., Gibson, J. G., and McCormick, W. O.: 3,4-Dimethoxyphenylethylamine in schizophrenia. Nature 211: 1195, 1966.

112. Winter, C. A., Flataker, L., Boger, W. P., Smith, E. V. C., and Sanders, B. E.: The effects of blood serum and of serum fractions from schizophrenic donors upon the performance of trained rats. In Folch-Pi, J. (Ed.) Chemical Pathology of the Nervous System. Oxford, Pergamon Press, 1961, pp. 641-646.

113. Woolley, D. W.: The Biochemical Bases of Psychoses. New York, John Wiley & Sons, 1962.

114. Young, H. K., Berry, H. K., Beerstecher, E., and Berry, J. S.: Metabolic patterns of schizophrenic and control groups. In Biochemical Institute Studies IV, University of Texas Publication No. 5109. Austin, University of Texas, 1951, pp. 189-197.

115. Yuwiler, A., and Good, M. H.: Chromatographic study of "Reigelhaupt" chromogens in urine. J. Psychiat. Res. 1: 215-227, 1962.

6

Neurophysiological Studies

CHARLES SHAGASS, M.D.

Dr. Shagass is Professor of Psychiatry at Temple University Medical School, psychiatrist in charge of the Temple Clinical Unit at Eastern Pennsylvania Psychiatric Institute and directs, as well, a laboratory of Human Neurophysiology at this Institute.

Educated at McGill (from which he received a Diplomate in Psychiatry) and Rochester Universities, Dr. Shagass has served on the faculties of McGill and the University of Iowa. Subsequent to his early research on conditioned electroencephalographic responses in man, he has continued his investigation of brain-behavior relationships in psychiatric disorders. He has done a great deal of work in averaging technics for studying the electrical activity of the brain.

Dr. Shagass has published material in the areas of psychosomatic relationships, pharmacologic reactivity, pharmacotherapy of psychiatric illness, and on medical selection of military pilots.

It is not known whether the states encompassed under "schizophrenia" involve one disorder or many, and there are no clearly established etiologies. The task of delineating pathophysiology is, consequently, replete with uncertainties. Apart from the problems of defining criterion groups in human studies, there are no convincing animal models of schizophrenic states. This necessitates an extraordinary degree of dependence upon investigation in man, with inevitable limitation of observational scope.

Pathophysiologic studies involving biochemical and general biologic factors have been reviewed elsewhere in this volume. The focus of this chapter will be neurophysiologic. Since all behavior depends upon the detail of events in the central nervous system, pathogenetic phenomena originating in other parts of the body, or resulting from stressful experience, must modify brain function in order to produce disordered behavior. It should be clear, however, that brain activities relevant to psychopathology may lie toward the end of a long chain of pathophysiologic events. They could thus be relatively nonspecific with respect to etiology. For example, although it would be a great advance to discover an electroencephalographic (EEG) sign of hallucination, such a sign could occur equally well in a wide variety of disorders and have little specific relevance for schizophrenia.

There has been tremendous progress in the sciences concerned with nervous system function during the past decade. The technics of electron microscopy and microelectrode recording, coupled with sophisticated chemical and

172

pharmacologic analyses, have revealed a wealth of structural and functional detail concerning the modes of communication between nerve cells at the synapse.[25] The important role in higher mental functions of various ganglia lying at the base of the brain has been extensively documented by experimental evidence.[162] In particular, the parts played by the reticular formation in consciousness and the limbic system in emotional activities have received much attention. Older concepts of "telephone-type" connections within the nervous system have been replaced by concepts of circuits which allow for a series of complex transformations at each stage. However, although expanding neurophysiologic knowledge has clearly demonstrated that known functional properties of the central nervous system are sufficiently complex to account for the infinite variety of behavior, specific neural mechanisms for even relatively primitive functions, such as conditioned reflex formation, have not yet been established. Explanations for phenomena such as hallucinations, delusions, depersonalization, and all of the other complex manifestations of schizophrenic disorders in terms of known central nervous system properties are still in the realm of speculation.

As indicated previously, pertinent neural mechanisms must be verified in the schizophrenic patient himself, since there is no convincing experimental model. For obvious reasons, relatively few observations have been made in patients in whom electrodes have been inserted directly into the brain. The great bulk of available data on patients comes from recordings made from the outside of the cranium. Since extracranial electrical recordings reflect no more than a small fraction of total brain activities,[124] events of real pathophysiologic significance may go undetected.

ELECTROENCEPHALOGRAPHIC STUDIES

Interest in psychologic relationships to the EEG pattern started with Hans Berger, psychiatrist discoverer of the EEG. Early hopes that characteristic EEG patterns would be found in psychotic states were doomed to disappointment. Although many workers reported a higher incidence of EEG abnormality in schizophrenic populations than in comparison groups of non-patients, the data were open to criticism on many grounds. On the one hand, there was frequently failure to control for important factors, such as age and previous or concurrent treatment with electroconvulsive therapy (ECT) and drugs. On the other hand, the nature of the positive findings was essentially statistical, i.e., the patients displayed more fast and/or slow activity, but there was inadequate quantification of the data, thereby raising doubts about reliability. The development of methods for reducing the enormous quantity of EEG data to understandable, numerical measurements has been a long term development in electroencephalography; it may now be close to achieving its goal as a consequence of advances in applications of computer methods.

Waking EEG Patterns

Among pioneer workers Berger,[5,6] Lemere[95] and Travis and Malamud[170] reported that the EEG was normal in schizophrenia. Hoagland, Cameron and Rubin[69] reported that the per cent time occupied by delta slow waves in the frontal areas was significantly higher in untreated than in treated schizophrenics. MacMahon and Walter[99] also found the delta waves occurred less frequently as the patient recovered, but showed that they did not originate in the brain and were, in fact, produced by rhythmic eyeball movements.

Pauline Davis[18] described an EEG pattern with little or no alpha or slow rhythm, consisting of "disorganized" low voltage, very fast random frequencies at 25 to 50 c./sec. She called this the "choppy" pattern and found a 61 per cent incidence in schizophrenics.[19] Davis considered the "choppy" rhythm to be evidence of brain pathology in schizophrenia because the pattern was found in patients known to have suffered brain damage. Many workers regard the "choppy" pattern as an artifactual resultant of alpha blocking and muscle activity. However, in Hill's[68] view, it is still an EEG reality, although seen in less than 25 per cent of schizophrenic EEG's. Other workers reporting a high incidence of "choppy" records in schizophrenics are Hurst,[73] who found them in over half of schizophrenics, about 30 per cent of neurosyphilitics and in no control subjects, and Lester and Edwards[96] who observed fast, "choppy" records in about one third of waking schizophrenic EEG's. Kammerer et al.,[83] however, considered the "choppy" pattern to have no pathologic value. If the "choppy" pattern genuinely reflects cortical activity, it would suggest the presence of intense, continuous and abnormal activation by subcortical mechanisms.[68]

Epileptiform EEG Patterns in Schizophrenia

The issue of the relationship between schizophrenia and epilepsy continues to receive investigative attention. Pioneer workers[20,44,79] reported an unusual incidence of "epileptic" wave forms in the EEG of schizophrenics. These were generally described as "sharp" waves. Hill[68] found that about 25 per cent of schizophrenics, particularly young catatonics, displayed paroxysmal bilaterally synchronous combinations of spike and wave patterns or slow wave bursts in which the spike component is minimal. He observed the same relationship in catatonic forms of schizophrenia as had other workers,[117] and in one case showed that the incidence of such paroxysmal phenomena varied with the severity of the illness. Hill noted that treatment of such patients by anticonvulsants had no therapeutic effect, so that the issue of the relationship of these findings to epilepsy is in doubt. Furthermore, he was able to tabulate distinguishing characteristics between the spike and wave discharges of epileptic and schizophrenic patients, indicating that they differed in frequency, voltage, location, age of incidence, and response to hyperventilation.

Landolt[92] differentiated four types of psychotic episodes in epilepsy. The one of special interest was described as productive psychotic episodes with "forced normalization" in the EEG. Included in the category are the "oriented and lucid" twilight states in which the patients are quiet and composed, seemingly no more than slightly tense, and present a clinical picture which is almost indistinguishable from schizophrenic states. Further epileptic seizures do not appear during the twilight state, and the EEG becomes more normal or entirely normal. The phenomenon is often, but not always, associated with a temporal focus. Landolt's observations are of particular interest in relation to the findings of "hypernormal" EEG's in therapy resistant schizophrenia.

Treffert[171] compared psychotic patients with temporal lobe spikes and without clear evidence of epilepsy with matched epileptic patients and with other patients without either temporal lobe foci or clinical epilepsy. He found that aggressive symptomatology in the form of combative behavior, rage episodes, and paroxysmal symptoms in the form of blackouts and hallucinations characterized both temporal lobe groups, while the control groups were characterised by delusions and other classical psychiatric symptoms. The schizophrenic group with EEG foci resembled more clearly the known epileptic group than it did the other groups. Small et al.[160] and Small and Small[159] also found clinical differences between psychotic patients with and without epileptiform EEG's and clinical epilepsy; mental signs suggesting organic brain disease were more common in epileptics. Tucker et al.[172] reported a higher incidence of schizophrenia among 95 psychiatric patients found to have EEG abnormality on admission to a university psychiatric center than among matched patients with normal EEG's. EEG abnormality was more often associated with destructive-assaultive behavior, irritability, religiosity, impaired personal habits, increased psychomotor activity, flattened affect, impaired association, persecutory and somatic delusions, perseveration, vagueness, auditory hallucinations, time disorientation, recent memory difficulty and headache. The type of abnormal EEG was not well related to clinical variables.

A major difficulty in evaluating studies attempting to relate epilepsy and schizophrenia derives from the origin of the sample being studied. In relatively unselected large samples, e.g., that of Colony and Willis,[16] the incidence of epileptiform EEG's in a general schizophrenic population is quite small and no different from that in nonpatients. In contrast, where EEG's are performed only on referral there would probably be a higher incidence of abnormal recordings in individuals suspected of convulsive disorder, i.e., in whom actual convulsive manifestations or episodic disturbances suggest the possibility of epilepsy.

14 and 6 per sec. Positive Spiking

This EEG pattern was recognized by Gibbs and Gibbs in 1951[42] and interpreted as evidence of thalamic and hypothalamic epilepsy. There have been numerous clinical reports relating the 14 and 6 pattern to psychiatric symptoms such as aggressiveness, affective impulsivity and driven behavior. Henry[66] has reviewed the status of this EEG sign as a clinical correlate of disturbed behavior. He suggests that its highly variable incidence in various reported populations depends upon differing amounts of attention to essential technical requirements for observing it, namely recording during sleep and use of "monopolar" electrode montages. Niedermeyer and Knott[104] found that 14 and 6 per sec. positive spiking was most frequent in psychiatric patients, and Schmidt and Andrews[119] reported a relatively high incidence in schizophrenic patients. Walter et al.[179] and Small and Small[157] did not find associations between the 14 and 6 phenomenon and behavioral manifestations in psychiatric populations. Greenberg and Pollak[52] found nine cases with 14 and 6 patterns in a sample of 60 psychiatric patients. Of these, eight were diagnosed as schizophrenic by the hospital staff. Compared with matched patients who had no positive spiking, the 14 and 6 patients showed: impairment in affective relatedness, sensitivity to others, and understanding the consequences of wrong actions; greater suicidal risk, aggressive behavior, and management problems; less clinical improvement.

The relatively high incidence of the 14 and 6 per sec. positive spike phenomenon in young schizophrenic patients may make this EEG sign of some practical importance in the light of Greenberg and Pollack's findings. It may be that the clinical picture in schizophrenic disorders is significantly modified when the mechanisms underlying the 14 and 6 per sec. positive spike phenomenon are present.

EEG Deviations Related to Age

Hill[68] states that rhythmic EEG slow wave activity is more common in any group of psychiatric patients than in the normal population when age is controlled. The slow activity is often of the type found normally in the EEG of younger persons, thus leading to the concept of EEG maturation defect. However, all the EEG patterns described can reappear in later life following acquired dysfunction of the brain, either from local disease or from metabolic disorder. Hill classified four types of slow activity and reported on their incidence in various populations, including a group of 147 schizophrenics. Although two of these types, the alpha variant and the post-temporal focus, were more common among schizophrenics than normals, they occurred most frequently in individuals with severe conduct disturbances. At the older end of the age range, Turton and Warren[173] also failed to find specific deviations in schizophrenia. They studied 274 patients between the ages of 60 and 79. There was no one-to-one correspondence between assessment of dementia and presence of an EEG abnormality. Abnormalities, consisting mainly of slowing, were about as frequent in patients suffering from schizophrenia, senile paranoid psychoses, affective psychoses and in a group of normals of the same age.

EEG and the Evolution of Schizophrenic Disorders

Considerable attention has been devoted, particularly by European workers, to the relationship between EEG characteristics and the course of schizophrenic illness. Igert and Lairy[75] reported on 209 EEG studies of 62 female schizophrenic patients. Morphologically normal records, consisting of pure alpha rhythm without superimposed fast or slow activity, were found in 56 per cent. Successive records showed that the same electrical pattern persisted throughout the evolution of the illness, in spite of intensive treatments. They regarded this as psychobiologic hyperstability, and concluded that such an EEG picture, when combined with clinical presence of schizophrenia, has unfavorable prognostic significance. On the contrary, the illness of patients whose EEG's were dysrhythmic or abnormal was more often discontinuous, showing remissions and improved social adjustment, i.e., they were more sensitive to treatments. Similar conclusions were reached by Heuyer et al.[67] in a study of the EEG's of 50 schizophrenic children.

In 31 patients who developed schizophrenia at a very young age, Deglin[22] found that those with a marked alpha rhythm had more severe intellectual impairment. Small and Small[158] studied 88 patients hospitalized with acute schizophrenic illness and concluded that those with normal EEG recordings had a more severe and prolonged course of illness than those with distinct focal and paroxsymal EEG abnormalities. Yamada[185] examined schizophrenic patients grouped according to Mitsuda's geneticoclinical classification into 50 "nuclear" and 61 "peripheral" cases. The resting EEG was abnormal in 42 per cent of the "peripheral" group compared to only 10 per cent of the "nuclear" group. Similar differences between "nuclear" schizophrenic patients and those with paranoid and circular forms were described by Feigenberg.[28] The "nuclear" cases with poor prognosis showed more pronounced and diffuse alpha rhythms and less response to sensory stimuli. Feigenberg postulated that in "nuclear" schizophrenia the activating influence of the reticular formation on the cortex is weakened. Jus[82] similarly explained the findings of a slow alpha rhythm with diffuse slow activity in stuporous schizophrenic states as an inhibition of reticular activating effects.

The general agreement among different workers that a "well-regulated" EEG, resistant to displacement by various kinds of stimuli, is an unfavorable prognostic sign in the presence of schizophrenic psychosis, seems striking. The results suggest an electrophysiologic analogue of the "encapsulation" and withdrawal noted clinically.

Studies Employing Special Methods of EEG Analysis

Various quantification technics have been applied to the description of EEG records. These include: electronic frequency analysis, amplitude integration, period analysis, cross correlation, power density spectrum, and measures of phase relationships. Some of these methods have been applied to studies of psychiatric patient populations.

Kennard and Schwartzman[85] studied 62 patients, about half of whom were schizophrenic, and 25 normal controls repeatedly by means of frequency analyzed EEG's. The schizophrenic patients all received insulin coma therapy between their first and second tests. An important feature of the investigation was the quantification of data from eight different electrode placements. Patients showed less sharply defined alpha activity than nonpatients, with a greater frequency spread within the alpha range; they also showed more nonalpha activity. Furthermore, the gradient of activity from anterior to posterior derivations was less marked in patients. "Poor" organization of the EEG was more common amongst the patients, and there was also evidence of reduced synchrony between the right and left hemispheres. Clinical improvement in the patients was associated with a shift of the EEG frequency graph toward the nonpatient pattern. An abnormal, poorly organized frequency graph was associated with acute and severe onset of disturbance and greater degree of dissociation with immediate environment.

Fink et al.[35] compared schizophrenic and depressive psychotic subjects with respect to EEG frequency bands derived from electronic frequency analysis. A discriminant function analysis suggested that schizophrenics exhibited greater amounts of 3 to 4.5 c./sec. and less 22.5 to 33 c./sec. activity than the depressive subjects. However, further analyses showed that there were significant effects of age and sex, which may have led to spurious diagnostic differences.

Bruck[12] employed a hand method to measure amplitude and detect synchrony between records from different head areas. He compared chronic schizophrenic patients with nonpatients and with other patients, and found significantly lower amplitudes in the schizophrenics, particularly in the occipital area. He did not find significant differences between schizophrenics and nonpatients on his synchrony measures, but did find some between schizophrenic and nonschizophrenic patients. Although Bruck's results on synchrony were largely negative and are open to methodologic criticism, the reports of Soviet workers[2,10] who have found that spatial synchronization differs from normal in catatonia, suggests the desirability of further studies of synchrony. Under "inactive" conditions, schizophrenic patients have also been observed to show the heightened synchrony found in normals during mental activity.[98]

Goldstein and his co-workers[49,50,51,102,111,169] have used the Drohocki integrator for amplitude analysis of the EEG. This method automatically measures the area under the EEG curve and the display can be processed to yield the standard deviation. Comparison of analyses of monopolar EEG's from the left occipital area in male chronic schizophrenics with those from normal volunteers showed that the coefficient of variation for the patient group was one-half of that for the nonpatients. No significant differences could be detected with respect to the overall amplitude. Effective drug treatment increased the variability, i.e., shifted it toward normal. The reduced EEG variability in schizophrenics seemed comparable to the effects of a small dose of LSD in normals, which decreased the variability without significant change in mean EEG amplitude.[50] Pfeiffer et al.[110] presented a hypothesis concerning schizophrenia which rests heavily upon the evidence of marked EEG activation and hyper-regulation indicated by Goldstein's results. They believe that prolonged stimulation arising from any cause will produce hallucinatory states, and that the chronic schizophrenic is in a state of overstimulation.

Although it seems hopeful that comprehensive quantification of the EEG by means of computer methods may yet reveal important changes in electrical activity of the brain in schizophrenic disorders, relatively little use has so far been made of such methods. In the near future more widespread application may be anticipated.

EEG Reactivity in Relation to Attention

The rhythmic activity of the EEG, characteristically greatest in a state of waking relaxation with eyes shut, is attenuated or blocked when the eyes are open or attention is directed to a novel stimulus. In normal subjects, Lansing et al.[93] showed that reaction time to a visual stimulus was faster when alpha blockade preceded the stimulus, an effect attributed to increased reticular formation activity. Blum[9] found that the alpha activity of the schizophrenic's EEG was more resistent to change by external stimulation than that of nonpatients. Reaction time tends to be slower in schizophrenic patients generally.[74,116] These findings led Fedio et al.[27] to test the hypothesis that the reaction time impairment of the schizophrenic is related to his heightened resistance to alpha blockade. Although their schizophrenic subjects did show alpha blockade to the alerting signal, there was not an associated reduction in reaction time as found in nonpatients when the alerting signal produced alpha blockade. Fedio et al. interpreted their findings to suggest that arousal functions differed from normal in schizophrenia and that this could ultimately be related to reticular system dysfunction.

Hein et al.[64] found no significant differences between chronic schizophrenics and controls in alpha blocking to photic stimuli, although variability was much greater in the patients. Salamon and Post[118] did find less alpha blocking in schizophrenic patients, but most patients with poor alpha blocking had received phenothiazines during the preceding week.

The studies of Venables[176,177] although done independently of EEG recordings, are relevant to the problem of arousal in schizophrenia. Venables and Wing[178] showed that there is a high correlation between skin potential level and the threshold of fusion of paired light flashes. In schizophrenic subjects rated for degree of withdrawal and for delusional activity, a high correlation was found between arousal and withdrawal when marked coherent delusions were absent. The most withdrawn patients were the most aroused, i.e., showed the highest skin potential and the lowest two-flash threshold. In deluded patients without incoherence of speech the correlation between two-flash threshold and withdrawal was not significant.

EEG Sleep Studies in Schizophrenia

Recording of the EEG during sleep has become a useful, routine procedure in clinical laboratories, since sleep recordings may reveal convulsive discharges not seen in the waking record. Gibbs and Gibbs[43] have demonstrated an EEG pattern in sleep which appears to correlate with psychosis. They have called it the "mitten" pattern, because the slow wave and spike resemble the hand and thumb of a mitten. It occurs only during sleep, is found mainly in the frontal areas but usually spreads to the parietal areas, does not repeat rhythmically, and has not been seen under 15 years of age. Gibbs and Gibbs subdivide these patterns into the "A" mitten, in which the fast component lasts longer than 100 msec. and the "B" mitten, in which it lasts between 80 and 100 msec. Neither pattern was observed very frequently in healthy subjects, but Gibbs and Gibbs found that the B-mitten was frequent in psychotic patients without epilepsy, whereas A-mittens were most common in patients with Parkinson's disease. The B-mitten pattern was found in 37 per cent of schizophrenic subjects, and the incidence was nearly as high in patients with paranoid psychoses and higher in epileptic patients with psychosis. There was no difference in the incidence of B-mittens among the various subtypes of schizophrenia.

Sleep research was greatly stimulated by Aserinsky and Kleitman's discovery[1] that certain phases of sleep are associated with rapid eye movements (REM). Subjects awakened during REM sleep report dreams with much higher frequency than when awakened during other phases. Since the subjective world of the schizophrenic has often been compared to that of the dreamer, investigators sought to discover some relationship between waking physiologic indices in schizophrenics and the characteristics of dreaming sleep. Rechtschaffen et al.[114] studied the waking EEG, eye movements, and electromyographs (EMG) of five schizophrenic patients. They found that the physiologic recordings failed to show, even for short periods, any patterning which bore convincing resemblance to that of these variables during the REM period. They concluded that these parameters failed to support the hypothesis that the schizophrenic state has any obvious similarity to normal dreaming.

Feinberg et al.[30] studied 18 acutely ill schizophrenics, 4 schizophrenics in remission, and 10 controls for several nights. They found that the actively ill patients showed significantly less REM sleep than the control subjects, and that short term patients had significantly less REM than long term patients. Since the long term patients were similar to controls, the data did not suggest alteration in the neurophysiologic systems associated with dreaming as a basic or causal factor in schizophrenia. The alteration in dreaming could be considered secondary to the various stages of pathology. From additional analysis of the data, Feinberg et al.[29,89] reported significantly higher values for eye movement density in hallucinating patients than in nonhallucinating ones. Lairy et al.[91] studied 19 patients with periods of delusion at different times during their illness. The sleep of patients undergoing acute, brief delusional episodes was short in duration and almost entirely made up of the early stages I and II; stages III, IV, and REM were brief or absent. In the phase of remission, the findings were comparable to the normal individuals. In prolonged delusional episodes or in episodes occurring in chronically delusional cases, total sleep duration was quite constant at different periods of the episode, but REM phase duration was considerably increased at its beginning. These findings suggest that the EEG is more stable in the chronic patient during sleep, as it is in the waking.

Kodman et al.[87] compared auditory thresholds during sleep in catatonic and noncatatonic patients by means of EEG and galvanic skin responses. The results indicated that the psychotic patients were easily aroused. Lester and Edwards[96] found significant increases in the amount, amplitude and spindle-like appearance of precentral EEG fast activity in schizophrenic patients during drowsiness or REM sleep. They also found increases of this sort in patients with chronic alcoholism, in some neurologic patients and in asymptomatic relatives of schizophrenic patients. No differences in amount of fast activity were found during slow wave (stage IV) sleep. They believe that the fast activity reflects the modulation of cortical activity by a specific subcortical system.

Ornitz et al.[105,106] reported on dreaming sleep in autistic children. They found no EEG abnormalities in the all night records of their small sample, and noted no particular differences from controls in the amount or pattern of dreaming sleep in their autistic patients. White et al.[184] employed promazine to obtain drowsy and sleep EEG's in 149 child psychiatric patients and 13 controls, ranging in age from 1 to 15 years. They considered their data to indicate a significant organic concomitant in psychiatrically disturbed children, since they found 51 per cent abnormalities in the patients. The only subgroup with few abnormalities was composed of 10 neurotic children. The most frequent abnormalities were irregular paroxysmal spike and wave complexes, often seen during the transition from waking to sleep; one third of the patients had this complex either alone or with independent spikes.

Linked to the interest in the study of sleep are observations on sleep deprivation. Koranyi and Lehmann[88] kept a group of six chronic psychotic patients awake for 100 hours and noted psychologic and physiologic impairment by the fourth day. Snyder[163] reviewed the evidence concerning possible effects of sleep and concurrent "dream" deprivation in mental illness and concluded that available information was sufficient to suggest that REM deprivation does occur at some stages in mental illness and that this significantly alters brain function. It is, however, only one of many factors. Mandell and Mandell[100] have given some indication of the remarkable range of possible biochemical changes associated with REM sleep, many of which could modify brain function.

Reactivity of the EEG to Drugs and Other Agents

The idea that pharmacologic reactivity is impaired in schizophrenia is widely held and supported by many observations, such as the great tolerance to large doses of phenothiazines, compared to that observed in nonpsychotic individuals. A number of workers have employed the EEG changes induced by drugs as measures of cerebral reactivity to compare various psychiatric populations.

In 1954 Shagass[127] described the sedation threshold, which was measured by injecting amobarbital intravenously at a constant rate while recording the EEG, and also noting the development of dysarthria. Changes in amplitude of frontal fast activity provided the EEG indicator of threshold. Although the sedation threshold appeared to be correlated with the degree of manifest anxiety and anxiety-proneness in nonpsychotic subjects, no such correlation was found in the psychoses.[133] In schizophrenic patients the sedation threshold appeared to be correlated with the duration of psychotic symptoms.[129] Patients with symptoms under one year in duration were found to have low thresholds, indistinguishable from those of a normal population. Schizophrenic patients with symptoms of one year or more duration had significantly higher thresholds, but the average thresholds were not further increased with longer durations. An exception to this finding occurred in the simple subtype; all simple schizophrenics had thresholds below the median. The highest sedation thresholds were found in the group of "borderline" schizophrenic patients, presenting clinical findings like those described by Hoch and Polatin.[71] Thus, although the range of thresholds was very broad in a heterogenous schizophrenic population, it could be divided into component groups with reference to duration of illness and subtype. In schizophrenic patients treated with ECT the pretreatment threshold was related to the short-term therapeutic benefit; patients with low thresholds showed the greatest improvement rate, a finding similar to that in depressives.[137]

Although the EEG changes provided the main indicator of sedation threshold employed by Shagass and his collaborators, they later found that the clinical endpoint of unconsciousness or "sleep" yielded a measure reasonably well correlated with the EEG-determined sedation threshold and possessing similar clinical relationships.[134,136] It was also demonstrated that the sedation threshold was truly a reactivity measure, as it reflected the *rate* of EEG fast wave production by amobarbital.[128]

Claridge and Herrington[15] devised a method of determining sedation threshold which does not require EEG recording. It involves the impairment by amobarbital of ability to double numerical digits presented by a tape recording. They confirmed the differences found previously between hysterical and dysthymic psychoneurotic patients by Shagass and Kerenyi[135] and also showed that the sedation threshold was correlated with the duration of the Archimedes spiral afterimage in psychoneurotic subjects. In contrast to the findings in psychoneurotics, Claridge et al.[14] found that the correlation between sedation threshold and Archimedes spiral afterimage duration was negative in schizophrenics. Similar findings were obtained by Krishnamoorti and Shagass[90]; they verified Claridge and Herrington's positive correlation between sedation threshold and Archimedes spiral in nonpsychotic subjects, but found a negative correlation in psychotics. These results imply a difference in patterning of CNS reactivities in schizophrenic patients.

Another indicator of sedation threshold, lateral gaze nystagmus, was introduced by Fink.[33] Peck[107] measured the nystagmus threshold in a heterogeneous group of psychiatric patients. He found significant differences between acute and chronic schizophrenic patients; the thresholds of the chronic group were higher.

Goldman[45] developed a pentothal activation technic which appeared to give relatively specific results in schizophrenic states. In Goldman's technic the EEG is recorded while pentothal is injected intravenously, 100 mg. at a dose, as rapidly as possible. The cycle of effects produced by a single injection is, in most patients, completed within 1 or 2 min. The injection is repeated two or three times at 2 min. intervals. Activation effects, involving prolonged beta activity, high amplitude "bursts" of fast activity, and high amplitude 4-7 c./sec. activity, occurred more often in schizophrenic than in other patients. The effects of pentothal activation were no longer produced after improvement with chlorpromazine or similar drugs. In subsequent reports, Goldman[46,48] described similar findings in additional series of patients. Sila et al.[155] attempted a quantitative replication of Goldman's findings with an EEG frequency analyzer. They obtained equivocal results. Their total data showed a greater change in the EEG following pentothal in 39 schizophrenic patients as compared with 19 depressive patients, but when they reduced their samples to 12 in each group by elimination of patients with atypical symptoms, the difference between the groups disappeared.

Gastaut[38] measured the threshold for "convulsive" responses in the EEG by combining intermittent photic stimulation with graded injection of Metrazol. He reported that photo-Metrazol thresholds were low in schizophrenia, idiopathic epilepsy and hysteria. Ulett et al.[174] compared two excitant agents, hexazole and Metrazol and, on the basis of reliability data, concluded that hexazole was superior to Metrazol for determining the photopharmacologic threshold. Driver[24] employed the method of Ulett et al. to study groups of epileptic, schizophrenic, and depressive patients; he also evaluated a number of other factors, such as sex, age, height, weight, etc. Among Driver's subjects 40 per cent of schizophrenics, 75 per cent of epileptics and 6 per cent of depressives showed a photoconvulsive EEG end point. Driver interpreted his data to indicate that certain patients with schizophrenia displayed diencephalic sensitivity similar to that found in subcortical epileptics, but not of the same degree. However, Smith et al.,[161] also employing Ulett's method, found no significant difference between 40 schizophrenic and 20 nonschizophrenic patients and no concomitant change in threshold when the clinical status of the schizophrenics improved. Desai and Vahia[23] concluded that the photo-Metrazol threshold was too variable to be used in routine clinical work. The findings of Gerald[39] and Bradley and Jeavons[11] indicated that there is no simple relationship between sedation and photo-Metrazol thresholds in schizophrenia.

The well-known observation that catatonic stupor can be reversed with amobarbital was subjected to clinical and EEG study by Stevens and Derbyshire.[167] They found that amobarbital produced the fast rhythms characteristic of barbiturate sedation, decreased muscle tension, and produced a slight trend toward increase in pulse rate. Alpha activity decreased slightly in frequency following the drug. The results suggested that remission of the catatonic stupor was related to a temporary decrease in alertness and that the term "stupor" is a misnomer, since the psychic state in catatonic schizophrenia is one of great excitement.

Differential incidence of the parkinsonism side effect in therapy with phenothiazines and reserpine has been utilized by Goldman[47] to support the idea that psychotic illness is accompanied by a localized brain abnormality. His case material showed that asymmetrical parkinsonism was manifested in 45 per cent of 422 schizophrenics, 51 per cent of 51 psychotic depressive patients and only 14.4 per cent of 216 patients with other diagnoses. Goldman's report did not specify whether the drug dosage levels were equal in the groups compared.

EEG changes produced by drugs have been used in a number of psychopharmacologic studies in an attempt to relate clinical effects to alterations in electrical activity.[78] Ulett et al.[175] studied the effects of eight tranquilizing drugs over a period of 15 months in 21 patients and demonstrated that EEG changes occurred with all patients, that drugs could be distinguished by their EEG effects and that there was great individual variability in EEG response to drugs. An important methodologic point was that the drug effects are reversible within, at most, a ten week period. Fink[34] demonstrated that chlorpromazine, imipramine and placebo could be discriminated with respect to EEG effects. The effects of chlorpromazine would depend upon the pretreatment EEG; subjects with a low alpha index showed increased alpha, whereas those with a high initial alpha index showed reduced alpha. Pollack et al.[112] found that 6 of 29 imipramine-treated schizophrenic patients, who were rated as behaviorally worsened after five weeks of medication, showed increases in both slow and very fast EEG frequencies. Klein[86] employed their observations to support the formulation that some schizophrenic states result from chronic CNS disturbances associated with poor regulation of central activation. He postulated that both imipramine and phenothiazines remedied pathologic states of activation regulation rather than stimulating or inhibiting normal control mechanisms.

SENSORY EVOKED RESPONSES

In ordinary EEG recordings from the scalp, the electrical deflections evoked by sensory stimuli are usually obscured by the larger "spontaneous" rhythms. Dawson[21] demonstrated in 1947 that the evoked response could be extracted from scalp recordings by applying the principle of averaging. If the EEG's following many stimulus presentations are summed or averaged, the time-locked evoked response becomes augmented, whereas the activities unrelated to the stimulus tend to cancel out. Many kinds of instruments have been devised to automate the process of averaging or summation, and, although most apparatus is relatively expensive and complex, the procedures are quite feasible. There are, however, a number of important limitations and complications to the application of averaged evoked response recording, which should be considered in interpreting results. Among these are: the need to repeat stimuli many times; the limited significance of the brief elementary stimuli, such as clicks or flashes, usually employed; and problems of distinguishing events of extracranial from those of intracerebral origin.[7]

Shagass and Schwartz[138] apparently were the first to apply the method of recording averaged evoked responses to electrophysiologic studies of psychiatric patients. They employed brief electrical shocks over the ulnar nerve to elicit somatosensory cortical responses from the hemisphere contralateral to the stimulus. They were interested in studying the recovery function, determined by applying paired stimuli at varying interstimulus intervals. Their measure of recovery was the relative amplitude of response to the second of a pair of stimuli (peak to peak measurements of the initial components occurring from 15 to 30 msec. after the stimulus) compared to that of the response to the first stimulus. In nonpatient control subjects the second response usually equalled the first within intervals of 20 msec. or less. This initial peak of recovery or augmentation of response was followed by a period of suppression and a second recovery period which occurred at about 100 msec. They found that the initial peak recovery was lower than normal in a heterogeneous psychiatric population.[138] The psychiatric groups which showed the greatest diminution of initial recovery were those diagnosed as schizophrenics, psychotic depressives, and personality disorders.[139,140,141,142]

In addition to finding diminished recovery function in "functional" psychoses and personality disorders, Shagass and Schwartz[143,144] found that these patient groups displayed greater amplitude somatosensory responses to stimuli of a given intensity. In a study of visually evoked responses Shagass and Schwartz[146] also found that psychiatric patients generally had larger responses than nonpatient controls. However, the differences between schizophrenic patients and nonpatients were not statistically significant, although the schizophrenic group did show a significant tendency for earlier occurrence of some evoked response peaks. An attempt to relate various psychologic test findings to visual evoked responses[150] revealed that test results indicative of greater psychopathology, i.e., poor Bender-Gestalt performance and high neuroticism and low extraversion scores on the Maudsley Personality Inventory, were associated with increased amplitude of evoked responses.

Shagass and Schwartz[140] were able to demonstrate that normalization of the somatosensory recovery function occurred in patients with psychotic depression after effective treatment with ECT. No similar systematic study was done with schizophrenic patients, although individual examples of normalization of recovery and amplitude decreases after successful therapy were described.[149]

Shagass' more recent data suggest that the previously found amplitude differences were probably an effect of age. Evoked response amplitude tends to increase with age,[147,168] and the data in the earlier studies did not adequately control for interactions between age and presence of psychopathology. With the application of proper statistical controls for this factor, diagnostic differences in relation to amplitude were not found.[148,130,131] On the other hand, the recovery function differences found in the earlier studies were again confirmed.[131] Schizophrenic patients, as well as those in all other major diagnostic groups, were found to have diminished recovery when compared with nonpatient controls matched for age and sex.

The finding that recovery is diminished in schizophrenic patients, as well as in other groups, has been confirmed by Speck et al.[164] and Floris et al.[36] for visual responses. Speck et al. found no significant differences between schizophrenics and nonpatients in characteristics of their response to single visual flashes, but did find a decrement of amplitude in the response to paired flashes at 35 msec. interval. Heninger and Speck[65] also carried out an intensive study of 10 female schizophrenic patients in the original larger group of Speck et al. Before drug treatment, the schizophrenic patients had significantly less recovery than matched nonpatients. Following treatment, significant correlations were found between improvement in symptoms and evoked response shifts toward nonpatient values, with least improved patients showing the smallest shifts.

Heninger and Speck[65] speculatively related their data to the interpretation of other workers that there is increased activation in schizophrenia. They assumed that reduction of the recovery function is related to activation, citing as possible evidence the findings of Spinelli and Pribram,[165] who demonstrated reduced recovery following infratemporal lobe stimulation in monkeys. The validity of the assumption that diminished recovery indicates increased activation is open to question, since Schwartz and Shagass[120] found that recovery was augmented following electrical stimulation of the mesencephalic reticular formation, which also produced EEG activation. Heninger and Speck[65] also present data indicating that phenothiazines increase evoked response amplitude and that effects are evident within four hours after the initial dose. Since their published tracings taken at one month do not show much increase in amplitude, it may be the initial amplitude increase was associated with drowsiness.[151]

The consistent findings of impaired recovery function in schizophrenic disorders would be more exciting if they were specific for schizophrenic states. The studies of Shagass and Schwartz[145] and Speck et al.[164] indicate, however, that similar deviations are found in other psychiatric conditions, nonpsychotic as well as psychotic. Furthermore, in addition to the absence of specificity with respect to diagnosis, there appears to be no particular specificity with respect to the components of evoked responses which are deviant, since Shagass[131] found similar diagnostic trends for nearly all response peaks measured. Attempts by Shagass and Canter[132] to relate evoked response findings within a heterogeneous patient population to results of the Minnesota Multiphasic Personality Inventory, the Rod and Frame test of field-dependence and the Bender-Gestalt test also failed to reveal specific psychologic-physiologic relationships.

Rodin et al.[115] obtained findings somewhat different from those of other workers in a comparison of visual evoked responses in 20 normal and 20 schizophrenic patients. In general, their patients showed smaller amplitude responses. One of their groups of patients differed from the other on biochemical measurements of energy metabolism and also showed more deviant evoked responses.

A somewhat different approach utilizing evoked response measurement in the study of schizophrenia has been taken by Callaway and his group. Callaway et al.[13] employed the auditory evoked response as an indicator of differences in response set. Their work stems from Shakow's[152] conclusion that there is impairment in schizophrenia of integrating and organizing functions that provide for the establishment of generalized or major sets, so that patients employ multiple, enduring, minor or "segmental" sets for categorizing sensory inputs and directing action. Psychologic observations indicate that this defect is most prominent in chronic or process schizophrenia and least characteristic of coherent, paranoid schizophrenia. Callaway, therefore, predicted that the responses evoked by two tones of different frequency, 1000 and 600 c./sec., would be more dissimilar in schizophrenic patients than in nonpatients and most dissimilar in nonparanoid schizophrenics. His data[13] supported these predictions. They did not support predictions of difference between process and reactive or between acute and chronic schizophrenic patients. In subsequent studies, Jones et al.[80,81] demonstrated that the evoked response similarity index changed in relation to clinical improvement in schizophrenic patients. Improved patients were more like normals on repeat testing than were unimproved patients. Nonschizophrenic patients did not show similar shifts. They also presented data showing that scores derived from factor analysis of nurses' clinical ratings were correlated with evoked response shifts. The related factor scores were most loaded with items such as disorganized thinking, inappropriate affect, suspiciousness, craziness, withdrawal, and confusion. Their data also suggested that a normal two-tone response similarity, coupled with a highly disturbed clinical picture, would predict a poor prognosis for response to phenothiazines.

Walter et al.[182] described another evoked response event which has psychologic relevance. This has been named the "contingent negative variation" (CNV) or expectancy wave (E-wave). It may be demonstrated in averaged responses when an initial signal has the significance of indicating to the subject that he is to prepare for a response to a forthcoming stimulus, e.g., a warning tone indicates that a button is to be pressed when a light flashes. In recordings from the vertex to a reference electrode, and employing direct coupled or long time-constant amplifiers, there is a shift in the base line toward negativity of the vertex following the warning signal. Although a systematic study of CNV in schizophrenia has not yet appeared, the postulated relationships of the CNV to phenomena of attention and motivation[76] renders its exploration in schizophrenic disorders desirable.

It seems clear that averaged evoked responses reflect phenomena which are in some way related to the functional disturbance of brain activity in psychiatric disorders. The limited specificity of evoked response variables in relation to clinical findings may be as much a clinical or psychologic problem as a neuro-physiologic one. Significant advances at both levels probably must take place before more specific relationships are established. Nevertheless, it is important that positive findings have been obtained by several groups of workers at a relatively early stage in the development of evoked response methods and that such findings can lead to experimental tests of significant hypotheses involving phenomena at other levels. An example is the experiment of Gartside et al.[37] who tested the hypothesis that the somatosensory recovery function would be modified by lithium carbonate. They reasoned that lithium should increase intracellular sodium concentration; since sodium is raised in psychotic depression, they expected the somatosensory recovery cycle to shift toward the kind of curves found in depression. They did, in fact, demonstrate that such a shift occurred. However, they did not find consistent concomitant clinical depression in their normal subjects after lithium administration.

DIRECT BRAIN RECORDINGS

Electrical recording from the exposed human brain in the neurosurgical operating theater has yielded valuable information about cerebral functioning. The work of Penfield[108] on the "interpretive cortex" is of special psychiatric interest. In some epileptic patients at surgery under local anesthesia electrical stimulation of a certain portion of either temporal lobe has caused the patient to be aware of a previous experience, or to somehow change his own interpretation of what he is seeing, hearing or thinking at the moment. Penfield considers the interpretive cortex to have in it a mechanism for instant reactivation of a detailed record of the past, and also a mechanism for the production of interpretive signals.

Purpura et al.[113] recorded dendritic potentials at surgery in two schizophrenic patients scheduled for frontal lobotomy and two patients being operated for removal of neoplasm; recordings from the latter patients were over presumably normal cortex. They evoked responses by direct stimulation of the cortex and found that the second response to pairs of stimuli showed greater delay in recovery in the psychotics than in the tumor patients. They interpreted their observations to mean that inhibitory synaptic activity was prominent in the cortex of the psychotic patients. It is possible that similar mechanisms underlie the deviant recovery functions observed in averaged evoked response recordings from scalp leads.[145,164,36]

Although operating room observations are of great interest, more relevant psychiatric observations can be made in psychotic patients with electrodes implanted in the brain for lengthy periods of time. Such studies have been carried out in several laboratories, the justification for the implants being the anticipated facilitation of subsequent therapy, e.g., by leucotomy. However, the impossibility for ethical reasons, of making comparable observations in unquestionably normal brains presents serious limitations to the interpretation of these observations.

Bickford et al.[8] reported in 1953 that slow waves can be recorded from the depths of the frontal lobes of many psychotic patients at operation. Petersen et al.,[109] of the same Mayo Clinic group, shortly thereafter reported their observations in four schizophrenic patients with implanted depth electrodes. They also found slow waves from the deep frontal regions and eliminated the possibility that these waves were due to electrode artifact by showing that they were suppressed by thiopental. By 1959 Sem-Jacobsen[124] was able to describe the observations made in 136 patients with over 6500 implanted electrodes. A consistent finding made by these and other workers was the fact that the scalp EEG may give no indication whatsoever of high amplitude discharges and rhythms recorded from electrodes placed in the depths of the brain.

Sem-Jacobsen et al.[125] showed that arrhythmic waves of 2-4 c./sec. were recorded only from the ventro-medial part of the frontal lobe and were constantly present. Contacts in the lateral part of the frontal lobes gave entirely different, but consistent, recordings with frequencies about 25 c./sec. In contrast to the consistently present activity, these workers found in the frontal lobe paroxysmal rhythmic bursts of high voltage 2-5 c./sec. waves usually bilaterally synchronized and occasionally simulating slow sharp waves. The incidence of these was about 50 per cent in psychiatric patients, most of whom were schizophrenic. However, it is noteworthy that in one tabulation of 40 patients, such bursts were observed in three patients diagnosed as psychotic depressions. In 15 chronically psychotic patients, recordings of periodic focal high voltage discharges were closely related to acute episodes of psychotic behavior.[126] Focal spike discharges occurred during episodes of agitation, hallucinations, or both, and there were changes in the activity of the temporal lobe and probably the frontal lobe during hallucinations.

Sem-Jacobsen[124] states that electrical stimulation of the parietal area from which the spike focus was recorded during acute psychotic episodes started an acute psychotic episode in a number of patients. Also, the administration of mescaline and LSD often triggered a spike focus into continuous firing, lasting as long as the patient showed clinical drug effects. The clinical and electrical effects were reversed by intravenous chlorpromazine. The region which Sem-Jacobsen postulates to be connected with psychotic episodes in schizophrenic patients is in the parietal lobe on the border of the temporal lobe. Electrical stimulation to the ventro-medial part of the frontal lobe frequently resulted in temporary clinical improvement or even complete freedom from symptoms which could last from a few minutes up to three weeks, depending on the type of stimulation used. It is claimed that leucotomy limited to the region where strong electrical stimulation gave a prolonged therapeutic effect produced good clinical results.

Sem-Jacobsen[124] also described pleasant and unpleasant emotional responses resulting from electrical stimulation through implanted electrodes. The pleasant responses include reports of feeling easy and relaxed, a feeling of joy with smiling, and considerable satisfaction with request for further stimulation. Unpleasant, "negative" responses included anxiety, restlessness, depression, fright and horror. He attempted to map the "positive" and "negative" systems and note that opposite effects were obtained from electrodes placed 5 to 10 mm. apart. There appeared to be a topographic relation to intensity of affective responses, i.e., given areas yielded both "positive" and "negative" reactions, but these varied in strength from area to area.

Sherwood[154] reported abnormalities of electrical activity in ten cases whose frontal lobes were explored with depth recordings. Three of ten patients who were obsessionals had similar electrical patterns mainly confined to the cortex, internal capsule, and corona radiata. The other patients, all schizophrenics, presented widely variable abnormalities, such as paroxysmal activity in the cingulate area or in the neighborhood of the caudate nucleus. Sherwood attempted surgical disconnection of areas that manifested paroxysmal activity. The results in schizophrenics were variable, although all three obsessionals showed uniform and marked improvement. Sherwood also injected a variety of drugs into the ventricles of catatonic schizophrenic patients and observed that some of these drugs, including cholinesterase, banthine and serotonin, increased "adaptability" to a marked extent. He also observed that adrenaline injected intraventricularly produced relaxation and sleep in catatonics. Sherwood attempted to integrate these observations with EEG findings suggesting alterations in timing and topologic prominence of various rhythms in different clinical states. He argued that in schizophrenia, particularly in its catatonic form, there is a "blocking" of the passage of impulses or signals and that such failure of conduction occurs in the neighborhood of the periventricular gray matter.

Hori[72] and Ishibashi et al.[77] stimulated the cortex in deep temporal areas in schizophrenic patients to elicit and treat auditory hallucinations. The characteristics of hallucinations produced by temporal lobe stimulation were reported as considerably different from those occurring naturally in schizophrenics. Visual hallucinations were particularly frequent in response to electrical stimulation, and a change in emotion did not play a significant role in occurrence of the hallucinations. Some therapeutic effect on the auditory hallucinations associated with the psychosis was observed following temporal lobe stimulation.

The Tulane University group led by Robert Heath has conducted the longest continuous program of investigation into the brain activity of schizophrenic patients employing electrode implantation technics. They observed abnormal spiking and slow wave activity consistently in recordings from the septal region of patients during psychotic behavior.[62] By 1966 Heath[54] could report on observations in 42 patients who displayed psychotic symptoms consistently or intermittently and 15 nonpsychotic patients who were included for investigation and treatment of other diseases. The septal discharge observed in conjunction with waking psychotic behavior was typically a fast biphasic spike, sometimes superimposed on a slow wave. This spike appeared more often during sleep, when it was characterized by slowing and increasing amplitude. It was found to be focal in the septal region, although occasionally it was accompanied by abnormal recordings from the closely connected hippocampus and amygdaloid areas. However, abnormal recordings from the hippocampus and amygdaloid alone, without accompanying septal dysrhythmia, were not associated with psychotic behavior. Heath reports that no septal spiking has been observed in the nonpsychotic patient group. Monroe et al.[101] showed that psychotomimetic compounds given to monkeys produced catatonic manifestations. This was associated with septal spiking; the same was also true of psychotic patients. Heath[54] states that psychotomimetic agents, in addition to inducing spiking in the septal region, had more diffuse electrical effects than are usually observed in patients with schizophrenic psychoses.

In some patients Heath and his co-workers induced spiking and dysrhythmia in septal recordings by stimulation of the connecting cerebral region.[56] Stimulation of the hippocampus at slow frequencies (3-6 c./sec.) was particularly effective. The patients showed classical psychotic symptoms once the recording abnormality appeared. They became depersonalized, occasionally overtly delusional and later described the experience as dreamlike.

In addition to implanting electrodes for recording, the Heath team has implanted a cannula for the injection of small quantities of chemical substances into particular areas of the brain.[63] Of a large number of substances tried, only two induced psychotic symptoms; these were atropine and histamine, and they produced this effect only when they were introduced into the septal region. There was concomitant septal spiking. The effects were more consistent in monkeys, but were also observed in a few patients. The effects of histamine were not as consistent as those of atropine.

Heath's observations relating septal spiking to psychotic behavior provided a kind of bioassay for the effectiveness of a serologic fraction extracted from the blood of schizophrenics, which was named "taraxein."[60,61,62,63] When an active fraction was given to monkeys it induced severe behavioral symptoms of reduced awareness and waxy flexibility, together with septal spiking. Taraxein appeared to be related to ceruloplasmin in early work but was later proved to be distinct from it.[94] When given to nonpsychotic human subjects, taraxein appeared to produce clinical manifestations of schizophrenia. The taraxein fraction has proved difficult to extract in a consistent manner. Nevertheless, Hoagland et al.[70] reviewing the work from four different research groups concluded that all indicated the existence of an active globulin in human blood, probably associated with a tightly bound small molecule. By several test procedures this active complex displayed greater activity if extracted from the plasma of schizophrenic patients than if taken from normal controls. Bergen et al.,[4] using the indicator of delay in rat rope climbing, showed that the greater delays produced by taraxein-like extracts from schizophrenic patients could not be attributed to nonspecific effects of prolonged illness.

Similar plasma protein fractions from schizophrenics and normal persons differed in their effects upon visual evoked responses in the rabbit cortex;[3] schizophrenic fractions reduced the variability of the response, an effect also seen with LSD-25. The results of studies of alterations in animal brain activity by schizophrenic body fluids have not, however, been consistent, even though the experimental approach seems promising. German[40] found increased amplitude of somatosensory cortical evoked responses after schizophrenic serum was applied directly to the exposed cerebral cortex of the anesthetized rat. Later studies by German et al.[41] and Stenhouse et al.[166] failed to confirm these findings. Kemali[84] found that the urine of certain schizophrenics contains an undialysable factor capable of producing a focus of high voltage activity in the rabbits' cortex. On the other hand, other workers[26,103] have reported that blood serum from acute schizophrenic patients introduced into the third ventricle of the cat with implanted electrodes reduces the amplitude of evoked responses.

Heath and his co-workers[57,58,59] have recently obtained evidence suggesting that taraxein may be antibody to unique antigenic sites of the septal region. It is claimed that this has led to simplified methods for obtaining a specific, active gamma G immunoglobulin (IgG) apparently with psychosis-inducing activity. Fluorescent antibody technics showed globulin to be attached to nerve cell nuclei of the septal region of brains obtained within eight hours after death from psychotic schizophrenic patients, but not to the brains of nonschizophrenic control patients. There was enhanced fluorescence when tissues were reacted with sera of schizophrenic patients and then stained with FTA human gammaglobulin, but tissues similarly reacted with control sera before such staining showed no enhancement of fluorescence. Intraventricular or intravenous injections of the antibody IgG produced in sheep to tissues of the septal regions of the brains of monkey and man induced catatonic behavior and focal abnormal EEG's of the septal region of recipient monkeys with chronically implanted electrodes. In contrast, sheep antibody to other parts of monkey and human brain caused no discernible change in the EEG or behavior of test monkeys. These findings were similar to changes induced in monkeys with taraxein.

Using fluorescent antibody technics, Heath et al. detected antibody on the nerve cell nuclei of the septal region in monkeys that had been rapidly exsanguinated while displaying maximal EEG and behavioral aberrations in response to antiseptal antibody. Brains of monkeys killed after receiving sheep antibody to other brain locations did not show the effect. Similar attachment of antibody to septal neuronal nuclei was found in the brains of monkeys killed at peak response to intravenous injection of taraxein.

On the basis of these data, Heath postulated that schizophrenia represents an immunologic disorder. He believes that the schizophrenic patient, possibly because of hereditary influences, may have unique clones of antibody cells that produce IgG capable of combining with precise antigenic sites of nerve cell nuclei of the septal region. These would impair neurohumoral conduction and cause pathologic changes in activity of the septal region, resulting in reduced level of awareness and psychotic symptoms. Obviously, many aspects of this theory require confirmation and elucidation. It is noteworthy that the electrophysiologic sign of septal spiking has remained a guidepost observation through Heath's research.

The concept that schizophrenia may be an immunologic disorder is not new. Fessel[31,32] has written about auto-immunity in mental illness. Shaposhnikov[153] obtained evidence suggesting an allergic component in the pathogenesis of schizophrenia. Semenov and his co-workers[121,122,123] also believe thay have evidence for anticerebral antibodies in the serum of patients suffering from schizophrenia and other mental disorders. Skalickova and Jezkova[156] claimed to demonstrate antibodies against gray and white matter of the brain in the blood and cerebral spinal fluid of schizophrenic patients. However, the major contribution of Heath's work on the immunologic factor, if it can be confirmed, is its specificity with respect to the septal area, since this can be related to electrophysiologic and behavioral observations.

Another group of workers conducting studies on human brain activity with implanted electrodes is the one associated with Grey Walter. The therapeutic method consists of progressive electrocoagulation of small areas of brain tissue, carefully decided upon after various studies. This procedure results in minimal destruction to brain to achieve the desired clinical effect of reduction in anxiety. The concomitant physiologic and psychologic observations have made important contributions to basic knowledge in the field.[17,180,181] Few of their patients were classed as schizophrenic.

SUMMARY AND CONCLUSIONS

Many aspects of electrocerebral activity appear to deviate from normal in schizophrenic disorders. However, most of the positive findings are statistical and nonspecific, and many are unconfirmed and open to question on methodological grounds. The "choppy" pattern may be a reality, but it certainly occurs in a minority of schizophrenic patients. Epileptiform patterns may be more frequent in patients diagnosed as schizophrenic, but they are still relatively uncommon in a general population of such patients. The 14 and 6 per sec. positive spiking pattern and the B-mittens sleep pattern are not specific to schizophrenic disorders. Although the correlation of "hyperstability" with poor prognosis is of considerable interest, and perhaps practical value, the electrical sign is that of an unusually normal pattern. The observations concerning differences in organization and synchrony of patterns, prevalence of fast activity, and deviant alpha reactivity require confirmation; in common with the data on drug reactivity and evoked response differences, they are also statistical and nonspecific.

The information derived from direct brain recordings suggests that psychotic behavior may be associated with electrical discharges in various brain areas, particularly in the septal region, which in some ways resemble convulsive discharges, but are of a more localized character. These discharges, apparently poorly or not at all reflected in scalp recordings, may be general correlates of severe behavioral disturbance rather than specific ones of the states classified as schizophrenia. Nevertheless, they are of extraordinary interest, particularly in the light of Heath's findings on immunologic reactions in the septal area.

Critical issues in pathophysiologic studies concern locus of events, specific mechanisms, and the interactions between etiologic factors and clinical manifestations. The data on depth recording give some indications of the locus of pathophysiologic changes, whereas those recorded from the scalp do not. The specific mechanisms underlying deviant findings are not provided by correlative material and the data are generally of low relevance to issues of etiology. A very large number of mechanisms may underlie deviant electrical signs; they range from molecular changes in the cell membrane, as suggested by Grenell,[53] to variations in the timing of impulses in complex circuits involving large cortical and subcortical neuronal aggregates. Changes at all levels may well be involved at one time. Furthermore, even within the brain the relevant mechanisms may be outside of the neuron in glial or vascular structures.

From the etiologic point of view, the brain effects which underlie deviant behavior may be secondary to any of many possible pathologic processes: psychosocial, genetic, metabolic, endocrine, infectious, immunologic, etc. Weiner[183] has recently reviewed the status of the etiologic theories and indicated their inadequacies and the great problems involved in firmly establishing any one of them. There is virtually no proposed etiologic agent or combination of interacting agents, which could not modify brain function to produce psychotic behavior.

The studies reviewed here involve a relatively small number of dominant interpretive ideas. These may be stated as follows:

1. Schizophrenic disorders involve a chronic state of cerebral overstimulation or hyperarousal. Data which have been interpreted in this way include those on: "choppy" patterns; fast activity; reduced variability; "poor" organization; dissociation between reaction time and alpha blockade; lowered photo-convulsive threshold; reduced response to paired flashes; EEG response to barbiturates in catatonic stupor.

2. Some kinds of schizophrenia involve disordered brain activity resembling that found in epilepsy and this may involve a lesion, probably of biochemical nature, in certain brain areas. Abnormalities seen in both surface and depth recordings suggest this conclusion. Another interpretation is that epileptiform brain activity modifies the clinical expression of schizophrenia.

3. Schizophrenic patients with poor prognosis, i.e., "process" or "nuclear" cases, tend to show unusually normal and stable EEG patterns. This suggests impaired access of displacing stimuli to the structures generating the electrical activity. Reduced reactivity to drugs and sensory stimulation may reflect a similar change. At least superficially, this concept is not compatible with the idea of hyperarousal, but could be reconciled with it by postulating additional cerebral "adaptive" changes associated with chronicity.

4. The temporal and spatial organization of brain activity is altered in schizophrenic disorders, resulting in impairment of information processing.

These interpretations are not mutually exclusive. Although of relatively low power as explanatory hypotheses, they have generated fruitful research. As electrophysiologic methods become more sophisticated, they may produce data for more incisive formulations.

BIBLIOGRAPHY

(*Papers in foreign languages, except French, were not read in original form.*)

1. Aserinsky, E., and Kleitman, N.: Two types of ocular motility occurring in sleep. J. Applied Physiol. 8: 1-10, 1955.

2. Belenkaya, N. Ya.: Electrophysiological studies in the terminal stage of schizophrenia (Russian). Zh. Nevropat. I Psikhiat., 63: 1223-1228, 1963.

3. Bergen, J. R., Czicman, J. S., and Koella, W. P.: Influence of a plasma protein fraction from schizophrenic and normal persons upon the optic evoked response in the rabbit. J. Neuropsychiat. 4: 219-223, 1963.

4. Bergen, J. R., Gray, F. W., Pennell, R. B., Freeman, H., and Hoagland, H.: Taraxein-like extracts. Arch. Gen. Psychiat., 12: 80-82, 1965.

5. Berger, H.: Über das Elektrenkephalogramm des Menschen. Arch. f. Psychiat. 94: 16-60, 1931.

6. Berger, H.: Über das Elektrenkephalogramm des Menschen. Arch. f. Psychiat. 100: 301-321, 1933.

7. Bickford, R. G., Jacobson, J. L., and Cody, D. T.: Nature of average evoked potentials to sound and other stimuli in man. Ann. N.Y. Acad. Sci. 112: 204-223, 1964.

8. Bickford, R. G., Uihlein, A., and Petersen, M. C.: Electrical rhythms recorded from the depth of the frontal lobes during operations on psychotic patients. Proc. Staff. Meet., Mayo Clin. 28: 135-143, 1953.

9. Blum, R. H.: Alpha-rhythm responsiveness in normal, schizophrenic, and brain-damaged persons. Science, 126: 749-750, 1957.

10. Borisova, T. P., and Talavrinov, V. A.: Spatial synchronization of the alpha activity in the cerebral cortex of patients with the catatonic-oneiroid form of schizophrenia (Russian)., Zh. Nevropat. I. Psikhiat. 64: 420-427, 1964.

11. Bradley, P. B., and Jeavons, P. M.: The effect of chlorpromazine and reserpine on sedation and convulsive thresholds in schizophrenic patients. Electroenceph. Clin. Neurophysiol. 9: 661-672, 1957.

12. Bruck, M. A.: Synchrony and voltage in the EEG of schizophrenics. Arch. Gen. Psychiat. 10: 454-468, 1964.

13. Callaway, E., Jones, R. T., and Layne, R. S.: Evoked responses and segmental set of schizophrenia. Arch. Gen. Psychiat. 12: 83-89, 1965.

14. Claridge, G. S., Burns, B. H., and Foster, A. R.: Sedation threshold and Archimedes spiral after effect: A follow up of their use with civilian psychiatric patients. Behav. Res. Ther. 1: 363-370, 1964.

15. Claridge, G. S., and Herrington, R. N.: Sedation threshold, personality, and the theory of neurosis. J. Ment. Sci. 106: 1568-1583, 1960.

16. Colony, H. S., and Willis, S. E.: Electroencephalographic studies of 1,000 schizophrenic patients. Amer. J. Psychiat. 113: 163-169, 1956.

17. Cooper, R., Winter, A. L., Crow, H. J., and Walter, W. G.: Comparison of subcortical, cortical and scalp activity using chronically indwelling electrodes in man. Electroenceph. Clin. Neurophysiol. 18: 217-228, 1965.

18. Davis, P. A.: Evaluation of the electroencephalogram of schizophrenic patients. Amer. J. Psychiat. 96: 851-860, 1940.

19. Davis, P. A.: A comparative study of the EEG's of schizophrenic and manic-depressive patients. Amer. J. Psychiat. 99: 210-217, 1942.

20. Davis, P. A., and Davis, H.: Electroencephalograms of psychotic patients. Amer. J. Psychiat. 95: 1007-1025, 1939.

21. Dawson, G. D.: Cerebral responses to electrical stimulation of peripheral nerve in man. J. Neurol. Neurosurg. Psychiat. 10: 134-140, 1947.

22. Deglin, V. Ya.: The electrical activity of the cerebral cortex in schizophrenics who developed schizophrenia at a pre-school age (Russian). Zh. Nevropat. I Psikhiat. 62: 1837-1842, 1962.

23. Desai, A., and Vahia, N. S.: Use of photo-metrazol in electroencephalography with regard to epilepsy, hysteria and schizophrenia. Neurology (Madras) 5: 73-80, 1957.

24. Driver, M. V.: A study of the photoconvulsive threshold. Electroenceph. Clin. Neurophysiol. 14: 359-367, 1962.

25. Eccles, J. C.: The Physiology of Synapses. New York, Academic Press, Inc., 1964.

26. Faivyshevskii, V. A., and Nemtsov, A. V.: Effect of the blood serum from schizophrenics on the electrical activity of the brain in experimental animals. II. Study of blood serum from patients with nuclear forms of schizophrenia (Russian). Zh. Nevropat. I Psikhiat. 65: 247-250, 1965.

27. Fedio, P., Mirsky, A. F., Smith, W. J., and Parry, D.: Reaction time and EEG activation in normal and schizophrenic subjects. Electroenceph. Clin. Neurophysiol. 13: 923-926, 1961.

28. Feigenberg, I. M.: Comparative electro-encephalography of various clinical groups of patients with schizophrenia (Russian). Zh. Nevropat. I. Psikhiat. 64: 567-574, 1964.

29. Feinberg, I., Koresko, R. L., and Gottlieb, F.: Further observations on electrophysiological sleep patterns in schizophrenia. Compr. Psychiat. 6: 21-24, 1965.

30. Feinberg, I., Koresko, R. L., Gottlieb, F., and Wender, P. H.: Sleep electroencephalographic and eye-movement patterns in schizophrenic patients. Compr. Psychiat. 5: 44-53, 1964.

31. Fessel, W. J.: Autoimmunity and mental illness. Arch. Gen. Psychiat. 6: 320-323, 1962.

32. Fessel, W. J.: The "antibrain" factors in psychiatric patients' sera. Arch. Gen. Psychiat. 8: 614-621, 1963.

33. Fink, M.: Lateral gaze nystagmus as an index of the sedation threshold. Electroenceph. Clin. Neurophysiol. 10: 162-163, 1958.

34. Fink, M.: Quantitative EEG and human psychopharmacology. In Wilson, W. P. (Ed.) Application of Electroencephalography in Psychiatry. Durham, Duke University Press, 1965.

35. Fink, M., Itil, T., and Clyde, D.: The classification of psychoses by quantitative EEG measures. In Wortis, J. (Ed.) Recent Advances in Biological Psychiatry, Vol. VIII. New York, Plenum Press, 1966.

36. Floris, V., Morocutti, C., Amabile, G., Bernardi, G. and Rizzo, P. A.: Recovery cycle of visual evoked potentials in normal, schizophrenic and neurotic patients. In: N. S. Kline and E. Laska (Eds.), Computers and Electronic Devices in Psychiatry. New York, Grune & Stratton, 1968, pp. 194-205.

37. Gartside, I. B., Lippold, O. C. J., and Meldrum, B. S.: The evoked cortical somatosensory response in normal man and its modification by oral lithium carbonate. Electroenceph. Clin. Neurophysiol. 20: 382-390, 1966.

38. Gastaut, H.: Combined photic and Metrazol activation of the brain. Electroenceph. Clin. Neurophysiol. 2: 249-261, 1950.

39. Gerard, K. Z.: Studies on the metrazol-flicker threshold in schizophrenia (correlations with the sedation threshold). Neurol. Neurochir. Psychiat. Pol. 12: 247-253, 1962.

40. German, G. A.: Effects of serum from schizophrenics on evoked cortical potentials in the rat. Brit. J. Psychiat. 109: 616-623, 1963.

41. German, G. A., Antebi, R. N., Dear, E. M. A., and McCance, C.: A further study of the effects of serum from schizophrenics on evoked cortical potentials in the rat. Brit. J. Psychiat. 111: 345-347, 1965.

42. Gibbs, E. L., and Gibbs, F. A.: Electroencephalographic evidence of thala-

mic and hypothalamic epilepsy. Neurology. 1: 136-144, 1951.

43. Gibbs, F. A., and Gibbs, E. L.: The mitten pattern. An electroencephalographic abnormality correlating with psychosis. J. Neuropsychiat. 5: 6-13, 1963.

44. Gibbs, F. A., Gibbs, E. L., and Lennox, W. G.: The likeness of the cortical dysrhythmias of schizophrenia and psychomotor epilepsy. Amer. J. Psychiat. 95: 255-269, 1938.

45. Goldman, D.: Specific electroencephalographic changes with pentothal activation in psychotic states. Electroenceph. Clin. Neurophysiol. 11: 657-667, 1959.

46. Goldman, D.: Electroencephalographic changes brought to light under pentothal activation in psychotic (schizophrenic) patients with particular reference to changes produced by pharmacologic agents. Ann. N. Y. Acad. Sci. 96: 356-374, 1962.

47. Goldman, D.: The relationship of parkinsonism produced by drugs to psychotic reactions. In Wortis, J. (Ed.) Recent Advances in Biological Psychiatry, Vol. IV. New York, Plenum Press, 1962.

48. Goldman, D.: Electroencephalographic manifestations associated with psychotic illness: Pentothal activation technique and pharmacologic interrelationships. Compr. Psychiat. 5: 80-92, 1964.

49. Goldstein, L., and Beck, R. A.: Amplitude analysis of the electroencephalogram. Review of the information obtained with the integrative method. Int. Rev. Neurobiol. 8: 265-312, 1965.

50. Goldstein, L., Murphree, H. B., Sugarman, A. A., Pfeiffer, C. C., and Jenney, E. H.: Quantitative electroencephalographic analysis of naturally occurring (schizophrenic) and drug-induced psychotic states in human males. Clin. Pharmacol. Therap. 4: 10-21, 1963.

51. Goldstein, L., Sugerman, A. A., Stolberg, H., Murphree, H. B., and Pfeiffer, C. C.: Electro-cerebral activity in schizophrenics and nonpsychotic subjects: Quantitative EEG amplitude analysis. Electroenceph. Clin. Neurophysiol. 19: 350-361, 1965.

52. Greenberg, I. M., and Pollack, M.: Clinical correlates of 14 and 6/sec positive spiking in schizophrenic patients. Electroenceph. Clin. Neurophysiol. 20: 197-200, 1966.

53. Grenell, R. G.: Molecular biology and psychopathology. Ann. N. Y. Acad. Sci. 96: 345-352, 1962.

54. Heath, R. G.: Schizophrenia: biochemical and physiologic aberrations. Int. J. Neuropsychiat. 2: 597-610, 1966.

55. Heath, R. G., Cohen, S. B., Silva, F., Leach, B. E., and Cohen, M.: Administration of Taraxein in humans. Dis. Nerv. Syst. 20: 206-208, 1959.

56. Heath, R. G., and Guerrero-Figueroa, R.: Psychotic behavior with evoked septal dysrhythmia: Effects of intracerebral acetylcholine and gamma aminobutyric acid. Amer. J. Psychiat. 121: 1080-1086, 1965.

57. Heath, R. G., and Krupp, I. M.: Schizophrenia as an immunologic disorder: I. Demonstration of antibrain globulins by fluorescent antibody techniques. Arch. Gen. Psychiat. 16: 1-9, 1967.

58. Heath, R. G., Krupp, I. M., Byers, L. W., and Liljekwist, J. I.: Schizophrenia as an immunologic disorder. II. Effects of serum protein fractions on brain function. Arch. Gen. Psychiat. 16: 10-23, 1967.

59. Heath, R. G., Krupp, I. M., Byers, L. W., and Liljekvist, J. I.: Schizophrenia as an immunologic disorder. III. Effects of antimonkey and antihuman brain antibody on brain function. Arch. Gen. Psychiat. 16: 23-33, 1967.

60. Heath, R. G., Martens, S., Leach, B. E., Cohen, M., and Angel, C.: Effect on behavior in humans with the administration of Taraxein. Amer. J. Psychiat. 114: 14-24, 1957.

61. Heath, R. G., Martens, S., Leach, B. E., Cohen, M., and Feigley, C. A.: Behavioral changes in nonpsychotic volunteers following the administration of Taraxein, the substance obtained from serum of schizophrenic patients. Amer. J. Psychiat., 114: 917-920, 1958.

62. Heath, R. G., and the Department of Psychiatry and Neurology, Tulane University: Studies in Schizophrenia. Cambridge, Harvard University Press, 1954.

63. Heath, R. G., and Verster, F. B.: Effects of chemical stimulation to discrete brain areas. Amer. J. Psychiat., 117: 980-990, 1961.

64. Hein, P. L., Green, R. L., Jr., and Wilson, W. P.: Latency and duration of photically elicited arousal responses in the electroencephalograms of patients with chronic regressive schizophrenia. J. Nerv. Ment. Dis., 135: 361-364, 1962.

65. Heninger, G., and Speck, L.: Visual evoked responses and mental status of schizophrenics. Arch. Gen. Psychiat., 15: 419-426, 1966.

66. Henry, C. E.: Positive spike discharges in the EEG and behavior abnormality. In Glaser, G. H. (Ed.) EEG and Behavior. New York, Basic Books, 1963.

67. Heuyer, G., Lacasble, R. Lelord, G., and Fardeau, M.: A study of the correlations between clinical and EEG findings in cases of schizophrenia in children and adolescents. Rev. Neuropsychiat. Infant. Hyg. Ment. Enfance (Paris), 4: 436-441, 1956.

68. Hill, D.: Electroencephalogram in schizophrenia. In Richter, D. (Ed.) Schizophrenia: Somatic Aspects. London, Pergamon Press, 1957.

69. Hoagland, H., Cameron, D. E., and Rubin, M. A.: The delta index of the EEG in relation to insulin treatments of schizophrenia. Psychol. Record., 1: 196-202, 1937.

70. Hoagland, H., Pennell, R. B., Bergen, J. R., Saravis, C. A., Freeman, H., and Koella, W.: Studies of plasma protein factors that may be involved in psychoses. In Wortis, J. (Ed.) Recent Advances in Biological Psychiatry, Vol. IV. New York, Plenum Press, 1962.

71. Hoch, P., and Polatin, P.: Pseudoneurotic forms of schizophrenia. Psychiat. Quart., 23: 248-276, 1949.

72. Hori, H.: Hallucinations induced by electrical stimulation of the temporal lobes (Japanese). Psychiat. Neurol. Jap., 64: 1010-1016, 1962.

73. Hurst, L. A.: Electroencephalographic support for genetically oriented organic concept of schizophrenia. J. Nerv. Ment. Dis., 115: 95-120, 1952.

74. Huston, P. E., Shakow, D., and Riggs, L. A.: Studies of motor function in schizophrenia. II. Reaction time. J. Gen. Psychol., 16: 39-82, 1937.

75. Igert, C., and Lairy, G. C.: Prognostic value of EEG in the development of schizophrenics. Electroenceph. Clin. Neurophysiol., 14: 183-190, 1962.

76. Irwin, D. A., Knott, J. R., McAdam, D. W., and Rebert, C. S.: Motivational determinants of the "contingent negative variation". Electroenceph. Clin. Neurophysiol., 21: 538-543, 1966.

77. Ishibashi, T., Hori, H., Endo, K., and Sato, T.: Hallucinations produced by electrical stimulation of the temporal lobes in schizophrenic patients. Tohoku J. Exp. Med., 82: 124-139, 1964.

78. Itil, T.: Elektroencephalographische Studien Bei Psychosen Und Psychotropen Medikamenten. Istanbul, Ahmet Sait Matbassi, 1964.

79. Jasper, H. H., Fitzpatrick, C. P., and Solomon, P.: Analogies and opposites in schizophrenia and epilepsy; electroencephalographic and chemical studies. Amer. J. Psychiat., 95: 835-851, 1939.

80. Jones, R. T., Blacker, K. H., Callaway, E., and Layne, R. S.: The auditory evoked response as a diagnostic and prognostic measure in schizophrenia. Amer. J. Psychiat., 122: 33-41, 1965.

81. Jones, R. T., Blacker, K. H., and Callaway, E.: Perceptual dysfunction in schizophrenia: Clinical and auditory evoked response findings. Amer. J. Psychiat., 123: 639-645, 1966.

82. Jus, K.: Investigation of slow a rhythm in schizophrenia. Pol. Med. J., 2: 397-402, 1963.

83. Kammerer, T., Rohmer, F., Israel, L., and Wackenheim, A.: The EEG in schizophrenics. Strasbourg Med., 6: 20-30, 1955.

84. Kemali, D.: The effect of urinary fractions from schizophrenic patients on the electrical activity of the brain. Brit. J. Psychiat., 110: 576-581, 1964.

85. Kennard, M. A., and Schwartzman, A. E.: A longitudinal study of electroencephalographic frequency patterns in mental hospital patients and normal controls.

Electroenceph. Clin. Neurophysiol., 9: 263-274, 1957.

86. Klein, D. F.: Behavioral effects of imipramine and phenothiazines: Implications for a psychiatric pathogenetic theory and theory of drug action. In Wortis, J. (Ed.) Recent Advances in Biological Psychiatry, Vol. VII. New York, Plenum Press, 1965.

87. Kodman, F., Griffith, R., and Sparks, C.: Wakefulness in catatonic schizophrenia. Confin. Psychiat., 5: 189-195, 1962.

88. Koranyi, E. K., and Lehmann, H. E.: Experimental sleep deprivation in schizophrenic patients. A.M.A. Arch. Gen. Psychiat., 2: 534-544, 1960.

89. Koresko, R. L., Snyder, F., and Feinberg, I.: "Dream time" in hallucinating and non-hallucinating schizophrenic patients. Nature, 199: 1118-1119, 1963.

90. Krishnamoorti, S., and Shagass, C.: Some psychological test correlates of sedation threshold. In Wortis, J. (Ed.) Recent Advances in Biological Psychiatry. New York, Plenum Press, Vol. VI, 1964.

91. Lairy, G. C., Barte, H., Golstenas, J., and Ridjanovic, S.: The recording of night sleep during episodes of delusion. Electroenceph. Clin. Neurophysiol., 18: 96-97, 1965.

92. Landolt, H.: Serial electroencephalographic investigations during psychotic episodes in epileptic patients and during schizophrenic attacks. In Lorentz de Hass, A. M. (Ed.) Lectures on Epilepsy. Folia Psychiat. Neerl., Suppl. 4, 1958.

93. Lansing, R. W., Schwartz, E., and Lindsley, D. B.: Reaction time and EEG activation under alert and nonalerted conditions. J. Exp. Psychol., 58: 1-7, 1959.

94. Leach, B. E., Byers, L. W., and Heath, R. G.: In Heath, R. G. (Ed.) Serological Fractions in Schizophrenia. New York, Hoeber Medical Division, Harper and Row, 1963, pp. 7-22.

95. Lemere, F.: The significance of individual differences in the Berger rhythm. Brain, 59: 366-375, 1936.

96. Lester, B. K., and Edwards, R. J.: EEG fast activity in schizophrenic and control subjects. Int. J. Neuropsychiat., 2: 143-156, 1966.

97. Lief, H. I.: The effects of taraxein on a patient in analysis. Arch. Neurol. Psychiat. (Chic.), 78: 624-627, 1957.

98. Livanov, M. N., Gavrilova, N. A., and Aslanov, A. S.: Reflection of some mental states in the spatial distribution of human cerebral cortex biopotentials. Proc. XVIII Int. Cong. Psychol., Symposium No. 6, pp. 31-38, 1966.

99. MacMahon, J. F., and Walter W. G.: The electro-encephalogram in schizophrenia. J. Ment. Sci. 84: 781-787, 1938.

100. Mandel, A. J., and Mandell, M. P.: Biochemical aspects of rapid eye movement sleep. Amer. J. Psychiat., 122: 391-401, 1965.

101. Monroe, R. R., Heath, R. G., Mickle, W. A., and Llewellyn, R. C.: Correlation of rhinencephalic electrograms with behavior. A study on humans under the influence of LSD and Mescaline. Electroenceph. Clin. Neurophysiol., 9: 623-642, 1957.

102. Murphree, H. B., Goldstein, L., Pfeiffer, C. C., Schramm, L. P., and Jenney, E. H.: Computer analysis of drug effects on the electroencephalograms of normal and psychotic subjects. Int. J. Neuropharmacol., 3: 97-104, 1964.

103. Nemtsov, A. V., and Faivishevskii, V. A.: The effect of blood serum from patients with schizophrenia on the electrical activity of the brain in laboratory animals. I. Study of the blood serum of patients in the acute stage (Russian). Zh. Nevropat. I. Psikhiat., 64: 559-566, 1964.

104. Niedermeyer, E., and Knott, J. R.: Über die Bedeutung der 14 und 6/sec—positiven Spitzen im EEG. Arch. Psychiat. Nervenkr., 202: 266-280, 1961.

105. Ornitz, E. M., Ritvo, E. R., and Walter, R. D.: Dreaming sleep in autistic and schizophrenic children. Amer. J. Psychiat., 122: 419-424, 1965.

106. Ornitz, E. M., Ritvo, E. R., and Walter, R. D.: Dreaming sleep in autistic twins. Arch. Gen. Psychiat., 12: 77-79, 1965.

107. Peck, R. E.: Nystagmus threshold

as an office procedure in psychiatry. Int. J. Neuropsychiat., 1: 424-429, 1965.

108. Penfield, W.: The interpretive cortex. Science, 129: 1719-1725, 1959.

109. Petersen, M. C., Bickford, R. G., Sem-Jacobsen, C. W., and Dodge, H. W.: The depth electrogram in schizophrenic patients. Proc. Staff Meet., Mayo Clinic, 28: 170-175, 1953.

110. Pfeiffer, C. C., Beck, R. A., Goldstein, L., and Neiss, E. S.: Etiology of the stimulant nature of the schizophrenias. In Wortis, J. (Ed.) Recent Advances in Biological Psychiatry, Vol. IX. New York, Plenum Press, 1967.

111. Pfeiffer, C. C., Goldstein, L., Murphree, H. B., and Sugerman, A.: Time-series, frequency analysis, and electrogenesis of the EEGs of normals and psychotics before and after drugs. Amer. J. Psychiat., 121: 1147-1155, 1965.

112. Pollack, M., Klein, D. F., Willner, A., Blumberg, A., and Fink, M.: Imipramine-induced behavioral disorganization in schizophrenic patients: physiological and psychological correlates. In Wortis, J. (Ed.) Recent Advances in Biological Psychiatry, Vol. VII. New York, Plenum Press, 1965.

113. Purpura, D. P., Pool, J. L., Ransohoff, J., Frumin, M. J., and Housepian, E. M.: Observations on evoked dendritic potentials of human cortex. Electroenceph. Clin. Neurophysiol., 9: 453, 1957.

114. Rechtschaffen, A., Schulsinger, F., and Mednick, S. A.: Schizophrenia and physiological indices of dreaming. Arch. Gen. Psychiat., 10: 89-93, 1964.

115. Rodin, E., Zacharopoulos, G., Beckett, P., and Frohman, C.: Characteristics of visually evoked responses in normal subjects and schizophrenic patients. Electroenceph. Clin. Neurophysiol., 17: 458, 1964.

116. Rodnick, E. H., and Shakow, D.: Set in the schizophrenic as measured by composite reaction time index. Amer. J. Psychiat., 97: 214-225, 1940.

117. Rowntree, D. W., and Kay, W. W.: Clinical, biochemical and physiological studies in cases of recurrent schizophrenia. J. Ment. Sci., 98: 100-121, 1952.

118. Salamon, I., and Post, J.: Alpha blocking and schizophrenia (I. methodology and initial studies). Arch. Gen. Psychiat., 13: 367-374, 1965.

119. Schmidt, H. O., and Andrews, R. C.: Notes on the 6- and 14- positive spikes in the EEG. Psychol. Rep., 9: 399-400, 1961.

120. Schwartz, M., and Shagass, C.: Reticular modification of somatosensory cortical recovery function. Electroenceph. Clin. Neurophysiol., 15: 265-271, 1963.

121. Semenov, S. F.: The role of immunological changes in the clinical picture of pathophysiology of schizophrenia and other neuropsychic diseases (Russian)). In Voprosy Kliniki Patofiziologii i immunologii shizofrenii (Moscow), 1961, pp. 128-141.

122. Semenov, S. F.: Certain aspects of the clinical picture and of the course of schizophrenia with manifestations of auto-immunization brought about by cerebral antigens (Russian). Zh. Nevropat. I. Psikhiat., 64: 398-403, 1964.

123. Semenov, S. F., Morozov, G. V., and Kuznetsova, N. I.: Appraisal of the clinical significance of anticerebral antibodies in the serum of patients suffering from schizophrenia and other mental disorders (Russian) Zh. Nevropat. I. Psikhiat., 61: 1210-1215, 1961.

124. Sem-Jacobsen, C. W.: Depth-electrographic observations in psychotic patients. A system related to emotion and behavior. Acta Psychiat., 34: 412-416, 1959.

125. Sem-Jacobsen, C. W., Petersen, M. C., Dodge, H. W., Jr., Lazarte, J. A., and Holman, C. B.: Electroencephalographic rhythms from the depths of the parietal, occipital and temporal lobes in man. Electroenceph. Clin. Neurophysiol., 8: 263-278, 1956.

126. Sem-Jacobsen, C. W., Petersen, M. C., Lazarte, J. A., Dodge, H. W., and Holman, C. B.: Intracerebral electrographic recordings from psychotic patients during hallucinations and agitation. Amer. J. Psychiat., 112: 278-288, 1955.

127. Shagass, C.: The sedation threshold. A method for estimating tension in

psychiatric patients. Electroenceph. Clin. Neurophysiol., 6: 221-233, 1954.

128. Shagass, C.: A measurable neurophysiological factor of psychiatric significance. Electroenceph. Clin. Neurophysiol., 9: 101-108, 1957.

129. Shagass, C.: A neurophysiological study of schizophrenia. Report, 2nd Internat. Congress for Psychiatry, 2: 248-254, 1959.

130. Shagass, C.: Cerebral evoked response findings in schizophrenia. Proc. IV. World Congress of Psychiatry, Madrid, 1966, (in press).

131. Shagass, C.: Averaged somatosensory evoked responses in various psychiatric disorders. In Wortis, J. (Ed.) Recent Advances in Biological Psychiatry. New York, Plenum Press, Vol. X, pp. 205-219, 1968.

132. Shagass, C., and Canter, A.: Some personality correlates of cerebral evoked response characteristics. Proc. XVIII Internat. Congress of Psychology, Moscow, Symposium No. 6, pp. 47-52, 1966.

133. Shagass, C., and Jones, A. L.: A neurophysiological test for psychiatric diagnosis. Results in 750 patients. Amer. J. Psychiat., 114: 1002-1009, 1958.

134. Shagass, C., and Kerenyi, A. B.: The "sleep" threshold. A simple form of the sedation threshold for clinical use. Can. Psychiat. Ass. J., 3: 101-109, 1958.

135. Shagass, C., and Kerenyi, A. B.: Neurophysiologic studies of personality. J. Nerv. Ment. Dis., 126: 141-147, 1958.

136. Shagass, C., Muller, K., and Acosta, H. B.: The pentothal "sleep" threshold as an indicator of affective change. J. Psychosom. Res., 3: 253-270, 1959.

137. Shagass, C., Naiman, J., and Mihalik, J.: An objective test which differentiates between neurotic and psychotic depression. A.M.A. Arch. Neurol. Psychiat. 75: 461-471, 1956.

138. Shagass, C., and Schwartz, M.: Reactivity cycle of somatosensory cortex in humans with and without psychiatric disorder. Science, 134: 1757-1759, 1961.

139. Shagass, C., and Schwartz, M.: Cortical excitability in psychiatric disorder. Preliminary results. Proc. III World Congress Psychiat., U. Toronto Press, 1: 441-446, 1961.

140. Shagass, C., and Schwartz, M.: Cerebral cortical reactivity in psychotic depressions. A.M.A. Arch. Gen. Psychiat. 6: 235-242, 1962.

141. Shagass, C., and Schwartz, M.: Excitability of the cerebral cortex in psychiatric disorders. In Roessler, R., and Greenfield, N. S. (Eds.) Physiological Correlates of Psychological Disorder. Madison, U. Wisconsin Press, 1962.

142. Shagass, C., and Schwartz, M.: Psychiatric correlates of evoked cerebral cortical potentials. Amer. J. Psychiat., 119: 1055-1061, 1963.

143. Shagass, C., and Schwartz, M.: Cerebral responsiveness in psychiatric patients. A.M.A. Arch. Gen. Psychiat., 8: 177-189, 1963,

144. Shagass, C., and Schwartz, M.: Psychiatric disorder and deviant cerebral responsiveness to sensory stimulation. In Wortis, J. (Ed.) Recent Advances in Biological Psychiatry, Vol. V. New York, Plenum Press, 1963.

145. Shagass, C., and Schwartz, M.: Evoked potential studies in psychiatric patients. Ann. N.Y. Acad. Sci., 112: 526-542, 1964.

146. Shagass, C., and Schwartz, M.: Visual cerebral evoked responses characteristics in a psychiatric population. Amer. J. Psychiat., 121: 979-987, 1965.

147. Shagass, C., and Schwartz, M.: Age, personality and somatosensory cerebral evoked responses. Science, 148: 1359-1361, 1965.

148. Shagass, C., and Schwartz, M.: Somatosensory cerebral evoked responses in psychotic depression. Brit. J. Psychiat., 112: 799-807, 1966.

149. Shagass, C., Schwartz, M., and Amadeo, M.: Some drug effects on evoked cerebral potentials in man. J. Neuropsychiat., 3: S49-S58, 1962.

150. Shagass, C., Schwartz, M., and Krishnamoorti, S. R.: Some psychologic correlates of cerebral responses evoked by light flash. J. Psychosom. Res., 9: 223-231, 1965.

151. Shagass, C., and Trusty, D.: So-

matosensory and visual cerebral evoked response changes during sleep. *In* Wortis, J. (Ed.) Recent Advances in Biological Psychiatry, Vol. VIII. New York, Plenum Press, 1966.

152. Shakow, D.: Psychological deficit in schizophrenia. Behav. Sci., 8: 275-305, 1963.

153. Shaposhnikov, V. S.: Investigation of the biochemistry and pathophysiology of the allergic component in the pathogenesis of schizophrenia and infective psychoses (Russian). Zh. Nevropat. I. Psikhiat., 64: 1712-1716, 1964.

154. Sherwood, S. L.: Consciousness, adaptive behaviour and schizophrenia. *In* Richter, D. (Ed.) Schizophrenia: Somatic Aspects. London, Pergamon Press, 1957.

155. Sila, B., Mowrer, M., Ulett, G., and Johnson, M.: The differentiation of psychiatric patients by EEG changes after sodium pentothal. *In* Wortis, J. (Ed.) Recent Advances in Biological Psychiatry, Vol. IV. New York, Plenum Press, 1962.

156. Skalickova, O., and Jezkova, Z.: Immunological investigation of schizophrenia Čas Lěk Čes., 100: 1233-1240, 1961.

157. Small, J. G., and Small, I. F.: Fourteen- and six-per-second positive spikes. Arch. Gen. Psychiat., 11: 645-650, 1964.

158. Small, J. G., and Small, I. F.: Re-evaluation of clinical EEG findings in schizophrenia. Dis. Nerv. System, 26: 345-349, 1965.

159. Small, J. G., and Small, I. F.: A controlled study of mental disorders associated with epilepsy. *In* Wortis, J. (Ed.) Recent Advances in Biological Psychiatry, Vol. IX. New York, Plenum Press, 1967.

160. Small, J. G., Small, I. F., and Surphlis, W. R. P.: Temporal EEG abnormalities in acute schizophrenia. Amer. J. Psychiat., 121: 262-264, 1964.

161. Smith, K., Ulett, G., and Johnson, L. C.: A convulsive threshold in schizophrenia. Arch. Neurol. Psychiat. (Chic.) 77: 528-532, 1957.

162. Smythies, J. R.: The Neurological Foundations of Psychiatry. New York, Academic Press, 1966.

163. Snyder, F.: Progress in the new biology of dreaming. Amer. J. Psychiat., 122: 377-391, 1965.

164. Speck, L. B., Dim, B., and Mercer, M.: Visual evoked responses of psychiatric patients. Arch. Gen. Psychiat., 15: 59-63, 1966.

165. Spinelli, D. N., and Pribram, K. H.: Changes in visual recovery functions produced by temporal lobe stimulation in monkeys. Electroenceph. Clin. Neurophysiol. 20: 44-49, 1966.

166. Stenhouse, D., Antebi, R., Dear, E. M. A., Herrington, R. N., and Mc-Cance, C.: Effect of serum from schizophrenics on evoked cortical potentials in the rat. Brit. J. Psychiat., 111: 339-344, 1965.

167. Stevens, J. M., and Derbyshire, A. J.: Shifts along the alert-repose continuum during remission of catatonic "stupor" with amobarbital. Psychosomat. Med., 20: 99-107, 1958.

168. Straumanis, J. J., Shagass, C., and Schwartz, M.: Visually evoked cerebral response changes associated with chronic brain syndromes and aging. J. Gerontology, 20: 498-506, 1965.

169. Sugerman, A. A., Goldstein, L., Murphree, H. B., Pfeiffer, C. C., and Jenney, E. H.: EEG and behavioral changes in schizophrenia. Arch. Gen. Psychiat., 10: 340-344, 1964.

170. Travis, L. E., and Malamud, W.: Brain potentials from normal subjects, stutterers and schizophrenic patients. Amer. J. Psychiat., 93: 929-936, 1937.

171. Treffert, D. A.: The psychiatric patient with an EEG temporal lobe focus. Amer. J. Psychiat., 120: 765-771, 1964.

172. Tucker, J., Detre, T., Harrow, M., and Glaser, H.: Behavior and symptoms of psychiatric patients and the electro-encephalogram. Arch. Gen. Psychiat., 12: 278-286, 1965.

173. Turton, E. C., and Warren, P. K. G.: Dementia: A clinical and EEG study of 274 patients over the age of 60. J. Ment. Sci., 106: 1493-1500, 1960.

174. Ulett, G. A., Brockman, J. C., Gleser, G., and Johnson, A.: Determination of convulsive threshold by photo-

pharmacologic stimulation: a study of technique and reliability. Electroenceph. Clin. Neurophysiol., 7: 597-607, 1955.

175. Ulett, G. A., Heusler, A. F., and Word, T. J.: The effect of psychotropic drugs on the EEG of the chronic psychotic patient. *In* Wilson, W. P. (Ed.) Applications of Electroencephalography to Psychiatry. Durham, Duke University Press, 1965.

176. Venables, P. H.: Selectivity at attention, withdrawal, and cortical activation. Studies in chronic schizophrenia. Arch. Gen. Psychiat., 9: 74-78, 1963.

177. Venables, P. H.: The relationship between level of skin potential and fusion of paired light flashes in schizophrenic and normal subjects, J. Psychiat. Res., 1: 279-287, 1963.

178. Venables, P. H., and Wing, J. K.: Level of arousal and the sub-classification of schizophrenia. Arch. Gen. Psychiat., 7: 114-119, 1962.

179. Walter, R. D., Colbert, E. G., Koegler, R. R., Palmer, J. O., and Bond, P. M.: A controlled study of the fourteen- and six-per-second EEG pattern. Arch. Gen. Psychiat., 2: 559-566, 1960.

180. Walter, W. G.: Where vital things happen. Amer. J. Psychiat., 116: 673-694, 1960.

181. Walter, W. G.: The convergence and interaction of visual, auditory, and tactile responses in human nonspecific cortex. Ann. N.Y. Acad. Sci., 112: 320-361, 1964.

182. Walter, W. G., Cooper, R., Aldridge, V. J., McCallum, W. C., and Winter, A. L.: Contingent negative variation: An electric sign of sensorimotor association and expectancy in the human brain. Nature, 203: 380-384, 1964.

183. Weiner, H.: Schizophrenia. III: Etiology. *In* Freedman, A. M. and Kaplan, H. I. (Eds.) Comprehensive Textbook of Psychiatry. Baltimore, Williams and Wilkins, 1967.

184. White, P. T., Demyer, W. and DeMyer, M.: EEG abnormalities in early childhood schizophrenia: a double-blind study of psychiatrically disturbed and normal children during promazine sedation. Amer. J. Psychiat., 120: 950-958, 1964.

185. Yamada, T.: Heterogeneity of schizophrenia as demonstrable in electroencephalography. Bull. Osaka Med. Sch., 6 :107-146, 1960.

7

Psychological Studies

A. I. RABIN, Ph.D. and C. L. WINDER, Ph.D.

Dr. Albert I. Rabin is Professor of Psychology at Michigan State University, Consultant to the VA and Department of Corrections of the State of Michigan.

He was educated at Harvard and Boston Universities and subsequently served as Chief Psychologist at the New Hampshire State Hospital and Mental Hygiene Clinics and as research psychologist at Michael Reese Hospital in Chicago. Dr. Rabin also served as guest professor at the Hebrew University, Jerusalem and Bar-Ilan University, Israel (1962). He was visiting professor at the City University of New York (1964-1965).

Dr. Rabin's early work was concerned with perserveration and ·patterns of intellectual functioning in schizophrenia and manic depressive psychoses, and contributed the same chapter for the previous volume, Schizophrenia. *His later work deals with temporal experience and personality as well as with the effects of early childhood experience upon personality and development. He is co-editor of Projective Techniques With Children (Grune & Stratton, 1960) and author of* Growing Up in the Kibbutz (*Springer, 1965*).

C. L. Winder, Ph.D., is Professor of Psychology and Chairman of the Department of Psychology at Michigan State University; Consultant to the NIMH, the VA, and the Michigan Department of Mental Health.

Educated at U.C.L.A. and Stanford University, Dr. Winder subsequently served on the faculties of Stanford University and the University of Southern California. Dr. Winder was a Faculty Fellow at the Neuropsychiatric Institute, University of Illinois Medical School, Chicago (1952-1953).

Dr. Winder's early research on the developmental history and functioning of reactive and process schizophrenics has been followed by studies of personality and social adjustments of children in relation to parental attitudes. He is the author of several reviews of research literature in this field.

Research in the field of schizophrenia is continuing with undiminished vigor. Recent years have witnessed greater involvement of academic psychologists, and of theories and methods evolved by academic psychology in this research endeavor. Since the present authors have last reviewed the literature,[391,550] the amassed publications, which cannot be reviewed completely within the confines of the present brief chapter, point in the direction of greater methodologic sophistication and theoretical integration of schizophrenic behavior with that of general and developmental psychology.

In one of our reviews[550] the prediction was made that "the strategy of future research will be to test hypotheses regarding antecedents of these deficits and deviations and to find means of correcting, compensating for, and preventing them." The other review[391] emphasizes that: "The selection of a specific frame of reference in the determination of samples, such as chronicity, or reactive vs. process, or some other behavioral aspect (e.g., paranoia) tends to be a most fruitful avenue of approach pending a more revolutionary revision of the concept of schizophrenia." These trends are quite well reflected in the conduct of the subsequent research which is briefly discussed in the present chapter. With slight modifications it follows the pattern of the combined outlines of our previous attempts to order and organize the current literature.

INTELLECTUAL FUNCTIONING

Interest in intellectual deficit, demonstrated by means of standard measures of intelligence, continues unabated. The inconclusive results obtained via the use of scatter and pattern analysis of test components[187,185,390,391] during the past 25 years or more have stimulated new research directions. Instead of inferring deficit in schizophrenic intellectual functioning from cross-sectional data and pattern analysis (comparing tests which presumably are, or are not, affected by psychopathology), investigators have turned to longitudinal studies using the test-retest method.

Comparisons of premorbid with morbid test results indicate, as earlier cross-sectional research suggested, a reduction in I.Q. Veterans showed a drop of 6 I.Q. points after a mean interval of 10 years between the premorbid and morbid state.[448] However, the process seems reversible in ex-patients.[145,449] The relationship of indices of intellectual functioning to clinical status is further demonstrated in other studies. Thus patients who had a "work shop experience" showed no decline and even some improvement in mental level.[193] Similar results are reported in still another study of two matched groups of "improved" and "unimproved" schizophrenics.[204] After intervals of 16-42 months, the former showed an average gain of 7.30 points whereas the latter indicated a loss of 2.65 points. A discordant note is struck in another investigation reporting a "net *gain*" in I.Q. when the premorbid state is compared with the morbid condition.[180] However, the small difference and the fact that different tests were used under both conditions, detracts considerably from the credibility of these findings. The bulk of the evidence, reviewed here, and of earlier studies points to a reduction in intellectual functioning following the onset of schizophrenia. The loss, however, is reversible.[144,145,146]

A series of studies concerning the childhood intellectual status of schizophrenics is of interest at this juncture. Essentially, the findings indicate that children who later became schizophrenics achieve lower I.Q.'s than their nonpathological siblings,[281,282,384] showed a significant loss in functioning between early (5-8 years) and latter childhood (ages 11-14)[283] and, on the whole, produced below average I.Q. levels in childhood which are comparable to those they obtain upon reaching adulthood as schizophrenics.[3] A study by another investigator[101] who reports no relationship between the I.Q.'s of schizophrenic children and those of their mothers may be related to the differences in I.Q. between schizophrenics and their nonpsychotic siblings.[281,282] Generally, the notion that schizophrenics are below par intellectually even before the onset of the disorder is quite tenable. Hence the differences between I.Q.'s of schizophrenics, normals, and other groups. This is not to deny however, that some loss as a result of morbidity, temporary or reversible, does in fact take place. The test-retest studies mentioned in previous paragraphs support this conclusion. Some investigators note that improved test performance prior to the onset of the disorder is related to the experience of auditory hallucinations during schizophrenia.[241] Another study seems to contradict this notion by finding no relationship between intelligence and clinical form of the disorder.[280]

The possibility of differential impairment, that some intellectual functions are better preserved than others in schizophrenia, is still an intriguing topic. In two studies[158,345] patients were reexamined with the WAIS Vocabulary an average of 6 and 17 years after the original testing upon admission to a hospital. No significant changes in vocabulary performance were demonstrated. Confirmatory results are reported in a study on the "influence of hospitalization on the verbal behavior of chronic schizophrenics."[559] Whereas other measures of verbal behavior (e.g., free association, sentence completion, etc.) showed lower levels when long-term schizophrenics were compared with short-term ones, the measures comparable to the vocabulary test did not yield significant differences. Another retest study, however, reports that "Pattern Analysis and Mechanical Aptitude deteriorate less than Reading and Vocabulary etc."[314] These results were obtained when the Army Classification Battery scores of schizophrenic patients were compared with their previous enlistment data. The apparent inconsistencies with respect to vocabulary may lie in the differential requirements of different vocabulary tests employed in the sundry investigations.[145,196] Refinement of vocabulary tests to include the task of achieving unusual meanings of familiar words seems to be a promising method for spotting schizophrenics[548] who allegedly show impairment in this sphere. The notion that schizophrenics make greater literal misinterpretation of words failed to receive support in a recent study.[122]

Related to the issue of stability of vocabulary and differential impairment is the concept of scatter or discrepancy between different tests, subtests within the same test, and items within the same subtest. Although schizophrenics were found to have Wechsler I.Q.'s comparable to those of normals, they did more poorly on the Raven Progressive Matrices.[501] The latter finding is not confirmed, however.[271] A miscellany of reports on intertest patterns[264,277,271,521] yields slim pickings. Intratest scatter fails to differentiate between schizophrenics and organics[519] although close analysis of the information items of the WAIS tends to show that schizophrenics have greater difficulty with items requiring reasoning as compared with those demanding simple recall.[418] Continued interest in the analysis of types of errors on individual items demonstrated by schizophrenics and organics is found in a couple of additional studies.[418,520]

All in all, we have learned that schizophrenics manifest comparatively lower intelligence long before the onset of the disorder, that further impairment of a reversible nature tends to occur upon hospitalization and that the change in the course of impairment is probably related to the overall clinical picture and, possibly, to motivational factors in the testing situation.[107] Vocabulary levels as determined by the conventional methods remain fairly stable, but little support for the diagnostic value of scatter and pattern analysis has been added.

PERCEPTION

The study of perception, in a general sense, focuses on the organization of sensory input. Because a clear distinction between "the perceptual system" and "the response system" is attained only with the greatest care, studies and discussions of perception are often complex. Allowing for the difficulties of the subject matter, the research literature supports the conclusion that schizophrenic subjects tend to be deviant from normals in performance of perceptual tasks. A disquieting fact is the occasional but persistent occurrence of studies which contradict this conclusion.[263,325,373] The explanation of perceptual deviance and of occasional failures to find deviance are not clear or simple and should be the focus of future research efforts. There are many special effects of the particular experimental procedures used.[206,525] A problem for theories of behavior pathology is the fact that when groups of schizophrenics are found to differ from normal controls often they do not differ from other diagnostic groups.[173,202,147] But, on some tasks, schizophrenics differ from other patient groups such as organics.[325]

Schizophrenics are frequently deviant in perception of simple visual and auditory stimuli such as shape,[92,2] complex stimuli,[102] figural aftereffects,[538] monocular distance perception,[258] fusion of flashes of light,[437] pain,[161] constancy,[64,530,529,531,421] time,[298,165,186,289,556,536,298] apparent motion,[436,434,435] closure,[473] hidden pictures,[528] illusions,[533] visual vs. tactual exploration,[447] stimulus-seeking behavior,[461,330] perception of body size,[88] reaction to sensory deprivation,[471,399] reactions to human faces,[232] have difficulty with establishment and adherence to social perceptual norms,[342,446,110] and are influenced by details of experimental procedure to an unusual extent.[424]

Subgroups of schizophrenics often differ from each other, e.g., as regards size of afterimages,[201] constancy,[527] GSR reactions to lights,[513] threshold judgments,[411] responses to ambiguous pictures,[118] and reactions to novel stimuli.[330] The fact of some such differences among various subgroups of schizophrenics seems established; the explanation of this fact is not apparent and the theories offered are not compelling. Unreliability of the categorization into subgroups confounds the matter as does the instability of patterns of associations between subgroup and type of performance from study to study and from task to task.

Size constancy is a convenient illustration of the difficulties presented by diverse research findings. Some studies report no difference between chronic schizophrenics and normals,[292,381] other studies find overconstancy characteristic of schizophrenics[430,370] and still other researchers find underconstancy among schizophrenics.[194,526,97] In part, investigators have probably not been able to define their samples with precision so comparisons are inexact. When samples are carefully defined, several types of deviations are found but in different subgroups.[37] Paranoid schizophrenics are probably close to normals and tend to overconstancy.[396,530] In a recent and highly sophisticated study of size constancy, Price and Erikson[389] failed to find gross differences of the kinds described above between normals, nonparanoid schizophrenics, and paranoid schizophrenics. They did find nonparanoid schizophrenics low in perceptual sensitivity and paranoid schizophrenics unrealistic in subjective confidence in their judgments. In general, schizophrenics are likely to be deviant in performances on perceptual constancy tasks as compared with normals. Subgroups of schizophrenics probably show specific deviations or unique patterns. The great need is for much more definitive research on the origins and meaning of these deviant behaviors as well as others.

Many authorities are inclined to conclude on the basis of studies of perception that some cases and aspects of schizophrenia derive from biological-physiological-biochemical deficiencies or deviations.[60,59,58] In part, this is because the stimuli employed in some studies of perception are commonplace and uncomplicated, and because the responses required of the subjects are performed with ease, and to an extent because of the particular nature of the findings, e.g., Wertheimer's work related to the "neural satiability" hypothesis.[538] Given the nature of the experimental procedures and observations, these explanations are highly plausible, but the experimental procedures employed do not rule out explanations having to do with attention, set, motivation, dynamic or symbolic determinants, and experimenter influences. There are several complications which make interpretation of results uncertain. One example is the apparent heightened susceptibility of schizophrenic subjects to procedural or methods effects, e.g., schizophrenics show a usually large discrepancy between a threshold measure using a series of decreasing stimuli as contrasted with the threshold measure using increasing stimuli.[371] Another example of the marked effect produced by seemingly small changes in procedure is the significant effect of noise on the threshold for fusion of a flashing light for schizophrenic but not for normal subjects.[512] Yet another example is the heightened threshold for perception of speech among schizophrenic children.[219] In the fusion example, the interpretation emphasized hypothetical deficiencies in cortical functions of schizophrenics; in the latter the symbolic nature of speech was emphasized. It is easy to accept both theories as partially correct, but it is difficult to achieve a precise integration of the theories, and it is not possible to reject either theory on the basis of the evidence in hand. The literature lends support to those views which emphasize the variety and pervasiveness of the processes involved in the schizophrenic adaptations.

Motivational and dynamic hypotheses predict atypical responses to meaningful stimulus materials. For example, schizophrenics have special problems responding to conflict and affective stimuli,[504,257,368,348,6] pictures of interpersonal situations,[420,291] and perception of own body.[225,87] Because many researchers find these effects, the psychosocial hypotheses must continue to receive serious consideration.

Among schizophrenics there are individual differences, often very large individual differences, in the extent of deviations such as those noted above. This has stimulated studies of the relationship of particular deviations to variables such as withdrawal, the process-reactive continuum, good-premorbid and poor-premorbid a d j u s t m e n t and the acute-chronic dimension.[141,568,22,511,17,200,51,116,108,36,561,562,171,237,464] There are many positive findings but one can do little more than conclude that the ultimate explanation of schizophrenia will involve a large number of variables.

Because perceptual deviations are so obvious to the clinical observer and are so readily demonstrated in the laboratory, continued research in this area is clearly appropriate and necessary. One focus with high heuristic appeal is continued and intensified research on factors involved in attention.[463]

PSYCHOMOTOR FUNCTIONING

Schizophrenics have been studied primarily in terms of fine psychomotor performance with very little research on gross abilities.

Reaction time studies continue to yield evidence that schizophrenics respond differently from normals in many ways such as generally slower speed,[28,356] choice of less adaptive preparatory intervals,[96] inadequate maintenance of set,[564] less response to increased stimulus intensity,[262] unusual difficulty when the procedure requires shifts from one sensory modality to another,[493,563] deficient adaptation to lengthened preparatory intervals,[233,565] and response to the regularity of presentation of the stimulus.[233] In other words, schizophrenics are slow, variable, and adapt poorly to more complex procedures.

The meaning which attaches to these deviant responses is still obscure, and research results are open to alternative interpretations. For example, reaction time by schizophrenics to a verbal rather a nonverbal signal is disproportionately longer than for normals.[419] The study was done to support the view that schizophrenia reflects a disturbance of interpersonal relations but the results could be explained in other ways, e.g., selective cortical dysfunction. In addition to uncertainties about interpretation of differences, there are enough studies (e.g.,[213]), which fail to yield the expected differences to create some uncertainty about the prevalence of particular deviations. Another source of ambiguity is the rather frequent failure to find significant, specific differences between groups of schizophrenics and other pathological groups such as organics, severe neurotics, or psychotic depressives. On the basis of the evidence in hand, a relatively high frequency of deviations among hospitalized schizophrenics is confirmed; equally clearly, there is no one deviation which is assuredly typical of all schizophrenics. A remarkable fact is that Rodnick and Shakow[408] developed an index based on reaction times so that there was no overlap of a group of schizophrenics and a control group made up of individuals low in motivation and intelligence. There may be important differential deficits in different types of psychomotor performances, as suggested, for example, by a study in which schizophrenics were less handicapped in tapping than in reaction time tasks.[453]

Given the wide individual differences among schizophrenics, investigators have attempted to identify dimensions or subtypes which order this extreme variability. Reaction time or changes in reaction time have been related to dimensions such as general level of activity,[509] extent of withdrawal,[498] degree of disorganization,[418] and other variables. [412] The extent to which these variables are associated with reaction time in groups of nonschizophrenic subjects is obscure.

Schizophrenics often respond in a relatively normal way if special experimental manipulations are applied. Aversive conditions and critical or negative evaluations of specific responses rather consistently promote improved performances by schizophrenics.[413,174,285,67] The interpretation is in doubt, although many would adopt a motivational explanation. In regard to reaction time, explanations in terms of a stimulus-intensity dynamism[262] and in terms of reinforcement[174,250] are attractive. Schizophrenics may improve psychomotor performances with positive reinforcement.[174,29,491,31,99] Similar effects of a wide variety of special procedures are often found with normal groups and other deviant groups.[174,29,235,491,99] If procedures which change performance do not yield effects peculiar to schizophrenic subjects, interpretation of the effects as relevant to theories of schizophrenia are gratuitous. Nevertheless, any knowledge of ways to modify the responses of schizophrenics in the direction of normal behavior is surely of interest.

Studies to show in detail the influence of specific factors in the psychomotor performances of schizophrenics are all too infrequent. Zahn, Shakow, and Rosenthal[566] in a study of reaction time present evidence that it is specifically the long preparatory interval rather than the slow pace of events which is associated with the deviant performance of schizophrenics. In other words, schizophrenics seem to adopt a preparatory set based on the last trial rather than establishing a generalized preparatory set. As another example, Cromwell et al.[96] showed that in contrast with normals, schizophrenics perform best if they have little control of the experimental procedure while normals elected nearly optimum preparatory intervals. A series of studies by Tizard and Venables and their associates on parameters associated with reaction time performances and thresholds are analytical and significant.[509,498] Such studies are relatively difficult to design but are far more relevant at this point than further studies which simply show that schizophrenics tend to differ from normals.

Aspects of psychomotor performance other than reaction time have received little concerted study recently but a variety of findings keep interest alive.[405] Weaver,[523] found that a "less sick group" of schizophrenics tends to perform better than a more disturbed group on five psychomotor tasks. King[261] found that schizophrenics tend to show a positive constant error in attempting to coordinate a simple motor response with intermittent auditory stimuli whereas a negative error was more characteristic of the normals. With increasing task complexity, schizophrenics tended to sacrifice accuracy for speed in contrast to normals who decreased speed and preserved accuracy.[515] After working on a pursuit-rotor, schizophrenics dissipated reactive inhibition slowly.[329] In attempting to spin a wheel at a constant speed, schizophrenics are excessively distracted by an irregularly timed, intermittent auditory stimulus.[70] Schizophrenic children tend to make more whirling responses than normals given the "Romberg" test.[393] These diverse studies confirm earlier conclusions[391,550] that as with reaction time, schizophrenics tend to be slow, variable, and inclined to atypical responses in a variety of psychomotor tasks.

Lang and Buss,[57,286] on the basis of a detailed analysis of research on deficit and schizophrenia, concluded that schizophrenia involves a "fundamental sensorimotor defect." They suggest that "researchers in schizophrenia should concentrate on the processes by which stimuli adapt out or habituate and response competition is resolved".[286,p.98] Their analysis is impressive but seems to give very little weight to some highly relevant factors such as the strong correlation between level of performance and cooperativeness of schizophrenic subjects.[229]

The findings on psychomotor performance are subject to at least three alternative and overlapping psychological interpretations. Schizophrenics may be fundamentally deficient in maintaining attention, they may be relatively uninfluenced or influenced in unusual ways by the social reinforcements intrinsic in the experimental situation, and they may be responding intermittently to internal or other irrelevant stimuli with the result that irrelevant responses compete with the experimental response. Within any one of these views, there are conflicting subhypotheses. For example, attention deficit might be explained by some organic condition, or by unusual motivation, or by faulty learning.

In research on the schizophrenias, fundamentals of measurement and research design are too often neglected. The rather consistent results on reaction time from a variety of laboratories might be explained in a number of ways. It is a fact, however, that measures of reaction time cluster together as a coherent dimension of personal tempo.[402] Thus, the precise details of procedure assume relatively little importance because the procedures are interchangeable measures in large part. Other tasks, such as those used in studies of learning, cognitive processes, and interpersonal relationships are probably not interchangeable and comparisons of results from study to study are often inappropriate therefore. There is need for much more attention to this issue in research.

LANGUAGE AND COGNITIVE PROCESSES

Traditionally, much of the research on concept formation, thinking, and reasoning has been inspired by the regression or the abstract-concrete hypotheses. Much of this research suggested that these concepts prove vague under empirical analysis and consequently not precisely subject to test.[318] Other, usually less global, hypotheses have emerged and found expression in research during recent years.

Studies of cognitive processes often involve language and a definitive distinction between thinking and language is obviously difficult.[306] Studies of schizophrenic language are considered to be part of the study of cognitive processes here.

Clinicians and intelligent laymen produce reliable ratings of the degree of schizophrenicity of language such as responses to a vocabulary test.[226] The primary dimension of language reflected in these ratings is "communicability."[227] Clinicians make valid judgments of clinical severity of pathology from language[242] and detailed analyses to identify the cues underlying these judgments are needed. Process schizophrenics use a relatively restricted sample of words as compared with normals[319] and probably produce a low adjective-verb quotient,[307] but many schizophrenics are quite similar to both normals and other patient groups. Content analyses of schizophrenic language show a wide variety of deviations and schizophrenics differ from normals on many language tests[177,452,175,136,251,425,428,179,361,475,125,55,295,544,401,415] as expected from the finding that clinical judgments of schizophrenicity reflect communicability of language, primarily. There is evidence that language deviations are greater among chronic than acute schizophrenics.[216,367]

In some ways, the deviations observed in language use by schizophrenics are different from errors made by organics but these groups are similar in some ways, also. In a study by Chapman, schizophrenics made more literal misinterpretations and organics made more figurative misinterpretations.[74]

Milgram,[339] however, is an example of an investigator who found that in contrast to normals, schizophrenics, and organics show a preference for concrete as opposed to abstract word meanings. The trend was stronger among the organics but similar in kind for both pathologic groups. Often, the size and kind of differences among various groups of patients, as well as in contrast to normals, is a function of the task and other aspects of the experimental situation, in part.

Learned mediating verbal responses result in changed conceptual sorting of objects by both normals and paranoid schizophrenics.[139] Reactive schizophrenics, but not process schizophrenics, learn as well as nonpsychotic patients to respond with abstract rather than concrete words in a verbal learning task.[502] Such studies are more useful than a simple demonstration of group differences because there is clarification of ways in which inadequate verbal responses may be changed.

Schizophrenics are inferior to normals in interpretation of proverbs,[364] an effect not due just to number of words in answers,[170] and performed poorly in sorting of cards into groups in terms of object names written on the cards.[331] Thus verbal behavior of schizophrenics is found not only in spontaneous talk or written documents but also in response to verbal problems. Patients who responded best, clinically, to shock therapy gave improved postshock performances on a proverbs test.[40] This suggests that verbal behavior varies as part of the overall level of adjustment.

On the Object Sorting Test, open-private responses are more often given by schizophrenics than by other groups such as organics[326] and neurotics.[466] But, if the definition of the "response" is stringent and excludes seemingly irrelevant comments, the differences between medical patient controls and psychopathological groups, including schizophrenics, disappear.[492] This is illustrative of the general point that differences between the better cognitive efforts of schizophrenics and typical normal performances are often small.

The sophisticated researcher can find ways of demonstrating any number of deviations by groups of schizophrenics.[149,89] Interpretations of line drawings reveal that schizophrenics, as compared with normals, show high variability, lump very different drawings as though they were the same, and assign opposite mood terms to identical stimuli.[166,168] Analogous results appeared in response to auditory stimuli,[150] self concept and body concept,[124,49,26,188,320,211] performance on the Rorschach,[514,467] and the progressive matrices test.[134] Schizophrenics are especially inept on difficult problem-solving tasks, as are organics,[93] but are relatively less handicapped on more structured tasks.[192]

Cameron (e.g., Ref. 61) did much to stimulate a detailed, heuristic approach in the analysis of the thinking of schizophrenics. His concept of "overinclusion" has found much support and some refinement during recent years. Chapman and his associates contributed numerous studies which show that many errors made by schizophrenics in sorting tasks involve incorrect use of qualities or components common to both correct and incorrect answers.[72,71,80,73,75] Overinclusion, or more specifically, errors in response to associatively linked distractors, is a common finding in these studies and has been confirmed by other investigators.[117] Such errors are made by normals, of course, and are frequently observed with organics.[135] Schizophrenics tend to respond in terms of concepts of some preferred breadth[75] and this produces overinclusion or overexclusion depending on the nature of the experimental task. There are other deficiencies in the performance of schizophrenics, such as difficulty in forming concepts.[73]

Payne and his associates[362,366,363,364] have shown that overinclusion is a more effective basis for differentiation of schizophrenics from neurotics than is concreteness. It is acute schizophrenics who produce more overinclusive thinking on at least one test[363] and overinclusive thinking is correlated with delusional thinking.[364] Chronic schizophrenics tend to fewer usual responses than normals.[363]

Overall, it seems clear that there is no aspect of cognitive dysfunction which is found only among schizophrenics. Neither is there any deviation found among all schizophrenics. Rather, a large number of deviations occur among schizophrenics more frequently than among normals. And, cognitive dysfunction is frequently found among other pathological groups. Patients make more but the same kinds of errors as normals. Assuming that these generalizations are valid, the study of schizophrenics' thought processes is enlightened by studies such as that by Holtzman, Gorham, and Moran[221] which suggests that there are at least 7 dimensions which are reflected in the performance of paranoid schizophrenics on tests of cognitive functioning. These factors are: verbal ability, integrated ideation, stimulus sensitivity, pathologic verbalization, conceptual autism, concreteness in proverbs, sexual concern. These must be viewed as preliminary findings but the study does illustrate a potentially fruitful strategy for clarifying the scope and extent of the cognitive dysfunctions of schizophrenics.

While some investigators do not find differences among schizophrenics,[123] many studies do show that such variables as acute-chronic, good-premorbid vs. poor-premorbid, and reactive-process are predictive of individual differences on a large number of tasks and characteristics. For example, good-premorbid (acute, reactive) schizophrenics tend to use broad, vague or idiosyncratic concepts and poor-premorbid (chronic, process) schizophrenics show an inability to specify the common property of objects,[505] reactives tend to give abstract but illogical vs. concrete interpretations of proverbs;[42] abstract level shown by reactives is close to that of normals whereas process schizophrenics show low abstract ability;[212] reactives make better use of redundancy in a proverbs test[195] and give more common and more stable word association responses.[114] Other variables predict individual differences in conceptual deficits among schizophrenics, also.[310,557,558]

The perennial debate regarding the etiology of thought disorders continues and will probably be resolved only by experimental, longitudinal studies. There is, however, an increasing amount of evidence that contingent, selective reinforcements result in modifications of the level of cognitive functioning of schizophrenics. One recent study points to the conclusion that contingent positive reinforcement of abstract responses to proverbs increases the frequency of such responses and the effect transfers to other tests of thinking[336] In the same study, noncontingent positive and contingent negative reinforcements did not influence performance. Under at least some conditions, nonparanoid schizophrenics profit less from social-interpersonal reinforcement than from mechanical-impersonal rewards, paranoids show no differential effect, but the performance of normals is better in response to social than nonsocial reinforcements.[234] Negative interpersonal interaction seems to be followed by a decrease in the level of abstraction in interpretations of proverbs by schizophrenics but positive interaction is followed by an increase, particularly among female patients.[303] Specific, mild censure results in an increment in reasoning of good-premorbid schizophrenics[309] As in other areas of research on the schizophrenias, reports of failure to find the expected effects cloud the picture and suggest caution in reaching conclusions.[315]

Persons who prefer psychodynamic and other psychosocial explanations of schizophrenia expect to find that stimulus content influences performance. In general, the expectation is that human content and, more specifically, conflict related content, will tend to disrupt cognitive processes. Genetic, physiological, metabolic, toxic, and other biologically oriented hypotheses do not suggest this type of hypothesis, directly. Of course, one may reason that if cognitive processes are deviant, say by reason of a metabolic dysfunction of parts of the central nervous system, then the area of social interaction might be especially sensitized because of greater emotionality surrounded deficiencies of this kind. This is illustrated by the notion that the unresponsive infant tends to produce a distressed mother who then behaves in unfortunate ways in caring for the child with a deteriorating spiral of subsequent interaction within the dyad. The fact remains that it has been the psychosocial theorists who have stimulated the research on differential deficits related to stimulus content.

There is a sizable number of studies which support the view that if human, social events are depicted in the stimuli presented, schizophrenics are likely to perform even less well than they do on tasks involving impersonal stimuli such as numbers, geometric forms, and the like.[541,535,105,346,104] The effect is not always found, but this may be because schizophrenics give less attention to the social stimuli.[379] In a very significant study, Cavanaugh[66] found that escape from a noxious stimuli prompted a normal level of performance by schizophrenics on tasks involving social stimuli. The inference is that there is no fundamental, irreversible deterioration involved.

Heath[205] presents evidence that the degree of disruption of performance is related to rather specific content areas such as sex, aggression, and relationship to parents. Silverman[465] presents related evidence on aggression. Detailed analyses of this kind, coupled with studies on the modification of deficits using learning and reinforcement principles may permit significant change of thought dysfunctions of schizophrenics.

The reactive-process and similar conceptualizations have suggested studies of differences among schizophrenics in responsiveness to selected, socially relevant stimuli and results tend to support the heuristic value of this approach,[296,291,524] but the results obtained so far seem rather variable depending on both the specific task and the general social implications of the experimental situation.

All of these results must be viewed as tentative because a total over-view suggests that results obtained depend on: a) the characteristics of the patient, b) the nature of the task, c) the characteristics of the experimenter, and d) the nature of the reinforcement. And, there are very likely other important parameters.[483,35] What seems clear is the need for much more detailed studies of clearly defined, larger samples of patients, using a carefully ordered, varied array of tasks, and a variety of experimental procedures such as the nature of the reinforcements used.

Reports of failure to find expected differences between groups of schizophrenics and other groups such as normals, organics, and other psychopathological groups[272,137,546,123] continue to appear. Such failures can be rationalized, for example, in terms of unreliability of diagnoses, unreliability of tests used, and chance sampling variations, but these reports serve as forceful reminders of the relatively low power of our generalizations regarding the schizophrenias.

LEARNING

The number of studies of learning has been on the increase in recent years. In part, this reflects the interest of psychologists in so-called behavior modification or behavior therapy. Also, psychologists have studied learning as part of a strategy in which general principles of psychology are tested for applicability to patients. If the behavior of schizophrenics is acquired, learning is of focal interest. Two principal lines of investigation stem from the work of Rodnick and Garmezy on social censure[407] and from Mednick's theoretical articles in which he presents a learning theory explanation of important aspects of schizophrenic functioning.[333,334]

The amount of research on classical conditioning of schizophrenics is very limited despite interesting findings. (e.g., Ref. 275, 477, 224). Results available suggest that schizophrenics often differ from normals in rate of conditioning but that the nature of the deviation depends on degree of withdrawal and arousal, response and sensory modality, and type of conditioning, e.g., avoidance conditioning, autonomic conditioning, and conditioning of skeletal muscle responses.[224,477] Conditioning of eyelid closure to a puff of air to the eye is a procedure which often yields relatively rapid learning by schizophrenics.[477] Studies of GSR to shock suggest that chronic schizophrenics tend to condition less than normals.[224]

Operant learning or conditioning has been demonstrated repeatedly with schizophrenics (e.g., Ref. 426, 472, 403, 429, 231, 230, 404, 476, 11, 460, 312). The fact that schizophrenics may respond more slowly than normals is not emphasized as much as it probably should be,[52] and among schizophrenics there are large individual differences in responsiveness.[403,53] King, Armitage, and Tilton[259] found that compared with more usual therapy and no therapy, a group of severe schizophrenics given training with an operant-interpersonal training method showed more improvement in verbalization, motivation to leave the ward, and interest in occupational therapy. Their work suggests that secondary gains may accompany sophisticated operant training procedures. Ayllon and Azrin[10] report that a token reward system can be used to improve and sustain adaptive ward behaviors. The learning approach is used in work with autistic children[312,337] with some success.

There are many subtleties to operant principles and procedures, implications of which should be appreciated and explored. For example, elimination of a given response is easier if alternative responses for obtaining the reinforcement are available to the subject.[222]

The ultimate practical utility of operant learning principles as the basis for treatments of schizophrenics is obviously still in doubt but this approach merits further extensive and intensive exploration. In terms of short term, systematic control of behavior there is now no doubt of the effectiveness of operant procedures. Two major doubts regarding the practical effectiveness of training of schizophrenics using the operant learning approach are: a) the extent of generalization of these learned responses outside the treatment situation, and b) the persistence, or lack of persistence, of these responses in the absence of the original reinforcements.

Learning by schizophrenics often seems to proceed best under conditions of punishment of specific, undesired responses as contrasted with reward.[8,462,290,235] Under many conditions, verbal reinforcement of specific responses seems relatively ineffective[91] and this may be especially true of paranoids.[500] The effects of various positive and negative incentives depends upon many variables including the particular incentive, the task, chronicity, age, and personality variables such as dependency.[305,160,317,499,382,347,159,169,479] Furthermore, deviant reactions to various incentive conditions are probably not unique to schizophrenics. For example, schizophrenics and neurotic depressives were found to be very similar in a study by Knopf and Brown.[274] In their discussion, these investigators suggest that if variables such as chronicity, process-reactive, and paranoid-nonparanoid were taken into account, some deviations unique to selected schizophrenics might emerge.

Studies of the transfer and interference phenomena during learning have been stimulated especially by Mednick's[333] theory. For example, if the learning task is designed to produce high degrees of associative inference among elements of the lesson, Mednick's theory predicts that schizophrenics in the early phase of their disorder will have unusual difficulties learning. This prediction rests on the assumption that early schizophrenics are in a state of high drive and thus all responses—correct and incorrect—tend to occur. Several studies support this view,[215,253,472] others are not congruent[115,480,65] and others lend only partial support.[287,481] The peculiarities of association so apparent clinically in the verbalizations of many schizophrenic patients has not yet been explained satisfactorily as a result of laboratory researches.[495]

One study of the persistence of learned responses suggests a line of investigation which could be very instructive. Crumpton[98] found that schizophrenics are more likely than normals to continue learned complex responses when these become ineffective. To the clinical observer, repetitive, perseverative responses are obviously characteristic of schizophrenics, and Crumpton's approach offers an avenue for relevant systematic research.

Various dimensions of schizophrenia, such as paranoid-nonparanoid and reactive-process, seem useful in ordering the variability in learning and performance.[236,569] Learning studies have not yet yielded sufficient cumulative confirmations of results to justify any general substantive conclusions. Sufficient work has been done to show that many schizophrenics are responsive in learning studies. Theories of schizophrenic functioning may often be tested in analyses of aspects of learning. Treatment procedures of at least limited usefulness have been derived from the learning approach. Conditionability, the role of reactive inhibition, atypical stimulus generalization effects, and the consequences of various types of reinforcement—positive, negative, social, nonsocial, specific, and general—are topics deserving further investigations.

PERSONALITY PROCESSES

In the present context we are primarily interested in personality variables and processes of a substantive nature, with relatively little focus upon the methodological issues, which may be touched upon only in passing.

The discrepancy between the perceived self and ideal-self has been considered as an index of maladjustment. Two studies seem to counter this formulation. In one study, a "global apperception technique" rather than the Q-sort, has been utilized[409] with paranoid schizophrenics who were compared with hospital aides. The patients showed *less* self vs. ideal-self discrepancy than the controls. Failure to bring about the reduction of a self vs. ideal-self discrepancy by means of group psychotherapy and "intensive occupational therapy" has also been reported.[433] These results may not be as fatal to self theory as it may appear at first, for the first study employed a new and untried method of dubious validity, and the second, a method of therapy which may not be very insight-producing after a period of "10 weeks." On the other hand, one investigator[351] employing a self-image scale reports that, unlike normal controls, schizophrenics differ significantly, and show a dichotomous departure, from the central trend of the control group. The schizophrenics showed extreme self enhancement and self depreciation. Another study[203] also reports "unrealistic self enhancement" in a group of paranoid schizophrenics. A structured setting rather than a permissive one is reported to bring about enhancement in the "self value" of chronic schizophrenics.[439] It is not clear, however, whether this enhancement is realistic or not. A study of self satisfaction by means of the semantic differential (self, ideal, and least liked self) indicates that women patients who show high self satisfaction also have great discrepancy between level of aspiration and level of actual performance.[246] With respect to level of aspiration, it is reported that chronic female patients show little effect of censure upon level of aspiration or performance; however, the opportunity to set one's level of aspiration, and especially when combined with praise, tend to result in significant improvement of patients' performance.[537] The authors conclude that the opportunity to express and respect one's own estimate was the most important factor in improvement of performance. Another level of aspiration study shows some interesting relationships to social desirability and mental health status.[352] Social desirability correlates positively with performance, and the discrepancy between level of aspiration and performance is positive for the high mental health groups and negative for the low one.

Some hypotheses, relating to the etiology of schizophrenia and stemming from psychoanalytic theory, have been subjected to examination. Orality and narcissism have been found to be of more focal concern for process as compared with reactive schizophrenics.[140,354] Heterosexual fantasy, however, was greater in the reactives. These results were interpreted as being consonant with the psychoanalytic view of schizophrenic psychogenesis. Another point is the similarity between normal controls and reactives, whereas process patients differ from both groups in the aforementioned aspects of psychosexual development. A related finding involves an important degree of impairment in the abstracting ability of schizophrenics when dealing with oral proverbs as compared with anal and phallic ones.[297] On the other hand, investigators who employed "sketches representing Freudian psychosexual stages" with schizophrenics and controls[484] conclude that: "intensity of conflict rather than qualitative differences" may be the basis for the development of schizophrenia. The issue of sexual identification concerned some workers[140,535] who detect sex role confusion and inconsistency by means of different methods. Disturbances in the body-image[570,532] and the "fluidity of ego boundaries"[570] have been demonstrated in schizophrenics by a variety of projective and experimental methods. One investigator[417] argues that the absence of higher frequency of incidence of schizophrenia among twins dictates a rejection of the "confusion of ego identity" hypothesis.

A complex experimental design was employed in an attempt to assess the conformity behavior of schizophrenics.[85] The behavior was to conform to that of a negative (cold, domineering) maternal figure. "Nondrug poor premorbid" schizophrenics were more conforming than those treated with drugs, alcoholics, and normals. In a study using the "body-sway" method as a measure of suggestibility,[100] paranoids showed more sway than nonparanoids. The predictive value of suggestibility tests with respect to improvement is, however, in doubt.[543] The results concerning the verbal-behavior discrepancy in schizophrenia[94] appear to be consonant with the results on suggestibility, for the S's accepted questionnaire statements which did not conform to their actual attitudes and behavior. Role-taking ability of schizophrenics, however, is inferior to that of drug addicts.[111]

Two aspects, fantasy and motor activity, were studied by means of a variety of tests administered to schizophrenics of Irish and Italian descent.[569] The Irish subjects were characterized by more imaginative behavior and motor control as compared with the Italian schizophrenics. Relationships between these differences and subcultural child rearing patterns were discerned.

A scale for the measure of motivation did not distinguish between hospitalized patients and those on leave; both groups exhibiting a "passive" orientation.[191] In another, experimental, situation process patients showed higher motivation for viewing pictures of conflict while the reactives, seen as more defensive, tend to avoid them.[398] Paranoid schizophrenics do not seem to differ consistently with respect to their "need-attitudes."[68] Of course, defensive behavior of which schizophrenics are also capable, and the specific content of methods readily open to awareness may be important factors in the apparent similarity between groups within schizophrenia and between patients and normals, with respect to needs and motivations. One study[197] comparing improved chronic schizophrenics did achieve a relationship between positive mental health and "an orientation toward self actualization, achievement, responsibility, and goal-directed effort." Deviation of moral judgment in schizophrenics and its relation to "sociopsychological position" is reported in another study.[238]

Finally, mention should be made of several studies which report interest patterns of schizophrenics. Kuder Preference Record findings indicate that schizophrenics are lower than the norms in mechanical, scientific and computational scores and higher on social service and literary scores.[268] These results were generally confirmed; an additional finding is that sex differences, with respect to vocational preference, that obtain with normals are also found in the schizophrenics.[269] With another test, the Strong, schizophrenics are comparable to normals on the overall range of scores and evidence a relatively stable interest pattern.[133] They also show greater interest in skilled labor and business details while controls are more interested in "selling and linguistic occupations." The relationship obtained between motoric and ideational activity preference and time perspective[487] may have some relevance for the interest patterns just discussed.

INTERPERSONAL RELATIONSHIPS

This section has points of contact with the one that precedes it (personality) and the one that follows it (familial relationships). It will be concerned primarily with social aspects not directly involving, or based in, the familial context.

The classical description of the withdrawn schizophrenic who is impervious to his social surroundings[151] is readily dispelled by some research findings of recent vintage.[414] The evidence points to the effects of social reinforcement (encouragement or praise) upon the performance of schizophrenics in various motor tasks.[357,99] However, schizophrenics respond with enhanced performance to negative conditions as well as do normals whose performance is not enhanced by positive comment. Other experiments indicate that the schizophrenics do not differ from normals with respect to the effects of social pressure upon their performance in a group judgment situation.[542] Moreover, more regressed patients are reported to be more responsive to the social environment, but such responses do not conform "to either physical or social reality."[446] Conformity in group situations is found to interact with a "mental health" and an "affect" factor.[156] Also, "conformity and affect were more closely related to the factor of mental health than they were to each other." In more naturalistic hospital settings, patients are reported to improve while working under supervision and even more, with additional social incentiveness.[551] Less supervision of patients who worked at policing a dormitory brought about some group cohesiveness, lessened dependency on staff and some indications of increased job performance, despite the continuing avoidance of verbal communication.[294] Variations in role differentiation and status of schizophrenics via participation in a "patient council" were carefully assessed,[416] as was group membership in relation to status.[266] The significance of the socioeconomic factor in relation to the other variables was also considered. A factor analytic study of behavioral observations of a large number of patients[265] offers the major conclusion that "the mere rate of social interaction is not associated with 'health' or 'adjustment' by clinical criteria." This finding is consonant with the one mentioned above[446] that the greater responsivity of regressed patients to the social environment is out of step with reality. Additional results from several studies indicate the schizophrenics perform more rapidly on a nonverbal task in the presence of their peers (social facilitation)[293] and that regressed patients participate more effectively in problem-solving situations when placed in heterogeneous groups (including more active and less withdrawn patients) than when working in homogeneous groups.[483] The degree of verbal communication, however, does not seem to be affected by personal contact.[136] This finding yields some indirect corroboration in a comparative study of schizophrenic children and nonschizophrenic controls.[210] Good premorbid social and interpersonal relationship is related to rapid recovery.

Studies of affiliation among schizophrenics are most relevant to the foregoing discussion. It is not surprising that a heterogeneous group of patients indicates greater reluctance to social exposure than normals.[443] It is interesting to note that this reluctance is more characteristic of males than females. Data from an experimental situation as well as from staff ratings of affiliation were factor analysed and yielded a general Health Factor which was loaded on social functioning and positive social attitudes.[445] Further confirmation of data on birth order was obtained in that S's from the first half of the family were more sociable.

Finally, schizophrenics more poorly sort pictures showing people (perceptual defense) than neutral stimuli.[43] They are also found to be inferior in judging facial expressions on pictures in a forced choice test.[507]

It would appear, therefore, from the above, that schizophrenics are motivated in social situations, especially when nonverbal tasks are involved. Mere rate of social interaction does not seem, however, to be related to mental health, while conformity does. Yet, there is a greater reluctance to get involved in social situations and a greater tendency to withdraw from, and misperceive or misinterpret social stimuli. Thus, despite the reluctance with respect to social involvement and participation, when patients are exposed to such circumstances they are motivated by them and to some extent alter their behavior in accordance with the social demands or suggestions.

FAMILY ATTITUDES AND RELATIONSHIPS

Familial background of schizophrenics and, especially, the concept of the "schizophrenogenic mother" have received considerable searching attention by quite a number of investigators. This trend was accelerated by the introduction of the Parental Attitude Research Instrument (PARI). However, studies have, by no means, been confined to the employment of this questionnaire, but utilized case history materials, interviews and direct observation as well. Nor has the focus investigation been limited to the mothers of patients, but fathers and other family members and relatives have also received some consideration.

One group of investigators using the PARI compared the responses of mothers of schizophrenics with those of mothers of normals.[571] Of the 23 comparisons only one yielded a significant difference between the two groups of mothers. Another study[223] reports significant differences on two out of 19 comparisons (pathogenic scales only) between mothers of normal and schizophrenic females. Factor A (authoritarian control) showed differences in the expected direction (higher for mothers of schizophrenics than normal controls). Nencini's[349] results are similarly positive. That the negative responses of mothers are not related to the presence of schizophrenic pathology alone was pointed out by Heilbrun.[209] He highlighted the effects of social class membership since higher social class mothers of schizophrenics tended to be more authoritarian in their attitudes than higher social class mothers of normal controls. Moreover, the relationships were reversed in lower social class mothers.

The same investigator also employed the PARI in a different way, by having schizophrenic daughters answer the questionnaire the way they think their mothers would.[207,208] Compared with normal controls, the schizophrenic patients perceived their mothers as more authoritarian on most of the scales that comprise the "control" factor (Factor A). These results are interesting in view of the fact that the responses of the mothers of both groups on the PARI did not differ significantly.

An attempt was made to relate the PARI responses of mothers of schizophrenics to symptom factors in the patients.[184] The results, however, are not clear-cut or conclusive. Direct observation of interaction between mothers and their schizophrenic sons and the use of the F-scale (authoritarianism) yielded some congruent results.[119] The observations "supported the view that the mothers would be domineering and smothering, but also demanding of achievement." The F-scale yielded considerable similarity between the responses of mothers and sons, but differed markedly from controls in the authoritarian direction. The similarity between mothers and sons is interpreted by the authors to be related to dependence-independence conflict.

A variety of other questionnaires have been employed in the study of mothers and fathers of schizophrenics. A factor analysis of a 100 item instrument, concerned with attitudes toward children and family life and administered to mothers of 20 male schizophrenics, yielded *several* "schizophrenogenic patterns of motherhood."[459] Still another study comparing mothers of schizophrenics, neurotics and normals yields the conclusion that mothers of schizophrenics are overly controlling and "seem to fear sex."[328] Using a method similar to the one described above[207,208] patients were asked to reflect upon the time they were 13 or 14 and respond to a 75-item child rearing scale as they thought would reflect the attitudes of their parents at that time.[152] Parents were perceived as dominating, not overprotective or rejecting. The poor premorbid patients "reveal maternal dominance, whereas 'goods' ascribe heightened paternal dominance in their responses." These results are consistent with three other studies.[19,171,153]

An extensive study of the personal histories of schizophrenics and physically ill patients reports to have failed to confirm the hypothesis concerning the schizophrenogenic mother.[441] The authors call into question the "notion that any single circumstance, deprivation or trauma contributes uniformly and inevitably to the etiology of schizophrenia." Instead, "the patterning of life experiences" is suggested as an alternative. This may be consonant with such paradigms involving the somatically inadequate child evoking certain attitudes versus the deviant family's relationship to the healthy child,[162] both being important in the genesis of schizophrenic disorder. The single background trait inadequacy as an explanatory principle is also illustrated in the negative findings of overprotectiveness as a pathogenic factor in schizophrenia.[148] These doubts concerning overprotectiveness are echoed in still another study[327] based on interviews with mothers of 20 schizophrenics who were compared with normals and neurotics.

More recent studies show a shift of interest from the study of single parents to that of investigation of both parents and the familial interaction process.[302] The general hostile atmosphere in the home of the potential schizophrenic which blocks identification with either parent, rather than maternal dominance and paternal passivity, is emphasized in a study employing questionnaires and analyses of intrafamilial interaction.[62] These results are in direct contrast with the case study reports presented in an earlier study.[300] The findings regarding the dominant hostility pattern are also inconsistent with other findings[518] which emphasize the "extended symbiotic union between a parent and the preschizophrenic child."

Several reports are especially concerned with the different constellations of familial influences and their impingement upon male and female schizophrenics. An interview study involving parents of two groups, of male and female schizophrenics[16] reports comparable "amounts" of intrafamilial conflict in both. However, more interparental conflict was found in the families of the males whereas "a greater degree of participation in conflictual behavior" was noted in the females. Consistent with this finding is the greater activity of females in family interaction.[83] A group of other investigators[143] found that schizophrenic males tended to come from families where the fathers were "disturbed and ineffectual" and the mothers "engulfing." The females, however, were subjected to a "paranoid, seductive father and a cold mother." Wolman[554,555] presents a different conceptualization regarding the parents of schizophrenics. Based on case history data of 101 schizophrenics, hospitalized and ambulatory, he concludes that "each parent expected the other parent to be his parent"; moreover, the "parents turned children" expected the child to satisfy their emotional needs, thus casting him in an adult role which he, naturally, is incapable of fulfilling.

That social class membership can be a complicating factor in the study of familial background and attitudes is clearly illustrated by Lane and Singer.[284] Consideration of this issue is also incorporated in the complex design involving a comparison of the families of schizophrenic and well children.[20] In the latter study Beck isolated "source traits" by means of which "environments" may be defined. This greater complexity in defining familial antecedents is necessary in order to make some sense of the numerous conflicting results.

Still another dimension is introduced by considering differences within the schizophrenic category itself. Thus we are informed that fathers are more dominant in good premorbid schizophrenia, whereas mothers are more dominant in the poor premorbid cases.[126,128] Indirect confirmation of these findings comes from the report that the thematic responses of good premorbids who produce more anxiety-related imagery to the father while the poor premorbids show the same tendency with respect to the mother.[17] It was also found that parents of poor premorbids produce a "greater amount of immature defensive behavior" as compared with parents of good premorbids.[18] Further pathological behavior in parents of schizophrenics is reported. Thus letters of mothers of schizophrenics show incongruent communication consonant with the double bind hypothesis;[522] contradictory expectations along the dependence-responsibility dimensions are found;[313] schizophrenic pathology in the families;[410] varying degrees of congruence in attitudes between parents and their schizophrenic children;[278] maintenance of stereotyped roles in the family;[423] and great perplexity of mothers in view of the absence of neurologic pathology[338] are also reported. Therapeutic outcome seems to be unrelated to family pathology,[440] but appears to relate with father's greater involvement with the family.[84]

Some aspects regarding patients and their spouses have also been reported. Fewer unrecovered patients tend to be married.[129] The husbands of schizophrenic women display the same pattern of attitudes towards their wives which characterized their prehospitalization interaction[299] and relatives of schizophrenics, other than their mothers and husbands, have been judged to possess more "resourcefulness" in relation to the patients.[109]

Finally, the birth order of schizophrenics has also been investigated. Some studies find no such relationship[56,182] while others find that more patients were born in the "last half than in the first half of the birth order"[127] or indicate that a significantly higher rate of female schizophrenics are found among the last-born than first-born.[442] Social class factors complicate these relationships.[444]

In sum, it may be stated that a good many reports concerning the familial antecedents of schizophrenia contradict each other. It appears that concentration upon the future schizophrenic's interaction with one or, even, both parents without taking the entire family constellation into account, omits significant factors in the psychogenic process.[301] Moreover, as we indicated on a previous occasion,[391] retrospective reports regarding such interactions are suspect. The same applies to contemporaneous attitudinal assessments via questionnaires such as the PARI for, aside from the social desirability aspect to which such instruments are vulnerable, there is no guarantee that the child rearing attitudes currently elicited were dominant during the schizophrenic's childhood. The factors of the sex of the patient, premorbid picture and social class status are being recognized and contribute to marked improvement and greater sophistication in research design. It is also necessary to compare the family context of schizophrenics with that of other psychotics, not only neurotics or normals. Beginnings of such efforts are in evidence.[155]

METHODOLOGIES

In addition to the great variety of experimental and empirical procedures employed to study schizophrenic phenomena, a number of studies in which the method is most salient may be summarized in the present section. The MMPI employed with schizophrenics is reported to differentiate between "good social adjustment and severe behavioral disturbance." Females tend to admit pathology more readily than males who are prone to deny it.[120,181] The Sc score was found to relate to "life adjustment" estimates based on structured interviews,[217] and the Pa scale tends to identify some paranoids, but misses others who "attempted to deny their symptoms."[267] Data on a special MMPI scale considered to differentiate between schizophrenics and others with similar symptoms were also reported.[198] Rapid improvement of female schizophrenics was readily reflected in performance on the Rorschach, but not on the MMPI.[34] Three Rorschach scores, mainly color indices, are reported to be indicative of schizophrenia.[534] This finding is somewhat at variance with those of a factor-analytic study of Rorschach scores.[490] A series of reports by Piotrowski and his co-workers[378,375,376,377] produce evidence of the efficacy of a special index in the prognosis of schizophrenia. A prognostic Rorschach indicator of treatment failure is also reported.[344] Additional data concerning prediction of post-hospital adjustment by means of the Rorschach are reported in still another study.[244] By means of special Rorschach indices it was found that good and poor premorbid subjects operate at "levels closer to primary process" than normals, whereas good premorbids show similar levels of ego strength to those of normals. Both differ in this respect from poor premorbids.[573] Genetic level ratings based on Holtzman's inkblots correlate significantly with the Elgin Prognostic Scale[486] and a combination of the Rorschach and Howard tests is recommended for "difficult diagnostic cases."[450] Parallel findings between life history variables and Rorschach indices of pathology were also demonstrated.[249] A miscellany of other technics, such as the Hand test in differentiating aggressive from nonaggressive schizophrenics,[516] fingerpainting[304] and the Bender Gestalt[12] which differentiates normals from schizophrenics has been employed. Also, the Object Relations Test differentiates between hospitalized and outpatient schizophrenics and neurotics.[358] The Proverbs test has some value in differentiating borderline schizophrenics from other diagnostic groups[41] and from normals, but is not so effective with patients of high intelligence.[172]

A most comprehensive and well-documented treatment of differential diagnosis in schizophrenia is presented in Weiner's[534-a] recent volume. The author gives extensive consideration to the logic of testing by means of a battery consisting of the Rorschach, Draw-a-Person and the Wechsler Adult Intelligence Scale and relates test variables to personality constructs and behavior within an ego psychology theoretical framework. He marshals considerable empirical evidence and case study material to buttress his orientation and demonstrates convincingly the effectiveness of the tests in the diagnosis of schizophrenia. His demonstration and incisive analysis of the diagnostic process do much to restore confidence in this type of endeavor which has been dubiously regarded by many who prematurely draw conclusions from partial data in a number of research investigations.

Employing a "forced choice word association" technique, Gottesman[175] confirmed his prediction that schizophrenics will choose children's rather than adult responses; these findings are consonant with those reported in another study.[340] A composite index based on the Kent Rosanoff Free Association test which differentiates schizophrenics from normals is proposed by Shakow and Jellinek.[455] Estimation of social alienation and personal disorganization was attempted by using 3 minute speech samples[178] and of pathology, from 2 minute interview samples.[90] Activity patterns[81] and ward behavior[228] are the object of two other measuring devices.

A very high relationship between Elgin and Phillips ratings of process-reactive schizophrenia is reported[474] and a self-report measure of the same continuum has also been devised.[506] In addition, mention of the study of early memories of schizophrenics,[288] mental disorganization (based on a factor analysis of symptomatology) as the primary process in schizophrenia, and special technics for the study of motivation[191] and the selection of "drug free" schizophrenics,[76] rounds out the present section.

MISCELLANEOUS REPORTS

There is a large number of studies and theoretical essays which are not readily classifiable under the rubrics considered above. Yet they deserve some treatment in the context of this review.

Several physiological indices of dreaming were employed with a small group of schizophrenics in the waking state.[397] The patterning did not resemble results obtained during REM periods with normals. White sound is a noxious stimulus to schizophrenics as to normals. They respond to it physiologically but fail to respond to conditioning.[380] Under prolonged sleep deprivation schizophrenics manifest progressive deterioration and the acute psychotic symptoms similar to those present upon admission.[276] On the Nufferno speed test, patients whose illness was of longer duration were slower as were those who had physical treatment, but the ones with a favorable outcome were faster.[199] Prognostic studies indicated that demographic variables[321] and some behavior variables[321] are among the best predictors of outcome. Although premorbid social and sexual adjustment are only slightly related to patients' ability to stay out of the hospital on a trial visit, they seem to be more predictive of later adjustment (4 to 10 years) outside a hospital.[131] Men are reported to have gained a clearer insight than women upon release from the hospital to a rehabilitation program.[48] Factor analyses of nurses' ratings of ward behavior of 417 acute schizophrenics yield a constellation of factors similar to those reported by Lorr et al.[308]

The popularity of the reactive-process dichotomy,[23,154,213,214,247,248,95,218] which is still considered to hold great promise and heuristic value, has stimulated considerable focus on antecedent factors in the development of schizophrenia. Several retrospective studies involving the life histories of schizophrenics point to poor academic success,[38,386] greater stress[387] and anxiety,[38] and, generally, poorer adjustment than that of siblings[38] and co-twins[387] rather early in life. These are consonant with Fleck's[142] detailed psychodynamic analysis of the family settings. Beck[21] stresses the adaptive aspects of schizophrenic behavior from an ego-psychological viewpoint, while White[539] emphasizes the cumulative anxiety and inhibition of action resulting from frequent failure and low self esteem ultimately traceable to constitutional defect. The latter point is made more boldly in the speculation that schizophrenia is "fundamentally a neurological disease of genetic origin."[335] Shakow's[453] notion of the schizophrenic's inability to maintain major sets is probably related to White's theorizing mentioned above.

Concern with sociocultural aspects is reflected in a comparative study of Negro and white patients,[106] the former showing fewer symptoms due to under-recording by the therapist. Related problems of communication with patients from minority and bilingual groups and their effects on chronicity have also been reported.[54] Subcultural differences tend to insinuate themselves in rating scales of premorbid adjustment.[77] This is consonant with differences in premorbid competence of middle and working-class patients.[395]

A number of sundry studies on schizophrenic verbalization,[108,138,243,406] semantic generalization[369] and responses to verbal stimuli[240,524,567] should be mentioned. Finally, the surprising finding of *less* variability in performance of schizophrenics, on a task of drawing big and little objects,[496] was also reported.

OVERVIEW

Space does not permit a summary of all the findings detailed in the several sections of the review. It is our purpose, in these closing paragraphs, to note the general research and theoretical trends in the psychological studies of schizophrenia.

First, there is an increasing trend to pursue longitudinal research. Some of the alleged effects of schizophrenia upon intellectual functioning may, at least in part, be attributed to lower premorbid intelligence. It is hoped that similar approaches to the study of other functions such as perception, cognition, and others, will be exploited. In these areas wide individual differences within the schizophrenic group remain, and the differentiation from normal and other pathological groups is far from clear-cut.

Second, there is an upsurge in the investigation of antecedent conditions in the etiology of schizophrenia. Developmental (mostly retrospective) studies of earlier adjustment, intrafamilial relationships, and social class variables have been scrutinized in numerous reports. Clearly related to these issues is, of course, the reactive-process dichotomy or continuum.

Third, although there is a clearer definition of the experimental schizophrenic samples employed, too many studies still use the generic designation of schizophrenia without further qualification.

Fourth, more analytic approaches in the various experimental designs are in evidence and greater attention is being paid to such concomitant and complicating factors as, the interpersonal elements in the experimental situation, aspects of attention, social reinforcement, etc.

Fifth, recognition of the schizophrenic's responsiveness to environmental and social demands is growing, but the relationship of these phenomena to clinical status and prognosis require further delineation.

Sixth, the phenomenology regarding the self in schizophrenia is not simple nor does it permit clear differentiation from normals and other groups. The evidence of bimodal trends in the self versus ideal-self discrepancy demand utmost caution in drawing conclusions based upon group comparisons. The situation with respect to other personality variables is not dissimilar.

Previously, psychologists have done research on schizophrenia primarily within the context of psychiatric and psychodynamic theories. Recently, a significant amount of psychological research on schizophrenia reflects theories developed primarily within general psychology. Meehl[335] takes a biosocial position in his proposal that schizotaxia is a neurological state of genetic origin which is potentiated into clinical schizophrenia by certain interpersonal circumstances. Buss and Lang[58,286] conclude that a fundamental sensorimotor deficit is a critical factor in schizophrenia. The orientation of developmental psychology is represented in papers by Goldman[167] and Feffer.[132] Shakow[453,454] presents an eclectic, research based summary of important trends in inductive theory building.

Schizophrenic adaptations, according to Mednick[333] result primarily from anxiety which gives rise to a three-stage pattern as the patient attempts to cope with this problem. Initially, the patient experiences intense anxiety which operates to broaden the gradient of stimulus generalization. Anxiety attaches to more and more stimuli by generalization in a spiraling sequence such that the most intense level of anxiety is reached. Then, as the range of stimuli increases, there is an increasing probability that some of these stimuli will evoke previously learned responses which reduce anxiety. These responses are strongly reinforced by the reduction of severe anxiety. Thus, seemingly irrelevant responses and irrelevant thoughts become more and more characteristic of the patient. The final, chronic stage is reached when very frequent irrelevant thoughts and actions stabilize a low level of anxiety. The key idea in this formulation is that learning of seemingly nonadaptive, and bizarre responses is very likely if relevant anxiety reducing responses are absent in the repertoire of the individual. Learning to cope with anxiety emerges as a preventive measure. The importance of early treatment of an anxiety crisis is obvious, given Mednick's formulation.

McReynolds[329,332] has developed a conceptualization of anxiety in schizophrenia which emphasizes the process of assimilation of new information into the existing cognitive structure. New events are pleasurable provided the rate of input is neither too slow or too fast. An excessive rate of input, extreme novelty, uncertainty about future inputs, and percepts, which are incongruent relative to the prior system of interpretation and beliefs, are sources of anxiety. Schizophrenic withdrawal is a means to reduce stimulation and may result in functional sensory deprivation. The paranoid seems to attempt to assimilate all stimuli and to achieve maximum congruence of information from the external world and the belief system. Thus, McReynolds has contributed a theory which assumes that anxiety results from perceptual and cognitive processes.

Working within the personal construct theory of Kelly,[256] Bannister[13,14,15] proposes that the schizophrenic's language and thought disorder results from successive invalidations of his notions about reality, including himself. In the extreme, a highly capricious and inconsistent environment produces a fractionated, vague, unrealistic, and idiosyncratic conceptual schema characterized by loose and inconsistent constructs. This, in Bannister's view, is reflected in ineffective performance on tasks requiring a set of consensually valid concepts.

Venables[508] puts forward the hypothesis that chronic schizophrenics are in a state of extremely high arousal. Consequently, these patients seem unresponsive and in one sense they are because their level of arousal is not subject to significant modification. High arousal is offered as the explanation of a wide range of performance deficits which derive from narrowed attention. Venables exemplifies the great recent interest in attention in psychology and in psychological research on schizophrenia. To what extent and under what conditions and due to what processes are schizophrenic symptoms the result of unusually broad or unusually narrow or selective attention?

Broen and Storms[47,45,46,44] offer an ingenious hypothesis based in behavior theory without rejecting such dynamic hypotheses as the concept of anxiety reducing defensive behavior. These authors focus primarily on thinking and conceptual disorders, delusions, hallucinations, and regression. They recognize that arousal or stimulation activates a response system or response hierarchy, not just a single response. So long as arousal or drive is low or moderate, the several response tendencies within the system or hierarchy vary in strength or probability of occurrence. But, assuming there is a "response strength ceiling," if arousal is intense, the several response tendencies become equally strong. Thus, behavior becomes disorganized in the sense that the most adaptive response is no longer the dominant response. The key assumption in this formulation is that of the "response strength ceiling." Empirical validation of this hypothesis is very tentative but the approach has the appeal of organizing a large amount of data. Research based on this point of view will be of much interest. Of course, there are a very large number of theoretical contributions in research reports cited in this review. The examples mentioned here, are intended to show something of the nature of the trends in recent psychological theory. In many respects these trends are closely related to earlier theoretical views but these recent developments are characterized by a higher degree of precision and explicitness which promotes research more concerned with processes and conditions which may result in schizophrenic behavior.

BIBLIOGRAPHY

1. Abrams, S.: The effects of motivation upon the intellectual performance of schizophrenic patients. Amer. J. Clin. Hypnos. 8: 37-43, 1965.

2. Adams, H. E.: Statistical rigidity in schizophrenic and normal groups measured with auditory and visual stimuli. Psychol. Rep. 7: 119-122, 1960.

3. Albee, G. W., Lane, E. A., Corcoran, C., and Werneke, A.: Childhood and intercurrent intellectual performance of adult schizophrenics. J. Consult Psychol. 27: 364-366, 1963.

4. Alson, E.: Psychological correlates of capillary morphology in schizophrenia. Amer. J. Psychiat. 122: 444-446, 1965.

5. Apperson, L. B., and McAdoo, W. G., Jr.: Paternal reactions in childhood as described by schizophrenics and alcoholics. J. Clin. Psychol. 21: 369-373, 1965.

6. Arey, L. B.: The indirect representation of sexual stimuli by schizophrenic and normal subjects. J. Abnorm. Soc. Psychol. 61: 424-431, 1960.

7. Astrup, C.: Klinisch-experimentelle Untersuchungen bei verschiedenen Formen von Schizophrenie. (Clinical and experimental investigations of the different forms of schizophrenia.) Psychiat. Neurol. Med. Psychol., Leipzig, 10: 355-356, 1958.

8. Atkinson, R. L., and Robinson, N. M.: Paired-associate learning by schizophrenic and normal subjects under conditions of personal and impersonal reward and punishment. J. Abnorm. Soc. Psychol. 62: 322-326, 1961.

9. Ayllon, T.: Intensive treatment of psychotic behavior by stimulus satiation and food reinforcement. Behav. Res. Ther. 1: 53-61, 1963.

10. Ayllon, T., and Azrin, N. H.: The measurement and reinforcement of behavior of psychotics. J. Exp. Anal. Behav. 8: 357-383, 1965.

11. Ayllon, T., and Haughton, E.: Control of the behavior of schizophrenic patients by food. J. Exp. Anal. Behav. 5: 343-352, 1962.

12. Bambaren, V. C.: La prueba de la "Gestalt" de Bender, en esquizofrenicos. (The Bender Gestalt Test among schizophrenics.) Rev. Psicol. Gen. Apl., Madrid. 13: 481-509, 1958.

13. Bannister, D.: Conceptual structure in thought-disordered schizophrenics. J. Ment. Sci. 106: 1230-1249, 1960.

14. Bannister, D.: The nature and measurement of schizophrenic thought disorder. J. Ment. Sci. 108: 825-842, 1962.

15. Bannister, D.: The genesis of schizophrenic thought disorder: A serial invalidation hypothesis. Brit. J. Psychiat. 109: 680-686, 1963.

16. Baxter, J. C., Arthur, S., Flood, C. G., and Hedgepeth, B.: Conflict patterns in the families of schizophrenics. J. Nerv. Ment. Dis. 135: 419-424, 1962.

17. Baxter, J. C., and Becker, J.: Anxiety and avoidance behavior in schizophrenics in response to parental figures. J. Abnorm. Soc. Psychol. 64: 432-437, 1962.

18. Baxter, J. C., Becker, J., and Hooks, W.: Defensive style in the families of schizophrenics and controls. J. Abnorm. Soc. Psychol. 66: 512-518, 1963.

19. Baxter, J. C., Williams, J., and Zerof, S.: Child-rearing attitudes and discipline fantasies of parents of schizophrenics and controls. J. Nerv. Ment. Dis. 141: 567-579, 1966.

20. Beck, S. J.: Families of schizophrenic and of well children: Method, concepts and some results. Amer. J. Orthopsychiat. 30: 247-275, 1960.

21. Beck, S. J.: Psychological processes in the schizophrenic adaptation. New York: Grune & Stratton, 1965.

22. Becker, W. C.: A genetic approach to the interpretation and evaluation of the process-reactive distinction in schizophrenia. J. Abnorm. Soc. Psychol. 53: 229-236, 1956.

23. Becker, W. C.: The process-reactive distinction: A key to the problem of schizophrenia? J. Nerv. Ment. Dis. 129: 442-449, 1959.

24. Becket, P. G. S., Senf, R., Frohman, C. E., and Gottlieb, J. S.: Energy production and premorbid history in schizophrenia. Arch. Gen. Psychiat. 8: 155-162, 1963.

25. Bender, L., and Hitchman, I. L.: A longitudinal study of ninety schizophrenic women. J. Nerv. Ment. Dis. 124: 337-345, 1956.

26. Bennett, D. H.: The body concept. J. Ment. Sci. 106: 56-75, 1960.

27. Bennett, S., and Klein, H. R.: Childhood schizophrenia: Thirty years later. Amer. J. Psychiat. 122: 1121-1124, 1966.

28. Benton, A. L., Jentsch, R. C., and Wahler, H. J.: Simple and choice reaction times in schizophrenia. AMA Arch. Neurol. Psychiat. 81: 373-376, 1959.

29. Benton, A. L., Jentsch, R. C., and Wahler, H. J.: Effects of motivating instructions on reaction time in schizophrenia. J. Nerv. Ment. Dis. 130: 26-29, 1960.

30. Berger, A.: A test of the double-bind hypothesis of schizophrenia. Fam. Proc. 4: 198-205, 1965.

31. Berkowitz, H.: Effects of prior experimenter-subject relationships on reinforced reaction time of schizophrenics and normals. J. Abnorm. Soc. Psychol. 69: 522-530, 1964.

32. Billingberg, O., and Jonsson, C.: The ability of schizophrenic patients to interpret intonation. Acta Psychiatrica Scandinavia. 41: 218-226, 1965.

33. Birch, H. G., and Walker, H. A.: Perceptual and perceptual motor dissociation: Studies in schizophrenic and brain-damaged psychotic children. Arch. Gen. Psychiat. 14: 113-118, 1966.

34. Bloom, B. L., and Arkoff, A.: Role playing in acute and chronic schizophrenia. J. Consult. Psychol. 25: 24-28, 1961.

35. Blumenthal, R., Meltzoff, J., and Rosenberg, S.: Some determinants of persistence in chronic schizophrenic subjects. J. Abnorm. Psychol. 70: 246-250, 1965.

36. Boardman, W. K., Goldstone, S., Reiner, M. L., and Fathauer, W. F.: Anchor effects, spacial judgments, and schizophrenia. J. Abnorm. Soc. Psychol. 65: 273-276, 1962.

37. Boardman, W. K., Goldstone, S., Reiner, M. L., and Himmel, S.: Constancy of absolute judgments of size by normals and schizophrenics. J. Abnorm. Soc. Psychol. 68: 346-349, 1964.

38. Bower, E. M., Shellhamer, T. A., and Daily, J. M.: School characteristics of male adolescents who later became schizophrenic. Amer. J. Orthopsychiat. 30: 712-729, 1960.

39. Bowers, M.: The onset of psychosis: A diary account. Psychiatry. 28: 346-358, 1965.

40. Bratemo, C. E.: Changes in interpretation of proverbs in schizophrenic patients. Acta Psychol., Amsterdam. 20: 269-278, 1962.

41. Bratemo, C. E.: Differentiating borderline schizophrenics from other diagnostic groups by use of the proverbs test. Acta Psychol. 20: 279-284, 1962.

42. Bratemo, C. E: Interpretations of proverbs in schizophrenic patients: Further studies. Acta. Psychol., Amsterdam. 20: 254-263, 1962.

43. Brodsky, M.: Interpersonal stimuli as interference in a sorting task. J. Pers. 31: 517-533, 1963.

44. Broen, W. E., Jr.: Response disorganization and breadth of observation in schizophrenia. Psychol. Rev. 73: 579-585, 1966.

45. Broen, W. E., Jr., and Storms, L. H.: The differential effect of induced muscular tension (drive) on discrimination in schizophrenics and normals. J. Abnorm. Soc. Psychol. 68: 349-353, 1964.

46. Broen, W. E., Jr., and Storms, L. H.: Lawful disorganization: The process underlying a schizophrenic syndrome. Psychol. Rev. 73: 265-279, 1966.

47. Broen, W. E., Jr., Storms, L. H., and Goldberg, D. H.: Decreased discrimination as a function of increased drive. J. Abnorm. Soc. Psychol. 67: 266-273, 1963.

48. Brooks, G. W., and Deane, W. N.: Attitudes of released chronic schizophrenic patients concerning illness and recovery as revealed by a structured posthospital interview. J. Clin. Psychol. 16: 259-264, 1960.

49. Bruch, H., and Palombo, S.: Conceptual problems in schizophrenia. J. Nerv. Ment. Dis. 132: 114-117, 1961.

50. Bruch, H.: Psychotherapy with schizophrenics. Arch. Gen. Psychiat. 14: 346-351, 1966.

51. Buck, L., and Kates, S. L.: Perceptual categorizations of love and anger cues in schizophrenics. J. Abnorm Soc. Psychol. 67: 480-490, 1963.

52. Bullock, D. H.: Performances of psychiatric patients in a brief operant discrimination test. Psychol. Rec. 10: 83-93, 1960.

53. Bullock, D. H., and Brunt, M. Y., Jr.: The testability of psychiatric patients in an operant conditioning situation. Psychol. Rec. 9: 165-170, 1959.

54. Burke, J. L., Lafave, H. G., and Kurtz, G. E.: Minority group membership as a factor in chronicity. Psychiatry. 28: 235-238, 1965.

55. Burstein, A. G.: Some verbal aspects of primary process thought in schizophrenia. J. Abnorm Soc. Psychol. 62: 155-157, 1961.

56. Burton, A., and Bird, J.: Family constellation and schizophrenia. J. Psychol. 55: 329-336, 1963.

57. Buss, A. H., and Lang, P. J. Psychological deficit in schizophrenia: I. Affect, reinforcement, and concept attainment. J. Abnorm. Psychol. 70: 2-24, 1965.

58. Callaway, E.: The influence of amobarbitol (amylobarbitone) and metamphetamine on the focus of attention. J. Ment. Sci. 105: 382-392, 1959.

59. Callaway, E., and Dembo, D.: Narrowed attention. Arch. Neurol. Psychiat. 79: 74-90, 1958.

60. Callaway, E., and Thompson, S.: Sympathetic activity and perception: An approach to the relationship between autonomic activity and personality, Psychosom. Med. 15: 443-455, 1953.

61. Cameron, N., and Margaret, A.: Behavior pathology. Boston: Houghton Mifflin, 1951.

62. Caputo, D. V.: The parents of the schizophrenic. Fam. Proc. 2: 339-356, 1963.

63. Cardon, P. V., Sokoloff, L., Vates, T., and Kety, S. S.: The physiological and psychological effects of intravenously administered epinephrine and its metabolism in normal and schizophrenic men. J. Psychol. Res. 1: 37-49, 1961.

64. Carroll, F. M., Rivoire, J. L., Gallagher, P. J., and MacDorman, C. F.: Size constancy of adolescent schizophrenics. J. Abnorm. Soc. Psychol. 69: 258-263, 1964.

65. Carson, R. C.: Intralist similarity and verbal rote learning performance of schizophrenic and cortically damaged patients. J. Abnorm. Soc. Psychol. 57: 99-106, 1958.

66. Cavanaugh, D. K.: Improvement in the performance of schizophrenics on concept formation tasks as a function of motivational change. J. Abnorm. Soc. Psychol. 57: 8-12, 1958.

67. Cavanaugh, D. K., Cohen, W., and Lang, P. J.: The effect of "social censure" and "social approval" on the psychomotor performance of schizophrenics. J. Abnorm. Soc. Psychol. 60: 213-218, 1960.

68. Chambers, J. L., and Broussard, L. J.: Need-attitudes of normal and paranoid schizophrenic males. J. Clin. Psychol. 16: 233-237, 1960.

69. Chapman, J.: The early symptoms of schizophrenia. Brit. J. Psychiat. 112: 225-251, 1966.

70. Chapman, J., and McGhie, A.: A comparative study of disordered attention in schizophrenia. J. Ment. Sci. 108: 487-500, 1962.

71. Chapman, L. J.: Distractibility in the conceptual performance of schizophrenics. J. Abnorm. Soc. Psychol. 53: 286-291, 1956.

72. Chapman, L. J.: The role of type of distracter in the "concrete" conceptual performance of schizophrenics. J. Pers. 25: 130-141, 1956.

73. Chapman, L. J.: Intrusion of associative responses into schizophrenic conceptual performance. J. Abnorm. Soc. Psychol. 56: 374-379, 1958.

74. Chapman, L. J.: Confusion of figurative and literal usages of words by schizophrenics and brain damaged patients. J. Abnorm. Soc. Psychol. 60: 412-416, 1960.

75. Chapman, L. J.: A reinterpretation of some pathological disturbances in conceptual breadth. J. Abnorm. Soc. Psychol. 62: 514-519, 1961.

76. Chapman, L. J.: The problem of selecting drug-free schizophrenics for research. J. Consult. Psychol. 27: 540-542, 1963.

77. Chapman, L. J., and Baxter, J. C.: The process-reactive distinction and patients' subculture. J. Nerv. Ment. Dis. 136: 352-359, 1963.

78. Chapman, L. J., Burstein, A. G., Day, Dorothy, and Verdone, P.: Regression and disorders of thought. J. Abnorm. Soc. Psychol. 63: 540-545, 1961.

79. Chapman, L. J., Day, D., and Burstein, A.: The process-reactive distinction and prognosis in schizophrenia. J. Nerv. Ment. Dis. 133: 383-391, 1961.

80. Chapman, L. J., and Taylor, J. A.: Breadth of deviate concepts used by schizophrenics. J. Abnorm. Soc. Psychol. 54: 118-123, 1957.

81. Chapple, E. D., Chamberlain, A., Esser, A. H., and Kline, N. S.: The measurement of activity patterns of schizophrenic patients. J. Nerv. Ment. Dis. 137: 258-267, 1963.

82. Chatterjee, T. K.: Study of the personality of parents of schizophrenics. Council Soc. Psychol. Res. Bull., Calcutta. 2: 1961.

83. Cheek, F. E.: A serendipitous finding: Sex roles and schizophrenia. J. Abnorm. Soc. Psychol. 69: 392-400, 1964.

84. Cheek, F. E.: The father of the schizophrenic: The function of a peripheral role. Arch. Gen. Psychiat. 13: 336-345, 1965.

85. Clarke, A. R.: Conformity behavior of schizophrenic subjects with maternal figures. J. Abnorm. Soc. Psychol. 68: 45-53, 1964.

86. Clement, D. E.: Note on visual perception in schizophrenic patients. Percept. Mot. Skills. 21: 385-386, 1965.

87. Cleveland, S. E.: Judgments of body size in a schizophrenic and a control group. Psychol. Rep. 7: 304, 1960.

88. Cleveland, S. E., Fisher, S., Reitman, E. E., and Rothaus, P.: Perception of body size in schizophrenia. Arch. Gen. Psychiat. 7: 277-285, 1962.

89. Cobrinik, L., and Popper, L.: Developmental aspects of thought disturbance in schizophrenic children: A Rorschach study. Amer. J. Orthopsychiat. 31: 170-180, 1961.

90. Cohen, A. J.: Estimating the degree

of schizophrenic pathology from recorded interview samples. J. Clin. Psychol. 17: 403-406, 1961.

91. Cohen, E., and Cohen, B. D.: Verbal reinforcement in schizophrenia. J. Abnorm. Soc. Psychol. 60: 443-446, 1960.

92. Cooper, R.: Objective measures of perception in schizophrenics and normals. J. Consult. Psychol. 24: 209-214, 1960.

93. Cowden, R. C.: Problem-solving in schizophrenics as a function of motivation. Psychol. Rep. 10: 627-633, 1962.

94. Cowden, R. C., Reynolds, D. J., and Ford, L. I.: The verbal behavior discrepancy in schizophrenia. J. Clin. Psychol. 17: 406-408, 1961.

95. Coyle, F. A., Jr., and Coyle, G. F.: An operant explanation of the process-reactive differentiation. J. Psychol. 61: 39-45, 1965.

96. Cromwell, R. L., Rosenthal, D., Shakow, D., and Zahn, T. P.: Reaction time, locus of control, choice behavior, and descriptions of parental behavior in schizophrenic and normal subjects. J. Pers. 29: 363-379, 1961.

97. Crookes, T. G.: Size constancy and literalness in the Rorschach test. Brit. J. Med. Psychol. 30: 99-106, 1957.

98. Crumpton, E.: Persistence of maladaptive responses in schizophrenia. J. Abnorm. Soc. Psychol. 66: 615-618, 1963.

99. D'Alessio, G. R., and Spence, J. T.: Schizophrenic deficit and its relation to social motivation. J. Abnorm. Soc. Psychol. 66: 390-393, 1963.

100. Das, J. P., and O'Connor, N.: Body-sway suggestibility in paranoid and nonparanoid schizophrenics. Int. J. Clin. Exp. Hypnosis. 7: 121-128, 1959.

101. Davids, A.: Intelligence in childhood schizophrenics, other emotionally disturbed children, and their mothers. J. Consult. Psychol. 22: 159-163, 1958.

102. Davis, D. R., and Cullen, J. H.: Disorganization of perception in neurotics and psychotics. Amer. J. Psychol. 71: 229-237, 1958.

103. Davis, E. B.: Schizo-affective disease and periodic schizophreniform psychoses and their relation to schizophrenia. Acta Psychiatrica Scandinavica. 41: 313-327, 1965.

104. Davis, R. H., and Harrington, R. W.: The effect of stimulus class on the problem-solving behavior of schizophrenics and normals. J. Abnorm Soc. Psychol. 54: 126-128, 1957.

105. Deering, G.: Affective stimuli and disturbance of thought processes. J. Consult. Psychol. 27: 338-343, 1963.

106. de Hoyos, A., and de Koyos, G.: Symptomatology differentials between Negro and White schizophrenics. Int. J. Soc. Psychiat. 11: 245-255, 1965.

107. De Luca, J. N.: Cognitive task performance in schizophrenia as a function of premorbid history, evaluation, and set to improve. Dissertation Abstr. 24: 3834-3835, 1964.

108. DeWolfe, A. S.: The effect of affective tone on the verbal behavior of process and reactive schizophrenics. J. Abnorm. Soc. Psychol. 64: 450-455, 1962.

109. Deykin, E. Y., Klerman, G. L., and Armor, D. J.: The relatives of schizophrenic patients: Clinical judgments of potential emotional resourcefulness. Amer. J. Orthopsychiat. 36: 518-528, 1966.

110. Diamond, D.: The ability of schizophrenics to modify responses in an interpersonal situation. J. Consult. Psychol. 20: 441-444, 1956.

111. Diamond, M. D.: Role-taking ability and schizophrenia. J. Clin. Psychol. 14: 321-324, 1958.

112. Diggory, J. C., and Loeb, A.: Motivation of chronic schizophrenics by information about their abilities in a group situation. J. Abnorm. Soc. Psychol. 65: 48-52, 1962.

113. Docter, R. F.: Test-retest performance of schizophrenics on two forms of the Porteus Mazes. J. Clin. Psychol. 16: 185-187, 1960.

114. Dokecki, P. R., Polidoro, L. G., and Cromwell, R. L.: Commonality and stability of word association responses in good and poor premorbid schizophrenics. J. Abnorm. Psychol. 70: 312-316, 1965.

115. Donahoe, J. W., Curtin, M. E., and Lipton, L.: Interference effects with schizophrenic subjects in the acquisition and re-

tention of verbal material. J. Abnorm. Soc. Psychol. 62: 553-558, 1961.

116. Donovan, M. J., and Webb, W. W.: Meaning dimensions and male-female voice perception in schizophrenics with good and poor premorbid adjustment. J. Abnorm. Psychol. 70: 426-431, 1965.

117. Downing, R. W., Ebert, J. N., and Shubrooks, S. J.: Effects of three types of verbal distractors on thinking in acute schizophrenia. Percept Mot. Skills. 17: 881-882, 1963.

118. Draguns, J. G.: Responses to cognitive and perceptual ambiguity in chronic and acute schizophrenics. J. Abnorm. Soc. Psychol. 66: 24-30, 1963.

119. Dworin, J., and Wyant, O.: Authoritarian patterns in the mothers of schizophrenics. J. Clin. Psychol. 13: 332-338, 1957.

120. Eichman, W. J.: Discrimination of female schizophrenics with configural analysis of the MMPI profile. J. Consult. Psychol. 23: 442-447, 1959.

121. Eisenman, R.: Usefulness of the concepts of inferiority feeling and life style with schizophrenics. J. Indiv. Psychol. 21: 171-173, 1965.

122. Eliseo, T. S.: Figurative and literal misinterpretations of words by process and reactive schizophrenics. Psychol. Rep. 13: 871-877, 1963.

123. Eliseo, T. S.: Overinclusive thinking in process and reactive schizophrenics. J. Consult. Psychol. 27: 447-449, 1963.

124. Fagan, J., and Guthrie, G. M.: Perception of self and normality in schizophrenics. J. Clin. Psychol. 15: 203-207, 1959.

125. Faibish, G. M.: Schizophrenic response to words of multiple meaning. J. Pers. 29: 414-427, 1961.

126. Farina, A.: Patterns of role dominance and conflict in parents of schizophrenic patients. J. Abnorm. Soc. Psychol. 61: 31-38, 1960.

127. Farina, A., Barry, H. III, and Garmezy, N.: Birth order of recovered and nonrecovered schizophrenics. Arch. Gen. Psychiat. 9: 224-228, 1963.

128. Farina, A., and Dunham, R. M.: Measurement of family relationships and their effects. Arch. Gen. Psychiat. 9: 64-73, 1963.

129. Farina, A., Garmezy, N., and Barry, H. III.: Relationship of marital status to incidence and prognosis of schizophrenia. J. Abnorm. Soc. Psychol. 67: 624-630, 1963.

130. Farina, A., Garmezy, N., Zalusky, M., and Becker, J.: Premorbid behavior and prognosis in female schizophrenic patients. J. Consult. Psychol. 26: 56-60, 1962.

131. Farina, A., and Webb, W. W.: Premorbid adjustment and subsequent discharge. J. Nerv. Ment. Dis. 124: 612-613, 1956.

132. Feffer, M.: Symptom expression as a form of primitive decentering. Psychol. Rev. 74: 16-28, 1967.

133. Fein, A., Lipton, L., and Elton, C. F.: Comparison of Strong Vocational Interest patterns of schizophrenics and normals. Psychol. Rep. 13: 887-894, 1963.

134. Feinberg, I., and Garman, E. M.: Studies of thought disorder in schizophrenia: II. Plausible and implausible errors on a modification of the progressive matrices tests. Arch. Gen. Psychiat. 4: 191-201, 1961.

135. Feinberg, I., and Mercer, M.: Studies of thought disorder in schizophrenia. AMA Arch. Gen. Psychiat. 2: 504-511, 1960.

136. Feldstein, S.: The relationship of interpersonal involvement and affectiveness of content to the verbal communication of schizophrenic patients. J. Abnorm. Soc. Psychol. 64: 39-45, 1962.

137. Feldstein, S., and Jaffe, J.: Vocabulary diversity of schizophrenics. and normals. J. Speech Hear. Res. 5: 76-68, 1962.

138. Feldstein, S., and Jaffe, J.: Schizophrenic speech fluency: A partial replication and a hypothesis. Psychol. Rep. 13: 775-780, 1963.

139. Fenn, J. D., and Goss, A. E.: The role of mediating verbal responses in the conceptual sorting behavior of normals and paranoid schizophrenics. J. Genet. Psychol. 90: 59-67, 1957.

140. Figetakis, N.: Process-reactive schizophrenia, ego-strength and selected psychosexual dimensions. Unpublished

doctoral dissertation, Michigan State University, 1963.

141. Fine, H. J., and Zimet, C. N.: Process-reactive schizophrenia and genetic levels of perception. J. Abnorm. Soc. Psychol. 59: 83-85, 1959.

142. Fleck, S.: Family dynamics and origin of schizophrenia. Psychosom. Med. 22: 333-344, 1960.

143. Fleck, S., Lidz, T., and Cornelison, A.: Comparison of parent-child relationship of male and female schizophrenic patients. Arch. Gen. Psychiat. 8: 1-7, 1963.

144. Foulds, G. A., and Dixon, P.: The nature of intellectual deficit in schizophrenia and neurotics: I. A comparison of schizophrenia and neurotics. Brit. J. Soc. Clin. Psychol. 1: 7-19, 1962.

145. Foulds, G. A., and Dixon, P. The nature of intellectual deficit in schizophrenia: III. A longitudinal study of the sub-groups. Brit. J. Soc. Clin. Psychol. 1: 199-207, 1962.

146. Foulds, G. A., Dixon, P., McClellang, M., and McClelland, W. J. The nature of intellectual deficit in schizophrenia: II. A cross-sectional study of paranoid, catatonic, hebephrenic and simple schizophrenics: Brit. J. Soc. Clin. Psychol. 1: 141-149, 1962.

147. Fox, R. Rate of binocular rivalry alternation in psychotic and nonpsychotic patients. J. Abnorm. Psychol. 70: 34-37, 1965.

148. Freeman, H. E., Simmons, O. G., and Bergen, B. J. Possessiveness as a characteristic of mothers of schizophrenics. J. Abnorm. Soc. Psychol. 58: 271-273, 1959.

149. Friedman, G. Conceptual thinking in schizophrenic children. Genet. Psychol. Monogr. 63: 149-196, 1961.

150. Friedman, H. The structural aspects of schizophrenic responses to auditory stimuli. J. Genet. Psychol. 89: 221-230, 1956.

151. Gard, J. G. Interpersonal orientations in clinical groups. J. Abnorm. Soc. Psychol. 69: 516-521, 1964.

152. Garmezy, N., Clarke, A. R., and Stockner, C. Child-rearing attitudes of mothers and fathers as reported by schizophrenic and normal patients. J. Abnorm. Soc. Psychol. 63: 176-182, 1961.

153. Garmezy, N., Farina, A., and Rodnick, E. H. Direct study of child-parent interactions: I. The structured situational test. A method for studying family interaction in schizophrenia. Amer. J. Orthopsychiat. 30: 445-452, 1960.

154. Garmezy, N., and Rodnick, E. H. Premorbid adjustment and performance in schizophrenia: Implications for interpreting heterogeneity in schizophrenia. J. Nerv. Ment. Dis. 129: 450-466, 1959.

155. Gibson, R. W. The family background and early life experience of the manic-depressive patient: A comparison with the schizophrenic patient. Psychiatry. 21: 71-90, 1958.

156. Gill, W. S. Interpersonal affect and conformity behavior in schizophrenics. J. Abnorm. Soc. Psychol. 67: 502-505, 1963.

157. Gillis, L. S., and Keet, M. Factors underlying the retention in the community of chronic unhospitalized schizophrenics. Brit. J. Psychiat. 111: 1057-1067, 1965.

158. Ginett, L. E., and Moran, L. J. Stability of vocabulary performance by schizophrenics. J. Consult. Psychol. 28: 178-179, 1964.

159. Gladis, M. Age differences in repeated learning tasks in schizophrenic subjects. J. Abnorm. Soc. Psychol. 68: 437-441, 1964.

160. Gladis, M., and Wischner, G. J. Schizophrenic and normal response patterns to "aversive" and "neutral" associations in two paired-associate paradigms. J. Abnorm. Soc. Psychol. 64: 249-256, 1962.

161. Goldfarb, W. Pain reactions in a group of institutionalized schizophrenic children. Amer. J. Orthopsychiat. 28: 777-785. 1958.

162. Goldfarb, W. The mutual impact of mother and child in childhood schizophrenia. Amer. J. Orthopsychiat. 31: 738-747, 1961.

163. Goldfarb, W., and Goldfarb, N. Evaluation of behavioral changes of schizophrenic children in residential treatment. Amer. J. Psychother. 19: 185-204, 1965.

164. Goldfarb, W., Goldfarb, N., and

Pollack, R. C. Treatment of childhood schizophrenia: A three year comparison of day and residential treatment. Arch. Gen. Psychiat. 14: 119-128, 1966.

165. Goldfarb, W., and Mintz, I. Schizophrenic child's reactions to time and space. Arch. Gen. Psychiat. 5: 535-543, 1961.

166. Goldman, A. E. Symbolic representation in schizophrenia. J. Pers. 28: 293-316, 1960.

167. Goldman, A. E. A comparative-developmental approach to schizophrenia. Psychol. Bull. 59: 57-69, 1962.

168. Goldman, A. E. Symbol consensus and univocality in schizophrenia. J. Proj. Tech. 26: 288-294, 1962.

169. Goldman, A. R. Differential effects of social reward and punishment on dependent and dependency-anxious schizophrenics. J. Abnorm. Psychol. 70: 412-418, 1965.

170. Goldstein, R. H., and Salzman, L. F. Proverb word counts as a measure of overinclusiveness in delusional schizophrenics. J. Abnorm. Psychol. 70: 244-245, 1965.

171. Goodman, D. Performance of good and poor premorbid male schizophrenics as a function of paternal versus maternal censure. J. Abnorm. Soc. Psychol. 69: 550-555, 1964.

172. Gorham, D. R. Use of the Proverbs Test for differentiating schizophrenics from normals. J. Consult. Psychol. 20: 435-440, 1956.

173. Goodstein, L. D. Right-left discrimination and finger localization in schizophrenic subjects. Proc. Iowa Acad. Sci. 64: 504-507, 1957.

174. Goodstein, L. D., Guertin, W. H., and Blackburn, H. L. Effects of social motivational variables on choice reaction time of schizophrenics. J. Abnorm. Soc. Psychol. 62: 24-27, 1961.

175. Gottesman, L. E. Forced-choice word associations in schizophrenia. J. Abnorm. Soc. Psychol. 69: 673-675, 1964.

176. Gottesman, L., and Chapman, L. J. Syllogistic reasoning errors in schizophrenia. J. Consult. Psychol. 24: 250-255, 1960.

177. Gottschalk, L. A., and Gleser, G. C. Distinguishing characteristics of the verbal communications of schizophrenic patients. Disord. Commun. 42: 400-413, 1964.

178. Gottschalk, L. A., Gleser, G. C., Daniels, R. S., and Block, S. L. The speech patterns of schizophrenic patients: A method of assessing relative degree of personal disorganization and social alienation. Psychiat. Res. Rep. 10: 141-158, 1958.

179. Gottschalk, L. A., Gleser, G. C., Magliocco, E. B., and D'Zmura, T. L. Further studies on the speech patterns of schizophrenic patients. J. Nerv. Ment. Dis. 132: 101-113, 1961.

180. Griffith, R. M., Ester, B. W., and Zerof, S. A. Intellectual impairment in schizophrenia. J. Consult. Psychol. 26: 336-339, 1962.

181. Gross, L. R. MMPI, L-F-K relationships with criteria of behavioral disturbance and social adjustment in a schizophrenic population. J. Consult. Psychol. 23: 319-323, 1959.

182. Grosz, H. J., and Miller, I. Sibling patterns in schizophrenia. Science. 128: 30, 1958.

183. Guertin, W. H. Medical and statistical-psychological models for research in schizophrenia. Behav. Sci. 6: 200-204, 1961.

184. Guertin, W. H. Are differences in schizophrenic symptoms related to the mother's avowed attitudes toward child rearing? J. Abnorm. Soc. Psychol. 63: 440-442, 1961.

185. Guertin, W. H., Ladd, C. E., Frank, G. E., Rabin, A. I., and Hiester, D. S. Research with the Wechsler Intelligence Scales for adults: 1960-1965. Psychol. Bull. 66: 385-409, 1966.

186. Guertin, W. H., and Rabin, A. I. Misperception of time in schizophrenia. Psychol. Rep. 7: 57-58, 1960.

187. Guertin, W. H., Rabin, A. I., Frank, G. H., and Ladd, C. E. Research with the Wechsler Intelligence Scales for adults: 1955-1960, Psychol. Bull. 59: 1-26, 1962.

188. Guller, I. B. Stability of self-concept in schizophrenia. J. Abnorm. Psychol. 71: 275-279, 1966.

189. Gurel, L. Release and community stay in chronic schizophrenia. Amer. J. Psychiat. 122: 892-899, 1966.

190. Guthrie, D. M. Role structure in schizophrenic and normal adult males. Dissertation Abstr. 26: 493, 1965.

191. Haas, W. A. Motivation in schizophrenic patients. Psychol. Rep. 12: 199-802, 1963.

192. Hall, G. C. Conceptual attainment in schizophrenics and nonpsychotics as a function of task structure. J. Psychol. 53: 3-13, 1962.

193. Hamilton, V. I.Q. changes in chronic schizophrenia. Brit. J. Psychiat. 109: 642-648, 1963.

194. Hamilton, V. Size constancy and cue responsiveness in psychosis. Brit. J. Med. Psychol. 54: 25-29, 1963.

195. Hamlin, R. M., Haywood, H. C., and Folsom, A. T. Effect of enriched input on schizophrenic abstraction. J. Abnorm. Psychol. 70: 390-394, 1965.

196. Hamlin, R. M., and Jones, R. E. Vocabulary deficit in improved and unimproved schizophrenic subjects. J. Nerv. Ment. Dis. 136: 360-364, 1963.

197. Hamlin, R. M., and Nemo, R. S. Self actualization in choice scores of improved schizophrenics. J. Clin. Psychol. 18: 51-54, 1962.

198. Harding, G. F. Holz, W. C., and Kawakami, D. The differentiation of schizophrenic and superficially similar reactions. J. Clin. Psychol. 14: 147-149, 1958.

199. Harris, A., and Metcalfe, M. Slowness in schizophrenia. J. Neurol. Neurosurg. Psychiat. 22: 239-242, 1959.

200. Harris, J. G., Jr. Size estimation of pictures as a function of thematic content for schizophrenic and normal subjects. J. Pers. 25: 651-671, 1957.

201. Hartman, A. M. The apparent size of after-images in delusional and nondelusional schizophrenics. Amer. J. Psychol. 75: 587-595, 1962.

202. Harway, N. I., and Salzman, L. F. Size constancy in psychopathology. J. Abnorm. Soc. Psychol. 69: 606-612. 1964.

203. Havener, P. H., and Izard, C. E. Unrealistic self-enhancement in paranoid schizophrenics. J. Consult. Psychol. 26: 65-68, 1962.

204. Haywood, H. C., and Moelis, I. Effect of symptom change of intellectual function in schizophrenia. J. Abnorm. Soc. Psychol. 67: 76-78, 1963.

205. Heath, D. H. Individual anxiety thresholds and their effect on intellectual performance. J. Abnorm. Soc. Psychol. 52: 403-408, 1956.

206. Heath, H. A. Measurement of the inadequacy in schizophrenic patients for making difficult discriminative evaluations. AMA Arch. Neurol. Psychiat. 79: 675-680, 1958.

207. Heilbrun, A. B., Jr. Perceptual distortion and schizophrenia. Amer. J. Orthopsychiat. 30: 412-418, 1960.

208. Heilbrun, A. B., Jr. Perception of maternal child rearing attitudes in schizophrenics. J. Consult. Psychol. 24: 169-173, 1960.

209. Heilbrun, A. B., Jr. Maternal authoritarianism, social class, and filial schizophrenia. J. Gen. Psychol. 65: 235-241, 1961.

210. Hermelin, B., and O'Connor, N. The response and self-generated behavior of severely disturbed children and severely subnormal controls. Brit. J. Soc. Clin. Psychol. 2: 37-43, 1963.

211. Herner, T. Significance of the body image in schizophrenic thinking. Amer. J. Psychother. 19: 455-466, 1965.

212. Herron, W. G. Abstract ability in the process-reactive classification of schizophrenia. J. Gen. Psychol. 67: 147-154, 1962.

213. Herron, W. G. The process-reactive classification of schizophrenia. Psychol. Bull. 59: 329-343, 1962.

214. Higgins, J. The concept of process-reactive schizophrenia. Criteria and related research. J. Nerv. Ment. Dis. 138: 9-25, 1964.

215. Higgins, J., and Mednick, S. A. Reminiscence and stage of illness in schizophrenia. J. Abnorm. Soc. Psychol. 66: 314-317, 1963.

216. Higgins, J., Mednick, S. A., and Philip, F. J. Associative disturbance as a

function of chronicity in schizophrenia. J. Abnorm. Psychol. 70: 451-452, 1965.

217. Higgins, J., Mednick, S. A., and Philip F. J. The schizophrenia scale of the MMPI and life adjustment in schizophrenia. Psychology 2: 26-27, 1965.

218. Higgins, J., and Peterson, J. C. Concept of process-reactive schizophrenia: A critique. Psychol. Bull. 66: 201-206, 1966.

219. Hoberman, S. ,and Goldfarb, W. Speech reception thresholds in schizophrenic children. J. Speech Hear. Res. 6: 101-105, 1963.

220. Hobbs, G. E., Wanklin, J. M., Buck, C., and Egener, K. M. The prepsychotic characteristics of schizophrenic patients: A comparison with a nonpsychotic sibling of the same sex. Canad. Psychiat. Ass. J. 11: 140-145, 1966.

221. Holtzman, W. H., Gorham, D. R., and Moran, L. J. A factor-analytic study of schizophrenic thought processes. J. Abnorm. Soc. Psychol. 69: 355-364, 1964.

222. Holz, W. C., Azrin, N. H., and Ayllon, T. Elimination of behavior of mental patients by response-produced extinction. J. Exp. Aanal. Behav. 6: 407-412, 1963.

223. Horowitz, F. D., and Lovell, L. L. Attitudes of mothers of female schizophrenics. Child Develpm. 31: 299-305, 1960.

224. Howe, E. S. GSR conditioning in anxiety states, normals, and chronic functional schizophrenic subjects. J. Abnorm. Soc. Psychol. 56: 183-189, 1958.

225. Hozier, A. On the breakdown of the sense of reality: A study of spatial perception in schizophrenia. J. Consult. Psychol. 23: 185-194, 1959.

226. Hunt, W. A., and Arnhoff, F. The repeat reliability of clinical judgment of test responses. J. Clin. Psychol. 12: 289-290, 1965.

227. Hunt, W. A., and Jones N. F. Clinical judgments of some aspects of schizophrenic thinking. J. Clin. Psychol. 14: 235-239, 1958.

228. Hunter, M., Schooler, C., and Spohn, H. E. The measurement of characteristic patterns of ward behavior in chronic schizophrenics. J. Consult. Psychol. 26: 69-73, 1962.

229. Huston, P. E., Shakow, D., and Riggs, L. A. Studies of motor function in schizophrenia: II. Reaction time. J. Gen. Psychol. 16: 39-82, 1937.

230. Hutchinson, R. R., and Azrin, N. H. Conditioning of mental hospital patients to fixed-ratio schedules of reinforcement. J. Exp. Anal. Behav. 4: 87-95, 1961.

231. Isaacs, W., Thomas J., and Goldiamond, I. Application of operant conditioning to reinstate verbal behavior in psychotics. J. Speech Hear. Dis. 25: 8-12, 1960.

232. Izard, C. E. Paranoid schizophrenic and normal subjects' perceptions of photographs of human faces. J. Consult. Psychol. 23: 119-124, 1959.

233. Jentsch, R. C. Reaction time in schizophrenia as a function of method of presentation and length of preparatory interval. J. Pers. 26: 545-555, 1958.

234. Johannsen, W. J. Responsiveness of chronic schizophrenics and normals to social and nonsocial feedback. J. Abnorm. Psychol. 62: 106-113, 1961.

235. Johannsen, W. J. Effect of reward and punishment on motor learning by chronic schizophrenics and normals. J. Clin. Psychol. 18: 204-207, 1962.

236. Johannsen, W. J., Friedman, S. H., Leitschuh, T. H., and Ammons, H. A study of certain schizophrenic dimensions and their relationship to double alternation learning. J. Consult. Psychol. 27: 375-382, 1963.

237. Johannsen, W. J., and O'Connell, M. J. Institutionalization and perceptual decrement in chronic schizophrenia. Percept. Mot. Skills 21: 244-246, 1965.

238. Johnson, D. L. The moral judgment of schizophrenics. J. Nerv. Ment. Dis. 130: 278-285, 1960.

239. Johnson, R. E. Imaginative sensitivity in schizophrenia. Rev. Existent. Psychol. Psychiat. 4: 255-264, 1964.

240. Johnson, R. C., Weiss, R. L., and Zelhart, P. F. Similarities and differences between normal and psychotic subjects in responses to verbal stimuli. J. Abnorm. Soc. Psychol. 68: 221-226, 1964.

241. Johnson, R. L., and Miller, M. D. Auditory hallucinations and intellectual deficit. J. Psychiat. Res. 3: 37-41, 1965.

242. Jones, N. F. The validity of clinical judgment of schizophrenic pathology based upon verbal responses to intelligence test items. J. Clin. Psychol. 15: 396-400, 1959.

243. Jones, R. A. Some effects of emotion on the use of words by schizophrenics. Washington, D. C.: Catholic Univ. America Press, 39, 1957.

244. Kaden, S. E., and Lipton, H. Rorschach developmental scores and post-hospital adjustment of married male schizophrenics. J. Proj. Tech. 24: 144-147, 1960.

245. Kahn, E. Self-pity. Amer. J. Psychiat. 122: 447-451, 1965.

246. Kamano, D. K. Self-satisfaction and psychological adjustment in schizophrenics. J. Consult. Psychol. 25: 492-496, 1961.

247. Kantor, R. E., and Herron, W. G. Reactive and process schizophrenia. Palo Alto, Calif.: Science and Behavior Books, Inc., 1966.

248. Kantor, R. E., and Winder, C. L. The process-reactive continuum: A theoretical proposal. J. Nerv. Ment. Dis. 129: 429-434, 1959.

249. Kantor, R. E., and Winder, C. L. Schizophrenia: Correlates of life history. J. Nerv. Ment. Dis. 132: 221-226, 1961.

250. Karras, A. The effects of reinforcement and arousal on the psychomotor performance of chronic schizophrenics. J. Abnorm. Soc. Psychol. 65: 104-111, 1962.

251. Kates, W. W., and Kates, S. L. Conceptual behavior in psychotic and normal adolescents. J. Abnorm. Soc. Psychol. 69: 659-663, 1964.

252. Kaufman, I., Fran, T., Neims, L., Herick, J., Reiser, D., and Willer, L. Treatment implications of a new classification of parents of schizophrenic children. Amer. J. Psychiat. 116: 920-924, 1960.

253. Kausler, D. H., Lair, C. V., and Matsumoto, R. Interference transfer paradigms and the performance of schizophrenics and controls. J. Abnorm. Soc. Psychol. 69: 584-587, 1964.

254. Kavkewitz, H. The psycho-eco-

nomic evaluation of schizophrenic rehabilitants in a vocational training program. Psychiat. Quart. 39: 702-721, 1965.

255. Keehn, J. D. Repeated testing of four chronic schizophrenics on the Bender-Gestalt and Wechsler Block Design tests. J. Clin. Psychol. 13: 179-182, 1957.

256. Kelly, G. A. The psychology of personal constructs. Vol. I-II. New York: Norton, 1955.

257. Kidd, A. H. The effect of stimulus color and content upon schizophrenics. J. Psychol. 56: 29-41, 1963.

258. Kidd, A. J. Monocular distance perception in schizophrenics. J. Abnorm. Soc. Psychol. 68: 100-103, 1964.

259. King, G. F. Armitage, S. G., and Tilton, J. R. A therapeutic approach to schizophrenics of extreme pathology: An operant-interpersonal method. J. Abnorm. Soc. Psychol. 61: 276-286, 1960.

260. King, H. E. Some explorations in psychomotility. Psychiat. Res. Rep. 14: 62-90, 1961.

261. King, H. E. Anticipatory behavior: Temporal matching by normal and psychotic subjects. J. Psychol. 53: 425-440, 1962.

262. King, H. E. Reaction-time as a function of stimulus intensity among normal and psychotic subjects. J. Psychol. 54: 299-307, 1962.

263. King, H. E. Two-flash and flicker fusion thresholds for normal and schizophrenic subjects. Percept. Mot. Skills, 14: 517-518, 1962.

264. Kissel, S. Schizophrenic patterns on the WISC: A missing control. J. Clin. Psychol. 22: 201, 1966.

265. Klein, E. B., and Spohn, H. E. Behavioral dimensions of chronic schizophrenia. Psychol. Rep. 11: 777-783, 1962.

266. Kleiner, R. J., and Tuckman, J. Multiple group membership and schizophrenia. Behav. Sci. 6: 292-296, 1961.

267. Kleinmuntz, B. Two types of paranoid schizophrenia. J. Clin. Psychol. 16: 310-312, 1960.

268. Klugman, S. F. Comparison of total interest profiles of a psychotic and a normal group. J. Counsel. Psychol. 7: 283-288, 1960.

269. Klugman, S. F. Differential preference patterns between sexes for schizophrenic patients. J. Clin. Psychol. 22: 170-172, 1966.

270. Knapp, R. H., and Ehlinger, L. A. Sex differences among schizophrenics in the interpretation of the human diad. J. Psychol. 56: 473-478, 1963.

271. Knehr, C. A. Psychological assessment of differential impairment in cerebral organic conditions and in schizophrenics. J. Psychol. 54: 165-189, 1962.

272. Knehr, C. A. Thinking impairment in acute schizophrenic illness. J. Psychol. 53: 15-28, 1962.

273. Knehr, C. A., and Brown, N. L. Perseveration in schizophrenic and brain damaged patients. J. Psychol. 43: 269-275, 1957.

274. Knopf, I. J., and Brown, R. A. The effects of social and nonsocial censure on stimulus generalization in neurotics and schizophrenics. J. Consult. Psychol. 30: 315-319, 1966.

275. Kodman, F., Jr. Auditory incompatibility in catatonic schizophrenia. Arch. Gen. Psychiat. 4: 390-394, 1961.

276. Koranyi, E. K., and Lehmann, H. E. Experimental sleep deprivation in schizophrenic patients. Arch. Gen. Psychiat. 2: 534-544, 1960.

277. Kottenhoff, H. Metric determination of schizophrenic dementia. Psychol. Rep. 11: 646, 1962.

278. Krinsky, L. W. Personal beliefs of schizophrenics and their parents. J. Psychol. 53: 387-397, 1962.

279. Kritskaia, V. P. Characteristics of statistical organization in the speech process of schizophrenics. Zhurnal Neuropatologii i Psikhiatrii. 66: 102-109, 1966.

280. Lab, P. Le niveau intellectuel et les schizophrenies: Significations diagnostiques et evolutives. (Intellectual level and the schizophrenias: Diagnostic and evolutive indications.) Encephale. 49: 544-556, 1960.

281. Lane, E. A., and Albee, G. W. Early childhood intellectual differences between schizophrenic adults and their siblings. J. Abnorm. Soc. Psychol. 68: 193-195, 1964.

282. Lane, E. A., and Albee, G. W. Childhood intellectual differences between schizophrenic adults and their siblings. Amer. J. Orthopsychiat. 35: 747-753, 1965.

283. Lane, E. A., and Albee, G. W. Childhood intellectual development of adult schizophrenics. J. Abnorm. Soc. Psychol. 67: 186-189, 1963.

284. Lane, R. C., and Singer, J. L. Familial attitudes in paranoid schizophrenics and normals from two socioeconomic classes. J. Abnorm. Soc. Psychol. 59: 328-339, 1959.

285. Lang, P. J. The effect of aversive stimuli on reaction time in schizophrenia. J. Abnorm. Soc. Psychol. 59: 263-268, 1959.

286. Lang, P. J., and Buss, A. H. Psychological deficit in schizophrenia. II. Interference and activation. J. Abnorm. Psychol. 70: 77-106, 1965.

287. Lang, P. J., and Luoto, K. Mediation and associative facilitation in neurotic, psychotic, and normal subjects. J. Abnorm. Soc. Psychol. 64: 113-120, 1962.

288. Langs, R. J., Rothenberg, M. B., Fishman, J. R., and Reiser, M. F. A method for clinical and theoretical study of the earliest memory. Arch. Gen. Psychiat. 3: 523-534, 1960.

289. Lanzkron, J., and Wolfson, W. Prognostic value of perceptual distortion of temporal orientation in chronic schizophrenics. Amer. J. Psychiat. 114: 744-746, 1958.

290. Laventhal, A. M. The effects of diagnostic category and reinforcer on learning without awareness. J. Abnorm. Soc. Psychol. 59: 162-166, 1959.

291. Lebow, K. E., and Epstein, S. Thematic and cognitive responses of good premorbid schizophrenics to cues of nurturance and rejection. J. Consult. Psychol. 27: 24-33, 1963.

292. Leibowitz, H. W., and Pishkin, V. Perceptual size constancy in chronic schizophrenia. J. Consult. Psychol. 25: 196-199, 1961.

293. Lerner, M. Responsiveness of chronic schizophrenics to the social behavior of others in a meaningful task situ-

ation. J. Abnorm. Soc. Psychol. 67: 295-299, 1963.

294. Lerner, M., and Fairweather, G. W. Social behavior of chronic schizophrenics in supervised and unsupervised work groups. J. Abnorm. Soc. Psychol. 67: 219-225, 1963.

295. Lewinsohn, P. M., and Elwood, D. L. The role of contextual constraint in the learning of language samples in schizophrenia. J. Nerv. Ment. Dis. 133: 79-81, 1961.

296. Lewinsohn, P. M., and Riggs, A. The effect of content upon the thinking of acute and chronic schizophrenics. J. Abnorm. Soc. Psychol. 65: 206-207, 1962.

297. Lewis, J. M., Griffith, E. C., Riedel, A. F., and Simmons, B. A. Studies in abstraction: Schizophrenia and orality: Preliminary results. J. Nerv. Ment. Dis. 129: 564-567, 1959.

298. Lhamon, W. T., and Goldstone, S. The time sense; estimation of one second durations by schizophrenic patients. AMA Arch. Neurol. Psychiat. 76: 625-629, 1956.

299. Lichtenberg, J. D., and Pao, P. The prognostic and therapeutic significance of the husband-wife relationship for hospitalized schizophrenic women. Psychiatry. 23: 209-213, 1960.

300. Lidz, T., Cornelison, A. R., Fleck, S., and Terry D. The intrafamilial environment of the schizophrenic patient: I. The father. Psychiatry. 20: 329-342, 1957.

301. Lidz, T., Cornelison, A., Terry D., and Fleck, S. Intrafamilial environment of the schizophrenic patient: VI. The transmission of irrationality. AMA Arch. Neurol. Psychiat. 79: 305-316, 1958.

302. Lidz, T., Fleck S., Cornelison, A. R., and Terry, D. The intrafamilial environment of the schizophrenic patient: IV. Parental personalities and family interaction. Amer. J. Orthopsychiat. 28: 764-776, 1958.

303. Little, L. Effects of the interpersonal interaction on abstract thinking performance in schizophrenics. J. Consult. Psychol. 30: 158-164, 1966.

304. Long, J. A., and Dellis, N. P. Relationships between the fingerpaintings and

overt behavior of schizophrenics. J. Proj. Tech. 25: 193-198, 1961.

305. Long, R. C. Praise and censure as motivating variables in the motor behavior and learning of schizophrenics. J. Abnorm. Soc. Psychol. 63: 283-288, 1961.

306. Lorenz, M. Problems posed by schizophrenic language. Arch. Gen. Psychiat. 4: 603-610, 1961.

307. Lorenz, M., and Cobb, S. Language patterns in psychotic and psychoneurotic patients. Arch. Neurol. Psychiat. 72: 665-673, 1954.

308. Lorr, M., Klett, C. I., and McNair, D. M. Syndromes of psychosis. New York: The Macmillan Co., 1963.

309. Losen, S. M. The differential effects of censure on the problem-solving behavior of schizophrenic and normal subjects. J. Pers. 29: 258-272, 1961.

310. Lothrop, W. W. Psychological test covariates of conceptual deficit in schizophrenia. J. Consult. Psychol. 24: 496-499, 1960.

311. Lothrop, W. W. A critical review of research on the conceptual thinking of schizophrenics. J. Nerv. Ment. Dis. 132: 118-126, 1961.

312. Lovaas, O. I., Freitag, G., Gold, V. J., and Kassorla, I. C. Experimental studies in childhood schizophrenia: Analysis of self-destructive behavior. J. Exp. Child Psychol. 2: 67-84, 1965.

313. Lu, Y. Contradictory parental expectations in schizophrenia: Dependence and responsibility. Arch. Gen. Psychiat. 6: 219-234, 1962.

314. Lubin, A., Gieseking, C. F., and Williams, H. L. Direct measurement of cognitive deficit in schizophrenia. J. Consult. Psychol. 26: 139-143, 1962.

315. Lydecker, W. A., Piskin, V., and Martin, B. Effects of different feedback conditions on the concept identification of schizophrenics. Psychol. Rep. 9: 557-563, 1961.

316. Lynne, R. Russian theory and research on schizophrenia. Psychol. Bull. 60: 486-498, 1963.

317. MacDonald, W. S., and Sheehan, J. G. Responses of schizophrenics to dif-

ferent incentives. Psychol. Rep. 11: 211-217, 1962.

318. Maher, B. A. Principles of psychopathology. New York: McGraw-Hill Book Co., 1966.

319. Maher, B. A., McKean, K. O., and McLaughlin, B. Studies in psychotic language. In Stone, P. (Ed.), The general inquirer: A computer approach to content analysis. Cambridge, Mass.: M.I.T. Press, 1966.

320. Manasse, G. Self-regard as a function of environmental demands in chronic schizophrenics. J. Abnorm. Psychol. 70: 210-213, 1965.

321. Marks, J. Stauffacher, J. C., and Lyle, C. Predicting outcome in schizophrenia. J. Abnorm. Soc. Psychol. 66: 117-127, 1963.

322. May, A. E. Anxiety and overinclusion. Brit. J. Psychiat. 112: 41-42, 1966.

323. McConaghy, N. The use of an object sorting test in elucidating the hereditary factor in schizophrenia. J. Neurol. Neurosurg. Psychiat. 22: 243-246, 1959.

324. McConaghy, N. The measurement of an inhibitory process in human higher nervous activity: Its relation to allusive thinking and fatigue. Amer. J. Psychiat. 118: 125-132, 1961.

325. McDonough, J. M. Critical flicker frequency and the spiral after-effect with process and reactive schizophrenics. J. Consult. Psychol. 24: 150-155, 1960.

326. McGaughran, L. S., and Moran, L. J. Differences between schizophrenic and brain-damaged groups in conceptual aspects of object sorting. J. Abnorm. Soc. Psychol. 54: 44-49, 1957.

327. McGhie, A. A comparative study of the mother-child relationship in schizophrenia: I. The interview. Brit. J. Med. Psychol. 34: 195-208, 1961.

328. McGhie, A. A comparative study of the mother-child relationship in schizophrenia: II. Psychological testing. Brit. J. Med. Psychol. 34: 209-221, 1961.

329. McReynolds, P. Anxiety, perception, and schizophrenia. In Jackson, D. D. (Ed.), The Etiology of Schizophrenia. New York: Basic Books, 1960.

330. McReynolds, P. Reactions to novel and familiar stimuli as a function of schizophrenic withdrawal. Percept. Mot. Skills. 16: 847-850, 1963.

331. McReynolds, P., and Collins, B. Concept forming behavior in schizophrenic and nonschizophrenic subjects. J. Psychol. 52: 369-378, 1961.

332. McReynolds, P., Collins, B., and Acker, M. Delusional thinking and cognitive organization in schizophrenia. J. Abnorm. Soc. Psychol. 69: 210-212, 1964.

333. Mednick, S. A. A learning theory approach to research in schizophrenia. Psychol. Bull. 55: 316-327, 1958.

334. Mednick, S. A. Learning theory and schizophrenia: A reply to a comment. Psychol. Bull. 56: 315-316, 1959.

335. Meehl, P. E. Schizotaxia, schizotypy, schizophrenia. Amer. Psychologist. 17: 827-838, 1962.

336. Meichenbaum, D. H. Effects of social reinforcement on the level of abstraction in schizophrenics. J. Abnorm. Psychol. 71: 354-362, 1966.

337. Metz, J. R. Conditioning generalized imitation in autistic children. J. Exp. Child Psychol. 4: 389-399, 1965.

338. Meyers, D. I., and Goldfarb, W. Studies of perplexity in mothers of schizophrenic children. Amer. J. Orthopsychiat. 31: 551-564, 1961.

339. Milgram, N. A. Preference for abstract versus concrete word meanings in schizophrenic and brain-damaged patients. J. Clin. Psychol. 15: 207-212, 1959.

340. Milgram, N. A. Microgenetic analysis of word associations in schizophrenic and brain-damaged patients. J. Abnorm. Soc. Psychol. 62: 364-366, 1961.

341. Miller, M. D., Johnson, R. L., and Richmond, L. H. Auditory hallucinations and descriptive language skills. J. Psychiat. 3: 43-56, 1965.

342. Miller, M. H., and Chotlos, J. W. Spatial differentiation in chronic schizophrenia. J. Nerv. Ment. Dis. 125: 558-563, 1957.

343. Minkowski, E. A propos de la psychopathologie de la schizophrenie. (With regard to the psychopathology of schizophrenia.) Acta Neurologica et Psychiatrica Belgica, 65: 693-699, 1965.

344. Molish, H. B., Hanlon, T. E., and Kurland, A. A. A prognostic indicator of treatment failure in schizophrenia. AMA Arch. Neurol. Psychiat. 78: 177-193, 1957.

345. Moran, L. J., Gorham, D. R., and Holtzman, W. H. Vocabulary knowledge and usage of schizophrenic subjects: A six-year follow-up. J. Abnorm. Soc. Psychol. 61: 246-254, 1960.

346. Moriarity, D., and Kates, S. L. Concept attainment of schizophrenics on materials involving social approval and disapproval. J. Abnorm. Soc. Psychol. 65: 355-364, 1962.

347. Neiditch, S. J. Differential response to failure in hospital and non-hospital groups. J. Abnorm. Soc. Psychol. 66: 449-453, 1963.

348. Nelson, S., and Caldwell, W. E. Perception of affective stimuli by normal and schizophrenic subjects in a depth perception task. J. Gen. Psychol. 67: 323-335, 1962.

349. Nencini, R. Effetti di alcuni atteggiamenti materni sulla personalita dei figli. (The influence of some maternal attitudes on children's behavior.) Boll. Psicol. Appli. 37-39: 123-144, 1960.

350. Nikols, J. Mental deficit, schizophrenia and the Benton Test. J. Nerv. Ment. Dis. 136: 279-282, 1963.

351. Nickols, J. Self-image ratings of normal and disturbed subjects. J. Hlth. Hum. Behav. 7: 28-36, 1966.

352. Norman, R. P. Level of aspiration and social desirability in chronic schizophrenics. J. Consult. Psychol. 27: 40-44, 1963.

353. Norman, R. P., and Wilensky, H. Item difficulty of the WAIS I subtest for a chronic schizophrenic sample. J. Clin. Psychol. 17: 56-57, 1961.

354. Normington, C. Some aspects of psychosexual development in process-reactive schizophrenia. Unpublished doctoral dissertation, Michigan State University, 1964.

355. Nutenko, E. A., and Khitrik, L. A. Clinical comparisons and development of schizophrenia in the members of 111 families. Zhurnal Neuropatologii i Psikhiatrii. 65: 1547-1553, 1965.

356. O'Connor, N., and Venables, P. H. The response of chronic schizophrenics to verbal signals. Acta Psychol. 17: 218-225, 1960.

357. Olson, G. W. Failure and the subsequent performance of schizophrenics. J. Abnorm. Soc. Psychol. 57: 310-314, 1958.

358. Orme, J. E. O.R.T. performance in schizophrenia. J. Ment. Sci. 105: 1119-1122, 1959.

359. Overall, J. E., Gorham, D. R., Shawver, J. R. Basic dimensions of change in the symptomatology of chronic schizophrenics. J. Abnorm. Soc. Psychol. 63: 597-602, 1961.

360. Panteleyeva, G. P. Slowly progressing schizophrenia linked with clinical psychoasthenic changes. Zhurnal Neuropatologii i Psikhiatrii. 65: 1690-1696, 1965.

361. Parks, J. R. A committee report on schizophrenic language. Behav. Sci. 6: 79-83, 1961.

362. Payne, R. W. Some aspects of perception and thought disorder in schizophrenic subjects. Schweiz. Z. Psychol. Anwend. 17: 300-308, 1958.

363. Payne, R. W. An object classification test as a measure of overinclusive thinking in schizophrenic patients. Brit. J. Soc. Clin. Psychol. 1: 213-221, 1962.

364. Payne, R. W., Caird, W. K., and Laverty, S. G. Overinclusive thinking and delusions in schizophrenic patients. J. Abnorm. Soc. Psychol. 68: 562-566, 1964.

365. Payne, R. W., and Hewlett, J. H. Thought disorder in psychotic patients. In Eysenck, H. J. (Ed.), Experiments in Personality. Vol. II. London, Routledge, 1960.

366. Payne, R. W., Mattussek, P., and George, E. I. An experimental study of schizophrenic thought disorder. J. Ment. Sci. 105: 627-652, 1959.

367. Pearl, D. Language information processing ability of process and reactive schizophrenics. J. Psychol. 55: 419-425, 1963.

368. Pearl, D., and Berg, P. S. D. Time perception and conflict arousal in schizophrenia. J. Abnorm. Soc. Psychol. 66: 332-338, 1963.

369. Peastrel, A. L. Studies in efficiency:

Semantic generalization in schizophrenia. J. Abnorm. Soc. Psychol. 69: 444-449, 1964.

370. Perez, P. Size constancy in normals and schizophrenics. In Ittelson, W. H., and Kutash, S. B. (Eds.), Perceptual Changes in Psychopathology. New Brunswick, Rutgers University Press, 1961.

371. Perris, C. Recherches sur le seuil de fusion du papillotement lumineux a yeux fermes chez des subjets normaux et schizophrenes. (Study of flicker fusion threshold with closed eyes for normal and schizophrenic subjects.) Rev. Psychol. Appl. 9: 35-41, 1959.

372. Petrie, A., Holland, T., and Wold, I. Sensory stimulation causing subdued experience; audio-analgesia and perceptual augmentation and reduction. J. Nerv. Ment. Dis. 137: 312-321, 1963.

373. Petrovich, D. V. Pain apperception in chronic schizophrenics. J. Proj. Tech. 24: 21-27, 1960.

374. Philips, J. E., Jacobson, N., and Turner, W. J. Conceptual thinking in schizophrenics and their relatives. Brit. J. Psychiat. 111: 823-389, 1965.

375. Piotrowski, Z. A., and Bricklin, B. A long-term prognostic criterion for schizophrenics based on Rorschach data. Psychiat. Quart. Suppl. 32: 315-329, 1958.

376. Piotrowski, Z. A., and Bricklin, B. A second validation of a long-term Rorschach prognostic index for schizophrenic patients. J. Consult. Psychol. 25: 123-128, 1961.

377. Piotrowski, Z. A., and Efron, H. Y. Evaluation of outcome in schizophrenia. In Hoch, P. H., and Zubin, J. Psychopathology of Schizophrenia. New York: Grune & Stratton, 1966.

378. Piotrowski, Z. A., and Levine, D. A case illustrating the concept of the alpha schizophrenic. J. Proj. Tech. 23: 223-236, 1959.

379. Pishkin, V., and Blanchard, R. J. Stimulus and social cues in concept identification of schizophrenics and normals. J. Abnorm. Soc. Psychol. 67: 454-463, 1963.

380. Pishkin, V., and Hershiser, D. Respiration and GSR as functions of white sound in schizophrenia. J. Consult. Psychol. 27: 330-337, 1963.

381. Pishkin, V., Smith, T. E., and Leibowitz, H. W. The influence of symbolic stimulus value on perceived size in chronic schizophrenia. J. Consult. Psychol. 26: 323-330, 1962.

382. Pishkin, V., Smith, T. E., and Lundy, R. M. Verbal concept identification with schizophrenics and psychopaths. J. Clin. Psychol. 18: 198-203, 1962.

383. Poliakov, Y. F. O printsipakh podkhodak izucheniya narusheniya poznavatel nykh protessov pri shizotrenii. (Guiding principles for research on disturbed cognitive (principles) processes in schizophrenia.) Zhurnal Neuropatologii i Psikhiatrii. 66: 95-102, 1966.

384. Pollack, M. Comparison of childhood, adolescent, and adult schizophrenias. AMA Arch. Gen. Psychiat. 2: 652-660, 1960.

385. Pollack, M., and Goldfarb, W. The face-hand test in schizophrenic children. AMA Arch. Neurol. Psychiat. 77: 635-642, 1957.

386. Pollack, M., Woerner, M. G. Goodman, W., and Greenberg, I. M. Childhood development patterns of hospitalized schizophrenic and nonschizophrenic patients and their siblings. Amer. J. Orthopsychiat. 36: 510-517, 1966.

387. Pollin, W., Stabenau, J. R., Mosher, L., and Tupin, J. Life history differences in identical twins discordant for schizophrenia. Amer. J. Orthoypsychiat. 36: 492-509, 1966.

388. Pontius, A. A. Role of hallucinatory experiences of rhythmical movements during ego re-integration in a schizophrenic man. Percept. Mot. Skills. 14: 439-473, 1962.

389. Price, R. H., and Eriksen, C. W. Size constancy in schizophrenia: A reanalysis. J. Abnormal. Psychol. 71: 155-160, 1966.

390. Rabin, A. I. Diagnostic use of intelligence tests. In Wolman, B. (Ed.) Handbook of Clinical Psychology. New York: McGraw-Hill, 1965.

391. Rabin, A. I., and King, G. F. Psychological studies. In Bellak, L. L. (Ed.)

Schizophrenia: A review of the Syndrome. New York: Logos Press, 1958.

392. Rachman, S. Inhibition and disinhibition in schizophrenics. Arch. Gen. Psychiat. 8: 91-98, 1963.

393. Rachman, S., and Berger, M. Whirling and postural control in schizophrenic children. J. Child Psychol. Psychiat. 4: 137-155, 1963.

394. Raskin, A., and Clyde, D. J. Factors of psychopathology in the ward behavior of acute schizophrenics. J. Consult. Psychol. 27: 420-425, 1963.

395. Raskin, A., and Golob, R. Occurrence of sex and social class differences in premorbid competence, symptom and outcome measures in acute schizophrenia. Psychol. Rep. 18: 11-22, 1966.

396. Raush, H. L. Perceptual constancy in schizophrenia. J. Pers. 21: 176-187, 1952.

397. Rechtschaffen, A., Schulsinger, F., and Mednick, S. A. Schizophrenia and psychological indices of dreaming. Arch. Gen. Psychiat. 10: 89-93, 1964.

398. Reisman, J. M. Motivational differences between process and reactive schizophrenics. J. Pers. 28: 12-25, 1960.

399. Reitman, E. E., and Cleveland, S. E. Changes in body image following sensory deprivation in schizophrenic and control groups. J. Abnorm. Soc. Psychol. 68: 168-176, 1964.

400. Reznikoff, M., and Olin, T. D. Recall of the Bender-Gestalt designs by organic and schizophrenic patients: A comparative study. J. Clin. Psychol. 13: 183-186, 1957.

401. Richman, J. The effect of the emotional tone of words upon the vocabulary responses of schizophrenics. J. Gen. Psychol. 56: 95-119, 1957.

402. Rimoldi, H. J. A. Personal tempo. J. Abnorm. Soc. Psychol. 46: 283-303, 1951.

403. Robertson, J. P. S. The operant conditioning of speech and drawing behavior in chronic schizophrenics. Schweiz. Z. Psychol. Anwend. 17: 309-315, 1958.

404. Robertson, J. P. S. Effects of different rewards in modifying the verbal behavior of disorganized schizophrenics. J. Clin. Psychol. 17: 399-402, 1961.

405. Robertson, J. P. S. Perceptual-motor disorders in chronic schizophrenia. Brit. J. Soc. Clin. Psychol. 1: 1-6, 1962.

406. Robertson, J. P. S., and Shamsie, S. J. A systematic examination of gibberish in a multilingual schizophrenic patient. Lang. Speech. 2: 1-8, 1959.

407. Rodnick, E. H., and Garmezy, N. An experimental approach to the study of schizophrenia. In Jones, M. R. (Ed.) Nebraska Symposium on Motivation 1957. Lincoln, Nebraska University, Nebraska Press, 1957.

408. Rodnick, E., and Shakow, D. Set in the schizophrenic as measured by a composite reaction-time index. Amer. J. Psychiat. 97: 214-225, 1940.

409. Rogers, A. H. The self-concept in paranoid schizophrenia. J. Clin. Psychol. 14: 365-366, 1958.

410. Rosenbaum, C. P. Patient-family similarities in schizophrenia. Arch. Gen. Psychiat. 5: 120-126, 1961.

411. Rosenbaum, G., Flenning, F., and Rosen, H. Effects of weight intensity on discrimination thresholds of normals and schizophrenics. J. Abnormal. Psychol. 70: 446-450, 1965.

412. Rosenbaum, G., Grisell, J. L., and MacKavey, W. R. The relationship of age and privilege status to reaction time indices of schizophrenic motivation. J. Abnorm. Soc. Psychol. 55: 202-207, 1957.

413. Rosenbaum, G., MacKavey, W. R., and Grisell, J. L. Effects of biological and social motivation on schizophrenic reaction time. J. Abnorm. Soc. Psychol. 54: 364-368, 1957.

414. Rosenberg, B. G., Balogh, J. K., McDevitt, R., Gerjuoy, H., and Bond, J. An investigation of social interaction in schizophrenia. J. Clin. Psychol. 18: 54-57, 1962.

415. Rosenberg, B. G., and Langer, J. A study of nonverbal symbolic behavior of schizophrenics. J. Clin. Psychol. 21: 243-247, 1965.

416. Rosenberg, L. Social status and participation among a group of chronic

schizophrenics. Hum. Relat. 15: 365-377, 1962.

417. Rosenthal, D. Confusion of identity and the frequency of schizophrenia in twins. Arch. Gen. Psychiat. 3: 297-304, 1960.

418. Rosenthal, D., Lawlor, W. G., Zahn, T. P., and Shakow, D.: The relationship of some aspects of mental set to degree of schizophrenic disorganization. J. Pers. 28: 26-38, 1960.

419. Rosenthal, D., Zahn, T. P., and Shakow, D.: Verbal versus manual reaction time in schizophrenic and normal subjects. The Quart. J. Exp. Psychol. 15: 214-216, 1963.

420. Rosenthal, R.: Perception of success or failure in pictures of others. J. Clin. Psychol. 15: 216-217, 1959.

421. Rump, E. E.: A note on distance constancy in schizophrenic patients. J. Ment. Sci. 107: 48-51, 1961.

422. Russo, D. G.: On the onset of schizophrenia. Psychiatric et Neurologia, 149: 150-159, 1965.

423. Rychoff, I., Day, J., and Wynne, L. C.: Maintenance of stereotyped roles in the families of schizophrenics. AMA Arch. Gen. Psychiat. 1: 93-98, 1959.

424. Saltzinger, K.: Shift in judgment of weights as a function of anchoring stimuli and instructions in early schizophrenics and normals. J. Abnorm. Soc. Psychol. 55: 43-49, 1957.

425. Salzinger, K., and Hammer, M.: Some formal characteristics of schizophrenic speech as a measure of social deviance. Ann. N.Y. Acad. Sci. 105: 861-889, 1963.

426. Salzinger, K., and Pisoni, S.: Reinforcement of affect responses of schizophrenics during the clinical interview. J. Abnorm. Soc. Psychol. 57: 84-90, 1958.

427. Salzinger, K., and Pisoni, S.: Some parameters of the conditioning of verbal affect responses in schizophrenic subjects. J. Abnorm. Soc. Psychol. 63: 511-516, 1961.

428. Salzinger, K., Portnoy, S., and Feldman, R. S.: Verbal behavior of schizophrenic and normal subjects. Ann. N.Y. Acad. Sci. 105: 845-860, 1963.

429. Salzinger, K., Portnoy, S., and Feldman, R. S.: Experimental manipulation of continuous speech in schizophrenic patients. J. Abnorm. Soc. Psychol. 68: 508-516, 1964.

430. Sanders, R. S., and Pacht, A. R.: Perceptual size in known clinical groups. J. Consult. Psychol. 16: 440-444, 1952.

431. Sarro, R., and Caderch, J.: El pensamiento paleologico en la esquizofrenia. (Paleologic thought in schizophrenia.) Revista de Psiquiatria Y Psicologia Medica. 7: 144-153, 1965.

432. Sastry, M. N. C., and Kasturi, H. Y.: Conceptual error, vocabulary and level of abstraction. Trans. All-India Inst. Ment. Hlth. 2: 107-114, 1961.

433. Satz, P., and Baraff, A. S.: Changes in the relation between self-concepts and ideal concepts of psychotics consequent upon therapy. J. Gen. Psychol. 67: 291-298, 1962.

434. Saucer, R. T.: A further study of the perception of apparent motion by schizophrenics. J. Consult. Psychol. 22: 256-258, 1958.

435. Saucer, R. T.: Chlorpromazine and apparent motion perception by schizophrenics. J. Consult. Psychol. 23: 134-136, 1959.

436. Saucer, R. T., and Deabler, H. L.: Perception of apparent motion in organics and schizophrenics. J. Consult. Psychol. 20: 385-389, 1956.

437. Saucer, R. T., and Sweetbaum, H.: Perception of the shortest noticeable dark time by schizophrenics. Science 127: 698-699, 1958.

438. Schafer, R.: Bodies in schizophrenic Rorschach responses. J. Proj. Tech. 24: 267-281, 1960.

439. Scher, J. M.: The concept of self in schizophrenia. J. Existent. Psychiat. 1: 64-88, 1960.

440. Scherer, I. W., and Nidorf, L. J.: Familial psychopathology and environmental stress as prognostic signs. J. Clin. Psychol. 16: 60-62, 1960.

441. Schofield, W., and Balian, L.: A comparative study of the personal histories of schizophrenic and nonpsychiatric pa-

tients. J. Abnorm. Soc. Psychol. 59: 216-225, 1959.

442. Schooler, C.: Birth order and schizophrenia. Arch. Gen. Psychiat. 4: 91-97, 1961.

443. Schooler, C.: Affiliation among schizophrenics: Preferred characteristics of the other. J. Nerv. Ment. Dis. 137: 438-446, 1963.

444. Schooler, C.: Birth order and hospitalization for schizophrenia. J. Abnorm. Soc. Psychol. 69: 574-579, 1964.

445. Schooler, C., and Scarr, S.: Affiliation among chronic schizophrenics: Relation to interpersonal and birth order factors. J. Pers. 30: 178-192, 1962.

446. Schooler, C., and Spohn, H. E.: The susceptibility of chronic schizophrenics to social influence in the formation of perceptual judgments. J. Abnorm. Soc. Psychol. 61: 348-354, 1960.

447. Schopler, E.: Visual versus tactual receptor preference in normal and schizophrenic children. J. Abnorm. Psychol. 71: 108-114, 1966.

448. Schwartzman, A. E., and Douglas, V. I.: Intellectual loss in schizophrenia: Part I. Canad. J. Psychol. 1: 1-10, 1962.

449. Schwartzman, A. E., Douglas, V. I., and Muir, W. R.: Intellectual loss in schizophrenia: Part II: Canad. J. Psychol. 16: 161-168, 1962.

450. Scott, E. M., and Douglas F.: A comparison of Rorschach and Howard tests on a schizophrenic population. J. Clin. Psychol. 13: 79-81, 1957.

451. Sechehaye, M.: Les divers aspects du moi schizophrenique. L'Evolution Psychiatrique. 30: 299-316, 1965.

452. Seth, G., and Beloff, H.: Language impairment in a group of schizophrenics. Brit. J. Med. Psychol. 32: 288-293, 1959.

453. Shakow, D.: Segmental set: A theory of the formal psychological deficit in schizophrenia. Arch. Gen. Psychiat. 6: 1-17, 1962.

454. Shakow, D.: Psychological deficit in schizophrenia. Behav. Sci. 8: 274-305, 1963.

455. Shakow, D., and Jellinek, E. M.: Composite index of the Kent-Rosanoff Free Association Test. J. Abnorm. Psychol. 70: 403-404, 1965.

456. Shamanina, V. M.: O nekotorykh Uozrastnykh zakonomernostiakh v razvittii i techenii tsirkuliarnoi shizofrenii: I. (Concerning certain effects of age on the development and course of circular schizophrenia: I.). Zhurnal Neuropatologii i Psikhiatrii, 66: 259-266, 1966.

457. Shatin, L.: The influence of rhythmic drumbeat stimuli upon the pulse rate and general activity of long-term schizophrenics. J. Ment. Sci. 103: 172-188, 1957.

458. Sheiner, S.: The schizophrenic process: Some further considerations. Amer. J. Psychoanal. 25: 158-170, 1965.

459. Shepherd, I. L., and Guthrie, G. M.: Attitudes of mothers of schizophrenic patients. J. Clin. Psychol. 15: 212-215, 1959.

460. Sherman, J. A.: Use of reinforcement and imitation to reinstate verbal behavior in mute psychotics. J. Abnorm. Psychol. 70: 155-164, 1965.

461. Sidle, A., Acker, M., and McReynolds, P.: "Stimulus-seeking" behavior in schizophrenics and nonschizophrenics. Percept. Mot. Skills. 17: 811-816, 1963.

462. Silverman, J.: Psychological deficit reduction in schizophrenia through response- contingent noxious reinforcement. Psychol. Rep. 13: 187-210, 1963.

463. Silverman, J.: The problem of attention in research and theory in schizophrenia. Psychol. Rev. 71: 352-379, 1964.

464. Silverman, J., Berg, P. S., and Kantor, R.: Some perceptual correlates of institutionalization. J. Nerv. Ment. Dis. 141: 651-657, 1965.

465. Silverman, L. H.: A technique for the study of psychodynamic relationships: The effects of subliminally presented aggressive stimuli on the production of pathological thinking in a schizophrenic population. J. Consult. Psychol. 30: 103-111, 1966.

466. Silverman, L. H., and Silverman, D. K.: Ego impairment in schizophrenia as reflected in the Object Sorting Test. J. Abnorm. Soc. Psychol. 64: 381-385, 1962.

467. Silverman, L. N., Lapkin, B., and Rosenbaum, I. S.: Manifestations of

primary process thinking in schizophrenia. J. Proj. Tech. 26: 117-127, 1962.

468. Simon, W., and Wirt, R. D.: Prognostic factors in schizophrenia. Amer. J. Psychiat. 117: 887-890, 1961.

469. Singer, J. L., and Opler, M. K.: Contrasting patterns of fantasy and motility in Irish and Italian schizophrenics. J. Abnorm. Soc. Psychol. 53: 42-47, 1956.

470. Smith, A., Smith, R., Sanders, R., Weinman, B., Kenny, J., and Fitzgerald, B.: Predicting the outcome of social therapy with chronic psychotics. J. Abnorm. Soc. Psychol. 66: 351-357, 1963.

471. Smith, S., Thakurdas, H., and Lawes, T. G. G.: Perceptual isolation and schizophrenia. J. Ment. Sci. 107: 839-844, 1961.

472. Smock, C. D., and Vancini, J.: Dissipation rate of the effects of social censure in schizophrenics. Psychol. Rep. 10: 531-536, 1962.

473. Snyder, S., Rosenthal, D., and Taylor, I. R.: Perceptual closure in schizophrenia. J. Abnorm. Soc. Psychol. 63: 131-136, 1961.

474. Solomon, L., Zlotowski, M.: The relationship between the Elgin and the Phillips measures of process-reactive schizophrenia. J. Ment. Nerv. Dis. 138: 32-37, 1964.

475. Sommer, R., Dewar, R., and Osmond, H.: Is there a schizophrenic language? Arch. Gen. Psychiat. 3: 665-673, 1960.

476. Sommer, R., and Whitney, G.: Teaching common associations to schizophrenics. J. Abnorm. Soc. Psychol. 65: 58-61, 1962.

477. Spain, B.: Eyelid conditioning and arousal in schizophrenic and normal subjects. J. Abnorm. Psychol. 71: 260-266, 1966.

478. Spence, J. T.: Patterns of performance on WAIS S in schizophrenic, brain-damaged and normal adults. Psychol. Rep. 13: 431-436, 1963.

479. Spence, J. T., Goodstein, L. D., and Lair, C. V.: Rote learning in schizophrenic and normal subjects under positive and negative reinforcement conditions. J. Abnorm. Psychol. 70: 251-261, 1965.

480. Spence, J. T., and Lair, C. V.: Associative interference in the verbal learning performance of schizophrenics and normals. J. Abnorm. Soc. Psychol. 68: 204-209, 1964.

481. Spence, J. T., and Lair, C. V.: Associative interference in the paired-associate learning of remitted and nonremitted schizophrenics. J. Abnorm. Psychol. 70: 119-122, 1965.

482. Spohn, H. E., and Wolk, W.: Effect of group problem solving experience upon social withdrawal in chronic schizophrenics. J. Abnorm. Soc. Psychol. 66: 187-190, 1963.

483. Spohn, H. E., and Wolk, W. P.: Social participation in homogeneous and heterogeneous groups of chronic schizophrenics. J. Abnorm. Psychol. 71: 147-150, 1966.

484. Starer, E., and Tanner, H.: An analysis of responses of male schizophrenic patients to Freudian-type stimuli. J. Clin. Psychol. 18: 58-61, 1962.

485. Stauffacher, J. C., and Anderson, C. L.: The performance of schizophrenics on the Kuder Preference Record. Educ. Psychol. Measmt. 19: 253-257, 1959.

486. Steffy, R. A., and Becker, W. C.: Measurement of the severity of disorder in schizophrenia by means of the Holtzman Inkblot Test. J. Consult. Psychol. 25: 555, 1961.

487. Stein, K. B., and Craik, K. H.: Relationship between motoric and ideational activity preference and time perspective in neurotics and schizophrenics. J. Consult. Psychol. 29: 460-467, 1965.

488. Stephens, J. H., and Astrup, C.: Treatment outcome in "process" and "non-process" schizophrenics treated by "A" and "B" types of therapists. J. Nerv. Ment. Dis. 140: 449-456, 1965.

489. Storozhenko-Morozova, N. L.: Razlichnye klinicheskie varianty katatonicheskoi formy schizofrenii i prognoz trudosposobnosti pri nikh. (Different clinical variants of the catatonic form of schizophrenia and their prognosis with regard to working capacity.) Zhurnal Neuropatologii i Psikhiatrii. 66: 280-284, 1966.

490. Stotsky, B. A.: Factor analysis

of Rorschach scores of schizophrenics. J. Clin. Psychol. 13: 275-278, 1957.

491. Stotsky, B.: Motivation and task complexity as factors in psychomotor responses of schizophrenics. J. Pers. 25: 327-343, 1957.

492. Sturm, I. E.: "Conceptual area" among pathological groups: A failure to replicate. J. Abnorm. Soc. Psychol. 69: 216-223, 1964.

493. Sutton, S., Hakerem, G., Zubin, J., and Portnoy, M.: The effect of shift of sensory modality on serial reaction-time: A comparison of schizophrenics and normals. Amer. J. Psychol. 74: 224-232, 1961.

494. Sutton, S., Roehrig, W. C., and Kramer, J.: Delayed auditory feedback in schizophrenics and normals. Ann. N.Y. Acad. Sci. 105: 832-844, 1963.

495. Tamkin, A. S.: Selective recall in schizophrenia and its relation to ego strength. J. Abnorm. Soc. Psychol. 55: 345-349, 1957.

496. Taylor, I. A., Rosenthal, D., and Snyder, S.: Variability in schizophrenia. Arch. Gen. Psychiat. 8: 163-168, 1963.

497. Tiganov, A. S.: Klinicheskie osobennosti ostrykh parafrennykh sostoianii i ikh otnoshenie k formam rekurrentnoi shizofrenii. (Clinical features of acute paraphrenic conditions and their relations to the forms of recurrent schizophrenia.) Zhurnal Neuropatologii i Piskhiatrii. 66: 266-272, 1966.

498. Tizard, J., and Venables, P. H.: The influence of extraneous stimulation on the reaction time of schizophrenics. Brit. J. Psychol. 48: 299-305, 1957.

499. Thorpe, J. G.: The response of chronic female schizophrenics to monetary incentives. Brit. J. Soc. Clin. Psychol. 1: 192-198, 1962.

500. Topping, G. G., and O'Connor, N.: The response of chronic schizophrenics to incentives. Brit. J. Med. Psychol. 33: 211-214, 1960.

501. Torrigiani, G.: Rilievi psiconetrici sulla efficienza intellettiva nello schizofrenico. Arch. Psicol. Neurol. Psichiat. 22: 589-604, 1961.

502. True, J. E.: Learning of abstract responses by process and reactive schizo-phrenic patients. Psychol. Rep. 18: 51-55, 1966.

503. Tsutsul' kouskaia, M. Ia., and Druzhinina, T. A.: O sistematike nepreryuno tekushchei shizofrenii, uoznikaiushchei u iunosheskom uozraste. (Concerning the systematization of continuously evolving schizophrenia, beginning at an early age.) Zhurnal Neuropatologii i Psikhiatrii. 66: 273-280, 1966.

504. Turbiner, M.: Choice discrimination in schizophrenic and normal subjects for positive, negative and neutral affective stimuli. J. Consult. Psychol. 25: 92, 1961.

505. Tutko, T. A., and Spence, J. T.: The performance of process and reactive schizophrenics and brain-injured subjects on a conceptual task. J. Abnorm. Soc. Psychol. 65: 387-394, 1962.

506. Ullmann, L. P., and Giovannoni, J. M.: The development of a self-report measure of the process-reactive continuum. J. Nerv. Ment. Dis. 138: 38-41, 1964.

507. Vandenberg, S. G.: La mesure de la deterioration de la comprehension sociale dans las chizofrenia. (The measurement of deterioration of social understanding in schizophrenia.) Rev. Psychol. Appl. 12: 189-199, 1962.

508. Venables, P.: Input dysfunction in schizophrenia. In Maher, B. A. (Ed.), Progress in experimental personality research. Vol. I. New York: Academic Press, 1964.

509. Venables, P. H.: The effect of auditory and visual stimulation on the skin potential response of schizophrenics. Brain. 83: 77-92, 1960.

510. Venables, P. H.: Selectivity of attention, withdrawal, and cortical activation: Studies in chronic schizophrenia. Arch. Gen. Psychiat. 9: 74-78, 1963.

511. Venables, P. H., and Wing, J. K.: Level of arousal and the subclassification of schizophrenia. Arch. Gen. Psychiat. 7: 114-119, 1962.

512. Venables, P. H.: Changes due to noise in the threshold of fusion of paired light flashes in schizophrenics and normals. Brit. J. Soc. Clin. Psychol. 2: 94-99, 1963.

513. Venables, P. H.: The relationship between level of skin potential and fusion

of paired light flashed in schizophrenic and normal subjects. J. Psychiat. Res. 1: 279-286, 1963.

514. Vinson, D. B.: Responses to the Rorschach test that identify schizophrenic thinking, feeling, and behavior. J. Clin. Exp. Psychopath. 21: 34-40, 1960.

515. Wadsworth, W. V., Wells, B. W. P., and Scott, R. F.: A comparative study of chronic schizophrenics and normal subjects on a work task involving sequential operations. J. Ment. Sci. 108: 309-316, 1962.

516. Wagner, E. A., and Medvedeff, E.: Differentiation of aggressive behavior of institutionalized schizophrenics with the Hand Test. J. Proj. Tech. 27: 111-113, 1963.

517. Ward, T. F., and Hoddinott, B. A.: A study of childhood schizophrenia and early infantile autism: II. Selection of a group for inpatient treatment. Canad. Psychiat. Ass. J. 10: 382-386, 1965.

518. Waring, M., and Ricks, D.: Family patterns of children who became adult schizophrenics. J. Nerv. Ment. Dis. 140: 351-364, 1965.

519. Watson, C. G.: Intratest scatter in hospitalized brain-damaged and schizophrenic patients. J. Consult. Psychol. 29: 596, 1965.

520. Watson, C. G.: WAIS error types in schizophrenics and organics. Psychol. Rep. 16: 527-530, 1965.

521. Watson, C. G.: WAIS profile patterns of hospitalized brain-damaged and schizophrenic patients. J. Clin. Psychol. 21: 294-296, 1965.

522. Weakland, J. H., and Fry, W. F.: Letters of mothers of schizophrenics. Amer. J. Orthopsychiat. 32: 604-623, 1962.

523. Weaver, L. A., Jr.: Psychomotor performance of clinically differentiated chronic schizophrenics. Percept. Mot. Skills. 12: 27-33, 1961.

524. Webb, W. W.: Premorbid adjustment and the perception of meaning. Percept. Mot. Skills. 17: 762, 1963.

525. Webster, F. R., Goldstone, S., and Webb, W. W.: Time judgment and schizophrenia: Psychophysical method as a relevant contextual factor. J. Psychol. 54: 159-164, 1962.

526. Weckowitz, T. E.: Size constancy in schizophrenic patients. J. Ment. Sci. 103: 475-486, 1957.

527. Weckowicz, T. E.: Autonomic activity as measured by mecholyl test and size constancy in schizophrenic patients. Psychosom. Med. 20: 66-71, 1958.

528. Weckowicz, T. E.: Perception of hidden pictures by schizophrenic patients. AMA Arch. Gen. Psychiat. 2: 521-527, 1960.

529. Weckowicz, T. E.: Shape constancy in schizophrenic patients. J. Abnorm. Soc. Psychol. 68: 177-183, 1964.

530. Weckowicz. T. E., and Blewett, D. B.: Size constancy and abstract thinking in schizophrenic patients. J. Ment. Sci. 105: 909-934, 1959.

531. Weckowicz, T. E., and Hall, R.: Distance constancy in schizophrenic and nonschizophrenic mental patients. J. Clin. Psychol. 16: 272-276, 1960.

532. Weckowicz, T. E., and Sommer, R.: Body image and self-concept in schizophrenia. J. Ment. Sci. 106: 17-39, 1960.

533. Weckowicz, T. E., and Witney, G.: The Muller-Lyer illusion in schizophrenic patients. J. Ment. Sci. 106: 1002-1007, 1960.

534. Weiner, I. B.: Three Rorschach scores indicative of schizophrenia. J. Consult. Psychol. 25: 436-439, 1961.

534a. Weiner, I. B.: Psychodiagnosis in Schizophrenia. New York: John Wiley and Sons, 1966.

535. Weingold, H. P., Adams, H. E., and Wittman, F.: Sexual symbolism, abstract designs and the PRT. Psychol. Rep. 13: 90, 1963.

536. Weinstein, A. D., Goldstone, S., and Boardman, W. K.: The effect of recent and remote frames of reference on temporal judgments of schizophrenic patients. J. Abnorm. Soc. Psychol. 57: 241-244, 1958.

537. Weltman, R. E., and Wolfson, W.: The effect of praise, censure and a self-established goal on the functioning of chronic schizophrenics. Psychiat. Quart. Suppl. 37: 81-87, 1963.

538. Wertheimer, M., and Jackson, C. W., Jr.: Figural after-effects, "brain modifiability," and schizophrenia: A further study. J. Gen. Psychol. 57: 45-54, 1957.

539. White, R. W.: The experience of efficacy in schizophrenia. Psychiatry. 28: 199-211, 1965.

540. Whitehead, W. A., and Thune, L. E.: The effects of chlorpromazine on learning in chronic psychotics. J. Consult. Psychol. 22: 379-383, 1958.

541. Whiteman, M.: Qualitative features of schizophrenic thought in the formation of social concepts. J. Nerv. Ment. Dis. 124: 199-204, 1956.

542. Whitman, J. R.: Responsiveness to social pressures in schizophrenia. Psychol. Rep. 8, 238, 1961.

543. Whitman, J. R.: Suggestability in schizophrenia. J. Clin. Psychol. 17: 203-205, 1961.

544. Whitman, J. R.: Learning from social and nonsocial cues in schizophrenia. J. Gen. Psychol. 68: 307-315, 1963.

545. Wild, C., Singer, M., Rosman, B., Ricci, J., and Lidz, T.: Measuring disordered styles of thinking: Using the Object Sorting Test on parents of schizophrenic patients. Arch. Gen. Psychiat. 13: 471-476, 1965.

546. Williams, E. B.: Deductive reasoning in schizophrenia. J. Abnorm. Soc. Psychol. 69: 47-61, 1964.

547. Willis, J. H., and Bannister, D.: The diagnosis and treatment of schizophrenia: A questionnaire study of psychiatric opinion. Brit. J. Psychiat. 111: 1165-1171, 1965.

548. Willner, A.: Impairment of knowledge of unusual meanings of familiar words in brain damage and schizophrenia. J. Abnorm. Psychol. 70: 405-411, 1965.

549. Willner, G.: The role of anxiety in schizophrenia. Amer. J. Psychoanal. 25: 171-180, 1965.

550. Winder, C. L.: Some psychological studies of schizophrenia. In: Jackson, D. (Ed.) The Etiology of Schizophrenia. New York: Basic Books, 1960.

551. Wing, J. K., and Freudenberg, R. K.: The response of severely ill chronic schizophrenic patients to social stimula-tion. Amer. J. Psychiat. 118: 311-322, 1961.

552. Wishner, J.: Efficiency in schizophrenia. Bulletin de l'association Inter. de Psychologie Appliquee. 14: 30-46, 1965.

553. Wolff, S., and Chess, S.: A behavioral study of schizophrenic children. Acta Psychiatrica Scandinavia, 40: 438-466, 1964.

554. Wolman, B. B.: The fathers of schizophrenic patients. Acta Psychother. Psychosom. 9: 193-210, 1961.

555. Wolman, B. B.: Family dynamics and schizophrenia. J. Hlth. Hum. Behav. 6: 163-169, 1965.

556. Wright, D. J., Goldstone, S., and Boardman, W. K.: Time judgment and schizophrenia: Step interval as a relevant contextual factor. J. Psychol. 54: 33-38, 1962.

557. Wynne, L. C., and Singer, M. T.: Thought disorder and family relations of schizophrenics: I. A research strategy. Arch. Gen. Psychiat. 9: 191-198, 1963.

558. Wynne, L. C., and Singer, M. T.: Thought disorder and family relations of schizophrenics: II. A classification of forms of thinking. Arch. Gen. Psychiat. 9: 199-206, 1963.

559. Wynne, R. D.: The influence of hospitalization on the verbal behavior of chronic schizophrenics. Brit. J. Psychiat. 109: 380-389, 1963.

560. Yates, A. J.: Psychological deficit. In Ann. Rev. Psychol. 17: 111-144, 1966.

561. Zahn, T. P.: Acquired and symbolic affective value as determinants of size estimation in schizophrenic and normal subjects. J. Abnorm. Soc. Psychol. 58: 39-47, 1959.

562. Zahn, T. P.: Size estimation of pictures associated with success and failure as a function of manifest anxiety. J. Abnorm. Soc. Psychol. 61: 457-462, 1960.

563. Zahn, T. P., and Rosenthal, D.: Preparatory set in acute schizophrenia. J. Nerv. Ment. Dis. 141: 352-358, 1965.

564. Zahn, T. P., Rosenthal, D., and Shakow, D.: Reaction time in schizophrenic and normal subjects in relation to the sequence of series of regular pre-

paratory intervals. J. Abnorm. Soc. Psychol. 63: 161-168, 1961.

565. Zahn, T. P., Rosenthal, D., and Shakow D.: Effects of irregular preparatory intervals on reaction time in schizophrenia. J. Abnorm. Soc. Psychol. 67: 44-52, 1963.

566. Zahn, T. P., Shakow, D., and Rosenthal, D.: Reaction time in schizophrenic and normal subjects as a function of preparatory and intertrial intervals. J. Nerv. Ment. Dis. 133: 283-287, 1961.

567. Zax, M., Gardiner, D. H., and Lowy, D. G.: Extreme response tendency as a function of emotional adjustment. J. Abnorm. Soc. Psychol. 69: 654-657, 1964.

568. Zimet, C. N., and Fine, H. J.: Perceptual differentiation and two dimensions of schizophrenia. J. Nerv. Ment. Dis. 129: 435-441, 1959.

569. Zlotowski, M., and Bakan, P.: Behavioral variability of process and reactive schizophrenics in a binary guessing task. J. Abnormal. Soc. Psychol. 66: 185-187, 1963.

570. Zucker, L. J.: Ego structure in paranoid schizophrenia: A new method of evaluating projective material. Springfield, Ill.: Charles C. Thomas, 1958.

571. Zuckerman, M., Oltena, M., and Monashkin, I.: The parental attitudes of mothers of schizophrenics. J. Consult. Psychol. 22: 307-310, 1958.

572. Zuk, G. H.: On silence and babbling in family psychotherapy with schizophrenics. Confinia Psychiatrica, 8: 49-56, 1965.

573. Zukowsky, E.: Measuring primary and secondary process thinking in schizophrenics and normals by means of the Rorschach. Unpublished doctoral dissertation, Michigan State University, 1961.

8

Socio-Cultural Aspects

VICTOR D. SANUA, Ph.D.

Dr. Victor D. Sanua is an Associate Professor in the Department of Social and Psychological Foundations in the School of Education of The City College, City University of New York. Formerly, he was an Associate Professor at the Ferkauf Graduate School of Social Sciences and Humanities of Yeshiva University.

He received his Ph.D. degree from Michigan State University in clinical psychology with a minor in sociology and anthropology. After interning in clinical psychology at N.Y.U.-Bellevue Medical Center, he was awarded a post-doctoral fellowship by the Russell Sage Foundation. During this time, he worked on the Midtown Manhattan Mental Health Study in the Department of Social Psychiatry at the Payne Whitney Clinic of Cornell University Medical College. Subsequently, he became a research fellow in the Department of Social Relations at Harvard University where he initiated research in schizophrenia among different socio-cultural groups in the U.S.A. He is Vice President for North America of the Interamerican Society of Psychology.

During the 1965-1966 academic year, Dr. Sanua was a Fulbright Lecturer at the University of Paris (Sorbonne) where he taught at the Center of Social Psychiatry. He is a Fellow of the American Psychological Association (Clinical and Social Psychology Divisions), International Council of Psychologists and American Sociological Association.

During the last decade the labels of "social psychiatry," "transcultural psychiatry," "community psychiatry," "ethno-psychiatry," etc. have come to be used more frequently in psychiatric nomenclature. The abundance of new terminologies has created what Srole[400] labels the "Babel syndrome." In defining social psychiatry, Rennie[341] in the first issue of the *International Journal of Social Psychiatry*, states the following:

> "Social psychiatry tries to determine the significant facts in family and society which affect adaptation as revealed through the study of individuals or groups functioning in their natural setting. It concerns itself not only with the mentally ill, but with the problems of adjustment of all persons in society toward a better understanding of how people adapt, and what forces tend to damage or enhance their adaptive capacities." (p. 12)

Srole points out that the label of social psychiatry has been fluidly applied to two major discussions. One refers to *disciplines* identified with social psychiatry, and the other refers to *functions* identified with social psychiatry. At one end, clinicians contend that social psychiatry is exclusively the domain of, and for the psychiatrist, and, at the other end, sociologists claim social psychiatry to be a social science preserve. Service functions assigned to social psychiatry may include the following: a) therapy, where the sociocultural aspects of the patient's life is taken into account; b) group manipulations in the service of the patient, as "milieu therapy;" and c) the therapist who considers societies as being "sick." Functions further attributed to social psychiatry are: a) research in 1 : 1 therapy; b) psychiatric institutions; and c) basic etiologic investigation of large populations.

While British psychiatrists confine "social psychiatry" to the first three functions, Americans seem to prefer alternative terms, such as "community psychiatry." On the other hand, Americans seem to favor the use of "social psychiatry" in its research aspect.

The immense growth of the field is reflected by the number of publications which have compiled bibliographies: *Medical Sociology* (Simmons[389]) 1,700 items; *Medical Behavioral Science* (Pearsall[324]) 3,064 items; *Community Mental Health and Social Psychiatry,* (Harvard Medical School[79]) 1,158 items; *The Sociology and Anthropology of Mental Illness* (Driver[94]) 1,585 items; *Psychiatric Index for Interdisciplinary Research: A Guide to the Literature, 1950-1961* (Vocational Rehabilitation Administration[378]) 1,244 pages of references. Another publication of interest is the *Mental Health Book Review Index*[48] which started in 1955. It provides an annual list of books selected and reviewed by specialists and organized as a bibliography by librarians. It aims at a synthesis of the significant monographic literature in the behavioral sciences, as it is related to mental health. At least one third of the reviews mentioned originate outside the United States.

Since 1955, Wittkower and Fried[413] have edited the *Transcultural Psychiatric Research Review and Newsletter,* (formerly Transcultural Research in Mental Health Problems) reporting on research conducted in many parts of the world. Wittkower[439] regards cultural psychiatry as a branch of social psychiatry, which concerns itself with the cultural aspects of the etiology, frequency, and nature of mental illness and the care and after-care of the mentally ill within the confines of a given cultural unit. In *transcultural* psychiatry the observer's field extends beyond the scope of one cultural unit, while the term *cross-cultural* is applied to comparative aspects of psychiatry in many areas.

A similar newsletter, *International Mental Health Research Newsletter,* is published by the Postgraduate Center for Mental Health in New York, edited by Riess.[159a] This interest in international research and communication in the field of social psychiatry is expressed in the publication of new journals such as the *International Journal of Psychiatry,* edited by Jason Aronson and Ari Kiev; *Social Psychiatry,* edited by an international group of editors—Boeyer, Carstairs, Daumézon, Lindemann, and Redlich. Mention should also be made of the *International Journal of Social Psychiatry,* published in London.

Related to cultural psychiatry is "international psychiatry," which transcends geographical limits. This is the sort of psychiatry which concerns organizations such as the World Health Organization, World Federation for Mental Health, and World Psychiatric Association.

Another recent development is the publication of a number of volumes reporting on large-scale epidemiologic studies primarily conducted in the United States, Canada, and the Scandinavian countries. These include Srole et al.,[399] Langner et al.,[196] Leighton et al.,[156,211,217] Zubin,[443] and Hoch and Zubin.[153] Langner is presently conducting an epidemiologic study on mental illness among children, similar to the "Midtown Study."

For a general discussion of the field of social psychiatry and transcultural psychiatry, the following reports should be of interest: Ruesch,[359] Bell and Spiegel,[28] Opler,[304,310,313] Pepper and Redlich,[325] Wittkower,[439] Lin,[224] Frank,[120] Ellenberger,[107] Dunham,[100] Leighton,[207] Sandifer,[361] and Murphy and Leighton.[291]

Papers emphasizing the need for more cross-cultural and international studies have been written by: Lin,[223] Krapf,[193] Kaebling,[166] Leighton and Hughes,[210] Soddy (ed.),[393] Allinsmith and Goathals,[4] Opler,[309] and Linton.[227]

While all have emphasized the interdisciplinary approach, the relationships of the various social sciences and psychiatry in the study of mental disorders have been discussed by: Simmons and Davis,[390] Branch and Anderson,[39] Caudill,[58,61] Cohen,[74] Becker,[26] Mayo,[262] Lenz,[218] Opler,[308] and Goshen.[133]

The following have provided reviews or reports on the role of sociocultural factors in mental illness and treatment and research problems of the field: Carstairs,[55,56] Scott,[384] Bustamante,[51] Spiegel,[396] Pfanz,[326,327] Kennedy,[174] Sanua,[363,370,372] Giovacchini,[129] Hunt,[158,159] Ellenberger,[106,107] Opler,[311,312] Phillips and Draguns,[331] Dunham,[95,96,97] Mishler and Scotch,[281] Murphy,[286] Wittkower and Dubreuil,[441] and Kohn.[191]

Interest in cultural psychiatry was expressed by Kraepelin in the early 1900's. The question of the increase of mental illness and the progress of civilization, coupled with the observation that European Jewry showed different patterns of mental illness from other Europeans, provided the impetus for Kraepelin to explore the role of culture in mental illness (Lauter[204]). According to Carothers[54] literacy, or the lack of literacy in a society, is one factor, perhaps the major one, in shaping the minds of men and the patterns of their mental breakdowns.

Rosen[355] believes that current problems of mental illness may be illuminated by historical analysis. As culture changes in history, new styles of mental illness arise.

There have been a number of contributions pertaining to the etiology of mental illness, with specific emphasis on the role of culture. Wallace[426] in his biocultural theory, believes that schizophrenia is caused by some organic lesion leading to an inadequacy of social participation, and defenses against the social consequences of this incapacity are influenced by culture. Kline[189] presents a somewhat similar theory. He distinguishes two types of symptoms: "basic symptoms," such as distortion of memory, perception or feeling, which are produced directly by the organic disease, and "compensatory symptoms," which result from the organism's attempt to compensate for the disease. Thus, false memory leads to false choices. Chapman et al.[69] reverse the order. They say that, rejection and disapproval, being the greatest threat to man, result in impairment to organ functions, the brain in particular, which leads to serious disturbance of mood, thought, and behavior, including schizophrenia.

Arsenian[11,12] talks about "easy" and "tough" cultures. Simons[391] finds that in some social systems, some members are sacrificed because they do not fit into the slot of the system, or because they pay the price for the benefit or the folly of the whole, as in warfare, for example. Becker[27] feels that failure to maintain self esteem leads to the kind of behavior—largely forms of inhibited action—which has been labelled schizophrenia and depression. The upper class schizophrenic is in a more fortunate situation. He can effect some measure of correspondence between his fantasy world and certain specialized symbolic achievements provided by society, and he thus may have his identity validated.

McCaffrey[264] discusses the failure to meet role obligations and expectations; Kleiner and Tuckman,[184] the pervasive restriction of the social environment; Leighton[211] the fragmentation of the socio-cultural system or rate of acculturation; Burg,[50] starting with the double-bind hypothesis and its application to the Japanese, introduces a new concept of the "acculturationally rooted double-binds."

Montagu[282] goes even further by giving various examples of cultures that create group-learned schizoid or obsessive behavioral patterns. Whole nations may be considered "neurotic" or even "psychotic."

Bleuler[33] summarizes the status of research in schizophrenia in the following paragraph:

"The position as to schizophrenia research today may be summarized very simply: the personal influences of the patients' original disposition, his life history, physical peculiarities, and his attitudes towards his fellow men are known certainly to be important in the development of schizophrenia and its treatment. Whether in addition, impersonal, physical, or psychic, hereditary or noxal play a part in some or all forms of schizophrenia still remains to be proved."

With this voluminous literature available, it behooves us to read some sobering remarks by a few writers. Hunt[157] points out that no definite conclusion is possible from the study on the relationship between socio-cultural variables and functional mental disorders; the precise nature of the relationship is manifestly uncertain. Kohn[191] in his review of research studies in schizophrenia, reaches the startling conclusion that "there has not been a single well-controlled study that demonstrates any substantial difference between the family relationships of schizophrenics and those of normal persons *"from the same social class background"* (italics mine). Sanua[363] provides us with a review of the limitations of the various methodologies used in the study of schizophrenia and suggestions for future research. Murphy[286] has written an extensive review on the methodology of socio- and ethno-psychiatric research.

POVERTY, ECONOMIC MOBILITY, AND PROGNOSIS IN SCHIZOPHRENIA

Schizophrenia, in general, has been found to be more prevalent among the poorer classes than others. Differing interpretations have been propounded to explain this difference in rates. Some believe that no assumptions should be made about a cause and effect relationship. Since most epidemiologic studies have relied on "treated prevalence," it is possible that the poor are over-represented because upper class schizophrenics may be under private care, and thus are not included in the general vital statistics.

The incompleteness of the identification of schizophrenics is responsible for these different rates. Others believe that the stresses incurred in poverty are responsible for the higher rates among the lower classes. However, the relationship between schizophrenia and poverty is not found to be universal; a number of studies have shown that there is no relationship between the two, and have even shown that schizophrenia may be more prevalent among the upper classes than the lower.

A third set of studies has found a "drifting down" in the history of the schizophrenic, but again, there is the problem of interpretation. Some investigators believe that, following the "drifting down," the frustration encountered by the individual may lead to schizophrenia. On the other hand, others believe that, prior to the drifting itself, certain personality characteristics of the individual, or a predisposition towards schizophrenia, have made it impossible for the individual to assume a certain degree of necessary responsibility. As a result, he is forced to accept lower class positions more in line with the limitations imposed by his personality or illness. The studies that we shall now review will provide illustrations to the above hypotheses.

One of the large scale studies which has tried to relate social class and schizophrenia was conducted in New Haven by Hollingshead and Redlich.[155] They found that the incidence rate of schizophrenia for Class I and II was 6 per 100,000, while the incidence for Class V was 20 per 100,000. The prevalence figures were 111 and 895 respectively. This indicated that the lower class would tend to have more schizophrenics and a much lower rate of hospital discharge. Furthermore, they found that schizophrenic patients, in 91 per cent of the cases, remain in the same social class as their father's.

Some polemic has resulted from these findings. Reviewers concluded from this investigation that lower class living stimulates the development of schizophrenic symptomatology. However, this was disclaimed by Hollingshead and Redlich in later writings. They have been reluctant to state that their findings are of etiologic significance. Their purpose was to present information on "treated prevalence" rates obtained from psychiatric settings and from psychiatrists in private practice.

We have some further examples of studies which have found an inverse relationship between social class and the rate of mental disorders. Cooper,[80] in England, saw little evidence for the "drift hypothesis." He clearly states that conditions of socioeconomic stress suffered by lower class patients are important in the genesis of schizophrenia. Rennie et al.[342] in Manhattan, Hardt[142] in Syracuse, Bodian et al.,[36] Gardner and Bobigian,[125] Turner and Wagenfeld[416] in Rochester, Kaplan et al.[168] in Greater Boston, Warthen et al.[429] in Maryland, Achte and Seppala[1] in Helsinki, Finland, and Lowe and Garrat[233] in Birmingham, England, found that those belonging to the poorer social classes, or living in tenement type dwellings, were overrepresented in admissions to mental hospitals. Hardt found that the hebephrenics were somewhat overrepresented in the lowest class. Vail et al.[418] in a study in the 87 counties of Minnesota of the relationship between 77 socioeconomic and demographic variables and mental illness, found that half of the variance in state hospital load was associated with socioeconomic variables. One study in London, by Stein,[401] demonstrated, contrary to expectation, that more schizophrenics from well-to-do boroughs were admitted to mental hospitals, as compared to a number of poorer boroughs. She suggested that when several important features differ so much between areas, comparison by single index of social class is open to criticism. The two types of neighborhoods studies were not only different in social class, but also in family life and social and geographical stability.

A study by Clausen and Kohn[72,73] found no relationship between socioeconomic level of areas of the city of Hagerstown, Maryland, and rates of hospitalization for schizophrenia. Clausen and Kohn offer three possible explanations for the discrepancies in the two findings. Either the prepsychotic of the lower class had left the city prior to the outbreak of the illness, thus reducing the link between lower class status and schizophrenia, or, as may be the case in a small town, there is more tolerance for schizophrenia among the lower classes. The third explanation is that small towns offer greater possibilities for integration and social participation, and hence create an atmosphere more conducive to mental health, even among the lower class, while large cities with heterogeneous populations, foster a greater degree of social disorganization.

A number of studies have found that the schizophrenic suffers from economic mobility ("drift hypothesis"). However, the interpretation of such studies has given rise to two types of contrary opinions. One holds that schizophrenia develops after downward mobility, and the other that the schizophrenic illness or predisposition exists prior to the drifting.

Lystad[236] demonstrated that schizophrenics are more downwardly mobile than neurotics. Srole et al.[399] found that the downwardly mobile are characterized by poorer mental health, but this finding only applied to the psychotic. Tuckman and Kleiner[415] and Parker and Kleiner,[315] instead of using intergenerational movement from father's occupation to son's occupation, used an intragenerational index—that is, the discrepancy between one's educational status and one's occupational status. The authors feel that those who have higher goal strivings, and low self esteem, and who are not successful, suffer more frequently from mental illness. The philosophy of an open society, as emphasized in the United States, becomes maladaptive to those who, despite their efforts to go up the ladder, get nowhere. However, Parker and Kleiner[315] indicated that the concept of social mobility in itself is too gross a structural factor, and too variable in its psychologic implication to relate to mental disorder in a simple manner.

The most recent large-scale effort to study the relationship between schizophrenia and social class was conducted by Dunham[95,99,101] in Detroit. It is the first major epidemiologic study to concentrate on a single mental illness. According to Dunham, the evidence suggests that the class position of a given schizophrenic is a function of the disease. The potential schizophrenic, because of his limitations, is more likely to end up in a lower-class position. Thus, Dunham rejects both hypotheses that rates of prevalence are due to differences in community structure and social class. He believes that the differential rates are better explained by the "social selection" hypothesis.

Both Haag[137] and Rinehart[350] discuss this polemic. Among those who agree with Dunham are McCaffrey and Downing[263] who indicated that the economic conditions might be the result, rather than the cause of the disease. In other words, the sick selects his own environment.

Studies conducted in England corroborated the downward mobility of the schizophrenic. Morris,[283] Morrison,[284] and Goldberg and Morrison[131] demonstrated that schizophrenics move downward in the socioeconomic ladder. While fathers of schizophrenics conform to the expected frequency of social class distribution, 45 per cent of their children belong to social class V.

Recently, Brody[41] tried to combine the two hypotheses. There seems to be a dual "process of adverse selection (with individuals moving into areas permitting them maximum social survival without responsible community participation) and downward intergenerational occupational mobility due to failure to achieve in the prepsychotic state. Thus, both environmental vulnerability and a reduced repertory of coping mechanisms is translated into impaired capacity in the face of stress."

Probably some of the inconsistencies in these findings are attributable to the fact that: 1) there has been a lack of uniformity in the coverage of morbidity rates; 2) that social class criteria have been different in the various studies, such as social class of individuals, characteristics of the neighborhood, rentals, etc.; and 3) there has been a neglect of cultural values or special status of the lower class individual considered in the analysis of the relationship between social class and schizophrenia.

Carstairs and Brown[57] found that nonminers in a mining community had a higher prevalence of psychotic disorder than had miners. They conclude that the linking of social pressures to psychiatric disorders must await the analysis of the social system and value system of a community. Two further studies illustrate the need to control other variables besides social class, type of neighborhood, and rental level. A recent study by Mintz and Schwartz[280] has thrown some doubt on the relationship between poverty and schizophrenia. They found that in communities of "Italian" density, fewer "Italians" were admitted for schizophrenia than in communities with a lower density. There was no relationship between "Italian" incidence rates for schizophrenia and median monthly rental. They concluded that, in a homogeneous city, within a strongly stratified society, socioeconomic factors may be the most relevant dimension. However, the urban areas, lower class community integration achieved by ethnic groups in "Little Italies" or "Chinatowns" can relegate socioeconomic status to secondary importance. Thus, it would seem that many of the studies conducted in the past may have invalidated their results through neglect of the ethnic component in the population, and its density within the general population.

Sanua[365] tested the mobility hypothesis of a group of Jewish and Protestant paranoid schizophrenics, equated for socioeconomic status. The father's vocational status was taken as a basis for evaluating the direction of the mobility. Within the Jewish group, approximately one-third exhibited upward mobility, one-third had gone downward, and one-third had not moved. Within the Protestant group, one-fifth had moved upward, one-fifth downward, and three-fifths had remained in similar levels to their fathers. Thus, it would seem that a consideration of the ethnic, religious, and possibly the subcategory of the schizophrenic diagnosis, may provide us a more efficient way to study economic mobility. It is obvious that a normal control group of the same socio-economic background as the schizophrenics would indicate whether the latter have a social mobility dissimilar from the normal group, which could thus be attributed to the illness.

Another aspect of the relationship between social class and schizophrenia is prognosis. Hardt and Feinhandler[143] found that only 24.7 per cent of Class I patients were considered long term patients,—that is, had remained two years and beyond in mental hospitals—while 57 per cent of Class V patients were considered to be long term. Cooper[80] in England, also found that schizophrenics of the lower classes tended to stay longer in mental hospitals.

Mason[260] improved the prediction of discharge when social class was associated with marital status. Single schizophrenics of lower class had the worst prognosis.

The only study which has focused on social class, mental illness, and long-term treatment outcome is the follow-up study of the New Haven epidemiologic study conducted in 1950. Bean, Myers, and Pepper[25] compared the social adjustment of schizophrenics ten years after they had been released. Although they found a smaller percentage of lower class schizophrenics had been released, those who had been released manifested a much better mental status than upper class released schizophrenics. They believe that for a Class V patient to be released from a mental hospital, there must be almost complete remission, while a greater availability of all kinds of resources among the relatives of the upper-class schizophrenic facilitate his earlier return to the community, despite his condition.

Sanua,[373] in a study conducted in a small psychiatric hospital providing intensive psychotherapy, found that one-third of lower class Protestant and Jewish patients had been readmitted for any type of psychiatric care, while the percentage for readmission of the upper class patient was almost 70 per cent. Since the hospital was available for all patients in the neighborhood, it is believed that upper class patients were probably sicker at admission than lower class patients, assuming that the upper class patient had received treatment with private psychiatrists prior to commitment at the psychiatric hospital.

In recent years, this interest in the relationship between poverty and mental illness has been the subject of a number of publications (Greenblatt et al.,[134] Miller and Grigg,[277] Roman and Trice,[353] and Riessman et al.,[344]).

EDUCATION, VOCATION AND MENTAL HEALTH

Since it was found that schizophrenia was more prevalent among individuals belonging to the lower social classes, it could be assumed that the rate of schizophrenia would be higher among those with lower education and vocational achievement. However, a number of studies do not confirm this assumption.

Nurnberger et al.,[295] in a study in Indiana, confirmed that educational level and admission rate had an inverse relationship. However, they suggest that local circumstances may either enhance, reduce, or even neutralize the impact of education. Similar findings concerning the relationship between education and admission rates were found in Ohio (Locke et al.[230]).

Jaco,[163] who conducted his survey in Texas, found that this inverse relationship held only with the Anglo-American (correlation —.30). For the Spanish-American, it was +.90, and for the nonwhite it was +.38. Thus, while lack of education among the Anglo-Americans was related to psychiatric problems, extensive education among minority groups was found to be correlated with mental illness. For the total sample, he found that admission rates for schizophrenia was higher among those with no education (45 per 100,000) followed by those with college education (39 per 100,000). Those with lower education had, on the average, an incidence of 28 per 100,000.

Ødegard,[301] and Noreik and Ødegard[294] found that the rate of schizophrenia was raised by females who had graduated from high school. It is to be noted that high school education in Norway represents an achievement. They believe that females with high school education, as compared to those without it, may suffer more environmental stress. Among high school graduates, both males and females, the incidence of manic depression was twice as high as among the control group of nongraduates.

Frumkin[122] indicated that income per se is less important than the prestige associated with an occupation. Upon comparing different occupational groups, he found that upper class groups tend to develop psychopathology of "psychogenic origin," while lower class groups tend to develop psychopathology of "sociogenic origin." Lower social class status tends to promote social isolation and schizoid tendencies.

Locke[230] found that laborers and service workers had the highest incidence of schizophrenia. Employed females had more schizophrenia than had housewives.

Jaco[163] found a curvilinear relationship between occupation and psychosis in Texas. The highest incidence rates for schizophrenia were found among the unemployed (295 per 100,000) followed by rates for the professional and semiprofessional, (61 per 100,000), for service workers (64), manual workers (33), clerical and sales (54), agricultural (51), and managerial, official and proprietary occupations (19). It should be noted, however, that the above statistics include both the Spanish American and the nonwhite, and since the better educated in the two latter groups suffer more mental illness, the curvilinear relationship could be explained on that basis.

Studies of schizophrenia, vocation and education in other countries do not show this general consistency of higher rates of schizophrenia for those with poor education and low status professional positions, except for England, as shown by Brooke[44,45] and Folkard and Mandelbrote.[117] They found that kitchen hands and laborers have the highest admission rates o f schizophrenia.

Rose[354] found, contrary to expectations, that professional men in Lazio, Italy have a noticeable tendency toward schizophrenia, whether of the paranoid type or other.

Ødegard[296,297] found that schizophrenia is more frequent in the professional classes than among sales assistants, restaurant workers, and sailors in Norway. However, it was found to be highest for unskilled workers. He feels that most of the evidence points towards the reinforcement of the hypothesis of social selections as pointed out by Dunham in this country. Ødegard believes that schizophrenia may possibly be connected with individual life experience in early life, rather than with stress situations characteristic of larger social groups. He also found lower admission rates for children of business people, than for children of professionals and laborers.

Sundby and Nyhus[406] found the admission rate highest for sailors (71 per 100,000), followed by salesmen (36 per 100,000), and then workmen (10 per 100,000). Total admission rates vary considerably in the different areas of Oslo and among the sixteen different occupational groups. Thus, all these variations demonstrate that in Norway there is no linear relationship between socioeconomic status, education, vocation, and schizophrenia.

Ødegard[300] notes that class differential in mental illness is less marked in Norway. It may be attributable to the availability of similar facilities to everyone, or possibly to the fact that lower status in Norway is not related to a high stressful environment, as it is in the United States, where open opportunity is emphasized, but where achievement of one's aspirations is concomitantly more difficult.

GEOGRAPHIC MOBILITY AND SCHIZOPHRENIA

Since World War II, large population movements have occurred throughout the world. A question often raised is whether there is more schizophrenia among immigrants in their new environment because of the stress they encounter, or whether individuals who are already prone to mental illness tend to migrate. Four types of criteria are generally used to express geographical mobility: a) overseas emigration; b) movement within a continent; c) internal migration from one state to another, from rural to urban areas; and d) residential movement, i.e., within a city.

Listwan[229] found that migrants in Sydney, Australia develop paranoidal states. Cade and Krupinski[52] and Schaechter,[377] both in Melbourne, indicated that schizophrenia, mostly of the paranoid type, occurs more frequently among female immigrants who are of non-British birth. They feel that the paranoid tendencies are related to the difficulties of assimilation.

Cade and Krupinski discovered a correlation between schizophrenia and population density in Melbourne. Consistency of the relationship between migration and schizophrenia was also found by Tsung and Rin,[414] in Formosa, with paranoid psychosis being observed most frequently among female migrants from the mainland.

However, Ward,[428] studying the records of the Saskatchewan Mental Hospital, found that immigration and ethnicity had no effect on the incidence of mental disorders. It should be noted that the Saskatchewan area is considered to be a frontier society where fewer conflicts exist than in densely inhabited areas.

In Israel, whose population increase, mainly through immigration, has been threefold in the last two decades, Halevi[139] demonstrated that the immigrants from Europe, despite their war-time experience, had a lower incidence of schizophrenia than the native born Israelis. However, there has been a gradual increase in rates of schizophrenia among the later immigrant groups.

On the other hand, Eitinger,[105] in Norway, found psychosis, mostly paranoid, to be ten times higher among the refugees of different nationalities than in the indigenous population. Mezey,[275,276] in England, found that the stresses of immigration did not play an important causal role in Hungarian schizophrenics who had left their country following the revolution of 1956. He supports the "selection" hypothesis in the interpretation of differential incidence of schizophrenics in migrants.

In the United States, Malzberg[245] and Locke et al.[231] studied the relationship between incidence of schizophrenia and migration within the United States. Both Malzberg and Locke et al., in New York State and Ohio respectively, found a higher incidence among the migrants than among the native born. Lazarus et al.[205] found in Ohio, New York, and California, that admission rates for schizophrenia among the out-of-state migrants was higher than for native born, and even foreign born. Thomas and Locke[411] controlling for status, education, and occupation, in New York and Ohio, found that the rate for nonwhite migrants was higher than for nonwhite natives, although the difference was small. Lee[206] controlled for education in New York, and the difference between migrant and nonmigrant groups remained. Thus, most of the evidence in the United States tends to show that migration is related to a higher rate of admission for schizophrenia, at least in the three major states studies in New York, California, and Ohio. However, in all instances, increased standardization of the statistics reduced the differences.

Other studies have published contradictory findings. For example, Jaco[163] in Texas, showed a consistently higher incidence of schizophrenia among native-born males than three groups of migrants. However, with the females, the reverse was true. Thus, from the data reviewed, it would seem that migration is of greater consequence for the females.

In three large scale epidemiologic studies, (Hollingshead and Redlich,[55] Srole et al.;[399] and Leighton et al.,[217]) no relationship was found between normal foreign born, migrant and native born, and mental illness.

In a study of Negro migrants in Philadelphia, Kleiner and Parker[181] found that the Southern-born Negro who had moved to Pennsylvania was underrepresented in hospital statistics, as compared to the native-born Negro. In both instances, the incidence for schizophrenia was higher for the Negro female. Their hypothesis is that the discrepancy between level of aspiration and goal attainment for Negroes born in Pennsylvania is greater than for migrants, leading to greater stress among the former.

Turning to the role of migration in the Scandinavian countries, similar contradictory data are found. Astrup and Ødegard[16] demonstrated that only in Oslo do migrants have a higher rate of admission than native born. For all other parts of the country, people born locally have higher rates of admission than those born elsewhere. Sternbach[403] showed the reverse finding in Helsinki, Finland, as compared to Oslo. The rate of admission for schizophrenics was lower for migrants than for native born. In Iceland, Helgason[147] showed that schizophrenia was less frequent among migrants from the country than in the general rural population. It would seem that in Scandinavia, those who are on the move suffer less mental illness, which contrasts with findings in the United States.

Only one study by Keeler and Vitols[172] has tried to trace the psychologic adjustment of individuals prior to their migration. They found that 40 per cent of the patients admitted to an all-Negro mental hospital in North Carolina had moved between states or major districts in North Carolina prior to their hospitalization. Approximately two-thirds had been free of psychotic symptoms before migration. Such information was obtained from those who lived with the patient prior to the migration. Assuming that the reports of the informants were valid, we calculated that 14 per cent of the schizophrenic Negro population in the mental hospital in North Carolina had resided in areas other than those served by the hospital, thus indicating that hospital admissions may be inflated by sick individuals coming from other states.

The least extensive movement is residential mobility within a city. Here again, findings about change of residence and schizophrenia seem to be inconsistent. Lapouse et al.[203] in a study of admissions in state hospitals in Buffalo, rejected the "downward drift" hypothesis. They found no evidence that the concentration of psychotics in poorer areas was the product of recent movement. Hollingshead and Redlich[55] and Clausen and Kohn[7] likewise found no evidence that geographical mobility within the city is related to schizophrenia.

On the other hand, Plank[333] indicated that schizophrenics tended to remain on the residential level in which they are, while other people moved upward. In a control group of neurotics, 44 per cent of them had moved to better neighborhoods, while among the schizophrenics, it was only 12 per cent.

To summarize the findings, it would seem that overseas emigration, and intracontinental emigration, with some exceptions is related to an increase of mental illness. Migration within the same country seems to be deleterious in the United States, but related to good mental health in the Scandinavian countries. Recent studies of movement of schizophrenics within a city have shown that they tend to remain in the same neighborhoods.

Various hypotheses have been formulated to explain these findings. One is that individuals already predisposed to mental illness may relocate themselves in other parts of the country, and subsequently develop the psychiatric illness. The assumption is that they would have developed the illness even if they had not moved. The second hypothesis is that the mental illness is not related to actual relocation but is related to the difficulties encountered in the new environment due either to social isolation or to stress-caused cultural conflicts between old and new values. Another variable which has to be taken into consideration, is the type of environment in which the immigrant or migrant settles. Murphy[287] hypothesized that the rate of admission to mental hospitals may be related to the degree of group membership in the host country. In the United States and Australia, there is an emphasis on acculturation because of the "melting pot" policy. Canada has been more permissive with its immigrants, and French Canadians have been able to maintain their own identity. In Israel, it is to be noted that the immigrant group has been larger than the native-born group. This, coupled with the pioneering spirit, may have reduced the incidence of mental illness among the immigrants. As to the better mental health of migrants in the Scandinavian countries, we may hypothesize that in countries where opportunities for geographic mobility are limited, it is the more resourceful and capable who migrate, and those with better mental stamina who are less predisposed to mental illness.

SCHIZOPHRENIA AMONG DIFFERENT NATIONALITY, RELIGIOUS, AND ETHNIC GROUPS IN THE UNITED STATES AND CANADA

Epidemiologic Studies

A number of papers and books were published by Malzberg, giving incidence figures of hospital admissions for mental disorders in the State of New York. The following represent schizophrenia incidence rates per 100,000, for various ethnic and nationality groups:

NATIVE BORN		FOREIGN BORN	
Negro	109.0[239]	All Foreign-born (white)	52.7
Puerto Rican	99.4[238]		
White	41.3[249]		
German	42.0[251]	German	58.2
Norwegian	45.4[244]	Norwegian	26.7
Polish (50% Jewish)	55.7[243]	Polish (50% Jewish)	73.1
Russian (90% Jewish)	46.0[248]	Russian (90% Jewish)	65.4
Italian	36.3[247]	Italian	48.4
Irish	59. [246]	Irish	60.2
English	44.6[250]	English	26.6

Native-born of native parentage	Mixed Parentage	Foreign Parentage
33. [252]	59.2	49.1

The highest incidence is among Negroes and Puerto Ricans, where the rates are more than twice as high as for the general population. Malzberg explains this high incidence by the fact that 60 per cent of New York Negroes were born outside of New York, compared to 14 per cent of the white residents of the state.

In an earlier census of hospital admissions, Malzberg[241] found the rate for Negroes to be 71.8 per 100,000. With Puerto Ricans, Malzberg indicates that the high rate could be attributed either to difficult circumstances of living, or selection.

As indicated, large percentages among natives of Polish and Russian parentage are Jewish. Since the total Jewish rate for schizophrenia[243] was found to be lower (35.5) than the rate for Protestants (41.7) and Catholics (41.2) Malzberg concluded[248a] that non-Jewish Russian born and Polish born may have a rate of first admissions sufficiently high to raise the average for all Russian born.

Kleiner et al.[185] found a greater incidence of paranoid schizophrenia and other schizophrenias in "low status" religious groups (Methodist and Baptist) than in "high status" church groups. They found paranoid schizophrenia and other types of schizophrenia were lowest with the White Protestants and highest with Negro Catholics, the ratio being 1 : 4: In the latter group, there was a great prevalence of extreme aggressive and withdrawal behavior, and an earlier onset of mental disorders.

Levine and Delman[212] reported that the readmitted schizophrenic was more likely to be a Catholic than a Protestant, and to be of lower socioeconomic status. Myers and Roberts[293] found that the Jews, as a group, have a lower rate of schizophrenia than other groups. Since lower class members are more prone to schizophrenia, and Jews have a smaller percentage of their numbers in that category, they would accordingly show a lower incidence of schizophrenia.

Eichler and Lirtzman[104] found that while Jews represent 25 per cent of the population in New York, 50 per cent of the patients at a V.A. psychiatric clinic were Jewish. Percentages for Catholic and Protestant patients were 29.4 per cent and 12.5 per cent respectively, whereas the percentage for the total New York population of Catholics and Protestants was 45 per cent and 25 per cent respectively. Srole et al.[399] found that more non-Jews were admitted to state hospitals, but more Jews are treated in private hospitals and by private therapists. The disparity between the two groups is greatest for outpatients, where the ratio of Jew to non-Jew is 4 to 1.

Total rates, in general, are found to be higher for Negroes. However, in a number of other instances, they were found to be lower. In Louisiana, Pollack et al.[334] found that total admission rates among whites were higher than among nonwhites, except for schizophrenic reaction. In Maryland, total first admission rates were higher among nonwhites than whites. Rates for nonwhites in Maryland were higher than in Louisiana, particularly among urban groups. Schizophrenic rates were found to be higher for Negroes in North Carolina (Vitols[422]), in Pennsylvania (Kleiner et al.[182,183]), in Maryland (Bahn et al.[20]), and in Ohio (Locke[230]).

Jaco[163] found the highest rate for schizophrenia among the Anglo-

Americans (38 per 100,000) and the lowest among the Spanish Americans (23 per 100,000), with the rate for nonwhites falling between the two (31 per 100,000). Wilson and Lanz[434] found that while the admission rates for whites had not changed in the past 40 years in Virginia, it has almost doubled for Negroes. Their explanation is that with the drive for full equality, the Negro had lost his former security. Thus, by becoming more "acculturated" he has become more "marginal." These authors are taken to task by Pasamanik[321] since they seem to justify the old system of master-servant relations of white and Negro in the South.

Pasamanik believes that the higher rates for Negroes in Virginia may be due to the fact that lower class individuals are proportionately overinstitutionalized, since an ability to keep a sick person in the community is related to social class.

In his own study of Baltimore, Pasamanik[320,322] found that the rate for psychosis for institutionalized nonwhites is almost twice as high as for the whites. However, the number of noninstitutionalized white psychotics was almost ten times higher than nonwhites, making the total white rate higher than the rate for Negroes. Thus, according to Pasamanik, the usual higher rate found among Negroes could be attributed to urban conditions.

Hawaii presents an interesting area of research in schizophrenia, in view of the mingling of so many cultures. Schmitt[382,383] found schizophrenia to be lowest with the Chinese and Caucasians, and highest with the Hawaiian and Japanese. The high percentage of schizophrenia was also demonstrated by Ikeda, Ball and Yamamura.[159] They found 54 per cent of first admissions among the Japanese were diagnosed as schizophrenics, while 23 per cent of the non-Japanese were similarly diagnosed. Within the Japanese groups, Okinawans had a higher rate of admissions than mainland Japanese, despite similar ethnic background. The assumption is that Okinawans have not been able to maintain all of their traditional institutions. Okinawan women have a low rate of schizophrenia, which the authors assume is due to the fact that they marry outside the group.

For a number of years Murphy[258,288,289] has been studying subcultural groups in Canada. He has indicated that community conditions can affect both the onset and the later course of schizophrenia. He found the rate of schizophrenia to be very high for French Canadian women and Polish males, and lower for the Irish, British, and German groups. He formulated a "compromise theory" which includes familial, community, epidemiologic, sociologic and psychologic factors. On the basis of his analysis of schizophrenia among the various subcultural groups, he feels that schizophrenia is evoked or promoted when a community demands of its members lines of action which seem to be conflicting, or to be confusingly mapped out. The French Canadian female and the Polish male seem to have many such conflicts.

Clinical and Descriptive Studies

A number of studies using the clinical approach will now be reviewed. Opler[305] has shown that the Irish male schizophrenic is tortured by feelings of guilt and inadequacy, and suffers with paranoid delusions. The Italian is subject to moods of depression or uncontrolled elation. Fantl and Schiro[110] replicated the study with females, and the same differences were found, in most instances. Parsons[318] found that the South Italian schizophrenic in Naples tends toward a very close identity with family members, rather than the drift toward isolation, which is so characteristic of the schizophrenic in the United States. Piedmont[332] has found that the German schizophrenic shows more hostility and sado-masochistic, paranoid tendencies, while the Polish patient shows more anxiety, tends to be passive dependent, with somatic features, and presents more of the catatonic symptomatology.

Spitzer et al.[397] detected differences in the amount and kind of psychopathology between schizophrenics from urban New York and rural Kentucky. There was more psychopathology in the Kentucky group. The New York sample exceeded the Kentucky sample only with respect to flatness of affect, and anger, which was slightly higher.

Prange[335] shows how paranoid symptoms develop in the Chinese in the United States. With the Negroes, de Hoyos and de Hoyos[85] found that, except for hallucinations, white schizophrenics have more symptoms. They hypothesize that white psychiatrists probably see fewer symptoms in the Negro because they have a lower intensity of social involvement with the Negro. Prange and Vitols[366] suggest in a study of an all-Negro mental hospital in North Carolina, that stoicism and subtle defiance prevents depression in the Negro, who selects projection instead of introjection, as a defensive technic.

McGough et al.[265] indicate, however, that cultural factors and accessibility of treatment makes the lack of depression among Negroes "apparent" rather than "real."

In the Spring of 1963, Negro patients were accepted at an allwhite hospital in North Carolina. While the percentage of schizophrenia in the integrated hospital was almost twice as high for Negroes, psychotic depression was not significantly lower than among the white control group, but was four times higher than in the all-Negro hospital where Prange and Vitols conducted their study. The assumption is that, prior to integration, Negroes with psychotic depression were not likely to be referred to the all-Negro hospital. With more acculturation towards the values of the predominant white culture, the authors feel that the distribution of diagnostic categories among Negroes will more closely approximate the white norm.

Vitols[423] found that the incidence of hallucinations is higher with the Negro. He indicated that if hallucinations are considered evidence of a more severe schizophrenic state, it may be possible that Negroes are kept out of the hospital until the illness is more severe, or that the Negro culture predisposes to more severe schizophrenic illness.

Brody[40] finds three major characteristics in the Negro schizophrenic: the lack of well systematized delusion in the presence of a paranoid attitude, the prominence of perplexity and confusion, and somatic concern. He suggests that this type of symptomatology is also found among the nonliterate African schizophrenics, as reported by Carothers. In a recent study Brody[43] indicated that his data suggests the Negro in urban Baltimore must be sicker or more dramatically disturbed in order to receive hospital care comparable to the white, and therefore, may be underrepresented in admission rates.

Hammer[140] found greater self referral and family referral among Jews than among Negroes. Negroes tended to have shorter periods of hospitalization. Dohrenwend[90] has tackled the problem of "social causation" and "social selection" hypotheses, which have been plaguing psychiatric research. His basic assumption is that Jewish and Irish subjects represent the "advantaged minorities," while Negroes and Puerto Ricans represent the "disadvantaged minorities." The result of Dohrenwend's study showed that when income was controlled, Puerto Rican subjects had higher rates of symptoms than the Irish and Jewish, but that the Negro did not. This conformed to neither hypothesis, and after considering various explanations, it was asked whether the method of mental health assessment might be susceptible to cultural influences in response style. Answering "yes" or "no" to the same question might not have the same meaning among individuals belonging to different cultural groups. The Puerto Rican may be less reluctant to report on symptoms, even if he has experienced them in only minor degree.

Three papers have been devoted exclusively to mental illness among Jews. Freed[121] found no difference on ethnic identifications between psychotic and nonpsychotic Jews. Rinder[349] finds that while psychosis is low for Jews, neurosis is high. For the Jews, there is a high degree of security derived from parental affection. However, he believes that if there should be economic collapse, or an ascendance of racial-religious hostility, neurosis would decrease, and psychosis increase. Armstrong[9] does not believe that ethnic and religious aspects are causal affects in the incidence, or type of mental disturbance. It is the degree of acculturation to American norms which seems to have the greatest influence on the overall occurrence of mental illness.

Sanua[364,365,366,369,370,373] in a series of articles, compared the family background of Protestant, Irish, Italian and Jewish schizophrenics, with social class being controlled. It was shown that certain family characteristics which were associated with schizophrenia result simply from the sociocultural background of the schizophrenic sample studied. For example, it has been assumed that schizophrenics come from very large families. Sanua showed that in the various ethno-religious groups, the number of siblings is not any higher than would be expected in normal families of these groups. Small families exist among Jews and Protestants, and large families among the Italian and the Irish. A lack of consistency in former findings can largely be attributed to a partial or total neglect of sociocultural variables, including neglect to control for diagnostic subcategories of schizophrenia.

Meadow and Stoker[267] found that the Mexican-American schizophrenic is characterized by more affective symptomatology with catatonic tendencies. The Anglo-American had more paranoid delusions, despite the fact that jealousy is said to be a well-known characteristic of the Mexican.

Rogler and Hollingshead,[352] in a study of Puerto Rican schizophrenics, indicated that schizophrenia may bring about a reversal of roles. Males abandon the "machismo" pattern and become mild, meek and defenseless, whereas females become hostile, intolerant, and assaultive, which is the opposite of the traditional pattern. Maldonado-Serra[237] found that one way to make group psychotherapy meaningful with Puerto Rican schizophrenics was to have a three-member therapy team. Since the schizophrenic has repressed resentment and massive fear of paternal and maternal authority, there is the need to have a symbolic sibling who could help bridge the relationship with the mother and father figures, in the therapy sessions. Mehlman[271] has discussed the "Puerto Rican Syndrome," which is a collection of various disease processes that tend to be superficially and deceivingly similar in this particular culture.

Fernandez-Marina and Von Eckhardt[111] have diagnosed a pattern of relationship among the parents of schizophrenics which is specific to Puerto Rico.

Enright and Jaeckle[108,109] found that Japanese paranoid schizophrenics are more restrained and have more disturbance of thinking. Ideas of reference are frequent Japanese symptoms. The Filipino schizophrenic is violent, as he directs his anger actively and tries to remove outside obstacles. Finney[112] found that the Portuguese had the highest admission rates—more than four times their numbers in the total population. Using the M.M.P.I. with outpatients, he found that anxiety was highest with the Portuguese and lowest with the Chinese, who had the lowest admission rates.

STUDIES IN LATIN AMERICA AND THE CARIBBEAN ISLANDS

Weinstein[431] states that in the Virgin Islands catatonic psychoses were common, but rare among the French-speaking group who manifested a high incidence of paranoid reactions. Delusions about sex, food and color were frequent in French-speaking patients, but infrequent among the other patients.

Despinoy et al.[86] however, cites that 48 per cent of the schizophrenics in Martinique were paranoid. Bordeleau[38] had a similar finding in Haiti. Mars[258] observed that urban and rural lower classes in Haiti had delusions similar to French white schizophrenics. Sanseigne[362] observed two main features in psychotic outbreaks among Haitians. The most frequent was an acute psychosis *bouffée delirante aigue*, characterized by sudden attack, confusion, and hallucinations; the other was a picture of paranoid psychoses with voodoo delusions which was found even among upper-class patients. Kiev[175,176] studied the practices of native healers in Haiti and observed that with involvement of voodoo deities, the healer provides a familar means to reduce the maladaptive process. Under the auspices of the Research Institute for the Study of Man, in New York City[67] a one-day census of patients was conducted in ten mental hospitals in the Caribbean Islands. It was found that approximately 58 per cent of the patients had been classified as schizophrenics.

A number of studies were conducted in England with West Indians who had immigrated. Gordon[132] states they have a low incidence of personality disorders and neurosis, but that there was a high frequency of schizo-affective illness. Hemsi[148] found that schizophrenia was considerably higher among the West Indians than in the native population. Kiev[177,178] stresses that most of the West Indian schizophrenics committed to mental hospitals displayed religious delusions accompanied by hallucinatory command to preach and heal. These delusions are strongly related to the beliefs of normal West Indian immigrants.

Stein,[402] visiting a Peruvian hospital where 80 per cent of the patients were diagnosed as schizophrenics, reports that patients are rarely violent. A lone female nurse can take charge of a male ward because of the special position of women in a society where values supporting a "cult of the Virgin" play a role in structuring male-female relationships. The physician can be paternalistic and directive. He can put his arm around his patients, and this gesture is accepted as fatherly support.

The high percentage of schizophrenics in mental hospitals in Latin America was also confirmed by Seguin[386] in Peru, 66.7 per cent, with 52 per cent being of the paranoid type; by Leon[219] in Colombia, where the rate was 70 per cent. There was not a single case of true manic-depressive psychosis. The high percentages of schizophrenics in hospital facilities are probably due to the fact that only the very seriously ill are accepted because of limited facilities.

Draguns et al.[98] studied the symptomatology of Argentinian and American psychiatric patients, half of them being schizophrenics. They presented data to show that the Argentinian patient more frequently expressed more ideational impoverishment, apathy and a sense of interpersonal alienation. The American mental patient had a greater frequency of thought disorganization and tended to be overtly destructive.

Bonhour[37] reported on epidemiologic studies carried on by the National Institute of Mental Health of Argentina. The survey was conducted in three areas—urban, rural-urban, and rural. The total morbidity rate of impaired individuals was found to be 6.43 per cent, 12.30 per cent, and 19.9 per cent respectively. These figures include mental deficiency and disturbances of childhood. In the Midtown Manhattan Study, Srole et al. found a total impairment rate of 23.4 per cent for the total sample studied, a rate which is much higher than the findings in Argentina. Of the total sample of 4,422 individuals interviewed in the Argentinian study, only 5 were diagnosed as schizophrenics, thus giving a morbidity rate of 1.1 per 1000, which is a much lower figure than is ordinarily found in other parts of the world. In the Midtown Manhattan Study, 1 out of 4 of the impaired individuals were psychotic. Here again, the problem is whether mental illness is less frequent in Argentina, or whether the discrepancy can be explained on the basis of differential diagnosis in the two countries. As in the Midtown Manhattan Study, however, mental illness was found to be dominant among the lower social classes. More than 90 per cent of the impaired individuals in the Argentinian study belonged to Class IV or Class V.

Bastide[21] reported that the rate of schizophrenia in Brazil is highest with the white population, lowest with the Negro population. The rate for the mulatto is between these two extremes. Negroes suffer from the mental illnesses of the poor—those of organic origin, toxic and infectious. In contrast to the United States, the Negro in Brazil accepts an inferior status which insures him security in his dependence. Bastide hypothesizes that the low rates of psychoses and neuroses among the Negroes may be attributed to their practice of "lower spiritualism" of Yoruba or Dahomian origin which may fulfill a useful function in their lives.

STUDIES IN EUROPEAN COUNTRIES

Parsons[317,319] contrasted the schizophrenics in Naples and the United States. While the incidence of schizophrenia may be higher among the lower classes in Italy, the presence of strong family ties alters the course of the schizophrenic syndrome. She feels that in a highly technologically-evolved nation such as the United States, schizophrenics become more severely incapacitated mental patients.

Risso and Boker[351] indicated that workers from Southern Italy, working in Switzerland, often had overpowering delusions that they had been bewitched, and usually were diagnosed by Swiss psychiatrists as suffering severe acute schizophrenia. To their families, the transformation was considered to be a natural reaction to being bewitched. Comparing the reaction time of Italian and American schizophrenics, Rosenbaum[357] found that disorganizing anxiety was more pronounced with the Italian patient. Like Parsons, he found that Italian schizophrenics were more responsive than American schizophrenics, who tended to be more socially disarticulated. Rose[354] indicated that in the Province of Lazio (including Rome) 18 per cent of the admitted patients were schizophrenics. Manic-depressive psychosis was more frequent than schizophrenia. However, he found that with a rise in social status, as evaluated by education and migration to the nation's capital, the rate of paranoid schizophrenia went up. Camba and Bernardino,[53] on the other hand, showed that in the province of Cagliari, the highest incidence was with schizophrenic patients. In some areas, 75 per cent of the admitted patients were diagnosed as such. Aronson,[10] commenting on the handling of schizophrenics in the United States and the Soviet Union, indicates that the attitudes towards the mental patient in the latter country are affected by the dominant philosophy regarding the responsibility of man. In the United States, the orientation is individualistic. The patient is seen as important and responsible for himself. In the Soviet Union, the "group," the "collective" are primary, and the individual has to subject his egocentric wishes to them. The purpose of Soviet psychotherapy is not to enable the individual to fulfill his potential, but rather, to enable the individual to work within his collective. Since "work" is viewed as man's most important activity, treatment and rehabilitation of mental patients is always carried on within the framework of job activities.

Field[113,114] recently explored trends in the care of the mentally ill in the Soviet Union, where, according to him, mental illness does not receive the same emphasis as it does in this country. The general pronouncement on the subject is that mental illness can only decline in the Soviet Union because of the political system in force. However, accurate data from which such a conclusion can be drawn are not available. On the basis of his reading of the literature, and visits there, Field concludes that schizophrenia is a major and unresolved problem in the Soviet Union as it is in the United States.

Quoting a Soviet publication, Field points out that first visits by schizophrenic patients to a neuropsychiatric dispensary in Moscow were reduced by almost one half from 1940 to 1956. Kerbikov, who wrote the report, attributed this change to the constant improvement in material standards of living, and to the cultural level attained by Soviet citizens, leading to a general strengthening of mental health. Field cites some of the major differences between the USSR and the United States. In the Soviet Union there is a greater emphasis on an organic interpretation as to the etiology of schizophrenia (Lynn,[235] Gilyarovsky,[128]). This may mean a greater readiness on the part of Soviet psychiatrists to diagnose patients in organic rather than dynamic terms. The number of psychiatrists in the Soviet Union is greater than in the United States. It should be noted that the medical profession in the U.S.S.R. is primarily a female profession, with 75 per cent of the doctors being women. Undoubtedly, this could be a major factor in the rehabilitation of the mentally ill, since women psychiatrists are likely to give more help and emotional support than male psychiatrists. While there is one psychiatric bed for every 250 persons in the United States, the corresponding figure for the Soviet Union is one bed for each 1000 to 1500 persons. The policy in the U.S.S.R. is one of active treatment and the patient's return to the community as fast as possible. Field estimates that hospital beds in the Soviet Union are utilized nine times as intensively as in the United States. Physicians there normally carry 27.4 patients, whereas in the United States, the load is 183.9 patients.

The main contribution of Soviet psychiatry, according to Field, is probably their concept of not condemning psychiatric patients to the idle, demoralizing, desocializing, untherapeutic and wasteful life of a chronic patient in a large mental hospital. Soviet psychiatrists avoid the hospitalization of psychotics, but would be inclined to hospitalize neurotics. This is based on the assumption that neuroses are the result of environmental factors, and that the hospital is needed to enable the patient to recuperate. Since the mental hospital does not occupy a central position in the Soviet Union, the focus is on the psychoneurologic dispensary, which provides all types of psychiatric care except long-term hospitalization.

Two papers on Soviet psychiatry were recently published by Kolb[192] and Ziferstein.[442] Kolb suggests that economic security through immediate pensioning of the mentally ill, plus the offering of salaries for work during the rehabilitative process has the advantage of maintaining or expanding ego functions. The psychoneurological dispensary, according to Kolb, has features in common with the community mental health centers to be built in this country. However, he states that, contrary to the new organizational structure of psychiatric services in the Soviet Union, the system in the United States will have to lay aside antiquated boundaries of responsibilities now held by the vast number of governmental and voluntary boards, commissions, and professional organizations, which today in many cities fragment effective patient care. Ziferstein[442] indicates that the distinctive features of Soviet psychotherapists are their informality, availability and activity. A patient can see a therapist at any time he feels the need, without advance appointment. There are no standard psychotherapeutic hours.

Klein et al.[180] believes that the low overall rate of mental patients in the Soviet Union is due to the fact that a large percentage of citizens still live in the less demanding environment of rural communities, where the mentally ill can make a marginal adjustment. However, Krasik[194] found in Riazne, U.S.S.R. that although the rate for schizophrenia in urban areas was higher than in rural areas, the difference was not significant.

In Czechoslovakia, Ivanys et al.[161,162,163] found that psychiatric morbidity in Prague is significantly higher in unsatisfactory tenement areas inhabited by people living alone, or in broken families. Gerard[127] compiled a 106-item bibliography on research in social psychiatry in Poland. In one study by Gnat and Henisz,[130] it was demonstrated that the incidence of mental disorders is inversely related to education and also to the prestige of the respondent's occupational category.

Norway has been in the vanguard in the field of psychiatric epidemiology. Astrup[17] compiled a bibliography of research conducted by Scandinavian psychiatrists within the field of "social psychiatry", which includes "genetics, epidemiology, demography, ecology, and medical statistics." Ødegard[298] reviewed incidence and prevalence studies with control of demographic variables.

In Ireland, Walsh[427] agreed with Opler's description of the Irish schizophrenic. Browne[46] indicated that mental illness in Ireland is not likely to come to public attention until it has reached psychotic intensity. O'Doherty[302] found that admissions of schizophrenics in Ireland were 28 per cent higher than in England and Wales, while the total admission rate was twice as high. Emigration to cities, traditional abhorrence of suicide, long established tolerance for the psychotic which makes them more visible, and large number of single adults are all factors contributing to a higher mental hospitalization rate.

Brunetti[47] conducted a prevalence study in the rural area of Vaucluse in France. He found that 25 per cent of the population were significantly impaired in their functioning by a mental disorder. We note in a statistical report of the National Institute of Mental Health and Medical Research in France[49] that the percentage of schizophrenics in mental hospitals is 27.3 per cent, and the percentage for new admissions is 13.9 per cent, both of which are lower than figures for the United States. It is possible that there is less schizophrenia in France, or that the diagnosis is less frequently given. Our feeling is that the latter interpretation is more correct.

Crocetti et al.[81,82] in an epidemiologic study on the northern shore of the Adriatic part of Croatia, confirmed a long-standing belief that there is an unusual prevalence of schizophrenia in the region. Army rate discharge was also found to be twice as high for this region as for the rest of Croatia. Lopasic and Mikic[232] found the rate of schizophrenia in Susak, Yugoslavia, a small island, to be higher than on the mainland. Listwan[228] indicated that since the inhabitants of the Mediterranean countries are inclined to be emotional and excitable, they would tend to have more manic-depressive reaction when mentally deranged. In Eastern Europe, because of the slowness and languidness of the inhabitants, they would tend to become schizophrenics of the catatonic type. However, Hartocollis[144] found in Greece that 75 per cent of the mental patients are chronic schizophrenics. The general belief in Greece is that demons and evil spirits cause mental illness. Mental patients are often taken to altars of saints who are said to effect cure of the "possessed." This is the general practice in the whole of the Middle East as well.

STUDIES IN ASIATIC COUNTRIES

Israel, with its mingling of population from all corners of the world, presents an interesting laboratory for psychiatric research. A striking and unexpected finding is that the incidence rate for schizophrenia is highest for Israel-born males, (80.8 per 100,000, -Halevi,[139]) and low for Jews who emigrated from Eastern Europe, (34.2 per 100,000). In general, Jews from Muslim countries also had lower rates than Israel-born. Maoz et al.[253] found that psychosis not falling into any standard classification occurred especially among recently arrived Oriental Jews. Miller[278] believes that the rates for the latter group may be overestimated because of the difficulties and confusions in the diagnosis of patients from cultures unfamiliar to the Western psychiatrist. He also commented on the high rates for native-born Israelis, and pointed out the complicating factor that 40 per cent of the native-born are of Oriental descent. On the other hand, Miller believes that this high rate could be attributed to the fact that the schizophrenic symptomatology is likely to develop to a greater extent in the more advanced section of the population.

Over the course of the past ten years there has been a relatively large increase of research studies in Asia. Murphy et al.,[290] in a survey of schizophrenic symptomatology as reported by local psychiatrists in various parts of the world, found larger percentages of simple and catatonic type of schizophrenia, and a low percentage of paranoid type in Asian samples. However, the paranoid subtype was found to be more prevalent in urban areas of middle class population than in rural areas.

Zunin and Rubin[445] observed that foreign students from non-Western countries, who become psychotic while studying in the United States, seem to have a strong paranoid element. Wittkower and Fried[437] indicate that opinions differ as to whether the Eastern way of life, in general, predisposes to schizophrenia, conceals schizophrenia, or safeguards against schizophrenia.

Meerloo (270) compares the Western "psyche," burdened with a punishing conscience and fighting an inner battle alone, with the Oriental "psyche" where integration into group life provides a security often lacking in Western man. Mayer Gross[261] does not believe that the different social and cultural backgrounds in India and England are of major importance in the causation, prevention, or chronicity of schizophrenia. Gaitonde[123,124] compared mental patients in India and the United States, and concluded that while there may be an *international* surgery, there is only a *national* psychiatry. For example, he mentions that among the uneducated, catatonic schizophrenia is considered to be a result of divine grace.

Rao[340] in the Bihar province, found that 70 per cent of the admissions are due to schizophrenic breakdown, reflecting a salient feature of Indian culture, which encourages withdrawal in the face of stress.

The following represent other major findings by investigators studying schizophrenia in India. Sukthankar and Vahia[404] and Vahia[417] indicate that catatonic states are significantly more common in India. Of those who had hallucinations, 80 per cent had the auditory type. Sreenivasant and Hoenig[398] and Hoenig and Sreenivasant[154] found the Vaisyos group (merchants) to have the highest hospital admission rates, followed by Brahmins and Indian Christians, —that is, the more literate had more mental illness. Walker[425] observed an earlier onset of schizophrenia in Ranchu, India, as compared to the age of onset in the United States. Bhaskaran[32] likewise found an earlier onset of schizophrenia. Because of the family setup, he found that mothers-in-law and older brothers tended to be persecutors. While some patients may have sex conflicts, very few of the paranoid schizophrenics showed latent homosexuality.

Chakraborty[68] demonstrated that the eldest born, as in Japan, had a higher breakdown rate, and females exhibited more violence than males. Hoch[151] found a complete absence of infantile psychosis among the Muslims, as compared to the Hindus. However, the Muslims "catch up" with the Hindus after the age of sixteen. The predominance of fathers in academic and high positions in a group of patients suffering from infantile psychosis tends to confirm Western theories (Lowe[234]) about the sophisticated environment in which an autistic child is likely to develop. Sanua[368,370] has reviewed the literature on the influence of the sociocultural background in the symptomatology of childhood schizophrenia.

Hoch[150] has found that Indian patients seem to be far more flexible in their symptomatology than Europeans. They often seem to try out all the possibilities of psychiatric symptomatology consecutively, or even simultaneously. She noted, however, that Indian Christians most frequently show paranoid symptomatology.

In Thailand, as in other Asian countries, there is a high incidence of schizophrenia (72 per cent of all admitted cases) with paranoid symptomatology being extremely rare (Ratanakorn[338,339]) because of the very strict child rearing practices, the reaction of frustrations is one of withdrawal. Kelman[173] discussed a number of factors which seem to be associated with a schizophrenic-like personality in Thai patients.

Schizophrenics in Burma (Hitson and Funkenstein[149,] and Grewal[135]) do not seem to follow the usual pattern found in other Asian countries. Schizophrenia of the catatonic and simple types are rare, while paranoid schizophrenia is more frequent. Hitson and Funkenstein indicated that the patterns of family life of paranoid schizophrenics in Boston is similar to the general family pattern in Burma—complete domination by the parents. Accordingly, this results in aggression being directed against the outside world as evidenced by the homicide rate in Burma, one of the highest in the world. While some authors have indicated that complete subjugation to authority leads to withdrawal in most of the Asian countries, in Burma this seems to have the opposite effect.

In the Philippine Islands, as in Burma, paranoid schizophrenics have a great tendency to act out their impulses (Ventura[421]). It was found that the homicide rate in Manila is eleven times higher than in New York City (Sechrest[385])

On the basis of returned mailed questionnaires, Murphy, Wittkower, Fried, and Ellenberger[290] noted that simple schizophrenia and social withdrawal was more frequent than paranoid schizophrenia in Asia. With few exceptions, this seems to be corroborated by the studies reviewed here. The Asian tolerance for social withdrawal seems to make for a greater frequency of such cases.

A number of psychiatric studies on the Chinese were recently conducted, either in Formosa or Southeast Asia, where Chinese had been settling prior to the establishment of Communist China. Rin and Lin[346] found that the catatonic type was more prevalent among the Formosan aborigines than among the Chinese living in Formosa, who had come from the mainland. All types of psychoses tended to follow a relatively favorable clinical course and prognosis. It is believed that the social forces in the community itself act to reduce the deterioration of the patients. Rin, Wu and Lin[347] found more grandiose ideas among the Formosan male, with magic and superstitious content, probably because of their lower social and cultural status. Rin[345] showed that parental loss played no role whatsoever with the Chinese schizophrenic. As in other Asian countries, a greater number of first-born were admitted with a diagnosis of schizophrenia.

Schmidt[379,380] found that most of the hospital admissions in Sarawak, Borneo, were Chinese schizophrenics of the hebephrenic or simple types. Malayans had atypical schizophrenia, with a marked depressive, or more often, hypomanic coloring. Medlicott[268] indicated that Chinese in Indonesia, because of their ambitious nature and higher economic level, have more mental illness than Malayans, who presumably are protected by fatalism, a philosophic aspect of their Islamic faith.

Cerny,[65,66] a Czech psychiatrist, has reviewed psychiatry on the mainland of China. He found that 46 per cent of the schizophrenics are of the paranoid type, and 11 per cent are catatonic. Traditional Chinese medicine, such as acupuncture, iguipuncture, and breathing exercises for treatment of psychosis, is extensive. These methods have spread to other Asian countries, and even to Europe. Chu[71] found in Peking that the percentage of schizophrenia is higher for Chinese than for Manchu. Mental hospitals in China, contrary to Western hospitals, admit only a very small percentage of aged.

Dorzhadamere[91] found in Mongolia that schizophrenia is increasing, now that infectious psychosis has been reduced, while atypical types of psychoses are decreasing.

In Korea, guilt feelings were found to be rare, and euphoric delusions are more frequent than persecutory delusions. (Song[395]) In an epidemiologic study, Yoo[450] indicated that the symptomatology, incidence, and prevalence of functional mental disorders in Korea do not significantly differ from those in other countries. Oh[303] studied the family background of schizophrenics in Pusan, and found that rejection and broken homes were very frequent. Kahn et al.[167] compared American and Korean mental patients. The Americans concentrated on issues of authoritarian control and restrictions; the Koreans saw the hospital as a pleasant way to get away from problems, even though they harbored some fears about other patients.

There is little paranoid schizophrenia in Indonesia (Pfeiffer[328,329], and Kline[188]). The hebephrenic type is most frequent. Even when patients had hallucinations, they were not disturbing. Berne[30,31] has reported on patients in the Fiji Islands. After visiting thirty countries, he indicates he found the same reservoir of psychopathology in each. He feels that diagnosis can be independent of culture, and that there is a bias towards the "cultural viewpoint" at the expense of the genetic, and other aspects. He feels that rates of mental illness are the same the world over.

Cawte and Kidson[62,63,64] carried out epidemiologic studies on the north coast of Western Australia, and discuss the role that sorcery plays in mental illness. Statistics on mental illness among the Maori in New Zealand (Government Report) showed that paranoid forms are very rare.

Caudill[59,60] has written extensively on mental illness in Japan. Cultural changes, with the maintenance of certain traditional roles, produce more serious psychologic problems in the eldest male and the youngest daughter. He found a higher frequency of schizophrenia among the latter two than in the rest of the siblings. He was impressed by the greater degree of contact with other human beings exhibited by the Japanese schizophrenic.

In a more recent study, Schooler and Caudill[383] found the Japanese schizophrenic more likely to be physically assaultive than his American counterpart. Among the Americans, there was a greater disruption of reality testing. They hypothesized that in a society like Japan, which insists on decorum, a breach of the norm leads to hospitalization, while a lack of reality testing in the United States would lead to hospitalization. A high prevalence of schizophrenia (76.7 per cent) was found in the Okayama prefecture in Japan. Asai[13] and Hasuzawa[145] showed that the delusions of Japanese schizophrenics changed from the divine concept of the Emperor to powerful deities and Buddha during the postwar period.

In Okinawa, on the other hand, Hankoff[141] found that assaultive and agitated behavior was rare. Most of the patients were chronic schizophrenics, with hebephrenic schizophrenia being most frequent with the females.

It is to be noted that the Japanese schizophrenics in Hawaii were found to be restrained, but showed more disturbance of thinking. This is probably due to the acculturation process of the Japanese on the Islands. Antrobus and Bloom[6] tried to test the hypothesis that schizophrenia was more frequent with the older male sibling and the youngest daughter in Hawaii. However, no differences were found between the younger and older siblings. Terashima[410] has found that the second generation of Japanese schizophrenics in Canada, because of the conflict with the old traditions, tended to use withdrawal as a defense against overpowering guilt.

STUDIES IN AFRICA

Psychiatric research in Africa has been somewhat limited, when compared to the research conducted on other continents. However, there are few major writings which provide a reasonable introduction to the field. The Bukavu Conference[272] which was sponsored by the World Health Organization, presents short papers, summary statements, and bibliographic sources regarding psychiatric research in fourteen African states. Most of the writers believe that increased contact with Western modes of life has resulted in increased mental illness. Two major concerns were expressed—lack of accurate knowledge on incidence and prevalence, and the effect of physical disease upon mental health.

Two books discuss West African psychiatric literature, and report on present research. Field[115] found that schizophrenics in rural Ghana, whose hallucinations and delusions are within the bounds of culturally determined credibility, are not regarded as mentally ill. Leighton et al.[212] report on the psychiatric symptoms found in a representative sample from fifteen Yoruba villages in Nigeria, and the data is compared with a similar study that was conducted in Canada. They found 16 per cent of the adults in rural villages, and 17 per cent of the adults in a segment of a city had psychiatric symptoms to a significant degree. The impairment was found to be related to the degree of disintegration in the social environment, which is similar to the findings of their Stirling County research.

Forster[118,119] observed that most schizophrenics come from more Westernized environments, and suggests that radical culture change increases the admission of schizophrenia. Lambo[198] reviewed some of the work conducted in Africa. Contrary to popular belief, he found that catatonic schizophrenia is very common among the native population, although no subvariety is predominant. However, the assumption that paranoid schizophrenia is rare among Africans is unsupported by clinical findings, according to Lambo. He indicates[197] that African university students in Britain are most vulnerable to paranoid schizophrenia. He observes that the favorable social environment influences quick recovery among schizophrenics in Africa.

Lambo[199] studied two groups of paranoid schizophrenics—literate and nonliterate. In the illiterate group, he observed a symptom-complex which included anxiety state, neurotic depression, vague hypochondriacal symptoms, magic-mystical projection symptoms, episodic twilight or confusional states, atypical depersonalization phenomenon, emotional lability, and retrospective falsification of hallucinatory experiences. However, in the literate group, the variation in psychiatric symptomatology was minimal; the pattern of illness was quite similar to the pattern of illness usually described in Western Europe.

Vyncke's research[424] on mental disorders in the Congo found, as did

Forster, that schizophrenia was more frequent with the westernized Congolese. Wintrob and Wittkower[435] observed in Liberia that preliterate Africans are more, and not less, prone than members of advanced cultures to regress into psychotic states, which are more often than not transient in nature. In Guinea, Jakovljevic[164] found only 13 per cent of the patients at the Central Hospital in Conakry had been diagnosed as having functional psychosis.

Pavicevic[323] suggested that schizophrenics in Ethiopia tend to be paranoid with higher frequency than is usually found in Europe, but they are less aggressive. Paranoid grandiosity occurred only among Muslims. Collomb[76] reports that schizophrenia of the paranoid type is the most widespread psychosis in psychiatric hospitals south of the Sahara. However, in a later paper Collomb[78] found that the simple form was more numerous. Somatization is frequent in certain depressives, who also become autistic. Transitory delusional states seem to be the most typical form of Senegalese psychopathology.

Weinberg[430] found that the percentage of hospitalized depressives and of attempted suicides in Ghana tends to be high, while low rates are consistently reported for other countries in the sub-Sahara. A number of explanations offered, however, suggest that Ghanian social organization and culture, as they affect personality organization, are somewhat different than in the other African countries.

A number of papers have been published by Margetts[254,255,257] on the status of psychiatry in East Africa. He states that schizophrenia is the most frequent diagnosis at Mathari Hospital in Kenya. Edgerton[103] conducted a survey on the attitude towards psychosis in four East African societies. The role of witchcraft was dominant in two of these societies.

In South Africa Simons[391] warns that conclusions about the African's proneness or lack of proneness toward certain psychotic disorders, based on hospital statistics, would be misleading. Hospital admissions are more apt to reflect society's need to control the violent, uncontrollable, or destitute cases, than to indicate the true incidence and nature of mental health problems among Africans. Berman[29] feels that reliable information on a scientific level is conspicuously absent, although he states that catatonic schizophrenia seems to be more prevalent among the detribalized Africans. Blignault[35] found the Bantu, in transition, are likely to hear accusatory hallucinations, indicating an awareness of individual guilt.

In general, there seems to be less agreement about mental disorders in Africa than in Asia. Africa is obviously very different from Asia. Since the end of World War II independence has been achieved by a large number of former African colonies, at various rates and degrees. Among the Africans, there are many Christians and Muslims who maintain some of the traditional folk religion, with a large majority still not detribalized. As indicated by a number of writers, with this state of flux in Africa, disagreements are bound to occur regarding the observations of psychiatrists. However, as expressed by Bleuler, there seems to be some agreement that in Africa[34] patients with psychoses of schizophrenic symptomatology recover entirely much more frequently than in Europe.

Margett, a Canadian psychiatrist who was formerly director of the Mathari Mental Hospital in Kenya, is editing a book entitled *Mind of Man in Africa*[256] which will be an anthology relating to psychiatry and mental health in Africa.

STUDIES IN THE MIDDLE EAST

There are approximately 110 million Arabs in the whole Middle East and North Africa. While these countries are more accessible to the Western world, psychiatric studies in the area are limited in scope.

Kline[187] finds that paranoid schizophrenia in Kuwait is high among city dwellers and low among the isolated Bedouins. The fact that homosexual practices are frequent among both groups throws doubt on the conjectural relationship between paranoid reactions and homosexuality. Parhad[316] reporting from Kuwait, observes the passivity and nondestructiveness of schizophrenic patients in the hospital. He studied the ruling family of Kuwait, about 300 persons, and found not a single case of schizophrenia. He relates this to the family structure and the way in which the children are reared from the day of birth.

Lewin[221] pointed out that in Egypt the differential diagnosis of schizophrenia presents problems because of a prevailing belief in spirits, and the use of hashish which produces a clinical picture of schizophrenia; true schizophrenia is frequently masked by neurotic and hysterical symptoms and chronic intoxication.

In Iraq, Bazzaoui and Al-Issa[24] found that schizophrenia is the most common of psychoses. Psychotics tend to be noisy and aggressive. Such behavior is attributed by the authors to the cultural context which "encourages assertion and aggression." A thorough discussion on the "desert type" Arab is presented by a French psychoanalyst, Laforgue.[195] The following are his views:

> "The rigidity of the psyche is shown in the way every man inflexibly follows one direction and one idea, which often becomes a fixed idea or fanaticism. Concurrently, along with this strong tyrannical superego, there are strongly eroticized aggressive drives which sometimes break out in the form of a reckless bloodthirsty rage; they will crack an infant's skull against the wall, rip open a woman's womb, and kill animals. The oral, sadistic organization of their libido explains why blood-spilling is common among these people, and why they need such Draconian laws."

For a more recent evaluation of the psychology of the Arab, Sanua[374] has brought together research and observation on the Egyptian fellah which could also apply to other Muslims in the Middle East.

Baasher[18,19] found that females in the Sudan have a much higher incidence of schizophrenia than do males. He did not find any peculiar type of mental disease. However, he states that the environment has a definite influence on the onset of mental illness and on the ensuing psychological reaction.

In Lebanon, Katchadourian and Racy[170,171] conducted a large scale epidemiologic study for the whole of Lebanon. They found that the undifferentiated chronic type is most common. Prevalence rates are found to be much higher for males. They suggest that there might be a reluctance on the part of women to seek psychiatric care, because this would compromise their social standing in a culture where they are less secure. Lemkau's commentary on the paper suggested that bed shortage might lead to priority use for men, who, if violent, could require hospitalization more urgently than women.

Sutter et al.[407,408] discussed what they have called "nuptial psychosis" following weddings in Algeria, where unwanted and forced marriages are still prevalent. There are no systematic delusions. Among the psychotic, ideas of influence are poor, and events are explained by outside powers, particularly spirits. Assicot, Dequeker, and Fauer[15] found the catatonic forms more common among the Muslims in Algeria.

In Tunisia, however, Ammar[5] has found that the syndromes of schizophrenia with delusions of persecution have been increasing with socioeconomic changes. Alliez et al.[3] and Daumezon[84] have found that repatriates of white stock, and immigrant native males from North Africa have great difficulties in adjustment on the French mainland. However, six months following their arrival, their morbidity rate goes down. In 1957, Daumezon found that 14.5 per cent of the patients admitted to a major Parisian hospital were North Africans.

OTHER TYPES OF STUDIES

Exotic Psychosis

The number of studies devoted to what has been called "exotic psychosis" have been somewhat limited. Yap[447] has criticized the use of the term. These conditions, according to him, are atypical because of the pathoplastic influence of specific cultural conditions, but they are not exotic in the sense that they cannot be contained within widely accepted nosological categories. It is the illiterate, poorly developed logical habits of thought in a simple environment which predisposes to gross dissociative reactions which are difficult to diagnose.

Yap[448] and Rin[348] reviewed the Suk-Yeong, a Koro symptom usually found in the Far East. The presenting complaint is that of penile shrinkage. 25 per cent of the cases Yap saw were schizophrenics. The symptom was usually found among immature, young men of poor education.

Fischer and Fischer[116] reviewed the Kuru disease found in New Guinea, which kills 50 per cent of the patients. The patient is unable to walk, and is convinced he has been sorcerized. The illness has both possible organic and psychogenic etiology.

Teicher[409] has reviewed the Windigo psychosis found among Indians of Northwestern Canada. The chief symptom is a compulsive desire to eat human flesh. The victim is supposed to be possessed by the spirit of Windigo, a "gigantic cannibalistic monster with a head of ice." The seventy cases examined by Teicher displayed symptoms that ranged over the entire spectrum of psychiatric illness. The Windigo theme runs through all cases and serves as a uniting link. Parker[314] has provided an explanation of Windigo psychoses in the context of Ojibwa personality.

Other studies of unusual symptoms include the Piblobtoq of the polar Eskimo, (Gussow[136]). Attacks include the tearing of clothing, glossalalia, wandering off, rolling in snow, and occasional coprophagia.

In Latin America there is the Susto, a belief among highland Indian tribes of Bolivia and Peru that their soul has been stolen (Vellard,[420]; Soly Rosas,[360]; Rubel[358]), and this is precipitated by contact with supernatural beings or animals. The non-Indian (Mestizos or other rural population) diagnose the soul-loss as caused by a fright.

In Japan (Yonebayashi[449]) there is a belief in the rural areas that evil spirits in the form of a fox, dog, or snake attach themselves to human beings. Among the Navaho, there is the "moth sickness" (Kaplan, 169) where violence is associated with epilepsy, believed to be caused by incest, in which the person goes around and around like a moth, and finally destroys himself by leaping into a fire. A monograph was written by De Martino[87] on the tarantism, which is alleged to result from the bite of a tarantula spider. It is similar to the 15th century "choreomania" which is still found in Southern Italy. In another European country, a collective psychosis has been reported in Poland (Wiecek[433]) where fourteen members of three related families living in Kielce have been gradually affected. They keep silent and have to be fed artificially.

Other Variables

One area which has been neglected is the effect of hospitalization on the patient. Linn[226] found that patients reflected their social background before the onset of overt symptoms of mental illness. However, during the illness at the hospital, symptoms were little influenced by race, sex, education or other characteristics of the patients. Linn attributes this either to conformity or to the disease process. This type of finding seems surprising, in view of the number of studies which find behavior differences in the wards, among mental patients belonging to different socio-cultural backgrounds.

Sommer and Hall[394] do not agree that when the patient enters a hospital he has already rejected the values of society. Using a special scale of alienation, they found that mental patients in the admission wards were less alienated than were hospital physicians and psychiatrists. On the basis of their research, they feel that large mental hospitals produce more alienation than they treat. Discussion about alienated patients should be focused on the dis-culturating effect of the hospital, rather than on the relation between aliena-tion and psychopathology.

Mednick[269] has recently emphasized the limitations of the studies that have not taken into account the influence of hospitalization on the mental patient. Whatever differences were found between a control group leading a "normal life" and a group of patients in mental hospitals could be attributed to their custody. He gives an example of study which found that short term and long term convicts had restricted perceptual scanning and narrow concept width, which were found to be characteristic of schizophrenics tested in a mental hospital.

While there is widespread use of drugs, the number of studies in differential reactivity to the drugs, based on sociocultural variables, are somewhat scant. In 1958, the use of R1625 (haloperidol) was found to have strong effects on Europeans. However, when American psychiatrists used it in the United States, they did not obtain the same results. The difference in effect raised the question of whether chemicals might have a differential effect on patients of different nationalities. Collard, a Belgian psychiatrist[75] investigated these differences. He found that the threshold of pharmacologic and therapeutic reactivity of the American group was ten times greater than the corresponding threshold of the Europeans. He believes the great difference in response to a compound of identical chemical structure suggests there are probably differences in ecologic and genetic biologic structures between American and European patients.

Studies in the characteristics of the parents of schizophrenics have been the subject of intensive research during the last two decades. (Haley and Glick[138]) For a number of years studies regarding the relationship between dominance of the parents and type of premorbid adjustment of the schizophrenic have also appeared.

Investigators at Duke University (Garmezy, Farina, Rodnick[126]) have found that when the father is strongly ascendant and the mother is submissive, the son usually has a good premorbid history. However, when the mother is dominant and the father is submissive, the son usually has a poor premorbid history. Since father or mother dominance are characteristics of certain social classes, subcultural, and national groups, we might question the universality of these findings with other groups. In most cultures outside of the United States the usual pattern is male dominance. If we pursue the hypothesis of the Duke investigators, we could say that schizophrenics in male-dominant cultures have good premorbid histories. It is to be noted that the studies in the United States were conducted only with male subjects. One can assume that the pattern with families of female schizophrenics would be different. This hypothesis needs to be tested cross-culturally.

Chapman and Baxter[70] discussed the methodologic problems in using the concepts of "good premorbid" and "poor premorbid" history, without taking into account the social background of the patient. They pointed out that since the normal behavior of people from different social and cultural groups varies, then cultural differences may be confused for correlates of adjustment. To illustrate their point, they mention the Phillips Premorbid History Scale, which uses premorbid sexual and affiliative behavior to distinguish the two patterns of schizophrenia. Studies have shown that sex and affiliative experiences of a lower class and upper class male are different. The lower class individual experiences more premarital heterosexual activity, and more affiliative behavior through gangs, than the upper class individual. Query[337] found that schizophrenics from rural areas had a more favorable premorbid history than schizophrenics from urban areas. In the rural area, the favorable outlook could be attributed to the family structure, which is more patriarchial than it is in the cities. In contrast, large urban areas are characterized by nuclear rather than extended families, and the tendency would be for less contact between father and son than is usually the case in rural areas. However, further clinical studies, including control groups in both rural and urban setting, with different ethnic and religious, and nationality groups would be needed to relate dominance of parents and severity of schizophrenia in the children.

Recently Dohan[88,89] has provided us with an interesting hypothesis which relates schizophrenia to the type of food consumed by the populations of the world. He feels there is enough evidence to suspect that some cereals, and possibly other foods play a role in the onset of the disease. The highest rate of schizophrenia is to be found in those countries that have large consumption of wheat (Europe). Lower rates are to be found where the population eats relatively little wheat and large amounts of rice (Japan, Taiwan Chinese). The rate is quite low in a population whose staple foods are primarily sweet potatoes, millet and corn, and some rice (Taiwan aborigines), and may possibly be even lower among non-Westernized Africans, whose staple foodstuffs are maize or millet and sorghums. Dohan seems also to find evidence of changes in the rates of schizophrenia during war time, because of the changes in cereal consumption.

DISCUSSION

In this chapter we have reviewed numerous studies, from very simple clinical appraisals, to sophisticated methodologies which include hundreds of cases. The reader will have to bear in mind that the level of research sophistication varies a great deal, and he is cautioned at this point, therefore, not to draw definite conclusions from the findings. One generalization which can be made is that schizophrenia is to be found in all cultures, and that personal experience colors the symptomatology (Bustamante[51]). The contention of Van Loon[419] and Seligman[387] that psychosis is almost nonexistent among primitives no longer has adherents today.

In the previous review of the literature on the sociocultural aspects of schizophrenia, Benedict and Jacks and covered a wider scope of the literature on schizophrenia in underdeveloped areas, with less space on studies conducted in the Western world. This, we believe, reflected the interest of that time. Currently, however, more effort is being expended on studies which try to relate sociocultural variables to the existence of mental illness in advanced societies. This is seen in our own review. Within the last two decades there has been evidenced a greater awareness of the influence of social and cultural environment on the distribution of mental illness and its manifestations. A greater involvement of governmental efforts towards alleviating the consequences of mental illness and the establishment of community psychiatry are bound to increase this research trend.

Second in importance in this review are studies which have been conducted in developing nations that have recently acquired their independence. Since a number of native-born psychiatrists have been trained in the West, they are in a better position to make comparisons. However, because they are handicapped by limitations in the number of hospitals, and the lack of adequate vital statistics, truly epidemiologic studies are impossible. Except for the study conducted by Lin[222] in Formosa, and by Leighton et al.[212] in Nigeria, most of the available research is primarily clinical in approach.

In Africa, however, there is still open the question regarding the relationship between westernization and schizophrenia. Investigators seem to be more careful in attributing cause and effect relationship between these two variables. The line between what is considered acceptable in the culture, and what is considered pathological is still blurred. Yap[446] points out that all cultures offer conflicts, and that it would be naive to believe in the simplicity of interpersonal structures among the primitives, compared to the complexity of our own interpersonal structures. Simons[391] points out the need for more trained native psychiatrists who would be in a position to improve on studies which were limited by lack of communication, the use of interpreters, and lack of genuine understanding of a culture.

A general shortcoming of psychiatric studies in underdeveloped areas is the lack of case histories. Is it possible that child rearing practices and parental attitudes are so uniform that description of cases would not be worthwhile? Just as the study of family interaction has proven to be useful in the overall study of mental illness in the Western world, we may assume that case histories from emerging nations could be equally illuminating. Case histories collected by anthropologists in the course of their culture and personality studies have demonstrated their usefulness in the past. The general concept of

292   THE SCHIZOPHRENIC SYNDROME

"detribalization" would be made more explicit if supported by case histories. The recent upheavals in many African states, in their efforts towards self determination, open a most interesting field for intensive studies on the relationship between self identity, social change, and mental illness.

While some believe that the social environment may increase or decrease schizophrenia, others insist that true prevalence of schizophrenia is the same all over the world. Differences in statistics are to be attributed primarily to hospital facilities available, and general attitudes toward mental illness. Berne,[31] holding an extreme point of view, clearly states that the estimates of patients in each community "tend to support" the hypothesis that "the reservoir of endogeneous psychosis (true prevalence) maintains a constant ratio regardless of racial, cultural, geographical, and socioeconomic conditions."

Despite intensive efforts to cope with the problem of the etiology of schizophrenia, it is still considered one of man's major dilemmas. The lack of uniformity in psychiatric research, vested interests, and the tendency of investigators to ignore the findings from other disciplines hinders the efforts to solve this complex problem. Research in this area can become effective only if a genuine, concerted, interdisciplinary effort is directed toward its solution. More scientific answers can be assured if longitudinal studies are conducted on individuals facing different types of stresses and cultural demands over extended periods of time and space. Our goal should be to tackle the problems of mental health and illness on an international level, on a very large scale, and with intensive clinical studies. I suggest that an international *research* organization be established to coordinate research in mental illness. Under the auspices of such an international agency, it would be possible to set up research programs in various countries, staffed by polyglot scientists, in order to provide a basis for more effective communication. An integration of data from research conducted by similar methods and utilizing comparable samples in different countries would lead to greater validity and universality of findings.

BIBLIOGRAPHY

1. Achte, K. A., and Seppala, K. R.: Emergency cases at Hesperia Hospital, Helsinki, during 1962. Psychiat. Quart. 38: 537-543, 1964.

2. Adams, H. B.: The influence of social variables, treatment methods and administrative factors on mental hospital admissions. Psychiat. Quart. 35: 353-372, 1961.

3. Alliez, J., and Mayaud, R.: Role of displacement and of habitat in the psychopathological reactions of a group of repatriates of European stock, originally of Tunisia. Ann. Medicophychol. 118: 918-923, 1960.

4. Allinsmith. W., and Goathals, G. W.: Cultural factors in mental health: An anthropological perspective. Review of Educ. Research, 26: 429-450, 1956.

5. Ammar, S.: Psychic disorders in Tunisian society. Read at the First Int'l Cong. of Soc. Psychiat., London, 1964.

6. Antrobus, J. S., and Bloom, B. L.: Sibling rank among Japanese-American

male schizophrenics. Transcultural Psychiatric Research, Vol. II, 54-56, 1965.

7. Arieti, S., and Meth, J. M.: Rare, unclassifiable, collective and exotic psychotic syndromes. In Arieti, S. (Ed.) American Handbook of Psychiatry, Chapt. 27, New York: Basic Books, 1959.

8. Arieti, S.: Some socio-cultural aspects of manic-depressive psychosis and schizophrenia in Progress in Psychotherapy, Vol. IV, Social Psychotherapy. H. Masserman and J. L. Moreno (Eds.) N. Y., Grune & Stratton, 1959.

9. Armstrong, Renate G.: Mental illness among American Jews. Jewish Social Studies, 27: 103-111, 1965.

10. Aronson, J.: Schizophrenia in transcultural perspective. Read at First Int'l Cong. Soc. Psychiat., London, 1964.

11. Arsenian, J., and Arsenian, J. M.: Tough and easy cultures: a conceptual analysis. Psychiatry, 11: 377-385, 1948.

12. Arsenian, J.: Situational factors contributing to mental illness in the United States: A theoretical summary. Ment. Hygiene, 45: 194-206, 1961.

13. Asai, T.: The contents of delusions of schizophrenic patients in Japan: Comparison between periods from 1941-1961. Transcultural Psychiat. Research, 1: 27-28, 1964.

14. Asghar, G. A.: Problems of mental disorders in Pakistan. Pakistan J. Health, 10: 84-89, 1960.

15. Assicot, M., and al.: Main causes of psychiatric morbidity among Algerian Muslims. L'Hygiene Mentale, 50: 261-286, 1961.

16. Astrup, C., and Ødegard, O.: Internal migration and mental disease in Norway. Psychiat. Quart. Suppl. 34: 116-130, 1960.

17. Astrup C.: Scandinavian literature on psychiatric genetics and epidemiology. Acta Psychiat. Neurol. Scand. 32: 399-423, 1957.

18. Baasher, T.: Survey of mental illness in Wadi Halfa. World Mental Health, 13: 181-185, 1961.

19. ———: The influence of culture on psychiatric manifestations. Transcultural Psychiat. Research, 15: 51-52, 1963.

20. Bahn, Anita, Chandler, Caroline K., and Eisenberg, L.: Diagnostic and demographic characteristics of patients seen in outpatient psychiatric clinics for an entire state (Maryland): Implications for the psychiatrist and mental health program planner. Amer. J. Psychiat. 117: 769-778, 1961.

21. Bastide, R.: Mental illness and the Brazilian Negro. In Mental Disorders and Mental Health in Africa South of the Sahara, CCTA/CSA WFMH/WHO. Meeting of Specialists on Mental Health, Bukavu, 1958.

22. ———: La Sociologie des Maladies Mentales. Paris: Flammarion, 1965.

23. ———: Interdisciplinary approach to mental illness. Social Science Information, Vol. VI 4, Aug., 1967.

24. Bazzoui, W., and Al-Issa, I.: Psychiatry in Iraq. Brit. J. Psychiat. 112: 827-832, 1966.

25. Bean, Lee L., Myers, J. K., and Pepper, M. P.: Social class and schizophrenia: A ten-year follow-up. In Shostak, A. B., and Gomberg, W. (Eds.) Blue Collar World: Studies of the American Worker. Englewood Cliffs, N. J. Prentice-Hall, Inc. 1964.

26. Becker, E.: The relevance to psychiatry of recent research in anthropology. Amer. J. Psychother. 16: 600-617, 1962.

27.———: The Revolution in Psychiatry. Glencoe: The Free Press of Glencoe, and New York: Collier-MacMillan Ltd., 1964.

28. Bell, N. W., and Spiegel, J. P.: Social Psychiatry: Vagaries of a term. Arch. Gen. Psychiat. 14: 337-345, 1966.

29. Berman, S.: Letter to the Editor: Transcultural Research in Mental Health Problems. 4: 54-58, 1958.

30. Berne, E.: Difficulties of comparative psychiatry: The Fiji Islands. Amer. J. Psychiat. 116: 104-109, 1959.

31. ———: The cultural problem: psychopathology in Tahiti. Amer. J. Psychiat. 116: 1076-1081, 1960.

32. Bhaskaran, K.: A psychiatric study of paranoid schizophrenics in a mental hospital in India. Psychiat. Quart. 37: 734-751, 1963.

33. Bleuler, M.: International cooperation in research on schizophrenia. Bull. Menninger Clin. 22: 43-50, 1958.

34. ———: Conception of schizophrenia within the last fifty years and today. Int. J. of Psychiat., Vol. I, 3-30, 1966.

35. Blignault, W. J.: A Study of Auditory Verbal Hallucinations in Male Bantu Psychotics, M.D. Thesis of the University of Witwatersand, 1960.

36. Bodian, C., Gardner, E. A., Willis, E. M., and Bahn, A. K.: Socioeconomic indicators from Census Tract data related to rates of mental illness. Papers presented at the Census Tract Conference, Sept. 5, 1963; Working Paper No. 17. Washington, D. C. 1964.

37. Bonhour, A.: Epidemiologie Psychiatrica Instituto Nacional de Salud Mental. Republica Argentina, Buenos Aires, 1966.

38. Bordelau, J. M., Haitian medicine and psychiatry. L'Union Med. Canada 91: 115-119, 1962.

39. Branch, C. H., and Anderson, R.: Clinical and research collaboration in psychiatry and anthropology. Int. J. Soc. Psychiat. 6: 247-251, 1960.

40. Brody, E. B.: Social conflict and schizophrenic behavior in young adult Negro males. Psychiatry. 24: 337-346, 1961.

41. ———: Some conceptual and methodological issues involved in research on society, culture and mental health. J. Nerv. Ment. Dis. 39: 62-74, 1964

42. ———: Socio-cultural influences on vulnerability to schizophrenic behavior. Read at the First Rochester International Conference on Schizophrenia, March, 1967.

43. Brody, E. B., Derbyshire, R. L., and Schleifer, C.: How the young adult Baltimore Negro male becomes a Maryland mental hospital statistic. In Monroe, R. R., Klee, G. D., and Brody, E. B. (Eds.) Psychiatric Epidemiology and Mental Health Planning. Amer. Psychiat. Assoc. Research Reports No. 22, 1967.

44. Brooke, Eilleen M.: National statistics in the epidemiology of mental illness. J. Ment. Sci. 105: 893-908, 1959.

45. ———: A national study of schizophrenia patients in relation to occupation. Congress Report, Vol. 3, Second International Congress of Psychiatry, Zurich, 1957.

46. Browne, I. W.: Psychiatry in Ireland. Amer. J. Psychiat. 119: 816-819, 1963.

47. Brunetti, P. M.: A prevalence survey of mental disorders in a rural commune in Vaucluse: Methodological considerations. Acta Psychiat. Neurol. Scand. 40: 323-358, 1964.

48. Bry, Ilse (Ed.): Mental Health Book Review Index. Council on Research in Bibliography, Inc., New York.

49. Bulletin de l'Institut National de la Sante et de la Recherche Medicale, Statistiques Medicales des Etablissements Psychiatriques, Year 1963, 20, 4, 1965.

50. Burg, M.: Some East-West implications and integration of psychologic-communicational-sociopsychiatric considerations of schizophrenia. Transcultural Research in Mental Health Problems, 9: 26-29, 1960.

51. Bustamante, J. A.: Cultural factors in some schizophrenic patterns. Int. J. of Soc. Psychiat. 5: 50-54, 1959.

52. Cade, J. F., and Krupinski, J.: Incidence of psychiatric disorders in Victoria in relation to country of birth. Med. J. Aust. 49: 400-404, 1962.

53. Camba, R., and Bernardino, M. C.: The incidence of mental diseases in the Province of Cagliari (Statistical study on patients in the Ospedale Psichiatrico Provincial di Cagliari from 1901 to 1960. Rass. Med. Sarda 64: 609-627, 1962.

54. Carothers, J. C.: Culture, psychiatry and the written word. Psychiatry. 22: 307-320, 1959.

55. Carstairs, G. M.: Some problems of psychiatry in patients from alien cultures. The Lancet, 7: 1217-1220, 1958.

56. Carstairs, G. M.: Round Table Meeting on Transcultural Psychiatric Problems. Transcultural Research in Mental Health Problems, 4: 4-5, 1958.

57. ———, and Brown, G. W.: A cen-

sus of psychiatric cases in two contrasting communities. J. Ment. Sci. 104: 72-81, 1958.

58. Caudill, W.: Anthropology and Psychoanalysis: Some theoretical issues. In T. Gladwin and W. C. Sturtevant, (Eds.) Anthropology and Human Behavior. The Anthropological Society of Washington, Washington, D. C. 174-214, 1962.

59. ———: Sibling rank and style of life among Japanese psychiatric patients. Proceedings of the Joint Meeting of the Japanese Society of Psychiatry and Neurology and the American Psychiatric Association, Tokyo, 1963.

60. ———: Observations on the cultural context of Japanese psychiatry. In Opler, M. K. (Ed.) Culture and Mental Health, McMillan Company, New York, 213-242, 1958.

61. Caudill, W., and Doi, L. Takeo: Interrelations of psychiatry, culture and emotion in Japan. In Galdston, I. (Ed.) Man's Image in Medicine and Anthropology, New York: International Universities Press, 374-421, 1963.

62. Cawte, J. E.: Tjimi and Tiagolo: Ethnopsychiatry in the Kalumburu People of North Western Australia. Oceania 43: 170-190, 1964.

63.———: Australian ethnopsychiatry in the field: A sampling in North Kimberly. Med. J. Aust., 1: 467-472, 1964.

64. ———: Australian ethnopsychiatry: The Walbiri doctor. Med. J. Aust. 2: 977-983, 1964.

65. Cerny, J.: Chinese psychiatry. Int. J. Psychiat. 1: 648-649, 1965.

66.———: Psychiatry in China. Ces. Psychiat. 59: 273-282, 1963.

67. Census of Mental Hospitals in the Caribbean. Working paper for the Third Conference of the Caribbean Federation for Mental Health. Prepared by the Research Institute for the Study of Man.

68. Chakraborty, A.: An analysis of paranoid symptomatology. Transcultural Psychiatric Research, 1: 103-107, 1964.

69. Chapman, L. J., Hinkle, L. E., and Wolff, H. G.: Human ecology, disease, and schizophrenia. Amer. J. Psychiat. 117: 193-204, 1960.

70. Chapman, L. J., and Baxter, J. C.: The process-reactive distinction and patients' subculture. J. of Nerv. Ment. Dis. 136: 352-359, 1963.

71. Chu, L. W., and Liu, M. C.: Mental disease in Peking between 1933 and 1943. J. Ment. Sci. 106: 274-280, 1960.

72. Clausen, J. A., and Kohn, M. L.: Relations of schizophrenia to the social structure of a small city. In Pasamanik, B. (Ed.) Epidemiology of Mental Disorders. American Association for the Advancement of Science, No. 60, Washington, D. C., 69-95, 1959.

73. ———: Social relations and schizophrenia: A research report and a perspective. In Jackson, D. (Ed.) The Etiology of Schizophrenia. New York: Basic Books, 295-320, 1960.

74. Cohen, Y. A.: Social Structure and Personality. New York: Holt, Rinehart and Winston, 1961.

75. Collard, J.: Drug responses in different ethnic groups. J. of Neuropsychiat. 3: Suppl. No. 1, 114-121, 1962.

76. Collomb, H.: Problems of African psychiatry (South of the Sahara). Transcultural Research in Mental Health Problems. 6: 34-36, 1959.

77. Collomb, H., and Ayats, H.: Migrations in Senegal: A psychopathologic study. Cahiers d'Etudes Africaines, 2: 590-598, 1962.

78. ———: Psychiatric assistance in Africa: Senegalese experience. Psychopathologie Africaine, 1: 11-84, 1965.

79. Community Mental Health and Social Psychiatry: A Reference Guide. Harvard Medical School and Psychiatric Service, Massachusetts General Hospital. Harvard University Press, Cambridge, Mass., 1962.

80. Cooper, B.: Social class and prognosis in schizophrenia: Parts I, II. British J. Prevent. & Soc. Med. 15: 17-41, 1961.

81. Crocetti, G. M., Kulcar, Z., Kesic, B., and Lemkau, P. V.: Differential rates of schizophrenia in Croatia, Yugoslavia. Amer. J. Public Health, 54: 196-206, 1964.

82. ———: Selected aspects of the epidemiology of schizophrenia in Croatia

(Yugoslavia). The Milbank Mem. Fund. Quart. 42: 9-37, 1964.

83. Daumezon, G., et al.: Increases in the psychiatric hospitalization in Metropolitan France of immigrant native males from North Africa for the year 1957. Ann. Medicopsychol. 116: 1031-1033, 1958.

84. Daumezon, G., Champion, Y., and Champion-Basset, J.: The psychopathologic incidence on a transplanted population of North African origin. Monog. Inst. National d'Hygiene No. 7, Paris, 1955.

85. DeHoyos, A., and DeHoyos, Genevieve: Symptomatology differentials between Negro and White schizophrenics. Int. J. Soc. Psychiat. 11: 245-255, 1965.

86. Despinoy, M., Benoist, A., and Mares, J.: Schizophrenia in Martinique. Congres Medical des Antilles de Langue Francaise, Haiti, March, 1958.

87. DeMartino, E.: The Land of Remorse. II Saggiatore, 1961.

88. Dohan, F. C.: Wartime changes in hospital admissions for schizophrenia. Acta Psychiat. Scand. 42: 1-23, 1966.

89. ———: Cereals and schizophrenia; Data and hypothesis. Acta Psychiat. Scand. 42: 125-152, 1966.

90. Dohrenwend, B. P., and al.: The problem of validity in field studies of psychological disorder. Int. J. Psychiat. 1: 585-610, 1965.

91. Dorzhadamba, Sh.: The epidemiology of mental illness in the Mongolian People's Republic. Transcultural Psychiatric Research, 11: 19-22, 1965.

92. Draguns, J. C., Knobel, M., Fundia, Toba A. de, Broverman, Inge K., and Phillips, L.: Social competence, psychiatric symptomatology, and culture. Proceedings of the Ninth Interamerican Congress of Psychology, Miami, M. B. Jones (Ed.) Interamerican Society of Psychology, 610-615, 1964.

93. Draguns, J. G., Phillips, L., Broverman, Inge K., Caudill, W., and Nishimae, Shiro: Psychiatric symptoms in relation to social competence and culture: A study of Japanese patients. Paper read at the 10th Congress of the Interamerican Society of Psychology, Lima, Peru, 1966.

94. Driver, E. D.: The sociology and Anthropology of Mental Illness: A Reference Guide. The University of Massachusetts Press, 1965.

95. Dunham, H. W.: Methodology of sociological investigations of mental disorders. Int. J. Soc. Psychiat. 3: 7-17, 1957.

96. ———: Sociological Theory and Mental Disorders. Detroit: Wayne State University Press, 1959.

97. ———: Social structures and mental disorders hypotheses of explanation. In Causes of Mental Disorders: A Review of Epidemiological Knowledge; 1959. Milbank Memorial Fund Quarterly, 227-279, 1961.

98. Dunham, H. W.: Social class and schizophrenia. Amer. J. Orthopsychiat. 34: 634-644, 1964.

99.———: Community and Schizophrenia. Detroit; Wayne State University Press, 1965.

100. ———: Community psychiatry. Newest therapeutic bandwagon. Arch. Gen. Psychiat. 12: 303-313, 1965.

101. ———: A research note on diagnosed mental illness and social class. Amer. Soc. Rev. 31: 223-227, 1966.

102. ———: Epidemiology of psychiatric disorders as a contribution to medical ecology. Arch. Gen. Psychiat. 14: 1-19, 1966.

103. Edgerton, R. B.: Conceptions of psychosis in four African Societies. American Anthrop. 68: 408-425, 1966.

104. Eichler, R. M., and Litzman, S.: Religious background of patients in a mental hygiene setting. J. Nerv. Ment. Disease. 124: 514-517, 1956.

105. Eitinger, L.: The incidence of mental disease among refugees in Norway. J. Ment. Sci. 105: 326-338, 1959.

106. Ellenberger, H.: Cultural aspects of mental illness. Amer. J. of Psychotherapy. 14: 158-173, 1960.

107. ———: Ethno-pschiatrie: Theorique et générale. Partie descriptive et clinique. Encyclop. Medico-Chirurgicale. 37725 A10 and 37725 B10. Paris, 1965.

108. Enright, J. B., and Jaeckle, W. R.: Psychiatric symptoms and diagnosis in two subcultures. Int. J. Soc. Psychiat. 9: 12-17, 1963.

109. ———: Ethnic differences in psychopathology. Soc. Process, 25: 71-77, 1961.

110. Fantl, Berta, and Schiro, J.: Cultural variables in the behavior patterns and symptom formation of 15 Irish and 15 Italian female schizophrenics. Int. J. Soc. Psychiat. 4: 245-253, 1959.

111. Fernandez-Marina, R., and Von Eckardt, U. M.: Cultural stresses and schizophrenogenesis in the mothering one in Puerto Rico. Annals, New York Academy of Sciences. 84: 864-877, 1960.

112. Finney, J. C.: Psychiatry and Multiculturality in Hawaii. Int. J. Soc. Psychiat. 9: 5-11, 1963.

113. Field, M. G.: Approaches to mental illness in Soviet society: Some comparisons and conjectures. Social Problems, 7: 277-297, 1960.

114. ———: Soviet and American approaches to mental illness: A comparative perspective. Rev. of Soviet Med. Sci. 1: 1-37, 1964.

115. Field, Margaret J.: Search for Security: An Ethno-Psychiatric Study of Rural Ghana. Northwestern University Press, Evanston. African Studies No. 5, 1960.

116. Fisher, Ann, and Fischer, J. L.: Culture and epidemiology: A theoretical investigation of Kuru. J. Health & Human Behav. 2: 16-25, 1961.

117. Folkard, S., and Mandelbrote, B.: Some ecological aspects of schizophrenia in Gloucestershire. Int. J. Soc. Psychiat. 8: 256-271, 1962.

118. Forster, E. B.: The theory and practice of psychiatry in Ghana. Amer. J. of Psychother. 16: 7-51, 1962.

119. ———: Schizophrenia as seen in Ghana. Congress Report Vol. 1, p. 151. Int. Cong. of Psychiatry, Zurich, 1957.

120. Frank, L. K.: The emergence of social psychiatry in the United States. Read at the First Int. Cong. of Soc. Psychiat. London, 1964.

121. Freed, E. X.: Ethnic identification of hospitalized Jewish psychiatric patients: an exploratory study. Int. J. Soc. Psychiat. 11: 110-115, 1965.

122. Frumkin, R. M.: Occupation and mental disorders. In Rose, A. M. (Ed.) Mental Health and Mental Disorder. London, Routledge and Kegan, 136-160, 1956.

123. Gaitonde, M. R.: Cross-cultural study of the psychiatric syndromes in outpatient clinics in Bombay, India and Topeka, Kansas. Int. J. Soc. Psychiat. 4: 98-104, 1958.

124. ———: Psychiatry in India. In Progress in Psychotherapy, Vol. IV, Masserman, J. H., and Moreno, J. L. (Ed.) New York: Grune & Stratton, 289-295, 1960.

125. Gardner, E. A., and Babigian, H. M.: A longitudinal comparison of psychiatric services to selected socioeconomic areas of Monroe County, N. Y. Amer. J. Orthopsychiat. 36: 818-828, 1966.

126. Garmezy, N., Farina, A., and Rodnick, E. H.: The structured situation test: A method for studying family interaction in schizophrenia. Amer. J. Orthopsychiat. 30: 445-452, 1960.

127. Gerard, K.: Trends in socio-psychiatric research in Poland. Read at First Int. Cong. Soc. Psychiat., London, 1964.

128. Gilyarovsky, V. A.: The Soviet Union. In Bellak, L. (Ed.) In Contemporary European Psychiatry, New York: Grove Press, Inc. 283-323, 1961.

129. Giovacchini, P. L.: Ego adaptation and cultural variables. Arch. Gen. Psychiat. 5: 37-45, 1961.

130. Gnat, T., Heinsz, J., and Sarapata, A.: A psychiatric-statistical study of two Polish towns. Read at the First Inter. Cong. of Soc. Psychiat., 1964.

131. Goldberg, E. M., and Morrison, S. L.: Schizophrenia and Social class. Brit. J. Psychiat. 109: 785-802, 1963.

132. Gordon, E. B.: Mentally ill West Indian immigrants. Brit. J. Psychiat. 3: 877-887, 1965.

133. Goshen, C. E.: New interdisciplinary trends in psychiatry. Amer. J. Psychiat. 117: 916-921, 1961.

134. Greenblatt, M., Emory, P. E., and Glueck, B. C., Jr.: Poverty and Mental Health. Psychiatric Research Report of the American Psychiatric Association Washington, D. C. 1967.

135. Grewal, R. S.: Mental disorders

in Burma. (Thesis) Transcultural Res. Ment. Health Problems, 6: 20-21, 1959.

136. Gussow, Z.: Pibloktoq (Hysteria) among the Polar Eskimos. Psychoanal. Study of Society. 1: 218-236, 1960.

137. Haag, E. Van Den.: On diagnosed mental illness and social class. Amer. Sociol. Rev. 31: 544, 1966.

138. Haley, J., and Glick, Ida.: Psychiatry and the Family. An Annotated Bibliograph of Articles published 1960-1964. Published by Family Process, 777 Bryant St., Palo Alto, Calif.

139. Halevi, H. S.: Frequency of mental illness among Jews in Israel. Int. J. Soc. Psychiat. 9: 268-282, 1963.

140. Hammer, Muriel.: Social factors in mental hospital admission (preliminary report) Biometrics Research. N. Y. State Dept. of Mental Hygiene.

141. Hankoff, L. D.: Letter from Okinawa. Transcultural Res. Ment. Health Problems. 4: 19-21, 1958.

142. Hardt, R. H.: The ecological distribution of patients admitted to mental hospitals from an urban area. Psychiat. Quart. 33: 126-144, 1959.

143. ———, and Feinhandler, S. J.: Social class and mental hospitalization prognosis. Amer. Soc. Rev., 24: 815-821, 1959.

144. Hartocollis, P.: Psychiatry in contemporary Greece. Amer. J. Psychiat. 123: 457-462, 1966.

145. Hasuzawa, T.: Chronological observations of delusions in schizophrenics. Transcultural Psychiat. Research, 1: 27-28, 1964.

146. Heilbrun, A. B.: Maternal authoritarianism, social class, and filial schizophrenia. J. Gen. Psychol., 65: 235-241, 1961.

147. Helgason, T.: Epidemiology of Mental Disorders in Iceland: A psychiatric and demographic investigation of 5,395 islanders. Munksgaard, Copenhagen, 1964.

148. Hemsi, L. K.: Psychiatric morbidity of West Indian immigrants. Soc. Psychiat. II: 95-100, 1967.

149. Hitson, Hazel M., and Funkenstein, D. H.: Family patterns and paranoidal personality structure in Boston and Burma. Int. J. Soc. Psychiat. 5: 182-190, 1959.

150. Hoch, Erna M. (Lucknow, India) Comments on special issue on schizophrenia. Transcultural Res. Ment. Health Problems. 11: 65-71, 1961.

151. ———: Indian children on a psychiatric playground. Transcultural Psychiatric Res. 1: 40-44, 1964.

152. Hoch, P. H., and Zubin, J. (Eds.): Psychopathology of Schizophrenia. New York: Grune and Stratton, 1966.

153. ———: Comparative Epidemiology of the Mental Disorders. New York: Grune and Stratton, 1961.

154. Hoenig, J., and Sreenivasan, U.: Mental hospital admissions in Mysore State, India. J. Ment. Sci. 105: 124-141, 1959.

155. Hollingshead, A. B., and Redlich, F. C.: Social Class and Mental Illness. New York: John Wiley & Sons, Inc., 1958.

156. Hughes, C. C., Tremblay, M. A., Rapoport, R. N., and Leighton, A. H.: People of Cove and Woodlot Communities from the Viewpoint of Social Psychiatry, Vol. II. The Stirling County Study of Psychiatric Disorder and Sociocultural Environment. New York: Basic Books, 1960.

157. Hunt, R. G.: Sociocultural factors in mental disorders. Behav. Sci., 4: 96-106, 1959.

158. ———: Social class and mental illness: Some implications for clinical theory and practice. Amer. J. Psychiat. 116: 1065-1069, 1960.

159. Ikeda, Kiyoshi, Ball, H. V., and Yamamura, D. S.: Ethnocultural factors in schizophrenia: The Japanese in Hawaii. Amer. J. Sociol. 68: 242-248, 1962.

160. Ivanys, E., Drdková, S., and Vána, J.: Prevalence of psychoses recorded among psychiatric patients in a part of the urban population: I. Prevalence. Cs. Psychiat. 60: 152-162, 1964.

161. ———: Distribution of psychoses registered in psychiatric care in a part of inhabitants of the Capital: II. Year's incidence. Cs. Psychiat. 61: 47-57, 1965.

162. Ivanys, E., and Vána, J.: Distribution of psychoses registered in psychiatric health care in a part of the metropolitan

population: III. Some methodological remarks. Cs. Psychiat. 61: 145-155, 1965.

163. Jaco, E. G.: The Social Epidemiology of Mental Disorders: A Psychiatric Survey of Texas. Russell Sage Foundation, New York, 1960.

164. Jakovljevic, V. Transcultural-psychiatric experiences from the African Guinea. Transcultural Psychiatric Research, 1: 55-58, 1964.

165. Jores, A., and Puchta, H. G.: Diseases of civilization among the natives of French West Africa. Med. Klin. 55: 2145-2149, 1960.

166. Kaelbling, R.: Comparative psychopathology and psychotherapy. Acta. Psychotherap. 9: 10-28, 1961.

167. Kahn, M. W., Lee, Hyun-Soo, Jones, N. F., and Kee Jin, S.: A comparison of Korean and American mental patients' attitudes towards mental illness and hospitalization. Inter. J. Soc. Psychiat. 13: 14-20, 1966/67.

168. Kaplan, B., Reed, R. B., and Richardson, W.: A comparison of the incidence of hospitalized and non-hospitalized psychoses in two communities. Amer. Soc. Review, 21: 472-479, 1956.

169. Kaplan, B.: A study of Navaho psychopathology. Transcultural Res. Ment. Health Problems, 12: 68-72, 1962.

170. Katchadourian, H.: Mental Illness in Lebanon: Preliminary Report. Transcultural Psychiat. Res. II, 115-116, 1965.

171. Katchadourian, H., and Racy, J.: The diagnostic distribution of treated psychiatric illness in Lebanon. Unpublished paper. American University at Beirut, Lebanon, 1967.

172. Keeler, M. H., and Vitols, M. M.: Migration and schizophrenia in North Carolina Negroes. Amer. J. Orthopsychiat. 33: 554-557, 1963.

173. Kelman, H.: Psychotherapy in the Far East. In Progress in Psychotherapy, Vol. IV, J. H. Masserman (Ed.) 296-305, 1959.

174. Kennedy, D.: Key issues in the cross-cultural study of mental disorders. In Studying Personality Cross-Culturally, B. Kaplan (Ed.) Evanston, Ill.: Row, Peterson & Co., 405-426, 1961.

175. Kiev, A.: Folk Psychiatry in Haiti. J. Nerv. Ment. Dis. 132: 260-265, 1961.

176. ————: Brief Note: Primitive holistic medicine. Int. J. Psychiat. 8: 58-61, 1961/62.

177. ————: Beliefs and delusions of West Indian immigrants to London. Brit. J. of Psychiat. 109: 356-363, 1963.

178. ————: Psychiatric illness among West Indians in London. Race 5: 48-53, 1964.

179. Kimmich, R. A.: Ethnic Aspects of schizophrenia in Hawaii. Psychiatry, 23: 97-102, 1960.

180. Klein, R. H.: Visit to Kachenko Mental Hospital, Moscow. Mental Hospitals, December, 1958.

181. Kleiner, R. J., and Parker, S.: Migration and mental illness: A new look. Amer. Sociol. Rev. 24: 687-690, 1959.

182. Kleiner, R. J., Tuckman, J., and Lavell, Martha: Mental disorder and status based on religious affiliation. Human Relations, 12: 273-276, 1959.

183. ————: Mental disorder and status based on race. Psychiatry. 23: 271-274, 1960.

184. Kleiner, R. J., and Tuckman, J.: Multiple group membership and schizophrenia. Behav. Sci. 6: 292-296, 1961.

185. Kleiner, R. J., and Lavell, Martha: Mental disorder and status based on Protestant sub-group membership. J. Soc. Psychol. 58: 345-348, 1962.

186. Kline, N. S.: Psychiatry in the underdeveloped countries. Report of Round Table Meetings, Atlantic City, 116th meeting of the American Psychiatric Association, Washington, D. C. 1960.

187. Kline, N. S.: Psychiatry in Kuwait. Brit. J. Psychiat. 109: 766-774, 1963.

188. ————: Psychiatry in Indonesia. Amer. J. Psychiat. 119: 809-815, 1963.

189. ————: A theoretic framework for transcultural psychiatry. Amer. J. Psychiat. 123: 85-87, 1966.

190. Kline, N. S., Field, M. G., and Aronson, J. Soviet psychiatric nomenclature. Amer. J. Psychiat. 118: 178-180, 1961.

191. Kohn, M. L.: On the social epi-

demiology of schizophrenia. Acta Socio-logica, 9: 209-221, 1966.

192. Kolb, L. C.: Soviet psychiatric organization and the community: Mental health center concept. Amer. J. Psychiat. 123: 433-440, 1966.

193. Krapf, E. E.: The international approach to the problems of mental health. Int. J. Soc. Psychiat. 11: 63-71, 1959.

194. Krasik, E. D.: Data on comparative epidemiology of schizophrenia in cities and rural locations. Zh. Nevropat. Psikhiat. Korsakov. 65: 608-616, 1965.

195. La Forgue, R.: About psyche and constitution in analytic perspective. Fortschritte der Psychosoma. Med. 1: 128-143, 1960.

196. Langner, T. S., and Michael, S. T.: Life Stress and Mental Health: The Midtown Manhattan Study (Thomas A. C. Rennie Series in Social Psychiatry, Vol. II). New York: The Free Press of Glencoe, 1963.

197. Lambo, T. A.: A study of Social and Health Problems of Nigerian Students in Britain. Government Publications, Western Nigeria, 1957.

198. ———: Further neuropsychiatric observations in Nigeria, with comments on the need for epidemiological study in Africa. Brit. Med. J. 1696-1704, 1960.

199. ———: Schizophrenia and borderline states. In de Reuck, A. V. S., and Porter, Ruth (Eds.) Transcultural Psychiatry, London: J. A. Churchill, Ltd., 67-74, 1965.

200. ———: Psychiatry in the tropics. Lancet 2: 1119-1121, 1965.

201. ———: Socioeconomic change, population explosion and the changing phases of mental health programs in developing countries. Amer. J. Orthopsychiat. 36: 77-83, 1966.

202. Lane, R. C., and Singer, J. L.: Familial attitudes in paranoid schizophrenics and normals from two socioeconomic classes. J. Abnorm. & Soc. Psychol., 30: 328-339, 1959.

203. Lapouse, Rema, Monk, M. A., and Terris, M.: The drift hypothesis and socioeconomic differentials in schizophrenia. Amer. J. Pub. Health, 46: 978-987, 1956.

204. Lauter, H.: Kraepelin's importance for cultural psychiatry. Transcultural Psychiatric Research, II: 9-12, 1965.

205. Lazarus, J., Locke, B. I., and Thomas, D. S.: Migration differential in mental disease: State patterns in first admission to mental hospitals for all disorders and for schizophrenia; New York, Ohio and California as of 1950. Milbank Memorial Fund Quart. 41: 25-42, 1963.

206. Lee, E. S.: Socioeconomic and migration differentials in mental disease: New York State 1949-1951. Milbank Memorial Fund Quart. 41: 244-269, 1963.

207. Leighton, A. H., Clausen, J. A., and Wilson, R. N. (Eds.): Explorations in Social Psychiatry. New York: Basic Books, 1957.

208. Leighton, A. H.: Mental illness and acculturation. In Galdston, I. (Ed.) Medicine and Anthropology, N. Y. International Universities Press, Inc., 1959.

209. Leighton, A. H.: An Introduction to Social Psychiatry, Springfield, Ill.: Charles C. Thomas, 1960.

210. Leighton, A. H., and Hughes, Jane: Culture as causative of mental disorder. In Causes of Mental Disorders: A Review of Epidemiological Knowledge, 1959. Milbank Mem. Fund, New York, 341-383, 1961.

211. Leighton, A. H.: My Name is Legion: Foundations for a Theory of Man in Relation to Culture. Vol. I. The Stirling County Study of Psychiatric Disorder and Sociocultural Environment. New York: Basic Books, 1959.

212. Leighton, A. H., Lambo, T. A., Hughes, C. C., Leighton, D. C., Murphy, J. M., and Macklin, D. B.: Psychiatric Disorder among the Yorubas: A Report from the Cornell-Aro Mental Health Research Project. Ithaca, N. Y.: Cornell University Press, 1963.

213. ———: Psychiatric disorder in West Africa. Amer. J. Psychiat. 120: 521-527, 1963.

214. Leighton, A. H.: Social psychiatry and the concept of cause. Amer. J. Psychiat. 122: 929-930, 1966.

215. Leighton, Dorothea C., and Leighton, A. H.: Mental and social factors. In

Freedman, A. M., and Kaplan, Harold I. (Eds.) Comprehensive Text book of Psychiatry. Baltimore: Williams and Wilkins Co., 1967.

216. Leighton, Dorothea C., Harding, J. S., Macklin, D. B., Hughes, C. C., and Leighton, A. H.: Psychiatric findings of the Stirling County study. Amer. J. Psychiat. 119: 1021-1026, 1963.

217. Leighton, Dorothea C., Harding, J. S., Macklin, D. B., MacMillan, A. M., and Leighton, A. H.: The Character of Danger, Vol. III, The Stirling County Study of Psychiatric Disorder and Sociocultural Environment. New York: Basic Books, 1963.

218. Lenz, H.: Comparative Psychiatry: A Study of the Relationship between Culture, Sociology and Psychopathology. Wien: Wilhelm Maudrich Verlag, 1964.

219. Leon, C. A.: Annual Report of Studies conducted by the Dept. of Psychiatry of the Faculty of Medicine of the University of Valle, in Psychiatric Hospital "San Isidro", Aug. 1956 to Aug. 1957, Cali, Colombia. (mimeographed) Transcultural Research in Mental Health Problems Review and Newsletter, 5: 56, 1959.

220. Levine, D., and Delman, L.: Community adjustment of schizophrenics. J. Clin. Psychol. 17: 138-139, 1961.

221. Lewin, B.: Problems of differential diagnosis of schizophrenia in Egypt. Congress Report, Second Int. Cong. Psychiat., Zurich, 1957, Vol. III, 23-30.

222. Lin, T. Y.: A study of the incidence of mental disorder in Chinese and other cultures. Psychiatry, 16: 313-336, 1953.

223. ———: Social change and mental health. World Mental Health, 12: 65-73, 1960.

224. ———: The role of epidemiology in transcultural psychiatry. Acta Psychiat. Scand. 38: 158-163, 1962.

225. ———: Historical survey of psychiatric epidemiology in Asia. Ment. Hygiene, 47: 351-359, 1963.

226. Linn, E.: The association of preadmission symptoms with the social background of mental patients. Arch. Gen. Psychiat. 3: 557-562, 1960.

227. Linton, R.: Culture and Mental Disorders, Springfield, Ill.: Charles C. Thomas, 1956.

228. Listwan, I. A.: Paranoid states: Social and cultural aspects. Med. J. of Australia, 43(1): 776-777, May, 1956.

229. ———: Mental disorders in migrants: Further study. Med. J. of Australia, 46(1): 566-568, 1959.

230. Locke, B. Z., Kramer, M., Timberlake, C. E., Pasamanick, B., and Smeltzer, D.: Problems in interpretation of patterns of first admissions to Ohio State public mental hospitals for patients with schizophrenic reactions. Psychiatric Res. Rep. 10: 172-196, 1958.

231. Locke, B. Z., Kramer, M., and Pasamanick, B.: Immigration and insanity. Public Health Rep. 75: 301-306, 1960.

232. Lopasic, R., and Mikic, F.: Mental disturbance. Jugoslavenska Akademija Znanosti i Umjetnosti, Zagreb, 535-551, 1957.

233. Lowe, C. R., and Carrat, F. N.: Sex pattern of admissions to mental hospitals in relation to social circumstances. Brit. J. Prev. Soc. Med. 13: 88-102, 1959.

234. Lowe, L. H.: Families of children with early childhood schizophrenia: Selected demographic information. Arch. Gen. Psychiat. 14: 26-30, 1966.

235. Lynn, R.: Russian theory and research on schizophrenia. Psychol. Bull. 60: 486-498, 1963.

236. Lystad, Mary H.: Social mobility among selected groups of schizophrenic patients. Amer. Soc. Rev. 22: 288-292, 1957.

237. Maldonado-Serra, E. D., and Trent, R. D.: The sibling relationship in group psychotherapy with Puerto Rican schizophrenics. Amer. J. Psychiat. 117: 239-244, 1960.

238. Malzberg, B.: Mental disease among Puerto Ricans in New York City. J. Nerv. Ment. Dis. 123: 262-269, 1956.

239. ———: Statistical data for the study of mental disease among Negroes in New York State. Albany Research Foundation for Mental Hygiene and N. Y. State Dept. of Mental Hygiene, 1959.

240. ———: Important statistical data

about mental illness. *In* American Handbook of Psychiatry, Chapter 7, S. Arieti (Ed.) N. Y. Basic Books, 1959.

241. ———: Mental disease among Negroes; Analysis of first admissions in New York State, 1949-1951. Ment. Hyg. 43: 422-459, 1959.

242. Malzberg, B.: Mental Disease among Jews in New York State. New York: International Medical Book Corporation, 1960.

243. ———: The distribution of mental disease according to religious affiliation in New York State, 1949-1951. Ment. Hyg. 46: 510-522, 1962.

244. ———: Mental disease among Norwegian-born and native-born of Norwegian parentage in New York State, 1949-1951. Acta Psychiat. Scand. 38: 48-75, 1962.

245. ———: Migration and mental disease among the white population of New York State: 1949-1951. Hum. Bio. 34: 89-98, 1962.

246. ———: Mental disease among Irish-born and native whites of Irish Parentage in New York, 1949-1951. Ment. Hyg. 47: 12-42, 1963.

247. ———: Mental disease among the Italian-born and native whites of Italian parentage in New York State, 1949-1951. Ment. Hyg. 47: 300-332, 1963.

248. ———: Mental disease among Polish-born and native whites of Polish-born parentage in New York State, 1949-1951. Ment. Hyg. 47: 421-451, 1963.

248a. ———: Mental disease among Russian-born and native born of Russian-born parentage in New York State, 1949-1951. Ment. Hyg. 47: 649-678, 1963.

249. ———: Mental disease among the native whites in New York State, 1949-1951, classified according to parentage. Ment. Hyg. 48: 517-536, 1964.

250. ———: Malzberg, B.: Mental disease among English-born and native whites of English parentage in New York State, 1949-1951. Ment. Hyg. 48: 32-54, 1964.

251. ———: Mental disease among German-born and native whites of German parentage in New York State, 1949-1951, Ment. Hyg. 48: 295-317, 1964.

252. ———Mental disease among native and foreign-born whites in New York State, 1949-1951. Ment. Hyg. 48: 478-499, 1964.

253. Maoz, B., Levy, S., Brand, N., and Halevi, H. S.: An epidemiological survey of mental disorders in a community of newcomers to Israel. J. of the Coll. of Gen. Practitioners, II: 267-284, 1966.

254. Margetts, E. L.: The future for psychiatry in East Africa. East African Med. J. 37: 448-457, 1960.

255. Margetts, E. L.: The psychiatric examination of native African patients. Med. Proceedings, Mediese Bydraes, 4: 679-683, 1958.

256. ——— (Ed.): The Mind of Man in Africa: An integrated anthologia relating to psychiatry and mental health. Pergammon Press, (in process of publication).

257. ———: Clinical Psychiatry in an African Mental Hospital. Conference on Cross-Cultural Psychiatry and Psycho-Ethnology, University of Kentucky, Lexington, 1965. (in process of publication as proceedings).

258. Mars, L.: A few cases of mental illness in Haiti. La Semaine des Hopitaux de Paris, 30: 1-8, 1954.

259. ———: Schizophrenia in Haiti. Bull. du Bureau d'Ethnologie, Haiti, #15, 1958.

260. Mason, A. S., Tarpy, Eleanor K., Sherman, L. J., and Haefner, D. P.: Discharges from a mental hospital in relation to social class and other variables. Arch. Gen. Psychiat. 2: 1-6, 1960.

261. Mayer-Gross, W., Cross, K. W., Harrington, J. A., and Sreenivasan, U.: The chronic mental patient in India and in England. Lancet. 1: 1265-1267, 1958.

262. Mayo, J. A.: What is the social in social psychiatry? Arch. Gen. Psychiat. 14: 449-455, 1966.

263. McCaffrey, Isabel, and Downing, J.: The usefulness of ecological analysis in mental disease epidemiology. Amer. J. Psychiat. 113: 1063-1068, 1957.

264. McCaffrey, Isabel, Cumming, Elaine, and Rudolph, Claire: Mental dis-

orders in socially defined populations. Amer. J. Pub. Health 53: 1025-1030, 1963.

265. McCough, E., Williams, Edwina, and Blackley, J.: Changing patterns of psychiatric illness among Negroes of the Southeastern United States. Paper read at International Congress of Psychiatry, Madrid, 1966.

266. McPartland, T. S., and Cumming, J. H.: Self-conception, social class and mental health. Hum. Org. 17: 24-29, 1958.

267. Meadow, A., and Stoker, D.: Symptomatic behavior of hospitalized patients. Arch. Gen. Psychiat. 12: 267-277, 1965.

268. Medlicott, R.: Psychiatric impressions of South East Asia. Transcultural Research on Ment. Health Problems. 10: 33-35, 1961.

269. Mednick, S. A.: The children of schizophrenics: serious difficulties in current research methodologies which suggest the use of the "high-risk group" method. In Romano, J. (Ed.) The Origins of Schizophrenia. Amsterdam: Excerpta Medica Foundation, 1967.

270. Meerloo, J. A. M.: Psychological remarks on the East-West controversy. Transcultural Research in Ment. Health Problems, 4: 14-15, 1958.

271. Mehlman, R. D.: The Puerto Rican syndrome. Amer. J. Psychiat. 118: 328-332, 1961.

272. Mental Disorders and Mental Health in Africa South of the Sahara: Commission for Technical Cooperation in Africa South of the Sahara—WFMH-WHO Meeting of Specialists on Mental Health, Bukavu, 1958.

273. Mental Health Book Review Index: Ilse Bry (Editorial Chairman) N. Y. Council on Research in Bibliography, Inc., New York University.

274. Mental hospitalization rates for New Zealand Maoris. Transcultural Res. Ment. Health Problems. II: 18-19, 1961.

275. Mezey, A. G.: Personal background emigration and mental disorder in Hungarian refugees. J. Ment. Sci. 106: 618-627, 1960.

276. ———: Psychiatric aspects of human migrations. Int. J. Soc. Psychiat. 5: 245-260, 1960.

277. Miller, K. S., and Grigg, C. M. (Eds.): Mental Health and the Lower Social Classes. Florida State University Studies No. 49. Tallahassee: The Florida State University, 1966.

278. Miller, L.: The social psychiatry and epidemiology of mental ill health in Israel. Ministry of Health, Jerusalem, 1966.

279. ———: Psychiatry in Israel. Dis. Nerv. System 22: 467-469, 1961.

280. Mintz, N. L., and Schwartz, D. T.: Urban ecology and psychosis: Community factors in the incidence of schizophrenia and manic depression among Italians of Greater Boston. Int. J. Soc. Psychiat. 10: 101-118, 1964.

281. Mishler, E. G., and Scotch, N. A.: Sociocultural factors in the epidemiology of schizophrenia. Psychiatry, 26: 315-351, 1963.

282. Montagu, A.: Culture and Mental illness. Amer. J. Psychiat. 117: 15-23, 1961.

283. Morris, J. N. Health and social class. The Lancet 7: 303-305, 1959.

284. Morrison, S. L.: Principles and methods of epidemiological research and their application to psychiatric illness. J. Ment. Sci. 105: 999-1011, 1959.

285. Murphy, H. B. M.: Community variables and the prevalence of schizophrenia. Paper read at First Inter. Cong. Soc. Psychiatry, London, 1964.

286. ———: The methodology of socio- and ethno-psychiatric research. Encyclop. Med. Chir. Psychiatrie, Paris, 1965.

287. ———: Migration and the major mental disorders: A reappraisal. In Mobility and Mental Health, Kantor, Mildred B. (Ed.) Springfield, Ill.; Charles C. Thomas Publishers, 5-29, 1965.

288. ———: Socio-cultural factors in schizophrenia: A compromise theory. Paper read at American Psychopathological Society Meeting, New York, 1967.

289. Murphy, H. B. M., and Lemieux, M.: The problem of the high schizophrenic prevalence in one type of French-Canadian rural community. To be published by Canadian Journal of Psychiatry.

290. Murphy, H. B. M., Wittkower, E.

D., Fried, J., and Ellenberger, H.: A cross-cultural survey of schizophrenic symptomatology, Int. J. Soc. Psychiat. 9: 237-249, 1963.

291. Murphy, Jane N., and Leighton, A. H. (Eds.): Approaches to Cross-Cultural Psychiatry. Ithaca: Cornell University Press, 1966.

292. Myers, J. K., and Roberts, B. H., Some relationships between religion, ethnic origin and mental illness. In Sklare, M. (Ed.) The Jews: Patterns of an American Group, Glencoe, Ill.: The Free Press, 1958.

293. ———: Family and Class Dynamics in Mental Illness. New York: Wiley and Sons, 1959.

294. Noreik, K., and Ødegard, O.: Psychoses in Norwegians with a background of higher education. Brit. J. of Psychiat., 112: 43-55, 1966.

295. Nurnberger, J. M., Zukerman, M., Norton, J. A., and Brittain, H. M.: Certain sociocultural and economic factors influencing utilization of state hospital facilities in Indiana. Amer. J. Psychiat. 117: 1065-1074, 1961.

296. Ødegard, O.: Epidemiology of schizophrenia in Norway. Cong. Rep. III. Second Int. Cong. Psychiat. Zurich, 49-52, 1957.

297. Ødegard, O.: Occupational incidence of mental disease in single women. Transcultural Res. Ment. Health Problems 5: 68-69, 1959.

298. ———: Current studies of incidence and prevalence of hospitalized mental patients in Scandinavia. In Hoch, P. H., and Zubin, J. (Eds) Comparative epidemiology of the Mental Disorders. New York: Grune and Stratton, 1961.

299. ———: Patterns of discharge and readmission in psychiatric hospitals in Norway, 1926 to 1955. Ment. Hyg. 45: 185-193, 1961.

300. ———: Psychiatric epidemiology. Proc. Roy. Soc. Med. 55: 831-837, 1962.

301. ———: Mental disease in Norwegians with a high school background. Acta Psychiat. Scand. 39: 31-40, 1963.

302. O'Doherty, E. F.: The high proportion of mental hospital beds in the Republic (Ireland). Transcultural Psychiat. Res: II: 134-136, 1965.

303. Oh, Suk Whan, Chung, Kiu Han, Park, Cho Yul, and Bae, Kae Kioon: Family backgrounds of schizophrenia. Dept. of Neuropsychiatry, College of Medicine, Pusan National University, May, 1963, Vol. 3.

304. Opler, M. K.: Cultural anthropology and social psychiatry. Amer. J. Psychiat. 113: 302-311, 1956.

305. ———: Schizophrenia and Culture. Scient. Amer. 197: 103-110, 1957.

306. ———: The contribution of social psychiatry to preventive psychiatry. Dis. of the Nerv. Sys. Monograph Suppl. 20: No. 5, 22-29, 1959.

307. ———: Cultural perspectives in research on schizophrenia. A history with examples. Psychiat. Quart. 33: 506-524, 1959.

308. ———: Anthropological aspects of psychiatry. In Masserman, J. H., and Moreno, J. L. (Eds.) Progress in Psychotherapy, Vol. IV. New York: Grune and Stratton, 1959.

309. ———: Culture and Mental Health: Cross-cultural Studies. New York: MacMillan Co., 1959.

310. ———: Social Psychiatry-Evolutionary, existentialist and transcultural findings. Psychosomatics. 11: 430-434, 1961.

311. Opler, M. K.: Socio-cultural roots of emotional illness. Psychosomatics, 5: 55-58, 1964.

312. ———: Leading problems in cross-cultural psychiatry in data and research. In Rapoport, I. (Ed.) Social Aspects of Mental Disorder, Wisconsin Press, 1961.

313. ———: Culture and Social Psychiatry. Atherton Press, 1967.

314. Parker, S.: The Windigo psychosis in the context of Ojibwa personality. Amer. Anthrop. 62: 603-623, 1960.

315. Parker, S., and Kleiner, R. J.: Mental Illness in the Urban Negro Community. New York: The MacMillan Company and Free Press of Glencoe, 1966.

316. Parhad, L.: Report from Kuwait. Transcultural Res. in Ment. Health Problems 9: 36-37, 1960.

317. Parsons, Anne: Some comparative observations on ward social structure: Southern Italy and the United States. I' Ospedale Psichiatrico (Naples) II: April/June, 1959.

318. ———: Family dynamics in South Italian Schizophrenics. Arch. Gen. Psychiat. 3: 507-518, 1960.

319. ———: A schizophrenic episode in a Neapolitan slum. Psychiatry, 23: 109-121, 1961.

320. Pasamanick, B.: A survey of mental disease in an urban population. VII. An approach to total prevalence by race. Amer. J. Psychiat., 119: 299-305, 1962.

321. ———: Some misconceptions concerning differences in the racial prevalence of mental disease. Amer. J. Orthopsychiat. 33: 72-86, 1963.

322. ———: Myths regarding prevalence of mental disease in the American Negro: A century of misuse of mental hospital data and some new findings. J. Nat. Med. Assoc. 56: 6-17, 1964.

323. Pavicevic, M. B.: Psychoses in Ethiopia. Transcultural Psychiat. Res. III, 1966, pp. 152-54.

324. Pearsall, Marion: Medical Behavioral Science: A Selected Bibliography of Cultural Anthropology, Social Psychology and Sociology in Medicine. University of Kentucky Press, Lexington, 1963.

325. Pepper, M., and Redlich, F. C.: Social Psychiatry. Amer. J. Psychiat. 118: 609-612, 1962.

326. Pflanz, M.: The epidemiological method in medical sociology. Kolner Zeitschrift fur Soziologie und Sozialpsychologie Sonderheft. 3: 134-149, 1958.

327. ———: Sociocultural factors and mental disturbances. Fortschriftte der Neurologie-Psychiatrie und lhrer Grenzgebite, Stuttgart, 28: 471-508, 1960.

328. Pfeiffer, W. M.: Mental disturbance among the Sudanese. Psychiat. Neurol. 143: 315-333, 1962.

329. ———: Comparative Psychiatric Studies of different population groups in West Java. Arch. Psychiat. Nervenkr 204: 404-414, 1963.

330. ———: Psychiatric illness in Indonesia. AKT. Fragen Psychiat. Neurol. (Basel) 52: 102-142, 1967.

331. Phillips, L., and Draguns, J.: Some issues in intercultural research on psychopathology. Read at the Conference on Mental Health in Asia and the Pacific, March/April, 1966, Honolulu, Hawaii.

332. Piedmont, E. B.: Ethnicity and schizophrenia; a pilot study. Ment. Hyg., 50: 374-379, 1966.

333. Plank, R.: Ecology of schizophrenia: Newer research on the drift hypothesis. Amer. J. Orthopsychiat. 29: 819-826, 1959.

334. Pollack, E. S., Redick, R. W., Norman, Vivian B., Wurster, C. R., and Gorwitz, K.: Socioeconomic and family characteristics of patients admitted to psychiatric services. Amer. J. Pub. Health 54: 506-518, 1964.

335. Prange, A. J. Jr.: An interpretation of cultural isolation and alien's paranoid reaction. Int. J. Soc. Psychiat. 4: 254-263, 1959.

336. Prange, A. J. Jr., and Vitols, M. M.: Cultural aspects of the relatively low incidence of depression in Southern Negroes. Int. J. Soc. Psychiat. 8: 104-112, 1962.

337. Query, J.: Pre-morbid adjustment and family structure: A comparison of selected rural and urban schizophrenics. J. Nerv. Ment. Dis. 133: 333-338, 1961.

338. Ratanakorn, P.: Studies of mental illness in Thailand. Transcultural Res. Ment. Health Problems 7: 27-28, 1960.

339. ———: Schizophrenia in Thailand. Int. J. Soc. Psychiat. 5. 47-49, 1959.

340. Rao, S.: Caste and mental disorders in Bihar. Ranehi, India. Amer. J. Psychiat., 122: 1045-1055, 1966.

341. Rennie, T. C. A.: Social Psychiatry —A definition. Int. J. Soc. Psychiat. 1: 5-13, 1955.

342. Rennie, T. C. A., Srole, L., Opler, M. K., and Langer, T. S.: Urban life and mental health: Socio-economic status and mental disorders in the Metropolis. Amer. J. Psychiat. 113: 831-837, 1957.

343. Rezai, J.: Increase in the number of mental patients in the City of Teheran. Rev. Med. Moyen Orient. 20: 34-37, 1963.

344. Riessman, F., Cohen, J., and Pearl, L.: Mental Health and the Poor: New Treatment Approaches for Low Income People. New York: The Free Press, and Macmillan Co., 1964.

345. Rin, H.: Family study of Chinese schizophrenic patients: Loss of parents, sibling rank, parental attitude and short-term prognosis. Transcultural Psychiatric Research. II: 24-27, 1965.

346. Rin. H., and Lin, T. Y.: Mental illness among Formosan aborigines as compared with the Chinese in Taiwan. J. Ment. Sci., 108: 134-146, 1962.

347. Rin, H., Wu, K. C., and Lin, C. L.: A study of the content of delusions and hallucinations manifested by the Chinese paranoid psychotics. J. of the Formosan Med. Assn. 61: 47-57, 1962.

348. Rin, H.: A study of the aetiology of Koro in respect to the Chinese concept of illness. Int. J. Soc. Psychiat. 11: 7-14, 1965.

349. Rinder, I. D.: Mental health of American Jewish urbanites: A review of literature and predictions. Int. J. Soc. Psychiat. 9: 104-109, 1963.

350. Rinehart, J. W.: On diagnosed mental illness and social class. Amer. Sociol. Rev. 31: 545-546, 1966.

351. Risso, M., and Baker, W.: Delusions of being bewitched: A contribution to the understanding of delusional disorders in Southern Italian labourers in Switzerland. Bibliotheca Psychiat. Neurol. Basel 124: 1-79, 1964.

352. Rogler, L. H., and Hollingshead, A. B.: Trapped: Families and Schizophrenia. New York: John Wiley and Sons, Inc., 1965.

353. Roman, P. M., and Trice, H. M.: Schizophrenia and the Poor. New York State School of Industrial and Labor Relations Paperback No. 3, Cornell University, Ithaca, 1967.

354. Rose, A. M.: The prevalence of mental disorders in Italy. Int. J. Soc. Psychiat. 10: 87-100, 1964.

355. Rosen, G.: Social stress and mental disease from the 18th century to the present: Some origins of social psychiatry.

Milbank Mem. Fund Quarterly, 37: 5-32, 1959.

356. ———: Patterns of discovery and control in mental illness. Amer. J. Public Health. 50: 855-866, 1960.

357. Rosenbaum, G.: Reaction time indices of schizophrenic motivation: A cross-cultural replication. Brit. J. Psychiat. (in press) 1967.

358. Rubel, A. J.: The epidemiology of a folk illness: Susto in Hispanic America. Ethnology, 3: 268-283, 1964.

359. Ruesch, J.: Research and training in social psychiatry in the United States. Int. J. Soc. Psychiat. 7: 87-96, 1961.

360. Sal y Rosas, F.: The myth of Jani or Susto (Magic Fright) in the medical theory and practice of Peruvian Indians. Revista de la Sanidad de Policia (Lima) 18: 167-210, 1958.

361. Sandifer, M. G. Jr.: Social psychiatry 100 years ago. Amer. J. Psychiat. 118: 749-750, 1962.

362. Sanseigne, A., and Desrosiers, M.: Evaluation of psychopharmaceuticals in an under-developed country. Paper presented at the Amer. Psychiat. Assn. Meeting, 1960.

363. Sanua, V. D.: The sociocultural factors of families of schizophrenics: A review of the literature. Psychiatry, 24: 246-265, 1961.

364. ———. Comparison of Jewish and Protestant Paranoid and Catatonic Patients. Dis. of the Nerv. Sys. 28: 1-7, 1962.

365. ———: A comparative study of schizophrenics of different backgrounds; Italian, Irish, Jews and Protestants. Progress Report to the Scottish Rite Program in Schizophrenia, 1964.

366. ———: The sociocultural aspects of schizophrenia: A comparison of Protestant and Jewish schizophrenics. Int. J. Soc. Psychiat. 9: 27-36, 1963.

367. ———: The etiology and epidemiology of mental illness and problems of methodology. Ment. Hyg. 47: 607-621, 1963.

368. ———: The socio-cultural aspects of childhood schizophrenia: A review of the literature with special emphasis on methodology. Presented at the Second

Institute of Research Methodology in Childhood Schizophrenia, Amer. Orthopsychiat. Assoc., Chicago, March, 1964, 79 pp.

369. ———: Social disorganization in families of schizophrenics belonging to various ethno-religious groups. Psychiatry Digest, 26: 45-59, 1965.

370. ———: The sociocultural aspects of childhood schizophrenia: A discussion with special emphasis on methodology. In Zuk, G. H., and Boszormenyi-Nagy, I. Family Therapy and Disturbed Families. Palo Alto, Calif.: Science and Behaviour Books, 159-176, 1967.

371. ———: The epidemiology and etiology of mental illness and problems of methodology with special emphasis on schizophrenia and manic-depressive psychoses. A review of the literature. (mimeographed, 100 pp.)

372. ———: Sociocultural aspects of psychotherapy and treatment: A review of the literature. In Abt, L. E., and Riess, B. F. (Eds.) Progress in Clinical Psychology VII, New York: Grune & Stratton, 151-190, 1966.

373. ———: Parental loss and prognosis in schizophrenia: A comparative socio-cultural study. In Finney (Ed.) Culture, Mental Health, and Poverty. Lexington: University of Kentucky Press. (In process of publication.)

374. ———: The psychology of the Fellah. In Margetts, E. L. (Ed.) The Mind of Man in Africa: An Integrated Anthologia Relating to Psychiatry and Mental Health. Pergamon Press (In process of publication.)

375. Savage, C., Leighton, A. H., and Leighton, Dorothea, C.: The problem of cross-cultural identification of psychiatric disorders. In Murphy, J. M., and Leighton, A. H. (Eds.) Approaches to Cross-Cultural Psychiatry. Ithaca, N. Y.: Cornell University Press, 1965.

376. Saucier, J. F.: Essai sur l'aspect socioculturel de la maladie mentale. (Essay on the sociocultural aspect of mental illness.) L'Union Med. du Canada. 91: 627-637, 1962.

377. Schachter, Frieda: A study of psy-choses in female immigrants. Med. J. Aust. 49(2): 458-461, 1962.

378. Schermerhorn, R. A.: Psychiatric Index for Interdisciplinary Research: A guide to the literature 1950-1961. Vocational Rehabilitation Administration, Washington, D. C.: U. S. Dept. of Health, Education and Welfare, 1964.

379. Schmidt, K. E.: The racial distribution of mental hospital admissions in Sarawak. Transcultural Res. Ment. Health Problems. 11: 17-18, 1961.

380. ———: Management of schizophrenia in Sarawak mental hospital. J. Ment. Sci. 107: 157-160, 1961.

381. Schmitt, R. C.: Population densities and mental disorders in Honolulu. Hawaii Med. J. 16: 396-397, 1957.

382. ———: Psychosis and race in Hawaii. Hawaii Med. J. 16: 144-146, 1956.

383. Schooler, C., and Caudill, W.: Symptomatology in Japanese and American schizophrenics. Ethnology, 3: 172-177, 1964.

384. Scott, W. A.: Social psychological correlates of mental illness and mental health. Psychol. Bull. 55: 65-87, 1958.

385. Sechrest, Lee: Philippine Culture, Stress and Psychotherapy. Conf. on Mental Health in Asia and the Pacific. March, 1966.

386. Seguin, C. A.: The theory and practice of psychiatry in Peru. Amer. J. Psychother. 18: 188-211, 1964.

387. Seligman, C. G.: Temperament, conflict and psychosis in a stone age population. Brit. J. Psychol. 9: 187-202, 1929.

388. Simmons, L. W.: Impact of social factors upon adjustment within the community. Amer. J. Psychiat. 122: 990-998, 1966.

389. Simmons, O. G.: Social research in health and medicine: A bibliography. In Freeman, H. E., Levine, S., and Reeder, L. G. (Eds.) Handbook of Medical Sociology. Englewood Cliffs, N. J.: Prentice-Hall, 1963.

390. Simmons, O. G., and Davis, J. A.: Interdisciplinary collaboration in mental illness research. Amer. J. Sociol., 63: 297-303, 1957.

391. Simons, H. J.: Mental disease in

Africans: Racial determinism. Race Relations Journ. 24: 1958 and J. Ment. Sci. 104: 372-388, 1958.

392. Sirakov, A. A., and Popov, S. T.: On the problem of schizophrenia in Bulgaria. Zh. Nevropat. Psikhiat. Korsakov, 61: 1396-1401, 1961.

393. Soddy, K. (Ed.): Identity: Mental Health and Value Systems. Tavistock Publications, London, 1961.

394. Sommer, R., and Hall, R.: Alienation and mental illness. Amer. Sociol. Rev. 23: 418-420, 1958.

395. Song, Ro Chae: Observations on Mental Illness in Korea. Transcultural Res. Ment. Health Problems 5: 22-24, 1959.

396. Spiegel, J. P.: Some cultural aspects of transference and countertransference. In Masserman, J. H. (Ed.) Science and Psychoanalysis: Individual and Family Dynamics. New York: Grune & Stratton, 1959.

397. Spitzer, R. L., Fleiss, J., Kernohan, W., Lee, Joan C., Baldwin, I. T.: Mental status schedule, comparing Kentucky and New York schizophrenics. Arch. Gen. Psychiat. 12: 448-455, 1965.

398. Sreevivasan, U., and Hoenig, J.: Caste and mental hospital admissions in Mysore State, India. Amer. J. Psychiatry 117: 37-43, 1960.

399. Srole, L.: Social Psychiatry, the "Babel syndrome." Roche Rep. Frontiers of Hospital Psychiatry, April, 1967.

400. Srole, L., Langner, T. S., Michael, S. T., Opler, M. K., and Rennie, T. A. C.: Mental Health in the Metropolis: The Midtown Manhattan Study. Thomas A. C. Rennie Series in Social Psychiatry, Vol. I. New York: McGraw-Hill Book Co., Inc. 1962.

401. Stein, L.: Social class gradient in schizophrenia. Brit. J. Prev. Soc. Med. 11: 181-195, 1957.

402. Stein, W. W.: Patterns of a Peruvian Mental hospital. Int. J. Soc. Psychiat. 9: 208-215, 1963.

403. Sternback, A., and Achte, K.: An epidemiological study of the psychiatric morbidity in Helsinki. Acta Psychiat. Scand., Suppl. 180. 40: 287-307, 1964.

404. Sukthankar, H. K., and Vahia, N. S.: Influence of social and cultural factors in schizophrenia and hysteria. Read at the First Inter. Cong. of Soc. Psychiatry, London, 1964.

405. Sundby, P.: Occupation and insanity. Acta Psychiat. Neurol. Scand. Supp. 106: 276-287, 1956.

406. Sundby, P., and Nyhus, P.: Major and minor psychiatric disorders in males in Oslo. Acta Psychiat. Scand. 39: 519-547, 1963.

407. Sutter, J. M., Porot, M., and Pelicier, Y.: Algerian aspects of mental pathology. Algerie Med. 63: 891-896, 1959.

408. Sutter, J. M., Susini, R., Pelicier, Y., and Pascalis, G.: Some clinical observations of marriage psychoses among Algerian Moslems. Ann. Med. Psychol. 5: 907-913, 1959.

409. Teicher, M.: Windigo psychosis: A study of a relationship between belief and behavior among Indians of Northwestern Canada. Proceedings of the 1960 Annual Spring Meeting of the Amer. Ethnol. Soc., April, 1960, Stanford, Calif.

410. Terashima, S.: Schizophrenic Japanese Canadians and their sociocultural backgrounds. Canad. Psychiat. Assoc. J. 3: 53-62, 1958.

411. Thomas, D. S., and Locke, B. Z.: Marital status, education and occupation differentials in mental disease: State patterns in first admission to mental hospitals for all disorders and for schizophrenia, New York and Ohio as of 1950. Milbank Mem. Fund Quart. 41: 145-160, 1963.

412. Tokuhata, G. K., and Stehman, V. A.: Sociological implications, and epidemiology of mental disorders in recent Japan. Amer. J. Pub. Health, 51: 697-705, 1961.

413. Transcultural Psychiatric Research. Review and Newsletter, formerly Transcultural Research in Mental Health Problems, published by the McGill University Press, Montreal, Canada. Wittkower, E. D., Dubreuil, G., Murphy, H. B. M., and Chance, N. A. (Eds.)

414. Tsuang, M. T., and Rin, H.: An evaluation of social and migration factors among psychiatric out-patients in the Uni-

versity Hospital. J. of the Formosan Med. Assoc. 60: 30-36, 1961.

415. Tuckman, J., and Kleiner, R.: Discrepancy between aspiration and achievement as a predictor of schizophrenia. Behav. Sci. 7: 443-447, 1962.

416. Turner, R. J., and Wagenfeld, M. O.: Occupational mobility and schizophrenia: An assessment of the social causation and social selection hypothesis. Amer. Soc. Rev. 32: 104-113, 1967.

417. Vahia, N. S.: Cultural differences in the clinical picture of schizophrenia and hysteria in India and the United States. Transcultural Psychiat. Res., 14: 16-18, 1963.

418. Vail, D. J., Lucero, R. J., and Boen, J. R.: The relationship between socioeconomic variables and major mental illness in the counties of a Midwestern state. Community Ment. Health J. 2: 211-212, 1966.

419. Van Loon, H. G.: Protopathic instinctive phenomena in normal and pathologic Malay life. Brit. J. Med. Psychol. 8: 264-276, 1928.

420. Vellard, J.: The concept of soul and illness among the American Indians. Travaux de l'Institut Francais d'Etudes Andines, Vol. VI, 5-34, 1957-1958.

421. Ventura, P. A.: The Rorschach applied to Filipino paranoid schizophrenics. Paper read at the 1964 Convention of the Psychological Association of the Philippines.

422. Vitols, M. M.: The significance of the higher incidence of schizophrenia in the Negro race in North Carolina. N. Carolina Med. J., 22: 147-158, 1961.

423. Vitols, M. M., Waters, H. G., and Keeler, M. H.: Hallucinations and delusions in white and Negro schizophrenics. Amer. J. Psychiat. 120: 472-476, 1963.

424. Wyncke, J.: Psychoses and Neuroses in Central Africa. Academie Royale des Sciences Coloniales, Brussels, 1957.

425. Walker, R. G.: Comparison of age of onset of schizophrenia among patients hospitalized in Ranchi, India and in Brockton, U.S.A. J. Neuropsychiat. 2: 183-185, 1961.

426. Wallace, A. P.: The biocultural theory of schizophrenia. Int. Rec. Med. 173: 700-714, 1960.

427. Walsh, D.: Cultural influences in psychiatric illnesses in the Irish. J. Irish Med. Assn. 50: 62-68, 1962.

428. Ward, T. E.: Immigration and ethnic origin in mental illness. Canad. Psychiat. Assn. J. 5 and 6: 323-332, 1961.

429. Warthen, Frances J., Klee, G. D., Bahn, Anita, and Gorwitz, K.: Diagnosed schizophrenia in Maryland. In Monroe, R. R., Klee, G. D., and Brody, E. B. (Eds.) Psychiatric Epidemiology and Mental Health Planning. Psychiatric Research Reports of the A.P.A., No. 22, Washington, D. C., 1967.

430. Weinberg, S. Kirson: Cultural aspects of manic-depression in West Africa. J. of Health and Hum. Behav. 6: 247-253, 1965.

431. Weinstein, E. A.: Cultural Aspects of Delusions: A Psychiatric Study of the Virgin Islands. Free Press of Glencoe, Ill., 1962.

432. Whiteley, J. S.: Sociological aspects of schizophrenia. Ment. Hyg. 42: 497-503, 1958.

433. Wiecek, Z.: Results of observations for several years of a group of persons suffering from collective psychosis. Neurol. Neurochir. Pol. 15: 229-233, 1965.

434. Wilson, D. C., and Lantz, Edna: The effect of culture change on the Negro race in Virginia as indicated by a study of state hospital admissions. The Amer. J. Psychiat. 114: 25-32, 1957.

435. Wintrob, R., and Wittkower, E. D.: Magic and witchcraft in Liberia, its psychiatric implications. Presented at the Assoc. for the Advancement of Psychoth. Atlantic City, 1966.

436. Wittkower, E. D., and Fried, J.: Some problems in transcultural psychiatry. Int. J. Soc. Psychiat. 3: 245-252, 1958.

437. ———: A cross-cultural approach to mental health problems. Amer. J. Psychiat. 116: 423-428, 1959.

438. Wittkower, E. D., and Bijou, L.: Psychiatry in developing countries. Amer. J. Psychiat. 120: 218-221, 1963.

439. Wittkower, E. D., with the assistance of H. Rin.: Recent development in

transcultural psychiatry. In DeReuck, A. V. S., and Porter, Ruth (Eds.) Transcultural Psychiatry. London: J. and A. Churchill Ltd., 4-25, 1965.

440. Wittkower, E. D., and Rin, H.: Transcultural psychiatry. Arch. Gen. Psychiat. 13: 387-394, 1965.

441. Wittkower, E. D., and Dubreuil, G.: Cultural factors in mental illness. Prepared for Symposium on the Study of Personality: An interdisciplinary appraisal. Rice University, Houston, Texas, 1966.

442. Ziferstein, I.: The Soviet psychiatrist: His relationship to his patients and to his society. Amer. J. Psychiat. 123: 440-446, 1966.

443. Zubin, J. (Ed.): Field Studies in the Mental Disorders. New York: Grune & Stratton, 1961.

444. Zubin, J., and Kietzman, M. L.: A cross-cultural approach to classification in schizophrenia and other mental disorders. In Hoch, P. H., and Zubin, J. (Eds.) Psychopathology of Schizophrenia. New York: Grune and Stratton, 482-514, 1966.

445. Zunin, L. M., and Rubin, R. T.: Paranoid psychotic reactions in foreign students from non-Western countries. Presented at the American Psychiatric Assoc. Meeting, New York, 1965.

446. Yap, P. M.: The possession syndrome: A comparison of Hong Kong and French findings. J. Ment. Science. 106: 114-137, 1960.

447. ———: Words and things in comparative psychiatry, with special reference to the exotic psychoses. Acta Psychiat. Scand. 38: 163-169, 1962.

448. Yap, P. M., Suk Yeong or Koro: A culture-bound depersonalization syndrome. Brit. J. Psychiat. 111: 43-50, 1965.

449. Yonebayashi, T.: Kitsunetsuki (Possession by Foxes). Transcultural Psychiatric Research I: 95-97, 1964.

450. Yoo, P. S.: Mental disorders in the Korean rural communities. Proceedings of the Third World Cong. of Psychiat., 1961, Montreal, Canada.

9

Symptomatology, Diagnosis and Course

THOMAS FREEMAN, M.D.

Dr. Thomas Freeman is Consultant Psychiatrist to Holywell Hospital, Antrim, and the City Hospital, Belfast, Northern Ireland.

Graduated from the Queens University of Belfast, Northern Ireland in 1942, he proceeded, after military service, to the degree of M.D. in 1947, as well as a Diploma in Psychological Medicine from the University of London. Dr. Freeman trained in psychoanalysis at the British Institute of Psychoanalysis and in 1955 was elected to membership in the British Psychoanalytic Society. Dr. Freeman spent most of his medical career working as a clinical psychiatrist in mental hospitals in the London area, in Scotland, and most recently in Northern Ireland.

In addition to hospital work and private practise, Dr. Freeman has published two books and some thirty-five papers on various aspects of psychotic illness, the schizophrenias in particular ("Chronic Schizophrenia"). Dr. Freeman is the Editor of the British Journal of Medical Psychology and a member of the Royal College of Physicians of Edinburgh.

This chapter presents a review of the literature of the last decade on the symptomatology, diagnosis and course of schizophrenia. It is a particularly difficult and ambitious undertaking, for as yet no one has been able to answer the question: What exactly is schizophrenia, and what are the signs and symptoms of the illness? For some[80,85,103] schizophrenia is a disease entity with its own specific characteristics which sharply distinguish it from all other psychotic states. For others[12,95] it is a group of syndromes each bearing some resemblance to the other and with considerable overlap at each periphery. Then again there are those[75] who regard the schizophrenias as a series of separate diseases each with its own special pathology. Such theoretic speculations either excessively narrow or indiscriminately widen the range of what is to be designated schizophrenia. For this reason a wholly empirical attitude will be adopted in this chapter. All those signs and symptoms which have at some time been described as schizophrenic and which have again been referred to in the recent literature will be described here.

This review will be selective rather than critical. No attempt will be made to present every publication which has appeared during the last ten years. Special attention will, however, be given to papers and articles which seem to provide fresh standpoints from which schizophrenic psychoses can be viewed. Details

311

will also be provided of those studies which have clarified or amplified some aspect of the symptomatology, either as it occurs in the initial phase of the illness, or at a later time. As this review is concerned with clinical observations, with the subjective experience and behavior of the patient, no reference will be made to those publications which offer a psychoanalytic or existential interpretation of the phenomena. While all quoted papers are clinical in nature, there are a number which can be described as phenomenologic,[34] if by this term is meant the attempt to understand the essence of the patient's experience as well as describing the observable manifestations.

In the past, much of the information about the patient's symptomatology and about the manner in which the illness proceeded was obtained by the same means as that employed with the physically ill. The data was elicited in the course of a few consultations and additional material was gained from relatives or friends. Observations made on ward visits and factual reports from nurses describing the patient's utterances and behavior made up the remainder. Many of the classical descriptions are based on such sources of information. This method of data collection facilitated the exclusion of the effect of consultations, of admission to the hospital, hospitalization and treatment procedure, on form and content of the symptomatology. A consequence of this was to foster the belief that the clinical manifestations had a spontaneous generation within the patient and were without an external stimulus. It also led to the view that certain delusional experiences were without meaning in terms of the patient's personality and current life situation.

The first attempts to treat schizophrenic patients by psychoanalytic psychotherapy showed that the traditional methods of clinical observation had not revealed a complete picture of the symptomatology and the course of the illness. Phenomena in the sphere of object relations had received scant attention and the expression of the remaining healthy mental activity was generally ignored. The psychotherapeutic work of the past 25 years and of the past 10 years in particular[9,15,110,111,112,128] has resulted in increasing recognition of the fact that a comprehensive, realistic account of the symptomatology at any stage of the illness can only be obtained by a careful study of the patient in the course of his relationship with others over an extended period of time. Psychotherapists have made a fundamental contribution to the methodology of the clinical study of schizophrenic patients and in so doing they have exposed the artificiality of the consulting room approach.

No mention will be made in this review of psychophysiological studies beyond reference to reports which describe those alterations in bodily function which can be detected by clinical examination. While physiological, psychological and epidemiological aspects of schizophrenia provide the material for other chapters, it is inevitable that the account of the course of the illness to be described here will at times overlap with the problem of prognosis, which is to receive detailed treatment in a later part of this book. Similarly no reference will be made to therapy although the influence of treatment, whether physical or psychological, must exert a decisive influence on the expression of the symptomatology.

SYMPTOMATOLOGY

An account will be given of publications which have drawn attention to reports of patients' subjective experiences and, to the various behavioral phenomena which can occur in the schizophrenias. These will range from behavior which is entirely voluntary in nature to that which is entirely automatic and apparently outside the control of the individual. In addition to this, reference will be made to papers which report reactions to simple clinical tests and to those which describe observations found on physical examination.

At this point the phenomena reported will not be conceptualised in terms of specific syndromes. The data will not be identified and categorised as typically hebephrenic, catatonic or paranoid. Instead the clinical data will be described under such headings as "impairment of object relations," "disturbances of attention and concentration," "psychomotor phenomena," etc. Recent experience suggests that only when an illness becomes firmly established, do symptom groupings appear vividly enough to provide justification for allocating a patient to one or other of the diagnostic subgroups. Even then the close scrutiny of the clinical picture possible during individual or group psychotherapy, exposes the presence of phenomena inappropriate for the category to which the patient may have been allocated.

The empirical approach demands that the clinical phenomena be given their proper significance unprejudiced by reference to a classification which must inevitably be based on a particular theory of schizophrenia. On this account the clinical data will not be categorized as primary or secondary, or as process or reactive. For purposes of description they will be accorded an equality and regarded as the result of a disorganisation of mental functions. Sufficient has already been said to indicate that the observable clinical phenomena cannot be viewed *in vacuo*. They must be seen against a background of interpersonal contact from which they primarily arise.

The Sources of Clinical Data

Today there are several sources which contribute to an increasing knowledge of schizophrenic symptomatology. First, is the consulting room situation which in spite of its limitations has provided a rich harvest of new observations. This must be attributed to psychoanalysts[16,19,43,72,101,106,113,124] to phenomenologists and to descriptive psychiatrists.[17,21,22,38,39,40,41,81,128]

Second, is the exploitation of the hospital milieu as a means of gathering clinical data. This development had its origins in the introduction, primarily by American psychiatrists, of psychoanalysis into the mental hospital and in the appearance of the therapeutic community.[70] The nurse and occupational therapist were now explicitly recognised as individuals with therapeutic potential. This was a result of the spontaneous transferences displaced on to them, sometimes from the person of the psychiatrist. As a consequence the nurse and occupational therapist became a further source of information about the patient's illness. These data, in contrast to the formal reports of earlier times demonstrated how the symptomatology had the closest ties with interpersonal relationships reflected now in the interaction with the hospital personnel. A number of studies on symptomatology have been based on material obtained from nursing staff and ancillary therapists.[17,44,45,120]

Group psychotherapy[18] has provided a third source of information about symptoms. In the group, in contrast to the consulting room, the psychiatrist can observe the patient reacting with other patients and with himself. The patient is able to move about and there is less restraint upon spontaneity. This compensates to some extent for the paucity of information about past experience and phantasy. New symptoms frequently make their appearance and the repetition of established phenomena provides an opportunity to observe their possible stimulus. Free communication between psychiatrists and nursing staff who are involved with thes patients enables reactions which are carried into the ward to be fed back into the group situation.

Finally there are the data which are to be obtained from family studies.[3,13,88,131] These researches, which are often therapeutically orientated, have provided a new standpoint from which to observe the symptoms of the illness. They frequently demonstrate the stimulus for the expression of symptoms and the precondition for their expression. Above all these family groups bring together the principal actors in the drama of the patient's illness and in this provide a plethora of fresh material for clinical observation.

The Impairment of Object Relations

Impairment of the capacity to relate to others is an established sign of schizophrenia. It has been the practice for many years to identify this impairment with the characteristic indifference, loss of interest and volitional lack, restricting the concept to those phenomena. In more recent years it has become apparent, mainly through a closer study of patients, that there are a variety of symptoms which are the expression of the impairment of object relations.

There are five distinct forms of object relationship pattern which can be observed with schizophrenic patients. These patterns may appear at any point of the illness and on the basis of only the slightest acquaintanceship. Their expression is therefore independent of the establishment of a specific relationship and a lengthy period of interpersonal contact is not a prerequisite for their appearance. They may arise with psychiatrist or nurse or both or with occupational therapist and fellow patient. The first pattern is one in which the psychiatrist is involved in the patient's delusional preoccupations and is converted into a persecutor. This belief is not associated with visual misidentification for the patient clearly recognizes the correct identity of the psychiatrist. It is not uncommon to observe the displacement of this persecutory delusion from one psychiatrist to another after an initial period of friendliness.

It can also happen that, instead of the psychiatrist's becoming identified with a persecutor, his image may be condensed with a delusional object towards whom the patient has friendly feelings. This development is not uncommon in established cases, and the psychiatrist is misidentified and confused with the delusional object. This is the counterpart to the situation where the patient misidentifies the psychiatrist as a persecutor. There is no reason to deny the possibility that this form of "positive" equation of doctor and delusional object may also occur in early phases of the illness more often than is recognized. When this happens, the patient's management becomes much easier although it does not guarantee a better outcome.

The second pattern is that in which the patient misidentifies the individual with whom he is in contact. The latter may be confused with a real or delusional object. The misidentification does not remain static but can change from one figure to another. The psychiatrist may be confused with several real or delusional objects. In the early case it is the rule to find that the misidentifications do not entirely dominate the patient's mental life. From time to time he has insight into the misidentifications and will say so. This is less common with the chronic patient, and there it is clear that the delusional object has a greater reality and importance than the real person. This is borne out by the unmarried female patient who misidentifies the ward doctor as her husband giving him a new name and yet calling him doctor. This suggests that a correct perception of the world is not entirely lost. If the doctor is replaced, the patient misidentifies the new man in exactly the same way. Such instances show that object relations of this type are in no way specific for a particular patient/doctor relationship.

The third pattern falls within the category designated as failure of self-object discrimination. These disorders[9,45,101,110,112,113] are closely connected with disorders of the sense of autonomy and personal identity and with distractibility.[9,46,47,101,110,113] There are patients who fail to discriminate themselves from others and yet retain their identity. In such cases a weakened sense of autonomy and separateness from environmental objects becomes evident. Then there are patients who not only fail to discriminate adequately but have also lost, partially or completely, their personal identity.

This distinction can be used as a means of classification. First there are patients who retain their sense of identity. In some cases the defect of discrimination may effect the patient's perception of himself and not of others. He complains that his speech, thinking, emotions, needs and movements have been taken over by someone else. Here the loss of autonomy is apparent but personal identity is retained. Identity may also be preserved in cases where faulty discrimination effects the patient's perception of others. In such circumstances he believes that his thoughts, feelings, traits of character, and drives have flowed into another individual causing him to behave as he does, would like to do or as he fears to do. The dangers of classification become immediately apparent when patients are seen, especially in the early phases of the illness, who demonstrate such manifestations accompanied by a transitory loss of personal identity.

In the second group of patients where personal identity is deficient, the discriminatory defect may include one or both of the types described above. For the most part defects in identity, whether passing or permanent, are most common in established cases. In some patients the new identity is valued and at other times resented because of the belief that it has been imposed. In these cases the patient is in a state of confusion because he cannot discriminate between his old and new identity. There are cases, both recent and established, where the sense of identity alters in accordance with whomever the patient may be in contact. If the patient is with a doctor, he is that doctor, if a nurse, then that nurse and so on. This tendency is often accompanied by a trend towards the assimilation of irrelevant environmental stimuli thus once again pointing to a defective discriminating function. This distractibility usually involves some action, utterance or characteristic of the psychiatrist or nurse with whom the patient is in contact.[48]

The fourth form of anomalous object relationship comprises the merging or assimilation with the object leading to transient identifications. This category of impaired relating is closely connected with faulty self-object discrimination and from an interpretative standpoint can be regarded as the outcome of it. Nevertheless for descriptive purposes it requires separate treatment. Patients report a change in some aspect of the physical or mental self although retaining the sense of identity. Only a part of the body may be involved. Merging phenomena and self-object discrimination failure are frequently accompanied by anxiety and distress. These experiences lead to depression of mood, to a feeling of helplessness, and to suicidal intent.

The fifth category is that characterised by negativism and ambivalence. Once again these phenomena rarely appear without evidence of faulty self-object discrimination and merging phenomena, thus indicating that all the forms described are but aspects of a central defect in the sphere of relating to others. Negativism is rarely complete, ambivalence being a more frequent manifestation. This ambivalence may influence movement (ambi-tendency), thinking, or affect. A compulsive need to disagree or reverse an earlier statement is characteristic. In these circumstances it is difficult to separate out obsessive compulsive manifestations from ambivalence.[11,100] When negativism and ambivalence are the leading manifestations of anomalous relating capacity, they are usually associated with disturbances of speech and motor function.

Disturbances of Attention and Concentration

Although an account of the disturbances which affect attention and concentration involves consideration of the state of consciousness, this aspect is more appropriately discussed in conjunction with abnormalities of perception. Similarly the relation between attention and thinking must be postponed to a later section of this chapter.

There are a number of important phenomena which indicate the extent to which the schizophrenic patient has lost the capacity to selectively attend. They are inattention, a form of negative hallucination, denial, distractibility, and perseveration. Inattention has a double aspect. Not only is the patient unresponsive to a stimulus directed to him, but there are times when he pays little attention to his own thoughts as they occur in speech. This inattention can occur at the level of sensation, with simple percepts and with verbal communication. Instances are cited in the literature[31,49] which show that inattention is not due to faulty registration. Following a latent period the response appears but now in a different context. It is this which leads to what are apparently incomprehensible statements or replies to questions. Inattention is often associated with echo reactions and distractibility. When these phenomena appear together, a close examination reveals the presence of faulty self-object discrimination and transient identifications.

While it is very difficult to obtain an account of the subjective experiences which accompany inattention there is a similar phenomenon where this is possible. This phenomenon can, for want of a better term, be described as a form of negative hallucination.[33] In such cases the patient reports that disturbing needs, images, and affects can be dispelled by turning toward another form of external or internal stimulation. In one case visual hallucinations with an erotic content could be banished if the patient looked at herself in a mirror.[31]

Denial is also encountered in schizophrenic states, and there are occasions when a patient will provide details of this phenomenon as it occurs in the illness.[49] Such reports indicate that this form of denial is of a different order from that which occurs in the neuroses and in the healthy. In the latter categories denial is discrete and only effects specific items of affective significance. It does not lead to the kind of misinterpretation of environmental events which precludes adaptation. The denial of the schizophrenic patient would appear to be designed to preserve delusional ideas. Any external experience which might act as a threat to these ideas is blotted out. This inevitably leads to a distorted account of what actually occurred. Inattention, negative hallucination, and denial belong together and would appear to serve a similar function.

Perseveration is another expression of faulty attention and concentration. It is necessary to give it some consideration at this point. Perseveration has important connections with perceptual and motor functions. It has been known for many years that certain types of chronic schizophrenic patients are unable to disengage themselves from the effects of a stimulus and redirect their attention to a new one. This stimulus may be at the sensory or the perceptual level. They may be unable to relinquish a particular word or verbal theme or unable to refrain from compulsively writing a letter or word over and over again. The occurrence of this compulsive repetition in the verbal sphere makes communication quite impossible. Evidences of this defect of attention are to be found in the recent case but here these manifestations are transient and not persistent over a period of time as with the chronic patient. While patients cannot describe their experiences, it would seem reasonable to assume that perseveration reflects the fact that attention has lost its mobile quality.

Although Bleuler described the occurrence of distractibility in schizophrenia, this phenomenon has received relatively little attention until recent years.[15,21,22,46,50,91] The distractibility is not confined to one sensory modality. According to patients' reports[21,91] the capacity to direct attention is lost. Attention is governed rather by the pattern of environmental stimuli existing at the moment. The patient is unable to direct his attention as he wishes. Instead it is the change that is going on around him which determines the manner in which his attention operates. The patient, having the impression that he cannot contain the flood of incoming stimulation, thus feels insecure. Patients state that they find themselves compulsively attending to aspects of their perceptual field which ordinarily occupied a background position. The whole range of perceptual experiences is widened and selective attention becomes impossible. The authors who have described these manifestations[21,91] point out that the lack of selectivity also effects thoughts, and this in turn leads to disturbance of logical thinking. They also suggest that an important causal relationship exists between the faulty attention mechanism and voluntary movement.

There appear to be two distinct forms of distractibility in schizophrenic states. The first type has been briefly referred to in an earlier section. This distractibility has a passive quality insofar as the patient appears to assimilate the percepts into his stream of talk without the intervention of awareness.[45,46,48] This is accompanied by defects of self-object discrimination and sometimes by echo phenomena. In the second form of distractibility the patient appears alert and gives the impression of seeking out an understanding of whatever extraneous stimuli occur. Here the distractibility can be regarded as "active" insofar as the patient is trying to record all new stimuli in order to help him confirm or refute his current delusional preoccupations. Each new stimulus, which he sometimes mentions and questions, is regarded as a fresh proof of his conviction that he is the victim of a persecution or that the world is in fact disintegrating. In this second form self-object discrimination is intact. Both forms of distractibility can occur in the same patient in different phases of the illness.

Disturbances of Speech

In most descriptions of schizophrenic symptomatology little distinction is made between disorders of speech and disorders of thinking. This approach is based on the belief that speech disorders are wholly the outcome of the disturbance of thinking and that the speech function is quite intact. According to this view, speech disorders are only a facet of a disturbance of communication.[28] The facts of observation indicate that serious derangements of speech do occur, and on this ground alone they demand separate consideration. There are several writers[21,38,75] who believe that speech disturbances arise in schizophrenia because of a disorganisation and inaccessibility of verbal symbols and that they are not directly related to a disorder of thinking. According to one observer[21] schizophrenic patients have difficulty in word finding, and this applies to both the expressive and receptive aspects of speech. It is true that patients often demonstrate a faulty use of words and sometimes present a naming difficulty. It has been suggested[21,38,105] that a true aphasia occurs in schizophrenia but that this disturbance has only an intermittent appearance. It is this aphasia which leads to the verbal and literal paraphasias and to the agrammatism which can be observed. Perseveration and echo phenomena also disturb the formal aspects of speech.

For purposes of description, disorders of speech in schizophrenia can be grouped into those which are predominantly expressive in nature and those which are primarily receptive. Patients vary considerably in their speech capacity. There are many in whom the expressive aspects of speech are in no way disordered. The only exception to this may be found when they are describing their delusional or hallucinatory experiences. At the other end of the scale there are patients who present a fragmentation and disintegration of speech. These are the patients who display the classical obstruction of speech. In these cases the patients may express themselves on certain occasions and not at all on others. Variation in speech productivity will therefore occur within the one patient.

It is possible to recognise three overlapping categories of speech disturbance in schizophrenic states. First there are those schizophrenics in whom the speech disintegration parallels the disorganisation of all cognitive functions. Second are those in whom the volume of speech is adequate but the content is almost entirely incomprehensible. This jargon-like speech ignores all grammatical laws. Such a speech defect is not accompanied by gross cognitive upset. Patients of this kind are to be found in useful employment in mental hospitals. While thought disorder may be present to some extent it obviously does not interfere with adaptive behavior. This suggests that the speech confusion is not primarily caused by the thought disorder.[38] Such patients have been described as suffering from a special form of schizophrenia—schizophasia.[38,75] Third there are patients with a similar type of speech defect but they are solitary, uncommunicative, and disinclined to undertake work. Patients in the second and third categories differ in their attitude towards other people. The former are friendly and like to talk even though their speech is not understood, while the latter have no desire to make any kind of contact.

Disturbances of the capacity to comprehend speech are difficult to assess in schizophrenic patients. The response of the patient to instructions or questions is such as to leave the interviewer with the impression that the patient has either ignored him or has failed to understand. The question always remains whether this reaction is due to disinterest and inattention or whether there is indeed a loss of verbal symbols. The former view seems to be correct as patients often show later that they have understood what was said to them and sometimes they respond to the stimulus, now quite inappropriately. The cause for this latent period is not understood.

Before concluding this section, mention must be made of the fact that there are occasions when disordered speech can be replaced by normal utterances. This is often to be observed in early stages of the illness. Fluctuations in the organizational level of speech is but an aspect of a general tendency in the schizophrenias towards alterations in the quality of cognitive and affective functions under the influence of environmental circumstances.

Disorders of Thinking

Increased interest in the speech of schizophrenic patients has been accompanied by a change of emphasis in those clinical investigations concerned with the disorder of thinking. Earlier studies described characteristics of the abnormal thought processes as reflected in speech. (These descriptions were confined to the manner in which thinking proceeded—hence the concepts of asyndetic thinking, over inclusion (Cameron); omission, derailment (Schneider).) In more recent studies attempts have been made to make good the omissions of some of the earlier work.[15,46,47,110,128] These omissions arose from the fact that no allowance was made for the clinical observation that thought processes in the schizophrenias are neither typified by one particular form of disturbance, nor are they constant for the patient over a period of time. The facts of observation indicate that they can easily change their nature depending upon a number of circumstances. This change may be in the direction of even greater pathology or towards normal functioning. Thus later inquiries have taken as their starting point the concept of organizational levels of thought processes. They describe the formal characteristics of the organization of thought as it occurs in the patient at the time of observation. Most of the stimulus for these attempts have arisen from the works of Schilder, Rapaport, Piaget and Werner.

Available evidence suggests that an examination of schizophrenic thinking must take into account first, the formal aspects of the organizational level obtaining and second, the attendant phenomena, particularly those appertaining to the state of the object relationships.[11,15,48,101,106,113] Two major categories of thought organization are encountered in schizophrenic psychoses and their formal characteristics are as follows. In the first type thinking is not differentiated from percepts and motility. It is also closely bound to affect, to instinctual drives and their mental representations. This trend away from discrimination even between verbal ideas (overinclusion, condensation) leads to the appearance of a primitive form of abstraction. Selection of material for thinking, and sometimes for speech, is dependent on its sensory, affective, and drive characteristics.

Recognition of those features which would lead to reality directed thinking is impossible in the absence of an adequately functioning factor of discrimination. The result is the breakdown of grammatical construction which makes speech and writing difficult to comprehend. The syntactical fault results from the inappropriate use of words but it may also arise from a neologism or substitute word (paraphasia). The patient who says, "I didn't have a church wedding, I was history . . . " introduces the inappropriate second phrase because of ideas which have a special affective significance for him. They thus disrupt his logical train of thought. The word (history) which is really a substitute formation—a condensation product—has multiple meanings which can only be discovered through knowledge of the patient's past life, present experiences, preoccupations, and circumstances. Syntax can be further disrupted by a tendency for words to be fragmented—the part standing for the whole and in some cases words are referred to as if they were things (concretization).

In the second category of thought organization, the thinking disturbance does not lead to faulty grammatical structure and so the patient's communications are logical and coherent. In such cases the organization of thought is at a level which is characterized by egocentrism (Piaget) and omnipotence (Freud). In such circumstances ideas are valued for themselves and are endowed with a power to alter the environment or the self in either a constructive or destructive manner. The former leads to pleasure and elation, the latter to anxiety and dread. Ideas are no longer regarded primarily as a means of communicating thoughts to others or as a way in which adaptation to the world may be achieved. A degradation of thinking has taken place from the advanced level of abstraction and conceptualization. The trend is towards thinking becoming self orientated and closely linked to immediate perceptual experience and drives. Concrete attitudes appear, but they are only one facet of the organizational level. This form of thinking leads to delusional ideas, but they are presented without the emergence of syntactical errors. Although both forms of thought organization may appear in some cases of schizophrenia, the second type can exist alone.

Clinical material has been advanced[15,47,49,110,112] to show that the first category of thought organization (syncretic) is associated with object relationship patterns characterized by self-object discrimination failure, merging with the object, misidentification with the object and with loss of autonomy of the self. In the second form of thinking disturbance, the object relationship is of quite a different order. There is rarely a tendency towards merging, and the sense of identity is well retained. Further, the clinical reports clearly show that even where the organization of thinking operates in a syncretic manner the thought processes can reach a normal level even if only for a few minutes. This change in the direction of normalcy with the resolution of inertia and blocking can occur with the appearance of a strong affect—usually anger.

Disorders of Perception and Self Awareness

In the past ten years many reports have appeared describing faults in perceptual function in the schizophrenias. Disorders of visual perception, of perception of the body and of the self have received most attention.[21,45,51,91] Again these publications refer to the close association which these disturbances have with object relationships. At the most elementary level there are disorders which appear identical to the phenomenon of inattention. Here, the patient fails to perceive a prized object (cigarettes, chocolates) once it has passed outside his immediate visual field. He drops a cigarette and does not pick it up. He ignores it when it is placed beside him. Seconds later he asks for another cigarette.

In certain schizophrenic patients perception of the environment is largely conditioned by the needs. Many withdrawn and inactive patients come to life at meal times and for cigarettes. Individuals only exist as instruments for the satisfaction of needs, or as objects against whom hate can be directed when the needs are not met. In one report[51] in which an attempt is made to interpret perceptual disorders in Piagetian terms, it is suggested that patients are inattentive because they have lost the conservation of the object (Piaget). A description is given of a patient in whom the perceptual inattention was resolved as a consequence of continuous contact with a nurse over a period of several months. At the end of this time conservation of the object had been restored contemporaneously with a positive attachment to the nurse. These observations suggest that the state of visual perception and attention is closely linked with needs, interest, and the presence or absence of relationships.

Disturbances of perceptual constancies (size, shape and distance) and loss of figure-ground discrimination are further categories of perceptual upset to be encountered in the schizophrenias.[15,22,41,45,52,91,110] In contrast to the first

group of disorders the patient remains in reasonable contact with his surroundings. Many instances are described of such disturbances arising in
association with specific events in an interpersonal relationship. Patients
report that constancy could be restored by bodily movements of self or object.
Loss of differentiation between sensory modalities has also been described.[30]
Visual and auditory percepts have an equivalence. Synesthetic-like
phenomena appear where auditory stimuli evoke sexual sensations. No
reference will be made here to misidentifications as these perceptual disorders,
always associated with real or delusional object relations, have already been
described.

Federn's concept of ego feeling has been employed as a means of describing
and understanding the disorders of self awareness and perception of the body
in the schizophrenias. Self awareness is in turn an aspect of the state of consciousness existing in the patient at any one moment. In the past many attempts have been made to interpret schizophrenic symptoms on the basis of a
disordered state of consciousness. In the present context it is sufficient to say
that consciousness may be significantly altered, and some of the consequences
of this have already been described. There are some writers who support the
view that a special category of illness exists (oneirophrenia) in which consciousness is significantly altered.[5,97,121] This view is not shared by all. There
are psychiatrists who maintain that this clouding of consciousness does not
have any specific characteristics which might distinguish it from such
manifestations (misidentifications, perceptual symptoms) encountered in early cases of schizophrenia.

Schizophrenic psychoses are both fascinating and frustrating because objective information about bodily awareness is difficult to obtain in those patients where such disturbances are most strongly suspected. A distinction must
be drawn between reports of subjective experiences and data elicited by
examination. The former are most often presented by patients whose mental
function is still in a fair state of preservation. With respect to the latter the difficulty reaches its height in patients who are resistive and negativistic. As a
rule they do not seem to give any attention to the examiner's request, or when
they do, it is after a lapse of time, and then the instruction may not be fully
carried out. Often, the patient will not comply with the request because of
some delusional preoccupation, as with a woman patient who said, some
minutes after being asked to report awareness of a stimulus, "I am not allowed
to tell you, doctor."

Caution must therefore be exercised in interpreting clinical findings,
because of the difficulties which the patient has in cooperating. A patient who
apparently cannot identify his left hand or denies a tactile stimulus will at a second examination readily extend the correct hand and acknowledge the
stimulus. When patients are asked to identify the right and left ear with
appropriate hands and later asked to make the cross over (Head's test) they

often fail touching the right and left ear with the corresponding hands. During this test perseverative tendencies make their appearance, and the patient may retain the posture, grasping his ears with his hands, now being insensitive to any further instruction or command. A further observation can sometimes be made which suggests that there is a faulty awareness of the spatial relations of the body parts. When a patient is asked to imitate an examiner opening and closing his mouth, he opens and closes his eyes. This behavior is similar to that of the infant just under a year who cannot imitate movements which he is unable to see on his own body.

Some reference must be made to phenomena which result from the disturbance of the relationship which normally exists between percepts and memories on the one hand and perception and motility on the other. As the former are of a hallucinatory character they will be discussed later. With respect to the latter, cases have been described where the patient compulsively responds to visual or auditory percepts with motor behavior.[48,52] Echopraxia falls into this category. Finally there are the misinterpretations of perceived speech and vision. Recent clinical studies[48,53,54,67,107] substantiate Federn's assertion that such misinterpretations are associated with specific thoughts and feelings in the patient's mind. These thoughts which the patient fully recognized and experienced earlier are preconscious at the time of the misinterpretation. A latent period intervenes lasting for minutes or hours. Only when the latent period lasts a matter of minutes is the association between the patient's thoughts and the misinterpretation most clearly observed.

Disorders of Memory

Memory is no less affected than perception. Patients show a normal capacity to retain and recall experiences previously perceived, but it is in the temporal sequence of the experiences recalled, and their appropriateness to the present situation that the distortions are clearly apparent. Accompanying these temporal distortions patients frequently relate detailed memories as if they had been experienced by another person. In memory disturbances which entail an objective temporal distortion and a subjective lack of belongingness, it is possible to note the presence of a loss of self awareness. Memories in the schizophrenic patient also possess a vivid psychic and somatic reality for the patient. Reports are described of such phenomena.[44]

In some cases memories of life experiences prior to the illness[24,35,48] are repressed entirely so that there should be no contradiction to the new psychic reality. In other cases memories are reactivated as current experience as hallucinations. Often it is possible to observe that such a memory, usually with a significant interpersonal content, is associated temporarily with a stimulus arising from a doctor-patient or nurse-patient situation. German psychiatrists[38,40] describe a special form of paranoid schizophrenia—progressive confabulosis—on the basis of the patient consistently presenting falsifications of memory.

Psychomotor Phenomena

As disorders of voluntary movement in the schizophrenias cannot be easily separated from the accompanying psychopathology—using this term in its original sense—it is appropriate to describe such manifestations under the heading "psychomotor phenomena." Interruption of voluntary movement after its inception, is an exact counterpart to the obstruction of speech frequently described as blocking of thought. In this motor blocking patients become fixed at some stage of a voluntary movement, and it is not brought to completion. Sometimes it is easy to see that this interruption of movement is an expression of motor ambivalence (ambi-tendency); here the patient cannot decide whether to remain sitting or to get up and go. He stands, sits down and then ends up in a position which is half standing and half sitting. This difficulty which patients have in satisfactorily completing a voluntary act has been described as a form of apraxia[21] with the implication of an underlying neurological disorganization.

The posture of some patients is awkward and often unusual. Head, neck, and arms may be held rigidly in uncomfortable positions, and repetitive movements of the limbs are often to be seen. The tendency to maintain the hands, arms, and body in a fixed position instead of completing a voluntary act can be compared with the tendency to assume unusual postures. In all these instances there is an increase in the tone of the muscles involved. The term tone is used here to denote the presence of an increase in muscle tension whenever a limb is passively flexed or extended.

Postural persistence is only one of several phenomena to be included within the concept of catalepsy. Apart from the phenomenon of flexibilitas cerea there is the rigid form of catalepsy where both agonistic and antagonistic muscle groups are simultaneously innervated. In all cases there is a pronounced hypertonia of the muscles. A range of variation exists between minimal and extreme degrees of hypertonia. In the former, the increased tone is just sufficient to maintain a limb in its unusual posture for only a short period, while in the latter the position may be maintained for a long time. These motor manifestations are usually associated with inattention, echo phenomena, distractibility, and defects in self-object discrimination. The disturbances of voluntary movement and posture can be understood as resulting from the occurrence of tonic reactions, which are essential for posture, occurring in muscles which would ordinarily not be so effected. This leads to interference with movements which require phasic contractions for their efficient execution.

Many of the automatic movements and the stereotypies which occur in the schizophrenias can be regarded as due to motor (clonic or kinetic) perseveration. This form of perseveration consists of a compulsive repetition. The phenomenon may either arise spontaneously or as a response to an instruction. It can be elicited by asking the patient to perform a simple act. The patient will continue with the movement indefinitely continuing even when the response is no longer required. A second form of motor perseveration can also be found in schizophrenic states. Here a response which is evoked under a first stimulus continues when a second stimulus is offered. Although both types of motor perseveration occur the former is by far the most common.[55] Motor perseveration can be observed in early as well as in established cases, but it is usually associated with echo phenomena and distractibility.

A further psychomotor phenomenon which whas recently been subject to fresh examination is echopraxia.[23] In this study[23] echopraxia includes all forms of mimetic motor behavior which arise simultaneously with the perception of sensory data originating in the actions of another person. It is suggested that the phenomenon occurs in the earliest stages of the illness, but as subjective awareness of its presence precedes its overt expression, it can only be detected by active enquiry. The authors of this study propose that there are different degrees of echopraxia in the schizophrenias. In one form it is completely involuntary and automatic, in the other it is in awareness. The former is associated with an extensive disorder of cognition, while the latter only occurs when the cognitive organization is well preserved.

In the past, detailed descriptions were published of hyperkinetic states. This category of phenomena now attract much less interest, principally because their expression is, of necessity, drastically curtailed by the employment of phenothiazine drugs. The grosser forms of postural disturbance, motor automatisms and stereotypies are much less common, and this can partly be attributed to the changes which have taken place in mental hospital practice. Clinical observation of recent cases, however, reveals that psychomotor phenomena are common manifestations, and given adverse conditions, the gross phenomena described in earlier years could easily make their reappearance.

Sensory Motor Phenomena

Those patients who demonstrate psychomotor phenomena also present disturbances at the sensory-motor level. Although these manifestations are transient in nature and variable in expression, it is essential to record their presence. There have been a few publications dealing with this topic.[56,118,127] It has been noted that motor signs are much more common in schizophrenic patients than in the healthy population. Hypotonia, hypertonia, diminution or absence, accentuation and asymmetrical reactions of the tendon reflexes have been recorded. The hyper-reflexia is sometimes associated with a tonic reflex response which can most easily be elicited during the examination of the biceps tendon reflexes. The biceps muscle progressively shortens with successive blows of the tendon hammer until the forearm is quite unsupported, making an angle of various degrees with the upper arm. Here there is a persistence of posture akin to the cataleptic phenomenon. It can, like the latter, be regarded as due to tonic (Schilder) or static (Purves Stewart) perseveration. This can be contrasted with the other form of perseveration described above (clonic, kinetic) which occurs in the course of voluntary movement. One report[56] suggests that tonic perseveration is encountered more often in chronic (duration of illness over 2 years) hebephrenic and catatonic patients, than in those with a diagnosis of paranoid schizophrenia or paranoid psychosis.

Inattention to tactile stimuli has already been referred to. Sometimes a generalised analgesia can be encountered. The localization of stimuli is often disturbed, displacement occurring from one body part to another. This takes place at random, the stimulus not being transposed to the symmetrical opposite part of the body. With regard to sensory organization schizophrenic patients have been found to show a face dominance when examined by means of double simultaneous stimulation.[127] Sensory signs like the motor phenomena show a striking variability of response—a positive sign being obtained, disappearing and then reemerging at a later time. This variability is also characteristic of organic cerebral disease.[4,29]

Affective Reactions

Elation, depression of mood, anxiety, and dread are common manifestations at the onset of a schizophrenic illness.[8,71,114,115] Self criticism may appear and depression of mood may persist for some time before schizophrenic features arise. In the established case, depression of mood and a sense of hopelessness are sometimes reported when delusional experiences of a wish-fulfilling type are threatened by real circumstances. A depression of mood can occasionally be seen arising from the nonpsychotically involved part of the patient's mind, and this can be regarded as an appropriate reaction to his plight.

It is the absence of affectivity or inappropriate affective responses which are regarded as characteristic of the illness. A result of the psychotherapeutic work, which has been conducted over the past 25 years, has been to show that there is no impairment or weakening of affect in schizophrenic psychoses. Instead, it is the manner of expression which is disturbed. It is of some interest that anger is the most commonly observed affect, particularly in patients who are for the most part withdrawn and inaccessible. As in the case of thinking, perceiving and involuntary movements, a latent period is interposed between the stimulus and the overt reaction.

Hallucinations

Increased knowledge of hallucinatory phenomena has again accrued from intensive studies and from the psychotherapy of schizophrenic patients.[19,48,61,92] In one study[61] concerned with the placement of hallucinations in subjective space, it was noted that the hallucinatory object is sometimes experienced at a distance, close at hand or within the body. Movement between these positions occurred in the one patient with accompanying alteration in affect. These reports demonstrate that the content of auditory hallucinations consists of the patient's own thoughts, phantasies, wishes, judgements, and memories. The form in which they find expression depends upon the extent to which the cognitive functions are impaired by the illness.

An attempt has been made to produce a new classification based on the content of the hallucinations.[48] This classification depends upon the relationship of the hallucinations to real objects. It is not concerned with whether or not the content is advisory, admonishing, persecuting, observing, grandiose, or melancholic. In one category, there are those hallucinations which are clearly bound to real objects which the patient is either conflicted about, or which he has lost. The second category comprises those hallucinations which are part of a delusional reality. They bear no obvious relationship to real objects in the current life situation. The hallucinations arise from delusional objects. Nevertheless these hallucinations are influenced by the immediate environment insofar as they easily merge with real percepts. These percepts arise from medical and nursing staff who have also become condensed with delusional objects. The content of the hallucinations is thus influenced to some extent by the environment.

Finally reference must be made to the quite recent translations of the writings of the German psychiatrists Kleist and Leonhard.[38,39,40,41,75] These writers provide classificatory schemes utilizing the characteristics of hallucinations as one means of categorization of the different schizophrenic states.

Delusions

Grandiose, melancholic, and persecutory delusions can occur in schizophrenic psychoses. They have been divided into smaller units by the German writers[39,40,41] and as in the case of hallucinations have been used as a means of classification. It is generally accepted that complex delusions with an internal consistency are associated with those conditions in which cognition, affect, and volition are not too seriously disturbed. Where cognition is disordered, the delusional ideas are disconnected, and a central theme is absent. They are changing in content and ephemeral in nature. There would appear to be three factors operative in delusional thinking: 1) A pathological egocentrism which is reflected in the patient's belief that he is the focus and cause of all kinds of activity, 2) an omnipotence which he either attributes to others or to himself, and 3) an active denial of those facts which would damage the validity of his beliefs.

Persecutory delusions fall broadly into two groups. First, there are irrational beliefs which never extend beyond what might be possible, and second, are those in which the content is archaic and infantile in nature. Not only are powers of some kind working against the patient, but the persecutors employ all kind of secret, magical or scientific means to interfere with his body and mind. In the former category the patient still retains a good contact with the environment and with the people in it, although they are often the cause of much conflict and guilt feeling. In the latter group, the delusions appear to consume the whole of the patient's interest and he appears to be quite divorced from real objects. Delusional ideas, therefore, like hallucinations can be classified into those which are associated with existing relationships, and those which do not have this connection. However, even in patients who fall into this second category, it is clear that the delusions, although quite divorced from any real relationship, have important adaptive functions. Condensation of real objects with delusional objects provides a bridge to the real world.

Recent work[45,48] has demonstrated that while the nucleus of a delusion may remain constant and influence the perception of environmental events, the remaining content is not necessarily unalterable. Additions and deletions occur depending upon external circumstances. It is now widely recognized that the milieu in which the patient finds himself can be decisive for the manner in which delusional ideas find expression.

DIAGNOSIS

There are two aspects to the diagnosis of schizophrenic psychoses. One of these is straightforward, the other is fraught with problems and complexities. The first is the differentiation of schizophrenia from organic brain disease, drug reactions and metabolic disease. This facet of the diagnostic problem is simplified for the psychiatrist by the presence, in these conditions, of observable phenomena which are largely independent of the patient's subjective experiences and his own. The diagnosis can be arrived at on the basis of relatively objective phenomena—physical signs and laboratory tests. The differentiation of the schizophrenias from other functional psychoses is hindered by the absence of such objective information.

In recent years[7,26] there has been recognition of the fact that amphetamine taken over a long period of time may produce psychotic symptoms which are almost indistinguishable from a schizophrenic psychosis. The differential diagnosis is difficult because in both conditions persecutory delusions, hallucinations, and anxiety exist. The only distinguishing feature is the presence of visual hallucinations in some cases. Amphetamine addiction can also lead to the onset of a schizophrenic illness proper. The diagnosis is established by the detection of amphetamine in the urine.

Alcohol can also lead to a state characterised by persecutory delusions and hallucinations but here the history and the characteristic hallucinatory experiences assist in the diagnosis. Again it is not uncommon to find an associa-

tion between alcoholism and illnesses characterised by delusional preoccupations. These conditions can be differentiated from schizophrenia by the
absence of volitional disturbance, extensive cognitive defect, and the retention
of relationships in certain areas of living.

Epilepsy can present mental manifestations which r e s e m b l e
schizophrenia.[62,90,96,116] Psychomotor attacks may be accompanied by
hallucinatory experiences, motor symptoms, passivity feelings, misidentification and delusions. Additionally there are those psychotic states, almost
identical with schizophrenic psychoses in their expression, which appear at
some period in the life of certain epileptic subjects. These conditions have
recently been subject to exhaustive examination[116] with the aim of assessing
their relationship to the schizophrenias. Epileptic conditions can be
distinguished by the history, the occurrence of major seizures and
electroencephalographic examination. A further differentiating factor is that,
in contrast to the schizophrenias, the epileptic patient relates in a warm, often
friendly, cooperative manner. He has an awareness of the irrationality of his
ideas and frequently goes to some length to hide them from others. The retention of the capacity for rapport and affect characterize the patient suffering
from epilepsy.

Brain damage due to trauma, vascular and degenerative diseases can at
times produce symptoms which may make a psychiatrist, initially at least give
consideration to the diagnosis of schizophrenia. Recently two reports[68,69] have
been published in which nine cases eventually discovered to be Schilder's
disease were diagnosed as schizophrenic psychoses. In five of these cases no
physical signs of nervous system derangement were observed. Occasionally patients suffering from encephalitis or its sequelae present symptoms reminiscent
of a schizophrenic state.[84] In the majority of instances such organic brain
diseases can be distinguished on the basis of the physical signs which can be
observed on examination. The presence of fever and clouding of consciousness
suggests a pathological process other than schizophrenia. Finally, mention
should be made of the metabolic disease porphyria which may manifest itself
in mental symptoms. The diagnosis can be made with special laboratory tests.

The differentiation of the schizophrenias from the other functional
psychoses is difficult because this must be made on clinical grounds
alone.[27,58,102] Additionally the majority of the clinical phenomena consists of
the patient's subjective experiences. This inevitably leads to the problem of the
reliability of the recorded manifestations. The efforts made to correct this
source of error have been discussed in several publications.[78,79,108] It is clear
that the diagnosis is entirely dependent on the psychiatrist's conception of
schizophrenia. This may be very wide, very narrow, or somewhere in between.
A comparative study of psychiatric classifications[119] has shown that the
criteria employed in the diagnosis of schizophrenia can vary considerably

within the same hospital quite apart from the inevitable differences which exist within one country and from one country to another.

In recent years a reaction has set in against the broader conception of the disease which Bleuler introduced with his group of schizophrenias. Several authorities[6,75,80,85,104] have asserted that the concept of schizophrenia must be refined and made more exact, so that it can be distinguished from other psychotic states which present such phenomena as delusions, hallucinations, incoherence of speech, and affective disturbance. This approach does not imply that schizophrenia is to be regarded as a unitary condition. The German writers among others, have strongly advocated the view that there are several schizophrenias. According to these authors there are systematic and nonsystematic schizophrenias which have distinctive clinical characteristics and follow a different clinical course. These attempts to refine the nosology of schizophrenia have been offset by the necessity to postulate so many intermediate forms and by the contradictory results of long term follow-up studies.

A problem which has not been resolved is whether the diagnosis of schizophrenia should be based on the clinical phenomena presented at the time of examination, or whether it should depend on the course of the illness. According to the W.H.O. study group on schizophrenia,[99] the diagnosis should be made on the available evidence including the previous history of illness and the personality make up. When the diagnosis is decided in this way two conditions must be fulfilled. First, criteria for the diagnosis must be established. Here is a major difficulty because there are no universally agreed upon criteria on which a diagnosis can be based. An account of some of the diagnostic criteria which have been proposed will be described below. Secondly, it is absolutely essential that the diagnosis be made on data elicited at a number of consultations.[58] Supplementary information should be obtained from relatives and friends.

One writer[80] of great experience has pointed out that the main difficulty in making the diagnosis arises in those cases where paranoid delusions are the leading feature. Less difficulty is encountered with patients in whom a gradual personality change occurs in late adolescence or early adult life. Here there is a falling off of spontaneity and initiative and the appearance of unusual and peculiar behavior. It is not difficult to make the diagnosis when cataleptic signs and negativism are prominent clinical manifestations. In this author's opinion there are four diagnostic criteria, namely: a break-up in the development of the personality; catatonic stupor or excitement; symptoms of depersonalisation and derealisation (passivity experiences); primary delusions as seen in paranoid cases. He believes that the tendency to identify all cases manifesting hallucinations and delusions as schizophrenia is "an unfortunate trend in international psychiatry."

A further attempt has been made[109] to detail criteria which are diagnostic.

These criteria have been termed first rank symptoms and when present indicate a schizophrenic process. They are: thought echo or the hearing of one's own thoughts spoken aloud; hallucinatory voices in the form of statement and reply; hallucinatory voices which describe the patient's behavior; thought broadcasting, thought insertion and thought withdrawal; bodily passivity experiences; delusional perception; all impressions of control of movement, and motion, speech and drive. The remaining phenomena are classed as second rank symptoms. These include mood change, speech disturbances, motor symptoms, and many forms of delusion and hallucination. The second rank symptoms alone are not diagnostic of a schizophrenic psychosis. This scheme, as has recently been pointed out,[42] is not entirely successful. The patient's mental state at the time of the examination may mislead the examiner into believing that first rank symptoms are present when in fact they do not exist.

In keeping with the trend to narrow the concept of schizophrenia one German writer[86] has described a group of psychotic states—cycloid psychoses—which in his opinion are neither schizophrenias nor manic depressive psychoses. In his opinion these conditions always remit without a defect state. These conditions bear great similarities to the schizophrenias but they can be distinguished from each other on clinical grounds alone. Three different categories of cycloid psychosis have been described: motility psychosis, confusion psychosis, and anxiety-elation psychosis. A characteristic feature is that they are bipolar illnesses—two contrasting states can occur in the one illness.

In the motility psychosis, hyperkinesia and akinesia occur, but there is no mixture as in catatonia. This is a differentiating criterion. In confusion psychosis there is incoherent thinking. During the excited phase there is pressure of talk and misidentifications while in the inhibited phase there is retardation or stupor, affectivity is not effected. It is the inhibition of thought which leads to misinterpretation of the environment. However other significant schizophrenic signs are absent. The mood swings of the anxiety-elation psychosis help to make the diagnosis in spite of ideas of reference and delusions usually with a grandiose or melancholic content. Unfortunately for this formulation overlapping occurs between the different forms and thus atypical states have to be postulated. The author admits that there are times when it is difficult to make a distinction between schizophrenia and cycloid psychoses. This implies that the diagnosis of cycloid psychosis is eventually made on the outcome rather than on the clinical picture during the illness.

Awareness that misinterpretations, hallucinations, and delusions do not signify the presence of a schizophrenic illness or depressive manifestations, a manic depressive psychosis led to the introduction of the category of psychogenic psychoses in which complete recovery took place (Wimmer). This category was subdivided by Schneider into paranoid forms, disturbances of consciousness, and emotional syndromes. In a recent study[37] of 170 cases diagnosed as psychogenic psychoses sixteen years earlier, the diagnosis had to be revised in about half the cases. As might have been expected, the diagnosis had to be changed most often in the paranoid group and then to a diagnosis of schizophrenia. According to the author of this study psychogenic psychoses can be distinguished from the schizophrenias. Schizophrenic psychoses are characterised by autism, withdrawal of thought, pressure of thoughts, audible thoughts in the absence of disturbances of consciousness, and finally flattening of affect. Psychogenic psychoses are not commonly encountered. According to the criteria proposed in this study they do not amount to more than 2 per cent of all hospital admissions. The presence of a psychic trauma, affect, hallucinations, and paranoid features alone favor this diagnosis.

A further attempt to reduce the difficulties of diagnosis was to exclude the paranoid syndromes from the group of schizophrenias (Henderson and Gillespie). When this is done, a diagnosis of schizophrenia is not only easier but is made less frequently. One British author[6] suggests that paranoid psychoses and the schizophrenias should be considered as two separate types of psychosis. To support his contention this author advances the following differentiating factors: sex and social class; age of onset; previous personality; possibly body build; tendencies to systematization of thought and to mental deterioration; response to treatment. Although this is an attractive theory many arguments can be marshalled against it. Among these may be mentioned the trend towards deterioration which occurs in many cases, and the fact that although the disorder is apparently confined to delusions, it permeates the whole of cognition and volition.

The diagnosis of a schizophrenic psychosis is therefore dependent on the psychiatrist's conception of the illness. It is necessary not to make this too wide,[66,117] but it is equally important not to make it too narrow. While delusions and hallucinations do not necessarily signify the presence of a schizophrenic psychosis, the occurrence in a patient of disorders of speech, thinking, perception and voluntary movement should raise suspicions about the possibility such a diagnosis.[21] The terms schizophreniform psychosis,[2] pseudoneurotic schizophrenia,[63] atypical manic depressive psychosis, schizo-affective state and nuclear schizophrenia[93] reflect the current difficulties which beset diagnosis. There must be acceptance of the fact that at this stage of knowledge, the diagnosis can rarely be absolute unless it is to be based on the final outcome of the illness. This often means a revision of the original diagnosis, as the follow-up studies show. There will always be some doubt, particularly in those cases where the predominant manifestations are of a delusional nature. Steps towards improving the standard of diagnosis can be made by spending as much time as possible with the patient before coming to a decision, and by utilizing descriptive concepts which are solidly grounded in clinical observations.

COURSE OF THE ILLNESS

An account of the clinical course of an illness implies a discussion of its outcome. Thus in the case of the schizophrenias it is necessary at the outset to refer to some of the numerous publications which have appeared during the last decade dealing with the outcome of the illness.[14,25,59,64,65,76, 77,82,87,89,94,98,122,126,130] Follow-up periods ranged from one year[94,130] to 15 years.[77] These reports point to the fact that a large proportion of patients diagnosed as suffering from schizophrenia at first admission to a hospital are able to live in the community for months or years without further periods of hospitalization.

The question which is still left unanswered is the psychosocial state of these patients—the extent to which they are troubled by symptoms and the degree to which they are able to adjust to home and to work. Several publications indicate that all is not well in this respect. According to one study[89] 171 patients out of a total of 230 were living outside the hospital two years after their referral. Only three were seriously ill and only four families suffered severe stress on account of the illness. However the work record of these patients was poor—40 per cent of the men were not working and 33 per cent had not worked for at least one year. Relevant to this problem of the clinical state of the discharged patient is a report[57] dealing with factors underlying the retention of chronic schizophrenic patients in the community. The authors studied two groups of patients—all of whom had been ill for more than two years. One group had been kept at home, the other comprised patients still in hospital. The clinical features of the patients kept at home consisted of catatonic, hebephrenic, and paranoid manifestations.

It would appear from these follow-up studies that the adjustment of many patients living in the community is poor or marginal. They suffer from symptoms which are very similar to those found in patients who are confined to hospital.[20] The families are often under considerable stress and crises of various kinds arising from time to time causing difficulties with neighbors, police, and other social institutions. One author[129] of considerable experience in this area has pointed out that in the United Kingdom the proportion of schizophrenic patients in the hospital has fallen, while the number who are dependent on the community has increased. A follow-up undertaken by the same author[129] shows that five years after discharge following first admission to a hospital with the diagnosis of schizophrenia, one-half of the patient sample required little attention from psychiatrists or social agencies.

While the vast majority of these outcome studies have paid considerable attention to the diagnostic categories of the patients, varying conceptions of schizophrenia will influence psychiatrists in their assessment of these reports. Controversy will be bound to occur about the diagnosis of those patients who made a good recovery, particularly when reports continue to appear[74] which claim that only 10 per cent of 500 schizophrenic patients did not relapse, five years after discharge from the hospital.

These follow-up studies reflect the great change which has taken place in the treatment and management of schizophrenic psychoses. Periods of hospitalization are now much shorter. Conditions existing in the mental hospital are possibly more favorable for spontaneous remission, or remission obtained with the use of drugs[1,60,83] The fact that patients are discharged in a matter of weeks does not mean, as some would perhaps like to believe, that a specific cure has been found for the illness, but rather that a conviction has developed in psychiatric circles that hospitalization is bad for the patient and that his recovery will be expedited by his speedy return to the community. Some of the results obtained in the publications referred to above, show that this conviction is by no means justified.

In spite of the new developments in treatment and management, there are categories of patients whose illness does not remit and where all the phenomena described in the section on symptomatology are to be found. These cases differ only quantitatively from those end states described by Kraepelin many years ago. The low incidence of stereotypies, motor automatisms, and mannerisms which is now reported in mental hospitals, does not indicate that the precursors for such phenomena do not exist. The predisposition is present even in the earliest case, and this is betrayed by the postural persistence, perseverations, and ambitendency. There is little support for the belief that a schizophrenic illness, like an infection, eventually "burns" itself out. Psychotherapeutic work with long stay patients has demonstrated, unequivocally, that patients whose withdrawal and volitional lack suggest a destruction of affect and abandonment of delusions, are quite capable of exhibiting the very phenomena which characterized the illness at its outset.

Today, there is a clearer realization that at the beginning of the illness patients do not demonstrate clear cut patterns of symptomatology which enable them to be placed in one or other of the schizophrenic subtypes. This is one source of difficulty in diagnosis. It is particularly applicable to patients whose illness begins in late adolescence or early adult life, where in addition to the withdrawal, there are severe cognitive upsets, emotional lability, and motor signs. It is only after a period of months, failing remission, that the patient's state can be characterized as predominantly hebephrenic or catatonic. Most often combinations of phenomena occur. Thus it is difficult to assert that a patient who predominantly demonstrates catatonic signs will never manifest the deterioration of cognition, affective lability, and incongruity which is supposed to characterize hebephrenia. Here again, the psychiatrist's concept of hebephrenia or catatonia is the decisive factor in the classification. Once more it has been the psychotherapeutic work with patients which has demonstrated the variability of the symptomatology, particularly in the hebephrenic-catatonic group.

An outstanding feature of the illness in its early stages is the periodic return of judgment and insight. The patient, for brief periods of time, recognizes that much of his thinking and experiencing is irrational. For those inexperienced in clinical psychiatry it seems as if the patient is on the way to a speedy remission of the illness. However, a few hours later this insight is completely lost. As the illness continues these phases of awareness of illness become less frequent, until the time comes when the patient seems to have lost all insight into the fact that he is ill. However, even the most deteriorated patient will sometimes surprise an examiner by expressing, in quite striking terms, recognition of the extent of his mental disturbance.

The patient's occasional recognition of his mental disorder whether at the outset or late in the illness, reflects the presence of what has been variously described as "nonpsychotic layer" (Katan), the "nonpsychotic part" (Bion) and the "nonpsychotic residues" (Davie and Freeman). This an aspect of the phenomenology of the schizophrenias which has received little attention. It is described, now, because it bears an important relationship to the course of the illness. The nonpsychotic residues[32] refer to those mental processes which have escaped involvement by the psychosis.

Psychotherapeutic work, and reports of the interactions which occur between patients and nurses, have provided excellent illustrations of the activity of these healthy mental processes occurring in schizophrenic patients. Normal speech, thinking, perceiving in a cognitively disorganised patient occur only to disappear again. This development usually arises under two circumstances: 1) when a patient has made a tenuous attachment to a psychiatrist or nurse, and 2) when a patient becomes overtly angry. It is doubtful whether the mechanisms leading to the normal functioning are identical in both these instances. In the former there seems to be the reemergence of thinking and speech which is at the patient's command. The latter is reminiscent of the aphasic patient to whom word patterns become accessible again under the impact of emotion.

The expression of the nonpsychotic part[10] in a need for contact with another person is often difficult to detect—the more so in established cases. It is expressed in subtle and oblique ways and the slightest reference to it may lead to its disappearance. The presence of these nonpsychotic processes—in object relations, in cognition and in affect—indicate that the illness does not involve the entirety of the patient's mental life. This has led one authority[12] to state that, "a healthy life goes on in a concealed form in the schizophrenic." The presence of this "healthy life" has important consequences for the course of the illness, as some of the studies on outcome suggest.[87,94] The results of these investigations favor the view that the ability of patients to continue successfully in the community is dependent on the stimulation and support of the nonpsychotic part of the patient.

The course which the illness is to follow will be decided by the extent to which the "healthy life" existing in the patient can be widened and strengthened. When this happens, the psychotic phenomena diminish in number and intensity. The ability to enter into relationships improves and insight develops. As the nonpsychotic part fluctuates in power and influence, symptoms wax and wane. The range of these fluctuations is partly dependent on the patient's encounters with other individuals in his immediate environment. When these contacts stimulate unfavorable responses in the patient, the "healthy life" recedes and psychotic phenomena are intensified, or if absent, return. While the influence of contact with others does not provide a complete explanation for the appearance or disappearace of symptoms, it must be regarded as of considerable significance. Awareness of its importance may help a psychiatrist to avoid measures which aggravate, rather than ameliorate, the patient's condition.

Today the course of the illness cannot be considered apart from its treatment and management. The nature of the therapy and the hospitalization radically influence the manner of expression of the clinical phenomena.[12,73,123] Unfortunately the illness need not follow a favorable course and the symptoms may not remit—withdrawal, affect disorder, psychomotor symptoms and delusions remaining prominent. However, the therapeutic community approach, group therapy, drug treatment, and modern hospital practice, with its emphasis on encouragement of the nonpsychotic part, holds in check the development of the dramatic and distressing manifestations, which were described in the earlier literature as characteristics of the long stay schizophrenic patient.

SUMMARY

For many years the conception of schizophrenic psychoses was based on the model of somatic disease established towards the end of the nineteenth century. A specific etiology, pathology, and symptomatology were presumed as in physical illness. This predisposed to the idea that the signs and symptoms of the schizophrenias were not only comparable but identical in nature to the phenomena of somatic disease. The gradual abandonment of this view is due to a number of causes. It can partly be attributed to the employment of psychoanalytical psychotherapy in these conditions. Although these methods have not proved to be the effective treatment, their application has led to a better understanding of the nature of the symptomatology and the course of the illness.

The patient who suffers from a schizophrenic psychosis presents manifestations which are not fixed and constant after the manner of some physical diseases. The patient does not exhibit the symptomatology directly, consistently, or uniformly. This is due to the fact that the clinical data consists almost exclusively of the patient's subjective experiences. The phenomena are present one day and not the next. They are revealed to one examiner and not to another. This variability also occurs between one patient and another, and here again is a striking difference from physical disease, where interpatient variability is low in incidence. A complete account of a patient's symptomatology, therefore, demands that he be observed over an extended period of time.

The changing nature of the symptomatology, and the extent to which this is brought about by environmental circumstances and psychotherapy does not carry implications for etiology beyond underlying the sensitivity of the schizophrenic patient to his physical and psychological milieu. It indicates, however, that it is difficult, if not impossible, to draw hard and fast distinctions between one subtype of the illness and another. Hence no attempt was made in this chapter to group the clinical phenomena into hebephrenic or catatonic types or to draw up criteria for these syndromes. This would have been neither more nor less arbitrary than those already described in the earlier literature. The diagnosis itself, must, as has been emphasized above, depend almost entirely on the psychiatrist's conception of schizophrenia.[36,12] This has proved an obstacle to research into causation and treatment. It has also obstructed the free flow of meaningful communication between clinicians about these illnesses.

BIBLIOGRAPHY

1. Abrams, S., Hart, I. and Licht, L.: The Effects of Increasing Duration of Chronicity and Hospitalisation on Schizophrenics. Dis. Nerv. Sys. 26: 229-233, 1965.

2. Achte, K. A.: The Course of Schizophrenic and Schizophreniform Psychoses. Acta. Psychiat. et Neurol. Scand. Supp. 36, 1961.

3. Alanen, Y. O., Rekola, J. K., Stewen, A., Takala, K., and Tuovinen, M.: On Factors Influencing the onset of Schizophrenia in the Light of a Family Study. Proc. 6th Int. Cong. Psychotherapy. 3: 1-8. Basel, Karger, 1965.

4. Allison, R. S.: The Senile Brain, London, Arnold, 1962.

5. Akapova, I. L.: Typology of Oneiric Catatonia. Zh. Nevropat. Psikhiat. Korsakov 65: 1710-1716, 1965.

6. Batchelor, I. R. C.: The Diagnosis of Schizophrenia. Proc. Roy. Soc. Med. 57: 417-420, 1964.

7. Bell, D. S.: Comparison of Amphetamine Psychosis and Schizophrenia. Brit. J. Psychiat. 111: 701-708, 1965.

8. Benjamin, L. A.: Neurodynamic Disorders in Acute Stages of Schizophrenia. Sborn. Nauch. Rabot. Nevropat. Psikiat. Latv. 1: 7-40, 1956.

9. Bion, W. R.: On Hallucination. Int. J. Psychoanal. 39: 341-351, 1958.

10. Bion, W. R.: Differentiation of the Psychotic from the Non-Psychotic Personalities. Int. J. Psychoanal. 38: 266-273, 1957.

11. Blacker, K. H.: Obsessive Compulsive Phenomena and Catatonic States—A Continuum. Psychiatry 29: 185-194, 1966.

12. Bleuler, M.: Conception of Schizophrenia within the Last 50 Years and To-day. Proc. Roy. Soc. Med. 56: 945-953, 1965.

13. Bowen, M.: A Family Concept of Schizophrenia. In Jackson, D. (Ed.) Etiology of Schizophrenia. New York, Basic Books, 1960.

14. Brown, G. W., Carstairs, G. M., and Topping, G. C.: Post Hospital Adjustment of Chronic Mental Patients. Lancet 2: 685-688, 1958.

15. Burnham, D. L.: Autonomy and Activity Passivity in the Psychotherapy of a Schizophrenic Man. In Burton, H. (Ed.)

Psychotherapy of the Psychoses. New York, Basic Books, 1961.

16. Bychowski, G.: From Latent to Manifest Schizophrenia. 2nd Int. Cong. Psychiat. 3: 128-134, 1957.

17. Cameron, J. L.: Patient, Therapist and Administrator. Brit. J. Med. Psychol. 13-22, 1963.

18. Cameron, J. L., Freeman, T., and McGhie, A.: Clinical Observations on Chronic Schizophrenia. Psychiatry 19: 271-281, 1956.

19. Cameron, N.: Introjection, Reprojection and Hallucination in the Interaction between Schizophrenic Patient and Therapist. Int. J. Psychoanal. 42: 86-95, 1961.

20. Catterson, A. G., Bennet, D. H., and Freudenberg, R. K.: A Survey of Long Stay Schizophrenic Patients. Brit. J. Psychiat. 109: 750-758, 1963.

21. Chapman, J.: The Early Diagnosis of Schizophrenia. Brit. J. Psychiat. 112: 225-238, 1966.

22. Chapman, J., Freeman, T., and McGhie, A.: Clinical Research on Schizophrenia. Brit. J. Med. Psychol. 32: 75-85, 1959.

23. Chapman, J., and McGhie, A.: Echopraxia in Schizophrenia. Brit. J. Psychiat. 110: 365-374, 1964.

24. Ciompi, L.: Disturbance of Time Experience in a Female Schizophrenic. Psychiat. et Neurol. 142: 100-121, 1961.

25. Clark, J. A., and Mallet, B. L.: A Follow-up Study of Schizophrenia and Depression in Young Adults. Brit. J. Psychiat. 109: 491-500, 1963.

26. Connell, P. H.: Amphetamine Psychosis. Maudsley Monographs 5, London. Staples Press.

27. Cooper, H. N.: Problems in Application of the Basic Criteria of Schizophrenia. Am. J. Psychiat. 117: 66-72, 1960.

28. Critchley, M.: The Neurology of Psychotic Speech. Brit. J. Psychiat. 110: 353-364, 1964.

29. Critchley, M.: Psychiatric Symptoms and Parietal Disease. Proc. Roy. Soc. Med. 57: 422-430, 1964.

30. Davie, J. M.: Observations on Some Defensive Aspects of Delusion Formation. Brit. J. Med. Psychol. 34: 117-126, 1963.

31. Davie, J. M., and Freeman, T.: Disturbance of Perception and Consciousness in Schizophrenic States. Brit. J. Med. Psychol. 34: 33-42, 1961.

32. Davie, J. M., and Freeman, T.: The Non-Psychotic Residues in Schizophrenia. Brit. J. Med. Psychol. 34: 117-128, 1961.

33. Eissler, K.: Notes upon the Emotionality of a Schizophrenic Patient and its Relation to Problems of Technique. The Psychoanal. Study of the Child 8: 199-251, London, Imago, 1953.

34. Ellenberger, H.: A Clinical Introduction to Psychiatric Phenomenology and Existential Analysis. In May, R., Angel, E., and Ellenberger, H. (Eds.) Existence, New York, Basic Books, 1958.

35. Erentheil, O. F., and Jenney, P. B.: Does Time Stand Still for Some Psychotics? Arch. Gen. Psychiat. 3: 1-3, 1960.

36. Ey, H.: Unity and Diversity of Schizophrenia. Amer. J. Psychiat. 115: 706-717, 1969.

37. Faergeman, P.: Psychogenic Psychoses, London, Butterworth, 1963.

38. Fish, F. J.: The Classification of Schizophrenia. J. Ment. Sc. 103: 443-465, 1957.

39. Fish, F. J.: A Clinical Investigation of Chronic Schizophrenia. J. Ment. Sci. 104: 34-54, 1958.

40. Fish, F. J.: Leonhard's Classification of Schizophrenia. J. Ment. Sci. 104: 943-971, 1958.

41. Fish, F. J.: Senile Schizophrenia. J. Ment. Sci. 106: 444-458, 1960.

42. Fish, F. J.: The Concept of Schizophrenia. Brit. J. Med. Psychol. 39: 269-274, 1966.

43. Freeman, T.: The Concept of Narcissism in Schizophrenic States. Int. J. Psychoanal. 44: 273-303, 1963.

44. Freeman, T., McGhie, A., and Cameron, J. L.: The State of the Ego in Chronic Schizophrenia. Brit. J. Med. Psychol. 30: 120-132, 1957.

45. Freeman, T., Cameron, J. L., and McGhie, A.: Chronic Schizophrenia. New York, Int. Univ. Press 1958.

46. Freeman, T.: On the Psychopath-

ology of Schizophrenia. J. Ment. Sci. 106: 913-924, 1960.

47. Freeman, T.: A Psycho-Analytic Approach to the Diagnosis of Schizophrenic Reactions. J. Ment. Sc. 108: 286-299, 1962.

48. Freeman, T., Cameron, J. L., and McGhie, A. Studies on Psychosis. New York. Int. Univ. Press. 1966.

49. Freeman, T.: The Psycho-Analytic Observation of Chronic Schizophrenic Reactions. In Richter, D., Tanner, J. M. (Eds.) Aspects of Psychiatric Research, London, Oxford Univ. Press, 1962.

50. Freeman, T.: Clinical and Theoretical Notes on Chronic Schizophrenia. Brit. J. Med. Psychol. 33: 33-44, 1960.

51. Freeman, T., and McGhie, A.: The Relevance of Genetic Psychology for the Psychopathology of Schizophrenia. Brit. J. Med. Psychol. 30: 176-187, 1967.

52. Freeman, T.: The Contribution of Psycho-Analysis to the Problem of Schizophrenia. In Rodger, T. F., Mowbray, R. M., and Roy, J. R. (Eds.) Topics in Psychiatry, London, Cassel, 1958.

53. Freeman, T.: Psycho-Analysis and the Psychotherapy of Psychoses. Anglo-German Medical Review 2: 780-786, 1965.

54. Freeman, T.: Psycho-Analytic Aspects of Communication with Psychotic Patients. J. Soc. Issues 1: 21-30, 1965.

55. Freeman, T., and Gathercole, C. E.: Perseveration—the Clinical Symptoms—in Chronic Schizophrenia and Organic Dementia. Brit. J. Psychiat. 112: 27-32, 1966.

56. Freeman, T.: A Clinical Approach to Research in Schizophrenia. Brit. J. Med. Psychol. 39: 275-280, 1966.

57. Gillis, L. S., and Keet, M.: Factors underlying the Retention in the Community of Chronic Hospitalised Schizophrenics. Brit. J. Psychiat. 111: 1057-1070, 1965.

58. Gillies. H.: Clinical Diagnosis of Early Schizophrenia. In Rodger, T. F., Mowbray, R. M., and Roy, J. (Eds.) Topics in Psychiatry, London, Cassel, 1958.

59. Goldberg, E. M., and Morrison, S. L.: Schizophrenia and Social Class. Brit. J. Psychiat. 109: 785-799, 1963.

60. Greenblatt, M., York, H., and Brown, L.: From Custodial to Therapeutic Patient Care in Mental Hospital. Russel Sage Foundation, New York, 1964.

61. Havens, L. L.: Placement and Movement of Hallucinations in Space—Phenomenology and Theory. Int. J. Psychoanal. 43: 426-435, 1962.

62. Hill, D.: The Schizophrenia-like Psychoses of Epilepsy. Proc. Roy. Soc. Med. 55: 315-316, 1962.

63. Hoch, P., Cattell, J. P., Strahl, M. O.: and Pennes, H. H.: Course and Outcome of Pseudoneurotic Schizophrenia. Am. J. Psychiat. 119: 106-115, 1962.

64. Homboe, G., and Astrup, C.: A Follow-up Study of 225 Patients with Acute Schizophrenia and Schizophreniform Psychoses. Acta. Psychiat. Neur. Scand. 32, Supp. 115.

65. Huber, G.: Some Aspects of the Course of Schizophrenia. Dtch. Med. Wschr. 89: 212-216, 1963.

66. Irle, G.: The Praecox Feeling in the Diagnosis of Schizophrenia. Arch. Psychiat. Nervenkr. 203: 385-406, 1962.

67. Jackson, D.: The Monad, The Dyad and the Family Therapy of Schizophrenics. In Burton, H. (Ed). Psychotherapy of Psychoses. New York, Basic Books, 1961.

68. Jankowski, K., and Maczar, B.: Symptomatic Schizophrenia in the Course of Schilder's Disease. Neurol. Neurochir. Psychiat. Pol. 12: 737-742, 1962.

69. Jankowski, K.: A Case of Schilder's Diffuse Sclerosis diagnosed Clinically Schizophrenia. Arch. Neuropath. 2: 302-305, 1963.

70. Jones, M.: Social Psychiatry, Springfield, Thomas, 1962.

71. Kaczynski, M.: Symptomatology of Early Schizophrenia. Neurol. Neurochir, Psychiat. Pol, 7: 505-511, 1957.

72. Katan, M.: Dreams and Psychosis. Int. J. Psychoanal. 41: 273-303, 1963.

73. Kayser, H.: A Therapeutic Community with Chronic Schizophrenics. Proc. 6th Int. Cong. Psychoth., Basel, Karger, 1965.

74. Kerbikov, O. V.: Schizophrenia as a Nosological Problem. In Symposium—

Schizophrenia—Voprozy Nozologii, Patogeneza, Klinikii, 1 Anatomii. 5-18, 1962.

75. Kleist, K.: Schizophrenic Symptoms and Cerebral Pathology. J. Ment. Sc. 106: 246-253, 1960.

76. Kleist, K., Faust, E., and Schurman, C.: Further Clinical and Catamnestic Studies in Schizophrenia. Arch. Psychiat. Nervenkr. 200: 541-566, 1960.

77. Klonoff, H., Hutton, G. A., Gundry, G. A., and Coulter, T. T.: A Longitudinal Study of Schizophrenia. Amer. J. Psychiat. 117: 348-352, 1960.

78. Kreitman, N.: The Reliability of Psychiatric Diagnosis. J. Ment. Sc. 107: 876-886, 1961.

79. Kreitman, M., Sainsbury, P., Morrissey, J., Towers, J., and Scrivener, J.: The Reliability of Psychiatric Assessment. J. Ment. Sc. 107: 887-908, 1961.

80. Langfeldt, G.: Diagnosis and Prognosis of Schizophrenia. Proc. Roy. Soc. Med. 53: 1047-1055, 1960.

81. Laing, R. D.: The Divided Self, London, Tavistock, 1960.

82. Laskowska, K., Urbániak, K., and Jus, A.: The Relationship between Catatonic Delirious States and Schizophrenia in the Light of a Follow-up Study. (Stauder's Lethal Catatonia). Brit. J. Psychiat. 111: 254-562, 1965.

83. Lehrman, N. S.: Do our Hospitals Help Make Acute Schizophrenia Chronic? Dis. Nerv. Sys. 22: 439-443, 1961.

84. Lempf, R.: Catatonic Symptoms in Encephalitis. Arch. Psychiat. Nervenkr. 195: 193-198, 1956.

85. Leonhard, K.: Discussion of M. Bleuler's "Conception of Schizophrenia within the Last 50 years and To-day". Int. J. Psychiat. 1: 516-517, 1965.

86. Leonhard, K.: Cycloid Psychoses—Endogenous Psychoses which are neither Schizophrenic nor Manic Depressive. J. Ment. Sc. 107: 633-647, 1961.

87. Leyberg, J. T.: A Follow-up Study on Some Schizophrenic Patients. Brit. J. Psychiat. 111: 617-625, 1965.

88. Lidz, T., and Fleck, S.: Schizophrenia, Human Integration and the Role of the Family. In Jackson, D. (Ed.) Aetiology of Schizophrenia. New York,

Basic Books, 1960.

89. Mandelbrote, B., and Folkard, S.: Some Factors Related to Outcome and Social Adjustment in Schizophrenia. Acta. Psychiat. Scand. 37: 223-230, 1961.

90. Mirek, R.: Psychomotor Epilepsy and the Problem of Schizophrenia. Psychiat. Neurol. Med. Psychol. 14: 151-168, 1962.

91. McGhie, A., and Chapman, J.: Disorders of Attention and Perception in Early Schizophrenia. Brit. J. Med. Psychol. 34: 103-116, 1961.

92. Modell, A. A.: The Theoretical Implications of Hallucinatory Experiences in Schizophrenia. J. Amer. Psychoanal. Ass. 6: 442-458, 1958.

93. Nadsharow, R. A.: The Nuclear Group of Schizophrenia and the Problem of Reversibility. Psychiat. Neurol. Med. Psychol. 16: 262-264, 1964.

94. Orlinsky, N., and D'Elia, E.: Rehabilitation of the Schizophrenic Patient. Arch. Gen. Psychiat. 10: 147-154, 1964.

95. Parfitt, D. N.: The Neurology of Schizophrenia. J. Ment. Sc. 102: 671-695, 1956.

96. Pond, D.: The Schizophrenia like Psychoses of Epilepsy. Proc. Roy. Soc. Med. 55: 316-317, 1962.

97. Reardon, J. D.: Oneirophrenia—Entity or Enigma. Dis. Nerv. Syst. 25: 157-161, 1964.

98. Renton, A., Affleck, J. W., Carstairs, G. M., and Forrest, A. D.: A Follow-up of Schizophrenic Patients in Edinburgh. Acta. Psychiat. Scand. 39: 548-560, 1963.

99. Report on the W.H.O. Study Group on Schizophrenia. Amer. J. Psychiat. 115: 865-872, 1959.

100. Rosen, I.: The Clinical Significance of Obsessions in Schizophrenia. J. Ment. Sc. 103: 773-785, 1957.

101. Rosenfeld, H.: Psychotic States. London. Hogarth Press, 1965.

102. Rotshtein, G. A.: Diagnostic Criteria of Schizophrenia. In Symposium Schizofreniya—Voprozy, Nozologii, Patogeneza, Kliniki 1, Anatomii 49-55, 1962.

103. Rumke, H. C.: Clinical Distinctions within the Group of Schizophrenias.

Ned. T. Geneesk. 102: 1361-1366, 1950.

104. Rumke, H. C.: Contradictions in the Concepts of Schizophrenia. Comprehens. Psychiat. 1: 331-342, 1960.

105. Rumke, H. C., and Nijam, S. J.: Aphasia and Delusion. Folia Psychiat. Neurol. Neurochir Neel. 61: 623-629, 1958.

106. Rycroft, C.: An Observation on the Defensive Function of Schizophrenic Thinking. Int. J. Psychoanal. 43: 32-45, 1962.

107. Salzman, L.: Paranoid State—Theory and Therapy. Arch. Gen. Psychiat. 2: 679-693, 1960.

108. Schmidt, H. O., and Fonda, C. A.: The Reliability of Psychiatric Diagnoses. J. Ab. Soc. Psychol. 32: 262-273, 1956.

109. Schneider, K.: Clinical Psychopathology. New York, Grune & Stratton, 1959.

110. Searles, H. F: Integration and Differentiation in Schizophrenia. Brit. J. Med. Psychol. 32: 261-275, 1959.

111. Searles, H. F.: Anxiety concerning Change as seen in the Psychotherapy of Schizophrenic Patients. Int. J. Psychoanal. 42: 74-88, 1961.

112. Searles, H. F.: Transference Psychosis in the Psychotherapy of Schizophrenic Patients. Int. J. Psychoanal. 44: 249-265, 1963.

113. Searles, H. F.: Phases of Patient-Therapist Interaction in the Psychotherapy of Schizophrenia. Brit. J. Med. Psychol. 34: 169-191, 1961.

114. Shostakovich, V. V.: Nosological Entity of Schizophrenia. In Symposium Schizofrenja-Voprozy, Nozologii, Patogeneza Kliniki, 1, Anatomii 92-105, 1962.

115. Singer, L.: Some Pictures of Early Schizophrenia. Strasbourg Med., 8: 748-751, 1957.

116. Slater, E., and Beard, A. W.: The Schizophrenic like Psychoses of Epilepsy. Brit. J. Psychiat. 109: 95-127, 1963.

117. Spoerri, T.: Diagnosis of Schizophrenia and Praecox Feeling. Conf. Psychiat. 6: 53-63, 1963.

118. Stefanowskii, V. A.: Neurological Signs in Schizophrenia. Zh. Nevropat. Psikhiat. Korsakov. 64: 1365-1368, 1964.

119. Stengel, E.: A Comparative Study of Psychiatric Classification. Proc. Roy. Soc. Med. 53: 123-130, 1960.

120. Stierlin, H.: Individual Therapy of Schizophrenic Patients and Hospital Structure. In Burton, H. (Ed.) Psychotherapy of Psychoses. New York, Basic Books 1961.

121. Turner, W. S.: Schizophrenia and Oneirophrenia. Trans. N.Y. Acad. Sci. 26: 361-368, 1964.

122. Vaillant, G. E.: The Natural History of the Remitting Schizophrenias. Amer. J. Psychiat. 120: 367-376, 1963.

123. Vanderpol, M., and Stanton, A. H.: Observations on the effect of Environment on Schizophrenic Behaviour in the Psychiatric Hospital. Psychiatry. 29: 412-421, 1966.

124. Volken, V.: The Observation and Topographic Study of the Changing Ego State of a Schizophrenic Patient. Brit. J. Med. Psychol. 37: 239-256, 1964.

125. Walker, R. W.: Some Observations on the Concept of Reactive and Process type Schizophrenia. J. Clin. Expt. Psychopathol. 5: 432-465, 1962.

126. Waters, M. A., and Northover, J.: Rehabilitated Longstay Schizophrenics in the Community. Brit. J. Psychiat. 111: 258-264, 1965.

127. White, R. P.: Face-Hand Response of Psychotic and Mentally Defective Patients. Arch. Neurol. & Psychiat. 77: 120-128, 1957.

128. Will, O.: Process, Psychotherapy and Schizophrenia. In Burton, H. (Ed.) Psychotherapy of Psychoses. New York, Basic Books, 1961.

129. Wing, J. K.: Five Year Outcome in Early Schizophrenia. Proc. Roy. Soc. Med. 59: 17-24, 1966.

130. Wing, J. K., Monck, E., Brown, G. W., and Carstairs, G. M.: Morbidity in the Community of Schizophrenic Patients Discharged from London Mental Hospitals in 1959. Brit. J. Psychiat. 110: 10-22, 1964.

131. Wynne, L., and Singer, M.: Thought Disorder and Family Relations of Schizophrenics. Arch. Gen. Psychiat. 9: 191-199, 1963.

10

Psychoanalytic, Psychotherapeutic,* and Generally Psychodynamic Studies

LEOPOLD BELLAK, M.D. and LAURENCE LOEB, M.D.

For Dr. Bellak's biography, see Chapter 1.

Dr. Loeb is currently Clinical Assistant Professor of Psychiatry at the Cornell University Medical College, consultant to the Youth Consultation Service in White Plains, N.Y., and psychiatrist to Briarcliff College, Briarcliff Manor, N.Y., where he also teaches in the Department of Psychology.

A graduate of the State University of New York College of Medicine (Downstate) Dr. Loeb received his psychiatric training at the New York Hospital, Westchester Division, following which he was a Clinical Fellow in Adolescent Psychiatry at the Albert Einstein College of Medicine.

Though for the most part in private practice, (with emphasis on treatment of the adolescent) Dr. Loeb has taught at the Albert Einstein College of Medicine and at Cornell University Medical College. He was, for some time, Clinical Director of Education, Training and Research at the Division of Psychiatry of Grasslands Hospital, Valhalla, N.Y. During his military service (Captain, U.S. Army), he headed a Mental Hygiene Consultation Service, and in 1953 was awarded the Kings County Medical Society's Pediatrics Award. A Fellow of the American Psychiatric Association, Dr. Loeb has written on adolescence and on anorexia nervosa.

OVERVIEW

This rather broad group of studies is considered in this single chapter for at least two reasons. First, it was difficult in the previous volumes to separate papers of broad psychodynamic interest, including those considering psychodynamic etiology or pathogenesis, from papers concerned with psychotherapy because, frequently, the same paper would deal with both aspects. At the same time, it was often difficult to decide whether a paper was specifically psychoanalytic or not.

The second reason for the broad range of coverage in this chapter is that relatively fewer papers have been published during the last ten years in this area than was the case in the preceding decade. To be sure, this need not, and almost certainly does not, imply an actual decrease in the importance of psychodynamic or psychotherapeutic consideration. On the contrary, the decreased number of publications are probably reflections of the fact that

---

*For treatment, see also Chapter 2.

much of what was exciting in this field during the war years and in the immediate postwar decade has been generally accepted and widely used. Certainly, some overenthusiasm, existing in all forms of therapy, had to be given up. Therapeutic ventilation under intravenous sodium pentothal or amytal proved less effective than dramatic, as did "direct analysis," psychodrama, and other modalities. On the other hand, a deeper understanding of extension of complex dynamic treatment of schizophrenics has steadily continued. This understanding is widely applied, often without its being realized, and certainly without its being acknowledged, in many fields—those of social legislation, social planning, and even hospital architecture, where, finally, the need for and importance of a human milieu is being considered. Smaller hospitals are being built, and the patient is being kept closer to his family and community, and the daily role of the ward personnel is considered as an integral part of the patient's welfare and treatment.

Group psychotherapy of schizophrenics has attained an increasing importance over the last three decades, as Semrad et al. point out (Chapter 14). It commends itself, of course, for economic reasons. Faced with large numbers of patients in need of psychotherapy, it seems a practical way of providing the skills of one therapist to more than one patient at a time. There are other merits to group therapy, as well as some disadvantages, as will be discussed in Chapter 14.

Several other treatment approaches, apart from individual and group therapy, have moved to the fore. Some utilize psychotherapy within their frameworks, others replace it. Psychotherapy has been aided, in turn, by other therapeutic modalities. The extensive use of psychotropic drugs, for example, has opened new vistas in the psychotherapy of schizophrenics. It enables one to engage in psychotherapy generally, and in private practice or in a general hospital specifically, many patients who, formerly, would have been considered to be too ill to be reached or able only to utilize the most basic psychotherapeutic procedures. In this way, the advent of psychotropic drugs has played a role for psychotherapy similar to that which the anesthetics have played for surgery: it has produced the field within which the symbolic verbal operation can be performed.[8]

Again, sometimes rightly, sometimes wrongly, drug therapy has often replaced psychotherapy for reasons of expedience, economy, or for lack of psychotherapeutic competence.

Similarly, the community mental health movements and various community psychiatric endeavors have been utilized or substituted for psychotherapy. In a research project, Pasamanick[55] suggests, for instance, that home care of schizophrenics is a modality frequently preferable to limited hospitalization in the psychiatric division of a general hospital or the often insufficient care, with accompanying disadvantages of dislocation from the family and community, in the state hospital.

If one surveys the field of psychotherapy itself, looking for one main trend, one is, of course, in grave danger of overgeneralizing and oversimplifying. With this in mind, one is nevertheless tempted to conclude that the predominant theme of the recent literature is a concern with the *"self"* and its distortion in the schizophrenias. This interest cuts across most schools of thought within the field, as seems apparent in Arieti's most recent paper[3] and in Jacobson's important volume on *The Self and the Object World*.[39] Freeman et al.,[26] in their instructive volume on the psychoanalytic understanding of chronic schizophrenia, hold that impairment of the sense of self is primary to the disturbance of all other ego functions.

This point of view is certainly plausible for some schizophrenics, although it is doubtful that it would hold true for all, if the multiple etiology and pathogenesis concept of schizophrenia is accepted. It is as likely that a disturbance of the synthetic function, on organic or other grounds, leads to an impairment of the sense of self as well as the other way around. Searles[69] sees the fear of destruction of the self as the mainspring of schizophrenic pathology, and, in somewhat differing vocabulary, the Kleinian view, as stated by Rosenfeld,[62] is not much different; a fear of destruction, by projective identification, of devouring and other destructive impulses. Laing,[44] as an existentialist, sees the main problem of schizophrenics as being that of the self.

If our generalization is correct, it merits contemplation. One must wonder how much this trend of thought pertaining to psychopathology, plausible and useful as it may be, *sui generis,* is primarily a reflection of the general cultural concern with the self. Ours is, to a large degree, the era of existentialism which has gone beyond its strictly philosophic ground and is reflected in many fields; in literature, Camus as well as Sartre; in sociopolitical areas such as the young "anti-establishment," the self-seeking and self-exploring "hippies"; psychiatric and psychologic schools of existentialism in Europe and in the United States.

If the psychiatric preoccupation with the self is indeed but part of the general cultural concern, this implies no lessened merit. Technologic and economic changes brought about the age of enlightenment, which, in turn, was of benefit for the humane treatment of psychiatric patients. The development of physics corresponded to advances in physiology at the turn of the century: it is hard to consider Freud's general motivational theory of personality without Helmholtz' contributions to the concept of the conservation of energy. Thus, the concern with the self in schizophrenics may be merely an accentuated form of an appropriate concern with the self in those of us who are not schizophrenic. Above all, schizophrenia can be seen as an exaggerated form of general human foibles and problems.

SPECIFIC STUDIES

A book published just prior to this volume's going to press merits special attention, as it revives a trend more characteristic of the previous decade than that under consideration, yet makes some excellent points for its current importance. Boyer and Giovacchini[15] are classically-trained psychoanalysts, who are, by their own statement, iconoclastic, and not organization-bound. They are, in some ways, more than "classically" oriented toward their treatment of schizophrenics, as they insist that these patients may be treated in the ordinary psychoanalytic manner with a minimum of other parameters introduced. Boyer, reporting on his experience with seventeen patients, states that no drugs were employed, the couch was used, and free associations constituted the main vehicle of treatment. Reporting on the basis of twenty years of orthodox analytic work with schizophrenics, he feels that regression is possible, in a controlled manner in a psychotic transference, and is essential for real restructuring. Although he dealt primarily with rather acutely ill patients, he feels that few, if any, patients are inaccessible. In what he calls the "noisy period" of treatment, the patients cannot usually tolerate silence for long, and he makes some sort of noise to let them know he is there. He considers accurate and appropriate timing of interpretations essential, and, in relating his experiences is not only unusually straightforward, but replete with useful clinical observations. His statements about the therapist's feelings about some aspects of some patients (p. 195) is refreshingly realistic:

> "When the schizophrenic with his highly tuned sensitivity to the unconscious of the therapist says that he does not think that the therapist likes him, I think it is most helpful to both participants for the therapist to admit the simple truth that in many ways he does not like his patient any more than any doctor likes some manifestations of disease that he is called upon to face. I usually let the patient know about this negative feeling toward him by asking him (or its equivalent and when it is fitting), 'Am I supposed to like everything about you?' This is a countertransference problem having to do with the analyst's guilt feelings about his own aggressiveness."

Boyer prefaces his contribution to the volume (which also has a very useful paper by Hoedemaker) with a most extensive review of the historical development of the psychoanalytic treatment of schizophrenia. There is much that is not generally known in the review. At the same time, there are some shortcomings, such as too little an account of Federn's historical role and of Jung's work at the Burghölzli in Zurich.

Giovacchini, in his part of the book, states that character disorders are primarily characterized by ego defects which lead to distortion of various aspects of the world. He and Boyer apparently find enough common ground between schizophrenics, borderline states, and at least some character disorders to discuss their shared viewpoint within one volume. This may become more understandable if one keeps in mind Frosch's term "psychotic character",[30] relating to character disorder, as does psychosis to psychoneurosis; in one case the ego-syntonic characteristic of character disorder and psychotic character, in the other, the ego-alien characteristics of (at least some) psychotic and psychoneurotic conditions. Obviously, in psychodynamic terms, we are dealing with continua in both cases, and not with discreet entities.

Sechehaye[71] continued her pioneering "symbolic realization" psychotherapy in an article in which she describes four phases of her technique. In the first one, she speaks of the establishment of contact with a schizophrenic which she considers a pre-object relationship concerned with the recognition of the patient's needs and its polarization on the therapist. The second phase of treatment, she says, is taken up with the symbolic gratification of the needs of the patient and which she considers the crucial part of the cure. The third phase Sechehaye's translator calls graft transference (perhaps better called transference graft), that is, a grafting onto the patient of characteristics of the transference object relationship lived by the schizophrenic in a mode of symbiosis and with magical presymbolic participation. In another language, one might say that the patient learns within the setting of the transference situation. The fourth phase consists of the restoration of narcissism, the structuring of the ego, and the investment of reality. With regard to restoration of narcissism, Sechehaye reports that she was struck from the earliest experiences by the *lack* of narcissism found in schizophrenics, in distinction to Freud's affirmation that schizophrenia was primarily a narcissistic neurosis. In this context, she apparently fails to avail herself of the distinction most clearly made by Hartmann[34] between narcissism as an investment or overinvestment of the *self,* as distinct from an investment or overinvestment of the *ego functions.* In a schizophrenic we believe there is often overinvestment of some ego functions, especially of thinking, to the point where thought becomes concrete and equated with fact and action. In distinction, probably all concerned can agree that the normal libidinal investment of the self, as, for instance, acknowledged as crucial in Anna Freud's metapsychological profile,[28] is deficient in the schizophrenic.

When Sechehaye also speaks of the usefulness of having a nurse and a sociotherapist working with the patient with resulting lateral transferences, it becomes particularly obvious how useful it would be to consider her very valuable technique in a combination of psychoanalytic propositions and learning principles for optimal clarity: namely, to state the psychoanalytic propositions in terms of what a maximally regressed schizophrenic has to learn or relearn in this profound and complex method. Sechehaye's technique deserves more than passing reference, not solely because of its intrinsic value as a form of treatment, which, at least conceptually speaking, would be hard to doubt. It certainly seems to stand in this decade as being at one extreme of the therapeutic continuum, more even than do other treatment techniques for schizophrenics in that it is profoundly and intimately dedicated to the intensive and time consuming understanding of one person, and a meticulous, laborious, loving, carefully thought-out building and rebuilding of a severely defective personality. It stands in opposition to the mass methods of drug control and social manipulation (not to mention complete lack of treatment), which are so infinitely more practical and attainable and are so much more within the need and the spirit of our mass production era. Useles as Sechehaye's individual approach may be as a method for the millions of schizophrenics in the world, it is exceedingly valuable for learning from the few for the many. It may possibly lead, in the long run, to a variation of treatment in the form of mass treatment in groups, carefully preselected for some common denominators in their symbolic needs and carried out systematically through the four stages of treatment.

Bychowski[18] discusses the psychoanalysis of the psychotic core as crucial in the treatment of schizophrenics. He describes the psychotic core as a primitive, archaic ego, functioning on the primitive level, full of primitive narcissism, with grandiose features and non-neutralized aggression. Similarly, the superego is primitive and archaic, provoking classic guilt and destructive self punishment.

As the psychotic core may manifest itself in the transference and as a form of resistance, the analysis of schizophrenics may have to be interrupted at certain times, to resume at a more propitious future occasion.

Rosenfeld[63] continues to be the outstanding authority on the psychoanalysis of schizophrenia within the theory of Melanie Klein. Rather than insisting upon free associations or the use of the couch, he uses the entire behavior of the patient as analytic material, and actively and intensively relies on the transference psychosis. He emphasizes, however, that both a psychotic and a nonpsychotic transference might appear, which seems quite reasonable if one keeps in mind the generally accepted idea of the intact residue in the schizophrenic personality. Nobody is all schizophrenic or all normal, and, therefore, the transference phenomena are likely to involve various features.

In discussing the psychopathology of schizophrenics, Rosenfeld does not hold with the theory of a schizophrenogenic mother. He believes that psychotic parts of the personality may be split off in very earliest infancy, while other parts of the self may develop apparently normally. Under certain circumstances, the split-off psychotic part may break through to the surface, producing the acute psychosis. He assumes that certain predispositions to the psychosis exist from birth; and that in studying the question of disturbed mother-infant relationship in the first year of life, it is important to consider not only the influence of the mother on the child, but the reaction of the mother to a particularly difficult schizoid infant. Rosenfeld also discusses the object relations of the acute schizophrenic patient in the transference situation. He bases this discussion on the experiences of a group of analysts who have each treated a number of schizophrenic patients and who meet every two weeks for a discussion of cases. The technique for treatment has not changed during the last few years: the patient is seen five or six times a week at the analyst's office, at the hospital or at home. The patient does not usually use the couch in the acute stage and communications other than verbal ones are also interpreted. There is a specific attempt to help the transference to develop, and, as it branches out, it becomes clear that the schizophrenic personality is divided into many different parts related to different objects, having quite different functions and meanings. He concentrates on the most difficult transference of the patient on the basis of the projective identification, as is customary in Kleinian conceptualization. Projective identification implies, in his usage, not only the taking over of or identification with an envied role or function, but it also implies a projection of unwanted parts of the self into another object, causing this object to be identified with the projected parts of the self. This leads to a confusion of self in objects; omnipotent projections and omissions combined with projection play an important part; instead of getting rid of something omnipotently, the emphasis is on the patient's omnipotently asserting that certain attitudes, impulses, and states of mind exist in other people. This projection constitutes the main difficulty in analyzing severely ill delusional schizophrenic patients. He therefore suggests that projective identification forms one of the bases of the delusional transference which requires analysis.

Arieti,[2] in discussing the psychotherapy of schizophrenia, begins with a review of theoretical bases of the main methods of the psychotherapy of the schizophrenias, starting with Freud. Federn attempted to treat schizophrenics based on his concepts of ego feeling and attempts to establish ego boundaries; according to the views of Melanie Klein, psychotics must be treated in the same way as neurotics; Rosen's techniques of "direct analysis" and Sechehaye's techniques of "symbolic realization" are also briefly discussed. For Sullivan and Fromm-Reichmann, the therapists served as "ambassadors of reality." Arieti conceives of the treatment of schizophrenia as being divided into three parts. The first is the establishment of patient-therapist relatedness; the second, the acquisition on the part of the patient of insight; and the third, active intervention or involvement in the life of the patient outside of the ordinary therapeutic situation. With regard to the first, Arieti feels that the practise of the establishment of relatedness may be learned by many. His concept of relatedness does not mean only the establishment of rapport, but includes the classic psychoanalytic concepts of transference and countertransference. "A fight against relatedness is an inherent part of the schizophrenic condition. Attempts to establish contact made in the usual way increase the anxiety of the patient and make him disintegrate even more." "In the therapeutic situation relatedness will be reestablished if the therapist is able to elicit an atmosphere of basic trust." As for insight, Arieti feels that interpretations are beneficial: first, as enlightenment; secondly, as experiences; and third, as triggers to different patterns of behavior.

In another paper Arieti[1] describes techniques which apply only to an early stage of treatment—as soon as relationship has been established,—consisting chiefly of "making the patient aware of certain processes that he himself brings about or over which he retains some control. In other words, an attempt is made to make the patient realize that he no longer needs to transform or translate his psychodynamic conflicts into psychotic symptoms in spite of a strong tendency to do so. That is, both the 'world' of reality and the 'world' of psychosis are in certain circumstances still accessible to him."

He reviews ten cases of patients actively psychotic with hallucinations, delusions, and ideas of reference, but who were not hospitalized. In regard to hallucinations, Arieti says, "with the exception of patients who are in a very advanced state of the illness, or with whom no relatedness whatsoever can be reached, it is possible to recognize that the hallucinatory voices occur only in particular situations, that is, *when the patient expects to hear them.*"

Arieti states that the patient puts himself in a "listening attitude," and it may be pointed out to the patient that he does so. He then may be able to be helped to see that he puts himself into this attitude under certain circumstances. At that point "he will no longer see himself as a passive agent, as the victim of a strange phenomenon, or of persecutors, but as someone who still has a great deal to do with what he experiences."

He speaks of four methods of interpreting the formal mechanisms for ideas of reference and delusions. In a way similar to that described of hallucinations the patient puts himself into what Arieti calls the referential attitude, in which he looks for references corroborating a preexisting mood. Interpretation of this mood is often useful. The second method of therapy consists in "making the patient aware of his concretizing attitude." The third method consists in showing him "that in order to sustain his delusional or referential beliefs he must resort to a special form of abnormal cognition." Arieti describes a fourth method as "acquiring awareness of the punctiform insight." This refers to the grain of truth often found behind a delusion or a set of ideas of reference. Recognition of the grain of truth may represent a "consensual validation."

In a recent paper, Arieti[3] offers his new views on the psychodynamics of schizophrenia. He thinks of the patient's life pattern as consisting of four stages, of which only the last one can be considered psychotic. In the first stage, the child finds himself in a family situation in which the family does not offer him security or basic trust. There is intense anxiety, extreme hostility or a combination of the two, or extreme avoidance of these feelings. For a longer period than the average child, he experiences the world in accordance with immature cognitive processes, consistent with the Freudian "primary process." While the normal child is in a state of basic trust, these children are in a state of ominous expectancy, especially in view of a poor appreciation of causality in this early period of life. Nevertheless, he feels that these children do not become openly psychotic, and enter a second stage. The self may be preserved, now, either by a reduction of the intensity and number of object relations, or, affected by object relations of an unstable or undependable nature, with a stormy relationship, and with stormy feelings. Towards the end of childhood, he believes that the psychologic picture seems improved as the family has now learned to live with the patient, who is now less immature. The child does not feel any more that the family constitutes the whole world and is, therefore, able to feel more hopeful about the world and his ability to deal with it. In the majority of these cases there are no further pathologic stages, and the individual increasingly succeeds, more or less, in building up adequate defenses in coping with life, and no manifest psychosis occurs. The third stage, however, develops in some, when these defenses begin to be less effective. This may start around the time of puberty, but there may, of course, be many individual reasons for variations on the onset of further difficulties. Arieti also stresses here the concept-feelings of personal significance, of self identity, of one's role in life, and that the disturbance is primarily in the world of ideas and concepts about himself. The future patient comes to feel that the segment of the world which is important to him finds him unacceptable, and he feels alone. It is at this point that preschizophrenic panic occurs. The past early experiences of the first stage emerge, and with them some characteristics of the primary process. In turn, this primary process further destroys whatever was wholesome about the self image and the self concept. In the fourth stage, the further dissolution of the secondary process seems the best defense. Now the purely psychotic stage begins. Here the inner turmoil is translated into external reality.

In one of her last publications, Fromm-Reichmann[29] discusses the difficulties of intensive therapy with schizophrenics, stemming primarily from two sources—from the dynamics of schizophrenic patients, and from the kinds of transference reactions produced. She sees the schizophrenic's fear of closeness as a response to anxiety about his own hostility.

Also not long before his untimely death, Azima[4] stated his basic hypothesis to be: 1) The problems of orality and oral object relations are the core conflicts of all psychopathologic states where external traumatic events have not interfered with pregenital development. 2) The psychogenic pathogenesis of schizophrenic states can be conceptualized as having as its central point the persistence of memory traces of markedly frustrating experiences, i.e., "bad superego formations" or "bad introjects." 3) The immediate logically comprehensible therapeutic hypothesis would be that a change in the "introject" in these bad-mother memory traces and mothering techniques may lead to a reorganization of psychic structure and function. 4) This change can be brought about through reenactment, in action or in fantasy, of the infantile situations where the originally frustrated needs can be adequately gratified. His methodology is an attempt "to produce a state of attachment similar or symbolically perceivable to good mother-child relationships for the purpose of evoking early modes of oral experiences and of gratifying them." He describes maneuvers for establishing such a relationship, based on encouragement of reexpression in words and action, the patient being seen five to six times weekly and on "anaclitic interpretation." Object-relations therapy proper is an attempt to gratify previously unresolved, pregenital problems by actually giving the patient a baby bottle, mud pies, etc.

In a volume of his collected papers, Searles[69] presents his views, as seen from 1951 to 1964. Some of the papers included are described below. It provides an interesting opportunity to follow the developments of one psychiatrist's thinking about this group of disorders, and, as Searles is so cognizant of the mutual interaction of therapist and patient, as well as of his own professional development. Of particular interest is his description of supervision of treatment of the schizophrenias (Problems of Psychoanalytic Supervision, 1962, pp 584-604).

> "If I had to select any one supervisory problem as the most important, it would be that of how one helps the person under supervision to discover the extent to which his own previously unconscious ambivalence has been contributing to a prolonged stalemate in the relationship between the patient and himself . . . it gradually becomes quite clear to the supervisor that the student analyst's genuine striving to help the patient to grow and progress is matched by an unconscious determination to keep him ill and thereby to avert the loss of a mode of relatedness which is yielding deeply cherished, but deeply denied, infantile gratifications to analyst as well as patient."

Searles speaks of a "preambivalent symbiotic" stage in the psychotic transference-countertransference as crucial in the treatment of both neurotic and psychotic, but particularly with reference to the treatment of the schizophrenic. He parallels the resolution of this stage to developments in supervision, seeing the "extent to which the transference evolution of the course of treatment as a whole is paralleled by an unfolding in the supervisory relationship . . ." The importance of this stage in the transference is tied to his formulation that "I consider it valid to conceive of the patient's *transference to the therapist* as being in the nature, basically, of a relatedness to the therapist as a mother figure from whom the patient has never, as yet, become deeply differentiated." (Transference Psychosis, 1963, pp. 654-716.)

Searles is deeply concerned with the countertransference manifestations as well, and each page of this volume reflects his efforts to understand his own responses and feelings in his work with severely ill people. It is through his openness that one learns increasingly more about Searles' own professional development.

On the other hand, Searles discusses the anxiety concerning change in the psychotherapy of schizophrenics, particularly with reference to the problems of the sense of personal identity. He feels that the concept of therapeutic change is threatening to the schizophrenic because of his unstable sense of identity and ego integrity; a change for the better is even regarded as a threat to the accustomed status quo. In a sense, his belief seems to parallel Marx's sociologic beliefs about the perils of the very poor (Lumpen proletariat). Their hold on life in a primitive, feudal society, especially economically speaking, is considered so poor that they would not only be not the ones to start revolutions, but would rather fight on the side of the established feudal society out of fear of losing what little safety in life they perceive themselves to have, rather than take a chance on change. Searles pursues this thought of the fear of change in an article on the discussion of schizophrenia as an alternate defense against the knowledge of personal death. He states that the schizophrenic in treatment often signals his improvement by the acknowledgement of his eventual personal death as a reality . . . the thought suggesting itself that all change is feared by the schizophrenic as a form of dissolution and death. On the other hand, Searles pursues the idea concerning the development of an identity in another paper, (stressing the aspects of identity which are not touched upon by Edith Jacobson's monograph on *The Self and the Object World*). He speaks of ambivalence concerning identity, the role of the nonhuman environment in identity formation; healthy identity is seen as based in and expressive of internalized mother-infant symbiosis and the mutuality of parent-child dependency (or in the transference, analyst-patient dependency) in identity formation. He also mentions the child's accepting and identifying with the parents' individuality, the relationship between murderousness and identity formation, and the sense of identity as a perceptual organ.

Searles' basic view about the psychogenesis and dynamics of schizophrenia is stated in another article[70] where he describes how the shifting of the family roles makes it impossible for some children to develop a consistent, reliable picture of the world. As an unconscious defense against this process, the child identifies with the parents in a primitive, automatic, indiscriminate fashion. This process takes precedence over any developing capacity that may lie within the child. Searles' conception of the shifting family roles is quite consistent with the double bind theory advanced some years ago by Bateson and Ruesch,[5] explaining how an inconsistent use of language behavior may lead to semantic confusion and schizophrenia. His view is also not inconsistent with the ones of schizophrenic genesis advanced by Lidz and associates in a variety of publications. He concludes with six suggestions concerning psychotherapeutic technique: "1) We cannot ask the patient to relinquish his world readily" to embrace gratefully the view of reality which we offer him. 2) To endeavor to share the patient's *feelings about* the world as he perceives it, rather than to challenge the accuracy of his perceptual world itself. 3) The patient's perceptual experience is dominated by his immediate interpersonal environment far more than he or the therapist realize. 4) The patient's moment-by-moment, changing perception of the therapist, in the course of the therapeutic session, forms a crucial, ongoing theme for both participants to explore together. 5) The perceptions that the therapist comes to have of the patient . . . are of great therapeutic significance. 6) The therapeutic process requires that we alternatively, and in varying doses, look with the patient at *his* world . . . and give him glimpses of *our* view of the world."

In a volume on *Schizophrenia and the Family*, Lidz and his co-workers[47] report their studies on families of schizophrenics. Their theoretical considerations are summarized in Chapter XX, "Family Studies and a Theory of Schizophrenia," originally presented by Lidz and Fleck. They suggest the possibility that schizophrenia may represent a deficiency disease, rather than the result of "distorting or traumatic influences—a deficiency of the nurturance, guidance, and transmission of the basic adaptive techniques that must be provided . . ." They have divided these deficiencies into three groups: "1) Deficiencies of parental nurturance . . . 2) failures of the family as a social institution that directs the integrated development of the child by channeling drives and by providing conflict-free areas . . . the deficiencies in the family structure will be related to the faulty structuring of the patient's personality . . . 3) The defects in transmitting the communicative and other basic instrumental techniques of the culture to the child."

Indicating the importance of the father in the constellation of the child, they nonetheless focus on the role of the mother in the family. They see two arbitrarily grouped kinds of mothers, one group of which "cannot set boundaries, treating the child as an extension of herself." The other type is "unable to invest the mother-child relationship, tending to be apathetic toward the infant, and remaining emotionally withdrawn from the older child."

The first type causes the son's development a great deal of difficulty, preventing autonomous development and the ability to view the mother as an object in the development of sexual identity. The second, distant type, causes more difficulty for the daughter because of difficulty in identification with the female role.

With regard to the failures of the family as a social institution, they "posit that for spouses to form a family conducive to the integrated development of their offspring, they must form a coalition as parents, maintaining the boundaries between generations, and adhere to their respective gender-linked roles . . . None of the families (studied) with schizophrenic offspring met any of these several conditions." The passive, intellectual father and the cold, unyielding mother may well distort the family structure, causing deficient identity formation in the children.

Concerning instrumental techniques, the authors point out that the family forms the foundation of language for the individual, and that the culturally accepted and personal meanings of words derive ultimately from the family. In the failure of what the Sullivanian group would call "consensual validation" of language, distortion in the child may well arise. Thus, "the systematic investigations of the thought processes of parents of schizophrenic patients that are being carried out by our group at Yale and by the National Institute of Mental Health investigators are producing clear evidence that the thought disorder that forms a critical characteristic of schizophrenia does not arise *de novo* in the patient but has clear antecedents in one or both parents, and, further, that the deficiencies in that patient's thinking appear to relate specifically to the styles of communicating and ways of thinking of the parents."

In one of their papers, Lidz et al.[46] discuss details of their studies. Of special interest is a study of schizophrenic siblings in 16 families of schizophrenics, families studied from 6 months to 6 years. *All* families were found to be seriously disturbed. "We do not consider it likely that any single factor such as a faulty mother-infant relationship will prove to be responsible in itself in causing schizophrenia, but we have found that the structure and interaction of these families are highly detrimental to the ego development of children raised in them."

Eighteen of the 29 siblings were found to be disturbed. Those "healthy" siblings were often constricted and isolated. Many factors play a role within a family, i.e., changing family circumstances, mother's incapacity to provide "nutrient care" in infancy, the child's role in family dynamics, the child's role in "skewed" families, and the sibling's gender.

The existential-analytic approach to the problems of the schizophrenias is perhaps best exemplified by the writings of R. D. Laing, of England. Using the phenomonologic methodology of the existentialists (Jaspers, Heidegger, Boss), he believes the classic psychoanalytic terminology of ego, id, and superego to put unnecessary limitations on understanding of case material and patient. His work, *The Divided Self,*[44] is described as an attempt at an "existential-phenomonologic account of some schizoid and schizophrenic persons." "No one *has* schizophrenia, like having a cold. The patient has not 'got' schizophrenia. He is schizophrenic." (Ibid, p. 34). Laing feels that there are marked differences between people living in an existential position of *primary ontological security* and those whose position is that of *primary ontological insecurity*. The first case is that of the individual who "may experience his own being as real, alive, whole; as differentiated from the rest of the world in ordinary circumstances so clearly that his identity and autonomy are never in question; as a continuum in time; as having an inner consistency, substantiality, genuineness and worth, as spatially coextensive with the body; and, usually, as having begun in or around birth and liable to extinction with death." (p. 41)

"If a position of primary ontological security has been reached, the ordinary circumstances of life do not afford a perpetual threat to one's own existence. If such a basis for living has not been reached, the ordinary circumstances of everyday life constitute a continual and deadly threat." (p. 42) Three forms of anxiety are encountered by the ontologically insecure, to which Laing gives the names of *engulfment, implosion,* and *petrification.* By engulfment, he means the threat of the loss of identity and existence by being swallowed up in another, hence "the main maneuver used to preserve identity under pressure from the dread of engulfment is isolation." (p. 44) Implosion is correlated with the feeling of nothingness within a person: there may be a dread that the world will crush in on the person, thus, "reality, as such . . . is the persecutor." The term petrification may have many meanings, including the horror of being turned to stone, the dread of this, the being treated as a thing rather than as a person, and so forth. As a result of these anxieties, the individual tends toward increasing isolation and its opposite, "therefore, the polarity is between complete isolation or complete merging of identity rather than between separatedness and relatedness." (p. 53)

Such people, says Laing, do not have a sense of basic unity, but rather experience themselves as divided into a mind and a body, identifying with the mind fraction. Thus, there is a part, a self, which is an *embodied self,* and another, the *unembodied self.* In this position, "the body is felt more as one object among other objects in the world than as the core of the individual's own being. Instead of being the core of his true self, the body is felt as the core of a *false self* . . . the unembodied self, as onlooker at all the body does, engages in nothing directly . . . the unembodied self becomes hyperconscious. It attempts to posit its own imagos. It develops a relationship with itself and with the body which can become very complex." (p. 69)

For these people, this splitting is not a temporary dissociation, but a basic, profound orientation to life. With others, "there is a quasi-it-it interaction instead of an I-thou relationship." (p. 82) (This sounds very much like Helene Deutsch's concept of the "as-if" relationship.) "If there is anything the schizoid individual is likely to believe in, it is his own destructiveness." (p. 93)

This schizoid position can progress to the schizophrenic: Laing points out that "the divorce of the self from the body is both something which is painful to be borne, and which the sufferer desperately longs for someone to help mend, but it is also utilized as the basic means of defense. This in fact defines the essential dilemma. . . Its orientation is a primitive oral one, concerned with the dilemma of sustaining its aliveness, while being terrified to 'take in' anything. . . The 'inner self' becomes itself split, and loses its own identity and integrity." (p. 161)

Therefore, "The main agent in uniting the patient, in allowing the pieces to come together and cohere, is the physician's love, a love that recognizes the patient's total being, and accepts it, with no strings attached. This, however, is simply the threshold and not the end of the relationship with the doctor." (p. 165)

This book, then, represents a phenomonologic-existential approach to the question of the schizoid personality and the schizophrenic. As with many existential writings, it conveys in an unusually graphic (and useful) manner, the world as experienced by the schizophrenic. This humanistic view avoids excesses sometimes seen in the descriptive, and, at times, the analytic literature on the schizophrenias. At the same time, although the description of this world does present another view, it, too, remains descriptive; another dimension is presented, yet seems not to clarify the enigmas of the schizophrenias at base. The broad, unsystematized generalizations, the lack of clear conceptualization, (if not plain antirationalism) of existentialism makes it unlikely that this will prove to be of more than passing interest.

Betz[12] continued the studies originally started by her and Whitehorn on the relationship of the therapist's personality to the outcome of therapy in schizophrenia. Following up the earliest paper on this topic, Betz and Whitehorn reported in 1956 that although physicians from a certain Group A had better therapeutic results with schizophrenics than those from Group B, the same findings were not borne out with regard to therapeutic efficacy with patients with other diagnoses. In her latest publication, 100 schizophrenic patients were treated by 7 physicians, in Group A, with an improvement rate of 75 per cent; 7 physicians in Group B had only a 27 per cent improvement rate. She found that the Strong Vocational Interest Inventory discriminated well between Groups A and B.

It seems that the Group A doctors scored high in interest for lawyer and C.P.A. and low for mathematics and physical science teacher. Group A seemed more likely to grasp personal meaning and motivation of the patient's behavior and more likely to select personality-oriented rather than psychopathology-oriented goals. Group B was more passively permissive and interpreted behavior to the patient in an instructional sort of style. The A therapists were also more active.

She then made an attempt to predict in advance which therapists would work better with which patients and found that the predictions turned out to be 80 per cent correct for the A group and 67 per cent correct for the B group. She concludes that the results support the idea that determinants of success in the treatment of the schizophrenic patient lie in the physician, and that it may be the "fit" between therapist characteristics and patient characteristics, and not the therapist's personality alone which determines the mode of therapeutic behavior. The same difference between those two groups of physicians again did not predict the efficacy of treatment of other conditions.

Of course, these findings are subject to other interpretation. It might well be that schizophrenic patients as posited by the analytic school of thought need, primarily, at least at first, an object relationship, and it sounds as if the more active, more humanly interested doctors in Group A were better able to provide that than the ones in Group B. Regrettably, such improvement of schizophrenic patients is likely to correspond only to a first phase of treatment (comparable to bed rest and fluids in internal medicine) and not likely to represent stable enough changes or extensive enough changes; Sechehaye's work, as well as earlier work by Eissler, Fromm-Reichmann, Rosen, and others, suggests such nonspecific changes need to be followed by long, drawn out, highly conceptualized interventions in order to be of real value.

Rosen reviewed the entire history of his direct psychoanalysis in a chapter on Research on Schizophrenia.[59] Direct analysis originated in 1943, and he now sees it as having passed through several stages. He thinks of the first stage of study (1943-1953) as almost exclusively concerned with techniques of treatment, with the goal of complete recovery from psychosis, by attacking with direct psychoanalytical understanding, traumatic events of infancy and childhood. At that time he would sometimes even spend 24 hours a day continuously with one and the same patient—for instance, with a catatonic woman—trying to get her to make some sound or sign of acknowledgment. In 1952 he published many of his ideas in his first volume on Direct Analysis. In the second stage (1953-1956), he developed an interest in the theoretic basis of his procedure, and in the third stage (1956-1961) he worked especially in Philadelphia, at the Institute for Direct Analysis, Temple University. With the help of extensive funds, his method was studied by a variety of teams for various research purposes. This effort was followed by the current and fourth stage; trying to further explore the theoretical underpinnings of direct psychoanalysis, with heavy emphasis on the early maternal environment, both with regard to superego and the striving of the patient who also has a tendency to "seek the mother you knew." In discussing Rosen's paper, Scheflen, who played a prominent role in the research on Rosen's work at Temple University[68] suggests that to the best of his understanding, Rosen's success with patients is predicated on forcefully reestablishing a one-to-one relationship with a patient who has come to grief precisely in some previous one-to-one relationship. He feels that all the work at Temple did not give a sufficiently good idea of whether Rosen's treatment is effective or not, and in what ways.

Despite Rosen's intentions to contribute more to the theory of his approach, the outstanding contribution of his volume on Direct Psychoanalytic Psychiatry[60] lies in the practical clinical parts which describe his kind of treatment approach, and in the cataloging of various psychotic manifestations and his understanding and treatment of them. This part of the volume is very well organized and, as far as it goes, very useful for the immediate direct cathartic interpretations of psychotic manifestations, which is Rosen's real contribution. Though of necessity overgeneralized, it is a specific and detailed prescription for direct intervention into the psychotic symptomatology, at least for the purpose of establishing communication and preparing a base for other therapeutic work.

Honig[37] reported on the use of Rosen's direct analytic approach to the treatment of schizophenia. He says the aim of therapy is to reproduce anxiety and feels that the direct analytic approach to the interpretation after symptomatology is a very useful procedure.

Horwitz et al.[38] report a 10 year follow-up of 19 of Rosen's original patients. 12 had been diagnosed schizophrenic, 6 as psychoneurotic, 1 as manic-depressive; he concludes that the group failed to show any outstanding therapeutic response to his particular technique.

English,[24] in his review of Rosen's technique, sees both assets and drawbacks. While the patient receives care, love, and protection, and is being made aware of his illness, English sees primarily a failure to give the patient enough time to assimilate the learned material.

Edith Jacobson[40] stresses the importance of the differentiation of schizophrenic and melancholic states of depression. She stresses it by way of a case discussion of the importance of disturbances of self esteem. The patient's ideas of worthlessness involved her inability to make a living as did her mother. Unlike melancholics, the patient hardly showed any genuine guilt feelings about anything. Between the mother's complete neglect and cruel discipline and the father's overindulgence and seductiveness, she was kept from building up affectionate, stable object relations.

In distinction to her history, melancholics frequently recall an early period of parental overindulgence, followed by disillusionment and abandonment. Unlike depressives, her patient revealed a defectiveness of her superego. Jacobson considers the absence of feelings of moral worthlessness as characteristic of many, but not necessarily all, schizophrenic depressed patients. Jacobson also discusses the difference in paranoid features in melancholic and schizophrenic depressives, the schizophrenics being particularly parasitical in their demands of a psychopathic quality. Comparing compulsive traits in depression and in schizophrenia, she states that the schizophrenic's compulsiveness is characterized by cool formality and politeness, stiffness and remoteness, while a warm affectionate relationship usually returns in a depressed patient, despite his compulsive traits, as soon as the depressive period has ended. She defines the difference between the depressive conflicts of the schizophrenic and that of the melancholic from dynamic and structural points of view. The manic depressive may be, at the beginning, irritable and dissatisfied with himself as well as the rest of the world; by this process, his ambivalence increases, his destructive drive impulses tend to be completely absorbed by the superego and are then turned against the self, as a protection against discharge of hostility toward others. On the other hand, in schizophrenics, because of the defective superego this process does not succeed, and their hostility tends to break through (albeit without strong feeling tone): in structural terms the melancholic suffers from a conflict between the superego and the ego, and all the conflict is inter-systemic, reflecting the discrepancy between the inflated ego ideal and the pathologically distorted sinful image of his own self.

In the schizophrenic depressive, only part of the conflict is between the superego and the ego, the other part is *intra*-systemic, that is, within the ego.

The retransformation of the ego ideal into realified images of a ruthless self permits entry of aggressive fantasies into consciousness and sometimes their expression. Jacobson makes allowance for a great many individual variations and much greater complexities than can be stated in attempts at generalization. She discusses the therapeutic implications predicated upon clearly conceptualized diagnostic differences. The schizophrenics commonly show a rapid vacillation from clinging, to remote and hostile, attitudes toward the therapist. They may stop treatment even during a period of depression or look for another therapist, while manic-depressives, even with paranoid features, want to stay with the same therapist.

Jacobson, in her 1965 Freud anniversary lecture on Psychotic Conflict and Reality,[41,] reviews the variable nature of reality testing (and other ego functions) in schizophrenics.

> "There are delusional psychotics who, despite their impaired reality testing in the areas of their psychopathology, may be able, for instance, temporarily to engage in highly intellectual work. Other patients may show such a severe deterioration of their ego functions that they are incapable of working, even though they may not suffer from any overt psychotic symptoms such as delusions or hallucinations."

She emphasizes that neurotics also misuse external objects for defensive purposes; in neurotics however she finds a firmer repressive barrier and better defined boundaries between self and object representations, protecting them from defusion of drives.

She reviews and compares very usefully her own conceptions with those of other classically analytically oriented investigators like Freeman, Cameron, and McGhie, and also with Rosenfeld (as representing the Kleinian School), and Searles.

Of Freeman, Cameron, and McGhie, she says that:

> "they carefully distinguish the 'genuine, employable transferences (which are) similar to the transference neurosis of the neurotic reaction' from the 'so called "psychotic transferences" (which) result from an attachment of the predominant delusional complexes to the clinician.' In their opinion, a patient who regresses to a 'need-satisfying' level of mental functioning 'is incapable of transference, which is dependent upon neutralized object-libidinal cathexes'."

In agreeing with Freeman et al., she clearly indicates that she feels the loose use of the term transference to be misleading; this standpoint is not only in opposition then to all nonclassical Freudian points of view, but also in distinction to Boyer and Giovacchini.

Though she also uses the terms introjective and projective identification to characterize a psychotic's relations to the persons he needs as defensive aids, she doubts that her use of the term involves the same wishes, processes, and impulses which Rosenfeld (and other Kleinians) refers to in his case reports; she feels that the differences in types of introjective and projective identifications depend upon the patient's fixation to early narcissistic stages and upon the depth of narcissistic regression and dedifferentiation of psychic structures. Accepting terms there into her classical frame of reference, which are practically the exclusive property of the Kleinian School in that specific phraseology (we believe), she changes the dynamic implications of their propositions.

Going on to Searles, Jacobson considers him a brilliant observer with broad experience, especially with severe hospitalized cases where the treatment problems are quite different in nature than in the group of ambulatory psychotics she has treated. Although she admires his frank discussion of his own countertransference manifestations, she feels that countertransference problems are a private matter. Searles' description of the interrelationship and interaction between therapist and patient is the opposite of her therapeutic suggestions. She feels that if the therapist permits himself to establish an exaggerated parent-child relationship with the patient, the therapist is likely to regress along with the patient to mutually symbiotic dependency and will find himself in dangerous situations which are of no therapeutic value. Jacobson has found it useful to adapt her emotional attitudes and behavior to the patient's wishes only up to a certain point.

As the therapist has a reality testing function to perform and some technical interventions to observe, her point is well taken. The line between excessive rigidity and anxiety of some therapists of schizophrenics and the excessive fluidity of boundaries between primary and secondary process thinking in some others is a difficult one to hue: "classical" analysis at times belong with the former group and existentialists and some Neo-Freudians sometimes share a fuzziness of conceptual thinking which becomes attractive only if compared with the lack of any depth of conceptualization or feeling in behavioral therapists.

In a recent article on psychotherapy with schizophrenia, Bruch[16] stresses as a prerequisite the possibility of establishing a meaningful interpersonal communication. The main work, she feels, must be done in the postacute phase. She also sees schizophrenia primarily as distortion of the learning process in infancy and the therapy as a corrective learning process.

Ploeger[56] considers typical trigger constellations responsible for the repeated outbreaks of psychotic episodes in patients: when destructive family relationships are relived in contemporary social relationships, the patient responds with the schizophrenic reaction. He discusses case material and suggests that in some patients further schizophrenic episodes can be avoided if they are shown how to avoid social trigger situations.

Dellaert,[22] on the other hand, says that the schizophrenic patient is isolated from affective contact with the real world and tries to maintain power over the real world and by magic means. He too, therefore, stresses the need to establish a positive transference, with the therapist accepted in the autistic

world of the patient without negative reactions; only after that process (an im-
bibing in the symbolic sense of the therapist as the libidinous object with
moments of ecstatic pleasure, according to the author), can ordinary verbal
communication in a more ordinary setting be established.

Benedetti[9] reviews his experience and concept of psychotherapy with
schizophrenics over the years and formulates the following rules:

1) reinforcement of the weak ego
2) caution in analysis of resistance
3) less reductive-genetic interpretations than in therapy of neurosis with
   more of a relating to the patient's present life.

He also finds pharmacotherapy a useful adjunct and feels the success of a
therapy depends more upon the duration of the psychotherapeutic relationship
than the diagnosis. He feels that psychotherapy of adolescents after the first
schizophrenic attack would be especially valuable.

In another article,[10] he discusses similarities and differences between child
therapy and the therapy of regressed schizophrenic adults. Similarities are seen
in the ego weaknesses of both categories; in the partial regression of serious
schizophrenic patients to earlier stages of development and the resultant consequences; in the role which the consideration of the family constellation plays
in therapy; in the predominance of primary pathologic thought processes and
symbolizations over the normal adult's processes of reflection; and in the intensity and modes of expression of the affects.

The differences result from the fact that schizophrenic patients and neurotic
children are different types of patients with regard to disorder, age, life history, potentialities of identification and transference, affective reactions, and
family constellations.

Benedetti, in a volume concerned with general clinical psychotherapy[11] also
discusses psychotherapy of various disorders, including the one of
schizophrenia. He suggests that different patients bring different parts of their
personalities into contact with the therapist; some may find him the only
person they can relate to psychotically, other patients are eager to maintain
a good relationship with the therapist, seen as a good mother, and hesitate
to burden that relationship by unrealistic demands or other psychotic
manifestations.

The latter group seems to desire a reinforcement of the healthy part of the
self by virtue of controlling or denying the psychotic manifestations. He
describes some patients, in fact, who withdraw from treatment when they
become manifestly disturbed and willingly return to it when they have
recovered from it, either spontaneously or with the help of drugs. He suggests
permitting the patients to choose the type of relationships they want, provided
that contact with relatives and others continues so that the patient is offered
some indirect supervision and help while not in therapy, or, with regard to

those aspects of his problems which he does not bring to therapy. He sees the psychotherapist as having, basically, the role of facilitating transmission between the patient and his environment.

De Perrot and Lai[23] report their experiences with a therapeutic group of six schizophrenic patients, which they ran from 3 to 6 years and make some conclusions for therapeutic groups with more than one therapist. The triangular relationship which develops from the presence of two therapists in a group creates affective reactions among the group and each of the therapists and between the therapists themselves, which can be understood as transference and countertransference. From this point of view, each therapist experiences the common life of the group through these reactions of the group members towards the other therapist. It is therefore possible that rivalry may develop which is unfavorable for the therapeutic process. This conflict may be surpassed by integrating it into the analytic process itself.

In the psychotherapy of schizophrenic patients, especially in group therapy, three phases may be distinguished, Maugile and Ferron[51] suggest, from their experiences with a therapeutic group of six schizophrenic patients, the following:

1) First phase, or prepsychotherapeutic phase: (The six patients participate in three sessions during the week.) This is the assertive phase with the aim being to hold the patients back from the destruction of reality.

2) second phase, or psychotherapeutic phase. Patients stop to destroy reality. Their anxiety becomes overt. No more medicament; events in the group sessions are interpreted psychoanalytically.

3) third phase, or postpsychotherapeutic phase. After leaving the hospital, the six continued psychotherapy as outpatients (First, three times a week, later, once).

The results of this form of group therapy were good: the authors intend to further prove it by a similar form of group therapy with seven schizophrenic patients.

Lichtenberg[45] makes the useful point that initial improvement of a schizophrenic may lead to a facing of reality which in turn may trigger a temporary worsening of the patient until worked through again.

Davis[21] describes short-term psychoanalytic therapy with hospitalized schizophrenics. He sides with the resistance as a method of encouraging transference phenomena and thus facilitates a strong narcissistic transference. As he sees schizophrenia as a defense against primitive aggression and rage, he utilizes this transference for dealing with it.

Wyss,[78] in the treatment of a paranoid, hallucinating schizophrenic, stimulated the associations of the patients by exposing them to the Thematic Apperception Test and similar material, especially as the patient was not able to talk about dreams. In the first phase, he also discussed the content of the psychosis and the life history but found that the first phase was unsuccessful;

the patient became even more paranoid. In the second phase, the magic world of the patient was accepted by the therapist; experiences were explained to the patient on a magic-realistic level and on a psychologic level, and in that way the symptoms disappeared.

Feldmann[25] was also specifically interested in the magic and mythical delusional ideas of schizophrenics. He assumes that the choice of delusional content has some structural correspondence to the experience of the patient: this means that delusions are the way in which the patient overcomes aspects of his experience which he cannot understand, and that these delusions are the adequate inner model of the cognitive world.

Beyme[13] analyzes a schizophrenic psychosis during pregnancy. He believes that he can perceive the main phases of development of society described by Bachofen, namely, matriarchy without marriage, matriarchy with marriage, and patriarchy with marriage in the case history of a schizophrenic woman who was a patient in the University Clinic at Basel for twenty-two years. He believes that in the schizophrenic process a person traverses these phases in reverse order.

Savage[64] discusses countertransference as an integral part of the treatment of schizophrenics, and perhaps the most important part. He sees schizophrenia as consisting of distorted relationships where the therapist's identification with the patient is intense, primitive, and regressive: he feels it must be so if the analyst is to achieve an understanding of the patient. With his special sensitivity, the schizophrenic patient may act out the unconscious conflicts and impulses of the analyst.

Savage[65] also discusses the diffusion of the transference psychosis in the treatment of schizophrenia. In the hospital treatment of the schizophrenic the transference is diffused onto staff, attendants, and other persons in the hospital.

Knight[43] discusses the concept of autism. He feels that it is a process of shifting of the cognitive development from exteroceptive to interoceptive ego functioning which is a factor in the establishment of oral primacy.

Willner[77] discusses anxiety of an all-pervading nature as the primary symptom of schizophrenia, to which all other symptoms are seen to be secondary or attempts at restitution.

McCarley[48] discusses the similarity of the transference psychosis to the transference neurosis. When it occurs in the treatment of schizophrenics, it must be interpreted the way a transference neurosis is interpreted.

Wexler[74] discusses working through in the therapy of schizophrenia and considers the core of the schizophrenic fear the preservation of identity. Therapy must include education, restriction of destructive impulses, support, affection, and the provision of effective models for thought, feeling, and action.

Modell[53] is especially interested in the nature of the object relationships and suggests that borderline patients are those characterized by being arrested at the stage of transitional object relationships.

St. John[67] discusses the dynamic importance of regressive symptoms as a defense in schizophrenia.

Gittleson and Butterworth[31] observed 57 female schizophrenics (of which 41 were paranoids) and a control group of endogenous depressions for three months with regard to the subjective ideas concerning sexual change. They found that schizophrenics were more likely to exhibit hallucinations concerning the genital, to express delusions of change of size or shape of genitals, and to express delusions of changing sex.

Cameron[20] discussed the process of introjection, reprojection, and hallucination in the interaction between schizophrenic patient and therapist as handled in a detailed case report.

Bloch[14] feels that infanticidal desires in parents often play a decided role in the genesis of schizophrenia. The child may respond to the parents' hatred by creating the illusion of being loved, but he makes the parents hate him. Such a person is likely to devote his life to establishing his own worthlessness. The parents' murderous feelings evoke similar ones in him which he must conceal at all cost.

Richardson and Moore[57] studied manifest dreams of schizophrenics and control patients, letting them be evaluated blind by several analysts. The raters were 55 per cent accurate in designating correctly dreams of nonschizophrenics. This figure, while not very high, was significantly better than chance. The expectation that schizophrenic dreams would contain more unrepressed sexual and aggressive content than the nonschizophrenic dream was not borne out.

McGhie[49] was particularly interested in the distractability of schizophrenics, finding that they are unable to successfully screen data irrelevant to the task in hand. However, he also finds that this does not hold true for all patients labeled schizophrenic. He feels that this is sufficient to consider it unlikely that there is a single causal factor to explain all the symptoms in that which we call schizophrenia, though the acute-chronic dichotomy *might* explain the differences. He holds that the schizophrenic deficiency in selective attention and short-term storage might well be restated in the language of ego psychology.

Trunell and Semrad[73] discuss the nature of the schizophrenic anxiety in the light of Anna Freud's concept of object anxiety. Psychosis, according to them, serves to manage the otherwise overwhelming object anxiety and to secure actual restitution with objects. They present clinical material to show the schizophrenic's family participates with him in his psychotic behavior.

Mead and Rollins[52] attempted a "brainwashing" technique on chronic schizophrenics by exposing them to prolonged periods of isolation with constant verbal stimulation in rooms 6' x 10'. The light was cut off from the outside and loudspeakers placed in rooms with two-hour tape recordings set up with constant barrage of admonitions, five days a week, for two weeks. There were four patients and four controls. They found no conclusive results in regard to the symptomatology.

Wiekramasekera[75] used a learning theory derived technique in the treatment of a case of paranoid schizophrenia who had been unsuccessfully treated with E.C.T., chemotherapy, and analytic psychotherapy and had five psychotic breaks within four years. The therapy used over a six-week period (80 minutes daily) consisted largely of desensitization, acquisition of more adaptive responses, counter conditioning, externalization, clarification, labeling, and discrimination of feelings. The author describes in detail the course of treatment. Sixteen months after discharge, the patient, while receiving no treatment, had shown no reactivation of symptoms or symptom substitution.

Will[76] suggests a schizophrenic be regarded as someone who has learned to be the kind of person he is. The human can be considered as born with an orientation toward the fulfillment of his capacities. He sees the infancy of the future schizophrenic as determined by the relationship of intense closeness to the mother and his fear of being engulfed.

Hoedemaker[36] reported on the intensive psychotherapy of schizophrenia; a successful empathic contact was explained to the patient in detail, as well as some of the content of the psychopathology. He also suggests[35] the formation of a superego-like structure by introjection as aiding the countercathexes against the pleasure ego, prior to introduction of more classical analysis.

> "She introjected my attitude, and it became part of her own character structure, appearing to be a partial identification with me. This element, introjected and apparently subsequently incorporated, has served as a modifying influence on the pleasure ego, producing a self-regarding function which allows for delay between impact of perception and response, and for judgment to take place when she is threatened from within by explosive expression of instinctual drives . . ."

A single case report made by Cameron and Esterson,[19] based on Rosen's direct analysis and Abraham's genetic theory, relates the therapist's attempt to shift the patient from an oral to an anal to a genital phase. The comment is made that, "the authors feel that preverbal factors in the relationship influenced the course of the illness."

Johnsen[42] sees schizophrenia as a state of being "which is a consequence not of positive ideologic elements, but rather of the absence of those factors which ordinarily result in normal, rational thinking and behavior." He approaches the treatment of the schizophrenic utilizing learning theory.

A predominantly nonverbal therapeutic approach to the schizophrenic patient on an ego-psychological basis is described as the *body ego technique* by Goertzel et al.[32] Previously, also described in a paper by May et al., this approach focuses attention on body posture and movement as they relate to body image. It focuses on body ego boundaries, involves the patient's sense of time in relation to different speeds of movement and emphasizes reality contact. The approach is primarily concerned with the process of recathexis of ego functions. In a typical group, the patients are drawn into a circle barefoot and sit on the floor. The therapist demonstrates rhythms, which they are asked to follow by beating the floor in front of them, to the left, right, and back, with the therapist directing attention to these dimensions of space and to the variation in rhythms. At the simple levels, most patients are willing to participate. Later, clapping, stamping, different forms of breathing, and other exercises such as crawling, walking, running are introduced, and body awareness is stressed by having the patients touch and move different parts of the body separately, in different directions and at different speeds. The patients are also taught movements that accompany the motions of childhood, throwing, kicking, etc. There is a deliberate educational focus and in some ways, this approach is reminiscent of Sechehaye's. The patients are guided to relearn the parts of the body and their capabilities, and relationships to space and other people, to make a distinction between themselves and others. The method sounds like a well conceptualized one, which should hold a great deal of promise for working with whole groups of severely disturbed patients. Preliminary data suggest that the patients in *body ego technique* seemed to show improvement, when compared to a control group.

One publication which is also concerned with ego boundaries is the excellent study of chronic schizophrenia by Freeman, Cameron, and McGhie.[27] They found that, regardless of the presumed nature of the disorder, a disturbance of the development and maintenance of adequate ego boundaries is the essential feature of the schizophrenic process. With the disruption of the ego boundaries the schizophrenic patient experiences uncertainty with regard to his own existence. He loses a sense of reality, of himself as separate from the rest of the world, and all hierarchical sense of order and place breaks down. Because of this lack of differentiation, the patient easily incorporates extrinsic stimuli from the environment into a stream of thought. This process will often account for the apparent bizarreness and lack of purpose in the speech content. Similarly, the phenomenon of hallucinations can be understood primarily in relation to the breakdown of the outer and inner ego boundaries.

The case work treatment of schizophrenia is considered by Marcus,[50] especially in terms of the breakdown of ego functions in schizophrenia. She carefully conceptualizes her approach in terms of the ego functions impaired, suggests utilizing the ones still intact. She reviews the current literature as part of her discussion: combining the theoretic framework of Federn and other classical psychoanalysts as well as the orientation of Sullivan and Fromm-Reichmann with regard to the approach to the patient.

The need to treat schizophrenic patients in a highly individualized way, depending on their ego function disturbance, is stressed by Bellak.[6] He enumerates the ego functions, their disturbance, and some of the therapeutic measures useful in each instance. For instance, disturbances in adaptation to reality need reality testing, analysis of the apperceptive distortions. Disturbance in the sense of the self can sometimes be allayed by teaching a breathing technique if the feelings of depersonalization are particularly brought about by overbreathing, and secondary changes in the acid-base balance of the blood: the resulting changes in muscle tone, especially of the nuchal muscles, can be one of many pathways toward depersonalization.[7] He also recommends muscle reeducation of a particular kind, helping to develop awareness of proprioceptive stimuli and automatization of muscular functioning, especially in patients with an excessive impulsive charge. In instances of disturbances primarily in the regulation and control of drives he discusses the technique utilized in the Altro Workshop for acquiring frustration tolerance, as well as closeness to others.[5a] (See Chapter 18) Strictly psychotherapeutically, he suggests teaching the patient the recognition of the internal signals of anger and anxiety in order to respond to them appropriately, rather than defensively. He insists that it is necessary to formulate a precise statement of the individual problems of each patient to be matched by a precise prescription on how to meet these problems. In his opinion, a general understanding and establishment of rapport with the patient is comparable only to bedrest, fluids, and other general supportive measures of general medicine. Specific measures predicated on precise understanding are in his opinion the sine qua non of all rational treatment and vague generalizations basically useless.

In another paper,[8] he reviews more of the general theoretic psychoanalytic background of the treatment of the schizophrenic and discusses some particularly widely differing types of schizophrenics: some are best characterized as cases of infantilism because of an extreme lack of ego functioning. In them, very often, the ego functions have never developed, and much of therapy consists of actually teaching frustration tolerance, anxiety tolerance, and the complexities of behavior that stand between drive demand and drive gratification in our culture. In such cases therapy is a long, drawn-out process. If, however, it is a case of a patient who had attained high levels of functioning and suffers from a loss of functions previously acquired, the treatment is usually less difficult. In contrast, some schizophrenics may be people functioning at a high level in most of their personality, say, as professionals, but they have relatively selective but severe paranoid distortions. In such instances, extensive working-through of the early acquired identifications which contaminate the patient's contemporary apperceptions is indicated. For a long time the process of working-through involves conscious reality testing, conscious attempts at maintaining insight when in a situation especially suitable for distortion by past images and introjects until, hopefully, under most ordinary circumstances, reality is perceived "correctly," that is, within the social consensus, rather than in terms of the individual past experience of the patient.

Rosen (Joseph D.)[61] suggests that two therapists approach a patient: one pretends the validity of the patient's delusion, the other denies the delusion and represents reality, confronting the patient with a choice between delusion and reality.

> "When the patient is maneuvered into a position of choice, he has also the opportunity to assert his identity. He thus begins to think of himself as an individual in his own right.
>
> "In the case of two therapists, he shares the opinion of one of them and is permitted to be the deciding factor in the balance of opinions. The conflict between reality and unreality is somehow externalized. The patient is in a better position to differentiate between fantasy and reality while the delusion is confronted, again and again, with the real situation."

An extensive review of the relationship between neurosis and schizophrenia was offered by Parkin.[54] His paper includes a comprehensive historical review, a discussion of modern perspectives, as well as specific clinical considerations. In the latter, he reviews 25 cases of neurosis, of which 21 were searched out from the literature, examines the clinical data concerning the transformation from a manifestly neurotic condition to a manifestly schizophrenic condition, and concludes that we are not dealing with disease entities but with reaction sets.

In the context of psychotherapy, a consideration of the nature of schizophrenia can never be very distant. An illuminating discussion of the confusing aspects of Bleuler's concept of schizophrenia is offered by Stierlin[72] for those who have wrestled with the question, "What was Bleuler's real view of schizophrenia?" He suggests that Bleuler was caught in the center of two psychiatric mainstreams, namely, the one of which Kraepelin was the chief proponent on the one hand, and that of Freud and psychoanalysis on the other hand. Bleuler attempted to synthesize the two viewpoints. While Kraepelin provided his nosologic framework, Freud supplied the main ideas by which Bleuler could build the psychologic theory and understand schizophrenia, seeing a basic similarity between dreams as Freud had discussed them and schizophrenic symptomatology. It appears, however, that after Bleuler's first enthusiastic endorsement and use of Freud's ideas, he found himself increasingly under pressure from the psychiatric "establishment," as exemplified by Gruhle, Bumke, and Hoche, who took a dim view of permitting psychoanalysis to contaminate "respectable" psychiatry. Regrettably, Bleuler has seemed to capitulate increasingly over the years to the "establishment," in dramatic, if not nearly tragic, progression, as one gathers from excerpts by Stierlin.

In a volume edited by Alfred H. Rifkin,[58] one of the more relevant papers is by Eldred, discussing the selection of schizophrenic patients for office practice. In his practice, he chooses patients in whom he does not expect continuing sources of gross interpersonal anxiety in their external situation. A patient he did not take was one who lived alone with his paranoid mother and most likely would have continuous occasions for anxiety precipitation. From a descriptive clinical standpoint, the patients whom he selected for treatment did not differ from those he rejected. However, he found on retrospective examination that he excluded four who at the time of the initial interview produced a lack of interest and coldness in him, in distinction to the others. He feels that a variety of intuition was at play which he considers important. He feels that linguistic patterns of the patient's, the style of speaking, for instance, play a major role in the intuitive understanding and communication between patient and therapist. In discussing this paper, Ackerman points out that, apart from these facts mentioned, it is extremely necessary to estimate the extent of the personality defect of the patient, to what degree there is an intactness of the self and, for instance, the risk of uncontrolled destructiveness to self and others, as well as an appraisal of the degree of protection which the environment, especially family, is able to provide for the schizophrenic patient. He agrees with Eldred on the importance of the first encounter in deciding whether they will be able to have a good therapeutic relationship or not and suggests that in fact a mutual impression of each other before any spoken communication may be the essential one.

Another discussant, Janet Rioch, expressed particularly the need to work out the timing of interpretations beforehand (while remaining free to apply them when one feels that the interpretation is appropriate), and that in fact intuition is probably facilitated by preparatory planning and thinking. In another paper in the same volume, Chrzanowski discusses the treatment of asocial attitudes in ambulatory schizophrenic patients. Rather than discussing strategy and tactics of such treatment, he discusses primarily his belief that in the attempt to find solutions for the acute schizophrenic crisis, patients frequently find some salvation in asocial or antisocial attitudes. He suggests that such asocial or antisocial compromise solutions should be clearly understood as attempts at problem solving, and that they must be treated as symbols of profound insulation against an inner turmoil. The patient must be confronted with the full picture of his conflicts covered up by the asocial attitudes. At the same time, the analyst must not minimize or deny his own feelings or else he repeats the situation which the patient met in the traumatic parent-child relationship which originally had encouraged asocial solutions to emotional conflicts.

A volume on the *Psychotherapy of the Psychoses,* edited by Burton,[17] offers much material on the treatment of schizophrenics. The contributors include a large number of well known workers in the field, such as Will, Pious, Arieti, Sechehaye, Searles, and Jackson, who more or less state their well known positions. In that sense, the volume is a good introductory textbook to the field, offering a broad and broadminded panorama, somewhat at the cost of specific focus and specific contributions. Will, for instance, discusses in his chapter the schizophrenic in relation to his social milieu, or field. Arieti within his known theoretic framework, offers a list of specific psychotherapeutic interventions, of which the first is a suggestion of an attitude of active and intense intervention itself; the second, the attempt to remove the fear of contact in a schizophrenic; the third is a general attitude of reassurance; the fourth, a simple interpretation which conveys to the patient that he is being understood; fifth, some nonverbal acts (at least with some patients) such as walking together and, above all, establishing a basic trust. Jerome W. Perry offers a Jungian approach to the transference in schizophrenia: he sees as the principle of the Jungian approach that a theory be fitted to the psychotherapist on the one hand and to his patient on the other hand. He describes the theory as inherently polyglot. It is correspondingly difficult to give a specific account as the following quote will illustrate:"I believe it is no coincidence that a patient with a preponderance of feminine imagery such as this should be one to develop a strong transference from the very outset, since the feminine principle is involved with relationship."

An unusual and very scholarly volume was published in German in 1967 (and in French several years earlier) by Gabel, under the title of *Ideology and Schizophrenia, Forms of Alienation*.[30a] Gabel is a psychiatrist as well as a philosopher. He is a Marxist in the sense that he uses the dialectic method as his method of investigation. In his sense ideology is defined not merely as the sum total of ideas of a political movement, but rather as the expression of historical forms of thinking related to specific class interests. The thinking of German National Socialism seems a classical example. Gabel's main thesis is that such political-social ideologies attempt to deal with reality by concretistic thinking. Such reification often involves other primitive organization of thought as is described for children by Piaget and by Freud for the primary process. Such an ideology then leads to further distortion of reality and alienation from it. Gabel suggests that ideology may be seen as a social-political manifestation of schizophrenia, as well as schizophrenia as a manifestation of an individual ideology—a stereotyped dialectically (as well as logically) disturbance of awareness in the service of other needs. In the case of political ideology, the needs served are those of class interest, while presumably in schizophrenia they are some primitive affective needs or a lack of development of the subject-object relationship (which semanticists have also pointed out as one of the possible sources of schizophrenia). The conception of extreme social-political ideologies as delusional systems is a not unfamiliar one. (See for instance Brickner[15a])

Psychotic behavior as role playing within a theory of games and "set" is also not an unfamiliar one. Yet, Gabel's view may offer some useful thoughts to the psychotherapist of schizophrenia, maybe particularly in those instances where characterological features play a marked role.

DISCUSSION AND SUMMARY

Psychotherapy of the schizophrenic syndrome means different things to different people, depending upon their view of schizophrenia on the one hand and their general psychotherapeutic orientation on the other.

One of the basic premises all schools of thought seem to share is the importance of the patient-doctor relationship. Some would stop there, claiming the personality of the therapist and the establishment of good rapport to be paramount, as far as their conceptualization goes. This seems grossly oversimplified. The psychotherapeutic personality of the psychiatrist is as important as the medical-surgical dictum not to cause damage. Important as that is, it is not the whole story. Something positive must usually be done. The establishment of a good relationship is parallel to the creation of a beneficial therapeutic climate by bedrest, warmth, fluid intake. Usually, specific interventions by antibiotics, surgery, etc., are necessary. Similarly, specific psychotherapeutic interventions are necessary to attain more than transitory results: they are predicated upon some knowledge of the structure and dynamics of personality, much as general medicine is predicated upon a knowledge of anatomical structure and physiologic dynamics. Any other viewpoint must perforce be seen as prerational and nonscientific, however good the intentions or the occasional success.

Aside from the classical psychoanalytic school of thought, the Sullivanian, the Kleinian, combinations of these, and the work of eclectics, the existential school has attained more prominence in the last decade than it had had in the previous one, at least for the American public: in Europe the existential viewpoint became prominent as a post World War II phenomenon.

The specific schools of psychodynamic thought are divided on the conceptions of structure and dynamics and the interventions predicated upon them. Classical Freudians, Kleinians, and Sullivanians are probably more alike than different. In our bias, classical Freudian theory seems to provide the most internally consistent framework in general, and for the treatment of schizophrenia in particular, though it is by no means the ultimate and final word as yet.

The existential school has fascinating things to say about experiences of the self and offers much for a broader understanding of phenomena of depersonalization. Its verbiage, its sweeping philosophical generalizations, often bordering on the mystic and religious, make it likely that it represents regression rather than progress in the field.

Few, if any, papers addressed themselves explicitly to what must be considered the most important underlying question of any therapy, and thus of the therapy of schizophrenia, and in the narrower context of this chapter, of the psychotherapy of schizophrenia: *To what extent can be expected?* To avoid the complex pitfalls and problems of statistical appraisal of the effectiveness of any therapy, including psychotherapy, let us narrow the question to its logical nucleus within our conceptual framework.

Assuming that one subscribes to the proposition that "schizophrenia" is a syndrome of varied pathogenesis and etiology, what role can psychotherapy be expected to play?

Our review suggests that, whether the psychodynamics of the schizophrenic syndrome exists as a primary psychogenic constellation or develops secondarily to other factors, at all events the psychodynamic features can be understood and, to some extent, can be modified by psychodynamic propositions.

The key words in this statement may well be, "to some extent." In the light of our present knowledge, is the schizophrenic syndrome curable?[66]

This question implies two subsidiary questions: a) Is the disorder, of whatever nature, reversible? b) How stable can we expect such reversibility to be? The question of reversibility is the easier to answer. Few doubt, even in classical Kraepelinian terms, that the manifest clinical picture can be reversible for shorter or longer periods, often to the point at which, even by subtle means, at times one may not be able to discover that an individual had had a previous schizophrenic episode.

With regard to stability, it must be remembered that *all* life processes, be they biological, physical, sociological, or psychological, are resultants of the interplay of dynamic forces. This is so, whether one thinks of Selye's stress concept, the field concept of the physicists and of Kurt Lewin in psychology, or of psychoanalytic psychodynamics. It was suggested (Chapter 1) that the *schizophrenic syndrome is a more or less stable resultant of the interplay of a variety of forces:* it must be placed on a continuum which ranges from health on the one end, through neuroses, and extending to the psychoses on the other. Even as "normal" and "neurotic" attempts at adaptations may fail, leading to schizophrenic ones, so schizophrenic attempts may shift in the direction of neurotic and healthy ways of adapting and coping. It is inherent in the concept of *process* that we can speak only of relative stability of any constellation of forces. This certainly holds for the schizophrenic syndrome.

With this in mind, one need not hesitate to say that some schizophrenics are certainly curable; that is, the process is reversible to the point where, by any method, the personality may be indistinguishable from the relatively healthy. Further, this reversal may remain stable. However, in others, the reversibility may be only partial, or could result in only temporary episodes of good adjustment. In some, such episodes may leave the patient more regressed; in others, the patient may return to the same level of reintegration, and occasionally, even to a better one than before.

The degrees of reversibility and stability, external factors being constant, are likely to depend primarily on the contribution of the G factors of the affliction, of the synthetic function, and of the stimulus barrier function. (See Chapters 1 and 2) In addition, the degree of such reversibility and stability will be less, the earlier in the life history traumatic or pathogenic factors played a role, and the more severe these factors were. In turn, the relatively less that general factors of biological and other nature play a role, and the relatively less severe, and the relatively later in the individual life history the pathogenic constellations played a role, the more likely it is that schizophrenia be curable: that is, that someone at one time afflicted with the schizophrenic syndrome revert to, for all practical purposes, a form of functioning indistinguishable from the hypothetical normal.

BIBLIOGRAPHY

1. Arieti, S.: Hallucinations, delusions, and ideas of reference treated with psychotherapy. Am. J. Psychotherapy. 16: 1, 52-60, Jan. 1962.

2. Arieti, S.: Psychotherapy of schizophrenia. Arch. of Gen. Psy., Vol. 6, February, 1962.

3. Arieti, S.: New views on the psychodynamics of schizophrenia. Am. J. Psychiat. 124: 4, 453-466, October, 1967.

4. Azima, H.: Object relations therapy of schizophrenic states: Technique and theory. In Psychotherapy of schizophrenic and manic depressive states, Azima, H., and Glueck, B., Jr., Ed. Psychiat. Research Reports 17: 1963, Amer. Psychiat. Assoc.

5. Bateson, G., and Ruesch: Toward a theory of schizophrenia. Behav. Science, 1956, 1: 251-264.

5a. Bellak, L., with Black, B.: The rehabilitation of psychotics in the community. Am. J. Orthopsychiat. 30: 346-355, 1960.

6. Bellak, L.: The treatment of schizophrenia and psychoanalytic theory. J. Nerv. Ment. Dis. 131: 39-46, 1960.

7. Bellak, L.: Depersonalization as a variant of self-awareness. In Unfinished Tasks in the Behavioral Sciences. Abrams, A. (Ed.) Baltimore: Williams & Wilkins, 1964.

8. Bellak, L.: Methodology and research in the psychotherapy of psychoses. Am. Psychiat. Research Report 17, 1963.

9. Benedetti, G.: Entwicklung der Psychotherapie schizophrener, Zeitschr. f. Psychotherapie. 12: 2, 59-62, March, 1962.

10. Benedetti, G.: Analogien zwischen Kinderpsychotherapie und Psychotherapie von regredierten schizophrenen Erwachsenen. Acta Paedopsychiatrica. 29: 10, 320-330, 1962.

11. Benedetti, G.: Klinische Psychotherapie. Bern: Hans Huber, 1964.

12. Betz, B.: Studies of the therapists' role in the treatment of the schizophrenic patient. Am. J. Psychiat. 123: 8, 963-971, February, 1967.

13. Beyme, F.: Analyse eines schizophrenen Schwangerschaftswahns im Lichte der Forschungen von J. J. Bachofen, C. G. Jung, und E. Neumann, Schweizer Archiv für Neurologie und Psychiatrie, 1957, 80, parts 1-2, also, review in J. Analytic Psychol. 7: 1, 89-90, January, 1962.

14. Bloch, D.: Some dynamics of suffering: effect of the wish for infanticide in a case of schizophrenia. Psa. Rev. 53: 4, 531-554, Winter 1966/67.

15. Boyer, L., with Giovacchini, P.: Psychoanalytic Treatment of Characterological and Schizophrenic Disorders. New York: Science House, Inc., 1967.

15a. Brickner, R.: Is Germany Incurable? Philadelphia: Lippincott, 1943.

16. Bruch, H.: Psychotherapy with schizophrenics. Arch. Gen. Psy. 14: 346-351, 1966.

17. Burton, A., Ed. Psychotherapy of the Psychoses. New York: Basic Books, Inc., 1961.

18. Bychowski, G.: The psychoanalysis of the psychotic core in: Psychotherapy of

schizophrenic and manic depressive states, Azima, H., and Glueck, B., Jr., Ed. Psychiatric Research Reports 17, 1963, Am. Psychiat. Assoc.

19. Cameron, J. with Esterson, A.: The schizophrenic woman. Psy. Qrtrly. 32: 304-317, 1958.

20. Cameron, N.: Introjection, reprojection, and hallucination in the interaction between schizophrenic patient and therapist. Int. J. Psychoanal. 42: 86-96, 1961.

21. Davis, H.: Short-term psychoanalytic therapy with hospitalized schizophrenics. Psychoanal. Review. 52: 81-108, 1965/66.

22. Dellaert, R.: Psychotherapie des schizophrenes par la methode de la participation engagée. Psychother. Psychosom. 14: 2, 118-132, 1966.

23. de Perrot, E., with Lai, G.: Incidence de la co-therapie sur la psychotherapie d'un groupe de psychotique. Social Psychiat. 1: 4, 182-187, March 1967.

24. English, O.: Clinical observations on direct analysis. Compr. Psychiat. 1: 156-163, 1960.

25. Feldmann, H.: Die magisch-mythischen Wahngedanken Schizophrener, Part I, Confin. Psychiat. 8: 1, 20-34, 1966, Part II, Confin. Psychiat. 9:2, 78-92, 1966.

26. Freeman, T., with Cameron, J.: Chronic Schizophrenia, Tavistock Publications, Ltd., 1958.

27. Freeman, T., with Cameron, J., and McGhie, A.: The state of the ego in chronic schizophrenia. Brit. J. Med. Psychol. 30: 9-18, 1957.

28. Freud, A., Nagera, H., and Freud, E: A metapsychological assessment of the adult personality: the adult profile. In The Psychoanalytic Study of the Child. New York: International Universities Press, 1965, 22.

29. Fromm-Reichmann, F.: Basic problems in the psychotherapy of schizophrenia. Psychiatry 21: 1-6, 1958.

30. Frosch, J.: The psychotic character. Psy. Qrtrly. 38: 81-96, Jan. 1964.

30a. Gabel, J.: Ideology and Schizophrenia, Forms of Alienation. Frankfurt am Main: S. Fischer Verlag, 1967.

31. Gittleson, N., and Dawson-Butterworth, K.: Subjective ideas of sexual change in female schizophrenics. Brit. J. Psychiat. 113: 498, 491-494, May, 1967.

32. Goertzel, V., May, P., Salkin, J., and Schoop, T.: Body-ego technique: an approach to the schizophrenic patient. J. Nerv. Ment. Dis. Vol. 141, No. 1, 1965.

33. Grinspoon, L., Ewalt, J., and Shader: Long-term treatment of chronic schizophrenia. A preliminary report. Int. J. Psychiat. 4, 2: 116-127, 1967.

34. Hartmann, H.: Contribution to the metapsychology of schizophrenia. In The Psychoanalytic Study of the Child 8:177-198, 1954.

35. Hoedemaker, E.: Preanalytic preparation for the therapeutic process in schizophrenia. Psychiatry 21: 285-291, 1958.

36. Hoedemaker, E.: Intensive psychotherapy of schizophrenia. Canad. Psychiat. Assn. J. 12: 3, 253-261, June, 1967.

37. Honig, A.: The analytic treatment of schizophrenia. Psychoan. & Psychoan. Rev. 45: 51-62, 1958.

38. Horwitz, W., Polatin, P., Kolb, L., and Hoch, P.: A study of cases of schizophrenia treated by direct analysis. Am. J. Psychiat. 114: 780-783, 1958.

39. Jacobson, E.: The Self and the Object World. New York: International Universities Press, 1964.

40. Jacobson, E.: Problems in the differentiation between schizophrenic and melancholic states of depression. In Lowenstein, R. et al. (Eds.). Psychoanalysis —General Psychology. New York, International Universities Press, 1966, pp. 499-518.

41. Jacobson, E.: Psychotic Conflict and Reality. New York: International Universities Press, 1967.

42. Johnson, C.: The importance of patient-laid traps in the psychotherapeutic study of schizophrenia. J. Psychotherapy 19: 1, 75-86, 1965.

43. Knight, E.: Some considerations

regarding the concept autism. Dis. Nerv. Syst. 24: 224-229, 1963.

44. Laing, R.: The Divided Self (a) London: Tavistock Publications, Ltd., 1960 (b) Harmondsworth: Penguin Books, Ltd., 1965.

45. Lichtenberg, J.: The return to reality as a critical phase in the treatment of schizophrenic patients. Psychiatry 26: 26-38, 1963.

46. Lidz, T., Fleck, S., Alanen, Y., and Cornelison, A.: Schizophrenic patients and their siblings. Psychiatry 26: 1-18, 1963.

47. Lidz, T., Fleck, S., and Cornelison, A.: Schizophrenia and the Family. New York: International Universities Press, 1965.

48. McCarley, T.: Transference cure and transference psychosis. Dis. Nerv. Syst. 24: 602-605, 1963.

49. McGhie, A.: Psychological studies of schizophrenia. Brit. J. Med. Psychol. 39: 4, 281-288, December, 1966.

50. Marcus, E.: Ego breakdown in schizophrenia: some implications for casework treatment. Am. J. Ortho., Vol. XXXI, No. 2, April, 1961.

51. Maugile, D., and Ferron, L.: Les phases fondamentales de la psychotherapie collective des schizophrenes. Canad. Psychiat. Assn. J. 12: 2, 205-206, April, 1967.

52. Mead, B., and Rollins, J.: Response of schizophrenics to a brainwashing technique. Dis. Nerv. Syst. 22: 376-381, 1961.

53. Modell, A.: Primitive object relationships and the predisposition to schizophrenia. Int. J. Psychoanal. 44: 282-292, 1963.

54. Parkin, A.: Neurosis and schizophrenia. Psychiat. Qrtrly. Vol. 40, 203-235, July, 1966.

55. Pasamanick, B., Scarpitti, F., and Dinitz, S.: Schizophrenics in the Community. New York: Appleton-Century-Crofts, 1967.

56. Ploeger, A.: Auslösung einer Psychose durch verteilte übertragung. Z.f. Psychother. 16: 6, 219-228, November, 1966.

57. Richardson, G., and Moore, R.: On the manifest dream in schizophrenia. J. Am. Psychoanal. 11: 281-302, 1963.

58. Rifkin, A.: Schizophrenia in Psychoanalytic Office Practice. New York: Grune & Stratton, 1957.

59. Rosen, John: The study of direct psychoanalysis. In American Psychiatric Association Research Reports No. 19: Recent Research in Schizophrenia, ed. Solomon, P., and Blueck, B. Washington, D.C. Am. Psychiat. Assoc. pp. 41-55, 1964.

60. Rosen, John: Direct Psychoanalytic Psychiatry. New York: Grune & Stratton, 1962.

61. Rosen, Joseph: Some variations in the psychotherapeutic approach to schizophrenia. Am. J. Psychother. 12: 451-454, 1958.

62. Rosenfeld, H.: Notes on the psychoanalysis of the superego conflict in an acute schizophrenic patient. In New Directions in Psycho-Analysis, ed. Klein, M., et al. New York: Basic Books, Inc., 1955.

63. Rosenfeld, H.: Notes on the psychopathology and psychoanalytic treatment of schizophrenia. In Psychotherapy of schizophrenic and manic depressive states, Azima, H., and Glueck, B., Jr., ed. Psychiat. Research Reports No. 17: 1963, American Psychiat. Assoc.

64. Savage, C.: The diffusion of the transference-psychosis in the treatment of schizophrenia. Psychiatry 20: 419-421, 1957.

65. Savage, C.: Countertransference in the therapy of schizophrenics. Psychiatry 24: 53-60, 1961.

66. Spence, D.: The Broad Scope of Psychoanalysis—Selected Papers of Leopold Bellak. New York: Grune & Stratton, 1967.

67. St. John, R.: Regression as a defense in schizophrenia. Psychoanal. Qrtrly. 35: 414-422, 1966.

68. Scheflen, A.: A Psychotherapy of Schizophrenia: Direct Analysis. Springfield: C. C. Thomas, 1961.

69. Searles, H.: Collected Papers on Schizophrenia and Related Subjects. New York: International Universities Press, 1965.

70. Searles, H.: The schizophrenic individual's experience of his world. Psychiatry 30: 2, 119-131, May, 1967.

71. Sechehaye, M.: Principles and methods of symbolic realization. *In* Psychotherapy of schizophrenic and manic depressive states, Azima, H., and Glueck, B., Jr., ed. Psychiat. Research Reports No. 17: 1963, Amer. Psychiat. Assoc.

72. Stierlin, H.: Bleuler's concept of schizophrenia: a confusing heritage. Amer. J. Psychiat. 123: 996-1001, 8, February, 1967.

73. Trunnell, T., and Semrad, E.: Object anxiety and primitive defenses in schizophrenia. J. Nerv. Ment. Dis. 144: 2, 101-110, February, 1967.

74. Wexler, M.: Working through in the therapy of schizophrenia. Int. J. Psychoanal. 46: 279-286, 1965.

75. Wiekramasekera, I.: The use of some learning theory derived techniques in the treatment of a case of paranoid schizophrenia. Psychother. 4: 1, 22-26, February, 1967.

76. Will, O., Jr.: Psychotherapeutics and the schizophrenic reaction. J. Nerv. Ment. Dis. 126: 109-140, 1958.

77. Willner, G.: The role of anxiety in schizophrenia. Am. J. Psychoanal. 25: 171-180, 1965.

78. Wyss, D.: Psychotherapeutische behandlung einer halluzinatorisch-paranoiden Schizophrenie. Inst. f. Psychotherapie und Tiefenpsychologie, Almanach, 1959.

11

Childhood Schizophrenia

M. W. LAUFER, M.D. and D. S. GAIR, M.D.

Dr. Maurice W. Laufer is Director, Emma Pendleton Bradley Hospital; Member, Institute for the Health Sciences, Brown University; Adjunct Professor, Mental Health and Education, Rhode Island College, and past president of the Rhode Island District Branch of the American Psychiatric Association.

Educated at the University of Wisconsin and the Long Island College of Medicine, Dr. Laufer served residencies in Pediatrics and Psychiatry. He is an Affiliate Member of the Boston Psychoanalytic Society and Institute and various other professional associations.

In addition to his contribution to this volume, Dr. Laufer has authored several other textbook chapters and numerous articles.

Dr. Donald S. Gair is Chief of the Children's Ward and a principal psychiatrist on the staff of the Child Psychiatry Unit of the Massachusetts Mental Health Center, Director of the Metropolitan Training Program in Child Psychiatry at the Children's Unit of the Metropolitan State Hospital, and an instructor in Psychiatry at Harvard Medical School.

Graduated from Harvard Medical School (M.D. cum laude, 1950) Dr. Gair trained in child and adult psychiatry at the Boston Psychopathic Hospital (MMHC), and in neurology at the National Hospital, Queen's Square, London. On the staff of the MMHC since 1954, he has headed adult and adolescent services at various times.

His interests have been in the study of psychosis in children and residential treatment. He is Chairman of a continuing workshop begun in 1967 under the auspices of the American Orthopsychiatric Association for the study of "Clinical Criteria of Psychosis in Children."

THE UNIVERSE OF CHILDHOOD SCHIZOPHRENIA

Between birth and puberty there are an indeterminate number of children who manifest marked deviations from the norm in one or more of the following areas: i) in relatedness and responsiveness to people; ii) in relatedness and responsiveness to the physical environment and things in it other than people; iii) in the evenness of their maturation; in the acquisition and integrated use of iv) perceptual, v) motor, and/or vi) intellectual skills; and vii) in a combination of the above functions that can be called an awareness of self.

Some of these children demonstrate striking abnormalities of responsiveness beginning immediately after birth, alternating between states of maximal excitation with inconsolable screaming and extreme motor activity and states of

378

flaccid unresponsiveness, with abrupt shifts.[71] Others are persistently either minimally responsive or hyperactive.[5] Some children appear to the mothers to be wooden and not easy to cuddle—they lack the "anticipatory posture" and the smile of recognition that most infants develop by three months of age. Others are described as "melting into the mother's body" when held. These same or other infants do not fix their eyes on their mother's face, nor attend to sounds or, alternately, they may be hyperreactive to sound or other stimuli at first and later become unresponsive to them.

Some of the children with these early abnormalities persist in their deviance and at later ages in childhood develop various combinations of abnormal behaviors and other signs which other children, apparently normal previously, do not demonstrate until as late as the end of their fifth year. These signs include: bizarre posturing or gesturing; muteness in some or uncommunicative or primitive speech with absent or reversed pronouns, echolalia, sudden darting off, prolonged and aimless rocking, apparent inability to distinguish between animate and inanimate objects, confusion between self and nonself; soiling; repetitive stereotyped patterns of behavior; sudden outbursts of poorly directed violent behavior often apparently initiated in response to interruptions of their apparent inattentiveness; expressions of extreme fright without apparent or with trivial cause. The inattentiveness of many of these children is so marked as to make them appear deaf although they prove not to be. Some of these children have isolated hypertrophied skills involving memory feats or musical ability.

Those who develop such signs after several years of normal outward maturation and behavior may do so gradually without evident precipitation or rapidly after mild or moderately severe stress such as: the birth of a sibling; move to a new home; illness or absence of a parent; or physical illness of the child. When the children with appearance of the deviations in the first months of life reach the age of the children with later onset the two groups are often descriptively indistinguishable. There are some children who show the same severely disturbed picture but only transiently, but the majority persist in their abnormalities for prolonged periods, even for the duration of life.

Other children show little difficulty until well into their grade school years (ages 8-12 years) and then undergo breakdown of adaptation and personality organization. Most of these children have less global pictures of disorder, with organized symptomatology like that seen in schizophrenic reactions of adolescent and adult life.

The foregoing represents "the universe of childhood schizophrenia,"* and it includes the most seriously deviant children who come under the purview of children's mental health facilities. It is from this amalgam of disorders that

---

*A phrase coined by Goldfarb in 1960.[235]

various workers have separated out different syndromes or diseases. In some instances one condition may be designated by several conditions. When an author refers to "childhood schizophrenics" without further qualification, he may be referring to any of the possible clinical pictures subsumed within the first five paragraphs above.

In the 1958 edition of *Schizophrenia*, our predecessors summarized 1946-1956 in part thus: "In the area of differential diagnosis, the major contributions have led to increased clarification of the more precise and specific criteria which have aided in the establishment of childhood schizophrenia as an illness; it has also led to its differentiation from related and allied conditions".* The present writers can only state that the differentiation that appeared so clear then, has been subject to continuing efforts towards further clarification in the ensuing decade and that at the arbitrary point in time of the present review this work is still in its intermediate stage.

In the same chapter, Ekstein, Bryant and Freedman (relevant to the then, only recent, general acceptance of the existence of psychosis in children) speculated "as to whether the need to deny the designation of obvious psychotic states in children by both psychiatrists and lay individuals was not associated with the overwhelming threat that severe, psychotic personality disorganization posed to an adult world, still fearful of the primitive, archaic, and magical aspects of the infantile remnants of its own personality organization." The present authors speculate that the sometimes polemical assertions and counterassertions in this, as well as other areas of psychiatry, reflect exasperation with, if not fear of its lack of certainty. It is our impression, however, after reviewing the literature of the past decade that, with a very few exceptions, the extreme positions are less vehemently defended and optimistic belief in one or another theory and therapy, however reluctantly, has been tempered by the accumulated frustration of treatment attempts by the limited response of the majority of these very sick children (Szurek[540]). The problem of refinement and agreement on classification moves perhaps somewhat less slowly towards resolution because of this change. Although there has been a shift away from optimism there is no sign on the horizon of a spread of therapeutic nihilism.

DIAGNOSIS AND DIFFERENTIAL DIAGNOSIS

Diagnosis

Within the "universe of childhood schizophrenia" described above, the following diagnoses are currently employed:

a. *Inclusive terms* (age of onset 0-12)
   1. childhood schizophrenia

---

*Ekstein, Bryan, and Freedman. *In:* Schizophrenia, A Review of the Syndrome (New York: Logos Press, 1958 and Grune & Stratton, 1966) p. 683.

    2. childhood psychosis
    3. atypical development
    4. schizophrenic syndrome of childhood

b. *Specific diagnostic entity covering onset 0-12*
    1. childhood schizophrenia

c. *Specific clinical pictures or diagnostic entities with onset before six years.*
    1. early infantile autism
      a. primary
      b. secondary to organic factors
    2. childhood schizophrenia with early onset
    3. symbiotic psychosis
    4. infantile psychosis
    5. developmental psychosis
    (6. chronic brain syndrome with psychosis)
    7. protophrenia
    (8. propfschizophrenia [or mental deficiency with psychosis])
    (9. pseudoretardation)
   (10. pseudoschizophrenia)

d. *Specific clinical pictures or diagnostic entities with onset between six and twelve years.*
    1. Childhood schizophrenia; pseudoneurotic; pseudopsychopathic; pseudosomatic
    2. More benign childhood psychoses
    3. Schizophreniform psychosis of childhood
    (4. Propfschizophrenia [mental retardation with psychosis])
    5. Borderline psychosis
    6. Psychotic character
    (7. Pseudoschizophrenia)
    (8. Chronic brain syndrome with psychosis)

(Note: The conditions bracketed will be taken up under differential diagnosis.)

All of these categories with relevant historical review and conceptual exposition were extensively and well summarized through 1955 by Ekstein, Bryant, and Freedman (Bellak, 1958) except for four which have appeared since their review: 1) Developmental psychosis (Kamp[286]) is a generic term in use at the Utrecht Clinic covering psychoses of early onset and therefore overlapping with early infantile autism, symbiotic psychosis and atypical development. It is used to emphasize the interweaving of psychopathological processes with continuing development. 2) "Infantile psychosis" is a term proposed by Reiser[445] (1964) to cover the same group of children. 3) The third, "Psychotic character," is a nosological concept developed by Frosch and found applicable to children by Settlage.[498] It will be further elaborated below. 4) "Protophrenia" a term coined by Bourne[68] (1955) to characterize some among 154 mentally defective children admitted to the Fountain Hospital in London during a two year period. He conceives of it as a psychogenic amentia. It too will be described and discussed below.

Much confusion arises from the fact that "childhood schizophrenia" may mean different things. As already mentioned, it may refer to the very broad group of psychiatrically (and often neurologically) disordered children. It may, secondly, refer to a specific subgroup of these children. Thirdly it may refer to a postulated underlying causative process such as Bender's[29] "maturational lag" and Kaufman's[297] "core conflict." The use of the term "childhood psychosis" carries similar ambiguities.

Many authors have referred to the lack of adequate objective criteria for classification of apparent clinical entities within this broad group of children, among them Beck,[23] Caplan,[90] Delage,[121] Eisenberg,[142] Rutter,[471] Ward,[562] and Wing.[586] A few groups have questioned the significance of categorization, emphasizing the variability of the individual clinical problems even within similar groups of children (Szurek[540]) (Rank[440]); also considering the uncertainty of the cause (Reiser[444]). Szurek and Rank have been criticized for this attitude (as by Eisenberg,[142] and Kanner[295]). In the sense that the adaptive problems are similar regardless of basic cause and can be profitably studied independent of such causes, the criticism would appear unjustified. However, both Szurek and Rank explicitly emphasize the primary causative role of psychopathology in the parents and by thus minimizing the importance of other possible causes, which may vary between progressive (Creak[115]) brain degeneration and reversible metabolic defect (Yaker et al.[596]), they contribute to this controversy.

A large number of workers (Eisenberg,[142] Garcia,[215] Goldfarb,[232,236] Jackson,[281] Kanner,[292] Menolascino,[373] Rutter,[468,469] Stroh[536]), including also the present authors believe that refinement of classification remains essential for the evaluation of etiologic and therapeutic work within this broad group of seriously sick—"psychotic," "schizophrenic"—children.

Classifications

Classification schemes in psychiatry, no less than in other areas of human observation, can be endlessly elaborated, shuffled, and reshuffled. Menninger, in *The Vital Balance* (Viking, N.Y., 1963), has an 80 page appendix on classifications and an amusing and instructive chapter on "the urge to classify." The recent G.A.P. proposal for a classification in Child Psychiatry[253] has a similar appendix, representing persistent efforts to bring at least the illusion of order into the field. In the past decade there have been several formal proposals for subclassification of childhood psychosis with more or less necessity for revising the entire system of classification of all childhood disorders.

They are summarized as follows:

PSYCHOSES OF CHILDHOOD

1) Psychoses of Early Onset
   a) Infantile Autism (onset at birth or within first two years)
   b) Autistic Psychosis of Mahler
   c) Symbiotic Psychosis (onset at individuation phase of development)

2) Childhood Schizophrenia (onset after anywhere from one to eight years, with "previously normal development")

3) Borderline Psychosis

4) Psychosis in association with organic brain disease (including mental retardation)

It is necessary and helpful to point out the various uses of "autism" and "autistic" as they appear in the literature.

"Autistic" may be used as a behavioral description without a necessary implication of psychosis. Autism may refer to Kanner's "Early Infantile Autism," or to Mahler's subclassification of "Autistic Psychosis" in the first few months of life. It is also used as an equivalent for the term "schizophrenia." Finally, it is used by some to refer to psychoses of early onset which are meant to be differentiated from childhood schizophrenia (Rutter[469,470]).

Most of the articles on the subject present some variation of this outline.[4,8,120,125,356,371,372,557,558] The G.A.P. proposal[253] is in this format and reflects the practice current today. Some major points of dispute may be incorporated in it but it will be far more satisfactory than the current official nomenclature.* In the G.A.P. proposal the general definition of "Psychotic Disorders" is first given by a condensation of the nine points of the British Working Party (see pages 386-387 of this chapter). Absence of pertinent signs of brain damage is required for inclusion here, as is absence of mental retardation. The special categories are given as:

a) Psychoses of Infancy and Early Childhood
1) Early infantile autism (to be distinguished from autism secondary to brain damage or mental retardation)
(onset in first months or year)
2) Interactional psychotic disorder (to include symbiotic psychosis but also related disorders)
(onset second to fifth year)
3) Other psychosis of infancy and early childhood (equivalent to "atypical development" or Reiser's "Infantile Psychosis," see below)

b) Psychoses of Later Childhood
1) Schizophreniform psychotic disorder
(onset six-thirteen)

---

*Because of the vagueness of definition and the genuine disagreement with the concept of schizophrenia in childhood (perhaps, also because of reluctance by some to use a term regarded as so stark), many psychotic children are classified under "Psychotic Reaction without clearly defined structural change, other than above" although "this classification is introduced primarily for the use of librarians and statisticians in those instances where the diagnosis has been left incomplete" or under "Adjustment reaction of childhood (or infancy)" with the qualifying phrase "with psychotic reaction" added.

Diagnostic and Statistical Manual, Mental Disorders, American Psychiatric Association, Washington, D.C. 1952.

(Schizophreniform chosen to indicate parallel to schizophrenia but also to emphasize "developmental differences and the clinical impression that children with this disorder do not necessarily develop the later form.")

2) Other psychoses of later childhood (if any).

Anthony,[10,11] Fish,[188] Gold,[220,221] and Settlage[498] have proposed distinctive classifications which will be briefly outlined. Anthony's proposal is based on etiologic factors and is designed to circumvent disagreements and confusion that arise from arbitrary boundaries between related syndromes. He proposes five "continua," each ranging from nonpsychotic to psychotic: 1) normal continuum; 2) deficiency continuum; 3) organic continuum; 4) neurotic continuum; and 5) psychopathic continuum. He uses a set of 30 symptom rating scales ranging between absent symptom to extreme form and including such items as: withdrawal, relationship, evidence of organic disease.

Fish's proposal of a typology of children's disorders is similar to Anthony's in that each category (except her "Type I" which are all psychotics) ranges from nonpsychotic to psychotic degree. However her classification continua are all psychological and refer to personality structure types: Type I is "autistic-disjunctive" (all psychotic, includes autistic and symbiotic psychoses); Type II is "immature-labile" (fragmentary autistic, neurotic or paranoid features); Type III is "anxious-neurotic" (range from mild neurosis to psychotic pseudoneurotic schizophrenia); Type IV is "sociopathic-paranoid" (range from sociopathic personality disorders to psychotic paranoid schizophrenia). These two proposals for a new nosology are similar to proposals for evaluation of children by estimation of the competence of various ego functions without reference to specific diagnoses (see p. 388 in this chapter). They all have the value of incorporating a ready means of evaluating change if the rating scales prove to be reliable.

Gold and Vaughan[220,221] have proposed a classification that is essentially a chart of differential diagnoses. The major headings are: Childhood Schizophrenia; Organic state with Psychosis; Mental subnormality with Psychosis; Sensory deprivation; Neurosis; and Manic-depressive Psychosis. There are many further subheadings, for which the article should be consulted.

Finally, Settlage[498] proposed a six-stage classification of all childhood disorders in order of severity of deviation: 1) Developmental disorders, 2) Situational disorders, 3) Neurosis, 4) Neurotic character, 5) Psychotic character, 6) Psychoses. He added 7) Psychic disorders in association with organic disorders "for completeness." The major new suggestion in this article is the inclusion in child diagnoses of Frosch's "Psychotic character." (See p. 381 of this chapter)

In this chapter the authors do not follow a particular classification, but present the material in accordance with the trends in the literature. The reference to age of onset of psychotic disorder is one that the authors have tried to keep clear. It is not always clearly specified in the literature.

*Childhood Schizophrenia, A Semantic Convenience** (*Childhood Psychosis*) "Childhood Schizophrenia" is the label still in most general use to refer to this broad group of children. For many authors it is a generic term, equivalent to "childhood psychosis" and its existence as a natural nosologic entity uniting all of this group is seriously doubted (Bruch[82]). Kanner[295] in 1965 wrote. "There is, indeed, no 'disease entity' called childhood schizophrenia, just as there is no disease entity called mental deficiency." Anthony[10] (1958) does not use the term at all in his proposal for classification of psychosis on children nor does Settlage[498] (1964) in his proposed classification of childhood disorders. A number of writers would restrict the use of "childhood schizophrenia" to designating only the children with the onset of symptoms in middle childhood or prepuberty years (Rutter,[471] Despert,[124] G.A.P.,[253] Menolascino[371]).

However, the global designation is still implicitly or explicitly used as a nosological entity by Bender, Goldfarb, Blau and others. Childhood schizophrenia as a nosological entity is presented in the next subsequent section. Goldfarb[235] wrote (1964): "In recent years the criteria for the diagnosis of childhood schizophrenia have been delineated with increasing precision and agreement by child psychiatrists." But shortly before, Blau[63] (1962) characterized childhood schizophrenia as one disease "more or less synonymous" with all of the following designations: "atypical, prepsychosis, ego deviant, seriously deviant child, infantile anaclitic depression, preschizophrenic, autistic, symbiotic, brain-injured, incipient schizophrenia, pseudopsychosis, pseudoneurotic psychosis, abnormal child, schizoid personality, impulse-ridden character, and oligophrenia." He attributed reluctance, sentimentality, and evasiveness to those who do not assign the label of childhood schizophrenia to children for whom he believes it appropriate. At the opposite pole, Pollack[432] on the basis of a review of 13 studies reported between 1937 and 1965, challenged the appropriateness of the diagnosis of childhood schizophrenia altogether, on the grounds that the majority of these children give evidence of disordered brain function. He believed that "chronic brain syndrome with psychosis" should become the major diagnosis itself for the entire group, not a condition to be differentiated from "childhood schizophrenia." The evidence he emphasized is the high incidence of mentally retarded functioning reported for schizophrenic children. His culled statistics show that over three-fourths of the testable schizophrenic children have I.Q.'s below 90, with between one-third and one-half of the testable total scoring below 70. Although few go so far as Pollack, the extensive overlapping and

---

*Kanner.[295]

coincidence of mental retardation and psychosis has been a subject of increasing study and discussion during the past decade. This will be taken up
later on in sections on "pseudoretardation, mental retardation, and chronic
brain syndrome."

Despite the many criticisms and challenges it has received, the term
"schizophrenia" is not readily replaced or eliminated. The necessity of some
such term despite its ambiguity and the related dilemmas are well described by
many (see especially Kanner[292]). In 1960 a British Working Party was
convened to "clarify and describe what was meant by 'psychosis in childhood'
. . . (and) . . . after lengthy discussion it was agreed that the term
'schizophrenic syndrome in childhood' should be used" (Creak[114]). Apropos
of the all or nothing range of views summarized above, their balanced conclusion (Creak[116]) (1964) was "that the syndrome represents what is almost
certainly a heterogeneous group." In 1966 the Committee on Child Psychiatry
of the Group for Advancement of Psychiatry proposed the term
"schizophreniform psychotic disorder" for psychosis with onset between 6 and
12, "to indicate the parallels between this disorder and the adult form of
schizophrenia, but to emphasize as well the developmental differences . . ."[253]

Symptomatology and Criteria. Most authors have not committed
themselves to necessary and sufficient criteria for the inclusion of a child in
the broad group of childhood psychosis. Although long lists of symptoms have
been detailed and discussed and analyzed, the diagnostic decision has remained, remarkably enough, a matter of total clinical impression. Various inclusive lists of behavioral descriptions (Brown,[79,80] Reiser,[445] Goldfarb[232,235])
cover the same items sufficiently to indicate that equivalent groups of children
are being designated but the generality is such as to allow for wide divergence
between individual children.

Most diagnostic criteria are given for groups of children. Authors write, for
instance, of "higher incidence of decreased socialization, unusual play patterns, and neurophysiological disturbances in the schizophrenic group."[310]
Goldfarb's extensive findings at the Ittelson Center are largely reported by
group incidence.[232,235,236] His subdivision of the broad group of childhood
schizophrenics into "organic" and "nonorganic" will be discussed in the section on etiology.

Szurek[540] stressed variability in psychotic behavior *in the same child,* with
alternations between pathological extremes, such as between total urinary and
fecal incontinence and retention to the point of impaction, or gross pica
alternating with refusal even to bring the hands near the mouth.

The broad general criteria for psychosis in children, summarized by Ekstein
et al. (Bellak 1958) remain the same. The British Working Party's list of nine
criteria for "schizophrenic syndrome of childhood"[114] (1961) is a most important recent clinical outline and will be reproduced here.

"Point 1: *Gross and sustained impairment of emotional relationships with people.* This includes the more usual aloofness and empty clinging (so-called symbiosis): also abnormal behavior towards other people as persons, such as using them, or parts of them, impersonally. Difficulty in mixing and playing with other children is often outstanding and longlasting.

"Point 2: *Apparent unawareness of his own personal identity to a degree inappropriate to his age.* This may be seen in abnormal behaviour towards himself, such as posturing or exploration and scrutiny of parts of his body. Repeated, self-directed aggression, sometimes resulting in actual damage, may be another aspect of his lack of integration (see also Point 5), as also the confusion of personal pronouns (see Point 7).

"Point 3: *Pathological preoccupation with particular objects or certain characteristics of them, without regard to their accepted functions.*

"Point 4: *Sustained resistance to change in the environment and a striving to maintain or restore sameness.* In some instances behaviour appears to aim at producing a state of perpetual monotony.

"Point 5: *Abnormal perceptual experience* (in the absence of discernible organic abnormality), implied by excessive, diminished, or unpredictable response to sensory stimuli—for example, visual and auditory avoidance (see also Points 2 and 4), or insensitivity to pain or temperature.

"Point 6: *Acute, excessive and seemingly illogical anxiety.* This is a frequent phenomenon and tends to be precipitated by change, whether in material or in routine, as well as by temporary interruption of a symbiotic attachment to persons or things (compare Points 3 and 4, and also 1 and 2). Apparently commonplace phenomena or objects seem to become invested with terrifying qualities. On the other hand, an appropriate sense of fear in the face of real danger may be lacking.

"Point 7: *Speech may have been lost, or never acquired, or may have failed to develop beyond a level appropriate to an earlier stage.* There may be confusion of personal pronouns (see Point 2), echolalia or other mannerisms of use and diction. Though words or phrases may be uttered, they may convey no sense of ordinary communication.

"Point 8: *Distortion in motility patterns,* e.g., a) excess as in hyperkinesis; b) immobility as in catatonia; c) bizarre postures or ritualistic mannerisms, such as rocking and spinning (of themselves or of objects).

"Point 9: *A background of serious retardation* in which islets of normal, near normal or exceptional intellectual function or skill may appear."

In their 1964 progress report[116] it was underlined that the list of criteria was not meant as a specific diagnostic formula. Here again, as with most other reports, the criteria are guidelines only. However, the Working Party criteria have been widely read and adopted. Increasing numbers of articles refer to "the criteria of Creak et al." or of "the British Working Party" and they undoubtedly have contributed to a trend towards uniformity in designation. In 1966 Whittam et al.[581] reported a study in which "at least four" of the criteria were required for the diagnosis of psychosis. The list of Creak et al. is of descriptive items only and does not refer to etiologic factors nor does it refer to onset, course, or outcome. However, they make the important point that some interpretation must be included.

Even among these general criteria, including such central concepts as "social withdrawal" and "unresponsiveness," there are exceptions. The criteria are not firmly enough established for the absence of any single item or even of several significant items to suggest that the diagnosis is in error. Szurek[540] drew attention to the fact that no child that he has seen, regardless of the depth of pathology is totally unresponsive. Beres,[50,51] and Ekstein,[154] and others have stressed the variability in clinical states in many of these children. The most consistent finding with the highest reported incidence in all studies is that of absent or faulty verbal communication[32,79,80,116,212,225,232] and yet Weber[565] reports that one "severely autistic . . . schizophrenic child" used "communicative speech only," and "no bizarre language." The criteria were not sufficiently designated in this particular article to be certain, but the child may have been an instance of "autism without psychosis," a descriptive concept elaborated by Bender[36] and Menolascino.[373] (See below under "Psychoses of early onset").

Stroh[536] (one of the members of the British Working Party), in an excellent review of the problem, discussed the increasing frequency of the diagnosis of "childhood psychosis" and difficulties of delimitation and naming. He cited a reported incidence of 66 per cent improvement rate in one group as presumptive evidence that the group was different from most of those reported on as childhood psychosis or schizophrenia. He believed that the search for a single cause has prevented progress in nosology, which must be sought by agreement on frames of reference for collection of data and progressive reexamination of data, particularly by longitudinal studies in residential centers in order to create specific boundaries. He recommended inclusion of psychopathology and psychoanalytically oriented developmental concepts in diagnostic thinking.

There have been other suggestions that "childhood schizophrenia" be replaced by a broader concept of ego pathology, beginning with the introduction of the term "atypical development" by Putnam in 1948. Beres[50] made a major contribution to this thinking in 1956 when he wrote of deviations in ego function associated with the diagnosis of schizophrenia in children. He must also be credited with one of the few attempts at delineation of necessary and sufficient criteria for diagnosis of childhood schizophrenia. He specified that children diagnosed as schizophrenic had deviations in "more than one" of the seven major areas of ego function that he outlined. These areas are: 1) relation to reality, 2) regulation and control of instinctual drives, 3) object relationships, 4) thought processes, 5) defense functions of the ego, 6) autonomous functions of the ego, and 7) synthetic functions of the ego. Most of the 18 patients he described, had psychosis with onset over six and some of them can clearly be placed in the "borderline psychosis" category (see below). However he did not specify a diagnostic category since, recognizing existing diagnostic confusion, his intent was to provide another basis for evaluation and classification. Esman[162] has suggested replacing the assignment of a specific diagnostic label by the delineation of those ego functions which are impaired and those which are intact and a thorough assessment of possible etiologic factors. Most recently (1967),[101] using Beres' areas of ego function, Coddington and Offord have demonstrated that psychiatrists' reliability in judging ego functions in a group of children ranging from normal to psychotic on the basis of the usual unstructured clinical interview is of a similar order of magnitude to that of cardiologists' reliability in diagnosing cardiac dysfunction from murmurs and radiologists' reliability in reading films. They suggested that the establishment of an "ego-quotient" for each child would be "one way of dealing effectively with the diagnostic dilemma, and at the same time it provides a yardstick by which we can measure changes in a given child and differences or similarities between children."

Thomas[547] used Anna Freud's "diagnostic profile" in assessment of psychotic children and found it useful. Mack and Gair[350] compared 19 psychotic children with 19 neurotic or behaviorally disordered children and 12 "borderline" children. The age range was 3-12 years. They found that children who were diagnosed as psychotic on the basis of gross estimate of severity of disorder had symptoms indicative of three categories of disorder; bizarreness (lack of normal social responsiveness); poor object relations; and poor capacity for reality-testing. Assessing the 50 children in their study by 52 signs culled from the literature (1937-1961) on childhood psychosis they found that the psychotics could be distinguished from the other two groups by the occurrence of: *either* marked disturbances in distinction between animate and inanimate (particularly human and inanimate); *or* persistent aimless rocking (or both). The only symptoms occurring in *all* "psychotics" were: deviant affective expression, poor frustration tolerance, and fragmented thinking. These occurred, however in neurotic or borderline children as well.

Newly suggested, special, or research methods of evaluation Some of the new evaluative methods point out a special aspect of common procedures, others contribute something to diagnostic thinking even though the methods employed are not readily applied, still others suggest new approaches to clinical diagnosis.

The use of Beck's 170-item "trait universe" describing schizophrenia in children and adults (1954-ref.#36 in Bellak 1958) has not been widely reported in other hands, but he and Molish[24] have reported its use in the five-year course of treatment of a seven year old schizophrenic boy at the Orthogenic School. They show how the method allows the identification of the most severe degrees of behavior disruption and areas of higher potentialities, thereby providing a systematic means of knowing the patient and planning his treatment.

Spivack and Levine[530] (1964) developed a 68 item form, the Devereux Child Behavior Rating Scale, from a pool of 850 items studied for rater reliability. The scale was applied to 140 children, ages 5-12 years with diagnoses including neurotic, chronic brain syndrome, and schizophrenia. Each item had a five point scale for rating specific behavior. Data was analyzed by factor analysis. Rater reliability coefficients for 15 derived factor scores were high (.77-.93 with a median of .83). The fifteen factors in the profile were called: 1) proneness to anger and aggression, 2) autistic social unresponsiveness, 3) need for social contact, 4) arrested or regressed in self-care, 5) negativism, 6) cognitive coherence, 7) receptor hypersensitivity and avoidance, 8) disinhibition, 9) motor dysmaturity, 10) cleanliness, 11) language maturity, 12) the you-I confusion in language, 13) need for autonomy, 14) competence, 15) receptor hypersensitivity and fear of physical harm. They concluded that use of the scale may lead to a refinement in diagnostic groupings.

Wechsler and Iaros[567] reported a careful study indicating a means of identifying schizophrenic children from normals on the basis of W.I.S.C. test performance. They stated that 40 per cent of schizophrenic children were correctly spotted at "a cost of" only 2 per cent false positives, which, they say, is better than psychiatric examination and interview alone (not according to[350]). However, the next year Kissell[311] pointed out that in duplicating the work and using a second control of nonpsychotic but emotionally disturbed children, the schizophrenics could not be distinguished from the nonpsychotic disturbed children.

Fuller[208] reported using the Minnesota Percepto-Diagnostic test, which measures perceptual stability in degrees of rotation of a copied figure compared to the stimulus figure, in assessment of schizophrenic children (ages 12-13). He compared 150 schizophrenic children with 260 emotionally disturbed but nonpsychotic children, and 450 normal children. The groups were clearly distinguished. He stated that perceptual stability varies directly with personality organization. However, since a control group on nonpsychotic children with cerebral dysfunction was not included, the possibility of the results reflecting organic disorder is not ruled out.

Goldfarb and his co-workers[225] have studied the speech of schizophrenic children carefully. The general impression of "odd quality" speech was confirmed by prolonged observation by trained speech therapists. "Flatness" of tone, idiosyncratic and narrow changes of pitch, incorrect inflection, monotony, appeared to be objectifiable items contributing to the overall impression of oddness. Weiland and Legg (1964)[571] in a careful analysis of parts of speech employed in the conversation of psychotic children, compared with normal and brain damaged children, showed that the psychotic children used significantly more imperative verbs and fewer conjunctions and first person plural pronouns than the nonpsychotic controls.

Hospitalization was seen as a diagnostic aid by Kemph,[308] and Gair and Salamon.[212] The child's response to separation from the family, even if relatively brief (as with weekends spent at home regularly), as well as to the different environment can indicate potential for change and nature of relationship to parents. This is a variant of diagnosis by response to therapeutic trial. Lovatt[345] similarly used a four-week observation period in a nursery school by a trained nursery teacher.

Structured observations of children with standardized procedures or standardized recording of semi-standardized interviews have been reported by Loomis,[337,338] Jahoda and Goldfarb,[283] Steisel et al.,[533,534] Wortis and Choi,[594] and Wright et al.[595] Most of these reports indicate the possibility of indices important in differentiating between diagnostic categories in psychotic children and the work is being further refined. Loomis's and Steisel's work was with nonverbal psychotic children. Wortis' report was of an 8-channel polygraph recording of responses to positive, negative, and neutral stimuli (colored lights and lights associated with a buzzer). His results indicated that schizophrenic children have difficulty in developing and maintaining conditioning, tend to engage in repetitive stereotyped reactions and exhibit difficulty in respect to the interaction of both signal systems. Active inhibitory phenomena were readily induced in these children. Wright's report was of a pilot study employing a Q sort technique on observations of schizophrenic, retarded, and normal children. The Q sort items were based on statements concerning objective descriptions of overt behavior, subjective responses of adult to child, and inferred response to the adult from the child. Analysis of the initial data indicated that the schizophrenic subjects were rated low in mutual trust and constructiveness and high on retentiveness, activity, and orality.

Colbert and Koegler[103] believe that electroencephalographic study and psychological tests lack reliability as diagnostic aids in childhood schizophrenia.

Childhood Schizophrenia—designating a nosological entity, age of onset 0-12 years

LAURETTA BENDER'S CHILDHOOD SCHIZOPHRENIA

The most inclusive concept of childhood schizophrenia remains that of Bender. She views it as a process of dysmaturation, inborn, global, and, once established, ineradicable although modifiable in its protean manifestations. She has emphasized that childhood schizophrenia is not synonymous with psychosis,[30] "because many schizophrenic children are never psychotic, and many schizophrenic children who may have psychotic episodes recover from their psychotic episodes and are still schizophrenic but are not psychotic; so these two terms are not readily equivalent."

Her behavioral descriptions of schizophrenic children who are psychotic are equivalent to the general descriptions summarized earlier in this chapter, with the exception of her perception of the tendency of these children to cling to the adult, rather than to withdraw, and also with the exception of those aspects of description that are largely inferential. For instance: "Being terror-stricken by the disturbances in motility, perception and emotional responses, the child often clings to adults and attempts to melt into the adult body and to use the adult's motility, perceptual and emotional experiences."[356] The diagnosis of schizophrenia, for Bender requires findings indicative of maturational lag. Signs of maturational lag are the so-called "soft neurologic signs," including "whirling," "toe-walking," and various discoordinations of visual-motor integration, which exist in the absence of "hard" signs of pyramidal tract and sensory tract disruption.

The work of Fish et al.[180,187,189] on detection of schizophrenia in infancy is an extension of Bender's work and lends strong support to her concept, at least for some children. In this study, 16 infants were selected at random from the population at the Bellevue Hospital's Well-Baby Clinic. These children were examined serially, beginning at the age of one month. "Vulnerability to schizophrenia was defined in terms of abnormally uneven neurological development, characterized by unusual combinations of retardation and precocity as compared to Gesell's norms." Three of the infants (all boys) were judged to be "vulnerable" to schizophrenia by the results of the examination at one month. The description of the child with the most irregular development is dramatic. "His head control was advanced for his age (he was able to lift both head and chest when prone), but his trunk was so flaccid that he could not be pulled to sit, but had literally to be 'folded up.' He was abnormally underactive, showing none of the usual kicking or crawling, but only slow writhing, fish-like movements. Visual following was normal, but he showed no response to the examiner's voice. Muscle tone was doughy and he had peripheral mottling and cyanosis."[189] At nine years of age the children were evaluated by independent psychiatric and psychological examinations. The independent psychiatrist found the child described above to be clearly schizophrenic. A second of the three showed "predominantly a psychopathic personality organization resulting from early deprivation, with some schizophrenic features." The third child, the least irregular in neurological development at one month, appeared to be a well-compensated neurotic boy at nine years by psychiatric interview. On psychological examinations at nine years (W.I.S.C., Rorschach, T.A.T., Human Figure Drawings, Bender Gestalt), all three of the "vulnerable" boys "showed pathological disorders of thinking, identification, and personality organization." These were judged to be of more than neurotic severity and less organized than the two "nonvulnerable" children whose psychological test performances revealed "moderate neurotic problems." The remaining children were within normal limits both by psychiatric examination and psychological test.

Hellersberg[261] agreed that such infants as those described by Fish et al. have disruptions in ego growth but implied that such children may ultimately reach an even and harmonious pattern. Several reported studies[53,105,325,426,439,462,515] support Bender's views on the presence of maturational lag, revealed by soft signs, and the importance of this in schizophrenic children. Safrin[474] tested visual perception, visual motor performance, and performed neurological examination on 39 psychotic and 57 nonpsychotic 8-12 year old boys. She found that differences between these groups could be accounted for by correcting for "mental age functioning" and concluded that the study failed to support Bender's maturational lag hypothesis. It would appear, however, that the need to correct for immaturity points to association of impaired mental and biological maturation which would support, rather than refute Bender. But, in another study, Kramer et al.[318] administered the "whirling test" to schizophrenic children, normal middle-income white children, and normal lower-income Negro children. Schizophrenics demonstrated the highest incidence of whirling, though not all whirled. Continual whirling was significantly higher for the normal Negro children of lower income families than for the normal white children of middle income families. The authors concluded that whirling may be influenced by environment as well as age and that the whirling test is not a reliable diagnostic tool.

Bender's several clinical categories within childhood schizophrenia are:[32] "pseudo-defective or autistic, pseudo-neurotic, and pseudo-psychopathic." These subclassifications will be discussed below.

BETTELHEIM, GOLDFARB, KAUFMAN, DESLAURIERS

These authors are grouped here because they also use "childhood schizophrenia" as a specific diagnostic term.

Bettelheim's[56] pioneering achievements in residential treatment of seriously disturbed children are widely recognized. His view of the schizophrenic child reacting as to a chronically catastrophic situation is outlined later in this chapter under psychopathology. He does not make a fundamental distinction between psychoses of early onset and later onset and, although he recognizes the difficulties and imprecisions in diagnoses, his use of "schizophrenia" implies that it is the same relatively specific entity at whatever age it emerges. His major contributions have not been to diagnosis but to hypotheses of psychogenic causation and to treatment based on these hypotheses.

Goldfarb does not have an unequivocal unifying concept such as Bender's, although he postulates "catastrophic feelings of strangeness" and "primordial anxiety" secondary to "parental perplexity" as the core of childhood schizophrenia,[232,235] which are analogous to Bender's description of the schizophrenic child's "terror" at perception of inner disequilibrium. In his group of severely disturbed children, he has identified "organic" and "nonorganic" subgroups. "Soft neurological signs" are more prevalent in the "organic" group although also seen in the "nonorganic group." His assessment of parental psychosocial competence showed more disordered parents in the group of "nonorganic" children than in the group of "organic" children. He is not unequivocal, however, in postulating parental pathology as a diagnostic item in the child, tending more towards an etiologic theory of interaction between pathology in the child and pathology in the parent.

DesLauriers[123] was refreshingly direct. "Schizophrenia is not seen here as an illness, the symptoms of which have to be enumerated and dealt with piecemeal: schizophrenia is a defect in ego formation and development which finds expression in patterns of behavior that are aberrant." He stressed the centrality to the diagnosis of psychosis, of a seriously disordered relationship with reality. His treatment work is summarized later. It should be said that, although he does not make any distinction between early and late onset, his six cases were all verbal adolescents with histories of prior complex and active, though pathological, social adaptations. Adult type symptomatology was common, and none of the children were autistic.

Kaufman and his co-workers,[298,302] like Bender and Goldfarb, identified a core problem as essential to the diagnosis and understanding of childhood schizophrenia, and similarly it is a core of anxiety that is postulated. According to Kaufman this core anxiety is the fear of annihilation. Like Bender, he saw as diagnostic the core rather than the outer manifestations and also classified childhood schizophrenia into subgroups. The common characteristics that he listed for childhood schizophrenics are: core anxiety (fear of annihilation); object interaction at primary object or monadic level of development with little self-differentiation; affect disturbances—either inhibited or explosive; communication, both verbal and nonverbal, at a primary process level; ego organization at the most primitive level, with denial of reality; projection and introjection; massive inhibition and exclusion of sensory stimuli; psychosexual development at the oral level. Although he did not list parental psychopathology as diagnostic, he has reported it as an invariable[298] finding. His findings will be further elaborated in the section on etiologic hypotheses. His subclassification is based on overt severity, reflecting the same underlying causative and adaptive process in each instance. In order of decreasing severity, he groups the children as: 1) schizophrenic children with minimal ego developments, 2) schizophrenic children with fragmented ego development, 3) pseudodelinquent schizophrenics, 4) pseudopsychosomatic schizophrenics, 5) pseudoneurotic schizophrenia.[302]

Kanner's Early Infantile Autism. Mahler's Symbiotic Psychosis, and other designations for children with onset of disorder before six years Early infantile autism enjoys the most durable status as an entity sui generis of all diagnoses in the spectrum of "childhood schizophrenia," but even with this diagnosis, precise delineation is not everywhere the same. Kanner[295] (1965) and Rimland (1960), the latter in a far-ranging monograph, have reviewed the history of the entity and its diagnosis since Kanner first reported it and both referred to its frequent misapplication. Rimland held Kanner himself partially responsible for this on the grounds that he has emphasized the "aloneness" and "preservation of sameness" aspects of the diagnosis, thereby minimizing other elements initially deemed essential—pronoun reversal, delayed echolalia, intelligent facies, special skills, musical interest, unusual memory, intelligent compulsive parents, freedom from neurogical abnormality.

Eisenberg and Kanner[140] in 1956 and Kanner and Lesser[289] in 1958 did in fact emphasize the extreme isolation and obsessional insistence on sameness observed in 132 cases and wrote that they regarded the language problem as a derivative of the social isolation from people. Both Rimland and Kanner refer to European psychiatry as having adhered more strictly to the original criteria than the American groups. The situation is epitomized by a recent report. Wolff and Chess[590] (1964) carefully studied the behavior of 14 children whom they diagnosed as "Early Infantile Autism." Paradoxically, although they found avoidance of social contact, echolalia and delayed echolalia, and unusual discrimination or skills, they explicitly disagreed with the criteria of sustained resistance to change in the environment and a striving to maintain or restore sameness. In fact their disagreement with this criterion is cited as the basis for the study and the report. Their aim was precisely that of Kanner and Rimland, namely "to establish specific behavioral characteristics of schizophrenic (autistic) children." They referred to general neglect of the phenomenology of the condition and explained this on the basis of the ease with which the diagnosis can be made and the preference for speculation over description. Yet they explicitly disavowed one of the two aspects of the diagnosis that Kanner has persistently emphasized—insistence on preservation of sameness. They did observe stereotyped obsessional behavior in all of the children and believed that this may represent what appears in other children as preservation of sameness but they did not observe the protest at alteration of the environment described by Kanner. Clearly neither Kanner nor Rimland could remain consistent and still concur in the diagnosis of the children in this careful, detailed and informative study of "Early Infantile Autism," despite the many striking similarities in symptomatology. It appears that with "infantile autism" as with "childhood schizophrenia" the question of semantics arises.

In response to this problem of definition, Rutter,[470] while recognizing that the specific constellation delineated by Kanner (and insisted on even more rigorously by Rimland) may well exist, has introduced the less restrictive term, "psychosis with early onset." Few of the articles purportedly on "Kanner's Autism" are as explicit in presenting diagnostic findings as are Wolf and Chess. Therefore conclusions cannot be taken as necessarily supportive of the existence of the entity nor as applying solely to it. Rimland, by calling attention to the prevalence of many of the criteria of infantile autism in combinations less complete than in the original designation, may have contributed as much to the recognition of the importance of the mechanisms underlying the various items of symptomatic behavior as to his primary goal of ultimate crystallization of Kanner's group as a nosological entity. Rimland's etiologic hypothesis will be summarized later.

Polan and Spencer[424] prepared a 30 item check list of symptoms of early infantile autism and Rimland prepared a longer list based on this one. Research usefulness of the tool was demonstrated by Vaillant's[554] application of the Polan and Spencer list to a case reported by Haslam in 1809. On the basis of his review with the check list, Vaillant concluded that the early report was of a case of infantile autism.

Ruttenberg et al.[467] (1966) presented four "core" scales for the evaluation of autistic children: relationship, communication, mastery, and psychosexual development. Each ranged from most severe autistic behavior to normality at the six year old level. Three supplementary scales were also presented.

The extent to which liberties have been taken with Kanner's definition of autism is exemplified in an article by O'Connor and Hermelin.[402] They compared institutionalized psychotic and nonpsychotic imbecile children for social responsiveness to various social stimuli. They concluded that their findings do not support the widely-held view that autistic children are abnormally socially withdrawn and preoccupied with objects. The important studies summarized next, however, adhere very closely to Kanner's criteria.

Rutter[469] equated autism and "child psychosis." His criteria for this diagnosis in 63 children diagnosed by the age of six years are: disorder symptoms present at birth or in first few years; lack of warmth, detachment from people; intellectual retardation with islets of normal intelligence; serious abnormalities of communication, with half never developing useful speech; morbid preoccupation with objects; obsessionality; resistance to environmental change; hyperkinesis and ritualistic mannerisms; overreaction or lack of reaction to sounds; possible aggressiveness to others or self; commonly, eating and sleeping disturbances. Absence of a family history of schizophrenia in these children is another important item identifying this group as similar to Kanner's as is the high educational and intellectual status of the parents. Rutter regarded the manifest retardation as actual, despite islets of normal intelligence, and in this he differs from Kanner who specifies normal or high intellectual potential.

Mahler's articles[355,356] on symbiotic and autistic psychosis are summarized under etiology and psychopathology.

The "children with atypical development" studied at the Putnam Center were reclassified. Those in whom the diagnosis had been made before the age of five were designated "Infantile Psychosis" by Reiser[445] in 1963. These children can now be compared with other children with "psychosis of early onset." The list of descriptive criteria for the diagnosis was eclectic and nonobligatory, and most diagnostic descriptions (see above) are as in the British Working Party list, which it parallels. Reiser added the requirement of a history of severe disturbance in parent-child interaction in the first months of life. The age of onset was given as in the first two years, from infancy on but most commonly in the second year. The follow-up on 125 of these children is summarized later in this chapter. Reiser differentiated infantile psychosis from retardation, chronic brain syndrome, deafness, aphasia, and later-onset psychoses.

Menolascino[371,373] and Eaton and Menolascino[136,137] reported on autism discovered in a group of 616 suspected "retarded" children (1-8 years) referred to the Nebraska Psychiatric Institute. This excellent study will be discussed more fully later under differential diagnosis but at this point their comments on autism are important. They found 34 children (out of the 616) to have "autistic behavior," which Menolascino[373] defined as "behavior which is characterized by extreme self preoccupation, highly personalized and stereotyped approach to inanimate objects, and unrelatedness to people." Of these 34, only two fit the exacting criteria for Early Infantile Autism at the time of the first report.[373] Autistic behavior in the remaining 32 was associated with diagnoses of schizophrenia, encephalopathy with and without psychotic reaction, nonpsychotic stress reactions, and central language disorder. Their conclusion was that "autistic behavior" should be studied as a significant psychiatric phenomenon separate from the syndrome of Early Infantile Autism, that it may form a part of a psychosis, but also that it can exist by itself.

Bender[36] also argued for regarding autism as a phenomenon not synonymous with psychosis. This is not a parallel to her argument that schizophrenia is not equivalent to psychosis. Rather she pointed out that certain aspects of autistic reaction may be a primitive part of normal development. Persistent autism, it follows, would be another instance of maturational lag.

Other conditions in the group of psychoses of early onset are "protophrenia" and "pseudoretardation."

Bourne,[68] in 1955, presented an impressive study of severely retarded young children admitted to a hospital for mental defectives. Signs of neurological damage were thoroughly excluded. The children were matched for age and I.Q. with other children in the institution and statistical comparison of their parents were made. He presented striking evidence that the group he calls "protophrenia" came from families in which both parents exhibited a high degree of psychopathy, including arrests, immoral behavior and gross neglect of the child himself. Because of the lack of any evidence of even primitive personality organization in these children, he avoided the term "psychosis" (presumably because of an implication that psychosis implies regression) and coins "protophrenia." He further labelled them "mental dwarfs secondary to perverted rearing." He found that 10 per cent of admissions with extreme mental defect fit this category. It is a careful study, well worth reading. The author believes the prognosis to be hopeless, but the condition perhaps preventable.

Related to protophrenia in implication, but not in prognosis, is "pseudofeeblemindedness," a condition reported by Benton[49] in 1956. He called attention to children whose performance and behavior is feebleminded but who become socially competent adults of dull to high average intelligence. These all come from the "high grade" defective group. The author stated that "low grades" have an unrelievedly poor prognosis, frequently associated with manifest cerebral pathology. He summarized studies showing that one fourth to one half of the group of high grade defectives become socially adapted and bright or dull normal. He emphasized the necessity of omitting prognosis from diagnosis because of conditions just such as this. He presented an excellent outline of factors contributing to mentally defective behavior. Although potentially reversible, these conditions are not "pseudo" in the sense of being evanescent, as they may last forever. The possibility of psychologic causes was implied.

Psychosis with onset after six years and borderline psychosis   The group of children who become psychotic after the age of six have not been studied with the relatively precise delineation applied to those with earlier onset. Accordingly the discussion on diagnosis applying to "childhood schizophrenia" in general (see page 399) applies to most children with onset in this age period. As the children approach adolescence the clinical picture more closely resembles adult forms of schizophrenia.

There are children, primarily between six and twelve, who become seriously disturbed and may at times be totally withdrawn, and bizarre, but who do not maintain such a severe picture for long periods. Such children have been described by Szurek[540] as "children with psychotic episodes." Rosenfeld et al.,[459] Ekstein (Bellak 1958, ref. no. 167), have described children with variable integration with the environment which they have termed "borderline."

Marcus[363] related together: "borderline" of Geleerd, "benign psychoses" of Mahler, and the "borderline psychoses" of Weil. He described difficult children with tantrums, rages, overactivity, temporary losses of contact, negativism, impulsivity, and narcissism. He reported that these children have many and fluctuating neurotic symptoms. Rosenfeld and Sprince[458,459] also described labile reversibility of ego functions in these children, with anxiety related to feelings of disintegration and annihilation. Ekstein has written extensively about study of and therapy with these children (ref. no. 167 in, Bellak 1958) and also described the marked variability in ego functioning. All of the above agree that there is a well-preserved or relatively correct reality testing. The "brittle-eruptive schizoid" children that Reiser and Brown[444] found at follow-up of atypical children fit the general description as well.

Settlage[498] proposed that these children be categorized as "psychotic characters," a concept proposed for borderline adults by Frosch.[205,206] Frosch emphasized that the "psychotic character" has defects in "relationship to reality" (as evidenced by misperceptions, even hallucinations) and in the "sense of reality" (as evidenced by feelings of depersonalization, oddness, oceanic feelings), but that they retain an intact capacity to test reality including being aware of the unreality of their "reality relationship" and "sense." Cain's report of borderline psychotic children "playing crazy,"[85] to assure themselves that they are not, appears to fit in with Frosch's concept. In the articles referred to above there are many examples further substantiating the validity of this concept. The consensus of these authors is that these children have probably been affected psychologically by the same problems that have contributed to the more severe psychotic states in childhood but to a lesser extent and are therefore able to give imaginative and informative accounts of the nature of the developmental conflicts involved. The pseudoneurotic schizophrenic children of Bender and of Kaufman, referred to above, are descriptively similar to these. "Autistic psychopaths" (see under Etiology, constitutional, below) are sharply distinguished from the borderline, "psychotic character" group because of an apparent total lack of awareness of their malfunctioning, although their total adjustment is far better and nonpsychotic.

The present authors raise the possibility that the severe obsessional, which Despert[124] differentiated with difficulty from schizophrenia, may be regarded as psychotic characters. Her differential is that the psychotic-like thought of the obsessional are recognized by the children themselves as bizarre—and this test parallels that described for the "psychotic character."

Differential Diagnosis

The group of severely withdrawn children with psychosis of early onset (early infantile autism, symbiotic psychosis) are often mistakenly thought to be deaf. Walter,[560] reported that five to ten year old deaf-mute children frequently do present "autistic lack of affective contact" although others have reported a low incidence of this.

Rutter,[472] Eisenson,[145,146] Fowler and Kastein,[194] and others[52,60,148] reported on the differentiation of autism from aphasia. In some instances the initial picture is strikingly similar, but the child's urge to relate and communicate emerges rapidly. A particularly dramatic account was given by Bjorsen and Nylander[60] of a child institutionalized as an autistic (Kanner's criteria) from age four to eight, then taken into speech therapy on the strength of observing the child drawing representationally. Within one year he was back at home and at regular school and his five year follow-up found him normal.

Rutter emphasized (see below under Etiology) the fact that aphasia and autism can coexist. McGinnis et al.[368] also stressed this observation. Interestingly Rosenblut et al.[457] found that schizophrenic children had vestibular responses to caloric stimulation analogous to those of aphasic children. This was a secondary observation growing out of a comparison of deaf and aphasic children. The authors concluded that this suggested an overlap.

The problem of differentiation from children with brain damage or other causes of cerebral dysfunction is exemplifed by Pollack's assertion, referred to above[432] that the entire syndrome of childhood schizophrenia should be renamed "chronic brain syndrome" because of the evidence of cerebral dysfunction. There is unquestionably a large overlap throughout the different forms of psychosis in children with brain damage but the relationship is obscure. Baer,[14] for instance, pointed out that overlapping symptoms frequently occur. Eaton and Menolascino[136] reported the same from their own observations.

Birch[61] summarized the problem:

"In large part our difficulties derive from the fact that a considerable proportion of the children who now come to our attention have rather subtle disturbances of the nervous system. Many of them do not exhibit the gross motor disturbances and alterations of normal reflex patterns that have classically been correlated with damage to the central nervous system. Instead, they present varied pictures of developmental lag, of behavioral disturbance, of transient or persistent motor awkwardness, or minor perceptual disturbance . . ."

The problem of mental retardation and childhood psychosis is similar and very extensive. Both conditions may be created by or simulated by brain damage or other cerebral dysfunction. Furthermore, as many references indicate[364,373,429,470,566,588,593] they can coexist. It appears that the same child may be diagnosed first as one and then the other by successive examiners with differing orientation.[429]

The history of Heller's disease and its inclusion as a form of childhood schizophrenia, then its exclusion as a progressive dementia, is an interesting one. The diagnosis is again receiving increasing attention.[126,218,362,464] In an authoritative and thorough review, with presentation of one new case, Roy[464] marshalled convincing evidence that this is an entity. The description of the disease given by Heller is summarized: 1) begins in the third or fourth year after normal growth and adjustment; 2) starts with change in mood, development of morbid, angry behavior, destructive rage, anxiety; 3) progressive dementia; 4) hyperactivity, animal-like movement, grimaces, odd postures, incontinence; 5) intelligent facial expression remains. (It should be noted that this is a parallel description to that given by Despert in 1938 for childhood schizophrenia with acute onset.) Roy's conclusions were: 1) There is a syndrome of Heller's Infantile Dementia. 2) There are cases exactly fitting the description in which organic findings are a certainty. 3) There are closely related pictures with organic findings. 4) There are children with the clinical picture, with no evidence (even with brain biopsy) of organic pathology. 5) It is not yet certain that all cases are organic. This appears to the present authors to be further evidence of the overlap of clinical pictures from divergent causes.

ETIOLOGY

General Statement

An outstanding problem is one of identifying as clearly as possible all factors that appear to be correlated with the disease state. Here, however, the indefiniteness of diagnosis has hampered etiologic study.

Caplan[90] wrote (1961), "Schizophrenia for instance, however indefinite a diagnosis it may be in adults, is clearly a vague concept indeed as applied to childhood psychoses. In the absence of clearly definable consequent variables it is hardly surprising that our knowledge of specific antecedent etiologic variables is hazy." Furthermore, if one defines "childhood schizophrenia" as a functional disorder without organic precipitants, then one would use organic findings only to "rule out" the diagnosis rather than to add to its explanation. Conversely, if one defines it as organically based, then the clear demonstration of psychological causation would rule out the disorder rather than explain it. In fact, almost precisely this predicament has obtained with the syndrome, Dementia Infantilis of Heller, as was outlined above under Diagnosis and Differential Diagnosis.

In this section, the major contributions of the past decade to furthering etiologic understanding of this group of disorders will be reviewed. Although it should be clear as pointed out by Stroh,[536] that "multi-factorial" etiology is applicable to all of these conditions, this does not relieve the clinician of the responsibility of determining what particular group of factors is acting in the clinical problems here under consideration.

Physical Components

Genetic factors There remains general agreement that children who develop schizophrenia later in childhood have the same familial incidence of schizophrenia as obtains among adult schizophrenics (Rutter[469,470]). The finding of low familial incidence of schizophrenia in children with early infantile autism, first reported by Kanner 1946, has been extended by Rutter to all children with psychosis of early onset.

Kallman and Roth[285] studied genetic factors in "pre-adolescent" schizophrenia and concluded that it was genetically related to adult schizophrenia. However, since they did not separate out children with onset below six from those above, their results do not bear on this question.

The principles of genetic studies in childhood schizophrenia are identical with those for adult schizophrenia and other psychological problems, and the reader is referred to the section on genetics in this book and to Sheilds and Slater,[506] for coverage of the general principles involved and reviews of studies applicable to childhood schizophrenia.

Constitutional factors   Many observers have postulated a constitutional factor as being essential for the unusually severe psychological reactions in childhood schizophrenia; Bender;[34] Fish;[135] particularly in its early form, Mahler;[353] Kanner;[292] Gordon;[247] Van Krevelen;[319] Schopler;[493] Silberman.[512] This is sometimes postulated to be genetically carried, but there has been no sophisticated genetic study of this possibility and the basis for such a constitutional factor remains obscure. The studies and speculations of Rutter, and Menolascino suggest that there may be several such factors.

Rutter's study[469] of 63 autistic ("childhood psychosis") children followed up for nine to sixteen years, has been summarized earlier. He concluded that autism, retardation, and aphasia were all aspects of the clinical picture in "childhood psychosis" but that they were independent phenomena. He saw as evidence for this the fact that various children retained one or two of these dysfunctions while losing the other. The independence of each from the other was suggested, for instance, by the fact that retardation did not abate in those children who lost their autism; the same for aphasia. He postulated that whatever central nervous system component was operative it must involve early injury to or maldevelopment of particularly the central speech areas, although he recognized that the correlation was a loose one.

Menolascino[373] and Eaton and Menolascino[137] found "autistic behavior" as a clearly identifiable syndrome in the absence of the larger syndrome of Early Infantile Autism or even of psychosis. Their study was also cited above, under Diagnosis. Their findings reinforce Rutter's conclusion. Bender's comments on autism[36] as a phenomenon separate from the syndrome of Kanner were also supportive.

What has been identified and called "autistic psychopathy" by Asperger (referred to by Van Krevelen[556]) and "children with circumscribed interest patterns" by Robinson and Vitale (ref. no. 431, in Bellak, 1958) is another complex but circumscribed function of relatedness that was thought by Asperger and Van Krevelen to be hereditary or at least constitutional. It is unlike the old "constitutional psychopathic inferior" which referred to antisocial and self-defeating characters. This syndrome, which comes to light at between eight and eleven years, consists of a curious lack of the capacity for empathy or intuition. Other intellectual and psychological functions are well-preserved and such children grow to be successful adults. They have an associated lack of good spatial orientation, of the kind necessary for ball playing. Apparently "insolent" and "haughty" (Van Krevelen,[556]), in reality they simply do not know how to behave. This lack of social intelligence is similar to that described by Kanner and Weiland for recovered autistics, referred to above, and suggests still another possibility of a discrete constitutional factor that may exist and be a part of "schizophrenia" but can also exist in isolation.

Congenital constitutional factors may not manifest themselves until critical developmental times when the factor becomes central in the developmental process. (Fedor, Horkovic and Kovac[171])

Brazelton[71] has reported the earliest evidence of a constitutional factor. He describes infants who, from just after birth, manifest extreme states shifting between total frenetic and maximally stressful arousal and flaccid unresponsive sleep. This variation persists with gradual modulation. One such child, whose mother was painfully unsure of herself, appeared vulnerable to the development of autism. The mother responded to his remoteness as though it were proof of her inadequacy and tended to withdraw herself.

Alpert et al.[5] presented three extensive case studies exhibiting "unusual variations in drive endowment." One girl showed "hypolibidinal and hypoaggressive drive energies" from birth. She had been reported by the mother as having been "inactive" in utero. Her low activity continued from birth onward with limited responsiveness to mother or to feeding and early and persistent genital masturbation. At age six she had poor relationships, being "distant" and slow to respond, both with peers and adults.

Bergman and Escalona's descriptions of "children with unusual sensitivities" (ref. no. 58, Bellak) (1945) also suggested constitutional factors.

Hutts et al.[274,275] studied the electroencephalograms of ten young (three to four years) autistic children who had no evidence of cerebral dysfunction as it is usually diagnosed by E.E.G. (no spikes, no slow-waves, no asymmetry, etc.). Their observations on resting and telemetered E.E.G.'s suggested to them that at least some of these children had overactive reticular activating systems and were in a state of maximal arousal. The authors suggested that stereotypy, maintenance of sameness, and apparent inattention to stimuli all may be designed to prevent overloading in an already highly active reticular system and that when these defenses fail, a "catastrophic reaction" follows. These neurophysiological findings and interpretations very closely parallel Mahler's postulation. She speculated[355] that enteroproprioceptive over-stimulation due to illness or adverse maternal symbiotic milieu may generate great amounts of unneutralized drive energy with a resulting physiologic up-heaval. This process, she thought, might contribute to the development of autism.

MacMillan[352] critically reviewed Mahler's explanation of symbiotic psychosis. He proposed and explained a Pavlovian theory as a better alternate. The proposed mechanism involves reinforcement of a passive defensive reflex in the child by "continuous reinforcement" coming from "the mother's continued anxiety and dependence." The author stated that the initial appearance of the pathogenic reflex in the child could also follow from the mother's anxiety and dependence and could be innate. In its general outline it appears to the present authors that MacMillan's alternate is not materially different from Mahler's explanation.

Wortis and Choi,[594] using conditioning tests in children, found that active inhibitory phenomena were more readily induced in schizophrenic children than in neurotic and normal children.

Deajuriaguerra et al.[120] believed that an early and massive lack of interest in the environment from as yet unknown causes is a constitutional factor leading to language disorders in psychotic children.

Moloney,[389] has written a poetic, far-ranging psychoanalytic and cultural synthesis of concepts pertaining to the vital significance of the earliest mother-infant relationship. He stressed the indispensable nature of exercise and stimulation of the whole of the child's skin as part of the precognitive relatedness between a mature mother and her child. He said that mothers of schizophrenic children either fail to stimulate the whole of the child's skin or smother the child with too much attention. The constitutional factor here introduced is not specific to schizophrenic children but rather is postulated to be universal, that is, the need for stimulation of the whole skin. Shevrin and Toussieng,[505] in a most significant article, elaborated on the "need for tactile stimulation" which they saw, as does Moloney, as fundamental. They postulated a refinement of psychoanalytic drive instinct theory for the first three months of life and succeeded in bringing the concepts of psychoanalytic psychology and neurophysiology into close proximity.

Pertinent aspects of their article will be summarized. Certain deficits (food depletion, for instance) unlike other deficits (iron-deficiency, for instance) in the neonate give rise to *stimuli* which tend toward activity that may relieve the deficit. Such stimuli they call *cravings* and they exist without symbolic psychic representation because they predate the capacity for mental representation. If excessive they will disrupt the organizing function of the infant's nervous system (primitive ego). The mechanism of threshold-raising exists to guard against this. (This would be another way of talking about the "stimulus-barrier" postulated by Freud). The authors explain that thresholds function on an all-or-none principle. Once passed, the craving results in motor discharge. If an excessive amount of craving has accumulated before the threshold is passed, the flood of resultant motor discharge is threatening and a higher threshold is generated. The thresholds are nonspecific because the cravings are nonspecific (though from specific deficits). The effect of threshold raising to guard against one type of excessive craving is therefore a generalized stimulus avoidance. The damming effect results in a spiral increase in the problem.

Tactile stimulation deficit was suggested as of prime significance in the first three months. The authors postulated that this may result from a constitutional factor, from inadequate stimulation, or from excessive stimulation. They suggested that this may be the mechanism operating in autism and symbiotic psychosis. Goldstein's postulate[245] of a single defect with two alternate results dependent essentially on whether the mother overstimulates (symbiosis) or understimulates (autism) the affected child fits in with this theoretical formulation.

The writings cited above, especially those of Rutter,[469,471] Menolascino,[371,373] Eaton,[136,137] Mahler,[353,355,356] Goldstein,[245] Hutt and Hutt et al.,[274,275] Moloney,[389] and Shevrin and Toussieng,[505] represent a major contribution. The work has in many instances been concurrent and independent but the themes emerging are promising.

Other neurophysiological, metabolic, or organic factors The incidence of cerebral dysfunction concommitant with psychotic syndromes in children has been widely studied. Studies of "soft neurologic signs" have been reviewed under Diagnosis, above. Other inferences of cerebral dysfunction are drawn from: 1) histories of birth difficulties; 2) abnormal electroencephalograms; 3) metabolic abnormalities; and 4) gross neurological signs.

Pollack's views on the overriding etiologic significance of cerebral dysfunction in most children diagnosed as being schizophrenic have been stated above. In another study,[433] he reviewed five investigations on incidence of pre and perinatal complications in childhood schizophrenia or childhood psychosis. He pointed out the variability in criteria for psychiatric diagnosis and also the variable inclusion or exclusion of gross neurological disorders. He observed that these studies differ in whether or not information is obtained all, part, or none from parents' reports. Nonetheless he recounted a great agreement as to the significantly higher number of pregnancy complications in childhood psychosis, compared with controls. He also found that the reports indicated severe illness and/or prolonged feeding difficulty in early infancy as significantly greater in psychotics.

Rimland's monograph on Infantile Autism[450] provided more than a thorough marshalling of evidence supporting the specificity of the syndrome of Early Infantile Autism as originally described by Kanner. He argued persuasively against psychogenic causes, cites evidence for congenital causes. He went on, admittedly in free speculation, to postulate oxygen damage to the reticular activating system (analogous to oxygen damage to the retrolental tissue in retrolental fibroplasia) as a specific neuropathological cause of the condition. He further elaborated on this idea as to the role of the reticular activating system as central in the integration of memory into behavioral adaptation. In this light he interpreted the difficulty in and peculiarities of learning characteristic of such children as defects in integration of remembered events. He has been criticized by some (Connell[108]) for using a "procrustean" approach to the literature, selecting items of wide variance in scientific merit in order to support his far-ranging theses. However, his book has proved stimulating and was one of the earliest to focus on the reticular activating system in connection with infantile autism. He has directly influenced some writers, such as

Glavin.[219] Glavin repeated Rimland's suggestion that oxygen damage to the reticular area causes autism and also added that the occipital association areas may be similarly affected. Other studies and speculative articles, independent of Rimland, have implicated the reticular activating system, including Hutt and Hutt et al. cited just above. In the Hutts' work it appeared that the reticular activating system was overactive, resulting in "hyperalertness", while Rimland's suggestions implied a malfunctioning consisting of underactivity, with inadequate function for normal attention and recall.

Electroencephalographic abnormalities have often appeared later in life in autistic children initially considered free of neurologic abnormality. Rutter's study, already cited, indicates that the longer the follow-up, the higher the incidence of such abnormalities. (This does not preclude the possibility that the E.E.G. abnormalities result from the psychotic condition.) Bray[70] reported that of twenty children with temporal lobe foci from varying causes, six children were psychotic. Sarvis[481,482] and Garcia and Sarvis[215] emphasized the importance of perceptual distortion, similar to Bergman and Escalona's "children with unusual sensitivity," as contributing to the development of psychosis. They have found temporal lobe foci, cortical or subcortical thalamic foci in such children. In 100 autistic children, they found unequivocal evidence of such foci in 15 per cent and equivocal findings in an additional 5-10 per cent. Their theories integrate these findings with relationship factors as well. Bender discussed the interrelationship of convulsive states and schizophrenia.[38]

Schain and Yannet[486] found 42 per cent of fifty autistic mental defective children had a history of seizures and 22 per cent had a current convulsive disorder. They suggested the limbic system as the likely locus of the disorder.

The possibility of an as yet undiscovered metabolic deficiency is raised by Yaker and Goldberg's study[596] comparing children with phenylketonuria with organic and schizophrenic children, using a 46-item behavioral check list. They found that the P.K.U. children exhibited symptoms intermediate between the organic and the schizophrenic children, showing properties of both. They propose that the P.K.U. children may represent a "missing link" and suggested further studies.

Psychogenic Factors

Psychogenic causation, primary Bettelheim,[56,57] Boatman and Szurek,[65] Kaufman,[299,302] Eisenberg,[140] Goldfarb,[232,233] Meyers,[378] Moloney,[389] Williams,[584] Alanen,[3] Berlin,[54] Clerk,[99] Dunkel,[133] Pavenstedt,[412] Reiser,[446] Ross,[461] Lordi,[340] Winnicott,[587] Brody,[76] have all written with conviction, from moderate to almost absolute, about the psychogenic causation of childhood schizophrenia, in whole or in part, with early, middle, or late onset. Goldfarb,[233] and Eaton and Menolascino[136] have found differences between the families of "schizophenic" children of the "organic type" and those who were in the "psychogenic type." They reported the families of the "organic schizophrenics" of Goldfarb and the "chronic brain syndrome with psychosis" of Eaton and Menolascino, to be less psychiatrically disturbed and less pathogenic than the families of "nonorganic schizophrenic" children (Goldfarb,[233]) and schizophrenic and autistic children (Eaton and Menolascino[136]). In an early report on his cases, Menolascino found the most disturbed families among the (two) autistic children, with the disturbance reportedly having existed prior to the child's birth and therefore not reactive to anything in the child's behavior. However, in a five-year follow-up study reported (with Eaton[137]) one of these two autistic children had developed gross evidence of neurological disorder. The small number of cases in this instance does not allow firm conclusions but the example illustrates how tentatively one must view such assertions.

Although some authors are quite specific in their ascription of pathology to the parents and especially to their relationship with the child who becomes schizophrenic (Kaufman,[297,302] Bettelheim,[56,57] Goldfarb,[233] Reiser[446]), others, equally convinced of the psychogenic causation of the psychosis, find that they cannot determine any specific and unique etiologic factor in these families (Boatman and Szurek[65]).

In an illuminating article on necessary and sufficient conditions in psychiatric explanation, Wender[574] referred to several studies on incidence of psychopathology in parents of psychotic children. He explained clearly how the findings are limited as explanations without postulating a special sensitivity in the patient. He gave tuberculosis as an analogy (and subjected it to the same statistical analysis), in which instance the precisely *necessary* causative agent is known but is clearly not sufficient in itself to cause the disease. (In childhood schizophrenia the agent of parental pathology is not *always necessary*.) In the kind of data reported in all of the studies demonstrating psychogenic contribution to psychosis in children (or adults), there were rarely (and in the articles covered in this chapter there are none) parental findings that are invariably present in every instance of the disease, in this instance "childhood schizophrenia." This means that in addition to not being *sufficient* factors (they are present in some of parents of normal children) they are not universally *necessary* factors. Wender went on, however, to make it clear that these facts in no way detract from the importance of determining as many of these factors, "improbably due to chance," as one can, even though it cannot be said that they have an "appreciable" significance as necessary and sufficient explanations. Their importance lies in the fact that any one of these factors may be modified and, depending on its importance in that individual case, may therefore be a most significant area for treatment efforts. With this perspective in mind and with the absence of any study reported that overrides these considerations, the factors indicated by various authors will be briefly summarized with minimal individual commentary.

Mahler's strict clinical thoroughness took these factors into account from the first, and in all of her writings which have had such a profound influence on the psychoanalytic understanding of early development and psychosis she has postulated a constitutional vulnerability as necessary to the development of the severe psychotic states she has studied. Her additions to her theories are taken up later under Psychopathology.

Winnicott[587] reported the effect of a mother's period of depression causing her to drop off to sleep while holding her 14-16 month old son, which appeared to initiate a pseudoretarded psychotic development in the child. After the boy had "reconstructed" a frightening memory of the event indirectly through drawings in one interview at age six, Winnicott comfirmed the history from the mother.

Szurek,[540] and Boatman and Szurek[65] stressed the interplay of parental conflicts and onset or exacerbation of the child's psychosis. At times they have found evidence that the child appeared to incorporate the parental conflicts and his reaction to them. Reiser[446] stated that he no longer thinks of "maternal hostility and rejection of the child" but rather of a prolonged, subclinical, postpartum depression rendering the mother unable to provide "adequate mothering." Like Szurek,[540] Pavenstedt[412] found parallels between psychodynamics of mother and child sufficient to apply a concept of *folie-à-deux*. Kaufman et al.[299] classified parents, as well as their schizophrenic children, as pseudoneurotic, pseudopsychosomatic, pseudodelinquent, and overtly psychotic. By implication, he and his co-workers found severe contributory psychopathology in all parents of the children they have studied. The child's illness was viewed by Kaufman as being essential to the parents' emotional life. Dunkel[133] studied the homes of 34 schizophrenic children and found them materially adequate but so empty that the children are regarded as having been "homeless."

Bettelheim[57] drew a parallel between schizophrenic children and adults in concentration camps. He wrote that these children seem convinced "that they are threatened by total destruction all of the time and that no personal relations offered any relief. Thus the psychologic cause of childhood schizophrenia is the child's subjective feeling of living permanently in an extreme situation . . . of being totally helpless in the face of threats to his very life, at the mercy of insensitive powers which are motivated only by their own imcomprehensible whims, and of being deprived of any interpersonal, need-satisfying relationship." He provided convincing examples of noxious emotional treatment by parents of children who become schizophrenic.

The theories of parental pathogenicity can be divided roughly into two groups: in one the psychotic illness in the child is specifically necessary to the parent's psychic balance or arises from a malevolent (conscious or unconscious) reaction to the child; in the other the psychosis in the child arises from parental pathology which is not specifically directed at the child but which prevents the mother (or mothering person) from reacting properly to the child and providing the stimulation or responsiveness necessary to maturation. Bettelheim and Kaufman stressed the former situation while most other authors who emphasized the psychogenic role of the parents implied the second. A dramatic example of specific need for a child's pathology by family members was reported by Elles.[157]

MacAndrew and Geerstsma[348] summarized concepts of experienced psychiatrists, revealed by Q-sort data, on how mothers could help induce childhood schizophrenia: 1) *hostile rejecting mother*—excessive guilt, general insecurity leading to pervasive emotional isolation; 2) *unbending mother*—whose rigid superego controls and lack of flexibility reflect a neurotic strength of character; and 3) *fearful, inadequate-mother*—with excessive guilt and insecurity handled by flight into anonymity, conventionality, near-total suppression of self expression.

Lennard et al.[329] found fewer interactions between family members in families with a schizophrenic child. Perr[416] using a check list of attitudes towards self and others and items from the MMPI and TAT in comparing parents of normals and schizophrenic children found the parents of schizophrenics tended to misperceive their impact on others, provided conflicting identification for their children, saw the world and others as hostile, were more rigid and inflexible and self-deceptive.

Osterkamp and Sands[406] obtained data from hospital records and mothers of schizophrenic and neurotic children about breast feeding and birth difficulties. Children who had both birth difficulties and a short period of breast feeding tended to fall in the schizophrenic group while those who experienced neither problem tended to fall in the neurotic group. They interpreted the data, which included reference to negative feelings in the mothers, as supportive of a psychogenic etiology, Pasamanick[410] reviewed Osterkamp's and Sand's work and reinterpreted the findings as indicative of the probability of organic brain syndrome, with maternal feelings resulting from the child's illness rather than causing it.

The finding by Terris et al.[545] that childhood schizophrenia was not associated with prematurity but was definitely associated with a history of previous fetal loss can be interpreted as evidence of special psychologic significance attached to the child that survives.

Rice et al.[448] measured the impact on five judges of taped interviews with mothers of psychotic children and ten with mothers of nonpsychotic but disturbed children. The mothers of psychotics were consistently rated as "less likeable," "more pathogenic," and "less treatable." A second panel studied the reactions of the first panel and found a significantly greater incidence of reactions suggesting unclear and confused images of child and child-mother relationship in the psychotic group as compared with the control group. The authors concluded that there is confused communication between the mother and the child in childhood psychosis and also between these mothers and therapists.

Singer and Wynne[520] compared parents of autistic children, neurotic children and schizophrenics who became ill in late adolescence or later, using TAT and Rorschach test performances. They concluded that disorders of relationship, particularly a marked "disaffiliative" tendency, are especially pertinent in differentiation of families of both autistic and schizophrenic children from families of neurotic children.

Psychogenic causation related to other factors, (interactive, mixed) Mahler has elaborated on her views of the etiology of childhood psychosis in several articles in this decade. In one[355] she postulates the genesis of early infantile autism as involving either enteroproprioceptive overstimulation due to illness or adverse maternal symbiotic milieu, generating great amounts of unneutralized drive energy. She reasoned that the resulting physiologic upheaval may lead to inadequate function of the sensorium and impairment of self-discrimination. In another article[353] she ascribed to overwhelming maternal invasiveness, the same overstimulating effect on the child who develops symbiotic psychosis.

Weiland[570] has emphasized the vital importance of a critical phase of early development. Referring to the viewpoints of Mahler, Bender, Rank and Despert and Sherwin and citing Harlow's[257] work with monkeys, he reasoned that parental behavior or other factors that interfere with the proper formation of attachment behavior in the first year of life will distort all subsequent development of ego functions. He distinguished[569] two groups of autistic children: 1) those who have suffered traumatic experiences during the period when object relationships are learned and 2) those who fail to experience those operations essential in forming object relatedness. Weil[568] similarly wrote of "inappropriate timing" of ego-distorting experiences in deviational children.

Garcia and Sarvis[215] also considered age 6-18 months as an age when children are vulnerable to development of infantile autism if exposed to a variety of possible psychological or physical factors. Accordingly they regarded autism as a syndrome, not a disease. Escalona, in a classic study of early mother-infant interaction[159] documented different innate qualities of responsiveness among normal infants and also the effects of different mothering qualities and the various interactions. She wrote: "contradictory finding about the genesis of infantile psychosis are reconcilable in this manner. Children who suffer from this illness have in common the lack or distortion of a mutual relationship with a mother person . . . (which) may arise from maternal deficiency but may stem from intrinsic lack." Thus, "autistic psychosis . . . is caused by the absence of those vital experiences in early childhood which we regard as the necessary condition for ego synthesis."

Stroh and Buick[537] also referred to differences among infants in basic sensory capacities and hypothesized that failure of an orderly hierarchical development of perception may lead to psychotic conditions.

Bender's theory[32] is also a mixed psychogenic and constitutional theory although the psychogenicity is not stressed as much as the maturational lag. However the postulated psychologic reaction of terror at the postulated perception of inner dysequilibrium is central to her explanation of the secondary defenses which produce the overt picture of psychosis.

Goldfarb's many articles on parents and their role in the genesis of schizophrenia in children, also presented a view of the parent's involvement as partly reactive to the child and not solely pathogenic. His designation for their problem is "parental perplexity"[378] and his schema of etiology has as its center the interrelationship of a disoriented child and a perplexed parent. He postulated that the problem can therefore originate in the child or in the parent with the resultant pathogenic interaction being roughly the same. His discovery of a significantly lower incidence of incompetence in parents of "organic" schizophrenics than in parents of "nonorganic" schizophrenics has already been mentioned.

In his most interesting article referred to under Diagnosis, Goldstein[245] regarded the mother's handling of a child with a special defect as central to the differential development of autism or symbiosis. He postulated that the mother who allowed the child to withdraw contributes to the development of early infantile autism from the pathologic matrix in the child while the mother who was protective of the child caused the emergence of the symbiotic picture.

The following section will summarize a rather extensive literature[13,111,135,313,317,345,421,438,490,532] criticizing or purporting to refute hypotheses or allegations of parental pathogenicity in childhood psychosis. The positions taken are primarily of two types. First, the parents of psychotic children are not found to be significantly different from parents of other groups of children, including normal, (or, specific reported findings are not confirmed). Second, parental differences are found but accounted for as entirely reactive to the difficulty of rearing a psychotic child.

Rabkin[438] reviewed various concepts and studies in this area and concluded that the trait studies were inconsistent, inadequately controlled and lacked predictive power. He also criticized methodology in family studies. He focussed on the idea that the child's perception of parental attitudes might be a significant variable and reported his own research findings. "Schizophrenic" children were found to see mother as more dominant and punitive and father as more passive and less competent than normals. He did not specify how to distinguish cause from effect.

Creak and Ini,[111] Pittfield and Oppenheim,[421] and Klebanoff,[313] studied families by retrospective interviews, or attitude scales and did not find confirmation for theories of parental pathogenesis. Creak and Ini could find no distinguishing characteristics among the parents. Pittfield and Oppenheim found the mothers of psychotic children were more lax and indulgent than mothers of normal children. Klebanoff found fewer pathological attitudes among the schizophrenic children's mothers studied than among mothers of mentally retarded or brain-damaged children.

Arnstein[13] reporting on his experience with parents of children at the League School in Brooklyn, stated that the parents more often seem affected by rather than causing the problem. Lovatt[345] made the same observation about parents of schizophrenic children attending a nursery school. Easton[135] presented the case of a two-year-old autisic girl who was the product of parents described as warm, stable, concerned and loving and who had an older, healthy child. The author perceived this case as a point of evidence for considering autism as largely due to innate constitutional factors rather than to a cold and rejecting environment.

Ferreira and Winter[174] studied family decision-making and found that families with a schizophrenic child tended to arrive at inappropriate solutions by wasteful means. However they found no evidence to single out a particular member or two-member coalition as a source and no support for a hypothesis of symbiotic mother-child relationship in schizophrenia-producing families.

Stabenau et al.,[532] by psychological tests and clinical observations, studied families with a schizophrenic child, families with a delinquent child, and families with a well-adjusted child. Each family had, in addition, a control child in it. They found no significant differences.

Sanua[479] discussed inconsistencies and large gaps in findings of studies in this area and recommended more consistent methodology of investigation.

PSYCHOPATHOLOGY, PATHOPHYSIOLOGY, NEUROLOGY BIOCHEMISTRY, MECHANISMS

Just as considerations of possible causes of psychotic manifestations in children have covered a tremendously broad range, so must this section dealing with the mechanisms which may be operating within them. Some have already been discussed in the section on Etiology.

Psychological Studies

One source of information is the psychological studies reported in this decade. Beck[23] compared ratings derived from Rorschach analysis to those of psychiatrists using clinical data. The different values from this were compared and the virtue of collaborative research was stressed.

Cobrink[100] further elaborated upon Rorschach responses of schizophrenic children. Engel[158] described characteristic Rorschach patterns of borderline psychotic children, commenting also upon the intense emotional reaction these children evoke in the examiner. Meyer and Caruth[377] showed how Rorschach responses can demonstrate defects in "outer" as well as "inner" reality testing.

Davids[118] and Viitamaki[558] reported on psychological testing of schizophrenic children and their mothers, with a lack of correlation between these two (as the schizophrenic children had lower I.Q.'s than nonpsychotic, emotionally disturbed children, while the mothers of schizophrenics had higher I.Q.'s than did the general public)[118], and Kissel[311] reported that patterns and signs previously suggested by Wechsler and Jaros were not consistently present.[567]

Pollack[430,432] stressed the frequent presence of low intellectual functioning as characteristically present in children diagnosed as schizophrenic and that the frequently noted "islets of intelligence" were of no functional significance.

Birch and Walker[62] felt that modes of dealing with visual-perceptual and perceptual-motor tasks could differentiate between schizophrenic children and those with chronic brain syndrome.

Two relatively recent tests were reported by Fuller[208] and Tien[548] to reflect the frequent presence of perceptual deviation in schizophrenic children. However, Safrin[474] reported no significant differences in visual-perceptual and visual-motor functioning as between psychotic and nonpsychotic children when appropriate controls were established for differences in mental age functioning.

Berkowitz[53] demonstrated inferiority in motor and memory tests in psychotic versus nonpsychotic children, while visual perception results were variable.

Conceptual thinking in schizophrenic children was analyzed by Friedman[203] confirming previous statements of concrete forms of thinking and difficulties with abstraction. Halpern[256] pointed out that the use of standardized Piaget tasks may discriminate retardation in cognitive development and a conceptual lacuna which traditional intelligence scales do not reveal.

Making use of such scales, however, Wassing[564] was able to establish profiles in infantile autism suggesting (contrary to previous quotations) that they could perform superiorly on a purely perceptual basis, but could not reach a level of language development in which words can be used as symbols.

Finally, Ottinger et al.[407] were able to demonstrate some degree of visual discrimination learning in schizophrenic (autistic) children, warranting further study.

Ethology

A new theme has appeared, with the introduction of ethologic concepts, Hutt and Ounsted[276] have likened the aversion of gaze of autistic children to a signalling function such as the "appeasement postures" in animals which inhibit aggression on the part of others.

Physical Components

Reference should be made to the discussion under Etiology, of two speculative contributions, by Glavin[219] and Rimland[450] suggesting abnormal functioning of the reticular activating system as an important component of autistic and schizophrenic symptoms. In the same section, the description of the paper by Shevrin and Toussieng[505] offered significant hypotheses as to neurophysiological dysfunction in autistic children.

This thesis of deviations in sensory reception, stimulation, patterns and preferences appears in a number of other contributions. Schopler[493,494] pointed out that in normal infants, the near receptors of touch and taste are first dominant, but that the autistic infant fails to develop the normal shift to dominance of distant receptors of sight, smell and hearing. He too feels that this may result from deficiencies of the reticular activating system—but also from lack of effective, affective mothering.

Goldfarb[224,227,228,229] also describe preference of contact over distance receptors, exclusion of auditory stimuli in the form of speech, while pure tone thresholds were not impaired and also diminution of pain perception. Stroh and Buick[537] reaffirmed these points and their role in development of the psychotic process and picture.

O'Connor and Hermelin[401] found relatively little difference in responses to sound and to light stimuli (when kept at the same intensity) between autistic and subnormal controls, but felt the autistic children overall showed an inability to inhibit dominant patterns.

Freedman et al.[200] found that schizophrenic children only established a response set to light stimuli, while normal children did to both light and sound stimuli and that this discrepancy was reduced by treatment with hydroxyzine.

Nichtern,[399] elaborating upon the concepts of Bender, postulated global disturbances of central nervous and almost all other body systems as present and significant in childhood schizophrenia.

A more restricted view was offered by Fedor and Horkovic-Kovac[171] as to how aberrations in specific developmental phases produce psychotic processes. Rothman[462] postulated defects in the vestibular system and Schain[486] in the limbic system.

More specific descriptions were offered by Shapiro[500] of deviant hand morphology in childhood schizophrenia, and Colbert and Koegler[104] of persistent toe walking. Rachman and Berger[439] confirmed the presence of "whirling" and impaired postural control in schizophrenic children, while Pollack and Krieger[428] found altered postural and oculomotor patterns in half of the schizophrenic children they studied. Colbert et al.[105] found that a majority of the child schizophrenics they studied had depressed and unusually variable vestibular responses to caloric and rotational tests while optokinetic tests showed no differences!

Pollack and Goldfarb[427] failed to find any significant difference in orientation for time, place and person in a group of schizophrenic as compared with other emotionally disturbed children.

There has been a continuing interest in E.E.G. phenomena, (see also p. 403 under Etiology). Hutt et al.[274,275] reported either "flat" desynchronized E.E.G.'s, or higher frequencies than usual. Kennard[309] found that there were "organic signs" in 13 out of 18 children showing "thought disturbances," White et al.[578,579] found significant E.E.G. abnormalities in approximately 50 per cent of psychotic children and 19 per cent had seizures. An even higher proportion of other than normal E.E.G.'s was reported by Goldman and Rosenberg.[244]

Studies of sleep and dreaming by means of the E.E.G. were reported by Onheiber et al.[404] and Ortiz et al.[405] to show no significant differences as between psychotic children and normal controls.

Rubin[465,466] on the basis of pupillary studies concluded that autistic children demonstrated peripheral autonomic dysfunction with lower levels of adrenergic and cholinergic activity than normal.

As to physical growth, in the same issue of the same journal, Dutton[134] found that in schizophrenic children, the mean for the group fell within the normal range for height, weight and bone age, while Simon and Gillies[517] reported that, of a group of schizophrenic children, on the average, subjects were subnormal in height, weight and bone age!

Finally, using Pavlovian theory and techniques, Wortis and Choi[504] found that schizophrenic children have difficulty in developing and maintaining conditioning, engage in repetitive stereotyped reactions and have difficulty with interaction of signal systems.

There have been relatively few contributions on metabolism. At the beginning of the decade there had been much emphasis on the role of copper and ceruloplasmin in adults, with only dubious support as to children,[77] but a succession of reports[12,17,18] showed this to be without significance.

Gottlieb, Frohman, and his co-workers[204] had found a specific effect of adult schizophrenic serum on the lactate/pyruvate ration (L/P) in chicken erythrocytes. Not only did they not find this so in childhood schizophrenia, but it was also not found in adult schizophrenics who *had* been child schizophrenics!

Amines have attracted more attention. Heeley and Roberts[259] reported abnormalities in metabolism of a tryptophan load which, they felt, may be connected with the endogenous production of niacin. It may be significant that this was only true for children whose deviant behavior was noted from very early in life. However, Shaw et al.[502] reported no significant abnormalities in metabolism of a tryptophan load in schizophrenic children or in their amino acid excretion pattern.[503] Schain and Freedman's observations[487] on 5-hydroxyindole metabolism, with and without tryptophan loading suggested a possible correlation of any metabolic abnormality with some degree of central nervous system involvement. That such metabolic abnormality is not necessarily associated with autistic behavior was shown by Sutton and Read.[538] The question as to whether abnormal amine metabolism is a cause or a result of childhood psychosis was raised by Perry.[418]

A series of reports by Sankar and co-workers[475,476,477,478] emphasized the significance of plasma and erythrocyte inorganic phosphate levels and the uptake of serotonin by blood platelets. Values of these were different as between autistic and nonautistic schizophrenic children, with the former qualitatively similar to retardates! Another report on the sera of child schizophrenics was that by Syner and Shaw[539] which showed no interference in synthesis of glutamine and gamma-aminobutyric acid.

Lastly, Simon and Tarnoky[519] felt that results of insulin tolerance tests suggested psychotic children to be physiologically immature.

Speech and Language

Turning to the area of speech and language in schizophrenic children, most contributions[99,229] dealing with interactions of child and mother have stressed the psychological and emotional status of mother as being the primary mode of interference with a child's developing speech functions. To this, Goldfarb et al.[243] added the presence of actual speech impairment in the mother, thus adding a poor model for identification to a diminished ability to set up mutual communication.

Specifics of peculiarities of speech development and patterns and means of studying them were set forth.[117,120,152,225,436,437,571,597] Utilizing some of these techniques, Pronovost et al.[437] reported a longitudinal study of the speech of fourteen children, felt to be of normal intelligence, but psychotic (though the diagnostic criteria are not entirely clear).

Wolff and Chess[591] offered an interesting analysis of the language of fourteen children meeting most of the diagnostic criteria of early infantile autism. While language development generally was retarded, the ratio of original, nonrepetitive speech was more highly correlated with clinical status than was ratio of communicative to noncommunicative speech. The unusual use of metaphor and symbolic language in those least ill was felt due to repetitive clinging to former modes of expression with inability to modify in accordance with present reality.

Rutter[470] reported on the outcome of various aspects of speech disorder in an article previously quoted. Whittam et al.[581] using the criteria of Creak for diagnoses of psychotic children and comparing them with their siblings, reported that two thirds of the psychotic children showed marked, severe and persisting speech delay and then went on to normal development.

Ekstein[152] adapted the theories of Böhler concerning speech to the acquisition of speech in the autistic child. The autistic child, like the normal infant, displays only expressions of unintentional signals, whereas, with interaction with the mother, the normal infant goes on to develop intentional signals. As self consciousness of meaning develops, the normal, unlike the autistic, goes on to the phase of symbols.

Psychodynamics and Psychopathology

The next section deals with psychodynamics and psychopathology, often intermingled. Mahler et al.[356] in a wide-ranging article previously cited under Etiology, presented a review not only of psychoanalytic theories (so enriched by Mahler), but of many other major contributions as well, differing little from the accounts given in the previous edition of this book.

Shevrin and Toussieng's ingenious and thorough discussion,[505] which was described in detail also in the section on Etiology, discussed how originally constitutionally determined reactions to deficits or excesses of physical stimuli eventually become endowed with symbolic psychic significance.

Beres et al.[51] described disturbance of identity function in childhood. In a massive article[50] he used numerous case descriptions to support a detailed description and discussion of retardations and/or regressions creating ego deviations in the seven areas of ego function, with great variability in these areas.

A number of authors dealt with modes of origin and ego-disruptive effects of anxiety in psychotic children. Brody[76] offered the hypothesis that repetitions and agitated self-rocking may represent autoplastic efforts to reestablish body contact with mother in infants whose object cathexis of her is intense and who have experienced relatively great kinesthetic stimulation. Despert[124] stressed that anxiety in the schizophrenic child arises from the pregenital period. Goldfarb[234] felt such anxiety can arise from a defective self awareness and lack of consistent response to sensory stimuli, as well as to "parental perplexity."

Kaufman and co-workers, who have contributed so much to understanding of childhood psychosis, in a series of articles[297,301,302] indicated that fear of annihilation is the core anxiety of schizophrenic children and that their parents, as well as they, have inadequate ego development. Kaufman's further thoughts have been summarized above.

Weiland[572] explored both the literature and case material in characterizing symbiosis as a defense against primitive or excess anxiety in failures of perceptual discrimination or ability to generalize. The child fixates on clinging to the familiar mother and lacks the capacity to relate adequately to others. In another article[570] he has listed many sources for the conclusion that proper formation of attachment behavior is necessary for subsequent development of ego functions.

Esman et al.[163] regarded a severe degree of ego disorganization as characteristic of "childhood psychosis," with the basic problem being a complete loss of object contact which they equated with Erickson's "lack of basic trust."

In this decade, as in the last, the contributions of Mahler, alone and with others, continued to impress with their richness and variety. With Elkisch[354] and by Elkisch alone[155] an ego defect in the mechanism of repression was used to explain the ability to recall minute detail and Piaget's theories were also involved. In one article[353] she referred to a constitutional ego defect in the child, combining with overprotection by the mother to precipitate feelings of severe engulfment and separation anxiety. These result in restitutive autistic withdrawal. In another[355] she reviewed and elaborated on old themes, with an intricate and well reasoned account of how constitutional maldevelopment within the infant and/or inadequate mothering may interact through physical-psychologic reverberation and embodiments to constitute both early infantile autism and symbiotic psychoses, both representing fixations at or regressions to the first two developmental stages of undifferentiation within the child-mother unity. Auto-aggressive activities were seen as restitutive attempts at sharpening awareness of body-self boundaries. The symbiotic psychotic, faced with demand of development and sexuality, may respond by delusions or fantasy of oneness with the omnipotent mother, lessening of object-cathexis, alienation from own body and fragmentation of body image. Secondary recathexis leads to body delusions and hallucination as restitutive devices.

With Elkisch[156] she suggested that separation panic in the normal course of development may not be adequately handled by partial identification with the mother, resulting in total introjection of mother. A narcissistic focus on the interior of the child's own body then results in delibidinization of his ego boundaries and mechanization of the introject and of his inner functions.

She returned[358] to the theme of possible contributions from either mother or child. There may be repeated separations, overwhelming proprioceptive stimulation and painful illness, multiple traumata, maternally induced pathological closeness, grossly unpredictable alternations of overstimulation, seduction and abandonment—or there may be an essential defect within the child.

Her latest article[359] stressed the knowledge to be gained from studying of psychotic children for details of normal and pathological child-parent interaction and development of autonomous ego functions out of undifferentiated ego/id, stressing that this requires a "satisfactory symbiotic phase."

Goldfarb, whose contributions are as numerous and important, described[231] time-space orientation and defensive and restitutive adjustments. Lustman[347] depicted responses of infants to stimuli, postulated that a normal capacity to inattend when maximally stimulated may abnormally persist in autistics.

Knight[315] suggested that a failure in establishment of oral primacy caused a type of perceptual functioning which, in autism, results in a shift of cognitive development from exteroceptive to interoceptive ego organization.

Sarvis[480,481] has again called attention to how a variety of organic, inner personal and interpersonal factors, and especially perceptual distortions may result in a basic paranoid position. Autistic defenses may then develop.

Wexler[577] focussed on object relationships, stating that in infantile autism there is a developmental failure with difficulty in the establishment of internal representations, while in schizophrenia they are first established and then abandoned. A grand old man of neuropsychiatry, Kurt Goldstein,[245] on the other hand, viewed autism and symbiosis as both being results of innate defects in development and maturation. Autism is seen if the child is allowed to withdraw and symbiosis if he is overprotected.

Szurek[540] described the deficiency of executive ego in psychotic children as directly related to repression of earlier libidinal impulses, superego being savage and defective, id impulses raw, intense and violent, the whole conglomeration resulting in psychic paralysis.

A new version of an old theme emerged in the article of Pollack.[425] He discussed the biological utility of various forms of partnership arrangements in different species and in the stage of postnatal symbiosis in humans. Both child and mother fulfill each other's needs and trigger innate mechanisms in a manner suggesting the mutual "releasers" of the ethologists. Deviation on either side and resulting disruption engender a depressive constellation within the child as the nuclear conflict.

Van Krevelen and Kuipers[556] also reviewed the psychopathology of the autistic child, while Anthony[11] offered an experimental approach to the psychopathology of childhood, presenting a five-point continuum ranging from nonpsychotic to psychotic.

Benjamin[46] devised a research aspect, by presenting a protocol for prediction of psychopathology in children on the basis of prenatal assessment of the family. MacMillan[351] presented a social and historical perspective.

Smolen,[522] in an article so rich and extensive that it can scarcely be summarized but must be consulted, offered a remarkable review and conceptual framework, including the psychopathology of childhood psychosis.

There are several narrower areas of special interest. One deals with hallucinatory phenomena. Eisenberg[144] discussed hallucinations in children, differentiates them from "phantasy and pretend play" and described hallucinations in a psychotic child like those of an adult except for their simplicity, lack of systematization and obvious reference to current life situations. Furer et al.[209] found hallucination of introjected objects to be twice as common in schizophrenic children as in adolescents, representing primitive restitutional mechanisms to deal with anxiety stemming from overwhelming impulses, with few defenses. Weiner,[573] too, viewed hallucinations as an adaptive mechanism. The schizophrenic child deals with feeling states he cannot accept or apprehend by translating or misperceiving them as concrete external happenings, to which he can then react. Wilking and Paoli[583] described differences in hallucinations in psychotic and nonpsychotic states. Those of the schizophrenic children were characterized by incoherent, fragmented form and autistic, bizarre content. There might be peculiar complaints about viscera and persecutory objects, while in auditory hallucinations, there were apt to be reflections of grandiose or paranoid delusions.

Wolfensberger[588] suggested concerning schizophrenia in mental retardates, that low capacity for symbol formation makes it difficult for them to flee into phantasy and that, for them, delusions may be due to forced attempts to give meaning to events. Considering Weiner's view above,[573] this may offer a clue as to similarity of phenomena in retardates and psychotics.

Niederland[400] discussed narcissistic ego impairment in patients with physical malformations.

Greenacre[250] reported on a propensity for focal symbiotic relation to objects, displaced from the original symbiotic tie, a tendency previously suggested by Mahler.

Sachs[473] described a five year old boy who developed catatonic features after a tonsillectomy, seeming to "act dead" (equated to being a "machine") to prevent murderous retaliatory acts directed to others (especially mother) and to self.

Another special area has been "borderline" children. Brask[69] offered a description while Engle[158] delineated their unstable ego organization. Lewis[334] gave an absorbing account of the psychic structure of a highly sensitive borderline child whose analysis revealed fear of oral destruction by mother herself. Gordon[247] reported a single case of a borderline child who, having a defective stimulus barrier, failed to develop ego organization, differentiation and integration. There was impaired ability to introject a love object to serve as a model and enable inhibition of instinctual tendencies and protection from stimuli.

Cain[85] felt that in "playing crazy," borderline children test psychotic states, reassure themselves that they are not psychotic and are enabled to reach out to people in ways the child can tolerate.

Frosch[205,206] described the "psychotic character" in adults in ways which Settlage[498] suggested as applicable to the borderline child. There are defects in relationship to reality and in sense of reality, but reality-testing is mostly intact and regressions are transient and reversible, often with conscious effort.

Geleerd[216] reviewed the views of others and her own work with patients who fall under this classification. She felt they are hypersensitive to real or fancied loss of love and unable to relinquish omnipotent fantasies for more adequate reality testing. The love objects may be seen as malign and the ego feels helpless, which, to her, is pathognomonic of the borderline state.

Rosenfeld and Sprince[458,459] stressed the lability and reversability of ego functions in borderline children, who at the same time have a greater capacity for object relationships than do schizophrenics. These children are basically "pre-Oedipal." Bisexual conflict, though present, is not central and Oedipal material has an "as-if" quality. Ego apparatus displays a faulty capacity to select and inhibit stimuli. Higher functioning is possible, but unstable. Anxiety, relating to feelings of disintegration and annihilation, is overwhelming rather than alerting. Object cathexis, as suggested by Anna Freud, is precarious and easily converted into identifications. With all this, relatively correct reality-testing is maintained.

TREATMENT AND MANAGEMENT

General

Just as concepts of etiology in these multitudinous conditions subsumed under the headings of schizophrenia, childhood psychosis, etc. cover a very wide range, so do the treatment modalities explored and advised. With each decade, too, some major approaches come into prominence, and others wane. The last edition pointed to the increased interest in psychotherapy which has continued unabated. The use of such physical methods as insulin and electroshock has diminished markedly. Medications continued to be explored, but with interest in specific indications for specific phenomenologic subtypes or symptom pictures. A trend of increasing prominence was that of family therapy. The literature concerning this has dealt chiefly with adolescent or adult schizophrenics, but this is being applied more and more to children and their families, and it is anticipated that much more can be said about this in the next edition.

A relatively new theme was that of behavior therapy, reflecting the increasing concern of clinical psychologists, both with theory and practice in this area. Overall, the literature on treatment suggested a greater consideration for experimental design and precise analysis of the results of treatment. There was less of a tendency for sweeping claims and global statements. There seems also to have been more of a differentiation between short term, symptomatic results and long term cure. With this, there was an appreciation for the worth of symptomatic improvement, even though absolute cure cannot be attained.

In accord with consideration of multiple etiologic factors, many of the contributions dealt with multiple therapeutic approaches. Eisenberg[142] and Chapman[96] advocated this, but offered relatively gloomy outlooks as to the efficacy of treatment, particularly for the severely impaired. A number of other articles described pluralistic approaches with more optimism.[7,15,16,30,32,37,215,273,489,514,525]

A particularly vivid account was that of La Vietes et al.[324] recounting seven years of experience with combined psychiatric, psychologic casework, and special educational services on a day basis. They stressed that the total therapeutic prescription must be known to all staff, which must respond to emergencies with a concentration of any and all useful measures—psychological and medical for the child, and help for the parent. They were quite flexible as to which staff member relates to the child—who often, in some way, makes the choice himself. A concluding comment was that while 76 per cent improve in some way, the I.Q. often does not and the basic schizophrenic process seems unchanged.

Psychotherapy

As for psychotherapy, Mahler et al.[356] in a textbook section summarized the role and goals of psychotherapy as: enhancing body-image integrity; enhancing relationships and creating or restoring missing or distorted ego functions—themes which, in one way or another, appear in many of the contributions to follow. Escalona[160] based treatment approaches on the belief that what has been done, can be undone. However, she characterized the two major modes of therapy as "expressive" (uncovering) and "suppressive." She pointed out that the dramatic improvements associated with "expressive" therapy were usually not maintained. On the other hand, "suppressive" therapy tended to leave the underlying psychotic process intact, with the most favorable outcome, a "pseudo-adjustment." This, again, poses the dichotomy between "cure" and "relief" earlier alluded to, with long term and follow-up studies more and more suggesting that the latter is what is generally accomplished.

Other broad reviews of psychotherapy were presented by Berliner,[55] Bruch,[82] Gianascol,[217] and Kanner.[294]

The group of Szurek and his co-workers at the Langley Porter Clinic have continued to relate therapeutic experiences supporting their views that psychosis in childhood, having an entirely psychogenic causation, is to be treated successfully only through psychotherapy of child, of parents, and of family groups.[54,65,540,541]

A number of papers deal with work with the mother-child unit. Call[86,87] reported two such cases, with favorable outcome. Gordon[248] described simultaneous treatment as allowing alteration of the disturbed child-mother relationship, then making possible the institution of individual therapy. Kawabata[303] was able through simultaneous work with mother and autistic child, to allow transition from schizophrenic to neurotic symptoms, but with still a lingering underlying residue of isolation.

This observation was supported by Weiland[569] whose findings suggested that, regardless of psychotherapeutic techniques (which he reviewed), results rarely went beyond a pseudo-object-type of relationship.

Several papers have dealt with countertransference aspects of treatment of psychotic children. Ekstein, alone and with co-workers[91,152,153] pointed out how the therapist may be limited in using interpretation in dealing with such situations, after long periods of having to assume distorted roles assigned him by the child, the therapist may be overwhelmed by lethargy when having to function as an extension or echo of the patient. He pointed out how such children may evoke "rescue fantasies" in the child therapist who may have residual feelings of hostility and rebelliousness toward parental, authority figures. One of these articles[150] showed in a clear and sensitive way how such countertransference feelings played a large role in accepting a psychotic child into treatment and then in its termination. Christ[97] recounted how unawareness of his own countertransference reactions hampered therapy with a psychotic girl. Rice and Klein[447] echoed this theme and stressed the importance of feelings aroused in the therapist as a means of understanding the child's behavior. Prall and Dealy[435] supported some of Ekstein's comments with their own experiences, as to how rescue fantasies and expectations for rapid improvement may disrupt the course of treatment.

Kemph et al.[306] offered an intriguing observation, that using multiple long term therapists diminishes the likelihood of hampering countertransference reactions.

Details of therapeutic technic were presented by Bettelheim,[59] Caruth and Ekstein,[92] Ekstein and Wallerstein,[148] Ekstein and Caruth,[153] summarized in Ekstein,[154] Ford,[193] Furer,[210] Furman,[211] Hafilena,[255] Kemph et al.,[307] Morrow,[393] Pavenstedt[412] and Shugart.[508] Stewart and Sardo[535] discussed the special aspects of treating a blind schizophrenic child. King[310] illustrated a focus in therapy upon defensive aspects of a child's play communications, rather than its content. Miller[384] viewed the child's silence as an adaptational mechanism, suggesting that the therapist accept this and not try to press the child into speech. Perl and Goldberg[415] illustrated the progress of therapy by a child's successive drawings. Livermore[336] presented most interestingly, a schizophrenic child's view of her own treatment.

Morgan[390] made use of the technic introduced by Sechehaye, "symbolic realization" as a means of removing hallucinations. Spotnitz et al.,[531] feeling that schizophrenic children need help in building a protective barrier, used "mirroring" as a technic for so doing. The Kleinian technic of interpretation of what are deemed to be the earliest traumata was illustrated by Sousz[526] and Tustin.[552] Hirsch[267] attempted a balance between autistic and symbiotic positions of the psychotic child and helped him to test reality.

In a series of articles, Kaufman, who has contributed so much to this field, along with his co-workers,[297,302] offered means of dealing with what he feels is the "core problem," that of anxiety relating to fear of annihilation, always associated with psychopathology in the parents. He presented means of dealing with this, modified according to the classifications he has developed. In another article,[300] he recounted those factors which seem associated with success and with failure of therapy.

Maslow[365] had a variant to offer, relating symptomatic improvement after a brief period of intensive therapy by an untrained student receiving one hour of supervision weekly!

Garcia and Sarvis[215] presented a view of the therapist's role which is contrary to that recommended by many. They felt the therapist should remain a representative of reality, not encouraging regression, or participating in the child's magical or delusional world. He should avoid reinforcing the child's "basic paranoid attitude" by assuming familial psychopathology to be the major etiologic factor.

Goldfarb[239,240] suggested it is inappropriate to offer psychoanalytic interpretations of what he feels is the essentially preconflictual, "preneurotic" schizophrenic problem. He observed that therapists tend to see "significant improvement" on the basis of increasing understanding of the patient, but without objective evidence.

Hirsch[268] related a poignant account of long term, extensive and intensive treatment of a schizophrenic child (about whom much had been written in the literature) without accomplishing any fundamental change. He questioned the utility of continuing such unsuccessful modes of treatment, but wondered how else to proceed. Less use of the spoken word? Some more concrete modality? But what?

A possible answer was offered by DesLauriers.[123] He felt that schizophrenia represents an inability to establish contact with reality, rather than a withdrawal from or conflict with it. Thus, he advocated forceful intrusion and bodily contact by the therapist, clarifying the patient's feelings and experiences as his own, establishing boundaries, limits, orientation in time and space and suppression of delusional or autistic behavior. Eickhoff[139] emphasized bodily contact between therapist and patient, as also did Schopler.[492] White[580] viewed such techniques as valuable in helping to develop a feeling and experience of "efficacy."

A number of contributions were addressed to the problems of the borderline patient. Rosenfeld and Sprince[459] indicated that the therapist, while seeking causes for sudden panic, must provide missing ego supports, at times quite actively and concretely. The therapist must carefully gauge interpretations and frustrations, while encouraging displacement of direct primitive expressions. The therapist has to withstand the hurt of being ignored and avoided and, later, anger over being placed in the parent role. Physical contact is hard to handle, being at the same time, both needed and a threat to the patient.

Cain[85] discussed the many possible significances and uses of "playing crazy" by borderline children. Ekstein and Wallerstein[148] recommended gearing interpretations to the level tolerable to the child at the moment, or "interpretation within the regression" until secondary process reasoning is well established. While staying within the symbolic metaphors produced by the patient in the regressed phase, contact is maintained.

Details of treatment were given by Knowlton[316] and Shore et al.[507] The latter wrote a most interesting account of phases of transition from external, imposed controls, through phases of mastery alternating between therapist and patient, to a flexible internalization of controls displaying and requiring adequate integration of all aspects of ego functioning. Winnicott,[587] reported on the remarkable effects of a single consultation in a child who might be regarded as borderline or psychotic.

Frostig and Horne,[207] Loomis and Meyer[338,376] presented modes of evaluation of therapy and therapeutic approaches.

III. Physical Methods

Physical modalities of treatment have also been vigorously explored and in wide variety. Considerations of evaluation of effects of treatment were given by Fish[188] emphasizing the need to differentiate what is due to treatment from what is due to maturation and to natural evolution of the disease process. Fish and Shapiro[190] offered a typology, utilizing severity and patterns of integrative defect to provide a classification, baseline, prognosis, and means of measuring the effects of medication upon children's behavior. Tesarova[546] also presented a rating scale for evaluating pharmacotherapy of childhood schizophrenia.

An exhaustive and widely ranging survey of clinical experiences with medication in children and indications for combinations with other therapeutic approaches was presented by Corboz.[109]

Fish[182] reported the effects of tranquilizers, an antihistamine and amphetamine on children with psychosis, organic brain disorders and primary behavior disorders. She observed that medications were the only regime which helped the schizophrenic children.

Michaux and Flavigny[381] wrote an encyclopedic article on schizophrenia in childhood reporting pessimistically on the effects of insulin coma, electroconvulsive therapy, tranquilizers and, for good measure, psychotherapy also!

Boatman and Berlin[66] believed their observations suggested that psychological factors contribute both to apparent success and apparent failure of medication.

One article only, by Rees[443] reported atropine as useful in two cases. Several articles[167,172,272,408] described chlorpromazine as helpful in childhood schizophrenia. These ranged from general statements as to symptomatic usefulness, to specific recommendations in agitated, hyperactive cases—or the contrary, in severely withdrawn children.

In pursuit of his theory on the role of the reticular activating system, Rimland[450] referred to the use of deanol (2 dimethylaminoethanoethanol), an acetylocholine precursor.

At the beginning of the decade, Beaujard[22] reflected current French opinion that electroconvulsive therapy and insulin coma could be symptomatically helpful in childhood schizophrenia, while Hift et al.[264] later decried its use. Mechlow[369] after describing favorable results with ambulatory insulin, speculated that it artificially created a situation like that of the infant, dependent upon outside sources for survival and gratification with a resulting primary transference upon the therapist. The child described, however, seemed to have achieved prior to treatment, a degree of ego development greater than and different from most children classified as psychotic.

Glutavite[330] was found not useful, but there were two reports on the utility of haloperidol,[258,271] one being in a single case of Maladies des tics in an autistic child.

The use of LSD in psychotic children received some attention. Theories as to mode of action were given by Abramson,[2] while Sankar et al.[475,477,478] related this to its effect upon phosphate metabolism.

Simmons et al.[516] did a careful study on a pair of identical, retarded, autistic twins, suggesting an increase in social behavior and contact with humans and decrease in nonadaptive behavior. However, less retarded children showed responses suggesting social withdrawal and disorganization. Freedman et al.[201] reported somewhat similar experiences—increased body awareness but also suggestion of hallucinations, panic, etc., which they felt discouraging.

The favorable reports of Bender et al.[39,42] as to effects of both LSD and UML as to the symptom picture in autistic and nonautistic psychotic children were noted by Rolo et al.[454] to be based upon largely clinical, descriptive comments. Therefore an elaborate method was devised and presented to make possible a more systematic pattern of judging. In a single reference, Marsilid[197] was described as symptomatically useful and meprobamate[442] as not. Faretra and Gozun,[168] however, suggested a combination of meprobamate and promazine as being symptomatically useful.

Ferster and DeMyer[178] described improved experimental performance of an autistic boy with the use of prochlorperazine. Two observations on reserpine[326,382] reported decrease in tension, anxiety and uncontrolled behavior, but no basic improvement in the psychotic process. Thioridazine was felt to be helpful in a similar way[167,483] especially for agitated, hyperactive schizophrenic children.

In contrast, Eveloff[164] found trifluoperazine to be more useful for withdrawn and autistic children. Fish et al.[186] used the scales previously described as means of matching treatment and control children and evaluating treatment response to trifluoperazine (4-20 mg. day in children aged 2-6 years) and also response to nonpharmacologic treatment. With medication, the originally most impaired children improved, while the others did not, or became worse. With nonpharmacologic treatment, those originally least impaired in language improved the most. Silberstein et al.[513] felt that trifluoperazine up to 4-5 mg. t.i.d. brought about enough symptomatic improvement (possibly due to suppression of anxiety) to enable eight psychotic children to keep from being hospitalized.

A single report[504] listed symptomatic improvement in two psychotic children after the use of triiodothyronine, while exchange transfusion[198] was of no utility whatever.

Behavior Therapy

A newer modality which received increasing attention was that of "behavior-therapy" in its various forms. Breger[72,73] criticized some of its underlying assumptions and in particular, the work reported by Lovaas et al.[341] on the use of painful electric shocks in alleviating self-destructive behavior. In another article Lovaas et al.[343] gave a very detailed report of a program to enhance acquisition of imitative speech in two psychotic children, based upon rewarding desired behavior and punishing autistic distraction. Here, the reinforcement was largely of positive physical contact with the therapist and the work was intensive, six days per week, seven hours per day, but the results described as remarkably successful. In another study, Lovaas et al.[342] investigated and manipulated the variables controlling the self-destructive behavior of a schizophrenic child, feeling that specific environmental control was more useful than attempts at control from alternating internal states.

Metz[375] reported on conditioning generalized imitation, Davison[119] on social conditioning and Wetzel[576] on behavior therapy in outpatient treatment.

Hewett[263] described an operant conditioning speech training program which was said to have established a basic speaking vocabulary in a four and a half year old, nonverbal, autistic boy, with conditioned speech later showing characteristics of meaningful language.

Hingtgen[265] used methods of operant conditioning to shape cooperative behavior in schizophrenic children and felt modifications of this could be useful in schizophrenic ward behavior.

Ferster and DeMyer have been most active in this field. They[178] reported operant conditioning methods of analysis of behavior which can lead to treatment methods to alter these. In one article[122] they showed how child care workers can use social reinforcement methods—involving much, but controlled interpersonal interaction, while in another[175] they described the use of an automatically controlled, nonhuman environment for developing performance. Yet Ferster[177] did report that a child exhibited aversive behavior when exposed to this inanimate environment, which could be countered by the use of human reinforcement! Finally, Ferster[179] offered ways to use behavior theory in understanding the development of the autistic child and his behavior.

Speech and Language

There have been some contributions on speech and language therapy. Rutter[470] who thinks aphasia and autism are separate states, even though they resemble each other, but may be mixed in the same child, believed that successful treatment of the aphasia may improve the psychotic aspect. McGinnis et al.[368] gave the specifics of a method for teaching of aphasics. Scanlon et al.[484] had a preliminary report dealing with autistic children functioning on a retarded level. They felt that intensive individual speech therapy resulted in noteworthy changes in communication, behavior and interpersonal relationships.

Educational Therapy

One consistent theme has spanned the last decade, and this has been emphasis on the great importance and utility of educational approaches in the treatment of psychotic children. Abbate et al.[1] recommended: for symbiotic children, emphasizing testing and accepting of reality; with autistic children, the establishment of a primary love object. Involvement of mother was necessary.

Alpert[6] described "Corrective Object Relations" (COR) as used by a special teacher serving as a "need-satisfying object," applicable to schizoid and borderline, but not autistic children. She also[7] described a nursery school program for an autistic child.

Lovatt[344] reported an interesting variant in which psychotic children, by means of an individual, one to one, relationship with a nursery-teacher-therapist were gradually introduced into and became part of a normal nursery school group.

Arnstein[13] and Fenichel et al.[172] described the principles and practice of the League School of Brooklyn which attempts to: a) relieve the child's fears, anxiety and confusion; b) help him get along with others; c) teach him skills and increase his confidence. This begins individually, "where the child is," followed by bringing into the group, structuring an academic program, setting kind but firm limits, reassurance that he will not be allowed to hurt or be hurt by others. Further education and widening experiences may lead to ego-building successes.

Specifics of teaching approaches, often stressing perceptual aspects and self awareness were presented in a number of other articles.[84,98,102,284,387,449,468]

La Vietes et al.,[323] describing the school aspect of their multiple treatment approach, provided much valuable discussion as to problems, questions, and potentials in the role of the teacher. Wolfenstein[589] differentiated roles and gave guidelines for teacher versus therapist.

Mahler and Furer[357] offered a warning in relating a case in which a symbiotic, psychotic child became disturbed in a school setting but functioned better with individual tutoring.

Eisenberg and Kanner[140] reiterated that a tolerant and helpful school and teacher seem to be the most helpful agents for Early Infantile Autism.

Nichtern[397,398] described the favorable results obtained by the "Teacher-Mom" program, using untrained mother-volunteers on a two to one basis in a public school system.

Toomey and Allen[551] reported the Vineland Social Maturity Scale as valuable for evaluating the progress of psychotic children in a nursery school and Berlin[54] emphasized the vital role of educational technics in the treatment of schizophrenic children.

Work with Families

The long term concern over the role of the parents in childhood psychosis was reflected by articles on family therapy and on direct work with the parents. Bruch[82] refered to this. Brown[81] described in detail therapy of two families, one with a two year old autistic and the other with a three year old atypical child. He recounted the many sets giving rise to resistance to change and the great utility of family therapy. Both individual and small group dynamics are pertinent and the "set" of the therapist is distinct from that in individual therapy. The child's psychotic state, whatever its etiology, functions as a vehicle for resistance to any change in a complementary, neurotic, marital interaction.

Elles[157] found that a three year old boy's muteness was important to the entire family organization, with improvement in the boy upsetting the family structure and capable of being tolerated only as the rest of the family was involved in treatment.

Colbert[106] reported on a relatively unsuccessful project of group psychotherapy of mothers of hospitalized schizophrenic children, suggesting that diminished parental motivation, because the child was no longer in the home, contributed to this. In contrast, Gordon's report[248] of simultaneous treatment of mother and child was much more encouraging.

There were a number of contributions[129,317,367,387,499,510] which emphasized the need for help for the parents. In some because their emotional disturbance was secondary to that of the child, rather than causative. In others because of the belief that parental ego defects might have helped to create the child's problem and/or limit their capacity to deal with it.

Regardless of these specifics, most authors point out, and the present authors concur, that the parent needs respectful, delicate, and flexible support and intensive help rather than assault and condemnation, overt or concealed, on the part of the professional.

One of the major aspects of the last edition, with a section all its own, was that of residential treatment. Interest in this has continued, buttressed by consideration of both hospital and day hospital aspects.

Day hospitals were discussed by Freedman,[199] who pointed out their differential values versus outpatient clinics and full hospitalization. These include: avoidance of institutionalization of the child; of the family excluding the child from family life; of the family being overburdened if he is home all day; of problems in public school placement.

Goldfarb et al.[242] suggested that there is no preference between day and residential treatment for the "organic" child, while residential treatment is better for the "nonorganic" child, who may profit from separation from the pathogenic family.

As for hospital treatment, Falstein[166] described the contribution of nursing and Kemph[306] gave the details of a hospital program and how it may diminish countertransference reactions. He also[308] discussed the virtues of brief hospitalization for evaluative purposes. Peet[414] listed the use of "remotivation" techniques in a hospital program. Ward[563] described a relatively brief hospital program, which seemed to have been more useful diagnostically and symptomatically than effecting any basic change.

Bettelheim[57] and Brown[78] emphasized the need for and virtue of removing the child from the pathogenic parent-home environment and providing him with a total treatment environment.

Ekstein et al.,[150] pointed out how countertransference aspects can disrupt successful treatment in a residential setting.

Goldfarb et al.[231] described how the child's difficulty with orientation in time and space required the institution to prepare routines to counteract this. Maier and Campbell[361] echoed this thought. Goldfarb and Pollack[237] discussed the integration of schooling in such a program. Goldfarb and Radin[238] pointed out the actuality of group formation in schizophrenia and the need and means of using this in treatment, rather than opposing it. Levy[332] emphasized the need of structuring activities and helping the child to recognize and respond to "the end" of an act or activity.

Hafilena,[255] May and May,[366] and Morrow[393] gave treatment details, and Robinson[452] presented a broad overview of residential treatment.

Group Therapy, Outpatient Treatment

Treatment outside the hospital was something that is more readily contemplated in the literature of this decade than of the past.

In part, this has been contributed to by the development of work with schizophrenic children in groups—something which would once have been looked upon as an inherently contradictory statement!

Smolen and Lifton[335,523] for instance, felt that group therapy was the key factor in the unusual degree of success encountered in outpatient treatment of childhood psychotics. Their basic plan was to establish contact with the children at whatever level possible, building from there, pushing the child toward facing reality and encouraging the parents to do likewise, rather than fostering or accepting regression.

Scheidlinger[488] wrote on a prepsychotic group of severely deprived, latency-age children, with promising results. The group was structured, provided a "benign family setting," with the therapist being direct and protective. In this setting, the boys were able to reenact early conflicts and accept parental figures.

Speers and Lansing,[528,529] acting upon a suggestion of E. J. Anthony, undertook group psychotherapy with young psychotic children, accompanied by collateral group therapy with their parents. The results with the children were most promising. The mothers, generally, responded more favorably than the fathers.

Jensen et al.[282] reported on a "total push" program for schizophrenic children in the community utilizing a variety of modalities.

Klapman[312] described work in the community around children who had been treated at and discharged from a children's psychiatric hospital.

Seidman[497] presented a detailed account of outpatient treatment of a four year old girl, using the modality of once-weekly interviews.

There have been two articles noted, dealing with treatment of the children at home. One, by Schulman,[495] argued that residential treatment is unnecessary and keeping the child at home preferable with work directed at support for and guidance of parents. Egan and Robison[138] reviewed and contrasted the advantages and disadvantages of the actual locus of treatment being in the home, rather than office, clinic or hospital.

Kaplan and Turitz[296] reported significant success in the use of a foster home program for five childhood schizophrenics. This involved subsidized foster homes, most for multiple children, only one for just one child, combined with continuing psychotherapy and use of community services and facilities.

Innovations

A final section, on different modes of treatment, is appropriately introduced by the report of Langdell[321] on recent observations in Great Britain. At High Wick children were left completely alone until they expressed a desire for companionship which was immediately gratified. This was felt responsive to the schizophrenic child's need to escape from people, sounds, and sights. With this the children seemed to seek more attention and to be less anxious.

At Smith Hospital (see also[403]) the use of mentally retarded girls as mother figures seemed beneficial to both sides. When this was no longer possible, children's mothers were substituted, which resulted in many difficulties but overall seemed rewarding.

Dundas[132] reported on use of volunteers as "substitute mothers" in a day hospital program, providing cuddling, bottle feeding and helping child to regress to and to receive satisfactions appropriate to developmental level at which initial psychological trauma was deemed to have occurred.

Rappaport[441] attempted to reproduce one of the characteristic concomitants of the earliest period of development by the use of Salk's "heart beat machine," with a group of autistic girls. This use was said to be associated with a decrease in restlessness and screaming and change in physiological measures.

Dreikurs[130] and Farmer[169] described favorable symptomatic effects and an increase in learning associated with the use of music therapy. Miles[383] and Rousos[463] gave details of two different occupational therapy programs for schizophrenic children.

Finally, Robertson[451] reported on an intriguing technique used with autistic and retarded children who went (individually) with the therapist into a dark room in which there were shadows cast by the subject and shadows of the environment and shadows, controlled by the therapist which were cast by silhouettes. This method seemed to allow much greater fluidity and freedom of response than in standard play therapy and allowed the therapist some control over levels of reality and unreality.

FOLLOW-UP AND PROGNOSIS

Follow-up of "Childhood Schizophrenia" with Varying Degrees of Specificity of Diagnosis at Outset

Early in this decade Eisenberg[142] reviewed the world literature on childhood schizophrenia and summarized the follow-up studies. He specified the lack of comparability of criteria. He found that a similar outlook was forecast by most, namely a 20 to 30 per cent chance of social recovery.

Kane[287] and Ward[562] and others have also pointed to characteristic limitations and errors in follow-up studies. Difficulties specified include: inadequate diagnostic criteria; lack of relationship of follow-up criteria to diagnostic criteria, inconsistency of and limited validity of reports on improvement from parents; and the complex problem of quantifying improvement. The use of profiles of ego functioning or "ego quotients" and of typologies such as Fish's, both referred to earlier, may help with this in future follow-up studies.

In 1966 Bennet and Klein[47] gave a follow-up report on the original childhood schizophrenic cases reported in the American Literature. Six cases had been reported by Potter in 1933[434] in an article previously quoted, and an additional eight were added in 1937 when the first follow-up on the original six was published. In 1937, one-third of the fourteen showed early evidence of organicity but in the follow-up in 1966 this issue was not clarified. Adult criteria for schizophrenia had been applied in making the original diagnosis and as Bennett and Klein point out the diagnostic category has broadened since then to include less severely impaired children. Still it is most unlikely that these fourteen would be excluded from the category by more recent standards.

Of the fourteen, two were not found, two were dead. One had committed suicide by hanging at the age of 29 in 1950. His diagnosis prior to death had been dementia praecox, paranoid type. One had died of a coronary occlusion at the age of 31 in 1962. His diagnosis had been mental deficiency, undifferentiated. Only one of the remaining ten was maintaining himself outside of a hospital. He was an isolated, awkward, emotionally flat dishwasher. Nine were in a state hospital and seven of these were "regressed and deteriorated," with diagnoses of dementia praecox, catatonic, or hebephrenic type. Two were in institutions for the mentally defective and were uncommunicative.

Follow-up studies of 100 "pre-adolescent schizophrenics" who had been treated at the Langley-Porter Clinic were reported by Boatman and Szurek[65] in 1960. Twenty (20 per cent) had shown major improvements and were living independent lives although three of these had had relapses. Thirty-four more had improved but still required special supervision. Forty-six had not improved. Of twenty-one children who had been seen for diagnosis and had not been treated, only three were found to have improved. But this would make a spontaneous improvement rate of almost 15 per cent!

Creak reported one hundred cases of "childhood psychosis" in 1963.[115] Two of these had died and were found at autopsy to have cerebral lipoidosis, clinically unsuspected. Twelve of the one hundred had epilepsy as well as psychosis. Of the one hundred cases seventeen were attending ordinary schools, forty were living at home or attending special schools, and the remaining forty-three were "permanently" institutionalized at the time of follow-up.

Weiland[570] wrote of the persistence of social inappropriateness in schizophrenic children as they grow up, even when they are able to make productive adjustments to school and work. Bashina[20] followed up one hundred and forty-eight patients admitted to a hospital with "schizophrenia" in childhood or adolescence. Of the eight who were children at the time of admission five were incapable of working 10-14 years later. Annell[9] followed-up one hundred and fifteen children who had presented "a psychotic syndrome" before the age of ten years. Study showed sixteen subjects were completely healthy at the age of fifteen to twenty-three years. Forty-three had schizophrenia, five were organically demented, one had manic-depressive psychosis, and the others showed various forms of mental disturbances of a non-psychotic nature.

Eaton and Menolascino[137] reported a five-year follow up on patients described in articles refered to above (under Diagnosis and Etiology). Five of six childhood schizophrenics were followed. One remained in a symbiotic relationship with a disturbed mother who had withdrawn the child from treatment. A second, with multi-factored therapy improved in I.Q., speech, and awareness of environment but deviant affect remained. Three others were worse, functioning on a severely retarded level. Twenty-two children with "chronic brain syndrome with psychosis" (which they viewed as phenomenologically the same as childhood schizophrenia but due to reactions to an organic process) were followed up. Seven showed no improvement or were worse, two improved in speech alone. Of nineteen in this group with severe initial speech impairment, most were speaking better. Mildly retarded and low normal children remained the same but those who tested moderately retarded were severely retarded on follow-up. Five with "scattered test findings suggestive of higher potential" initially, were all severely retarded eventually.

Articles by Bender and her associates on follow-up of schizophrenic children as originally diagnosed by Bender, published during this decade were elaborations on findings extensively reported before. Freedman and Bender in 1957[196] cited a previous study in which they had reported that 87 per cent of 143 childhood schizophrenics were later diagnosed as adolescent or adult schizophrenics. In this and two other articles[32,35] Bender described the process by which some schizophrenic children tend to reorganize their defenses during puberty with a tendency to shift toward antisocial behavioral characteristics and psychopathic defenses when exposed to the greater demands of later adolescent life and early adulthood. In 1963[40] she presented the life histories of two schizophrenic patients first seen when they were in their late twenties. Both exhibited a lag in maturation and plasticity in all areas of functioning.

Fish's important article has been extensively summarized earlier in this chapter. It represented more the prediction of overt schizophrenia than the follow-up of childhood schizophrenics in adolescence (100-1961). Three groups of adolescents (12 to 17) were compared, those who had been childhood schizophrenics, those in whom schizophrenia had developed during adolescence and a third group with behavior problems. Abnormalities such as twirling, distortion of body image, and poverty of thought were frequent among the former childhood schizophrenics. The adolescent schizophrenics showed fewer of these and the adolescents with behavior problems showed none.

Follow-up Studies on Children with Early Infantile Autism, and Other Psychoses with Onset Before Six Years.

Eisenberg and Kanner[140] and Eisenberg[141,142] reported the follow-up in adolescence or adult life of sixty-three cases of early infantile autism. Fifty per cent of those who had had speech before the age of five years made adequate social scholastic adaptation while only 5 per cent of children with no speech by five years made even a limited social adjustment. Most "recovered" autistics in this series showed persistence of social unawareness even in their late teens. This was also reported by Weiland (see above). It is of interest that both Weiland and Kanner[295] reported an almost identical story of such a youngster at a college pep rally on the eve of a big football game advising his classmates to expect defeat (which was realistic) and being unable to understand the response he received.

Bruch[82] reported seeing a twenty-one year old boy, thirteen years after she had first treated him. He had been one of Kanner's early cases. At twenty-one he was quite child-like, had a phenomenal memory, was still dependent on and living with his family. She reported her feeling that he was "odd" and that the follow-up made her more inclined to an "organic" view of his problem than her earlier psychogenic, bias. Jackson[280] reported a follow-up on two symbiotic and one autistic child. One symbiotic child became essentially normal while the other, though improved, required a protective environment. The autistic child displayed hebephrenic mannerisms and was inaccessible to ordinary human intercourse.

Varley[557] reported a follow-up of sixty autistic children in England who showed an increasing frequency of seizures as the children grew older. He preferred the term "psychosis" to "autistic."

Rutter, in the significant article already referred to (Etiology—Diagnosis)[469] and another[470] followed sixty-three children of the early onset type for nine to sixteen years. At the time of follow-up they were from fifteen to twenty-two years old. None of the patients' conditions resembled adult schizophrenia. Eight had developed seizures. Originally half of the children had an I.Q. below 50. Most of the rest were between 50 and 80 and one in five had above 80. The brighter ones remained the same at follow-up, the duller ones became worse. At follow-up only one-fifth had a normal I.Q. and half were now below 45. A number showed variability, with peaks on block design and object assembly, while the rest of performance and verbal skills were depressed. This variability was found primarily in the cases with poor speech. Some lost signs of autism without change in an initially low I.Q. This finding and the general close correspondence of initial and follow-up I.Q. led Rutter to believe that the low I.Q. was not a function of withdrawal. At follow-up five children showed clear aphasia, and fourteen others had a suggestive picture of aphasia. Three-fourths of the speaking children had echolalia and pronoun reversal. His conclusions from his study were that there was a coexistence in these children of several phenomena, some of which became separated out at follow-up namely: autism, retardation; and aphasia.

Reiser,[445] in 1963 and Reiser and Brown[444] in 1964 reported on 125 children who had initially been diagnosed "atypical development" under the age of five. These are the children for whom Reiser proposed the term "infantile psychosis." This represented a follow-up of all but eleven of the children so diagnosed at the Putnam Center between 1943 and 1963. They defined "atypical development" as "ego fragmentation" secondary to distortion of the "parent-child axis." Over half of the children (nine to twenty-two years old at time of follow-up) were able to function at least moderately well in society. Most of the remainder were more "retarded" than "disturbed." More specifically they classified seven groups of clinical states at follow-up: "normal-neurotic, (16); brittle-schizoid (13); eruptive-schizoid (21); schizophrenic (9); over-grown children (4); (minimal) passive-retarded (8), moderate (9), and severe retardation (17); regressed-arrested (28)." Children in the first three groups and in the minimal and moderately retarded of the passive-retarded group were functioning moderately well to normally. By school placement, 35 per cent of the total group were in regular schools, 32 per cent in special schools, 25 per cent in custodial settings, and 6 per cent restricted to home. In learning, 37 per cent were at or close to age level, 22 per cent were mildly retarded, 14 per cent were markedly retarded, and 25 per cent manifested no learning at all.

It is apparent that some children diagnosed as childhood schizophrenics do become schizophrenic adolescents and adults and that some, notably those diagnosed as early infantile autism, with close adherence to Kanner's criteria, do not. A related question which has been studied is the prediction of adult schizophrenia in childhood or, put another way, the discovery of regular antecedents in the childhood of those who became schizophrenic as adults. In a retrospective study of records at the Judge Baker Center of adult schizophrenics seen there as children, Nameche et al.[396] found that as children they had not been psychotic. The significant correlations they found were between severity of adult schizophrenia (as measured by being in or out of hospital at the time of the study) and 1) psychotic or schizoid mother; 2) close tie to a pathogenic family; 3) duration of treatment and 4) "acting-out" in the community. Adult schizophrenics who had had psychotic or schizoid mothers, close ties to a pathogenic family, remained in treatment less than three months, and did little "acting-out" in the community were more likely to be found in a mental hospital than others.

Morris did a follow-up study on 606 boys initially evaluated at the Dallas Child Guidance Clinic.[392] He concluded that there was no adequate justification for an assertion that introverted children are more likely to develop schizophrenia than extroverted children. Moriarty[391] postulated "psychosis-vulnerability" in children but did not demonstrate it. Brask,[69] describing "borderline schizophrenia" in children as ranging from near normal to manifest psychosis, concluded that every adult schizophrenic has been a borderline schizophrenic child.

Prognosis—All Groups

Szurek[540] referred to the multiplicity of factors that appear to enter into outcome of childhood schizophrenia, such as family cooperation and consistency of therapists. His impression was that severe illness from very early in life not treated until late pre-adolescence; older parents; and the child's having been institutionalized or otherwise out of the home for several years were all poor prognostic factors. Many changes, particularly involving a succession of inexperienced therapists for parents, also impressed him as correlated with poor outcome. He also reported unexpected and dramatic improvement several years after cessation of apparently fruitless treatment that has been conducted for years.

Pollack, whose proposal to replace "childhood schizophrenia" with the diagnosis of "chronic brain syndrome with psychosis" has been cited above,[432] believed that low intelligence correlates with poor outcome and that "islets of intelligence" do not foretell an eventual higher I.Q. (Eaton and Menolascino's findings agreed with this).

In early infantile autism and other psychoses with onset before six, the poor prognosis of absent speech at five years, first reported by Eisenberg and Kanner,[140] has been widely corroborated. Brown reported the same prognostic significance when the age with absent speech was lowered to three years.[79]

Rutter,[469,471] referring to children with psychosis of early onset, believed, as does Pollack, that low I.Q. scores are a poor prognostic sign. He disputed the widespread belief that I.Q. scores in psychotic children are unreliable and, specifically, that "untestable children" were manifesting psychopathology and not intellectual impairment.[470] He cited his studies of consistency in I.Q. ratings over long follow-up periods. He considered rises in I.Q., sometimes obtained if the Binet is used initially, as being spurious since the Binet relies heavily on verbal skills. He emphasized that testing must be done by experienced psychologists and spread over several sessions. He found that none of the nine children in his series who made a good adjustment had an initial I.Q. below 60 and that only six of thirty-eight who had a poor adjustment at follow-up had an initial I.Q. above sixty. Severity of the disorder, particularly acting as though deaf, was correlated with poor outcome.

Reiser and Brown, in studies already mentioned,[444,445,79,80] found that physical handicaps, neurological abnormalities, psychotic parents, widespread withdrawal, mutism after three years, and inability to use play materials appropriately or to direct aggression outward at all, were all correlated with poor outcome. Although they reported that they sense a "catalytic" influence of treatment, they also admit that their findings did not allow the assertion of real treatment benefit.

Absence of incontrovertible evidence for benefit from various treatment methods was also concluded by Eisenberg[144] and Rutter,[469] both after extensive review of the literature.

EPIDEMIOLOGY AND PREVENTION

Wing[586] said (in 1963) that the determination of epidemiology for early childhood autism is difficult because of lack of objective diagnostic criteria. As of this writing there is no adequate epidemiologic study extant for any of the groups of children in the spectrum of "childhood schizophrenia."

In 1957 (Robinson[452]) in a report of a conference on psychiatric inpatient treatment of children stated that there is a need for hospital beds but "no statistically valid data on the number."

In 1960 (Plunkett and Gordon[423]) in the Joint Commission on Mental Illness and Health report on Epidemiology and Mental Illness did not include any report of systematic case finding in the children's field.

In 1965, Mishler[385] reported on sociocultural factors in epidemiology of schizophrenia. This is a most careful and instructive review of the problems limiting accuracy in epidemiologic study of schizophrenia, starting with ambiguity of clinical definition. By extrapolation, many of his inferences are applicable to childhood schizophrenia but in this, as in the other major epidemiological studies and reviews published during the past decade, childhood schizophrenia is not included.

Rutter[468] stated (1965) that childhood psychosis (early onset) occurs at the rate of four or five out of nine to ten thousand children.

Despite the dearth of information on incidence, there were a few guides towards prevention based on early detection. Fish[182] and Brazelton[71] both reported very early observation of abnormalities (see above) that should alert physicians to the possibility of psychosis developing in the child who displays them.

Pasamanick[409] observed (1961) that "a significant rise in rate of schizophrenia in individuals born following hot summers, as contrasted to cool summers, similar to the picture discovered for mental deficiency." What preventive use can be made of this finding is not immediately clear. Rose[455] suggested that decreasing "fetal wastage" may contribute to a larger pool of schizophrenic children.

Pavenstedt[413] wisely summarized signs of trouble in a child that should mobilize early intervention: 1) absence of well established patterns for communicating needs by three to four months; 2) hypersensitivity to certain perceptual stimuli; 3) extreme sensitivity and distress when minor changes are made at about three to four months; 4) absence of responsive smile in the third month; 5) no or little mouthing of objects in the sixth month; 6) poor handling and exploration in tenth and eleventh month; 7) absent self assertion, eighteen to twenty-four months; 8) absence of stranger or separation anxiety in first two years; 9) absence of definite speech progress in the third year; and 10) absence of biting and chewing solid foods by age three.

CONCLUSION

This chapter has attempted to characterize the kinds of phenomena which have been gathered together in what Goldfarb felicitously termed the "universe of childhood schizophrenia" and pointed out the confusion of terms used to classify both its totality and its possible component parts. Frustration with any scheme is inevitable when the items classified are confusing or poorly understood. The names assigned will always assume an aura of greater certainty than is justified. When the actuality of the uncertainty becomes clear, it is usually projected onto the label, rather than on the object or area that is ill-defined.

This emphasizes the need to delimit, clarify, and specify the populations and diagnostic criteria in studies in this field. This, unfortunately, has often not been done.

The question as to whether "childhood schizophrenia" represents one condition or many is still unresolved, but receiving much attention.

The articles reviewed suggest a need for a classification scheme, both with regard to and also independent of etiology.

It is necessary to have a better knowledge of the natural history of the conditions described. While there have been few presentations in this area, there have been relatively more attempts to provide for accurate baselines, both for diagnosis and for ways of evaluating treatment.

There has been increasing emphasis that etiologic factors and psychopathological mechanisms are multiple, that the physical and the psychological are intertwined and interacting. Overall, contributions have been more holistic, less dogmatic and polemic.

Considerations of diagnosis have suggested that these need to be twofold, taking into account both the ego maladaptation and the causative factors. The latter may remain obscure, but even when manifest, the management and treatment of the child is largely dictated by the former.

It is striking how, regardless of orientation and theories as to causation, most of the major workers in the field use generally similar methods of treatment.

Concerning treatment with physical modalities, in this decade they have been essentially limited to the use of antipsychotic medication. Behavior therapy has assumed increased prominence. This in part may reflect as increased willingness to value symptomatic aid and not to scorn anything less than a "cure."

Individual approaches have continued to dominate within psychotherapy. There is a persisting dichotomy between those who seek to enter into the child's psychosis, accept his world and help to lead him out and those who feel that the therapist should safely remain on the side of reality and push, pull or entice the child into it.

Group therapy and family therapy are assuming increasing prominence, and there has been much attention to the specifics of education—for therapeutic as well as learning purposes.

Follow up studies have increased. Overall, the results have supported optimism for individual cases but provide a pessimistic outlook for the majority.

Clarity and consensus for prevention remain the hope for the next decade.

BIBLIOGRAPHY

1. Abbate, G.: A pilot study of schizophrenic children in a nonresidential school. Amer. J. Orthopsychiat. 27: 106-116, 1957.

2. Abramson, H. A.: Lysergic acid diethylamide. J. Asthma Res. 2: 257-262, 1965.

3. Alanen, Y. O.: Some thoughts on schizophrenia and ego development in the light of family investigations. Arch. Gen. Psychiat. 3: 650-656, 1960.

4. Alderton, H. R.: A review of schizophrenia in childhood. Canad. Psychiat. Ass. J. 11: 276-285, 1966.

5. Alpert, A., Neubauer, P., Weil, A.: Unusual variations in drive endowment. In Eissler et al. (Eds.) Stud. Child 11: 125-163, 1956.

6. Alpert, A.: Reversibility of pathological fixations associated with maternal deprivation in infancy. In Eissler et al. (Eds.) Psychoanal. Stud. Child 14: N.Y. Int. Univ. Press, 1959.

7. Alpert, A.: Treatment of an autistic child. J. Amer. Acad. Child. Psychiat. 3: 591-616, 1964.

8. Andrews, E., and Cappon, D.: Autism and schizophrenia in a child guidance clinic. Canad. Psychiat. Ass. J. 2: 1-23, 1957.

9. Annell, A. L.: The prognosis of psychotic syndromes in children. Acta Psychiat. Scand. 39: 235-297, 1963.

10. Anthony, E. J.: An aetiological approach to the diagnosis of psychosis in childhood. Acta Paedopsychiat. 25: 89-96, 1958.

11. Anthony, J.: An experimental approach to the psychopathology of childhood. Brit. J. Med. Psychol. 31: 211-223, 1958.

12. Aprison, H. M., and Drew, A. L.: N. N - Dimethyl - p - phenylene-diamine oxidation by serum from schizophrenic children. Science 127: 758-760, 1958.

13. Arnstein, H. S.: An approach to the severely disturbed child. In Weston, P.T.B. (Ed.) Some Approaches to Teaching Autistic Children. London, Pergamon Press, 1965.

14. Baer, P. E.: Problems in the differential diagnosis of brain damage in childhood schizophrenia. Amer. J. Orthopsychiat. 31: 728-737, 1961.

15. Bakwin, H.: Dementia praecox, home management of children. J. Pediat. 47: 514-519, 1955.

16. Bakwin, H., and Bakwin, R.: Schizophrenia in childhood. Pediat. Clin. N. Amer. 5: 699-709, 1958.

17. Bakwin, R. M.: Ceruloplasmin activity in the serum of children with schizophrenia. Pediatrics. 22: 905-909, 1958.

18. Bakwin, R. M., Mosbach, E. H., and Bakwin, H.: Concentration of copper in serum of children with schizophrenia. Pediatrics 27: 642-643, 1961.

19. Bakwin, R. M.: Somatic basis for behavior problems in children. J. Amer. Med. Wom. Ass. 20: 142-147, 1965.

20. Bashina, V.: The work capacity and social adaptation of schizophrenic patients who became ill in childhood and adolescence. Int. J. Psychiat. 1: 248-257, 1965.

21. Beach, W. B., Jr.: Psychosis in childhood. Northwest Med. 56: 438-442, 1957.

22. Beaujard, M.: Les Therapeutiques de choc en psychiatrie infantile. Pediatrie 11: 765-771, 1956.

23. Beck, S. J.: Current status of the Rorschach test, Symposium, 1955. Amer. J. Orthopsychiat. 26: 792-800, 1956.

24. Beck, S. J., and Molish, H. B.: Course in the individual patient as traced in the six schizophrenias. J. Nerv. Ment. Dis. 125: 403-411, 1957.

25. Beck, S. J.: Families of schizophrenics and of well children. Amer. J. Orthopsychiat. 30: 247-275, 1960.

26. Beck, S. J., and Nunnally, J. C.: Parental attitudes in families. Arch. Gen. Psychiat. 13: 208-213, 1965.

27. Behrens, M. L., and Goldfarb, W.: A study of patterns of interaction of families of schizophrenic children in residential treatment. Amer. J. Orthopsychiat. 28: 300-312, 1958.

27a. Bellak, L.: Schizophrenia: A Review of the Syndrome. New York, Logos

Press, 1958 and Grune & Stratton, 1966.

28. Benda, C., and Melchoir, J.: Childhood schizophrenia, childhood autism, Heller's disease. Int. Rec. Med. 172: 137-154, 1959.

29. Bender, L.: Twenty years of clinical research on schizophrenic children with special reference to those under six years of age. In Caplan, G. (Ed.) Emotional Problems of Early Childhood. New York, Basic Books, 503-515, 1955.

30. Bender, L.: Treatment of juvenile schizophrenia. Res. Publ. Ass. Res. Nerv. Ment. Dis. 34: 462-477, 1955.

31. Bender, L., and Nichtern, S.: Chemotherapy in child psychiatry. New York J. Med. 56: 2791-2795, 1956.

32. Bender, L.: Schizophrenia in childhood—its recognition, description and treatment. Amer. J. Orthopsychiat. 26: 499-506, 1956.

33. Bender, L., and Grugett, A.: A study of certain epidemiological factors in a group of children with childhood schizophrenia. Amer. J. Orthopsychiat. 26: 131-143, 1956.

34. Bender, L.: Genesis in schizophrenia in childhood. Z. Kinderpsychiat. 25: 101-107, 1958.

35. Bender, L.: The concept of pseudopsychopathic schizophrenia in adolescents. Amer. J. Orthopsychiat. 29: 491-509, 1959.

36. Bender, L.: Autism in children with mental deficiency. Amer. J. Ment. Defic. 64: 81-86, 1959-1960.

37. Bender, L.: Treatment in early schizophrenia. Progr. Psychother. 5: 177-184, 1960.

38. Bender, L.: Childhood schizophrenia and convulsive states. Recent Advances Biol. Psychiat. 3: 96-103, 1961.

39. Bender, L., Goldschmidt, L., and Sanker, S. D. V.: Treatment of autistic schizophrenic children with LSD-25 and UML-491. Recent Advances Biol. Psychiat. 4: 170-179, 1962.

40. Bender, L.: The origin and evolution of the Gestalt function, the body image and delusional thoughts in schizophrenia. Recent Advances Biol. Psychiatry 5: 38-62, 1963.

41. Bender, L.: Mental illness in childhood and heredity. Eugen. Quart. 10: 1-11, 1963.

42. Bender, L., Faretra, G., and Cobrinik, L.: LSD and UML treatment of hospitalized disturbed children. Recent Advances Biol. Psychiat. 5: 84-92, 1963.

43. Bender, L., and Andermann, K.: Brain Damage in blind children with retrolental fibroplasia. Arch. Neurol. 12: 644-649, 1965.

44. Bender, L.: The concept of plasticity in childhood schizophrenia. In Hoch and Zubin Psychopathology of Schizophrenia. New York, Grune & Stratton, 354-365, 1966.

45. Bene, E.: A Rorschach investigation into the mothers of autistic children. Brit. J. Med. Psychol. 31: 226-227, 1958.

46. Benjamin, J. D.: Prediction and psychopathological theory. In Jessner, L., and Pavenstedt, E. (Ed.) Dynamics of Psychopathology in Childhood. New York, Grune & Stratton, 1959.

47. Bennett, S., and Klein, H. R.: Childhood Schizophrenia: 30 years later. Amer. J. Psychiat. 122: 1121-1124, 1966.

48. Bental, E.: Acute psychoses due to encephalitis following Asian influenza. Lancet 2: 18-20, 1958.

49. Benton, A. L.: Concept of pseudofeeblemindedness. Arch. Neurol. 75: 379-388, 1956.

50. Beres, D.: Ego deviation and the concept of schizophrenia. In Eissler et al. (Eds.) Psychoanal. Stud. Child 11: 164-235, 1956.

51. Beres, D. et al.: Disturbances of identity function in childhood. Amer. J. Orthopsychiat. 30: 369-381, 1960.

52. Berg, I. S.: A case study of developmental auditory imperception. J. Child Psychol. Psychiat. 2: 86-93, 1961.

53. Berkowitz, P. H.: Some psychophysical aspects of mental illness in children. Genet. Psychol. Monogr. 63: 103-148, 1961.

54. Berlin, I. N.: Aspects of creativity and the learning process. Amer. Imago. 17: 83-99, 1960.

55. Berliner, O. A.: Childhood schizo-

phrenia, diagnosis and rehabilitation. Jour. Rehab. 32: 10-12, 1966.

56. Bettleheim, B.: Ref. from Bettleheim, B. Truants From Life, Free Press. New York, 1955.

'57. Bettleheim, B.: Schizophrenia as a reaction to extreme situations. Amer. J. Orthopsychiat. 26: 507-518, 1956.

58. Bettleheim, B.: Feral children and autistic children. Amer. J. Sociol. 64: 455-467, 1959.

59. Bettleheim, B.: Joey: a mechanical boy. Sci. Amer. 200: 117-127, 1959.

60. Bjorsen, A., and Nylander, J.: A case of severe developmental motor aphasia with psychotic symptoms successfully treated by speech therapy. Acta Paedopsychiat. 30: 59-70, 1963.

61. Birch, H. G.: The Biological and Social Aspects. In Brain Damage in Children, Baltimore, Williams and Wilkins, 1964.

62. Birch, H. G., and Walker, H. A.: Perceptual and perceptual-motor dissociation. Arch. Gen. Psychiat. 14: 113-118, 1966.

63. Blau, A.: Nature of childhood schizophrenia. J. Amer. Acad. Child Psychiat. 1: 225-230, 1962.

64. Block, J. et al.: A study of the parents of schizophrenic and neurotic children. Psychiatry 21: 387-397, 1958.

65. Boatman, M. J., and Szurek, S. A.: A clinical study of childhood schizophrenia. In Jackson, D.D. (Ed.) The Etiology of Schizophrenia. New York, Basic Books, 1960.

66. Boatman, M. J., and Berlin, I. N.: Some implications of incidental experiences with psychopharmacologic drugs in a children's psychotherapeutic program. J. Amer. Acad. Child Psychiat. 1: 431-442, 1962.

67. Book, J. A.: Cytogenetical investigations in childhood schizophrenia. Acta Psychiat. Scand. 39: 309-323, 1963.

68. Bourne, H.: Protophrenia, a study of perverted rearing and mental dwarfism. Lancet 2: 1156-1163, 1955.

69. Brask, B. H.: Borderline schizophrenia in children. Acta Psychiat. Scand. 34: 265-282, 1959.

70. Bray, P. F.: Temporal lobe syndrome in children. Mod. Med. 30: 117, 1962.

71. Brazelton, T. B.: Observations of the neonate. J. Amer. Acad. Child Psychiat. 1: 38-58, 1962.

72. Breger, L., and McGaugh, J. L.: Critique and reformulation of "learning theory" approaches to psychotherapy and neurosis. Psychol. Bull. 63: 338-358, 1965.

73. Breger, L.: Comments on Lovaas et al., "Building Social Behavior in Children by use of electric shock". J. Exp. Res. 1: 110-113, 1965.

74. Brody, S.: Patterns of Mothering. New York Univ. Press, 1956.

75. Brody, S.: Signs of disturbance in the first year of life. Amer. J. Orthopsychiat. 28: 362-368, 1958.

76. Brody, S.: Self-rocking in infancy. J. Amer. Psychoanal. Ass. 8: 464-491, 1960.

77. Brown, B. S.: Serum Akerfeldt for schizophrenia in children: preliminary reports. J. Pediat. 51: 46-48, 1957.

78. Brown, G. T.: Schizophrenia in children. J. Indiana Med. Ass. 53: 1906-1916.

79. Brown, J. L.: Prognosis from presenting symptoms of preschool children with atypical development. Amer. J. Orthopsychiat. 30: 382-390, 1960.

80. Brown, J. L.: Follow-up of children with atypical development (infantile psychosis). Amer. J. Orthopsychiat. 33: 855-861, 1963.

81. Brown, S. L.: Family therapy viewed in terms of resistance to change. Psychiat. Res. Rep. Amer. Psychiat. Ass. 20: 132-139, 1966.

82. Bruch, H.: The various developments in the approach to childhood schizophrenia. Acta Psychiat. Scand. 34: 1-48, 1958.

83. Bruch, H.: Developmental obesity and schizophrenia. Psychiatry 21: 65-70, 1958.

84. Bruch, H.: Psychotherapeutic aspects of teaching emotionally disturbed

children. Psychiat. Quart. 34: 648-657, 1960.

85. Cain, A. C.: On the meaning of "playing crazy" in borderline children. Psychiatry 27: 278-289, 1964.

86. Call, J. D.: Prevention of autism in a young infant in a well-child conference. J. Amer. Acad. Child Psychiat. 2: 451-459, 1963.

87. Call, J. D.: Interlocking affective freeze between an autistic child and his "as-if" mother. J. Amer. Acad. Child Psychiat. 2: 319-344, 1963.

88. Cameron, K.: Diagnostic categories in child psychiatry. Brit. J. Med. Psychol. 28: 67-71, 1955.

89. Cameron, K.: A group of twenty-five psychotic children. Z. Kinderpsychiat. 25: 117-122, 1958.

90. Caplan, G.: Prevention of Mental Disorders in Children. In Caplan, A. (Ed.) New York, Basic Books, 1961.

91. Caruth, E., and Ekstein, R.: Certain phenomenological aspects of the counter-transference in treatment of schizophrenic children. Reiss Davis Clinic Bull. 1: 80-88, 1964.

92. Caruth, E., and Ekstein, R.: Interpretation within the metaphor: further considerations. J. Amer. Acad. Child Psychiat. 5: 35-45, 1966.

93. Cassel, R. H.: Differentiation between mental defective with psychosis and childhood schizophrenic functioning as mental defective. Amer. J. Ment. Defic. 62: 103-107, 1957.

94. Chao, D.: The autistic child. Med. Rec. Ann. 56: 247-248, 1963.

95. Chapman, A. H.: Early infantile autism in identical twins. Arch. Neurol. Psychiat. 78: 621-623, 1957.

96. Chapman, A. H.: Early infantile autism. J. Dis. Child. 99: 783-786, 1960.

97. Christ, A.: Sexual countertransference with a psychotic child. J. Amer. Acad. Child Psychiat. 3: 298-315, 1964.

98. Clar, G. D.: An Education Program for Psychotic Children. In Weston, P. T. B. (Ed.) Some Approaches to Teaching Autistic Children. London, Pergamon Press, 1965.

99. Clerk, G.: Reflections on the role of the mother in the development of language in the schizophrenic child. Canad. Psychiat. Ass. J. 6: 252-256, 1961.

100. Cobrink, L.: Developmental aspects of thought disturbance in schizophrenic children: a Rorschach study. Amer. J. Orthopsychiat. 31: 170-180, 1961.

101. Coddington, R. D.: Psychiatrists' reliability in judging ego functions. Arch. Gen. Psychiat. 16: 48-55, 1967.

102. Cohen, R. S.: Some childhood identity disturbances: educational implementation of a psychiatric treatment plan. J. Amer. Acad. Child Psychiat. 3: 488-497, 1964.

103. Colbert, E. G.: Diagnosis of schizophrenia in young children. Calif. Med. 89: 215-216, 1958.

104. Colbert, E. G., and Koegler, R. R.: Toe walking in childhood schizophrenia. J. Pediat. 53: 219-220, 1958.

105. Colbert, E. G. et al.: Vestibular function in childhood schizophrenia. Arch. Gen Psychiat. 1: 62/600-79/617, 1959.

106. Colbert, E. G.: Group psychotherapy for mothers of schizophrenic children in a state hospital. Int. J. Group Psychother. 9-10: 93-98, 1959-1960.

107. Colbert, E. G., and Koegler, R.: The childhood schizophrenic in adolescence. Psychiat. Quart. 35: 693-701, 1961.

108. Connell, P.: Review of "Infantile Autism." Develop. Med. Child Neurol. 8: 635-636, 1966.

109. Corboz, R. F.: Clinical experiences with psychopharmacological agents in childhood. Acta Paedopsychiat. 1: 24-39, 1965.

110. Cowan, P. A. et al.: Compliance and resistance in the conditioning of autistic children: an exploratory study. Child Develop. 36: 914-923, 1965.

111. Creak, M., and Ini, S.: Families of psychotic children. Child Psychol. Psychiat. 1: 156-175, 1960.

114. Creak, M. et al.: Schizophrenic syndrome in childhood. Progress Report (April 1961) of a working party. Brit. Med. J. 2: 889-890, 1961.

115. Creak, M.: Childhood psychosis:

a review of 100 cases. Brit. J. Psychiat. 109: 84-89, 1963.

116. Creak, M. et al.: Schizophrenic syndrome in childhood. Further progress report of a working party. (April, 1964) Develop. Med. Child Neurol. 6: 530-535, 1964.

117. Cunningham, A.: A study of the language of an autistic child. J. Child Psychiat. 2: 193-202, 1961.

118. Davids, A.: Intelligence in childhood schizophrenia, other emotionally disturbed children, and their mothers. J. Consult. Psychol. 22: 159-163, 1958.

119. Davison, G. C.: A social learning therapy programme with an autistic child. Behav. Res. Ther. 2: 149-159, 1964.

120. Deajuriaguerra, J. et al: Difficulties in the development of language in the course of childhood psychosis. Psychiatria Enfant 2: 1-65, 1959.

121. Delage, J.: Considerations sur L'Identile Clinique et Diagnostique de la Schizophrenic es Infantile. Canad. Psychiat. Ass. J. 6: 261-271, 1961.

122. DeMyer, M. K., and Ferster, C. B.: Teaching new social behavior to schizophrenic children. J. Amer. Acad. Child Psychiat. 1: 443-461, 1962.

123. DesLauriers, A. M.: The Experience of Reality in Childhood Schizophrenia. New York, International Universities Press, Inc., 1962.

124. Despert, J. L.: Differential diagnosis between obsessive-compulsive neurosis and schizophrenia in children. Psychopath. Child. 30: 240-253, 1955.

125. Despert, J. L., and Shervin, A. C.: Further examination of diagnostic criteria on schizophrenic illness and psychoses of infancy and early childhood. Amer. J. Psychiat. 114: 784-790, 1958.

126. Dietze, H. J.: Dementia infantilis-Heller. Amer. J. Ment. Defic. 80: 114-116, 1959.

127. Dobson, J. R.: Childhood psychoses. New Zeal. Med. J. 56: 647-653, 1957.

128. Donnelly, E. M.: The quantitative analysis of parent behavior toward psychotic children and their siblings. Genet. Psychol. Monogr. 62: 331-376, 1960.

129. Dowd, D. D.: Medical practice and treatment of schizophrenia in childhood. J. Amer. Med. Wom. Ass. 10: 47-50, 1955.

130. Dreikurs, R.: Music therapy with psychotic children. Psychiat. Quart. 34: 722-734, 1960.

131. Duffy, J. H.: Childhood schizophrenia. Med. Rec. Ann. 57: 344-345, 1964.

132. Dundas, M. H.: Autistic children. Nurs. Times 60: 138-139, 1964.

133. Dunkel, M. L.: Homelessness as a major problem of hospitalized children. Soc. Ser. Review 37: 12-16, 1963.

134. Dutton, G.: The growth pattern of psychotic boys. Brit. J. Psychiat. 110: 101-103, 1964.

135. Easton, K.: Considerations on autism in infancy and childhood. New York J. Med. 62: 3628-3633, 1962.

136. Eaton, L., and Menolascino, F. J.: Psychotic reactions of childhood: experiences of a mental retardation pilot project. J. Nerv. Ment. Dis. 143: 55-67, 1966.

137. Eaton, L., and Menolascino, F. J.: Psychotic Reactions of Childhood: A Follow-Up Study. Amer. J. Orthopsychiat. 37: 521-529, 1967.

138. Egan, M. H., and Robinson, O. L.: Home treatment of severely disturbed children and families. Amer. J. Orthopsychiat. 36: 729-734, 1966.

139. Eickhoff, L. F. W.: Treatment. J. Ment. Sci. 101: 399-403, 1955.

140. Eisenberg, L., and Kanner, L.: Early infantile autism 1943-1955. Amer. J. Orthopsychiat. 26: 556-566, 1956.

141. Eisenberg, L.: Autistic child in adolescence. Amer. J. Psychiat. 112: 607-612, 1956.

142. Eisenberg, L.: The course of childhood schizophrenia. Arch. Neurol. Psychiat. 78: 69-83, 1957.

143. Eisenberg, L.: The fathers of autistic children. Amer. J. Orthopsychiat. 27: 715-724, 1957.

144. Eisenberg, L.: Hallucinations in children. In West, L. J. (Ed.) Hallucinations, Grune & Stratton, 1962.

145. Eisenson, J.: Disorders of language in children. J. Pediat. 62: 20-24, 1963.

146. Eisenson, J.: Developmental pat-

terns of non-verbal children and some therapeutic implications. J. Neurol. Sci. 3: 313-320, 1966.

146a. Ekstein, Bryan, and Freedman: In Bellak, L.: Schizophrenia: A Review of the Syndrome. New York, Logos Press, 1958 and Grune & Stratton, 1966.

147. Ekstein, R., and Wallerstein, J.: Observations on the psychotherapy of borderline and psychotic children. In Eissler et al. (Eds.) Psychoanal. Stud. Child 11: 303-311, 1956.

148. Ekstein, R. and Wallerstein, J.: Choice of interpretation in the treatment of borderline and psychotic children. Bull. Menninger Clin. 21: 199-207, 1957.

149. Ekstein, R., and Friedman, S. W.: On the meaning of play in childhood psychosis. In Jessner, L., and Pavenstedt, E. (Eds.) Dynamics of Psychopathology in Childhood. New York, Grune & Stratton, 1959.

150. Ekstein, R. et al.: Countertransference in the residential treatment of children: treatment failure in a child with symbiotic psychosis. In Eissler et al. (Eds.) Psychoanal. Stud. Child. New York, Int. Univ. Press, 1959.

151. Ekstein, R.: Special training problems in psychotherapeutic work with psychotic and borderline children. Amer. J. Orthopsychiat. 32: 569-583, 1962.

152. Ekstein, R.: The acquisition of Speech in the Autistic Child. Reiss Davis Clinic Bull. 1: 63-79, 1964.

153. Ekstein, R., and Caruth, E.: The working alliance with the monster. Bull. Menninger Clin. 29: 189-197, 1965.

154. Ekstein, R.: Children of Time and Space, action and impulse: Clinical studies on the psychoanalytic treatment of severely disturbed children. New York, Appleton-Century-Crofts, 1966.

155. Elkisch, P.: Struggle for ego boundaries in psychotic child. Amer. J. Psychother. 10: 578-602, 1956.

156. Elkisch, P., and Mahler, M. S.: On infantile precursors of the "Influence Machine". In Eissler et al. (Eds.) Psychoanal. Stud. Child 14: New York, Int. Univ. Press, 1959.

157. Elles, G.: The mute sad-eyed child: collateral analysis in a disturbed family. Int. J. Psychoanal. 43: 40-49, 1962.

158. Engel, M.: Psychological Testing of Borderline Psychotic Children. Arch. Gen. Psychiat. 8: 426-434, 1963.

159. Escalona, S. K.: Patterns of infantile experience and the developmental process. In Eissler et al. (Eds.) Psychoanal. Stud. Child. 18: 197-244, 1963.

160. Escalona, S.: Some considerations regarding psychotherapy with psychotic children in Haworth, M. R. (Ed.) Child Psychotherapy. New York, Basic Books, 1964.

161. Esman, A. H. et al.: The family of the schizophrenic child. Amer. J. Orthopsychiat. 29: 455-459, 1959.

162. Esman, A. H.: Childhood psychosis and "childhood schizophrenia". Amer. J. Orthopsychiat. 30: 391-396, 1960.

163. Esman, A. H.: Visual hallucinations in young children. In Eissler et al. (Eds.) Psychoanal. Stud. Child. 17: 334-343, 1962.

164. Eveloff, H. H.: The autistic child. Arch. Gen. Psychiat. 3: 66-81, 1960.

165. Eveloff, H. H.: Psychopharmacologic agents in child psychiatry. Arch. Gen. Psychiat. 14: 471-481, 1966.

166. Falstein, E. I., and Sutton, H. A.: Childhood schizophrenia. Amer. J. Nurs. 58: 666-670, 1958.

167. Faretra, G.: Pseudoneurotic schizophrenia in childhood. J. Amer. Med. Wom. Ass. 16: 603-606, 1961.

168. Faretra, G., and Gozun, C.: The use of drug combinations in pediatric psychiatry. Curr. Ther. Res. 6: 340-343, 1964.

169. Farmer, R.: A musical activities program with young psychotic girls. Amer. J. Occup. Ther. 17: 116-119, 1963.

170. Faure, J. L., and Abric, J.: Clinical studies of indications for use of chlorpromazine and reserpine in infantile neuropsychiatry. Pediatrie 11: 773-776, 1956.

171. Fedor, P. et al.: Childhood schizophrenia and the problem of autism in childhood. Cesk. Psychiat. 60: 311-317, 1964.

172. Fenichel, C. et al.: A day school for schizophrenic children. Amer. J. Ortho-

psychiat. 30: 130-143, 1960.

173. Fenichel, C.: Psycho-educational approaches for seriously disturbed children in the classroom. *In* Knoblock, P. (Ed.) Intervention Approaches in Educating Emotionally Disturbed Children. Syracuse, Univ. Press, Syracuse, New York, 1966.

174. Ferreira, A. J., and Winter, W. D.: Family interaction and decision-making. Arch. Gen. Psychiat. 13: 214-219, 1965.

175. Ferster, C. B.: The development of performance in autistic children in an automatically controlled environment. J. Chronic Dis. 13: 312-345, 1961.

176. Ferster, C. B.: Increased performances of an autistic child with prochlorperazine administration. J. Exp. Anal. Behav. 4: 84-87, 1961.

177. Ferster, C. B.: Positive reinforcement and behavioral deficits of autistic children. Child Develop. 32: 437-456, 1961.

178. Ferster, C. B., and DeMyer, M. K.: A method for the experimental analysis of the behavior of autistic children. Amer. J. Orthopsychiat. 32: 89-98, 1962.

179. Ferster, C. B.: Psychotherapy by machine communication in disorders of communication. Res. Publ. Ass. Res. Nerv. Ment. Dis. 12: 317-333, 1964.

180. Fish, B.: The detection of schizophrenia in infancy. J. Nerv. Ment. Dis. 125: 1-24, 1957.

181. Fish, B.: Longitudinal observations of biological deviation in a schizophrenic infant. Amer. J. Psychiat. 116: 25-31, 1959.

182. Fish, B.: Drug therapy in child psychiatry: pharmacological aspects. Compr. Psychiat. 1: 212, 1960.

183. Fish, B.: Involvement of the central nervous system in infants with schizophrenia. Arch. Neurol. 2: 115-121, 1960.

184. Fish, B.: The study of motor development in infancy and its relationship to psychological functioning. Amer. J. Psychiat. 117: 1113-1118, 1961.

185. Fish, B., and Alpert, M.: Abnormal states of consciousness and muscle tone in infants born to schizophrenic mothers. Amer. J. Psychiat. 119: 439-445, 1962.

186. Fish, B.: Evaluation of psychiatric therapies in children. Proc. Amer. Psychopath. Ass. 52: 202-220, 1964.

187. Fish, B. et al.: The prediction of schizophrenia in infancy. Amer. J. Psychiat. 121: 768-775, 1965.

188. Fish, B., and Shapiro, T.: A typology of children's psychiatric disorders. J. Amer. Acad. Child Psychiat. 4: 32-52, 1965.

189. Fish, B. et al.: The prediction of schizophrenia in infancy. A ten year follow-up report of predictions made at one month of age. *In* Hoch and Zubin (Eds.) Psychopathology of Schizophrenia. New York, Grune & Stratton, 1966.

190. Fish, B. et al.: Long term prognosis and the response of schizophrenic children to drug therapy: A controlled study of trifluoperazine. Amer. J. Psychiat. 123: 32-38, 1966.

191. Fisher, S.: Child Research on Psychopharmacology. Springfield, C. C. Turner, 1959.

192. Forbing, S. E.: The teaching of schizophrenic children. *In* Berlin, I., and Szurek, S. (Eds.) Learning and Its Disorders. Palo Alto, Science and Behavior Books, 1965.

193. Ford, E. S.: Psychotherapy with child psychotics. Amer. J. Psychother. 14: 705-718, 1960.

194. Fowler, E. P., Jr., and Kastein, S.: Hypoacusis, dysacusis, and retardation. *In* Kolb, L. C., Masland, R. L., and Cooke, R. E. (Eds.) Mental Retardation. Baltimore, Williams and Wilkins, 1962.

195. Freedman, A. M. et al.: Psychiatric aspects of familial dysautonomia. Amer. J. Orthopsychiat. 27: 96-106, 1957.

196. Freedman, A. M., and Bender, L.: When the childhood schizophrenic grows up. Amer. J. Orthopsychiat. 27: 553-565, 1957.

197. Freedman, A. M.: Treatment of autistic schizophrenic children with Marsilid. J. Clin. Psychopath. 19: Suppl. 1, 138-142, 1958.

198. Freedman, A. M. et al.: Exchange transfusions in schizophrenic patients. J. Nerv. Ment. Dis. 126: 294-301, 1958.

199. Freedman, A. M.: Day hospitals for severely disturbed schizophrenic chil-

dren. Amer. J. Psychiat. 115: 893-899, 1959.

200. Freedman, A. M. et al.: Effects of hydroxyzine hydrochloride on the reaction time performance of schizophrenic children. Arch. Gen. Psychiat. 3: 153-159, 1960.

201. Freedman, A. M. et al.: Autistic schizophrenic children. Arch. Gen. Psychiat. 6: 203-213, 1962.

202. Freud, A.: Normality and Pathology in Childhood. In Assessment of Development. New York, Int. Univ. Press, 1965.

203. Friedman, G.: Conceptual thinking in schizophrenic children. Genet. Psychol. Monogr. 63: 149-196, 1961.

204. Frohman, C. E. et al.: The isolation of an active factor from serum of schizophrenic patients. Ann. N.Y. Acad. Sci. 96: 438-447, 1962.

205. Frosch, J.: The psychotic character. Psychoanal. Quart. 30: 314-316, 1961.

206. Frosch, J.: The psychotic character. Psychiat. Quart. 38: 81-96, 1964.

207. Frostig, M., and Horne, D. Changes in language and behavior in psychotic children during successful therapy: method of evaluation and findings. Amer. J. Orthopsychiat. 33: 734-737, 1963.

208. Fuller, G. B.: The objective measurement of perception in determining personality disorganization among children. J. Clin. Psychol. 21: 305-307, 1965.

209. Furer, M. et al.: Internalized objects in children. Amer. J. Orthopsychiat. 27: 88-95, 1957.

210. Furer, M.: The development of preschool symbiotic psychotic boy. In Eissler et al. (Eds.) Psychoanal. Stud. Child. 19: 448-469, 1964.

211. Furman, E.: An Ego Disturbance in a Young Child. In Eissler et al. (Eds.) Psychoanal. Stud. Child. 11: 312-335, 1956.

212. Gair, D. S., and Salomon, A. D.: Diagnostic Aspects of Psychiatric Hospitalization of Children. Amer. J. Orthopsychiat. 32: 445-461, 1962.

213. Galdston, R.: Observations on children who have been physically abused and their parents. Amer. J. Psychiat. 122: 440-443, 1965.

214. Galdston, R.: Personal Communication. 1967.

215. Garcia, B. et al.: Evaluation and treatment planning for autistic children. Arch. Gen. Psychiat. 10: 530-541, 1964.

216. Geleerd, E. R.: Borderline states in childhood and adolescence. Psychoanal. Stud. Child. 13: 279-295, 1958.

217. Gianascol, A. J.: Psychodynamic approaches to childhood schizophrenia: a review. J. Nerv. Ment. Dis. 137: 336-348, 1963.

218. Gibson, R.: Dementia infantilis, report of a case. Canad. Med. Ass. J. 80: 114-116, 1959.

219. Glavin, J. P.: Rapid oxygen change as possible etiology of RLF and Autism. Arch. Gen. Psychiat. 15: 301-309, 1966.

220. Gold, S., and Vaughan, G. F.: Classification of childhood psychosis. Lancet 2: 1058-1059, 1964.

221. Gold, S., and Vaughan, G. F.: Childhood psychosis. Guy Hosp. Rep. 113: 273-279, 1964.

222. Goldberg, B. R.: Pseudo-retardation. J. Med. Soc. New Jersey 57: 579-583, 1960.

223. Goldberg, B., and Soper, H.: Childhood psychosis or mental retardation: A diagnostic dilemma. Canad. Med. Ass. J. 89: 1015-1019, 1963.

224. Goldfarb, W.: Reactions to delayed auditory feedback in schizophrenic children. Proc. Amer. Psychopath. Ass. 49-63, 1956.

225. Goldfarb, W. et al.: A study of speech patterns in a group of schizophrenic children. Amer. J. Orthopsychiat. 26: 544-555, 1956.

226. Goldfarb, W., and Dorsen, M. M.: Annotated Bibliography of Childhood Schizophrenia and Related Disorders. New York, Basic Books, 1956.

227. Goldfarb, W.: Receptor preferences in children. Arch. Neur. Psychiat. 76: 643-652, 1956.

228. Goldfarb, W.: Pain reactions in a group of institutionalized schizophrenic children. Amer. J. Orthopsychiat. 78: 777-785, 1958.

229. Goldfarb, W. et al.: An approach to the investigations of childhood schizophrenia: the speech of schizophrenic children and their mother. Amer. J. Orthopsychiat. 29: 481-490, 1959.

230. Goldfarb, W.: Mutual Impact of Mother and Child in Childhood Schizophrenia. Amer. J. Orthopsychiat. 31: 738-747, 1961.

231. Goldfarb, W., and Mintz, I.: Schizophrenic child's reaction to time and space. Arch. Gen. Psychiat. 5: 535-543, 1961.

232. Goldfarb, W.: Childhood Schizophrenia, Cambridge, Mass. Harvard Univ. Press, 1961.

233. Goldfarb, W.: Families of schizophrenic children. Res. Publ. Ass. Res. Nerv. Ment. Dis. 39: 256-269, 1962.

234. Goldfarb, W.: Self-awareness in schizophrenic children. Arch. Gen. Psychiat. 8: 47-60, 1963.

235. Goldfarb, W.: Childhood Schizophrenia. Int. Psychiat. Clin. 1: 821-845, 1964.

236. Goldfarb, W.: An investigation of childhood schizophrenia; a retrospective view. Arch. Gen. Psychiat. 11: 620-634, 1964.

237. Goldfarb, W., and Pollack, R. C.: The childhood schizophrenic's response to schooling in a residential treatment center. Proc. Amer. Psychopath. Ass. 52: 221-246, 1964.

238. Goldfarb, W., and Radin, S. S.: Group behavior of schizophrenic children. Int. J. Soc. Psychiat. 10: 199-208, 1964.

239. Goldfarb, W. et al.: Evaluation of behavioral changes of schizophrenic children in residential treatment. Amer. J. Psychother. 19: 185-204, 1965.

240. Goldfarb, W.: Corrective socialization: a rationale for the treatment of schizophrenic children. Canad. Psychiat. Ass. 10: 481-496, 1965.

241. Goldfarb, W. et al.: Evaluation of behavioral changes of schizophrenic children in residential treatment. Amer. J. Psychother. 19: 185-204, 1965.

242. Goldfarb, W. et al.: Treatment of childhood schizophrenia. A three year comparison of day and residential treatment. Arch. Gen. Psychiat. 14: 119-128, 1966.

243. Goldfarb, W. et al.: Speech of mothers of schizophrenic children. Amer. J. Psychiat. 122: 1220-1227, 1966.

244. Goldman, D., and Rosenberg, G.: EEG observations in psychotic children. Compr. Psychiat. 3: 93-112, 1962.

245. Goldstein, K.: Abnormal mental conditions in infancy. J. Nerv. Ment. Dis. 128: 538-557, 1959.

246. Gordon, F. F.: The world of the autistic child. Virginia Med. Monthly 88: 469-471, 1961.

247. Gordon, K. H., Jr.: Child with a defective stimulus barrier. Arch. Gen. Psychiat. 4: 77-87, 1961.

248. Gordon, K. H., Jr.: An approach to childhood psychosis. Simultaneous treatment of mother and child. J. Amer. Acad. Child Psychiat. 2: 711-724, 1963.

249. Green, M. R., and Schecter, D. E.: Autism and symbiotic disorders in three blind children. Psychiat. Quart. 31: 628-646, 1957.

250. Greenacre, P.: On focal symbiosis. In Jessner, L., and Pavenstadt, E. (Eds.) Dynamics of Psychopathology in Childhood. New York, Grune & Stratton, 1959.

251. Gregory, I.: Genetic factors in schizophrenia. Amer. J. Psychiat. 116: 961-972, 1960.

252. Gross, H. P., and Schlange, H.: "Autistic" behavior in childhood and its causes. Z. Kinderheilk. 92: 343-353, 1965.

253. Group, A. P.: Psychopathological disorders in childhood. Theoretical considerations and a proposed classification. Group Advance. Psychiat. 6: 251-256, 1966.

254. Grunes, W. F., and Szyrunski, V.: Secondary pseudoautism caused by physiological isolation. J. Consult. Psychol. 29: 455-459, 1965.

255. Hafilena, F. P.: A case of child psychosis. J. Phillipp. Med. Ass. 33: 473-480, 1957.

256. Halpern, E.: Conceptual development in a schizophrenic boy. J. Amer. Acad. Child Psychiat. 5: 66-74, 1966.

257. Harlow, H. F., and Harlow, M. K.:

Effect of rearing conditions on behavior. Int. J. Psychiat. 1: 43-49, 1965.

258. Healy, N. M.: Giles de la Tourette Syndrome in an autistic child. J. Irish Med. Ass. 57: 93-94, 1965.

259. Heeley, A. F., and Roberts, G. E.: Tryptophan metabolism in psychotic children. Develop. Med. Child. Neurol. 7: 46-49, 1965.

260. Heilburn, A. B.: Maternal authoritarianism, social class and filial schizophrenia. J. Gen. Psychol. 65: 235-241, 1961.

261. Hellersberg, E. F.: Unevenness of growth in its relation to vulnerability, anxiety, ego weaknesses and the schizophrenic pattern. Amer. J. Orthopsychiat. 27: 577-586, 1957.

262. Hermelin, B., and O'Connor, N.: The response and self-generated behavior of severely disturbed children and severely subnormal controls. Brit. J. Soc. Clin. Psychol. 2: 37-43, 1963.

263. Hewett, F. M.: Teaching speech to an autistic child through operant conditions. Amer. J. Orthopsychiat. 35: 927-936, 1965.

264. Hift, E. et al.: Results of Shock Therapy in childhood schizophrenia. Schweiz. Arch. Neur. Psychiat. 86: 256-272, 1960.

265. Hingtgen, J. N.: Shaping cooperative responses in early childhood schizophrenics. In Ullman, L., and Krasner, L. (Eds.) Case Studies in Behavior Modification. New York, Holt, Rinehart, and Winston (in press).

266. Hinton, G. G.: Childhood psychosis or mental retardation: a diagnostic dilemma. II. Pediatric and neurological aspects. Canad. Med. Ass. J. 89: 1020-1024, 1963.

267. Hirsch, E. A.: Interpretive flexibility or a condition set by schizophrenic children in psychotherapy. Amer. J. Orthopsychiat. 30: 397-399, 1960.

268. Hirsch, E. A.: Basic mistrust and defensive omnipotence in a severely disorganized child. J. Amer. Acad. Child Psychiat. 5: 243-254, 1966.

269. Hirschberg, J. C., and Bryant, R. N.: Problems in the differential diagnosis of childhood schizophrenia. In Mc-

Intosh, R., and Hare, C. C. (Eds.) Neurology and Psychiatry in Childhood. Res. Publ. Ass. Nerv. Ment. Dis. 34: Baltimore, Williams and Williams, 1956.

270. Hoberman, S. E., and Goldfarb, W.: Speech reception thresholds in schizophrenic children. J. Speech Hearing Res. 6: 101-106, 1963.

271. Holstein, A. P. et al.: Haloperidol, a preliminary clinical study. Amer. J. Psychiat. 122: 462-463, 1965.

272. Hunt, B. R. et al.: Chlorpromazine in treatment of severe emotional disorders. Amer. Med. Ass. J. Dis. Child. 91: 268-277, 1956.

273. Hunt, B. R.: Schizophrenia in childhood. Pediat. Clin. N. Amer. 493-512, 1958.

274. Hutt, C. et al.: Arousal and childhood autism. Nature (London) 204: 908-909, 1964.

275. Hutt, S. J. et al.: A behavioral and electroencephalographic study of autistic children. J. Psychiat. Res. 3: 181-197, 1965.

276. Hutt, C., and Ounsted, C.: The biological significance of gaze aversion with particular reference to the syndrome of infantile autism. Behav. Sci. 11: 346-356, 1966.

277. Ingram, T. T. S., and Reid, J. F.: Developmental aphasia observed in department of child psychiatry. Arch. Dis. Child 31: 161-172, 1956.

278. Ishizima, T.: The low-grade idiot and so-called early infantile autism. J. Jap. Child Psychiat. 2: 226-237, 1961.

279. Jackson, D. D. et al.: Psychiatrists' conceptions of the schizophrenic parent. Arch. Neur. Psychiat. 79: 448-459, 1958.

280. Jackson, L.: Non-speaking children: seven years later. Brit. J. Med. Psychol. 31: 92-103, 1958.

281. Jackson, D. D.: Introduction to Jackson, D. D. (Ed.) The Etiology of Schizophrenia. New York, Basic Books, 1960.

282. Jensen, S. E. et al.: Treatment of severely emotionally disturbed children in a community. Canad. Psychiat. Ass. J. 10: 325-331, 1965.

283. Johada, H., and Goldfarb, W.: Use

of a standard observation for the psychological evaluation of nonspeaking children. Amer. J. Orthopsychiat. 27: 745-754, 1957.

284. Johnson, J. L.: Learning problems in a schizophrenic child. Exceptional Child 27: 135-138, 1960-1961.

285. Kallmann, J., and Roth, B.: Genetic aspects of preadolescent schizophrenia. Amer. J. Psychiat. 112: 599-606, 1956.

286. Kamp, L.: Autistic syndrome in one of a pair of monozygotic twins. Psychiat. Neurol. Neuroschir. 67: 143-147, 1964.

287. Kane, R. P. et al.: Improvement —real or apparent? A seven year follow-up of children hospitalized and discharged from a residential setting. Amer. J. Psychiat. 117: 1023-1027, 1961.

288. Kanner, L.: General concept of schizophrenia at different ages. Res. Publ. Ass. Nerv. Ment. Dis. 34: 451-453, 1955.

289. Kanner, L., and Lesser, L.: Early infantile autism. Pediat. Clin. N. Amer. 5: 711-730, 1958.

290. Kanner, L.: History and present status of childhood schizophrenia in the U.S.A. Z. Kinderpsychiat. 25: 138-149, 1958.

291. Kanner, L.: The specificity of early infantile autism. Z. Kinderpsychiat. 25: 108-113, 1958.

292. Kanner, L.: Schizophrenia as a concept. In Scher, S. C., and Davis, H. R. (Eds.) The Outpatient Treatment of Schizophrenia. New York, Grune & Stratton, 1960.

293. Kanner, L.: Emotionally disturbed children: an historical review. Child Develop. 33: 97-102, 1962.

294. Kanner, L.: The scope and goal of psychotherapy with children. Amer. J. Psychother. 17: 366-374, 1963.

295. Kanner, L.: Infantile autism and the schizophrenias. Behav. Sci. 10: 412-420, 1965.

296. Kaplan, L. K., and Turitz, L. L.: Treatment of severely emotionally traumatized children in a foster home setting. Amer. J. Orthopsychiat. 27: 271-285, 1957.

297. Kaufman, I. et al.: Childhood psychosis. I. Childhood schizophrenia; Treatment of children, and parent. Amer. J. Orthopsychiat. 27: 683-690, 1957.

298. Kaufman, I. et al.: Four types of defense in mothers and fathers of schizophrenic children. Amer. J. Orthopsychiat. 29: 460-472, 1959.

299. Kaufman, I. et al.: Treatment implications of a new classification of parents of schizophrenic children. Amer. J. Psychiat. 116: 920-924, 1960.

300. Kaufman, I. et al.: Success and failure in the treatment of childhood schizophrenia. Amer. J. Psychiat. 118: 909-1015, 1962.

301. Kaufman, I.: The defensive aspects of impulsivity. Bull. Menninger Clin. 27: 24-32, 1963.

302. Kaufman, I. et al.: Adaptation of treatment techniques to a new classification of schizophrenic children. J. Amer. Acad. Child Psychiat. 2: 460-483, 1963.

303. Kawabata, T.: A case of a child with autism due to the disturbance of mother-child relations. J. Jap. Child Psychiat. 2: 184-189, 1961.

304. Kawabata, T. et al.: A symptomatological study of a psychotic child with brain injury. J. Jap. Child Psychiat. 4: 73-74, 1963.

305. Kay, P.: The phenomenology of schizophrenia in childhood: a review of the literature and clinical material. J. Hillside Hosp. 11: 206-216, 1962.

306. Kemph, J. P. et al.: New directions in the inpatient treatment of psychotic children in a training center. Amer. J. Psychiat. 119: 934-939, 1963.

307. Kemph, J. P. et al.: Promoting the development of ego functions in the middle phase of treatment of psychotic children. J. Amer. Acad. Child Psychiat. 4: 401-412, 1965.

308. Kemph, J. P.: Brief hospitalization in treatment of psychotic child. Psychiat. Dig. 27: 35-43, 1966.

309. Kennard, M. A.: Characteristics of thought disturbances as related to EEG findings in children and adolescents. Amer. J. Psychiat. 115: 911-921, 1959.

310. King, P. D.: Theoretical consid-

erations of psychotherapy with a schizophrenic child. J. Amer. Acad. Child Psychiat. 3: 638-649, 1964.

311. Kissell, S.: Schizophrenic patterns on the WISC: A missing control. J. Clin. Psychol. 22: 201, 1966.

312. Klapman, H. et al.: Rehabilitation of children discharged from a psychiatric hospital. Amer. J. Orthopsychiat. 34: 942-947, 1964.

313. Klebanoff, L. B.: Parental attitudes of mothers of schizophrenic, brain-injured and retarded and normal children. Amer. J. Orthopsychiat. 29: 445-454, 1959.

314. Kloss, M. et al.: Difficulties of differentiation between the child schizophrenias and the schizophrenia-like syndromes on the basis of organic changes in the brain. Neurol. Neurochir. Psychiat. Pol. 15: 207-212, 1965.

315. Knight, E. H.: Some considerations regarding the concept "autism". Dis. Nerv. Syst. 24: 224-229, 1963.

316. Knowlton, P.: Treatment of a borderline psychotic five-year old girl. In Caplan, G. (Ed.) Emotional Problems of Early Childhood. New York, Basic Books, 1955.

317. Koegler, R. R., and Colbert, E. G.: Childhood schizophrenia: role of family physician. J. Amer. Med. Ass. 171: 1045-1050, 1959.

318. Kramer, Y. et al.: Whirling as a clinical test in childhood schizophrenia. J. Pediat. 52: 295-303, 1958.

319. Krevelen, D. A.: Autismus infantum. Z. Kinderpsychiat. 27: 97-107, 1960.

320. Kucera, O. et al.: Psychopathologic manifestations in children with mild encephalopathy. Prague: Statni' Zdravotnicke' Naklodetelstvi' 235-247, 1961.

321. Langdell, J. I.: Child psychotherapy in Britain. Amer. J. Psychother. 20: 489-498, 1966.

322. Langsley, D. G. et al.: Schizophrenia in triplets: A family study. Amer. J. Psychiat. 120: 528-532, 1963.

323. LaVietes, R. L. et al.: A Psychiatric day treatment center and school for young children and their parents. Amer. J. Orthopsychiat. 30: 468-482, 1960.

324. LaVietes, R. et al.: Day Treatment Center and school: Seven Years Experience. Amer. J. Orthopsychiat. 35: 160-169, 1965.

325. Lebowitz, M. H. et al.: Schizophrenia in children. The frequency and quality of certain motor acts in diagnosis. Amer. J. Dis. Child. 102: 25-27, 1961.

326. Lehman, E. et al.: Use of reserpine in autistic children. J. Nerv. Ment. Dis. 125: 351-356, 1957.

327. Lempp, R.: Schizophrenia in childhood and adolescence. Landarzt. 42: 94-98, 1966.

328. Leonhard, K.: Uber Kindliche Katatonien. Psychiat. Neurol. Med. Psychol. 12: 1-12, 1960.

329. Lennard, H. L. et al.: Interaction in families with a schizophrenic child. Arch. Gen. Psychiat. 12: 166-183, 1965.

330. Leven, S., and Impastato, A. S.: A pilot study of L-Glutavite in hospitalized "autistic" and "hyperactive" children. Amer. J. Psychiat. 118: 459, 1961.

331. Levy, D. M.: Early infantile deprivation. In Kolb, L. C., Masland, R. L., and Cooke, R. S. (Eds.) Mental Retardation, Baltimore, Williams and Williams, 1962.

332. Levy, D. M.: The "Act" as an operational concept in psychodynamics. Psychosom. Med. 24: 49-57, 1962.

333. Lewis, H. B.: A case of watching as defense against an oral incorporation fantasy. Psychoanal. Rev. 50: 68-80, 1963.

334. Lewis, S. R., and Van Ferney, S.: Early recognition of infantile autism. J. Pediat. 56: 510-512, 1960.

335. Lifton, N., and Smolen, E. M.: Group psychotherapy with schizophrenic children. Int. J. Group Psychother. 16: 23-41, 1966.

336. Livermore, J. B.: A schizophrenic child reviews her own treatment. Amer. J. Orthopsychiat. 26: 365-373, 1956.

337. Loomis, E. A. et al.: Play patterns as non-verbal indices of ego functions; a preliminary report. Amer. J. Orthopsychiat. 27: 691-700, 1957.

338. Loomis, E. A., and Meyer, L. R.: Observation and recording: a simultaneous process. Amer. J. Orthopsychiat. 29: 574-582, 1959.

339. Loomis, E. A.: Autistic and symbiotic syndromes in children. Monogr. Soc. Res. Child Develop. 25: 39-48, 1960.

340. Lordi, W. M.: Infantile autism: a family approach. Int. J. Group Psychother. 14: 360-365, 1964.

341. Lovaas, O. I. et al.: Building social behavior in autistic children by use of electric shock. J. Exp. Res. Personal. 1: 99-109, 1965.

342. Lovaas, O. I. et al.: Experimental studies in childhood schizophrenia. Analysis of self-destructive behavior. J. Exp. Child Psychol. 2: 67-84, 1965.

343. Lovaas, O. I. et al.: Acquisition of imitative speech by schizophrenic children. Science 151: 705-707, 1966.

344. Lovatt, M.: Autistic children in a day nursery. Children 103-108, 1962.

345. Lovatt, M.: Some approaches to Teaching Autistic Children. In Weston, P.T.B. (Ed.) Pergamon Press, London, 1965.

346. Lowe, L. H. Families of children with early childhood schizophrenia. Selected demographic information. Arch. Gen. Psychiat. 14: 26-30, 1966.

347. Lustman, S. L.: Psychic energy and mechanisms of defense. In Eissler et al. (Eds.) Psychoanal. Stud. Child 12: 151-165, 1957.

348. MacAndrew, C., and Geertsma, R. H.: A reanalysis of "Psychiatrists' Conceptions of the Schizophrenogenic Parent", J. of Clin. Psychol. 17: 82-87, 1961.

349. MacGillivray, R. C.: Larval psychosis of idiocy. Amer. J. Ment. Defic. 60: 570-572, 1956.

350. Mack, J., and Gair, D. S.: Clinical criteria of psychosis in children, presented at Harvard Medical School, Dept. of Psychiatry Research Conf. 1965.

351. MacMillan, M. B.: Extra-scientific influences in the history of childhood psychopathology. Amer. J. Psychiat. 116: 1091-1096, 1960.

352. MacMillan, M. B.: A Pavlovian approach to symbiotic psychoses. J. Nerv. Ment. Dis. 132: 397-403, 1961.

353. Mahler, M. S.: On symbiotic child psychosis: genetic, dynamic, and restitution aspects. In Eissler et al. (Eds.) Psychoanal. Stud. Child. 10: 195-214, 1955.

354. Mahler, M. S., and Elkisch, P.: Some observations on the disturbances of the ego in a case of infantile psychosis. In Eissler et al. (Eds.) Psychoanal. Stud. Child. 8: 252-261, 1958.

355. Mahler, M. S.: Autism and symbiosis, two extreme disturbances of identity. In Eissler et al. (Eds.) Int. J. Psychoanal. 39: 77-83, 1958.

356. Mahler, M. S. et al.: Severe emotional disturbances in childhood: psychoses. In Arieti, S. (Ed.) American Handbook of Psychiatry. New York, Basic Books, 1959.

357. Mahler, M. S., and Furer, M.: Observations on research regarding the "symbiotic syndrome" of infantile psychosis. Psychoanal. Quart. 29: 317-327, 1960.

358. Mahler, M. S.: On sadness and grief in childhood. In Eissler et al. (Eds.) Psychoanal. Stud. Child. 16: 332-351, 1961.

359. Mahler, M. S.: "Cruel experiments of Nature", Foreword to Reiss Davis Clin. Bull. 1: 54-56, 1964.

360. Mahler, M. S.: On early infantile psychosis. The symbiotic and autistic syndromes. J. Amer. Acad. Child Psychiat. 4: 554-565, 1965.

361. Maier, H. W., and Campbell, S. G.: Routines: a pilot study of three selected routines and their impact upon the child in residential treatment. Amer. J. Orthopsychiat. 27: 701-709, 1957.

362. Malamud, N.: Heller's disease and childhood schizophrenia. Amer. J. Psychiat. 116: 215-218, 1959.

363. Marcus, J.: Borderline states in childhood. J. Child. Psychol. Psychiat. 4: 207-218, 1963.

364. Masland, R. L., and Sarason, S. B.: Mental Subnormality. New York, Basic Books, 1958.

365. Maslow, A. R.: A concentrated therapeutic relationship with a psychotic child. J. Amer. Acad. Child Psychiat. 3: 140-150, 1964.

366. May, J. M., and May, A. M.: The treatment and education of the atypical autistic child in a residential school situ-

ation. Amer. J. Ment. Defic. 64: 435-443, 1959.

367. McCollum, A. T.: Circular interaction between the young psychotic child and his mother. Social Work 9: 50-59, 1964.

368. McGinnis, M. et al.: Teaching aphasic children. Volta Rev. 50: 239-244, 1956.

369. Mechlow, J.: Psychobiological implications in insulin therapy with children. J. Nerv. Ment. Dis. 123: 432-447, 1956.

370. Mednick, S. A. et al.: A preschizophrenic sample. Acta Psychiat. Scand. 40: Suppl. 180: 135-140, 1964.

371. Menolascino, F.: Psychoses of childhood. Amer. J. Ment. Defic. 70: 83-92, 1965.

372. Menolascino, F.: Emotional disturbance and mental retardation. Amer. J. Ment. Defic. 70: 248-256, 1965.

373. Menolascino, F.: Autistic reactions in early childhood: differential diagnostic consideration. J. Child Psychol. Psychiat. 6: 203-218, 1965.

374. Menolascino, F. J.: The facade of mental retardation: its challenge to child psychiatry. Amer. J. of Psychiat. 122: 1227-2135, 1966.

375. Metz, J. R.: Conditioning generalized imitations in autistic children. J. Exp. Child Psychol. 74: 389-399, 1965.

376. Meyer, L. R.: A methodological approach to the evaluation of treatment in young non-verbal children. Amer. J. Orthopsychiat. 31: 748-756, 1961.

377. Meyer, M., and Caruth, E.: Inner and outer reality testing on the Rorschach. Reiss Davis Clin. Bull. 1: 100-106, 1964.

378. Meyers, D. I., and Goldfarb, W.: Studies of perplexity in mothers of schizophrenic children. Amer. J. Orthopsychiat. 31: 551-563, 1961.

379. Meyers, D. I., and Goldfarb, W.: Psychiatric appraisals of parents and siblings of schizophrenic children. Amer. J. Psychiat. 118, 902-908, 1962.

380. Michaux, L. et al.: The difficulty of distinguishing between dementia precocissima and evolutive backwardness. With reference to a case. Rev. Neuropsychiat. Infant. 4: 397-401, 1956.

381. Michaux, L., and Flavingy, N.: Traitement de la schizophrenic infantile. Presse Med. 64: 865-867, 1956.

382. Miksztal, M. W.: Chlorpromazine, (Thorazine) and Reserpine in Residential Treatment of Neuropsychiatric Disorders in Children. J. Nerv. Ment. Dis. 123: 477-479, 1956.

383. Miles, D. J.: The treatment of emotionally disturbed children. Canad. J. Occup. Ther. 24: 115-124, 1957.

384. Miller, B. M.: Communication with a non-verbal child. Amer. J. Psychoanal. 20: 79-82, 1960.

385. Mishler, E. G., and Scotch, N. A.: Socio-cultural factors in the epidemiology of schizophrenia. Int. J. Psychiat. 1: 258-305, 1965.

386. Mishler, E. G.: Families and schizophrenia. Ment. Hyg. 50: 552-556, 1966.

387. Mittler, P.: Education of psychotic children. In Weston, P.T.B. (Ed.) Some Approaches to Teaching Autistic Children. London, Pergamon Press, 1965.

388. Mittler, P. et al.: Prognosis in psychotic children: Report of a Follow-up Study. J. Ment. Defic. Res. 10: 73-83, 1966.

389. Moloney, J. C.: The precognitive cultural ingredients of schizophrenia. Int. J. Psychoanal. 38: 325-340, 1957.

390. Morgan, P. K.: Application of "symbolic realization" to the removal of hallucinations in childhood schizophrenia. Amer. J. Psychother. 18: 59-65, 1964.

391. Moriarty, D. M.: Psychosis-vulnerable. Psychiat. Quart. 36: 121-128, 1962.

392. Morris, D. et al.: Follow-up studies of shy, withdrawn children. II: Relative incidence of schizophrenia. Amer. J. Orthopsychiat. 27: 331-337, 1957.

393. Morrow, T., and Loomis, E.: Symbiotic aspects of a seven-year-old psychotic. In Caplan, G. (Ed.) Emotional Problems of Early Childhood. New York, Basic Books, 1955.

394. Mosse, H. L.: The misuse of the diagnosis of childhood schizophrenia. Amer. J. Psychiat. 114: 791-794, 1958.

395. Nagera, H.: Early Childhood Dis-

turbances. The Infantile Neurosis, and the Adulthood Disturbances. New York Intnat. Univ. Press, 1966.

396. Nameche, G. et al.: Early indicators of outcome in schizophrenia. J. Nerv. Ment. Dis. 139: 232-240, 1964.

397. Nichtern, S. et al.: A Community education program for the emotionally disturbed child. Amer. J. Orthopsychiat. 34: 705-712, 1964.

398. Nichtern, S.: The education and rehabilitation of childhood schizophrenics within a regular school setting. Curr. Psychiat. Ther. 5: 67-70, 1965.

399. Nichtern, S.: Developmental disturbances in childhood schizophrenia. Psychosomatics 6: 189-191, 1965.

400. Niederland, W. G.: Narcissistic ego impairment in patients with early physical malformations. In Eissler et al. (Eds.) Psychoanal. Stud. Child 20: 518-534, 1965.

401. O'Connor, N., and Hermelin, B.: Sensory dominance in autistic children and subnormal controls. Percept. Motor Skills. 16: 920, 1963.

402. O'Connor, N., and Hermelin, B.: Measures of distance and motility in psychotic children and severely subnormal controls. Brit. J. Soc. Clin. Psychol. 3: 29-33, 1964.

403. O'Gorman, G.: A hospital for the psychotic defective child. Lancet 2: 951-953, 1958.

404. Onheiber, P. et al.: Sleep and dream patterns of childhood schizophrenics. Arch. Gen. Psychiat. 12: 568-571, 1965.

405. Ortiz, E. M. et al.: Dreaming sleep in autistic and schizophrenic children. Amer. J. Psychiat. 122: 419-424, 1965.

406. Osterkamp, A., and Sands, D. J.: Early feeding and birth difficulties in childhood schizophrenia: a brief study. J. Gent. Psychol. 101: 363-366, 1962.

407. Ottinger, D. R. et al.: Visual discrimination learning in schizophrenic and normal children. J. Clin. Psychol. 21: 251-253, 1965.

408. Paleologos, M.: Treatment of childhood schizophrenia with chlorpromazine in details. G. Psichiat. Neuropat. 87: 1171-1766, 1959.

409. Pasamanick, B., and Knobloch, H.: Epidemiologic studies in the complications of pregnancy and the birth process. In Caplan, G. (Ed.) Prevention of Mental Disorders in Children, New York, Basic Books, 1961.

410. Pasamanick, B., and Knobloch, H.: Early feeding and birth difficulties in childhood schizophrenia: an explanatory note. J. Psychol. 56: 73-77, 1963.

411. Patterson, V. et al.: The relation between intention to conceive and symptoms during pregnancy. Psychosom. Med., 22: 373-376, 1960.

412. Pavenstedt, E.: History of a child with an atypical development, and some vicissitudes of his treatment. In Caplan, G. (Ed.) Emotional Problems of Early Childhood. New York, Basic Books, 1955.

413. Pavenstedt, E.: A study of immature mothers and their children. In Caplan, G. (Ed.) Prevention of Mental Disorders in Children, New York, Basic Books, 1961.

414. Peet, D. S.: Children reborn. Amer. J. Nurs. 64: 102-106, 1964.

415. Perl, W. R., and Goldberg, F. A.: Graphic demonstration of receding schizophrenia. Arch. Gen. Psychiat. 14: 48-54, 1966.

416. Perr, H. M.: Criteria distinguishing parents of schizophrenic and normal children. Arch. Neurol. Psychiat. 79: 217-224, 1958.

417. Perron, L.: The psychoses of childhood. Canad. Nurse. 60: 42-43, 1964.

418. Perry, T. L.: N-Methylmetanephrine: excretion by juvenile psychotics. Science, 139: 587-589, 1963.

419. Phillips, E. E.: Contributions to a learning theory account of childhood autism. J. Psychol. 43: 117-124, 1957.

420. Philips, I.: Children, mental retardation and emotional disorder. In Philips, I. (Ed.) Prevention and Treatment of Mental Retardation. New York, Basic Books, 1966.

421. Pittfield, M., and Oppenheim, A. N.: Child rearing attitudes of mothers of psychotic children. J. Child Psychol. Psychiat. 5: 51-57, 1964.

422. Pivovarova, Von G.: Symptomatology of the onset of Hebephrenia in

adolescence. Psychiat. Neurol. Med. Psychol. (Leipzig) 17: 185-191, 1965.

423. Plunkett, R. J., and Gordon, J. E.: Epidemiology and Mental Illness. New York, Basic Books, 1960.

424. Polan, C. C., and Spencer, B. L.: Check list of symptoms of autism in early life. W. Virginia Med. J. 55: 198-204, 1959.

425. Pollock, G. H.: On symbiosis and symbiotic neurosis. Int. J. Psychoanal. 45: 1-30, 1964.

426. Pollack, M., and Goldfarb, W.: Face-hand test in schizophrenic children. Arch. Neurol. and Psychiat: 77: 635-642, 1957.

427. Pollack, M., and Goldfarb, W.: Patterns of orientation in children in residential treatment for severe behavior disorder. Amer. J. Orthopsychiat. 27: 538-540, 1957.

428. Pollack, M., and Krieger, H. P.: Oculomotor and postural patterns in schizophrenic children. Arch. Neurol. Psychiat. 79: 720-726, 1958.

429. Pollack, M.: Brain damage, mental retardation and childhood schizophrenia. Amer. J. Psychiat. 115: 422-428, 1958.

430. Pollack, M.: Comparison of childhood, adolescent and adult schizophrenias. Arch. Gen. Psychiat. 2: 652-660, 1960.

431. Pollack, M., and Gittelman, R. K.: The Siblings of childhood schizophrenics: A Review. Amer. J. Orthopyschiat. 34: 868-874, 1964.

432. Pollack, M.: Mental Subnormality and "Childhood Schizophrenia". In Zubin, J., and Jervis, G. (Eds.) Psychopathology of Mental Development, New York, Grune and Stratton, 1966.

433. Pollack, M., and Woerner, M. G.: Pre and Perinatal Complications and "Childhood Schizophrenia". Pre-publication copy, in press in J. Child Psych. and Psychiat. 1967.

434. Potter, H. W.: Schizophrenia in children. Amer. J. Psychiat. 12: 1253-1270, 1933.

435. Prall, R., and Dealy, M. N.: Countertransference in therapy of childhood psychosis. J. Hillside Hosp. 14: 69-82, 1965.

436. Pronovost, W.: The speech behavior and language comprehension of autistic children. J. Chronic Dis. 13: 228-233, 1961.

437. Pronovost, W. et al.: A Longitudinal study of the speech behavior and language comprehension of fourteen children diagnosed atypical or autistic. Exceptional Child. 32: 19-26, 1966.

438. Rabkin, L. Y.: The Patient's family. Research Methods. Family Process 4: 105-132, 1965.

439. Rachman, S. and Berger, M.: Whirling and postural control in schizophrenic children. J. Child Psychol. Psychiat. 4: 137-155, 1963.

440. Rank, B.: Intensive study and treatment of preschool children who show marked personality deviations of "atypical development", and their parents. In Caplan, G. (Ed.) Emotional Problems of Early Childhood. New York, Basic Books, 1955.

441. Rappaport, J.: A study of the influence of the normal heartbeat on a group of autistic girls. J. Amer. Med. Wom. Ass. 18: 982-984, 1963.

442. Rawitt, K. C.: The usefulness and effectiveness of Equanil in children. Amer. J. Psychiat. 115: 1120-1121, 1959.

443. Rees, E. L.: Metabolism of schizophrenic child. J. Amer. Med. Wom. Ass. 11: 11-16, 1956.

444. Reiser, D. E., and Brown, J. L.: Patterns of later development in children with infantile psychosis. J. Amer. Acad. Child Psychiat. 3: 650-657, 1964.

445. Reiser, D. E.: Psychosis of infancy and early childhood, as manifested by children with atypical development. New Eng. J. Med. 269: 790-798, 844-850, 1963.

446. Reiser, D. E.: Infantile psychosis. Ment. Hyg., Special Sci. Issue 50: 588-589, 1966.

447. Rice, G., and Klein, A.: Getting the message from a schizophrenic child. Psychiatry 27: 163-169, 1964.

448. Rice, G. et al.: Differences in communicative impact between mothers of psychotic and non-psychotic children.

Amer. J. Orthopsychiat. 36: 529-543, 1966.

449. Richards, J. E.: Techniques used in a school program for children emerging from early infantile autism. Exceptional Child. 29: 348-357, 1962-1963.

450. Rimland, B.: Infantile Autism. New York, Appleton-Century-Crofts, 1964.

451. Robertson, M. F.: Shadow therapy. Ment. Retard. 2: 218-223, 1964.

452. Robinson, J. F. (Ed.): Psychiatric In-patient Treatment of Children. Washington, J. Amer. Psychoanal. Ass. 1957.

453. Robinson, J. F.: The psychoses of early childhood. Amer. J. Orthopsychiat. 31: 536-550, 1961.

454. Rolo, A. et al.: Preliminary method for study of LSD with children. Int. J. Neuropsychiat. 1: 522-555, 1965.

455. Rose, J. A.: Stress outcome: schizophrenia or creativity? Pediatrics. 28: 472-479, 1961.

456. Rosenberger, L., and Woolf, M.: Schizophrenic development of two children in the 4-6 age group. Psychoanal. Rev. 57: 469-530, 1964.

457. Rosenblut, B. et al.: Vestibular responses of some deaf and aphasic children. Ann. Otol. 69: 747-755, 1960.

458. Rosenfeld, S. K., and Sprince, M. P.: An attempt to formulate the meaning of the concept "borderline". In Eissler et al. (Eds.) Psychoanal. Stud. Child. 18: 603-635, 1963.

459. Rosenfeld, S. K., and Sprince, M. P.: Some thoughts on the technical handling of borderline children. In Eissler et al. (Eds.) Psychoanal. Stud. Child. 20: 495-517, 1965.

460. Rosenthal, D.: Confusion of identity and the frequency of schizophrenia in twins. Arch. Gen. Psychiat. 3: 297-304, 1960.

461. Ross, A. O.: Schizophrenic child and his mother. J. Abnorm. Psychol. 51: 133-139, 1955.

462. Rothman, E. P.: Some aspects of the relationship between perception and motility in children. Genet. Psychol. Monogr. 63: 67-102, 1961.

463. Rousos, I. C.: Planning occupational therapy for schizophrenic children.

Amer. J. Occup. Ther. 14: 137-139, 1960.

464. Roy, I.: Zur Frage der Dementia Infantilis Heller (on the problem of dementia Infantile of Heller), Helvetia Paediatrica 14: 288-301, 1959.

465. Rubin, L. S.: Patterns of pupillary dilation and constriction in psychotic adults and autistic children. J. Nerv. Ment. Dis. 133: 130-142, 1961.

466. Rubin, L. S.: Autonomic dysfunction in psychoses: adults and autistic children. Arch. Gen. Psychiat. 7: 1-14, 1962.

467. Ruttenberg, B. A. et al.: An instrument for evaluating autistic children. J. Amer. Acad. Child Psychiat. 5: 453-478, 1966.

468. Rutter, M.: Medical aspects of the education of psychotic (Autistic) children. In Weston, P.T.B. (Ed.) Approaches to Teaching Autistic Children, London, Pergamon Press, 1965.

469. Rutter, M.: Influence of organic and emotional factors on origins, nature and outcome of childhood psychosis, Develop. Med. Child. Neurol. 7: 518-528, 1965.

470. Rutter, M.: Speech disorders in a series of autistic children. In Franklin, A. W. (Ed.) Children with Communication Problems, London, Pitman, 1963.

471. Rutter, M.: Prognosis: Psychotic children in adolescence and early adult life. In Wing, J. (Ed.) Childhood Autism, London, Pergamon Press, 1966.

472. Rutter, M.: Behavioral and Cognitive Characteristics of a series of psychotic children. In Wing, J. (Ed.) Childhood Autism. London, Pergamon Press, 1966.

473. Sachs, L. J.: On changes in identification from machine to cripple. In Eissler et al. (Eds.) Psychoanal. Stud. Child. 12: 356-375, 1957.

474. Safrin, R. K.: Differences in visual perception and in visual-motor functioning between psychotic and nonpsychotic children. J. Consult. Psychol. 28: 41-45, 1964.

475. Sankar, S. D. V., and Sankar, D. B.: Biochemical studies on childhood schizophrenia and autism. Fed. Proc. 21: 348, 1962.

476. Sankar, S. et al.: General metabolic

studies on schizophrenic children. Ann. N. Y. Acad. Sci. 96: 392-398, 1962.

477. Sankar, D. V. S., et al.: Metabolic effects of psychoactive drugs. Recent Adv. Biol. Psychiat. 4: 247-256, New York, Plenum Press, 1962.

478. Sankar, S. D. V., et al.: Biochemical parameters of childhood schizophrenia (autism) and growth. Recent Advances in Biol. Psychiat. 5: 176-183, 1963.

479. Sanua, V. D.: Sociocultural factors in families of schizophrenics: a review of the literature. Psychiatry, 24: 246-265, 1961.

480. Sarvis, M. A.: Etiological variables in autism. Psychiatry. 24: 307-317, 1961.

481. Sarvis, M. A.: Paranoid reactions. Arch. Gen. Psychiat. 6: 157-162, 1962.

482. Sarvis, M. A., and Rauch, S.: Longitudinal study of a patient with premature ego development. J. Amer. Acad. Child. Psychiat. 3: 46-64, 1966.

483. Saski, I. et al.: Clinical effect of Thioridazine (Mellaril). J. Yamaguchi Med. Ass. 12: 154-162, 1963.

484. Scanlon, J. B. et al.: Language training in the treatment of the autistic child functioning on a retarded level. Ment. Retard. 1: 305-310, 1963.

485. Schacter, F. et al.: Childhood schizophrenia and mental retardation: differential diagnosis before and after one year of psychotherapy. Amer. J. Orthopsychiat. 32: 584-595, 1962.

486. Schain, R. J., and Yannet, H.: Infantile autism: an analysis of 50 cases and a consideration of certain relevant neurophysiological concepts. J. Pediat. 57: 560-567, 1960.

487. Schain, R. J., and Freedman, D. X.: Studies on 5-hydroxyindole metabolism in autistic and other retarded children. J. Pediat. 58: 315-320, 1961.

488. Scheidlinger, S.: Experimental group treatment of severely deprived latency-age children. Amer. J. Orthopsychiat. 30: 356, 1960.

489. Schneer, H. I.: Recent advances in the treatment of childhood schizophrenia. J. Hillside Hosp. 11: 199-205, 1962.

490. Schofield, W., and Balian, L.: A comparative study of the personal histories of schizophrenic and nonpsychiatric patients. J. Abnorm. Psychol. 59: 216-225, 1959.

491. Schooler, C.: Birth order and schizophrenia. Arch. Gen. Psychiat. 4: 91-97, 1961.

492. Schopler, E.: The development of body image and symbol formation through bodily contact with an autistic child. J. Child. Psychol. Psychiat. 3: 191-202, 1962.

493. Schopler, E.: Early infantile autism and receptor processes. Arch. Gen. Psychiat. 13: 327-335, 1965.

494. Schopler, E.: Visual vs. tactual receptor preference in normal vs. schizophrenic children. J. Abnorm. Psychol. 71: 108-114, 1966.

495. Schulman, J. L.: Management of the child with early infantile autism. Amer. J. Psychiat. 120: 250-254, 1963.

496. Schumann, W.: Zur Problematik des kindlichen Autismus und der psychologischen Nosologie. Prax. Kinderpsychol. 15: 168-175, 1966.

497. Seidman, F.: Outpatient treatment of a seriously disturbed child in a child guidance center. J. Clin. Psychol. 17: 220-225, 1961.

498. Settlage, C. F.: Psychoanalytic theory in relation to the nosology of childhood psychic disorders. J. Amer. Psychoanal. Ass. 12: 776-800, 1964.

499. Shapiro, M. I., and Shugart, G.: Ego therapy with parents of the psychotic child. Amer. J. Orthopsychiat. 78: 786-793, 1958.

500. Shapiro, T.: Hand morphology in some severely impaired schizophrenic children. Amer. J. Psychiat. 122: 432-435, 1965.

501. Sharoff, R. L.: Enforced restrictions of communication, its implications for the emotional and intellectual development of the deaf child. Amer. J. Psychiat. 116: 443-446, 1959.

502. Shaw, C. R. et al.: Effects of tryptophan loading on indole excretion. Arch. Gen. Psychiat. 1: 366-370, 1959.

503. Shaw, C. R., and Sutton, H. E.: Metabolic studies in childhood schizophrenia; II. Amino acid excretion patterns.

Arch. Gen. Psychiat. 3: 91/519-94/522, 1960.

504. Sherwin, A. C. et al.: Treatment of psychosis in early childhood with triodothyronine. Amer. J. Psychiat. 115: 166-167, 1958.

505. Shevrin, H., and Toussieng, P. W.: Vicissitudes of the need for tactile stimulation in instinctual development. In Eissler et al. (Eds.) Psychoanal. Stud. Child. 20: 310-339, 1965.

506. Shields, J., and Slater, E.: Heredity and Psychological Abnormality. In Eyseuck, H. J. (Ed.) Handbook of Abnorm. Psychol., Basic Books, New York, 1961.

507. Shore, M. F. et al.: Stages in the Evolution of Internalized Impulse Controls as Revealed in the Treatment of an Atypical Child. Amer. J. Orthopsychiat. 310: 187-189, 1961.

508. Shugart, G.: Preventive and treatment methods for psychotic children. In Progress in Psychotherapy, Grune and Stratton, New York, 1956.

509. Shugart, G:. History-taking in infantile psychosis. J. Soc. Work, 1: 84-88, 1956.

510. Shugart, G.: Casework with parents of psychotic children. Social Casework 38: 8-15, 1957.

511. Shulman, J. L.: Management of the child with early infantile autism. Amer. J. Psychiat. 20: 250-254, 1963.

512. Silbermann, I.: Two types of pre-Oedipal character disorders. Int. J. Psychoanal. 38: 350-358, 1957.

513. Silberstein, R. M. et al.: Avoiding institutionalizing psychotic children. Int. J. Neuropsychiat. 1: 144-148, 1965.

514. Silver, A. A.: Management of children with schizophrenia. Amer. J. Psychother. 9: 196-215, 1955.

515. Silver, A. A. et al.: The association of schizophrenia in childhood with primitive postural responses and decreased muscle tone. Develop. Med. Child. Neurol. 6: 495-497, 1964.

516. Simmons, J. et al.: Modification of autistic behavior with LSD-25. Amer. J. Psychiat. 122: 1201-1211, 1966.

517. Simon, G. B., and Gillies, S. M.: Some physical characteristics of a group of psychotic children. Brit. J. Psychiat. 110: 104-107, 1964.

518. Simon, N. M., and Senturia, A. G.: Adoption and psychiatric illness. Amer. J. Psychiat. 122: 858-868, 1966.

519. Simon, G. B., and Tarnoky, A. L.: Insulin tolerance in psychotic children. Amer. J. Ment. Defic. 70: 829-834, 1966.

520. Singer, M. T., and Wynne, L. C.: Differentiating characteristics of parents of childhood schizophrenics, childhood neurotic and young adult schizophrenics. Amer. J. Psychiat. 120: 234-243, 1963.

521. Singer, M. T. et al.: Thought disorder and family relations of schizophrenics, three methodologies using projective techniques. Arch. Gen. Psychiat. 12: 187-200, 1965.

522. Smolen, E. M.: Some thoughts on schizophrenia in childhood. J. Amer. Acad. Child Psychiatry. 4: 443-472, 1965.

523. Smolen, E. M., and Lifton, N.: A special treatment program for schizophrenic children in a Child Guidance Clinic. Amer. J. Orthopsychiat. 36: 735-742, 1966.

524. Sobel, D. E.: Children of schizophrenic patients: preliminary observations on early development. Amer. J. Psychiat. 118: 512-517, 1961.

525. Soddy, K.: The autistic child. Practitioner. 192: 525-533, 1964.

526. Souza, D. S.: Annihilation and reconstruction of object relationship in a schizophrenic girl. Int. J. Psychoanal. 41: 554-558, 1960.

527. Souza, D. S.: Schizophrenic syndrome in childhood. Brit. Med. J. 5257: 945-947, 1961.

528. Speers, R. W., and Lansing, C.: Group psychotherapy with preschool psychotic children and collateral group therapy of their parents: preliminary report. Amer. J. Orthopsychiat. 34: 659-666, 1964.

529. Speers, R. W., and Lansing, C.: Group Therapy in Childhood Psychoses. Chapel Hill, N. C., Univ. North Carolina, 1965.

530. Spivack, G., and Levine, M.: The Devereux child behavior rating scale: A study of symptom behaviors in latency

äge atypical children. Amer. J. Ment. Defic. 68: 700-717, 1964.

531. Spotnitz, H. et al.: Ego Reinforcement in the schizophrenic child. Amer. J. Orthopsychiat. 26: 146-164, 1956.

532. Stabenau, J. R. et al.: A comparative study of families of schizophrenics, delinquents and normals. Psychiatry 28: 45-49, 1965.

533. Steisel, I. M. et al.: Measuring interaction in non-verbal psychotic children. Amer. J. Orthopsychiat. 30: 405-411, 1960.

534. Steisel, I. M. et al.: Interaction in non-verbal psychotic children. II. Measuring by a differential diagnostic instrument. Arch. Gen. Psychiat. 5: 141-145, 1961.

535. Stewart, R. H., and Sardo, R.: The psychotherapy of a blind schizophrenic child. J. Amer. Acad. Child Psychiat. 4: 123-132, 1965.

536. Stroh, G.: On the diagnosis of childhood psychosis. J. Child Psychol. Psychiat. 1: 238-243, 1960.

537. Stroh, G., and Buick, D.: Perceptual development and childhood psychosis. Int. J. Med. Psychol. 37: 291-299, 1964.

538. Sutton, H. E., and Read, J. H.: Abnormal amino acid metabolism in a case suggesting autism. Amer. J. Dis. Child. 96: 23-28, 1958.

539. Syner, F. H., and Shaw, C. R.: Effect of schizophrenic serum on in vitro synthesis of glutamine and gamma aminobuyric acid. Compr. Psychiat. 3: 309-313, 1962.

540. Szurek, S.: Psychotic episodes and psychotic maldevelopment. (Symposium on Childhood Schizophrenia). Amer. J. Orthopsychiat. 26: 519-543, 1956.

541. Szurek, S. A., and Berlin, I. N.: Elements of psychotherapeutics with schizophrenic child and his parents. Psychiatry 19: 1-9, 1956.

542. Taft, L. T., and Goldfarb, W.: Prenatal and perinatal factors in childhood schizophrenia. Devel. Med. Child Neurol. 6: 32-43, 1964.

543. Takahaski, A.: Supplement on psychic symptoms of mentally retarded children. J. Jap. Child Psychiat. 1: 50-57, 1960.

544. Tec, L.: Vicissitudes in guidance of parents of schizophrenic children. J. Nerv. Ment. Dis. 124: 233-238, 1956.

545. Terris, M. et al.: Relation of prematurity and previous fetal loss to childhood schizophrenia. Amer. J. Psychiat. 121: 476-481, 1964.

546. Tesarova, O., and Fedor, P.: Quantitative evaluation of psychopharmacological treatment in pedopsychiatry. Activ. Nerv. Sup. 6: 197-198, 1964.

547. Thomas, R.: Comments on some aspects of self and object representation in a group of psychotic children. An application of Anna Freud's Diagnostic Profile. In Eissler et al (Eds.) Psychoanal. Stud. Child. 21: 527-580, Int'l. Univ. Press, New York, 1966.

548. Tien, H. C., and Williams, M. W.: Organic integrity test (OIT) in children. Arch. Gen. Psychiat. 12: 159-165, 1965.

549. Tilton, J. R., and Ottinger, D. R.: Comparison of the toy play behavior of autistic, retarded, and normal children. Psychol. Rep. 15: 967-975, 1964.

550. Toler, A., and Rafferty, W.: Incidence of symptoms of early infantile autism in subsequently hospitalized psychiatric patients. Dis. Nerv. Syst. 24: 423-429, 1963.

551. Toomey, L. C., and Allen, C. E.: Use of the Vineland Social Maturity scale for evaluating progress of psychotic children in a therapeutic nursery school. Amer. J. Orthopsychiat. 35: 152-159, 1965.

552. Tustin, F.: A significant element in the development of autism. A psychoanalytic approach. J. Child. Psychol. Psychiat. 7: 53-67, 1966.

553. Uschakov, G. K.: Early diagnosis of schizophrenia in children and adolescents. I. Early diagnosis of early childhood schizophrenia. Deutsch. Gesundh. 20: 1922-1925, 1965.

554. Vaillant, G. E.: John Haslam on early infantile autism. Amer. J. Psychiat. 119: 376, 1962.

555. Vaillant, G. E.: Twins discordant for early infantile autism. Arch. Gen. Psychiat. 9: 163-167, 1963.

556. Van Krevelen, D. A., and Kuipers,

C.: The psychopathology of autistic psychopathy. Acta Paedopsychiat. 29: 22-31, 1962.

557. Varley, J.: The autistic child. Speech Path. Ther. 8: 46-51, 1965.

558. Viitamaki, R. O.: Psychoses in childhood and psychological follow-up study, II. Acta Psychiat. Scand. Suppl. 174: 33-73, 1964.

559. Vorster, D.: An investigation into the part played by organic factors in childhood schizophrenia. J. Ment. Sicence 106: 494-522, 1960.

560. Walter, B.: Over het kinderhjk autisme, in het bizoner' bij doofstomment. Tijd Sehr. Opvoedk 3: 224-251, 1958.

561. Ward, T. F., and Hoddinott, B. A.: Early infantile autism in fraternal twins. A case report. Canad. Psychiat. Ass. J: 7: 191-196, 1962.

562. Ward, T. F.: The course of childhood schizophrenia. Dis. Nerv. Syst. 24: 211-220, 1963.

563. Ward, T. F. et al.: A study of childhood schizophrenia and early infantile autism. Canad. Psychiat. Ass. J. 10: 377-386, 1965.

564. Wassing, H. E.: Cognitive functioning in early infantile autism. Acta Paedopsychiat. (Basel) 32: 122-135, 1965.

565. Weber, J. L.: Speech and language abilities of emotionally disturbed children. Canad. Psychiat. Ass. J. 10: 417-420, 1965.

566. Webster, T. G.: Problems of emotional development in young retarded children. Amer. J. Psychiat. 120: 37-43, 1963.

567. Wechsler, D., and Jaros, E.: Schizophrenic patterns on the WISC. J. Clin. Psychol. 21: 288-291, 1965.

568. Weil, A. P.: Some evidence of deviational development in infancy and early childhood. Psychoanal. Stud. Child. 11: 293-299, 1956.

569. Weiland, I. H., and Rudnik, R.: Considerations of the development and treatment of autistic childhood psychosis. In Eissler et al. (Eds.) Psychoanal. Stud. Child. 16: 549-563, 1961.

570. Weiland, I. H.: Development of object relationships and childhood psychosis. J. Amer. Acad. Child. Psychiat. 3: 317-329, 1964.

571. Weiland, I. H., and Legg, D. R.: Formal speech characteristics as a diagnostic aid in childhood psychosis. Amer. J. Orthopsychiat. 34: 91-94, 1964.

572. Weiland, I. H.: Considerations on the development of symbiosis, symbiotic psychoses, and the nature of separation anxiety. Int. J. Psychoanal. 47: 1-5, 1966.

573. Weiner, M. F.: Hallucinations in children. Arch. Gen. Psychiat. 5: 540-544, 1961.

574. Wender, P. H.: On necessary and sufficient conditions-psychiatric explanation. Arch. Gen. Psychiat. 16: 4-47, 1967.

575. Werkman, S.: Present trends in schizophrenia research: implications for childhood schizophrenia. Amer. J. Orthopsychiat. 29: 473-480, 1959.

576. Wetzel, R. J. et al.: Outpatient treatment of autistic behavior. Behav. Res. Ther. 4: 169-177, 1966.

577. Wexler, M.: Hypotheses concerning ego-deficiency in schizophrenia. In Scher, S. C. and Davis, H. R. (Eds.) The Outpatient Treatment of Schizophrenia, New York, Grune and Stratton, 1960.

578. White, P. T. et al.: The neurologic status of children with early infantile autism: an EEG survey. Electroenceph. Clin. Neurophysiol. 17: 461-462, 1964.

579. White, P. T. et al.: EEG abnormalities in early childhood schizophrenia: a double-blind study of psychiatrically disturbed and normal children during promazine sedation. Amer. J. Psychiat. 120: 950-958, 1964.

580. White, R. W.: The experience of efficacy in schizophrenia. Psychiatry, 28: 199-211, 1965.

581. Whittam, H. et al.: The early development of psychotic children and their siblings. Develop. Med. Child. Neurol. 8: 552-560, 1966.

582. Wilcox, D. E.: Speech disturbances. Dis. Nerv. Syst. 17: 20-23, 1956.

583. Wilking, V. N., and Paoli, C.: The hallucinatory experience. J. Amer. Acad. Child. Psychiat. 5: 431-440, 1966.

584. Williams, J. F.: Childhood schizophrenia. Med. J. Aust. 1: 224-226, 1956.

585. Wills, D. M.: Some observations on blind nursery school children's understanding of their world. *In* Eissler et al. (Eds.) Psychoanal. Stud. Child. 20: 340-364, 1965.

586. Wing, J. K.: Epidemiology of early childhood autism. Develop. Med. Child. Neurol. 5: 646-647, 1963.

587. Winnicott, D. W.: A clinical study of the effect of a failure of the average expectable environment on a child's mental functioning. Int. J. Psychoanal. 46: 81-87, 1965.

588. Wolfensberger, W.: Schizophrenia in mental retardates: three hypotheses. Amer. J. Ment. Defic. 64: 704-706, 1960.

589. Wolfenstein, M.: Some observations on atypical children in school. J. Amer. Acad. Child. Psychiat. 2: 693-710, 1963.

590. Wolff, S., and Chess, S.: A behavioural study of schizophrenic children. Acta Psychiat. Scand. 40: 438-466, 1964.

591. Wolff, S., and Chess, S.: An analysis of the language of fourteen schizophrenic children. J. Child. Psychol. Psychiat. 6: 29-41, 1965.

592. Woodward, K. F. et al.: Psychiatric study of mentally retarded children. Arch. Gen. Psychiat. 2: 156-173, 1960.

593. Wortis, J.: Schizophrenic symptomatology in mentally retarded children. Amer. J. Psychiat. 115: 429-431, 1958.

594. Wortis, J., and Choi, S. M.: Psychophysiological factor analysis in retarded, neurotic and psychotic children. Recent Advances Biol. Psychiat. 5: 63-71, 1963.

595. Wright, B.: Observational Q sort differences between schizophrenic, retarded and normal pre-school boys. Child Develop. 34: 169-185, 1963.

596. Yaker, H. M., and Goldberg, B. R.: Some preliminary comparisons of phenylketonuria with childhood schizophrenia. Penn. Psychiat. Quart. 4: 10-17, 1963.

597. Zhezlova, L.: Speech pecularities of schizophrenic children in the preschool age group. Zh. Nevropat. Psikhiat. Korsakov 65: 1063-1065, 1965.

598. Zublin, W.: Drug Treatment of Severe Affective Contact Disorders in children. Schweiz. Med. Wschr. 93: 84-86, 1963.

599. Tilton, J. R., DeMyer, M. K., and Loew, L. H.: Annotated Bibliography on Childhood Schizophrenia 1955-1964. National Clearing house for Mental Health Information, National Institute of Mental Health, Chevy Chase, Maryland.

12

Adolescent Schizophrenia

LAURENCE LOEB, M.D.

For Dr. Loeb's biography, see Chapter 10.

Since the term "dementia praecox" was replaced by those of "schizophrenia" and "schizophrenic reactions", attention has shifted from the emphasis of this early concept of this group of disorders as praecox, i.e., as pubertal and adolescent in time of onset. As a consequence, there is remarkably little in the current literature pertaining specifically to the schizophrenias in adolescence.

Although it was Emil Kraepelin,[48] following Morel and Wundt, who codified this group of disorders as dementia praecox, he pointed out that "there can be no talk of an inviolable connection of dementia praecox with the period of youth." He did state that, "from this time (age 15) on we see the frequency of dementia praecox increasing with extraordinary rapidity; more than two-thirds of the cases begin between the fifteenth and thirtieth year." In short, Kraepelin never thought of dementia praecox as solely a "praecox" condition, but strove rather to emphasize the frequency with which the condition begins in adolescence. Bleuler,[8] commenting on the need for change of name as well as thought about these states, said that, "as the disease needs not to progress as far as dementia and does not always appear *praecociter,* i.e., during puberty, or soon after, I prefer the name schizophrenia."

With increased interest in this time of life, attention is again being paid to questions of adolescent schizophrenias, and it is hoped that this interest may clarify some of the concepts of schizophrenia as a whole.

Not only had adolescent schizophrenia been largely ignored by the clinician and research worker, but, until recent years, the entire subject of adolescence had received scant attention. The subject is of far greater importance now than heretofore, as nearly half of the population of the United States is under 25 years of age.

Adolescence was glossed over, for the most part, by psychiatrists and by psychoanalysts until the publication of *The Ego and the Mechanisms of Defense* by Anna Freud[27] in 1936. This work served not only to reawaken interest in the study of adolescence, but also played a major role in ushering in current concepts of ego psychology. Interest in adolescence, then, paralleled the reawakened interest in ego functions; the history of inquiry into adolescence since parallels that of ego psychology.

THE EGO IN ADOLESCENCE

In order to view current concepts of adolescent schizophrenia, it is useful to put them in the context of ego function in this age range, as the schizophrenias are generally seen as disorders of ego functioning.

Most who work with adolescents find it convenient to divide the age range into three subranges: early adolescence, mid-adolescence and late adolescence. Early adolescence, in current usage, is not synonymous with puberty. Puberty is conceptualized as that group of physiochemical changes responsible for accelerated growth and the development of secondary sexual characteristics; adolescence is thought of as that group of psychological events joining childhood to adulthood. Puberty, then, may antedate the onset of adolescence, may coincide with it, or may follow the psychological event. For example, puberty in the girl is usually thought of as beginning with menarche. However, breast development has begun approximately one year prior to the onset of menstruation, and is the subject of much interest in the developing girl and those around her, and may usher in the psychologic phase of early adolescence. Conversely, in spite of the establishment of menstruation, adolescence may be postponed because of emotional difficulties.

The first ejaculation is seen by some as the analogue of menarche for the male. This event, however, generally occurs long after male adolescence has begun: the onset of puberty in the male, then, is more difficult to determine with certainty as compared to the female. It should not be overlooked that, in response to physiological changes, the time of the subranges of adolescence differs in the sexes. It is commonplace to state that the adolescent boy is emotionally two years behind the development of the girl.

It is necessary to avoid the trap of conceptualizing the ego as a "thing" rather than as a set of functions. Although one could list ego functions as one would wish, it is convenient to use those designated by Beres[7] as: 1) relation to reality, 2) regulation and control of instinctual drives, 3) object relationships, 4) thought processes, 5) defense functions, 6) autonomous functions, and 7) synthetic functions. Even as growth and development never follow a straight line, each ego function may develop at a rate independent of the others. This is all the more true in adolescence, characterized as it is by unevenness, spurts, and temporary regressions, with little stabilization.

The so-called late latency period of childhood is one of relative quiescence of instinctual drive and of a gradual increase of strength of all ego functions. In early adolescence, ego strength seems to increase still further. Josselyn[41] accounts for this on the basis of increased muscular strength, serving to augment the youth's defenses.

In early adolescence, the relation to reality is little altered from that which obtained in latency. Regulation and control of instinctual drives is good: it may be that the drives have not yet reached a position of strength relative to that of the ego to upset an equilibrium, or, that the augmentation of defensive function assists the ego. Object relationships begin to change: closeness to the "best friend" of childhood may begin to waver, and there is beginning flight from the parental domain. Thought processes vary little from those of late latency, but, in our culture, this phase is coincident with entrance into high school and increased educational demands. Autonomous functions are not greatly invaded by conflict, and there is greater capacity to deal with things in the conflict-free ego sphere. Synthetic functions are greater now than in latency, but have not yet achieved those characteristics indicative of later adolescence. In sum, then, early adolescence differs little from late latency in regard to ego functions. Such differences which do exist are in the direction of increased ego strength and stronger ego boundaries.

Mid-adolescence is the period of turmoil ordinarily associated with the teen years. If early adolescence may be arbitrarily described as ages 12 to 14, making allowances for sexual differences, mid-adolescence would include the fifteenth through seventeenth years.

The whole of the child's relation to reality now undergoes considerable change. Questions of "ego identity" now come to the fore. Alienation from the parents often increases, largely under the impact of the pressures of and response to instinctual drives. Because of accelerating body changes, the body image is subject to change with almost bewildering rapidity. As body image is integral to the ego boundaries, normative distortion puts additional strain on the ego's relation to reality. Regulation and control of instinctual drives becomes more difficult. In this period, the upsurge in sexual and aggressive drives, manifested by changing secondary sexual characteristics and growth of the entire body, indicates a relative increase in the strength of the drives as compared to that of the ego.

Sexual drive, held in relative check prior to this point, increases alienation from the previously-known self. The oedipal conflict is revived with perhaps greater force than was present originally. As a consequence, object relationships, with the parents and others, undergo massive changes at this time. Close ties to members of the same sex weaken as heterosexual interests begin. It is at this time that the intimacy characteristic of later relationships begins to be developed. Under the influence of all these changes, the processes of thought are put under stress and stimulation.

Piaget[40] and others[9,28,73] have commented on the mid-adolescent's increased awareness, changes in perception and in perceptiveness, and speak of the development of alternatives in thought that could not have occurred earlier. Defensive functions become increasingly important. Intellectualization, not previously present, appears at this time and augments the other defenses in their struggles with instinctual drives and the pressures of the external world. Repression becomes still less sufficient, and all defenses fluctuate to a marked degree. Functions previously autonomous may be invaded conflictually. For example, walking may become sexualized or aggressivized, as may speech and other ego functions.

The synthesizing function of the ego now becomes more prominent. Inhelder and Piaget[40] speak of the development of "formal structures" of thought indicative of greater synthesizing capability.

Late adolescence, perhaps from ages 18 to the mid-twenties, is more difficult to define. At its onset, its features are similar to those of mid-adolescence, at its close, to those of early adult life. The disharmony of ego functions present during mid-adolescence gives way to the smoother functioning of early adulthood. Relation to reality improves, and the regulation and control of instinctual drives eases as ego strength consolidates. Object relationships now tend to center about the kind of individual with whom one could hope to lead a happy life, and there is a return to the parents on an adult-to-adult level. Thought processes are no longer so inundated by sexual and aggressive concerns, and the late adolescent is far better able to pursue intellecutal tasks than could have been the case earlier. Defensive functions are strengthened, and those defenses typical of consolidated character structure are in evidence.

The conflict-free ego sphere widens, formerly-invaded ego functions regaining their autonomy. The synthesizing function becomes increasingly important. Fountain[25] and Nixon[61] describe characteristics they feel to be important in the transition from late adolescence to early adulthood in normal college populations, and include the establishment of new introjects and an ego-ideal more in accord with reality.

There are many deviations from this scheme of ego development in adolescence. This material is not, however, presented as an exhaustive review of the literature on the subject, but, rather, is intended to serve as a frame of reference for the understanding of the work done during the past decade on the schizophrenias of adolescence.

REVIEW OF LITERATURE, 1956-1966: ADOLESCENT SCHIZOPHRENIA: FROM CHILDHOOD TO ADOLESCENCE

In the past decade, there have been several studies on the development of the childhood schizophrenic as he approaches adolescence and on the early phases of schizophrenia in this age range. Freedman and Bender,[25] in studying the later development of patients diagnosed as schizophrenic in childhood, conclude that the childhood schizophrenic becomes the adult schizophrenic. This is supported by Eisenberg,[20] who studied 63 children having been previously diagnosed as having had early infantile autism. From 4 to 20 years later, only 3 were seen as having a good adjustment in adolescence: 14 had a fair adjustment, and that of the remainder was said to be poor. He concluded that "the separation of early infantile autism from other cases of childhood schizophrenia continues to be justified clinically." Freedman and Bender[26] had further suggested the possibility that most adults demonstrating disturbances of motility would prove to have been, on closer examination, childhood schizophrenics.

In these cases of early infantile autism and childhood schizophrenia, ego deviations and pathology of ego functions are so marked that they evidently do not permit these functions to approach a normal developmental pattern of adolescence, and those in these groups may differ from those whose schizophrenic illnesses begin in adolescence.

Less pronounced ego deviations were evaluated by Bower, Shellhamer and Daily,[10] who studied school characteristics of male adolescents who later became schizophrenics. They found that these boys tended to have less interest in girls, in group activities and athletics compared to the controls: most tended toward a shut-in, withdrawing kind of personality. Their object relationships were apparently poor, and their tendencies to fantasy great. These deviations of ego function accord with the idea of the schizoid personality a "predisposing" to schizophrenia. Yet, clinical experience is such that not all schizoid children became schizophrenic, and other personality organizations may give way to schizophrenic psychoses. There must be other factors involved: the question of the relation of schizoid personality to schizophrenia has never been resolved, and it would seem that this is worthy of continued study.

Colbert and Koegler[13] examined physical characteristics of childhood schizophrenics in adolescence. They commented on the apparent youthfulness of their group, saying that, "the average adolescent childhood schizophrenic in the 12 to 14 year old group still appeared markedly younger, both physically and psychically, than his peers."

It is difficult to fit these observations into current ego psychology. Rosenbaum's study[68] of growth inhibition in a nonschizophrenic adolescent is suggestive of the possibility that emotional factors may interfere with the growth process through as yet unknown pathways. In this connection, Loeb[52] considers anorexia nervosa as another form of growth inhibition, the acting-out of the wish to not grow.

The apparent improvement of some childhood schizophrenics in early adolescence is often noted in the literature. This apparent improvement is frequently accompanied by acting-out behavior. Tec[76] pointed to the absence of schizophrenic symptomatology in some juvenile delinquents, who, nonetheless, were basically schizophrenic. His observations arose from the follow-up of schizophrenic children, whose behavior as puberty approached resembled that thought of as typical of the character disturbance of the psychopathic personality. This finding was reinforced by the work of Davidman and Preble,[16] who found a high degree of emotional disorder, particularly the schizophrenias, among adolescent street gang leaders. More will be discussed concerning the apparent alteration from the schizophrenias to the psychopathies in the next section of this chapter.

Pollack,[66] in a comparison of childhood and adult schizophrenias, studied intellectual functioning through the Stanford-Binet tests. He found that, the greater the age of onset of the schizophrenias, the higher the I.Q., "as the age of onset increases for schizophrenic disorders, there is less evidence of neurological defect." He posits some form of neurologic defect, yet these findings could be understood in terms of earlier interference with thought processes continuing to interfere with intelligence as tested.

In England, Fitzherbert[24] reported three cases in thirteen and fourteen year old girls in whom there was a marked increase in I.Q. at the onset of their schizophrenic disorders: in one case, there was a 40 per cent rise. She suggests the possibility of a facilitation of associations in early schizophrenia to account for this.

The question of preschizophrenic states is far from clear. Stein[75] is of the opinion that there are recognizable preschizophrenic states, and that these are characterized by a marked difficulty in establishing and maintaining interpersonal relationships, a tendency toward seclusiveness and daydreaming, a withdrawal from work responsibility, personal neglect, and a tendency toward delinquency. On the other hand, Heuyer et al.[35,36,37] feel that the concept of "preschizophrenia" is both invalid and misleading. He attempted to describe ten forms of behavior which might be considered preschizophrenic, but which he did not think of as pathognomonic. These included youngsters with apparent intellectual deficit, with decreased attention, difficulty in concentration, and easy fatigability, obsessional manifestations and perfectionist needs. Others were characterized by affective defects, intellectual preoccupations, family problems, excitation, and so forth.

To again present the other point of view, Male and Green[54] discuss preschizophrenic states in adolescence, seeing such states analytically as weaknesses of the ego or attempts to deal with such weaknesses. Male states that, in these states, "authenticity, lively resonance, adaptive movements" are affected. "The preschizophrenic has not completely assumed his feelings and is not able to integrate them. His personality demonstrates the absence of cohesion of an ego which has split or which has never been achieved." In short, he feels that, in adolescence, before classic Bleulerian signs may be elicited, an organization similar to that of the concept of "borderline state" is present: it is this organization that he considers preschizophrenic.

Thus, even as the question of the relationship of the schizoid personality to the schizophrenias persists, so too does the question of the presence of identifiable preschizophrenic states in adolescence. It is possible that further detailed study of specific ego functions in the adolescent schizophrenic may provide valuable information in identifying those who are likely to become schizophrenic.

DIAGNOSIS: THE ADOLESCENT AND THE SCHIZOPHRENIC

There is confusion in distinguishing schizophrenia in adolescence from other disorders in this age range. In the last edition of this volume, Weiner[79] said, "a neglected but very important area in clinical psychiatry is the differential diagnosis between the turbulent behavior of adolescence and the early symptoms of schizophrenia which so commonly begin in this period of life." He described differential points, the persistence, pervasiveness, and surface inexplicability which point toward the schizophrenias.

Most feel that adolescence is characterized by turbulence and turmoil, Anna Freud[28] stating that the adolescent upset is both inevitable and predictable, and that such upset is largely responsible for the difficulty in drawing the line between psychopathology and normality at this time. She states that:

"adolescence constitutes by definition an interruption of peaceful growth which resembles in appearance a variety of other emotional upsets and structural upheavals. The adolescent manifestations come close to symptom formation of the neurotic, psychotic, or dissocial order and merge almost imperceptibly into borderline states, initial, frustrated, or fully fledged forms of almost all the mental illnesses."

Voegele and Dietze[78] feel that in the differential diagnosis of schizophrenia in adolescence, acute and chronic brain syndromes, mental deficiency, neurotic reactions and adjustment reactions of adolescence are commonly mistaken for the schizophrenic disorders. They feel that the diagnosis should be based on the cardinal symptoms as set down by Bleuler and on the absence of signs of organic illness. Edelston[19] commented on the confusion of schizophrenia and transient disturbances in adolescence, stating that "schizophrenic disorders notoriously originate during adolescence . . . it should be remembered, however, that adolescence is normally an age of emotional turmoil and instability and much that would be classed as pathologic in later adult life may prove to be but a temporary exaggeration of normal trends of character and not necessarily the harbinger of a psychosis."

Neubauer and Steinert[59] added that "schizophrenia in adolescence requires the keenest sensitivity and clinical acumen in differentiating psychotic disturbances and disturbances of puberty that are within normal limits and in differentiating schizophrenia in adolescence proper from recurrent childhood schizophrenia accentuated in puberty." Kestenberg[45] said that "to compound the confusion, in some latency children and adolescents psychotic-like periods may occur. In these, reality testing does not break down, but in some of these individuals there may be a wish for a psychosis because of their problems."

Not all workers see the diagnosis of schizophrenia as being exceptionally difficult in this age group. Masterson and Washburne,[57] in a study of 101 "relatively healthy" and 101 "psychiatrically ill" adolescents, concluded that "the relatively healthy adolescents, though they be in turmoil, did not show symptoms that simulate a psychiatric illness, and differed quite distinguishably from those with a psychiatric illness. This suggests that adolescent symptomatology may not be as confusing as theory implies." This view is given support by Annesley,[2] in England, who feels that there is no difference in the way schizophrenia in adolescence presents itself compared to that in the adult. Again, to present the other side of this argument, Sands,[69] in England, stated that "even pathological degrees of regression at this age fail to carry the ominous prognosis associated with the same change in the adult . . . these psychoses can develop from a setting of conduct disorder in a manner unusual in adults." He attempts to distinguish the characteristics of the adolescent schizophrenias as their capacity for variation in intensity, form and duration, and adds that another main feature is the readiness with which the adolescent may regress to earlier forms of behavior.

Wilson[81] points out that the interviewer's reaction may aid in the differential diagnosis of the turbulence of adolescence from the schizophrenias, saying that "the distinction from an unusually turbulent adolescence, with impulsive and thoughtless acts, wild actions, scenes and psychopathic behavior rests upon the maintenance of affective sympathy. If we accept the youth's premises (false though they be) might we have done the same? With the neurotic we should answer 'yes'. With the schizophrenic we should answer 'no'." Spotnitz[74] feels that one of the most reliable differentiating criteria in adolescence is the persistence of a symptom picture. He added that "adolescent schizophrenia as it appears clinically is some combination of the less familiar childhood schizophrenic reaction with the more familiar adult schizophrenic reactions."

In Russia, Lupandin[53] described 30 patients between the ages of 12 and 16 and attempted to divide them into three descriptive groups. Of these 30 schizophrenic adolescents, he described a group of 15 presenting primarily an oneiroid-catatonic form which differed little from the adult form. Five patients in his group had illnesses characterized by transient delerious episodes of two to three week's duration, accompanied by fear. The third group of 10 patients were intermediate between the first two groups. In France, Heuyer and Laroche et al.[34,35,36,37] in their work with the adolescent schizophrenic, see certain cardinal signs, including alterations of intelligence, of affectivity, of comportment and a spontaneous tendency to chronicity which need not be constant. They feel that these criteria define the adolescent schizophrenic in a manner similar to that of the adult. They feel, in effect, that there is only one form of schizophrenia whose nucleus is constant and whose clinical expression varies within limits. The function of the individual, in their view, depends on the maturational degree, both neurologic and psychologic, of the individual. On the basis of psychologic testing, including the Wechsler Bellevue, the TAT, and Rorschach, tests attempted to delineate the adolescent schizophrenias further. They report the almost constant finding of a higher verbal score on intelligence testing than performance score and found on their projective tests that the adolescent schizophrenic fell into a "grave" group in which the young person does not refuse to work but does stop short of exposing his delusions. The second group they call "restrictive" in which the poverty of ideas is manifest. A third group they call "diverse."

In sum, then, there is a diversity of opinion concerning the clinical appearance of schizophrenias in adolescence. Some see this group as difficult to distinguish from normal adolescent turmoil on the one hand, and other psychiatric disorders on the other; whereas others feel that there is no basic difference between the schizophrenias as they appear in adolescence and those which appear in later life.

There is, however, one further form that the schizophrenias may take during this period of life that does seem to be largely different from the adult form. I here refer to the so-called "pseudo-psychopathic" forms of schizophrenic reactions. Sands[69] had referred to this group in his article previously alluded to, in which he states that "in retrospect it may be found that stealing, truanting, refusal to attend school, screaming attacks and behavior sometimes involving court appearances have marked the onset of a disorder that subsequently is diagnosed schizophrenic." Bender,[6] in 1959, in attempting to clarify the concept of "pseudopsychopathic" schizophrenias listed six groups of schizophrenic reactions in adolescence. The first of these were those psychotic disturbances often beginning with a pseudoneurotic picture that apparently had their onset in adolescence. The second group, which she referred to as "pseudodefective" or autistic, had been ill from infancy or very early childhood. These, she stated, run a chronic course. During adolescence, an increase in impulsivity, aggression and sexual behavior was noted. The third group were those who were schizophrenic before puberty and continued to be schizophrenic. A fourth group were known to be schizophrenic in childhood. As puberty approached there was a change in symptomatology, often "by a suppression of anxiety and neurotic or psychotic behavior and continuing for a shorter or longer period with nothing more disturbing than the mild behavior disorders." A fifth group was similar to the foregoing, which starts with apparent childhood schizophrenic features; this group passes through early adolescence almost completely symptom-free, but develop during adolescence psychopathic-like behavior characteristics, including acting out against others with no apparent anxiety or guilt; the last group first became known during their adolescence because of delinquency and antisocial or behavioral disorders . . . this group is felt to be basically schizophrenic.

In the Soviet Union, Dzhartov[18] published a study in which he found that during the initial period of schizophrenia in children and adolescents, syndromes resembling psychopathy were prominent. He said that "some of these features resemble the behavior of adolescents at the age of puberty but in the schizophrenic these features are distinguished by considerable disharmony, a caricature-like aspect and a curious mixture of infantilism and precocious maturation.[11]

There were three studies of organic factors in adolescent schizophrenias. Larsen[49] studied the physical characteristics of disturbed adolescents, and found that the incidence of physical and neurological defects among adolescent patients in the state hospital population he studied were significantly higher than would be expected. In Russia, Alexaniantes[1] studied the indoles in the blood and urine of mentally ill children and adolescents. He established to his own satisfaction that an indolemia and indoluria were inherent in those psychotics whose clinical manifestations were schizophrenic.

Heuyer[38] and his group studied electroencephalographic responses to simple and combined stimuli in adolescent schizophrenics. They felt that the schizophrenic patients differed in their reactivity to simple stimuli on the EEG, vis-a-vis normal.

COURSE

Symonds and Herman[70] reported on 50 cases of schizophrenia in adolescent girls at Bellevue Hospital. They stated that the group fell into three types. Type 1 consisted of those with short term illnesses on a "good" personality substrate. Type 2 were those "whose histories indicated many serious personality and behavior problems in childhood." Type 3 had long histories from infancy or early childhood of bizarre behavior suggestive of childhood schizophrenia. They felt that those in type 2 group were the most difficult to diagnose. The course lengthens and prognosis worsens in descending order of these three types. Errera,[23] reporting on a 16 year follow-up of 54 adolescent patients seen in an outpatient clinic (schizophrenics) found that only 25 per cent had a "good adjustment to life." The rest remained severely handicapped. Tiganov[77] studied 25 schizophrenics whose disorder developed in adolescence (in Russia). In all, the illness began between the ages 13 and 15 and his group had been ill from 4 to 45 years. In his entire group, the illnesses ran a continuous course without remission so that manic and depressive states succeded each other without a lucid interval.

He found that the worse prognoses were those in which psychopathic-like changes of personality were present in the initial stage. Masterson,[55] studying 201 adolescents at the Paine-Whitney Clinic in New York City, found that 67 per cent had a poor outcome. The prognosis seemed to be better in those whose illness began after age 15 and was worse than those whose disorder began before they were 14 years old. Beckett,[5] in a follow-up study of hospitalized adolescent schizophrenics said that approximately 50 to 60 per cent of them were improved or recovered at the time they were discharged from the hospital. On follow-up several years later, however, many had relapsed. He estimates the improvement rate at about 33 per cent. In the Soviet

Union, Bashina,[4] in describing working capacity and social adaptations of patients acquiring schizophrenia in childhood or adolescence, found that 43.2 per cent of his group were unable to work.

Pitt, Kornfeld and Kold[64] attempted to utilize adolescent friendship patterns as indicators of prognosis for schizophrenic adults. They studied 33 white male schizophrenics between the ages of 20 and 30, hospitalized after age 18. This group was interviewed for an evaluation of their leisure time activities in adolescence. The study group was divided into those who were hospitalized over a long term, a second group of those hospitalized for a short term and a third, a relapsing group. In the first group, deterioration in interpersonal relationships apparently began between ages 12 and 15, in the third group, between ages 15 and 17.

Two papers appeared in the literature on the schizophrenic in college. Kiersch and Nikelly[46] studied 108 schizophrenic college students at the University of Illinois during a five year period. This group was matched with random control, and the authors found that three times as many patients diagnosed as psychotic dropped out of college compared to the random group without mental illness; that twice the number of students who were not psychotic eventually graduated compared to the group that was psychotic, and concluded "that both intellectual productivity and scholarly thinking are not generally characteristic of the schizophrenic process." Podolsky[65] felt that the schizophrenic college group showed certain common features. First, "they were not quite goal-directed as to life's vocation," having rather vague ideas as students of what they might want to be and that this vague idea usually involved an occupation far beyond the student's capability. Second, "his methods of studying are bizarre." Third, "perfectionistic, he always attempts to get an 'A'." Fourth, "this group does not seem to be able to discuss any topic for any length of time and are easily distracted." Fifth, there is a tendency on the part of the schizophrenic to make himself conspicuous in his dress. Sixth, they are not able to form close interpersonal relationships and seventh, they seek special attention from instructors.

TREATMENT

Most of the literature concerning treatment of the adolescent schizophrenic is that of psychotherapeutic intervention. One paper on organic treatment, by Darling,[15] noted a 72 per cent improvement rate in the treatment of ambulatory adolescent schizophrenics with acetophenazine.

Wilkins,[80] in speaking of the meaning of external control to a 14 year old schizophrenic girl, commented that, in treating such badly disturbed adolescents, the therapist may have to impose controls, and perhaps even resort to force, by way of controlling aggressive behavior. Such controls are, at times, apparently reassuring to the patient, and aid in reestablishing ego boundaries.

Perhaps one of the most remarkable works on psychotherapy was that of Parker,[62] who presented verbatim material concerned in her treatment of a severely disturbed adolescent boy. In this work, she found that it was necessary to have recourse to the patient's private language, which was highly symbolic. Originally stating that "my language is me," through the interpretive understanding of his therapist, he found it less and less necessary to use this language for understanding. Most, working with schizophrenics, emphasize the necessity of making contact primarily in the schizophrenic's own language as a bridge toward psychotherapeutic work. Most, working with the non-schizophrenic adolescent, find it necessary to comprehend the adolescent's language: for the treatment of the adolescent schizophrenic, this is essential.

The bibliography would not be complete without reference to a work, not of the psychiatric literature, but of fiction, by an author named Hannah Green.[32] This book, entitled "I Never Promised You a Rose Garden," is a description of a schizophrenic girl, her illness, and her treatment as seen by the patient, and is remarkable for its lucidity and for its ability to convey to the general reading public the world of the schizophrenic adolescent. For us, as professionals, the patient's view of the treatment process, focusing on the relationship of patient and therapist, suggests a model worthy of study.

SUMMARY AND CONCLUSIONS

Amid this welter of material it appears that certain trends in the study of schizophrenia in adolescence are beginning to clarify. Most authors agree, although this agreement is far from universal, on the existence of so-called preschizophrenic states before schizophrenia is clinically manifest in the adolescent group. This would seem to be a necessary aspect for research. Within the framework afforded by ego-psychology it might be postulated that the child who is later to become schizophrenic in his adolescence has already manifested some disturbances in ego function. Of these, perhaps the most amenable to study would be that of the interpersonal relationships of the child. The work of Piaget[40] indicates that there is one alteration in structure of thought at about eight years of age and a second in midadolescence. As indicated earlier, these alterations seem to have to do largely with those characteristics which we associate with the synthesizing function of the ego. At the present state of our knowledge (or ignorance), it is far from clear as to whether this alteration is organically based or based in sociopsychological developmental factors. In either case, the question could legitimately be asked, "What would happen if this necessary developmental stage were not to occur?" Whether arising from developmental or maturational aspects, such an individual might then be unable to effectively and affectively synthesize aspects of his experience into a meaningful whole. Object relationships would then be one of the early ego functions showing an apparent disruption. If our hypothetical child is bright, he will recognize this defect within himself and will, in all likelihood, feel different when comparing himself to other children. He may then, in an attempt to be like others, act "as if" he acts, feels and reacts as the others do and may even establish apparently good relationships which, on close examination, will prove to have a "pseudo" character. Overt symptomatology could then be the result if this mechanism, largely defensive, gives way. It is likely that acquaintances and friends of our hypothetical patient will recognize that there is "something wrong," but will not be able to define exactly what it is. In our terms we would think of this as the "lack of affective resonance" described by Male[54] and would be perceived by the clinician as a feeling of distance.

If this hypothesis is correct, in some cases it should be possible to study other ego functions as well. Those functions which are thought of as autonomous or in a conflict-free sphere seem little affected. In point of fact, some of the studies indicated in this chapter suggest that at the beginning of adolescence, coincident with the increased ego strength, there is a strengthening of autonomous functions. This would correspond with Fitzherbert's[24] three cases, exhibiting an increase in intellectual functioning as tested on standard intelligence tests as well as that of Bender[6] who, in describing the pseudopsychopathic schizophrenic mentioned the dropping of overt symptomatology in the schizophrenic child as he approaches early adolescence.

Another question presents itself, that of the relationship of the "identity crisis" described by Erikson and others, and its relationship to schizophrenia. Erikson considers "identity crisis" as a normative period of development. Other writers, however, and clinicians in some areas, consider the "identity crisis" to fit a badly needed diagnostic lacuna by way of describing mid-and late adolescence with difficulties in ego functioning that do not yet appear schizophrenic. It would be of interest to know how many adolescents so diagnosed would, on further study, turn out to have a schizophrenic illness and in how many the "crisis" is in fact a normative change.

Work with and study of the adolescent schizophrenic remains in an early phase. There is much to be studied and much to be learned by further inquiry into disorders of this age and period of life.

BIBLIOGRAPHY

1. Alexaniants, R. A.: Study of indole-like substances in children and adolescents having schizophrenia or other psychoses. Zh. Nevropat i Psikhiat. Korsakov 63: 1022-1028, 1963.

2. Annesley, P. T.: Psychiatric illness in adolescence: presentation and prognosis. J. Ment. Sc. 107: 268-278, 1961.

3. Auerwald, E., M.D.: Society for Adolescent Psychiatry, Inc. Scientific Meeting 4/20/66—N.Y. Ac. of Sc. N.Y.C. Subject—Adolescent Schizophrenia.

4. Bashina, V. M.: Working capacity and social adaptation of patients acquiring schizophrenia in their childhood or

adolescence (catamnestic data). Zh. Nevropat i Psikhiat. Korsakov.

5. Beckett, Peter: Adolescents Out of Step. Wayne State U. Press, Detroit, 1965.

6. Bender, L.: The concept of pseudopsychopathic schizophrenia in adolescents. Amer. J. Orthopsych. 29: 491-513, 1959.

7. Beres, D.: Ego Deviation and Concept of Schizophrenia (from Psychoanalytic Studies of the Child). II: 164-235, N. Y. Int. U. Press, 1956.

8. Bleuler, E.: Textbook of Psychiatry. Macmillan, New York, 1924.

9. Blos, P.: On Adolescence. Free Press of Glencoe, New York, 1962.

10. Bower, E. M., Shellhamer, Thomas A., and Daily, John M.: School characteristics of male adolescents who later became schizophrenic. Amer. J. Ortho. 30: 712-729, 1960.

11. Braaten, L. J.: A descriptive study of schizophrenia in a college setting. Student Med. 9: 298-312, 1961.

12. Brody, Claire: A study of the personality of normal and schizophrenic adolescents using two projective tests; a differentiation on the basis of structural and behavioral rigidity using the Loenfeld Mosaic and Rorschach tests. Diss. Abstract 16. 381, 1956.

13. Colbert, E. G., and Koegler, R. R.: The schizophrenic child in adolescence. Psych. Quart. 35: 693-701, 1961.

14. Curtis, Glen R.: Self concept and identification in preschizophrenic adolescents. Diss. Abstract 24(1): 389-390, 1963.

15. Darling, H. F.: The treatment of ambulatory adolescent schizophrenics with acetopheniazine. Amer. J. Psych. 120: 68-69, 1963.

16. Davidman, H.: Schizophrenia among adolescent street gang leaders (in) Psychopathology of Schizophrenia. Hoch, P. (Ed.) Grune and Stratton, New York, 1966.

17. Dax, E. C.: Major psychiatric problems of adolescence. Med. J. Australia 1: 913-916, 1956.

18. Djartov, L. B.: Les estats psychopathosimilies dans la periode initiale de la schizophrenie chez les adolescents. Zh.

Nevropat i Psikhiatrii Korsakov 65: 1045-1047, 1965.

19. Edelston, H.: Differential diagnosis of some emotional disorders of adolescence (with special reference to schizophrenia). J. Ment. Sc. 95: 960-967, 1949.

20. Eisenberg, L.: The autistic child in adolescence. Amer. J. Psychiat. 112: 607-612, 1956.

21. Ekstein, R., Bryant, Keith, and Friedman, Seymour W.: Childhood Schizophrenia (in) Schizophrenia, L. Bellak (Ed.) Logos Press, N. Y. 1958.

22. Ekstein, R.: Cross-sectional views of the psychotherapeutic process with an adolescent recovering from a schizophrenic episode. Amer. J. Orthopsychiat. 31: 757-775, 1961.

23. Errera, Paul: A sixteen year follow-up of schizophrenic patients seen in an outpatient clinic. AMA Arch. Neurol. Psychiat. 78: 84-87, 1957.

24. Fitzherbert, J.: Increase in I.Q. at onset of schizophrenia: three adolescent cases. Brit. J. Med. Psychiat. 28: 191-193, 1955.

25. Fountain, G.: Adolescent into Adult: An Inquiry. J. Amer. Psychiat. Ass. 9: 417-433, 1961.

26. Freedman, A. M., and Bender, L.: When the childhood schizophrenic grows up. Amer. J. Orthopsychiat. 27: 553-565, 1957.

27. Freud, Anna: The Ego and the Mechanisms of Defense. Int. Univ. Press, 1946.

28. Freud, Anna: Adolescence (in) Psychoanalytic Studies: Child. 13: 255-278, 1958.

29. Garner, H. H., and Waldman, I.: The confrontation technique as used in the treatment of adolescent schizophrenia. Amer. J. Psychother. 17: 210-253, 1963.

30. Gidro-Frank, L.: Society for Adolescent Psychiatry, Inc. Scientific Meeting 4/20/66 N. Y. Academy of Sciences, N.Y. City. Subject—Adolescent Schizophrenia.

31. Gould, Robert E.: Society for Adolescent Psychiatry, Inc. Scientific Meeting 4/20/66 N.Y. Academy of Sciences,

N. Y. City. Subject—Adolescent Schizophrenia.

32. Green, H.: I Never Promised You a Rose Garden—Holt, Rinehart, Winston, 1964.

33. Green, Maurice, R.: Common problems in the treatment of schizophrenia in adolescents. Psychiat. Quart. 40: 294-307, April 1966.

34. Heuyer, G., Lelord, G., and Laroche, J. et al.: La schizophrenie de l'adolescence. Zschr. Kinderpsychiat. 25: 226-236, 1958.

35. Hueyer, G., and Laroche, J.: La schizophrenie de l'adolescence; essai de definition et de deliniation nosologique. Zschr. Kinderpsychiat. 25: 190-191, 1958.

36. Heuyer, G., Duranton, P., and Laroche, J.: Aspects clinique de la schizophrenie de l'adolescence. Zschr. Kinderpsychiat. 25: 191-193, 1958.

37. Heuyer, G., Shentoub, V., Rausch, N., and Jampolsky, L.: L'examen psychologique dans la schizophrenie juvenile. Zschr. Kinderpsychiat. 25: 193-195, 1958.

38. Heuyer, G., Popv, C., and Lelord, G.: Etudes EEG de responses aux stimuli simples et combines chez les schizophrenes adolescents. Zschr. Kinderpsychiat. 25: 232-234, 1958.

39. Hoffer, W.: Diaries of adolescent schizophrenics (hebephrenics) Psychoanalytic studies—Child. 2: 293-312, 1956.

40. Inhelder, B., and Piaget, H.: The Growth of Logical Thinking from Childhood to Adolescence. Basic Books, N. Y., 1958.

41. Josselyn, I.: The ego in adolescence. Amer. J. Orthopsychiat. 22: 223-237, 1954.

42. Jacobson, E.: The Self and the Object World. Int. Univ. Press, New York, 208-214, 1964.

43. Kanner, L.: Problems of adolescence. J. Ped. 55: 397-404, September 1959.

44. Kaufman, S. S.: Adolescence and Schizophrenia. Psychotherapy, 1: 321-350, 1956.

45. Kestenberg, J. S.: Pseudo-schizophrenia in childhood and adolescence. New Child. 10: 146-160, 1953.

46. Kiersch, T. A., and Nikelly, A. G.: The schizophrenic in college. Arch. Gen. Psychiat. 15: 54-58, 1966.

47. Kisker, K. P., and Stroetz, L.: (On a comparative analysis of situation in incipient schizophrenia and faulty developments in reactive experiences in adolescents, I) Arch. Psychiat. 202: 1-30, November 1961.

48. Kraepelin, Emil: Dementia Praecox and Paraphrenia, Edinburgh E and S. Livingston 1919 .

49. Larsen, V. L.: Physical characteristics of disturbed adolescents. Arch. Gen. Psychiat. 10: 55-64, 1964.

50. Lebovici, Serge, Roumajon, Y., and Morin, Bournea: Deux cas de schizophrenie de l'adolescence, presentation de malades. Arch. Med-Psychol. 112: 195-197, 1954.

51. Lidz, T., and Fleck, S.: Schizophrenia, Human integration and the role of the family in the etiology of schizophrenia. Jacobson, D. (Ed.) New York, Basic Books, 1960.

52. Loeb, L.: Anorexia nervosa Jr. Nerv. & Ment. Dis. 131: 447-451, 1960.

53. Lupandin, V. M.: (A clinico-psychopathological analysis of periodic schizophrenia in adolescents) (Russian) Zh. Nevropat i Psikhiatrii Korsakov 65. 1056-1062, 1965.

54. Male, P., and Green, A.: Les preschizophrenies de l'adolescence (Adolescent Preschizophrenia) Evolut. Psychiat. 1: 323-375, 1958.

55. Masterson, Jas. F. Jr.: Prognosis in adolescent disorders: schizophrenia. J. Nerv. & Ment. Dis. 24: 219-232, September 1956.

56. Masterson, J. F., Tacker, K., and Beck, G.: Psychopathology in Adolescence IV: Clinical and dynamic characteristics. Amer. J. Psychiat. 120: 357-365, 1963.

57. Masterson, J. F., and Washburne, A: The symptomatic adolescent; psychiatric illness or adolescent turmoil? Amer. J. Psychiat. 122:141 1240-1247.

58. Mertz, A. W.: Follow-up study of adolescent patients admitted to Hawaii State Hospital 1957-1958. Hawaiian Med.

J. 23: 189-197, January-February, 1964.

59. Neubauer, P. B., and Steinert, J.: Schizophrenia in adolescence. New Child 10: 129-134, 1953.

60. Nickling, G., and Toolan, J. (Ed.): 20 year follow-up of an adolescent service in a psychiatric hospital. Psychiat. Quart. Suppl. 33: 311-316, 1959.

61, Nixon, R.: The Art of Growing. Random House, 1962.

62. Parker, B.: My Language is Me. Basic Books, New York, 391, 1962.

63. Pearson, A.: Adolescence and the Conflict of Generations. Norton, New York, 1958.

64. Pitt, R., Kornfeld, D. S., and Kold, L.: Adolescent friendship patterns as prognostic indications for schizophrenic adults. Psychiat. Quart. 37: 499-508, 1963.

65. Podolsky, E.: A note on the schizophrenic college student. Amer. J. Psychiat. 119: 783-787, 1963.

66. Pollack, M.: Comparisons of childhood, adolescent and adult schizophrenia. Arch. Gen. Psychiat. 2: 652-660, 1960.

67. Rolla, E. H.: Analisis de una esquizofrenia. Revuista de Psicoanalisis, Buenos Aires 14(1-2): 72-77, January-June, 1957.

68. Rosenbaum, M.: The role of psychological factors in delayed growth in adolescence: A case report. Amer. J. Orthopsychiat. 29: 762-771, 1959.

69. Sands, D. E.: The psychoses of adolescence. J. Ment. Soc. 102: 308-318, 1956.

70. Simonds, A., and Herman, M.: Patterns of schizophrenia in adolescence; report on 50 cases of adolescent girls. Psychiat. Quart. 31: 521-530, June, 1957.

71. Shentoub, V., and Lang, L. L.: Les schizophrenies juveniles (anamnese) Zschr. Kinderpsychiat. 25(5): 234-236, 1958.

72. Singer, L.: Quelques formes de debut de schizophrenie. Strasbourg Med. 8(9): 748-751, October, 1957 .

73. Solnit, A. J.: The vicissitudes of ego development in adolescence. J. Amer. Psychoanalytic Asoc. 7(3): 523-536, July, 1959.

74. Spotnitz, Hyman: Adolescence and Schizophrenia; problems in differentiation (in) Adolescents, (Lorand, S. Schneer, H. I. (Ed.) Psychoanalytic approach to problems and therapy. Paul B. Hoeber, Inc., New York, 217-237, 1961.

75. Stein, Erich: Praeschizophrene zustande (preschizophrenic states) Prax. Kinderpsychologie Kinderpsychiat. 5, 273-284, 1956.

76. Tec, Leon: A schizophrenic child becomes adolescent. J. Nerv. Ment. Dis. 122: 105, 1955.

77. Tiganov, A. S.: Clinical features of cyclic schizophrenia developing in adolescence (Russian) Zh. Nevropat i Psikhiatrii Korsakov 63/11: 1695-1702, 1963.

78. Voegele, G. E., and Dietzer, H. J.: Differential diagnosis of schizophrenia in adolescence. Psychiat. Dig. 26: 36-48, April, 1965.

79. Weiner, Herbert: Diagnosis and Symptomatology (in) Schizophrenia. Bellak, L. (Ed.) Logos Press, New York, 171-172, 1958.

80. Wilkins, Ann: The meaning of external control to a schizophrenic adolescent girl. Bull. Menninger Clinic 21: 140-152, 1957,

81. Wilson, H.: The early diagnosis of schizophrenia. Brit. Med. J. 1: 1502, 1951.

82. Wilson, H.: Psychological and psychiatric disturbances in adolescence. Practitioner 184/1101: 301-307, 1960.

13

Antipsychotic Drugs

JONATHAN O. COLE, M.D. and JOHN M. DAVIS, M.D.

Dr. Cole is Chief of the Psychopharmacology Research Branch of the NIMH.* In his capacity as head of this branch, he has been instrumental in developing a comprehensive program of grants and contracts directed toward improving our knowledge about the efficacy of psychoactive drugs and their mechanisms of action. His program has given special emphasis to the development of collaborative clinical drug studies and to the application of psychometric and statistical procedures to the area of clinical drug evaluation.

A graduate of Cornell University Medical College, trained in psychiatry at the Payne Whitney Clinic of the New York Hospital, Dr. Cole taught at Cornell, later joining the NIMH. Interested in the application of drugs to psychiatric disorders, he has been council member and president of the American College of Neuropsychopharmacology. He is also on the Editorial Board of the American Journal of Psychiatry.

Dr. John M. Davis is Chief, Unit on Clinical Pharmacology, Laboratory of Clinical Science, at the National Institute of Mental Health in Bethesda, Maryland. His primary field of interest is psychotropic drugs and their interactions with mental illness.

Dr. Davis received his medical training at Yale University, interned at Massachusetts General Hospital, and was a resident in psychiatry at Yale University School of Medicine. He has worked as a clinical associate in the Adult Psychiatry Branch of the National Institute of Mental Health, where he was involved in studies of biochemical factors in mental illness.

His recent publications include: The Efficacy of Tranquilizing and Antidepressant Drugs, *and* Norepinephrine in Depressive Reactions. *In addition he has had numerous other articles published in psychiatric and other professional journals.*

HISTORICAL INTRODUCTION

This chapter was made possible by the recent discovery of two classes of drugs having a beneficial effect on schizophrenia. It is remarkable that, after many centuries during which there was no known effective treatment for schizophrenia, two quite independent and different therapies were discovered at approximately the same time, and both in part by serendipity. The *Rauwolfia* plant, from which reserpine is derived, had been used in India[593] for many years in the treatment of a variety of mental ills. When tried in the

---

*At final press time, Dr. Cole has become Superintendent, Boston State Hospital, Boston, Massachusetts.

treatment of schizophrenia by Kline at the Rockland (N.Y.) State Hospital in 1954, it was found to have definite antipsychotic properties.[401,402] Chlorpromazine, a phenothiazine derivative, was synthesized in an attempt to produce a better antihistamine. It was first used in anesthesia and only tried as an antipsychotic agent by Delay and Deniker in 1952.[155,156,158-160] These discoveries marked the beginning of the psychopharmacologic revolution in psychiatry and made the clinical use of drugs a valuable part of the psychiatrist's therapeutic armamentarium.

Since the discovery of these two drugs, many others have been developed. Today there are at least a dozen antipsychotic drugs available for general prescription use here and abroad, and many more in various stages of clinical evaluation. The question must then be posed: Which drug does what, and which drug should be used for what kind of patient?

Many factors enter into the decision regarding the use of a particular drug in a given patient. Certainly, clinical hunches and judgments based on the individual clinician's past experience are important factors in that decision. However, it is also important to take into consideration the results of research studies, particularly those which utilize a double-blind design. Therefore, it would be helpful to have a box score of the efficacy of the various antipsychotic drugs as determined by the results of controlled studies (Tables 1-5). It would also be important to have evidence available on the interactions of these drugs with other forms of treatment, such as social therapy, and one should know something about the mode of action of these drugs.

Uncontrolled studies may give misleading evaluations of the clinical effectiveness of drugs. It has been shown by several authors[235,236,269] that uncontrolled studies give a generally more positive evaluation of drug effects than do controlled studies. Since many patients will show improvement when treated with placebo alone, in an uncontrolled study one does not know whether the improvement shown is due to placebo effect or to the drug in question.* Thus, unless otherwise stated, all studies mentioned in this chapter are controlled evaluations. All of the studies mentioned were reviewed in detail, and a decision was made as to whether or not the authors had unequivocally shown the drug to be more effective than placebo or other control medication. This judgment was based on all the evidence presented in the studies reviewed. In some cases, the statistics in the original studies were recalculated using different methods to arrive at the proper classification.

A series of questions for investigation can be framed as follows: 1) Is a given drug or class of drugs more effective than placebo? 2) Given several effective drugs for a particular condition, is one drug more effective than the others? 3) Given equally effective drugs, are some effective with less risk of

---

*References 48, 49, 237, 269, 313-317, 603.

severe side effects than others? 4) Given equal group effectiveness and an equal incidence of side effects for several drugs, do subgroups of the patient populations respond differentially to different drugs? 5) Will patients who fail to respond to one drug respond to another drug, either of the same class or of a different class? 6) Are drug combinations more effective than single drugs in certain populations? 7) What are the relationships between drug therapy and other therapies?

METHODOLOGIC PROBLEMS OF DRUG EVALUATION

Fox,[236] Foulds,[235] and Glick[269] have previously noted that, in general, greater improvement was found in uncontrolled studies than in controlled drug evaluations. This plus our data suggests that, perhaps, if one were to plot the degree of rigor with which a study was done against the amount of therapeutic efficacy, one would obtain a U-shaped relationship. Uncontrolled studies show a high degree of therapeutic efficacy because of the placebo effect and other nondrug factors. Poorly done, controlled studies show the least amount of therapeutic effect because of low dose levels, inadequate measuring instruments, the use of a severely chronic population, or possibly the antitherapeutic effects of an unduly skeptical staff.[483] Large, very carefully done studies, which used reasonably sensitive populations, do show a good amount of therapeutic effectiveness when clearly active drugs are evaluated. Thus, both completely uncontrolled studies and very well designed controlled studies are likely to show high improvement rates, while poorly designed controlled studies show less improvement.

If an inadequate dose is used, either because the prescribing physician prescribes an inadequate dose or because some of the patients do not take the full amount of their medication (this can occur, particularly in outpatients), the results of the study are meaningless, since one does not know whether the drug is truly ineffective or whether no effect was shown simply because of inadequate dose. If the wrong patient population is used, or if inadequate measuring instruments are used, or if the study is conducted for too short a period, false negative results will probably be found also. The results of a poorly done double-blind study can be just as wrong as the overpositive results from an uncontrolled study.

In the physical sciences, when an investigator obtains negative results, the question is raised as to whether his technique is sensitive enough to show the proper effects.[234] Similar criteria should apply to clinical psychopharmacological studies, and a reasonable burden of proof should be placed on the investigator showing the negative result, particularly in hypothesis-confirmation research. The investigator should show that his measuring instruments and populations are sensitive enough to rule out the possibility that negative results are dosage artifacts, measurement artifacts, population effects, duration of study artifacts, etc. Obviously, in the first few double-blind studies done on a particular drug, the variables may not be clear enough to enable one to make a definitive statement. Later and larger studies should be designed to answer unequivocally the questions raised by contradictions found in earlier results. In this regard, it would be particularly important to build in controls for adequacy of measurement as well as to rule out the placebo effect, and such studies should also have controls in terms of dosage, duration of treatment, and sensitivity to therapeutic effect. This can be partially achieved by the use of biochemical tests, which show whether or not the patient has actually taken his drug, and pharmacologic tests which will show that the pharmacologic effects of the drug appear in patients, even though the patients may not manifest any clinical reactions. This would indicate whether or not the patients are getting an approximately therapeutic dose. In addition, the inclusion in the study of an active drug which clearly has effects different from placebo effects would be a further indication of the sensitivity of the measuring instruments. These considerations of control for double-blind studies are necessary in order to rule out the possibility of double-blind studies achieving false negative results.

CLINICAL EFFECTIVENESS

Table 1 shows the number of studies in which the various drugs have been shown to be more effective than placebo,* contrasted with the numbers of studies in which the drug effect was equal to the placebo effect.† It is preferable to use this classification scheme rather than per cent improvement since both the criteria for improvement and the base rate for per cent improvement vary considerably from population to population; e.g., per cent improvement would be low in chronic populations and high in acute populations.

One will note that in Table 1, with the exception of mepazine (Pacatal) and promazine (Sparine), most of the antipsychotic drugs are clearly shown to be more effective than placebo. One should also note that there are a fair number of studies which show chlorpromazine (Thorazine) and reserpine (Serpasil) to be no more effective than placebo. Since these were the first of the modern antipsychotics to be used in the treatment of schizophrenia, one might wonder if these negative results occurred during initial clinical trials when adequate dose levels had not yet been worked out, and when there was insufficient sophistication in the application of psychological measurement techniques to drug effects. In order to test the first portion of this hypothesis,

---

*References 1, 6, 41, 46, 52, 98, 99, 111, 113, 120, 127, 146, 149, 151, 170, 183, 194, 197, 209, 228, 242, 256, 267, 278-280, 304, 305, 309, 311, 329-331, 334, 346, 348, 357, 360, 394, 396, 405, 409, 412, 464, 524, 533, 537, 545, 546, 548, 555, 559, 567, 570, 578, 586, 592, 600, 612, 613, 615, 616, 618, 622, 635, 636, 648, 650, 660, 661, 668, 674, 677, 692.

†References 31, 98, 120, 121, 134, 149, 228, 264, 267, 394, 412, 434, 441, 460, 491, 617, 628, 657, 660, 672.

the effect of dose schedules on therapeutic results was studied. The studies on chlorpromazine were rated on a scale for adequacy of dosage, ranging from small fixed doses to moderate or large flexible doses. Most of those studies which did not show a therapeutic effect were found to have used small fixed doses (chi-square test significant at the .001 level). Studies which used a moderate or large dose of chlorpromazine, almost without exception, demonstrate a clear-cut therapeutic improvement. It is in those studies which utilized a very low dose level (400 mg./day or less) that equivocal results are found (see Table 2). Most of these studies were done early in the phenothiazine era, before adequate dose relationships had been worked out, and when psychiatrists were very concerned about the effects of excessive dosages. In the studies which used low fixed doses, it might be assumed that in many cases the dose was too low to be of any help to the patient. Dosage will be discussed in more detail in a subsequent section.

A second comparison was made between those studies which had adequate

Table 1.—Double-Blind Placebo Controlled Studies of the Efficacy of the Tranquilizing Drugs on Hospitalized Psychotic Patients, Comparing the Numbers of Studies in Which the Drug Was More Effective Than Placebo to the Numbers of Studies Finding the Placebo Equal in Effectiveness.

Drug		Number of Studies in Which	
Generic Name	Trade Name	Drug Was More Effective Than Placebo:	Drug Was Equal to Placebo:
Chlorpromazine	Thorazine Largactil	50	11
Reserpine	Serpasil	20	9
Triflupromazine	Vesprin Vespral	8	1
Perphenazine	Trilafon Fentazine	5	0
Prochlorperazine	Compazine Stemetil	7	2
Trifluoperazine	Stelazine	16	2
Fluphenazine	Prolixin Permitil	9	0
Thioridazine	Mellaril	6	1
Mepazine	Pacatal Pecazine	2	3
Promazine	Sparine	3	4
Phenobarbital	......	0	3

dose levels, duration of treatment, design, and methodology of measurement of clinical improvement, and those studies which were rated below average in at least one of these areas. Those studies which suffered from one or more of these methodological difficulties tended to find drugs ineffective in comparison to placebo. Even though these studies showed methodological faults, they were included in this review in order to eliminate the possibility of reviewer bias.

To complement this approach, those studies which were felt to be entirely methodologically correct, regardless of their results, were selected for a separate analysis. The choice of studies to be included in this separate analysis was based on such criteria as large patient samples, random assignment of treatment, double-blind control, careful qualitative and quantitative assessment of patient change, adequate dosage, reasonable durations of treatment, and an adequate statistical analysis of the data.

Table 3 presents the results of some of those studies. It is to be emphasized that the results quite unequivocally indicate that most phenothiazines have a therapeutic effect on schizophrenia.

Since there are many drugs which are more effective than placebo in the treatment of schizophrenia, the question arises as to whether a given drug is more effective than reserpine. Twenty-six studies were reviewed which compared reserpine with chlorpromazine.[149] In order to increase the number of studies included in this review, some comparative studies which were not double-blind were included.[149] Twelve of these studies showed chlorpromazine to be more effective than reserpine, while the other fourteen studies showed the two drugs to be about equal in effectiveness. There were no studies which

Table 2.—Comparison of the Therapeutic Effectiveness of Chlorpromazine as Compared to That of Placebo, Using Controlled Studies, Indicating the Number of Studies in Which Chlorpromazine was Found to be More Effective, Slightly More Effective, or Equal to Placebo, Indicating the Dose of Chlorpromazine Used.

Dose Range	More Effective Than Placebo:	Slightly More Effective Than Placebo:	Equal to Placebo:
300 mg./day or less	10	6	9
301-400 mg./day	4	3	1
401-500 mg./day	4	0	1
501-800 mg./day	14	0	0
More than 800 mg./day	9	0	0
Totals (all doses):	41	9	11

showed reserpine to be clearly more effective than chlorpromazine. Worthy of particular note is a carefully controlled, large, cooperative Veterans Administration study in which reserpine was compared with chlorpromazine, thioridazine, fluphenazine, and triflupromazine.[420] Reserpine was shown to be

Table 3.—Controlled Studies of Drug Effects
(All studies were double-blind with random allocation of treatment)
Part I

Study Length of time	Patient Population	Measuring Instrument	Drug Effectiveness		
VA Coop. Studies 1 & 2 (Casey et al.) 12 weeks	N=805 Acute and chronic schizophrenic men	MSRPP	Chlorpromazine	> Promazine	> Phenobarbital, Placebo
VA Coop. Study 3 (Casey et al.) 12 weeks	N=640 Newly admitted schizophrenic men	MSRPP CEPS	Chlorpromazine Prochlorperazine Triflupromazine Perphenazine	> Mepazine	> Phenobarbital
Spring Grove State Hospital (Kurland et al.) 6 weeks	N=238 New admissions	PRP MSRPP Psychiatric Scale of Target Symptoms	Perphenazine Prochlorperazine Triflupromazine Chlorpromazine	> Promazine	> Placebo Phenobarbital Mepazine
California State Hospital (Adelson & Epstein) 34 weeks	N=312 Chronic schizophrenic	MSRPP	Chlorpromazine Prochlorperazine Trifluopromazine Perphenazine	>	Placebo Scopolamine-chlorprophenpyridamine maleate (active placebo)
VA Coop. Study* (Lasky et al.) 24 weeks	N=512 Newly admitted schizophrenic men	IMPS PRP	Chlorpromazine Thioridazine Fluphenazine	> Reserpine	

*Chlorprothixene (a thioxanthene derivative) and triflupromazine were also included in this study. They were found to be less effective than the three phenothiazines but more effective than reserpine, although the differences were not significant.

Table 3.—Controlled Studies of Drug Effects
(All studies were double-blind with random allocation of treatment)
Part II

Study Length of time	Patient Population	Measuring Instrument	Drug Effectiveness
VA Hospital (Pearl et al.) 8 weeks	N=170 Chronic and acute schizophrenic men	MSRPP Global Clinical Rating Scale	Reserpine > Placebo
NIMH-PSC Coop. Study I 6 weeks	N=344 Newly admitted global acute schizophrenics	IMPS WBRS	Thioridazine Fluphenazine > Placebo Chlorpromazine
Vestre, Hall, Schiele (Minn.) 12 weeks	N=93 Hospitalized schizophrenics	PRP MMPI Clin. Eval.	Triflupromazine Fluphenazine > Phenobarbital
Schiele et al. (Minn.) 16 weeks	N=80 Male schizophrenics	MMPI Manifest Behavior Scale, and Clin. Eval.	Chlorpromazine Thioridazine > Placebo Trifluoperazine
VA Hospital (Hollister et al.) 17 weeks	N=60 Male hospitalized schizophrenics	Hospital Adjustment Scale, Clin. Eval.	Chlorpromazine Trifluoperazine > Phenobarbital
Spring Grove State Hospital (Hanlon et al.) 4 weeks	N=322 New admissions with high MSRPP morbidity scores	MSRPP PRP MACC IMPS	Prochlorperazine Fluphenazine Perphenazine > Thioridazine Chlorpromazine Thiopropazate Trifluoperazine Triflupromazine
NIMH-PSC Coop. Study II 26 weeks	N=480 Newly admitted schizophrenics	Clin. Eval. IMPS WBRS BPRS	Acetophenazine* > Chlorpromazine Fluphenazine

*All three of the phenothiazines compared in this study were found to be therapeutically
effective, and on some of the variables analyzed, chlorpromazine was found to be more
effective than acetophenazine.

less effective than all of these phenothiazine derivatives in reducing excitement, symptoms of withdrawal, and agitated depression. Overall, it was definitely less effective on a multivariate measure of general morbidity.[420]

Table 4 shows the number of studies in which chlorpromazine was equal to or better than other phenothiazine derivatives, compared to the number of studies in which the other drugs were found to be more effective than chlorpromazine. Mepazine (Pacatal) and promazine (Sparine) were less ef-

Table 4.—Comparative Effectiveness of Phenothiazine Drugs Compared to Chlorpromazine as a Standard Using Controlled Studies, Indicating Number of Studies in Which a Drug was Found More Effective, Equally Effective or Less Effective than Chlorpromazine.

Drug		Number of Studies in Which		
Generic Name	Trade Name	Drug Was More Effective Than Chlorpromazine:	Drug Was Equal to Chlorpromazine:	Chlorpromazine Was More Effective:
Mepazine	Pacatal	0	0	4
Promazine	Sparine	0	2	4
Triflupromazine	Vesprin	0*	10	0
Perphenazine	Trilafon	0	6	0
Prochlorperazine	Compazine	0	10	0
Trifluoperazine	Stelazine	0†	8	0
Thioridazine	Mellaril	0‡	12	0
Fluphenazine	Prolixin	0	7	0
Acetophenazine	Tindal	0	1	0
Thiopropazate	Dartal	0‡	1	0
Phenobarbital	......	0	0	6

*In VA Cooperative Study No. 3, the predominant statistical analysis showed no significant difference between the effectiveness of chlorpromazine, triflupromazine and perphenazine. However, supplementary statistical analysis showed the latter two drugs equal to each other but more effective than the former. Since this is only a finding in one study, found only by certain statistical techniques, not verified in other studies, it can only be viewed as tentative and not proven. In addition, in a subsequent large double-blind VA study, triflupromazine proved to be slightly less effective than chlorpromazine, thioridazine and fluphenazine. However, this difference did not reach the satisfactory statistical level. It should be pointed out that when one does a large number of studies, using a large number of measuring instruments, occasionally one finds differences that are significant by chance alone.

†In one study, there was no difference between trifluoperazine and chlorpromazine on most measures. However on one variable (withdrawal) trifluoperazine (Stelazine) was found superior to chlorpromazine, which itself was better than placebo. This finding, since it has not been found in other studies, can only be regarded as tentative until it is cross validated.

‡One study found thioridazine and thiopropazate to be inferior to chlorpromazine in a selected group of high morbidity patients. However, for the patient population as a whole, this difference was not significant.

Table 5.—The Comparative Effectiveness of Phenothiazine Derivatives. Data are Taken from Double-Blind Studies Which Utilized Trifluoperazine (Stelazine) as a Standard, and Which Did Not Include Chlorpromazine or Placebo as Control Medications.

Drug		Number of Studies in Which		
Generic Name	Trade Name	Drug Was More Effective Than Stelazine:	Drug Was Equal to Stelazine:	Stelazine Was More Effective:
Thioridazine	Mellaril	0	2	0
Fluphenazine	Prolixin	0	3	0

fective than the chlorpromazine standard.* Numerous studies showed other phenothiazine derivatives to be approximately equal to chlorpromazine in their therapeutic effects.† Similarly, thioridazine (Mellaril), fluphenazine (Prolixin), and triflupromazine (Vesprin) were shown to be equal to the trifluoperazine (Stelazine) standard (Table 5) in studies which did not include chlorpromazine.

A multiple variate analysis in the Veterans Administration study[98,99,282,520] showed no difference between perphenazine, triflupromazine, prochlorperazine, and chlorpromazine. These same results were obtained with a state hospital population in the carefully done studies of Kurland et al.[411,412] In a second study by Hanlon et al.,[319] chlorpromazine, thioridazine, triflupromazine, prochlorperazine, perphenazine, thiopropazate (Dartal), trifluoperazine and fluphenazine were found to be of approximately equal effectiveness. The first NIMH cooperative study,[127] which included among its cooperating hospitals both private and general municipal institutions, found chlorpromazine, thioridazine and fluphenazine to be about equally effective, and all clearly more effective than placebo even though one drug was a so-called activating tranquilizer and the others so-called sedative tranquilizers.

Granted the antipsychotic drugs produce improvement, is this improvement only a slight statistical quantity or is it clinically significant? The data from the first NIMH-PSC collaborative study was examined in an attempt to answer this question. Clinical improvement was evaluated, both in patients who had completed the six-week study and in patients who had been dropped from the study as treatment failures before the six-week evaluation period had been completed. The judgments of the study psychiatrists showed that two-thirds of

*References 51, 52, 98, 99, 149, 228, 267, 411, 412, 428, 636.

†References 6, 42, 51, 52, 99, 111, 113, 114, 127, 134, 149, 180, 207, 249, 305, 318, 319, 321, 332, 333, 348, 394, 412, 420, 428, 503, 529, 559, 567, 586, 612, 613, 615, 617, 618, 619, 630, 651, 655, 657, 674.

the phenothiazine-treated patients were considered to be much improved, while only one-fourth of the placebo-treated patients showed comparable improvement. One-half of the placebo-treated patients were judged by the study psychiatrists to be unchanged or worse, while only one-tenth of the phenothiazine treated patients had as poor an outcome.

The second NIMH collaborative study[503] compared chlorpromazine, fluphenazine, and acetophenazine (Tindal), and no one drug showed any clear-cut superiority over any other on all of the 57 dependent variables measured. There was a significant superiority of acetophenazine on both of the doctors' global ratings after five weeks of treatment, but this superiority was not clearly shown on the other 55 measures. However, inspection of the rank orders of therapeutic efficacy on the various measures shows a trend for acetophenazine to be more effective than the other two drugs. In addition, the idea that chlorpromazine was more effective with the overactive belligerent patient was not supported, nor was fluphenazine more effective with the withdrawn patient.

With certain types of statistical analyses, the VA cooperative study III showed perphenazine and triflupromazine to be superior to chlorpromazine.[99,]

Table 6.—Visual Representation of the Rank Order of Efficacy of the Phenothiazine Derivatives in Carefully Done Studies Which Utilized Rating Scales as a Measure of the Reduction of Psychopathology

Schiele et al. (Manifest Behavior Scale)	Vestre, Hall, & Schiele (PRP)	Hanlon et al. (High Group) (MSRPP)	Hanlon et al. (Low Group) (MSRPP)	Adelson & Epstein (MSRPP-mean diff.)	Kurland et al. (MSRPP)	Lasky et al. (IMPS-PRP)	Casey et al. (change on PRP)	Casey, Lasky, Klett, & Hollister (MSRPP)	NIMH Collab. Study I (Global Rating Scale)	NIMH Collab. Study II (Global Rating Scale)	Other Studies Combined (BPRS)
PCB	PBT			Inactive PCB / Active PCB	PBT		PBT	PBT		PCB	
					PCB / MZ		PCB	MZ		MZ	
						RP	PZ	PZ			TDZ / PPZ
CPZ		TPZ	PPZ / TFluPZ / PCPZ / TFluPZ / PPZ	PZ / CPZ / PCPZ / TFluPZ / CPZ / TFluPZ / PCPZ		PZ / PPZ / CPZ / TFluPZ / PCPZ		PCPZ / CPZ / PPZ	CPZ / PCPZ / CPZ / PPZ	CPZ / TDZ / FPZ	CPZ / APZ
TDZ	FPZ	TDZ / TFluoPZ / TFluPZ / CPZ / PPZ / FPZ / PCPZ	TPZ / TDZ / TFluoPZ			TFluPZ / CPT / FPZ / TDZ / CPZ		TFluPZ	TFluPZ	FPZ	FPZ / APZ
TFluoPZ	TFluPZ						CPZ				

PCB = Placebo	PBT = Phenobarbital	PPZ = Perphenazine	RP = Reserpine
CPZ = Chlorpromazine	FPZ = Fluphenazine	PCPZ = Prochlorperazine	CPT = Chlorprothixene
TDZ = Thioridazine	TPZ = Thiopropazate	TFluPZ = Triflupromazine	APZ = Acetophenazine
TFluoPZ — = Trifluoperazine	MZ = Mepazine	PZ = Promazine	

279,282,520 Since, in doing many statistical tests, a few such tests will be significant by chance alone, one should not accept these findings until they have been crossvalidated. It is interesting to inspect the findings of many studies on phenothiazines to see if any one drug consistently shows a slight superiority to the other drugs, even if the superiority is not statistically significant. In Table 6, a visual representation of the rank order of efficacy of the phenothiazine derivatives in a number of carefully done studies is shown.

The rough quantitative position of the phenothiazine derivatives on the scales showing reduction of psychopathology is presented. This provides a rough comparison between studies so that one can see by inspection if the trends are consistent for the slight superiority of any one drug. Since the different studies used different populations of psychotic patients, dosage levels, measuring instruments, duration of treatment, etc., it is important not to be overprecise in interpreting small differences which for statistical and methodologic or clinical reasons are insignificant. This scale should not be considered as being on a common axis, but rather only showing the relative positions of the drugs in a given study, compared with the relative differences found in other studies. The ordinate in this table consists of the average drug scores on the various measuring instruments (shown in the top row). Although this type of table has its limitations, it does provide a way to represent data taken from many studies. For a more exact comparison the

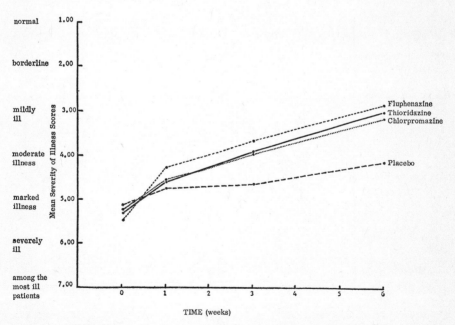

FIG. 1.—Severity of illness over time in patients treated with phenothiazines. (Data from NIMH-PSC Collaborative Study I.)

reader is encouraged to compare the actual data from the original studies. The rating on the far right is taken from several studies, and although it is not as precise a measurement as those within a single study, it does provide data on the same measuring instrument for several more drugs.

Again, those studies were selected which were methodologically the best, and they indicated that chlorpromazine, perphenazine, triflupromazine, acetophenazine, fluphenazine, prochlorperazine and thioridazine were about equally effective and clearly better than mepazine and promazine, which in turn were more effective than placebo or phenobarbital. (See Table 6).

Thus we have made two comparisons of the various drugs; one is based on a consideration of all the studies included in this report (Tables 1, 2, 4, and 5), and one is based on selected studies (Tables 3 and 6). In general, the results of the analysis of the selected studies are similar to the results obtained when all the studies were analyzed, but with more consistent drug effects shown for the more active phenothiazine derivatives.

The kinetics of patient improvement with phenothiazines is a matter of considerable interest. Figures 1-4 present improvement over time from several large studies. Figure 2 shows that patients on chlorpromazine improve continuously from the beginning of treatment to 26 weeks.[503] Similarly, in the Veterans Administration cooperative studies (Figures 3 and 4), improvement also takes place gradually over a long period of time.[98,99] To give a patient 25

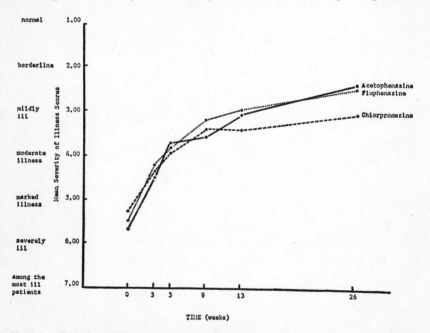

FIG. 2.—Severity of illness over time in patients treated with phenothiazines. (Data from NIMH-PSC Collaborative Study II.)

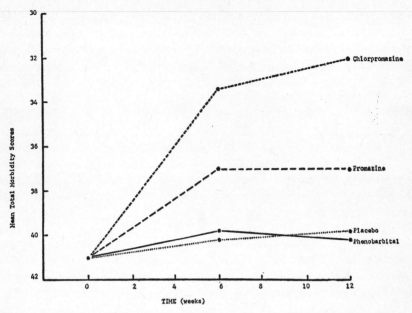

FIG. 3.—Severity of illness over time in patients treated with phenothiazines. (Data from VA Studies 1 and 2.)

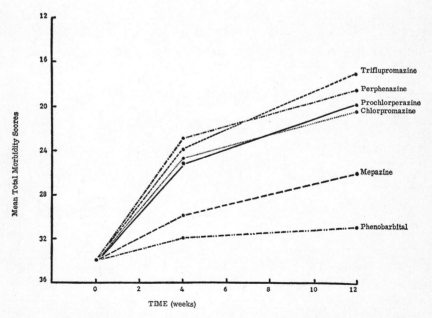

FIG. 4.—Severity of illness over time in patients treated with phenothiazines. (Data from VA Study 3.)

mg. of chlorpromazine for one or two days and then claim that phenothiazines do not help him would be giving him an ineffectual dose for too short a period of time, and any conclusions drawn from this treatment episode would, in all probability, be incorrect. To obtain the maximum clinical effect, one should treat patients with reasonable doses of the drug for a long enough period of time to allow the drug to have its maximum effect.

EFFECTS OF WITHDRAWAL OF PHENOTHIAZINES

Two questions can be asked regarding the withdrawal of phenothiazine medication: 1) Is there a significant risk of a recurrence or reemergence of psychotic symptomatology following the discontinuance of phenothiazine medication?* 2) Do side effects or acute withdrawal effects occur when phenothiazine medication is abruptly stopped?[308,374]

Reemergence of psychotic symptomatology can be a serious problem. It is quite clear from an examination of studies on phenothiazine withdrawal that relapses do occur (Table 7). Often relapses do not occur until three to six months after the discontinuance of medication. Obviously, if one studies patients who do not really need phenothiazines, who have not been taking their medication (as verified by urinary analyses), who were prescribed inadequate doses, or who were not followed for a sufficient period of time after drug cessation, it is difficult to demonstrate the occurrence of relapses. However, in studies of chronically ill severe schizophrenic patients who clearly need phenothiazine medication and who are studied for at least four to six months, the results show that a significant number of the patients do have a recurrence of their psychoses when phenothiazines are withdrawn.[63,91,120,171,189,194,195,244,277,299,456,671] Caffey and his collaborators[91] studied phenothiazine withdrawal in 348 schizophrenic patients, some being treated with chlorpromazine or thioridazine daily (no withdrawal), others transferred to an intermittent dose of phenothiazine medication such that they would receive a lower total dose per week (partial withdrawal), and a third group transferred to placebo. The relapse rate at the end of four months was 45 per cent for the placebo group in contrast to a 5 per cent relapse in the continuous treatment group. These results are consistent with a number of other studies summarized in Table 7. If the withdrawal of maintenance phenothiazine therapy, at least in chronic schizophrenic patients, leads to reexacerbation of symptoms, is it valuable to continue maintenance medication indefinitely? The long term value of phenothiazine treatment in patients over a ten or fifteen-year period has not been studied in well controlled, double-blind studies and may never be. It is difficult to do this type of study because of dropouts, because nondrug-related factors may contribute to acute exacerbations of illness, and

---

*References 82, 244, 255, 268.

Table 7.—Results of Phenothiazine Withdrawal: Controlled Studies

Author(s)	Patient Population	Length of Study	Design	Results	Comments
Blackburn & Allen (63)	60 Open-Ward Chronic Schizophrenics	16 weeks	Random allocation into three groups: 1. Phenothiazine for 16 weeks (N=30) 2. Phenothiazine for 16 weeks. (N=15) 3. Placebo for 8 weeks followed by placebo for 8 weeks (N=15)	12 patients in placebo group deteriorated and required resumption of medication or transfer to a closed ward. 1 patient in drug group deteriorated to the same degree.	Patients' self ratings showed no significant differences between the three groups.
Good et al. (277)	112 chronic male schizophrenics	6 months	Double-Blind Design Patients assigned to four groups: 1. Placebo for 6 months (N=28) 2. Chlorpromazine for 6 months (N=28) 3. Chlorpromazine-Placebo Crossover (N=28) 4. Placebo-Chlorpromazine Crossover (N=28)	At 3 months no significant differences were found between groups. At 6 months the 6 month placebo group showed a significant increase in total morbidity.	No relationship was found between duration of previous drug treatment and tendency to regress on withdrawal.
Diamond & Marks (171)	40 chronic schizophrenics receiving maintenance doses of chlorpromazine (N=20) or triflupromazine (N=20).	6 months	Double-Blind Design Placebo was substituted for 50% of the patients receiving each drug.	At six months, 14 of 20 on placebo had worsened, while only 5 of 20 on drugs worsened. (Sig. at 0.01 level)	At 3 months, the placebo group showed more deterioration than the drug group, but the difference became definitely significant at 6 months.

Table 7—Results of Phenothiazine Withdrawal: Controlled Studies (continued)

Author(s)	Patient Population	Length of Study	Design	Results	Comments
Freeman & Alson (244)	94 long-term psychotics receiving chlorpromazine	6 months	Double-Blind Design Patient sample divided into 2 groups: 1. placebo group (N=46) 2. chlorpromazine group (N=48)	At 6 months, 13 of 46 placebo patients had relapsed. 6 of 48 chlorpromazine-treated patients had relapsed.	No significant differences between groups was found on the Lyons Behavior Rating Scale. Authors indicate that patients with initially higher morbidity scores, especially those with confusion and lack of interest, are generally poorer risks for withdrawal.
Caffey et al. (91)	348 chronic schizophrenics	4 months	Double-Blind Design Patients divided into 3 groups: 1. Placebo group (N=171) 2. Reduced Dosage Group (N=89) 3. Drug Group (N=88)	At 4 months, 77 of 171 (45%) patients in placebo group had relapsed, 13 of 89 (15%) of the patients in the reduced dosage group had relapsed, and 4 of 88 (5%) in the drug group had relapsed.	Relapses in general were more severe when they occurred in patients receiving placebo.
Clark et al. (121)	57 chronic schizophrenic women	32 weeks	Double-Blind Design Patients received placebo, phenobarbital or chlorpromazine. Maximum dose was given for 16 weeks, reduced doses for 4 weeks, and no dose for final 12 weeks.	4 weeks after drugs were stopped, there were significant differences between the drug group and the nondrug groups on same measures. Some significant differences persisted for 8 weeks.	Data from this study indicates a 4-8 week lag period in the dissipation of the effects of chlorpromazine.

Table 7 (continued)

Author(s)	Patient Population	Length of Study	Design	Results	Comments
Marjerrison et al. (456)	78 chronic hospitalized psychotics receiving long term phenothiazine treatment	7 months	Double-Blind Design Random assignment to phenothiazine group (N=47) or placebo group (N=31).	After 7 months, the placebo group had significantly lower scores than the active-drug groups on the behavioral inventory.	Significant differences did not appear until the 5th month.
Whittaker & Hoy (671)	39 male chronic schizophrenics	10 weeks	Random assignment to 3 groups: 1. Placebo group (N=13) 2. Perphenazine group (N=13) 3. No Medication group (N=13)	17 of 26 patients not receiving drug relapsed. 1 of 13 drug patients relapsed.	After 2 weeks only 19% of the nondrug groups had relapsed. By 10 weeks, 64% had relapsed.
Gross et al. (299)	90 released chronic psychotics. (82/90 were schizophrenic).	7 months	Double-Blind Design Patients were assigned to 2 groups: 1. Control group (N=34) 2. Experimental group (N=56) Dose in experimental patients was gradually reduced to none and placebo was substituted (Usually over 2 month period).	At 7 months, 41 of 56 (73%) patients in the experimental group had relapsed. 3 of 34 (9%) of the patients in the control group had relapsed.	Authors suggest that long term phenothiazine medication should be continued after release from hospitalization.

because many patients stop taking drugs without medical advice or knowledge. In addition, if a significant portion of the placebo group in such a study relapses, the portion of patients with good prognoses becomes higher in the residual placebo group. Hence, after several years, the withdrawal and non-withdrawal groups will no longer be matched for psychopathology.

In a very important series of studies, Engelhardt and his group have demonstrated that chlorpromazine, in comparison to placebo, can significantly prevent hospitalization in schizophrenic patients treated on an outpatient basis.[189,193,195,196]

Several studies have reported that, upon the sudden withdrawal of phenothiazine medication in chronic patients maintained on high doses, withdrawal effects occurred beginning the second and the fourth day after withdrawal. Brooks,[82] Gallant et al.,[252] and Simpson et al.[608] found that following abrupt withdrawal, patients exhibited such symptoms as nausea, vomiting, increased sebaceous secretion, tension, restlessness, and physical complaints. Simpson and his collaborators have suggested that at least some of the immediate withdrawal symptoms such as perspiration, insomnia, and restlessness may in part relate to the withdrawal of the antiparkinsonian drugs frequently given in conjunction with the phenothiazines. To test this hypothesis, they withdrew patients from an antipsychotic medication (butaperazine) and an antiparkinsonian medication (benztropine methanesulphate), and compared this group to another group of patients withdrawn from the phenothiazine medication alone. The group withdrawn from both drugs showed a higher incidence of withdrawal effects than the group which was kept on the antiparkinsonian drug. These authors speculated that, since the antiparkinsonian medication is excreted more rapidly than the phenothiazines, there is a return of phenothiazine-caused extrapyramidal side effects. Furthermore, they suggest that the antiparkinsonian drugs may have a synergistic or additive effect with the phenothiazines in controlling the acid output of the stomach; hence, withdrawal of these drugs may result in a rebound phenomenon causing the observed withdrawal vomiting. Whatever the mechanism of these effects, it would be advisable to withdraw medication over the course of several days to a week and to continue the patient on antiparkinson drugs for a few days after the phenothiazines have been withdrawn. In general clinical practice, such effects as withdrawal vomiting are not observed to any significant degree, and, in general, they do not constitute a problem, but they may occur.

PHENOTHIAZINE COMBINATIONS

Clinicians sometimes feel that a combination of several drugs is better than a single psychotropic drug, and some combine two, three, or even more drugs in an attempt to meet the needs of various patients.* One cannot predict the effect of a combination of drugs with certainty from the properties of the individual drugs involved in the combination, since certain properties may be additive, may potentiate each other, or may cancel each other out. For purposes of study and comparison, dosage is another important variable, since the dose of the combination should be pharmacologically equivalent to the doses of single medications. If this factor is not taken into account, results of studies may reflect simply a high dose versus a low dose rather than a combination versus a single drug effect. For the best interpretation of results, it is important to have each single drug, as well as a placebo, to compare with the combination-treated patients.

Michaux, Kurland, and Agallianos[482] studied the use of drug combinations in the treatment of 131 newly hospitalized acutely ill patients at a state-supported mental institution. The patients were treated with chlorpromazine-imipramine (Thorazine-Tofranil), chlorpromazine-chloridiazepoxide (Thorazine-Librium), or chlorpromazine-placebo. A fourth group received whatever single drug or combination of these three drugs the physician viewed as most suitable. In this study, patients assigned randomly to receive the chlorpromazine-chlordiazepoxide combination did not receive adequate chlorpromazine dosage, possibly because they appeared sedated from the effects of the chlordiazepoxide, and their physician then (inappropriately) felt that they had received sufficient medication. No combination of drugs showed an unqualified superiority to chlorpromazine alone. However, this study presents several leads for further research which may lead to the identification of subtypes of disorders which are sensitive to particular combinations of drugs.

For example, chlorpromazine-imipramine seemed to be particularly effective in the treatment of patients with high levels of depression and low levels of agitation, a group which included some catatonic schizophrenics. Chlorpromazine-chlordiazepoxide was less effective than chlorpromazine-imipramine in the treatment of schizophrenic disorganization, but was effective in the treatment of patients with considerable behavior disturbance, including highly agitated and highly retarded patients. Chlorpromazine alone was effective against the "core" symptoms of schizophrenia, showing superiority to other treatments in the reduction of schizophrenic disorganization. The reader is referred to the original monograph[482] for further detail.

In a comparative, but not double-blind study, Hollister[341] showed that perphenazine (Trilafon) combined with amitriptyline (Elavil) in newly admitted schizophrenics produced an improvement rate that was comparable to

---

*References 17, 29, 53, 86, 88, 203, 205, 303, 354, 369-370, 406, 407, 432, 458, 476, 482, 493, 508, 609, 651, 676.

that of perphenazine alone. However Hanlon et al.[320] did observe the combination to be useful in chronic patients.

Many chronic schizophrenics residing in mental hospitals have been treated with and are maintained on chlorpromazine, and yet have failed to respond sufficiently to be discharged. To see whether drug combinations could help these "chlorpromazine failures," Casey et al.[101] gave chlorpromazine to a sample of patients and, in addition, gave some of the patients chlorpromazine-dextroamphetamine (Thorazine-Dexedrine), chlorpromazine-isocarboxazid (Thorazine-Marplan), chlorpromazine-imipramine (Thorazine-Tofranil) or chlorpromazine-trifluoperazine (Thorazine-Stelazine). No combination of drugs was found to be more effective than chlorpromazine alone. There was some evidence that amphetamine made the patients worse. Although it has been said that trifluoperazine has an alerting effect, adding this drug to chlorpromazine did not significantly increase the activity level or the excitement level.

The combination marketed abroad under the trade name of Parstelin, consisting of tranyclypromine (Parnate) and trifluoperazine (Stelazine), has been shown to be slightly more effective than trifluoperazine alone in a few patients, but quantitatively the difference is small.[582-584] A few patients seem to respond dramatically to this combination who are often treatment-resistant to standard chlorpromazine therapy. It would be important to cross-validate this finding of a subgroup of patients uniquely sensitive to tranylcypromine-trifluoperazine, and to develop methods of identifying this subtype of disorder.

COMPARISON WITH SOMATIC THERAPIES

In a well-controlled study of insulin coma[4] with a three-year follow-up, a placebo condition was provided by treating the control group with barbiturate-induced periods of unconsciousness equal to the number of insulin coma treatments of the experimental group. The investigators did not find a significant difference between the control (sedated) and the experimental (insulin) groups. Trifluoperazine and chlorpromazine, however, were found to be equal to insulin coma therapy in the treatment of schizophrenia,[30,223,475] and chlorpromazine was found to be equal to or slightly superior to electroconvulsive treatment (ECT) in the initial treatment o f schizophrenia.[30,416,565] Miller et al.[484] found no appreciable difference in the improvement of catatonics and a group of mixed psychotics with ECT over the control groups of patients who received anesthesia alone. Furthermore, ECT was not found to be more effective than placebo in chronic schizophrenic patients.[276,506] Although ECT and insulin coma treatments have been widely used, their efficacy in the treatment of schizophrenia has not been clearly established by systematic, controlled investigation, and controlled studies have not proven these treatments to be more effective than drug treatments. In addition, insulin coma treatment is expensive and a potentially dangerous treatment in experienced hands.[37,54,79,375,388,395,437,484,565] There have been no controlled studies which have isolated a subtype of schizophrenia differentially sensitive to ECT using pretreatment psychiatric assessment, a possibility suggested by clinical experience. ECT combined with antipsychotic drugs may be helpful.[613a]

PHENOTHIAZINES, SOCIAL THERAPY, AND PSYCHOTHERAPIES

Over the past fifteen years, there has been a striking alteration in many state mental hospitals involving a change from custodial to active methods of treatment such as occupational therapies, active treatment units, group therapy, and total push units.* In many cases, the use of tranquilizers may make it possible for a patient to participate in these social therapies.

Greenblatt and his collaborators[87,287] did a revealing study serving to clarify the relationship between drugs and social therapy. One hundred fifteen chronic schizophrenic patients were divided into four matched groups: 1) twenty-seven patients who received intensive social therapy without drugs, 2) thirty-three patients who received both intensive social therapy and drug therapy, 3) twenty patients who received a normal course of social therapy and no drugs, and 4) thirty-five patients who received a normal course of social therapy and also received antipsychotic drugs. After six months, the patients in all groups were given drugs if their physician felt it would be desirable. The patients in each group were evaluated and comparisons were made at intervals of six, eighteen, and thirty-six months after the study began. One very important aspect of the high social therapies groups was the active and aggressive discharge policy which prevailed at the institution where these groups were studied. This may have been as important as the social therapies per se in increasing discharges within these groups. The results are summarized in Table 8.

After six months, there was a striking difference between the groups which had received drugs and the groups which had not, regardless of whether or not the patients had received intensive social therapy. The authors state that, at six months, differences attributable to contrasting milieu appear to be relatively small. Of the two groups which were treated with drugs, 28 per cent had improved, while only 4 per cent of the nondrug groups showed comparable improvement. The least improvement was found in the group which had received intensive social therapy unaccompanied by drugs, and the greatest improvement was found in those patients who had received both antipsychotic drugs and intensive social therapy.

After thirty-six months the differences between the drug groups and the

---

*References 87, 135, 176, 287, 294, 297, 310, 393, 464-467.

nondrug groups were somewhat blurred, since all patients had been permitted to receive drugs after the initial six months. Again, the group showing the greatest improvement was the group which received both drug therapy and intensive social therapy. The group showing least improvement was the group which had received neither intensive social therapy nor drugs for the first six months.

Furthermore when the rates of discharge between six and nine months were compared, it was observed that the greatest number of patients were discharged from the group which received both drugs and social therapy (27 per cent), while all of the other groups showed low rates of discharge. From this evaluation, it appeared that neither drug therapy alone nor intensive social therapy alone was enough to cause a significant increase in the percentage of patients discharged.

The groups which received drugs clearly did better than the groups which did not receive tranquilizers in regard to amelioration of their psychopathology. However, the group given both drugs and intensive social

Table 8.—Results of Treatment of Chronic Schizophrenia with Four Treatment Regimes. (Greenblatt et al.)

| Per Cent High Improvement at Six Months Evaluation | | |
High Social Therapy Transferred to MMHC	Low Social Therapy State Hospitals	Total
Drug Therapy	33%	23%	28%
No Drug Therapy	0%	10%	4%
Total	18%	18%	

| Per Cent Discharged After Six to Nine Months | | |
High Social Therapy Transferred to MMHC	Low Social Therapy State Hospitals	Total
Drug Therapy	27%	9%	15%
No Drug Therapy for 6 Months	7%	5%	6%
Total	18%	7%	

| Per Cent High Improvement After Thirty-Six Months | | |
High Social Therapy Transferred to MMHC	Low Social Therapy State Hospitals	Total
Drug Therapy	35%	19%	27%
No Drug Therapy for 6 Months	26%	6%	17%
Total	31%	11%	

therapy had a significantly greater number of discharges than any other group, and based on the follow-up evaluations, did better than the other groups. It appears, then, that social therapies and drug therapies potentiate each other in terms of ultimate prognosis. Apparently, the drugs make for symptomatic improvement, while the social therapies allow more patients to be discharged and form more meaningful relationships within the community. Social therapies appear to consolidate and put to good use the drug-initiated and drug-sustained improvement.

The effects of group treatment, adjunctive social therapies, and drug therapy were compared in a group of chronic patients by Evangelakis.[197] The groups that received group therapy and/or adjunctive social therapies, but no drug therapy, did poorly. All of the groups which were treated with the various combinations of group, nongroup, adjunctive, and nonadjunctive treatment, in combination with drug treatment, did consistently better. The discharge, trial visit, and boarding-home visit rates of the groups receiving adjunctive treatments in combination with drug therapy seemed slightly higher than those of the other groups.

King[393] found no significant difference in frequency of discharge between the effects of group therapy with chlorpromazine medication, and chlorpromazine alone. Cooper[135] compared two groups of ten chronic schizophrenics, the first receiving chlorpromazine (Thorazine) therapy, and the second receiving group therapy. The chlorpromazine group showed a greater trend toward improvement than the group which was receiving group therapy, but this trend failed to reach statistical significance. May and Tuma[467] studied the effects of drug therapy alone, drug therapy combined with psychotherapy, and psychotherapy alone, with a control group, in acute schizophrenic reactions (Table 9).[464-497] The drug treatments, whether given alone or in combination with psychotherapy, increased the release rate, shortened the hospital stay, decreased the necessity for the use of sedatives or hydrotherapy, and produced a more beneficial change in clinical status.

Grinspoon and Ewalt[294,297] studied a group of chronic schizophrenic patients treated by experienced senior psychoanalysts. The patients were taken

Table 9.—Comparison of Four Methods of Treatment of Acute Schizophrenics (May and Tuma)

Treatment	Percentage of Patients Released in Study Period
Control	65%
Psychotherapy Only	70%
Drug Only	90%
Drug and Psychotherapy	95%

off drugs for a three-month period, during which time placebo was substituted for any active medication they had been receiving. A group of patients were then given thioridazine (Mellaril), while the other group received continued placebo treatment. All patients were treated throughout the two year study period with intensive psychotherapy by experienced psychoanalysts. The patients given thioridazine did better than the patients treated with placebo, even though both groups received intensive psychotherapy. The drug treated group also showed a much greater involvement with their therapists, and a more intense reaction to such events as their therapists' vacation, ward administrators leaving the ward, President Kennedy's death, etc. Psychoanalytic psychotherapy alone was ineffective in curing these schizophrenics. Many psychoanalytically-oriented therapists have objected to phenothiazine treatment because it is said to block emotional involvement, yet this study showed that the drug treated group manifested more emotional involvement than the nondrug treated group.

In a cooperative study done at nine Veterans Administration Hospitals, 150 patients were randomly assigned to treatments with group therapy alone, thioridazine therapy alone, and combined therapy (thioridazine combined with group therapy) for a period of twelve weeks. Drug therapy, either alone or with group therapy, produced a marked improvement in the reduction of symptoms commonly associated with schizophrenia. The drug effect was seen on global measures of improvement. Of interest also is the finding that group psychotherapy was effective in relieving tension and reducing somatization, with or without medication, while group therapy with medication was effective in the reduction of motor retardation and anxiety.[281]

The studies reviewed above indicate that drug therapy combined with social therapies can often be a more effective treatment mode than either drug or social therapy by itself. Further studies are badly needed concerning the possible interactions between the psychotherapies, adjunctive therapies, and drug treatment.[310] Further investigation the usefulness of antipsychotic agents both in the outpatient situation and in conditions other than schizophrenic is desirable.[165,166,221,335,444,551,558,640,667]

PREDICTION OF RESPONSE

An idea is widespread that hyperactive patients show the best response to treatment with the phenothiazines, while withdrawn patients do not respond, but, rather, become more withdrawn. This is not supported by the facts. In general, withdrawn patients become more active on phenothiazine therapy, while patients who are overactive tend to become less so. That is, psychotics showing the extremes of withdrawal and inactivity versus hyperactivity tend to move toward the mean when given antipsychotic medication.[420] The various phenothiazines have similar effects on populations of schizophrenic patients, but it would be of interest to know whether patients showing different types of

Table 10.—Prediction of Drug Response from Predrug Patient Variables

Author, Study, and Measuring Instruments	Drugs	Predrug Variables, Predictions of Successful Treatment	Cross-Validations
Marks, J., VA Co-Operative Study No. 3, MSRPP	Chlorpromazine	less resistiveness* less paranoid projection	Similar patterns existed on Spring Grove State Hospital Study (Kurland et al.), but individual predictions were not tested separately.
	Triflupromazine	manic excitement paranoid projection tension* perceptual distortion	
	Prochlorperazine	activity,* sociability	
	Perphenazine	sociability*	
Mosley & Klett VA Co-Operative Study IMPS	Chlorpromazine Fluphenazine Thioridazine	Multiple regression equations were used to predict excitement vs retardation, schizophrenic disorganization, and paranoid process from predrug variables.	Does not replicate
Overall et al. VA Co-Operative Study BPRS and Computer Analysis of Predrug BPRS scores	Acetophenazine	Paranoid schizophrenic (anxious, tense, suspicious, with unusual thought content).	Does not replicate
	Perphenazine	Core schizophrenic (disorganized, withdrawn, with blunted affect).	

*Indicates statistically significant predictors.

initial psychiatric symptomatology would respond differently to different drugs. It has been a common clinical assumption that the withdrawn patient responds better to the more alerting phenothiazines such as trifluoperazine (Stelazine) and fluphenazine (Prolixin). However, this has not been definitely proven.

Overall et al.[521] compared the effectiveness of acetophenazine (Tindal) with that of perphenazine (Trilafon), using 98 newly admitted schizophrenic men from five V.A. hospitals. When one looks at the total improvement as a whole, it appears that the patients improved equally on both medications. Through computer analysis of initial ratings on the Brief Psychiatric Rating Scale (BPRS), two groups of patients were separated and classified as paranoid and "core" schizophrenics. The paranoid patients had profiles with peaks in anxiety, tension, suspiciousness, and unusual thought content. The "core" schizophrenics had profiles with peaks in conceptual disorganization, withdrawal, and flattened affect. Acetophenazine was a more effective drug in treating the paranoid group, while perphenazine was more effective in treating the core group. Marks,[457] using data from a large co-operative study, investigated whether initial evaluation of the patient could predict response to drugs. In a total of forty-four comparisons predicting differential drug effectiveness from initial evaluation, he found four significant comparisons (see Table 10). Chlorpromazine (Thorazine) was effective in patients who showed less resistiveness. Patients who were more sociable had a differential improvement with perphenazine, patients with high activity improved on prochlorperazine (Compazine), and tense patients improved differentially with triflupromazine. Marks did not find that patients who were withdrawn responded better to the more activating phenothiazines such as perphenazine, or that patients with excitement responded better to more sedating phenothiazines such as chlorpromazine. A limited type of cross-validation is provided by the Kurland-Spring Grove Hospital group which made its data available to Marks, who found significant agreement between the two studies.[457] Mosley[500] has found that predrug behavior can predict better than chance the differential response of some patients to chlorpromazine and fluphenazine. It is important to note that several of the predictive classifications have not held up on cross-validation.[291,342]

The data from the NIMH Collaborative Studies I and II[127,503] were combined and a multivariate analysis was carried out. The multiple regression approach was used to determine whether any combination of pretreatment symptom ratings could predict clinical improvement at five or six weeks. Improvement on all four drugs, analyzed separately, could be predicted at a statistically significant level. The multiple regression equations are significantly different from each other beyond the .001 level, indicating that there are different bases for the prediction of improvement with each of the four drugs in these studies. Table 11 lists a summary of some of the better individual predictors; for example, "good self-care" predicts acetophenazine improvers, and "guilt feelings" predicts fluphenazine improvers. It is worthy of particular note that in the NIMH studies, not one drug-treated patient worsened during the period of the study, in contrast to the patients on placebo, many of whom did worsen.

Since it is possible to a certain extent to predict which drug will improve which patient, the question arises as to whether or not such predictions will be clinically useful, i.e., is the increment of improvement significant clinically? Since many patients improve with any phenothiazine, is the extra increment of improvement made by the differential selection enough to result in substantially more improvement if the patient is given the optimum drug? Since, in these NIMH studies, the patients were randomly assigned, one would expect that in certain cases patients would be randomly assigned to the drug which would have been predicted to do best from the multiple regression equation, had it been used, and in other cases patients would have been assigned to a drug which would not have been predicted to do well. To determine the extent of the increment caused by the patients' being assigned to the predicted "best" drug, a comparison was made between those patients who, by chance, were assigned to the drug on which they had been predicted to improve the most, and those patients who had been randomly assigned to the drug for which the least improvement was predicted. The observed difference was as great as the difference between all phenothiazines and placebo.

The authors state that the actual difference may be somewhat exaggerated because prediction equations developed from these patients' data were reapplied to the same patients. The use of an independent sample, unfortunately not yet available, would have eliminated this potential problem.

Since there is some increase in drug effectiveness if optimal prediction is used, one wonders if this extra improvement is worth the time it takes. Newly admitted patients are ordinarily interviewed by psychiatrists or psychologists and observed on their ward behavior by the nurses or nursing assistants. The completion of the Inpatient Multidimensional Psychiatric Scale (IMPS) and the Ward Behavior Rating Scale (WBRS), on which the above predictions are based, would take perhaps an additional ten minutes. The solving of the multiple regression equations would take a few minutes more, but this could be done by a ward secretary or some other clerical personnel. Thus, the extra time involved in making predictions would be negligible in comparison with the time already expended on the patient, especially if one considers that the drug of choice may significantly improve the patient's chance of recovery.

It is worth noting that in this study, patients who were assigned to the drug on which they were predicted to improve least still did better than those patients who received placebo. This indicates that any phenothiazine is better than no phenothiazine in the treatment of schizophrenia.

If one looks qualitatively at Table 11, one can see that the acetophenazine improver is hostile, hears voices, is agitated and confused, and has feelings of unreality, but has good self care habits. The chlorpromazine improver hears voices, is agitated, slow, indifferent, has ideas of persecution, is irritable, has poor self care, has feelings of unreality, shows poor social participation, and is confused. The chlorpromazine improver seems to have a greater number of core symptoms of schizophrenia than the improvers on other drugs, while the clinical picture of the acetophenazine improver seems to resemble paranoid excitement with a definite absence of such core schizophrenic symptoms.

The notion that agitated and aggressive schizophrenic patients respond to phenothiazine therapy while patients who do not have these disagreeable characteristics do not particularly respond to these drugs has been consistently demonstrated to be false in a series of studies. No author has isolated a group of patients who are positive on these target symptoms and shown that these patients respond better to phenothiazines than patients who lacked these symptoms.[249,342] Prediction of response from predrug assessment is an important area of investigation. The use of slogans such as "target symptoms" does not provide answers and is harmful insofar as it blocks further thinking and research. It is hoped that empirical research will advance beyond symptom lists and arrive at some rational means of classifying patients into categories.* The next step in the above investigations would be to cross-validate this research[249,342] with attention to quantitative detail, so that one could give a quantitative statement as to how much more effective differential treatment is, using a multidimensional conditional probability approach to gain a measure of the utility of the match of subpatient populations to their optimal drug therapies.

One of the most promising developments in the prediction of drug response is the work of Donald Klein who emphasizes the value of developmental and activation status as predictors of optimal drug response. He has found that schizo-affective schizophrenics respond differently better to chlorpromazine than other diagnostic subtypes. Furthermore, if schizophrenic patients are subdivided according to their activation levels both the retarded and the manic patients did better on chlorpromazine than the normactive group. It is also of interest to note the finding that imipramine may be useful in pseudoneurotic schizophrenia. Many of the relationships between diagnostic dimensions and differential outcome are curvilinear, and could be missed by linear methods of analysis.[398a]

PHENOTHIAZINE ACTION

The practicing psychiatrist may have an implicit notion or model of how phenothiazines affect his patients, and he may prescribe drugs to various types of patients, at various dose levels, for varying lengths of time, based upon this

---

*References 5, 271, 316, 380, 382, 500, 504, 519, 521, 522, 555.

Table 11.—Predictors of Drug Response Derived from Multiple Regression Coefficients of Pretreatment Symptoms on Doctor's and Nurse's Improvement Composites (NIMH-PSC Publication Report Number 4a, April 1966).

Variable:	Acetophenazine	Chlorpromazine	Fluphenazine	Thioridazine
IMPS:				
Hostility	−DD			
Disorientation				
Guilt		N	−D	
Auditory Hallucinations	−D	D, NN		
Agitation and Tension	−D	−D, −NN		
Slowed Speech and Movements		−DDD		−N
Delusions of Grandeur		−D		
Indifference to Environment				
Incoherent Speech	N	−DD		
Pressure of Speech		DDD	D, N	
Ideas of Persecution		−DDD		−DDD
Hebephrenic Symptoms				
Nonauditory Hallucinations		−N		
Memory Deficit				
WBRS:				
Social Participation		−DDD, −NNN	−DD, −NNN	
Irritability		−D, −NNN	−NN	
Self Care	DDD		−D	
Appearance of Sadness		−D		
Feelings of Unreality	−NN	−D, D		
Resistiveness			−DDD, −NN	−N
Confusion	−DDD, −NNN	−N		−N

N or D indicates p greater than .05 on Nurse's or Doctor's improvement composite.
NN or DD indicates p greater than .01 on Nurse's or Doctor's improvement composite.
NNN or DDD indicates p greater than .001 on Nurse's or Doctor's improvement composite.

model. These models have important implications for clinical practice, and it is necessary to consider in detail what is known about the action of the phenothiazines. Some psychiatrists regard the phenothiazines as merely sedatives, and often feel that it is not good medical practice to use these drugs because one does not want to sedate a patient's sensibilities.

DiMascio, Havens, and Klerman[174,175] studied the effects, on normal males, of the administration of four phenothiazines, three of which had antipsychotic properties (chlorpromazine, perphenazine, and trifluoperazine), and the fourth (promethazine), having no definite antipsychotic effect. If these drugs were merely sedatives, it would be anticipated that the three phenothiazines with antipsychotic properties would have definite sedative effects, and the phenothiazine with no antipsychotic effect would have no sedative effect. This was not found to be the case. Only one of the three antipsychotic phenothiazines (chlorpromazine) was found to produce sedation, and, in addition, the drug which was not an antipsychotic was found to have sedative effects. Both of these drugs produced definite psychomotor inhibition, mental confusion, and sedation. The other two phenothiazines, both effective antipsychotics, produced only minimal changes in measurements of cognitive impairment, and, in fact, a slight improvement was noted on some measures. The results of this study thus show a clear dissociation between mental sedation and antipsychotic action.

The Veterans Administration Cooperative Studies[98,99,420,520] and the study of Kurland et al.[411,412] conclusively demonstrate that the action of the phenothiazines is different from that of the sedative phenobarbital, which itself is no better than placebo in the reduction of psychotic symptomatology. (See Fig. 3)

There have been relatively few studies of the psychological changes produced in schizophrenic patients treated with phenothiazines. Most of the studies that have been done focus on symptomatic changes. Do the drugs first affect the primary symptoms of schizophrenia or the secondary symptoms? Do they affect anxiety first and psychotic symptoms secondarily, if at all? Do they really make patients more manageable? Do they affect a patient's drive to his ego structure? Some of the answers to these questions can be obtained from studies which have used rating scales to measure the therapeutic efficiency of the phenothiazines.

Gorham and Overall[282] showed that the variables most sensitive to phenothiazine derivatives were suspicion, tension-anxiety, conceptual disorganization, mannerisms-posturings, guilt, and dread. Pearl et al.[531] found reserpine to be effective when it was compared with placebo on the following scales of the Multidimensional Scale for Rating Psychiatric Patients (MSRPP): resistiveness, conceptual thinking disturbance, belligerence, mannerisms (motor disturbance), perceptual distortion, and withdrawal. The similarity of the effects of the phenothiazine derivatives and reserpine on these variables is worth noting.

Another method of measuring the psychological effects of the antipsychotic drugs is to study their effects on measures of psychopathology typical of schizophrenia. It has been stated that schizophrenics differ from normals in that they use more concrete than abstract thinking. If the phenothiazines act, at least in part, by an alteration of the thought disorder of schizophrenia, one would expect that an intelligent patient who does show concreteness as a result of his schizophrenia would improve his ability to think in terms of abstractions as a result of phenothiazine treatment. A subsample of the schizophrenic patients studied in the NIMH Psychopharmacology Service Center study was examined using the Gorham Proverbs Test, and, indeed, in the high IQ group, there was a definite improvement in the ability to abstract and a decrease in the amount of concrete thinking.[602]

In addition, these investigators scored the test for bizarre, circumstantial, and inappropriate responses and showed that the medication decreased the number of these responses. It is of interest to note that schizophrenics are found to be inferior to normals on conceptual tasks because of over-inclusiveness (over-responsiveness to an inappropriate stimulus). Bizarre, circumstantial, and inappropriate responses might fall into this category of over-inclusive pathology, and this type of psychopathology shows a definite response to phenothiazine treatment.

Chapman and Knowles[107] studied the effects of phenothiazines on disordered thought in chronic schizophrenics, testing those who did and did not receive phenothiazines, using tests of cognitive function. Phenothiazines apparently reduced errors of excessive breadth of concepts, providing evidence that phenothiazines reduce thinking disorders in schizophrenia. However, clinical experience shows that anxiety promotes concreteness of thought and that the reduction of anxiety alone may improve thought processes. A study of the effect of chlordiazepoxide (Librium)[49] also supports this proposition. Thus the specific effect of phenothiazines on thought concretization is in some doubt.

Data from five large, controlled studies of phenothiazines in schizophrenia which used placebo, phenobarbital, or psychotherapy control groups have been examined.[98,99,127,281,412] From these data, it can be seen that certain symptoms are more sensitive to phenothiazine treatment than others. The results of this analysis are presented in Table 12. In this table, certain liberties have been taken with the specific names for the variable factors or cluster scores to make them more compatible with the Bleulerian division of schizophrenic symptoms into primary and accessory categories. Inspection of Table 12 reveals that most of the primary symptoms are consistently helped by the phenothiazines. Symptoms typical of schizophrenia such as hallucinations and paranoid ideation, are also helped, while anxiety, tension, and agitation are less responsive to phenothiazine treatment. These data clearly support the notion that the phenothiazines are not in any sense purely anti-anxiety agents, but in a broad sense are antipsychotic. They affect the primary symptoms of schizophrenia and also those secondary symptoms characteristic of the schizophrenic.

The phenothiazines and the barbiturates, while they may have some similar behavioral effects, do differ widely in many of their pharmacological actions. These cannot all be detailed here because of space limitations, but they are briefly summarized below.

Data are provided by studies of normal and abnormal humans, animals, and neurophysiological preparations. Mirsky and Kornetsky[490] showed that chlorpromazine and barbiturates have differential effects on continuous performance tests and on digit symbol substitution tests. In general, chlorpromazine can be viewed as interfering with tasks requiring continual attention, such as watching for aperiodic stimuli which require a response, while the barbiturates interfere more with performance on tasks requiring a sustained self-paced cognitive effort. Several animal experiments using the escape-avoidance model have shown chlorpromazine to decrease avoidance behavior differentially in comparison with the barbiturates which suppress avoidance only at a dose which also suppresses escape behavior. There are a number of animal test systems which differentiate barbiturates from the phenothiazines.*

Barbiturates and minor tranquilizers (meprobamate, chlordiazepoxide), on the other hand, enable animals to brave an aversive stimulus (usually a shock) to obtain a food reward.[55,56,170] Chlorpromazine does not have this effect. Irwin[368] conceptualizes the differences between the two drugs as follows: the phenothiazines decrease motor activity, exploratory behavior, and responses to environmental stimuli; barbiturates and minor tranquilizers at appropriate doses increase motor activity, response to environmental stimuli, exploratory behavior, and generally act as disinhibiting agents. He feels that both animal studies and observed clinical effects reflect these pharmacological differences. These results suggest that there are real differences between these two classes of drugs.

Neurophysiological studies by Killam and Killam[390,392] and Bradley[72] support the concept that chlorpromazine and the barbiturates have differing neurophysiological effects. The reader is referred to the above articles for a more detailed discussion. Chlorpromazine can be viewed as enhancing the filtering out of irrelevant stimuli while preserving the brain's ability to respond to more urgent meaningful stimuli.

Chlorpromazine has only a small effect on the arousal threshold to direct

---

*For example: avoidance behavior versus discrimination behavior,[359] approach-avoidance conflict,[7,170,450,523,649] multiple schedules of reinforcement[662] web building of spiders[117,678,679] DRL behavior,[66] protection against amphetamine toxicity, activity of mice individually and in groups,[54] intracranial stimulation,[513,515] and aggressive behavior etc.[73,109,132,153,170,212,329,363,364,371,358,485,488,574,632,633,649,654,687]

Table 12.—Analysis of Symptom Sensitivity to Phenothiazines[125]

BLEULER'S CLASSIFICATION OF SCHIZOPHRENIC SYMPTOMS	V.A. Study No. 1	V.A. Study No. 3	Kurland 1962	NIMH-PSC No. 1	Gorham 1964 (vs. Group Psychotherapy)
FUNDAMENTAL SYMPTOMS:					
Thought Disorder	++	++	++	++	++
Blunted Affect–Indifference		++		++	+
Withdrawal-Retardation	++	++	0	++	++
Autistic Behavior-Mannerisms	++	++	0	++	+
ACCESSORY SYMPTOMS:					
Hallucinations	++	++	+	+	0
Paranoid Ideation	0	++	0	+	+
Grandiosity	0	0	0	0	++
Hostility-Belligerence	++	++	H.R.	+	+
Resistiveness-Uncooperativeness	++	++	H.R.	++	++
NONSCHIZOPHRENIC SYMPTOMS:					
Anxiety-Tension-Agitation	0	0	H.R.	+	0
Guilt-Depression	++	0	0	0	0
Disorientation				0	
Somatization					0

H.R.=Heterogeneity of regression was found on analysis of covariance of the measures indicated. (This invalidates this particular statistical procedure but does not mean that there was no drug effect)

++=Symptom areas showing marked differences between drug and control groups.

+=Symptom areas showing significant but less striking differences.

0=Areas not showing differential drug superiority.

electrical stimulation in the cat *encephalé isolé* preparation, while the barbiturates have a marked effect. However, chlorpromazine does have a definite effect on arousal induced by actual auditory stimulation. The hypothesis can be formulated from this and other data[569] that chlorpromazine acts on the reticular system causing the filtering and gating mechanisms to be enhanced, thereby reducing the flow of certain types of information to the cortex. There are profound differences between the neuropharmacological actions of the phenothiazines and the barbiturates; however this along with their metabolism, falls outside the scope of this review.

In a rough way, both the phenothiazines and the barbiturates function in some situations as sedatives. However, since in a great number of cases their actions are either qualitatively very different or show quite different dose-response curves, the two drug classes can be assumed to be pharmacologically quite separate.[70-72,80,164,177,219,221-222,240-241,272-273,390-393,492,528,569,668]

Since in the normal nondrugged human, in animals, or in neurophysiologic preparations, there is no analogue of psychosis, generalizations from the types of investigations reviewed above should be made with caution. However, when combined with data from clinical studies, it can be said that there is strong evidence that the predominant action of the phenothiazines is not sedation. Even when sedation occurs with some phenothiazines, it has behavioral consequences quite separate from those of the barbiturates. The phenothiazines have rather a broad "antischizophrenic" effect. It can be argued that this "antischizophrenic" effect sometimes falls short of major improvement, but the nature and direction of the effect is clear.

PHENOTHIAZINE STRUCTURE A N D STRUCTURE-ACTIVITY RELATIONSHIPS

The phenothiazine nucleus consists of three six-membered rings with an S and an N in place of the two interlocking middle carbon atoms, and with substitutions on the 10-nitrogen and the 2-carbon (see Figure 5). Promazine has a side chain attached to the 10-nitrogen consisting of a three carbon straight chain with a terminal nitrogen atom to which two methyl groups are attached. All of the other derivatives follow from promazine, in terms of both name and structure. Two substitutions are usually found at the 2-carbon position: a chlorine atom or a CF_3 group. There are three primary variations of the side chain attached to the nitrogen: the promazine, perazine, and phenazine side chains. Thus, one can usually determine the structure from analyzing the name. Chlorpromazine, for instance, has a chlorine atom attached at the 2-carbon position and a promazine side chain attached at the nitrogen. Triflupromazine has the same promazine side chain, but has a CF_3 group. Similarly, prochlorperazine has a perazine side chain and a chlorine atom as substituents. Trifluoperazine has a CF_3 group, plus the perazine group. The same pattern is repeated with the phenazine group: perphenazine has a chlorine and fluphenazine has a CF_3 group.

Figure 5 illustrates the structures of seven of the most common phenothiazine derivatives. The phenazine and perazine groups also have the side chain with three carbon atoms and the terminal nitrogen atom, but instead of ending in two methyl groups, the ring is completed, ending in another nitrogen atom, and followed either by a methyl group or a two carbon chain with a terminal OH.These variations are quite important to research scientists who try to synthesize better phenothiazines by altering the side chains of the phenothiazine nucleus. From the point of view of structure-activity relationships, some of the correlations prove interesting and may be of relevance to the psychiatric practitioner as well as to the basic research scientist.

Varying the length of the side chain alters the antipsychotic properties of the phenothiazine derivatives. Side chains with two carbon atoms, such as that present in promethazine cause decreased antipsychotic properties and increased antihistaminic properties, while chains of four or more carbon atoms also decrease antipsychotic properties. In terms of side effects, the dimethylamine side chain tends to be more sedating with more agranulocytosis, jaundice, convulsions, skin reactions, and hypotension. The piperazine group attached to the side chain decreases the side effects more

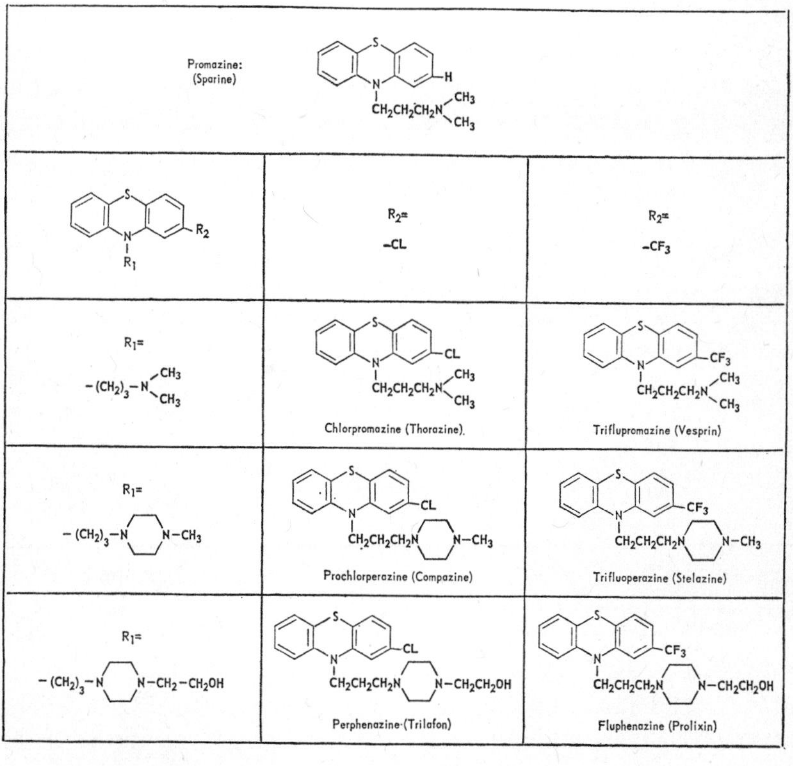

FIG. 5.—Phenothiazine structure.

typical of the dimethylamine group, but increases extrapyramidal effects. Mepazine and thioridazine have a piperidyl group on this side chain.

For comparative purposes, the structures of some of the non-phenothiazine antipsychotic agents are given in Figures 6 and 7.

DOSAGE

Dosage is a particularly important variable in phenothiazine treatment. It is unfortunate that it is often difficult to do dose-response curves in psychiatry, since maximum improvement occurs weeks after the initiation of treatment, and the data would be contaminated by the effects of time alone on the course of the schizophrenic illness.

In the early days of clinical drug evaluations, there were a number of studies done which used small fixed-dose levels. In contrast to this, there have been a number of studies done more recently which used flexible dose levels, and in which some patients received high doses, usually at the discretion of the physician. It would seem that those studies which used low doses of chlorpromazine (below 400 mg./day) and failed to find the drug effective did so because too low a dose was used (see Table 2).

Clinicians have noted that some patients do better on a moderate phenothiazine dosage than on a high dose level. It may be that, in high doses, phenothiazines might behaviorally impair certain adaptive faculties, hence, there could well be an optimal effective dose, with higher or lower doses both being less effective. In addition, of course, higher doses are usually accompanied by greater behavioral toxicity and greater frequency of other side effects.

In looking at the published results of drug studies, one should remember that one is looking at populations and not individual patients. This fact has important consequences. The fact that patients treated with low doses of chlorpromazine (200-400 mg./day) do not do well as a group may simply be indicative of the fact that the majority of the patients require a higher dosage for therapeutic effectiveness. There may be patients in this group who are benefited by these dose levels, but the fact that the majority of the group is not significantly improved may obscure their individual responses when the population is considered as a whole.

In evaluating patient improvement, it is important to think of dosage as well as of drug. In patients not improving on a drug, it is important to consider the dosage, since such a patient could be receiving an inadequate dose even though manifesting sedation. The reverse of this case is that of the patient who does not respond to phenothiazines readily, who is placed on a high dose level and kept there for long periods of time. Perhaps this patient would respond to lower doses of the same phenothiazine, to another phenothiazine, to a phenothiazine used in combination with other drugs, or to a drug of a different type.

Table 13. Dose Levels Used in Controlled Studies of Drug Effects (All Doses are in mg./day).

Note: The figures given below are average doses. The maximum and minimum doses are given in parentheses, except in those cases when a constant fixed dose was used.

Study	Chlorpromazine	Promazine	Triflupromazine	Mepazine	Prochlorperazine	Perphenazine	Thioridazine	Fluphenazine	Trifluoperazine	Acetophenazine
Casey et al. (VA I & II)	400 (fixed)	400 (fixed)								
Casey et al. (VA Study III)	635 (50-1200)		175 (25-300)	190 (25-300)	90 (10-150)	50 (8-96)				
Kurland et al. (Spring Grove)	401 (75-1200)	439 (150-1600)	110 (75-300)	135 (75-450)	45 (15-125)	31 (15-96)				
Adelson & Epstein	1800 (Max 3000)		621 (Max 750)		338 (Max 450)	181 (Max 240)				
Lasky et al. (VA Co-Op.)	746 (200-1600)		208 (50-400)				848 (200-1600)	10 (2.5-20)		
NIMH-PSC Co-Op. Study	655 (50-1600)						700 (50-1600)	6.4 (1.0-16)		
Vestre, Hall, & Schiele			137 (25-250)					9.5 (2.5-25)		
Schiele et al.	894 (200-1000)						958 (200-1000)		35 (10-50)	
Hollister et al. (VA)	300 (100-900)								15 (5-45)	
Hanlon et al. (Spring Grove)	396 (300-1200)		96 (75-200)		51 (37.5-150)	39 (24-144)	193 (150-440)	5.9 (3.75-20)	11.5 (7.5-40)	
NIMH-PSC Study II	690 (Min 200)							7.6 (Min 2)		152 (Min 40)
Average For All Studies:	692	420	224	162	131	75.5	675	7.9	20.5	152

There are wide individualities in drug response.[13,14,115,415,585] Hence, there is no standard dose in phenothiazine treatments, although to a certain extent there may be a useful standard dose range. The clinician aims to achieve the optimal improvement with phenothiazine treatment. Very low doses are not used in psychiatry merely to achieve some lessening of the aggressive and overtly psychotic behavior, but, rather, one tries to use the optimal dose to cause the greatest antipsychotic effect with the least side effects. Practically speaking, patients having mask-like facies may not necessarily be overmedicated, but should have antiparkinsonian drugs added to their medication, since these may be extrapyramidal side effects which could be quickly eliminated.

Chlorpromazine dosage may often be pushed as high as 2-3 Gm. per day, although it is doubtful that in most patients one would get much more improvement after one has tried 1.5 Gm. per day. It is clear that most acute psychotic patients require more than 600 mg./day and some may require up to 1500 mg. Doses such as 25 mg. t.i.d. are clearly inadequate for most acutely psychotic patients.

Table 13 lists the dose levels used in some of the better double-blind studies. From this table, one can get a rough idea of the effective dose ranges of the various phenothiazine derivatives. For comparative purposes, chlorprothixene (Taractan), reserpine, and phenobarbital doses are also included. As one can see, most of these studies used flexible dose schedules with considerable variation, reflecting the absence of any single optimum dose level for all patients.

SIDE EFFECTS

Most of the phenothiazine-produced side effects are relatively mild and do not complicate treatment or cause significant problems. Most of these side effects are subject to control by altering the dose levels or by treatment with antiparkinsonian medication. An excellent series of studies of side effects has been done by Hollister and his collaborators,[336-340,344,345,348] and the reader is referred to these studies for additional detailed information.

In this brief review, tabular data on the incidence of side effects will be presented first, followed by a discussion of selected phenothiazine side effects.* The relative incidence of side effects caused by different phenothiazines will then be considered and the discussion will conclude with a section on rare and unusual side effects.

In evaluating side effects, it is useful to have some idea of the relative frequency of the different side effects. To provide an estimate of the incidence of side effects, Table 14 was prepared, based on a number of large, well controlled studies in which systematic quantitative records of side effects were

---

*References 91, 92, 97, 102, 123, 143, 144, 186, 199, 202, 214, 216, 518, 525.

Table 14. Differential Incidence of Side Effects (Percentages):

	Chlorpromazine	Promazine	Triflupromazine	Mepazine	Prochlorperazine	Perphenazine	Thioridazine	Fluphenazine	Trifluoperazine	Acetophenazine	Phenobarbital
CENTRAL NERVOUS SYSTEM:											
Extrapyramidal Effects	11.9	26.0	6.5	1.9	33.4	21.1	11.8	15.4	23.7	10.1	0.0
Dystonia	2.8	..	1.3	0.97	1.8	2.8	0.88	8.0	3.5	2.9	1.0
Akathisia	12.1	..	10.4	11.6	11.5	27.3	8.9	21.6	4.8	4.3	10.8
Seizures & Convulsions	1.3	16.2	0.56	0.97	1.0	0.67	1.2	0.0	1.3	1.4	0.0
Drowsiness, Somnolence	23.8	6.6	11.8	27.2	10.1	16.3	36.2	19.5	20.8	7.2	31.0
Toxic Confusion	8.6	20.0	..	..	..	..	5.2	..	..	..	..
Depression	13.9	..	4.8	14.6	5.2	6.2	0.0	..	4.3	..	18.2
AUTONOMIC NERVOUS SYSTEM:											
Dizziness, Faintness, & Weakness	6.0	6.6	11.5	17.5	7.2	12.0	23.3	7.0	21.2	15.9	18.6
Dry Mouth & Throat	27.8	6.6	10.0	23.3	20.0	18.8	28.1	8.0	2.3	..	11.6
Disturbed Sexual Function	..	..	..	..	..	..	..	..	3.4	..	..
Urinary Disturbance	3.0	..	0.0	..	..	..	..	1.3	0.64	..	..
Nasal Stuffiness	2.5	..	3.1	..	0.45	0.97	5.5	9.2	1.8	2.9	8.5
Visual Disturbance	14.4	13.3	8.3	23.3	14.0	17.8	16.3	4.3	0.79	1.4	..
Hypotension	3.4	..	..	..	..	0.99	2.4	0.79	..	..	8.5
Constipation	13.9	..	4.5	22.3	1.8	4.6	16.8	9.6	1.1	..	..
Diarrhea	1.1	..	1.2	..	..	..	3.3	1.1	1.1	..	..
GASTROINTESTINAL EFFECTS:											
Anorexia	2.9	..	0.0	..	..	4.2	0.0	..	12.3	..	..
Nausea & Vomiting	5.0	3.3	4.5	4.8	3.6	2.9	29.3	4.3	2.4	..	5.4
BLOOD DISTURBANCES:											
Agranulocytosis	0.32	..	0.0	..	..	0.0	0.0	0.0	3.4	..	..
Eosinophilia	..	..	..	..	..	..	0.0	0.0	..	..	..
Leukocytosis	..	..	..	..	..	..	2.4	0.0	..	..	..
Leucopenia	0.32	..	..	..	..	..	1.5	..	0.0	..	..
ENDOCRINE EFFECTS:											
Menstrual Changes	16.3	..	..	..	..	..	3.3	4.4	..	..	..
Breast Swelling	1.1	..	0.0	..	0.15	0.97	0.60	2.2	..	..	..
Lactation	0.72	..	0.44	..	2.4	0.77	3.1	3.3	1.4	2.9	..
Edema	2.8	..	4.5	..	13.6	5.9	2.3	0.0	1.1	..	..
Weight Gain or Loss	29.8	..	3.2	1.9	1.6	0.83	3.2	2.6	4.2	2.9	3.0
ALLERGIC REACTIONS:	6.6	..	..	..	..	..	..	..	..	..	..
LIVER ABNORMALITIES:											
Abnormal Hepatic Tests	3.7	..	..	..	..	0.0	0.51	0.39	..	..	..
Jaundice	0.64	..	0.0	..	0.0	0.0	0.0	0.0	0.0	..	..

.. indicates that either there was no data available or the available data was considered extremely unreliable.

kept.† However, because of the different terminology and classifications used by different investigators, it should be remembered that the data presented in this table can only be considered as estimates of the probable incidence of such effects in practical clinical settings. Five side effects of clinical importance have been subjected to a separate analysis (Table 15). This table shows the percentages of patients in different studies who developed these effects. As one can see from this table, there is a great variation in the reported incidence of certain side effects. For example, the incidence of chlorpromazine-induced drowsiness has been reported by different authors to be as high as 95 per cent[64] or as low as 2 per cent.[274] Extrapyramidal effects are frequently masked since many patients are customarily given antiparkinsonian medication concurrently with phenothiazine therapy. Falsely low incidence figures for extrapyramidal effects may occur because of this,

Table 15.—Analysis of Side Effects of Clinical Importance

Drowsiness & Somnolence	Dry Mouth & Throat	Hypotension	Constipation	Seizures & Convulsions
Chlorpromazine, Thioridazine, Prochlorperazine, Trifluoperazine, Perphenazine, Triflupromazine, Fluphenazine	Chlorpromazine, Thioridazine, Prochlorperazine, Trifluoperazine, Perphenazine, Triflupromazine, Fluphenazine	Chlorpromazine, Thioridazine, Prochlorperazine, Trifluoperazine, Perphenazine, Triflupromazine, Fluphenazine	Chlorpromazine, Thioridazine, Prochlorperazine, Trifluoperazine, Perphenazine, Triflupromazine, Fluphenazine	Chlorpromazine, Thioridazine, Prochlorperazine, Trifluoperazine, Perphenazine, Triflupromazine, Fluphenazine

Per Cent of Patients Showing Side Effect

80— 60— 40— 20—

Horizontal lines indicate the percentages of patients showing these effects in different studies.

†References 6, 21, 26, 41, 42, 64, 89, 96, 127, 180, 202, 239, 274, 321, 325, 332, 345, 353, 358, 360, 398, 411, 420, 481, 483, 524, 563, 586, 615, 619, 630, 650, 655.

Table 16.—Side Effects Which Were Serious Enough to Cause Patients to be Dropped from Treatment Programs.

Side Effect	Thioridazine	Trifluoperazine	Perphenazine	Chlorpromazine	Prochlorperazine	Triflupromazine	Mepazine	Fluphenazine	Thiopropazate	Promazine	Chlorprothixene	Acetophenazine	Total
CNS Symptoms	1												1
Neurologic Effects		3	8	1	1	4							17
Severe Parkinsonism			1					3					4
Akathisia				1									1
Dystonic Reaction		1											1
Dyskinesia				1									2
Seizures				1							1		2
Depression	1												1
ANS Symptoms								1					1
Weakness								1					1
Dizziness	1												1
Sleepy-Dry Mouth				3		3				2			8
Hypotension			1	2				1		1			5
Vasomotor Episodes					1								1
Visual Disturbances					1	1	1						3
Aches & Pains	2					1							3
Insomnia-Weight Loss		1											1
Sleepless-Tense	1												1
Nausea & Vomiting				1									4
Gastrointestinal Upset		1		1				2					4
Ulcer or GI Bleeding				1									1
Leucopenia											1	1	3
Acute Cholecystitis													
Abnormal Liver Tests				1		2							3
Skin Rashes and Allergies		2		11	1	2		2			1	1	20
Photosensitivity				1									1
Edema			1										1
Drug Intoxication				1									1
Oral Monilid Infection				1									1
Total Number of Side Effects	6	8	11	27	4	13	1	10	0	3	3	3	89
Number of Patients	141	191	174	351	115	205	27	347	39	29	86	161	1866
Per Cent	4.2	4.2	6.3	7.7	3.5	6.3	3.7	2.9	..	10.3	3.5	1.9	4.8

since patients receiving drugs which are associated with frequent extrapyramidal effects might be more likely to be given antiparkinsonian medication.

Since many patients complain of side effects even when they are on placebo, some of the side effects are actually not drug-caused. Because of this, it is desirable to separate out the more serious side effects for further discussion. This has been done in Table 16. All of these side effects were regarded by the authors as at least serious enough to have caused the patient to be dropped from their studies.

Central Nervous System Effects

Although extrapyramidal side effects can usually be controlled without difficulty by the administration of antiparkinsonian medication, on occasion they can prove to be troublesome.[18,19,68,83,105,247,421,527,664] These effects can be classified as follows: 1) parkinson-like effects (mask-like facies, tremor, shuffling gait, rigidity, loss of associated movements, hypersalivation, drooling, etc.); 2) dystonia and dyskinesia (arching of the back, twisting posture of neck and body, oculogyric crises); and 3) akathisia (constant pacing, fidgeting, chewing and lip movements, finger and leg movements). The severe extrapyramidal effects such as dystonias with dysphasia, sometimes require intensive nursing care. Patients with extrapyramidal effects often respond dramatically to the IV or IM administration of antiparkinsonian drugs such as benztropine methanesulfonate (Cogentin), trihexyphenidyl HCl (Artane), or procyclidine (Kemadrin). Since agitation can often be confused with akathisia, administration of an antiparkinsonian drug can permit a differential diagnosis to be made within minutes and should be used in this manner, since the treatments for agitation and akathisia are radically different.*

Cole and Clyde[130] reviewed the association of extrapyramidal side effects with the drugs' clinical effectiveness and found no evidence to support the belief that the more effective drugs were associated with a greater incidence of such side effects. Thioridazine (Mellaril), which tends to produce extrapyramidal effects slightly less often than the other phenothiazines, was found to be as effective as fluphenazine (Prolixin), a drug which produced a much greater number of extrapyramidal symptoms.

Extrapyramidal effects are produced by other classes of antipsychotic

---

*Crane[139-141] and others have described a type of extrapyramidal side effect, the so-called "tardive dyskinesias" which can occur after long-term high-dose phenothiazine therapy. This side effect is clinically distinguishable from acute extrapyramidal effects, and is characterized by bucco-facial-mandibular movements. It is not responsive to antiparkinsonian drugs. It is important to consider the possibility of occurrence of this effect in patients receiving long-term phenothiazines, and more research is needed on this important problem.[23,105,152,184,198,201,307,365,497,539,588,643,664]

agents besides the phenothiazine derivatives. Reserpine-like drugs, the thioxanthene derivatives, and the butyrophenones all produce these effects. Thus, there may be some connection between the mechanism of these drugs' antipsychotic action, and the production of extrapyramidal effects. This topic deserves further investigation. The hypothesis that the most effective therapeutic dose is that dose which produces the earliest signs of extrapyramidal disorder also deserves investigation. Antiparkinsonian medications should be given with caution in the presence of prostate difficulties, glaucoma, or paralytic ileus. Since the antiparkinsonian drugs, as well as the phenothiazines and the tricyclic antidepressants all possess anticholinergic properties,[90] the parasympathetic stimulation resulting from combinations of these drugs can precipitate urinary retention or small bowel stasis, and can aggravate glaucoma in susceptible individuals.

One of the most common central nervous system effects which occurs with phenothiazine treatment, as well as with other antipsychotic drugs, is a drowsiness which usually occurs within the first few days of treatment, sometimes lasting as long as a week or two. Most patients develop a tolerance to this effect after the first few days of therapy.

Unfortunately, because of the drowsiness produced early in phenothiazine therapy, the physician often lowers the dose level below the level of therapeutic effectiveness, and the patient thus shows no clinical improvement because he is receiving an inadequate dose. Had the patient been kept at an adequate dose level, he would have developed a tolerance to this side effect and would have benefited from the treatment. Often, if a patient who has been taking phenothiazines for a long period of time develops undue sedative effects, close questioning will reveal that the patient had temporarily stopped taking his medication or had been taking it irregularly, and, therefore, has lost his tolerance to this effect. It is generally not wise to give amphetamine to counteract the sedative effects of phenothiazines, since this may cause a worsening of the patient's psychotic symptomatology. However, according to Lehmann,[423,427] the patient can safely increase his consumption of coffee. It has been found that chlorpromazine produces more sedation than other phenothiazines such as perphenazine (Trilafon) or trifluoperazine (Stelazine) (see Tables 14 and 15).

Convulsions may occur with phenothiazine treatment, particularly in patients given high doses of chlorpromazine or promazine (Sparine), but these are relatively rare. Reduction of phenothiazine dosage can also be used to control seizures or convulsions, although it is not wise to reduce the dose to a level below that necessary for therapeutic effectiveness.

Autonomic Nervous System Effects

A number of autonomic effects are produced by the phenothiazine derivatives.[445,590,631,641] These include dizziness, faintness or weakness, nasal congestion, dry mouth and throat, nausea and vomiting, diarrhea, constipation, blurred vision, urinary disturbances, hypotension, and other effects. The following discussion will be brief and will only consider some of these effects, since, for the most part, they pose no serious problem to the patient's health and are easily controlled.

One minor, though sometimes uncomfortable, side effect produced by the phenothiazines is dry mouth and throat.[376-378] This can be controlled by frequently rinsing the mouth with water, or by pilocarpine.[568,590] Orthostatic hypotension can occur with phenothiazine therapy and does so most often within the first five days of treatment. In some treatment centers, patients receiving high doses of phenothiazines are kept in bed during this time, and care should be taken, if the patient does show severe postural hypotension that he does not go unaccompanied in situations where he may fall and injure himself. Tolerance to this effect develops rapidly. Lehmann[423] feels that the arbitrary dividing line to define significant hypotension should be when the pulse pressure falls 30 mm. or more, or when the systolic pressure falls below 90, and under these circumstances he feels that the dosage should be reduced. However, many clinicians feel that the blood pressure readings are of relatively little importance in the absence of symptoms attributable to hypotension.

EKG changes have been observed with many phenothiazine derivatives but most often with thioridazine (Mellaril), and consist of increased Q-T intervals and flattened T-waves.[358] These effects have been observed to occur at doses as low as 300 mg./day within the first week of therapy. One case of ventricular tachycardia has been reported in a patient who was taking a minimum of one gram of thioridazine per day.[35,36,169,283,385,575,634,663]

Inhibition of ejaculation may also occur with phenothiazines, again most commonly with thioridazine.[507] Ejaculation may be delayed or completely blocked without interfering with erection. This effect has been used by some physicians in the treatment of ejaculatio praecox.[178,594]

Menstrual irregularities and galactorrhea can occur with the phenothiazines. Constipation can be a problem, particularly in the elderly patient. Weight gain may prove to be troublesome, particularly to female patients, and may necessitate the patient's being placed on a reducing diet. Although blurred vision, due to accommodatio difficulties, often develops in patients being treated with phenothiazines, a tolerance usually develops to this side effect after a time. Other autonomic effects produced by the phenothiazines are usually benign and do not require any special countermeasures.

Skin and Eye Effects

Skin rashes sometimes result from phenothiazine therapy, and these often yield to treatment with antihistamines. Corticosteroids may be used if antihistamines prove ineffective. These reactions may often be eliminated entirely by replacing the offending drug with a phenothiazine having a different side chain. Many phenothiazine derivatives, particularly chlorpromazine, produce photosensitivity and patients can develop painful sunburns with only a few minutes' exposure to sunlight. Patients should be warned of this hazard.[433,454,611]

Skin changes resulting from long-term, high-dose chlorpromazine therapy were first described by Perrot and Bourjala.[534] These changes have been described as consisting of a blue-gray discoloration of the skin over areas exposed to sunlight, such as the face and nose, sometimes the neck and open collar area of the chest, the dorsum of the hand, etc. They often start with a tan or golden brown color and progress to such coloration as slate-gray, metallic blue or purple, or even to a marked purple color. Skin biopsies indicate that an accumulation of golden brown pigment granules is present in the dermis.

The eye changes which accompany long-term, high-dose chlorpromazine therapy consist of bilateral whitish-brown granular deposits, which are concentrated in the anterior subcapsular area, and, in more severe cases, may be found in the anterior lens cortex. Posterior corneal changes and endothelial changes may also be present. The lens changes begin with bilateral, fine dot-like particles found in the anterior capsular and subcapsular portions of the pupillary area, generally visible only by slit-lamp examination. These progress to opaque white or yellow-brown granules, often stellate in shape. These changes are associated with corneal opacities occurring on the posterior surface (endothelium in axial region), but progress to the stroma and epithelial layer. In some patients, the conjunctiva is discolored by a brown pigment. These lens changes are quite different from those of senile cataracts and are in no way related to them. It should be noted that these eye changes almost never affect visual acuity, are usually detectable only by slit-lamp examination, and are almost invariably found only during routine examinations or research surveys. We have heard of no case identified initially because of complaints of visual disturbances.

The results of a number of studies of skin and eye effects after chlorpromazine therapy are summarized in Table 17. As can be seen from this table, many patients with eye changes also showed skin reactions.* These side effects can be seen to be dose-related with a much greater incidence at high doses. It is worth noting that in all of the cases involving chlorpromazine, no cases of pigmentary retinopathy were seen, although this effect has occurred with thioridazine (Mellaril).[131]

Greiner and Berry[292] and other authors have noted an association between

---

*References 33, 34, 38, 43-45, 78, 93, 163, 185, 211, 230-232, 250, 289-294, 327, 328, 426, 455, 462, 463, 469, 505, 540-543, 579, 604, 627, 639, 641, 645, 666, 690, 691.

Table 17.—Studies of Skin and Eye Effects After Chlorpromazine Therapy

Author (No. of Subjects)	Average Daily Dose (mg.)	Average Total Dose (Gm.)	Average Length of Therapy (months)	Eye Effects			Skin Effects
				% Showing Lens Changes	% Showing Corneal Changes	Effect on Visual Acuity	
Barsa et al. (N=658)	400	not given	24 or more	27%	5% (also showed lens changes)	not appreciably impaired	purple skin=5% gray skin=9.7% accelerated suntan=3% accelerated sunburn=15.6%
NIMH (Cole et al.) (N=834)	high group= 2000	high group= 360	6	High Group=22% Low Group=11% Placebo=7.2% Regular=5.2%	High Group=29% Low Group=2.8% Placebo=1.9% Regular=1.9%	not given	High Group=22.8% Other Groups=5% (74% of patients with skin effects also had eye effects)
Galbraith et al. (N=51) High Group and Low Group	not given	High= pts. on 5000 mg. per day or more	48	Low Group=52% High Group=84%	23% showed corneal effect 14% showed epithelial changes	no visual handicap	not given
DeLong et al. (N=131)	300 or more	1250	more than 36	37% showed lens changes	18% showed corneal changes (all also showed lens effects)	no decrease in visual acuity	not given
Siddall (N=50)	large doses	large amts.	up to 8 years	78% showed lens changes (32% showed stellate pattern)	76% showed corneal changes (19 epithelial 33 endothelial)	visual acuity reduced in 28% of pats.)	84% showed pigmentation of lids.
Valentine & Jardine (N=15)	not given	933	84 months	6.6% showed lens pigmentation (one case)	none found	not given	not given

Table 17.—Studies of Skin and Eye Effects After Chlorpromazine Therapy* (continued)

Author (No. of Subjects)	Average Daily Dose (mg.)	Average Total Dose (Gm.)	Average Length of Therapy (months)	Eye Effects			Skin Effects
				% Showing Lens Changes	% Showing Corneal Changes	Effect on Visual Acuity	
Lehmann et al. (22 pts. with skin effects)	600	not given	72 (other drugs also given)	not given	In all cases skin effects were accompanied by corneal opacity.	not given	Pigmentation (slate gray to dark purple) occurred only in areas exposed to the sun.
Tredici, et al. (N=18 pts. with eye & skin effects)	1200 to 5000	533 to 4000	35 to 95 (other drugs also given)	62% of patients had eye changes. (9/11 of these had skin pigmentation also.)	not given	not given	66% of patients had skin pigmentation (9/12 of these also has eye effects).
Feldman & Frierson (one case)	high dose	not given	118	no significant changes were noted.	Corneal opacities were present.	not given	Skin discolored in sun exposed areas, gradually becoming more intense.
Greiner & Berry (N=70 pts. with skin changes)	500 to 1500	not given	36 to 60	All 70 patients had corneal and lens opacities.	All 70 patients had corneal and lens opacities.	not given	All patients showed purple pigmentation on exposed areas.
Funk (N=77) pts. with skin pigmented	885	1517	57	Eye pigmentation was noted in 12 pts. (16%) who had skin pigmentation.	not given	not given	Pigment was localized in areas exposed to sunlight. Visceral pigmentation was observed in 5 pts. with skin pigmentation and 7 without pigmentation who died.

Table 17.—Studies of Skin and Eye Effects After Chlorpromazine Therapy (continued)

Author (No. of Subjects)	Average Daily Dose (mg.)	Average Total Dose (Gm.)	Average Length of Therapy (months	Eye Effects			Skin Effects
				% Showing Lens Changes	% Showing Corneal Changes	Effect on Visual Acuity	
Barnes & Cameron (N=30) Group A	not given	99 to 1363	more than 12	All patients (100%) showed eye changes. (16% had skin changes also)	None	Visual acuity was not affected	16% showed colored skin, another 20% had accelerated suntan.
Cairns et al. (N=4)	642	1916	96	All patients showed lens haze.	All patients show fine diffuse haze of cornea.	No diminished visual acuity	All cases showed varying degrees of melanosis of light exposed areas.
Wetterholm et al. (N=384)	300 to 1600	up to 2000	6 to 108	32.5% showed lens or corneal changes	32.5% showed lens or corneal changes.	3.6% of patient population had slight reductions.	not given
Mathalone Group I (N=275) Groups II, III & IV (N=189)	300 or more less than 300	not given	36 or more most less than 36	36% of high dose group (I) had lens changes; 6.3% of other groups had ocular effects.	16% of high dose group had corneal changes (all also had lens changes).	Little effect on visual acuity.	not given
Margolis & Goble (N=31)	not given	not given	36 to 120	26% of patients developed lens abnormalities after trifluoperazine or chlorpromazine.	3.2% showed corneal effect (1 patient).	No change in visual acuity.	No patients showed cutaneous pigmentation.

the occurrence of skin changes and the incidence of eye effects (see Table 17). In addition, Greiner and Nicolson[289] have described melanin-like pigmentation occurring in the internal organs of twelve autopsied patients who showed skin changes.[289-293] These patients had all received high-dose, long-term chlorpromazine therapy.

It is difficult to arrive at an accurate incidence figure for skin and eye effects, since hospitals differ in their reported incidence figures from less than 1 per cent to more than 30 per cent. Until these discrepancies are resolved, the actual incidence figures for these side effects must remain unknown. One possible reason for these differences in reported incidence figures may be that some hospitals use high doses of chlorpromazine and expose their patients to high amounts of sunlight, while other hospitals may use low doses and a lesser amount of sun exposure.

Treatment for these side effects may be helpful when carried out on the theory that blocking melanin synthesis would be helpful. This can be attempted by giving patients the copper chelating agent d-penicillamine (300 mg. t.i.d. for six days with a mineral supplement on the seventh day); the d-penicillamine depresses tyrosinase activity. A second method is to confine the patients to darkness and thereby increase melotonin production.

Since visual acuity is almost never affected, neither routine eye examinations nor specific therapy for the eye changes, if observed, would usually be indicated, but these may be desirable in patients known to have received very high doses of chlorpromazine or other phenothiazines for several years.

These skin and eye effects do not present any real contraindication for phenothiazine treatment but rather, are indicative of the necessity for monitoring for side effects. Future research in this field could focus on such topics as: 1) controlling dose levels, 2) use of other phenothiazines besides chlorpromazine, 3) the use of dark glasses by chlorpromazine-treated patients, 4) protection of patients from excessive sun exposure, and 5) the development of special window glass which admits a minimum amount of ultraviolet light. Although the great majority of cases of skin and eye effects have been reported to have occurred with chlorpromazine, this may simply be a reflection of the greater usage of this drug, and therefore, it would be important to study the other phenothiazines to see if they also produce these side effects to an appreciable extent.

Relative Incidence of Side Effects Caused by Different Phenothiazines

As one can see from Tables 14 and 15 and as mentioned earlier in the text, there is a large amount of variation in the reported incidence of side effects. This can be due to many causes, such as different methods of observing and reporting side effects, poor experimental procedures, different definitions of medical terminology, or the use of antiparkinsonian medications. Also, the per cent incidence of side effects would vary with the type of patient population studied, the dose levels of the drugs given, and the length of therapy. Therefore, for the purpose of comparing the relative incidence of side effects caused by a number of different drugs, it would not be preferable to utilize pooled data collected from a number of separate studies, all of which would be subject to the limitations mentioned above. In the subsequent section, the phenothiazines are compared for relative incidence of side effects, based on data from several large, double-blind studies, treated as individual evaluations.

The Veterans Administration Cooperative study[99] found that there was relatively little difference among the four so called "active" phenothiazines (chlorpromazine, triflupromazine, perphenazine, and prochlorperazine) as far as the incidence of side effects was concerned. No significant differences were found among the four drugs in the incidence of eosinophilia, leukopenia, abnormal liver function tests, or drowsiness. The only statistically significant differences found out of a great many comparisons made among these four phenothiazines was that perphenazine had slightly more extrapyramidal effects associated with its use than either triflupromazine or chlorpromazine and produced more akathisia than prochlorperazine.

Adelson and Epstein,[6] in another study of side effects, classified certain effects as serious (convulsions, anorexia, toxic confusion, weight loss, reduced resistance to infection), and found that chlorpromazine produced significantly more serious side effects than either perphenazine or triflupromazine, and prochlorperazine showed significantly more serious side effects than triflupromazine. In our review of the double-blind studies, it was our impression that trifluoperazine and fluphenazine showed an approximately equal incidence of serious side effects and that both of these drugs were found to produce more extrapyramidal effects than any of the other drugs.

In the fourth Veterans Administration Cooperative study,[420] fluphenazine and reserpine were found to produce more akathisia than the other drugs studied, with chlorprothixene and thioridazine producing the least amount of this effect. Triflupromazine, reserpine, and chlorpromazine produced the most dizziness, faintness, and weakness, while perphenazine produced the least amount. Fluphenazine was found to produce the least amount of nausea and vomiting.

In a study of drug combinations in acute patients,[482] chlorpromazine alone was compared with chlorpromazine—imipramine and chlorpromazine-chlordiazepoxide combinations. Little difference in side effects was noted. The female patients in the various treatment groups experienced a greater number of side effects than the male patients. There was no significant difference in the numbers of side effects produced by each treatment, nor were any significant differences found on laboratory test results for the different groups.

Rare Side Effects

It is difficult to compute an accurate incidence figure for rare side effects such as agranulocytosis and jaundice, since it is necessary to have both an accurate number of diagnosed cases and an accurate count of the patients receiving medication. We reviewed a large series of studies which give both total number of patients studied and the number who did or did not develop jaundice. The results of this analysis confirm the opinion of Hollister[335] that the incidence of chlorpromazine jaundice is decreasing, possibly because of changes in the populations of patients receiving chlorpromazine or to some factor associated with the manufacture of the drug, such as a greater purity.

Since, in any population of patients, a certain number will have or will develop abnormal laboratory values, even without the administration of any medication, one should be careful when interpreting laboratory results and assigning drug therapy as the cause of any observed abnormalities.

Our estimate of the incidence of jaundice is in rough agreement with that of Chalmers et al.[104] who reviewed ten studies reporting side effects on a total of 2902 patients and found that approximately 1 per cent of these patients developed jaundice. When the phenothiazine-induced jaundice does occur, it generally is seen within the first few weeks of treatment, is of the benign cholangetic type, and is probably due to a hypersensitivity reaction resulting in a blockage of the small bile ducts. Most patients show a spontaneous recovery within two weeks or months if their medication is discontinued. Jaundice due to phenothiazine derivatives is usually preceded by an elevated fever in a flu-like syndrome. For screening purposes, Chalmers does not recommend the cephalin flocculation test or the thymol turbidity test, but would use bilirubin, transaminase, and alkaline phosphatase as screening liver function tests. Bromosulphalein is not recommended as a routine testing procedure because of the one in 100,000 patients who develop fatal reactions to this test. No evidence has been found which indicates that the incidence of chlorpromazine-induced jaundice is in any way related to a past history of liver disease. Cohen[124] states that preexisting liver disease does not predispose patients to phenothiazine jaundice. Sporadic cases of jaundice have been reported with phenothiazines other than chlorpromazine, although the majority of cases occur with this drug.*

Agranulocytosis occurs most commonly within the first six weeks of phenothiazine therapy, usually developing in the course of a few hours, and accompanied by a sore throat, ulcerations, and a generally high fever.†

---

*References 47, 60, 65, 75, 77, 154, 162, 172, 188, 262, 298, 367, 386, 387, 389, 403, 431, 440, 451, 470, 472, 479, 501, 509, 510, 554, 576, 596, 597, 614, 618, 620, 623, 629, 647, 652, 653, 670, 689, 693.

†References 10, 11, 59, 116, 137, 187, 210, 265, 361, 447, 470, 512, 538, 547, 562, 573, 681, 682, 685, 688, 693.

Energetic treatment with antibiotics and other supportive measures when indicated and the assistance of an internist are recommended. When the drug is stopped, the WBC count usually returns to normal within seven to ten days, and if the initial phase is not fatal, recovery is fairly rapid thereafter. Patients who develop this side effect often have normal WBC counts a week prior to its onset, and then develop high fever and ulcerations. When the WBC count is done, it is found to be below 500 with almost no polymorphonuclear leukocytes. The phenomenon of agranulocytosis should not be confused with a gradual decline in WBC counts over a long period of time. This is a quite different phenomenon of different etiology.

A white cell count and a blood smear as baseline measurements before drug therapy is started can be useful. Since agranulocytosis develops abruptly, if one were doing white counts once or twice a week, one would probably miss the onset. In general, in hospitals with alert and adequate nursing staffs, the clinical symptoms such as sore throat and fever will be noticed before any alteration in WBC counts is seen.

Since the decrease in WBC counts is often to levels as low as 500 or 1500, it is often unnecessary to do an actual count. One can make a smear, screen it to see if the count is approximately normal, and then store it for possible future examination. In cases where low counts are observed, one can perform a regular chamber count as well as an appropriate hematologic workup, and in this case one might have a hematologist go over the previously-done smears more thoroughly.

Table 18 shows the number of cases of agranulocytosis reported to the A.M.A. blood dyscrasia registry as of December 1963. One can see from this table that the greatest number of cases were reported with chlorpromazine, although this may simply be a reflection of the fact that 50 per cent of the prescriptions written in the United States for phenothiazines are for chlorpromazine. Promazine (Sparine) and mepazine (Pacatal) also have been reported to cause cases of agranulocytosis with some relative frequency.

Although the fact that more cases of liver damage and blood dyscrasias have been reported with chlorpromazine than with any other phenothiazine

Table 18.—Drug Induced Agranulocytosis: Total Numbers of Cases of Agranulocytosis Reported to A.M.A. Blood Dyscrasia Registry, December 1963

Drug	Total	Only Drug Administered
Chlorpromazine	183	74
Promazine	58	28
Mepazine	33	13
Prochlorperazine	19	2

may simply reflect a greater differential use of that drug, it does seem possible that the incidence of chlorpromazine-induced jaundice is higher than should be expected from chance alone (0.1-0.5 per cent vs. rare cases), and the much higher number of cases of agranulocytosis due to this drug suggests a greater incidence of these dangerous side effects with this drug. However, since both the measure of the base rate of incidence and the actual incidence figures of these side effects are crude and of doubtful accuracy, no firm conclusions can be drawn as to whether one phenothiazine produces these serious effects more frequently than other phenothiazines. Emphasis is placed on the need to obtain more accurate incidence figures, rather than relying on the present figures, which should be regarded only as tentative and subject to revision.

In conclusion, while chlorpromazine, triflupromazine, perphenazine, prochlorperazine, trifluoperazine, fluphenazine and thioridazine are all basically similar in their therapeutic effects, there are differential incidences of certain side effects with these drugs which would argue against their use in the absence of a definite reason for their use. The following drugs have differentially high levels of certain side effects associated with their use: promazine and mepazine (agranulocytosis, jaundice), t h i o r i d a z i n e (retinopathy, inhibition of ejaculation), fluphenazine and trifluoperazine (high extrapyramidal effects), and chlorpromazine (jaundice, excessive sedation, agranulocytosis).* There is a great need for more data on the differential prevalence of side effects caused by the phenothiazine derivatives since, due to their similarity of action, determination of the drug of choice may rest in part on the differential incidence of side effects.

NON-PHENOTHIAZINE ANTIPSYCHOTICS

It would seem from the evidence mentioned in the preceding sections that most of the phenothiazines are roughly equally effective in the treatment of schizophrenic patients. It is necessary to ask whether other classes of drugs also show antipsychotic activity, and if so, are they equal to the phenothiazines? Unfortunately, not enough evidence is available to state whether or not some of the newer non-phenothiazine antipsychotics are equal in therapeutic efficacy to the phenothiazines.

It is clear, however, that several other types of drugs do have antipsychotic properties. The major categories of non-phenothiazine antipsychotics are the reserpine (rauwolfia) preparations, the thioxanthene derivatives, the benzoquinolizine derivatives, and the butyrophenones. There is a fair amount of clinical experience with these drugs and several well-controlled studies have been done.

---

*References 6, 89, 94, 123, 126-130, 214, 336, 337, 411, 412, 420, 483.

Rauwolfia Derivatives

The evidence concerning reserpine has been considered previously because reserpine's discovery coincided with that of chlorpromazine. The structure of reserpine is shown in Figure 7. Many studies show reserpine to be a therapeutically effective drug, although, statistically, it seems to be somewhat less effective than chlorpromazine.*

Benzoquinoline Derivatives

Some of the benzoquinolines share with reserpine the ability to deplete biogenic amines from the brain. One of these, tetrabenazine, has received considerable attention from basic scientists, but has not yet been subjected to extensive clinical investigation. However, several evaluations indicate that it does have antipsychotic activity, and is approximately equal in effectiveness to the other antipsychotic drugs. Since no study has yet been done with a large group of patients using sufficiently sensitive measuring instruments and patient populations, one cannot say at this time how effective this drug is. Lingjaerde[438] reports that some patients who show no response to phenothiazine derivatives will respond to tetrabenazine and vice versa. This drug might be valuable in the treatment of patients who show no improvement with phenothiazine therapy.

Thioxanthene Derivatives

Structurally, the thioxanthene derivatives (chlorprothixene, flupentixol, clopenthixol) closely resemble the phenothiazine derivatives. In these drugs, the nitrogen atom of the phenothiazine nucleus has been replaced by a carbon atom. The structures of the thioxanthene derivatives and their phenothiazine analogues are shown in Figure 6.

The thioxanthene analogue of chlorpromazine, chlorprothixene (Taractan), has been shown to be more effective than placebo,[379] and in a large VA study,[420] it was shown to be slightly more effective than reserpine, although no significant differences were found, possibly due to the relatively low doses of chlorprothixene used in this study (average 225 mg./day). In a wide variety of uncontrolled trials, this drug has been reported to be useful in both schizophrenia and depression.[166,206,216,563]

There is insufficient evidence to compare chlorprothixene with the phenothiazines, except to say that it is apparently effective within roughly the same range as the phenothiazines.

SKF-10812, the thioxanthene analogue of triflupromazine (Vesprin), has

---

*References 2, 3, 39, 95, 138, 147, 148, 179, 191, 200, 213, 229, 238, 243, 256, 276, 278, 326, 343, 401, 402, 405, 414, 429, 430, 435, 448, 506, 530, 531, 545, 587, 600, 605, 606, 673, 692.

been shown in uncontrolled studies by several investigators to be an effective antipsychotic agent.[598] Thiothixene (Navane), the thioxanthene analogue of thioproperazine, has also been found to be effective.[607] One study[254] found

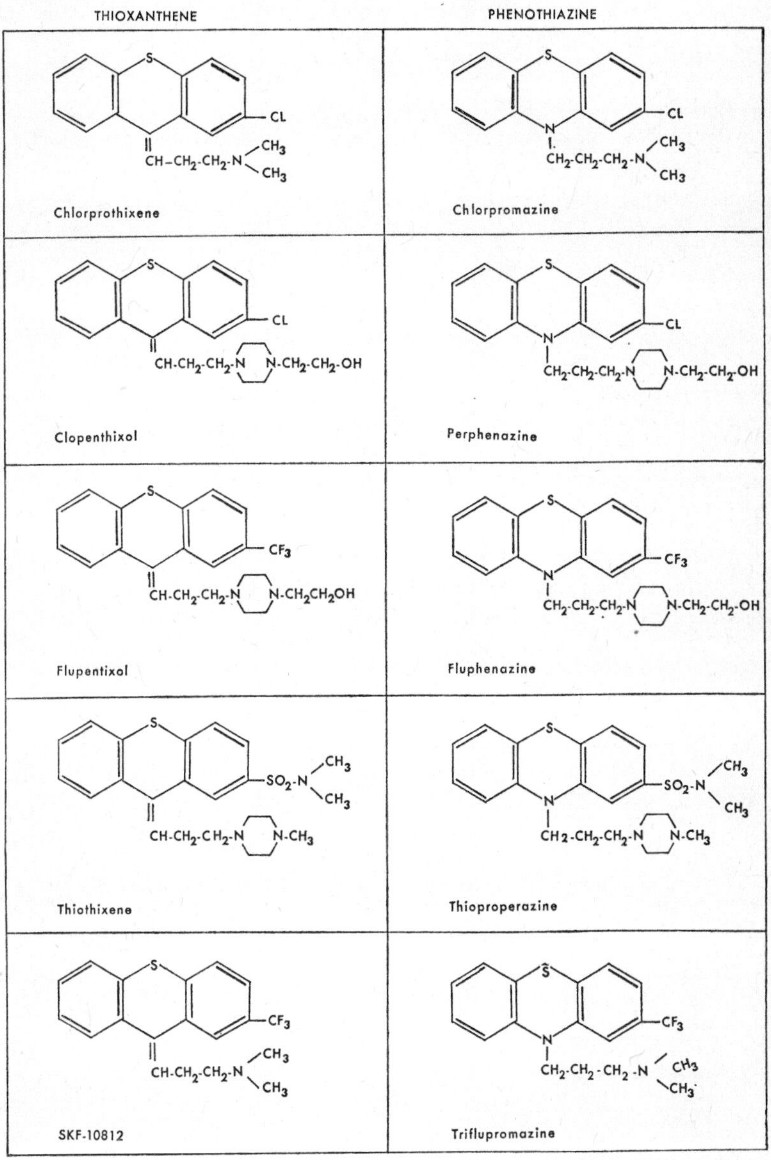

FIG. 6.—The thioxanthene derivatives and their phenothiazine analogues. (E = effective antipsychotic properties, S = slight antipsychotic effects, N = no effect, I = insufficient information available, EQ = equivocal evidence available.)

this drug to be approximately equal to thioridazine (Mellaril) in effectiveness. Clopenthixol (Sordinol), the thioxanthene analogue of perphenazine (Trilafon), has been shown to be an effective antipsychotic agent by reliable investigators.[624] There is suggestive evidence that flupentixol, the thioxanthene analogue of fluphenazine (Prolixin), is also effective.[556] Controlled data does not yet exist on a large enough sample of patients to enable one to make an exact calculation of the relative effective doses of these thioxanthenes. Thiothixene has been found to be effective in doses of 6-60 mg./day, while higher doses (300-600 mg./day) are required of chlorprothixene for therapeutic effectiveness. The therapeutic doses of clopenthixol and SKF-10812 are probably intermediate between the doses of these two drugs. It is difficult to specify the exact incidence of extrapyramidal side effects with these drugs. The structures of the thioxanthene derivatives and their phenothiazine analogues are shown in Figure 6.

Oxypertine

Oxypertine is an indolealkylphenylpiperazine derivative which is chemically related to tryptophan by the presence of an indole nucleus. Calwell et al.[94] studied schizophrenics given oxypertine or trifluoperazine in a double-blind crossover evaluation, and noted a statistically significant superiority of oxypertine on ratings of poverty of speech and on some behavioral scale items rated by nurses. Contrasted to this, Skarbeck and Jacobsen[610] review a study which compared oxypertine to chlorpromazine in a double-blind crossover trial and which found the drugs to be quite similar except that chlorpromazine was superior to oxypertine in decreasing posturing and mannerisms. In a study of chronic schizophrenics, oxypertine found to cause a decrease in isolation and withdrawal and an increased ability to communicate.[181] However, in another such study,[225] oxypertine resulted in a significant increase in laughter and talking to self, and in conversation, as compared with placebo. In this study, increased activity and noisiness was noted in the men's ward. Friedhoff and Hekimian,[246] in an early trial, also found this drug to be more agitating and stimulating than the typical tranquilizer, and this property has been noted by other authors. Flament and his collaborators[225] studied oxypertine in nine schizophrenics and demonstrated a therapeutic improvement in several patients. These authors felt that the drug was less effective than the phenothiazines, but suggested that it might have a mood elevating and activating property. Hollister[351] found the drug to be highly effective in schizophrenics and depressed patients, but less effective in paranoid patients. It may be that this drug could be useful in certain types of patients, while of limited effectiveness in others.

The discrepancies between the various studies of oxypertine may in part reflect the fact that this is a new clinical drug studied in a number of small samples of patients who may differ substantially from one another. It does seem to have interesting properties which may be significantly different from those of the phenothiazines, and it may have an activating or antidepressant effect as well.

Butyrophenone Derivatives

The butyronphenone derivatives (haloperidol, triperidol, benzperidol), are a class of drugs so structurally dissimilar in many ways from the phenothiazines that their antipsychotic properites must be of considerable interest from the structure-activity point of view. The structures of haloperidol (haldol) and triperidol, the butyrophenones which have been most extensively investigated, are shown in Figure 7.

Crane[142] has reviewed the literature and found 98 studies of haloperidol in 5300 patients. Most of the studies report improvement with this drug in 40 to 70 per cent of the cases. Maximum dosage used in these studies varied from 1 to 200 mg./day. However, for psychotic patients, the dosage was generally in the range of 8 to 32 mg./day. This drug is particularly effective against overactivity; and it is said to be effective against withdrawal, agitation, and paranoid ideation. It is also said to be less effective against retardation, depression, and apathy.[24,74,157,215,258,259,306,323,349,350,362,511,546]

Haloperidol is effective in the therapy of the manic patient. It can be administered as an oral tablet, or as a tasteless liquid, and may also be given

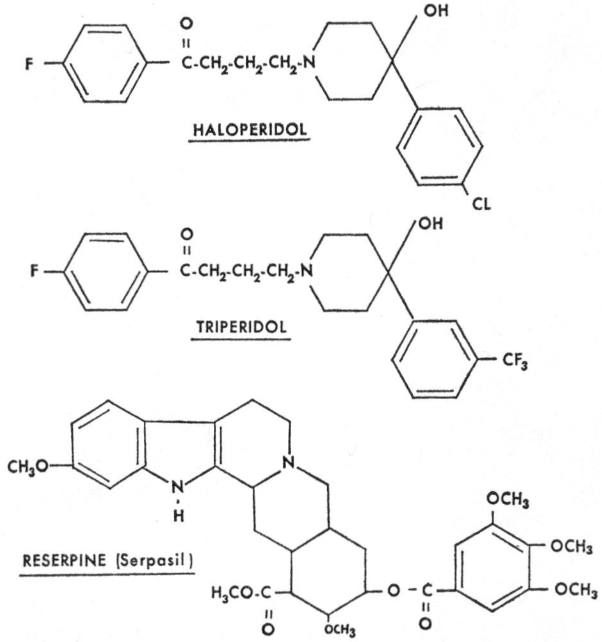

FIG. 7.—Structures of nonphenothiazine antipsychotics.

intramuscularly or intravenously. Crane[142] found the incidence of parkinsonian symptoms to be dose-related. Other side effects were about the same as those caused by the phenothiazine derivatives (e.g., hypotension, tachycardia, fever, vomiting, GU difficulties, stupor, confusion, liver impairment, urticaria). Since these side effects occurred in only a few patients in a minority of the studies reviewed by Crane, one cannot necessarily assume that these effects are drug-caused. It may be that haloperidol has fewer autonomic side effects than the phenothiazines.

Crane[142] notes nine cases of jaundice or hepatitis in his review; however, he also mentions that six of these nine cases occurred in one study of 240 patients. Gerle et al.[259] has reviewed side effects caused by haloperidol and notes that hypotension may occur, but generally does not prove to be a problem. No endocrine disorders have been reported. Haloperidol does not usually seem to alter laboratory tests such as blood or liver function tests. One case of agranulocytosis has been reported in a patient who was also receiving phenobarbital; the etiologic relationship of haloperidol to this case cannot be firmly established. Several cardiovascular incidents have occurred while patients were receiving haloperidol, but, again, there is no definite etiologic relationship between these effects and the drugs.

A syndrome consisting of confusion, perspiration, dehydration, and hyperthermia has occurred in patients treated with haloperidol, although it is not clear that the drug plays a causative role in this condition. Discontinuance of drug therapy, and treatment with fluids is indicated for this condition.

A number of studies indicate that haloperidol is effective in Gilles de la Tourette's disease,[32,103,106] and Huntington's chorea[40,161] as well as in certain cases of impulsive and destructive behavior in mental defectives with or without organic brain pathology.[306,323,362]

Haloperidol has consistently been proven superior to placebo in eight controlled studies.[142] In five comparisons with chlorpromazine, it was found to be approximately equal to that drug in therapeutic effectiveness, and two studies found haloperidol to be slightly more effective. Haloperidol has also been shown to be equal in effectiveness to other phenothiazines such as thioproperazine (Majeptil) or trifluoperazine (Stelazine). Since this drug has not been used in any large double-blind studies, its exact antipsychotic potential cannot be stated, but there is no doubt that this is a potent antipsychotic drug.

Triperidol is another butyrophenone derivative which has proven of value in the treatment of schizophrenia. In several small double-blind studies, this drug has been shown to be either slightly superior or approximately equal to phenothiazines. In three studies, triperidol was either slightly superior to chlorpromazine or equivalent to it, while it was equated with trifluoperazine in two studies. It has also been shown to be approximately equal to haloperidol in antipsychotic action. It would be important to see if phenothiazine failures would respond to the butyrophenone derivatives, since the two classes of drugs are structurally unrelated.

NEW PHENOTHIAZINES

Since chlorpromazine was discovered, there has been a continuing search for more effective phenothiazines with fewer side effects. In this section, some of the newer phenothiazine derivatives will be discussed. The evaluations of these drugs are still in the preliminary stages. In many cases, while uncontrolled studies may show the drug to have considerable clinical effectiveness, controlled studies have yet to be done. In addition, while one may have strong indications that these drugs are effective, in most cases, exact comparisons with the conventional phenothiazines are matters for future research.

Carphenazine (Proketazine) has proven to be an effective antipsychotic agent in many uncontrolled studies. It is more effective than placebo and has been found to be equal in effectiveness to thioridazine (Mellaril),[50] and to trifluoperazine (Stelazine),[618] in the treatment of schizophrenia. The data available on the quantitative incidence and severity of extra-pyramidal effects is not sufficient to enable one to make an exact comparison with other phenothiazines. This drug has been found to be effective within a dose range of 50 to 200 mg./day although doses as high as 450 mg./day have been used without serious effects.[517]

Hanlon et al.[319] studied another phenothiazine, thiopropazate (Dartal), in a well done, controlled, double-blind evaluation of eight phenothiazines. Thiopropazate was found to be more effective than chlorpromazine, prochlorperazine, perphenazine, triflupromazine, and fluphenazine, in less severely ill patients. However, in the high morbidity group (severely ill patients), this drug was very slightly inferior to the other seven studied in the reduction of psychotic symptomatology.

TPS-23 (mesoridazine) is the side chain sulfoxide of thioridazine, and this new drug has demonstrated some interesting pharmacological and clinical properties. Gallant, Bishop, and Sprehe[253] carried out a preliminary investigation of TPS-23, and found that severely ill chronic schizophrenics showed significant improvement on such variables as thinking disorganization, agitated depression, paranoid withdrawal, and belligerence. The authors noted one case of transitory agranulocytosis occurring during the seventh week of treatment. Shelton, Gallant, and Bishop[599] observed an additional 23 patients treated with TPS-23 and again found it to have antipsychotic properties. Sugerman[626] compared TPS-23 and thioridazine in a double-blind study. Although both drugs were shown to have roughly similar antipsychotic effects, TPS-23 caused considerably more side effects at the dose level used, including extrapyramidal effects and hypotension. It was recommended that the dose of TPS-23 should be approximately 2/3 that of thioridazine. Prusmack, Hollister,

Overall, and Shelton[549] studied the effects of TPS-23 on hospitalized male patients with fundamental thinking disturbances. Analysis of covariance of the mean changes in total pathology scores on the Brief Psychiatric Rating Scale (BPRS) showed that TPS-23 was most effective in hostile and withdrawn patients, while a less marked improvement was noted with depressed patients. Side effects were similar to those observed with thioridazine. The authors suggest that mesoridazine (TPS-23) and thioridazine are approximately equal in effectiveness.

Butaperazine (Megalectil) has been found to be superior to placebo in the treatment of chronic schizophrenic patients[61] and to be of approximately equal therapeutic efficacy to the other phenothiazines such as trifluoperazine[61,452] and perphenazine[595] and perhaps slightly inferior to prochlorperazine,[553] although the doses of butaperazine used in this last study were possibly too low for therapeutic effect. This drug consistently produces a high incidence of extrapyramidal effects. The effective dose range for this drug is between 50 and 200 mg. per day.

Thioproperazine methanesulfonate (RP-7843, Majeptil) is a phenothiazine derivative which resembles prochlorperazine, but the chlorine atom of prochlorperazine has been replaced by a dimethylsulfonyl group.[167,535] It has been found to be an effective antipsychotic agent in many uncontrolled studies and is in general use in Europe. It is used both in the conventional continuous dosage method of administration, and in an intermittent dosage regimen which consists of increasing dosage of thioproperazine for five to ten days until extrapyramidal effects occur, followed by an abrupt withdrawal for a similar period of time. This is repeated for several courses of treatment. Thioproperazine is generally, but not always, superior to placebo in therapeutic effect, and it produces a high incidence of extrapyramidal side effects. The therapeutic dose range for this drug is subject to a considerable amount of variation, but usually is to be found between 10 and 150 mg./day.

The Hungarian neuroleptic methophenazine (Frenolon) is the trimethoxybenzoic acid ester of perphenazine, trimethoxybenzoic acid being bound to the hydroxyl group of perphenazine. This drug has some antipsychotic action and causes extrapyramidal effects. In the absence of controlled studies, comparison of its efficacy and side effects is difficult. Those studies which have been done indicate that the therapeutic dose of this drug is between 40 and 60 mg./day, with some patients possibly requiring higher doses.

The cyanated phenothiazine, propericiazine (RP-8908, SKF-20716) has been found to have some tranquilizing effect in small uncontrolled evaluations, but some authors feel that it does not have major neuroleptic or antipsychotic properties. Others feel that it may be of value in the treatment of psychoses. Rajotte et al.[551] have suggested that it is effective in *les troubles charactériels* (social behavior disorders of an aggressive nature without clouding of consciousness). In this double-blind, comparative twelve-week study, both chlorpromazine and propericiazine were found to be of equal value in reducing the aggressive behavior of patients whose behavior was not controlled by their usual neuroleptics or anticonvulsants. Parkinsonian symptoms have been reported to occur with this drug. It has not been found to be more effective than control barbiturates in the treatment of outpatient neuroses. Data at present available are insufficient to make any firm conclusions as to its antipsychotic properties or its usefulness in character disorders.

Levomepromazine (Nozinan), also known as methotrimeprazine (Veractil), has as yet been subjected only to uncontrolled evaluations. Most of the studies which have been done have found it to be effective in the treatment of schizophrenia at doses ranging as high as 1000 mg./day, but usually falling between 200 and 500 mg. per day. This drug has also been found to be somewhat effective in the therapy of depression, and it has been found to be of use in many situations not directly related to mental illness, such as in the treatment of sleep disorders and in pre-operative treatment of surgical patients.

Piperacetazine (Quide) in doses of 50-100 mg./day, has been suggested, but not proven, to have antipsychotic properties. Extrapyramidal side effects are observed. Another new phenothiazine which causes extrapyramidal effects and which has been found to have antipsychotic effects in uncontrolled studies is SKF-7261. Dixyrazine (Esucos) has been subjected to a number of clinical trials in Europe, most of which were uncontrolled. The therapeutic dose of this drug seems to be between 25 and 200 mg./day. It has been found to be of value in the treatment of child psychiatric disorders as well as in adults. Prothipendyl is an azaphenothiazine derivative which has been subjected to a few uncontrolled studies with conflicting results. Some investigators have reported finding this drug useful in psychoses, while others have found it less useful than chlorpromazine.

A promising variant on an older drug, fluphenazine (Permitil, Prolixin) deserves comment. Fluphenazine has been coupled with fatty acid side chains as either fluphenazine enanthate or fluphenazine decanoate.[182] When injected, these compounds form a depot which slowly releases fluphenazine, providing adequate control of psychotic symptoms for one or two weeks. Generally these variations appear as effective as fluphenazine itself, and have the same general side effects.[42,46,413] The dosage required may be lower with a single 10 mg. injection of the enanthate replacing perhaps ten days of the oral medication at 6 mg./day. These preparations offer the potential advantage over oral medication of reduced nursing time and far greater assurance that the drug is ingested and absorbed. They may be particularly useful in aftercare clinics for schizophrenic patients who repeatedly fail to take prescribed oral medication with resulting relapses and rehospitalizations.

In summary, a number of the newer phenothiazine derivatives have been reviewed. Most of these have been subjected only to uncontrolled study; however, some of the newer phenothiazines have been shown to have definite antipsychotic properties and may prove to be of great value in the treatment of psychoses. The identification of newer antipsychotic drugs continues to be a necessary and valuable area of investigation.

SUMMARY

On the basis of evidence cited above, it can be firmly asserted that a number of phenothiazines have been shown in controlled studies to have real clinical value in the treatment of both acute and chronic hospitalized schizophrenic patients. The drugs, as contrasted with placebo therapy, substantially reduce a wide spectrum of symptoms found in the heterogeneous group of psychotic patients usually diagnosed as schizophrenic. Although the effect on certain target symptoms such as hallucinations or agitation may be quite striking, effects on withdrawal, indifference, and poor self-care are equally significant statistically and clinically. Generally secondary symptoms such as hostility, ideas of persecution, and hallucinations improve over a longer time period than do primary symptoms such as indifference and withdrawal. In acute patients, improvement continues to occur for at least 26 weeks, although change is most dramatic in the first few weeks.

These drugs have also been shown to be useful in averting hospitalization in both acute and chronic ambulatory schizophrenics, enabling them to be adequately treated in the community. In general, the drugs appear to be much more effective than psychotherapy or social therapy alone in reducing psychopathology. The combination of both approaches, in two major studies, has suggested little additional benefit over drug therapy alone in terms of symptom reduction. Social therapies may facilitate return to the community in chronic patients.

Newer antipsychotic drugs such as the butyrophenones, which are chemically quite different from the phenothiazines, are being studied. To date, none has shown clear superiority to the phenothiazines in the treatment of schizophrenic patients.

Although many clinicians believe that combining phenothiazines with antidepressant, stimulant, or sedative drugs has definite value, this has yet to be clearly demonstrated in controlled studies.

The side effects and toxic effects of these phenothiazines, although occasionally troublesome, are generally either mild and controllable, or, where more serious, are quite rare.

In short, these phenothiazines are valuable therapeutic agents and certainly deserve credit for making a significant contribution toward the reduction in the numbers of patients resident in our public mental hospitals and toward the development of new and improved patterns of patient care—open hospitals, day care centers, after-care programs, and community mental health centers.

BIBLIOGRAPHY

1. Abrams, J.: Chlorpromazine in the treatment of chronic schizophrenia. Dis. Nerv. Syst. 19: 20-28, 1958.

2. Abse, D. W. et al.: Evaluation of tranquilizing drugs in the management of acute mental disturbance. Amer. J. Psychiat. 116: 973-980, 1960.

3. Abse, D. W. et al.: The use of reserpine in the management of acute mental disturbance on an inpatient service: preliminary report. J. Nerv. Ment. Dis. 124: 239-247, 1956.

4. Ackner, B., and Oldham, A. J.: Insulin treatment of schizophrenia. Lancet, 1: 504-506, 1962.

5. Adelson, D., and Turner, A.: A note on the relation of somatotype to outcome after phenothiazine therapy in chronic schizophrenic patients. J. Nerv. Ment. Dis. 137: 242-245, 1963.

6. Adelson, D., and Epstein, L. J.: A study of phenothiazines with male and female chronically ill schizophrenic patients. J. Nerv. Ment. Dis. 134: 543-554, 1962.

7. Ader, R., and Clink, D. W.: Effects of chlorpromazine on the acquisition and extinction of an avoidance response in the rat. J. Pharm. Exp. Ther. 121: 144-148, 1957.

8. Amdisen, A.: Drug-produced obesity. Experiences with chlorpromazine, perphenazine and clopenthixol. Danish Medical Bull. 11: 182-189, 1964.

9. Andermann, K., and Lindsay, J. S. B.: Chlorpromazine. Med. J. Austral. 2: 80-82, 1955.

10. Anglejan, G. d'., Dausset, J., and Bernard, J.: Blood disorders induced by phenothiazines. Bull. Soc. Med. Hop. Paris. 116: 507-518, 1965.

11. Anglejan, G. d'. et al.: Les accidents sanguins provoqués par les phénothiazines. Nouvelle Revue Française d' Hématologie 4: 291-304, 1964.

12. Appel, K. E., Myers, J. M., and Scheflen, A. E.: Prognosis in psychiatry. Arch. Neurol. and Psychiat. 70: 459-468, 1953.

13. Appleton, W.: Massive doses of chlorpromazine: Effectiveness in controlling psychotic behavior. Arch. Gen. Psychiat. 9: 586-592, 1963.

14. Appleton, W. S.: The snow phenomenon: Tranquilizing the assaultive. Psychiatry 28: 88-93, 1965.

15. Arneson, G. A.: Phenothiazine derivatives and glucose metabolism. J. Neuropsychiat. 5: 181-185, 1964.

16. Ashcroft, G. W. et al.: A Comparison of tetrabenazine and chlorpromazine in chronic schizophrenia. J. Ment. Sci. 107: 287-293, 1961.

17. Atkinson, R. M., and Ditman, K. S.: Tranylcypromine: A review. Clin. Pharm. & Ther. 6: 631-655, 1965.

18. Ayd, F. J. Jr.: A survey of drug-induced extrapyramidal reactions. J.A.M.A. 175: 1054-1060, 1961.

19. Ayd, F. J. Jr.: Chlorpromazine: Ten years' experience. J.A.M.A. 184: 51-54, 1963.

20. Ayd, F. J., Jr.: A critical appraisal of chlordiazepoxide. J. Neuropsychiat. 3: 177-180, 1962.

21. Ayd, F. J., Jr.: Fluphenazine: Its spectrum of therapeutic application and clinical results in psychiatric patients. Cur. Ther. Res. 1(2): 41-48, 1959.

22. Ayd, F. J., Jr.: Perphenazine: Reappraisal after eight years. Dis. Nerv. Syst. 25: 311-317, 1964.

23. Ayd, F. J., Jr.: Persistent dyskinesia: neurologic complication of major tranquilizers. Int. Drug Therapy Newsletter 1: 6, 1966.

24. Azima, H., Durost, H., and Arthurs, D.: The effect of R-1625 (haloperidol) in mental syndromes: A multiblind study. Am. J. Psychiat. 117: 546-547, 1960.

25. Azima, H., and Ogle, W.: Effects of Dargactil in mental syndromes. Canad. Med. Ass. J. 71: 116, 1954.

26. Azima, H. et al.: The effect of thioridazine (Mellaril) on mental syndromes. Comparison with chlorpromazine and promazine. Canad. Med. Ass. J. 81: 549-553, 1959.

27. Bacon, G. A.: Compounding of symptoms with prochlorperazine (Compazine). Wisconsin Med. J. 63: 475-476, 1964.

28. Bacon, H. M.: Eosinophilia associated with chlorpromazine therapy. Am. J. Psychiat. 120: 915-916, 1964.

29. Bacsik, E. J.: Treatment of depression-anxiety in office patients with combination of tranylcypromine and trifluoperazine. Dis. Nerv. Syst. 21: 626-628, 1960.

30. Baker, A. A. et al.: Physical treatment for schizophrenia. J. Ment. Sci. 104: 860-864, 1958.

31. Baker, A. A., and Thorpe, J. G.: Placebo response. Arch. Neurol. Psychiat. 78: 57-60, 1957.

32. Balducci, M., and Frascella, G.: Un Caso di Malattia di Gilles de la Tourette Trattato con haloperidol (R1625). Symp. Int. Sull. Haloperidol e Triperidol. 177-180, 1960.

33. Ban, T. A., and Lehmann, H. E.: Skin pigmentation, a rare side effect of chlorpromazine. Canad. Psychiat. Ass. J. 10: 112-124, 1965.

34. Ban, T. A. et al.: Relationship between photosensitivity and pathological pigmentation of the skin with large doses of chlorpromazine. Union Med. Canada. 94: 305-307, 1965.

35. Ban, T. A., and St. Jean, A.: The effect of phenothiazines on the electrocardiogram. Canad. Med. Ass. J. 91: 537-540, 1964.

36. Ban, T. A., and St. Jean, A.: Electrocardiographic changes induced by phenothiazine drugs. Am. Heart J. 70: 575-576, 1965.

37. Barker, J. C., and Baker, A. A.: Deaths associated with electroplexy. J. Ment. Sci. 105: 339-348, 1959.

38. Barnes, G. J., and Cameron, M. E.: Skin and eye changes associated with chlorpromazine therapy. Med. J. Austral. 1: 478-481, 1966.

39. Barrett, W. W. et al.: Study of the differential behavioral effects of reserpine, chlorpromazine, and a combination of these drugs in chronic schizophrenic patients. Dis. Nerv. Syst. 18: 209-215, 1957.

40. Barrios, S. F.: Corea de Huntington tratada con haloperidol. Medicamenta. 19: 154, 1961.

41. Barron, A. et al.: A "double-blind" study comparing RO-4-0403, trifluoperazine and a placebo in chronically ill mental patients. Am. J. Psychiat. 118: 347-348, 1961.

42. Barsa, J. A., and Saunders, J. C.: A double-blind study of fluphenazine enanthate. Dis. Nerv. Syst. 26: 496-498, 1965.

43. Barsa, J. A., Newton, J. C., and Saunders, J. C.: Lenticular and corneal opacities during phenothiazine therapy. J.A.M.A. 193: 10-12, 1965.

44. Barsa, J. A., and Saunders, J. C.: A peculiar photosensitivity reaction with chlorpromazine. Psychopharmacologia 7: 138-143, 1965.

45. Barsa, J. A., Newton, J. C., and Saunders, J. C.: Lens and cornea changes during phenothiazine therapy: A preliminary report. Am. J. Psychiat. 122: 331-332, 1965.

46. Bartholomew, A. A., and Holt, N. F.: A long-acting phenothiazine (fluphenazine enanthate): A preliminary communication. Med. J. Austral. 1: 12-18, 1966.

47. Bartholomew, L. G., and Cain, J C.: Chlorpromazine hepatitis without clinical jaundice. Proc. Staff Meet. Mayo Clin. 31: 201, 204, 1956.

48. Beecher, H. K.: Measurement of subjective responses; Quantitative effects of drugs. Oxford Univ. Press, New York, 1959.

49. Bellak, L., and Chassan, J. B.: An approach to the evaluation of drug effect during psychotherapy: A double-blind study of a single case. J. Nerv. Ment. Dis. 139: 20-30, 1964.

50. Bellville, T. P., Heistad, G. T., and Schiele, B. C.: A comparative study of thioridazine and carphenazine using sequential analysis. Psychopharmacologia 4: 53-65, 1963.

51. Bennett, I. F.: Clinical studies with phenothiazine derivatives in psychiatry. From the effect of pharmacologic agents on the nervous system. Proc. of the Assoc. for Research in Nervous and Mental Disease. Williams and Wilkins Co., Baltimore. 1959, p. 37.

52. Bennett, J. L., and Kooi, K. A.: Five phenothiazine derivatives. Arch. Gen. Psychiat. 4: 413-418, 1961.

53. Benson, W. M., and Schiele, B. C.: Tranquilizing and antidepressant drugs. Charles C. Thomas, Springfield, 1962.

54. Berg, S. et al.: Comparative evaluation of the safety of chlorpromazine and reserpine used in conjunction with ECT. J. Neuropsychiat. 1: 104-107, 1959.

55. Berger, F. M.: The pharmacological properties of 2-methyl-2-n-propyl-1, 3-propanediol dicarbamate (Miltown), a new interneuronal blocking agent. J. Pharmac. Exp. Ther. 112: 413-423, 1954.

56. Berger, F. M.: The similarities and differences between meprobamate and barbiturates. Clin. Pharmac. Ther. 4: 209-231, 1963.

57. Berlet, H. H. et al.: Endogenous metabolic factor in schizophrenic behavior. Science 144: 311-313, 1964.

58. Berlet, H. H. et al.: Biochemical correlates of behavior in schizophrenic patients. Arch. Gen. Psychiat. 13: 521-531, 1965.

59. Bhaskaran, K. et al.: Fatal bone-marrow aplasia complicating prochlorperazine therapy. Amer. J. Psychiat. 119: 373-374, 1962.

60. Birch, C. A.: Jaundice due to phenobarbital. Lancet. 230: 478-479, 1936.

61. Bishop, M. P. et al.: A controlled evaluation of butaperazine in chronic schizophrenic patients. Dis. Nerv. Syst. 25: 674-683, 1964.

62. Blachly, P. H., and Starr, A.: Treatment of delirium with phenothiazine drugs following open heart surgery. Dis. Nerv. System 27: 107, 1966.

63. Blackburn, H. L., and Allen, J. L.: Behavioral effects of interrupting and resuming tranquilizing medication among schizophrenics. J. Nerv. Ment. Dis. 133: 303-308, 1961.

64. Blair, D., and Brady, D. M.: Recent advances in the treatment of schizophrenia: Group training and the tranquilizers. J. Ment. Sci. 104: 625-664, 1958.

65. Block, S. L.: Jaundice following thioridazine administration. Amer. J. Psychiat. 119: 77, 1962.

66. Blough, D. S.: New test for tranquilizers. Science 127: 586-587, 1958.

67. Blois, M. S., Jr.: On chlorpromazine binding in vivo. J. Invest. Dermat. 45: 475-481, 1965.

68. Bockner, S.: Neurological symptoms with phenothiazines. Brit. Med. J. 2: 876, 1964.

69. Boswell, J. I. et al.: Failure rate of tranquilizers as an index of drug effect. J. New Drugs 3: 96-105, 1963.

70. Bourgeois-Gavardin, M., Nowill, W. K., Margolis, G., and Stephen, C. R.: Chlorpromazine: A laboratory and clinical investigation. Anesthesiology 16: 829-847, 1955.

71. Bovet, D., Longo, V. G., and Silvestrini, B.: Electrophysiological methods of research in the study of tranquilizers—contribution to the pharmacology of reticular formation. Psychotropic Drugs. (Garattini, S., and V. Ghetti, Editors.) Elsevier, Amsterdam, 1957, pp. 193-206.

72. Bradley, P. B.: Tranquilizers. I. Phenothiazine derivatives. In Physiological Pharmacology. Volume I: The nervous system—Part A: Central nervous system. (Root, W. S., and Hofmann, F. G., Editors.) Academic Press, Inc., New York, 1963.

73. Brady, J. V.: Assessment of drug effects on emotional behavior. Science 123: 1033-1034, 1956.

74. Brandrup, E., and Kristjansen, P.: A controlled clinical test of a new psycholeptic drug (haloperidol). J. Ment. Sci. 107: 778-782, 1961.

75. Breuer, R. I.: Chlorpromazine hepatotoxicity manifested by a selective and sustained rise of serum alkaline phosphatase activity. Report of a case. Am. J. Digest. Dis. 10: 727-731, 1965.

76. Brill, H.: Trifluoperazine: Clinical and Pharmacological Aspects. Lea & Febiger, Philadelphia, 1958.

77. Brill, H., and Patton, R. E.: Chlorpromazine jaundice: statistical-clinical study. Arch. Neurol. 3: 459-461, 1960.

78. Brill, H., Scheie, H. G., and DeLong, S. L.: Phenothiazines, skin pigmentation and related eye findings. Am. J. Psychiat. 122: 326-327, 1965.

79. Brill, N. Q. et al.: Relative effectiveness of various components of electroconvulsive therapy. Arch. Neurol. Psychiat. 81: 627-635, 1959.

80. Brimer, A., Schnieden, H., and Simon, A.: The effect of chlorpromazine and chlordiazepoxide on cognitive functioning. Brit. J. Psychiat. 110: 723-725, 1964.

81. Brook, C. P. B., and Stafford-Clark, D.: Psychiatric treatment in general wards. Lancet 1: 1159-1162, 1961.

82. Brooks, G. W.: Withdrawal from neuroleptic drugs. Am. J. Psychiat. 115: 931-932, 1959.

83. Brooks, G. et al.: The effect of potassium on phenothiazine-induced extrapyramidal system dysfunction. Am. J. Psychiat. 119: 1096-1097, 1963.

84. Brown, C. R.: CNS drug actions and interaction in mice. Arch. Internat. Pharmacodyn. 128: 391-414, 1960.

85. Bucci, L.: Phenomenological vs. nosological approach in early therapy of mental illness. Dis. Nerv. Syst. 23: 461-466, 1962.

86. Buffaloe, W. J., and Sandifer, M. G., Jr.: A study of combined therapy with Stelazine and "Parnate" (SKF 385) in chronic anergic schizophrenics. Am. J. Psychiat. 117: 1030-1031, 1961.

87. Bullard, D. M., Jr.: The relative value of tranquilizing drugs and social and psychological therapies in chronic schizophrenia. Paper presented at the annual meeting of the American Psychiatric Association, Philadelphia, May 1, 1959.

88. Burke, C. W.: Collapse after "Parstelin." Brit. Med. J. 2: 998-999, 1963.

89. Caffey, E. M., Jr., and Klett, C. J.: Side effects and laboratory findings during combined drug therapy of chronic schizophrenics. Dis. Nerv. Syst. 22: 370-375, 1961.

90. Caffey, E. M., Rosenblum, M. P., and Klett, C. J.: Side effects and laboratory findings in a study of antidepressant drugs. V.A. Cooperative Studies in Psychiatry, Report No. 31, 1962.

91. Caffey, E. M., Jr. et al.: Discontinuation or reduction of chemotherapy in chronic schizophrenics. J. Chron. Dis. 17: 347-358, 1964.

92. Cahn, C. H.: Complication during reserpine therapy. Am. J. Psychiat. 112: 64, 1955.

93. Cairns, R. J., Capoore, H. S., and Gregory, I. D. R.: Oculocutaneous changes after years on high doses of chlorpromazine. Lancet 1: 239-241, 1965.

94. Calwell, W. P. K. et al.: A comparative study of oxypertine and trifluoperazine in chronic schizophrenia. Brit. J. Psychiat. 110: 520-530, 1964.

95. Campden-Main, B. C., and Wegielski, Z.: The control of deviant behavior in chronically disturbed psychotic patients by the oral administration of reserpine. Ann. N.Y. Acad. Sci. 61: 117-122, 1955.

96. Cares, R. M. et al.: Therapeutic and toxic effects of chlorpromazine among 3,014 hospitalized cases. Am. J. Psychiat. 114: 318-327, 1957.

97. Cares, R. M., and Buckman, C.: A survey of side effects and/or toxicity of newer psychopharmacologic agents. Dis. Nerv. Syst. 22: 97-106, 1961.

98. Casey, J. F. et al.: Drug therapy in schizophrenia. A controlled study of the relative effectiveness of chlorpromazine, promazine, phenobarbital, and placebo. Arch. Gen. Psychiat. 2: 210-220, 1960.

99. Casey, J. F. et al.: Treatment of schizophrenic reactions with phenothiazine derivatives. A comparative study of chlorpromazine, triflupromazine, mepazine, prochlorperazine, perphenazine and phenobarbital. Amer. J. Psychiat. 117: 97-105, 1960.

100. Casey, J. F., and Lindley, C. J.: Recent advances in Veterans Administration Psychiatry. In Masserman, J. H. (Ed.), Current Psychiatric Therapies, Vol. 2, Grune & Stratton, New York, 1962, pp. 233-246.

101. Casey, J. F. et al.: Combined drug therapy of chronic schizophrenics. Controlled evaluation of placebo, dextro-

amphetamine, imipramine, isocarboxazid and trifluoperazine added to maintenance doses of chlorpromazine. Amer. J. Psychiat. 117: 997-1003, 1961.

102. Chaffin, D. S.: Phenothiazine-induced acute psychotic reaction: The "psychotoxicity" of a drug. Am. J. Psychiat. 121: 26-32, 1964.

103. Challas, G., and Brauer, W.: Tourette's Disease: Relief of symptoms with R1625. Am. J. Psychiat. 120: 283-284, 1963.

104. Chalmers, T. C. et al.: Symposium on adverse reactions to psychotropic drugs. Psychopharm. Serv. Cent. Bull. 3(2): 3-23, 1965.

105. Chamberlin, R. T., and Trembly, B.: Dystonia phenothiazorum. J. Maine Med. Ass. 56: 30-31, 1965.

106. Chapel, J. L. et al.: Tourette's Disease: Symptomatic relief with haloperidol. Am. J. Psychiat. 121: 608-610, 1964.

107. Chapman, L. J., and Knowles, R. R.: The effects of phenothiazine on disordered thought in schizophrenia. J. Consult. Psychol. 28: 165-169, 1964.

108. Chaudhury, R. R., Chaudhury, M. R., and Lu, F. C.: The mechanism of the reserpine induced antidiuresis in the rat. Can. J. Biochem. Physiol. 40: 1465-1472, 1962.

109. Chen, G., and Bohner, B.: A study of certain CNS depressants. Arch. Internat. Pharmacodyn. 125: 1-20, 1960.

110. Chen, G., and Bohner, B.: The anti-reserpine effects of certain centrally-acting agents. J. Pharm. Exp. Ther. 131: 179-184, 1961.

111. Childers, R. T. Jr.: Response of schizophrenia to phenothiazines and placebo. J. Clin. Exp. Psychopath. 22: 223-225, 1961.

112. Childers, R. T. Jr.: Procyclidine and benztropine methanesulfonate compared in drug-induced extrapyramidal reactions. Amer. J. Psychiat. 119: 462-463, 1962.

113. Childers, R. T. Jr., and Therrien, R.: A comparison of the effectiveness of trifluoperazine and chlorpromazine in schizophrenia. Amer. J. Psychiat. 118: 552-554, 1961.

114. Childers, R. T. Jr.: Comaprison of four regimens in newly admitted female schizophrenics. Amer. J. Psychiat. 120: 1010-1011, 1964.

115. Childers, R. T.: Controlling the chronically disturbed patient with massive phenothiazine therapy. Am. J. Psychiat. 118: 246-247, 1961.

116. Chirico, A., Carfagno, S., and Lytel, F.: Agranulocytosis after promazine therapy: Report of a case. New Eng. J. Med. 256: 899-900, 1957.

117. Christiansen, A. et al.: Changes in spider webs brought about by mescaline, psilocybin and an increase in body weight. J. Pharm. Exp. Ther. 136: 31-37, 1962.

118. Clare, N. T.: A photosensitized keratitis in young cattle following the use of phenothiazine as an anthelmintic. II. Australian Vet. J. 23: 340, 1947.

119. Clark, L. D.: Further studies of the psychological effects of Frenquel and a critical review of previous reports. J. Nerv. Ment. Dis. 123: 557-560, 1956.

120. Clark, M. L. et al.: Chlorpromazine in chronic schizophrenic women: I. Experimental design and effects at maximum point of treatment. Psychopharmacologia 2: 107-136, 1961.

121. Clark, M. L. et al.: Chlorpromazine in chronic schizophrenic women: Rate of onset and rate of dissipation of drug effects. Psychosom. Med. 25: 212-217, 1963.

122. Clark, J. A., and Mallett, B. L.: A follow-up study of schizophrenia and depression in young adults. Brit. J. Psychiat. 109: 491-499, 1963.

123. Cohen, I. M.: Complications of chlorpromazine therapy. Amer. J. Psychiat. 113: 115-121, 1956.

124. Cohen, S.: Effects and side effects of the phenothiazines. In Lectures in Psychopharmacology. Clark, W. G., and Ditman, K. S., Sepulveda, California, Veterans Administration, 1964, p. 10.

125. Cole, J. O., Goldberg, S. C., and Davis, J. M.: Drugs in the treatment of psychosis: Controlled studies. Psychiatric Drugs, Grune & Stratton, New York, 1966, 153-180.

126. Cole, J. O.: Evaluation of drug treatments in psychiatry. Psychopharm. Serv. Cent. Bull. 2(3): 28-38, 1962.

127. Cole, J. O.: Phenothiazine treatment in acute schizophrenia. Arch. Gen. Psychiat. 10: 246-261, 1964.

128. Cole, J. O., and Gerard, R. W. (Eds.): Psychopharmacology: Problems in Evaluation, National Research Council, National Academy of Sciences, Washington, D.C., 1959.

129. Cole, J. O., Jones, R. T., and Klerman, G. L.: Drug therapy 1960. In Progress in Neurology and Psychiatry, Vol. 16 Spiegel, E. H. (Ed.) Grune & Stratton, New York, 1961, pp. 539-574.

130. Cole, J. O., and Clyde, D.: Extrapyramidal side effects and clinical response to the phenothiazines. Rev. Canad. Biol. 20: 565-574, 1961.

131. Connell, M. M., Poley, B. J., and McFarlane, J. R.: Chorioretinopathy associated with thioridazine therapy. Arch. Ophthal. 71: 816-821, 1964.

132. Cook, L., and Weidley, E.: Behavioral effects of some psychopharmacological agents. Ann. N.Y. Acad. Sci. 66: 740-752, 1957.

133. Cook, L., and Kelleher, R. T.: Effects of drugs on behavior. Ann. Rev. Pharmac. 3: 205-222, 1963.

134. Coons, W. H. et al.: Chlorpromazine, trifluoperazine, and placebo with long-term mental hospital patients. Canad. Psychiat. Assoc. J. 7: 159-163, 1962.

135. Cooper, B.: Grouping therapy and tranquillizers in the chronic ward. Brit. J. Med. Psychol. 34: 157-162, 1961.

136. Corneille, H. J.: Allergic purpura in a patient treated with carphenazine. Am. J. Psychiat. 121: 814-815, 1965.

137. Council on Pharmacy and Chemistry. Blood dyscrasias associated with chlorpromazine therapy. J.A.M.A. 160: 287, 1956.

138. Cowden, R. C. et al.: Reserpine, alone and as an adjunct to psychotherapy in the treatment of schizophrenia. Arch. Neurol. Psychiat. 74: 518-522, 1955.

139. Crane, G. E., and Paulson, G.: Involuntary movements in a sample of chronic mental patients and their relation to the treatment with neuroleptics. Int. J. Neuropsychiat. 3: 286-291, 1967.

140. Crane, G. E.: Tardive dyskinesia in schizophrenia patients treated with psychotrophic drugs. Aggressologic. In press.

141. Crane, G. E.: Tardive dyskinesia in patients treated with major neuroleptics: A review of the literature. Submitted for publication, Amer. J. Psychiat.

142. Crane, G. E.: A review of clinical literature on haloperidol. Internat. J. Neuropsychiat. 3 (Suppl. 1): S110-S123, 1967.

143. Cranswick, E. H. et al.: An abnormal thyroid finding produced by phenothiazine. J.A.M.A. 181: 554-555, 1962.

144. Cranswick, E. H., and Simpson, G. M.: Perphenazine and thyroid function. Am. J. Psychiat. 120: 1133-1134, 1964.

145. Current concepts in therapy. I. Tranquilizers. New Eng. J. Med. 260: 766-769, 1959.

146. Cutler, R. P. et al.: Effects of "tranquilizers" upon pathological activity in psychotic patients. I. Chlorpromazine Arch. Neurol. Psychiat. 77: 616-622, 1957.

147. Cutler, R. P. et al.: Effects of "tranquilizers" upon pathological activity in psychotic patients. II. Reserpine. Arch. Neurol. Psychiat. 78: 61-68, 1957.

148. Davies, D. L., and Shepherd, M.: Reserpine in the treatment of anxious and depressed patients. Lancet 269: 117-120, 1955.

149. Davis, J. M.: Efficacy of tranquilizing and antidepressant drugs. Arch. Gen. Psychiat. 13: 552-572, 1965.

150. Dawkins, M. J. R., Judah, J. D., and Rees, K. R.: The effect of chlorpromazine on the respiratory chain. Biochem. J. 72: 204-209, 1959.

151. Dean, E. F., and Buker, S.: Schizophrenia treated with and without chlorpromazine. Rocky Mt. Med. J. 55(4): 47-50, 1958.

152. Degkwitz, R. et al.: Zum Problem der terminalen extrapyramidalen Hyperkinesen an Hand von 1600 langfristig mit neuroleptica Behandelten. Arzneimittel-Forschung 16: 276-279, 1966.

153. Degkwitz, R. et al.: Über die wirkungen des L-Dopa bein Menschen und deren Beeinflussung durch Reserpin, Chlorpromazin, Iproniazid und Vitamin B₆. Klin. Wschr. 38: 120-123, 1960.

154. DeLamerens, S. et al.: Neonatal bilirubin levels after use of phenothiazine derivatives for obstetrical analgesia. J. Pediat. 65: 925-928, 1964.

155. Delay, J., and Deniker, P.: Trentehuit cas de psychoses traitées par la cure prolongée et continué de 4560 RP. Le Congres des Al. et Neurol. de Langue Fr. In Compte Rendu du Congres. Masson et Cie, Paris, 1952.

156. Delay, J., Deniker, P., and Harl, J. M.: Utilisation en thérapeutique psychiatrique d'une phénothiazine d'action centrale elective (4560 RP). Ann. Med.-Psychol. 110: 112-117, 1952.

157. Delay, J. et al.: Haloperidol et chimiotherapie des psychoses. Presse Med. 68: 1353-1355, 1960.

158. Delay, J., and Deniker, P.: Le traitment des psychoses par une methode neurolytique derivée de l'hibernothérapie. Congres des médecins alienistes et neurologistes de France, 497-502, Luxembourg, Julliet, 1952.

159. Delay, J., and Deniker, P.: 38 cas de psychoses traités par la cure prolongée et continué de 4568 RP. Ann. Med.-Psychol. 110-564, 1952.

160. Delay, J., Deniker, P., and Harl, J. M.: Traitment des états d'excitation et d'agitation par une methode medicamentense derivée de l'hibernothérapie. Ann. Med.-Psychol. 110: 267-273, 1952.

161. DeLerma Penaso, J. L.: Treatment of Huntington's Chorea with haloperidol. Medicamenta 19: 348, 1961.

162. Deller, D. J. et al.: Jaundice during prochlorperazine therapy. Brit. Med J. 2: 93, 1959.

163. DeLong, S. L., Poley, B. J., and McFarlane, J. R., Jr.: Ocular changes associated with long-term chlorpromazine therapy. Arch. Ophth. 73: 611-617, 1965.

164. DeMaar, E. W. J., Martin, W. R., and Unna, K. R.: Chlorpromazine. II: The effects of chlorpromazine upon evoked potentials in the midbrain reticular formation. J. Pharmac. Exp. Ther. 124: 77-85, 1958.

165. Denber, H. C. B., and Bird, E. G.: Chlorpromazine in the treatment of mental illness. III: The problem of depression. Amer. J. Psychiat. 112: 1021, 1956.

166. Denber, H. C. B., Rajotte, P., and Ross, E.: Some observations on the chemotherapy of depression: Results with "Taractan." Comp. Psychiat. 1: 308-312, 1960.

167. Denham, J., and Carrick, D. J. E. L.: Therapeutic value of thioproperazine and the importance of the associated neurological disturbances. J. Ment. Sci. 107: 326-345, 1961.

168. Denzel, H. A.: Fluphenazine in the treatment of psychotic patients. J. Clin. Expt. Psychopathol. 22: 34-37, 1961.

169. Desautels, S., Filteau, C., and St. Jean, A.: Ventricular tachycardia associated with administration of thioridazine hydrochloride (Mellaril): Report of a case with a favourable outcome. Canad. Med. Ass. J. 90: 1030-1031, 1964.

170. Dewar, R., and Ross, H.: The Use and Abuse of Tranquillizing Drugs for Mental Patients. Canad. Med. Ass. J. 87: 1375-1377, 1962.

171. Diamond, L. S., and Marks, J. B.: Discontinuance of tranquilizers among chronic schizophrenia patients receiving maintenance dosage. J. Nerv. Ment. Dis. 131: 247-251, 1960.

172. Dickes, R., Schenker, V., and Deutsch, L.: Serial liver-function and blood studies in patients receiving chlorpromazine. New Eng. J. Med. 256: 1-7, 1957.

173. Dierks, M.: A comparison of two phenothiazines in the treatment of schizophrenics. Amer. J. Psychiat. 119: 775-776, 1963.

174. DiMascio, A. et al.: The psychopharmacology of phenothiazine compounds: A comparative study of the effects of chlorpromazine, promethazine, trifluoperazine and perphenazine in normal males. I: Introduction, aims, and methods. J. Nerv. Ment. Dis. 136: 15-28, 1963.

175. DiMascio, A. et al.: The psychopharmacology of phenothiazine compounds: A comparative study of the effects

of chlorpromazine, promethazine, trifluo-perazine, and perphenazine in normal males. II: Results and discussion. J. Nerv. Ment. Dis. 136: 168-186, 1963.

176. Dinitz, S. et al.: An experimental study in the prevention of hospitalization of schizophrenics. Am. J. Orthopsychiat. 35: 1-9, 1965.

177. Dobkin, A. B., Gilbert, R. G. B., and Lamoureux, L.: Physiological effects of chlorpromazine. Anaesthesia 9: 157-174, 1954.

178. Doepfmer, R.: Der Thioridazin-Aspermatismus (Beitrag zur Behandlung der Ejaculatio praecox). Zeitschrift für Haut und Geschlectskrankheiten 36: 265-273, 1964.

179. Dransfield, G. A., and Browne, M. W.: A clinical trial of deserpidine and reserpine in the treatment of the chronic schizophrenic. J. Ment. Sci. 105: 1112-1118, 1959.

180. Dransfield, G. A.: A clinical trial comparing prochlorperazine ("Stemetil") with chlorpromazine ("Largactil") in the treatment of chronic psychotic patients. J. Ment. Sci. 104: 1183-1189, 1958.

181. Durell, J., and Pollin, W.: A trial on chronic schizophrenic patients of oxy-pertine, a psychotropic drug with an indole ring. Brit. J. Psychiat. 109: 687-691, 1963.

182. Ebert, A. G., and Hess, S. M.: The distribution and metabolism of fluphena-zine enanthate. J. Pharm. Exp. Ther. 148: 412-421, 1965.

183. Edisen, C. B., and Samuels, A. S.: The effects of promazine on psychiatric symptoms. J. Louisiana State Med. Soc. 110: 164-169, 1958.

184. Editorial. Phenothiazine dyskinesia after leucotomy. Lancet 2: 245, 1964.

185. Editorial. Phenothiazine pigmenta-tion and visceral infiltration. Lancet 2: 331, 1965.

186. Editorial. Side effect of pheno-thiazines. Canad. Med. Ass. J. 92: 135-136, 1965.

187. Ekblom, B., and Wälinder, J.: Agranulocytosis and thrombocytopenia after treatment with thioridazine hydro-chloride. Lancet. 1: 1450, 1964.

188. Elliott, H. W., Hilts, S. V., and Gilkey, J. V.: Hepatotoxicity of chlorpro-mazine and its response to cortisone. Stanford Med. Bull. 13: 536-540, 1955.

189. Englehardt, D. M. et al.: Preven-tion of psychiatric hospitalization with the use of psychopharmacological agents. J.A.M.A. 173: 147-149, 1960.

190. Engelhardt, D. M. et al.: Changes of social behavior in chronic schizophrenic outpatients under phenothiazine treat-ment. Comp. Psychiat. 1: 313-316, 1960.

191. Engelhardt, D. M. et al.: The treatment of schizophrenic out-patients with promazine and reserpine. Psychiat. Quart. 33: 102-114, 1959.

192. Engelhardt, D. M. et al.: The in-fluence of previous hospitalization on the clinical course of psychopharmacologically treated schizophrenic outpatients. Comp. Psychiat. 4: 337-342, 1963.

193. Engelhardt, D. M., and Freedman, N.: Maintenance drug therapy: the schizo-phrenic patient in the community. Psycho-pharmacology. Little, Brown & Co., Bos-ton, 1965.

194. Engelhardt, D. M. et al.: Long-term drug-induced symptom modification in schizophrenic outpatients. J. Nerv. Ment. Dis. 137(3), 231-241, 1963.

195. Engelhardt, D. M. et al.: Pheno-thiazines in prevention of psychiatric hos-pitalization. II. Duration of treatment ex-posure. J.A.M.A. 186: 981-983, 1963.

196. Engelhardt, D. M., Rosen, B., Freedman, N., and Margolis, R.: Pheno-thiazines in prevention of psychiatric hos-pitalization. Arch. Gen. Psychiat. 16:98-101, 1967.

197. Evangelakis, M. G.: De-institu-tionalization of patients. Dis. Nerv. Syst. 22: 26-32, 1961.

198. Evans, J. H.: Persistent oral dys-kinesia in treatment with phenothiazine derivatives. Lancet 1: 458-460, 1965.

199. Fatteh, A.: Death from chlorpro-mazine poisoning. J. Forensic Med. 11: 120-124, 1964.

200. Faucett, R. L., Litin, E. M., and Achor, R. W. P.: Neuropharmacologic action of Rauwolfia compounds and its

psychodynamic implications. Arch. Neurol. Psychiat. 77: 513-518, 1957.

201. Faurbye, A. et al.: Neurological symptoms in pharmacotherapy of psychoses. Acta Psychiat. Scand. 40: 10-27, 1964.

202. Feldman, P. E.: Safety and toxicity of trifluoperazine In: Trifluoperazine-Clinical and Pharmacological Aspects. Lea and Febiger, Philadelphia, 1958.

203. Feldman, P. E.: Treatment of anergic schizophrenia with nialamide. Dis. Nerv. Syst. 20 (Suppl. 8): 41-46, 1959.

204. Feldman, P. E.: Clinical evaluation of Pacatal. Am. J. Psychiat. 114: 143-146, 1957.

205. Feldman, P. E.: Psychotherapy and chemotherapy (amitriptyline) of anergic states. Dis. Nerv. Syst. 22: 27-31 (May Suppl.), 1961.

206. Feldman, P. E.: Clinical evaluation of chlorprothixene. Amer. J. Psychiat. 116: 929-930, 1960.

207. Feldman, P. E.: Drug therapy of psychotic patients, Scientific exhibit presented at the Annual Meeting of the American Psychiatric Association, Los Angeles, May 4-7, 1964.

208. Feldman, P. E.: Comparison of effect of 2-methyl-3-piperidinopyrazine on target symptoms of anergic schizophrenia. Ann. N.Y. Acad. Sci. 107: 1117-1130, 1963.

209. Feldman, P. E. et al.: A controlled, blind study of effects of thorazine on psychotic behavior. Bull. Menninger Clin. 20: 25-47, 1956.

210. Feldman, P. E., Bertone, J., and Panthel, H.: Fatal agranulocytosis during treatment with Pacatal. Amer. J. Psychiat. 113: 842-843, 1957.

211. Feldman, P. E., and Frierson, B. D.: Dermatological and ophthalmological changes associated with prolonged chlorpromazine therapy. Am. J. Psychiat. 121: 187-188, 1964.

212. Feldman, R. S., and Liberson, W. T.: The effects of reserpine on behavior fixation in rats. J. Comp. Physiol. Psychol. 53: 483-487, 1960.

213. Ferguson, R. S.: A clinical trial of reserpine in the treatment of anxiety. J. Ment. Sci. 102: 30-42, 1956.

214. Fernandes, B., and Leitão, G.: Incidents and accidents in chloropromazine therapy. J. Clin. Exp. Psychopath. 17: 70-76, 1956.

215. Ferraro, M.: Due casi di latah curati con "Seranase". Symp. Int. Sull' Haloperidol e Triperidol. 357-362, Milano, Nov. 18, 1962.

216. Fier, M., and Goldberg, M. A.: Convulsive seizures in chlorprothixene overdose. Am. J. Psychiat. 121: 76-77, 1964.

217. Fine, R. H.: Clinical experience with trifluoperazine in the severely retarded. J. Neuropsychiat. 5: 370-372, 1964.

218. Fink, M. et al.: Comparative studies of chlorpromazine and imipramine. In Neuro-Psychopharmacology, P. B. Bradley, F. Fluegel, and P. H. Hoch (Ed.) Vol. 3, Elsevier, Amsterdam, 1964, pp. 370-372.

219. Fink, M.: Quantitative electroencephalography and human psychopharmacology. Med. Exp. 5: 364-369, 1961.

220. Fink, M., Klein, D. F., and Kramer, J. C.: Clinical efficacy of chlorpromazine-procyclidine combination, imipramine and placebo in depressive disorders. Psychopharmacologia 7: 27-36, 1965.

221. Fink, M.: Significance of EEG pattern changes in psychopharmacology. Electroenceph. Clin. Neurophysiol. 11: 398, 1959.

222. Fink, M. et al.: Neuropsychologic response patterns of some psychotropic drugs. In Neuropsychopharmacology II, Rothlin, E., (Ed.) Elsevier, Amsterdam, 1961, pp. 381-384.

223. Fink, M. et al.: Comparative study of chlorpromazine and insulin coma in therapy of psychosis. J.A.M.A. 166: 1846-1850, 1958.

224. Flach, F., and Regan, P.: Chemotherapy in Emotional Disorders. McGraw Hill, New York, 1960.

225. Flament, et al.: Clinical investigation of the psychopharmacological effects of Winthrop 18,501-2. Neuropsychopharmacology 3: 275-278, 1963.

226. Fleeson, W. et al.: The ataraxic

effect of two phenothiazine drugs on an out-patient population. Univ. Minn. Med. Bull. 29: 274-286, 1958.

227. Fleming, B. G., and Currie, J. D. C.: Investigation of a new compound, B.W. 203, and of chlorpromazine in the treatment of psychosis. J. Ment. Sci. 104: 749-757, 1958.

228. Fleming, B. G., Spencer, A. M., and Whitelaw, E. M.: A controlled comparative investigation of the effects of promazine, chlorpromazine, and a placebo in chronic psychosis. J. Ment. Sci. 105: 349-358, 1959.

229. Foote, E. S.: Combined chlorpromazine and reserpine in the treatment of chronic psychotics. J. Ment. Sci. 104: 201-205, 1958.

230. Forrest, I. S. et al.: Free radicals as metabolites of drugs derived from phenothiazine. Biochim. Biophys. Acta. 29: 441-442, 1958.

231. Forrest, F. M.: Phenothiazines: Skin and eye complications. Paper presented at 9th Annual Meeting of the Western Pharmacology Society, San Francisco, Jan. 24-25, 1966.

232. Forrest, F. M. et al.: Clinical biochemical and post mortem studies on a patient treated with chlorpromazine. Revue Agressologie. 4: 259, 1963.

233. Forrest, F. M. et al.: Review of rapid urine tests for phenothiazine and related drugs. Am. J. Psychiat. 118: 300-307, 1961.

234. Forrester, M. E.: Disturbed chronic psychotic patients: Pilot trial of "Stelazine." Brit. Med. J. 2: 90-91, 1958.

235. Foulds, G. A.: Clinical research in psychiatry. J. Ment. Sci. 104: 259-265, 1958.

236. Fox, B.: The investigation of the effects of psychiatric treatment. J. Ment. Sci. 107: 493-502, 1961.

237. Frank, J. D.: Persuasion and Healing: A Comparative Study of Psychotherapy. Johns Hopkins Press, Baltimore. 1961.

238. Fraser, H. F., and Isbell, H.: Chlorpromazine and reserpine: (A) Effects of each and of combination of each with morphine; (B) Failure of each in treatment of abstinence from morphine.

Arch. Neurol. Psychiat. 76: 257-262, 1956.

239. Freed, S. C.: Thioridazine, a neuroleptic in general practice. Internat. Rec. Med. 172: 644, 1959.

240. Freedman, N., et al.: Communication of body complaints and paranoid symptom change under conditions of phenothiazine treatment. J. Pers. Soc. Psychol. 1: 310-318, 1965.

241. Freedman, N., et al. Patterns of verbal group participation in the drug treatment of chronic schizophrenic patients. Int. J. Group Psychother. 11(1): 60-73, 1961.

242. Freeman, H., and Cline, H. S.: Effects of chlorpromazine on chronic lobotomized schizophrenic patients. Arch. Neurol. Psychiat. 76: 500-507, 1956.

243. Freeman, H., Arnold, A. L., and Cline, H. S.: Effects of chlorpromazine and reserpine in chronic schizophrenic patients. Dis. Nerv. Syst. 17: 213-219, 1956.

244. Freeman, L. S., and Alson, E.: Prolonged withdrawal of chlorpromazine in chronic patients. Dis. Nerv. Syst. 23: 522-525, 1962.

245. Freeman, W.: Frontal lobotomy 1936-1956. A follow-up study of 3000 patients from one to twenty years. Amer. J. Psychiat. 113: 877-886, 1957.

246. Friedhoff, A. J., and Hekimian, L.: A pilot study of Win 18,501. Dis. Nerv. Syst. 24: 241-242, 1963.

247. Friedman, A. N., and Everett, G. M.: Pharmacological aspects of Parkinsonism. In Advances in Pharmacology (Ed.) by S. Farattini and P. A. Shore, New York, Academic Press, pp. 83-128, 1964.

248. Funk, H. U.: Pigment deposits in the eye, skin, and internal organs following long-term chlorpromazine treatment. Schweizer. Med. Wochenschrift. 95(13), 438-439, 1965.

249. Galbrecht, C. R., and Klett, C. J.: Predicting response to phenothiazine: the right drug for the right patient. J. Nerv. Ment. Dis. 147: 173-183, 1968.

250. Galbraith, J. E. K. et al.: The Mont Park survey for ocular changes in chlorpromazine therapy. Med. J. Austral. 1: 481-483, 1966.

251. Gallant, D. M. et al.: A preliminary

evaluation of SKF 20,716 (propericiazine) in chronic schizophrenic patients. Curr. Ther. Research. 6: 597-598, 1964.

252. Gallant, D. M. et al.: Withdrawal symptoms after abrupt cessation of antipsychotic compounds: clinical confirmation in chronic schizophrenics. Am. J. Psychiat. 121(5): 491-493, 1964.

253. Gallant, D. M. et al.: TPS-23: A new thioridazine derivative. Curr. Therap. Res. 7: 102-104, 1965.

254. Gallant, D. M. et al.: Thiothixene (P-4657B): A controlled evaluation in chronic schizophrenic patients. Curr. Therap. Res. 8: 153-158, 1966.

255. Gantz, R. S., and Birkett, D. P.: Phenothiazine reduction as a cause of rehospitalization. Arch. Gen. Psychiat. 12: 586-588, 1965.

256. Gardner, M. J., et al. Objective measurement of psychiatric changes produced by chlorpromazine and reserpine in chronic schizophrenia. Psychiat. Res. Rep. 1: 77-83, 1955.

257. Garry, J. W., and Hill, E. J.: Trial of a new phenothiazine in chronic schizophrenia. J. Ment. Sci. 108, 521-524, 1962.

258. Garry, J. W., and Leonard, T. J.: Haloperidol: a controlled trial in chronic schizophrenia. J. Ment. Sci. 108: 105-107, 1962.

259. Gerle, B. et al. Clinical experiences with haloperidol. Svensk. Läkartidn. 58: 1415-1422, 1961.

260. Gershon, S., and Yuwiler, A.: Lithium ion: A specific psychopharmacological approach to the treatment of mania. J. Neuropsych. 1: 229-241, 1960.

261. Gey, K. F., and Pletscher, A.: Influence of chlorpromazine and chlorprothixene on the cerebral metabolism of 5-hydroxytryptamine, norepinephrine and dopamine. J. Pharmacol. Exp. Ther. 133: 18-24, 1961.

262. Giambescia, J. M. et al.: Jaundice associated with the administration of chlorpromazine. Gastroenterology 30: 735-751, 1956.

263. Giarman, N. J., and Freedman, D. X.: Biochemical aspects of the actions of psychotomimetic drugs. Pharm. Rev. 17: 1-25, 1965.

264. Gibbs, J. J., Wilkens, B., and Lauterbach, C. G.: A controlled clinical psychiatric study of chlorpromazine. J. Clin. Exp. Psychopath. 18: 269-283, 1957.

265. Giles, C., and Vereker, R.: Fatal agranulocytoses due to chlorpromazine. Brit. Med. J. 2: 289-290, 1958.

266. Gilligan, J.: Review of literature. In Drug and Social Therapy in Chronic Schizophrenia. (Ed.) Milton Greenblatt, Charles C. Thomas, Springfield, 24-76, 1965.

267. Gilmore, T. H., and Shatin, L.: Quantitative comparison of clinical effectiveness of chlorpromazine and promazine. J. Ment. Sci. 105: 508-510, 1959.

268. Gittelman, R. K., Klein, D. F., and Pollack, M.: Effects of psychotropic drugs on long-term adjustment: A review. Psychopharmacologia 5: 317-338, 1964.

269. Glick, B. S., and Margolis, R.: A study of the influence of experimental design on clinical outcome in drug research. Amer. J. Psychiat. 118: 1087-1096, 1962.

270. Glowczewska, E., and Jankowski, K.: A case of pseudoencephalitis toxica during the course of treatment with chlorpromazine. Neurol., Neurochir. i Psychiat. Polska. 14: 709-710, 1964.

271. Goldberg, S. C., Cole, J. O., and Klerman, G. L.: Differential prediction of improvement under three phenothiazines. In Prediction of Response to Pharmacotherapy. (Ed.) Wittenborn, J. R., and May, P. R. A. Charles C. Thomas, Springfield, 1966.

272. Goldberg, S. C. et al.: Changes in schizophrenic psychopathology and ward behaviour as a function of phenothiazine treatment. Brit. J. Psych. 111: 120-133, 1965.

273. Goldberg, S. C., and Schooler, N. R.: Sex and race differences in schizophrenic prognosis. Paper presented at Annual Meeting of the American Psychol. Assoc., Los Angeles, Sept., 1964.

274. Goldman, D.: The results of treatment of psychotic states with newer phenothiazine compounds effective in small doses. Amer. J. Med. Sci. 235: 67-77, 1958.

275. Goldstein, L. et al.: Quantitative

electroencephalographic analysis of naturally occurring (schizophrenic) and drug-induced psychotic states in human males. Clin. Pharmac. Ther. 4: 10-21, 1963.

276. Goller, E. S.: A controlled trial of reserpine in chronic schizophrenia. J. Ment. Sci. 106: 1408-1412, 1960.

277. Good, W. W., Sterling, M., and Holtzman, W. H.: Termination of chlorpromazine with schizophrenic patients. Amer. J. Psychiat. 115: 443-448, 1958.

278. Gordon, H. (Ed.): The New Chemotherapy in Mental Illness. Philosophical Library, New York, 1958.

279. Gorham, D. R., and Overall, J. E.: Dimensions of change in psychiatric symptomatology. Dis. Nerv. Syst. 22: 576-580, 1961.

280. Gorham, D. R., and Betz, B. J.: Characteristics of change of schizophrenic patients during treatment. Am. J. Psychiat. 119: 164-167, 1962.

281. Gorham, D. R. et al.: Effects of a phenothiazine and/or group psychotherapy with schizophrenics. Dis. Nerv. Syst. 25: 77-86, 1964.

282. Gorham, D. R., and Overall, J. E.: Drug-action profiles based on an abbreviated psychiatric rating scale. J. Nerv. Ment. Dis. 131: 528-535, 1960.

283. Graupner, K. I., Murphree, O. D., and Meduna, L. J.: Electrocardiographic changes associated with the use of thioridazine. J. Neuropsychiat. 5: 344-350, 1964.

284. Greenblatt, M. et al.: Placebo effects, social milieu, and the evaluation of psychiatric therapies. J. Chronic Dis. 9: 327-333, 1959.

285. Greenblatt, M. et al.: Mental Patients in Transition. Charles C. Thomas, Springfield, 1961.

286. Greenblatt, M. et al.: The Prevention of Hospitalization; Treatment without admission for psychiatric patients, Grune and Stratton, New York, 1963.

287. Greenblatt, M. et al.: Drug and Social Therapy in Chronic Schizophrenia. Charles C. Thomas, Springfield, 1965.

288. Greengard, P., and Quinn, G. P.: Metabolic effects of tranquilizers and hypophysectomy. Ann. N.Y. Acad. Sci. 96: 179-184, 1962.

289. Greiner, A. C., and Nicolson, G. A.: Pigment deposition in viscera associated with prolonged chlorpromazine therapy. Canad. Med. Ass. J. 91: 627-635, 1964.

290. Greiner, A. C., and Nicolson, G. A.: New side effects in prolonged chlorpromazine therapy. Canad. Psychiatric A. J. 10: 109-111, 1965.

291. Greiner, A. C., and Nicolson, G. A.: Schizophrenia-melanosis: Cause or side-effect? Lancet. 2: 1165-1167, 1965.

292. Greiner, A. C., and Berry, K.: Skin pigmentation and corneal and lens opacities with prolonged chlorpromazine therapy. Canad. Med. Ass. J. 90: 663-664, 1964.

293. Greiner, A. C., Nicolson, G. A., and Baker, R. A.: Therapy of chlorpromazine melanosis: A preliminary report. Canad. M. A. J. 91: 636, 1964.

294. Grinspoon, L. et al.: Psychotherapy and pharmacotherapy in chronic schizophrenia. Am. J. Psychiat. 124: 1645-1652, 1968.

295. Grinspoon, L. et al.: Side effects and double-blind studies. I. A. clinical comparison between thioridazine hydrochloride and a combination of phenobarbital and atropine sulfate. J. Psychiat. Res. 2: 247-256, 1964.

296. Grinspoon, L., and Greenblatt, M.: Pharmacotherapy combined with other treatment methods. Comp. Psychiat. 4: 256-262, 1963.

297. Grinspoon, W., and Ewalt, J. R.: A study of long-term treatment of chronic schizophrenia. Paper presented at IV World Congress of Psychiatry, Madrid, Sept. 5-11, 1966.

298. Grolnick, W.: Psychological consequence of drug jaundice. Psychosomatics 6: 40-43, 1965.

299. Gross, M., Hitchman, I. L., Reeves, W. P., Lawrence, J., and Newell, P. C.: Discontinuation of treatment with ataractic drugs. Am. J. Psychiat. 116: 931-932, 1960.

300. Gross, M. et al.: Objective evaluation of psychotic patients under drug therapy: A symptom and adjustment index. J. Nerv. Ment. Dis. 133: 399-409, 1961.

301. Gross, M. et al.: The repetitive administration of two psychological tests during withdrawal from ataractic drugs. J. Nerv. Ment. Dis. 137(6): 574-576, 1963.

302. Grosz, H. J.: Phenothiazine effect on human antibody synthesis. Brit. J. Psychiat. 110: 603-604, 1964.

303. Guertin, W. H. et al.: Response of chronic schizophrenics to a monoamine oxidase inhibitor. Dis. Nerv. Syst. 21: 330-332, 1960.

304. Grygier, P., and Waters, M. A.: Chlorpromazine used with an intensive occupational therapy program: A controlled study. Arch. Neurol. Psychiat. 79: 697-705, 1958.

305. Gwynne, P. H. et al.: Efficacy of trifluoperazine on withdrawal in chronic schizophrenia. J. Nerv. Ment. Dis. 134: 451-455, 1962.

306. Haberlandt, W. F.: Treatment with haloperidol in child psychiatry. Med. Welt. 4: 210-212, 1963.

307. Haddenbrock, S.: Prolonged hyperkinetic syndromes following long term treatment with high doses of neuroleptic agents. Begleit. Misser. Psychiat. Pharmakother. Georg Thieme, 1964, p. 54.

308. Haden, P.: Gastrointestinal disturbances associated with withdrawal of ataractic drugs. Canad. Med. Ass. J. 91: 974-975, 1964.

309. Hall, R. A., and Dunlap, D. J.: A study of chlorpromazine: Methodology and results with chronic semi-disturbed schizophrenics. J. Nerv. Ment. Dis. 122: 301-314, 1955.

310. Hamilton, M. et al.: A controlled trial on the value of prochlorperazine, trifluoperazine, and intensive group treatment. Brit. J. Psychiat. 109: 510-522, 1963.

311. Hamilton, M. et al.: A controlled trial of thiopropazate dihydrochloride (Dartalan), chlorpromazine and occupational therapy in chronic schizophrenics. J. Ment. Sci. 106: 40-55, 1960.

312. Hankoff, L. D. et al.: Fluphenazine treatment in a receiving hospital setting. Dis. Nerv. Syst. 21: 467-472, 1960.

313. Hankoff, L. D. et al.: The prognostic value of placebo response. Am. J. Psychiat. 115: 549-550, 1958.

314. Hankoff, L. D.: Incidental factors in psychopharmacologic treatment: Findings in the long-term phenothiazine treatment of schizophrenic outpatients. Psychiat. Digest 26(9): 33-39, 1965.

315. Hankoff, L. D. et al.: Placebo response in schizophrenic outpatients. Arch. Gen. Psychiat. 2: 33-42, 1960.

316. Hankoff, L. D. et al.: Denial of illness in relation to differential drug response. J. Nerv. Ment. Dis. 137:29-41, 1963.

317. Hankoff, L. D., Heller, B., and Galvin, J. W.: The setting in psychopharmacological treatment. (The outpatient usage of antidepressants.) Psychosomatics 3: 201-208, 1962.

318. Hanlon, T. E. et al.: Chlorpromazine, triflupromazine, and prochlorperazine in chronic psychosis, Arch. Gen. Psychiat. 1: 223-227, 1959.

319. Hanlon, T. E. et al.: The comparative effectiveness of eight phenothiazines. Psychopharmacologia 7: 89-106, 1965.

320. Hanlon, T. E. et al.: The comparative effectiveness of amitriptyline, perphenazine, and their combination in the treatment of chronic psychotic female patients. J. New Drugs 4: 52-60, 1964.

321. Hanlon, T. E. et al.: A comparative study of chlorpromazine and triflupromazine in the management of the chronic hospitalized psychotic patient. J. Nerv. Ment. Dis. 127: 17-20, 1958.

322. Hanson, H. M.: The effects of amitriptyline, imipramine, chlorpromazine and nialamide on avoidance behavior. Fed. Proc. 20: 396, 1961.

323. Harder, A.: Clinical experiences with haloperidol: A chemically and clinically original neuroleptic drug. Prazis 50: 868-875, 1961.

324. Hare, H. P., Jr.: Comparison of diazepam, chlorpromazine and a placebo in psychiatric practice. J. New Drugs 3: 233-240, 1963.

325. Hargreaves, M. A.: An evaluation of the double-blind trial as a method of assessing promazine ("Sparine") in the treatment of chronic psychotic patients. J. Ment. Sci. 107: 529-537, 1961.

326. Hauck, P., Philips, H., and Armstrong, R.: The effects of reserpine on psychotic patients of varying degrees of illness: A pilot study. J. Clin. Psychol. 13: 188-190, 1957.

327. Hashimoto, K., Wiener, W., and Albert, J.: Electron microscopic studies of chlorpromazine pigmentation. Clin. Res. 13: 530, 1965.

328. Hays, G. B., Lyle, C. B., Jr., and Wheeler, C. E., Jr.: Slate-gray color in patients receiving chlorpromazine. Arch. Dermat. 90: 471-476, 1964.

329. Hegarty, J. G., and Dabbs, A. R.: A controlled study of the effectiveness of triflupromazine hydrochloride. J. Ment. Sci. 105: 811-814, 1959.

330. Heilizer, F.: A critical review of some published experiments with chlorpromazine in schizophrenic, neurotic, and normal humans. J. Chronic Dis. 11: 102-148, 1960.

331. Heilizer, F.: The effects of chlorpromazine upon psychomotor and psychiatric behavior of chronic schizophrenic patients. J. Nerv. Ment. Dis. 128: 358-364, 1959.

332. Herman, E., and Pleasure, H.: Clinical evaluation of thioridazine and chlorpromazine in chronic schizophrenics. Dis. Nerv. Syst. 24: 54-59, 1963.

333. Hindley, J. P. et al.: Comparison of three phenothiazines on chronic psychotic behavior. Dis. Nerv. Syst. 26: 91-98, 1965.

334. Hine, F. R.: Chlorpromazine in schizophrenic withdrawal and in the withdrawn schizophrenic. J. Nerv. Ment. Dis. 127: 220-227, 1958.

335. Hollister, L. E.: Chlorpromazine jaundice. J.A.M.A. 169: 181-182, 1959.

336. Hollister, L. E.: Adverse reactions to phenothiazines. J.A.M.A. 189(4): 311-313, 1964.

337. Hollister, L. E.: Complications from psychotherapeutic drugs. Clin. Pharmacol. Ther. 5: 322-333, 1964.

338. Hollister, L. E.: Current concepts in therapy. Complications from psychotherapeutic drugs. I. New Eng. J. Med. 264: 291-293, 1961.

339. Hollister, L. E.: Current concepts in therapy. Complications from psychotherapeutic drugs. II. New Eng. J. Med. 264: 345-347, 1961.

340. Hollister, L. E.: Current concepts in therapy. Complications from psychotherapeutic drugs. III. New Eng. J. Med. 264: 399-400, 1961.

341. Hollister, L. E. et al.: Perphenazine combined with amitriptyline in newly admitted schizophrenics. Amer. J. Psychiat. 120: 591-592, 1963.

342. Hollister, L. E., et al.: Specific therapeutic actions of acetophenazine, perphenazine, and benzquinamide in newly admitted schizophrenic patients. Clinical Pharmacol. Therap. 8: 249-255, 1967.

343. Hollister, L. E., Traub, E. L., and Beckman, W. G.: Psychiatric use of reserpine and chlorpromazine: Results of double-blind studies. In Kline, N. S. (Ed.) Psychopharmacologia. American Association for the Advancement of Science, publication No. 42, 1956, pp. 65-74.

344. Hollister, L. E.: Complications from the use of tranquilizing drugs. New Eng. J. Med. 257: 170-177, 1957.

345. Hollister, L. E., Caffey, E. M., Jr., and Klett, C. J.: Abnormal symptoms, signs, and laboratory tests during treatment with phenothiazine derivatives. Clin. Pharmacol. Ther. 1: 284-293, 1960.

346. Hollister, L. E., Traub, L., and Prusmack, J. J.: Use of thioridazine for intensive treatment of schizophrenics refractory to other tranquillizing drugs. J. Neuropsychiat. 1: 200-204, 1960.

347. Hollister, L. E., and Kosek, J. C.: Sudden death during treatment with phenothiazine derivatives. J.A.M.A. 192: 1035-1038, 1965.

348. Hollister, L. E. et al.: Trifluoperazine in chronic psychiatric patients. J. Clin. Exp. Psychopathol. 21: 15-24, 1960.

349. Hollister, L. E. et al.: Controlled comparison of haloperidol with thiopropazate in newly admitted schizophrenics. J. Nerv. Ment. Dis. 135: 544-549, 1962.

350. Hollister, L. E., and Motzenbecker, F. P.: Haloperidol in schizophrenic reactions. J. Neuropsychiat. 4: 386-387, 1963.

351. Hollister, L. E. et al.: Oxypertine

in newly admitted schizophrenics. J. New Drugs 3: 26-31, 1963.

352. Hollister, L. E.: Allergy to chlorpromazine manifested by jaundice. Amer. J. Med. 23: 870-879, 1957.

353. Honigfeld, G. et al.: Behavioral Improvement in the older schizophrenic patient. J. Am. Geriatrics Soc. 13: 57, 1965.

354. Hordern, A. et al.: Does chronic schizophrenia respond to a combination of a neuroleptic and an antidepressant? J. Nerv. Ment. Dis. 134: 361-376, 1962.

355. Hordern, A., and Somerville, D. M.: Clinical trials in chronic schizophrenia. Med. J. Austral. 1: 40-43, 1963.

356. Hordern, A. et al.: Thioproperazine in chronic schizophrenia. Brit. J. Psychiat. 110: 531-539, 1964.

357. Howell, R. J. et al.: A comparison of fluphenazine, trifluoperazine and a placebo in the context of an active treatment unit. J. Nerv. Ment. Dis. 132: 522-530, 1961.

358. Hudton, J. R., and Bell, S. C.: The effect of thioridazine and chlorpromazine in the electrocardiogram. J.A.M.A. 134-138, 1966.

359. Hughes, F. W., and Kopmann, E.: Influence of pentobarbital, hydroxyzine, chlorpromazine, reserpine, and meprobamate on choice-discrimination behavior in the rat. Arch. Intern. Pharmacodyn. 126: 158-170, 1960.

360. Hughes, F. W.: A comparative evaluation of two phenothiazines in the management of chronic schizophrenia. Canad. Med. Ass. J. 84: 268-271, 1961.

361. Huguley, C. M., Jr.: Drug-induced blood dyscrasias. II. Agranulocytosis. J.A.M.A. 188: 817-818, 1964.

362. Humbeek, L.: Clinical study of R1625 (Haloperidol), Acta Neurol. Psychiat. Belg. 60: 75-81, 1960.

363. Hunt, H. F.: Physiology and drug action: behavioral implications. Fed. Proc. 19: 629-634, 1960.

364. Hunt, H. F.: Methods for studying the behavioral effects of drugs. Ann. Rev. Pharmacol. 1: 125-144, 1961.

365. Hunter, R., Earl, C. F., and Thornicroft, S.: An apparently irreversible syndrome of abnormal movements following phenothiazine medication. Proc. Roy. Soc. Med. 57: 758-762, 1964.

366. Hurst, L.: Phenothiazine derivatives in the treatment of schizophrenia. J. Ment. Sci. 106: 755-770, 1960.

367. Hurt, P., and Wegman, T.: Prolonged jaundice resulting from Largactil administration, with development into a primary biliary cirrhosis. Acta Hepato-Splenologica 8: 87-95, 1961.

368. Irwin, S.: Considerations for the pre-clinical evaluation of new psychiatric drugs: A case study with phenothiazine-like tranquilizers. Psychopharmacologia 9: 259-287, 1966.

369. Janecek, J. et al.: Differential effects of psychotrophic drugs. Dis. Nerv. Sys. 26: 292-301, 1965.

370. Janecek, J. et al.: The effects of withdrawal of trifluoperazine on patients maintained on the combination of tranylcypromine and trifluoperazine: A double-blind study. Curr. Therap. Res. 5: 608-615, 1963.

371. Janssen, P. A. J. et al.: Effects of various drugs on isolation-induced fighting behavior of male mice. J. Pharm. Exp. Ther. 129: 471-475, 1960.

372. Johnson, F. P. et al.: Sudden death of a catatonic patient receiving phenothiazine. Amer. J. Psychiat. 121: 504-507, 1964.

373. Johnson, R. F., and Lee, H.: Rehabilitation of chronic schizophrenics. Arch. Gen. Psychiat. 12: 237-240, 1965.

374. Judah, L. N., Josephs, Z. M., and Murphree, O. D.: Results of simultaneous abrupt withdrawal of ataraxics in 500 chronic psychotic patients. Amer. J. Psychiat. 118: 156-158, 1961.

375. Kalinowsky, L. B., and Hoch, P. H.: Somatic Treatments in Psychiatry. Grune & Stratton, New York, 1961.

376. Kane, F. J., Jr., and Anderson, W. B.: A fourth occurrence of oral moniliasis during tranquilizer therapy. Amer. J. Psychiat. 120: 1199-1200, 1964.

377. Kane, F. J., Jr.: Severe oral moniliasis complicating chlorpromazine therapy. Amer. J. Psychiat. 119: 890, 1963.

378. Kane, F. J., Jr.: Oral moniliasis following the use of Thorazine. Amer. J. Psychiat. 120: 187-188, 1963.

379. Karn, W. N., Mead, B. T., and Fishman, J. J.: Double-blind study of chlorprothixene (Taractan), a panpsychotropic agent. J. New Drugs 1: 72-79, 1961.

380. Katz, M. M. et al.: Nonspecificity of diagnosis of paranoid schizophrenia. Arch. Gen. Psychiat. 11: 197-202, 1964.

381. Katz, M. M., and Cole, J. O.: Research on drugs and community care. Arch. Gen. Psychiat. 7: 345-359, 1962.

382. Katz, M. M., and Cole, J. O.: A phenomenological approach to the classification of schizophrenic disorders. Dis. Nerv. Syst. 24: 147-154, 1963.

383. Keller, D. L., and Umbreit, W. W.: Chemically altered "permanent" behavior patterns in fish and their cure by reserpine. Science 124: 407, 1956.

384. Kelly, D. H. W., and Sargant, W.: Present treatment of schizophrenia: A controlled follow-up study. Brit. Med. J. 1: 147-150, 1965.

385. Kelly, H. G. et al.: Thioridazine hydrochloride (Mellaril): Its effect on the electrocardiogram and a report of two fatalities with electrocardiographic abnormalities. Canad. Med. Ass. J. 89: 546-554, 1963.

386. Kelsey, J. R., Jr. et al.: Chlorpromazine jaundice. Gastroenterology 29: 865-876, 1955.

387. Kemp, J. A.: Jaundice occurring during administration of promazine. Gastroenterology 32: 937-938, 1957.

388. Kennedy, A.: The treatment of mental disorders by induced convulsions. J. Neurol. Psychiat. 3: 49-82, 1940.

389. Keup, W.: Effect of phenothiazine derivatives on liver function. Dis. Nerv. Syst. 20 (Suppl. 5): 161-175, 1959.

390. Killam, K. F., and Killam, E. K.: Drug action on pathways involving the reticular formation. In Jasper, H. H., Proctor, L. D., Knighton, R. S., Noshay, W. C., and Costello, R. T. (Eds.) Reticular Formation of the Brain. Little, Brown and Co., Boston, 1958.

391. Killam, E. K.: Drug action on the brain-stem reticular formation. Pharmac. Rev. 14: 175-223, 1962.

392. Killam, E. K., and Killam, K. F.: Neurophysiological approaches to an understanding of the action of tranquilizing drugs. In Internat. Psychiat. Clinics 2 (4): 845-859, 1965.

393. King, P. D.: Controlled study of group psychotherapy in schizophrenics receiving chlorpromazine. Psychiat. Dig. 24(1): 21-23; 26, 1963.

394. King, P. D., and Weinberger, W.: Comparison of prochlorperazine and chlorpromazine in hospitalized chronic schizophrenics. Amer. J. Psychiat. 115: 1026-1027, 1959.

395. Kino, F. F., and Thorpe, F. T.: Electrical convulsion therapy in 500 selected psychotics. J. Ment. Sci. 92: 138-145, 1946.

396. Kinross-Wright, J., and Charalampous, K. D.: A controlled study of a very long-acting phenothiazine preparation. Int. J. Neuropsychiat. 1: 66-70, 1965.

397. Kinross-Wright, J., and Ragland, J. B.: Clinical pharmacology of some newer phenothiazine analogues. In Proceedings Third World Congress of Psychiatry. Univ. Toronto Press and McGill Univ. Press, Montreal, 2: 901-905, 1961.

398. Kinross-Wright, V.: Complications of chlorpromazine treatment. Dis. Nerv. Syst. 16: 114-119, 1955.

398a. Klein, D. F.: Importance of psychiatric diagnosis in prediction of clinical drug effects. Arch. Gen. Psychiat. 16: 118-126, 1967.

399. Klett, C. J., and Moseley, E. C.: The right drug for the right patient. J. Consult. Psychol. 29: 546-551, 1965.

400. Klett, C. J., and Caffey, E. M., Jr.: Weight changes during treatment with phenothiazine derivatives. J. Neuropsychiat. 2: 102-108, 1960.

401. Kline, N. S.: Uses of reserpine, the newer phenothiazines, and iproniazid. In Effects of Pharmacologic Agents on the Nervous System. Braceland, F. J. (Ed.) Williams and Wilkins, Baltimore, 1959, pp. 218-244.

402. Kline, N. S.: Use of Rauwolfia serpentina Benth. In neuropsychiatric con-

ditions. Ann. N.Y. Acad. Sci. 59: 107-132, 1954.

403. Kohn, N. N., and Myerson, R. M.: Xanthomatous biliary cirrhosis following chlorpromazine. Amer. J. Med. 31(4): 665-670, 1961.

404. Kornetsky, C. et al.: Comparison of psychological effects of chlorpromazine and secobarbital in schizophrenia. Fed. Proc. 17: 385, 1958.

405. Kovitz, B., Carter, J. T., and Addison, W. P.: A comparison of chlorpromazine and reserpine in chronic psychosis. Arch. Neurol. Psychiat. 74: 467-471, 1955.

406. Kruse, W.: Trifluoperazine and tranylcypromine in chronic refractory schizophrenics. Amer. J. Psychiat. 117: 548-549, 1960.

407. Kurahara, K.: Treatment of neurosis with combination use of pulverized prochlorperazine and promethazine. Seishin Igaku (Clinical Psychiatry, Tokyo). 3: 523-530, 1961.

408. Kurland, A. A.: Comparison of chlorpromazine and reserpine in treatment of schizophrenia. Arch. Neurol. Psychiat. 75: 510-513, 1956.

409. Kurland, A. A. et al.: Fluphenazine in the treatment of the hospitalized psychiatric patient. Dis. Nerv. Syst. 22: 339-343, 1961.

410. Kurland, A. A. et al.: Chlorpromazine-chlordiazepoxide and chlorpromazine-imipramine treatment: Side effects and clinical laboratory findings. J. New Drugs 6: 80-95, 1966.

411. Kurland, A. A. et al.: The comparative effectiveness of six phenothiazine compounds, phenobarbital and inert placebo in the treatment of acutely ill patients: Global measures of severity of illness. J. Nerv. Ment. Dis. 133: 1-18, 1961.

412. Kurland, A. A. et al.: The comparative effectiveness of six phenothiazine compounds, phenobarbital and inert place bo in the treatment of acutely ill patients: Personality dimensions. J. Nerv. Ment. Dis. 134: 48-61, 1962.

413. Kurland, A. A. et al.: Fluphenazine (Prolixin) enanthate — a phenothiazine preparation of prolonged activity. Curr. Ther. Res. 6: 137-147, 1964.

414. Kurland, A. A. et al.: The response of chronically hospitalized, lobotomized patients to treatment with chlorpromazine and reserpine. Psychiat. Quart. 33: 647-663, 1959.

415. Kushner. T.: Experience with greater than recommended doses of fluphenazine and triflupromazine. Amer. J. Psychiat. 122: 1061-1062, 1966.

416. Langsley, D. G. et al.: A comparison of chlorpromazine and EST in treatment of acute schizophrenic and manic reactions. Arch. Neurol. Psychiat. 81: 384-391, 1959.

417. Lapolla, A., and Nash, L. R.: A comparative clinical study of prochlorperazine, SKF 4579, perphenazine, triflupromazine, chlorpromazine, and reserpine. Clin. Med. 72: 495-503, 1965.

418. Lapolla, A.: A study of Stelazine. Western Med. 6: 240-245, 1965.

419. Laskowska, D., and Brzezinska, I.: Acute paralytic ileus as a complication in the treatment with phenothiazine derivatives. Polski Tygodnik. Lek. 20: 1242-1243, 1965.

420. Lasky, J. J. et al.: Drug treatment of schizophrenic patients. A comparative evaluation of chlorpromazine, chlorprothixene, fluphenazine, reserpine, thioridazine, and triflupromazine. Dis. Nerv. Syst. 23: 698-706, 1962.

421. Leeman, C. P.: Acute dystonic reactions to small doses of prochlorperazine. Report of three cases misdiagnosed as hysteria. J.A.M.A. 193: 839-840, 1965.

422. Lehmann, H. E.: Combined pharmaco-fever treatment with imipramine (tofranil) and typhoid vaccine in the management of depressive conditions. Amer. J. Psychiat. 117: 356-358, 1960.

423. Lehmann, H. E.: Use and abuse of phenothiazines. Appl. Ther. 5: 1057-1069, 1963.

424. Lehmann, H. E., and Hanrahan, G. E.: Chlorpromazine. New inhibiting agent for psychomotor excitement and manic states. Arch. Neurol. Psychiat. 71: 227-237, 1954.

425. Lehmann, H. E.: Therapeutic results with chlorpromazine (largactil) in

psychiatric conditions. Canad. Med. Ass. J. 72: 91, 1955.

426. Lehmann, H. E. et al.: Pigmentation of the skin: A rare side effect subsequent to prolonged administration of high doses of chlorpromazine. Ann. Derm. Syphiligraphie 92: 287-289, 1965.

427. Lehmann, H. E.: Drug treatment of schizophrenia. In Psychopharmacology. Little Brown and Co., Boston, 1965.

428. Leitch, A., and Seager, C. P.: A clinical trial of our tranquilizing drugs. J. Ment. Sci. 106: 1093-1098, 1960.

429. Lemere, F.: Combined chlorpromazine-reserpine therapy of psychiatric disorders. Arch. Neurol. Psychiat. 74: 1-2, 1955.

430. Lemieux, G., Davignon, A., and Genest, J.: Depressive states during rauwolfia therapy for arterial hypertension. A report of 30 cases. Canad. Med. Ass. J. 74: 522-526, 1956.

431. Lemire, R. E., and Mitchell, R. A.: Regurgitation type jaundice associated with chlorpromazine ("Thorazine," SKF-2601-A) administration. J. Lab. Clin. Med. 44: 825, 1954.

432. Lentz, R. E.: Evaluation of antidepressant-tranquilizer combination in office practice. Clin. Med. 8: 75-79, 1961.

433. Levan, N. E.: Chlorpromazine dermatitis: Occupational and immunochemical aspects. New Eng. J. Med. 256, 651-652, 1957.

434. Levin, M. L.: A comparison of the effects of phenobarbital, promethazine, chlorpromazine, and placebo upon mental hospital patients. J. Consult. Psychol. 23, 167-170, 1959.

435. Lewis, J. J.: Rauwolfia derivatives. In The nervous system—Part A: Central nervous system. Root, W. S., and Hofmann, F. G. (Eds.) Academic Press, Inc., New York, 1963.

436. Lewis, R. A.: Inhibition of sickling by phenothiazines: Review of published studies and report on recent progress. J. Trop. Med. 67: 307-310, 1964.

437. Lingl, F. A.: Combined drug therapy compared with electric shock in psychotic depressions. Amer. J. Psychiat. 120: 808-810, 1964.

438. Lingjaerde, O.: Tetrabenazine (Nitonan) in the treatment of psychoses. Acta Psychiat. Scand. 39 (Suppl. 170): 1-109, 1963.

439. Lloyd, D. N., and Newbrough, J. R.: Sensory changes with phenothiazine medication in schizophrenic patients. J. Nerv. and Ment. Dis. 139: 169-175, 1964.

440. Loftus, L. R. et al.: Jaundice caused by chlorpromazine (Thorazine). J.A.M.A. 157: 1286-1288, 1955.

441. Loftus, T. A. et al.: Negative results with chlorpromazine and benactyzine in a group of chronic psychotics. Psychiat. Quart. 35: 121-133, 1961.

442. Lomas, J.: Uses of chlorpromazine in mental hospital patients. Brit. Med. J. 1: 879-882, 1955.

443. Lomas, J., Boardman, R. H., and Markowe, M.: Complications of chlorpromazine therapy in 800 mental-hospital patients. Lancet 268: 1144-1147, 1955.

444. Lorr, M. et al.: Meprobamate and chlorpromazine in psychotherapy. Arch. Gen. Psychiat. 4: 381-389, 1961.

445. Lund-Johansen, P.: Shock after administration of phenothiazine in patients with pheochromocytoma. Acta Med. Scand. 172: 525-529, 1962.

446. Lutz, E. G., and Rotov, M. D.: Angioneurotic edema of the tongue with phenothiazine administration. Report of two cases. Dis. Nerv. Syst. 25: 419-422, 1964.

447. Lutz, E. G.: Monocytosis, blood dyscrasia, and chlorpromazine toxicity. Internat. J. Neuropsychiat. 1: 76-79, 1965.

448. McDonald, R. E. et al.: Behavioral changes of chronic schizophrenics in response to reserpine. Arch. Neurol. Psychiat. 75: 575-578, 1956.

449. Macdonald, R., and Watts, T.: Trifluoperazine dihydrochloride (Stelazine) in paranoid schizophrenia. Brit. Med. J. 1: 549-550, 1959.

450. Maffii, G.: The secondary conditioned response of rats and the effects of some psychopharmacological agents. J. Pharm. Pharmacol. 11: 129-139, 1959.

451. Maier, C., and Rüttner, J. R.: Toxische Hepatose unter dem Bild des intrahepatischen Verschlussicterus nach

Chlorpromazin (Largactil), Atophan, Salvarsen, und Methyltestesteron-Medikation. Schweiz. Med. Wchnschr. 85: 445-448, 1955.

452. Mandel, W., and Evans, P.: Comparison of butyrylperazine and trifluoperazine in chronic schizophrenic subjects. Amer. J. Psychiat. 119: 70-71, 1962.

453. Margolis, L. H. et al.: Effects of decamethonium bromide (C 10) and d-tubocurarine on electroconvulsions. Arch. Neurol. Psychiat. 65: 174-180, 1951.

454. Margolis, L. H., Butler, R. N., and Fischer, A.: Nonrecurring chlorpromazine dermatitis. Arch. Dermat. 72: 72-73, 1955.

455. Margolis, L. H., and Goble, J. L.: Lenticular opacities with prolonged phenothiazine therapy. A potential hazard with all phenothiazine derivatives. J.A.M.A. 193: 7-9, 1965.

456. Marjerrison, G. et al.: Withdrawal of long-term phenothiazines from chronically hospitalized psychiatric patients. Canad. Psych. Ass. J. 9: 290-298, 1964.

457. Marks, J.: Predrug behavior as a predictor of response to phenothiazines among schizophrenics. J. Nerv. Ment. Dis. 137: 597-601, 1963.

458. Marksfield, W. C.: Tranylcypromine and trifluoperazine in the treatment of psychosomatic complaints. Psychosomatics. 2: 130-131, 1961.

459. Marley, E.: Response to drugs and psychiatry. J. Ment. Sci. 105: 19-43, 1959.

460. Mason-Browne, N. L.: Perphenazine—A drug modifying consciousness. Amer. J. Psychiat. 114: 173-174, 1957.

461. Mason-Browne, N. L., and Borthwick, J. W.: Effect of perphenazine (Trilafon) on modification of crude consciousness. Dis. Nerv. Syst. 18: 300-306, 1957.

462. Massey, L. W. C.: Skin pigmentation, corneal and lens opacities with prolonged chlorpromazine treatment. Canad. Med. Ass. J. 92: 186, 1965.

463. Mathalone, M. B. R.: Oculocutaneous effects of chlorpromazine. Lancet 2: 240, 1965.

464. Matheu, H., and Fogel, E. J.: Clinical effects of fluphenazine dihydrochloride in chronic schizophrenia. J. Neuropsychiat. 3: 105-111, 1961.

465. May P. R., and Tuma, A. H.: Choice of criteria for the assessment of treatment outcome. J. Psychiat. Res. 2: 199-209, 1964.

466. May, P. R., and Tuma, A. H.: Treatment of schizophrenia. An experimental study of five treatment methods. Brit. J. Psychiat. 111: 503-510, 1965.

467. May, P. R., and Tuma, A. H.: The effect of psychotherapy and stelazine on length of hospital stay, release rate and supplemental treatment of schizophrenic patients. J. Nerv. Ment. Dis. 139(4): 362-369, 1964.

468. McCabe, W. S., and Habovick, J. A.: Thorazine as an epileptogenic agent. Amer. J. Psychiat. 120: 595-597, 1963.

469. McClanahan, W. S. et al.: Ocular manifestations of chronic phenothiazine derivative administration. Arch. Ophth. 75, 319-325, 1966.

470. McFarland, R. B.: Fatal drug reaction associated with prochlorperazine (Compazine). Report of a case characterized by jaundice, thrombocytopenia, and agranulocytosis. Amer. J. Clin. Path. 40: 284-290, 1963.

471. Mead, B. T. et al.: The treatment of drug-resistive chronic schizophrenics. J. Nerv. Ment. Dis. 127: 351-358, 1958.

472. Mechanic, R. C., and Meyers, L.: Chlorpromazine-type cholangitis. Report of a case occurring after administration of prochlorperazine. New Eng. J. Med. 259: 778-780, 1958.

473. Mefferd, R. B., Jr. et al.: Influence of chlorpromazine on certain biochemical variables of chronic male schizophrenics. J. Nerv. Ment. Dis. 127: 167-179, 1958.

474. McLaughlin, R. F., Jr., Tyler, W. S., and Edwards, D. W.: Chlorpromazine-induced emphysema. Results of an initial study in the horse. Amer. Rev. Resp. Dis. 92: 597-608, 1965.

475. McNeill, D. L. M., and Madgwick, J. R. A.: A comparison of results in schizophrenics treated with (1) insulin, (2) trifluoperazine (Stelazine) J. Ment. Sci. 107: 297-299, 1961.

476. Mena, A. et al.: A comparison of tranylcypromine alone with tranylcypro-

mine plus trifluoperazine in the treatment of chronic outpatients: A double-blind controlled study. J. Neuropsychiat. 5:542-550, 1964.

477. Mendels, J. Transient toxicity with carphenazine hydrochloride. Amer. J. Psychiat. 121: 185-187, 1964.

478. Mendels, J.: Thioproperazine-induced lactation. Amer. J. Psychiat. 121: 190-191, 1964.

479. Menguy, R. B. et al.: Biliary stasis produced by chlorpromazine: An experimental study. Proc. Staff Meet. Mayo Clin. 30: 601-606, 1955.

480. Merlis, S. et al.: A double-blind comparison of diazepam, chlordiazepoxide and chlorpromazine in psychotic patients. J. Neuropsychiat. 3(Suppl. 1): S133-S138.

481. Michaux, M. et al. Phenothiazines in the treatment of newly admitted state hospital patients: Global comparison of eight compounds in terms of an outcome index. Curr. Ther. Res. 6(5): 331-339, 1964.

482. Michaux, M. H., Kurland, A. H., and Agallianos, D. D.: Chlorpromazine-chlordiazepoxide and chlorpromazine-imipramine treatment of newly hospitalized, acutely ill psychiatric patients. Curr. Ther. Res. 8: 117-152 (Suppl.), 1966.

483. Michaux, W. W.: Side effects, resistance and dosage deviations in psychiatric outpatients treated with tranquilizers. J. Nerv. Ment. Dis. 133: 203-212, 1961.

484. Miller, D. H. et al.: A comparison between unidirectional current nonconvulsive electrical stimulation given with Reiter's Machine, standard alternating current electroshock (Cerletti Method), and pentothal in chronic schizophrenia. Amer. J. Psychiat. 109: 617-620, 1953.

485. Miller, N. E.: Effects of drugs on motivation: The value of using a variety of measures. Ann. N. Y. Acad. Sci. 65: 318-333, 1956.

486. Miller, N. E.: Some recent studies of conflict behavior and drugs: Problems which illustrate some general problems in psychopharmacology. Amer. Psychol. 16: 12-24, 1961.

487. Miller, N. E., and Barry, H.: Mo-tivational effects of drugs. Psychopharmacologia 1: 169-199, 1960.

488. Miller, N. E., Murphy, J. V., and Mirsky, I. A.: The effect of chlorpromazine on fear-motivated behavior in rats. J. Pharmacol. Exp. Ther. 120: 379-387, 1957.

489. Milne, H. B., and Fowler, D. B.: A clinical trial of Largactil (chlorpromazine), Stemetil (prochlorperazine), and Veractil (methotrimeprazine). J. Ment. Sci. 106, 1105-1110, 1960.

490. Mirsky, A., and Kornetsky, L.: On the dissimilar effects of drugs on the digit symbol substitution and continuous performance tests. Psychopharmacologia 5: 161-177, 1964 .

491. Mitchell, P. H.: Chlorpromazine in the treatment of the chronic disturbed schizophrenic patient. J. Ment. Sci. 102: 151-154, 1956.

492. Monroe, R. R., Kramer, M. D., and Goulding, R.: EEG activation of patients receiving phenothiazines and chlordiazepoxide. J. Nerv. Ment. Dis. 141: 100-107, 1965.

493. Monroe, R. R., and Wise, S. P., III: Combined phenothiazine, chlordiazepoxide and primidone therapy for uncontrolled psychotic patients. Amer. J. Psychiat. 122: 694-698, 1965.

494. Moran, N. C., and Butler, W. M., Jr.: The pharmacological properties of chlorpromazine sulfoxide, a major metabolite of chlorpromazine. A comparison with chlorpromazine. J. Pharmacol. Exp. Therap. 118: 328-337, 1956.

495. Morganstern, F. V., Funk, I. C., and Holt, W. L.: Comparative short-term evaluation of triflupromazine hydrochloride, chlorpromazine hydrochloride, and placebo in acutely disturbed patients. New York State J. Med. 60: 254-258, 1960.

496. Moriarty, J. D.: Drug therapy versus psychotherapy. J. Neuropsychiat. 2: 82-85, 1960.

497. Morphew, J. A., and Barber, J. E.: Persistent oral dyskinesia in treatment with phenothiazine derivatives. Lancet 1: 650-651, 1965.

498. Morpurgo, C.: Influence of phenothiazine derivatives on the accumulation of

brain amines induced by monoamine oxidase inhibitors. Biochem. Pharmacol. 11: 967-972, 1962.

499. Morrow, L. E.: The effects of long-term use of fluphenazine in non-hospitalized patients with mental and emotional disorders. Psychosomatics 6: 371-374, 1965.

500. Mosley, E. C.: Selection of the most appropriate tranquilizer on the basis of pretreatment symptoms. Mimeograph, VA Hospital, Perry Point, Md., 1964.

501. Movitt, E. R. et al.: Jaundice associated with the administration of chlorpromazine, SKF-2601-A (thorazine). Report of three cases, with biopsies of the liver. Gastroenterology 28: 901-913, 1955.

502. NIMH Psychopharmacology Service Center Collaborative Study Group (Cole, J. et al.). Phenothiazine treatment in acute schizophrenia: Effectiveness. Arch. Gen. Psychiat. 10: 246-261, 1964.

503. NIMH Collaborative Study Group 2. Clinical effects of three phenothiazines in "acute" schizophrenia. Prepublication Rep. No. 6. Biol's. Psychopharm. Res. Branch, NIMH, Bethesda, Md. April, 1966.

504 NIMH - PSC Collaborative Study Group. Social and psychiatric history in the assignment of schizophrenic patients to drug treatment. Prepublications Report No. 5. Psychopharmacology Service Center, NIMH, Bethesda, Md. 1965.

505. Nahum, L. H.: The purple-people syndrome. Conn. Med. 29: 332, 1965.

506. Naidoo, D.: The effects of reserpine (Serpasil) on the chronic disturbed schizophrenic: A comparative study of Rauwolfia alkaloids and electroconvulsive therapy. J. Nerv. Ment. Dis. 123, 1-13, 1956.

507. Nistri, M., and De Luca, P. L.: Apropos of the inhibition of ejaculation during thioridazine treatment. Its possible therapeutic value. Encephalé. 53: 203-206, 1964.

508. Noble, R. C., and Castner, C. W.: Evaluation of prochloperazine and a prochloperazine-chlorpromazine combination in disturbed patients. Dis. Nerv. Syst. 19: 531-533, 1958.

509. Nørredam, K.: Chlorpromazine jaundice of long duration. Acta Med. Scan. 174(2): 163-170, 1963.

510. Norris, T.: Promethazine and drug-induced jaundice. Lancet 1: 394, 1963.

511. Okasha, A., and Tewfik, G. I.: Haloperidol: A controlled clinical trial in chronic disturbed psychotic patients. Brit. J. Psychiat. 110: 56-60, 1964.

512. Oldershausen, H. F., and Von Wiik, K.: On the clinical aspects of agranulocytosis. Med. Klin. 59: 50-55, 1964.

513. Olds, J., Killam, K. F., and Bach-y-Rita, P.: Self-stimulation of the brain used as a screening method for tranquilizing drugs. Science 124: 265-266, 1956.

514. Olds, J., Killam, K. F., and Eiduson, S.: Effects of tranquilizers on self-stimulation of the brain. In Psychotropic Drugs (Ed. Garattini, S., and Ghetti, V.) Author: Princeton or Amsterdam, Elsevier Publishing Co. Princeton, N. J. 235-243, 1957.

515. Olds, J.: Neuropsychopharmacology. Author: Princeton or Amsterdam, Elsevier Publishing Co., Princeton, N. J. 20-32, 1957.

516. Olson, G. W., and Peterson, D. B.: Sudden removal of tranquilizing drugs from chronic psychiatric patients. J. Nerv. Ment. Dis. 131: 252-255, 1960.

517. Oltman, J. E., and Friedman, S.: Treatment of schizophrenia with Proketazine. Amer. J. Psychiat. 117: 745-746, 1961.

518. Oltman, J. E., and Friedman, S.: Further report on protein-bound iodine in patients receiving perphenazine. Amer. J. Psychiat. 121: 176-178, 1964.

519. Overall, J. E., and Hollister, L. E.: Computer procedures for psychiatric classification. J.A.M.A. 187: 583-588, 1964.

520. Overall, J. E., and Gorham, D. R.: Factor-space D^2 analysis applied to the study of changes in schizophrenic symptomatology during chemotherapy. J. Clin. Exp. Psychopath. 21: 187-195, 1960.

521. Overall, J. E. et al.: Comparison of acetophenazine with perphenazine in schizophrenics: Demonstration of differential effects based on computer-derived

diagnostic models. Clin. Pharmacol. Ther. 4: 200-208, 1963.

522. Overall, J. E. et al.: Imipramine and thioidazine in depressed and schizophrenic patients. Are there specific antidepressant drugs? J.A.M.A. 189: 605-608, 1964.

523. Owen, J. E., Jr. et al.: Effects of secobarbital on escape and avoidance behavior: A replication using a cross-over design. Psychol. Rep. 4: 527-528, 1958.

524. Oybir, F.: Trifluoperazine in chronic, withdrawn schizophrenics. Dis. Nerv. Syst. 23: 348-350, 1962.

525. Pant, S. S. et al.: Tolerance of chlorpromazine by severely anemic and cirrhotic patients. Indian J. Med. Sci. 15: 345-350, 1961.

526. Pate, W. H.: Chlorpromazine therapy following transorbital lobotomy. J. Nerv. Ment. Dis. 125: 44-50, 1957.

527. Paulson, G.: Phenothiazine toxicity, extrapyramidal seizures, and oculogyric crises. J. Ment. Sci. 105: 798-802, 1959.

528. Pautler, E. L., and Clark, G.: The effect of chlorpromazine on the discrimination between intermittent photic stimulation and a steady light in normal and brain-damaged cats. J. Comp. Physiol. Psychol. 54: 493-497, 1961.

529. Pearl, D.: Phenothiazine effects in chronic schizophrenia. J. Clin. Psychology 18: 86-89, 1962.

530. Pearl, D. et al.: Differential effects of chlorpromazine and reserpine. Psychiat. Quart. 32: 565-573, 1958.

531. Pearl, D. et al.: The effects of reserpine on schizophrenic patients. Arch. Neurol. Psychiat. 76: 198-204, 1956.

532. Pennington, V. M.: A two year comparative study of ataraxics in neuropsychiatric patients. J. Amer. Geriat. Soc. 5: 421-429, 1957.

533. Pennington, V. M.: Clinical results of prochlorperazine. Med. Times 87: 1432-1437, 1959.

534. Perrot, and Bourjala: Cas pour diagnostic: Un visage mauve. Bull. Soc. Franc. Derm. Syph. 69: 631, 1962.

535. Pimley, K. G.: Thioproperazine: A study of its uses in psychotic excita-tion. Psychopharmacologia 4: 377-384, 1963.

536. Pisciotta, A. V., Santos, A. S., and Keller, C.: Studies on agranulocytosis. V. patterns of recovery from drug-induced bone marrow damage. J. Lab Clin. Med. 63: 445-458, 1964.

537. Pleasure, H.: Chlorpromazine (Thorazine) for mental illness in the presence of pulmonary tuberculosis. Psychiat. Quart. 30: 23-30, 1956.

538. Pollack, B.: Recurrent Thorazine induced agranulocytosis. Amer. J. Psychiat. 113: 557-558, 1956.

539. Pollack, B. et al.: An oral syndrome complicating psychopharmacotherapy: Study II. Amer. J. Psychiat. 121: 384-386, 1964.

540. Potts, A. M.: The concentration of phenothiazines in the eye of experimental animals. Invest. Ophth. 1: 522-530, 1962.

541. Potts, A. M.: Uveal pigment and phenothiazine compounds. Tr. Am. Ophth. Soc. 60: 517, 1962.

542. Potts, A. M.: Further studies concerning the accumulation of polycyclic compounds on uveal melanin. Invest. Ophth. 3: 399-404, 1964.

543. Potts, A. M.: The reaction of uveal pigment in vitro with polycyclic compounds. Invest. Ophth. 3: 405-416, 1964.

544. Porteus, S. D.: Specific behavior changes following chlorpromazine. J. Consult. Psychol. 21: 257-263, 1957.

545. Prange, A. J., Jr. et al.: A double-blind clinical trial of chlorpromazine and reserpine in acute mental disturbance. J. New Drugs (3)2: 85-95, 1963.

546. Pratt, J. P. et al.: Comparison of haloperidol, trifluperidol, and chlorpromazine in acute schizophrenic patients. Curr. Ther. Res. 6: 562-571, 1964.

547. Pretty, H. M. et al.: Agranulocytosis: A report of 30 cases. Canad. Med. Ass. J. 93: 1058-1064, 1965.

548. Prien, R. F., and Cole, J. O.: High dose chlorpromazine therapy in chronic schizophrenia. Arch. Gen. Psychiat. 18: 482-495, 1968.

549. Prusmack, J. J. et al.: Mesoridazine (TPS-23), A new antipsychotic drug. J. New Drugs 6(3): 182-188, 1966.

550. Quinn, P. J. G. et al.: A comparative controlled trial of methotrimeprazine (Veractil) in chronic schizophrenia. J. Ment. Sci. 106: 160-170, 1960.

551. Rajotte, P., Giard, N., and Tetreault, L.: A controlled trial of propericiazine and chlorpromazine in "behaviour disorders." Curr. Ther. Res. 8: 166-174, 1966.

552. Rajotte, P., and Denber, H. C. B.: Long-term community follow-up of formerly hospitalized psychotic patients. J. Nerv. Ment. Dis. 136: 445-454, 1963.

553. Rajotte, P. et al.: Comparative study of butaperazine and prochlorperazine in the chronic schizophrenic. Can. Psychiat. Ass. J. 10: 25-34, 1965.

554. Ranek, L.: A fatal case of prolonged chlorpromazine jaundice. Ugesk. Laeger. 126: 1271-1274, 1964.

555. Rathod, N., and Rees, L.: A controlled study of the prognostic significance of autonomic responses in the chlorpromazine treatment of disturbed psychotic patients. J. Ment. Sci. 104: 705-712, 1958.

556. Ravan, J., and Rud, C.: Patients suffering from neuroses treated with flupenthixol. Nord. Psychiat. Tidsskrift 19: 66-70, 1965.

557. Ravaris, C. L. et al.: A controlled study of fluphenazine enanthate in chronic schizophrenic patients. Dis. Nerv. Syst. 26: 33-39, 1965.

558. Raymond, M. J. et al.: A trial of five tranquillizing drugs in psychoneurosis. Brit. Med. J. 2: 63-66, 1957.

559. Reardon, J. D., and Abrams, S.: Acute paranoid schizophrenia (Treatment with chlorpromazine, trifluoperazine, and placebo). Dis. Nerv. Syst. 27: 265-270, 1966.

560. Rees, W. L., and Lambert, C.: The value and limitations of chlorpromazine in the treatment of anxiety states. J. Ment. Sci. 101: 834-840, 1955.

561. Rees, W. L.: Electronarcosis in the treatment of schizophrenia. J. Ment. Sci. 95: 625-637, 1949.

562. Report to the Council on Pharmacy and Chemistry: Blood dyscrasias associated with chlorpromazine therapy. J.A.M.A. 160: 287, 1956.

563. Reznikoff, L.: Clinical observations of therapeutic effect of chlorprothixene (Taractan) in psychoses. Amer. J. Psychiat. 118: 348-350, 1961.

564. Rickels, K. et al.: Evaluation of tranquilizing drugs in medical outpatients —meprobamate, prochlorperazine, amobarbital, sodium, and placebo. J.A.M.A. 171: 1649-1656, 1959.

565. Riddell, S. A.: The therapeutic efficacy of ECT. Arch. Gen. Psychiat. 8: 546-556, 1963.

566. Robin, A. A.: Pecazine ("Pacatal") compared with amylobarbitone sodium in anxiety states. J. Ment. Sci. 105: 1064-1069, 1959.

567. Roebuck, B. E. et al.: An evaluation of the therapeutic use of triflupromazine in mental disease. J. Nerv. Ment. Dis. 129: 184-192, 1959.

568. Rogers, G. A.: Use of pilocarpine nitrate for relief of dryness with phenothiazines. Amer. J. Psychiat. 122: 1316, 1966.

569. Root, W. A. P.: Physiological Pharmacology. Academic Press, New York, 1960.

570. Rosner, H. et al.: A comparative study of the effect on anxiety of chlorpromazine, reserpine, phenobarbital, and a placebo. J. Nerv. Ment. Dis. 122: 505-512, 1955.

571. Rothstein, C.: An evaluation of the effects of discontinuation of chlorpromazine. New Eng. J. Med. 262: 67-69, 1960.

572. Rothstein, C. et al.: Discontinuation of maintenance dosage of ataractic drugs on a psychiatric continued treatment ward. J. Nerv. Ment. Dis. 134: 555-560, 1962.

573. Rotstein, J., Frick, P. S., and Schiele, B. C.: Agranulocytosis associated with chlorpromazine therapy. Arch. Intern. Med. 96: 781-786, 1955.

574. Rutledge, L. T., and Doty, R. W.: Differential action of chlorpromazine on reflexes conditioned to central and peripheral stimulation. Amer. J. Physiol. 191: 189-192, 1957.

575. Saint-Jean, A., and Desautels, S.: Electrocardiographic changes with thioridazine. Un. Med. Canada. 95: 554-557, 1966.

576. Salač, M., and Svestka, J.: Liver damage in the course of phenothiazine treatment. Activitas Nervosa Superior 7(3): 250, 1965.

577. Salisbury, B. J., and Hare, E. H.: Ritalin and chlorpromazine in chronic schizophrenia: A controlled clinical trial. J. Ment. Sci. 103: 830-834, 1957.

578. Sandison, R. A., Whitelaw, E., and Currie, J. D. C.: Clinical trials with Melleril (TP21) in the treatment of schizophrenia. J. Ment. Sci. 106: 732-741, 1960.

579. Satanove, A.: Pigmentation due to phenothiazines in high and prolonged dosage. J.A.M.A. 191: 263-268, 1965.

580. Saunders, J. C., and Muchmore, E.: Phenothiazine effect on human antibody synthesis. Brit. J. Psychiat. 110: 84-89, 1964.

581. Sharpley, P. et al.: Comparison of butaperazine and perphenazine: A double-blind controlled study. Psychopharmacologia 5: 209-216, 1964.

582. Schiele, B. C.: The unique therapeutic properties of tranylcypromine and trifluoperazine (Parstelin). Amer. J. Psychiat. 117: 245-246, 1960.

583. Schiele, B. C.: Treatment of pseudoneurotic schizophrenics and chronic neurotics. Canad. Psychiat. Ass. J. 7: 560-566, 1962.

584. Schiele, B. C., Vestre, N. D., and MacNaughton, D. V.: Treatment of hospitalized schizophrenics with trifluoperazine plus tranylcypromine: A double-blind controlled study. Comprehens. Psychiat. 4: 66-79, 1963.

585. Schiele, B. C. et al.: Comparison of low and high dosage procedures in chlorpromazine therapy. Psychiat. Quart. 33: 252-259, 1959.

586. Schiele, B. C. et al.: A comparison of thioridazine, trifluoperazine, chlorpromazine, and placebo: A double-blind controlled study on the treatment of chronic, hospitalized, schizophrenic patients. J. Clin. Exp. Psychopath. 22: 151-162, 1961.

587. Schmidt, K. E.: Combined treatment with chlorpromazine and reserpine. J. Ment. Sci. 103: 200-208, 1957.

588. Schmidt, W. R., and Jarcho, L. W.: Persistent dyskinesias following phenothiazine therapy. Arch. Neurol. 14: 369-377, 1966.

589. Schooler, N. R. et al.: One year after discharge-community adjustment of schizophrenic patients. Paper presented at the Annual Meeting of the American Psychiatric Association, Atlantic City, N.J., 1966.

590. Scopp, I. W. et al.: Dryness of the mouth with use of tranquilizers: chlorpromazine. J. Amer. Dental Ass. 71(1): 66-69, 1965.

591. Scriabine, A. et al.: Benzquinamide. A new antianxiety drug. J.A.M.A. 184: 276-279, 1963.

592. Seager, C. P.: Chlorpromazine in treatment of elderly psychotic women. Brit. Med. J. 1: 882-885, 1955.

593. Sen, G., and Bose, K. C.: Rauwolfia serpentina. A new Indian drug for insanity and high blood pressure. Indian Med. Wld. 2: 194-201, 1931.

594. Shader, R. I.: Sexual dysfunction associated with thioridazine hydrochloride. J.A.M.A. 188: 1007-1009, 1964.

595. Sharpley, P., Heistad, G., and Schiele, B. C.: Comparison of butaperazine and perphenazine: A double-blind controlled study. Psychopharmacologia 5: 209-216, 1964.

596. Shay, H., and Siplet, H.: Study of chlorpromazine jaundice, its mechanism and prevention: Special reference to serum alkaline phosphate and glutamic oxalacetic transaminase. Gastroenterology 32: 571-591, 1957.

597. Shay, H., and Siplet, H.: Relation of chemical structure of chlorpromazine to its liver-sensitizing action. Gastroenterology 35: 16-24, 1958.

598. Shelton, W. et al.: SKF-10,812: A thioxanthene derivative. Curr. Ther. Res. 7(7): 415-416, 1965.

599. Shelton, W. H. et al.: Further observations on TPS-23, A thioridazine derivative. J. New Drugs 5: 343-344, 1965.

600. Shepherd, M., and Watt, D. C.: A controlled clinical study of chlorpromazine and reserpine in chronic schizophrenia. J. Neurol. Neurosurg. Psychiat. 19: 232-235, 1956.

601. Sheppard, C. et al.: Effects of acetophenazine dimaleate on paranoid symptomatology in female geriatric patients: Double-blind study. J. Amer. Geriatrics Society 12: 884-888, 1964.

602. Shimkunas, A. M., Gynther, M. D., and Smith, K.: Abstracting ability of schizophrenics before and during phenothiazine therapy. Arch. Gen. Psychiat. 14: 79, 1966.

603. Sherman, L. J.: The significant variables in psychopharmaceutic research, Amer. J. Psychiat. 116: 208-214, 1959.

604. Siddall, J. R.: The ocular toxic findings with prolonged and high dosage chlorpromazine intake. Arch. Ophth. 74: 460-464, 1965.

605. Simon, W. et al.: Long-term follow-up study of schizophrenic patients. Arch. Gen. Psychiat. 12: 510-515, 1965.

606. Simon, W. et al.: A controlled study of the short-term differential treatment of schizophrenia. Amer. J. Psychiat. 114: 1077-1086, 1958.

607. Simpson, G. M., and Iqbal, J.: A preliminary study of thiothixene in chronic schizophrenics. Curr. Ther. Res. 7: 697-700, 1965.

608. Simpson, G. M. et al.: Withdrawal effects of phenothiazines. Comp. Psychiat. 6: 347-351, 1965.

609. Singh, H., and Free, R. M.: A preliminary report on the use of Stelazine and Parnate in chronic regressed and withdrawn patients. Amer. J. Psychiat. 117: 364-365, 1960.

610. Skarbeck, A., and Jacobsen, M.: Oxypertine. A review of clinical experience, Brit. J. Psychiat. 111: 1173-1179, 1965.

611. Sletten, I. W. et al.: A new topical spray agent to protect patients on chlorpromazine from sunlight. Amer. J. Psychiat. 119: 991-992, 1963.

612. Smith, J. A. et al.: A comparison of triflupromazine (Vesprin), chlorpromazine and placebo in 85 chronic patients. Amer. J. Psychiat. 115: 253-254, 1958.

613. Smith, K. et al.: ETC-chlorpromazine and chlorpromazine compared in the treatment of schizophrenia. J. Nerv. Ment. Dis. 144: 284-290, 1967.

614. Solomon, F. A., and Capagna, F. A.: Jaundice due to prochlorperazine (Compazine). Amer. J. Med. 27: 840-843, 1959.

615. Somerville, D. M. et al.: Phenothiazine side effects. Comparison of two major tranquillizers. J. Ment. Sci. 106, 1417-1424, 1960.

616. Sommerness, M. D. et al.: Chlorpromazine: A controlled study with highly disturbed patients. Dis. Nerv. Syst. 18: 16-20, 1957.

617. South-East Region (Scotland) Therapeutic trials Committee: Controlled trial of prochlorperazine ("Stemetil") in schizophrenia. J. Ment. Sci.: 107: 514-522, 1961.

618. Spiegel, D., and Keith-Spiegel, P.: The effects of carphenazine, trifluoperazine and chlorpromazine on word behavior. J. Nerv. Ment. Dis. 144: 111-116, 1967.

619. Stabenau, J. R., and Grinols, D. R.: A double-blind comparison of thioridazine and chlorpromazine. Psychiat. Quart. 38: 42-63, 1964.

620. Stacey, C. H. et al.: Jaundice occurring during the administration of chlorpromazine. Canad. Med. Ass. J. 73: 386-392, 1955.

621. Stanley, W.: Prolonged hypotension due to chlorpromazine. Am. J. Psychiat. 115: 1124-1126, 1959.

622. Stanley, W. J., and Walton, D.: Trifluoperazine ("Stelazine"). A controlled clinical trial in chronic schizophrenia. J. Ment. Sci. 107: 250-257, 1961.

623. Stein, A. A., and Wright, A. W.: Hepatic pathology in jaundice due to chlorpromazine. J.A.M.A. 161: 508-511, 1956.

624. Sugerman, A. A. et al.: A pilot study of clopenthixol in chronic schizophrenics. Curr. Ther. Res. 8: 220-224, 1966.

625. Sugerman, A. A., and Rosen, E.: Absorption efficiency and excretion profile of a prolonged-action form of chlorpromazine. Clin. Pharmacol. Therap. 5: 561-568, 1964.

626. Sugerman, A. A.: Comparison of TPS-23 and thioridazine in chronic schizophrenic patients. Curr. Ther. Res. 7: 520-527, 1965.

627. Sulman, F. G.: Skin pigmentation following chlorpromazine treatment. Lancet. 2: 592-593, 1964.

628. Sulzer, E.: The effects of promazine on MMPI. Performance in the chronic psychiatric patient. Psychopharmacologia 2: 137-140, 1961.

629. Sussman, R. M., and Sumner, P.: Jaundice following administration of 50 Mg. of chlorpromazine. New Eng. J. Med. 253: 499-502, 1955.

630. Svendsen, B. B. et al.: Comparison of the effect of thioridazine and chlorpromazine on chronic schizophrenic psychosis using double blind technique. Psychopharmacologia 2: 446-455, 1961.

631. Swanson, D. W.: Hypotension associated with thioridazine HCl. Amer. J. Psychiat. 117: 834-835, 1961.

632. Tedeschi, R. E., Tedeschi, D. H., and Fellows, E. J.: Neuropharmacology of tranylcypromine and trifluoperazine. Canad. Psychiat. Ass. J. 7: S55-S59, 1962.

633. Tedeschi, R. E. et al.: Effects of various centrally acting drugs on fighting behavior of mice. J. Pharmacol. Exp. Ther. 125: 28-34, 1959.

634. Teitelbaum, I.: Electrocardiographic changes associated with phenothiazine. Lancet 1: 115, 1963.

635. Tenenblatt, S. S., and Spagno, A.: A controlled study of chlorpromazine therapy in chronic psychotic patients. J. Clin. Exp. Psychopath. 17: 81-92, 1956.

636. Thorpe, J. G., and Baker, A. A.: A research method to assess a new tranquillizing drug. J. Ment. Sci. 102: 790-795, 1956.

637. Tipton, D. L. et al.: Effect of chlorpromazine on blood level of alcohol in rabbits. Amer. J. Physiol. 200: 1007-1010, 1961.

638. Tourlentes, T. T. et al.: Chlorpromazine and communication processes. Arch. Neurol. Psychiat. 79: 468-473, 1958.

639. Tredici, L. M., Schiele, B. C., and McClanahan, W. S.: The incidence and management of chlorpromazine skin-eye syndrome. Minn. Med. 48: 569-574, 1965.

640. Trethowan, W. H., and Scott, P. A. L.: Chlorpromazine in obsessive-compulsive and allied disorders. Lancet 268: 781-785, 1955.

641. Turnbull, J. M.: Hypotensive effect of phenothiazines. Canad. Med. Ass. J. 94: 918, 1966.

642. Tuteur, W. et al.: Chlorpromazine: Five years later. In Recent Advances in Biological Psychiatry. Wortis, J. (Ed.) New York. Grune & Stratton, Inc., pp. 35-43, 1961.

643. Uhrbrand, L., and Faurbye, A.: Reversible and irreversible dyskinesia after treatment with perphenazine, chlorpromazine, reserpine, and electroconvulsive therapy. Psychopharmacologia 1: 408-418, 1960.

644. Vallat, J. N.: Attempted suicide with chlorpromazine. Presse Med. 62: 752, 1954.

645. Valentine, M., and Jardine, P.: Phenothiazines and eye complications. Brit. Med. J. 2: 586, 1966.

646. Van Ketel, W. G. et al.: Skin lesions caused by chlorpromazine. Nederl. Tijdschr. v. Geneesk. 102: 1799-1804, 1958.

647. Van Ommen, R. A., and Brown, C. H.: Obstructive-type jaundice due to chlorpromazine (Thorazine). Report of three cases. J.A.M.A. 157: 321-325, 1955.

648. Vaughan, G. F., Leiberman, D. M., and Cook, L. C.: Chlorpromazine in psychiatry. Lancet 268: 1083-1087, 1955.

649. Verhave, T. et al.: Effects of chlorpromazine and secobarbital on avoidance and escape behavior. Arch. Int. Pharmacodyn. 116: 45-53, 1958.

650. Vestre, N. D. et al.: A comparison of fluphenazine, triflupromazine, and phenobarbital in the treatment of chronic schizophrenic patients: A double-blind controlled study. J. Clin. Exp. Psychopath. 23: 149-159, 1962.

651. Vinar, O. et al.: Controlled comparison of 6 neuroleptic drugs. 7: 241-242, 1965.

652. Waitzkin, L.: Hepatic disfunction during promazine therapy. New Eng. J. Med. 257: 276-277, 1957.

653. Waitzkin, L., and MacMahon, H. E.: Hepatic injury found during chronic

chlorpromazine therapy. Ann. Int. Med. 56: 220-232, 1962.

654. Walaszek, E. J., and Abood, L. G.: Effect of tranquilizing drugs on fighting response of Siamese fighting fish. Science 124, 440-441, 1956.

655. Waldrop, F. N. et al.: A comparison of the therapeutic and toxic effects of thioridazine and chlorpromazine in chronic schizophrenic patients. Compr. Psychiat. 2: 96-105, 1961.

656. Walkenstein, S. S., and Seifter, J.: Fate, distribution and excretion of S^{35} promazine. J. Pharmac. Exp. Ther. 125: 283-286, 1959.

657. Walsh, G. P., Walton, D., and Black, D. A.: The relative efficacy of Vespral and chlorpromazine in the treatment of a group of chronic schizophrenic patients. J. Ment. Sci. 105: 199-209, 1959.

658. Walters, G. M. et al.: Jaundice following administration of fluphenazine dihydrochloride. Amer. J. Psychiat. 120: 81-82, 1963.

659. Wase, A. W., Christensen, J., and Polley, E.: The accumulation of S^{35} chlorpromazine in brain. Arch. Neurol. Psychiat. 75: 54-56, 1956.

660. Weckowicz, T. E., and Ward, T.: Clinical trial of RO 15-0690 and chlorpromazine on disturbed chronic schizophrenic patients. Dis. Nerv. Syst. 21: 527-528, 1960.

661. Weckowicz, T. E., and Ward, T. F.: Clinical trial of "Stelazine" on apathetic chronic schizophrenics. J. Ment. Sci. 106: 1008-1015, 1960.

662. Weissman, A.: Interaction effects of imipramine and d-amphetamine on non-discriminated avoidance. Pharmacologist 3(2): 60, 1961.

663. Wendkos, M. H.: The significance of electrocardiographic changes produced by thioridazine. J. New Drugs 4: 322-332, 1964.

664. Wertheimer, J.: Syndromes extra-pyramidaux permanents consecutifs a l'administration prolongee des neuroleptiques. Schweizer Arch. Neurologie, Nuerochirurgie Psychiatrie 95: 120-173, 1965.

665. Wessler, M. M., and Kahn, V. L.: Can the chronic schizophrenic patient remain in the community?: A follow-up study of twenty-four long-term hospitalized patients returned to the community. J. Nerv. Ment. Dis. 136: 455-463, 1963.

666. Wetterholm, D. H., Snow, H. L., and Winter, F. C.: A clinical study of pigmentary change in cornea and lens in chronic chlorpromazine therapy. Arch. Ophth. 74: 55-56, 1965.

667. Wheatley, D.: Evaluation of psychotherapeutic drugs in general practice. Psychopharmacol. Serv. Cent. Bull. 2(4): 25-31, 1962.

668. Whitehead, W. A., and Thune, L. E.: The effects of chlorpromazine on learning in chronic psychotics. J. Consult. Psychol. 22: 379-383, 1958.

669. Whitely, J. S.: The indications for combined treatment with trifluoperazine and amylobarbitone. Brit. J. Clin. Pract. 5: 613-615, 1961.

670. Whitfield, A. G. W.: Correspondence: Chlorpromazine jaundice. Brit. Med. J. 1: 784, 1955.

671. Whittaker, C. B., and Hoy, R. M.: Withdrawal of perphenazine in chronic schizophrenia. Brit. J. Psychiat. 109: 422-427, 1963.

672. Whittier, J. R. et al.: Mepazine (Pacatal): Clinical trial with placebo control and psychological study. Psychopharmacologia 1: 280-287, 1960.

673. Wilkins, R. W.: Clinical usage of Rauwolfia alkaloids, including reserpine (Serpasil). Ann. N. Y. Acad. Sci. 59: 36-44, 1954.

674. Wilson, I. C. et al.: A double-blind trial to investigate the effects of Thorazine, Compazine, and Stelazine in paranoid schizophrenia. J. Ment. Sci. 107: 90-99, 1961.

675. Winkelman, N. W., Jr.: A clinical and socio-cultural study of 200 psychiatric patients started on chlorpromazine ten and one half years ago. Amer. J. Psychiat. 120: 861-869, 1964.

676. Winkelman, N. W., Jr.: Three evaluations of a monoamine oxidase inhibitor and phenothiazine combination. Dis. Nerv. Syst. 26: 160-164, 1965.

677. Winter, W. D., and Frederickson, W. K.: The short-term effects of chlorpromazine on psychiatric patients. J. Consult. Psychol. 20: 431-434, 1956.

678. Wirt, R., and Simon, W.: Differential Treatment and Prognosis in Schizophrenia. Charles C. Thomas, Springfield, Ill. 1959.

679. Witt, P. N.: Tranquilizers: Experimental proof for their specific effects. Trans. Coll. Phys. Philadelphia 29: 9-16, 1961.

680. Witt, P. N.: Construction of spider webs as a test for drugs with CNS action. Arzneimitt. Forsch. 6: 628-635, 1965.

681. Witts, L. J.: Adverse reactions to drugs. Brit. Med. J. 2: 1081-1086, 1965.

682. Woodward, D. J., and Soloman, J. D.: Fatal agranulocytosis occurring during promazine (Sparine) therapy. J.A.M.A. 162: 1308, 1956.

683. Worthington, J. J.: Parotid enlargement bilaterally in a patient on thioridazine. Amer. J. Psychiat. 121: 813-814, 1965.

684. Wright, R. L. D., and Kyne, W. P.: A clinical and experimental comparison of four antischizophrenic drugs. Psychopharmacologia 1: 437-449, 1960.

685. Wrobec, T.: Blood dyscrasias associated with antituberculosis and/or tranquilizing chemotherapy. A long-term clinical observation. Dis. Chest. 47: 208-217, 1965.

686. Wurtman, R. J., Axelrod, J., and Fischer, J. E.: Melatonin synthesis in the pineal gland. Effect of light mediated by the sympathetic nervous system. Science 143: 1328, 1964.

687. Yen, C. Y. et al.: Ataractic suppression of isolation-induced aggressive behavior. Arch. Int. Pharmacodyn. 123: 179-185, 1959.

688. Yules, J. H., and Baker, H.: Agranulocytosis during chlorpromazine therapy. Bull. Tufts New Eng. Med. Ctr. 1: 224, 1955.

689. Zatuchini, J., and Miller, G.: Jaundice during chlorpromazine therapy. New Eng. J. Med. 251: 1003, 1954.

690. Zelickson, A. S., and Zeller, H. C.: A new and unusual reaction to chlorpromazine. J.A.M.A. 188: 394-396, 1964.

691. Zelickson, A. S.: Skin pigmentation and chlorpromazine. J.A.M.A. 194: 670, 1965.

692. Zeller, W. W. et al.: Use of chlorpromazine and reserpine in the treatment of emotional disorders. J.A.M.A. 160: 179, 1956.

693. Ziegler, H. R., Patterson, J. N., and Johnson, W. A.: Death from sulfadiazine with agranulocytosis, jaundice and hepatosis: report of a case. New Eng. J. Med. 223: 59, 1945.

14

Somatic Therapies Other Than Psychotropic Drugs

LEO ALEXANDER, M.D.

Dr. Alexander's colorful background and varied affiliations are too numerous to set forth here in their entirety. In addition to private practice he is consultant in Neurology and Biological Psychiatry to Boston State Hospital, Assistant Clinical Professor of Psychiatry at Tufts University Medical School, Consultant in Psychiatric Research to Northampton Veterans' Administration Hospital and consultant in psychiatry to the U.S. Army Hospital at Fort Devens, Mass.

Graduated from the University of Vienna Medical School in 1929, Dr. Alexander became a faculty member of the Peiping Union Medical College, Peiping, China, having served four years residency at the University Hospital in Frankfort, Germany. In 1934 he joined the staff of the Harvard Medical School as Instructor in Neurology, and spent the next seven years participating in clinical and research work in the Boston area. In 1941 he became Associate Professor of Neuropsychiatry at Duke University Medical School, Durham, N.C.

His subsequent service with the U.S. Army Medical Corps for the next four years took him to Germany on special medical intelligence duty, securing information on German neuropsychiatric practices. This experience, and his continuance in the active reserve after World War II (Dr. Alexander holds the rank of Colonel) resulted in recall to duty during the war crimes trials at Nuremberg, Germany. At that time he was appointed Consultant to the Secretary of Defense of the U.S.A.

The new psychotropic drugs, since Laborit's[32] introduction of Chlorpromazine, have enhanced so greatly the recovery rate of mental patients, especially schizophrenics, that the trend of increase in mental hospital

---

This chapter differs from most of the other chapters in being less of a review and more of a personal account by the author. Having consistency of style in mind, the editors nonetheless decided to include this chapter with only some editing of the original version because it performs a necessary service which could not very well be rendered were the chapter to follow rigidly the format of the others: there is not enough literature to survey at present regarding insulin treatment, ECT, and lobotomies. Doctor Alexander has had extensive experience in these areas and has observations on the possibly continued value of some of these treatment techniques in specified circumstances. As psychiatrists trained in the last ten years, (since the previous volume on schizophrenia) may have had little experience with these somatic methods, now so vastly overshadowed by the use of psychotropic drugs, we want to acquaint them with these methods in this chapter. (Eds.)

populations has been reversed, not only in this country[14] but throughout the world. Doubts that this reversal was due chiefly to the introduction of the psychotropic drugs and not to other improvements in management may be assuaged by the fact that the change in trend of hospital populations occurred with corresponding delay[45] in countries in which the psychotropic drugs were introduced two years after their introduction in France and in the United States.

Yet in treating severely ill patients we are faced with the apparent paradox that the older physical treatments, namely electroshock therapy and insulin coma therapy, frequently are more effective than the new psychotropic drugs, although the introduction of insulin coma therapy and electroshock had not modified the mental hospital statistics. This paradox may be ascribed to the fact that the ease of administration of the new psychotropic drugs had made them available to a far greater number of patients than had electroshock and insulin coma therapy, the administration of which required skill, specially

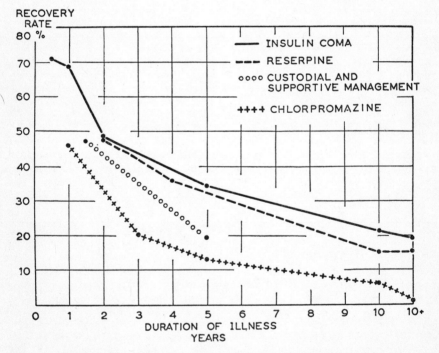

FIG. 1.—Recovery rate as a function of duration of illness separately for spontaneous recovery on custodial and supportive management, insulin coma therapy, Reserpine treatment and chlorpromazine treatment. (From Alexander, L., and Moore, M.: Multiple approaches to treatment in schizophrenia and discussion of indications. Am. J. Psychiat. 114: 577-582, 1958.)

*Admissions with no prior admission to any inpatient psychiatric facility.

trained personnel, and time, and therefore remained limited in their application to relatively small selected groups of patients.

In the treatment of schizophrenic reactions, the advantages of electroshock are largely limited to the catatonic states and to the schizo-affective reactions with depressive features. In all other types of schizophrenic illnesses, insulin coma treatment, particularly when combined with electroshock therapy, is vastly superior. The overall recovery rate with electroshock alone, which is similar to the recovery rate obtainable with psychotropic drugs during the first year of illness, is 49 per cent (Fig. 1).[3,8] This rate is greatly surpassed by insulin coma therapy, with its recovery rate of 72 per cent during the first year, which is maintained in 54 per cent for five or more years.[3] The only advantage of the new psychotropic drugs over the older treatments is that recoveries can be maintained by maintenance dosage; thus, although not a fully adequate substitute, they are a welcome addition to insulin coma therapy and/or electroshock.

Nevertheless, because of reduction in hospital populations, as the result of the new psychotropic drugs, many hospital administrators have discontinued the use of insulin coma therapy. In a recent survey published by Bennett,[9] of 214 institutions surveyed known to have active insulin clinics in the 1950's 69 had discontinued insulin clinics in 1960, another 24 by 1966; the remaining 63 units are fairly evenly distributed throughout the country. These institutions are employing a variety of techniques, many of them combining the treatment with electroshock and psychotropic drugs. The facilitation of coma and of resuscitation by Glucagon, to be described further below, is widely utilized.

Against the background of the effect of the new psychotropic drugs, the advantages of insulin coma therapy are becoming even more clearly recognized in many countries. Remy[42] of Switzerland stresses its long lasting effects. This is not the case with the other substances introduced in recent years which depend upon maintenance therapy. Dunlop[16] emphasizes the dramatic reversal of the patient's behavior which can be produced by insulin coma therapy, especially in younger patients in whom psychopharmaceuticals alone had failed to produce results. He suggested the return to insulin coma therapy as the primary type of treatment and recommended controlled research of the effectiveness of insulin in comparison with drug therapy instituted at the beginning of the illness, as well as their combination. Pichot,[39] working at the same university and hospital department in which the psychotropic drugs had been introduced immediately after their discovery, and their technic of administration refined and developed,[15] reports that the use of insulin coma treatment and electroshock therapy had been reduced at this important clinic, but had not been given up. The number of patients treated with insulin coma treatments had been cut down to one-third, those treated with electroshock to one-half of their predrug therapy utilization, while chemotherapy had increased sixfold. The opinion of psychiatrists throughout France was consistent with this change. Inasmuch as Pichot's opinion is derived from a particularly authoritative vantage point, I am quoting his conclusions:

> "Since 1952 psychopharmaceuticals have found increasing employment, to the point where treatment by psychotropic drugs currently represents at least two-thirds of all biological treatment methods employed. This growth has taken place at the expense of electric shock therapy and the insulin shock therapy of Sakel.
> Nevertheless, the last two methods are still indicated in a restricted number of well-defined cases.
> In the opinion of French psychiatrists, insulin shock therapy retains its value in the treatment of acute schizophrenia and, to a lesser extent, of chronic schizophrenia. For acute schizophrenia those who regard insulin therapy as the preferred treatment are almost as numerous (34 per cent) as the advocates of chemotherapy (39 per cent). For chronic schizophrenia, on the other hand, while 50 per cent of psychiatrists regard chemotherapy as the preferred treatment method, only 25 per cent would make insulin therapy their first choice."

Insulin coma therapy has survived in Germany as well. Ehrhardt[19] concludes that the general statistics of state hospital populations over the last 10 years do not yet prove the general superiority of the effects of pharmacotherapy over those of shock treatments. He states: "Insulin coma therapy and electroshock therapy are still today important tools in our therapeutic armament on behalf of the psychotic patients, and the metabolism of the brain in insulin coma therapy, as well as the physiology of electrically-induced convulsions, remain most timely subjects for research." Two reports from India are confirmatory of the above opinions. Vahia[44] of Bombay concludes that insulin coma treatment is still of value in resistant cases of schizophrenia. With further advances in drug therapy and increasing facilities for individual and group therapy, insulin treatment may become obsolete; but at present it has a definite place in the total therapeutic resources of the practicing psychiatrist. Parkash and Sagar[37] of Amritsar, Punjab, also point to the long lasting effects over several years of insulin-induced recoveries. (See also Remy.[42]) Lukomsky[35] of Moscow, Russia, concurred that recent achievements of psychopharmacology do not justify underestimation of insulin therapy. The latter should occupy a definite place in the psychiatric armamentarium for the treatment of psychosis, as an independent method and in combination with other modes and agents.

The greatest obstacle to the full and general acceptance of insulin coma therapy, or of shock treatments as a whole, has been their primarily empirical design, in spite of the fact that many important and lastingly accepted treatments—such as, for example, the quinine therapy of malaria—had been introduced as empirical panaceas. As a rule, physicians and scientists mistrust empiricism. In this connection, it is of interest that the new psychotropic drugs, with their more readily ascertainable physiologic action, and their more narrowly and specifically definable psychophysiologic effects and clinical rationale, have revitalized research on its older and more obscure precursors. Gellhorn[23,24] has established convincing evidence of the actions of electroshock and insulin coma upon the various components of the autonomic nervous system, as well as of their effects upon conditional behavior. Winnik and his collaborators,[46] by means of microvascular observations of the eyegrounds and nailbeds, have established an interesting sequence of vascular changes during insulin coma therapy, in which successfully treated patients differed from treatment failures. In successfully treated patients, the arterioles of the eyegrounds and the nailbeds constricted during somnolence (the cortical phase), while the capillary blood pressure and the vasomotor count increased. During agitation (the thalamic phase), the venules of the eyegrounds and the nailbeds dilated, while capillary blood pressure and vasomotor count continued to increase. In deep coma there was a sudden fall of the capillary blood pressure and the vasomotor count, while eyegrounds and nailbeds became edematous. From these observations, the authors concluded that they constituted evidence of stimulation of the diencephalo-hypophysioadrenal axis in the course of insulin coma therapy. They considered this an important basis of its effect upon the adaptive functions of the organism. Another observation suggesting a prolonged and progressive improvement in autonomic functioning was obtained by Dussik and his collaborators[18] by means of serial Glucagon tests in schizophrenic patients. They found a progressive increase in Glucagon-induced glucose mobilization in the course of insulin-coma therapy, which was correlated with clinical psychiatric improvement. Dussik et al[18] regarded this as a manifestation of a better balanced and more harmonious adjustment to emergency situations, an example of one of the ways in which the organism of the schizophrenic individual "learns" to respond in a more harmoniously balanced fashion to internal and external stresses of a physiological and psychological nature. The results of these facts in schizophrenics while under treatment seem to reflect the improvement of the adjustive ability of the organism.

THE TECHNIQUE OF INSULIN-COMA THERAPY

The most important addition to the technique of insulin-coma therapy during the past decade was the introduction of Glucagon by Braun and Parker.[13] The technic was further elaborated by Laqueur and LaBurt,[34] Dussik et al.[17] and Ramirez et al.[40] The action of Glucagon in insulin-coma therapy is twofold: administered one to four hours before administration of insulin, it facilitates insulin induced hypoglycemia and thus allows coma to supervene at a dosage less than that necessary without such pretreatment.[17] It is also a very effective measure for overcoming insulin resistance, often associated with acute schizophrenic psychoses.[3] Secondly, Glucagon is the simplest, safest, and most effective way to terminate the coma. Restoration of the blood sugar level and arousal will usually take place within 10-20 minutes after the injection of 1 mg. of Glucagon; however, immediately after arousal, an adequate amount of glucose has to be supplied by mouth, preferably 400 cc. of 50 per cent glucose flavored with orange juice. If not followed by adequate administration of sufficient amounts of glucose, the Glucagon-induced awakening will be of short duration.[33] The method of terminating coma by intravenous injection of glucose or by gavage no longer is used except in rare cases when injection of Glucagon was unsuccessful.

In all other respects the technique of insulin-coma therapy has not changed significantly. However, since publication of my earlier report,[3] fourteen years ago, a fact I emphasized at that time, has continued to impress me, namely that successful insulin coma treatment depends upon adequate depth and duration of the treatment. A full course of insulin-coma therapy should include 60 deep comas. A deep coma is defined as a coma deep enough to have affected the midbrain and thus to have abolished the light reaction of the pupils. The physician should ascertain that the pupillary light reaction has been abolished during the last 15 minutes of each full-hour coma before counting this coma as an effective treatment. As Holt[29] originally pointed out, insulin treatment is aided and rendered more effective by the ancillary use of electroshock. My practice is to administer one electroshock at the height of every third coma. Consequently, the full course administered by me consists of 60 deep comas and 20 electroshock treatments.

Insulin coma treatments are administered once daily for five to six days during each week, every sixth and/or seventh day being days of rest, which may be utilized for reevaluation of the patient, psychotherapy, and home visits. It is important to realize that the depot effect of the insulin may keep it potentially active for 18 hours; therefore, the patient should not be allowed to leave the hospital until 19 hours after termination of the last coma.

Prior to the beginning of treatment the patient should have a glucose tolerance test and, if pretreatment medication by Glucagon is contemplated, a Glucagon tolerance test[18] should be included. The following day the treatment should be initiated at a dose of 10 units and the daily dose raised gradually by 10 to 20 units per day until coma levels are reached. An experienced therapist may at times regard it as safe to increase the daily dose by 30-40 units per day, especially in insulin-resistant patients. Thus, the series of insulin comas is likely to be preceded by 6 to 20 subcomas and the total series is likely to require 70 to 90 treatments, extending over a period of about three to four months. A fact which has impressed me is that patients with a significant element of hysterical features tend to go into coma with a much smaller dose than classically schizophrenic patients. This may give an early hint as to prognosis and the type of associated psychotherapy required.

During the subcoma phase of the series, interruption by oral administration of glucose in orange juice should be carried out at first three hours after the injection of insulin, later during the fourth hour, finally at the end of the fourth hour. Approximately 1 Gm. of sugar must be given for every unit of insulin injected.

As the daily dose of insulin gradually increases, coma finally supervenes, at first usually at the end of the third or during the fourth hour after injection. Coma generally will supervene at doses between 100 and 400 units of insulin. Once an adequate coma dose has been reached, that same dose may again be given on subsequent treatment days without requiring much modification; however, the physician must at all times be alert in continually reevaluating the dose and its effects in terms of the treatment needs and the safety requirements of his patient. Thorough familiarity with the neurophysiologic aspects of insulin coma is required.[3] Four important phases need to be distinguished:

The Decorticate Phase

This begins when the patient has lost contact with the environment.

The Thalamic Phase

This manifests itself by increased automatic activity and agitation, with predominantly sympathetic autonomic release, which may be enhanced by nonspecific sensory stimuli.

The Midbrain Phase

During this phase signs of decerebration at the level of the red nuclei appear, as does abolition of the light reflex of the pupils. The latter is most easily ascertainable. Autonomic reactivity shifts to the parasympathetic-cholinergic, manifested by copious watery perspiration. A well established midbrain phase is essential for the therapeutic efficacy of the coma, especially in paranoid patients. It should be allowed to last an average of 15 minutes.

The Medullary Phase

In its beginnings this phase is characterized by a renewed shift to sympathetic reactivity. The pulse accelerates and the still nonreacting pupils dilate, while perspiration turns viscous. It is generally safe to leave the patient in this phase only as long as the pulse rate remains fast, i.e., usually not longer than 15 minutes. Any decline of the pulse rate during this phase heralds the approach of its safety limits, because it is an indication that the nucleus of the vagus—by nature the most resistant to hypoglycemia of all the parts in the brain stem—is being released preceding suspension of its activities, thus exposing the patient to the danger of irreversible coma.

The total time of the therapeutic coma should be one hour from its inception to its termination, with the exception of the first and second comas. Only 30 minutes should be allowed for the first, while the second coma of the series should be terminated after 45 minutes. If arousal is uneventful on these two occasions, one full hour may be allowed from then on. Whenever arousal is delayed, the coma dose for the subsequent day should be appropriately reduced (approximately by 15 per cent of the preceding dose).

Arousal from coma has been greatly simplified by the introduction of Glucagon. One-third mg. of Glucagon injected intramuscularly will be sufficient to terminate all comas in better than 90 per cent of the patients. I prefer administration of one mg. which, as a rule, will induce arousal within 10-20 minutes. If patient is not aroused within 20 minutes, the dose of Glucagon should be repeated. In most patients this results in arousal within another 10-15 minutes. Arousal should be followed immediately by an adequate supply of glucose by mouth and should contain at least 1 Gm. of sugar for every unit of insulin used during the treatment. Usually I administer 400 cc. of a 50 per cent solution. If the administration of oral glucose is delayed, or the amount is insufficient, the patient may lapse into coma again. Sometimes, if the deficit is only slight, there may be a most interesting revival of the original schizophrenic symptomatology of the patient. A 37-year-old paranoid schizophrenic female, whose symptoms had subsided in the early part of her course of insulin treatments, developed a striking reexacerbation of her hostile, aggressively projecting attitudes during partial arousal from her ninth treatment. This episode promptly subsided after administration of 25 cc. of 50 per cent glucose by vein, followed by 400 cc. of 50 per cent glucose by mouth. Similarly, a 32-year-old female patient, while still hypoglycemic and only semi-awake after her 16th coma treatment, went through a phase of cataclysmic annihilation panic. This was practically a reenactment of her original symptom which had brought her to the hospital. These observations may suggest a most interesting relationship of hypoglycemia to the psychophysiologic etiology of schizophrenic symptoms.

Whenever resuscitation by Glucagon is either delayed or incomplete, glucose by intravenous injection should be administered promptly. Usually we give 50 cc. of 50 per cent dextrose.

The two chief dangers of insulin coma therapy are: 1) irreversible coma, and 2) delayed coma.

TREATMENT OF IRREVERSIBLE COMA

Resuscitation measures in the event of irreversible coma consist, first of all, of prompt diagnosis of the condition. Time must not be futilely spent hoping that the patient may still arouse in response to the obviously inadequate routine dose of Glucagon and glucose. If the coma has not been terminated within 15 minutes after the second injection, given 20 minutes after the first attempt of interruption by Glucagon, and 5 minutes after one subsequent dose of 50 cc. of 50 per cent dextrose (25 Gm. of dextrose) by vein, an additional dose of 25 Gm. of dextrose should be administered promptly, again by vein. If the patient fails to regain consciousness within five minutes after this additional dose, the diagnosis of irreversible coma must be made and the full regimen for relief of his condition, as outlined below, must swing into action.

1. The most vital aspect of this regimen is the continued supply of adequate amounts of glucose so as maximally to facilitate uptake on the part of the brain. As soon as possible, continuous intravenous drip infusion should be initiated, administering 10 per cent glucose (dextrose) in saline. This should be supplemented by repeated additional injections of 25 per cent glucose through the infusion tube, sufficient to bring the hourly administered dose of dextrose to 50 Gm. Addition of concentrated dextrose is particularly helpful whenever the need seems indicated by a deepening of hypoglycemic symptoms, such as the recurrence of profuse perspiration after it had once abated following the previous administration of hypertonic dextrose. The fact that after a time during irreversible coma, the blood sugar may return to its normal level or rise above it, should not deter the therapist from continued administration of dextrose during this period. The vital fact that the ability of the brain to utilize glucose is sharply reduced, both during coma and subsequent to coma, must always be borne in mind.[3] For this reason it is essential that an overabundant supply of glucose be offered continually during this crucial phase. As a general rule, it may stated that the total amount of glucose in grams which must be supplied within the first twenty-four hours of irreversible coma is approximately three to four times that of the dose of insulin in units which had been given. Continued administration of glucose is also required during this period because intramuscular pools of such large amounts of insulin as are used in insulin coma treatments appear to remain active up to 18 hours or more, depending upon the amount of the dose (depot-effect). In addition, as a result of the rise of the blood sugar level during resuscitation by glucose, the patient's own pancreas or, rather, his entire parasympatho-insulin system, becomes stimulated to activity, i.e., to additional production of insulin, which again abrogates the brain's priority over the circulating glucose. For this reason it is necessary to assure, by continued administration, abundant supplies of glucose to the brain throughout the period of resuscitation. While, as a general rule, 50 Gm. per hour should be given by vein through the first twenty-four hours of coma, this dose can be modified later in accordance with the ability of the patient to take other forms of nourishment. With such prompt and adequate treatment, however, most cases of prolonged coma will be resuscitated successfully within the first twenty-four hours.

2. Thiamine chloride and other vitamins, particularly convenient in the form of ampules of Lyo-B-C (Sharp and Dohme), should be added to the infusion fluid in order to supply enzyme systems (particularly cocarboxylase which is diphosphothiamine) necessary for the oxidation and utilization of sugar by the central nervous system.

3. The patient should be placed in an oxygen tent to facilitate oxygen supply to the central nervous system, and to ease respiration, thus preventing exhausting hyperkapnia and its complication, hyperventilation tetany.

4. As soon as the patient has been resuscitated from the deepest (medullary) level of coma (during resuscitation the patient passes through the successive phases of coma in reverse order), he should be kept warm with the aid of heating pads or warm water bottles to guard against vascular collapse.

5. If signs of tetany, usually due to hyperventilation, develop, 30 cc. of 10 per cent calcium chloride should be added to the infusion fluid or should be injected independently.

6. Respiratory or circulatory stimulants may be added if and when the condition of the patient requires them.

Additional measures recommended are[3]: blood transfusions, using about 500 cc. of citrated blood; 3 to 10 cc. of adrenal cortical extract administered intravenously, or 200 mg. of cortisone in four divided doses intramuscularly.

In cases of severe respiratory embarrassment, tracheotomy should be decided upon as promptly as possible, so that it may be performed electively, rather than as an emergency procedure later, when the patient's general condition may have worsened.

PREVENTION AND TREATMENT OF DELAYED COMA

After resuscitation from therapeutic coma, the patient should be observed carefully throughout the remainder of the day and the subsequent night. Secondary comas should be prevented as much as possible, first, by administration of adequate amounts of glucose at termination of the original coma; second, by prompt diagnosis and treatment of secondary hypoglycemic reactions as soon as they appear and before they deepen into secondary coma. This is particularly important at night, when secondary comas may be easily overlooked unless the patients are awakened every three hours. At these awakenings they should be given small amounts of glucose (100 Gm. in orange juice) by mouth. These should be increased whenever the patients are found to be perspiring or unusually difficult to arouse.

TECHNIQUE OF ELECTROSHOCK THERAPY

Little needs to be added to well known techniques of electroshock therapy, as described by others and myself in the 1950's.[3,6,7] It should be emphasized that the use of Succinyl Choline Chloride (Anectine) is now accepted as a necessary protective premedication to soften the seizure to minimal proportions, thereby eliminating danger to the musculo-skeletal system and those dangers to the heart which are based on convulsive closure of the glottis and the resulting Valsalva phenomenon. This premedication is also necessary when the treatment is given at the height of insulin coma; however, anesthesia by sodium pentothal or brevital is not necessary at this time. Whenever electroshock therapy is given other than at the height of insulin coma, the paralyzing injection of Anectine should always be preceded by adequate anesthesia with sodium pentothal or brevital intravenously. I believe that most psychiatrists are well advised to administer the treatment in collaboration with an anesthesiologist, or a well trained nurse-anesthetist, unless they themselves have been trained in all the technics of anesthesiology.[5]

HORMONE TREATMENT OF SUBSTITUTIVE OR CORRECTIVE TYPE

Endocrine stigmata and borderline endocrine abnormalities are not uncommon in schizophrenic patients. Bleuler, Kind, and their co-workers[10,31] have carried out an extensive clinical and statistical study of their incidence and their relationship to prognosis. They found, surprisingly, that schizophrenics with acromegaloid bodily changes showed a more favorable clinical course, with more recoveries and less deterioration than schizophrenic patients not so stigmatized. By contrast, schizophrenic patients with adipose dysplasia showed a severer progressive course and fewer recoveries. Kind[31] concluded that these endocrine abnormalities, although not etiologically related to schizophrenia, exerted an illness-shaping or pathoplastic effect. Schizophrenic patients stigmatized by infantalism did not differ in their clinical course from the average. He and Bleuler considered infantalism to be a psychosomatic effect, secondary to the mental illness transmitted through hypothalamic mechanisms. Reiss,[41] who studied the problem of psychoendocrinology by means of modern laboratory methods, felt that if rational endocrinologic treatment were to be developed, it would have to be guided by highly individualized clinical and laboratory investigations, since there was no direct or specific relationship of any clinical psychiatric picture with any specific endocrine abnormalities. His opinion was that endocrine imbalance merely contributed a nonspecific impairment of a patient's adaptability to stress, thus facilitating the mental breakdown to which his personality was predisposed.

A persistent endocrine abnormality, such as primary hypothyroidism, may not only be a predisposing factor, but may also prevent response to treatment and recovery, even if it does not appear to be severe by clinical or laboratory standards. If the hypothyroidism is of a secondary nature, due to reduction of thyrotropic hormone, electroshock or insulin coma may relieve it without specific hormone therapy because of the stimulation to the hypothalamo-pituitary system incidental to these treatments. Primary hypothyroidism, however, is not affected by these treatments. In 1953 I reported such a case. The patient was a 52-year-old female suffering from a severe schizophreni-form psychosis[3] with paranoid and catatonic features, who manifested clinical signs of myxedema, although the laboratory findings were only borderline abnormal. Electroshock treatment failed to produce sustained results, not followed by early relapse until thyroid medication was added to her therapeutic regimen, after which her recovery became sustained. I concluded that although thyroid deficiency could not be regarded as a direct single cause of a schizophreni-form psychosis of this kind, there was nevertheless suggestive evidence that it may have been a predisposing and recovery-preventing factor.

There is, however, one condition in the field of schizophrenic psychoses—that of periodic catatonia (Gjessing's disease), in which a direct relationship of the psychosis with hypothyroidism has been established. Gornall et al.[25] confirmed this relationship in a well controlled clinical and laboratory study of 5 cases of this rather rare condition. These authors found treatment with high doses of thyroid extract, as well as with Triiodothyronine to be effective. Although these authors also found abnormalities in adrenocortical functioning, they regarded them as secondary. The authors favored the hypothesis that the underlying defect in these patients is probably metabolic and that the endogenous effort to effect a compensation can be assisted by raising the metabolic level with thyroid hormone.

In puerperal psychoses, most of which are schizophrenic or schizo-affective in type, the relationship of the psychosis to endocrine abnormalities appears to be more complex. The significantly beneficial effect of progesterone, first established by Blumberg and Billig,[11] was confirmed by Bauer and Altschule,[12] and most recently by Tucker.[43] Tucker accomplished his results with intramuscular injections of Delalutin, 125 mg. once weekly, to be reduced gradually as improvement supervened. Hamilton,[26] in his important study of postpartum psychoses, established a similar effect for thyroid and emphasized the likelihood of the equally-important role of the adrenal cortex. He called attention to the study of Jacobides,[30] who demonstrated that measurement of the adrenal steroids, especially of the 17-hydroxycorticoids, showed a great scattering of values. This observation is identical with findings which we have obtained in ACTH-induced psychoses.[4] We demonstrated by means of daily determinations of 17-hydroxycorticoid excretion levels, under high ACTH dosage, that marked day-to-day variations in 17-hydroxycorticoid output (averaging 44.9 mg. per 24 hours) characterized the patients who became psychotic in the course of ACTH therapy, while the day-to-day differences in output averaged only 15.1 mg. per 24 hours in patients treated with identical ACTH dosage who remained mentally well under ACTH therapy. We found that the ACTH-induced psychoses responded well to treatment with Cortisone or a Cortisone equivalent drug. This treatment reversed the psychotic episodes within 6 to 16 days, in spite of continuation of ACTH therapy in 7 of 9 patients. In only two of the patients with manic symptoms did ACTH have to be discontinued. The erratic day-to-day variation of adrenocortical output in our patients with ACTH-induced psychosis was regarded as being due to relative adrenal exhaustion.

In view of these findings and their concordance with the findings of Jacobides and Hamilton, I decided to treat two patients suffering from treatment-resistant puerperal psychoses in the manner patterned after our treatment of the ACTH-induced psychoses.[2] The first of these patients had failed with electroshock treatment, psychotherapy, Delalutin (125 Mg. once weekly), and a variety of psychotropic drugs, administered in the course of 13 months, during which she had remained unremittingly ill. When a Cortisone equivalent drug (Dexamethasone, 0.75 mg. 4 times daily) was added to her medicinal regimen, there was striking and marked improvement within two days, social recovery 24 days later. The dose of Dexamethasone was reduced gradually as improvement supervened, and discontinued after five months. ACTH (40 units once weekly) which had been administered concurrently, to prevent inhibition of adrenal cortex, was discontinued at the same time. In the second similar patient, who had been ill two and one-half years, in spite of a total of 40 electroshock treatments administered during that period, in addition to psychotherapy and psychotropic drugs, marked improvement supervened within three days, social recovery within two weeks. I also treated in a similar manner two patients suffering from chronic depressive reaction (one a male, the other a female), in whom clinical and laboratory findings suggested stress-induced adrenal disturbance. A 29-year-old male patient suffering from a chronic schizophrenic reaction of paranoid type responded strikingly to the same treatment. In his case, indication for this treatment was not merely that he had not responded to any other treatment for the past six years, but the unusual fact that he was also suffering severely from atopic eczematous dermatitis, and had been suffering from asthma as well. Within six days of initiation of treatment with dexamathasone, combined with one weekly intramuscular injection of 40 units of ACTH, he showed marked improvement of his paranoid psychosis and his skin had improved greatly. Within two weeks the patient appeared clinically recovered from mental illness and his skin was practically clear. One month after initiation of therapy the patient returned to full time work, and within four months he returned to college. Ten months after steroid treatment had been initiated, he continued to be well on a small maintenance dosage of dexamathasone, and was referred back to the psychotherapist who had referred him to me.

This case is of interest in view of Heath's recent suggestion of an allergic sensitization of certain brain areas to abnormal proteins as an etiologic factor in schizophrenia.[27]

TREATMENT WITH NICOTINIC ACID AND NICOTINAMIDE ADENINE DINUCLEOTIDE

This treatment has been advocated by Hoffer and his collaborators,[28] but conclusive data as to efficacy are not yet available.

FRONTAL LOBOTOMY

Frontal lobotomy may produce recoveries of high quality in severely and chronically-ill patients after all other treatments applied over many years have failed. In its capacity to produce such recoveries against these great odds, it still ranks high in our therapeutic armamentarium in spite of recent animadversions. The physician who sees such recoveries take place in patients whom rightfully he would have to consider incurable by all other measures, can appreciate why frontal lobotomy is one of only two therapeutic measures in psychiatry which received the Nobel Prize (the other having been given to Wagner-Jauregg for his malaria treatment of paresis.) An important fact often lost sight of is that full recovery without personality defect is obtainable, although not predictable.

The method of choice, in all except the most severe cases, is to perform a minimal operation at first and to increase its extent by means of a second or third reoperation if necessary. Freeman[22] in his 20-year survey, published ten years ago, pointed out that sustained high level performance was possible after a major frontal lobotomy. This was more frequently obtained after less radical operations, an experience consistent with the experience of Poppen, and Greenblatt and their co-workers[38] after bimedial lobotomy. Freeman[22] gives specific figures for complete and/or social recovery (employed or keeping house). This grade of recovery was achieved by a major frontal lobotomy in 40 per cent of schizophrenic patients operated on, in 60 per cent of involutional depressions, and in 65 per cent of psychoneurotics. For transorbital lobotomy, the figures are: 60 per cent for schizophrenics, 75 per cent for involutional depressives, and 80 per cent for psychoneurotics.

Harry Freeman[21] reanalyzed the combined treatment results of Greenblatt-Arnot-Solomon, Freeman-Watts, Walker and the Great Britain Board of Control, and reported a complete and/or social recovery rate of 18 per cent of 1211 lobotomized patients. If we consider that these lobotomies were performed exclusively on the residuum of chronically-ill patients who had failed to respond to any other form of treatment—a patient material, so well described as the chronic failures of psychiatric treatment[36]—this treatment result is impressive. It is important to realize that for a comparable patient material treated with the new psychotropic drugs the complete and/or social recovery rate is only 5 per cent.[8] Frontal lobotomy, therefore, should continue to be regarded as a very effective treatment for patients of this type; that is, as a treatment that may bring about recoveries of a surprisingly high quality after all other treatments, including treatment with the new psychotropic drugs, have failed.

A further advantage of the operation in such chronic cases is that the successfully lobotomized patient may become truly free and able to regulate his own life, a state which the patient on maintenance drug therapy can never achieve, even with the best possible results obtainable by this method, since the patient has to be motivated to continue drug therapy, and the dosage required has to be continually readjusted to meet the demands of the patient's still fluctuating condition.

The disadvantages of lobotomy are the limitation of predictability—common to all treatments—combined with relative irreversibility of the result. The decision to operate therefore requires great courage on the part of the physician, the patient, and his relatives. There must also be an objective knowledge allowing some prediction of possible results on the part of the physician.

The basic therapeutic process by means of which the operation achieves its results is probably similar to that of the shock therapies, namely, reduction in excitability of the higher cortical substrates of the ego. While in the shock therapies this is accomplished by a temporary extinction process which imposes a new "set" upon the nervous activity, probably akin to a learning or training process, lobotomy achieves this reduction in excitability by the actual reduction in the number of neuronal circuits that connect the higher (cortical) and intermediate (diencephalic) centers. The reduction in excitability resulting from the operation may be excessive if the mental disturbance to be relieved were not actually maximal, i.e., not inaccessible to sustained relief by any measures short of the operation. The only objective test capable of ascertaining the fact that the illness is actually of such maximal degree, is that of subjecting the patient to all other treatments offering a reasonable chance to relieve his illness before recommending the operation. Once this fact is ascertained beyond all reasonable doubt, the physician need not hesitate to recommend lobotomy. In planning the extent of the operation, however, he should consider carefully all other quantitative aspects of the disturbance that previous therapeutic experiences with the patient have revealed.

INTEGRATION OF PHYSICAL TREATMENT WITH PSYCHOTHERAPY

A sufficiency of effective physical treatment, irrespective of the modality used, makes two main contributions to the processes and the attainment of the goals of psychotherapy:[1]

1. It shifts sharply the focus of interest of the patient from the past or the remote future to the present, the "here and now." Refocusing of the patient's interest from the past to the present is the first crucial step or intermediate goal of psychotherapy which enables the patient to respond to the challenges of the present and to resume current adaptive tasks.

2. It restores the primacy of the drive for happiness, pleasure and gratification, i.e., the life instinct operating through the pleasure and reality principles over the competing and interfering destructive drives.

These gains will have to be furthered and made meaningful to the patient by concurrent and subsequent psychotherapy. In schizophrenic patients this psychotherapy should be both supportive and interpretive. It should be so designed as to aid the patient in reality testing and in improving his interpersonal relationships. This improvement may first appear in his relationship to the therapist, and then generalize to his relations with other persons in his environment. In psychotherapy with schizophrenic patients, I have come to regard a strong transference as unnecessary and undesirable because it tends to foster infantile dependency; I prefer to bring about identification with the therapist.

APPENDIX

As a practical demonstration of the unfolding process of recovery, as it proceeds through the *interacting effects* of physical and psychologic treatment, I should like to append the case report of a typical favorably responsive patient:

Case Report

This patient was a petite, attractive, and personable 30-year-old single female, who was referred by a fellow psychiatrist because her chronic schizo-affective reaction, perhaps best described as pseudoneurotic schizophrenia with hysterical and paranoid trends, had not yielded to nine years of psychoanalytically oriented psychotherapy in his hands. During these years she had to be hospitalized in a mental hospital five times for periods of 2 to 40 days for varying degrees of panic reaction with the diagnoses of personality disorder or anxiety reaction.

Her father was an educated and accomplished, energetic, hard-working, dapper and sociable man of small stature and a violent temper who, in the circle of family and close associates, liked to spice his verbal communications with vulgar and obscene expressions and allusions, which were in distinct contrast to his otherwise elegant and impeccable manner. The patient was obviously identified with her father in this regard because she occasionally lapsed into violent and vulgar language, which contrasted with her otherwise dainty and demure demeanor. Her mother was a solid, down-to-earth, but somewhat remote and cheerless person who, while attending to her children's needs to the point of overprotectiveness, tended to delegate a great deal of their management to others, thus reducing areas of close contact and relationship. Her only brother, nine years her senior, went overseas on Army service during World War II, when she became ten years old, and on return was married and moved to the Middle West. The patient believed that she never had a real relationship with her brother; in childhood she admired and adored him, while he, in her opinion, considered her "just a brat." She first disliked—later pitied—his "domineering, demanding, and efficient type of wife," who soon became chronically ill from a collagen disease. However, she related very well to and was very much liked by her brother's three young children.

Her school and work history was characterized by many interruptions and changes. She worked for a time as a nursery school teacher, subsequently as an airlines stewardess before completing high school. She attended three different colleges for short periods, in the intervals working as physical education instructor and general biology teacher in a girls' school, and as a day camp counselor. At the time of her referral to me she was again in college studying toward a degree in physical education.

The patient's chief complaint at intake was that she was "terribly frightened" and continuously obsessed with the fear of death, to the point of being afraid of falling asleep at night for fear of dying in her sleep.

Her psychiatrist wrote in his letter of referral: "Perhaps one of the outstanding difficulties has been her difficulty in maintaining any adequate or satisfactory relationship with people in general or with me in particular. Her relationship generally has been superficial, with a strong tendency to be based on dependency. She has verbalized many times over the years her feelings of hostility toward both parents, perhaps more intentionally directed at her mother, who she feels has been rather overpowering, domineering and unaffectionate. Her hostility toward her father appears to be based on her fear of him sexually and she relates perhaps as a fantasy a recollection of his alleged sexual play with her before she was six or seven."

"She has had a strong "homosexual" type of relationship with an older woman who has been a friend and neighbor. It perhaps typifies her in that discussing going to you she says, "I guess I am afraid of you. You know too much about me. You're like God.—I liked another psychiatrist whom I saw briefly at one time because he was friendly, like a high school kid. I guess I am just afraid of anyone or could be—of course you know I am going to be afraid of Dr. Alexander too."

In her subsequent sessions with me she remained totally preoccupied with the many emotional injuries inflicted upon her in the past, to which she ascribed her plight. She related with a great deal of violent emotion, "what happened between my father and me—he wanted to kill me when I was nine years old. I ran out of the house and he landed on top of me with a razor blade." She called him murderer for some time after this episode and had many angry, screaming altercations with him; but at the same time she began to initiate masturbation with the fantasy that her father was forcing her to have sexual intercourse with him, a fantasy that still plagues her: "I feel guilty and I hate it and I'm hostile." During her adolescence the patient experienced several crushes on women to whom she attached herself. These women usually were of the self-assured, independent, outdoorish type. In her fantasies she longed to be hugged by these women like a baby, wanting them to be her mother. When actual homosexual involvement threatened, the patient usually became frightened and broke off further contact. She reacted in the same way whenever she became attracted to a man. At age 19, however, she had become involved with a homosexual woman, who succeeded in inducing the patient to participate in sexual acts. During two years of this relationship, guilt and panic erupted with increasing intensity, which made her terminate this relationship. She would have preferred to continue to play the part of a baby, being hugged and petted only. This preference is characteristic of the type of female homosexuality which is based on persistence of the archaic primary fixation on the mother.[20] It may be more appropriately termed pseudohomosexuality, since sexuality in its full meaning is absent and in fact vigorously defended against. She then became friendly with a clergyman whom she had contacted for instruction preparatory to conversion to his faith. She spent a great deal of time with him for about five months. When she finally managed, by her coy, hysterical affection-demanding ways, to seduce him to make what she considered a sexual approach, she recoiled in horror and rejected him with venomous hatred. She relived this episode, which had occurred more than nine years previously, and her reaction to it with violently vivid emotion, exclaiming, "I hate his guts and hope he goes to hell for it." It was then that she had sought psychiatric treatment, in her opinion, to no avail.

Thinking tests revealed distortions in terms of her paranoid sensitivities. For instance, she explained the proverb, "A rolling stone gathers no moss" as meaning "If you don't stay in a place long enough you won't gather any enemies—keep moving, always on the run." Neurologic examination revealed psychomotor tension with difficulty in relaxing muscles on the examination table and minimal intentional tremor with goal-directed movements. The patient was admitted to Bournewood Hospital.

As it had during the preceding nine years of psychotherapy with my colleague, the focus of her attention remained rigidly fixed on the past and the experiences of emotional suffering it had entailed, although the most recent of these had occurred nine years ago. In view of the fixed rigidity of her emotions, attitudes, and projections, which became evident to me during the next five days, I became convinced that the results of further psychotherapy, unaided by physical treatment measures, would not differ from those of the past nine years.

I decided to administer Insulin coma therapy, reinforced by an electroconvulsive treatment after every third to fifth coma, beginning after the sixth coma. Psychotherapy was continued to be administered daily throughout the first 20 days of subcoma treatment, during which the dose of Insulin was gradually increased, after beginning with ten units. The first coma was obtained at the dose of 475 units on the twenty-first treatment day, but the coma dose had to be raised to 575 units daily to obtain consistent midbrain comas, was stabilized at 550 units from the seventh coma on, until it could be gradually reduced from the thirty-third coma on, to a final dose of 350 units from the fortieth to the sixtieth coma. A total of twenty-three convulsive electroshock treatments was administered, each one given at the height of the coma chosen, throughout the coma series. Psychotherapy sessions were held once or twice weekly during this phase of the physical treatment period, apart from the daily brief supportive and reassuring contacts on awakening from coma.

Throughout the physical treatment period, which lasted three months, her orientation toward the past remained unaltered, although there was gradual diminution of overt anxiety and distress. After her twelfth coma and fourth electroshock she appeared smiling and animated, but on question how she felt, she stated that she was miserable, unhappy, and bored: "There was nothing the matter with me in the beginning, except the miserable things I had been through, which cannot be changed—so why should I be any better?" When she was told that there must have been something she complained of, otherwise she would not have come for treatment, she replied: "I was frightened." When she was asked whether she was still frightened now, she answered, "No".

After her nineteenth coma and sixth electroconvulsive treatment, she was cheerful and reported delightedly that she no longer felt sick, that she slept like a rock, and was free from palpitations. When she was asked about her fears, she replied: "I will always be frightened. I'll bet I could go home tonight and be scared to death. . . ."

Two days after completion of the physical treatment series (sixty deep

Insulin comas, twenty-three electroconvulsive treatments), the patient for the first time felt free from her anxiety: "I am not frightened any more. You remember how frightened I used to be? I sleep like a rock now! Beautifully! I hope it continues—I am not frightened any more!"

Two weeks later, however, she wondered whether this happy state could last, and expressed apprehension about how things would go at home. Nineteen days after the completion of the physical treatment series she made her first attempt to cope with the adaptive tasks of living in terms of the present and the immediate future. After a weekend visit at home she stated that her task would be to control overwhelming inner feelings and to disclose them to the therapist rather than just hiding them, as she had done before. "But I'm afraid you won't continue to be as nice—because I like you, and because I feel you are a warm person—coldness is not good for me—I can be very warm and affectionate with children but I can't with adults—I just don't know. . . ." In reporting about her visit at home she referred in passing to her father, stating: "My father irks the holy hell out of me," but she no longer referred to the past.

One month after completion of the physical treatment series, she reported that she had been seeing many of her old friends, "All married—not an old maid like I am." Two weeks later she was animated, cheerful, and during her session exhibited a good sense of humor. At the end of the session she stated: "You can be quite proud of me that I did not go into hysterics when I realized I had been drinking too much this weekend, but decided simply to do something about it." Her mother reported that she no longer talked about death or the fear of death, and had even offered to donate blood for a neighbor who required transfusions after an operation, which her mother was sure she never would have offered before.

Forty-nine days post-treatment the patient stated she felt "wonderful" and that she had decided to go home and to go to work. She had found a job as a physical education instructor at a girls' camp. Three days later she came to the psychotherapy session in a somewhat flippant mood. She criticized the doctor for talking in an encouraging manner, since he probably gave everybody the same "bull." (She had become jealous of a fellow patient who had just completed the same course of treatment.) She also had found out that the doctor smoked cigars and she was surprised that he needed "pacifiers." She then told the therapist that what she really wanted was to hug him and to sit on his lap, but she knew that she had to resign herself to regard music and a bottle as the only relaxation available to her. She then told him that her mother had caught her masturbating at age eight, and told her that she would definitely go out of her mind as a consequence. Her mother then delegated the job of watching her to her brother so that she would not masturbate. The patient then corrected her previous version of her father's "sexual play" with her at age six or seven. She emphatically denied that it was intended as sex play on his part. She stated that in playing with her he merely caressed her on her stomach . . . "An immature need for contact . . . I knew it was wrong . . . all the women in my family are bosses, the men the pacifiers. . . ."

Three days later, on her fifty-fifth post-treatment day, the patient was discharged from the hospital. A week later she reported she felt "great." She was teaching full time at the girls' camp, was free from anxieties, slept well, because—she believed—the work made her wholesomely tired. She also enjoyed reading again, and read a great deal. "I do very well . . . extremely well." She thought that the only thing that might upset her present happy state was drinking, and she had decided not to drink.

It appeared that the patient's orientation, sixty-three days post-treatment, had swung effectively to the present and its adaptive challenges, and that after the long reign of the hostile drives manifested by hatred and panic the primacy of the pleasure and reality principles had reasserted itself. Not only had she achieved a measure of happiness, but she also understood and appreciated it and set out to do everything she could to render it lasting within the framework of the existing external and internal realities.

By the seventy-fifth post-treatment day she had remained cheerful and was working full time. She made a point then of correcting another misconception of the past, namely, what she now knew to be the real version of what she called the most traumatic incident in the long history of constant friction between her and her father which had occurred at age nine and which had led her ever since to ascribe actual murderous intent to him, until her recent recovery, and which had plagued her and had rendered her furious and hostile for so many years. She recalled that on this particular occasion her parents were entertaining friends at home, drinking moderately. When the patient came to regret the company her father asked her to give everyone a kiss. She refused, whereupon her father became angry. The patient then ran away outdoors and around the neighborhood, her father in pursuit. As her father caught her, she fell to the ground and her father landed on top of her. She got up and ran into the house screaming: "He tried to kill me with a razor blade." Actually, he had no razor blade, and she believes now that he probably had no more aggressive intent than to spank her. However, after she came back to the house, the only reproach the father made was to say, "Do you realize how embarrassed I am because of what you did tonight? Go right down there and apologize." She emphasizes that, in actuality, her father never made any sexual approach to her. However, she remembers going through his drawers at age ten or eleven and finding a nudist magazine and some pornographic drawings, made by an artist friend who had given them to her father as a present.

Two weeks later, three months after the completion of the physical treatment series, patient stated that she was more logical, more rational, and not as frightened; but that she had again begun to feel miserable and full of hatred. She struggled with these feelings over the next three weeks, during which she applied for various jobs while continuing to work effectively at the summer camp. At the end of this period, 109 days post-treatment, she stated: "I have myself under good to excellent control", but was still bothered by feelings of hostility toward her parents. However, she referred to present annoyances of living with them and no longer to the past. A week later she received two excellent job offers in reply to her applications and accepted a position as recreational therapist in an outstanding rehabilitation centre. She planned to continue to live at home for a time, although she believed she had very little in common with her parents, but hoped to find a place of her own with opportunities for social contacts with contemporaries. During this period of planning she had an argument with her mother, in the course of which the patient struck her mother, then sobbed disconsolately, scratching her chest with her nails. She was still stricken with remorse during an interview two weeks later. The incident was worked through with her and remained the last open outburst of hostility against her parents. Three weeks later she was doing well, working full time and enjoying her work. She was also going to night classes at a college working toward a B.S. degree.

During the ensuing two months she remained reality-oriented, calm, cheerful, and her employers considered her work excellent. Six months post-treatment she reported that she no longer harbored feelings of hatred, even against people she does not like. Eight months post-treatment she continued to do fine work and found herself appreciated. Friends told her that she had become "much more lovable and spontaneous." She also related with some pride that fellow workers had approached her for advice in personal problems, and she felt she has been able to be helpful. It appears that the patient had achieved a good level of unselfconscious functioning. But during her next interview she criticized the therapist, in quite an aggressive and hostile manner, for not insisting that the fellow patient of whom she had been jealous during her period of hospitalization go to work also. Her approval-seeking behavior was worked through with her. A month later the patient dropped in for an unscheduled interview to tell the therapist that she had succeeded in remaining abstinent and that alcohol was no longer a problem for her, adding "I still want to get soused but I have too much to lose." She was working full time and enjoying it.

It became increasingly clear from the topic of her interests that she was no longer trying to undo the past but was intent on building a happy present and future. Two weeks later she reported an interesting discovery, namely, that she could still "play-act the hostile nasty little brat," but no longer felt like it. When the therapist made a note of this she remarked jocularly "don't write it down because in five minutes I'll probably kill you." She added that she also would like to get drunk right here, drink and talk, but won't do it because no one likes a drunk.

Eleven months post-treatment she reported increasing congeniality between her and her parents. A week later, however, there began a sensitive-paranoid reaction against a superior at work, in whom she soon insightfully recognized many traits similar to her own. This was worked through with her during the next seven months. Throughout most of this time she continued to work most efficiently. She achieved tenure sixteen months post-treatment and her work was praised in the monthly publication of the center. There was a time, however, when her control seemed to break down. Seventeen months post-treatment she became quite tense, began drinking again to excess, was arrested for driving under the influence, and lost her license. Her reaction to this distressing episode illustrated the full measure of the recovery of her capacity to rise to the adaptive challenges of the day. She recognized and concluded that she was a periodic drinker, realized "alcohol has given me nothing but trouble, and the best alcohol has ever done for me was two hours of relaxation." She stated that this realization has given her a great deal of emotional security. She consulted the head of a committee on education on alcoholism and joined Alcoholics Anonymous two weeks later, one and one-half years after completion of the physical treatment series. She has remained totally abstinent since that time, except for one brief lapse on a Saturday night four months later.

Within the next two weeks she achieved insight into the paranoid projections against the supervisor, which the therapist had been working through with her throughout the preceding seven months. Throughout all of these sessions the therapist had taken an uncompromising stand, refusing to accept any of her projections as reality, refusing in any way to sympathize with her, and taking the stand that what a supervisor does is his privilege and problem, while it is the duty of the subordinate to accept criticism gracefully and to comply. The patient had stubbornly resisted the realization that her problems with her supervisor were due entirely to her own projections, getting angry whenever the therapist confronted her with the evidence and the weight of his uncompromising opinion. Her first acceptance came from the restored core of her self interest, powered by her renewed allegiance to the pleasure and reality principles. She conceded: "I got a lot at stake, so I might as well get back in her good graces." When her hostility and tendency to project were thus dampened, she was able to report, "I don't feel anything toward her now." Finally, she accepted the therapist's interpretation with good grace: "I thought you did not understand—but you did." There was one last flurry of paranoid reactivity two months later, 20 and a half months post-treatment, when she thought that a patient whom she had seen in the waiting room was a social worker from the hospital who knew something about her case. When this was worked through with her, she instantly abandoned this brief upwelling of delusion formation, explaining that she always used to get upset and paranoid before her period. This was the last manifestation of mental disease in this patient. From the twenty-second month post-treatment this patient has remained entirely well and what problems she continued to discuss with me were those of any normal sensitive and hardworking person intent on performing a difficult job that involved diligent and tactful management of interpersonal relationships well and efficiently. Fifty-four psychotherapeutic sessions had been held during the period of twenty-six months post-treatment. Twenty-seven months post-treatment she commented: "I have to be mature, kind, and helpful all day long—I am probably not mature enough because I am still bothered occasionally, but yet I'm doing a darn good job." She was quite proud that her supervisor, by whom she had felt discriminated, was now drinking heavily and she was not; that the supervisor was still sadistic which, I had told the patient before, was the supervisor's problem, and not hers, and that she, the patient, was no longer either sadistic or masochistic. She no longer believed she was homosexual, and she wondered whether she could fall in love and be happy. She had become attracted to a man whom she had met at Alcoholics Anonymous, but she was reality-oriented enough to realize that a man with such a problem could not give her happiness. She had noticed that attendance at Alcoholics Anonymous had made it possible for her to talk more honestly and freely also to the therapist. She stated that sometimes she still feels lonely and rejected but it passes quickly. At no time since the clarification of her past projections against her father two years previously, on the seventy-fifth post-treatment day, did she ever refer to the emotional injuries and hatreds of her past life which had preoccupied her for nine years prior to the institution of physical treatment, namely, Insulin Coma and electroshock therapy. When she was asked specifically two years after completion of the physical treatment series, what had happened with her former preoccupation with the past and her hatreds, she answered: "Since the insulin treatment, I find myself living much more in the present than in the past, than I had before—and if I find myself drifting back into the past, I find myself less anxiety-and-guilt ridden, less frightened; there's no more hyperventilation—even if I try to think of the past and try to recapture the hatred and anger, I cannot do it."

BIBLIOGRAPHY

1. Alexander, L.: Contribution of physical treatment to the processes and goals of psychotherapy. Am. J. Psychiat., 123: 87-91 (July), 1966.

2. Alexander, L.: Steroids in the treatment of chronic mental disorders. Read at the Annual Meeting of The American Society of Medical Psychiatry, Atlantic City, N.J., June 18, 1967.

3. Alexander, L.: Treatment of Mental Disorder. Philadelphia and London, W. B. Saunders, i-xi, 1-507, 1953.

4. Alexander, L., Cass, L. J., Frederik, W. S., and Ireland, P.: ACTH-induced psychoses in the light of daily determinations of 17-hydroxycorticoid excretion levels under high ACTH dosage. In Recent Advances in Biological Psychiatry. (Wortis, J., Ed.). New York, Plenum Press, VI: 242-255, 1964.

5. Alexander, L., Gilbert, I. E., and White, S. E.: Function of the anesthetist in electroshock therapy. Dis. Nerv. Syst. Monograph Supplement 19(2): 41-43 (July), 1958.

6. Alexander, L., Gilbert, I. E., and White, S. E.: Succinylcholine Chloride and Thiopental preparatory to electroconvulsive therapy. Dis. Nerv. Syst., Monograph Supplement 19(2): 72-73 (July), 1958.

7. Alexander, L., Gilbert, I. E., and White, S. E.: Unidirectional electroshock relaxed by succinylcholine chloride. Confinia Neurologica 13: 324-332, 1953.

8. Alexander, L., and Moore, H.: Multiple approaches to treatment in schizophrenia and discussion of indications. Am. J. Psychiat. 114: 577-582 (Jan.), 1958.

9. Bennett, I. F.: Changing concepts in insulin coma therapy. In Biological Treatment of Mental Illness (Rinkel, M., Ed.). New York, Farrar, Straus and Giroux, pp. 782-792, 1966.

10. Bleuler, M.: Endokrinologische Psychiatrie. Stuttgart, G. Thieme, 1954.

11. Blumberg, A., and Billig, O.: Hormonal influence upon "puerperal psychosis" and neurotic conditions. Psychiat. Quart. 16: 454-462, 1942.

12. Bower, W. H., and Altschule, M. D.: Use of progesterone in the treatment of post-partum psychoses. New England J. Med. 524: 157-160 (Jan.), 1956.

13. Braun, M., and Parker, M.: The use of Glucagon in the termination of therapeutic insulin coma. Am. J. Psychiat. 115: 814, 1959.

14. Brill, H., and Patton, R.: Clinical statistical analysis of population changes in New York State since the introduction of psychotropic drugs. Am. J. Psychiat. 119: 1 (July), 1962.

15. Delay, J., Deniker, P., and Harl, J. M.: Utilisation en therapeutique psychiatrique d'un phénothiazine d'action centrale élective (4560 RP). Medico-Psychol. Paris, 110-2: 112-117 (June), 1952.

16. Dunlop, E.: Concomitant use of insulin therapy and pharmacology. In Biological Treatment of Mental Illness (Rinkel, M., Ed.). New York, Farrar, Straus, and Giroux, pp. 800-807, 1966.

17. Dussik, K. T., Giddon, D. B., Watson, P. D., and White, J. J.: Increased control of insulin coma by prior administration of Glucagon: A preliminary communication. Am. J. Psychiat. 118: 66-69 (July), 1961.

18. Dussik, K. T., Greaney, J. F., Grunberg, E., and Schneller, P.: Serial Glucagon tests in schizophrenics. In Biological Treatment of Mental Illness (Rinkel, M., Ed.). New York, Farrar, Straus, and Giroux, pp. 715-730, 1966.

19. Ehrhardt, H.: Present status of insulin coma and electric convulsive treatment in Germany. In Biological Treatment of Mental Illness (Rinkel, M., Ed.). New York, Farrar, Straus, and Giroux, pp. 837, 847, 1966.

20. Fenichel, O.: The Psychoanalytic Theory of Neurosis. New York (W. W. Norton), ix, 1-703, 1945.

21. Freeman, H.: A critique of the tranquilizing drugs, chlorpromazine and reserpine, in neuropsychiatry. New England J. Med. 255: 877-883, 1956.

22. Freeman, W.: Frontal lobotomy 1936-1956. A follow-up study of 3000

patients from one to twenty years. Am. J. Psychiat. 113: 877-866, 1957.

23. Gellhorn, E.: Principles of Auto-nomic-Somatic Integrations: Physiological Basis and Psychological and Clinical Implications. Minneapolis, Univ. of Minneapolis Press, i-xiii, 1-318, 1967.

24. Gellhorn, E., and Loofbourrow, G. N.: Emotions and Emotional Disorders: A Neurophysiological Study. New York, Harper & Row, Hoeber Medical Div., i-xii, 1-496, 1963.

25. Cornall, A. G., Eglitis, B., and Stokes, A. B.: Endocrine studies and hormonal effects in periodic catatonia. In Psychoendocrinology (Reiss, M., Ed.). New York and London, Grune & Stratton, pp. 152-167, 1958.

26. Hamilton, J. A.: Postpartum Psychiatric Problems. Saint Louis, C. V. Mosby, 1-156, 1962.

27. Heath, R. G.: Antibrain-Antibody (Taraxein) in acute schizophrenic patients. Read at the 123rd Annual Meeting of the American Psychiatric Association, Detroit, Michigan, May 11, 1967.

28. Hoffer, A., Osmond, H., Callbeck, M. J., and Kahan, I.: Treatment of schizophrenia with nicotinic acid and nictoinamide. J. Clin. Exptl. Psychopath. 18: 131, 1957. (See also New York Times, March 31, 1966.)

29. Holt, W. L., Jr., Landau, D., and Vernon, T.: Insulin coma treatment of schizophrenia. J. Nerv. & Ment. Dis. 112: 375-383, 1950.

30. Jacobides, G. M.: Adrenocortical Function in Puerperal Psychoses. Athens, University of Athens thesis, 1961.

31. Kind, H.: Investigations on endocrine stigmatized schizophrenics and their families. In Psychoendocrinology (Reiss, M., Ed.). New York and London, Grune & Stratton, 120-128, 1958.

32. Laborit, H., Huguenard, P., and Alluaume, R.: Un nouveau stabilisateur végétatif; le 4560 RP. Presse méd. 60: 206-208 (Feb.), 1952.

33. Laqueur, H. P., Dussik, K. T., La-Burt, H. A., and McLaughlin, W. F.: Tactical and strategical considerations in the use of insulin therapy: a joint study of two mental hospitals. In Biological Treatment of Mental Illness (Rinkel, M., Ed). New York, Farrar, Straus and Giroux, 731-767, 1966.

34. Laqueur, H. P., and LaBurt, H. A.: Use of Glucagon in insulin coma therapy. Dis. Nerv. Syst. 22(4) Suppl.: 112-114, 1961.

35. Lukomsky, J. I.: The Place of insulin therapy in contemporary treatment of psychosis. In Biological Treatment of Mental Illness (Rinkel, M., Ed.). New York, Farrar, Straus and Giroux, 884-904, 1966.

36. Morgan, N. C., and Johnson, N. A.: Failures in psychiatry: The chronic hospital patient. Amer. J. Psychiat. 113: 824-830, 1957.

37. Parkash, A., and Sagar, V.: Present status of insulin shock therapy in Punjab (India). In Biological Treatment of Mental Illness (Rinkel, M., Ed.). New York, Farrar, Straus and Giroux, 873-883, 1966.

38. Paul, N. L., Fitzgerald, E., and Greenblatt, M.: The long-term comparative results of three different lobotomy procedures. Amer. J. Psychiat. 113: 808-814, 1957.

39. Pichot, P.: Psychopharmacology and the use of insulin shock therapy in France. In Biological Treatment of Mental Illness (Rinkel, M., Ed.). New York, Farrar, Straus and Giroux, 830-836, 1966.

40. Ramirez, E., Mariategui, J., and Bachmann, C.: Glucagon in terminating insulin coma: clinical and biochemical aspects. In Biological Treatment of Mental Illness (Rinkel, M., Ed.). New York, Farrar, Straus and Giroux, 694-714, 1966.

41. Reiss, M.: Psychoendocrinology. New York and London (Grune & Stratton), i-vii, 1-208, 1-40, 1958.

42. Remy, M.: Lasting value of insulin-shock treatment. In Biological Treatment of Mental Illness (Rinkel, M., Ed.). New York, Farrar, Straus and Giroux, 793-799, 1966.

43. Tucker, W. I.: Progesterone treatment in postpartum schizo-affective reac-

tions. J. Neuropsychiat. 3: 150-153, Feb., 1962.

44. Vahia, N. S.: Insulin treatment in India. *In* Biological Treatment of Mental Illness (Rinkel, M., Ed.). New York, Farrar, Straus and Giroux, 848-872, 1966.

45. Vinar, O.: Psychotropic drugs: their use and abuse. Comparison of their effects on hospitalized patients in Czechoslovakia and the United States. Read at the monthly staff meeting of Brooks Hospital, Brookline, Mass. on April 27, 1966.

46. Winnik, H. Z., Landau, I., Assael, M., and Tomim, B.: Microvascular changes during insulin-coma treatment. *In* Biological Treatment of Mental Illness (Rinkel, M., Ed.). New York, Farrar, Straus and Giroux, 680-693, 1966.

15

Group Psychotherapy of Schizophrenics

HENRY E. SCHNIEWIND, JR., M.D., MAX DAY, M.D., and ELVIN V. SEMRAD, M.D.

Dr. Schniewind is a Teaching Fellow in Psychiatry, Harvard Medical School, and collaborates with Doctors Semrad and Day in this interesting chapter of our volume.

Graduated from Harvard University (B.A. Germanic Languages and Literature), and receiving his M.D. from Harvard Medical School in 1965, Dr. Schniewind interned at Grady Memorial Hospital, Atlanta, Georgia, and is serving his residency at the Massachusetts Mental Health Center.

Dr. Max Day is Assistant Clinical Professor of Psychiatry, Tufts Medical School; Instructor of Psychiatry, Harvard Medical School.

After receiving his M.D. in 1947 (University of Toronto), Dr. Day interned at Metropolitan Hospital, New York City (1947-1948), and served his residency at Boston State Hospital, (1948-1949).

Dr. Day's considerable experience and past work in the field of group therapy is well known. He has authored numerous articles on various aspects of group therapy in all of its manifestations. Dr. Day is a member of the American Group Psychotherapy Association, and the American Psychoanalytic Association, among others.

Dr. Semrad is Director of Psychiatry, Massachusetts Mental Health Center, Clinical Professor of Psychiatry, Harvard Medical School, and Lecturer on Clinical Psychiatry, Simmons College.

Educated in Nebraska (A.B. Peru State Teachers College, Peru, Nebraska, 1932; B.Sc. in Medicine, University of Nebraska, Omaha, Nebraska, 1932; M.D. University of Nebraska, 1934) Dr. Semrad served his residency in psychiatry at Boston Psychopathic Hospital and the McLean Hospital. He returned to the Massachusetts Mental Health Center as Director of Psychiatry in 1952 and continues to date. He is generally considered a pioneer in the field of group therapy of the psychoses. Aside from many other professional affiliations which cannot in their entirety be listed here, Dr. Semrad is a member of the Boston Psychoanalytic Society and the American Psychoanalytic Association.

Preceding Dr. Semrad's contribution to this volume, he has authored some sixty-odd articles in his field, including two extensive works on the psychotherapy of psychoses.

The purpose of this chapter is to review the work done with group psychotherapy of schizophrenics from 1956 to 1966. Most of the material comes from the English and German speaking countries.

There seem to be two general and equally emphasized approaches to group psychotherapy with schizophrenic patients. The first uses *analytic* methods and focuses on interpretation of transference feelings in the group. The second method is more *synthetic* and task oriented with a focus on the development of adaptive behavior. Many authors feel that the synthetic approach is particularly useful with schizophrenics as opposed to other types of patients. Unfortunately wide variation in experimental design and the selection of patients renders a comparison between methods very difficult.

In a review of the decade 1936 to 1946, Bellak[27] did not mention group psychotherapy as a major form of treatment in schizophrenia. In a subsequent review of the decade 1946 to 1956, Bellak and Benedict[28] maintained that the group decreases *anxiety in resistance* and provides a broad choice of multiple transference interaction. They mentioned that group therapy had made great strides during that decade, increasing in status, range of application, and value. The importance of integrating psychotherapy and milieu therapy with other aspects of a total treatment program was stressed. They summarized by saying that group psychotherapy occupies a position in between individual psychotherapy and group work activities. Doubt was expressed that even good group therapy when used alone could produce permanent reconstruction of lasting therapeutic value. They felt it possible, however, that group therapy might produce some therapeutic changes where individual therapy could not be effective at all. They asserted that felicitous, strategical, and tactical employment of all therapeutic measures in various combinations was probably the most fruitful approach. Here, too, a comparison of methods was rendered difficult by lack of clearly defined criteria and description of specific group methods.

Standish and Semrad[353] classify the principle types of group psychotherapy with psychotics according to method as follows: the "repressive-inspirational," the "didactic," and the "analytic." The repressive-inspirational and the analytic approaches are seen as opposite extremes by Schilder.[316] The repressive-inspirational technique exploits the force of suggestion exerted on the group by its leader because of the strong collective transference to him. The didactic method emphasizes lecturing to patients; the therapist is a teacher who interprets mental mechanisms in order to impart conscious intellectual insight. The analytic or investigative technique, on the other hand, makes use of productions and interplay within the group, while the therapist maintains a neutral role. A miscellaneous group of techniques involves some combination of the above three methods, or emphasizes some aspect inherent in them, such as family therapy, psychodrama, and social club therapy.

Masserman's summary[254] on "Evolution" versus "Revolution" in psychotherapy refers to the various media for group communication and activity utilized from Greek times to the present. Music provided an opportunity for feelings of conjoint rhythm and harmony, esthetic expressions, and group belonging. Calisthenics and dancing offered similar possibilities of group catharsis and communion. Competitive athletics allowed opportunity for the joy of action and public recognition and reward through nondestructive competition. Drama was cherished and utilized for its deep human empathies and meanings. The Greeks endlessly varied their themes and were deeply involved as players, chorus, or affectively moved audience. They thus explored the basic individual-group interactions now utilized in psychodrama and other forms of group therapy. These offered a transition between a passive dependence on the sanatorium to an eventual recognition of an obligation to return to a place in the community.

Feldman[112] considers group therapy well suited to the treatment of psychotics, particularly those who are in a state of depression, and maintains that the group session should include discussions of psychopathology. The patients should be given an opportunity to voice fears relating to the treatment program at the hospital. This would apply particularly to patients who are anxious about possible dangers of shock therapy.

Geller[141] describes the widely used dynamic psychoanalytic approach initially based on the principles of individual psychotherapy in which the leader remains neutral and employs the interplay within the group to help the group members work through their emotional problems. Johnson[197] noted modifications of the dynamic approach to group treatment of psychotic patients to strengthen ego structure, improve reality-testing and reintegrate defensive patterns of behavior. He expanded the concepts of a group contract.

Kramer[215] felt group psychotherapy especially suited in the treatment of psychotic patients because it involves an educational as well as an emotional and social stabilizing factor. He covered the fundamental precepts of group psychotherapy with psychotic patients including the setting, techniques, modes of discussion and evaluation of treatment. The basic principles of group psychotherapy apparently lie in the modification of the transference and countertransference situation as a corrective ego experience.

Carletti[60] discusses the group treatment of regressed schizophrenic patients selected because they cannot tolerate a one to one relationship. He maintains that the interpersonal experience must be created and sustained on whatever terms and whatever levels are acceptable to the patients. Goals are gradually advanced as the members show that they possess the capacity to modify maladjustive behavior and engage in tasks of greater and greater complexity, setting goals for themselves, so that ultimately direction comes not only from the leader but also from the members of the peer group. Reality-testing is stimulated in their experience of social interaction within a group, and members help one another alter socially unacceptable behavior. Improvement results in a better overall hospital adjustment and frequently some members of the group become able to make effective use of other treatment measures. The group treatment of chronic schizophrenic patients can lessen emotional isolation and enable them to reestablish communications with their surroundings. Klapman[208] feels that group psychotherapy is the means par excellence of bringing psychotherapy to patients in large mental institutions. It re-enfranchises the patient as a distinct individual and is an effective antidote to the usual regimentation. Group therapy casts into sharp relief the milieu needs of the patient. It is no accident at this time when group psychotherapy is gaining vogue in institutional practices that a rebirth of interest in the therapeutic milieu is occurring simultaneously.

Benedetti et al.[29] present an extensive survey of group therapy with schizophrenics from 1956 to 1961. The papers reviewed are divided into three major categories: 1) general papers concerned with the development of basic insights into communication and socialization through group therapy, 2) papers using the psychological and developmental approach, and 3) those with a psychoanalytic orientation. Stotsky and Zolik[360] have reviewed group psychotherapy with psychotics, covering the period 1921 to 1963.

Preuss has edited a book, *Analytische Gruppenpsychotherapie,*[293] which gives an account of the historical development of analytic group psychotherapy, discussing theory, technique, group dynamics, and indications for group psychotherapy in schizophrenics. Dumont and Christ[97] review group methods in the treatment of psychoses in one chapter. They found that a great deal was accomplished particularly in institutions, to further the exchange of thoughts, and affectively significant human relationships. Treatment in small groups in a surrounding especially designed for psychotherapy has shown itself successful. Their personal experience shows that group psychotherapy with schizophrenics is a burdensome task which can be successful if used properly. The most important element is, as elsewhere, the building and understanding of human relationships.

Macnab,[246] a theologian with an existentialist point of view, tries to bridge the gulf between theology and clinical psychiatry. In his book he describes a group study with schizophrenic patients and their relatives, gives a general survey of schizophrenia, and summarizes modern forms of treatment. It is a fine, brief description of individual and group psychiatry. He then attempts to deal with the contribution of existentialism to psychotherapy. The group situation is seen as a religious fulfillment. The author describes his attempt to bring to the patient an awareness of the primacy of the self-world relation. He feels that the expressions of the schizophrenic would remain a closed book if one did not understand their existential context. The essential value of this is the stress on humanizing the patient.

There are other review articles pertaining to our subject which need to be mentioned. Stein[354] describes the history of the use of group psychotherapy in a small, intensive treatment hospital in the United States from 1910 to the present. In another review, Hulse[182] deals with the applications and modifications of group therapy in contemporary hospital psychiatric practice. A review from Amsterdam by Meyering[259] discusses the place of group therapy in the treatment of schizophrenia. Poser[289] surveys group therapy practice in Canada; Mowbray and Timbury[262] in Scotland; and Ivanov[191] in Russia. Genis[143] has written a general historical review.

GENERAL THEORETICAL CONSIDERATIONS

When group psychotherapy is used with schizophrenics certain modifications are necessary. According to Agara[270] special consideration should be given to such problems as group composition, the development of the therapeutic process, and the therapist's attitude towards transference. Specific features of the schizophrenic's personality deserve attention: the conservation of childhood, the substitution of fantasy for reality, the ability to animate and personify the surrounding world, emotional unresponsiveness to others, and an ability to keep narcissistic love as a basis for establishing relationships. Hora[178] speaks of a double dread of being involved in a relationship, coupled with a fear of exclusion.

Therapy of schizophrenics is much more a matter of relationship than of techniques, and hence Murthy[266] feels that it depends more on the devotion of the therapist than on his technique. Group psychotherapy acts effectively in unraveling double binding modes of communication. In Rifkin's book[302] the important role of reality-testing in group psychotherapy is stressed. To interpret reality is frequently met with by reactions of severe anger and abuse. Patients react to members of a group, however, with less fear. The transference neurosis in group therapy is triangular, with both parent figures simultaneously reenacted rather than transferred. Grotjahn[158] maintains that group psychotherapy repeats the setting of the family and offers daily opportunity for spontaneous maturation and growth.

A psychological approach described by Cameron,[58] based on the work of Freud and Federn, gives the best framework for understanding and handling very chronic schizophrenic patients. In order to deal with symptoms resulting from loss of ego function, and symptoms due to the emergence of primary process, there should be a staff member available for each small group of patients so that primary identifications can be fostered. This person should be constantly in the patient's environment. Care should be taken to insure that every part of the day's activities has some therapeutic aim.

Several years of experience in psychoanalytic psychotherapy and several experimental studies in social psychology led Wolman[399] to suggest a classification of mental disorders based on the balance of inter-individual and intra-individual libido cathexis. The roots of schizophrenia were characterized by a vectoriasis praecox or a too early and severe object hyper-cathexis. In order to correct this imbalance, group therapy was indicated for latent and manifest ambulatory schizophrenics. In the composition of groups, the emphasis was put on balancing of the inter-individual cathexis. The patient-therapist and the patient-patient transferences were fostered in such a way as to enable the latent schizophrenic to enter social relationships on a balanced give-and-take basis. Expressions of hostility were interpreted in a way that would reduce the latent schizophrenic's guilt feelings. Extreme caution and careful timing were required in handling unconscious material.

The possibility of multiple transferences is advantageous according to Lindinger,[234] and ample time should be allowed for it to develop. A closed group is recommended to achieve stability. A group with patients of mixed diagnoses is recommended because it provides a variety of transference objects. It is essential that the activity of the group develop spontaneously and be affectively shared. Interpretation should be limited to that which occurs within the group. The author's own experience with 18 groups,[233] some mixed, some with only schizophrenics, enables her to say that modest results are possible. Bleuler[37] feels that the most important thing in the treatment of schizophrenics is to help them, in spite of their difficulties, to be like healthy people, to realize their abilities, and to associate with other people again. Lindinger[234] has found that schizophrenics do better in the mixed groups. The purely schizophrenic groups are characterized by a rigidity in the transference and a general slowing down of all group processes. In one group of chronic schizophrenics the transference was particularly rigid and inflexible; the process was very slow. It lacked any ability to lessen anxiety. There was frequent acting out, and the patients stereotyped themselves in order to hide from the other members and from the world.

Abrahams[1] included one or two schizophrenics, usually of mild or borderline type in a group of neurotic patients.

Glatzer[148] finds that when patients develop insight during analytic therapy but cannot synthesize it, the trouble is rooted in the narcissistic oral substructure of these patients. Repeated insights are not always curative in themselves, and the therapist must help the patient build up new powers. Such patients repeat the infantile yearning to remain unchanged and may derive narcissistic satisfaction from defeating the therapist. They have felt narcissistic hurt by the frustrations of growing up and have attempted to outwit the parents' efforts to impose the reality principle on them by resorting to the masochistic solution of unconsciously enjoying punishment. In therapy every gain is followed by removal of symptoms and hopelessness. It is unproductive to use the neutral passive analytic approach with strongly narcissistic patients. Unresolved masochism in the therapist may deprive a taciturn patient of a much needed common sense intervention.

Much of the behavior of chronic schizophrenics in group psychotherapy is dynamically meaningful according to Alikakos.[3] Although expressed in a multitude of incomprehensible symbolic words, overt acts which accompany unconscious feelings often correlate with observations on the role of the superego in the schizophrenic process. Artiss[10] feels that the fundamental function of a psychotic symptom is the avoidance of group status. When a patient is able to "join" the patient group, a reciprocal symptom loss follows.

The role of the father in the etiology and group treatment of chronic schizophrenia is discussed by DaSylva.[84] He discusses the thought disorders of the schizophrenic and their relationship to language in shaping experience, concept formation, and ego structure. The function of words and the way in which meaning is established is outlined by Lidz[229] with a presentation of evidence, including clinical examples, of how irrationality is transmitted in the families of schizophrenics, of how words are used to obscure meanings for defensive purposes, and how the schizophrenic comes to reside ultimately in a meaningless world.

Clark and Biscardi[68] describe chronic patients, who in their speech simultaneously disclose and cover up ideas and feelings. In patients who lack the restitutive elements and present primarily communications that are negative and defensive, the chronic patient's preference for his view of things, and his unwillingness to check his views against facts and alternatives is self evident. The infinite and determined attempts to speak in terms of mutually observable facts of interaction are brought out. The objective of therapy is to provide the patient with an opportunity to develop a capacity for expression and/or sublimation of emotional needs and drives, to acknowledge, bear and keep in perspective real life object experiences. Individually, in groups, with or without the use of vehicles and activities, this means providing a corrective ego experience for the return to optimum ego functioning and continuing personal growth. Beran[30] sees a specific value for group therapy preceding individual therapy with guarded and suspicious patients.

Longabough et al.[236] speak of the interpersonal behavior of chronic schizophrenic patients as a process of social exchange in which a person is influenced by another's actions. A system for categorizing the behavior of schizophrenic patients in terms of this interpersonal exchange process shows him to be socially bankrupt. A sensitive understanding of the interaction between psychological and interpersonal events in the life of the schizophrenic patient may be achieved through careful analysis of his current resource exchange processes. In contrast to the psychoanalytic view, Astrup[13] advocates a commonsense approach based on "rational psychotherapy" considering the influence of language and words not only as a psychic but also a physiologic stimulation through the "second signal system" of Pavlov. The idea is to correct reaction patterns that impede social adaptation. In schizophrenics the most characteristic disturbances consist of inhibition of unconditioned reflexes and dissociations at higher activity levels of the nervous system. The influence of complex structures is slight. Long-standing cases of schizophrenia with severe impairment of the "second signal system" seem to benefit more from occupational therapy and other nonverbal socializing activities than from group discussions. Severe dissociative disturbances, especially as in hebephrenics, do not benefit much from group therapy and may be disturbing to others in the group. According to Astrup catatonics and some types of hebephrenics have fluctuating inhibitions of the cortical processes. They are by and large rather passive group members but may benefit from treatment. Group activity may contribute to counteracting their inhibited and autistic behavior and responses. Paranoid schizophrenics with systematized delusions regularly react with strong affect to their own psychotic ideas. Experimentally this is paralleled by violent respiratory and plethysmographic reactions. It is useless to try and convince them that their delusions are unreal. In the group they experience people who are friendly to them and who understand such ideas, although they may not accept them. The group offers them an opportunity to react to their delusions in other ways, making social adaptation possible. The purpose of the approach is to accelerate the "encapsulation" of psychotic ideas which is regularly found in improved paranoid schizophrenics. In paranoid patients who are dominated by projection symptoms, general affective changes in the direction of depression, ecstacy or perplexity are prominent. These patients do not react with great affect to their delusions and experimental mention of their delusions was found to produce only slight vegetative reactions. There are strong inhibitions of the unconditioned reflexes but good performances in the second signal system. These patients especially benefit from group therapy. They often feel isolated in their fantasy world of delusion. When their stories are accepted by friendly fellow group patients who may talk of similar experiences, their attention becomes more concentrated on problems leading to their breakdown. This helps them derive a common sense understanding of their disease which contributes to the correction of psychotic ideas and to facing the problems in the real world. Emotional contact with other group members might possibly act as a physiologic stimulation to schizophrenics, counteracting the inhibition of subcortical structures. This process can be experimentally demonstrated. At first schizophrenics cannot reveal any personal problems or other factors that may have precipitated their illness, and they have difficulty in verbalizing their reaction to their experimental performances. With clinic improvement, they grow able to talk about their problems. This makes one suspect that schizophrenics who seemingly deny personal problems are actually unable to verbalize adequately their reactions to experiences.

Illing[184] states that all theories and practices "must be based on an infinite quantity of observations and experiences, and only he who repeats these observations on himself and on others has found the way to his own direction." Haden[164] feels that group therapy affords a corrective emotional experience for many traumatic events of early life. Battegay[22] finds that regression as a result of the emotional participation of the members of the group allows schizophrenic a sense of security that may be new to him. The feelings of sharing and of being cared for can result in regression to infantile stages, and the patients often live out conflicts which they were unable to resolve with their parents or their family's children. Thus Schindler[321] holds that the experience of regression can in itself set in motion processes of maturation.

Kotov[214] identifies three distinct levels of psychotherapeutic achievement in group psychotherapy: social participation based chiefly upon symptom identification; increased confidence based chiefly upon ego identification; and emotional insight based chiefly upon modified superego identification. The therapist must be primarily a humanist well schooled in psychopathology and psychodynamics and capable of appreciating that he is a central figure in a dramatic reliving, reintegrating experience for all patients who come under his treatment. Clinical reports by Schultz and Ross[325] and Boe et al.[38] consistently show that schizophrenic patients in group therapy show increased self-expression, diminished anxiety, and improved reality-testing. However, studies by Illing and Brownfield[186] of central themes of delusional productions in group psychotherapy with newly released schizophrenic patients, report their uncertainty to the effectiveness of treatment and its measurements. In group psychotherapy with schizophrenics, the call to reality, the emotional participation, the regression, the identification, the tension between stereotyped behavior and group pressures, and the transference feelings are stronger than in individual treatment but also less permanent. Group cohesion is variable. In a group, Battegay[22] feels that schizophrenics become part of a nexus which prepares them for the real world. Slavson[337,338] sees group therapy conservatively as being in the nature of "psychonursing" or hospital community psychotherapy.

The use of Kleinian concepts in group psychotherapy with six psychotic patients in an Argentinian mental hospital is discussed by Resnik.[300] The schizophrenic requires the therapist to identify with him, so as to help him recover from panic and doubt. Success with such primitive identification in the therapist leads to the establishment of dependency on the therapist. Intense transference reactions can be analyzed only in graduated doses so as to reach the patient's inner core of helplessness. This author uses the group approach as a stepping-stone to "real work in individuation, which is psychoanalysis."

Alikakos[4] maintains that analytic group therapy is an effective and specific method in the treatment of the posthospital schizophrenic, primarily because the schizophrenic's intense and mercurial transference reactions are diluted and attenuated in group therapy. Also group dynamics tend to reduce anxiety and guilt feelings, to provide support and escape, to limit regression, to enhance reality-testing and self-esteem, and to provide graded socializing experiences. A number of patients were able to work steadily on their personality problems over a period of several years and to alter them. The five and one-half year treatment of one of these patients demonstrated the progress she made in working on her personality problems.

Several additional articles, from the German literature not available for review, also discuss theoretical considerations.[20,162,168,206,240]

In summary, the main theoretical considerations for the use of group therapy with schizophrenic patients also reveal two orientations: the analytic and the synthetic. The analytic approach, expressed for example by Lindinger, emphasizes the advantages of multiple and diluted transferences within the group. The more synthetic approach emphasizes socialization. A further dimension is added by the physiologic approach of Astrup.

DEVELOPMENTS IN TECHNIQUE

Various workers have reported their experiences and their thoughts about technical problems. The therapy group serves as an important source of emotional reference for the patient in terms of establishing reality values of emotional responsiveness. Geller[141] advocates that the role of a therapist should be more in the direction of therapeutic resource person than of active leadership. Special awareness of inattention to the prominence of symbolic communication by the schizophrenic patient is essential. Dream interpretation, analysis of transference and countertransference, and mechanisms of distortion are all applied.

Horwitz and Weisberg[180] used active, directive, even charismatic and manipulative measures to ameliorate the estrangement, confusions, and anxiety of acute psychosis. These techniques work provided they are used in an atmosphere of psychodynamic understanding. By being authoritarian, they encourage dependency which the authors found to be short-lived. During the acute psychosis the patients did incorporate, introject, and identify with the therapist and developed a variety of fluctuant transferences. They used him as an alter ego and even developed a kind of conditioned responsiveness. This produced an umbrella of trust under which anxiety and confusion were reduced, permitting time and energy for the reconstitution of prepsychotic defenses. Following recovery the emotional attachment to the therapist was dropped but the useful behavioral alternatives the patient had learned remained as part of a reestablished integrity. The authors warn against countertransference misuse of manipulation to work on the therapist's problems or to avoid areas to which the therapist is sensitive.

Deutsch et al.[90] describe the treatment of seven paranoid women in a group over three years through two changes of therapists. The institution of cotherapists, weekly supervision, and the handing on of the group from one set of therapists to another to focus on reactions to loss were some of the efforts to deal with the enormous oral craving and rage of these women. Reading minutes from the previous session to a psychotherapeutic group of hospitalized psychotic patients is viewed by Golner[149] as of value in improving reality testing and accuracy of self concept through confrontation of the patient with his own behavior. The differing roles and reactions of the therapist and recorder are discussed.

The diversity of patients found on an acute locked service and the transiency of group membership made it necessary for Forer[220] to deal with varying levels of pathology at the same time. Treatment was oriented toward advancing each patient one step along in the direction of adequate adjustment. The major techniques employed were: pointing out emotional concomitance of behavior in the group, and reasoning with patients who present unrealistic ideas or pathological behavior.

Klapman[209] maintains that the more disorganized the personality, and the more primitive and archaic the ego, the more directive in structure the group psychotherapy needs to be. With ego-deficient characters, as with regressed schizophrenics, it is necessary to rebuild, educate or reeducate the ego, and this requires a directive, didactic approach to treatment. The directiveness required can enable each patient to find a point of optimal benefit.

For the organization of different types of groups in accordance with the degree of personality integration Parker[273] recommends that group activities take into account the variability between patients and that a variety of approaches be made available. In the treatment of acute emotional disorders in an acute ward Blacker[35] found that the group therapist should be active, that structured technics should be used, and that the interpretations should be based primarily on pattern analysis and analysis of interactions. The evidence suggests that the use of group psychotherapy facilitated the goals of brief-term hospitalization. A "group balance," including instigators and passive personalities in the social milieu, was stressed by Ogara.[270] Therapy took place twice a week, and the function of the auxiliary ego was found to be very valuable. The therapist was essentially a participant-observer who helped repress again what came into consciousness. His chief function was to be that of a kindly paternal figure so as to increase the positive transferences first toward himself and later on towards the others. Most interpretations were directed toward the group as a whole. The chief aim was to increase sociability, and better mechanisms of projective and introjective identification. A relatively nonauthoritarian milieu is reported by Comer[73] to be more effective with depressed, withdrawn patients who tend to act out.

An article by Spitz and Kopp[348] on multiple psychotherapy states that two authority figures represent a family setting especially well for schizophrenics who, they consider, think symbolically. In group therapy the members may take on parental or sibling roles. In contrast to many other writers, these authors state that the therapist need not be of the opposite sexes to be given father or mother roles. Schizophrenics in particular respond to subtle psychologic differences in the therapist. The more aggressive therapist is equated with the masculine role, the more protective with the feminine. The implication here is that the personality of the therapist not only determines the role he plays but also the role given him by the patient who will have a primary reaction to one of the two therapists. Once this reaction is fixed, the second therapist assumes in the patient's mind the secondary qualities associated with the less dominant parent. In the previous decade the importance of the relationship was stressed. Here the techniques of interpretation and the role of the therapist, the therapist's verbal as well as his non-verbal and inadvertent behaviors, are considered as important determiners of the patient's behavior. Behymer[25] reports that when a psychiatrist and a social worker served as co-workers in a state hospital setting, the social worker, in her role as a passive recorder, was perceived as a mother figure.

Cowden[76] recommends a more aggressive role on the part of the therapist for producing changes in behavior by obtaining control over the patients, destroying psychotic symptoms, and breaking dependency. To deal with the chronic schizophrenic's resistance to change, the therapist must accept the patient, relax, walk around, and use other unorthodox methods. Drennen and Wiggins[94] describe an attempt to manipulate verbal behavior in a group of withdrawn, chronic schizophrenic patients on the assumption that more verbal behavior produces more activity in their general behavior. Mainord et al.[247] discuss the use of confrontation of schizophrenics in group psychotherapy.

The value of combining activity group treatment and individual treatment is upheld by Lieberman and Taylor.[230] They feel it enables the patient to achieve a better understanding of inner conflicts and their relationship to past traumata and allows them to synthesize the good and bad parts of self. The group experience helps to strengthen ego functioning by providing an arena for reality-testing, a feeling of acceptance and belonging, and release of hostility without fear of annihilation and desertion. The patient obtains understanding in individual treatment and thus is able to give up the destructive pathological defenses that isolate him from the world. The insight can be put to use in the group setting and from there it can be carried over to the wider arena of the community and the home.

Tauber[364,365] recommends that the hospitalized patient participate in the planning and evaluation of group psychotherapy. Soliciting the patient's assistance thus elicits his aid in evaluating how well he feels group therapy is meeting his needs. After the group has been meeting for some time, individual evaluative structured interviews are used. In this way the patient can feed back a special kind of information that may not be available to either the therapist or his supervisor. This can be used to clear up misconceptions about the purpose of group therapy. This was an attempt to counteract the generalized lack of motivation and great passivity found in long term patients. The basic goal of these planning interviews was to determine the expressed need of the patient by giving him an opportunity directly and indirectly to indicate areas of concern and importance to him. The focus was not on pathology. Once the therapist obtains and evaluates the expressed needs of the patients, group therapy can be planned with content based upon these needs, thus giving a "face validity" to the therapy session.

Schindler[318] reviews his ten years of experience with "bifocal group therapy." His work was guided by the general principle that a balance has to be struck between *interpretation* (analysis), which has to be carefully measured according to what the patient can bear, and *ego building* measures. A group was felt to be a suitable setting on the boundary between model and reality. It is a highly real experience, and also a model family. He emphasizes that the meaning of defense mechanisms is of much more vital consideration in schizophrenics than in neurotics, and the schizophrenic must be given room to avoid the consequences of his thinking as long as necessary. One pattern of avoidance is "generalization," or "anonymous thinking." It is helpful to focus generalizations onto one or more group members as a gradual means of helping them to give up this defense. Transference and projection are seen as more important in schizophrenics than repression. The therapist has to try and produce a positive transference. He is seen transiently as an enemy, but eventually a group is formed with him against the patient's other "enemies." Since parental ties have a very strong meaning in schizophrenics, Schindler feels that parents have to become actively involved in the therapeutic work. Often the family's "balance" depends upon the patient being sick and a great deal of resistance is met with when any change is attempted. To conquer this, two groups were formed; one with patients to *represent* a family to the patient, another was composed of only the parents of these patients who met with the same doctor. Patients and family were not allowed to visit at first. Somatic therapies were used where indicated, as part of a comprehensive treatment plan. This form of therapy necessitated a high investment of personal interest and time. The goal was not "cure," but the achievement of stability and a "higher level" of adjustment in personal and social spheres. There was no essential differences between the composition of the control and treated populations. Most were clearly diagnosed schizophrenics; about half were paranoid, the rest were hebephrenic, catatonic, or mixed. The patients were mostly between 20 and 35 since work with parents was a condition for their acceptance. There were more women than men, but this was due entirely to administrative factors. The amount of somatic therapy was the same in both groups. Schindler concludes that the results can therefore be explained only on the basis of psychotherapeutic influence, and claims that of 100 patients, 43 additional patients can become able to work who otherwise would become chronically hospitalized.

In breaking through the resistance in a group of psychotic patients Chesteen[65] feels that the therapist should try to give permission to all expressions of hostility, generally relating them to himself whether the basis for the hostility is reality or fantasy. In a sense he also tries to relate hostility to transference reactions towards himself in a very systematic way. His hope is that this will release the patients enough so that they can adjust better in the hospital atmosphere and in the outside world.

O'Hearne[271] contrasts the laissez faire and let's-try-and-make-sense-out-of-a-delusion approach with the more active approach of trying to deny the reality of delusions. The focus is to make sense out of delusions as a response to stresses of the moment in the group. By making sense out of this and universalizing these stresses, the patient involved and the other members of the group obtain relief. Cowden[76] encourages attempts to "dejoy" the defenses of chronic schizophrenic patients to make them aware of the degree of their pathology and needs for treatment. Ruiz-Agara[311] used group analysis with schizophrenics in Spain.

Boenheim[40] reviewed the role of group psychotherapy in a mental hospital, the theoretical positions, and types of groups. The usefulness of co-therapists was detailed. He feels it valuable to give protocols of actual sessions. Illovsky[187] used group hypnotherapy with eighty chronic schizophrenic women who had been hospitalized for an average of seven years, and reports discharge of 60 per cent after one year of treatment.

CLINICAL EXPERIMENTS IN GROUP PROCESSES

Some new and interesting studies focus on the dynamics of interactions within schizophrenic groups. Small et al.[340] discuss the evolution of large group meetings in a psychiatric hospital and propose a method of studying the interaction phenomena in such a group. Brant[47] expresses the conviction that group psychotherapy with larger groups of twenty to twenty-five psychotic patients is feasible and successful. Bros[50] found advantage in including a silent schizophrenic patient in a group of neurotics. This patient's silence, helplessness, and dependency generated within the group a continuous affect-laden stream of interaction.

Systematic observations of six patients participating in a therapeutic community program in a general hospital psychiatric ward by Prosen and Lamberd[294] demonstrated that the patient's physical movements in group meetings bear a dynamic relationship to his change in clinical status. They are also related to his attitudes towards the group leader and the staff according to Lamberd.[222] In particular, the balance between the patient's needs to express aggression over frustrated dependency needs and his need to placate authority figures seems to determine positioning, movement and perseveration in the group. Basham[17] in an investigation of the role of the group therapist as a determinant of the verbal behavior of schizophrenic patients demonstrates the relationship between the verbal behavior of the therapist and that of the patients. This study was not concerned with the improvement of the patient as a function of the two verbal techniques. Two well defined verbal techniques were formulated to enable the therapist to use statements of reflection, of content, and of feeling. Marked relationships existed between the category activity of the therapist and patients of each group. Under these controlled conditions, it was shown that within limits apparently set by the nature of verbal interaction itself, marked differences were attributable to the differing classes of statements consciously employed by the therapist. This suggests the operation of "laws" of verbal interaction which should be tested through the use of other systems of categories and other types of patients, and point to the possibility of controlling the verbal behavior of the patient through the use of specific kinds of therapist activity.

Drennen and Wiggins[94] studied manipulation of verbal behavior of chronic hospitalized schizophrenics in a group therapy situation. Two pairs of cotherapists attempted to react in a clearly differential manner toward the patients, one pair being hypercritical and the other being supportive and congenial. The results of the experiment were as follows: Two chronic patients who initially exhibited a zero interaction rate did not change; seven patients increased only in terms of patient-therapist verbal interaction; four patients increased in terms of patient-therapist verbal interaction as well as patient-patient interaction, and differential therapist treatment resulted in temporary differential effects.

The problems of experimental study of the effects of group therapy are well discussed by Kraus.[218] The effects were evaluated, using a time-sampling method, by ward physician and a psychiatrist independently based on therapists' reports and impressions, and psychological group tests. The results were treated by appropriate nonparametric statistics. The conclusion was drawn that psychotherapeutic group sessions with chronic psychotic patients, even in the form of short term therapy, seemed to constitute a therapeutic instrument of considerable value.

The effects of changes of milieu on body chemistry were studied in the community of a metabolic ward by Schottstaedt et al.[323] who found that the excretion of water, sodium, potassium, calcium, nitrogen, and creatine fluctuated with changes in milieu, demonstrating conclusively that we are dealing with a real force.

Anker and Walsh[5] specially designed an activity program, and evaluated homogeneity and heterogeneity as therapeutic modalities in the treatment of chronic schizophrenic patients. These variables were studied simultaneously in a $2\times2\times2$ factorial design with multiple covariance with initial level of behavioral adjustment and length of stay in the therapeutic program. Group psychotherapy produced relatively minor positive results and the group structure variable produced none. Refinements in design and suggestions for future use for research were presented.

Vernaillis and Reinert[376] studied the allocation of administrative responsibility to patients to increase treatment effectiveness. Holzberg and Knapp[175] found that as college students engage themselves as companions to chronically ill mental patients, the patients derive benefit from the interaction, and the students undergo an enlargement of their concept of mental illness, manifesting at the same time therapeutic personality changes. Query[295] studied performance and group cohesiveness and found that chronically ill schizophrenics are responsive to some of the same social stimuli as normals. A concurrent comparison was made by Semon and Goldstein[328] of the therapist in "active-participant" and "active-interpretive" roles. No difference in relative merits of these two methods was demonstrated. Lerner and Fairweather[225] state that schizophrenics "will exhibit appropriate social motivation and responsiveness in a meaningful situation which does not depend on the use of language or complex cognitive skills." Spohn and Wolk[350] found that chronic schizophrenics alter their behavior slightly from withdrawal to passive cooperation as a result of sustained problem solving activities. Derwort[89] discusses the behavior of schizophrenics in a group setting.

A study was made by Hirschman[174] of a group experience incident to the closing of a ward so that the space could be used for centralized offices. All reactions of patient and personnel seemed to indicate the wish that this situation continue indefinitely. Eight patients were selected from among the more active and communicative patients to work out these issues in a group and carry them back to the rest of the ward. The patients were transferred from the ward in groups of three over a period of time. At first there was massive denial. Gradually there was a great storm of hostility and blaming of the administration for the helplessness of the therapists. A certain amount of acting out on the ward occurred, including somatizations in the large ward group. In the small group there was a clear splitting into subgroups to preserve the ideal of group integrity. Gradually a depression descended on the ward. The patients who worked on the other hand adhered strictly to rules and regulations, recognized the authority figure as infallible, and used intellectual devices to comfort themselves. After the ward was closed, the small work group also disintegrated. The closing of the ward was accomplished without any massive self-destructive behavior. Healthy people as well as patients reacted similarly except that patients reacted in a more intense form. In face of a common threat deteriorated patients who were preoccupied with themselves reacted with the others.

Magazu et al.[244] describe the reactions of a group of chronic psychotic patients to the departure of their therapist. Dumont[96] studied a therapy group of chronic schizophrenics who had lost a previous leader through suicide. The intense feelings of fear and isolation that resulted had never been recognized until an interchange on President Kennedy's assassination permitted their expression in a displaced form. As the issue of the lost leader was ambiguously interjected into the discussion, an undercurrent of group cohesiveness was identified. Subsequently, forces in the group tended toward a much more unified and meaningful organization.

A study by Wolk[398] using Q-sort techniques correlated ego ideal and self evaluation among hospitalized schizophrenic patients. He found that self-ideal discrepancies are characteristic of psychological malfunctioning, but that ten weeks of group psychotherapy increased rather than decreased these discrepancies. As a result of this study, they question whether the period of group treatment between tests was too short and whether reduction of self-ideal discrepancies is a valid indicator of psychological improvement.

Shellhase[335] presents research on the group life of the schizophrenic patient which substantiates the clinical hypothesis that hospitalized schizophrenic patients can and do respond to and in a social structure, decidedly so when that structure has meaning for them. He assumes that patient government is a "creative group experience," and that group psychotherapy is a "corrective group experience;" that the former is focused on social functioning and the latter on psychic functioning; and that roles are explicitly consciously assumed and ascribed, rarely implicitly unconsciously assumed.

A study giving patients lysergic acid at the time they participated in permissive group meetings is reported by Spencer.[349]

Ugelstad[371] explored dream activity in psychotic patients. After six months of therapy, almost all patients had direct dream representations of other group members and the therapist, and it was relatively easy to see in the dreams connections between special transferences and relationships in the groups. In one group with more severe pathology they asked about the patient's dreams at the beginning of treatment and then again after three and six months. There was a considerable amount of recollected dream material which gave interesting insight into the intrapsychic state of the patients; in contrast with the less severely ill group where there was no direct representation of other group members or of therapist in the dreams. This began to show itself only later on and then to a small degree.

Zolik[404] demonstrated a method for conducting detailed content analyses of patient statements for studying the process of group therapy over successive sessions and in terms of individual patients.

MacDonald,[241] in dealing with the problem of applicability, considers the makeup of the chronic population. The first is what is truly an open ward and what is truly a closed ward. The second issue consists of two parts and has to do with selectivity through reputation. The first part of this is that one avoids sending patients from the continued treatment service to the small group wards. The other part of this issue is that mostly new patients are sent to the small group treatment from admission wards, including particularly acting out and alcoholic patients.

Diggory[91] found that chronic schizophrenic subjects vary their level of expected performance in another task directly with their manipulated perceived ability. Their rate of volunteering was related to perceived ability only when the expected task was harder but one in which their abilities had already been tested. By contrast incidents of voting for others were related to their presumed ability regardless of type of expected task. Better adjusted patients volunteered more often than sicker ones for competition on the same tasks and same but harder tasks, but voting had no association with the presumed sickness of the person voted for.

Spear[344] pertinently questions intensive resocialization programs including the formation of therapeutic groups and the treatment of chronic schizophrenia. He points to the "rejection effect" in control groups and the consequent deterioration which may contribute to difficulty in the interpretation of results. He suggests that no schizophrenic should be excluded from treatment for the "hypothetical benefit" of any form of psychotherapy and further that if positive results are to be obtained, group treatment of schizophrenics should be applied for periods of about six months, followed by a rest period for patients and staff.

Murray[264] studied variations in amount of talking by patients during group therapy sessions. Very similar, statistically significant patterns in quantity of speech were found for three groups of chronic psychotic male patients. This similarity of patterns held despite differing racial composition of the three groups, differences in profession, theoretical orientation and measured activity of the two therapists involved, the use of two different recorders or observers in collecting the data on the group, and the fact that two of the groups were just starting and the third group had been together for over a year. Suggestions were made for further research to establish the stability of the obtained pattern and delineate the degree to which the results are generalizable to other types of groups.

Scher[315] studied attendance fluctuations in an after-care group. He showed a correlation with the attendance pattern of the resident-co-therapist. When a resident was new in his group, the absences were unaffected. As the time approached for his departure, they dropped. Subsequent to his departure they rose even higher than the usual. Finally there were several times when one of the therapists knew in advance that he would be unable to attend a meeting because of conflicting commitments and was able to announce his impending absence to the group. These meetings which the patients did not expect them to attend showed a significantly higher percentage of absences than average.

Spear[344] concluded that much more research is needed on the effective ways of utilizing group treatment and on the ways in which it might work. One attempt was made by Wax[384] to organize the complex observations of a therapeutic community meeting in four categories—institutional context, social transactions, content, and latent content. Another group of workers, Peck et al.[282] tried to study the convergence of intrapsychic and intragroup processes by focusing study on the morning group meeting with emphasis on levels of communication, structural differentiation, latent themes and informal roles. Similar efforts were made by Lippman and Deutsch[235] in other experiments to involve the whole patient population and nursing and medical staff in various intersecting groups to propagate a psychotherapeutic program.

In these studies some effort has been made to correlate variations in technique with differences in the dynamics of group interaction. One experimental difficulty, the "rejection effect" of the control group was pointed out. Taking this difficulty and the difficulty of comparing results from different studies into account it would seem that a relatively fruitful and controllable approach to the study of group dynamics is possible by varying technique over time in one group that is stable and has learned to work together.

SOCIAL AND CULTURAL FACTORS IN GROUP PSYCHOTHERAPY

The danger of universalizing on sociological grounds what is true on intrapsychic grounds persists as a problem. Maldonado-Sierra et al.[249,250] describe how the group psychotherapeutic process was made more culturally relevant for Puerto Rican schizophrenics by harking back to the traditional child-rearing patterns of the patient's families. In the main it is similar in purpose, principles, and methods to usual group therapy but emphasizes the creation of a therapy team representing the significant members of a healthy family, i.e., the father, the mother, and the older brother. They aimed at clarification of the patients' blurred perception of others including the sibling figure, the clarification of the roles of mother and father, and study of the interactions and transactions between the healthy sibling figure and the patient who represented the younger, dependent figures. The authors feel that the principle of sibling relationship may be more significant than has been previously assumed by therapists. This is especially relevant to and consistent with the family experiences of the Puerto Rican. These children tend to confide more readily in their peers than in their parents, and they turn to their peers for confort when the parents do not supply adequate emotional support. The sibling's transaction[250] in verbalizing the unconscious of the schizophrenic to the mother and father figures resulted in a rapid resolution of resistance for what was formerly deemed dreadful and secret, but which through repeated sibling verbalizations gradually acquired the appearance of the commonplace.

In reviewing the literature from the German-speaking countries, a definite geographic and cultural distribution of orientation was observed. The analytically inclined papers tended to come from university centers such as Vienna, Basel, and Heidelberg. The synthetic approach was representative of nonuniversity, state hospitals in Wiesloch, Krefeld, Göppingen, and Gutersloh. There is also a striking north-south distribution. The analytic orientation is found in the southern, less industrialized areas; the synthetic approach was mainly confined to northern and industrial areas. This general pattern is an example of how social and cultural factors may enter into the structure of group therapy with schizophrenics.

A comparison of Negro participation in an all-Negro group led by white therapists, as well as Negro participation in a mixed Negro-white group with a white therapist was made by Murray and Brown.[265] For the first few meetings of the group the Negroes participated more heavily and even dominated the whole group. This put to rest the old intuition that Negroes would verbalize less in the presence of whites. Gradually the white patients also began to participate more freely.

The New Haven community was studied by Myers and Roberts[268] from the point of view of Hollingshead's Class 3, the white-collar high school graduates, and Class 5, the economically depressed, irregularly employed, unskilled grammar school graduates. The most disorganized families which provide the least opportunity for meaningful, supportive relationships with the community and with parents and siblings tend to produce patients with the most disorganized pathological forms of behavior. Poorly integrated Class 5 families isolated from major community institutions with overworked, neglectful mothers and remote impulsively brutal fathers, tend to produce schizophrenic patients. On the other hand, rigidly organized, mother-dominated Class 3 families, sensitive to status in the community, tend to produce psychoneurotic patients. In the world of the Class 5 child there is a pervasive and unpredictable aggression, and this may be a precondition for the psychotic response.

Burke and Lafave[53] describe a program to utilize existing, but as yet untapped resources for rehabilitation within the limited budgetary allowances of state institutions. It involves working with available personnel rather than with a numerically enlarged staff or with personnel specifically chosen for demonstrated talents in rehabilitation work. Basic requirements for the implementation of such a program seem to be administrative support, a competent team leader who is able to effectively utilize potential of personnel from the number of disciplines within the hospital, active recruitment, and use of community resources and volunteers.

Psychoanasynthesis is a term used by Vlavianos and Fink[378] to describe the operational procedure permitting readjustments and release from the hospital of previously unresponsive mental patients. The procedure makes dynamic use of an integrated team which includes the patients themselves, clergy, psychologists, social workers, occupational and recreational therapists, nursing and other employees under the guidance of a psychiatrist with the framework of the entire physical setup of mental hospital.

A total approach in France, described by Chen[64] is based on the assumption that mental illness is the consequence rather than the cause of the disturbance in the relationship between the individual and his environment. It emphasizes work, expression of aggression and interpersonal relationships. Work is a social responsibility, not merely something to be done with as little effort as possible. It is disgraceful not to work and it is a source of pride to work. In their weekly meetings with the staff, expression of aggression is encouraged and channelized in constructive activities. Group activity occurs when five or six patients meet twice a week with the physician-therapist. Physical exercises are encouraged and developed. The hospital assumes minimal responsibility in imposing expectations or setting limitations on the population. Each patient creates his own milieu. After hospitalization, employment graded to suit each patient's ability, as well as family placements and family colonies, permits the integration of each subject in a society modified to meet his capabilities. These artificial societies are felt to be indispensable for taking care of patients.

Jacoby[195] wrote about patient government organized in response to fire-setting and other problems of discipline in a state hospital. The administration resisted trying to tamper with the ballots in the elections and found the unstable patients elected to office responded to the challenge and improved. Business was conducted formally as in other organizations, and ordinary, everyday matters, such as food, privileges, were taken up. Private matters were referred elsewhere. Displays of temper were dealt with socially, by disapproval. This stimulated the growth of self respect among the patients.

Luchins[239] worked with 311 Negro and white psychotic patients, 119 of whom remained in closed wards. Group treatment was divided into two phases. In phase I, the leader presented in a dramatic manner for thirty to forty minutes part of a special topic for discussion. In phase II, the patients then formed small discussion groups, led by a social worker. Emphasis was on orientation toward life, information concerning mental illness and orientation to the treatment process. The groups consisted of ten to fifteen members in the first phase of treatment, and three to five in the second phase of treatment. In Germany, Schulte[324] emphasizes the value of a discussion group, a hospital newspaper, and a chess group for schizophrenics.

Projective group therapy described by Azima and Azima[15] allows the sequential combination of free creation with free association, and provides a group setting for the initiation of therapeutic movement and the uncovering and reorganization of unconscious processes. Some parts of the relating ego system and need system are sought through presentation in available medium such as plasticene, crayon and paper.

Activity group therapy reported by Beard et al.[24] and King[204] postulates that there remains in the patient a core of essential ego strengths which can be utilized therapeutically through the establishment of an activity group structure, provided the activities are relevant to these strengths. Because the requirements of the activities do not surpass the patient's ego capacity, he is able to participate effectively in social relationships. Participation in such an activity structure tends to isolate socially the patients symptomatology and pathology. The patient's new experience in participation with others on a basic reality level seems to promote a process of reinstitution of lost ego capacities.

Activity group therapy can serve as a useful adjunct prior to, simultaneous with, or following other therapeutic efforts. For the discharged psychiatric patient, it can play an important part in facilitation adjustment in the community and thereby potentially lessen the probability of rehospitalization. Anker and Walsh[5] compared the effectiveness of group psychotherapy and a specially designed activity program in the treatment of chronic, hospitalized, schizophrenic patients. The activity program produced significant and consistent positive changes, while the therapy group did not.

Hughes[181] taught outpatient psychotic children in three areas—communication-language, social-emotional, and conceptual-abstract reasoning. He found that how something was presented was more important than what was presented. The teachers became treatment-oriented, and the educational activities became vehicles for therapy. Moderately chronic mental patients receiving goal-directed group psychotherapy described by Vernaillis and Reinert,[374] were able to spend more time in the community with fewer breakdowns than were similar patients in a control group not receiving group therapy.

Aronson and Field[9] describe mental health programming in the Soviet Union. The collective interest is valued above the individual. A socialized medical program is provided with a range of outpatient services. They emphasize physiological rather than psychological concepts. This has resulted in a rejection of psychodynamics, an emphasis on work therapy, and the maintenance of psychiatric patients within the community in so far as possible.

DIFFERENT FORMS OF GROUP PSYCHOTHERAPY

The basic principles of group therapy have been modified and adapted for children and families, for short term group therapy, and for work therapy.

Speers and Lansing[345] and Smollen and Lifton[342] feel that group therapy is useful in staving off hospitalization or preparing the child for object-relations and possible individual therapy.

In a child guidance clinic[342] schizophrenic children met in therapy groups three to four times a week while their parents met weekly for two and one-half hours. In the summer the program was modified to be camplike. This group experience prepared the patients to enter into individual therapy at a later date. Speech therapy was also provided. Such a program seemed to be a program of choice.

DeMyer and Ferster[87] describe the technique of social reinforcements to teach new social behavior to autistic and symbiotic children, and maintain that it can be learned successfully by untrained psychotherapists, and changes in behavior directly attributable to the reinforcement program can be predicted. Changes are more likely to be closer to age appropriateness in the very young children than those older than 6. The first step was for the adult to insinuate himself into the behavior pattern of the child without upsetting him and thereby resolve autistic barrier. As soon as the social overture were accepted, the adult, who was generally most successful, was selected to do individual work with the child.

Speers and Lansing[345,346] placed psychotic children between the ages of 3½ and 4½ were into a group. As one child interfered with another's autism, there were panic reactions which had to be dealt with by bodily contact with the therapist. After trying to make contact by many aggressive attacks on one another, the children were able to unite about water and soap bubble play and then only cleaning and plasticene play. Feeding was particularly useful. Originally children escaped to the bathroom, but soon acceptance of fecal play led to self-toilet training. After eighteen months of therapy, group formation was possible. As panic reactions decreased, the meaning of material could be understood. The mothers were urged to hire full-time nannies for their children. After coming to terms with their jealousy, they began to look at their deepest feelings of deprivation. The fathers were invited to the group but were more persistent in keeping themselves out in various ways.

The family treatment of childhood schizophrenia described by Langdell[223] includes long term individual psychotherapy, conjoint family interviews, collaborative individual therapy of various family members, or concomitant individual or conjoint family interviews. In 200 children improvement in the child follows therapeutic loosening of intrapersonal and interpersonal parental conflicts. This required extravagant investment of time with uncertain and infrequent dividends.

Gunther et al.[160] gave children who were recommended for institutionalization and who were inaccessible to the usual clinic approaches, a test of treatment for three to six months in groups of six with a social worker. Within three months one could usually estimate if the child had sufficiently developed to have organizational capacity as an individual and capacity for self observation, the two qualities deemed essential for treatment in this setting. Sixty per cent of the children could then continue into individual treatment.

Munzer[263] worked for more than two years with a closed group consisting of ten parents of psychotic children. Increased acceptance by the parents of their own unconscious processes was found to be related to increased acceptance of the psychotic child by the family. Where the former did not occur, the latter also did not occur, and correspondingly there was no evidence of improvement in the children.

The British experience at The Maudsley, reviewed in a book by Foulkes and Anthony[123] sees group therapy with psychotic children as a way of arresting and reversing regression and with tolerance for frequent regression, the emergence of the individual personality. First panic reactions at closeness must be met with comforting physical contact. Gradually as infantile impulses are accepted and feelings are named, the mothers deal with their frustrations in parallel groups and the fathers with their rivalries in their own group; as a result the child matures. When he becomes neurotic and the group becomes neurotic, the child is entered in individual therapy. Chaplin[62] reports a fathers' group and a mothers' guidance group in relation to psychotic children.

Criteria of group selection and the extensive use of didactic methods of therapy groups in a mental hospital is described by Boenheim and Dillon.[43] Klapman[207,209] uses autobiographies in group psychotherapy with psychotics. The more primitive and archaic the ego the more directive in structure the group treatment needs to be. Preston[292] describes a class method of group psychotherapy and refers to its economy and facilitation of early rapport. The letter-reading techniques described by Kramish[217] extends participation and enhances interaction in the group. A form of group therapy called "Patient society," described by Freund,[127] is a voluntary group functioning under its own constitution with observance of strict parliamentary rules. The society has taken over many responsibilities within the functions of institutional life and in doing so has given patients who responded favorably to the tranquilizing drugs opportunities to regain self respect and take over responsibilities to make decisions and to show initiative and competitive spirit. It brought about a better understanding by the personnel of the personalities and trends of the members and has established closer and better understanding and relationship between members and personnel.

There are several papers dealing with the use of short term group psychotherapy with schizophrenics.

A statistical study by Buxbaum and Hrebicek[57] of the effects of short term group psychotherapy for female psychotic patients treated at a Czechoslovakian rehabilitation center indicates that group psychotherapy significantly lowered the duration of hospitalization and the dependence on drugs during the hospitalization. Pine et al.[285] feel that short term group psychotherapy increases motivation, reduces dependency ties, serves as a stimulus both in emotional expression and psychotherapy and aids an adjustment to hospital living. In more general ways it has shed many new lights on hospitalization so that the functioning of medical staff and other personnel has been given a greater impetus for more interaction with the patient. Within the total milieu program, short term group psychotherapy serves as a basic hospital experience which helps patients gain some understanding of their problems. Due to limitation of time with consequent restriction of goals to be attained, the therapist serves as a catalytic agent who stimulates and extends group discussions. In thus promoting group interaction, the therapist is aware of the need for rechanneling transference relations with little or no directing or interpreting. The goals that can be achieved in dynamically oriented short term group psychotherapy are interpreted by Kotov[213] in the light of levels of interlocking relationships and identifications which allow loss of fear or releasing speech and/or feelings, loss of isolation, increased confidence and symptomatic relief.

Hiler and Berkowitz[171] feel that this can be enhanced by the "family setting" atmosphere which often follows from the use of male-female therapists. Their group evolved through three stages, each lasting approximately three months. During the first period the level of therapy was superficial with the usual generalities, intellectualization, and inhibition of feelings. The second period was more uneven. There were intervals when more individual problems and feelings were expressed, along with greater patient interaction, but the overall level remained quite superficial with little insight. The last period found the group showing a surprising capacity to work at greater depths on key problems, to express unacceptable feelings, and particularly to relate to each other.

Sadock and Gould[313] describe short term group psychotherapy on acute adolescent male admitting ward dealing mostly with schizophrenics. Attendance was voluntary and total. The therapist was goal directed, nonpunitive, noncritical yet set limits on the behavior of the group as a whole. This first contact ward-positive response enabled effective relating with therapists. Major attainments are, according to Pine et al.[285] stimulate motivation, lessen dependency, develop attitudes toward psychotherapy, and adjustment to hospital living. Short term group therapy is used by Partridge[274] to prepare hospitalized schizophrenics for leaving the hospital and adjusting in the community.

Family therapy, one of the new frontiers of the mental health field is discussed by Hildreth[170] in a symposium on family process. It comes from direct-on-the-spot-observations of families in their own milieu and calls attention to the problems and mechanisms of close family relationships and the total interactional field of the family, with special emphasis on the determining influences exerted on the patient by the unconscious motivation of the other family members. He examined some hypotheses according to which schizophrenic personality development may in part be perpetuated by reciprocal interpersonal need complementaries between parent and offspring. Interactional dynamics could be either understood in terms of observable patterns of communications or analyzed as to the underlying intentions of the participants. Paul and Grosser[276] feel that family group therapy may be most productive when it revolves primarily around issues of loss and mourning.

The family relationship conduct of the schizophrenic suggests a compromise between internal-external relational ties.[170] One of the fundamental considerations pertains to the assignment of the sick role itself to a family member to be designated later as the psychotic patient. This presentation stresses the significance of the pathogenic expectations themselves which the members may have toward the schizophrenic, and interlacing between the unconscious need figurations of the parents and of the primary patient. One of the fundamental problems concerning the relative strength of a person's various motivational aims is whether his autonomous growth aspirations are stronger than his "symbiotic" strivings. Can the patient's psychosis in itself satisfy an important unconscious need in the parent? What configurational need leads to this destructively possessive and symbiotic parental attitude pattern? Considerable clinical evidence has been gathered from the observations of families in support of the assumption that the parents tend to regard the preschizophrenic or schizophrenic child as a parent-like figure. An explanation is needed for the willingness of the child to surrender his autonomous life goal unless a constitutional underendowment of his autonomous potential is assumed. It appears that once a counterautonomous superego structure has been built up in the preschizophrenic child, a simple, apparently innocuous trigger signal from the parent or even from others is sufficient to produce a painful and perplexing feeling of guilt over any semblance of emancipation. No doubt the confusing injunctions originally must have been of a double bind type. But later the structure of the patient's own motivational forces become such that the greatest inner resistance is mobilized against anything that could lead to independence and the parents' communication at this stage may only represent a comment on the patient's impotent and general situation. The "need-complementarity" hypothesis uses schizophrenic family pathology as an epiphenomenon of characteristic structural needs (identity defects) of the personalities of the members. The most important structurally determined needs pertain to the experiences of relatedness. It is largely out of relationship needs with respect to early important object relationships that the ego came to have its identity. Keeping the ego-constitutive function of relationships in mind, it is conceivable that a symbiotic attachment is maintained between family members; among other reasons, the economic one of keeping anxiety connected with threatening identity dissolution at a minimum level. Thus what appears to be a mutually possessive and captive relational feedback between parent and child may represent a game which brings satisfaction on a regressive level of ego integration, even if independent growth of both participants is hindered.

Wynn's[401] concept of pseudomutuality emphasizes that aspect of schizophrenic family living which is permeated with an illusion that rigid relationship ties among members secure them against the recognition of divergent aspirations. Whereas the concept of pseudomutuality connotes a "sense of relation" which becomes a "hollow and empty experience" the concept of need-complementarity suggests and stresses a regressive, but meaningful experience of relatedness between family members. According to Bateson et al.[18] and Jackson[193] complementarity of deep needs among the various family members, along with other factors such as specific communication patterns or the internalization of the overall "family role structure," help to make up a homeostasis. The end result of this type of adaptation is in part accountable for the characteristic socialized relationships in the family of schizophrenics. The psychotic state of the primary patient on the other hand often represents a rebellion against the rigid family ties which are manifestations of the powerfully binding need-complementarities. It is clinically observable that inner feelings of loneliness do not depend on outside circumstances; this has little to do with loneliness in a physical sense. In other words the total network of relationship possibilities is complicated by the fact that the ego can react to the more or less personified introjects with a subjunctive experience of relatedness. The psychotic condition produces many instances of an apparent exclusive preoccupation with aggressively gratifying introjects, perhaps as the only resort from the bind of symbiotic ties on the one hand and threatening personality disintegration on the other.

Midelfort[260] used some members of the family in the treatment of schizophrenia, as companions, constant attendants, and nurses, who took part in therapeutic interviews with the patient and psychiatrist. There is a predictable series of stages described by Framo[124] that the family sessions go through. Things happen much faster in family treatment than in individual treatment or even in group psychotherapy. In general focus on the feeling between family interactions is to acquaint the family with what is going on. To deal with the stalemate in doing group therapy with parallel groups of schizophrenics and their relatives, Lewis and Glasser[228] placed several patients and their families together in one group. This led to explosions of affects and dissolving of the conventional view of patients and relatives. All members began to look at their own feelings and anxieties and to communicate with them more directly. Focus was on how people dealt with each other here and now, and unconscious conflicts, especially incestuous ones, were dealt with more in terms of their derivatives in the form of dependency. This led to the strengthening of family ties and to greater independence.

Differential criteria are used by Gralnick[154] to determine when family interviewing is therapeutically indicated, and differences between conjoint treatment and group therapy are discussed along with emphasis that the person who does family treatment must have some basic conviction about the value of intact family life.

Friedman et al.[130] feel that schizophrenia is defined and fostered by the pathology of the family system and consequently must and can be treated within this system. Hospitalization was avoided in the majority of the 100 cases they studied. Co-therapists uncovered the central pathology of each family system, attempted to work through unconscious conflicts and simultaneously confront each family member with his rigid, provocative behavior toward the others. The homeostatic pathology focusing on one member who becomes the schizophrenic victim seems to protect the rest of the family from overt psychotic symptoms. While many of the parents showed some psychotic degrees of denial and paranoid projection, they were still able to function in the social and vocational areas, only as long as the child was actually regressed and symptomatic. The study reconfirms the pathologic symbiosis between mother and child and the role of the father in promoting overall family pathology. These isolated families maintain rigid boundaries between themselves and the outside world. The family's preoccupation with the schizophrenic patient seals this symbiosis.

Family group therapy with a schizophrenic during the crisis of his return to the family described by Glasmann et al.[146] showed twin themes of the father's inadequacy and the family's attempts to systematically sabotage their own pleasures. Towards the end, both patient and father were especially moved by having had an opportunity to see each others' feelings and hoped not to lose this. What seemed to hold this family together was the fathers' inadequacy and passivity, the concomitant understanding that the younger son would also become schizophrenic, and the mother's related aggression unleashed on the whole family. In family therapy they seemed to be able to tolerate much more hostility than in an ordinary therapy group because the members were already interrelated. This tolerance for the aggression found in this family was increased by the therapists generally benevolent attitude.

Peck[280] noted that a day-hospital program offered the opportunity to study families during decompensation, with the possibility of effective therapeutic intervention during the family crisis. Friedman[129] found that the process of family therapy was altered when it moved into the home setting because of the heightened reality context.

Farber[108] feels that we need deeper understanding of the various defensive maneuvers families use to maintain their primitive state of ego diffusion and the dubious pleasures of narcissistic excitement. Families' concerted efforts to maintain semantic chaos and affective vacuums may eventually increase the stalemate. The "absent member" maneuver described by Mack and Barnum[343] as a family resistance to treatment serves to maintain fixed and stereotyped dyadic relationship patterns within the family. The fixed and stereotyped relationship patterns maintained in the schizophrenic families were found to be unresolved oedipal patterns. The schizophrenic families have great difficulty tolerating the anxiety and instability of a three-person relationship composed of two members of one sex and one of the opposite sex in which one heterosexual relationship is resolved symbolically. This three-person relationship, instead of being resolved, fragments into fantasy heterosexual and homosexual relationships which are extremely conflictual, poorly repressed, and maintained with use of denial and projection. Three-way triadic relationships are much less well developed in the schizophrenic family than in normal families. Bowen[44] postulates that the passive father in the schizophrenic family may have been cut out of the significant relationship with his children, thus impairing the child's reality-testing from an early age and also setting up the early model of the intense binding of the schizophrenic patient to the mother. According to Wolf and Simmel[397] the three-person tension occurring in transition from dyad to triad which is necessary for growth and development, is dissipated repeatedly, and the oedipal conflicts remain unresolved. Interpersonal patterns among the family members are primarily dyadic, symbiotic, and static rather than triadic and maturational. Wahl[383] writes that failure to conceptualize the possibility of a three-person growth experience is shown in a family member's inability to believe that a three-person heterosexual experience can be had without incest, homosexuality, or murder. Hence there is difficulty in developing an internalized image of a three-person heterosexual growth experience over a prolonged period of time. The intense one-to-one relationships occur with great frequency in these families and interfere markedly with the multitude of shared relationships seen in more normal families. This family image may be an important need for maturation without which the family member is crippled. Anxiety is generated when these intense binding, paired relationships are threatened. The "absent member" maneuver is a resistance encountered in family therapy which allows the maintenance of psychopathological dyads and serves as a way of avoiding the anxiety which is inherent in the construction of a three-person, heterosexual growth experience over a prolonged period of time which may be called, intrapsychically, a family image.

Concepts relevant to helping the family as a group are outlined by Coyle[78] and emphasize family relationships, social science, small group theory, framework for understanding group processes, the process of group formation or establishment of group identity, interpersonal relations or interaction, group control, and the exercise of authority. "What we perceive or overlook in the field of our potential experience depends on the framework of concepts we have in our minds."

Davies et al.[85] describe conjoint family group therapy in which the members of a family increased their awareness of other families' processes and applied this knowledge to understanding their own family processes. If the families are homogeneous, that is, each has a psychotic child rather than that one family having a psychotic child and another a psychotic parent, interaction among group members was markedly increased. The groups were led by a medical man and a female social worker. How one's own family role is conceived of and handled can be understood as it is explored with several families where these same roles are handled similarly or differently. Seeing these problems in other families was a help in trying to understand problems rather than to deny their existence or blame others for them. Paul and Bloom[275] feel that by reciprocating recognition of observable interfamilial conflicts the primary emphasis should be on empathic understanding. This permits a wide array of identifications. In a studies of conjoint family therapy of hospitalized schizophrenic patients, by Wiedhorn[386] and by Jackson and Weakland,[192] the patient's mother, father, and sometimes siblings, were seen together for weekly therapy sessions.

Rabner[296] maintains that individual psychotherapy is not effective with hospitalized schizophrenic patients because of the schizophrenic's tendency toward withdrawal and his compulsory dependence on his family with whom he lives in an atmosphere of mutual misunderstanding and recrimination. Conjoint family therapy is felt to be an effective way of altering some of the family patterns which contribute to the patient's recurring pattern of self defeat. They also note that this form of treatment may promote countertransference problems, since the therapist tends to see himself as the sole judge and arbiter for the entire family.

Paul and Grosser[277] find that families with a psychotic child manifest greater fixity in structure and interpersonal relationships, as well as more intense parent-child symbiosis and parent-grandparent dependency than other families. Such families require more support and sensitive posing of therapeutic interventions. A transactional therapeutic process for the treatment of disturbed families described by Wilkinson and Reed[387] is based on the patient member acting out the family psychopathology by way of recognizable clinical symptoms. They divide the therapeutic process into three phases: absolving the patient of the burden of change; the honeymoon phase, because after years of confusion the serenity that occurs at this time does resemble the early alleged connubial bliss and is short-lived; and the reality phase. Families thus far terminated have established a new and different equilibrium devoid of the former role-deviation and communication distortions. Curry[81] brings together several family units into one large group. The depth is limited but offers family units an opportunity to examine their ways of functioning in a meaningful way with the support and help of a therapist.

Twenty male and twenty-two females schizophrenics were treated by Esterson et al.[103] in conjoint family and milieu therapy in two mental hospitals with reduced use of tranquilizers. All patients were discharged within one year of admission. The average length of stay was three months. Seventy per cent were sufficiently well adjusted socially to be able to earn their own living for a whole year after discharge. This type of therapy with hospitalized schizophrenics involves a systematic clarification and undoing of communication patterns that are recognized as being "schizogenic" within the family, between patients, and between staff and patients. Continuity of personnel working with the family during and after the patient's stay in the hospital is noted.

Work therapy, according to Jones,[201] can become a form of group therapy when the interaction between the individuals in the work situation are studied and discussed. The workshop supervisor-instructor requires a formal training in group therapy for this method to be effective, but at best it should only be seen as an extension of group therapy to a relatively unstructured work group.

At this stage of our experience, work therapy is seen as complementary to adding much from the field of social relationships which would otherwise be lost to the treatment situation. Hamilton[167] studied the behavioral effects of workshop activation as against the effects of occupational therapy, and favors workshop therapy. He feels that it is well worth while to continue introducing industrial work into mental hospitals so that its effect may be assessed over a number of years on groups of differential clinical status with a variety of incentive conditions over varying periods of time.

McCormick[255] maintains that the work program is an experimental setting in which the disabilities of patients can be characterized. Work can be a useful pragmatic guide and rehabilitative aid according to Jones.[201]

The conjunctive use of psychodrama and group psychotherapy in a group living program with schizophrenic patients described by McGee et al.[256] proved mutually reinforcing and tended to minimize problems of countertransference. The combined treatment facilitated discharge in a maximum number of patients and appeared to ameliorate the recidivistic tendencies.

Scillatani[326] employs extended groups. Winkler[395] describes "bifocal" therapy as does Brack.[46] Copp[74] uses pictures as projective techniques in group therapy. Boenheim[42] and Butler[56] write on music group therapy.

Berzon and Solomon[32] review the literature on self-directed groups and describe three studies undertaken by them in which they believe that members were able to help each other achieve therapeutic change. Rothaus et al.[307,308] describe a leaderless group of mentally ill patients focused on art, and describe ways in which patients on hospital wards help each other deal with crises. Lindinger[234] also describes a group in which psychotic patients alleviate each other's anxiety and Indin[188] writes of an antisuicide club for patients in a hospital.

GROUP THERAPY IN SPECIAL SETTINGS

Wilmer[389] describes an experimental "therapeutic community" in a naval psychiatric setting and puts emphasis on group living and the human contact theme in which group psychotherapy is a basic tool.

Tuttle and Peters[370] made similar efforts in an army setting. Schizophrenic patients, randomly selected, were studied for up to six months. A serious attempt was made to use current psychoanalytic knowledge and relatively intensive treatment methods as well as the social environment to change the schizophrenic illness of a small group (ten per ward) of patients. The analysis of the problem of schizophrenia and the operational model for the group of schizophrenic patients indicates the richness of this learning experience. It is an excellent plan. They assume that the difference between the normal and the schizophrenic is one of degree and that disturbances in feeling and acting can be readily recognized in the ordinary population.

Shaskan[330] placed an index of growth on the utilization of group therapy in a Veterans Administration Mental Hygiene Clinic. This stabilized the clinic program. They have never needed to resort to a waiting list for the patients to enter group therapy. Training has been aided and stabilized. Research has been stimulated. Because of the group psychotherapy program, they have been able to provide leadership in the community mental health and psychiatric programs and have received national and international recognition of their studies on leadership. Half of eighty patients in a VA hospital were assigned by Levine et al.[226] to traditional occupational therapy, and the other half was assigned to lawn-mowing detail. Those who were mowing the lawn showed significantly more improvement than those working in traditional O.T.

Group psychotherapy with psychotic and borderline military wives was instituted by Hartog[169] in a relatively closed military community and was distinctive because of the severity of illnesses represented, the involvement of husbands in the establishment of a rather firm treatment contract, and the influence of the military environment. These twenty-nine military wives were treated for varying lengths of time over a period of more than one and one-half years. Sixteen patients improved clinically, seventeen socially. Three became worse clinically and four socially. Ten were unchanged clinically, and eight were unchanged socially. Of the fifteen patients in treatment more than six months, thirteen improved. Almost all patients received tranquilizing medication before and during this period of treatment.

Welch and Robbins[385] describe short term group therapy with acutely psychotic patients. Garner et al.[462] consider groups in mental health connected with a general hospital. Towey[368] describes the range of groups conducted in inpatient settings, as well as how the settings may in themselves be consciously considered and planned for as groups.

SUPERVISION AND THE GROUP THERAPIST

Geller[140] describes the result of a series of seminars designed to furnish supervision of the work being done in group psychotherapy by the staff of a large mental hospital. There was discussion of the technical arrangements for group therapy groups and the theoretical considerations of both group therapy and psychotherapy in general. Interactions of the patients within the therapy groups presented were discussed and studied. The roles played by each therapist within his particular therapy group were investigated. Also useful were the interactions of the various therapists within the seminar group. The conclusions reached during the supervisory seminar were seen both from the standpoint of the supervisor and that of the participants who were given a questionnaire at the end of the seminars. It was the general feeling that the use of the seminar setting and the use of the participants' reactions, as well as the study of the content material, was a useful way to handle the supervision desired.

Cutter[83] describes patient leadership of discussion groups in a state hospital an important supplement to treatment. There was similar staff-led group supervision of the patient leaders.

Lay group psychotherapists who have been specially trained to work with psychotics compare favorably to regular professional group psychotherapists working with this population, according to Poser.[288] He goes so far as to question professional training.

Brown[52] discusses how a visiting consultant can focus the attention of the staff group members on the nature of the underlying themes and characteristic interactions in their ward group meetings. This increases staff self awareness in certain limited areas, and can lead to a reduction of the amount of unrecognized or unverbalized intrastaff tension and the creation of an atmosphere conducive to change.

The emotional position of the group psychotherapist has been discussed by Ross and Brissenden.[306] The therapist has greater opportunity than in individual therapy to see himself as others see him. There are reactions inherent in selecting a particular type of group (motivation by neurotic conflicts), reactions to individuals in the group (aggressive drives), and libidinal conflicts. These were found to be stimulated in a subtle fashion by the dependent, good patient who is willing to talk about symptoms more than by the more openly seductive ones. The therapist, writes Fidler,[113] must keep the interpersonal responsiveness of psychotics in mind as they go through the evolutionary phases of group life so as to help them to communicate and cooperate with other people. After initial reactions to the group setting, psychotics will begin to reveal psychotic material and gradually take an interest in that of other members. As they accept their own anxieties and those of others, they can begin to make plans for returning home, albeit with manifestations of pathology. He found an appreciation of the patient's psychological dilemma to be more important than deep interpretations.

Coleman[72] describes an acute treatment inpatient setting where the emphasis is on group and family treatment. The resident, he finds, experiences difficulty in separating his functions as individual therapist and group worker, in addition to the usual difficulties of being a helper for feelings rather than for physical problems. The staff, too, are torn between jealousy of his powers in individual work and need of him as a support. The different kinds of experience each has with the patients leads to staff and resident needing each other in making reasonable decisions about the patients.

Schindler[320] also writes on the position of the group therapist in the group.

GROUPS FOR THE BORDERLINE SCHIZOPHRENIC

Kadis et al.[202] feel that patients with long-standing psychoses find it difficult to follow the rapid shift of communication in group therapy. Unlike borderlines, they find it difficult to identify with other patients. The presence of overtly psychotic patients leads other group members to ward off their own fugitive fantasies and to shore up their own defenses. In a well-integrated group, the individual attributes of a psychotic member may prove invaluable for the others and for himself.

Spotnitz[351] feels that the group setting is a valuable means of treating borderline schizophrenics, either alone or in combination with individual therapy. However, it is still a question for the future to determine when group treatment is indicated, and group therapy ought not to be considered a catch-all for individuals difficult to treat by other means. One advantage of group treatment is that it helps to counteract seclusiveness. The author stresses that in working with borderline schizophrenics in group therapy, one should first support and reinforce the resistance and prevent the patient from using resistance as a weapon for self attack. These patients have excessive accumulations of latent destructive energy which facilitate regression. By all means he tried to avoid the mobilization of destructive energy. Because the patients' identifications are extremely defective, he chose patients with similar backgrounds to facilitate identifications. Five to ten individuals, mixed in sex, with divergence in personality structure were selected. He feels that along with instigators of emotional intensity, a group needs regulators of emotional release. The first six weeks of group therapy were an opportunity to test out the capacity of the assembled members to work together effectively. Gradually the members were educated to approach free association in the group. Interpretation was found not to be particularly therapeutic for the borderline patient. There seemed to be three basic types of resistance: resistance to spontaneous verbal communication, marked rivalry, and poor manners. The therapist was often given voluntary and deliberate help by the less seriously ill individuals in the group in their display of feeling for their sicker associates. The more severely disturbed the patients were, the less research-oriented the therapist could afford to be. The borderline patient is looking for direct and immediate satisfaction. The patient is more willing to discharge his destructive energy verbally when he realizes that he will not damage the significant object present. The opportunities which group treatment may provide to experience different sets of reactions to other individuals may enable the patient to learn how to temper this all-or-none tendency. As one member talks about a traumatic experience or intimate relationship, this has an explosive or contagious effect on other members, who will begin to relate similar experiences or relationships. This is invaluable for borderline patients. All in all, analytic group psychotherapy provided an excellent instrument for the treatment of borderline schizophrenia to promote ego growth and repair and stress the importance of individualization.

Hora[177] maintains that the borderline patient can proceed from interpersonal processes to contributing to the group's advance. The borderline's primary dilemma is to simultaneously crave for and dread the object. This conflict poses severe strain on his psychic economy and leads him to prefer the status quo and to avoid change. Preparatory individual therapy and a period of combined therapy is seen as indicated to lead the patient from relative isolation towards multiple relations. As a medium gear towards ego growth, an ego repair group psychotherapy is a favorable adjunctive method in the rehabilitation of this kind of patient. Hora focuses treatment preferably on relatedness and affect, and secondarily on content.

Forer[120] describes the outpatient schizophrenic's insistence that the therapist be a structed and real person helping his patients see enough of the reality of his life, emotions, motives and anxieties, to hasten their relating to and identifying with the real person rather than another construction of fantasy. This approach worked with patients in fair remission having moderately stable and structured egos even in the presence of hallucinatory and mild delusional material. It has not been successful with severely regressed, confused patients who require largely a supportive approach. To combat the schizophrenic's refusal to test the reality of the conviction that all relationships are dangerous, Forer uses an all-out approach, including his own emotions, in an appeal to the ego of the schizophrenics to test the irreality of their convictions. Acceptance and love are not enough and can merely lead to dependency. Schizophrenics develop their own methods for getting gratification. At times their activity is so great that it may to some extent impede group solidification. A direct interpretive approach rather than a passive one is used. Generous in praise at constructive steps, he has to build in missing ego functions when patients studiously avoid understanding other people around them. This forcing technique diminishes projection of blame for frustration and lessens denial of wishes, so that patients begin to tolerate anxiety. Because of this active attack on psychotic defenses, the therapist becomes the focus of transference feelings and resistances to social identification. Gradually he is trusted, at first ambivalently. When the defenses against their wishes lessen, the patients are no longer satisfied by the empty protection which psychosis offers. They are "hooked" on gratification. The therapist must align himself with the ego so that primary process motivation and psychotic superego functions eventually diminish to a point where they are manageable.

Pinney[286] reports considerable work on reactions of outpatient schizophrenics to group psychotherapy. Studies by Shattan et al.[332] show that the group approach bears wider application in improving outpatient programs for an ever increasing population of exhospital patients.

One of the major problems confronting the psychiatric facilities of a municipal general hospital is, according to Wong,[400] the treatment of a large population of schizophrenic patients. Group psychotherapy is a feasible and effective approach in the treatment of a large outpatient group of schizophrenic patients to provide adequate and intensive care using a limited number of personnel. Members of a spontaneously formed subgroup achieve better results when measured by their ability to remain in a group setting in outpatient treatment. They seem to require fewer readmissions, and adjust more successfully to social, family and work relationships than nonsubgroup patients with similar backgrounds and clinical syndromes.

Greenbaum[155] feels that combined psychoanalytic therapy and group therapy provide specific elements such as opportunities for multiple transference identification, reality-testing and activation of the socializing process.

The adjustment of the borderline schizophrenic in analytic group psychotherapy presents a complex dynamic interplay within the group which appears to permit the borderline patients to accept interpretations to a much higher degree than is possible in individual therapy according to Hulse.[183] Feldberg[111] finds that the borderline patient in turn contributes significantly to the group by his facility in offering lucid observations on ego-threatening feelings and ego defenses which aid in the development of insight by neurotics in a group.

Combined psychoanalytic therapy as described by Greenbaum[155,156] in the treatment of borderline cases of schizophrenia with negative therapeutic reactions encompasses individual psychoanalysis, group psychotherapy with the psychoanalyst present, and group psychotherapy without the psychoanalyst. The two group settings provided interaction on the peer level which interaction can be considered a specific technic of treatment for schizophrenics. Combined therapy decreases transference resistance through the mechanism of multiple transference interaction and the splitting of transference, increases reality-testing, improves the socializing process and intensifies the process of gaining insight and self esteem.

Hora[179] finds that the borderline schizophrenic patient reveals himself in a most typical way through the phenomenon of "double bind." This is a special mode of communication characterized by simultaneous contradictory messages conveyed through verbal and nonverbal channels. The impact of such mode of existence is an experience of enslavement and confusion on the part of the recipient of the patient's attention. One of the main aspects of the group psychotherapeutic rehabilitation lies in the systematic unraveling of the enslaving and double binding modes of their communication with the aim of exposing them to an experiential process through which they develop the capacity to participate in human relationships under conditions of freedom. They gain their freedom to be by learning to let-be.

MILIEU GROUP PROGRAMS

There has been increasing use of group approaches in the treatment of hospitalized patients. Patient government is described by Wachspress.[382] Leadership is usually given to the more responsible members. If it is given to deviant members, however, it diverts aggressive energy into constructive channels. The responsibility taken by patients remains at a relatively low level, and the term "patient government" is not entirely accurate, since patients depend on staff for all major decisions. Work groups, limited in scope, are useful as the first step in a more extensive vocational rehabilitational program. Problem-centered discussion groups can be helpful in more direct, practical ways.

Peck,[281] Battegay,[23] and Lamberd[221,222] report that the use of groups for physicians, nurses, wards and intensive therapy can change the flavor of a whole hospital community. It increases direct humane therapeutic contact with patients, studies the hospital as a society in miniature, increases the sense of community, increases communication among patients, increases the assumption of responsibility, and provides a group situation for relatives of patients. According to Kole and Daniels[212] it also releases and renders harmless old repressed emotions. For schizophrenics, the group is often the first setting in which they have been able to form genuine human relationships. Battegay[23] finds that they sit at first rather anxiously along the walls and make no contact, but they gradually approach one another in a genuine group experience because of the impossibility of avoiding one another.

A one year experience in Heidelberg with analytically-oriented group discussions on a rehabilitation ward is described by Von Zerssen.[380] The schizophrenic patients were under drug therapy as well. Most of the work was based on milieu therapy fostering the principle of the therapeutic community. Daily rounds, twice weekly ward meetings, staff discussions, exchange of thoughts and feelings between the patients in the group became the pattern. Change of patients, intensive group contact outside of the therapeutic group hours and considerations of the ego weakness of the patients were felt to hinder the continuity of experience from one therapeutic hour to the next. The initiative for discussion was very seldom taken over by the group leader. Deep interpretation was avoided and discussion of relatively concrete issues or opinions, or reactions, which were so obvious to the patients that they could not be denied, tied together what was going on in the group with other things that were going on in the ward milieu. The author felt that it would have been better if a combination of group therapy and individual therapy had been available to all. The more intensive the individual therapy was, the higher the status of the patient was in the group. Themes intensively worked through were: feeling of belonging to a group considered in Germany to be social outcasts, being locked up, having failed in life, the difficulty of living together with the other patients on the ward, the concern that by living in the clinic one will lose contact with the real tasks of life, anxiety of becoming chronically ill, anxiety about repeated failure, the wish to learn by the experiences which one has both inside and outside the clinic, and to learn new ways for the carrying out of life's tasks. The author has the impression that patients with group therapy are more likely to be rehabilitated in a social sense than to have their total personality traits definitively altered.

Spotnitz[351] outlines the concept of the therapeutic community which hopefully replaces the traditional role of the patient as sick with a new role in which he is expected to show self control. Expectations are based on actual happenings rather than on projected fears as responsibility is shared, and there is participation in the overall program within the limitations of the hospital structure. This opens up the possibilities of therapy through social interaction. The vigorous use of activities of normal living as a means of bringing about close interpersonal relationships tends according to Von Mering and King[379] to reverse the regressive symptoms so frequently found in large mental hospitals. This can be done largely by using relatively untrained personnel, giving them simple objectives and methods, and making them feel part of the treatment team. The most successful programs seem to have been woven around the personalities of particularly imaginative and dedicated people, often with a minimum of formal training. Such people cannot be created but should be sought out and their natural talents developed and utilized to the best advantage.

Edelson[98] sums up the experience of developing a therapeutic community and teaching psychiatry and psychotherapy in a small private mental hospital. The author synthesizes the theoretical principles of individual ego psychology with the applied concepts of the therapeutic community through the use of principles of group dynamics and the interplay between the two.

Rosen[305] defines milieu therapy as the use of the human and physical environment of the patient as a treatment tool. The significant components of the milieu are: 1) the beliefs, attitudes and orientations of the human beings in the institution or community, 2) the organization of this conglomerate, 3) the communication within it and with other conglomerates and the individuals outside it, 4) leadership, 5) the grouping of the patients, 6) the ways of using the team, 7) the roles flexible and stereotyped assumed by the members of the team and the patients, 8) and the nature of their motivations. Mako's[248] program includes daily ward meetings between the patients and hospital staff to discuss hospital policy and increased patient participation in community life. Tölle[367] uses certain synthetic methods such as discussion groups, play, psychodrama, puppet theatre, etc., on the psychiatric ward.

Community living is the basis for the method of Morgan.[261] Meals, occupational therapy, readings, group gymnastics, singing, listening to records, daily walks, outings and parties are included. Leadership of the group is shared by nurses and doctor. Krepinski[203] feels that group psychotherapy should not be separated from the general communal life of the ward. His goal is for each patient to become a psychotherapist for his neighbor, and have some understanding of his sufferings.

Patients who share a room in a mental hospital for two or more weeks are very likely to receive similar discharges from the mental hospital according to a study by Rule et al.[312] Type of discharge was unrelated to length of stay. Resident therapists judged as improved patients they had previously diagnosed as psychotic and judged as unimproved those they had diagnosed as having personality disorders.

Therapeutic leadership is used by Baak et al.[161] to implement policy, communicate treatment values to the staff, set limits on destructive competition and scapegoating, and promote the growth of the staff and patients. The success of this method rests on: 1) the recognition that good administration and good treatment share in common the need to deal with feelings and unconscious resistance; 2) the communication by the leaders of a set of treatment values to the staff; 3) the consistent effort and commitment to obtain consensus in meetings; 4) the establishment of formal communication channels for the explicit purpose of working through feelings at both horizontal and vertical administrative levels.

A British experiment by Martin[252] shows the value of changing the approach to a democratic equalitarian kind and details the problems of tremendous resistance aroused in the staff. Jones[200] has developed a method of treatment by daily examination of what is being done and why it is being done at all levels of staff and patient interaction. Esquibel and Bower[102] describe similar efforts in America.

The British experience with group and administrative therapy is summarized by Taylor[366] from the historical point of view. He finds swings between the two extremes of dealing with the mentally ill from impersonal segregation to the current so-called democratic interest in the individual and his feelings. Present methods are seen as more current versions of agelong swings between these two extremes.

Ishiyama and Grover[190] designed an approach to utilize the skills, attitudes, and personality quirks of every member of the staff, professional and nonprofessional, to provide a social context whereby desirable interpersonal contacts would be fostered. The model provides for a varied number of social structures suitable to the needs of a variety of patients or suitable for one patient at varying stages in his progress. Spivak[349] and Wing and Freudenberg[393] find that the patient experiences the mental hospital as an almost total society. Through the processes of social interaction different facets of the social organization facilitate, inhibit or redirect the patient's deviant behavior. Spivak[349] and Ugelstad[371] feel that a collaboration of the sociopsychological sciences organization, group theory, and technique of research and psychiatry can prove particularly fruitful. Where the main emphasis of care was on the "long-stay" patient there was least clinical disturbance and most personal freedom, useful occupation, and optimism among the nursing staff. Where reform had not progressed so far, there was most clinical disturbance among patients and least personal freedom, useful occupation and optimism. A hospital industries therapeutic placement program according to Fink and Dunning[114] involves careful evaluation of the patient by the physician and coordinator before assignment, prescription like any other treatment procedure, systematic followup, evaluation and upgrading from less responsible, less difficult jobs to more responsible, more difficult jobs, a link in the rehabilitation continuum which begins at the reception service and ends once more in the community.

Rothwell and Doniger[310] describe the experience of two professional women trained in occupational therapy who lived in a half-way house with forty-four patients, ten at a time. They dealt with the problems of the blurring of roles of staff and the importance of preservation of human dignity and the assignment of responsibility for self care, as well as the intimate details of psychotic and antisocial behavior, including suicides and runaways. The administration was much simpler than that of a psychiatric hospital. Every patient had his own therapist. The milieu treatment consisted of the informal give and take between staff and patients with focus on problems of everyday living, the sharing of such simple housekeeping tasks as grocery shopping, cooking, washing, and ironing, the small talk and common experiences.

According to Forrer and Grisell,[121] Goodson,[150] and Pinsky and Levy[287] the addition of psychiatric nurses shows, if patients are to be introduced to more activities, that it can be accomplished by additional nurses with patients who are slower in responding to the regular hospital program. Williams et al.[388] feel that this is an important group to reach because it is from this group that the additional remissions must come if there is to be an appreciable increase in a mental hospital discharge rate. A book by Armstrong and Rouslin[8] designed to teach nurses the practical and clinical implications of group psychotherapy on hospital wards is available. Boenheim[41] asserts that group therapy, indeed any form of psychotherapy, is hindered if the nursing staff is not drawn into the program.

In today's practice nurses are taking an ever increasing part in the supervision of mentally ill patients, and according to Brown[51] and Clark and Wackerman[66] often lead groups in hospitals. Discussion of the development and resolution of the intense rivalry between patients is encouraged. LaFave and Burke[219] examine the effort of different nursing approaches to the patients. Black[34] describes the effective combination of professional discipline and the industrial convalescent setting for the mentally ill.

One promising approach has been the day treatment of schizophrenics. It has been found to be superior to conventional outpatient psychotherapy particularly in the most poorly adjusted, prognostically least hopeful patients. Freeman[126] focuses on rehabilitation using the patients' strengths and democratic participation in the milieu. There exist various forms of day treatment such as the "drop in" center and intensive small group services described by Lucas[238] in Detroit.

Schnore[322] has reevaluated an activity program of intensive social, recreational, and occupational activities for regressed schizophrenics two years after its inception, and discusses the successes and limitations of this approach. The original objectives of decreasing the acute psychopathology in order to improve the ward adjustment of a group of seriously regressed male chronic schizophrenics appeared to be more than achieved. Although several patients were doing productive work, none could be considered "cured," with adjustment achieved to the point of discharge in the near future. These findings seem to bear out that the progressive regression and deterioration are due to the relative lack of social and physical stimulation on the typical back wards. This is a reversible process. Cohen[69] describes the effect of participation in social activity by two psychotherapeutic groups of hospitalized female chronic schizophrenics. He found that the increased pleasure and tension resulting from the social events served to heighten group unity and to motivate discussion of personal problems whereas previously there had been great resistance. In a second group of more withdrawn women, social events induced no apparent change.

Brant[48] reports that self government over a one year period on a psychiatric ward facilitated maturation and acceptance of responsibility on the part of the patients. Hoover et al.[176] report increased responsiveness, better social adjustment, and reduced distance between staff members instead of previous concepts of hierarchy and authority. Distance and isolation, were replaced by mutual stimulation and collaboration in the therapeutic teams, resulting in definite improvement of the patients. Krepinski et al.[203] found that a group therapy program in a mental hospital can be used for feedback information and create a psychotherapeutic community in which every patient becomes a therapist for every other patient.

When four group psychotherapy methods were compared by Glad[145] it was found that behavior and progress in psychotherapy are functions of the kind of operations employed by the group leader and the kind of personality composition of the patient. The therapy operations derived from interpersonal psychiatry appear to have generally socializing effects, but only if the patients were still struggling for adjustment. Therapist operations most closely representative of the client-centered approach appear to evoke individuality in paranoid schizophrenics. When behavior disturbance was high in the patients, projected material included the assumed aspects of the personality. When behavior included some comfortable acceptance of the desired but feared satisfactions, the disturbed quality was symbolized other than expressed in behavior.

Stamos[352] describes an experimental program of group therapy with hospitalized psychiatric patients chosen for provisional release to a nursing home. The group meetings increased socialization and reduced anxiety about leaving the hospital.

In one experiment by Gumrucku and Mikels,[159] schizophrenics and people who were not patients lived together. Treatment was concerned with helping patients work out real world problems in a sheltered environment.

Fairweather[106] found that the formation of small task groups of patients on the hospital ward in which each group is held responsible as a unit for the behavior and progress of its members results in an increase in active, socially oriented, goal-directed behavior. During large group meetings, small task group patients came on time more frequently, were more talkative, talked to other patients rather than just to the staff leader, discussed particular topics with less frequent changes of subject, tended to bring up problems about which the group could do something, and carried out a greater number of group projects. Small group ward patients chose a larger number of other patients as acceptable and desirable to have some relationship with, were more hopeful about the future, spent a relatively shorter time in the hospital, and following discharge were more frequently employed. They were more likely to meet regularly with friends and to talk to others. Artiss[11] feels that education in the rudiments of successful social behavior should be made a part of the treatment regimen. The patient should be placed in a position where he has regular opportunity and responsibility to interact with a healthy group. Ward aide personnel can serve as active psychotherapists by being available to the patients for discussion of and reflecting upon his feelings. Inpatient government the group selects its own leaders, plans, and decides the social activities for the evening and all periods of time not reserved for patient psychotherapy.

Discussion groups can be used to create a therapeutic milieu in psychiatric wards, for example by making it possible to work through resistance to the establishment of an open door policy. Vargas[373] found that informal, voluntary discussion groups in the admitting ward of a mental hospital decreased anxiety and increased sociability. The use of "psychiatric technicians" to lead nonauthoritarian discussions on a disturbed ward is reported by Stevens.[355] According to Eisen[100] a therapeutic milieu can be created and patients' orientation to reality improved by forming many different types of groups including ward councils, situational groups, peer-oriented groups, and work groups. Stotland and Kobler[357] describe how group dynamics affected the fate of a mental hospital.

Perrow[283] writes of the changeover from a custodial to a therapeutic model. Shrader and Beckenstein[336] describe reality therapy in the hospital. Eicke[99] describes therapy groups within the hospital.

Hinckley[172,173] on the basis of experience at Chestnut Lodge describes how psychoanalytically-oriented intensive psychotherapy can profitably give attention to the therapeutic consequences of work group activity and patient participation in community responsibility. The work group activity—the building of a kiosk by patients for patients—filled many desires and needs. It integrated the whole hospital community and provided the setting for experiments in friendship and group membership. It offered opportunity to master many new media and to satisfy curiosity. Unpaid patient workers were the forerunners of salaried patient managers, bookkeepers, and clerks. New roles of increased status opened for the patients after they had created the structure for these roles. This introduced a new dimension into the community. Out of group membership, work, and other ingredients the patients built a whole new community facility for the community's benefit. Some schizophrenics rose out of their torpor to participate actively in this concrete, useful, satisfying work only to fall back into their schizophrenic torpor after the work was over.

In Sullivan's milieu, as discussed by Rioch and Stanton,[303] the recovery rate measured by return to home or work of young, first-break male schizophrenic patients was better than 85 per cent and continued at this level for several years. Day-hospitalization for the social rehabilitation of the schizophrenic effects, according to Valliant,[372] rapid return to the community. Vernallis and Reinert[375] describe the use of group therapy in a weekend hospital program. Pinsky and Levy[287] discuss social workers, interest in running groups. Pace[272] reports significant improvement by a milieu approach, although the use of tranquilizers weakens the validity of the results.

Burke and Lee[55] discuss an acting-out patient in a psychotic group. The success of the inclusion of the sociopath appeared to hinge on the strict separation of responsibilities among ward personnel with the therapist having no ward discipline duties.

Clark and Hog,[67] Friedman and Lewis,[299,227] and Redlich and Carstairs[61] consider the best therapy to consist of a highly individualized system patient reeducation in a stable, reliable setting using individual and group therapy, controlled experiences in group living, occupational and recreational therapy, adult education, all coordinated with organic therapy as indicated. Performance has been equated by Shellhase[334] with the patient's acceptance or rejection of the role of patient within the treatment situation.

Galioni et al.[131] discuss a host of new problems opened up by the milieu approach. Such fruitfulness helps to justify a new idea. The milieu acts as a conditioning agent in often unintended ways. Noted are marked differences in schizophrenic behavior, in language and religious manifestations. Frequent references by patients to people "sucking their blood" may possibly be correlated with the milieu. Quite probably the milieu can potentiate or obstruct the effects of other treatment. Certainly results do vary from hospital to hospital and with patients given identical treatment.

A method of milieu therapy and vigorous physical activity was used by Suess[362] with a group of chronically disturbed female patients who had been unresponsive to other therapies, including group therapy. Seventy-eight patients, some hospitalized up to thirty-seven years, were studied for a period of thirty months between September 1955 and March 1957. There was obvious clinical improvement: 14 per cent returned home; 13 per cent live in less supervised hospital areas; 45 per cent can comfortably engage in common social activities; 97 per cent show decreased destructiveness and negativism. He feels that the daily use of both male and female authority figures presents a healthy milieu for therapy, and that the opportunity for, and the presentation of adequate interpersonal relationships is of prime and vital importance in the treatment.

A ten months' experience is reported by Wilmer[390] on an acute admissions service which dealt with severely disturbed schizophrenics and disruptive character neurotics in a closed thirty-four bed ward. The major therapeutic instrument was a forty-five minute community meeting of patients and staff held on the ward six days a week. The group meetings had a profound effect in improving patients' socialization both in the meetings and on the ward. Edelson[98] recommends daily staff meetings to convey belief in the individual dignity and importance of each patient.

The impact of the arrival of new patients and new staff members on the functioning of a therapeutic community in a voluntary psychiatric hospital is described by Small and Small.[339] They found that group and individual meetings can be used to limit destructive reactions and to reestablish the free flow of information and feeling on the ward.

Pratt and DeLange[291] feel that there are advantages to having a patient enter an on-going therapy group immediately after admission to the hospital. The value lies in reducing the patient's initial anxiety about hospitalization and in establishing an immediate diagnostic and treatment program.

Group therapy was introduced on an acutely disturbed ward by Weich and Robbins[385] to effect in the patient a strengthening of ego boundaries and ego controls through reality-testing, a working through of the patient's denial of illness by helping him to understand why he is in the hospital, a reduction in his sense of estrangement, a feeling of confidence in the staff demonstrated by the doctor's interest, increased verbalization rather than acting out of impulses, sociability and goal-directed activity, and through ventilating grievances and hostility. Repeated patterns of progression with some variations were discernible.

Mack[242] describes the evolution of patient ward meetings from the discussions of complaints about the hospital to group psychotherapy with discussion of personal problems and interpersonal relations. Gottsegen[153] feels that the Hunter Process Index may be useful in selecting patients who have significantly better potential to benefit from a program of social therapy in a psychiatric hospital. An admixture of diagnostic categories may be "quite advantageous" according to Battegay.[19]

Lapp[224] recommends that sociometric findings be taken into account when new patients are reassigned from one unit to another, and whenever patients become co-workers. Group psychotherapy in the form of group discussions, the application of sociometric insights, and group discussions were found to establish a more favorable therapeutic milieu.

Finkelstein and Berrent[115] found that in a psychiatric receiving hospital group therapy sessions structured as social meetings with doctors in attendance but not in leadership roles provided special diagnostic possibilities and a unique opportunity for human interchange between patients and staff.

In dealing with chronic hospitalized psychotics after about ten sessions in which "gripes" were exhausted, Bindelglas and Gosline[33] found that the group came to a therapeutic halt. However, when various ataractics were utilized, therapeutic movement was resumed.

Fifteen articles in a volume edited by Greenblatt[157] describe an experimental study of the comparative effects on long-hospitalized schizophrenic patients of chemotherapy in social or milieu therapy. Wilmer,[391] working in a naval hospital therapeutic community, reports that tranquilizers did not improve morale and activity beyond the level achieved by management alone.

Burke and Lafave[54] and Crocket and St Blaize-Molony[80] emphasize the coordination of staff efforts in the development of a therapeutic climate. "Grouping" is described by Flegel[118] as a method for manipulating the milieu in order to control patients. This seems to be akin to an old method segregation used for many years as part of custodial treatment. Rothenberg and Vogel[309] analyzed the value of patient cliques in a therapeutic community.

Ramsey[297] has written about the value of "sociotherapeutic camping" for the mentally ill. Jacobs[194] describes a social action approach to milieu therapy in a mental hospital. A weekend hospital program is reported and discussed by Marler.[251] Finally, Geert-Jørgensen[139] presents work with the group treatment of paranoid schizophrenics in the milieu of a Scandinavian mental hospital.

GROUPS FOR RELATIVES

Corsini[75] and Schindler[319] describe parallel, "bifocal," groups for the parents and mates of schizophrenics. The rationale for such groups is the assumption that family relationships are pathogenic and maintain the schizophrenic behavior patterns. The hope is that by insight, these family patterns may be changed enough to provide a better environment for the disturbed member, and possibly to act prophylactically on other members of the family. These groups are distinguished from family therapy groups by the absence of the patient.

Colbert[71] reviewed a psychotherapeutic group for mothers of schizophrenic children hospitalized in a distant state hospital. He contrasted this group to one composed of mothers whose children were receiving outpatient treatment, and found that the absence of the stimulus of having the child in the home markedly diminished parent motivation. One had to view the mother independently from the fact that she had a schizophrenic child. The validity of this form of therapy where the parent-child relationship is severed, probably for years, has been questioned.

Sculthorpe and Blumenthal[327] found that a combined patient-relative group reduced the number of relatives' complaints to a minimum although direct benefits to the patients were not striking.

A group casework approach with relatives of adult schizophrenic patients described by Mass and Odaniell[253] was found to reduce irritating occurrences between patients and family members.

Along lines resembling family therapy, Kirby and Priestman[205] worked with schizophrenic mothers and their daughters in a group. The parent-child relationship could be examined in a less static way and alternate patterns of behavior considered. It also gave the therapist an excellent opportunity to observe variations in parent-child relationships. The group members began, in addition, to learn about parent-parent and parent-self relationships which increased their general flexibility in dealing with life.

Kramer and Daniels[116] similarly describe a group composed of several families with a schizophrenic son. An atmosphere was created in which members could scrutinize their own forms of interaction and compare them with both constructive and destructive patterns present in other families. A consistently noted pattern was, for example, the tendency of some parents to support and reinforce their son's psychotic symptoms. The focus of the group was on the examination of reality, social interaction and family communication, rather than on the recovery of repressed material. In this, the continuing interaction between group members and the therapist was found to be all important.

SPECIAL AIDS TO GROUP PROGRAMS

Moving pictures, originally intended as recreation, were found to have therapeutic possibilities by Berman.[31] Even some of the most disturbed psychotic patients who had been noisy and hyperactive on the ward immediately prior to the showing of the films became quiet and watched the pictures in an orderly fashion, revealing in most cases some degree of identification with the characters on the screen. Women who were in the habit of wetting and soiling themselves had no incident of this sort during the performance. Uninterested, mute and apathetic patients were found in many instances to follow the continuity of the story and ask questions. Klapman and Meyer[210] describe how mental health films on group psychotherapy exerted a marked catalytic effect on the group process by loosening resistances, arousing feelings of curiosity, and complementing other treatment procedures. In the initial stages the material stimulated by the film appeared especially effective in reducing isolation and in providing a common focus of interaction.

Music alters the frequency and quality of verbal participation in psychotherapeutic groups according to Shatin and Zimet.[331] They observed differential effects by varying the type of background music. Music made a catatonic verbally accessible and indicated to Ishiyama[189] that music can be a medium of communication. Applied in a therapeutic atmosphere by Gillis et al.[144] music led to clear-cut clinical improvement in chronic hospitalized schizophrenics. There was no definite advantage of quick rhythmic music (rock and roll) over nonrhythmic music, although women tended to derive more benefit from rhythmic music than men. Winick and Holt[394] used music to stimulate free expression of feelings and to evoke dream and fantasy material with borderline and schizophrenics in group psychotherapy. Muskatevd[267] applied a combination of group psychotherapy, psychodrama and music therapy in treating hospitalized mental patients.

Occupational therapy cannot function successfully as an independent unit and has very little meaning without close coordination with the psychiatric staff, assert Ellis and Bachrach.[101] The potential value to the patient is limited only by the skill and resourcefulness of the psychiatric staff and the occupational therapists. Brigl and Lindinger[49] treated ten groups simultaneously with group psychotherapy and occupational therapy. Friedman[129] describes how planning of and participation in such group activities as putting out a newspaper can be effective indirect froms of psychologic treatment. A two-way television connection made it possible for Wittson and Affleck[396] to meet with groups who were geographically distant.

Exercise is used by Niver et al.[269] as a form of group therapy. Mack and Barnum[243] find that when an occupational therapy activities program is extended to include less structured group therapy discussions, the group meetings deepen the therapeutic impact of the hospital experience. This was reflected in the wide range of the emotionally significant issues approached in the meetings, in the development of close object ties with the leader and one another, in greater cohesion on the ward, in more productive, gratifying work, and in recreational performances. Insofar as activity is intrinsic to the early development of object relations and the formation of the most primitive defense mechanisms, it may be especially useful in the initial phases of the treatment of psychotic patients where the establishment of confident object-relationships and the reconstitution of familiar defenses are essential. To enable such patients to develop more mature relationships and defensive patterns, it is essential to encourage the postponement of tension-discharge and impulse gratification. It is possible that the capacity for such postponement may be developed in an occupational therapy setting if traditional reliance upon activity is modified and less structured group therapy sessions are introduced.

Gottsegen[153] found that an assessment group expanded the group therapy services in a psychiatric hospital. Zolik, et al.[403] used supervised lay persons as group discussion leaders with family members of patients who were either in the hospital or had returned to the community. He reports the value of such groups from the point of view of both family members and lay group leaders.

GROUP THERAPY AND DRUG TREATMENT

Several studies attempt to evaluate the effect of drugs on group therapy. Blair and Brady[36] studied chronically hospitalized patients during a period when there was only group therapy to offer, a time when reserpine was used, and a time when chlorpromazine was used. The effects of four years of group training proved beyond a doubt the important part this method played in ameliorating the patient's behavior and the general ward conditions. The value of occupational therapy or the total push program was accepted. Group training methods in themselves can almost completely abolish the need for restraint and seclusion, and the results affected by group training may often be mistakenly ascribed to the use of chlorpromazine. Alanen and Takha[2] and Magherini and Zuloni[245] combined somatic treatment, group therapy, occupational therapy, and socialization procedures.

An exploratory study by Freedman et al.[125] attempted to assess the effect of chlorpromazine on verbal participation in group therapy. Two groups were defined: one autistic, one interacting. The study had its own control. It was a double-blind experiment using a crossover design with one-half of the patients in each group receiving chlorpromazine and one-half receiving a placebo. Evaluation was by nonparticipant observers. With chlorpromazine autistic patients showed an increase in impaired control. Interacting patients showed a decrease in impaired control in communication. With chlorpromazine, autistic patients who moved away from the group-participating mean, showed an increase in impaired control and also showed decreased activities and increased seclusiveness on the ward, as rated by the nurses. Interacting patients who moved toward the group mean showed a decrease in impaired control of communication and seemed to show an increase in motor activity. With placebo this "spread" of the group drug effect on the ward was not observed. Chlorpromazine tended to reinforce the patient's typical mode of participation and its effect operated in contrasting patterns, depending on the patient group to whom it was administered. There is little evidence that the drug rendered patients more responsive to group participation. For the autistic group, group and drug seemed to be pulling in opposite directions, with the group facilitating involvement, and the drug facilitating withdrawal. The view that ataractics make schizophrenic patients more "accessible" to verbal interpersonal communications should be regarded with caution.

Cowden[77] reports a study in which eight schizophrenic patients received chlorpromazine and group psychotherapy, eight received only chlorpromazine, and seven patients acted as control. The two groups receiving drugs showed greater improvement than the drug, group alone or the drug only group.

Faure[109] describes a method in which groups of patients spend an average of twenty days in a sleep treatment ward, an "artificial paradise" where in action or fantasy patients experience relatively complete gratification of their needs. The sleep is induced by barbiturates and chlorpromazine so that it is a light sleep, and patients can communicate with each other and with the therapist. There are four stages; adaptation, regression, tension and reharmonization. This approach is most effective with acute psychotic episodes.

In another article[110] Faure describes how sleep-induced group psychotherapy was instituted because in individual sleep therapy patients became hallucinated and deluded. To get around this, patients were allowed to sleep together in the same room for treatment periods of three weeks in groups of seven at a time. Varying amounts of barbiturates and thorazine were given so that the patients slept about sixteen hours a day. There were opportunities for group interaction at mealtime, on awakening, and after meal-time, as well as individual sessions. After an initial consideration of personal problems that led to hospitalization, there was intense regression into childlike behavior and games. Soon states of tension and aggression broke out when people were openly hostile and very childish in their ways. When a definite time for termination was announced, there was a period of reharmonization. The greatest therapeutic benefit occurred at that time. The best results were obtained in anxiety neurosis and acute psychotic attacks. Chronic schizophrenics were provided with a means of brief contact but remained regressed.

Astrup and Harzstein,[14] through studies of the "high and nervous" activity of schizophrenics, established that psychotherapy has considerable influence on the nervous process of schizophrenics. It was felt that paranoid schizophrenics best benefited from psychotherapy. A rational psychotherapy based on simple, commonsense assumptions without any attempts at psychoanalytic sophistication and interpretation was used. In some individual sessions, discussion concentrated on the psychopathogenic experiences. In other, the authors tried to discuss plans for the future and how to obtain an optimal social adaptation. During one month the patients took part in eighteen group sessions, and each patient had several individual interviews. In addition, patients received somatic treatment including ataratic drugs which according to the authors decreased the pathological excitation of the pathodynamic structures and allowed for the establishment of new cortical connections, as well as the strengthening of healthy dominance and new interests. Psychotherapy consisted of sympathetic understanding. They felt that activation is likely to improve the high and nervous activity as judged by conditioned reflex investigations. Initial discussions of psychotic ideas seemed to have an unfavorable effect, but later on turn out favorably clinically as well as experimentally. This was explained as a weakening of the autonomic correlates of the delusions. They found that the autonomic reactions to pathodynamic structures are less influenced by drugs than the verbal and motor reactions.

Payn[278] saw schizophrenic patients, previously receiving only drugs, together in a group. Without expenditure of more time than is required for pharmacotherapy, he brought a form of psychotherapy to patients who had been found unsuitable for conventional psychotherapy, and made clinic visits more meaningful to them. This approach enabled the psychiatrist to get to know the patients better than is possible in brief individual contacts, and gave him opportunity to help the patients with difficulties in interpersonal relations. This method was more gratifying to the therapist than mere pharmacotherapy, and his increased interest in the patients was communicated to them.

A study in which one hundred fifteen chronic schizophrenics were observed for up to six years, half in a custodial care center and half in an acute treatment center, is reported in Greenblatt's book.[157] All had been sick between five and ten years and were under 50 years of age without evidence of organic deterioration or mental retardation. Half of the group in each of the settings was given drugs. In the acute treatment center those who received drugs showed more improvement than those who were in the acute treatment center only. Similarly in the purely custodial hospitals there was a higher improvement rate among patients who received drug therapy.

Evangelakis[104] found that female hospitalized psychiatric patients receiving a combination of trifluoperazine, group therapy, and adjunctive therapy showed far greater improvement as measured by ability to return home than do patients participating in none, one, or even two of these treatment methods. Bindelglas and Gosline[33] maintain that the effects of reserpine and chlorpromazine on the group process in two groups of hospitalized mental patients are associated with increased relatedness, loss of isolation, decreased hostility and improved social awareness. Gorham and Pokorny[151] review the effects of phenothiazines used alone and in conjunction with group psychotherapy.

GROUP PSYCHOTHERAPY AND REHABILITATION

Most of the papers in this section have the "synthetic", adaptive, task-oriented approach to group work with schizophrenics. This follows from the expressed therapeutic goal of rehabilitation and adjustment to living in the community.

Winkler[395] describes a controlled study of activity groups led by rehabilitation, recreational, and nursing personnel. Patients from the same wards, engaging in an equal number of activities, served as controls. The patients who belonged to the groups showed a significant increase in work performance and personal responsibility, but no increase in socialization or interpersonal relationships. The author feels that involvement in an equivalent number of activities, lessened the "rejection effect," although there was no way of compensating for the experimental group.

Stotsky et al.[358] used group counseling with an experimental group of chronic schizophrenics and evaluated change by means of the Q-sort (self-rating), behavioral rating scales, and other indices. They found greater change in the experimental group than in the controls. There were several possible sources of error such as pressure by the counselor to move patients and the "rejection effect" on the controls. Although elaborate measures were taken to prevent discovery of the experimental design by the psychiatric team, it is probable that these efforts were not entirely successful.

Annesley[7] found group therapy of value in reversing trends toward chronicity and institutionalization, especially with the framework of a rehabilitation unit. He[6] organized a rehabilitation ward for patients who had been in the hospital for more than two years. Patients were permitted to work in this ward and in group therapy for at least two years. The groups were composed of patients who were withdrawn and unproductive, patients who were over-reactive with free-floating delusions, and paranoid patients with frequent delusions. The emphasis in the group meetings was on social adjustment. Neither chronicity nor intelligence had any bearing on the outcome. Mixing the sexes was felt to be stimulating and useful in the therapy. The groups therefore consisted of six men and six women. This approach gave the members an opportunity to look at their current life situation and what had led up to it. In a number of cases this gave them a reevaluation of how they had gotten into such a state, and helped relieve them of some of their symptoms so that they were able to leave the hospital and reintegrate themselves in the community. First, there was a discussion of mental illness with an attempt to find common psychopathology and meaning of symptoms. Then friction between members of the community was analyzed, and the patients were given the responsibility for the best way of dealing with this. Finally patients' work records were discussed in detail to help them leave the hospital and find employment. An increased discharge rate, especially among male schizophrenics, who had been hospitalized for a long time in a state mental hospital was thus obtained by opening a mixed ward for the purpose of rehabilitation.

Group psychotherapeutic rehabilitation programs were used by Kramer and Daniels,[216] Hackstein[161] and Lindinger[232] to encourage interpersonal relations and improve ego integration among hospitalized chronic psychotic patients. Patient participation in a series of rehabilitation service meetings weekly between staff and patients were helpful in promoting communication and relationships between staff and patients according to Deane.[86]

Talmadge[363] describes a group therapeutic approach used to help former hospitalized mental patients adjust to leaving the hospital and handling the problems of going back into the community. The support and encouragement obtained by being in a therapeutic group with people in the same boat provided impetus to the patient to verbalize his feelings and was beneficial in preventing the necessity for repeated hospitalization.

Sixty families of chronic schizophrenic patients undergoing treatment with drugs and social therapy were studied by Evans et al.[105] to determine their potential role in the patient's rehabilitation and discharge. Many of these families maintained an active interest in the patients, expressed by continuing visits to the hospital. Their attitude toward the patient's illness was optimistic and many families favored discharge. Their expectations were realistic and in accord with the patient's capacities. Their ability to help the patient was compromised by a low annual income, insufficient room at home for another family member and inability to help the patient find a job. The importance of the increased use of the psychiatric social worker and of additional community resources was emphasized.

Rehabilitation and prevention of recurrent hospitalization were the general goals set by Freeman[126] and Dincin[93] for a day center. Each day began with a meeting of all the patients and staff. Twice a week group therapy, an activity program ranging from crafts to social activities, as well as many informal therapeutic contacts, were programmed. Following each day's session the staff would meet to discuss their observations. Minority group crisis, unfavorable family situation, long standing unemployment, inability to obtain sufficient help from verbal psychotherapy, were referral factors. Volunteers were used extensively in the program. There is evidence that group integration was the key to effectiveness in this setting. The individuals, modified, guided and advanced the social structure of which they were a part.

Black[34] maintains that the combination of professional disciplines and an industrial convalescent setting, such as a protected workshop, is effective for the mentally ill. The necessity of a team approach with reintegration of professional and vocational services is stressed. Industrial therapy in a large psychiatric hospital depends on close working relations with the hospital administration and cooperation among all disciplines involved in order to be successful according to Clark and Biscardi.[68]

A pressing problem in the comprehensive treatment of the schizophrenic patient is his rehabilitation into society after discharge from the mental hospital. Because inadequate bridges exist to fill the gap between hospital and society approximately 30 per cent are rehospitalized within the first year. The Fountain House described by Fisher[117] is a facility with small group activities in the community, utilizing community resources.

Gastager[134] and Gastager and Schindler,[138] working at the neuropsychiatric clinic of the University of Vienna, modified group psychotherapy to suit each of two clinical pictures of schizophrenia as an means of enhancing personality change induced by somatic therapies and as a good basis for social rehabilitation. The course of 100 patients, 41 "phasic" and 59 "process," their illness, and rehabilitation was reviewed with a follow-up of 5 to 11 years. The goal in all treatment was functional and social *Rehabilitation,* rather than *cure* in the usual medical sense. The somatic therapies were used to support a move in the direction of personality change. In the "phasic" schizophrenics, who mainly tend to encapsulate the psychotic material, shock therapy was used to support this tendency, and was followed immediately by participation in an open group of 15 patients, meeting at least once a week. The group supported encapsulation in a new human framework and provided the patient with a "milieu" which was neither "at home" nor totally "hospital." It helped each individual deal with difficulties in adjustment, and allowed him to share in other's problems. It provided the doctor with a means of assessing tendencies to relapse, absence from the group being often the first signal. The "process" types were much more difficult to rehabilitate. The defense of encapsulation was almost never sufficient, and there was a strong tendency to delusions. Somatic therapies consisted of sedation, insulin coma and ECT. Group therapy with such patients was more task oriented: occupational therapy, music, and gymnastics in formal groups. This was felt to keep transference conflicts from getting out of hand. For the process patients who somatized with grimaces, buffoonery, etc., the authors concentrated on dance, massage, gymnastics and bodily relaxation. Verbal contact, as for example in a discussion group was impossible in those cases. Their results showed 93 per cent of the "phasic" and 66 per cent of the "process" schizophrenics rehabilitated by these methods. There were no controls.

Carletti,[60] Glass,[147] and Yoshimura[402] found that the group treatment of chronic regressed schizophrenic patients can lessen emotional isolation and enable them to establish communication with the environment. Chen and Chu[63] report on the significance of patient meetings, and measurement of the patients' attendance in open group psychotherapy sessions on a psychiatric ward.

Häfner and VonZerssen[166] feel that work therapy, occupational therapy, and play therapy, have been very useful as activities which counteract the schizophrenic's tendency to withdraw and regress. This type of group has relatively little emotional stress attached. Battegay[19,21] describes the use of group psychotherapy since 1955 at the University of Basel, Switzerland. Large groups, small groups, staff groups, and doctor groups, as well as group work with families is described. He found work with relatives particularly indicated in schizophrenics.

Viefhues[377] states that although the problems of group psychotherapy are usually discussed in reference to analytically-oriented group psychotherapy, the simpler form, namely, the occupational therapy group, deserves study. The sense of belonging, and the opportunities provided to relate to others in the group, favor occupational therapy group with schizophrenic patients who can use the task at hand as a means of gradually dealing with others. He maintains that group therapeutic institutions outside of the hospital, such as sheltered workshops and patient clubs are useful.

Cohen[70] describes a group organized in the firm belief that chronic, regressed psychotics can be rehabilitated with the appropriate use of group technique.

His group meetings focused on specific behavioral patterns with the therapist making demands for behavioral changes. His patients' symptoms included muteness, and disheveled, manneristic, hallucinating, assaultive and soiling behavior. Gastager[135] and Wong[100] describe efforts to continue to develop outpatient group psychotherapy with schizophrenics. Fleischl[119] and Gastager[136] discuss the nature of therapeutic social clubs. Some therapists such as Geller[142] still defend the use of group analytic techniques with schizophrenic patients. Belinkoff et al.[26] find that in the case of an ambivalent, clinging, demanding, anaclitic types of transference of borderline to the therapist, the group can lessen the need to repeat this anaclitic pattern. Other patients are available as objects and for identification so that patients can become aware of, express, and deal with their guilt and anger.

Scher and Johnson[315] and Häfner[165] investigated attendance patterns in psychotherapy groups during after care. McGriff[257] used group counseling as a preparation for discharge to the community. Gardner[132] discusses continuity of care.

Chronic, rehabilitated psychiatric patients attending an outpatient clinic in order to receive renewal of prescription medication were seen by Cretekos et al.[79] in open-ended groups of six to ten persons for one hour a week in place of the previous procedure of seeing each person individually in a brief interview. Attitudes of patients and therapists to this modification are described, along with a brief description of some of the specific advantages. There seems to be no doubt that conducting a medication clinic as a group procedure is of value in that it engenders an atmosphere of increased therapeutic dynamism.

Janecek and Mandel[196] and Post and Salamon[290] make attendance at groups conditional for the prescription of drugs in the outpatient treatment of schizophrenia. Instead of merely seeing patients to prescribe drugs in follow-up clinic for 10 minutes apiece, Payn[279] began to see groups of six an hour. This was more meaningful to the patients, the psychiatrist got to know them better, and was more gratified in his work.

Fairweather[106] compared a small group program with individual work to traditional treatment and found that it produced a greater feeling of unity and social attractiveness among its members. Patients became more involved in the program, becoming therapist for each other. Regardless of their behavior, the attitude of patients to mental illness did not change. Forty fewer days were spent in the hospital by the small group as compared to the traditional ward. Medication, passes, visitors, recreation, and attrition were unaffected. Nevertheless, 50 per cent of the nonpsychotic and long-term psychotic patients returned to the hospital in six months. The study stresses the need for adequate leadership as well as the need for the patient to work without the staff. Groups of socially active and socially inactive members in a ratio of two thirds to one third solved the problems best at the ward level. McGee et al.[256] report a related experiment using group psychotherapy, psychodrama, and group living. Curry[82] discusses the phenomenologic issues in working with chronic patients.

STUDIES OF RESULTS

In group therapy of psychotic patients the most important changes according to Bower and Miller[45] seem to be training in meaningful communication, learning to appraise other people in a more undifferentiated way, and the regaining of parts of authoritarian identity. Artiss[12] emphasizes the modification of psychotic ideation.

Group therapy is described by Shear[333] as a socializing experience for chronically ill, formerly hospitalized, psychiatric outpatients whose intense feelings of egocentricity and omnipotence have previously barred them from satisfying participation in social and work groups. Semon and Goldstein[328] report improved interpersonal functioning, Satz and Baroff[314] report better adjustment to society after release. Tucker[369] found a great reduction in soiling behavior in chronic patients and feels that group therapy is a sufficiently potent technique to modify early, learned behavior patterns such as toilet habits. The study was designed to test the efficacy of group psychotherapy under controlled experimental conditions with an objective criterion. Annesley[6] reports an increased discharge rate for long-stay patients in a state mental hospital by opening a mixed ward for the specific purpose of rehabilitation and group psychotherapy. Straight[361] compared the social adjustment of twenty-four previously hospitalized patients, fourteen of whom had received group therapy while hospitalized and ten control subjects. He found no statistically significant difference in social functioning, but reports that "by inspection" the treatment group is doing slightly better both quantitatively and qualitatively than the controlled group. Carletti[60] maintains that patients can lessen emotional isolation and reestablish communication with the environment through group therapy.

Peyman[284] concludes that group psychotherapy plus electric shock therapy produces better results than either form of treatment alone. Higher levels of ego integration, lessened withdrawal in isolation, and decrease in psychotic fantasies, delusions and bizarre behavior were noted by Lifton and Smolen.[231] Better self control, less rigidity, more spontaneity, and movement from autistic to interpersonal modes of relating, made it possible for 70 per cent of the children to remain in public schools with almost all earning promotion to higher grades.

Stojilykovic and Savicevic[356] examined by interview a limited number of treated schizophrenics in order to learn the condition of their health and their ability for community, occupational, family and economic adjustment. They found the most improvement in the area of occupational adjustment, followed by economic and family adjustment. The poorest results were achieved in community adjustment. They maintain that the treatment of a schizophrenic patient should not stop with the disappearance of symptoms and his discharge from the hospital. It should be continued by reintroducing him into his family, occupation and community, and by preparing his environment for his reception as long as satisfactory family, occupational, economic, and community adjustments are reached. The cooperation of psychiatrists, social workers, social organizations, family members, work companions and closest friends becomes indispensable. The psychiatrist must remain an important support to the patient during his adaptation and resocialization. In a follow-up study of group psychotherapy patients by Boenheim[39] whose treatment had been terminated at least two years previously, seventeen responded for follow-up interviews. He found that in some instances, group therapy with these borderlines and schizophrenics helped. Illing and Brownfield[185] made an attempt to involve previously hospitalized schizophrenic patients in group psychotherapy. It produced uncertain results after 100 meetings, in spite of some growth, group interaction, and changes in work adjustment.

Rosen[304] feels that the value of groups for patients and for administration is ample reward for the perseverance needed to establish group therapy programs in mental hospitals. Lucas and Ludwik[237] report that group work reduces panic and suspiciousness in some hospitalized patients. Shellhase[334] maintains that the amount of benefit is dependent on the degree to which patients are aided to accept their role as mental hospital patients and to order their behavior appropriately. Canter[59] found that group psychotherapy facilitated transition and adjustment both on admission and discharged, as well as being essential for the ultimate adjustment to society.

Rickard[301] reviewed twenty-five studies of group psychotherapy and compared them in terms of patient characteristics, types of group psychotherapy, evaluative criteria, and tests and measures of those criteria. He divided the studies according to which of three improvement criteria were used: 1) hospital status changes—ward transfers, discharge rates, etc., 2) specific changes in personal behavior—talkativeness, anger, etc., 3) test performance criteria. He found such variability of patient populations, range of group psychotherapies, and multiplicity of measures that any comparisons had to be most tentative. He felt that the efficacy of group therapy still remained to be empirically validated, and suggested that more attention be given to questions uniquely related to group psychotherapy evaluation. He noted that many of the evaluative studies appeared to have been designed without awareness of other studies in the same area suggesting the need for more effective communication in the literature.

Gorham et al.[152] differentiate between group activity therapy, milieu group therapy, and group psychotherapy. Although all three approaches had measurable therapeutic effect, the authors found it difficult to differentiate any unique contribution from each type of group. Each treatment modality in a multi-approach unit produced significant changes in some measures. For example, they considered group psychotherapy specifically responsible for improvement on scales measuring somatization and tension, whereas a synergistic effect was found on scales of anxiety and motor retardation. DiGiovanni[92] used large batteries of standard tests, none of which demonstrated significant changes. Goram et al.[152] found a demonstrated discrimination between therapy and control group using behavioral rating scales, while no discrimination was shown by concomitant psychological tests. Forsyth and Fairweather[122] found that one's group behavior may only reflect social adaptation rather than therapeutic movement.

Fairweather et al.[107] report an investigation to evaluate the relative efficiency of four psychotherapeutic programs with three patient groups—nonpsychotic, short term psychotic, and long term psychotic: 1) all-group living and treatment; 2) group treatment and individual work; 3) individual treatment and individual work; and 4) control group of individual work and no treatment. The number of days was different for both treatment and diagnostic groups. Individual treatment took the greatest time, group living next, with group treatment and control the least and almost equivalent. Long term psychotics were in treatment longest, with short term psychotics and nonpsychotics in treatment the least. On tests the control groups had the least variance. In all three forms of treatment nonpsychotics and short term psychotics showed moderate to large adaptive change, while long term psychotics showed moderate to large maladaptive change. The three groups receiving treatment had a higher percentage of full time employment in the follow-up period. Overall short term psychotics made the best post-hospital adjustment and long term psychotics the poorest.

Friedemann[128] feels that because it is itself, a miniature society, a psychiatric hospital provides an almost ideal setting for assessing social behavior and interaction, either qualitatively or quantitatively with the aid of sociemetric tests. Schindler,[317] evaluating the results of the work at the Vienna clinic, feels that the failure rate of somatic therapy can be definitely decreased by the use of group psychotherapy. Dührssen[95] evaluates his results with group treatment after 5 years.

In general, the multiplicity of methods, and imprecise definitions of patient populations make comparisons of results between studies unproductive. A well controlled, standardized study with many clinics participating is needed.

SUMMARY

Most of the available literature in English and German on the use of group psychotherapy with schizophrenics between 1956 and 1966 has been reviewed. One outstanding feature of these papers is the emphasis on group work in hospital settings with rehabilitation and problems of after-care. This is consistent with the epidemiology of schizophrenic patients, and is reflected by developments in the areas of milieu and family group therapy. There also seems to be a general feeling that task-oriented, goal-directed, synthetic group work aimed at adaptation is more useful with this particular type of patient than the strictly analytic approach. Some work has been done to evaluate the usefulness of drug therapy in a group setting.

The authors have the general impression that group work is useful to schizophrenic patients. The question of which type, for which patients, in what setting, and with what goals remains unanswered. A well defined and controlled comparative study with long term follow-up seems to be the research area requiring attention at this point.

BIBLIOGRAPHY

1. Abrahams, J.: Group methods in the treatment of schizophrenic out-patients. *In* Scher, Samuel Charles, and Davis, Howard R. (Eds.). The Out-patient Treatment of Schizophrenia. New York, Grune & Stratton, 146-155, 1960.

2. Alanen, Y., and Takha, V.: On Somatic Methods, Group Therapeutic Procedures and Allied Measures in the Treatment of Schizophrenia. Duodecim (Finland), 77: 254, 1961.

3. Alikakos, L. C. et al.: Observations of the Meaning of Behavior in Groups of Chronic Schizophrenics. Internat. J. Group Psychother., Vol. 6, 1956.

4. Alikakos, L. C.: Analytical group treatment of the post-hospital schizophrenic. Int. J. Group Psychotherapy 15: 492-504, 1965.

5. Anker, J., and Walsh, R.: Group Psychotherapy, A Special Activity Program and Group Structure in the Treatment of Chronic Schizophrenics, J. Consult. Psychol. 25: 476-481, 1961.

6. Annesley, P. T.: Group Psychotherapy and Rehabilitation of Long-Stay Patients. Int. J. Group Psychother. 9: 167-174, 1959.

7. Annesley, P.: A rehabilitation unit on group therapy lines for long-stay patients. Psychiat. Quart. 35: 231-257, 1961.

8. Armstrong, S. W., and Rouslin, S.: Group Psychotherapy in Nursing Practice. New York, McMillan, 1963.

9. Aronson, J., and Field, M. G.: Mental Health Programming in the Soviet Union. Amer. J. Orthopsychiat. 34: 913-924, 1964.

10. Artiss, K. L.: The Symptom As Communication in Schizophrenia. New York, Grune & Stratton, 1959.

11. ———: Milieu Therapy in Schizophrenia. New York, Grune & Stratton, 1962.

12. ———: Group Psychotherapy in a Mental Hospital with Special Regard to Schizophrenics. Acta Psychiat. Scand. 33: 1-20, 1958.

13. Astrup, C.: A Note on Clinical and Experimental Observations of the Application of Group Therapy, Int. J. Group Psychother. 11: 74-77, 1961.

14. ———, and Harzstein, N. G.: The Influence of Psychotherapy on the High and Nervous Activity of Schizophrenics. Int. J. Group Psychother. 10: 394-407, 1960.

15. Azima, H., and Azima, F.: Projective Group Therapy. Int. J. Group Psychother. 9: 176-182, 1959.

16. Baak, W. W., Clover, C. G., Kalman, G. J., Mittel, N. S., and Stern, S.: Therapeutic leadership in milieu treatment. Int. J. Group Psychother. 16: 163-173, 1966.

17. Basham, J.: An Investigation of the Role of the Group Therapist As A Determiner of the Verbal Behavior of Schizophrenic Patients. Psychology 20: 3825, 1960.

18. Bateson, G. et al.: Toward A Theory

of Schizophrenia. Behav. Sci. 1: 251-264, 1956.

19. Battegay, R.: Unsere Methoden und Erfahrungen mit Gruppensychotherapie. Schweiz. Arch. Neur. Psychiat. 80: 1-37, 1957.

20. ———: Gruppenpsychotherapie als Behandlungsmethode bei hospitalisierten Patienten. Act. Psychother. (Basel) 7: 24-30, 1959.

21. ———: Gruppenpsychotherapie und moderness Psychiatrishes Spital. Nervenarzt 36: 250-253, June, 1965.

22. ———: Psychotherapy of Schizophrenia in Small Groups. Int. J. Group Psychother. 15: 3, 316-320, July, 1965.

23. ———: Group psychotherapy and the modern psychiatric hospital. Int. J. Group Psychotherapy 16: 270-278, 1966.

24. Beard, J. et al.: The Effectiveness of Activity Group Therapy with Chronically Regressed Adult Schizophrenics. Int. J. Group Psychother. 8: 128, 1958.

25. Behymer, A. et al.: Mental Health Films in Group Psychotherapy. Psychiatry 20: 27, 1957.

26. Belinkoff, J., Bross, R., and Stein, A.: The effect of group psychotherapy on anaclitic transference. Int. J. Group Psychotherapy 14: 474-481, 1964.

27. Bellak, L.: Dementia Praecox: The Past Decade's Work and Present Status: A Review and Evaluation. New York, Grune & Stratton, 1948.

28. ———, and Benedict, P. K.: Schizophrenia, A Review of the Syndrome. New York, Logos Press, 1958.

29. Benedetti, G. et al.: Forschungen zur Schizophrenielehre. 1956-61. Fortschr. Neurol. Psychiat. 30: 445-505, 1962.

30. Beran, M.: Combined individual and group therapy within the hospital team set up. Int. J. Group Psychotherapy 11: 313-318, 1961.

31. Berman, H. H.: Audio-visual Psychotherapeutics; Portable Moving Pictures with Sound as a Rehabilitation Measure. Psychiat. Quart. (Suppl.) 20: 197, 1946.

32. Berzon, B., and Solomon, L. N.: The self-directed therapeutic group; three studies. J. Counseling Psychol. 13: 491-497, 1966.

33. Bindelglas, P. M., and Gosline, E.: Differential Reactions of Patients Receiving Group Psychotherapy with Concomitant Somatic and Drug Therapies. Int. J. Group Psychother. 7: 275-280, 1957.

34. Black, B. J.: The Protected Workshop in the Rehabilitation of the Mentally Ill. Psychiat. Quart. (Suppl.) 33: 107-117, 1959.

35. Blacker, K. H.: Group Psychotherapy in the Treatment of Acute Emotional Disorders. Int. J. Group Psychother. 13: 355-359, 1963.

36. Blair, D., and Brady, D. M.: Recent Advances in the Treatment of Schizophrenia: Group Training and the Tranquilizers. J. Ment. Sci. 104: 625-663, 1958.

37. Bleuler, M.: Ursache und Wesen der schizophrenen Geistesstörungen. Deutsch. Med. Wschr. 89: 1947-1952, 1964.

38. Boe, E. E., Gocka, and Kogan: The effect of group psychotherapy on interpersonal perceptions of psychiatric patients. Multivar. Beha. Res. 1: 177-187, 1966.

39. Boenheim, C.: A Follow-Up Study of Group Psychotherapy Patients. Int. J. Group Psychother. 9: 463-474, 1959.

40. ———: On Goals in Problem Training As the Role of Group Psychotherapy in a Mental Hospital. Columbus State Hospital, Columbus, Ohio, 55, 1962.

41. Boeheim, C.: Expansion of the group psychotherapy program in mental hospitals. Paper delivered at the International Congress for Group Psychotherapy, Mailand, May 18-21, 1963.

42. Boenheim, C.: Music and Group therapy. J. Music Ther. 3: 49-52, 1966.

43. ———, and Dillon, L.: Group Psychotherapy in a Mental Hospital. Ment. Hosp. 13: 380, 1962.

44. Bowen, M. et al.: Study and Treatment of Five Hospitalized Family Groups, Each with a Psychotic Member. Am. J. Psychiat. 115: 1017-1020, 1959.

45. Bower, H., and Miller, G.: An Experiment in Resocialization of Patients with Long-Standing Psychoses. Med. J. of Australia, 1959.

46. Brack, E.: Bifocal group therapy

of schizophrenics. Zeitschrift Psychosom. Med. 8: 133-141, 1962.

47. Brant, H.: Group Therapy with Large Groups of Psychotic Patients. Int. J. Group Psychotherapy 10: 129, 1957.

48. ———: Values of Self-Government on the Psychiatric Ward. Int. J. Group Psychotherapy 9: 822-823, 1959.

49. Brigl, H., and Lindinger, H.: Über bisherige Erfahrungen mit Gruppen-psychotherapie in Kombination mit Arbeitstherapie in der psychiatrischen Heilanstalt. Wien. Z. Nervenheilk. 21: 169-176, 1964.

50. Bros, R.: The Silent Patient Among Severe Neurotics in Group Psychotherapy, Acta Psychotherapeutica, Vol. 7 Supplement, 69, 1959.

51. Brown, B.: Nurses Participate in Group Therapy. Am. J. Nursing 62: 68, 1962.

52. Brown, D. T.: Staff development through ward-group consultation. Int. J. Group Psychotherapy 16: 405-412, 1966.

53. Burke, J. L., and Lafave, H. G.: Rehabilitation: Comprehensive and Inexpensive. Dis. Nerv. Syst. 24: 612-619, Oct. 1963.

54. Burke, J. L., and Lafave, H. G.: A structured group programme for patient-staff communication. Int. J. Social Psychiatry 10, 142, 1964.

55. Burke, J. D., and Lee, H.: An acting-out patient in a psychotic group. Int. J. Group Psychotherapy 14: 194-201, 1964.

56. Butler, B.: Music group psychotherapy. J. Music therapy 3: 53-56, 1966.

57. Buxbaum, H., and Hrebicek, S.: The Effectiveness of Group Psychotherapy in the Treatment of Female Psychotic Patients at a Rehabilitation Center. Int. J. Sociometry and Sociatry 3: 25, 1963.

58. Cameron, J. L.: Some Indications of Ego Psychology for Group Psychotherapy of Chronic Schizophrenia. Int. J. Group Psychotherapy 7: 355-362, 1957.

59. Canter, A.: Observations of Group Psychotherapy with Hospitalized Patients. Am. J. Psychotherapy, 10: 66, 1956.

60. Carletti, J.: Group Treatment of Chronic Regressed Psychiatric Patients. J. Soc. Casework 44: 68-74, 1963.

61. Carstairs, M.: Industrial Work as a Means of Rehabilitation for Chronic Schizophrenics. Congress Report, Second International Congress of Psychiatry. Zurich 1: 99, 1957.

62. Chalpin, G.: The fathers' group: an effective therapy medium for involving fathers in a child psychiatric clinic treatment program. J. Am. Acad. Child Psychiatry 5: 25-133, 1966.

63. Chen, C., and Chu, H.: The Evaluation of Patients' Attendance in Open Group Psychotherapy Sessions on a Psychiatric Ward. J. Formosa Med. Ass. 61: 345, 1963.

64. Chen, R.: French Mode of Sociotherapy. Am. J. Psychiat. 121: 17-20, 1964.

65. Chesteen, H. E.: Breaking Through the Resistance in a Group of Psychotic Patients. Int. J. Group Psychotherapy 11: 462-467, 1961.

66. Clack, J., and Wackerman, E.: Five Patients in Group Therapy. Am. J. Nurs. 62: 70, 1962.

67. Clark, D. H., and Hoy, R. M.: Reform in the Mental Hospital. Int. J. Soc. Psychiat. 3: 211, 1957.

68. Clark, E. D., and Biscardi, A.: Industrial Therapy in a Large Psychiatric Hospital. Psychiat. Quart. 37: 631-641, 1963.

69. Cohen, L.: The Use of Extramural Activities in Group Psychotherapy with Hospitalized Female Chronic Schizophrenics. Int. J. Group Psychotherapy 12: 315, 1959.

70. Cohen, L.: How to reverse chronic behavior. Mental Hospital 15: 39, 1964.

71. Colbert, E. G.: Group Psychotherapy for Mothers of Schizophrenic Children in a State Hospital. Int. J. Group Psychotherapy 9: 93-98, 1959.

72. Colman, A. D.: The effect of group and family emphasis on the role of the psychiatric resident of an acute treatment ward. Int. J. Group Psychotherapy 15: 516-525, 1965.

73. Comer, M. et al.: Experiences with Milieu Therapy in a General Hospital. J. Nat. Med. Ass. 53: 36, 1961.

74. Copp, L. A.: The use of pictures as a projective technique in group therapy.

Perspectives in Psychiat. Care 4: 24-31, 1966.

75. Corsini, R. J.: Methods of Group Psychotherapy. New York, Blakiston Division of McGraw Hill Book Company, Inc. 105-106, 1957.

76. Cowden, R.: Group Psychotherapy with Chronic Schizophrenics. J. Group Psychotherapy 14: 209-214, 1961.

77. ———: et al.: Chlorpromazine Alone and As An Adjunct to Group Psychotherapy in the Treatment of Psychiatric Patients. Am. J. Psychiat. Vol. 112, Part II, 898-902, 1956.

78. Coyle, G. L.: Concepts Relevant to Helping the Family As A Group. Social Casework 43(7): 347-355, July, 1962.

79. Cretekos, C., Halperin, D., and Fidler, J.: Group communication with chronic "rehabilitated" psychiatric patients. Int. J. Group Psychotherapy 16: 51-57, 1966.

80. Crockett, R., and St. Blaize-Molony, R.: Social ramification of the therapeutic Community approach in psychotherapy. Brit. J. Med. Psychol. 37: 153, 1964.

81. Curry, A. S.: Therapeutic Management of Multiple Family Groups. Int. J. Group Psychotherapy 15(1): 90-95, Jan. 1965.

82. Curry, A. E.: Group psychotherapy: phenomenological considerations. Rev. Exist. Psychol. and Psychiatry 6: 63-70, 1966.

83. Cutter, F.: Discussion Groups in a State Hospital. Ment. Hyg. 44: 545, 1960.

84. DaSylva, G.: The Role of the Father with Chronic Schizophrenics. Canad. Psychiat. Assn. J. 8: 190, 1963.

85. Davies, R. J. et al.: Therapy with a Group of Families in a Psychiatric Day Center. Am. J. Orthopyschiat. 36: 134-136, 1966.

86. Deane, W.: Patient Participation in a Series of Rehabilitation Service Meetings. Ment. Hyg. 46: 121, 1962.

87. DeMyer, M. K., and Ferster, C. B.: Teaching New Social Behavior to Schizophrenic Children. J. Am. Acad. Child Psychiat. 1(3): 443-461, 1962.

88. Denber, H.: Group process in a state hospital. Am. J. Orthopsychiatry 33: 900-911, 1963.

89. Derwort, A.: Experimentelle Untersuchungen des Verhaltens von Schizophrenen bei der Arbeit in der Gruppe. Zbl. ges. Neurol. 140: 26, 1957.

90. Deutsch, A. L., Ainbinder, M., Becker, E., and Blumenfield, M.: Group therapy of schizophrenics in an out-patient clinic. J. of psychoanalysis in groups 2: 30-37, 1966-67.

91. Diggory, J. C., and Loeb, A.: Motivation of Chronic Schizophrenics by Information About Their Abilities in a Group Situation. J. Abnorm. Soc. Psychol. 65(1): 48-52, 1962.

92. DiGiovanni, P.: A comparison between group psychotherapy and activity group therapy in the treatment of chronic hospitalized schizophrenics. Unpublished doctoral dissertation: University of Illinois.

93. Dincin, J.: Utilization of a Professional staff in psychiatric rehabilitation. Soc. Work 10: 51, 1965.

94. Drennen, W. T., and Wiggins, S. L.: Manipulation of Verbal Behavior of Chronic Hospitalized Schizophrenics in a Group Therapy Situation. Int. J. Group Psychother. 14: 189-193, 1964.

95. Dührssen, A.: Catamnestic studies on group therapy results in 270 treated patients 5 years after termination of therapy. Zeitschrift. Psychosom. Med. 10: 120-126, 1964.

96. Dumont, M. P.: Death of the leader in a therapy group of schizophrenics. Int. J. Group Psychotherapy 16: 209-216, 1966.

97. Dumont, M., and Christ, J.: Gruppenpsychotherapie mit schizophrenen Patienten: I. Die therapeutische Gruppe als neue Dimension in der Behandlung von Psychosen. In Hans. G. Preuss: Analytische Gruppenpsychotherapie. Munich-Berlin-Vienna, Urban and Schwarzenberg, 159-165, 1966.

98. Edelson, M.: Ego psychology, group dynamics and the therapeutic community. Grune & Stratton, New York, 242, 1964.

99. Eicke, D.: Problems encountered with clinical indications of psychotherapy of schizophrenic patients with references to modern Sociopsychiatric aspects. Z. Psychother. Med. Psychol. 16: 70-78, 1966.

100. Eisen, A. et al.: Group Process in a Voluntary Psychiatric Hospital. Am. J. Orthopsychiat. 33: 750, 1963.

101. Ellis, M., and Bachrach, A. J.: Psychiatric Occupational Therapy: Some Aspects of Roles and Functions. Am. J. Psychiat. 115: 318-322, 1958.

102. Esquibel, E. V., and Bower, W. H.: Changeover of a mental hospital unit into a therapeutic community. Int. J. Group Psychotherapy 15: 11-16, 1965.

103. Esterson, A. et al.: Results of Family-Oriented Therapy with Hospitalized Schizophrenics. Brit. Med. J. 2/5476: 1462-1465, 1965.

104. Evangelakis, N.: De-Institutionalization of Patients. Dis. Nerv. Syst. 22: 26, 1961.

105. Evans, A. et al.: The Family as a Potential Resource in the Rehabilitation of the Chronic Schizophrenic Patient: A Study of Sixty Patients and Their Families. Am. J. Psychiat. 117: 1075-1081, 1960-61.

106. Fairweather, G. W.: Social Psychology in Treating Mental Illness: An Experimental Approach. New York, Wiley, 1964.

107. Fairweather, G. W., Simon, R., Gebhard, M. E., Weingarten, E., Holland, J. L., Sanders, R., Sonte, G. B., and Reahl, J. E.: Relative effectiveness of psychotherapeutic programs: a multicriteria comparison of four programs for three different patient groups. Psychological monographs: general and applied. 1-26, Vol. 74, #5, Whole #492, 1960.

108. Farber, L. H.: The Therapeutic Despair, Psychiatry 21: 7-20, 1958.

109. Faure, H.: Cure de Sommeil Collective. Paris, Maison and Cie, 1958.

110. ———: Sleep-Induced Group Psychotherapy: A New Utilization of Prolonged Sleep with Pharmacological Sleep Induction, Monotonous Environment and Psychosocial Interactions. Int. J. Group Psychotherapy 10: 22-37, 1960.

111. Feldberg, T.: Treatment of Borderline Psychotics in Groups of Neurotic Patients. Int. J. Group Psychotherapy 8: 76-84, 1958.

112. Feldman, F.: Group Techniques in a General Hospital. Psychiat. Quart. (Suppl.) 20: 276, 1946.

113. Fidler, J. W.: Group Psychotherapy of Psychotics. Am. J. Orthopsychiat. 35: 688-694, 1965.

114. Fink, L., and Dunning, E.: Therapeutic Utilization of Mental Hospital Industries. Psychiat. Quart. (Suppl.) Vol. 34, 76, 1960.

115. Finkelstein, L., and Berrent, I.: Group Therapy in a Receiving Hospital, Ment. Hosp. Vol. 11: 43, 1960.

116. Fischer, J.: Group Treatment with Schizophrenic Sons. Social Casework 47(7): 438-446, July, 1966.

117. Fisher, S. H.: The Rehabilitation of the Schizophrenic Patient: Fountain House Programme, Vol. III, International Congress for Psychiatry, Zurich (Switzerland), Sept. 1 to 7, 1957, p. 405. Congress Report Vol. III. Zurich, Orell Fussli Arts Graphique, S.A. 1959.

118. Flegel, H.: Regrouping in a psychiatric unit as a form of social therapy. A contribution to the sociology of institutional psychiatry. Nervenarzt (Dusseldorf) 34: 384, 1964.

119. Fleischl, M.: Special problems encountered in social rehabilitation, American J. Psychotherapy 18: 660, 1964.

120. Forer, B. R.: Group Psychotherapy with Out-patient Schizophrenics. Int. J. Group Psychotherapy 11: 188-195, 1961.

121. Forrer, G. R., and Grisell, J. L. Patient Improvement and Psychiatric Nursing Care. Dis. Nerv. Syst. 20: 357-363, August, 1959.

122. Forsyth, R. P., and Fairweather, G. W.: Psychotherapeutic and other hospital treatment criteria: the dilemma. J. Abnorm. Soc. Psychol. 62: 598-604, 1961.

123. Foulkes, S. J., and Anthony, E. J.: Group Psychotherapy, Penguin Books, Baltimore, 1957-1965.

124. Framo, J. L.: The Theory of the Technique of Family Treatment of Schizophrenia. Symposium: Family Treatment of Schizophrenia, Family Process 1(110): 119-131, 1962.

125. Freedman, N. et al.: Patterns of Verbal Group Participation in the Drug Treatment of Chronic Schizophrenic Pa-

tients. Int. J. Group Psycotherapy 11: 60-73, 1961.

126. Freeman, P.: Treatment of Chronic Schizophrenia in a Day Center. Arch. Gen. Psychiat. 7: 259-265, 1962.

127. Freund, R.: A Patient's Autonomous Society as a Method of Group Psychotherapy. Psychiat. Quart. (Suppl.) 33: 317, 1959.

128. Friedmann, A.: Gruppenpsychotherapie. In Frankl, V. E. et al., Handbuch der Neurosenlehre und Psychotherapie. Munich and Berlin: Urban und Schwarzenberg, 1958.

129. Friedman, A.: Group Psychotherapy as a Way of Life. Int. J. Group Psychotherapy 14: 78, 1961.

129a. Friedman, A. S.: Family Therapy as Conducted in the Home. Family Process 1(110): 133-139, 1962.

130. Friedman, A. S.: Boszormenyi-Nagy, I., Jungreis, J. E., Lincoln, G. Mitchell, H. E., Sonne, J. C., Speck, R. V., and Spivack, G.: Psychotherapy for the whole family: case histories, techniques, and concepts of family therapy of schizophrenia in the home and clinic. New York, Springer Publishing Co., 354, 1965.

131. Galioni, E. F. et al.: Intensive treatment of Back Ward Patients. Am. J. Psychiat. 109: 576, 1953.

132. Gardner, W. J.: A handful of people. J. Kansas Med. Soc. 67: 22-25, 1966.

133. Garner, H. H., Falk, and Feinerman: A general hospital approach to community mental health. Gen. Practitioner 34: 110-117, 1966.

134. Gastager, H.: Zur Methode und Organization der Rehabilitation in der psychiatrischen Klinik. Wien. Med. Wschr. 111: 61, 1961.

135. ———: Group Psychotherapy in a Psychotherapeutic Out-patient Service, Zeitschrift. Psychosom. Med. 9: 115-118, 1963.

136. ———: Der therapeutische Klub und die Nachbetreung von Psychosen. Wien. Z. Nervenhelk. 21: 159-165, 1964.

137. ———: Experience with the principle of the therapeutic community in a psychiatric ward. Wien. Med. Wschr. 114: 301-308, 1964.

138. Gastager, H., and Schindler, R.: Rehabilitationstherapie bei Schizophrenen, Nervenarzt 32: 368-374, 1961.

139. Geert-Jorgensen, E.: Group treatment of patients suffering from paranoid psychosis. Acta Psychiat. Scan., 39 Suppl. 169, 152, 1963.

140. Geller, J. J.: Supervision in a Hospital Group Psychotherapy Program. Int. J. Group Psychotherapy 8: 313-322, 1958.

141. Geller, J. J.: Group Psychotherapy in the Treatment of the Schizophrenic Snydromes. Psychiat. Quart. 37: 710-721, 1963.

143. Genis, A.: The group concept in psychotherapy. Revista Psiquiat. & Psicol. Med. 7: 394-398 (Suppl.) 1966.

144. Gillis, A. et al.: A Comparison of Rhythmic and Nonrhythmic Music in Chronic Schizophrenia. Am. J. Psychiat. 114: 1111-1112, 1958.

145. Glad, D. D. et al.: Schizophrenic Factor Reactions to Four Group Psychotherapy Methods. Int. J. Group Psychother. 13: 196-210, 1963.

146. Glasmann, R. et al.: Group Discussions with a Hospitalized Schizophrenic and His Family. Int. J. Group Psychother. 9: 204-212, 1959.

147. Glass, M.: A group leader program for regressed patients. Psychotherapy 2: 73, 1965.

148. Glatzer, H. T.: Handling Narcissistic Problems in Group Psychotherapy. Int. J. Group Psychotherapy 12: 448, 1962.

149. Golner, J. et al.: Notes on the Use of Recorded Minutes in Group Therapy with Chronic Psychotic Patients. Psychiat. Quart. 33: 312, 1959.

150. Goodson, M. D.: Group therapy with regressed patients. Perspectives in Psychiat. Care 2: 23, 1964.

151. Gorham, D. R., and Pokorny, A. D.: Effects of a phenothiazine and/or group psychotherapy for schizophrenics. Dis. Nerv. Syst. 25: 77-86, 1964.

153. Gottsegen, M.: The Role of an As-

sessment Group in a Hospital Setting. Am. J. Psychother. 17: 94, 1963.

154. Gralnick, A.: Conjoint Family Therapy: Its Role in Rehabilitation of the Inpatient and Family. J. Nerv. Ment. Dis. 136: 500, 1963.

155. Greenbaum, H.: Combined Psychoanalytic Therapy with Negative Therapeutic Reactions. *In* Schizophrenia and Analytic Office Practice, edited by A. H. Rifkin, New York, Grune & Stratton, 1957.

156. ———: The Role of Combined Psychoanalytic Therapy in the Treatment of Borderline Cases of Schizophrenia with Negative Therapeutic Reactions. International Congress for Psychiatry, Zurich (Switzerland), Sept. 1 to 7, 1957. P. 403 in: Congress Report, Vol. III, Zurich, Orell Fussli Arts Graphique S. A., 1959.

157. Greenblatt, M., Editor, et al.: Drug and Social Therapy in Chronic Schizophrenia. Springfield, Illinois, Charles C. Thomas, 1965.

158. Grotjahn, M.: Transient Contemporary Psychotherapy and the Future of Mental Health. Brit. J. Med. Psychol. 33: 263-267, 1960.

159. Gumrucku, M. A., and Mikels, E.: Combating post-hospital bends: patterns of success in a psychiatric halfway house. Mental Hygiene 49: 244, 1965.

160. Guntur, G. et al.: Intermediary Group Treatment of Inaccessible School Children. Am. J. Orthopsychiat. 35: 739-746, 1965.

161. Hackstein, F. G.: Rehabilitation bei schizophrenen Defektzustanden. Nervenarzt 36: 14-18, 1965.

162. Hackstein, F. G.: Die Gruppentherapie Schizophrener. (Vortrag). Psychiatertagg. des Landschaftsverbandes Rheinland, Rheinlandverlag, Düsseldorf, 1966.

163. Hackstein, F. G.: Rehabilitation Schizophrener—die Gruppentherapie und ithre Voraussetzungen. Nervenarzt. 37: 164-168 April, 1966.

164. Haden, S. B.: Dynamics of Group Psychotherapy. Dis. Nerv. Syst. 20: 258-262 June, 1959.

165. Häfner, H.: Experiences with schizophrenics in a transitional clinic treatment aftercare system. Z. Psychother. Med. Psychol. 15: 97-116, 1965.

166. Häfner, H., and Zerssen, D. V.: Soziale Rehabilitation. Nervenarzt. 35: 242-247, 1964.

167. Hamilton, V.: Psychological Changes in Chronic Schizophrenias Following Differential Activity Programs: A Repeat Study. Brit. J. Psychiat. 110(465): 283-286 March, 1964.

168. Harlfinger, H., Gruppengespräche mit psychotisch Kranken in der Heilanstalt. Z. Psychother. 8: 51-66, 1958.

169. Hartog, J.: Group Therapy with Psychotic and Borderline Military Wives. Am. J. Psychiat. 122: 1125-1131, 1966.

170. Hildreth, H. M.: Symposium, Family Treatment of Schizophrenia, Family Process, Vol. 1, 101-152, 1962.

171. Hiler, E. G., and Berkowitz, A.: Expanding Goals of Short-Term Group Psychotherapy. Dis. Nerv. Syst. 21: 573-574 Oct. 1960.

172. Hinckley, W. W.: The Chestnut Lodge Kiosk: Observation from a Psychiatric Hospital's Work Project—Part I. Int. J. Group Psychotherapy 7: 327-336, 1957.

173. ———: The Chestnut Lodge Kiosk: Observation from a Psychiatric Hospital's Work Project—Part II. Int. J. Group Psychotherapy 7: 437-449, 1957.

174. Hirschman, B.: The Closing of a Ward: A Group Experience. Int. J. Group Psychotherapy 11: 305-312, 1961.

175. Holzberg, J. B., and Knapp, R. H.: The Social Interaction of College Students and Chronically Ill Mental Patients. Am. J. Orthopsychiat. 35: 487-492, 1965.

176. Hoover, V. B., Raulinatis, V. B., and Spaner, F. E.: Therapeutic democracy: group process as a corrective emotional experience. J. Soc. Psychiat. 11: 26, 1965.

177. Hora, T.: Group Psychotherapy in the Rehabilitation Process of the Borderline Patient. Int. J. Group Psychotherapy 7: 406-413, 1957.

178. ———: The Schizophrenic Patient in the Therapy Group. J. Hillside Hosp. 7: 110, 1958.

179. ———: The Role of Group Psychotherapy in the Rehabilitation Process

of the Borderline Schizophrenic Patient. From International Congress for Psychiatry, Zurich (Switzerland), Sept. 1 to 7, 1957. P. 404 in: Congress Report, Vol. III, Zurich, Orell Fussli Arts Graphique S. A., 1959.

180. Horowitz, M. J., and Weisberg, P. S.: Techniques for the group psychotherapy of acute psychosis. Int. J. Group Psychotherapy 16: 42-50, 1966.

181. Hughes, R. B.: Teaching—A Treatment for Outpatient Psychotic Children. Am. J. Orthopsychiat. 35: 367-368, 1965.

182. Hulse, E.: Applications and modifications of group psychotherapy in contemporary psychiatric and mental hospital practice. J. Hillside Hospital 12: 140, 1963.

183. Hulse, W.: Psychotherapy with Ambulatory Schizophrenic Patients in Mixed Analytic Groups. A.M.A. Arch. Neurol. and Psychiat. 79: 681, 1958.

184. Illing, H.: Transference and Countertransference in Analytical Group Counseling. Acta Psychotherapeutics 10(1): 13-25, 1962.

185. Illing, H., and Brownfield, B.: Delusions of Schizophrenic Patients in Group Psychotherapy. J. of Social Therapy 6: 35, 1960.

186. Illing, H., and Brownfield, B.: Central Times of Delusional Productions in Group Psychotherapy with Schizophrenic Patients. Acta Psychother. (Basel) 9: 1, 1961.

187. Illovsky, J.: Experiences with Group Hypnosis on Schizophrenics. J. Ment. Sci. 108: 685, 1962.

188. Indin, B. M.: The crisis club: a group experience for suicidal patients. Ment. Hyg. 50: 280-290, 1966.

189. Ishiyama, T.: Music As a Psychotherapeutic Tool in the Treatment of a Catatonic. Psychiat. Quart. 37: 437-459, 1963.

190. ———, and Grover, W. L.: A Model for a Sociotherapeutic Approach in the Treatment of Psychotics. Psychiat. Quart. 35. 445-457, 1961.

191. Ivanov, N. V.: A Soviet view of group therapy. Int. J. Psychiatry 2: 201-228, 1966.

192. Jackson, B. and Weakland, J.: Conjoint Family Therapy. Psychiatry (Suppl.) 24: 30, 1961.

193. Jackson, D. D.: The Question of Family Homeostasis. Psychiat. Quart. (Suppl.) 31: 79-99, 1957.

194. Jacobs, J. D.: Social action as therapy in a mental hospital. Social work 9(1): 54, 1964.

195. Jacoby, M. G.: Patient Government. Am. J. Psychiat. 115: 943-944, 1959.

196. Janecek, J., and Mandel, A.: The combined use of group and pharmacotherapy by collaborative therapists. Comprehensive Psychiatry 6: 35, 1965.

197. Johnson, J. A., Jr.: Group Therapy: A Practical Approach. New York, McGraw Hill & Co., 1963.

198. Jones, M.: Work with Large Groups in Mental Hospitals. J. Indian Psychology 19: 61, 1963.

199. Jones, M.: A passing glance at the therapeutic community. Int. J. Group Psychotherapy 15: 5-10, 1965.

200. Jones, M.: Group work in mental hospitals. Brit. J. Psychiatry 112: 1007-1011, 1966.

201. Jones, N.: Social Rehabilitation with Emphasis on Work Therapy as a Form of Group Therapy. Brit. J. Med. Psychol. 33: 67, 1960.

202. Kadis, A. L., Krasner, J. D., Winick, C., and Foulkes, S. J.: A practicum of group psychotherapy. Hoeber Medical Division, Harper and Row, New York, 195, 1963.

203. Kepinski, A. et al.: Group Psychotherapy as an Approach to a Psychotherapeutic Community. Group Psychotherapy 13. 182, 1960.

204. King, C. H.: Activity Group Therapy with a Schizophrenic Boy. Follow-Up Two Years Later. Int. J. Group Psychotherapy 9: 184-194, 1959.

205. Kirby, K., and Priestman, S.: Values of a Daughter (Schizophrenic) and Mother Therapy Group. Int. J. Group Psycotherapy 7:281-288, 1957.

206. Kisker, K. P.: Erfahrungen und Methodisches zur Gruppenbildung im psy-

chiatrischen Krankenhaus. Nervenarzt 31: 392-402, 1960.

207. Klapman, J. W.: Use of Autobiography in Pedagogical Group Psychotherapy. Dis. Nerv. Syst. 8: 175-181, 1947.

208. Klapman, J. W.: Group Psychotherapist as Catalyst in Mental Hospital Treatment. Int. J. Group Psychotherapy 6: 80-85, 1956.

209. ———: The Unselected Group in Mental Hospitals and Group Treatment of Chronic Schizophrenics. Dis. Nerv. Syst. 20: 17-23, Jan. 1959.

210. ———, and Meyer, R.: The Team Approach in Group Psychotherapy. Dis. Nerv. Syst. 18: 95, 1957.

211. Knapp, R., and Holzberg, J. D.: Characteristics of College Students Volunteering for Service to Mental Patients. J. Consult. Psychol. 28(1): 82-85, 1964.

212. Kole, C., and Daniels, R. S.: An operational model for a therapeutic community. Int. J. Group Psychotherapy 16: 279-290, 1966.

213. Kotkov, B.: Goals of Short-Term Group Psychotherapy. J. Nerv. Ment. Dis. 123: 546, 1956.

214. ———: Psychoanalytical Applications to Levels of Group Psychotherapy with Adults. Dis. Nerv. Syst. 19: 379-385, Sept. 1958.

215. Kramer, H.: Group Psychotherapy with Psychotic Patients. J. Nerv. Ment. Dis. 125: 36-43, 1957.

216. Kramer, M., and Daniels, R.: A Group Psychotherapeutic Program for Chronic Psychotics. Psychiat. Quart. (Suppl.) 33: 119-127, 1959.

217. Kramish, A.: Letter Reading in Group Psychotherapy. Group Psychother. 9: 40-43, 1956.

218. Kraus, A. R.: Experimental Study of the Effect of Group Psycotherapy with Chronic Psychotic Patients. Int. J. Group Psychotherapy 9: 293-302, 1959.

219. LaFave, H. G., and Burke, J. L.: Two intensive treatment programes: nursing attitudes and evaluations. Brit. J. Psychiat. 3: 541, 1965.

220. Laffel, J., and Sarason, I.: Limited Goal Group Psychotherapy on a Locked Service. Dis. Nerv. Syst. 18: 63, 1957.

221. Lamberd, W. G.: The therapeutic community and the mental hospital. Manitoba Med. Rev. 40: 438-442, 1960.

222. Lamberd, W. G.: A therapeutic community in a general hospital psychiatric ward. Med. Services J. Canada 21: 389-397, 1965.

223. Langdell, J. I.: Family Treatment of Childhood Schizophrenia. Am. J. Orthopsychiat. 36: 335-336, 1966.

224. Lapp, E. A.: Sociometry and Group Therapy in the Mental Hospital. Group Psychotherapy 13: 135-151, 1960.

225. Lerner, M. J., and Fairweather, G. W.: Social Behavior of Chronic Schizophrenics in Supervised and Unsupervised Work Groups. J. Abnorm. Soc. Psychol. 67: 295-299, 1963.

226. Levin, D. et al.: Differential Effect of Factors in an Activity Therapy Program. Am. J. Psychiat. 114: 532-535, 1957.

227. Lewis, Sir Aubrey: Resettlement of the Chronic Schizophrenic. Congress Report, Second International Congress of Psychiatry, Zurich, 1957. In: Congress Report, Vol. 1. 1959, Zurich, Orell Fussli Arts Graphiques, S. A.

228. Lewis, J. C., and Glasser, N.: Evolution of a treatment approach to families: group family therapy. Int. J. Group Psychotherapy 15: 505-515, 1965.

229. Lidz, T.: The Family and Human Adaptation. International Universities Press, N. Y., 1963.

230. Lieberman, F., and Taylor, S.: Combined Group and Individual Treatment of A Schizophrenic Child. Social Casework, Feb. 1965, 80-86.

231. Lifton, N., and Smolen, E. M.: Group Psychotherapy with Schizophrenic Children. Int. J. Group Psychother. 16(1): 23-39, Jan. 1966.

232. Lindinger, H.: Zur Rehabilitation in der psychiatrischen Heilanstalt. Wien. Z. der Nervenheilk. 20: 349-359, 1962.

233. ———: Zur Zusammenstellung psychotherapeutischer Gruppen. Arch. Psychiat. Nervenkr. 207: 45-51, August, 1965.

234. ———: Zur Frage der Prinzipien einer Psychotherapie schizophrener Psy-

chosen. Nervenarzt. 37: 168-173, April, 1966.

235. Lippman, A., and Deutsch, A. L.: Multiple relationships in a group setting on a closed ward. J. of psychoanalysis in groups 1: 95-108, 1964.

236. Longabough, R. et al.: The Interactional World of the Chronic Schizophrenic Patient, Psychiatry 28(1): 78-100, Feb. 1966.

237. Lucas, D., and Ludwik, R.: A Case History of Panic. Ment. Hosp. 12: 37, 1961.

238. Lucas, L.: The Detroit Group: An Evaluative Study of a Social Activity Group for Convalescent Mental Patients. 1959, Detroit, Michigan, United Community Service of Metropolitan Detroit.

239. Luchins, A. S.: Experiences with Closed Ward Group Psychotherapy. Am. J. Orthopsychiat. 17(3): 511-520, 1947.

240. Maas, L. A. J. M.: Gruppenpsychotherapie bei Schizophrenen, T. Psychol. Kring. Nijmeegse. Univ. 6: 137-146, 1958.

241. MacDonald, W. S.: Small Groups Treatment of Chronic Mental Patients: The Problem of Applicability. Am. J. Psychiat. 122: 1298-1301, 1966.

242. Mack, J.: The Evolution of Patient Ward Meetings into Group Psychotherapy. Int. J. Soc. Psychiat. 9: 51, 1963.

243. Mack, J. E., and Barnum, M. C.: Group activity and group discussion in the treatment of hospitalized psychiatric patients. Int. J. Group Psychotherapy 16: 452-462, 1966.

244. Magazu, P., Golner, J., and Arsenian, J.: Reactions of a group of chronic psychotic patients to the departure of the group therapist. Psychiatric Quart. 38: 292, 1964.

245. Magherini, G., and Zuloni, G.: Combination of Neuroplegics in Group and Occupational Therapy in the Treatment of Chronic Psychotics. Rass. Stud. Psichiat. 50: 305, 1961.

246. Macnab, F. A.: Estrangement and Relationship. Bloomington, Ind., Indiana University Press, 1966.

247. Mainord, W. A., Burk, H. W., and Collins, L. G.: Confrontation versus diversion in group therapy with chronic schizophrenics are measured by a "Positive Incident" criterion. J. Clin. Psychol. 21: 222-225, 1965.

248. Mako, A. et al.: Defining and Applying Milieu Therapy. Ment. Hosp. 13: 516, 1962.

249. Maldonado-Sierra, E. D. et al.: Cultural Factors in the Group Psychotherapeutic Process for Puerto Rican Schizophrenics. Int. J. Group Psychotherapy 10: 373-382, 1960.

250. ———, and Trent, R. D.: The Sibling Relationship in Group Psychotherapy with Puerto Rican Schizophrenics. Am. J. Psychiat. 117: 239-244, 1960.

251. Marler, D. C.: A follow-up study of a week-end hospital program. Mental Hospital 15: 204, 1964.

252. Martin, D. V.: Adventure in Psychiatry. London, Faber and Faber, 1962.

253. Mass, P., and Odaniell, J.: Group Casework with Relatives of Adult Schizophrenic Patients. Ment. Hyg. 42: 504-510, 1958.

254. Masserman, J. H.: Group Relationships: Part VI. Summation. Evolution Versus "Revolution" in Psychotherapy: A Biodynamic Integration. In Progress in Psychotherapy (pp. 239-240), J. L. Moreno and J. H. Masserman, Editors, Vol. 2, N. Y. Grune & Stratton, 1957.

255. McCormick, W. O.: The Work Program in Research, Prognosis and Therapy. Am. J. Orthopsychiat. 34: 955-959, 1964.

256. McGee, T. F. et al.: Conjunctive Use of Psychodrama and Group Psychotherapy in a Group Living Program with Schizophrenic Patients. Group Psychother. 18(3): 127-135, Sept. 1965.

257. McGriff, D.: A Co-ordinated approach to discharge planning. Soc. Work 10(1): 45, 1965.

258. Meltzoff, J., and Blumenthal, R. L.: The Day Treatment Center: Principles, Application, and Evaluation. Springfield, Illinois, Charles C. Thomas, 1966.

259. Meyering, W. L.: The place of group therapy in the treatment of schizophrenia. Psychiat., Neurol., Neurochir. (Amsterdam) 67: 137, 1964.

260. Midelfort, C. F.: Family Treat-

ment of Schizophrenia. Family Process 1(110): 115-118, 1962.

261. Morgan, P. M.: A Project on Re-socialization of Patients in a Mental Hospital: Use of Group Work Techniques, Social Casework 42(2): 60-65, Feb. 1961.

262. Mobray, R. M., and Timbury, G. C.: Opinions on psychotherapy: an enquiry. Brit. J. Psychiatry 112: 351-361, 1966.

263. Munzer, J.: Group therapy with parents of psychotic children in a co-ordinated research program. Int. J. Group Psychotherapy 12: 107-112, 1962.

264. Murray, D. C., and Brown, J.: A Consistent Pattern in Variations in Amount of Talking by Patients During Group Therapy Sessions. Int. J. Group Psychotherapy 11: 456-461, 1961.

265. ——— et al.: Verbal Participation of Negro Psychotics in Combined as Contrasted to All-Negro Groups. Int. J. Group Psychotherapy 14: 221-223, 1964.

266. Murthy, H. N.: Group therapy with schizophrenics. Pratibha 2: 14-19, 1959.

267. Muskatevd, L.: Principles of Group Psychotherapy and Psychodrama as Applied to Music Therapy. J. Group Psychotherapy 14: 77, 1961.

268. Myers, J. L., and Roberts, B. H.: Family and Class Dynamics in Mental Illness. New York, John Wiley & Sons, Inc., 1959.

269. Niver, E. O. et al.: Exercise as group therapy. Mental Hospitals 16: 112, 1965.

270. Ogara, C. R.: The Principles of Group Psychotherapy with Schizophrenic Patients. Int. J. Group Psychotherapy 9: 53-61, 1959.

271. O'Hearne, J. J.: Some Methods of Dealing with Delusions in Group Psychotherapy. Int. J. Group Psychotherapy 12: 35-40, 1962.

272. Pace, R. E.: Situational Therapy. J. Personality 25: 578, 1957.

273. Parker, R. S.: Patient Variability as a Factor in Group Activities. Psychiat. Quart. 39(2): 264-270, 1965.

274. Partridge, W.: Deadline for Family Care. Ment. Hosp. 11: 21, 1960.

275. Paul, N. L., and Bloom, J. D.: Outpatient Multiple Family Group Therapy, Am. J. Orthopsychiat. 36. 333, 1966.

276. Paul, N. L., and Grosser, G. J.: Family resistance to change in schizophrenic patients. Family Process 3: 377-401, 1964.

277. ———, and Grosser, G.: The Diagnostic Significance of Comparative Findings in Conjoint Family Therapy in Families with Psychotic and Neurotic Children. Unpublished.

278. Payn, S. B.: Group Methods in the Pharmacotherapy of Schizophrenia. Psychiat. Quart. 39(2): 258-263, 1965.

279. ———: Group Methods in the pharmacotherapy of chronic psychotic patients. J. of psychoanalysis in groups 1: 31-35, 1965.

280. Peck, H.: The role of the psychiatric day hospital in a community mental health program: a group process approach. American J. Orthopsychiatry 33: 482-493, 1963.

281. ———: Group-Therapeutic approaches within the hospital community. Int. J. Group Psychotherapy 16: 267-269, 1966.

282. Peck, H. B., Roman, M., Kaplan, S., and Bauman, G.: An approach to the study of the small group in a psychiatric day hospital. Int. J. Group Psychotherapy 15: 207-219, 1965.

283. Perrow, C.: Reality adjustment: a young institution settles for humane care. Soc. Problems 14: 69-79, 1966.

284. Peyman, D.: An Investigation of the Effects of Group Psychotherapy on Chronic Schizophrenic Patients. Group Psychotherapy 9: 35, 1956.

285. Pine, I. et al.: Experiences with Short-Term Group Psychotherapy. Int. J. Group Psychotherapy 8: 276-284, 1958.

286. Pinney, E. L.: Reactions of Outpatient Schizophrenics to Group Psychotherapy. Int. J. Group Psychotherapy 6: 147-151, 1956.

287. Pinsky, S., and Levy, E. S.: Social group work in a private hospital. Mental Hospitals 15: 516, 1964.

288. Poser, E. G.: The effect of therapists' training on group therapeutic out-

come. J. Consult. Psychol. 30: 283-294, 1966.

289. ———: Group therapy in Canada: a National Survey. Canadian Psychiatric Ass. J. 11: 20-25, 1966.

290. Post, J. M., and Salamon, I.: Group drug supervision saves staff time. Mental Hospitals 16: 241, 1965.

291. Pratt, S., and DeLange, W.: The Admission Therapy Group. Ment. Hosp. 14: 222, 1963.

292. Preston, B.: Group Activities with Patients in a Mental Hospital, Int. J. Group Psychotherapy 8: 459, 1968.

293. Preuss, H. G. (Editor): Analytische Gruppenspychotherapie. Grundlagen und Praxis Privatklin. fur Psychosom. Krankh., Ebenhausen/Isartal—Urban and Schwarzenberg (Munchen) 1966.

294. Prosen, H., and Lamberd, W. G.: Movement in a ward community group as a reflection of patient change. Int. J. Group Psychotherapy 16, 291-303, 1966.

295. Query, W. T. et al.: Social Factors in Chronic Schizophrenia. Psychiat. Quart. 40(3): 504-512, 1966.

296. Rabiner, E. et al.: Conjoint Family Therapy in the Inpatient Setting. Am. J. Psychother. 16: 618, 1962.

297. Ramsey, G. V.: Sociotherapeutic camping for the mentally ill. Social work 9: 1-45, 1964.

298. Rashkis, H. A. et al.: Drug and Milieu Effects with Chronic Schizophrenics. Arch. Neurol. & Psychiat. 78: 89, 1957.

299. Redlich, F. C., and Freedman, D. X.: The Theory and Practice of Psychiatry. New York, Basic Books, Inc., 1966.

300. Resnik, S.: Experience with a group of chronic psychotics. Brit. J. Med. Psychol. 36: 327, 1963.

301. Rickard, H. C.: Selected group psychotherapy evaluation studies. J. Gen. Psychol. 67: 35-50, 1962.

302. Rifkin, A. H. (Editor): Schizophrenia in Psychoanalytic Office Practice. New York and London, Grune & Stratton, Inc., 1957.

303. Rioch, D. M., and Stanton, A. H.: Milieu in Psychiatric Treatment, Vol. 21, Proceedings of the Associates for Research in Nervous and Mental Diseases, Baltimore, Williams & Wilkins Co. 1953.

304. Rosen, I.: Developing and Sustaining Group Therapy Programs. Ment. Hosp. 10: 28, 1959.

305. ———: Milieu Therapy Appraised. Dis. Nerv. Syst. 20: 89-92, 1959.

306. Ross, W. D., and Brissenden, A.: Some Observations on the Emotional Position of the Group Psychotherapist, Psychiat. Quart. 35: 516-521, 1961.

307. Rothaus, P. et al.: Art and group dynamics. Amer. J. Occup. Ther. 20: 182-187, 1966.

308. Rothaus, P. et al.: The anticipation and management of crisis on an open psychiatric ward. J. Applied Behav. Sci. 2: 431-447, 1966.

309. Rothenberg, A., and Vogel, E. F.: Patient cliques and the therapeutic community. Brit. J. Med. Psychol. 37: 143, 1964.

310. Rothwell, N. D., and Doniger, J. M.: The Psychiatric Half-Way House. Springfield, Illinois, Charles C. Thomas, 1966.

311. Ruiz-Agara, C.: Group Analysis with Schizophrenic Patients. Medicina (Madrid) 27: 77, 1961.

312. Rule, B. G., Krieger, M. H., and Scher, M.: Patient group membership and outcome of psychiatric hospitalization. Int. J. Group Psychotherapy 16: 304-312, 1966.

313. Sadock, B., and Gould, R. E.: The Preliminary Report on Short-Term Group Psychotherapy on an Acute Adolescent Male Service. Int. J. Group Psychotherapy 14: 465-473, 1964.

314. Satz, P., and Baroff, A.: Changes in the Relation between Self-Concepts and Ideal Concepts for Psychotics Consequent Upon Therapy. J. Gen. Psychol. 67: 291, 1962.

315. Scher, M., and Johnson, N. H.: Attendance Fluctuations in an After-Care Group. Int. J. Group Psychotherapy 14: 223-224, 1964.

316. Schilder, P.: Psychotherapy, New York, Norton, 1958.

317. Schilder, R.: Ergebnisse und Erfolge der Gruppenpsychotherapie mit

Schizophrenen nach der Methoden der Wiener Klinik. Wien. Z. der Nervenheilk. 15: 250-261, 1958.

318. ———: Zehn Jahre "Bifokaler Gruppentherapie." II International Congress for Psychiatry, September, 1957, Zurich. Congress Report, Vol. 3, pp. 379-386, 1959.

319. ———: Der soziodynamische Aspekt in der "bifokalen" Gruppentherapie. Acta Psychother. Psychosom. Orthopaedagogica, Suppl. 3: 337, 1959.

320. ———: Der Gruppentherapeut und seine Position in der Gruppe., Prax. Psychother. 6: 1-8, 1961.

321. Schindler, W.: "Family Patterned" Group Psychotherapy. Acta Psychother. Supplement 3345, 1955.

322. Schnore, M. M.: Re-Evaluation of a Treatment Activity Program with Regressed Schizophrenic Patients. Canad. Psychiat. Ass. J. 6: 158-162, 1961.

323. Schottstaedt, W. W. et al.: Sociologic, Psychologic and Metabolic Observations on Patients in the Community of a Metabolic Ward. Am. J. Med. 25: 248, 1958.

324. Schulte, W.: Gruppentherapie als legitime Tochter der Arbeitstherapie bei schizophrenen Erkrankung. II International Congress for Psychiatry, September, 1957, Zurich. Congress Report, Vol. 3, 375-379, 1959.

325. Schultz, I. M. and Ross, D.: Group Psychotherapy with Psychotics in Partial Remission. Psychiat. Quart. 29: 273-279, 1955.

326. Scillitani, B.: 'Extended' group psychotherapy. Minerva Med. 57: 2805-2806, (It.) 1966.

327. Sculthorpe, W., and Blumenthal, I. J.: Combined Patient-Relative Group Therapy in Schizophrenia. Ment. Hyg. 49: 569-576, 1965.

328. Semon, R., and Goldstein, N.: The Effectiveness of Group Psychotherapy with Chronic Schizophrenic Patients and An Evaluation of Different Therapeutic Methods. J. Consult. Psychol. 21: 317, 1957.

329. Semrad, E. V.: Long-Term Therapy of Schizophrenia (Formulation of the Clinical Approach). In Psychoneurosis and Schizophrenia, (pp. 155-173), G. L. Usdin, Editor, Philadelphia, Lippincott, October, 1966.

330. Shaskan, D. A.: Group Psychotherapy as an Index of Growth in a Veterans Administration Mental Hygiene Clinic. Int. J. Group Psychotherapy 8: 285-292, 1958.

331. Shatin, L., and Zimet, C.: Influence of Music Upon Verbal Participation in Group Psychotherapy. Dis. Nerv. Syst. 1: 966, 1958.

332. Shattan, S. P. et al.: Group Treatment of Conditionally Discharged Patients in a Mental Health Clinic. Am. J. Psychiat. 122: 798-805, 1966.

333. Shear, H.: Group Therapy with Chronic Psychiatric Outpatients. Delaware Med. J. 32: 113, 1960.

334. Shellhase, L.: Acceptance of Role and Resultant Interaction in the Group Psychotherapy of Schizophrenia. J. Group Psychotherapy 13: 208-229, 1960.

335. ———: The Group Life of the Schizophrenic Patient: Social Work Investigation. Washington, D. C., Catholic University of America Press, 1961.

336. Shrader, W. K., and Beckenstein, L.: Reality-oriented group therapy. Hosp. and Commun. Psychiatry 17: 239-240, 1966.

337. Slavson, S. R.: Psychotherapy and the nature of schizophrenia. Int. J. Group Psychotherapy 11: 3-32, 1961.

338. ———: A textbook in analytic group psychotherapy. International Universities Press, New York, 563.

339. Small, I., and Small, J.: The Significance of the Introduction in Large Group Psychotherapy. Int. J. Soc. Psychiat. 9: 127, 1963.

340. ——— et al.: Total Ward Therapy Groups in Psychiatric Treatment. Am. J. Psychotherapy 17: 254, 1963.

341. Smith, A. et al.: Predicting the Outcome of Social Therapy with Chronic Psychotics. J. Abnormal. Soc. Psychol. 66: 351, 1963.

342. Smolen, E. M., and Lifton, N.: A Special Treatment Program for Schizophrenic Children in a Child Guidance

Clinic. Am. J. Orthopsychiat. 36: 736-742, 1966.

343. Sonne, J. C. et al.: The Absent Member Maneuver As A Resistance in Family Therapy of Schizophrenia. Family Process 1: 44-62, 1962.

344. Spear, G.: Deterioration in Schizophrenic Control Groups. Brit. J. Med. Psychol. 33: 143-148, 1960.

345. Speers, R. W., and Lansing, C.: Group Psychotherapy with Pre-School Psychotic Children and Collateral Group Therapy of Their Parents. Am. J. Orthopsychiat. 34: 659, 1964.

346. Speers, R. W., and Lansing, C.: Group therapy in childhood psychosis. Chapel Hill, North Carolina, University of North Carolina Press, 186, 1965,

347. Spencer, A.: Permissive Group Therapy with Lysergic Acid. Brit. J. Psychiat. 109: 37, 1963.

348. Spitz, H., and Kopp, S.: Multiple Psychotherapy. Psychiat. Quart. (Suppl.) Part II, Vol. 31, 295-331, 1957.

349. Spivak, M. et al.: An Experimental Social Interaction Approach to Milieu Treatment of Schizophrenia. Psychiat. Quart. 36: 484-501, 1962.

350. Spohn, H. E., and Wolk, W.: Effect of Group Problem Solving Experience upon Social Withdrawal in Chronic Schizophrenics. J. Abnorm. Soc. Psychol. 66: 187-190, 1963.

351. Spotnitz, H.: The Borderline Schizophrenic in Group Psychotherapy. Int. J. Group Psychother. 7: 155-174, 1957.

351. ———: The Importance of Individualization. The Borderline Schizophrenic in Group Therapy. Int. J. Group Psychotherapy, 7: 155-174, 1957.

352. Stamos, T.: An Experimental Pre-Placement Therapy Group. Ment. Hosp. 14: 286, 1963.

353. Standish, C. T., and Semrad, E. V.: Group Psychotherapy with Psychotics. Chapter 38 in Group Psychotherapy and Group Function, edited by M. Rosenbaum and M. M. Berger, New York, Basic Books, Inc. 1963.

354. Stein, A.: Hillside hospital and group psychotherapy. J. Hillside hospital 12: 131, 1963.

355. Stevens, S.: Talking It Over On A Disturbed Ward. J. Ment. Hosp. 12: 11, 1961.

356. Stojilykovic, S., and Savicevic, M.: On the Problem of Re-Adaptation and Social Adjustment of the Patients Treated for Schizophrenia. From International Congress for Psychiatry, Zurich (Switzerland), Sept. 1-7, 1957. Congress Report, Vol. III, Zurich, Orell Fussli Arts Graphiques S. A. 1959.

357. Stotland, E., and Kobler, A. L.: Life and death of a mental hospital. Seattle, Washington, University of Washington, 1965.

358. Stotsky, B. A., Daston, P. G., and Vardack, C. N.: An evaluation of the counseling of chronic schizophrenics. J. Counseling Psychol. 2: 248-255, 1955.

359. Stotsky, B. A., Mason, A. S., and Samaras, M.: Significant Figures in the rehabilitation of chronic mental patients. J. Chronic Diseases 7: 131-139, 1958.

360. Stotsky, B., and Zolik, E. F.: Group Psychotherapy with Psychotics: A Review 1921-1963. Int. J. Group Psychotherapy 15: 321-345, 1965.

361. Straight, E. M.: Evaluation of Group Psychotherapy by Follow-Up Study of Formerly Hospitalized Patients. Group Psychotherapy 13: 110-118, 1960.

362. Suess, J. F.: Milieu and Activity Therapy with Chronically Disturbed Female Patients, Psychiat. Quart. 32: 1-12, 1958.

363. Talmadge, M.: Values of Group Interaction for Discharged Mental Patients. Int. J. Group Psychotherapy 9: 338-344, 1959.

364. Tauber, L. E.: Participation of the Patient in the Planning and Evaluation of Group Psychotherapy. Int. J. Group Psychotherapy 14: 224-226, 1964.

365. ———, and Isaacson, L.: Group-Need Therapy: An Approach to Group Planning. J. Counsel. Psychol. 8: 260-262, 1961.

366. Taylor, F. K.: A history of group and administrative therapy in Great Britain. Brit. J. of Med. Psychol. 31: 153-173, 1958.

367. Tölle, R.: Die psychiatrische Sta-

tion Als Gruppe: Zur Gruppen-Psychotherapie von Schizophrenen. Nervenarzt 31: 264-267, 1960.

368. Towey, M. R. et al.: Group activities with psychiatric in-patients. Soc. Work 11: 50-56, 1966.

369. Tucker, J. E.: Group Psychotherapy with Chronic Psychotic Soiling Patients. J. Consult. Psychol. 20(6): 430, 1956.

370. Tuttle, J. F., and Peters, J. J.: Group techniques and ward administration in a military hospital. Int. J. Group Psychotherapy 15: 97-120, 1965.

371. Ugelstad, A.: Some Experiences in Group Psychotherapy with Psychotic Patients. Pp. 259-264, Report of the 14th Congress of Scandinavian Psychiatrists, 1964, Bengt. Janson, Editor, Acta Psychiatrica Scandinavica Supplementus 180 (ad volumen 40, 1964). Munksgaard, Copenhagen, 1965.

372. Vaillant, G. et al.: Current Therapeutic Results in Schizophrenia. New Eng. J. Med. Vol. 271, #6, pp. 280-283, Aug. 6, 1964. Abstract: Amer. J. Psychother. 19(2): 341-342, April, 1965.

373. Vargas, N.: A Group Therapeutic Project Involving a Total Admission Ward. Group Psychotherapy 13: 173, 1960.

374. Vernallis, F., and Reinert, R.: An Evaluation of a Goal-Directed Group Psychotherapy with Hospitalized Patients. Group Psychotherapy 14: 5, 1961.

375. ———, and ———: The Week-End Hospital. Ment. Hosp. 14: 254, 1963.

376. ——— et al.: The Group Therapist in the Treatment of Chronic Schizophrenics. Group Psychotherapy 18(4): 241-246, Dec. 1965.

377. Viefhues, H.: Group Therapeutic Institutions Outside of the Hospital: The Protected Working Place for Mental Patients and the Patient Club. Nervenarzt 32: 211, 1961.

378. Vlavianos, G., and Fink, L.: Psychoanasynthesis in Action in a Mental Hospital. Dis. Nerv. Syst. 22(3): 127-132, March, 1961.

379. Von Mering, O., and King, S. H.: Remotivating the Mental Patient. New York, Russell Sage Foundation, 1957.

380. Von Zerssen, D.: Hospital Group Psychotherapy of Relatively Young Schizophrenics. Psyche (Stuttgart) 18: 532-545, Dec. 1964.

381. Wachspress, M.: The use of groups in various modalities of hospital treatment. Int. J. Group Psychotherapy 15: 17-22, 1965.

383. Wahl, C. W.: The Psychodynamics of Consummated Maternal Incest. Arch. Gen. Psychiat. 3: 188-193, 1960.

384. Wax, J.: Analyzing a therapeutic community meeting. Int. J. Group Psychotherapy 15: 29-36, 1965.

385. Weich, M. J., and Robbins, E.: Short-Term Group Psychotherapy with Acutely Psychotic Patients. Psychiat. Quart. 40(1): 80-87, 1966.

386. Wiedorn, W.: Group Therapy for Families. Ment. Hosp. 12: 21, 1961.

387. Wilkinson, C. B., and Reed, C.: An Approach to the Family Therapy Process. Dis. Nerv. Syst. 26(11): 705-714, Nov. 1965.

388. Williams, W. et al.: An Evaluation of the Effects of a "Group Living" Program with Withdrawn Schizophrenic Patients. Group Psychotherapy 10: 161-169, 1957.

389. Wilmer, H.: A Therapeutic Community in a U. S. Navy Psychiatric Ward. Ment. Hyg. 41: 163, 1957.

390. ———: Social Psychiatry in Action—A Therapeutic Community. Springfield, Illinois, Charles C. Thomas, 1958.

391. ———: Towards a Definition of the Therapeutic Community. Am. J. Psychiat. 114: 824-834, 1958.

392. Wing, J. K., and Brown, G. W.: Social Treatment of Chronic Schizophrenia: A Compartive Survey of Three Mental Hospitals. J. Ment. Sci: 107(405): 847-861, Series 414, Sept. 1961.

393. ———, and Freudenberg, R. K.: The Response of Severely Ill Chronic Schizophrenic Patients to Social Stimulation. Am. J. Psychiat. 118(4): 311-322, Oct. 1961.

394. Winick, C., and Holt, H.: Uses of Music in Group Psychotherapy. Group Psychotherapy 13: 76, 1960.

395. Winkler, W. T.: Indication and

666 THE SCHIZOPHRENIC SYNDROME

prognosis for psychotherapy of the psychoses. Zeitschr. für Psychother. & Med. Psychol. 16: 42-51, 1966.

396. Wittson, C., and Affleck, C.: Two-Way Television in Group Therapy. J. Ment. Hosp. 12: 22, 1961.

397. Wolf, C. H., and Simmel, G.: *In* The Sociology of Georg Simmel. Glencoe, Illinois, Free Press, 1950.

398. Wolk, R.: The Relationship of Group Psychotherapy to Institutional Adjustment. Group Psychotherapy 16: 141, 1963.

399. Wolman, B. B.: Group Psychotherapy with Latent Schizophrenics. Int. J. Group Psychotherapy 10: 301-312, 1960.

400. Wong, N.: Outpatient Group Psychotherapy with Paranoid Schizophrenic Patients. Psychiat. Quart. 38(4): 665-678, Oct. 1964.

401. Wynne, L. C. et al.: Pseudomutuality in the Family Relations of Schizophrenics. Psychiatry 21: 205-220, 1958.

402. Yoshimura, P.: Psychotherapy and Patient Meetings. Iryo, (Tokyo) 17: 285, 1963.

403. Zolik, E. S., Des Lauriers, A., Graybill, J., Hollon, T: Fulfilling the needs of "Forgotten" families. Am. J. Orthopsychiat. 32: 176-185, 1962.

404. Zolik, E. S., Reevy, W., and Lowry, E. J.: A method for describing group therapy through content analysis. Paper presented a the 1963 conference of the American Group Psychotherapy Association.

16

Hospital and Community Psychiatric Approaches

MARVIN E. PERKINS, M.D., M.P.H., and
HARVEY BLUESTONE, M.D.

Dr. Perkins served as New York City's first Commissioner of Mental Health Services since 1961, and also as Director of Community Mental Health Services for the New York City Community Mental Health Board since 1960. His earlier positions include that of Chief, Bureau of Mental Health, Department of Public Health in Washington, D.C.

Educated at Harvard Medical School (M.D.) and Johns Hopkins University School of Hygiene and Public Health (M.P.H.), Doctor Perkins is Professor of Psychiatry, Mount Sinai School of Medicine and Director of Psychiatry, Beth Israel Medical Center.

Doctor Perkins was the Chairman of the New York City Regional Mental Health Planning Committee (1963-1965) and served on the New York State Planning Committee on Mental Disorders. His publications include "The Organization and Administration of the New York City Community Mental Health Board," Handbook of Community Psychiatry, *L. Bellak, Editor;* Public Image of Mental Health Services *(with Elena Padilla and Jack Elinson), (1967), a report of a community mental health research survey in New York City; and* Viewpoint on Mental Health *(1967), a volume of edited transcripts of the television series, Robert Ziskind, Editor.*

Doctor Bluestone is Director of Psychiatry at the Bronx Lebanon Hospital Center and Assistant Professor of Psychiatry at the New York School of Psychiatry. Educated at Columbia and Middlesex Universities (M.D. 1947), Doctor Bluestone trained in psychiatry at Overbrook Hospital, and in psychoanalysis at the New York Medical College. He has been, in the past, chief psychiatrist at Sing Sing Prison, senior psychiatrist at Rockland State Hospital, and on the faculty of the New York Medical College.

Doctor Bluestone is a Diplomate of the American Board of Psychiatry and Neurology, a Fellow of the American Psychiatric Association and the American Academy of Psychoanalysis, in addition to many other professional affiliations, and has published numerous articles in psychiatry and related fields.

1958, the year of publication of the previous edition of *Schizophrenia*[24] was the fiftieth anniversary of the formation of the Connecticut Society for Mental Hygiene, the first state association in what was to become the organized mental health movement in the United States.[297] In 1958, Solomon,[337] in his presidential address before the American Psychiatric Association, attacked

667

the concept of the large mental hospital. Hollingshead and Redlich[138] directed critical attention toward relationships between social class, mental illness, and the practice of psychiatry. Two other books, published that year, were representative of the existing conditions of psychiatric treatment and practice: Caudill[54] set forth the impact of the culture of the hospital staff on patient care, and Freeman, Cameron, and McGhie[103] related a responsiveness of the ego disturbances in chronic schizophrenia to a form of milieu treatment in which the nursing personnel played a central part. Thus, the decade 1958-1968 opened with concern about the obsolescent state of the institution primarily charged with care of the chronic schizophrenic patient, with renewed interest in socioeconomic factors as determinants of psychiatric practice, and with the promise of continued exploration of the salient features of the environment of treatment. In short, the patient was being seen in the context of two communities: that from which the patient emerges for care and that in which he receives his care. Additionally, two new developments had already begun to be established which would have impact upon both communities: the introduction of the use of tranquillizers on a large scale; and, the conversion of mental hospitals to open systems.

PUBLIC HEALTH RESPONSIBILITY

Notwithstanding such promise, Aldrich,[2] summarizing the events in psychiatry, wrote that schizophrenia continued to be "the major problem" for psychiatry, for the cause had not been clearly defined; prevention, not successfully demonstrated; and incidence, not appreciably altered for a century. Jackson,[145] was essentially in agreement when he described schizophrenia as "one of our major medical problems," noting, however, that public interest still was not widespread. Thus, at the beginning of the sixties, schizophrenia had not yet been seen as a public health responsibility, even though it was considered a major problem for psychiatry and medicine. Perhaps this assertion is dependent upon an acceptance of Mustard's[245] formulation:

"A health problem becomes a public health responsibility if or when it is of such character or extent as to be amenable to solution only through systematized social action. Its relative importance varies with the hazard to the population exposed. This hazard, may be qualitative, in terms of disability or death; quantitative, in terms of proportion of the population affected; it may be actual or potential."

One might imagine that schizophrenia ought to have become a public health responsibility, within Mustard's definition, on the basis of hazard to the population exposed, if for no other reason. Perhaps the impediment has been that the problem has not seemed amenable at all, to say nothing of being "amenable to solution only through systematized social action." From the time of Pinel, systematized social action has seemed less to offer solutions to the problem (whether it be *Manie sans Délire,* monomania, dementia praecox or schizophrenia), than to underscore continuing insolubility. G. Rosen[304] points out that, by the mid-nineteenth century, a widely accepted theory held mental disorders to be related to social instability and maladjustment, with rapid social change an important factor. He added that John Hawkes,* in 1857, recognized the significance of the association between diseases of the mind and the consequences of an industrialized society, and proposed a type of "preventive program for community mental health." He[305] also cites the suggestion of Erwin Ackerknecht that one aspect of the belief in progress during the nineteenth century was the belief in a progressive increase of insanity, "because the greater prevalence of mental illness was evidence of more advanced civilization, since civilization was considered a basic element in its causation." Whether out of rejection of beliefs formerly held, or perhaps out of vexation with the inadequacies of systems invented by predecessor physicians, each new generation has sought to reform the established systems, while fashioning new symbols and searching for the therapeutic keys to a complicated and ancient puzzle.

REFORMATION

Efforts at reformation of the systems of mental patient care have proceeded on both sides of the Atlantic, during the past decade. In discussing these throughout the rest of the chapter it will be virtually impossible to single out specific measures concerning schizophrenia from general ones concerning psychiatry—especially as schizophrenia constitutes such a large share of all psychiatric concern. In Britain, the *National Health Service Act, 1946* had given to psychiatric patients and psychiatric hospitals a kind of equality with other patients and hospitals, in that practically all hospitals were brought under one part of the national administration. Great disadvantages still obtained in the way of prejudice, neglect, staff shortages, isolation and custodial atmosphere.[185] England's *Mental Health Act, 1959*[228] created greater flexibility in the systems for securing care, and opened ways to the community for psychiatry. Hays[132] reviews this legislation, citing as advantages the humanized, simplified and flexible admission procedures. He points to a disadvantage, in that, under the informal admission procedure, some patients tend to leave the hospital prematurely, chronic schizophrenics being especially prone to readmission after trouble with the police. Compulsory admission under the Act is largely a psychiatric matter, with review vested in a tribunal of medical and legal members. *A Hospital Plan for England and Wales,*[139] in 1962, perhaps led toward a greater decentralization of inpatient facilities through the encouragement of the psychiatric unit of the general hospital. The Hospital Plan was criticized[293] and defended[276] and the

---

*Hawkes, J.: On the increase of insanity. J. Psychol. Med. and Ment. Path. 10:508-521, 1857 (cited by Rosen, 1959[304]).

controversy continues. The Ministry of Health has issued a memorandum outlining the essential elements of a comprehensive service in a mental hospital.[239]

In the United States, the *Final Report of the Joint Commission on Mental Illness* and *Health*.[148] (1961) set forth a number of recommendations some of which found voice at the national level. On February 3, 1963, President John F. Kennedy,[158] in his message to Congress relative to mental illness and mental retardation, called for the end of a "tradition of neglect" and the initiation of a concerted national attack on mental disorders. In his message, the President observed that the States had depended on custodial hospitals and homes, while the Federal Government, "despairing of solution" had largely left the solutions to the States. Care by the States was depicted in terms of: "a social quarantine" in institutions "from which death too often provided the only hope of release"; "cold mercy of custodial isolation"; and "desultory interest in confining patients."

The new attack was to be aimed at seeking causes and eradicating these by means of preventive efforts, at strengthening manpower training and research efforts, and at improvement of community based programs and facilities. To accomplish this, a new type of health facility, one which would return mental health care to the main stream of American medicine, was required. The ideal location for the proposed comprehensive community mental health center was the general hospital. The State mental institutions were to be improved, performing a valuable transitional role, until the center program was fully developed. An entirely new, systematic approach to mental illness as a national problem was being proposed. *The Community Mental Health Centers Act*[363] (Title II of Public Law 88-164) authorized appropriations for the construction of community mental health centers. *The Amendments of 1965*[364] (Public Law 89-105) authorized grants for initial cost of professional and technical personnel for centers. *The Mental Health Amendments of 1967*[367] (Public Law 90-31) extended both the earlier laws for construction and staffing, projecting the program into 1970.

The sense of being on the threshold of a new period of psychiatric development, similar to that experienced with the advent of psychoanalytic concepts and later with the renascence of psychiatry following the Second World War, is conveyed in Robbins'[299] reflections upon 25 years in psychiatry. In addition to the surges of enthusiasm which have followed other reforms, Robbins cites as factors: the emergence of psychoanalytic interests as part of the social psychiatry field; an aversion to the nondiscriminate use of hospitalization; a recognition of the value of the therapeutic community development in hospitals; an acknowledgement that the limitations of state hospitals often preclude giving the best of care; concern because one-to-one psychotherapy cannot meet the needs of the many; a tacit conclusion that present methods are more often ameliorative than curative; and the pervasive influence of factors of change from every quarter. These, with the developments from the fields of psychopharmacology, sociology and ego psychology, have found expression in the community mental health concept. The objective expression of the concept in the United States is the new system of comprehensive community mental health centers.

INTERNATIONAL EXCHANGE

Note should be made in brief to the transatlantic traveling which characterized the ten year period just concluded. Visitors from the United States found much of interest in the health services of Britain[133] and European nations, giving published reports of their visits to the United Kingdom and elsewhere.[20,97,163] For instance, the North American itinerant in Amsterdam might have visited Professor A. Querido whose works in public health care and municipal government,[283] in sociomedical science,[284] and in evaluation of medical care[286] have been so stimulating. He might have stopped to see Dr. Phillippe Paumelle, co-director of a comprehensive mental health center in the XIIIe arrondissement in Paris,[294,309] learning that psychoanalytically oriented psychiatrists, while not numerous, are influential in the development of community psychiatry in France; that the regional approach to community psychiatry is arranged by contract between a private corporation and the public agency, the Departement of the Seine,[281,290,295] and that a method of treatment little known in the United States is usefully applied in France (the "relaxation method" of Schultz.)[172,185,314] He might have met with Dr. Jan Blanpan of the Faculty of Medicine, The Catholic University of Louvain, there learning of the impressive history and recent developments;[71] in Brussels discussing with a top official in the Ministére de la Santé Publique et de la Famille the "doctors' strike[143] and at Gheel becoming acquainted at first hand with the place of the celebrated tradition of St. Dymphna and family care.[108,288,298,308]

Visitors to the United States from abroad enriched American programs by contributing their observations on developments in Denmark.[149,346] The Netherlands,[226,287] Great Britain,[199,220,310] Australia,[16,17] Israel,[237] Nigeria,[170] to cite only a few. Readers interested in the international perspective of community mental health will appreciate a recent book on the subject by Williams and Ozarin.[376]

THE MODERN HOSPITAL: PSYCHIATRIC

In *Action for Mental Health*, [148] major problems besetting the large state hospitals were tersely summarized: "Isolated from their communities and characterized by the negative features of mass-custodial institutions, they tend to compound the basic difficulty of providing effective treatment to their patients. Desocialization adds to the problems the patients bring with them, and the disabling effects of their illnesses are increased and prolonged." Schwartz and Schwartz[316] identify three major trends in the inpatient system of care of the mentally ill: 1) individualizing care and treatment, 2) breaking down the barriers between hospital and community, and 3) developing a therapeutic milieu. Four measures to alter the mass and custodial features of mental hospitals are discussed: 1) reducing hospital size; 2) eliminating homogeneous wards and services; 3) establishing direct contact between patient and physician; and 4) providing more depth and range in the relationship between patients and personnel.

One may "reduce" the size of the hospital by decentralization, as in the patterns noted below. The other choice is to plan for the construction of smaller units. The former method may be a more immediately attainable objective; the latter, a more desirable long-range one. The New York State Mental Health Planning Report of 1964[247] called for the construction of State hospitals of no more than 1,000 beds.

On the question of size, after observing that state hospitals were five to 50 times as great as the desirable limit of 250 beds suggested in 1880 by Thomas Kirkbride, a report called for small units with a high degree of autonomy as a possible remedy.[125] Various patterns of decentralization and the problems of continuity of care became subjects of interest.[231] Hunt et al.[142] had described the Dutchess County (N.Y.) Program as a part of the Hudson River State Hospital; Bloomberg[37] had advanced the concept of a community-based hospital as a branch of a state hospital in Connecticut; and Jackson and Smith[146] had reported the reorganization of the Kansas hospitals upon a geographic basis.

The observation may be made here that of eleven model facilities studied by Glasscote, Sanders, Forstenzer and Foley,[111] five were state hospitals having community mental health center programs: Yorkton Psychiatric Center, Yorkton, Saskatchewan;[382] The Dutchess County Project, N.Y.;[82] Fort Logan Mental Health Center, Denver, Colorado;[96] Massachusetts Mental Health Center, Boston, Massachusetts;[213] Nebraska Psychiatric Institute, Omaha, Nebraska.[246] Three of the model facilities studied were primarily based upon a voluntary or private psychiatric organization with some linkages to a nearby general hospital facility: The Penn Foundation, Sellersville, Pennsylvania;[264] The Psychiatric Receiving Center of the Greater Kansas City Mental Health Foundation, Kansas City, Missouri;[85,280] Prairie View Hospital, Newton, Kansas.[278] Evaluation of the Dutchess County services has been published, together with critical discussion, in the proceedings of a round table of the Milbank Memorial Fund.[127] At the same conference, evaluations of the Plymouth Nuffield Clinic[272] and the Chichester District psychiatric services[244] were similarly transacted.

Redlich et al.[291] have described The Connecticut Mental Health Center in which the State Department of Mental Health and the Yale University are joined by contractual agreement. A part of the Yale-New Haven Medical

Center,[66] this mental health facility conducts work in patient care, research and training in community psychiatry, as an affiliated facility of the Connecticut State Department of Mental Health, administered by the Yale Department of Psychiatry.

Breaking down the barriers between hospital and community is brought about in several ways. This is effected by the open door policy, by having psychiatric inpatient units in general hospitals, by decreasing the social and cultural differences between the hospital and community, and by increasing the interaction between the hospital and the community.[316] The open hospital development, probably accelerated by the successful application of new medications, was aimed at reducing the isolation of the hospital from the community. W. Barton[19] identifies the assumptions upon which the extensive use of open wards is based:

"Stigma diminishes when locks, barred windows, heavy doors, and security no longer characterize the image of the mental hospital.

"The open hospital encourages early treatment for there is greater willingness to seek and accept help when compulsion is not a principal instrument of management.

"Improvement that follows intensive individualized therapy is maintained with greater ease and the gains reenforced on the open ward. Respect for the individual is increased.

"More normal behavior is the product of the expectation for achievement and the expressed confidence of staff that the patient can accept responsibility for his own management. Open ward residence is followed by decreased disturbed behavior, lessened aggressiveness, and diminished destructiveness and violence.

"A shift in the time spent by staff in moving patients about through closed doors to keep appointments and in conducting operations for patients occurs. Freedom of movement enables patients to do many things for themselves that others previously did for them. Nursing personnel have more time available for the promotion of active treatment—more time to spend with individuals and with groups—and more time to devote to patient activities and work programs."

W. Barton points out that, by 1958, two-thirds of all the wards in English mental hospitals were unlocked by day, and a few mental hospitals were entirely opened. He observes that the Massachusetts Mental Health Center opened its doors in 1956, and that St. Lawrence (New York) State Hospital in 1960, became the first large public mental hospital to open its doors 100 per cent. Some of the early experiences in New York were described almost a decade ago by Hoch,[136] O'Neill,[252] and Snow.[335,336]

Eliminating homogeneous wards and services present many administrative, housekeeping, and medical problems, as well as staff resistance to change.[316] McGahee[221] discusses this issue stating that transition from a custodial institution to an active rehabilitation agency has been difficult. Traditionally arranged groupings in large patient-populations seldom lend support to active treatment programs. Grouping patients on a hospital ward according to condition is not necessarily therapeutic. He advocates patients being placed where they may reasonably expect to remain throughout their hospital stay. In that circumstance, all ward personnel are more readily enabled to establish therapeutic relationships with the patient, and all patients on the unit are under the care of the same psychiatrist and auxiliary personnel.

Therapeutic community, in the sense of involvement of the entire staff-patient complex, has been extensively employed at Fulbourn Hospital, near Cambridge. Clark[57] describes the marked reactions throughout the hospital to the establishment of a therapeutic community on a disturbed female ward; and Clark et al.[59] report a similar project on a woman's convalescent ward. A benefit derived from the work is the insight obtained by workers into the thought disorder of the schizophrenic.

Increasing contact of the patient with his responsible physician is too often hampered. The large number of patients per doctor in many institutions is of paramount importance. Additional problems are those of the use of physicians in nonmedical tasks and the barriers between physician and patient set up by administrative procedures and other hospital personnel. Cognizance of and attention to these issues are important in improving patient care. More effective use of other personnel in therapeutic activity is suggested by the work of Freeman, Cameron and McGhie.[103] They theorize that schizophrenia—a gross disturbance in the continuum between ego and outside world—may be treated in a milieu in which the nursing personnel are engaged as physically constant presences, who, by training or capability are able to meet as many needs of the schizophrenic patient as possible. They state:

"In essence our treatment centre simply presented the nurses with an opportunity to form durable relationships with their patients. Such relationships are formed first as primary identifications towards the nurse and it is therefore a first essential to ensure that the nurse can be constantly in the patients' environment."

Smith, Gibb and Martin[334] point to the use of the general practitioner for geriatric cases. They describe the reorganization of the Lancaster Moor Hospital to provide a psychiatric admission unit, and opine that the 200 bed unit serves a catchment area of 500,000 people, with provision of 800 beds for geriatric cases (which would otherwise soon block admissions).

Developing a "therapeutic milieu" has been written about in some detail.[58] The precursor of the present "therapeutic milieu" is the "moral treatment" of over a century ago. The theory and practice of environmental therapy is discussed in detail by Cumming and Cumming,[69] who state that, "the therapeutic milieu defines the patient as actor, initiator, cooperator, and manager of his own affairs and everyone else as assistants in this process." This definition necessitates restructuring the patient role as well as that of "everyone" with whom he comes into contact during his hospital stay. The authors make many cogent points and practical suggestions. They emphasize that the hospital should *not* be a self-contained entity supplying all services, but that many of these should be obtained from the surrounding community. The patient should *not* be isolated and disconnected from his family and community. Retention of clothes and personal objects as wedding rings and eyeglasses is emphasized, as is the importance to the retaining of one's identity by being respectfully addressed by last name.

Full application of the principles of milieu therapy appear to necessitate the relocation of large components of patient care into the community. While this has to a large extent happened for various pre-and post-hospital phases in the care of the schizophrenic patient, the inpatient phase of treatment is still largely accomplished in self-contained hospitals geographically isolated from, and relatively inaccessible to the patient's community. Patients with schizophrenia, according to Lambo,[169] the most common of psychoses in Nigeria, are treated in four villages near the psychiatric hospital at Aro. He reports 48 per cent of 906 patients treated in 1957-58 were diagnosed as schizophrenic. The "village system" is an integral part of the day hospital; patients, without regard to severity of symptoms, are boarded in the villages, coming to the hospital for treatment. The economic importance to the villagers and to the economy of a nation unable to support a large hospital system have been expressed by Lambo.

The distinction between ambulatory and hospital schizophrenia appears to Fisch and MacDonald[94] to be increasingly artificial, but "willingness to accept treatment" is one dimension that cuts across any classification and is of great significance. Of 100 patients followed for one full year, only four remained continuously hospitalized for that length of time. Problems of treatment include those of the treatment center, those of the community, and those of the patient's response.

Rehabilitation of the long-term schizophrenic patient presents a problem in severe disability. Wing[378] holds the view that these patients are slow to move and to think; nor can they exercise judgment in complicated situations; moreover they lack initiative and cannot be given responsibility. Though socially withdrawn, they are not usually unfriendly and are amenable, given plenty of supervision. He maintains that many patients when first seen by a psychiatrist have these characteristics so that their behavior cannot be entirely due to institutionalism.

Reporting on over three years' experience with an Admission Unit at Lancaster Moor Hospital, Lancaster, Smith[333] calls it a rare case of chronic schizophrenia which neither responds to any form of treatment nor to available community care. In this regard, he believes his experiences correlate well with psychiatric units attached to general hospitals.

Wing[377] points to the need for considering four facts when community care for schizophrenic patients is being planned: 1) long-term services will be needed; 2) a fluctuating course with crises must be anticipated; 3) slowness of thought and movement will be often present, with little initiative or judgment; and, 4) the family milieu must be given attention.

Goldberg[115] has prepared a review of developments in England, beginning in 1941 with appointment of the Tomlinson Committee on rehabilitation and resettlement. The background of industrial rehabilitation units (IRU's), government training centers (GTCs) and Remploy Limited are given. Other organizational and program developments are referred to: Glenside Hospital's Industrial Therapy Organization; the resettlement unit, Netherne Hospital; the community emphasis at Henderson Hospital; and, at St. Wulstan's, the rehabilitation hospital. Social incentives, cash, sheltered workshops IRUs, ITOs and community care are reviewed.

Programs that introduce patients to work in jobs that are valued in the community gives responsibility to patients. *The Vermont Story*[55] is an account of a comprehensive approach to rehabilitation of the chronic schizophrenic patient as undertaken by a State mental hospital. A cooperative program in New York has been reported[35] between a State mental hospital and a sheltered workshop, Altro Health and Rehabilitation Services. The use of the halfway house as an instrument in transitional aftercare is the basis of monographs on Rutland Corner House, Boston[171] and Woodley House,[306] Washington, D.C.

Papers by May and associates[216,217,219] describe the utilization of mental health nurses in the extramural treatment of psychotic patients; the operation of the rehabilitation unit; and problems of industrial resettlement as experienced in Warlingham Park Hospital in Croydon. Concerning the latter, Kiev[375] mentions it as an exemplary model of the combined use of part-time hospital programs with community facilities which he describes as a striking feature of English developments. He points to the complementary relationship these uses have held to the open door hospital development. He also mentions the examples of Graylingwell Hospital, Chichester, and Mapperley Hospital, Nottingham.

The whole rehabilitative effort, which may be considered as tertiary prevention,[160] provides a variety of difficult operational problems in discharge planning, flanking facilities, and community and family considerations[123] and attendant research requirements.[150,102,302]

Increasing the interaction between the hospital and the community can also be enhanced by the use of volunteers, which is a method of bringing the "community" into the hospital. Corollary to that is participation of hospital staff in educational and other community activities, bringing the hospital into the community. Concerning the former point, in the case of work with children, the same would appear to be a by-product of the program in the Cassel Hospital, Surrey. Here, continuity in the mother-child relationship is preserved for the inpatient treatment of severe neurosis by admitting both. T. F. Main[201] gives an account of the care of mothers with severe problems centering about the mother-child relationship, including the ambulatory schizophrenic patient. Furman[97] briefly describes the psychoanalytic focus and flexible program at Cassel Hospital.

In a preliminary study of the patients at the psychiatric hospital at Aarhus, Denmark, conducted in January 1953, referred to by Strömgren,[346] schizophrenic patients constituted half of the resident population there. There were concerns that some mental hospital patients were receiving full care who might need less. McKeown,[222] by analysis of Birmingham hospital patient needs, had determined that only 54 per cent needed full hospital facilities. Of a total of 9,505 patients in Birmingham hospitals 3,555 were mental patients. Only 459 of these required full hospital care, with mental supervision. He had recommended hospitals be planned as a group of buildings with common medical and nursing staffs and a range of services for all patients—the concept of a "balanced hospital community." Cooper and Early,[64] in their survey of patients in Glenside Hospital, Stapleton, Bristol, had found that a little more than half of 1,012 patients needed psychiatric care. They advocated a realistic employment and discharge policy so that the chronically ill might maintain themselves in the community.

Concerning the problem of desocialization, an untoward response to hospital care, the hospital as a "total institution" was critically studied,[114] the institutional milieu being evaluated along the lines of the therapeutic community orientations.[18,316]

To describe the adverse effects of hospitalization, the term "social breakdown syndrome" was proposed,[279] and the possible importance of this in the understanding of schizophrenia suggested.[129] Zusman,[385] in a review article, has summarized the theories developed to explain observed institutional behavior including those of R. Barton,[18] Miller,[233] Wing,[377] Sommer and Witney,[338] Martin,[211] Goffman,[113] and Gruenberg. The papers by Brandon and Gruenberg,[42] Gruenberg, Brandon and Kasius,[128]and Kasius[151] provide a research dimension to the concept.

Alteration in the movement of patients has continued to be of interest, together with the implications for planning. Brill and Patton[44,45,46] have reported on the experience in the hospitals of the New York State Department of Mental Hygiene for the period 1955-1960 inclusive. Coincident with the introduction of large-scale therapy with tranquilizing drugs, there was a decrease in resident patient population. Annually, for the next five years, the fall continued to be witnessed at about one and one-half per cent per year. Schizophrenic patients accounted for the largest population of the decrease in numbers, 3,376 of a total of 4,545. At the same time, first admissions rose 17 per cent and readmissions, 50 per cent. Wing and Brown,[379] in a study of three mental hospitals, found that the number of admissions had not increased; but the chances of readmission had increased. They also observed that the average length of stay for schizophrenics admitted to hospitals had decreased from 17 to 11 months. A somewhat similar trend appears to have been established during the last decade in New York State hospitals. Median lengths of stay of newly admitted schizophrenic patients are available for two years, showing the decreasing length of hospital stay per new admission of the mentally ill: in 1955, this stay was eight months; in 1962, four months. The development pertains only to newly admitted patients; long-term schizophrenic patients tend to continue to remain in the hospitals, representing an increasing proportion of the state hospital population.[248]

To give some perspective to the admissions phenomena, Brenner[43] tested an hypothesis, that a significant relationship exists between economic conditions and admission to mental hospitals in New York. By asking when, over time, mental illness appears most frequently in the population, he found an inverse correlation for large numbers of mental hospital admissions and the State's employment index, for the years 1910-1960.

Epstein,[86] enumerated the advantages of the private psychiatric hospital: absence of a time limit for residence, the noninstitutional character of the buildings and surrounding, the possibility of complete removal from home and threatening elements of the patient's environment, the complete range of treatment methods available for individualized application. Among the groups best treated in such a situation, he lists schizophrenic reactions of insidious onset. Much of the experience of Searles in psychoanalytic psychotherapy with schizophrenics was gained in a private hospital with long-term cases.[318]

In North America, the past decade has seen the development of such changes as to clearly identify the psychiatric hospital to be the terrain of a "therapeutic revolt," part of, and party to, the general revolution involving the community approach to psychiatric delivery of service.[268] Maclay,[197] in his preface to the book on the day hospital movement in Great Britain by Farndale,[91] refers to "a revolution in psychiatric practice and in the outlook of the public."

In the United States, in Canada[174] and in Britain,[307] various organizational futures were being considered. In Denmark, a commission appointed to consider the State Mental Health Service of Denmark, recommended that psychiatric hospitals be built in proximity to general hospitals, rejecting the development of smaller psychiatric units within regional general hospitals. The first of the new series of hospitals and nursing homes was opened at Glostrup in 1960, a description of which is reported by Furman,[97] who gained the impression that the unit was less closely related to the adjacent general hospital than were the English counterparts.

During the decade, the American Psychiatric Association has reprinted articles on new perspectives on mental patient care,[5] the future of mental hospitals[6] and the private psychiatric hospital.[7] Of great importance in the changing patterns of care for the schizophrenic patient have been changes in the public attitude[301] and image of mental health,[84] changes in the attitude of the mental health and hospital administrator, and changes in procedures.[270] In another part of the field, the development of new programs for care in the community general hospitals has emerged.

THE MODERN HOSPITAL: GENERAL

In the United States, in Canada, and in the United Kingdom the development of psychiatric practice in the general hospital has been on the increase. To some, the modern hospital and the general hospital are now synonymous. Tompkins[351] states:

"When I speak of the general hospital, I mean the modern hospital, which is gradually deemphasizing what previously was a too great preoccupation with inpatient beds for the already ill, and stressing extramural care, prevention and rehabilitation. I tried to indicate the organization of the community hospital and its clinics as it faces these multi-faceted tasks imposed upon it by community forces, exemplified by the treatment mission of the ordinary community hospital's psychiatric services, whatever they may be, almost exclusively predicated on short-term therapy; hence, my emphasis. If you accept this as a proper function of psychiatry in this setting, and most people do, there is a question what we have to offer presently to meet this responsibility. The manner in which we approach this problem will, to an appreciable extent, help fashion the future of psychiatry. I do not believe I exaggerate."

Cain and Ozarin[51] in their paper present two cardinal reasons for giving special consideration to general hospitals under the national program of community mental health centers in the United States: 1) the need for further integration of mental health with physical health; and, 2) the necessity for optimum manpower utilization. Both of these aims the general hospital may help the centers to realize. As to financing, they point to the fact that 21 states had passed community mental health services acts permitting state and local sharing of expenditures for mental health services, while taking note of the increasing availability of insurance plans for payment of psychiatric care. In connection with the latter point, the interested reader will want to refer to a study on the insuring of short term-treatment,[12] a review of community mental health by an insurance carrier[38] and a brief statement with recommendations on developments for the future.[359] As for the first fact, the state-local financing pattern has now been altered by federal legislation in the United States[365] which extends the benefits of social insurance to health care costs for those over age 65 (Title XVIII) and expands public assistance so that the states may provide recipients with a comprehensive psychiatric treatment program (Title XIX), while removing a prohibition against federal assistance to patients over 65 in mental institutions.[61]

The decade during which the general hospital was selected in the United States for a prominent place in the development of the new facility for mental health saw substantial enlargement in the concept of a modern general hospital.

The modern hospital is a complex organization, as befits an institution engaged in the provision of treatment for the bed patient and also for the ambulatory ill; maintaining special facilities and highly trained personnel for complicated diagnostic procedures; conducting research; engaging in professional education; and extending preventive services. So complex a set of missions calls for specialized personnel—medical and nonmedical—arranged in a team effort with specified tasks and responsibilities. "The hospital is, therefore, no longer simply a facility in the sense of providing a physical plant and special services at the disposal of physicians for use in the care of their patients. It has come to be a program of care with a set of objectives, goals, standards, and procedures adopted by the institution as a whole—as an institution."[321]

By and large, the modern hospital in the United States is an urban institution, which must be planned to carry out the institutional missions in relation to other urban developments. The radical nature of change produced by urban planning, the marked differences in the characteristics of the people reconstituting the urban population through migration, the strikingly uneven distribution of health, manpower and the economic problems attendant on providing a coordinated quality system of care mandate the development of area-wide plans. Although this imperative seems self evident, the fact is that city planning and health planning in cities more often than not proceed independently with but little formal interaction between the interested governmental offices.[322]

Administration of the modern hospital in the urban setting must ensure the accomplishment of a dual purpose: patient care and community service. When the hospital is affiliated with a medical school, the teaching purpose must be accomplished so that the twin purposes of the hospital are enriched rather than diminished. Clark and Sheps have reported eight key issues to be resolved for affiliation to be effective.[56] The issues were developed out of a study of affiliations, published as a monograph in which appears a chapter on each crucial area: shared goals; dual appointments; patients and teaching; students and patients; interns and residents; patient care; research; and affiliation agreements.[324]

The modern hospital is in an important and increasingly inextricable relationship with nonhospital based ambulatory services. The latter are frequently organized as parts of the local health department service system. An insistent, and evermore irresistible, call is being sounded for an organization of services which will bring all elements into a rational pattern. To close the gap between the knowledge of service needs and the application of practice, actionable requirements must be fulfilled in new ways: 1) the essential unity of health services expressed in organizational terms; 2) additional health personnel linked in more effective patterns of care; 3) greater epidemiologic intelligence gathered toward an improved determination of problems and more appropriate methodology; 4) more regionalization of delivery of service coupled with greater centralization of planning management; 5) finer appreciation of financing action reconciled with the costs of inaction and public leadership deliberately allied with health leadership toward improvement of services.[323]

In the developments in Great Britain, the *Hospital Plan* prescribes a new emphasis. Four years before issuance of the *Hospital Plan* in January 1958, at the First Canadian Mental Hospital Institute, Maclay[196] directed attention toward the achievements of the psychiatric organization of care in the Manchester Region, where psychiatric units of 100 to 200 beds were attached to general hospitals: "Each has its own catchment area, from which it admits all types of mental illness and provides appropriate treatment; each is linked with a big mental hospital to which it was anticipated they would send a stream of patients. To our surprise they are sending only a very small number and seem to be able to deal with their case load without getting silted up."

Hays[131] sets forth a whole series of reservations about the proposed direction of development: that chronic schizophrenics—rehabilitated, treated and discharged—do not necessarily do well in the community; that the family, in course of time, will refuse return of the dilapidating chronic patient; that misbehavior of the insane may lead to withdrawal of legislative support for liberal discharge policies; that staffing of comprehensive outpatient and general hospital facilities will be inadequately met; that general hospitals might take up half of the work of the mental hospitals (the more interesting half), leaving the chronic hospitals with even greater staffing problems than these presently have. He concludes that general hospital units will provide some gain for the psychiatrist; but, as for patients, he does not know. Heron[134] expresses the opinion that the general hospital is an "antitherapeutic" community, in that its orientation is authoritarian with the patient viewed as a passive object to which the necessary investigations and bodily manipulations are directed. He proposed that this is oppositional to the requirements of the mental patient and that general hospital management and administration may be expected to be torn between needs of the organization and the psychiatric patient.

PSYCHIATRY IN THE GENERAL HOSPITAL

In 1956, an admirable little book was published on the practice of psychiatry in general hospitals.[31] The arguments were direct. Every general hospital should be equipped for psychiatric care. Patients needing such care should promptly be provided it; psychiatric treatment—not temporary detention—should be given patients. Thus, communities would be served, and the burden of care and treatment of the psychiatric patient shared between the specialized and the general hospitals. The authors had found by survey that, although mental patients occupied more than half of all hospital beds in the United States and Canada, general hospitals accommodated less than one per cent. The book was intended to advocate the increased use of, and provide help in the establishment, organization and administration of, the psychiatric unit in the general hospital. Certain general references are of value to the planner of the general hospital psychiatric unit.[3,4,112,340,358]

In 1965, a survey was conducted jointly by the National Institute of Mental Health and the American Hospital Association.[271,362] The questionnaire was mailed to 5,964 general hospitals of which 88.7 per cent returned usable information: 467 reported having separate psychiatric inpatient units; and 579 hospitals indicated that on a routine basis psychiatric patients were admitted for diagnosis and treatment. A total of 1,046, thus, were committed to a planned psychiatric inpatient activity for diagnosis and treatment.

A major advantage of the treatment of the schizophrenic patient in the general hospital is that the difference between the hospital and the community is minimized. The advantage is achieved by its location, open ward policies, easy accessibility to visitors, short stay, and emphasis on "treatment' as against "custody." The day hospital geographically located so that it is readily accessible to the population served, has the same advantage with enablement of the patient to work while on a part-time patient status, added. Easy availability of this service is crucial to proper utilization. The day hospital at the Bronx-Lebanon Center demonstrates the relevant characteristics:

1. *Small size.* The maximum number of patients in care at any time is 35. This number is small enough to enable the physician in charge, as well as all other staff members, to know the patients well and to respond as needed on an individual basis.

2. *Heterogeneous composition.* With but few exceptions, all age groups and all diagnostic entities are accepted. Approximately 80 per cent of those participating have been women. A number of factors contribute to this preponderance. More women live in the area serviced by this hospital, the one parent family being common. The men from this section of the city wait until their symptoms are more severe before applying for treatment. In this impoverished area many men manifest antisocial and criminal activity including drug addiction which tends to prevent their becoming a patient in a voluntary hospital setting. The women on the other hand, most of whom are on welfare, can utilize a day hospital both as a method of receiving psychiatric treatment and as an escape from the intolerable combination of poverty, serious family problems, and social isolation. The majority of the patients are adults from 20-40 years of age. Adolescents and older people are acceptable for treatment but younger children have had to be excluded because adequate supervision is unavailable. While patients in all diagnostic categories are treated, most have chronic mental illness: many are schizophrenics and others show depressive

symptoms. Severity of symptoms, such as delusions and hallucination, is not a reason for exclusion, nor is severe depression, unless there is an immediate suicidal risk.

3. *Accessibility of staff.* The physician-in-charge, and all other professional staff are available to patients at all times. In effect, all doors to offices are left open except when patients are being individually seen. This policy includes physicians, nurses, social workers, psychologists, and occupational therapists.

4. *Free access of the unit.* Patients are encouraged to return for follow-up care after hospitalization is completed and the unit is freely accessible from the street. In fact, in certain instances patients use this facility as a second, and more pleasant, home returning regularly, and in effect, readmitting themselves to the service without formal steps being taken.

5. *Community contact.* Staff members, particularly the nurses, make home visits when patients do not appear as expected or when needed for illness or other reasons. The ethnic composition reflects that of the community served: approximately 45 per cent Negro, 45 per cent Puerto Rican and 10 per cent white patients.

Successful application of day hospital care of the schizophrenic patient at Bronx-Lebanon Center is aided by the symptomatic response obtained in many patients by the use of the phenothiazines and other medications. Of the schizophrenic patients treated in this fashion, 90 per cent have been returned to their homes, but 10 per cent have had to be admitted to a state hospital, although in most instances, continued outpatient treatment has been necessary. Follow-up activity has ranged from an infrequent visit to a medication clinic to the requirement of readmission to the day hospital.

Lebensohn has written on the development of general hospital psychiatry in the United States.[177] He discusses general principles employed in the planning of the psychiatric unit of Sibley Memorial Hospital, Washington, D.C.,[179] drawing upon the ideas of Osmond[254] and Izumi;[144] giving guidelines for establishing and operating a unit,[178] and describing the Sibley Memorial Hospital unit.[175,176] From the same city, Schultz[313] describes the municipal hospital psychiatric program at District of Columbia General Hospital. From other parts of the United States general hospital psychiatric unit developments have been reported: Puerto Rico;[104] Albany, New York;[74] Pennsylvania;[83] Maryland;[88] North Carolina;[140] Minnesota;[50] Illinois;[124] Missouri;[122] Louisiana;[319] Oregon[312] and California.[141,72,159] The Veterans Administration has determined to build no more neuropsychiatric hospitals, concentrating new building programs hereafter in general hospital units,[36] psychiatric activities of two of the latter have been described.[289,374]

Pauly, Saslow and Brown[260] describe a program for training in treatment, utilizing the patient, his family and community, encouraging innovation in treatment procedures and roles, and demonstrating the effectiveness of the psychiatric unit in the general hospital.[312] A description of psychiatry in University Hospital of the Boston University School of Medicine has been published as an issue of International Psychiatry Clinics.[15] An account is available in book form relative to the practice of general hospital psychiatry in Beth Israel Hospital, Boston.[383]

Canadian programs have been reported from Montreal;[240,241] in Yorkton,[382] Saskatoon,[330,331] Moose Jaw,[253] and in Vancouver.[296] A survey of general hospital units in Canada is given by McKerracher and Smith.[223]

Schwartz and Schwartz[316] point out that the voluntary general hospital was developed primarily for the privately practicing physician, and hence the psychiatric unit might be anticipated to operate within that perspective. Like the rest of the hospital, then, we would note, the inpatient unit is most likely to be operated within the open door concept, efforts being made, of course, to protect patients potentially dangerous to themselves or others. However, as the voluntary general hospital psychiatric units, in the main, take only patients who admit themselves willingly, no more effort would be made to retrieve patients who elope from the hospital or leave against medical advice, than would be expended to retrieve patients who would leave any other unit of the hospital under the same conditions.

West[373] believes that any kind of patient may be admitted to the psychiatric service of the general hospital which provides: 1) acute receiving and diagnostic service; 2) continuous treatment service; 3) day-night service; and 4) inpatient unit for emotionally disturbed children.

In New York, the circumstances of admission to the psychiatric wards of voluntary general hospitals is apt to be different from those as seen in the municipal and state public mental hospitals.[229] Patients, who are usually referred from the outpatient service of the voluntary hospital, from other hospital services, or by attending physicians of the patients, do not of necessity, have to be admitted. This ability to be selective tends to give a different character to the patient population in a voluntary general hospital service than in either the large state mental or municipal general hospital each of which has less freedom to refuse to admit patients, many of whom may be grossly disturbed, and involuntary. Sometimes the patient is brought by the police, with very little information obtainable.

The importance of financing to development of the inpatient services may be alluded to here. In 1946, Kaufman opened a 22-bed ward, as a part of a new independent Department of Psychiatry, in The Mount Sinai Hospital in New York City.[155] Eighteen years later, in 1964, an Institute of Psychiatry was dedicated,[154] a project which was to have been realized within five years from the founding of the department. Kaufman acknowledged the importance of current and prospective financial support in the establishment of the Institute of Psychiatry, this having been made possible by the New York State Community Mental Health Services Act of 1954.[342] Other voluntary general hospitals in addition to Mt. Sinai, supported by the City of New York under terms of the same State Act include the following: St. Vincent's Hospital;[147,348,349,350,352] St. Luke's Hospital;[67,68] Montefiore Hospital;[23,265,266] Roosevelt Hospital;[167,168] Maimonides Hospital,[356,357] Payne-Whitney Clinic; Bronx-Lebanon Hospital[190] and Beth Israel Hospital. New York City also supported an extensive program of psychiatric services in its general hospitals; of particular interest are those with both inpatient and outpatient services: Bellevue Hospital Center;[384] Kings County Hospital; Metropolitan Hospital;[98] Harlem Hospital;[49] City Hospital at Elmhurst;[26,25,28] Bronx Municipal Hospital Center;[1,62,63,386] Queens General Hospital. Many of these hospitals were affected by a program affiliating the municipal hospitals to medical schools of the city.[353]

On a matter of importance to community-oriented service, Mannucci and Kaufman[208] comment upon an aspect of the selective admission process relating to the ethnic composition of patients admitted. The reports were not a result of any formal admission policy. Yet, they observed that 93 per cent of the patients were white, despite the location of the hospital near to areas having large numbers of Puerto Rican and Negro Americans. The authors account for the small numbers of Puerto Rican patients in that there may have been a selective screening "policy" which by placing emphasis upon individual psychotherapy limited admissions of individuals with a language problem. Regarding Negro patients, where there is no language barrier, the authors suggested that requests for admissions from this segment of the population had been much fewer than from the white community.

In their study of 1,264 admissions to The Mount Sinai Hospital, during the period 1947 to 1957, Mannucci and Kaufman reported that schizophrenia was diagnosed in 15 per cent or 204 instances, generally in the younger patients. The median length of stay for all patients was 50 days; 43 per cent of the schizophrenic group were discharged in 30 days, and 67 per cent were discharged in 60 days. About 60 per cent of all patients were improved at discharge; for the schizophrenic patients 50 per cent were improved; only 8 per cent of all patients were transferred to long-term care facilities; 79 per cent were discharged home. Of these, about half were referred for outpatient care. They believe that their study shows the general hospital unit has the capability of treating a wide variety of patients, with different illnesses, attaining sufficient improvement, in a relatively short period of time so that return to the community is possible for most, many still needing ambulatory care.

The larger psychiatric units of general hospitals tend to resemble the small psychiatric hospital, which resemblance, according to Schwartz and Schwartz[316] increases as separation is greater from the general hospital, administratively and geographically. The units are engaged in treatment of acute disorders, with relatively short patient stays, and may serve a population like that of the private psychiatric hospital—to wit, "a relatively greater proportion of women, of psychoneurotic reactions, and of depressive psychoses than one finds in the admissions to state hospitals." This would appear to be supported in part by the study of the characteristics of the patient population of the 22-bed psychiatric unit of The Mount Sinai Hospital in New York City described by Mannucci and Kaufman.[208] Information was obtained by examining 1,264 hospital records during eleven years. A preponderance (68 per cent) were female; 39 per cent were diagnosed as psychoneurotic; 15 per cent, as schizophrenic. The ages of patients ranged from pre-adolescence to over 70 years, the group between 20-49 comprising 67 per cent of the admissions. The median length of stay was approximately 50 days, the authors stressing that the length of stay may have been "partly influenced by the emphasis placed on psychotherapy in the teaching program for the residents. The average older patient had a shorter hospitalization and a shorter duration of illness prior to admission. Of all patients, 68 per cent showed previous psychiatric illness. Two main findings are stated: "1) the essential 'chronicity' of psychiatric illness; and 2) the very useful role that the general hospital psychiatric unit plays in caring for and treating patients during exacerbations of the underlying chronic condition."

One of the important activities for psychiatry in the general hospital is that of providing consultative support through liaison with other inpatient services.[34,152,156,157,207] In his summary of the York Clinic Experience, Stafford-Clark[341] reported that, during a three year period, 151 of 222 referrals came from the medical service; 42 patients had psychiatric symptoms associated with other nonpsychiatric conditions; of 175 patients diagnosed as having psychiatric syndromes, 11 were classified as having schizophrenia. During a twelve month period, Shepherd, Davies and Culpan[320] studied consultations requested of psychiatry for 87 inpatients (1.34 per cent of 6,500 admissions) and 86 outpatients (3.4 per cent of all new patients seen in medical, surgical, and gynecological outpatient clinics). Schizophrenic reactions were *uncommon* among the referred inpatient group; neurotic reaction and personality disorders, depressive reactions, and toxic and organic reactions constituting three nearly equally sized groups. Among the outpatient referrals, schizophrenic reactions were again uncommon. The proportion of neurotic reaction and personality disorders the highest, with depressive reaction next, and toxic and organic reaction the least numerous. Querido,[285] discussing the psychiatric contribution to the treatment of the nonpsychiatric patient, found a few cases to be diagnosed as schizophrenic, "notably those admitted for accidents."

As to the recent history of British events, Brook[47] reviews the development of the general hospital psychiatric unit, observing that the first existed at Guy's Hospital from 1720 to 1861. However, it was not until after the Second World War that psychiatric units in general hospitals became well established. In addition to the community psychiatric service based on a mental hospital, he describes five types of general hospital based units: psychiatric beds on general wards; the teaching hospital unit; the general hospital unit with parent mental hospital; general hospital centered psychiatric service; and a unit accepting all types of patients. Each of these forms present problems, administrative, operational, and professional. Fundamentally, the five types of general hospital-based services are likely to be variations of local authority and hospital cooperative arrangement, perhaps following the Manchester example of arrangement. Brook and Stafford-Clark[47a] describe how the general hospitals may provide care for certain types of psychiatric patients on the general wards, including some schizophrenic patients. Their six years' in London's New Cross General Hospital is set forth.

Some developments in the general hospital field were the consequence of the enactment of *The Mental Health Act, 1959,* which opened the way for urgent admissions willing to accept treatment informally. Benady and Denham[30] of London describe the influence upon admission, management and immediate outcome of psychiatric patients admitted to St. Clement's Hospital Emergency Unit during 1960-1961, citing a comparison with the 1955-1956 experiences. They observe that the traditional ward is being influenced toward active treatment and discharge home from the emergency unit. Schizophrenics comprised the largest diagnostic group in the 1960-1961 series, 134 of 348. Of the entire number of schizophrenics, 70 were discharged home and 64 to a mental hospital, after an average stay of 24.2 days. This compares to 192 schizophrenic patients of a total of 473, in 1955-1956, 36 of the schizophrenic group having been discharged home, 156 to a mental hospital after an average stay of 15.2 days. The authors conclude that the lengthened average stay, and the reduction in numbers annually dealt with, are a result of the change to early treatment from observation. Although the experience is from a small psychiatric hospital, the authors conclude that the engagements of the unit is relevant to planning for general hospitals.

St. Pancras' Hospital also experienced an acceleration of change from observation ward to therapeutic unit as a result of *The Mental Health Act.* The advantages, disadvantages, patients' special needs, architectural considerations and staff requirements relative to the general hospital psychiatric service are developed in some detail in the report of Dunkley and Lewis.[81] In this they follow Cohen and Haldane[60] who discuss the special requirements for psychiatric treatment in the general hospital in terms of regime, staffing and space.

A large general hospital reported a similar evolution from observation to treatment. The St. James' Hospital, Leeds,[191] with 1,683 beds, was the first in the area to have a psychiatric unit. Of 1,200 admissions during 1961, when the unit had 120 beds, 116 were schizophrenic. With a bed complement increased to 180, the unit was expected to service the population of the city of about 500,000 people for most of the needed admissions.

The psychiatric unit at The West Hill Hospital, Dartford, (56 beds with day-patient services as part of the inpatient activity) has not found the acute schizophrenic patient to be difficult. They conclude that only a small proportion of patients need to be transferred to a long-stay unit.[52] A four year follow-up study was done of a general hospital psychiatric unit under a grant from the Manchester Regional Hospital Board.[137] The conclusions were that long-term stay in the mental hospital and admissions could largely be avoided, even though many patients remained unemployed and had a high rate of morbidity. Of the schizophrenic patients 22 per cent were symptom-free for two years or more. From St. Thomas' Hospital, London, Sargant[311] communicates his view that modern empirical, mechanistic, and physiologic treatments are essential to the restoration of normal brain function, being prerequisite to application of other methods. A two-year follow-up of cases of schizophrenia treated in the general hospital teaching unit disclosed that 86 per cent were home two years after discharge, having had an average inpatient stay of only six weeks. Those in the study had had "good previous personalities," a point considered vulnerable to criticism by correspondents whose letters were subsequently published.

Smith[332] points out that only in the Manchester region is there an integrated scheme covering the whole area, providing 12 psychiatric units attached to upgraded municipal hospitals. Each unit serves a population ranging from 120,000 to 260,000. The number of beds in the units varies from 42 to 252. He states that only 32 people from a total population of 500,000 had to be transferred in 1958 to a mental hospital. The two districts reported as having contributed such an arresting performance were Burnley and Oldham. Freeman[100] has described the experience of the latter. Another district of the Manchester region, Bolton, has been treated in the literature by Leyberg.[188] He concludes that the general hospital unit can never provide the best for rehabilitation for chronic schizophrenic patients—especially female schizophrenics. Smith suggests that a psychiatric unit of 120 beds could serve a population of 250,000, if geriatric facilities are available.

A somewhat lower estimate comes from Queen's Park Hospital, Blackburn, whence Silverman[325] reports, on the basis of a period of one year's experience, that his nearly 100-bed department was able to handle about 95 per cent of the total psychiatric inpatient load from a population of 250,000, provided a geriatric department is also available. He underscores the importance of home visits, early treatment, day-care facilities and the cooperation of ancillary nursing, welfare and other personnel. Silverman, who has reported on the problem of the inpatient case load of the comprehensive department of psychiatry which he directs, has concerned himself with assaying attitudes of non-patients toward the day-care program.[326,327] In 50 per cent of the nonpatient informants queried, the gravity of the burden at home was thought to have been reduced; 57 per cent thought that the patients frank psychotic state had improved, and 78 per cent thought that the regime had helped. He had reported 36 per cent of the day-patient case load to be patients with schizophrenia.

A different direction of community development, in a situation without long term psychiatric facilities is given by Vyncke.[371] He describes the formation of a psychiatric service in a general hospital at Usumbra, in which patients with schizophrenia and other mental disorders were intermingled with patients having other medical conditions. Of the first 509 cases, 350 were psychotic, 11 per cent of which were diagnosed as having schizophrenia. The experience of treating the mentally ill in this general hospital led to adoption of a plan to build a village of twenty-five little farmhouses, each accommodating six or eight patients. Both activities, that of the general hospital and that of the village, were to be under single direction.

Moll[242] describes the Day and Night Treatment Center at the Montreal General Hospital, of 500 patients treated in the night hospital, 56 were diagnosed as schizophrenic reactions. The treatment program, as in the day hospital, includes psychotherapy, modified insulin therapy, electroconvulsive therapy, pharmocotherapy, psychodrama, and social therapy. He observes that only ten per cent of 3,000 psychiatric patients treated in the hospital had received partial hospitalization in the day and night units, but asserts such facilities are necessary to an adequate general hospital service.[243] Tannenbaum, Pinsker and Sager[347] report a modification of the partial hospitalization concept. By including former patients in the activities for patients on the ward, service to the community is increased. Benefits include an improvement in milieu, a rise in optimism among inpatients and more comfortable adjustment to the community of those already discharged. The cost is negligible. Although the authors disclaim prevention of rehospitalization, they believe it is a justifiable extension of the inpatient service. The psychiatric day hospitals at Harlem Hospital[49] and Bronx Municipal Hospital[263] have been described. The principle of treating a patient close to his home and in the community can be carried out by means of the day psychiatric hospital,[165] with a preservation of community links[166] and avoidance of the successive degrees of separation from the family community, which occurs with remote hospitalization.[251]

OUTPATIENT EMERGENCY CARE

In their study of the outpatient system of care, Schwartz and Schwartz[316] develop three themes: providing immediate help; extending outpatient services in the community; and broadening conceptions of help. All three themes are evident in the paper by Pumpian-Mindlin[282] who observes the need for restructuring of outpatient services in the general hospital toward more effective use of the psychiatrist, psychologist and social worker. He points to the limitations of psychiatry with regard to various behavior disorders and advocates the use of: social clubs; specialized groups (as Synanon, Alcoholics Anonymous;) activity therapies; socializing therapies (marital, vocational counselling;) individual therapy based on recognition of environmental conflict; and psychoanalytic psychotherapy. He encourages use of home visits and mobile emergency units.

The *mobile approach* to handling emergencies still does not appear to be widespread of application, notwithstanding steady interest in the Amsterdam Plan of A. Querido.[186,287] Mobility of clinic personnel has characterized the mental hygiene consultation service of the Army since World War II. Glass[109] describes the Mental Hygiene Consultation Service as the main facility for carrying out the early identification and treatment phase of Army psychiatry. An outpatient unit, with a field approach to the interviewing of a referred soldier, it is directed by a psychiatrist who, "to insure uniformity of patient care . . . heads the small inpatient service of the local army hospital."

The idea of emotional first aid being available when needed—and not sometime later—led Bellak to establish the Trouble Shooting Clinic in 1958 at City Hospital at Elmhurst, New York.[25,117] A reasonable outgrowth has been the provision of psychiatric personnel to serve in the hospital medical-surgical emergency clinic.[29] The emergency psychiatric clinic[62] or the walk-in clinic[63] of the Bronx Municipal Hospital Center has been reported.

In their study of psychiatric emergencies, Fisch, Gruenberg, and Bandfield[93] focussed attention upon the age group of 15 to 44. This selection was made because of their finding of over half of the total admissions in their series (554 of 923) coming from within the age range, most of which were out of a crisis situation. As to the age group at greatest risk, the males, 25-44 years, had the highest rate (6.9 per thousand, compared to 3.4 for the whole group; Negro males within the group had a rate of 12.2 per thousand). Schizophrenia accounted for the largest number of admissions by clinical category, 177 of 394, and more females than males were in the schizophrenic group (perhaps because of the utilization of veterans hospitals by males). Well over half of the admissions were for emergencies: suicide attempt, gesture or major threat; assaultive or violent behavior; bizarre behavior; unmanageable household behavior; acute confusion; and delerium tremens. The authors made a number of observations anent schizophrenia and the psychiatric emergency: that suicidal behavior was more apt to be associated with schizophrenia, and hallucinations in women was more likely to be associated with schizophrenia than alcohol; that simple withdrawal requiring hospitalization was associated usually with schizophrenia; and somatic complaints were not infrequently so associated.

New Haven authors,[87,315] reporting on psychiatric care in a general hospital emergency room, found schizophrenia in 26.7 per cent of 1,130 cases, and noted that the proportion remained constant for all social classes, although the diagnosis was somewhat more common in Negroes than whites. Wayne and Koegler[372] have produced a book on brief therapy and the emergency. The social factors of involvement in the urgent admissions to a London hospital, St. Francis, are the subject of a Maudsley Monograph by Lawson.[173] She found that nonmedical factors played an extensive, if not governing role, in admission to observation units, and yet earlier, in the recognition and labelling of a disorder in the breakdown of tolerance and in the request for help.

In the United States the period from 1958 saw an expansion in the number of outpatient facilities, increasingly engaged in the treatment of adult psychotic patients,[13] even though community clinics were considered slow to discover the psychopharmacological revolution in care of the mentally ill.[161] Study of clinic functions, in view of the prospect of development of community mental health centers, were of greater interest[303] and the potential in the employment of area-wide psychiatric case registers more adequately demonstrated.[106,107,120] The international prospects for camparative study have been given notice. Three case registers, in Maryland, Aberdeen and Camberwell,[380] were used to compare "reported" prevalence in contact with a psychiatrist. Rates per 100,000 were developed, prevalence by type of service studied, distribution made of inpatients by length of stay to the teaching, general hospital or the mental hospital, and diagnostic comparisons charted. Baltimore reported more schizophrenics and addicts, but fewer affective psychoses and neuroses.

COMMUNITY PSYCHIATRY

The discipline of psychiatry continued to define the terms of a broader commitment than to individual patient care alone. In the introduction to his *Handbook of Community Psychiatry and Community Mental Health,* Bellak[27] calls community psychiatry "the third psychiatric revolution," acknowledging the psychiatric events during World War II to be important in creating awareness of need for services. Some appreciation of the changing breadth of psychiatric interests may be discerned in the content of recent annual reviews. In one annual review series, *Current Psychiatric Therapies,* instituted in 1961, sections have been devoted to papers on institution and community aspects of psychiatry from the beginning. And, beginning with 1962, the annual review, *Progress in Neurology and Psychiatry,* has contained a chapter on mental health,[41,192,193,194,195,225] successor to a chapter previously called "mental hygiene." The materials covered in the chapters are increasingly concerned with the sociologic aspects of psychiatry.

M. Ullman, who went from private practice of psychoanalysis into general hospital work,[355] and his associates[357] have given a view of community psychiatry as applied social psychiatry. In this, they appear to be in basic agreement with the distinction made by Redlich and Pepper[292] and Bernard[32,33] that community psychiatry emphasizes applied practice and evaluation at the community level, while social psychiatry connotes more attention to theory and research. Daniels' paper[70] details a definition which calls social psychiatry the body of theory upon which community psychiatric knowledge and practice are based. Zwerling, who has described a continuum along which four elements of individual and community psychiatry may be differentially located,[386] accepts the reasoning of M. Ullman and co-workers, recasting it in the positive statement: community psychiatry is applied social psychiatry.[387]

Although he designates the area as social psychiatry, Leighton[183] sets forth five concerns which would appear to bear upon the emerging concept of community psychiatry. The five are concerned with: 1) people in numbers; 2) relationships between mental disorder and sociocultural processes; 3) responsibility to society or a subgroup, which takes precedence over obligations to the individual patient; 4) conduct of knowledge out of clinical practice into strategic places in the sociocultural system; and 5) conduct of relevant knowledge into clinical psychiatry.

Melehov[227] provides an English summary of developments in social psychiatry in Russia during the past 50 years. He refers to the development of social psychiatry in fields of the military, in forensics, in prophylaxis and hygiene, in industrial therapy, in district psychiatry and in industrial resettlement, citing soviet authorities by name.

Gordon, O'Rourke, Richardson and Lindemann[121] in a major review article observed that human ecology relating to health and disease is medical ecology, which as it concerns communities of people is epidemiology. Duhl[78] has reminded us of the ecologic frame of reference for understanding causality in human behavior, observing that man "is not only part of an ecological network, but he modifies it, creates large parts of it, has giant technical tools to cope with it, and is in turn modified by it . . . fellow man, groups—creations of man even his by-products and his wastes, become tremendously important variables. Thus the changed patterns of cities, the armies, the satellites circling the globe, smog, insecticides, the automobile, cigarettes, and IBM machines are variables. . . ."

Community psychiatry was the subject in June, 1964, of a University of Wisconsin symposium, the proceedings of which were published,[300] including papers on such varied subjects as theoretical models, barriers to establishment of centers, training for community psychiatry in a psychoanalytically oriented department, ideational basis of a state program, community care for schizophrenic patients, and others. One month earlier, community psychiatry had been characterized as "the newest therapeutic bandwagon" by Dunham. A useful group of critical discussions, together with the original paper, make most interesting reading. Of interest is the fact Dunham[80] finds a compatability of views with those of Lebovici, of the XIIIe Arrondissement of Paris, who places community psychiatry in the mainstream of psychiatry while employing the ecological dimension.

Hausman and Rioch[130] observe, in their review of the field, that, in fact, contemporary military psychiatry as practiced in the United States Army[110] is a form of community psychiatry.[269] The contribution of the military to the advancement of knowledge in this connection is frequently overlooked. For instance, in the useful book edited by Goldston,[116] military psychiatry does not appear among the selected definitions; nor does the military contribution to "community mental health and social psychiatry" appear to be given much notice in a reference guide on the subject.[65] Two books by Artiss based upon work in schizophrenia at Walter Reed Army Institute of Research appeared during the past decade: in 1959[10] and in 1962.[11] The possible applications to treatment of patients extend beyond the military situation in terms of goals, socializing education, and specialized group therapy.

Developments in community psychiatry lead Becker, Murphy and Greenblatt[22] to say that the possibility of a therapeutic milieu beyond the hospital no longer seems to be as unrealistic of attainment than before, although Cumming and Cumming[69] remind that there are greater difficulties in attempting to structure a therapeutic milieu in a natural setting than in a hospital.

Leighton[184] predicts a major change in thinking about psychiatric disorder, given the proposition that society is a dynamic system, with individuals occupying various positions in it, so that relationships exist between the system and the positions, and between the conditions of mental health and mental illness, the nature of the relationships being subject to inquiry. Four clusters of ideas will undergo change: 1) a shift in emphasis from pathologic dynamics to disability control, with the matter of nomenclature being rethought; 2) a move from preoccupation with single cause toward the "concept of salient cause;" 3) greater attention to "sociocultural disintegration," as salient cause; and 4) "congruent planning" as a method of preventive psychiatry. Leighton suggests that the first point is germane to the phenomenon of the social breakdown syndrome; that the second is related to the critical relationship which social conditions, or virus, or diet, may have to a disability; that the third is a more fundamental disturbance than poverty or affluence, each of which may lead to impairment of processes necessary for group survival; and that the fourth is aimed toward reversing the downward spiral of sociocultural disintegration. The latter calls for a patterning of local coordination which binds together the social structures or bureaucracies in a congruent, effective way. He asks whether the mental health centers might evolve toward such a function. Marcus and Edelson[209] raise the question whether the integration and coordination function might be the crucial contribution of the community mental health program.

COMMUNITY MENTAL HEALTH CENTER: A REGIONAL APPROACH

A decade since publication of Bellak's *Schizophrenia,* and looking toward the seventies, one again might use the estimate of Aldrich or Jackson to describe the contemporary situation, except for the possibility that a new system for action may have been invented. Invention of the new system of community mental health centers with a regional approach may allow for a hitherto insoluble problem to become amenable to solution. If so, in the instant case, what have been long-standing problems in schizophrenia may be addressed in new and more fruitful ways.

The regional district or area approach to center development characterizes the current effort in the United States and elsewhere.* Marshall outlines a plan for Nova Scotia,[210] while Baldwin and Millar[14] present a collection of papers on the development of the regional program of services for the mentally ill in northeast Scotland. Millar[232] outlines the transformation of psychiatry in the general hospital into a regional center, part of a regional system of community services integrating social welfare and psychiatry. Stewart and associates[343] describe the role of Bilbohall Hospital, Elgin, in the development of services in northeast Scotland, commenting upon the remarkable similarity between the Elgin district pattern and the comprehensive mental health center proposed by President Kennedy.

Miller[235] examines various trends in the emerging centers, and reports upon the regional development[234] and use of the mental health center[236] in Israel. From Croydon, Surrey, district psychiatry developments have been communicated by May, Sheldon and MacKeith;[218] by May and Gregory[215] and May.[214]

In Paris, the XIIIe Arrondissement is a district having a population of 175,000, and being served by teams, one for children and one for adults, for every 30,000. Services are organized around the guiding principle of continuity of care. Paumelle[262] describes the organization and staffing. Other papers relating to the *service psychiatrique de secteur,* as developed in Paris, have been published by Duchene[76,77]; Paumelle[261]; Lebovici[180]; and Bonnafé and associates.[39,40] Le Guillant has reported upon socio-medical services[181] and with associates[182] upon the functioning of the sector facility. Sivadon and

---

*In England, the *Hospital Plan* does not replace the regional hospital structure where decisions may be made as to decentralization patterns and the locus of psychiatric services. The mental hospital is a service over which the local authority has no control. A basic problem remains, possibly the major operational problem in the organization of comprehensive mental health services: that of bridging the divisions between the local authority service and the mental hospital service. Administrative patterns to attain coordination between hospitals and local authorities have been described as being of three types by Freeman[99,101]: 1. The mental hospital takes on nearly all community work, leaving basic statutory functions and transport to the local authority; 2. The hospital and local authority join together as equal partners, establishing a new administrative structure for community service; 3. The hospital and local authority work closely together, without a joint managerial entity being elaborated, although staff are jointly used.

Baumé[328] and Sivadon and associates[329] have written on the social club approach in an aftercare center. In Italy the sector approach is debated pro[21] and con.[257]

The term, mental health center, has been in contemporaneous use at least since 1953, when the Boston Psychopathic Hospital became the Massachusetts Mental Health Center.[213] Ten years later, in the United States, the term began to take on more precision with the special message to Congress by President Kennedy and subsequent enactment of the Federal legislation for construction and staffing of community mental health centers. Felix[92] outlined the concept of the mental health center in the framework of a national program; the comprehensive aspect of center planning and development was sketched by Brown and Cain;[48] the emergence of new patterns of service reported by Ozarin and Brown.[255] The issues and policies at stake in the development of the new program were discussed by Yolles,[381] with emphatic recognition made of the mental health centers program as a new system of mental health care in a paper by Ozarin and Levenson.[256]

The "center" is not conceived of as a building, or a particular arrangement of staff, but as a *program* of services, hence the psychiatric hospital or the general hospital may be the locus. Foley and Sanders[95] make the point explicitly. Their paper refines two trends of thought from the contributions of a number of workers: 1) the view that early intervention, especially in response to crisis, results in not only resolution of the problem in context, but also in positive personality change; and 2) the view that treatment near family, friends and community, avoids the untoward effects of alienation and estrangement which geographical dislocation seems to promote. While the center is neither a building, nor a staff, and is a program, it is also a facility providing services for: 1) the prevention or diagnosis of mental illness; or 2) care and treatment of mentally ill patients; or 3) rehabilitation of such persons, which services are provided principally for persons residing in a particular community or communities in or near which the facility is situated. To put it another way, a mental health center is a facility by means of which persons residing in or near the location of the center are provided preventive, treatment and rehabilitative services, directed toward: 1) anticipatory interception of disease or disability; 2) therapeutic intermission of episodes of mental illness, emotional disturbance or adaptational impairment; and 3) remedial interdiction of pathogenic forces—social, cultural, familial, occupational, and personal.

For the purpose of qualifying for assistance, federal regulations set forth adequate mental health service elements for comprehensive care: 1) inpatient, 2) outpatient, 3) partial hospitalization, 4) emergency services, 5) consultation and education, 6) diagnostic services, 7) rehabilitative services, 8) precare and aftercare, 9) training, and 10) research and evaluation. The first five are the essential elements for comprehensive mental health services. Other desiderata include: the essential services of the center are to be coordinated, to be accessible, to insure continuity of care and to be compatible with the state plan. Further, regulations define a community of service (or "catchment area") to include between 75,000 and 200,000 population, by reference to most recent official population data.[360,361]

PLANNING FORECAST

If, standing alone, schizophrenia had failed to attain acceptance as a public health responsibility, the past decade had seen the emergence of "mental illness" in this light. Possibly what had failed to be won in the specific sense, may have been attained as a result of winning the more generalized campaign. As a major contributor to the numbers of the mentally disabled, schizophrenia might receive attention in the coming decade as a public health responsibility, on a scale never before possible. Whether this result obtains, will be dependent upon the extent to which the newer facilities are capable of giving *concerted attention to schizophrenia* in terms of treatment, research and training. This calls for new planning efforts which will take into account the requirements of the program, as seen in the light of recent experience.[164]

The comprehensive psychiatric community service provides an opportunity to develop criteria for the service programs specifically needed by schizophrenic patients. Mandelbrote[204] has touched on many matters of significance in the planning of facilities. His experiences in rapid conversion of a closed mental hospital into an open door hospital[202] and in development of a comprehensive psychiatric community service[203] have been reported. Mandelbrote and Folkard[205] conducted a study of 171 schizophrenics living in the community in Gloucestershire. Of the total, 96 appeared to be well; 36 to have slight impairment; 36, moderate; and 3, severe. The families of 65 were disturbed by the presence of the patient, but in only 4 instances was the degree severe. Unemployment was the lot of 24 out of 60 males, 20 of whom had been without work for a year. Of importance to planing of service is the community adjustment problem. The authors observed that the patients were apparently more aware of personal and social inadequacies than of problems related to work or to family. The same authors[206] point to the increased burden on the community, resulting from present dispositional trends, and emphasize the need for supportive and follow-up services. They state that their evidence shows a reduction in the number of schizophrenics staying in hospital more than 12 months. In 1947, the percentage was 50 to 60 per cent; in 1958, 6 to 15 per cent. Other facts highlighting the trend are reported: 60 per cent of schizophrenic patients were discharged in 4 months; 70 per cent were not readmitted within one year; 80 per cent were out of hospital a year after admission; and 88 per cent were discharged within one year.

In planning the new center approach, one must clearly take into account such trends and observations, having specifically to do with schizophrenic patient needs in relation to the community. The view taken by the planner may well be crucial as to the nature of the condition for which public responsibility is to become better defined. Without regard to etiology, schizophrenia may be viewed as a descriptive term for a group of conditions which may present a chronic course requiring, at various times, inpatient care or other types of organized treatment. In his foreword to the publication of a symposium on psychoneurosis and schizophrenia, Usdin[370] writes:

> "If schizophrenia is viewed as a disease with a predominant organic component (or organic defect disease), the therapeutic potential must be recognized as exceedingly limited. If schizophrenia is viewed in terms of social maladaptation, with some constitutional factors, then there is reasonable hope that the illness can be modified to the extent that the patient is relatively indistinguishable from the average person."

Psychiatric architecture[119] will give way to a new kind of collaboration with architects, engaging private and public hospitals in mental health.[118,187] A collection of articles in planning and construction of mental health facilities emphasize the broad dimensions of the joint planning effort.[274] Papers by Ng,[249] Dorsett,[75] Falick[89,90] and McLaughlin[224] are representative. Other more extensive references to the San Francisco Mental Health Center Planning Project[275] and to six representative center planning concepts, engaging the team approach,[9] have been published. A similar working approach in the XIIIe Arrondissement has been employed.[339]

The planners of services and facilities will need to take into account, not only the therapeutic requirements of the individual, of the community within the hospital, and of the community outside of the hospital.[79,259] The planners will also have to address themselves to larger issues of urban planning,[126] metropolitan development[366] and the megalopolis.[317] Issues of poverty and health,[277] the problem of financing all medical care[273] and need for responsible financial management[105] will call for use of intelligence based upon comparative studies,[354] of program budgeting[250,368,369] and of new systems of control.[8,238,258] Such issues as these require a contribution to planning from the field of political science.[344,345]

In summary, the community mental health center and the regional approach offers a base for work upon schizophrenia in the context of important urban or rural activities and experiences. A group of centers provides a complex, general management issue, in which prospective developments can be approached only through a management system effectively relating planning, programming, and budgeting. If an organized, systematic approach to the problem of schizophrenia is to be realized, a management concept will be required such that a facilitation results of all intergovernmental, interdepartmental and interagency relationships necessary to accomplish a complex mental health mission.

BIBLIOGRAPHY

1. Albert Einstein Medical Center—Bronx Municipal Hospital, Bronx, New York. In Glasscote, R., Sanders, D., Forstenzer, H. M., and Foley, A. R.: The Community Mental Health Center: An Analysis of Existing Models. Washington, D. C.: American Psychiatric Association, 201-213, 1964.

2. Aldrich, C. K.: Psychiatry. In 1959 Britannica Book of the Year. A Record of the March of Events of 1958. Chicago: Encyclopedia Britannica, 566, 1959.

3. American Hospital Association: Psychiatric Services in General Hospitals. Chicago, 1961.

4. American Psychiatric Association: Standards for Hospitals and Clinics. Washington, D. C. 1958.

5. American Psychiatric Association: New Perspectives on Mental Patient Care. Reprinted from Mental Hospitals, Washington, D. C., 1961.

6. ———: The Future of the Mental Hospital. Reprinted from Mental Hospitals, Washington, D. C., 1962.

7. ———: The Private Hospital. A Vital Element in the Progress of Psychiatry. Reprinted from Mental Hospitals, Washington, D. C., 1962.

8. Anthony, R. N.: Planning and Control Systems: A Framework for Analysis. Boston, Massachusetts: Harvard University Graduate School of Business Administration, 1965.

9. Architecture for The Community Mental Health Center. New York: Mental Health Materials Center, 1967.

10. Artiss, K. L.: The Symptom as Communication in Schizophrenia. New York: Grune & Stratton, 1959.

11. ———: Milieu Therapy in Schizophrenia. New York: Grune & Stratton, 1962.

12. Avnet, H. H.: Psychiatric Insurance. New York, Group Health Insurance, 1962.

13. Bahn, A. K., Norman, V. B., Hench, C. L., McCarty, C. L., and Rippy, M. A.: Gains in outpatient psychiatric clinic services, 1961. Ment. Hyg. 47: 177-188, 1963.

14. Baldwin, J. A., and Millar, W. M. (Eds.): Community Psychiatry. Int. Psychiat. Clin. Vol. 1, No. 3, Boston: Little, Brown & Co., 1964.

15. Bandler, B. (Ed.): Psychiatry in the General Hospital. Int. Psychiat. Clin. Vol. 3, No. 3. Boston: Little, Brown, 1966.

16. Barclay, W. A.: Mental Health Services in the United States. A Report on a Harkness Fellowship of the Commonwealth Fund. Sidney, Australia: V. C. N. Blight, Government Printer, 1966.

17. ———: Transcript of an interview by M. E. Perkins. In Ziskind, R. (Ed.) Viewpoint on Mental Health, 246-251. New York: New York City Community Mental Health Board, 1967.

18. Barton, R.: Institutional Neurosis, Bristol, Wright and Sons, 1959.

19. Barton, W. E.: Administration in Psychiatry. Springfield, Ill.: Charles C. Thomas, 1962.

20. Barton, W. E. et al.: Impressions of European Psychiatry. Washington, D. C.: American Psychiatric Association, 1961.

21. Barucci, M.: Arguments pour une organisation sectorielle psychiatrique. Social Psychiat. 1: 103-104, 1966.

22. Becker, A., Murphy, N. M., and Greenblatt, M.: Recent advances in community psychiatry. N. Eng. J. Med. 272: 621-626; 674-679, 1965.

23. Beckerman, A., Perlin, S., and Weinstein, W.: The Montefiore program: Psychiatry integrates with the community. Ment. Hosp. 14: 8-13, 1966.

24. Bellak, L. (Ed.): Schizophrenia: A Review of the Syndrome. New York, Logos Press, 1958.

25. Bellak, L.: A general hospital as a focus of community psychiatry. J.A.M.A. 174: 2214-2217, 1960.

26. Bellak, L.: A general hospital becomes a focus of community psychiatry. Ment. Hosp. 12: 8-10, 1961.

27. Bellak, L.: Handbook of Community Psychiatry and Community Mental Health. New York: Grune & Stratton, 1964.

28. Bellak, L.: Transcript of an inter-

view by M. E. Perkins. *In* Ziskind, R. (Ed.) Viewpoint on Mental Health. New York: New York City Community Mental Health Board, 22-28, 1967.

29. Bellak, L., Prola, M., Meyer, E. J., and Zuckerman, M.: Psychiatry in the medical-surgical emergency clinic. Arch. Gen. Psychiat. 10: 267-269, 1964.

30. Benady, D. R., and Denham, J.: Development of an early treatment unit from an observation ward. Brit. Med. J. 2: 1569-1572, Dec. 21, 1963.

31. Bennett, A. E., Hargrove, E. A., and Engle, B.: The Practice of Psychiatry in General Hospitals. Berkeley University of California, 1956.

32. Bernard, V. W.: A training program in community psychiatry. Ment. Hosp. 11: 7-10, 1960.

33. ———: Education for community psychiatry in a university medical center with emphasis on the rationale and objectives of training. In Bellak, L. (Ed.) Handbook of Community Psychiatry and Community Health. Chapt. 4. New York: Grune & Stratton, 1964.

34. Bernstein, S., and Kaufman, M. R.: The psychiatrist in a general hospital. J. Mount Sinai Hosp. 29: 385-394, 1962.

35. Black, B. J. (Ed.): Guides to Psychiatric Rehabilitation: A Cooperative Program with a State Mental Hospital. New York: Altro Health and Rehabilitation Services, Inc., 1963.

36. Blasko, J. J.: The general hospital psychiatric unit—a VA success story. Ment. Hosp. 13: 198-202, 1962.

37. Bloomberg, W.: A proposal for a community based hospital as a branch of a state hospital. Am. J. Psychiat. 116:814-817, 1960.

38. Blue Cross Association: New directions toward community mental health. Blue Cross Reports. 2, No. 3, July-Sept., 1964.

39. Bonnafé, L., and Daumerzon, G.: Pour réfléchir á la relation medecin malade dans le futur service psychiatrique public de secteur. Information psychiatrique 35: 451, 1959.

40. Bonnafé, L. et al.: Rapport sur l' equipment psychiatrique d'un territoire, dépourvu de toute formation spécialisée. Information psychiatrique 33: 299-311, 1957.

41. Bradlow, P. A., McLeod, S. W., and Brownstein, E. J.: Mental health. *In* Spiegel, E. A. (Ed.) Progress in Neurology and Psychiatry. Volume XXI. Chapter 21. New York & London: Grune & Stratton, 479-486, 1966.

42. Brandon, S., and Gruenberg, D.: Measurement of the incidence of chronic severe social breakdown syndrome. *In* Gruenberg, E. (Ed.) Evaluating the Effectiveness of Mental Health Services. New York: Milbank Mem. Fund Quart. 44: 129-142, Part 2, Jan. 1966.

43. Brenner, M. H.: Economic change and mental hospitalization: New York State, 1910-1960. Social Psychiat. 2: 180-188, 1967.

44. Brill, H., and Patton, R. E.: Analysis of 1955-1956 population fall in New York State Mental Hospitals in first year of large-scale use of tranquilizing drugs. Am. J. Psychiat. 114: 509-517, 1957.

45. Brill, H., and Patton, R. E.: Analysis of population reduction in New York State Mental Hospitals during the first four years of large-scale therapy with psychotropic drugs. Am. J. Psychiat. 116: 495-509, 1959.

46. Brill, H., and Patton, R. E.: Clinical-statistical analysis of population changes in New York State Mental Hospitals since introduction of psychotropic drugs. Am. J. Psychiat. 119: 20-35, 1962.

47. Brook, C. P. B.: Psychiatric units in general hospitals. Lancet 2: 684-686, Sept. 26, 1964.

47a. Brook, C. P. B. and Stafford-Clark, D.: Psychiatric treatment in general wards. Lancet 1: 1159-1162, May 27, 1961.

48. Brown, B. S., and Cain, H. P., II: The many meanings of 'comprehensive': underlying issues in implementing the community mental health center programs. Am. J. Orthopsychiat. 34: 834-839, 1964.

49. Butts, H. F.: The organization of a psychiatric day hospital. J. Nat. Med. Ass. 56: 381-389, 1964.

50. Byrne, M. E., Sr.: A psychiatric unit enters its second quarter century. Ment. Hosp. 11: 16-20, 1960.

51. Cain, H. P., II, and Ozarin, L. D.: Hospitals and the community mental health centers program. Hospitals 38: 19-22, 1964.

52. Capoore, H. S., and Nixon, J. W. G.: Short-stay psychiatric unit in a general hospital. Lancet 2: 1351-1352, Dec. 16, 1961.

53. Carse, J.: The Worthing experiment: A home care program. In Linn L. (Ed.) Frontiers in General Hospital Psychiatry. Chapt. 15. New York: International Universities Press, 1961.

54. Caudill, W.: The Psychiatric Hospital as a Small Society. Cambridge, Mass., Harvard University Press, 1958.

55. Chittick, R. A., Brooks, G. W., Irons, F. S., and Deane, W. N.: The Vermont Story: Rehabilitation of Chronic Schizophrenic Patients. Burlington, Vermont, Queen City Printers, 1961.

56. Clark, D. A., and Sheps, C. G.: On the administration of university teaching hospitals. J. Med. Educ. 39: 527-530, 1964.

57. Clark, D. H.: The ward therapeutic community and its effects on the hospital. In Freeman, H. (Ed.) Psychiatric Hospital Care. Chapt. 9. London: Bailliere, Tindall & Cassel, 1965.

58. Clark, D. H.: Administrative Therapy. The Role of the Doctor in the Therapeutic Community. London: Tavistock Publications. J. B. Lippincott, 1964.

59. Clark, D. H., Hooper, D. F., and Oram, E. G.: Creating a therapeutic community in a psychiatric ward. Hum. Relat. 15: 123-147, 1962.

60. Cohen, N. A., and Haldane, F. P.: Inpatient psychiatry in general hospitals. Lancet 1: 1113-1114, May 26, 1962.

61. Cohen, W. J.: An outline of social security provisions for psychiatric illness. Ment. Hosp. 16: 301-304, 1965.

62. Coleman, M. D.: Problems in an emergency psychiatric clinic. Ment. Hosp. 11: 26-27, May 1960.

63. Coleman, M. D., and Rosenbaum, M.: The psychiatric walk-in clinic. Israel Ann. Psychiat. 1: 99-106, 1963.

64. Cooper, A. B., and Early, D. F.: Evolution in the mental hospital. Brit. Med. J. 1: 1600-1603, June 3, 1961.

65. Community Mental Health and Social Psychiatry: A Reference Guide. Cambridge, Mass.: Harvard University Press, 1962.

66. Connecticut Mental Health Center: Yale Medicine 1: 2-5, 1966.

67. Cotton, J. M.: The function of a psychiatric service in a general hospital. Ment. Hosp. 12: 4-7, 1961.

68. ———: Transcript of an interview by M. E. Perkins. In Ziskind, R. (Ed.) Viewpoint on Mental Health. New York: New York City Community Mental Health Board, 35-40, 1967.

69. Cumming, J., and Cumming, E.: Ego and Milieu. New York, Atherton Press, 1962.

70. Daniels, R. S.: Community psychiatry—a new profession, a developing subspecialty, or effective clinical psychiatry? Community Ment. Health J. 2: 47-54, 1966.

71. Denis, V.: Catholic University of Louvain, 1425-1958. Louvain, Catholic University of Louvain, 1958.

72. dePaul, M. Sr.: Psychiatric center in a general hospital. Hosp. Prog. 42: 85-88, 1961.

73. Detre, T. P., Kessler, D. R., and Jarecki, H. G.: The role of the general hospital in modern community psychiatry. Am. J. Orthopsychiat. 33: 690-700, 1963.

74. Donohue, W. V., and Holt, W. L.: A psychiatric service in an all purpose general hospital. Dis. Nerv. Syst. 24: 562-566, 1963.

75. Dorsett, C.: New directions in mental health facilities. J. Am. Inst. Architecture 42: 65-69, November 1964.

76. Duchéne, H.: Le service de prophylaxie mentale de l'office public d'hygiéne sociale du Départment de la Seine. L'hygiene mentale 47: 245-255, 1958.

77. Duchéne, H.: Les services psychiatriques publics extra-hospitaliers. Comptes-Rendus. LVIIe Congrés de psychiatrie et neurologie de langue francaise. Tours

1959, Masson et Cie., edit. 583-665 (bibliographie).

78. Duhl, L. J.: The Changing Face of Mental Health. *In* Duhl, L. J. (Ed.) The Urban Condition. Chapt. 16. New York and London: Basic Books, 1963.

79. Duhl, L. J., Soskin, W. F., and Chayes, A. H.: Psychiatry and the urban community. Am. J. Psychiat. 122: 999-1001, 1966.

80. Dunham, H. W.: Community psychiatry: the newest therapeutic bandwagon. *In* Current Issues of Psychiatry. Selections from the Int. J. of Psychiat. 1:289-320, New York: Science House, 1967.

81. Dunkley, E. W., and Lewis, E.: North Wing. A psychiatric unit in a general hospital. Lancet 1: 156-159, Jan. 19, 1963.

82. Dutchess County Project: *In* Glasscote, R., Sanders, D., Forstenzer, H. M., and Foley, A. R.: The Community Mental Health Center: An Analysis of Existing Models. Washington, D. C.: American Psychiatric Association, 105-120, 1964.

83. Eaton, J. W. et al.: Resistance to psychiatry in a general hospital. Ment. Hosp. 16: 156-160, 1965.

84. Elinson, J., Padilla, E., and Perkins, M. E.: Public Image of Mental Health Services. New York, Mental Health Materials Center, 1967.

85. Epps, R. L., Barnes, R. H., and McPartland, T. S.: A Community Concern. Experiences with Management of Major Mental Illness in the Community. Springfield, Illinois: Charles C. Thomas, 1965.

86. Epstein, J.: The impact of the general hospital on the private psychiatric hospital. *In* Linn, L. (Ed.) Frontiers of General Hospital Psychiatry Chapt. 21, New York: International Universities Press, 1961.

87. Errera, P., Wyshak, G., and Jarecki, H.: Psychiatric care in a general hospital emergency room. Arch. Gen. Psychiat. 9: 105-112, 1963.

88. Esquibel, A. J.: Psychiatric services of Prince Georges General Hospital. Maryland Med. J. 13: 61-65, 1964.

89. Falick, J.: Good planning can make hospitals good neighbors. Hospitals 41: 40-45, July 16, 1967.

90. ————: Team planning: translating needs into physical facilities. Hospitals 42: 69-74, February 1, 1968.

91. Farndale, J.: The Day Hospital Movement in Great Britain. New York, Oxford, London, Paris, Pergamon Press, 1961.

92. Felix, R. H.: Community mental health. Am. J. Orthopsychiat. 33: 788-795, 1963.

93. Fisch, M., Gruenberg, E. M., and Bandfield, C.: The epidemiology of psychiatric emergencies in an urban health district. Am. J. Public Health 54: 572-579, 1964.

94. Fisch, M., and MacDonald, L.: Community-centered treatment of schizophrenia. Am. J. Orthopsychiat. 34: 652-658, 1964.

95. Foley, A. R., and Sanders, D.: Theoretical considerations for the development of the community mental health center concept. Am. J. Psychiat. 122: 985-990, 1966.

96. Fort Logan Mental Health Center. *In* Glasscote, R., Sanders, D., Forstenzer, H. M., and Foley, A. R.: The Community Mental Health Center: An Analysis of Existing Models. Washington, D. C.: American Psychiatric Association, 133-148, 1964.

97. Furman, S. S.: Community mental health services in northern Europe: Great Britain, Netherlands, Denmark, and Sweden. Public Health Service Publication No. 1407. Washington, D. C.: United States Government Printing Office, 1965.

98. Freedman, A. M.: Transcript of an interview by M. E. Perkins. *In* Ziskind, R. (Ed.) Viewpoint on Mental Health. New York: New York City Community Mental Health Board 359-363, 1967.

99. Freeman, H.: The inter-relationship of local authority and hospital services. *In* Freeman, H. (Ed.) Psychiatric Hospital Care. Chapt. 15. London: Bailliére, Tindall & Cassel, 1965.

100. ————: Oldham and district psychiatric service. Lancet 1: 218-221, Jan. 23, 1960.

101. Freeman, H., and Farndale, J. (Eds.): Trends in the Mental Health Services: A Symposium of Original and Reprinted Papers. Oxford, London, New York, Paris: Pergamon Press, 1963.

102. Freeman, H. E., and Simmons, O. G.: The Mental Patient Comes Home. New York and London, John Wiley and Sons, 1963.

103. Freeman, T., Cameron, J. L., and McGhie, A.: Chronic Schizophrenia. New York, International Universities Press, 1958.

104. Fuentes, C. E.: The first open psychiatric unit in a general hospital in Puerto Rico. Am. J. Psychiat. 121: 473-475, 1964.

105. Gabis, S. T.: Mental Health and Financial Management: Some Dilemmas of Program Budgeting. Department of Political Science Report No. 3 East Lansing, Michigan: Michigan State University, 1960.

106. Gardner, E. A., Miles, H. C., Bahn, A. K., and Romano, J.: All psychiatric experience in a community. Arch. Gen. Psychiat. 9: 369-378, 1963.

107. Gardner, E. A., Bahn, A. K., and Miles, H. C.: Patient experience in psychiatric units of general and state mental hospitals. Public Health Rep. 79: 755-767, 1964.

108. Geel: How to Visit Colony of Geel with a table "Movement of Population of the Colony during the year 1960 n.p. 1961.

109. Glass, A. J.: Advances in military psychiatry. In Masserman, J. H. (Ed.) Current Psychiatric Therapies. Volume 1. New York and London: Grune & Stratton, 159-167, 1961.

110. Glass, A. J., Artiss, K. L., Gibbs, J. J., and Sweeney, V. C.: The current status of army psychiatry. Amer. J. Psychiat. 117: 673-683, 1961.

111. Glasscote, R. M., Sanders, D. S., Forstenzer, H. M., and Foley, A. R.: The Community Mental Health Center: An Analysis of Existing Models. Washington, D. C.: American Psychiatric Association, 1964.

112. Glasscote, R. M., and Kanno, C. K.: General Hospital Psychiatric Units. A national survey. Washington, D. C.: Joint Information Service American Psychiatric Association — National Association for Mental Health, 1965.

113. Goffman, E.: Characteristics of total institutions. In Symposium on Preventive and Social Psychiatry. Washington, D. C.: Walter Reed Army Institute of Research 43-84, 1958.

114. Goffman, E.: Asylums. Essays on the Social Situation of Mental Patients and other Inmates. Chicago: Aldine Publishing Co., 1961.

115. Goldberg, D.: Rehabilitation of the chronically mentally ill in England. Social Psychiat. 2: 1-13, 1967.

116. Goldston, S. E. (Ed.): Concepts of Community Psychiatry: A Framework of Training. Bethesda, Md.: National Institute of Mental Health, 1965.

117. Golen, M.: This trouble shooting clinic is strengthening a community. J.A.M.A. 171: 1697-1699, 1959.

118. Good, L. R., Siegel, S. M., and Bay, A. P. (Eds.): Therapy by Design. Springfield, Illinois: Charles C. Thomas, 1965.

119. Goshen, C. E. (Ed.): Psychiatric Architecture. Washington, D. C.: American Psychiatric Association, 1959.

120. Gorwitz, K., Bahn, A. K., Chandler, C. A., and Martin, W. A.: Planned uses of a statewide psychiatric register for aiding mental health in the community. Am. J. Orthopsychiat. 33: 494-500, 1963.

121. Gordon, J. E., O'Rourke, E., Richardson, F. L. W., Jr., and Lindemann, E.: The biological and social sciences in an epidemiology of mental disorder. Am. J. Med. Sci. 223: 316-343, 1952.

122. Greco, J. T.: Case for the psychiatric unit. Ment. Hosp. 12: 10-12, 1961.

123. Greenblatt, M., Levinson, D. J., and Klerman, G. L.: Mental Patients in Transition. Springfield, Illinois, Charles C. Thomas, 1961.

124. Grinker, R., and Gordon, E.: The Simon Wexler Psychiatric Research and Clinic Pavilion. Ment. Hosp. 14: 473-479, 1963.

125. Group for the Advancement of Psychiatry. Administration of the Public Psychiatric Hospital. Report No. 46. New York, 1960.

126. Group for the Advancement of Psychiatry: Urban America and the Planning of Mental Health Services. Symposium No. 10. New York, 1964.

127. Gruenberg, E. M. (Ed.): Evaluating the Effectiveness of Mental Health Services. The Milbank Mem. Fund Quart., 44, Part 2, Jan. 1966.

128. Gruenberg, E. M., Brandon, S., and Kasius, R. V.: Identifying cases of social breakdown syndrome. In Gruenberg, E. M. (Ed.) Evaluating the Effectiveness of Mental Health Services. New York: Milbank Mem. Fund Quart. 44, 150-155, Part 2, Jan. 1966.

129. Gruenberg, E. M., and Zusman, J.: The natural history of schizophrenia. In Kolb, L. C., Kallman, F. J. and Polatin, P. (Eds.) Schizophrenia. Int. Psychiat. Clinics Vol. 1: No. 4, 699-710, October 1964.

130. Hausman, W., and Rioch, D. McK.: Military psychiatry: a prototype of social and preventive psychiatry in the United States. Arch. Gen. Psychiat. 16: 727-739, 1967.

131. Hays, P.: The future of psychiatric services. In New Horizons in Psychiatry. Chapt. 6. Baltimore: Penguin Books, 1964.

132. Hays, P.: The law relating to psychiatric patients. In New Horizons in Psychiatry. Chapt. 15. Baltimore: Penguin Books, 1964.

133. Health Services in Britain: Central Office of Information, Reference Pamphlet 20. London: Her Majesty's Stationery Office, 1964.

134. Heron, M. J.: Functions and problems of psychiatric units in general hospitals. Brit. Med. J. 2: 1529-1531, Dec. 8, 1962.

135. Hill, D.: Introduction. In Freeman, H. (Ed.) Psychiatric Hospital Care. London, Bailliere, Tindall & Cassell, 1-4, 1965.

136. Hoch, P. H.: Observations on the British 'open' hospitals: introduction. Ment. Hosp. 8: 5-6, September 1957.

137. Hoenig, J., and Hamilton, M. W.: Extramural care of psychiatric patients. Lancet 1: 1322-1325, June 19, 1965.

138. Hollingshead, A. B., and Redlich, F. C.: Social Class and Mental Illness. New York, John Wiley & Sons, 1958.

139. Hospital Plan for the England and Wales (Cmnd. 1604) London: Her Majesty's Stationery Office, 1962.

140. Hudgens, R. W.: Psychiatric inpatients at a teaching hospital. Arch. Gen. Psychiat. 9: 384-389, 1963.

141. Hume, P. B., and Rudin, E.: Psychiatric inpatient services in general hospitals. Calif. Med. 93: 200-207, 1960.

142. Hunt, R. C., Gruenberg, E. M., Hacken, E., and Huxley, M.: A comprehensive hospital-community service in a state hospital. Am. J. Psychiat. 117: 817-821, 1961.

143. Institute de Socoilogie: Universite Libre de Bruxelles. Corps Medical et Assurance Maladie. Revue de l'Institut de Sociologie, Bruxelles, 1964-3.

144. Izumi, K.: An analysis for the design of hospital quarters for the neuropsychiatric patient. Ment. Hosp. 8: 30-32.

145. Jackson, D. D. (Ed.): The Etiology of Schizophrenia. New York: Basic Books, 1960.

146. Jackson, G. W., and Smith, F. V.: The Kansas Plan. A proposal for mental hospital reorganization. Ment. Hosp. 12: 5-8, 1961.

147. Jacob L. Reiss Mental Health Pavilion: St. Vincent's Hospital of the City of New York. In Glasscote, R. M., Sanders, D. S., Forstenzer, H. M., and Foley, A. R. The Community Mental Health Center: An Analysis of Existing Models. Washington, D. C.: American Psychiatric Association, 165-181, 1964.

148. Joint Commission on Mental Illness and Health: Action for Mental Health. New York: Basic Books, 1961.

149. Juel-Nielsen, N.: Transcript of an interview by M. E. Perkins. In Ziskind, R. (Ed.) Viewpoint on Mental Health. New York: New York City Community Mental Health Board 231-236, 1967.

150. Kandel, D. B., and Williams, R. H.: Psychiatric Rehabilitation: Some

Problems of Research. New York and London, Prentice-Hall, 1964.

151. Kasius, R. V.: The social breakdown syndrome in a cohort of long-stay patients in the Dutchess County Unit, 1960-1963. *In* Gruenberg, E. M. (Ed.) Evaluating the Effectiveness of Mental Health Services. New York: Milbank Mem. Fund Quart. 44: 156-183, Part 2, Jan. 1966.

152. Kaufman, M. R.: A psychiatric unit in a general hospital. J. Mount Sinai Hosp. 24: 572-579, 1957.

153. Kaufman, M. R.: The role of the general hospital in community psychiatry. Comp. Psychiat. 4: 426-432, 1963.

154. Kaufman, M. R. (Ed.): The Psychiatric Unit in a General Hospital. Its Current and Future Role. New York: International Universities Press, 1965.

155. ———: Transcript of an interview by M. E. Perkins. *In* Ziskind R. (Ed.) Viewpoint on Mental Health. New York: New York City Community Mental Health Board 9-15, 1967.

156. Kaufman, M. R., Franzblau, A. N., and Kairys, D.: The emotional impact of ward rounds. J. Mount Sinai Hosp. 23: 782-803, 1956.

157. Kaufman, M. R., Lehrman, S., Franzblau, A. N., Tabbat, S., Weinroth, L., and Friedman, S.: Psychiatric findings in admissions to a medical service in a general hospital. J. Mount Sinai Hosp. 26: 160-170, 1959.

158. Kennedy, J. F.: Message from the President of the United States Relative to Mental Illness and Mental Retardation. February 5, 1963. 88th Congress, 1st Session. House of Representatives Document No. 58.

159. Khlentzos, M. T.: Role of a psychiatric unit in a general hospital. Hosp. Prog. 44: 54-55, 1963.

160. Kiev, A.: Community psychiatry: observations of recent English developments. Compr. Psychiat. 4: 291-298, 1963.

161. Kline, N. S.: Drugs and community mental hygiene clinics. Am. J. Public Health 52: Supplement 1-8, Sept. 1962.

162. Koegler, R. R., and Baill, N. Q.: Treatment of Psychiatric Outpatients. New York: Appleton-Century-Crofts, 1967.

163. Kolb, L. C.: Soviet psychiatric organization and the community mental health center concept. Am. J. Psychiat. 123: 433-440, 1966.

164. Kolb, L. C., Kallmann, F. J., and Polatin, P. (Eds.): Schizophrenia. Int. Psychiat. Clin. 1: No. 4, October, 1964.

165. Kramer, B. M.: Day Hospital. New York: Grune & Stratton, 1962.

166. ———: Links and barriers between hospital and community. Comm. Ment. Health J. 1: 69-72, 1965.

167. Laidlaw, R. W.: Organizational problems: the story of Tower 9. *In* Linn, L. (Ed.) Frontiers in General Hospital Psychiatry. Chapt. 3. New York: International Universities Press, 1961.

168. ———: Transcript of an interview by M. E. Perkins. *In* Ziskind, R. (Ed.) Viewpoint on Mental Health. New York: New York City Community Mental Health Board 53,-59, 1967.

169. Lambo, T. A.: A plan for the treatment of the mentally ill in Nigeria: the village system at Aro. *In* Linn, L. (Ed.) Frontiers in General Hospital Psychiatry. Chapt. 17, New York: International Universities Press, 1961.

170. ———: Transcript of an interview by M. E. Perkins. *In* Ziskind, R. (Ed.) Viewpoint on Mental Health. New York: New York City Community Mental Health Board, 259-264, 1967.

171. Landy, D., and Greenblatt, M.: Halfway House: A Sociocultural and Clinical Study of Rutland Corner House, a Transitional Aftercare Residence for Female Psychiatric Patients. Washington, D. C.: Vocational Rehabilitation Administration, 1965.

172. La Relaxation (Rééducation psychotonique) Aspects théoriques et pratiques. 3e édition augmentée. Aboulker, P., Chertok, L., Sapir, M. (Eds.) Paris: L'expansion Scientifique Francaise, 1964.

173. Lawson, A. R. L.: The Recognition of Mental Illness in London. London, New York and Toronto: Oxford University Press, 1966.

174. Lawson, F. S.: Mental hospitals:

their size and function. Canad. J. Public Health 49: 186-195, May, 1958.

175. Lebensohn, Z. M.: A new role for the psychiatric unit of the community hospital. Compr. Psychiat. 4: 375-380, 1963.

176. ———: Form and function in the general hospital psychiatric unit. Ment. Hosp. 14: 245-250, 1963.

177. Lebensohn, Z. M.: American psychiatry and the general hospital. Med. Ann. D. C. 33: 47-52, 1964.

178. ———: The psychiatric unit of the general hospital. Its organization and design as a therapeutic instrument. *In* Masserman, J. (Ed.) Current Psychiatric Therapies. New York: Grune & Stratton, 208-217, 1965.

179. Lebensohn, Z. M.: Facilities and organization. *In* Kaufman, M. R. (Ed.) The Psychiatric Unit in a General Hospital. New York: International Universities Press, 3-25, 1965.

180. Lebovici, S.: Quelques reflexions sur l' assistance extra-hospitaliere en psychiatrie infantile. Comptes-Rendus. LVIIe Congrés de psychiatrie et neurologie de langue francais, Tours 1959, Masson et Cie., edit. 688-690.

181. Le Guillant, L. Le service médico-social de secteur. Information psychiatrique 35: 9-39, 1959.

182. Le Guillant, L. et al.: Remarques sur trois ans de fonctionnement d'un dispensaire de secteur. Ann. medico-psychol. 116: 764-776, 1958.

183. Leighton, A. H.: An Introduction to Social Psychiatry. Springfield, Ill. Charles C. Thomas, 1960.

184. Leighton, A. H.: Is Social Environment a Cause of Psychiatric Disorders? *In* Monroe, R. R., Klee, G. D., Brody, E. B. (Eds.) Psychiatric Epidemiology and Mental Health. Psychiatric Research Report 22, American Psychiatric Association, 1967.

185. Lemaire, J. G.: La Relaxation. Relaxation et rééducation psychotonique. Paris: Petite Bibliothéque Payot, 1964.

186. Lemkau, P. V., and Crocetti, G. M.: The Amsterdam municipal psychiatric service: a psychiatric-sociological review. Am. J. Psychiat. 117: 779-783, 1961.

187. Levenson, A. I., Brown, B. S., and Knee, R. I.: The joint role of public and private hospitals in community mental health. Hospitals 42: 52-60, February 1, 1968.

188. Leyberg, J. T.: A district psychiatric service. The Bolton pattern. Lancet 2: 282-284, Sept. 5, 1959.

189. Linn, L. (Ed.): Frontiers in General Hospital Psychiatry. New York: International Universities Press, 1961.

190. Linn, L.: Transcript of an interview by M. E. Perkins. *In* Ziskind, R. (Ed.) Viewpoint on Mental Health, New York: New York City Community Mental Health Board, 60-65, 1967.

191. Little, J. D.: Development of a psychiatric unit in a large general hospital. Lancet 1: 376-377, Feb. 16, 1963.

192. Loftus, T. A., Crouse, F. R., and Pandelidis, P. K.: Mental Health. *In* Spiegel, E. A. (Ed.) Progress in Neurology and Psychiatry. Volume XVII. Chapter 22. New York & London: Grune & Stratton 412-420, 1962.

193. Loftus, T. A., and Mashikian, H. S.: Mental Health. *In* Spiegel, E. A. (Ed.) Progress in Neurology and Psychiatry. Volume XIX. Chapter 21. New York & London: Grune & Stratton 505-512, 1964.

194. Loftus, T. A., Preble, E., Bradlow, P. A., and McLeod, S. W.: Mental Health. *In* Spiegel, E. A. (Ed.) Progress in Neurology and Psychiatry. Volume XX. Chapter 23. New York & London: Grune & Stratton 600-607, 1965.

195. Loftus, T. A., Whitcomb, D. T., and Plutzky, M.: Mental Health. *In* Spiegel, E. A. (Ed.) Progress in Neurology and Psychiatry. Volume XVIII. Chapter 23. New York & London: Grune & Stratton 505-515, 1963.

196. Maclay, W. S.: Experiments in mental hospital organization. Academic Lecture. First Canadian Mental Hospital Institute, Toronto, Canada, January 20-24, 1958. Ottawa, Ontario: Department of National Health & Welfare, 1958.

197. Maclay, W. S.: Preface. *In* Farndale, J., The Day Hospital Movement in Great Britain. New York, Oxford, London, Paris, Pergamon Press, 1961.

198. Maclay, W. S.: After the Mental Health Act: an appraisal of English psychiatry. Ment. Hosp. 14: 100-106, No. 2, February, 1963.

199. Maclay, W. S.: The Adolf Meyer Lecture: A mental health service. Am. J. Psychiat. 120: 209-217, 1963.

200. MacMillan, D.: Hospital-community relationships. In An Approach to the Prevention of Disability from Chronic Psychosis. New York: Milbank Memorial Fund 29-39, 1958.

201. Main, T. F.: Mothers with children on a psychiatric unit. In Linn, L. (Ed.) Frontiers in General Hospital Psychiatry. Chapt. 12, New York: International Universities Press, 1961.

202. Mandelbrote, B.: An experiment in the rapid conversion of a closed mental hospital into an open-door hospital. Ment. Hyg. 42: 3-16, 1958.

203. Mandelbrote, B.: Development of a comprehensive psychiatric community service around the mental hospital. Ment. Hyg. 43: 368-377, 1959.

204. Mandelbrote, B. M.: Basic needs of psychiatric patients. In Freeman, H. (Ed.) Psychiatric Hospital Care. Chapt. 1. London: Bailliere, Tindall & Cassell, 1965.

205. Mandelbrote, B., and Folkard, S.: Some problems and needs of schizophrenics in relation to a developing psychiatric community service. Compr. Psychiat. 2: 317-328, 1961.

206. ———: The outcome of schizophrenia in relation to a developing community psychiatric service. Ment. Hyg. 47: 43-56, 1963.

207. Mannucci, M., Friedman, S., and Kaufman, M. R.: Survey of patients who have been attending non-psychiatric outpatient department services for ten years or longer. J. Mount Sinai Hosp. 28: 32-52, 1961.

208. Mannucci, M., and Kaufman, M. R.: The psychiatric unit in a general hospital: a functional analysis. Am. J. Psychiat. 122: 1329-1343, 1966.

209. Marcus, M. G., and Edelson, M.: Priorities in community mental health programs: a theoretical formulation. Social Psychiat. 2: 66-71, 1967.

210. Marshall, C.: The Nova Scotia mental health plan. Ment. Hosp. 13: 306-318, No. 6, June, 1962.

211. Martin, D. V.: Institutionalism. Lancet 2: 1188-1190, 1955.

212. Martin, M.: The Mental Ward. A Personnel Guidebook. Springfield, Illinois: Charles C. Thomas, 1962.

213. Massachusetts Mental Health Center: In Glasscote, R., Sanders, D., Forstenzer, H. M., and Foley, A. R. The Community Mental Health Center: An Analysis of Existing Models. Washington, D. C.: American Psychiatric Association, 149-163, 1964.

214. May, A. R.: Developing a community mental health service. (Mimeographed).

215. May, A. R., and Gregory, E.: An experiment in district psychiatry. Public Health 78: 19-25, 1963.

216. May, A. R. Gregory, E., Jones, D. M. H., and Bruggen, P.: Restoring the psychiatrically disabled to the community. Lancet 2: 241-243, 1963.

217. May, A. R., and Moore, S.: The mental nurse in the community. Lancet 1: 213-214, 1963.

218. May, A. R., Sheldon, A. P., and MacKeith, S. A.: Future of district psychiatry. Lancet 2: 1319-1320, 1962.

219. May, A. R., and Smith, J. A.: Problems in industrial resettlement of the mentally disabled. Occupational Therapy 22-28, 1965.

220. Mayer-Gross, W.: Adolf Meyer Research Lecture: Model psychoses, their history, relevancy and limitations. Am. J. Psychiat. 115: 673-682, 1959.

221. McGahee, C. M.: The ward community: a new route toward longstanding goals. Ment. Hosp. 12: 37-39, 1961.

222. McKeown, T.: The concept of a balanced hospital community. Lancet 1: 701-705, April 5, 1958.

223. McKerracher, D. G., and Smith, C. M.: A survey of psychiatric units in general hospitals in Canada. Canad. Med. Assn. J. 90: 1032-1033, 1964.

224. McLaughlin, H.: Programming and planning a community mental health center. Hospitals 41: 55-62, May 16, 1967.

225. McLeod, S. W.: Mental Health. *In* Spiegel, E. A. (Ed.) Progress in Neurology and Psychiatry. Volume XXII. Chapter 20, New York & London: Grune & Stratton, 402-410, 1967.

226. Meijering, W.: Recent developments in social psychiatry in the Netherlands. *In* Symposium on Preventive and Social Psychiatry. Washington, D. C.: Walter Reed Army Institute of Research, 409-418, 1958.

227. Melehov, D. E.: Some debatable problems in social psychiatry. Social Psychiat. 2: 107-110, 1967.

228. Mental Health Act, 1959: 7 & 8 Eliz. 2. Chapt. 72. London: Her Majesty's Stationery Office, Reprinted 1963.

229. Mental Illness and Due Process: Report and Recommendations on Admissions to Mental Hospitals under New York Law. Ithaca, New York: Cornell University Press, 1962.

230. Mickle, J. C.: Psychiatric home visits. Arch. Gen. Psychiat. 9: 379-383, 1963.

231. Milbank Memorial Fund: Decentralization of Psychiatric Services and Continuity of Care. New York, 1962.

232. Millar, W. M.: Psychiatry and the general hospital: emergence of the regional mental health center. *In* Baldwin, J. A., and Millar, W. M. (Eds.) Community Psychiatry. Int. Psychiat. Clin. 1: No. 3, July 1964. Boston: Little Brown & Co. 593-615.

233. Miller, D. H.: Psycho-social factors in the etiology of disturbed behavior. Brit. J. Med. Psychol. 34: 43-52, 1961.

234. Miller, L.: Mental health and social psychiatry. Medical and Biological Research in Israel. Moshe Prywes: Jerusalem 106-114, 1960.

235. Miller, L.: Community centers: emerging trends. An integrative overview. (Mimeographed)

236. ――――: Community psychiatry in Israel. Israel Ann. Psychiat. 2: 41-46, 1964.

237. ――――: Transcript of an interview by M. E. Perkins. *In* Ziskind, R. (Ed.) Viewpoint on Mental Health. New York: New York City Community Mental Health Board 252-258, 1967.

238. Miller, R. W.: How to plan and control with PERT. Harvard Business Review 40: 93-104, March-April, 1962.

239. Ministry of Health, National Health Service: Improving the Effectiveness of Hospitals for the Mentally Ill. F/M 121/1 June 25, 1964, Enclosure.

240. Moll, A. E.: Night and day treatment units in a general hospital. *In* Linn, L. (Ed.) Frontiers in General Hospital Psychiatry. Chapt. 9. New York: International Universities Press, 1961.

241, Moll, A. E.: Evolution of psychiatry in a general hospital and the community. Compr. Psychiat. 4: 394-408, 1963.

242. Moll, A. E.: The day and night treatment center. *In* The Psychiatric Unit in a General Hospital. Kaufman, M. R. (Ed.) New York: International Universities Press, 136-154, 1965.

243. ――――: Discussion: The patient. *In* The Psychiatric Unit in a General Hospital. Kaufman, M. R. (Ed.) New York: International Universities Press 155-174, 1965.

244. Morrissey, J. D.: The Chichester and district psychiatric service. *In* Gruenberg, E. M. (Ed.) Evaluating the Effectiveness of Mental Health Services. Milbank Mem. Fund Quart., 44: 28-36, Part 2, Jan. 1966.

245. Mustard, H. S.: An Introduction to Public Health. 2nd edition. New York: MacMillan, 1944.

246. Nebraska Psychiatric Institute: *In* Glasscote, R. M., Sanders, D. S., Forstenzer, H. M., and Foley, A. R. The Community Mental Health Center: An Analysis of Existing Models. Washington, D. C.: American Psychiatric Association 183-199, 1964.

247. New York State Department of Mental Hygiene. Report to the Governor by the New York State Planning Committee on Mental Disorders: A Plan for a Comprehensive Mental Health and Mental Retardation Program for New York State. 7 vols. July 1, 1965.

248. ――――: Unpublished data. Personal communication to H. Bluestone.

249. Ng, V.: Design concepts for a

comprehensive community mental health center. Hospitals 39: 56-59, August 16, 1965.

250. Novick, D. (Ed.): Program Budgeting: Program Analysis and the Federal Budget. Cambridge, Massachusetts: Harvard University Press, 1965.

251. Oast, S. P., and Perkins, M. E.: Changing patterns of psychiatric care in New York City. New York J. Med. 64: 2435-2441, 1964.

252. O'Neill, F. J.: Laying the foundation for the open door hospital. (Symposium) Ment. Hosp. 9: 10-12, May 1958.

253. O'Reilly, P. O.: The development and function of a comprehensive psychiatric service in the Moose Jaw Union Hospital (a five year study). Canad. Med. Ass. J. 88: 512-517, 1963.

254. Osmond, H.: Function as a basis of psychiatric ward design. Ment. Hosp. 8: 23-29, April 1957.

255. Ozarin, L. D., and Brown, B. S.: New directions in community mental health programs. Am. J. Orthopsychiat. 35: 10-17, 1965.

256. Ozarin, L. D., and Levenson, A. I.: The community mental health centers program in the U.S.: a new system of mental health care. Social Psychiat. 2: 145, 1967.

257. Padovani, G.: Objections a l'organisation sectorielle de l'assistance psychiatrique. Social Psychiat. 1: 105-106, 1966 (bibliographie).

258. Paige, H. W.: How PERT-Cost helps the general manager. Harvard Business Review. 41: 87-95, November-December, 1963.

259. Palmiere, D.: Problems in local community planning of mental illness facilities and services. Am. J. Public Health 55: 561-569, 1965.

260. Pauly, I. B., Saslow, G., and Brown, J. S.: A psychiatric service in a general hospital: ten years' experience in a setting for social learning. Int. J. Soc. Psychiat. 13: 85-92, 1967.

261. Paumelle, P.: Réflexions á propos de la création d'un service psychiatrique de secteur. Comptes-Rendus. LVIIe Congrés de psychiatrie et neurologie de langue francaise, Tours 1959, Masson et Cie., edit. 681-687.

262. Paumelle, P. L'organisation du travail d'équipe dans le 13° arrondissement de Paris. Social Psychiat. 2: 43-49, 1967.

263. Peck, H. B.: The psychiatric day hospital in a mental health program. Am. J. Orthopsychiat. 33: 482-493, 1963.

264. Penn Foundation: In Glasscote, R. M., Sanders, D. S., Forstenzer, H. M., and Foley, A. R. The Community Mental Health Center: An Analysis of Existing Models. Washington, D. C.: American Psychiatric Association 31-43, 1964.

265. Perlin, S.: Transcript of an interview by M. E. Perkins. In Ziskind, R. (Ed.) Viewpoint on Mental Health. New York: New York City Community Mental Health Board 16-21, 1967.

266. Perlin, S., and Kahn, R. L.: The development of a community mental health center model. In Psychiatric Research Report 22. Chapt. 14. Washington, D. C.: American Psychiatric Association, 1967.

267. Perkins, M. E.: The general hospital: local agency for community mental health services. Psychiat. Quart. Suppl. 37: Part 1, 111-118, 1963.

268. Perkins, M. E.: Meeting the needs of the mentally ill in the community through a community mental health services act. Missouri Med. 60: 1013-1018, 1026, 1963.

269. Perkins, M. E.: The concept of community psychiatry. J. Hillside Hosp. 14: 211-226, 1965.

270. Perkins, M. E.: Viewpoint on Mental Health. Transcripts, 1963-1965. New York: New York City Community Mental Health Board, 1967. R. Ziskind (Ed.)

271. Person, P. H., Hurley, P. L., and Giesler, R. H.: Psychiatric patients in general hospitals. Hospitals 40: 64-68, January 16, 1966.

272. Pilkington, F.: The Plymouth mental health service. In Gruenberg, E. M. (Ed.) Evaluating the Effectiveness of Mental Health Services. Milbank Mem. Fund Quart. 44: 37-54, Part 2. Jan. 1966.

273. Piore, N. K.: Metropolitan medical

economics. Sci. Amer. 212: 3-11, January 1965.

274. Planning and Construction Issue: Mental Health Facilities. Hospitals 38: 1-54, February 1, 1964. (Reprinted)

275. Planning, Programming, and Design for The Community Mental Health Center. New York: Mental Health Materials Center, 1966.

276. Planning the psychiatric services. The Hospital 59: 123-125, 1963.

277. Poverty and Health in the United States: A bibliography with abstracts. New York: Medical and Health Research Association, 1967.

278. Prairie View Hospital: In Glasscote, R. M., Sanders, D. S., Forstenzer, H. M., and Foley, A. R. The Community Mental Health Center: An Analysis of Existing Models. Washington, D. C.: American Psychiatric Association 121-132, 1964.

279. Program Area Committee on Mental Health of The American Public Health Association: A Guide to Control Methods. New York, 1961.

280. Psychiatric Receiving Center. In Glasscote, R., Sanders, D., Forstenzer, H. M., and Foley, A. R. The Community Mental Health Center: An Analysis of Existing Models. Washington, D. C.: American Psychiatric Association 83-103, 1964.

281. Psychiatrie de secteur dans la "communauté" du XIIIe a Paris Numéro spécial dirigé par P. Béquart. Information Psychiatrique, No. 7, 535-645, Juillet 1965.

282. Pumpian-Mindlin, E.: Types of outpatient services. In The Psychiatric Unit in a General Hospital. Kaufman, M. R. (Ed.) New York: International Universities Press 123-135, 1965.

283. Querido, A.: Gezondheidszorg en Gemeentelijke Overheid. Alphen aan den Rijn: N. Samson 1956.

284. ———: Voordrachten over Sociale Geneeskunde. Leiden: H. E. Stenfert Kroese, 1958.

285. Querido, A.: The role of emotional factors in readmissions to general hospitals. In Linn, L. (Ed.) Frontiers in General Hospital Psychiatry. Chapt. 22, New York: International Universities Press, 1961.

286. ———: The Efficiency of Medical Care. Leiden: H. E. Stenfert Kroese, 1963.

287. Querido, A.: Transcript of an interview by M. E. Perkins. In Ziskind, R. (Ed.) Viewpoint on Mental Health. New York: New York City Community Mental Health Board 280-287, 1967.

288. Rademaekers, H.: Geel et le placement familial. Allocution presidentielle du Dr. Rademaekers a la Societe Belge de Medecine Mentale, Seance du 31 Janvier 1953. Kolonie, Administratieve Drukkerij Merksplas, 1957.

289. Rakusin, M., and Fierman, L. B.: Five assumptions for treating chronic psychotics. Ment. Hosp. 14: 140-148, 1963.

290. Rapport de Monsieur le Docteur Bailly Salin, Medecin-Chef Adjoint du service d'hygiene mentale, sur l'etablissement d'un programme d'organisation et d'equipement du departement de la Seine en matiére de lutte contre les maladies mentales en application des directives de la circulaire ministerielle du 15 mars 1960. Paris: Prefecture de la Seine, Direction de l'Hygiene Sociale, 1965. (Mimeographed.)

291. Redlich, F. C., Klerman, G. L., McDonald, R., and O'Connor, J. F.: The Connecticut Mental Health Center. A joint venture of state and university in community psychiatry. Conn. Med. 30: 656-662, 1966.

292. Redlich, F. C., and Pepper, M. P.: Social psychiatry. Am. J. Psychiat. 116: 611-616, 1960.

293. Rehin, G. F., and Martin, F. F.: Psychiatric Services in 1975. London: PEP, 1963 Broadsheet No. 468.

294. République Francaise: Prefecture de la Séine. Direction de l'hygiéne mentale. Le service d'hygiene mentale et la coordination fonctionnelle en secteurs dans de département de la Seine. Introduction par J. Riviére. 2517. Paris: Imprimerie municipale, Hotel de Ville, 1961. (bibliography of 133 items.)

295. République Francaise. Prefecture de la Seine. Les maladies mentales dans le departement. Lés besoins et les moyens.

par M. Jean Benedetti. 4290. Paris: Imprimerie municipale, Hotel de Ville, 1962.

296. Richman, A., and Tyhurst, J. S.: Psychiatric care in a general hospital. Canad. Hosp. 42: 45-48, 1965.

297. Ridenour, N.: Mental Health in the United States: A Fifty-year History. Cambridge, Mass., Harvard University Press, 1961.

298. Rijkskolonie te Geel. Voor de vrije gezinsuerpleging van geesteszieken en zenuwlijders. Oorsprong en geschiedenis. Bruxelles, Maison Ern. Thill (n.d.).

299. Robbins, L. L.: Reflections 1940-1946. Bull. Menninger Clin. 30: 190-202, 1966.

300. Roberts, L. M., Halleck, S. L., and Loeb, M. B.: Community Psychiatry. Madison: University of Wisconsin Press, 1966.

301. Robinson, K.: The public and mental health in Freeman H., and Farndale, J. (Eds.) Trends in the Mental Health Services. Chapt. 2. Oxford, London, New York, Paris: Pergamon Press, 1963.

302. Rogler, L. H., and Hollingshead, A. B.: Trapped: Families and Schizophrenia. New York, London, Sydney, John Wiley and Sons, 1965.

303. Rosen, B. M., Wiener, J., Hench, C. L., Willner, S. G., and Bahn, A. K.: A nationwide survey of outpatient psychiatric clinic functions intake policies and practices. Am. J. Psychiat. 122: 908-915, 1966.

304. Rosen, G.: Social stress and mental disease from the eighteenth century to the present: Some origins of social psychiatry. Milbank Mem. Fund Quart. 37: 5-32, 1959.

305. Rosen, G.: Patterns of discovery and control in mental illness. Am. J. Public Health 50: 855-866, 1960.

306. Rothwell, N. D., and Doniger, J. M.: The Psychiatric Halfway House: A Case Study. Springfield, Illinois, Charles C. Thomas, 1966.

307. The Royal Medico-Psychological Association: memorandum on amalgamation of psychiatric with general hospital groups. Brit. J. Psychiat. 113: 235-237, 1967.

308. Sano, F.: Assistance familiale des enfants anormaux mentaux á la Colonie de Geel. Conférence donnée le 18 mai 1937 sous les auspices de la Ligue Nationale Belge d'Hygiéne Mentale. Extrait du "Service Social" nqs 7-8, juillet-août 1937.

309. Santé Mentale et Lutte contre L'Alcoolisme, L' expérience de santé mentale du 13e arrondissement. Paris: (1964).

310. Sargant, W.: Drugs or psychotherapy. Am. J. Psychiat. 121, June 1965 Suppl. xxvi-xxix.

311. Sargant, W.: Psychiatric treatment in general teaching hospitals: a plea for mechanistic approach. Brit. Med. J. 2: 257-262, 1966.

312. Saslow, G., and Matarazzo, J.: A psychiatric service in a general hospital: a setting for social learning. Int. J. Soc. Psychiat. 8: 5-18, 1962.

313. Schultz, J. D.: The treatment of psychiatric patients in a general hospital and the new psychopharmaceutical agents. J. Am. Coll. Neuropsychiat. 1: 36-44, 1962.

314. Schultz, J. H.: Le Training autogéne. Troisiéme édition revue et augmentée. Paris: Presses Universitaires de France, 1965. (Bibliothéque de psychiatrie.) English edition—Autogenic training, a psycho-physiological approach in psychotherapy. New York and London: Grune & Stratton, 1959.

315. Schwartz, M. D., and Errera, P.: Psychiatric care in a general hospital emergency room. Arch. Gen. Psychiat. 9: 113-121, 1963.

316. Schwartz, M. S., and Schwartz, C. G.: Social approaches to mental patient care. New York and London: Columbia University Press, 1964.

317. Scientific American: Cities. September, 1965.

318. Searles, H. F.: Collected Papers on Schizophrenia and Related Subjects. New York: International Universities Press, 1965.

319. Shannon, J., Jr.: The psychiatric service in a general hospital. J. Louisiana Med. Soc. 117: 261-264, 1965.

320. Shepherd, M., Davies, B., and Cul-

pan, R. H.: Psychiatric illness in the general hospital: Acta Psychiat. Scand. 35: 518-525, 1960.

321. Sheps, C. G.: Hospitals, health services, and patients. In Medical Education and Practice: Relationships and Responsibilities in a Changing Society. Evanston, Ill.: Association of American Medical Colleges, 1965.

322. ———: Interface between health facilities planning and total city planning. In Areawide Planning: Report of the First National Conference on Areawide Health Facilities Planning. Chicago: American Medical Association, 1965.

323. ———: Conference summary and the road ahead. Bull. N.Y. Acad. Med. 2nd series. 41: 146-156, 1965.

324. Sheps, C. G., Clark, D. A. et al.: Medical Schools and Hospitals: Interdependence for Education and Service. Evanston, Ill.: Association of American Medical Colleges, 1965.

325. Silverman, M.: A comprehensive department of psychological medicine. The problem of in-patient case-load: a 12-months review. Brit. Med. J. 2: 698-701, Sept. 9, 1961.

326. Silverman, M.: A comprehensive department of psychological medicine. The problem of the day-patient case-load. Int. J. Soc. Psychiat. 11: 204-209, 1965.

327. ———: Community attitudes to psychiatric day care, Int. J. Soc. Psychiat. 13: 67-70, 1967.

328. Sivadon, P., and Baumé, S.: Le club de post-cure de l'Elan. Ann. medico-psychol. 110: 489-492, 1952.

329. Sivadon, P., Amiel, R., and Baumé, S.: Trois années de fonctionnement d'un centre de post-cure pour malades mentaux. Ann. medico-psychol. 118: 160-167, 1960.

330. Smith, C. M., and McKerracher, D. G.: The comprehensive psychiatric unit in the general hospital. Am. J. Psychiat. 121: 52-57, 1964.

331. Smith, C. M., McKerracher, D. G., and Demay, M.: A follow-up study of comparable mental and general hospital patients. Canad. Psychiat. Ass. J. 9: 155-163, 1964.

332. Smith, S.: Psychiatry in general hospitals. Manchester's integrated scheme. Lancet 1: 1158-1159, May 27, 1961.

333. Smith, S.: The role of the admission unit in mental hospital work. In Freeman, H. (Ed.) Psychiatric Hospital Care. Chapt. 5. London: Bailliere, Tindall & Cassell, 1965.

334. Smith, S., Gibb, G. M., and Martin, A. A.: Metamorphosis of a mental hospital. Lancet 2: 592-593, Sept. 10, 1960.

335. Snow, H. B.: The open door concept. (Symposium) Ment. Hosp. 9: 33-35, May 1958.

336. Snow, H. B.: The open door and the community. Am. Pract. 13: 403-409, June 1962.

337. Solomon, H. C.: The American Psychiatric Association in relation to American psychiatry. Am. J. Psychiat. 115: 1-9, 1958.

338. Sommer, R., and Witney, G.: The chain of chronicity. Amer. J. Psychiat. 118: 111-117, 1961.

339. Sonolet, N.: Un centre de santé mentale urbain. Proposition d'une expérience. Social Psychiat. 2: 137-143, 1967.

340. Special Report on Psychiatric Units in General Hospitals. Modern Hosp. 93: 79-93, 1959.

341. Stafford-Clark, D.: The integration of services: a summary of the York Clinic experience. In Linn, L. (Ed.) Frontiers in General Hospital Psychiatry. Chapt. 1, New York: International Universities Press, 1961.

342. State of New York: Chapter 10 of the Laws of 1954, as amended by Chapters 145 and 805 of the Laws of 1954 (Mental Hygiene Law, subdivisions 10 and 11 of section 7; and article 8-A).

343. Stewart, R. A. Y., Faulkner, G. E., and Henderson, J. H.: Role of the mental hospital. In Baldwin, J. A., and Millar, W. M. (Eds.). Community Psychiatry. Int. Psychiat. Clin. 1: 617-634. No. 3, Boston: Little, Brown & Co. 1964.

344. Straetz, R., and Padilla, E.: Problem oriented political science in mental health. Comm. Ment. Health J. 2: 109-113, 1966.

345. ———: Social phenomena and the

physician. J. Med. Soc. New Jersey 63: 519-521, 1966.

346. Strömgren, E.: Mental health service planning in Denmark. In Linn, L. (Ed.) Frontiers of General Hospital Psychiatry. Chapt. 32, New York: International Universities Press, 1961.

347. Tannenbaum, G., Pinsker, H., and Sager, C. J.: The "shoestring" day hospital. Am. J. Orthopsychiat. 35: 729-732, 1965.

348. Tompkins, H. J.: The Jacob L. Reiss Mental Health Pavilion. In Psychiatric Architecture. Washington, D. C.: American Psychiatric Association 49-50, 1959.

349. ———: Experiences in a psychiatric unit in a large general hospital. Ment. Hosp. 12: 47-49, 1961.

350. ———: Psychiatric treatment in general hospitals and private practice. Am. J. Psychiat. 122: 1011-1014, 1966.

351. ———: Short-term therapy of the neuroses. In Usdin, G. L. (Ed.) Psychoneurosis & Schizophrenia. Chapt. 5. Philadelphia and Montreal: J. B. Lippincott, 1966.

352. ———: Transcript of an interview by M. E. Perkins. In Ziskind, R. (Ed.) Viewpoint on Mental Health. New York: New York City Community Mental Health Board 3-8, 1967.

353. Trussell, R. E.: The municipal hospital system in transition. Bull. N.Y. Acad. Med. 38: 221-236, 1962.

354. Ullman, L. P.: Institution and Outcome: A Comparative Study of Psychiatric Hospitals. Oxford, Pergamon Press 1967.

355. Ullman, M.: On the transition from private practice to general hospital psychiatry. Arch. Gen. Psychiat. 14: 261-269, 1966.

356. Ullman, M.: Transcript of an interview by M. E. Perkins. In Ziskind, R. (Ed.) Viewpoint on Mental Health. New York: New York City Community Mental Health Board 47-52, 1967.

357. Ullman, M., Gelb, L. A., Weber, W. F., and Tarail, M.: Theoretical and practical issues in a community psychiatric program. Science and Psychoanalysis 8: 198-207, New York and London: Grune and Stratton, 1965.

358. United States: Department of Health, Education and Welfare. Planning of Facilities for Mental Health Services. Report of the Surgeon General's Ad Hoc Committee. Public Health Service Publication No. 808. Washington, D. C.: Government Printing Office, 1961.

359. United States: Department of Health, Education and Welfare. National Institute of Mental Health. Improving Mental Health Insurance Coverage. Public Health Service Publication No. 1253. Washington, D. C.: Government Printing Office, 1963.

360. United States: Department of Health, Education and Welfare. Public Health Service. Community Mental Health Centers Act of 1963. Title 11, Public Law 88-164. Regulations. Federal Register 5951-5956, May 6, 1964.

361. ———: Department of Health, Education and Welfare. Public Health Service. Mental Retardation Facilities and Community Mental Health Centers Construction Act Amendments of 1965. Public Law 89-105. Regulations. Federal Register 3246-3248, March 1, 1966,

362. United States: Department of Health, Education and Welfare. Survey of General Hospitals Admitting Psychiatric Patients. Public Health Service No. 1462. Washington, D. C., Government Printing Office, 1966.

363. United States of America: Eighty-eighth Congress. Public Law 88-164. Mental Retardation Facilities and Community Mental Health Centers Construction Act of 1963. October 31, 1963.

364. ———: Eighty-ninth Congress. Public Law 89-105. Mental Retardation Facilities and Community Mental Health Centers Construction Act Amendments of 1965. August 4, 1965.

365. ———: Eighty-ninth Congress. Public Law 89-97. Social Security Amendments of 1965. July 30, 1965.

366. United States of America: Eighty-ninth Congress, Second Session. Metropolitan America: Challenge to Federalism. A Study . . . by the Advisory Committee

on Intergovernmental Relations. Washington, D. C.: Government Printing Office, 1966.

361. ———: Ninetieth Congress. Public Law 90-31. Mental Health Amendments of 1967.

368. United States Government: Ninetieth Congress. First Session. Planning-Programming-Budgeting. Office Documents. Washington, D. C.: Government Printing Office, 1967.

369. ———: Planning-Programming-Budgeting. Selected Comment. Washington, D. C.: Government Printing Office, 1967.

370. Usdin, G. L. (Ed.): Psychoneurosis & Schizophrenia. Philadelphia and Montreal: J. B. Lippincott, 1966.

371. Vyncke, J. C.: The psychiatric service of the general hospital "Prince Regent Charles" at Usumbra (Ruanda-Urundi), Africa. In Linn, L. (Ed.) Frontiers of General Hospital Psychiatry. Chapt. 35, New York: International Universities Press, 1961.

372. Wayne, G. J., and Koegler, R. R. (Eds.): Emergency Psychiatry and Brief Therapy. Int. Psychiat. Clin. Vol. 3. No. 4, 1966.

373. West, L. J.: Types of inpatients. In The Psychiatric Unit in a General Hospital. Kaufman, M. R. (Ed.) New York: International Universities Press 113-122, 1965.

374. Williams, M., and Halperin, L.: Work therapy for psychiatric patients in a general hospital. Ment. Hosp. 15: 572-573, 1964.

375. Williams, R. H. (Ed.): The Prevention of Disability in Mental Disorders. Mental Health Monograph 1, Public Health Service Publication No. 924. Washington, D. C., U. S. Government Printing Office, 1962.

376. Williams, R. H., and Ozarin, L. D. (Eds.): Community Mental Health: An International Perspective. San Francisco: Jossey-Bass, 1968.

377. Wing, J. K.: Institutionalism in mental hospitals. Brit. J. Soc. Clin. Psychol. 1: 38-51, 1962.

378. Wing, J. K.: The family management of schizophrenia and the principles of community care. In Freeman, H. (Ed.) Psychiatric Hospital Care. Chapt. 20. London: Bailliere, Tindall & Cassell, 1965.

379. Wing, J. K., and Brown, G. W.: Social treatment of chronic schizophrenia: a comparative survey of 3 mental hospitals, J. Ment. Sci. 107: 847-861, 1961.

380. Wing, L., Wing, J. K., Hailey, A., Bahn, A. K., Smith, H. E., and Baldwin, J. A.: The use of psychiatric services in three urban areas: an international case register study. Social Psychiat. 2: 158-167, 1967.

381. Yolles, S. F.: Community mental health: issues and policies. Am. J. Psychiat. 122: 979-985, 1966.

382. Yorkton Psychiatric Centre, Yorkton, Saskatchewan: In Glasscote, R. M., Sanders, D. S., Forstenzer, A. M., and Foley, A. R. The Community Mental Health Center. An Analysis of Existing Models. Washington, D. C.: American Psychiatric Association, 67-81, 1964.

383. Zinberg, N. E. (Ed.): Psychiatry and Medical Practice in a General Hospital. New York: International Universities Press, 1964.

384. Zitrin, A: The psychiatric division —Bellevue Hospital Center. In Linn, L. (Ed.) Frontiers in General Hospital Psychiatry. Chapt. 34. New York: International Universities Press, 1961.

385. Zusman, J.: Some explanations of the changing appearance of psychotic patients. Antecedents of the social breakdown syndrome concept. Milbank Memorial Fund Quart. 44: 363-394. Part 2, Jan. 1966.

386. Zwerling, I.: Transcript of an interview by M. E. Perkins. In Ziskind, R. (Ed.) Viewpoint on Mental Health. New York: New York City Community Mental Health Board 29-34, 1967.

387. ———: Some implications of social psychiatry for psychiatric treatment and patient care. Institute of Pennsylvania Hospital Award Lecture. Strecker Monograph Series, No. 2, 1965.

17

Prognosis

H. KIND, M.D.

As "Privatdozent" (a position equivalent to Associate Professor in an American university), Dr. Hans Kind lectures and teaches clinical psychiatry at the University of Zurich. Dr. Kind studied medicine at the Universities of Geneva and Zurich, and received postgraduate training in pathology and internal medicine. He received his training in clinical psychiatry under Professors Manfred Bleuler and Ernst Kretschmer; in psychoanalytic psychotherapy at the Institut für ärztliche Psychotherapie at Zurich.

Psychoendocrinology and schizophrenia have thus far been the main topics of Dr. Kind's work. A member of the regular staff of Burghölzli Psychiatric University Hospital, Dr. Kind currently heads its outpatient department. He is Dr. Manfred Bleuler's "First Assistant."

Real progress with regard to the possibility of predicting the course of schizophrenic disorders has not been made during the past ten years, though many authors have devoted their attention to the problem. This fact, however, will not surprise anybody who has kept himself informed on research in this field during the past decades. Reliable prognoses are as a rule only to be arrived at when illnesses can be classed as disease entities with reliable diagnoses. If in addition the possibilities of pathogenetic and pathoplastic influences are known, the course of the disease will be ascertainable. All these requirements, however, either do not apply or apply only to a limited extent to those mental disturbances classed under the heading of schizophrenia. Research workers who nowadays regard schizophrenia as a disease entity are rare and diagnostic frontiers vary considerably from one country and school to another. In England and the United States, for example, the limits set by diagnosis are wider than those of the Scandinavian countries or of the school of von Kleist and Leonhard. Moreover there is still considerable uncertainty with regard to pathogenetic factors. Though since World War II the interconnections between onset and course of schizophrenic disorders and possible environmental influences have aroused increasing interest, results acknowledged as valid by a majority of investigators are still not forthcoming. For such reasons little progress has been made where our knowledge of the predictability of schizophrenic disorders is concerned, and it cannot be otherwise so long as the problems associated with the nature of these mental disturbances remain far in excess of our factual knowledge.

In the chapter devoted to the prognosis of schizophrenia in the last edition of this book, Huston and Pepernik[10] published a list drawn up by L. Small contrasting prognostically favorable and unfavorable factors. This list, at least where clinical and social factors are concerned, still holds good. The prognostic value of test results, especially those based on physiologic data, leaves room for controversy and these problems will require our closer attention. However, even though there have been no basic changes of viewpoint, numerous studies on the problem of prognosis have been published during the past ten years. There is furthermore a much larger number of publications which mention other aspects of research in the field of schizophrenia and touch on individual prognostic criteria which crop up in connection with the specific material under investigation or the special angle from which the problems are being studied. However the space at our disposal requires that we concentrate in the main on those authors who have more or less dealt explicitly with the prognosis of schizophrenic disorders.

There are two basic approaches which for the most part have been treated in isolation. The first concerns itself with the prognosis of schizophrenic disorders in general, i.e., with the numerical possibility in cases of first onset of recovery or unfavorable course, large-scale statistics being employed. The second approach seeks to establish criteria which would make it possible to predict with relative certainty whether a favorable or unfavorable course is to be expected in the individual case. Such criteria may be sought in the sphere of psychopathologic symptoms, in the peculiarities of the previous course, in physiologic accompaniments, in the characteristics of the somatic constitution or of the premorbid personality as well as in sociologic data. In line with these varying approaches we have arranged our survey of the literature under the following headings:

1. Statistics concerned with the general prognosis of schizophrenic disorders, these as a rule comparing larger groups of patients with others. It is frequent in such studies that special attention is given to the general influence of the methods of treatment on the prognosis.

2. Studies which deal with the prognostic criteria as applied to a single patient or group of patients. Those investigations, however, which attempt to set diagnostic limits to malignant, "genuine" cases and those benign psychoses "similar to schizophrenia" will be summarized in a special section. This chapter will furthermore be split up under the following headings:

   Prognosis on the basis of psychopathologic and clinical symptoms.
   Prognosis aided by social and psychodynamic factors.
   Prognosis employing physiologic methods of investigation and somatic factors.
   Prognosis of special clinical types.

STATISTICS AS TO THE HISTORIC VARIABILITY OF THE PROGNOSIS OF SCHIZOPHRENIC DISORDERS

The application of new and more effective methods of treatment in the past decade has stimulated fresh interest in acquiring more precise knowledge of the course of schizophrenic disorders. In like manner the problems of prognosis were taken in hand because general predictability is only possible when facts are available as to the numerical proportion of cases with favorable or unfavorable outcome within a circumscribed pathologic group. Numerous investigators have taken the trouble to compare groups of patients admitted to psychiatric hospitals before the modern therapeutic era with groups of recent years. Achté[2] in Finland conducted a most careful follow-up study in 1959-60, selecting two random groups, each with a hundred patients, the first having been admitted between 1933-35 and the second between 1953-55. Within the period covered, 36 per cent of the patients of the 1933-35 group had not been discharged, i.e., they had become chronic cases permanently institutionalized. Of the 1953-55 group only 5 per cent had become permanent inmates. Of the patients admitted between 1933-35, 70 per cent belonged diagnostically to the group Langfeldt describes as nuclear, but only 54 per cent of the 1953-55 group fit into this category. There had been an increase in the paranoid types and a decrease in the catatonic. These shifts lead the author to the conclusion that between 1953-55 fewer serious cases were admitted, the course being, on the whole, more favorable. Pharmacotherapy made no contribution whatsoever to this improvement in prognosis as it was at that time in its initial stages. Similar findings were reported by a group of French investigators, Ey and collaborators.[26] They compared the course of an acute psychotic group of 1929-30 with a similar group of 1947-49, the follow-up covering in each case ten years. The risk of developing a chronic psychosis falls from 35 to 20 per cent and the difficult courses of the 1947-49 group are often more undulatory than was formerly the case. In France therefore, as elsewhere, the general prognosis of a schizophrenic disorder has improved during the therapeutic period under review. The authors, however, are of the opinion that this development is not to be traced to any one therapeutic approach but reflects the entire therapeutic activity of the psychiatric hospital.

A similar improvement in the general prognosis is reported by Schipkowensky in Bulgaria.[91] He compares a 1925-34 group with one of 1945-54. The percentage of complete remissions increases in the second ten-year period from 8 to 32 per cent as compared with the first and the proportion of schizophrenics remaining impervious to treatment dropped from 46 to 21 per cent.

Freyhan's well-known investigations[30] belong to this type of research, his work following course variations of patients at the Delaware State Hospital. The discharge rate between 1900 and 1950 increases from 38.8 to 84 per cent and the percentage taking a favorable course is progressive throughout the period. Kroiss[55] reports similar results in Germany and comes to the conclusion that the prognosis of chronic schizophrenics hospitalized for a period exceeding three years has considerably improved on the basis of 1925-28 and 1955-58 groups. Mental deterioration after a simple acute course made up 44 per cent of the 1925-28 group, but only 18 per cent of the 1955-58 group. Formerly simple chronic courses implied a very unfavorable prognosis, but nowadays the prospects even for this type have improved.

Leiberman, Hoenig, and Auerbach[39,58] in England have compared groups that were hospitalized before and during the new therapeutic era. In the 1934-35 group there were fewer atypical and more catatonic cases than in that of 1948-49 and the proportion of cures or improved cases after three years of hospitalization was lower. In 1948-49 even patients without therapy carry a better prognosis than in 1934-35, a fact suggesting other factors are at work apart from modern therapeutic methods. Freudenberg and collaborators[29] after comparing groups of patients covering 1935-37 and 1945-48 likewise announce a progressive increase in the number of patients moderately ill. However it is only the prognoses of the moderately ill that have improved; those of the severe cases remain unchanged.

The conclusion to which all these comparative studies lead is that the general prognosis of schizophrenic disorders has improved during the last three or four decades. Whether this is to be traced to modern therapeutic methods, to changes in the therapeutic atmosphere of psychiatric hospitals or to changes in the general course of the disorders that are independent of either still remains uncertain. It is not so easy to find a satisfactory answer to this question and it is still less easy to decide which general psychopathologic and sociologic factors in the population have contributed to reducing the frequency of the more serious types of schizophrenic illness. In this connection Müllers[73] comparative course study is of interest. In 1950 he compared one hundred first admissions in Berne in 1917-18 with the same number in 1933 and found there was no marked difference between the two groups with regard to their course. The total figures for the two groups were 66 with favorable outcome, of which 33 cures, over against 82 with unfavorable outcome. The remaining cases had initially appeared more favorable and then took a turn for the worse. Where these figures are concerned, we are certainly justified in speaking of spontaneous prognosis as at that time it was not possible to talk of therapeutic method in this field.

A further series of publications presents us with comparative studies based on various periods of the modern therapeutic era, the patients having been treated before and after the introduction of pharmacotherapy.[3,20,25,61,80,111,115,116] Without going into detail, it can be said that pharmacotherapy has definitely increased the chances of discharge of persons hospitalized because of schizophrenic disorders. Furthermore the duration of hospitalization has been shortened although, on the other hand, the possibility of readmission is greater. This more favorable prognosis of the course of the illness is doubtless to be ascribed to numerous factors which cannot easily be dealt with in isolation.

INVESTIGATIONS AS TO PROGNOSTIC CRITERIA APPLIED TO INDIVIDUALS OR GROUPS

Differentiation between benign and malignant courses

Since Eugen Bleuler widened the scope of Kraepelin's concept of dementia praecox by substituting for it the group of schizophrenias, the discussion as to the existence of differentiable subgroups with their own unique prognostic evaluation has remained open. Numerous studies have attempted to isolate a nuclear group of so-called genuine schizophrenias with unfavorable course from those types with a favorable course and schizophrenic characteristics. The differentiation between these two groups assumes crucial significance in terms of prognostic evaluation, and the criteria which permit the assignment of the individual case to one or the other group point direct to the long-term prognosis. The studies concerned with this differentiation are therefore to be mentioned in connection with the prognosis. It is particularly in Scandinavian psychiatry that the distinction between the malignant-genuine and benign types has been adopted more or less throughout. A further series of studies has appeared during the past ten years which, on the basis of long-term follow-ups employing new material, have sought to establish the basic division into two large course groups.[23,24,27,28,45,112,121,124,126] It has been confirmed again and again that the atypical schizophrenias which present a motley array of symptoms and are more influenced by exogenous factors are more frequently periodic and even episodic in their course. The terminology employed, however, is far from being consistent throughout. Writing under the title "psychogenic psychoses" Faergeman[27] describes disorders which are definitely not to be classed as schizophrenias and follow a favorable course. However for this author, an unfavorable course leading to dementia or defect belongs by definition to his concept of schizophrenia; in other words criteria that establish a good prognosis would be just those that question the validity of the diagnosis. In the front line of those Scandinavian authors who have conducted extensive follow-up studies to establish the distinction between benign and malignant courses are Astrup and collaborators[5] and Eitinger.[23,24] Astrup has taken especial pains to spread these ideas in the English-speaking world. Both authors have taken their basic ideas from Langfeldt who even in the thirties advocated division into two large groups in his studies on prognosis. Where German is spoken it is mainly Leonhard[59] and his school who are in favor of a stricter definition of the concept of schizophrenia and insist that the favorable cycloid psychoses should be excluded from the group. He considers these cycloid psychoses under which, to use his terminology, he includes anxiety-ecstasy-psychoses, motility psychoses etc. as independent types that are to be separated from schizophrenia. All these disorders carry a good prognosis, a fact that amounts to saying that the so-called "genuine" schizophrenias carry per definitionem a bad prognosis. This makes evident that prognostic studies not based on clear-cut diagnostic criteria can do little to clarify the situation.

Prognostic investigations in the narrower sense based mainly on psychopathologic symptoms and criteria of the course

Such investigations require no introduction and were mentioned in previous editions of this book; there is in fact nothing new to be reported. Most recent studies in this field were carried out retrospectively, i.e., earlier case histories were chosen for follow-ups and investigation of the final stage. The results were then related to factors of the initial clinical picture from which prognostic criteria were then deduced. There are indeed very few prospective investigations which apply prognostic criteria hypothetically formulated to contemporary cases and then test the reliability of such criteria after a certain lapse of time. Of course such prospective investigations carry considerably more weight than prognostic criteria formulated on the basis of the follow-up. Vaillant[104,105] has produced such a study and was able to formulate seven prognostic criteria that are usually accepted as valid. He then applied the criteria to 103 successive admissions of schizophrenic patients during the first few days of hospitalization. Among the criteria are acute onset, precipitating factors, depression, nonschizoid premorbid adjustment, confusion, concern with death and heredity positive for affective psychoses. After one or two years these patients were again examined and the validity of the initial prognosis put to the test. The author stresses that course criteria are much more important than those of contemporary symptom-formation and, above all, that isolated individual factors are of less significance. It is the entire range of prognostic indications that is important if we are to differentiate between favorable and unfavorable courses. A further prospective investigation has been carried out by Marks and collaborators,[67] but is based on hospital discharges and not on admissions. The results of psychologic tests were employed as prognostic factors, supplemented by interview and behavior rating in the clinic before discharge. Furthermore use was made of demographic data. The conclusion reached was that the length of hospitalization, the type of legal status in the clinic and the possession or lack of competency provided, when controlled after one year, are better prognostic criteria than the test results.

The large-scale investigations of Astrup and collaborators[5,6,40,100,102,127] and those of Leonhard,[59,125] Eitinger and collaborators[23,24] must be counted among these retrospective studies, not forgetting Arnold[4] who has devoted special attention to the subject.

Arnold has studied 500 case histories and carried out reexamination after about 10 years. He classifies the symptoms in related groups and compares them with the type of course. The author maintains on the basis of his results that the symptomatologic cross section enables him to deduce the subsequent course and, in particular, the extent of defect in the final stage. Insulin is strongly indicated on the basis of this prognosis because if this cure is omitted where courses are purely of the nature of a process there is no possibility of making up for the oversight at a later date.

Various authors[100,105,123] have formulated prognostic criteria for favorable or unfavorable course using their own follow-up material or findings of other research workers. The criteria, however, are usually very similar and rarely go beyond what for long has been common knowledge. Individual symptoms are stressed on occasion because they are regarded as having special significance.[122] Vaillant[105] for example holds that concern with death among the symptoms indicates a good prognosis. In like manner Stephens and Astrup[100] list twenty clinical signs that promise a favorable and twenty-two an unfavorable prognosis. Among the latter are: introverted schizoid personality prior to psychosis, chronic schizophrenia in near relations, poor premorbid social, work and sexual adjustment, insidious onset, long duration of symptoms, absence of precipitating factors, inability of patients to give any sort of psychologic reason for the psychosis, lack of apparent relationship of psychotic symptoms to past psychologic conflict, intense affective blunting, delusions which appear primary, delusions of bizarre fantastic type and so on. Those which indicate a good prognosis are: absence of process traits, extraverted personality prior to psychosis, absence of any gradual personality change, good premorbid work, social and sexual adjustment etc. In a later study Astrup and collaborators[6] stress above all the prognostic value of disturbances of verbal functions. Close runners-up as isolated symptoms are emotional blunting and passivity.[5] It is stressed again and again that the time factor is of great importance. Acute onset and short duration of illness before first admission are indications of a good prognosis, while continuous duration of manifest symptoms is a bad sign.[5,62,128]

A great deal of work has been done to arrive at exact statistical correlations. Stephens, Astrup, and Mangrum[102,127] have calculated that acute onset, precipitating factors, being married at the time of admission, and good premorbid social adjustment and work history are highly significant in that they serve to differentiate between a group of remissions and the chronic cases. Other factors which largely correspond to those of Vaillant[104,105] have received less statistical support but they still carry weight, e.g., schizophrenic heredity. However, with regard to the significance of schizophrenic disorders in the family circle, common agreement has not been reached, some authors regarding this as negative[57,100,102] while others state that psychotics with a neutral background carry the worst prognosis.[82] There are some authors, however, who announce that their experience has not enabled them to reach a definite conclusion.[5,86]

Molish and collaborators[70] and Marks and collaborators[67] have attempted to establish a prognosis on the basis of test results, but the outcome in both cases is not very convincing. French authors[7,57,87] employing a survey of the literature as their sole basis have studied the problem of prognosis in great detail. They do not, however, mention any prognostic criteria that are not to be found in the publications under review, though their figures as to spontaneous prognosis[57] are perhaps worth mentioning: 30-40 per cent of the cases undergo spontaneous remission during the first year after onset, i.e., without intensive treatment of any kind. Especially where cyclic types are concerned, 15-20 per cent of the cases achieve cures that are practically effective even after a course of several years duration. The dividing line between new cases with a good prognosis and the chronic cases that are less favorable is about one year. Application of the various types of therapy improves this spontaneous prognosis considerably, especially in cases that tend towards a chronic course. It is hardly necessary to stress that when course and symptoms approximate to manic-depressive psychosis, the prognosis is even more favorable, a fact mentioned or taken for granted by many authors.

Finally there are some writers who concern themselves with the prediction of relapses in the case of the schizophrenic psychoses. Danziger[21] in particular comes to the conclusion, on the basis of statistical evidence, that a schizophrenic successfully treated and discharged after insulin stands 55 per cent chance of rehospitalization, whereas the chance is 45 per cent after electroshock treatment. These figures stem from the time before the pharmacotherapy era. A Japanese[1] has done similar work on undulatory courses and provides evidence that undulatory schizophrenics are subject to seasonal influences. The graphic method he has developed to show how the course is influenced by the seasons enables prognostic deductions to be made on the basis of the previous course pattern. Huber[41] points out that a long-term prognosis is only possible one to two years after cessation of a psychotic relapse as the "pure" defect can only be ascertained after withdrawal of the specific psychosis. He bases this view on his earlier, well-known studies of chronic schizophrenics, but the very idea of a pure defect, defined as a lowering of the level of psychic energy per se, is one about which there is much controversy. However for prognostic purposes it would be of the utmost value if this hypothesis could be confirmed. Russian authors[32,103] have examined the prognostic significance of transitory psychopathologic syndromes in the course of schizophrenic psychoses. It is stated, for example, that a hypomanic state is prognostically favorable after insulin, whereas a hebephrenic reaction is considered as rather unfavorable. Furthermore the incidence of oneiroid states in the course of a schizophrenic psychosis is regarded as a good omen. This observation conforms to the general prognostic rule that acute psychotic phases with confusion and intense affective participation indicate a benign course.

The prognostic significance of social and psychodynamic factors

During the past few decades much attention has been paid by all concerned to the dependence of schizophrenic courses on the conditions of the psychic milieu in which patients grow up and have their being.

This has furthermore given rise to investigations which have sought to determine the prognostic significance of environmental factors. Nameche and collaborators[74] have examined fifty test cases of patients who in childhood were in treatment at a child guidance center and later became schizophrenic. The patients were divided into two groups—chronic cases and those that had undergone remission—the attempt then being made to ascertain the correlates between assignment to one of the groups and psychodynamic factors in childhood. The conclusion reached was that psychotic or schizoid behavioral disturbances on the part of the person who was mainly responsible for exercising the maternal function—the person was not necessarily the child's physical mother—were correlated with a chronic schizophrenic psychosis in the test case. Likewise unfavorable was the impossibility of breaking out of the pathogenic family during puberty and adolescence. Further negative factors were: poor social adaptation and erotic-sexual relationships in youth; inability to tolerate psychotherapeutic treatment for a duration exceeding three months during childhood; the lack of the possibility of abreaction and expression of affective tensions in a social group. It is interesting to note that test cases with even criminal types of behavior carried a better prognosis. The authors also list further prognostic criteria similar to those formulated by Vaillant[104,105] and others. Simon and Wirt[95] also draw attention to the fact that the lack of consistent parental figures indicates an unfavorable outcome in the case of schizophrenics.

In this connection we can also mention the interesting investigations of Whitehorn and Betz.[114] These authors are of the opinion that the personality of the therapist is an important prognostic factor where schizophrenics are concerned. There are, however, others[101] who doubt this hypothesis and stress that the long-term prognosis is more influenced by the entire clinical setup than by the person of the therapist.

There is, however, more or less general agreement that the nature of the patient's relationships to the members of his family and the degree of socioeconomic pressure to which he is exposed exercise an important influence on the course of the psychosis. Married schizophrenics who are affectively supported by their families and were doing responsible work before the onset of the psychosis stand a much better chance of remission than those who lack this background, and the chances are even better when, even after prolonged hospitalization, they return to the family fold and take up their professional activity again.[5,13,18,53,67,71,72,79,93,109,117] This does not imply, of course, that environmental influences can be considered in isolation from the type of premorbid personality. It has long been an accepted fact that a well-integrated premorbid personality has a much better prognosis than one with behavioral disturbances, and this fact is stressed again and again in all modern studies on the theme of prognosis. The individual creates the environment that corresponds to his make-up, for which reason one could say that the patient's good affective relationships to his family, considered as prognostically favorable, are merely the consequence of his socially well-integrated personality which is quite independent of the psychosis. The obvious conclusion in this case is that the decisive prognostic factor is the premorbid personality. However, Cooper's investigations[18] tend to show that the patient's social status is of importance for the prognosis, quite apart from the individual premorbid personality. He finds that people on the lower rungs of the social ladder stand much less chance, both professionally and privately, of social rehabilitation after discharge. Patients from the upper social classes with high occupational prestige and good employment records carry a good prognosis. The contrary is true of lower-class patients who have not been very successful in an occupation lacking prestige; here the prognosis is bad, though it is true that rehospitalization in the case of members of the lower classes is not more frequent than in the case of the upper social classes. It must be said, however, that the total duration of hospitalization among the lower levels of society is considerably longer. Nowadays it can be taken as an established fact that a patient's chances of remission and social rehabilitation are in direct ratio to the stability and reliability of the environment from which he stems. Even the distance separating the psychiatric hospital from the patient's home is of importance as Freudenberg and collaborators[29] have shown. Brun[13] has demonstrated, however, that about 50 per cent of the patients in a group of severe cases of chronic schizophrenia, all of whom had proved refractory to every kind of treatment, would have been faced with extremely difficult and even tragic circumstances had they responded to therapy, a fact which in any case would have cast doubts on the advisability of social rehabilitation. Similar observations have been made elsewhere.[72] It has frequently been stressed that a higher level of intelligence is correlated both with a more favorable prognosis and facility in resuming social status.[53,102,109] Simmons and Freeman[94] have drawn attention to the fact that the course after discharge may be influenced by members of the family if, as is often the case, too much is expected of the patient. Burdock and collaborators[14] mention another important factor: the "goodness" of the family circle is an extremely variable quantity that does not easily lend itself to statistical correlations. Hasty prognostic assumptions are therefore to be avoided if exact data as to the patient's affective relationships with his family have not been gathered. In any case the general impressions of a welfare officer are not a sufficient basis for operations.

To round off this section, mention should now be made of those studies which report on observations of patients living in special circumstances or exposed to specific stress situations, the attempt then being made to assess the influence of such factors on the prognosis of the course. It has already been mentioned above that exogenous factors, which play an obvious role in pathogenesis, usually indicate a more favorable prognosis, this being an opinion that is generally held to be true. It is therefore not surprising to hear that schizophrenics who suffered onset during military service carried a better prognosis than similar cases among a group of civilians.[118] It seems rather more likely, however, that such findings are not of general validity as numerous factors could influence the selection. Nuns, however, in contrast to the soldiers, show a more unfavorable psychotic course than other sectors of the population,[31] though here too selective factors may have been at work from the start. Yarden and collaborators[120] have examined the influence of pregnancy and confinement on the course of schizophrenic psychoses. After comparing their material with that of a control group they reached the conclusion that pregnancy after psychotic onset is usually a negative factor prognostically in that hospitalization is prolonged and the course tends to be more difficult. Such variations, however, are not on very safe ground statistically.

The investigations of Niswander and collaborators deserve mention here.[75,76,77] They found that schizophrenics in psychiatric hospitals have a shorter life-span than patients who after one or more periods in hospital could be discharged. Early schizophrenic onset implies a corresponding reduction of the life-span. As a rule schizophrenics in psychiatric hospitals die from the same causes as the general run of the population, and the percentile distribution of the various causes shows little variation. As might be expected deaths among schizophrenics due to infectious diseases have considerably decreased, while deaths brought about by cardiovascular troubles have become more frequent during the past decades. Whereas among the general population cardiovascular troubles occur more in men than women, the opposite is true among schizophrenics, the probable reason being that hospitalized women are not so physically active. In this connection, the way work and occupational therapy are organized in the mental hospital can be seen to be of prognostic importance for life duration. The authors furthermore discovered on the basis of their material that the diagnosis of catatonia correlates a considerably reduced life-span as compared with other schizophrenic subgroups.

Prognosis on the basis of physiological methods of investigation and somatic factors

Houston and Pepernik, in the last edition of this book, gave detailed information on the so-called Funkenstein test. It is only necessary here to remind the reader of Funkenstein's main thesis, i.e., that vegetative reactions after injections of mecholyl or epinephrine, especially the effect on blood pressure, indicated whether the patient would respond to the various methods of treatment. It was hoped, in other words, that this method would enable the therapist to distinguish between favorable and unfavorable courses. The publication of the findings concerning this prognostic test caused quite a stir among specialists and prompted numerous research workers to investigate the validity of Funkenstein's results. Rose[84] has produced a critical survey of the literature up to 1961 and has come to the conclusion that the modified test with mecholyl alone is certainly more reliable than the entire original test with epinephrine and mecholyl. It appears that the blood pressure reaction to mecholyl has some bearing on the success of electroshock treatment. However no proof has so far been forthcoming that the test has general clinical and prognostic significance. This cautious assessment is justified owing to the large number of contradictory findings. The following publications speak more or less in favor of the test,[16,46,51,81,83,85,106,108] though there are frequent reservations and restrictions imposed. However the studies listed below reach the opposite conclusion and state that Funkenstein's hypothesis does not bear closer investigation, the prognostic indications, in particular those for electroshock treatment, being insufficiently reliable.[17,35,48,54,56,63,64,65,66,69,89,92,96,99] In recent years the discussion about this test has almost dwindled to nothing, a fact which leads us to deduce that the test is not suitable for general clinical application in the prognosis of probable courses of schizophrenic disorders.

Of late research has been done on the electroencephalogram in connection with prognostic investigations. Small and collaborators[97,98] have pointed out that acute schizophrenic psychoses which show EEG modifications in the sense of a temporal focus take a more favorable course than patients in a comparative group with normal EEG. Yamada's[119] earlier findings in this field were similar. Other authors[33,42] believe that prognostic conclusions can be reached on the basis of the type of reaction in the EEG to pentothal injection. However other substances besides pentothal were employed, for example amobarbital[49] and meratran.[9] Jones and collaborators[47] have furthermore shown that the auditory evoked response in EEG is correlated to the clinical course. They were able to predict an improvement of the psychotic condition in the case of schizophrenic patients whose contemporary behavior was disturbed by depressions, anxiety, or aggressiveness. The fact remains, however, that these electroencephalographic investigations have not had any marked effect on actual practice.

Other investigators have taken physiologic processes or morphologic peculiarities as their points of departure for prognostic studies. Van Der Kamp and collaborators[107] have worked out a pulse-frequency index after mecholyl injection and find it useful for the prognosis of insulin treatment. Jugoslavian writers[44] employ a series of vegetative-humoral functions such as blood sugar, changes in the white blood picture, blood potassium and blood pressure in order to discover which patients will undergo prognostically unfavorable or favorable courses. Norris[78] has recently demonstrated in a prospective investigation on a large number of patients that the existence of a capillary plexus on the fingernail fold of schizophrenics is significantly correlated with an unfavorable course. As even in the case of healthy people the frequency of plexus formations increases with the years, the influence of age among the persons examined was accordingly taken into account. However the causal relationship between the phenomenon of plexus formation in the capillary area with the course of the psychosis remains for the present inexplicable.

In research on possible somatic causes of schizophrenic psychoses the presence of toxic substances in the body fluids plays an important part. It has long been known that serum of schizophrenics has a considerably greater toxic effect on animals than that of healthy people. With regard to the nature of these toxic substances nothing is definitely known at present. Benedetti, Kind and collaborators can be referred to for literature on the subject.[11] In this connection Walinder's study should be mentioned.[110] He has carried out a follow-up investigation over a period of twenty to twenty-five years on schizophrenics whose serum had caused a toxic reaction on white mice. The conclusion reached was that the presence or lack of serum toxicity was of no prognostic significance for the course of the psychosis.

Investigations on the prognostic importance of constitutional and body-build factors are seldom met with nowadays. They usually confirm well-established facts, i.e., that pyknic and athletic types carry a better prognosis than the leptosome-asthenic physique. Pyknics with athletic traits are said to carry the best prognosis.[82] Women with late menarche tend to develop more unfavorable course types than women with early menarche.[113] Late menarche is prognostically unfavorable especially when the onset of schizophrenia was in adolescence. Finally De Wet's work[20] in connection with the prognostic significance of body constitution can be mentioned. He discovered that the same prognostic criteria apply both to the white and Negro population in Africa.

Investigations on the prognosis of special clinical types

It is to the schizophrenias of childhood and adolescence that the greatest amount of attention has been devoted. There is more or less general agreement that the earlier the psychotic onset the more unfavorable the prognosis. Correspondingly, the prospects that treatment will show positive results are poor.[18,37,43,60,68,88,90] The more the symptomatology approximates to catatonia, the quicker the course, though one author questions this conclusion.[88] Children and adolescents who already show signs of somatic developmental disturbances suffer an earlier onset and the course of the psychosis will be more complicated.[90] However no new knowledge can be reported where the prognosis of the schizophrenias in childhood and adolescence is concerned.

Individual authors have devoted attention to the prognosis of special types of schizophrenia. Hoch and collaborators[38] have carried out follow-up studies on pseudoneurotic schizophrenia. 20 per cent of the patients investigated developed overt schizophrenic symptoms in the course of time. There is no method, especially no psychotherapeutic method, that can be regarded as effective for all such patients. The greater the number of symptoms, the less patients react positively to therapy, and the outcome is proportionately negative. Following on this investigation of pseudoneurotic schizophrenia comes a Russian study[34] on the influence of obsessional symptoms on the course of schizophrenic psychoses. It was discovered that patients with a monosymptomatic obsession carry a more unfavorable prognosis than those with polymorphous symptoms. Other authors have drawn attention to the fact that the same prognostic criteria which apply to cases with an unequivocal diagnosis of schizophrenia also hold good for borderline cases.

Cornu[19] has carried out follow-up studies on the long-term course of cases of schizophrenia simplex, such cases having up to now received little attention. Contrary to what would generally be expected the prognosis of these patients was not quite so unfavorable as is usually assumed. After an average of twenty years, four out of 27 patients had undergone remission and were fully able to work, while five others were slightly changed in personality though without loss of ability to work. Klages[52] has written a detailed study of late schizophrenia. The majority of his cases carried a rather unfavorable prognosis after acute onset, whereby a cyclothyme premorbid personality improved the prognosis. Genuine schizophrenias in childbed are said to carry a bad prognosis almost without exception, in contrast to childbed psychoses that are not schizophrenic.[36,50]

SUMMARY AND CONCLUSIONS

In the preliminary remarks to this paper, attention was already drawn to the fact that, during the past ten years since the last edition of this book appeared, there has not been a really new contribution to our knowledge of the prognosis of schizophrenic psychoses. That will certainly only be possible when the etiology and pathogenesis of the schizophrenic psychoses have been clearly stated. Meanwhile the prognostic criteria discovered by individual investigators on the basis of their own clinical material remain valid. Even if, however, it is true that the diagnosis of schizophrenic disorders is everywhere subject to certain variations, there are nevertheless, in circles where scientific psychiatry is demanded, prognostic statements which are generally accepted and which, in actual fact, have remained unchanged during the past ten years. In line with such criteria the following factors are regarded as prognostically favorable: acute onset; symptomatology accompanied by intense affect; a well-integrated premorbid personality which has proved its worth at work and in the family; onset caused by outer circumstances. In recent years attention has been directed to the prognostic significance of environmental factors to which the patient is exposed. On the basis of research done up to the present it may be assumed that the course of a schizophrenic psychosis will have better prospects insofar as the family is prepared to accept the patient as a member of the community and society facilitates resumption of social status. Furthermore it appears that the socioeconomic status of a patient is not without importance for the prognosis; numerous findings indicate that an unfavorable course is more often correlated with a lower social level.

Though a good deal of hard work has been done in the somatic sector, there have not resulted findings of general significance for the prognosis of schizophrenic disorders. No straightforward tests have so far been discovered that would enable the course to be predicted. Hopes cherished during the past few decades in this connection have been completely shattered. That which characterizes research in the field of the schizophrenias has been confirmed again and again, i.e., findings valid for one patient need on no account be valid for the majority.

More interest has been shown in the attempts to establish a basic division between two types of courses of schizophrenic psychoses, i.e., between the malignant, unfavorable courses which produce chronic illness and a complicated final outcome and those courses which are benign, lead to remissions and follow a development which is wavelike or runs in phases, the final outcome being without serious complications. Some schools, however, refuse to group these benign psychoses, even nosologically, under the heading schizophrenia. Generally speaking discussion nowadays turns less around the nosologic problem and the special status of the various types of courses; the present focus of attention is rather on speedy recognition of the possible course on the basis of prognostic criteria. However all the factors at our disposal for such differentiation are at present only to be applied in terms of greater or lesser statistical probability; their validity for the individual case is restricted. Those engaged in research will very likely take this for granted. It must, however, be brought home to the psychiatrist in his daily practice; he must always, that is, keep in mind that therapeutic optimism and unflagging effort on behalf of the patient exercise no small influence on the long-term course of the disorder.

Translated by J. Hull, Zurich

BIBLIOGRAPHY

1. Abe, K.: Patterns of relapse in remitting psychotics. Psychiatr. Neurol. (Basel) 150: 120-140, 1965.

2. Achté, K. A.: Der Verlauf der Schizophrenien und der schizophreniformen Psychosen. Acta Psychiat. Scand. 36; Suppl. 55: 1-273, 1961.

3. Alexander, L., and Moore, M.: Mul-

tiple approaches to treatment in schizophrenia and discussion of indications. Am. J. Psychiat. 114: 577-582, 1958.

4. Arnold, O. H.: Schizophrener Prozess und schizophrene Symptomgesetze. Eine prognostisch-statistische Grundlagenstudie. Wien, W. Maudrich, 1955.

5. Astrup, C., Fossum, A., and Holmboe, R.: Prognosis in functional psychoses: Clinical, social and genetics aspects. Springfield, C. C. Thomas, 1962.

6. Astrup, C., Haseth, K., and Ofstad, P.: Prognostic models in functional psychoses based on studies of higher nervous activity. Activ. Nerv. Sup. (Praha) 8: 81-86, 1966.

7. Barrès, P., Ey, H.: et Laboucarié, J. L'évolution des schizophrénies. (les rémissions spontanées et thérapeutiques et les critères évolutifs d'après les données statistiques) Evolution Psychiat. 239-279, 1953.

8. Baschina, W. M.: Besonderheiten der Klinik in der Spätperiode der Schizophrenie. Nach dem Katamnestischen Material im Jugendalter Erkrankter. Psychiat. Neurol. Med. Psychol. 17: 131-135, 1965.

9. Belenkaya, N. Y.: Etudes électro-encéphaloscopiques des malades de schizophrénie de forme paranoide à l'application du mératran. (Russian text with french summary) Z. Nervropat. Psichiat. 60: 224-233, 1960.

10. Bellak, L.: Schizophrenia; a review of the syndrome. New York, Logos Press, 1958.

11. Benedetti, G., Kind, H. und Wenger, V.: Forschungen zur Schizophrenielehre 1961-1965 Uebersicht. Fortschr. Neurol. Psychiat. 35: 1-34 and 41-121, 1967.

12. Bojanovsky, J., and Soucek, Z.: Possibilities of determining the prognosis of incipient schizophrenia and borderline schizophrenic states. (Chechish text with english summary) Csl. Psychiatr. 54: 170-172, 1958.

13. Brun, O.: Schwere schizophrene Verläufe. Zürich, Med. Diss. 1956.

14. Burdock, E. I., Sutton, S., and Zubin, J.: Prognosis in schizophrenia. II. Int. Congr. Psychiat. Zürich 1957, Congr. Rep.

4: 26, Zürich, Orell Füssli, 1959.

15. Chabert, G.: Aspects cliniques de la schizophrénie après dix ans d'évolution. Thèse présentée à la Faculté de Médecine, Marseille, 1966.

16. Charatan, B.: Effect of various drugs in the Funkenstein test. Dis. Nerv. Syst. 19: 352-353, 1958.

17. Childers, R. T.: Funkenstein test in newly admitted female schizophrenics. Am. J. Psychiat. 119: 259-260, 1962.

18. Cooper, B.: Social class and prognosis in schizophrenia. Part I and II. Brit. J. Prev. Soc. Med. 15: 17-41, 1961.

19. Cornu, F.: Katamnestische Erhebungen über den Verlauf einfacher Schizophrenien. Psychiatr. Neurol. (Basel) 135: 129-175, 1958.

20. Cross, K. W., Harrington, J. A., and Mayer-Gross, W.: A survey of chronic patients in a mental hospital. J. Ment. Sci. 103: 146-171, 1957.

21. Danziger, L.: Probability of relapse in dementia praecox. Dis. Nerv. Syst. 13: 111-116, 1952.

22. De Wet, J. S. D. T.: Evaluation of a common method of convulsion therapy in Bantu schizophrenics. J. Ment. Sci. 103: 739-757, 1957.

23. Eitinger, L.: Prognosis and therapeutic results in schizophrenia and the schizophreniform states. II. Int. Congr. Psychiat. Zürich 1957, Congr. Rep. 2: 150-153, Zürich, Orell Füssli, 1959.

24. Eitinger, L., Laane, C. L., and Langfeldt, G.: The prognostic value of the clinical picture and the therapeutic value of physical treatment in schizophrenia and the schizophreniform states. Acta Psychiat. Neurol. Scand. 33: 33-53, 1958.

25. Epstein, L. J., Morgan, R. D., and Reynolds, L.: An approach to the effect of ataraxic drugs on hospital release rates. Am. J. Psychiat. 119: 36-47, 1962.

26. Ey, H., Igert, C. et Rappard, Ph.: Psychoses aigues et évolutions schizophréniques dans un service de 1930à 1956. Ann. Méd. Psychol. 115/11. 231-240, 1957.

27. Faergeman, P. M.: Psychogenic psychoses. London, Butterworth & Co. 1963.

28. Filippini, V.: La prognosi della

schizofrenia. Rass. Studi Psichiat. 51: 1-30, 1962.

29. Freudenberg, R. K., Bennet, D. H., and May, A. R.: The relative importance of physical and community methods in the treatment of schizophrenia. II. Int. Congr. Psychiat. Zürich 1957, 1: 157-158, Zürich, Orell Füssli, 1959.

30. Freyhan, F. A.: The impact of somatic therapies on course and clinical profile of the schizophrenias. J. Clin. Psychopath. 19: 195-201, 1958.

31. Gamna, G., e Villata, E.: Studio statistico-clinico d'un gruppo di religiose psicotiche. Neuropsichiatria (Genova) 15: 237-252, 1959.

32. Gindis, I. Z.: Transitional (pre-remission) states in schizophrenia. (Russian text with french summary) Z. Nevropat. Psichiat. 62: 1868-1873, 1962.

33. Goldman, D.: Electroencephalographic manifestations associated with psychotic illness: pentothal activation technique and pharmacologic interrelationships. Comprehens. Psychiat. 5: 80-92, 1964.

34. Golovane, L. I.: Sur l'importance pronostique des phénomènes obsessifs observés au cours de la schizophrénie. (Russian text with french summary) Z. Nevropat. Psichiat. 65: 1218-1224, 1965.

35. Hamilton, M.: Quantitative assessment of the mecholyl (Funkenstein) test. Acta Psychiat. Scand. 35: 156-162, 1960.

36. Hemphill, R. E.: Schizophrenia and Childbirth. II. Int. Congr. Psychiat. Zürich 1957. 3: 433-437, Zürich, Orell Füssli, 1959.

37. Hift, E., Hift, St., and Spiel, W.: Ergebnisse der Schockbehandlungen bei kindlichen Schizophrenien. Schweiz. Arch. Neurol. Psychiat. 86: 256-272, 1960.

38. Hoch, P. H., Cattell, J. P., Strahl, M. O., and Pennes, H. H.: The course and outcome of pseudoneurotic schizophrenia. Am. J. Psychiat. 119: 106-115, 1962.

39. Hoenig, J., Leiberman, D. M., and Auerbach, I.: The effect of insulin coma and ECT on the short-term prognosis of schizophrenia. J. Neurol. Neurosurg. Psychiat. 19: 130-136, 1956.

40. Holmboe, R., and Astrup, C.: A follow-up study of 255 patients with acute schizophrenia and schizophreniform psychoses. Acta Psychiat. Scand. 32: Suppl. 115, 9-61, 1957.

41. Huber, G. Schizophrene Verläufe. Dtsch. Med. Wschr. 89: 212-216, 1964.

42. Itil, M. T.: Elektroencephalographische Studien bei endogenen Psychosen und deren Behandlung mit psychotropen Medikamenten unter besonderer Berücksichtigung des Pentothal-Elektroence phalogramms. Ahmet Sait Matbaasi, Istanbul, 1964.

43. Jay, M.: Les traitements de la schizophrénie infantile. Rev. Neuropsychiat. Infant. 8: 134-138, 1960.

44. Jevtic, N. und Babic, B.: Prognostisches Syndrom elektro-schockbehandelter Schizophrener mit besonderer Rücksicht auf den gebundenen Zucker. (Croatian text with german summary) Neuropsihijatrija (Zagreb) 5: 259-268, 1957.

45. Johanson, E.: A study of schizophrenia in the male: A psychiatric and social study based on 138 cases with follow-up. Acta Psychiat. Scand. 33: Suppl. 125, 7-132, 1958.

46. Jones, Ch. H.: The Funkenstein test in selecting methods of psychiatric treatment. Dis. Nerv. Syst. 17: 37-43, 1956.

47. Jones, R. T., Blacker, K. H., Callaway, E., and Layne, R. S.: The auditory evoked response as a diagnostic and prognostic measure in schizophrenia. Am. J. Psychiat. 122: 33-41, 1965.

48. Judson, A. J., and Katahn, M.: The relationship of autonomic responsiveness to process-reactive schizophrenia and abstract thinking. Psychiat. Quart. 37: 19-24, 1963.

49. Jus, A., Gerard, K., Gogol, Z., and Piotrowski, A.: Investigations upon the sedation threshold in schizophrenia. (Polish text with english summary). Neurol. Neurochir. Psychiat. Pol. 11: 497-503, 1961.

50. v. Keyserlingk, H.: Zum Krank-

heitsbild der Wochenbettpsychosen. Arch. Psychiat. Nervenkr. 203: 632-647, 1962.

51. King, G. F.: Differential autonomic responsiveness in the process-reactive classification of schizophrenia. J. Abnorm. Soc. Psychol. 56: 160-164, 1958.

52. Klages, W.: Die Spätschizophrenie. Biographie und Klinik schizophrener Ersterkrankungen des mittleren Lebensalters. Stuttgart, F. Enke, 1961.

53. Klonoff, H., Hutton, G. H., Gundry, G. H., and Coulter, T. T.: A longitudinal study of schizophrenia. Am. J. Psychiat. 117: 348-353, 1960.

54. Kramer, M., and Goldman, D.: Combination electroshock and drugs for severe chronic psychotic patients. (Prognostic value of Funkenstein rest). Dis. Nerv. Syst. 19: 161-164, 1958.

55. Kroiss, K. O.: Probleme bei der Behandlung chronisch verlaufender Psychosen. Zbl. Ges. Neurol. 155: 247, 1960.

56. Laane, C. L.: Adrenalin- and mecholyl test performed in schizophrenia and schizophreniform states. Acta Psychiat. Scand. 31: 467-476, 1956.

57. Laboucarie, J. et Barres, P.: Le pronostic des schizophrénies. Toulouse Med. 55: 167-181, 1954.

58. Leiberman, D. M., Hoenig, J., and Auerbach, I.: The effect of insulin coma and E.C.T. on the three-year prognosis of schizophrenia. J. Neurol. Neurosurg. Psychiat. 20: 108-113, 1957.

59. Leonhard, K., und v. Trostorff Sieglinde: Prognostische Diagnose der endogenen Psychosen. Jena, G. Fischer, 1964.

60. Levy, S., and Southcombe R. H.: Variability of deterioration in schizophrenia. Dis. Nerv. Syst. 13: 76-80, 1952.

61. Linn, E. L.: Drug therapy, milieu change and release from a mental hospital. Arch. Neurol. Psychiat. (Chicago) 81: 785-794, 1959.

62. Linn, E. L.: The relation of chronicity in the functional psychoses to prognosis, J. Nerv. Ment. Dis. 135: 460-467, 1962.

63. Lotsof, E. J., and Yobst, J.: Electric shock therapy and the mecholyl-test. Psychosomatic Med. 19: 374-378, 1957.

64. Lunde, F., Mansfield, E., and Smith, J. A.: Mecholyl chloride as a prognostic test in psychiatric patients. J. Nerv. Ment. Dis. 127: 430-436, 1958.

65. Maas, J. W.: Reliability of the methacholine (mecholyl) test. Variation in results when performed upon the same patient by different examiners. Arch. Psychiat. Neurol. (Chicago) 79: 885-889, 1958.

66. Marks, J. B., Stauffacher, J. C., Diamond, L. S., and Ax, A. F.: Physiological reactions and psychiatric prognosis. J. Nerv. Ment. Dis. 130: 217-223, 1960.

67. Marks, J., Stauffacher, J. C., and Lyle, C.: Predicting outcome in schizophrenia. J. Abnorm. Soc. Psychol. 66: 117-127, 1963.

68. Masterson, J. F., Jr.: Prognosis in adolescent disorders. Schizophrenia. J. Nerv. Ment. Dis. 124: 219-232, 1956.

69. Meregalli, E. e Bianchi, G.: La validitá del test di Funkenstein in psichiatria. Sistema Nervoso. 13: 141-147, 1961.

70. Molish, H. B., Hanlon, T. E., and Kurland, A. A.: A prognostic indicator of treatment failure in schizophrenia. Arch. Neurol. Psychiat. (Chicago) 78: 177-193, 1957.

71. Monck, E. M.: Employment experiences of 127 discharged schizophrenic men in London. Brit. J. Prev. Soc. Med. 17: 101-110, 1963.

72. Morgan, N. C., and Johnson, N. A.: Failures in psychiatry: the chronic patient. Am. J. Psychiat. 113: 824-830, 1957.

73. Müller, V.: Katamnestische Erhebungen über den Spontanverlauf der Schizophrenie. Mschr. Psychiat. Neurol. 122: 257-276, 1951.

74. Nameche, G., Waring, M., and Ricks, D.: Early indicators of outcome in schizophrenia. J. Nerv. Ment. Dis. 139: 232-240, 1964.

75. Niswander, G. D., Haslerud, G. M., and Mitchell, G. D.: Changes in cause of death of schizophrenic patients. A cross-sectional and Longitudinal study over a

60-year period. Arch. Gen. Psychiat. (Chicago) 9: 229-234, 1963.

76. Niswander, G. D., Haslerud, G. M., and Mitchell, G. D.: Effect of catatonia on schizophrenic mortality. Arch. Gen. Psychiat. (Chicago) 9: 548-551, 1963.

77. Niswander, G. D., Haslerud, G. M., and Mitchell, G. D.: Differences in longevity of released and retained schizophrenic patients. Dis. Nerv. Syst. 24: 348-352, 1963.

78. Norris, A. S.: Prognosis and capillary morphology. J. Nerv. Ment. Dis. 142: 369-375, 1966.

79. Ødegard, O.: A statistical study of factors influencing discharge from psychiatric hospitals. J. Ment. Sci. 106: 1124-1133, 1960.

80. Pacheco E Silva, A. C.: The prognosis of schizophrenia. II. Int. Congr. Psychiat. Zürich 1957. 1: 267-268, Zürich, Orell Füssli, 1959.

81. Pandelidis, P. K., and Busiek, R. D.: The epinephrine-mecholyl test applied to a state hospital population. Am. J. Psychiat. 117: 154-155, 1960.

82. Polonio, P.: A structural analysis of schizophrenia. Psychiat. Neurol. (Basel) 133: 351-379, 1957.

83. Rathod, N., and Rees, L.: A controlled study of the prognostic significance of autonomic responses in the chlorpromazine treatment of disturbed psychotic patients. J. Ment. Sci. 104: 705-712, 1958.

84. Rose, J. T.: The Funkenstein test— a review of the literature. Acta Psychiat. Scand. 38: 124-153, 1962.

85. Rouleau, Y., and Coulombe, M.: Clinical applications of the Funkenstein test to psychiatric patients. Canad. Med. Ass. J. 77: 116-121, 1957.

86. Ruckdeschel, K. Th.: Zur Prognose schizophrener Erkrankungen. Weitere Ergebnisse unserer Langstreckenkatamnesen. Dtsch. Med. Wschr. 82: 2166-2168, 1957.

87. Sadoun, R.: Le pronostic de la schizophrénie. Encéphale (Paris). 46: Plans de question de psychiatrie, XV-XXI, 1957.

88. Sakaoka, U.: A study of the prognosis of schizophrenia, with emphasis on childhood vs. adult schizophrenia. Psychiat. Neurol. Jap. 66: 30-45, 1964.

89. Satterfield, J. H.: Prediction of improvement by use of epinephrine-methacholine (mecholyl) test. Study of immediate response in twenty-six treated patients and one-year follow-up of forty-eight treated patients. Arch. Neurol. Psychiat. (Chicago) 81: 513-516, 1959.

90. Saumench, D.: Infantile somatic development in schizophrenia. Inform. Psiquiat. 2: 55-66, 1957.

91. Schipkowensky, N.: Die Behandlung der Schizophrenie und der Zyklophrenie mit Heilkrampf, Insulinschock und Chlorpromazin. Wien. Med. Wschr. 110: 745-747, 1960.

92. Schneider, R. A., Costiloe, J. P., Yamamoto, J., and Lester, B. K.: Estimation of central sympathetic reactivity using the blood pressure response to metacholine (mecholyl). Psychiat. Res. Rep. Am. Psychiat. Ass. 12: 149-160, 1960.

93. Sherman, J., Moseley, C., Ging, R., and Bookbinder, L. J.: Prognosis in schizophrenia. A follow-up study of 588 patients. Arch. Gen. Psychiat. (Chicago) 10: 123-130, 1964.

94. Simmons, O. G., and Freeman, H. E.: Familial expectations and posthospital performance of mental patients. Hum. Relat. 12: 233-242, 1959.

95. Simon, W., and Wirt, R. D.: Prognostic factors in schizophrenia. Am. J. Psychiat. 117: 887-890, 1961.

96. Sloane, R. B., and Lewis, D. J.: Prognostic value of adrenaline and mecholyl responses in electroconvulsive therapy. J. Psychosomatic Res. 1: 273-286, 1956.

97. Small, J. G., Small, J. F., and Surphlis, W. R. P.: Temporal EEG-abnormalities in acute schizophrenia. Am. J. Psychiat. 121: 262-264, 1964.

98. Small, J. G., and Small, J. F.: Re-evaluation of clinical EEG findings in schizophrenia. Dis. Nerv. Syst. 26: 345-349, 1965.

99. Stemmermann, M. G., and Owen, T. V.: Serial autonomic testing in psychi-

atric disorders. J. Clin. Exper. Psychopath. 18: 236-247, 1957.

100. Stephens, J. H., and Astrup, C.: Prognosis in "Process" and "Non-Process" schizophrenia. Am. J. Psychiat. 119: 945-953, 1963.

101. Stephens, J. H., and Astrup, C.: Treatment outcome in "process" and "non-process" schizophrenics treated by "A" and "B" types of therapists. J. Nerv. Ment. Dis. 140: 449-456, 1965.

102. Stephens, J. H., Astrup, C., and Mangrum, J. C.: Prognostic factors in recovered and deteriorated schizophrenics. Am. J. Psychiat. 122: 1116-1121, 1966.

103. Stoyanov, S. T.: Clinical features and psychopathology of oneiroid states arising in the course of schizophrenia. (Russian text with french summary). Z. Nevropat. Psichiat. 61: 1370-1377, 1961.

104. Vaillant, G. E.: The prediction of recovery in schizophrenia. J. Nerv. Ment. Dis. 135: 534-543, 1962.

105. Vaillant, G. E.: Prospective prediction of schizophrenic remission. Arch. Gen. Psychiat. (Chicago) 11: 509-518, 1964.

106. Van der Kamp, H.: Prognostic determinants in schizophrenia. J. Neuropsychiat. (Chicago) 5: 118-122, 1963.

107. Van der Kamp, H., Norgan, A., Wilkinson, G., and Pearl, D.: Methacholine reaction indices as prognosticators for insulin coma therapy. J. Clin. Psychopath. 19: 303-308, 1958.

108. Van der Kamp, H., Berghorst, J., and De Jong, R. N.: Neurophysiologic variants in schizophrenia. Arch. Gen. Psychiat. (Chicago) 1: 250-252, 1959.

109. Walker, R. G., and Kelley, F. E.: Predicting the outcome of a schizophrenic episode. Arch. Gen. Psychiat. (Chicago) 2: 492-503, 1960.

110. Walinder, J.: Serum toxicity in schizophrenic psychoses. A follow-up after 20-25 years. Acta Psychiat. Scand. 40: 307-322, 1964.

111. Walter Mc., H. S., Mercer, R., Sutherland, M., and Watt, A.: Outcomes of treatment of schizophrenia in a north-east scottish mental hospital. Am. J. Psychiat. 118: 529-533, 1961.

112. Welner, J., and Strömgren, E.: Clinical and genetic studies on benign schizophreniform psychoses based on a follow-up. Acta Psychiat. Scand. 33: 377-399, 1958.

113. Wertheimer, N. M.: Schizophrenic sub-diagnosis and age at menarche. J. Ment. Sci. 108: 786-789, 1962.

114. Whitehorn, J. C., and Betz, B.: Further studies of the doctor as a crucial variable in the outcome of treatment with schizophrenic patients. Am. J. Psychiat. 117: 215-223, 1960.

115. Wing, J. K.: Five-year outcome in early schizophrenia. Proc. Roy. Soc. Med. 59: 17-18, 1966.

116. Wing, J. K., Denham, J., and Munro, A. B.: Duration of stay in hospital of patients suffering from schizophrenia. Brit. J. Prev. Med. 13: 145-148, 1959.

117. Wirt, R. D., and Simon, W.: Differential treatment and prognosis in schizophrenia. Springfield, C. C. Thomas, 1959.

118. Wyss, R.: Zur Katamnese exogen beeinflusster Schizophrenie fälle. Praxis. (Bern) 45: 736-738, 1956.

119. Yamada, T.: Heterogeneity of schizophrenia as demonstrable in electroencephalography. Bull. Osaka Med. School 6: 107-146, 1960.

120. Yarden, P. E., Max, D. M., and Eisenbach, Z.: The effect of childbirth on the prognosis of married schizophrenic women. Brit. J. Psychiat. 112: 491-499, 1966.

121. Zharikov, N. M.: The criteria of prognosis in schizophrenia. (Russian text). Vestn. Akad. Med. Nauk. SSSR. 1: 14-17, 1962.

122. Dawson, J. G. and Weingold, H. P.: Prognostic significance of delusions in schizophrenia. J. Clin. Psychol. 22: 275-277, 1966.

123. Garfield, S. L. and Sundland: Prognostic scales in schizophrenia. J. Consult. Psychol. 30: 18-24, 1966.

124. Jansson, B. and Alström, J.: The relation between prognosis and back-

ground factors in suspected schizophrenic insufficiencies in young people. Acta Psychiat. Scand. Suppl: 198, Munksgaard Copenhagen, 1967.

125. Leonhard, K.: Prognostische Diagnostik der endogenen Psychosen unter Bezugnahme auf die zykloiden Psychosen. Wien. Z. Nervenheilk. 24: 282-296, 1967.

126. Mitsuda, H.: Clinico-genetic study of schizophrenia. Bull. Osaka Med. School. Suppl. 12: 49-90, 1967.

127. Stephens, J. H., Astrup, Ch. and Mangrum, J. C.: Prognosis in schizophrenia. Prognostic scales crossvalidated in American and Norwegian patients. Arch. Gen. Psychiat. (Chicago) 16: 693-698, 1967.

128. Walker, R. and Kelley, F. E.: Sudden and gradual onsets in schizophrenia. Dis. Nerv. Syst. 27: 515-521, 1966.

18

Rehabilitation

BERTRAM J. BLACK, M.S.W., and CELIA BENNEY, M.S.S.

Mr. Black, formerly Executive Director, Altro Health and Rehabilitation Services, Inc. and President, Altro Work Shops, Inc., is now Professor of Psychiatry (Rehabilitation), Albert Einstein College of Medicine, New York, and Executive Consultant to Altro Health and Rehabilitation Services.

Educated at Washington University, St. Louis, Mo. (B.S.-1937, M.S.W.-1398), Mr. Black has worked extensively in all phases of psychiatric rehabilitation and case work. He has served on study groups of the NIMH, and, in this capacity, recently researched and subsequently authored a monograph entitled, Industrial Therapy for the Mentally Ill—Observations on Developments in Western Europe and Significance for Programs in the United States (*Altro Work Shops, Inc., August 1966). Mr. Black has also authored numerous articles reflecting the many aspects of this field.*

Mr. Black is Co-Chairman, Citizens' Subcommittee, Mayor's Committee on Mental Retardation, a Fellow of the American Orthopsychiatric Association, the American Public Health Association, The American Association for the Advancement of Science, a member of the National Association of Social Workers (ACSW), the Royal Society of Health, the New York Academy of Sciences, and many others.

Mrs. Celia Benney, M.S.S. is the Associate Executive Director, Altro Health and Rehabilitation Services, Inc., and Associate Project Director for a NIMH project, "Rehabilitation of the Mentally Ill Older Adolescent and Young Adult."

A graduate of Smith College (B.A. 1932 Magna Cum Laude, Phi Beta Kappa) and the Smith College for Social Work (M.S.S. 1933), Mrs. Benney has taught in the field of social work in its many aspects at Smith College, Columbia University and the Wm. A. White Institute of Psychiatry, Psychoanalysis and Psychology.

Mrs. Benney has authored considerable material on case work and rehabilitation. Her articles have been published in Social Casework, Mental Hygiene, Journal of Rehabilitation, and Rehabilitation Record.

The term rehabilitation has been variously used to describe a method or technic, a system of delivering treatment to patients, and a set of specialties incorporated within the health helping professions. In its application to schizophrenia, the writers prefer to consider rehabilitation as an all-out, concerted, dynamic process involving the use of a variety of professional and technical skills and a variety of community resources to help handicapped people achieve the maximum functioning of which they are capable.[7] More than a decade ago, Maxwell Jones[40] in a classic study for the World Health Organization, defined rehabilitation as:

"a particular aspect of the process of adjustment to or recovery from an

735

illness. Treatment may be said to be any interference which aims to bring about or hasten this process. The term rehabilitation has come to imply the sociologic aspects of the recovery period, although there is no reason why such aspects should be thus confined. Clearly there are degrees of recovery. The double amputee or the schizophrenic can hardly be said to make a complete recovery, although rehabilitation may with advantage be applied to both. Rehabilitation is at present conceived as something in addition to the more specific methods. It may be defined as the attempt to provide the best possible community role which will enable the patient to achieve the maximum range of activity, compatible with his personality and interest and of which he is capable. This definition can be applied with equal facility to the schizophrenic or the simple fracture case."

In this same report, Jones observed, "The fact is that rehabilitation is a convenient term which draws attention to a relatively neglected area in our present medical, educational, and social organization. The use of the term may conceivably become obsolete in time, just as one hopes that it will not always be necessary to stress the psychological component by using the term psychosomatic." Over the years more and more of what can be labeled "rehabilitation" as so defined has been incorporated in treatment regimens for the mentally ill. However, the term does not show signs, as yet, of vanishing from the nomenclature.

The special modalities that are still identifiable as rehabilitation are the resocialization and remotivation programs which have developed from the older concept of "moral treatment," milieu rehabilitation procedures, the aftercare and "halfway house" services, and the industrial therapies.

MORAL TREATMENT

Many of the essential elements in rehabilitation of the mentally ill have existed at various stages in the evolution of treatment programs. Early in the nineteenth century, Pinel, Benjamin Rush, and Dorothea Dix were associated with the development of what is referred to as moral treatment. Menninger in *The Vital Balance*[46] notes that, "The moral treatment of the mentally ill is used today in a more ambitious and extensive way than its first proponents could have imagined. In the good psychiatric hospitals today, there are assignments, there are exercises for the mind and for the body, there are programs of activities and programs of inactivity. Instead of moral treatment, it is today called milieu treatment or rehabilitation. This not necessarily represents an improvement in terms, but the idea in back of it is the same, namely, to guide or lead or instruct the patient into a way of life and then gradually withdraw the instruction and the supports and permit him to take up an independent existence, once more using his own assets and his techniques. Along with the normative factors in moral therapy go many intangible factors that are largely psychological—the give and take of daily life with others in difficulty, seeing other patients improve, the model of living set by doctors and nurses, the attention given to psychological matters by staff and patients alike." The early era is described by Hobbs[37] as the first revolution in the treatment of the mentally ill. He ascribes a second revolution to the Freudian era and a third to the concept of mental illness as a social problem for which the whole community shares responsibility. Rehabilitation comes to the fore in this "third revolution." Attesting to this development is the fact that in 1964, the World Health Organization scientific group on mental health research[27] gave "top rank to promotion of epidemiologic studies on distribution of mental disorders in different countries and on assessing the effectiveness of rehabilitation and preventive services." There has evolved a shifting emphasis from concern for the person as a patient in a hospital to a much broader concern for those social problems which affect mental health and those facilities and services in the community which are needed to help the posthospitalized or nonhospitalized live and function at highest capacity. We note the heightened emphasis on interpersonal relationships with the recognition that schizophrenia is a manifestation of deficits and impairments in ego structure. Though a person might be mentally ill, there is some portion of the ego which remains conflict-free and intact, and many societal attitudes are involved in interpretation of symptoms.

In our current era of rehabilitation, the delivery of services to the schizophrenic is the concern of many institutions (schools, general hospitals, mental hospitals, halfway houses, industrial rehabilitation agencies) and an equally wide variety of professional disciplines. If the goal of rehabilitation (as well as treatment) is social adjustment, it follows that the psychiatrist alone cannot do the job. Among the professionals who have taken increased responsibility are nurses, psychologists, social caseworkers, and the relatively new profession of rehabilitation counseling.

It must be noted that, though the United States had legislation sponsoring rehabilitation for the physically handicapped since World War I, it was only in 1943 under the terms of the Barden-La Follette Act that services were made available through the Office of Vocational Rehabilitation to people with mental illness. Both the 1954 and 1965 amendments to the Vocational Rehabilitation Act have extended those services.

RESOCIALIZATION AND REMOTIVATION

It has long been recognized that effective rehabilitation should begin as close to the onset of the illness as is possible. The next ten years, it is hoped, will see a heightened emphasis on the development of community services that will prevent, for many, the need for hospitalization, and, for others, reduce the length of hospitalization significantly. Nevertheless, at the present time, we are still coping with a large number of schizophrenics, many of whom have been hospitalized for long periods of time. During the past ten years, resocialization programs within hospitals have made available a variety of services designed to counteract the desocialization or residual effects of life within a mental hospital, as well as to prevent these sequelae for the newly admitted. "Milieu therapy"[26] and more recently "milieu rehabilitation" have been added to the treatment armamentarium.

In a significant book entitled *Social Approaches to Mental Patient Care,* Charlotte and Morris Schwartz prepared a report on "the major developments, problems, and issues regarding the care of mental patients" for the Joint Commission on Mental Health and Illness.[54] The authors group their observations into major systems for breaking down the barriers to effective treatment: 1) the open door, and 2) the psychiatric inpatient unit in a general hospital. They see these developments "not simply as new methods of treatment but as new forms of social organization." "The major locus of organizational changes in the transformation of a custodial institution into an open hospital is in the ward itself and the role relationships of ward patients and personnel." They stress attempts being made to reverse the process by which a patient becomes dependent and powerless. These include a program of self government, ward meetings, the diminutions of total medical control by the sharing of tasks with psychiatric aides, nurses, etc. Volunteer programs are prescribed as a method of bringing the community to the hospital and vice versa.

The trend of involving all hospital personnel more totally in treatment is discussed under the concept of "broadening the base of therapeutic relevance." The Schwartzes identify three orientations as "implicit in the idea of therapeutic milieu." The first orientation relates to the social structure of the institution as a whole; the second orientation refers to the specific forms of interaction or interpersonal relations that are engaged in, facilitated, or hindered; and the third refers to the specific effects upon patients which the personnel try to achieve. The net effect of all orientations is to increase patient participation, either in their own care and treatment or in the administration of the hospital, or in the therapy of other patients. In some settings the therapeutic milieu effort is considered primary and in others, ancillary. Hamburg[55] summarized the characteristics of a therapeutic milieu as follows: "An intense dedication to the understanding of their patients as people and of mental illness; a respect for other human beings that pervades their relationships with both patients and staff members; a vigorous optimism coupled with a fundamental belief in progress and the perfectability of individuals; and a determination almost amounting to relentlessness in the pursuit of their goals."

In *Chronic Schizophrenia,* Freeman, Cameron, and McGhie[33] describe a milieu approach to the resocialization of the chronic schizophrenic patient. This study took place in the Glasgow Royal Mental Hospital. The authors selected a group of patients who had suffered with diagnosed schizophrenia for more than two years. Their patients were between the ages of 20 and 40 and had been treated with insulin or electroshock therapy. Those who had been leucotomized or who were mentally defective were excluded. The diagnosis had to be approved by independent consultant psychiatrists not directly concerned with the project. A treatment center was set up within the hospital, which allowed 12 patients and two nurses to "develop a relationship of as prolonged a nature as was administratively possible." In general, it was the task of the nurses to encourage identification of the patients with the staff. This was accomplished by the involvement of the nurses in many of the usual activities of daily living such as washing dishes, sometimes just sitting beside a withdrawn patient. Other measures for enhancing identification included the nurses leaving parts of their uniforms around, such as their white aprons, which patients then picked up. Considerable attention was paid to individual clothing and to feeding. Tasks had to be meaningful. It was noted, for example, that patients quickly lost interest in knitting unless it had some goal value. They noticed, too, that rug-making was not successful at first, but when the rugs were actually used on the ward, it became meaningful. Patients were encouraged to make articles which could be used on the wards. As a result of the program, there was obviously increased communication with chronic schizophrenic patients and establishment of ego boundaries. Though the authors make no great claims for their method and see it as complementary to individual forms of therapy, they did feel that the approach permitted the dissolution of many of the characteristic behavior patterns associated with chronicity. Though no statistics are given, they do note that some of the severely regressed patients improved to the point of being able to leave the hospital.

More highly structured research programs designed to encourage resocialization are described in several project reports by Sanders and Weinman.[53] These were based on studies sponsored by the National Institute of Mental Health at Philadelphia State Hospital. In a project proposal to the National Institute of Mental Health, Sanders and Smith, Co-Directors[52] summarized the experience of the psychology department of the Philadelphia State Hospital beginning in 1957. They felt that the treatment approach used in their rehabilitation efforts were basically socio-environmental. The project established three treatment units. These were housed in an area of the hospital previously used for domicile of attendant personnel. The physical design made possible increased "freedom of movement, more privacy, and the assumption of greater responsibility on the part of the patients." The purpose of the three-treatment units was to determine how much pressure would have to be exerted to obtain a sustained increase in social behavior. This was controlled by varying the degree of structure in the treatment situation. The three units were called: 1) therapeutic community, 2) core interaction program, and 3) intensified interaction program. In the therapeutic community neither the living situation nor the therapeutic program was structured to elicit interaction. The treatment program consisted of an assigned job in the hospital industry system and individual conferences with the unit administrator, a psychologist. In the core interaction program, patients were required to attend a program of structured group activities, each patient receiving approximately ten hours of program group interaction per week. The group leaders were instructed to "stimulate interaction among the participants and to selectively reinforce socially adaptive behavior." No special changes were made in the social living situation. In the intensified interaction program, "both the living situation and the therapeutic program were structured to promote interaction." In addition to the programs utilized in the core interaction program, the social living situation "was structured to promote interaction through the introduction of patient government." The overall objective of the rehabilitation project was to encourage the emergence of appropriate social behavior among patients who were essentially isolated from each other and from society. It was felt that social recovery alone might enable many such patients to return to the community. In addition, it seemed reasonable to expect that learning to interact with others more effectively might ultimately reduce the need to withdraw from reality through psychotic mechanisms such as delusions and hallucinations. The result of this project revealed that over 50 per cent were returned to the extramural community. The fact that these patients had been hospitalized for more than eight years on the average, and in some cases for as long as twenty or thirty years, indicated that there was no inverse ratio between length of hospitalization and response to socio-environmental treatment approaches. The researchers noted that actually the longer the patient had been hospitalized, the better his chance of being released. Research in that setting is continuing to determine more specifically those variables which contribute to the effectiveness of socio-environmental therapy.

Fairweather,[31] a social psychologist at the Veterans Administration Hospital, Palo Alto, California, set out to reverse the passive dependent role of patients in mental hospitals through "test groups" of patients. These groups were conducted by the patients themselves, and through a system of rewards and punishments, patients were made responsible for in-hospital privileges, leaves of absence, and even discharge planning. Though the staff did not totally abdicate its responsibility, considerable responsibility was delegated to patients. It was possible to contrast this ward with one which was run in the traditional manner. The effectiveness of the program in terms of socialization and rapid discharge was unquestioned. However, the success was not sustained after discharge, and it became obvious that elements of structure and service were needed in the community if the progress of the patients was to be sustained.

Sivadon,[56] working in France, has made available to his patients a variety of social environments, permitting them to move between large and small groups, homogeneous and heterogeneous groups, and offering them a range of activities from play to work. His institution is designed architecturally to permit patients to live in smaller or larger quarters with greater or fewer numbers of people, depending upon their needs.

MILIEU REHABILITATION IN THE HOSPITAL

Most hospitals in the United States now incorporate some element of milieu rehabilitation techniques. Milieu rehabilitation is a relatively new term coined by a group at the Butler Health Center.

In an excellent article entitled "Milieu Rehabilitation and the Role of the Counselor," Myers[47] notes nine characteristics of milieu rehabilitation: 1) It attempts to establish a more normal, meaningful, and accepting environment than that which the individual has been accustomed to. It is able to utilize a variety of work or educational situations for the core of the program. 2) Social and recreational activities are easily added. The goal is not so much productivity or educational achievement as it is the rehabilitation of individuals in a comprehensive sense. 3) It seeks to achieve both psychosocial growth and the acquisition of competitive skills needed to get along in society. Group dynamics provide an important source of motivation, support, and emotional growth. 4) Skills and growth factors potentiate each other in a reciprocating interaction. Meaningful relationships with members of the group, staff, and trainees foster the development of skills such as self care, communication, and the social amenities. 5) Many forms of cognitive training may be used to supplement experiences and interpersonal relationships. Professional and subprofessional workers, maintenance workers, and volunteers may all function as teacher-therapists in addition to their other responsibilities. 6) Earned income through sheltered employment may be used for motivation, to meet the financial needs of the trainee, to teach him to handle and budget money, and to provide a financial cushion for him after he leaves the program and until he earns his first salary check. 7) Activities may be graded in terms of demands made upon the individual—responsibility, hours worked, decision-making, independent thinking, and supervision. Success in an activity tends to increase the individual's level of aspiration. 8) To the extent possible, the outside community is used to teach community adaptability. 9) The anxiety and aspirations of the client, the physical resources and facilities of the unit, the personalities and talents of the participating personnel, and the opportunities offered by the surrounding community must be brought together in an integrative way for effective rehabilitation to occur.

Day hospitals have been particularly cognizant of this approach. Hyde, Bockoven, Pfautz, and York[38] describe a program of milieu rehabilitation carried on at the Butler Health Center in Providence, Rhode Island. This book, *Milieu Rehabilitation for Physically and Mentally Handicapped* describes the joint effort on the part of the health center and the local Division of Vocational Rehabilitation to rehabilitate a group of mentally and physically ill or handicapped people on a day basis. Since the physical facilities were those for a former private mental institution established in the days of moral treatment, they offered wide possibilities for rehabilitation activities. In addition to a large occupational therapy and crafts building with an auditorium, there was a green house, a hobby shop (which included printing, carpentry, and jewelry-making), and a paint shop. The gymnasium included bowling alleys, a pool table, and a nature study room. Farm areas and maintenance, industrial, kitchen, cafeteria, and service facilities were also available. Individual and group psychotherapy and casework service were made available to the client group. It was recognized that the client related to a great many other people in the setting and that it was the totality of these contacts which formed "a new Gestalt of group experience which could contribute to an alteration in the client's personality structure and attitudes which increases his usefulness to himself and others." Conventional personnel roles were carried by social worker, nurse, psychiatrist, rehabilitation counselor, coordinator, occupational therapist, psychologist, and sociologist. Others actively involved were volunteers and nonclinical personnel. Conflicts did occur among the personnel, but a high degree of success in the total project was noted.

Specifically, 77 per cent of those treated and discharged were either much improved or mildly improved, while only 23 per cent of those who were recommended and did not come to the Center improved at all. Among the interesting technical approaches were the arrangements made for total evaluation for admission on one day, during which the applicant was seen by various professional people. Attempts were made to match personalities of clients to staff. "For example, the sprightly, alert, quick-thinking, fast-talking members of the staff are often found to be especially able to establish warm relationships with patients in acute turmoil if they are also warm, friendly, and cheerful. The slow-moving, docile, placid individuals with infinite patience, who are thoughtful and reflective, can establish a relationship with those having anxiety reactions. On the other hand, the blunt, forthright, challenging person, who is at home with cynicism, is often able to establish a corrective relationship with paranoid patients."

SOCIAL AND DOMICILIARY REHABILITATION

Continuity of care for people with chronic mental illness has been long recognized as an essential need. More often than not, this concept has remained an elusive abstraction. It is true that for many years hospitals have been providing foster home care for discharged patients and have instituted follow-up systems, originally termed parole and now called convalescent care. The follow-up system has always been time-limited. A few rural halfway houses such as Gould Farm, established in Massachusetts in 1913, Spring Lake Ranch, in Vermont in 1932, and Meadow Lark Homestead, in Kansas in 1952, were precursors of the more recent developments as were the social clubs established by Dr. Joshua Bierer in the 1930's for his patients at Marlboro Hospital in England.

We have come to view schizophrenia not only as a medical but as a social entity or process. We have become increasingly concerned with the structuring of a former patient's life situation in the community. Many former patients cannot return to familial homes, either because they no longer exist, or because they are now considered antitherapeutic. The latter may be so, because some families have extremely low expectations of the patient's ability to function or because they provide too much stress.[34]

During the past decade, we have seen a persistent growth in expatients' clubs, social rehabilitation facilities, and halfway houses. These are not necessarily discrete entities. Associations such as Recovery, Inc., have 300 clubs but do not have residential facilities. The Hillside Hospital's Educational Alliance program is based in a community center.[24] On the other hand, programs—using Fountain House as one model—offer a range of services. It is difficult to obtain an accurate statement as to how many halfway houses now exist, partly because of the problem of definition but also because of their rapid development. Ghan[36] in 1962, made a comparative analytical survey of North American examples. At that time he noted that there were only two halfway houses, the Venture and the Vista in British Columbia, and he refers only to a "considerable number" in the United States.

Rutman,[51] in December, 1963, made an educated guess that there were at that time "100 transitional centers in the United States operating under the direction of at least one professionally-trained worker." Further, he estimated that there were at least another 75 to 100 groups that met under semiprofessional or volunteer leadership. Rutman summarized the shared characteristics of the group of halfway houses which participated in the Chicago Institute and noted that 80 per cent of the halfway houses were operating no more than five years. He noted "great variations in programs, procedures, staffing, auspices, use of volunteers and professional techniques that were employed." Services were, however, community-oriented and transitional in character. Most facilities were described as informal, humanitarian settings in which there was an "absence of traditional distance between worker and client."

THE SOCIAL CLUB AND THE HALFWAY HOUSE

Louis Reik[49] wrote, "The mental hospital with emphasis on illness and psychopathology is admirably equipped for the study and care of the sick, but for those with potentialities for healthy living, it can foster, as Eugen Bleuler taught long ago, morbid dependency and has an adverse effect. A halfway house, on the other hand, emphasizing health rather than disease, might offer a certain class of patients, not sick enough for the hospital or well enough to go home, an optimum environment for testing and realizing potentialities for health."

H. Wechsler,[63] in "Halfway Houses for Former Mental Patients: A Survey," defines a halfway house as "a residence for mental patients who no longer need to remain hospitalized but who are as yet unable to establish independent residence in the community." A report of the Woodley House Conference on Halfway Houses[69] noted that "what a halfway house is and does were considered inseparable—the process of life in the house, sharing with the physical entity of the house, and providing the opportunity for working with the emotional and environmental problems of the residents." Among the notions of a halfway house described by the participants at this Conference were the following: A halfway house was described as a place where exhospitalized or emotionally upset people live in order to avoid the necessity of hospitalization; "a place which encourages and forces normal patterns of living; a place relatively free from stigma; a place which provides temporary supports and provides an arena for trying different roles and behaviors, etc." In general, this group thought that there was value to having the halfway house physically separate from the hospital.

It was emphasized that, generally, it was not possible to provide the personal atmosphere that would be necessary if the house contained more than 30 people. It was found that professional participation was necessary, though often this came after the initial establishment of the house.

The size of halfway houses differs considerably. Fountain House offers apartments to two patients each as a minimum, whereas the halfway house of Gateways in Los Angeles accommodates sixty. In a recent verbal communication, it was learned that Fountain House now has twenty-five apartments for ex-patients. The agency secures, furnishes, and guarantees the lease for the apartments, which are considered transitional, although some clients have taken over the leases and have continued as independent tenants.

In a paper, "A "High-Expectations" Halfway House: A Follow-Up,"[64] the writers note that "halfway houses in the United States vary in several respects: in setting, more likely urban than rural; in type of structure, usually a large residential house; in sponsorship, usually private; in funding, more require some subsidy; in census, accommodating from five to thirty tenants, more often of one sex than of both sexes; and in average length of stay, usually between four and eight months."

One of the earliest halfway house models which incorporates perhaps the highest degree of comprehensive services of any of the halfway houses is Fountain House. In "Three Aspects of Psychiatric Rehabilitation at Fountain House,"[4] the authors note that Fountain House has a membership of 500 men and women, known as members rather than patients. Fountain House offers "a diversified program of social and recreational activities during evenings and weekends. Work opportunities exist within the house, and a program of transitional employment, developed in cooperation with commerce and industry, is offered to further the members' vocational recovery." The third aspect, the housing arrangement, has already been described. Fountain House is also committed to training graduate students in social work and vocational counseling. The staff consisted of eight caseworkers, a group worker, two sociologists, a psychologist, a psychiatric nurse, and four lay workers. Two psychiatric consultants were engaged on a part-time basis, and a group of 100 volunteers are active in all phases of the program. In 1966, Fountain House opened its new facility in New York City, a large, attractively furnished building in which everything is designed to create a homelike, pleasant atmosphere. In each of their activity areas, be it "the lunch program, the clerical office, the cleaning and maintenance of the house, professionals assume direct responsibility with members and volunteers working next to them in the performance of all tasks." There is a good deal of emphasis on members helping each other.

The membership of Fountain House is helped to establish better interpersonal relationships by a more intimate kind of relationship with professionals than one normally expects. Fountain House, as well as other social rehabilitation institutions, is still coping with the problem of dropouts.[3]

Another well established halfway house was initiated by the Vermont Division of Vocational Rehabilitation with the cooperation of the Vermont State Hospital.[22] Residential facilities are provided along with vocational counseling services and psychiatric treatment. At Horizon House, in Philadelphia, residential facilities are combined with a day center program; and Thresholds, in Chicago, has a day center and features use of ex-patients in employment as volunteers. Conrad House, in San Francisco, and Wellmet, in Cambridge, Massachusetts, combine healthy persons with ex-patients. At Wellmet, Harvard and Radcliffe students live with ex-patients.

Although all halfway houses are designed to encourage patients' responsibility for their own lives, Wilder, et al.[64] differentiate between a "nurturing approach and one of high expectations." Representative of a high expectation approach are the Overing Apartments, an urban halfway house under the aegis of the Division of Social and Community Psychiatry, Department of Psychiatry, Albert Einstein College of Medicine, New York, established by a private foundation, Pibly Fund. Inc., in 1964. The residence is located in the Bronx, New York, and consists of two semi-attached houses, each with two three-bedroom apartments. Each of the four apartments houses four to six men or women. Two recreation rooms are available to all.

There are some similarities between the philosophy and operation of Overing Apartments and Woodley House, in Washington, D. C. Rothwell and Doniger in a recent book describing Woodley House, *The Psychiatric Halfway*

House[50] note that "physically a halfway house is a home with bedrooms rather than beds, parlors or living rooms rather than day rooms, and studies rather than offices. Both Woodley and Overing are removed from the hospital grounds, are urban halfway houses, do not take primary responsibility for therapy (In both, residents must have their own therapists), and have high expectations of patients, with rewards built in for tenants who are productive (for example, both reduce the rental when tenants work full time). Overing has a direct connection with a psychiatric facility. As in most halfway houses, admissions of drug addicts and overt homosexuals are discouraged. The professionals differ in that Woodley House was started by occupational therapists; Overing is administered by a social worker. Patients do their own cooking at Overing; staff takes responsibility for cooking at Woodley House. Overing House has expanded its services to include apartments in regular apartment houses, and it is presently establishing one, where, it is hoped, the group of patients will remain indefinitely, whereas the house mother will move on.

In general, the Overing House experience, analyzed in terms of successful and unsuccessful cases, indicated that, on the whole, their failures were with younger people, more poorly motivated to move into a transitional residence than were those who succeeded. Since little attempt was made to screen out the severely ill, it is interesting that the percentage of success, at least in terms of employment, at the end of six months was comparable to that of other follow-up studies. Fifty-five per cent of women and fifty per cent of the men were employed. Regarding independent living, at the six-month follow-up forty-five per cent of all tenants were living on their own. One issue which Overing House, as well as other halfway houses, is now beginning to face is that of the length of stay. Most were organized as limited stay facilities and are now beginning to recognize that a longer supportive relationship may be necessary for many patients. Overing is trying to meet this through a newsletter, monthly alumni meetings, and a weekly social activity program in the community.

Not all attempts at establishing halfway houses have been successful.[43] At the Massachusetts Mental Health Center[44] an experiment was undertaken to establish a men's halfway house. The initiative came from a patient-group with strong leadership on the part of one patient. By the time the State Commissioner for Mental Health approved the house, half of the initial group of six had made other plans. Little structure was provided in terms of supervision, house rules, and little support was offered to the men who were expected to obtain and hold jobs without help. Though a doctor from the hospital was assigned a supervisory role, no consistent psychotherapeutic services were offered. The experiment failed, and the house closed after considerable acting-out behavior and destructive episodes. Interestingly enough, the destructive episodes were directed not towards persons but towards things.

It was also noted that the patient group had included a disproportionate number of sociopathic characters. In addition to these factors explaining the failure, many members of the staff were opposed to the project and indirectly contributed to its failure, almost like "a self-fulfilling prophecy."

The article contrasts this experiment with a successful venture, Rutland Corner House, developed by the same institution for discharged female patients. There selective screening was done by professional staff; a housekeeper was provided; rules were clear; and provisions for support of patients were prearranged.

A review of the literature would certainly indicate that some professional services readily available must be provided. There is also indication for a variety of halfway houses offering different degrees of structure and supervision as well as variable time limits. The quantitative inadequacy of present resources must be noted.

A different approach to transitional or permanent residential services is noted in the village settings of Gheel in Belgium and in Nigeria.[28] The Belgian plan, in existence for more than a century, utilizes foster home care among the families resident in the village. The village system in Nigeria permits "full treatment of the mentally ill by utilizing inherent dynamic resources of social environment as the principal therapeutic technique. Kinship groups, with their prescribed mutual obligation, came with the patient." The psychiatrists in Nigeria collaborate with the local witch doctors. There is considerable question as to the applicability of these two small village programs to situations in the industrialized countries.

REHABILITATION THROUGH WORK

History

The utilization of work processes in the rehabilitation of schizophrenic patients has a long history. The earliest recognition of the value of performing productive tasks was in using patients to assist in the maintenance activities within the mental hospital. Productive work is an important aspect of contemporary life, and return of the patient's ability to function in this area has been for generations one of the primary goals of rehabilitation.

In the nineteenth century, work for patients was looked upon as part of the "moral therapy" then in vogue in the treatment of the mentally ill.[20,21] Landy and Raulet[45] point to Dr. Benjamin Rush's quotation from Cowper in 1812 in substantiating Rush's treatment approach to work therapy: "Absence of occupation is not rest; a mind quite vacant is a mind distrest." With the growth of the tremendous state hospitals in the twentieth century, the "moral treatment" approach gave way to medically-oriented methods.

Occupational therapy came into being during World War I and was quickly transposed to the mental hospitals. While better functioning patients were assigned tasks aiding the hospital's maintenance and service programs, many more were placed on occupational therapy crafts by "medical prescription."[66] Wittkower and Azima[67] explain that "occupational therapy came into use on empirical grounds." It was taken for granted that "work and recreation per se have a remedial effect on the mentally ill" and that occupational therapy is the means for supplying them. No tests or evaluation to prove this assumption have ever been made. Patients, asked about their attitudes to and opinions of occupational therapy[68] generally felt that it had brought them relief. They nevertheless believed that the therapy had little to do with their treatment. In the patients' opinions, "It helps pass the time," or "It keeps you busy."

The use of patients in hospital service and maintenance quickly crosses the line to exploitation of labor. With no goal other than a niche in the custodial milieu, the tasks become neither therapeutic nor "work-a-day." They too, like much of the occupational therapy, fill time and "keep the patient busy." With the advent of modern therapies the numbers of patients functionally able to participate in work activities increased. Attention then turned to other modalities which might be both therapeutic and utilize the patients' time. The modern concepts of rehabilitation and industrial therapy came into application.[25]

During the late 1920's and early 1930's, a few Englisn mental hospitals brought in simple contract assembly work for their patients to do.[9] While rehabilitation for return to normal society was not the aim (for few patients in those years were expected to leave the hospital), any test of rehabilitation potential was lost when the Great Depression dried up the sources of work. It was not until the 1950's, following the success of sheltered work for the physically disabled after World War II, that the British hospitals tried this system again. This time the concern was with preparing patients for return to the world of work, along with the therapeutic goal of increasing the functioning capacity of even severely-regressed chronic schizophrenic patients. Interestingly enough, such "industrial therapy" programs, as they came to be known in England ("ergo-therapy," in France; and "beschützende" work, in Germany), were set up in mental hospitals in a number of European countries at about the same period.[10]

By 1965, Kidd[41] reported that in the majority of Great Britain's mental hospitals, between 30 and 35 per cent of the patients were on industrial therapy, while in 13 per cent of the hospitals, as many as 50 per cent of their patients were so involved. A year later, Kidd[39] surveyed 90 hospitals and found 78 of them serving long-term schizophrenics and other chronic psychotics in shops which, in many places, had supplanted conventional occupational therapy. Visitors to France, Holland, Germany, Russia, Yugoslavia, and other countries, bring back reports of an increasing number of mental hospitals trying industrial therapy programs.[11,32]

Community-based industrial work programs for post-mental hospital patients actually began before the hospital programs referred to above. The

Altro Work Shops' cooperative service with Hillside Hospital and the State Hospitals serving New York City began in 1953. A number of sheltered workshop-hospital ventures across the United States developed as demonstration rehabilitation programs under support of the 1954 amendments to the Federal Vocational Rehabilitation Act.[48] Perhaps the oldest and most continuous community-based industrial shop in the world for the post-mentally ill patient is Thermega, Ltd., outside of London, England. Thermega was established by the Ex-Service Mental Welfare Society after World War I to show that "shell-shocked" veterans could function in the work-a-day world. In recent years its program has paralleled that of Altro Work Shops in taking psychiatric patients from the neighboring mental hospitals.[12]

Most recently, in connection with psychiatric day hospitals and as extensions of hospital industrial therapy outside the hospital, has come the development of newer patterns in industrial therapy, closer to treatment of the patient in the community. These are in line with changes in medical treatment and are based upon experience with "in-hospital" rehabilitation.

Purposes and Design

The writers[17] find it helpful to think of the process of rehabilitation as "following a spectrum, beginning with onset of illness and ending with return to as near normalcy in the community as is possible for the handicapped person." "The structural services . . . may be introduced at any point along this spectrum. The medical, social, and vocational programs that are used in rehabilitation may be built into the hospital, the outpatient clinic, the aftercare clinic, or closer to the real world and industry, and in each case they can be vitally useful in returning more mental patients to useful living and keeping them there." Though the structure, machinery, and products of industrial therapy may be very similar, the programs introduced at different points in the spectrum will differ widely, at least with the differing symptomatology and needs of the patients served.

Some elements are common to all points, however. As was hinted in Dr. Rush's quotation from Cowper, the removal of a worker from his work through illness disturbs a major portion of his physical energy and emotional patterns. A vacuum exists for the patient, time-wise, money-wise, and psychologically. The loss of work also carries with it the loss of what has elsewhere been called the "S" values of a job—Salary, Status, and Success.[19] These losses present hazards particularly for schizophrenic patients, for loss of or lowered ego strengths play a large part in the dynamics of their illness.[6]

The sheltered or protected work setting provides a medium through which reestablishment of these losses may be started. There is a compendium of several uses to which such programs can be put for schizophrenic patients. The sheltered workshop can be used to evaluate the occupational potential of the patient or ex-patient, or it can be used to test the ego strengths of the individual. "It can become a preparatory-to-work setting in which proper habits of work and attitudes to work, supervision, and peers can be taught or reestablished. It can also be a place where basic job skills can be learned, or, depending upon the level of work available, on-the-job training can be provided for industry. Finally, for those individuals whose residual handicap may be too great for 'normal' industry but who can be at least partially productive, the sheltered workshop can become an occupational haven on a permanent basis."[18]

There has been accumulating evidence[6] that the proper work environment itself provides a form of therapy. The experience at Altro Work Shops over thirteen years can still be summed up in the words of one of its earlier reports: ". . . It (the rehabilitation workshop) offers restructuring of object relations by providing an environment which allows for trial and error in relearning in an actual life situation . . . but without the immediate dire consequences of error in the real world—where one quickly gets fired from a job or ostracized, etc. . . . In addition, the workshop has available its staff to structure the psychological life space, can vary the nature of the task and the nature of the co-workers, and can help the patient to bear conflict in the object relations." A more recent report of discussions on industry in the mental hospital[35] repeats these themes, pointing out that the therapeutic value of such programs results in improvement for even severely ill or chronically regressed schizophrenics.

Notwithstanding the elements in common to all industrial therapy for psychotics, it should be kept in mind[5] that, like other people, schizophrenics differ a great deal from one another, and quite highly individual approaches may be required for their rehabilitation. "If an extremely weak ego is the common denominator of schizophrenics, it must be remembered that different ego functions are involved to a differing degree in each case. The patient suffering from infantilism simpers, feigns, attracts attention, acts out impulsively, wishes to relate parasitically, symbiotically, or at best primitively, anaclitically; the intelligent, tense paranoid wants to maintain emotional isolation, is preoccupied with homosexual problems or more broadly with matters of activity and passivity. . . . The schizophrenic with hysterical character formation experiences wide mood swings, is given to dramatic, ominous-appearing symptomatology. . . . The schizophrenic with affective features will use excessive denial and be gay and apparently carefree, only to become suicidally depressed when the bubble bursts. Finally, there is the chronic 'burnt out' schizophrenic with many somatic delusions, quite bizarre symptom formation, apathy, but some remnant of a functioning ego." The "common" structure of industrial therapy must be flexible enough to adjust to the needs of most of these "types" if it is to be of service to schizophrenics.

Structure

Three main kinds of structured work settings have been developed over recent years to serve the needs of mental patients, including schizophrenics. One has been the utilization of patients, singly or in groups, on in-hospital tasks for which they may receive remuneration. A quite recent extension of this system is the placement of groups of patients, under the supervision of a hospital nurse or aide, in the production line of a commercial industry. Thus, Glenside Hospital in Bristol, England[13] has small groups of patients working in this fashion in a hygienic straw factory and a shoe manufacturing plant. A similar program has been described to the authors as run by the Fountain House Foundation in New York City.

The most familiar form of industrial therapy in the world is conducted in what are usually referred to in this country as "sheltered workshops." These are facsimiles of normal small businesses, most usually engaged in simple bench-type assembly under contract to industrial firms. In increasing numbers, these sheltered workshops are "upgrading" the types of work undertaken to include semiskilled occupations. The Altro Work Shops, for example, include power sewing machines, bench lathes, milling machines, key punches, and tabulating machines among its equipment. The CHIRP programs of the Veterans Administration hospitals include power presses and drill presses among other specialized tools.

Care must be exercised in using the terms "sheltered workshop" outside of the United States, for in Europe this title is restricted to permanently sheltered settings for handicapped persons not expected to move back into the normal work-a-day world.[14] The term "industrial therapy" seems to be a more generic one to also include the transitional workshops used in rehabilitation of the schizophrenic.

In brief, an industrial therapy program has all the attributes of a small business. It will either manufacture items for sale or subcontract to fabricate or assemble items for a commercial contractor. In either case, the industrial therapy unit must be concerned with obtaining work (selling or procuring), manufacturing (quantity and quality control), and delivery of merchandise (customer satisfaction). It has also to meet the wage needs of its "employees." In most of the industrialized nations of the world, there is now governmental regulation and supervision that these processes neither exploit the handicapped workers nor provide undue subsidization of the commercial supplier of work.

A third form of industrial therapy uses the medium of setting the patient up in a small business of his own under greater or lesser supervision. Glenside Hospital has developed a car wash unit, manned by patients. Glenside, as well as Fountain House, has established patient-operated shoe repair shops.[15,29]

From the therapeutic standpoint, there is general agreement among experts that in industrial therapy at least the following conditions be met:[23]

a) The work done must be productive work, real work, that has a real place in the industrial economy. Psychiatric patients must be able to feel that what they are doing is not just an extension of occupational therapy and that what they learn is related to existing job processes in the industrial or commercial world.

b) The work atmosphere, though real, should allow for a "low pressure system." It takes much longer for schizophrenic patients to rise to acceptable work tempos, and too much initial pressure can accentuate withdrawal.

c) There should be sufficient variety of work to offer, not only routinized occupations but also something more complex, so that a change of motion or pace is required from time to time. There should be work that can be done alone as well as work that can be done in groups.

d) It is also becoming clear that having a variety of fellow workers, persons with different handicaps or workers from the normal labor force, aids in insuring the real nature of the work environment.

e) The pay for the work done should be at the normal business levels per unit of time or product, but related to the actual productivity of the patient. In the United States this is now a legal requirement under the 1966 amendments to the Federal Wage and Hour Laws.

Experience in Europe and the United States has now made clear that industrial therapy services for schizophrenic patients should be available both within mental institutions and out in the general community. There is research evidence that many patients are actually employable during this hospitalization, even at very early stages.[2,57,58,59,60,61] The British Industrial Rehabilitation Unit[65] found that though most schizophrenic patients were socially withdrawn, lacking in skills, less pleasant in manner, and less industrious than nonschizophrenics, they were no more handicapped at work than their fellow, physically disabled, co-workers in the government sheltered workshops.

There are dangers, however, in having the industrial therapy unit within the hospital. These are most lucidly stated by Early[16] in a *Lancet* article of October 1, 1960. "To occupy consistently a third of the patients in a chronic hospital is obviously a desirable aim, but, it is not an end in itself. Patients tend to settle down as they have been encouraged to in the past, with a slightly better standard of living, and an 'industrial aristocracy' tends to replace the old, privileged, maintenance department worker. The ultimate aim of discharge may be lost sight of by patients and by staff." For this reason, Early initiated the first of what are known as Industrial Therapy Organizations in the British Isles. These are similar in structure to Altro Work Shops, the CHIRP programs, or the Goodwill Industries in the United States, except that the entire patient population is from the mental hospitals. Most recently, Altro Work Shops has reversed the Industrial Therapy Organization procedure in connection with newly-developing Comprehensive Community Mental Health Centers. In two of these, Soundview-Throgs Neck and the Lincoln Hospital psychiatric services, Altro has established "Partnerships in Industrial Therapy" that bring the sheltered work system for therapeutic purposes within the mental treatment institution while preserving the major business facsimile out in the general community.

Supporting Therapies and Aftercare

The rehabilitation of a disabled person to a useful role in society is a long and arduous process. This is particularly true of the "relapsing illnesses," which include schizophrenia. The best of industrial therapy programs without concurrent and follow-up services have but ephemeral value. The concomitant therapies include use of drugs, psychotherapy, and a variety of ego supportive techniques. Pasamanick and Wing[1] and their respective colleagues, have both demonstrated that smaller relapse rates result when there is regular aftercare. In a study of the effectiveness of preparation for employment of ex-schizophrenic veterans, Walker and McCourt[62] concluded that most discharged patients benefit from further support from mental health specialists on a follow-up basis.

In the experience of Altro Health and Rehabilitation Services,[8] a number of technics have been found to be necessary components to rehabilitation of the schizophrenics at Altro Work Shops. These include the following:

"1) Handling resistances to rehabilitation in the beginning stages of illness,

2) Reality testing,

3) Educational methods to help patients learn or relearn the elementary ways of coping with daily problems,

4) Helping the patient to live with his symptoms,

5) Working with the patients' families,

6) Follow-up to maintain "continuity of psychiatric service."

Else Kris[42] described the need for a similar array of services in her experience with rehabilitation at the Manhattan Aftercare Clinics in New York City. Similar experience has been reported from a number of other parts of the world.[30]

SUMMARY

Rehabilitation should be thought of as a concerted, dynamic process using a variety of professional and technical skills and of community resources to help handicapped people achieve the maximum functioning of which they are capable. While certain early approaches to dealing with schizophrenic patients, such as that of moral treatment, may be recognized as incorporating rehabilitation concepts, it is really only in the past two decades that formal rehabilitation programs and services for the mentally ill have been established.

By now it is recognized that rehabilitation of the schizophrenic embraces methods that are essentially elements of psychiatric treatment (e.g., milieu therapy, social remotivation) as well as methods that are apart from the clinical structure (e.g., halfway house, sheltered workshop). Each of these appears to be sufficiently effective in helping patients to warrant continuing the efforts, but it is still too early in the experience to be able to make differential judgments with regard to which element is more or most effective or as to which combination of services provides best for which kind of patients.

We are presently on the crest of great increases in the use of rehabilitation programs for the schizophrenic, and it is best to approach additional experience with an open and questioning mind.

BIBLIOGRAPHY

1. "Annotations — Rehabilitation in Schizophrenia," The Lancet 1(7386): 643, 1965.

2. Bashina, V. M.: The Work Capacity and Social Adaptation of Schizophrenic Patients Who Became Ill in Childhood and Adolescence," International Journal of Psychiatry 1(2): 248-257, 1965.

3. Beard, J., and Goldman, E.: "Major Problems," Rehabilitation Record, March-April, 1964.

4. Beard, J., Schmidt, W. J., Smith, M., Dincin, J.: "Three Aspects of Psychiatric Rehabilitation at Fountain House," Mental Hygiene, Vol. 48, No. 1, January, 1964.

5. Bellak, L., and Black, B. J.: "The Rehabilitation of Psychotics in the Community," American Journal of Orthopsychiatry, Vol. XXX, No. 2, April, 1960.

6. Bellak, L., Black, B. J., Lurie, A., and Miller, J. S. A.: "Rehabilitation of the Mentally Ill Through Controlled Transitional Employment," American Journal of Orthopsychiatry, Vol. XXVI, No. 2, April, 1956.

7. Benney, C.: "The Role of the Caseworker in Rehabilitation," Social Casework: 118-123, March, 1955.

8. Benney, C., Black, B. J., and Niederland, W. G.: "Rehabilitation of the Mentally Ill for the World of Work," Proceedings of the Institute on Rehabilitation of the Mentally Ill, Altro Health and Rehabilitation Services, New York, New York 52-63, 1962.

9. Black, B. J.: Industrial Therapy for the Mentally Ill in Western Europe, Altro Work Shops, New York 10, 1965.

10. Black, B. J.: Ibid 10-46, 65-70.

11. Black, B. J.: Ibid, see bibliography.

12. Black, B. J.: Ibid 12.

13. Black, B. J.: Ibid 37.

14. Black, B. J.: Ibid 17-18.

15. Black, B. J.: Ibid 39.

16. Black, B. J.: Ibid 44-46.

17. Black, B. J.: "The Protected Workshop," Rehabilitation of the Mentally Ill, A.A.A.S., Washington, D. C. 200, 1959.

18. Black, B. J.: "Psychiatric Rehabilitation in the Community," Chapter 12, Handbook of Community Psychiatry and Community Mental Health, Leopold Bellak, M.D. (ed.) Grune & Stratton, New York, 1964.

19. Black, B. J.: "The Work-a-Day World, Some Problems in Return of Mental Hospital Patients to the Community," Chapter 24, The Patient and the Mental Hospital, Milton Greenblatt, Daniel J. Levinson, and Richard H. Williams (eds.) The Free Press, Glencoe, Illinois, 1957.

20. Bockoven, J. S.: "Moral Treatment in American Psychiatry," Journal of Nervous and Mental Disease, Parts I-IV, Vol. 124, No. 2, 167-194, 1956.

21. Bockoven, J. S.: Ibid, Parts V-IX, Vol. 124, No. 3, 292-321, 1956.

22. Chittick, R. A., Brooks, G. W., Irons, F. S., and Deane, W. N.: The Vermont Story: Rehabilitation of Chronic Schizophrenic Patients, Vermont State Hospital, Waterbury, Vermont, January, 1961.

23. Chouinard, E. L., and Garrett, J. F. (eds.): Workshops for the Disabled, Rehabilitation Services Series No. 371, Office of Vocational Rehabilitation, U. S. Department of Health, Education, and Welfare, U. S. Government Printing Office, 95-96, 1956.

24. Chwast, J., and Lurie, A.: "The Resocialization of the Discharged Depressed Patient," Canadian Psychiatric Association Journal, Vol. 11, Special Supplement, 1966.

25. Cohen, G. L.: "The Sick in Mind. A Report on the Mental Health Service," New Statesman 70(1793): 119-122, 1965.

26. Cumming and Cumming: Ego and Milieu, Atherton Press, New York, 1962.

27. David, H. P.: International Trends

in Mental Health, McGraw-Hill, New York, 8, 1966.

28. David, H. P., Ibid., p. 147.

29. Early, D. R.: "Making Rehabilitation Work," New Society, 6: 18-19, June 3, 1965.

30. Examples: "Schizophrenics in the Community," British Journal of Psychiatry 3(472): 258-267, 1965.

Wilkins, G. D. et al.: "A Therapeutic Community Development in a State Psychiatric Hospital," Medical Journal of Australia 2(6): 220-224, 1963.

Charalampous, K. D. (ed.): "The Long-Term Care of the Chronic Mentally Ill Patient, a Medical Approach," Medical Record and Annals 56: 257-258, 1963.

Enss, H., and Hippius, H.: "Sozialpsychiatrische Aspektie der Modernen Psychosen-Therapie," Deutsches Medizinisches Journal 15(16): 529-533, 1964.

Bredamann, H.: "Klinik, Praxis und Soziolpsychiatrische Probleme der Pharmakotherapie," Deutsches Medizinisches Journal 15(16): 533-534, 1964.

Hofmann, G.: "Rehabilitaria Former Procesuale a Schizofreniei," Neurologia, Psihiatria, Neurochirurgia 5(5): 433-437, 1965.

31. Fairweather, G.: Social Psychology in Treating Mental Illness: An Experimental Approach, Wally & Sons, New York, 1964.

32. Field, M. G., and Aronson, J.: "Soviet Community Mental Health Services and Work Therapy—A Report of Two Visits," Community Mental Health Journal 1(11): 81-90, 1965.

33. Freeman, Cameron, and McGhie: Chronic Schizophrenia, International Universities Press, New York, 1958.

34. Freeman, H. E., and Simmons, O. G.: "Treatment Experiences of Mental Patients and Their Families," American Journal of Public Health, Vol. 51, No. 9, September, 1961.

35. Frost, E. S. (Ed.): Industry in the Mental Hospital—A Workshop. Proceedings, April 22-23, 1965, Veterans Administration Hospital, Brockton, Mass.

36. Ghan, S.: "The Halfway House: A Transitional Facility for the Rehabilitation of the Mentally Ill," Unpublished Master's Thesis, University of British Columbia, 13, 1962.

37. Hobbs, N.: "Mental Health's Third Revolution," American Journal of Orthopsychiatry, Vol. XXXIV, No. 5, October, 1964.

38. Hyde, Bockoven, Pfautz, and York: Milieu Rehabilitation for Physically and Mentally Handicapped, Butler Health Center, Providence, Rhode Island, April 19, 1962.

39. "Increase in Industrial Therapy Noted in British Survey," Frontiers of Hospital Psychiatry, 3(7): 1, 1966.

40. Jones, M.: "Rehabilitation in Psychiatry," World Health Organization, WHO/Ment/30, 4, July 7, 1952.

41. Kidd, H. B.: "Industrial Units in Psychiatric Hospitals," The British Journal of Psychiatry, 111(481): 1205-1209, 1965.

42. Kris, E. B.: "Aftercare and Rehabilitation of the Mentally Ill," Current Therapeutic Research, Vol. 5, 24-30, 1963.

43. Landy, D.: "Exploration of Residential Aftercare Psychiatric Patients: A Men's Halfway House," International Journal of Social Psychiatry, Vol. 6, Nos. 1 and 2, December, 1960.

44. Landy, D., and Greenblatt, M.: Halfway House, U. S. Department of Health, Education, and Welfare, Vocational Rehabilitation Administration, Washington, D. C., 1965.

45. Landy, D., and Raulet, H.: "The Hospital Work Program," Rehabilitation of the Mentally Ill, A.A.A.S., Washington, D. C. 72-73, 1959.

46. Menninger, K.: The Vital Balance, Viking Press, New York, 71, 1963.

47. Myers, J. S.: "Milieu Rehabilitation and the Role of the Counselor," National Rehabilitation Counseling Association/Professional Bulletin, Vol. VII, No. 5, October, 1966.

48. Rehabilitating The Mentally Ill, Report of Planning Conference, October, 1964, Vocational Rehabilitation Administration, Department of Health, Education, and Welfare, Washington, D. C., U. S.

Government Printing Office: 771-187, 1965.

49. Reik, L.: "The Halfway House: The Role of Laymen's Organizations in the Rehabilitation of the Mentally Ill," Mental Hygiene, 615, October, 1953.

50. Rothwell, N. D., and Doniger, J. A.: The Psychiatric Halfway House, Charles C. Thomas, Springfield, Illinois, 9, 1966.

51. Rutman, I.: "Origin and Present Status," Rehabilitation Record, March-April, 1964.

52. Sanders, R., and Smith, R. S.: NIMH Project Proposal OM 126, July, 1963, National Institute of Mental Health, Department of Health, Education, and Welfare, Washington, D.C.

53. Sanders, R., and Weinman, B.: NIMH Project No. OM 126, National Institute of Mental Health, Department of Health, Education, and Welfare, Washington, D. C.

54. Schwartz, C., and Schwartz, M.: Social Approaches to Mental Patient Care, Columbia University Press, New York and London, Chapter X, 136-162, 1964.

55. Schwartz, C., and Schwartz, M.: Ibid, Chapter XI, 163-189.

56. Sivadon, P.: "Technique for Socio Therapy," Symposium on Preventive and Social Psychiatry, U. S. Government Printing Office, Washingt2on, D. C., 1959.

57. Wadsworth, W. V., Wells, B. W. P., and Scott, R. F.: "A Comparative Study of Chronic Schizophrenics and Normal Subjects on a Work Task Involving Sequential Operations," The Journal of Mental Science, Vol. 108, No. 454, May, 1962, London, England, 309-316.

58. Wadsworth, W. V., Wells, B. W. P., and Scott, R. F.: "A Comparative Study of Fatiguability of a Group of Chronic Schizophrenics and a Group of Hospitalized Non-Psychotic Depressives," The Journal of Mental Science, Vol. 108, No. 454, May, 1962, London, England 304-308.

59. Wadsworth, W. V., Wells, B. W. P., and Scott, R. F.: "The Employability of Chronic Schizophrenics," The Journal of Mental Science, Vol. 108, No. 454, May, 1962, London, England 300-303.

60. Wadsworth, W. V., Wells, B. W. P., and Scott, R. F.: "An Experimental Investigation of the Qualitative Differences Between the Work Performance of Normals and Chronic Schizophrenics," Psychiatric Quarterly Supplement, Vol. 37, Part 2, 325-335, 1963.

61. Walker, R.: "Mistreatment of the Mentally Ill," American Journal of Psychiatry, 121(3): 215-220, 1964.

62. Walker, R., and McCourt, J.: "Employment Experience Among 200 Schizophrenic Patients in Hospital and After Discharge," American Journal of Psychiatry, 122(3): 316-319, 1965.

63. Wechsler, H.: "Halfway Houses for Former Mental Patients: A Survey," The Journal of Social Issues, 16:2, 20-26, 1960.

64. Wilder, J. F., Kessel, M., Caulfield, S. C., Davis, S., and Kent, J.: "A 'High-Expectations' Halfway House: A Follow-Up," Unpublished Paper, presented at the American Psychiatric Association Conference in Atlantic City, New Jersey, May 11, 1966.

65. Wing, J. K., Bennett, D. H., and Denham, J.: "The Industrial Rehabilitation of Long-Stay Schizophrenic Patients," Medical Research Council Memorandum No. 42, Her Majesty's Stationery Office, London, England, 1964.

66. Wittkower, E. D., and Azima, H.: "Dynamic Aspects and Occupational Therapy," Archives of Neurology and Psychiatry, Vol. 79, 706-710, 1958.

67. Wittkower, E. D., and Azima, H.: "Dynamic Aspects and Occupational Therapy," Rehabilitation of the Mentally Ill, A.A.A.S., Washington, D. C., 105, 1959.

68. Wittkower, E. D., and Azima, H.: Ibid, 106-107.

69. "Woodley House Conference on Halfway Houses," May 1963, Washington, D. C., U. S. Public Health Service Grant No. 5-R11 MH 454-3, 6.

19

Prevention

JACK R. EWALT, M.D. and
JOHN T. MALTSBERGER, M.D.

Dr. Ewalt is currently Bullard Professor of Psychiatry at Harvard Medical School, Chairman of the Executive Committee of the Department of Psychiatry, and Superintendent of the Massachusetts Mental Health Center. He is also Past Director and Past President of the American Board of Psychiatry and Neurology, Councilor and Past President of the American Psychiatric Association, and a Consultant to the Beth Israel and Cambridge City Hospitals.

Educated at the University of Colorado, Dr. Ewalt received his medical degree in 1933, following which he was a Commonwealth Fund Fellow at the Psychopathic Hospital in Colorado and held various teaching appointments there, including those of Instructor and Assistant Professor of Psychiatry.

Dr. Ewalt has in the past been Consultant to the Surgeon General of the Air Force, Consultant to the Surgeon General of the Army, Director of the Joint Commission on Mental Illness and Health, and was formerly Commissioner of the Department of Mental Health in the Commonwealth of Massachusetts.

Dr. Maltsberger is a graduate of Princeton University and Harvard Medical School, who interned at the Pennsylvania Hospital. He trained in both child and adult psychiatry at the Massachusetts Mental Health Center, where he is now the Associate Director of Psychiatry.

Dr. Maltsberger has been appointed by Harvard University as Instructor in Psychiatry; he is a Diplomate of the American Board of Psychiatry and Neurology.

The present state of psychiatric knowledge does not permit the claim that we can prevent the development of a schizophrenic illness in any given individual or population. The present chapter can offer no such happy prescription; its more modest intent is to describe the present status of efforts which may one day make that possible, and to outline those efforts now underway which aspire to reduce the incidence and prevalence of this terrible and elusive disease.

Three rubrics are commonly employed in describing efforts to eradicate and forestall illnesses—primary prevention, secondary prevention, and tertiary prevention. Primary prevention, those efforts directed to keep new cases from developing, will occupy our attention here. Secondary prevention refers to early detection and treatment, and will be discussed briefly—certain refinements in current practice should be forthcoming in the near future. For tertiary prevention, those efforts directed toward the optimum management of chronically ill persons, brief comment will be reserved, since in the strictest sense this work is preventive only in that it aims to forestall deterioration.

PRIMARY PREVENTION

Primary prevention, efforts directed to keep a disease from developing, is the chief goal of preventive medicine and a major concern of workers in public health. This kind of prevention is not possible without some understanding of the sources and circumstances from which a given disorder arises; inquiry into these origins comprises much of the current research on schizophrenia.

In those disorders of known etiology, primary preventive measures may be directed against such elements in the environment which invite spread, or they may aim to increase the resistance of the vulnerable population. In tuberculosis, for example, detection and treatment of chronic carriers has reduced the endemic source of infection; mosquito eradication programs have served a similar purpose in the reduction of malaria. Host resistance, increased by vaccination, is an effective primary preventive measure against smallpox and yellow fever.

Control of infection and reduction of infective source require varying degrees of social control and environmental manipulation when etiologic knowledge is applied to whole populations. Sanitary regulation of water supplies, regulation of food production and distribution, sewage and mosquito control have been achieved only after long efforts in public education. This always implies some measure of resistance because of the social and economic modifications such measures require. Such a program of education and the public resistance to it may now be seen in the fluoridation controversy—once again citizens raise the argument that constitutional rights are threatened by the legislation necessary to modify a public water supply.

Control measures of this sort have eventually been accepted by the public when sufficient numbers learn that the prevention of a disease is possible and in the general interest of all.

A second but less widely recognized means of primary prevention, related to the elimination of host factors which increase susceptiblity, also depends on public education. Preventoria for the children of tuberculous parents, weight and diet control to ward off the development of hypertension, arteriosclerosis, and associated coronary heart disease, and programs of immunization are examples of this work. Animal and plant breeders go one step further and develop strains resistant to some diseases, and in other instances follow genetic programs to produce individuals better equipped to flourish in extremes of climate.

It has been said that schizophrenia is a disease of multiple etiologies, and although there is much to suggest that this is true, candor requires us to state that we do not know with certainty what even one of these etiologies may be. Because we do not know the specific cause or causes of schizophrenia, it is possible only to make empiric applications of other knowledge to correct or eliminate certain social and psychologic conditions which are observed to be prevalent in the life situations of those who suffer from this disorder, and which we believe (but do not know) may play some role in its genesis. This application is fraught with difficulty and uncertainty, because we cannot demonstrate that such methods of primary prevention, as applied in the past two decades, have succeeded in diminishing the incidence of schizophrenic disorders.[12,13,20]

The array of studies and efforts in this direction is impressive, but we must repeat that we cannot honestly say that such measures are preventing schizophrenia. That they tend to eliminate some of the circumstances in which schizophrenia occurs we can be sure. These circumstances in themselves are often blots on the social scene—poverty, slum living, and ignorance are undesirable enough in themselves whether or not they play a part in the etiology of this disease. Measures directed toward the elimination of social ills are valuable in themselves; they contribute to the general welfare and reduce major causes of corrosive worry and concern which afflict many members of our society.[29] Even if we cannot be certain that such measures decrease the incidence of schizophrenia, we have evidence that some of the corrective measures improve the mental health and augment the personal development of some of our population.[3,4,26] To say, however, that general measures which improve health and hygiene contribute to the general good is not to say that they reduce the incidence of schizophrenia, or the incidence of any other mental disorder, for that matter.

Let us now turn our attention to some of the work which may in time make specific planning for the primary prevention of schizophrenia possible.

Genetics

To discover whether schizophrenia is an inheritable disorder has challenged many workers since the nineteenth century. There has been a recent reawakening of interest in this area of investigation, although the evidence for genetic transmission is not sufficiently convincing to recommend a eugenic approach to the problem. The tendency to view psychoses as hereditary degenerations has persisted since the days of Morel, and the search for supportive evidence has primarily involved investigations of pedigrees and identical twins. Kallman has led in the examination of affected families, and found a concordance rate of 86 per cent among identical twin pairs when schizophrenia was present, in contrast to a concordance of 15 per cent in dizygotic pairs. On this basis he did not hesitate to recommend eugenic measures as a primary preventive measure against this disorder.[36] Subsequent students have not found data to support such high rates of concordance and tend to deemphasize to some degree the importance of inheritance as a major factor.[70,61,42]

Another avenue of investigation, the study of the comparative incidence of schizophrenia in adopted children, with examination of the biologic parents for the disease, is now beginning to occupy some workers.[32,38] This subject has recently been reviewed by Jackson.[35] Although most students concur that genetic factors do have some determinative significance, certainly no specific metabolic error has been demonstrated that can point to the operation of a particular gene or group of genes for schizophrenia, nor is the mode of transmission for schizophrenic vulnerability, whether by a dominant or a recessive mode, clear at this time.[55] Certainly the evidence at hand cannot justify confident genetic counseling or sterilization laws. Even if some genetically determined enzymatic disturbance comes to light, many difficulties will remain to be overcome. Primary prevention in a free society becomes particularly difficult when eugenic programs are at issue. If the schizophrenia factor were detectable by some simple test and the remedy not burdensome, perhaps the obstacles in the way of a public health program would not be excessively great. This is the case in phenylketonuria, in which the metabolic error is detectable by a urine test and the oligophrenia preventable by special dieting. What, however, if the metabolic error is similar to that encountered in the Thalassemias?[49] In this instance it would be impossible to plan an effective program for primary prevention.

Biochemical Studies

Evidence for a specific metabolic etiology in schizophrenia is even more tenuous than that for a genetic explanation. The search for some intrinsic characteristic in the schizophrenic individual which renders him prone to psychosis, once concentrated in neuropathologic investigations, now proceeds in the chemical study of the nervous system and of the internal milieu. Griesinger took the view a hundred years ago that mental diseases were brain diseases; the search for specific anatomical lesions has thus far proven futile, although it has not yet been abandoned by some. The modern heirs of this nineteenth century hypothesis are the biochemical researchers who now pursue the elusive specific defect on the molecular rather than on the microscopic level.

The recent research of this kind has been extensively reviewed by Kety.[39] He points out that the biochemical studies have been particularly hampered by the difficulties in sampling from heterogeneous populations, and by certain sources of artifact. The infections endemic in mental hospitals, peculiarities of diet, hypnotic and ataractic drugs, and physiologic responses to stress all may produce biochemical changes easily mistaken for schizophrenia-specific phenomena. Although earlier workers had suggested that there was a disturbance in carbohydrate metabolism, no verification has been produced by more recent experiments.[62,63] Neither have claims that the blood glutathione level is diminished been substantiated. Still under investigation, however, are peculiarities in oxidative phosphorylation in the erythrocyte of schizophrenic subjects, and the suggestion that there is greater than normal anti-insulin or hyperglycemic activity in these patients.

Research tends to support the view that both serotonin and norepinephrine have some important central nervous system function, but just what the role of these substances may be is obscure; they are certainly not of proven importance in the genesis of schizophrenia.

The hypothesis that pathologic transmethylation of certain normal body metabolites has some evidence to support it, and the processes of methylation in schizophrenia are currently under investigation.

Reports that schizophrenic patients have a higher than normal level of ceruloplasmin have been discredited by the discovery that the atypical finding disappeared when the subject's ascorbic acid deficiency was corrected. Before the importance of ascorbic acid was appreciated in the oxidation studies of epinephrine (The ceruloplasmin hypothesis related to epinephrine oxidation), Robert Heath and his colleagues at Tulane University[30a,30b,30c,30d,30e] postulated the presence of a qualitatively different form of ceruloplasmin, Taraxein, which they felt was present in schizophrenic subjects, and which they claim to have isolated. Reports that this substance when given to normal subjects on a double-blind basis produces mental disturbances similar to those in schizophrenia have not been substantiated in other laboratories.

There is evidence, however, suggestive of an abnormal protein in schizophrenia which is not due to artifact. Studies based on plasma fractionation,[28a] animal experiments, and immunology are continuing in an effort to better define this substance.

Although it has not been substantiated that there is any special oxidative pattern for epinephrine that is characteristic for schizophrenia, there is no evidence against it.[33b,33c] This hypothesis remains an attractive one because it encompasses the contribution of psychologic factors as well as the chemical; the secretion of this compound is increased by psychologic stress, and a defect in its oxidation might conveniently account for schizophrenia.

The study of amino acids and amines[33a] in the genesis of schizophrenia has been plagued by failure to control against many possible artifacts, and though research, especially by utilization of chromatography, is proceeding, nothing has yet been proven characteristic of these patients.

The absence of any conclusive findings prevents biochemistry from contributing to the primary prevention of this disorder. It may be that further research will provide information which will be useful in this direction, but that it will do so is by no means certain. The usefulness of any future discovery of a specific metabolic error will depend on the exact nature of the error in question. If some substance is discovered to occur in excess, or another is shown to be lacking, if some abnormal variation of yet a third substance is being produced, perhaps production can be reduced, the deficiency remedied, or the abnormal variant suppressed by some means.

Such means might well prove highly complex to devise. Before any of them would be useful in a program of primary prevention, the biochemical defect would have to be demonstrable by a test sufficiently simple so that it could be employed on a wide scale. Without some treatment to remedy the biochemical defect and without some ready device for detecting it, that much to be desired biochemical discovery would be useful only as a basis for treatment in the phases of secondary or tertiary prevention.

Social measures

Of more immediate promise in the primary prevention of schizophrenia than the findings in genetics and biochemistry are certain conclusions from sociology. The specific etiology of this disorder remains obscure, but the social environment in which it is most likely to occur has become ever more clearly defined over the past twenty years. We now know, for example, that schizophrenic psychoses occur with great frequency in areas characterized by social and family disorganization.[21] It has been demonstrated that the highest incidence and prevalence of these disorders occur among the lower classes.[68,45] A tentative hypothesis can be entertained that the occurrence of schizophrenia (as well as other mental ills) might be substantially reduced by measures which would promote greater stability and reduce deprivation in the population particularly vulnerable, i.e., the slum dwellers in the city centers. It has been objected, however, that the high prevalence of the disorder in the city centers is the consequence of schizophrenia rather than a true indicator of something schizophrenogenic in these areas—namely, that schizophrenic persons are likely either to move away from their families or else be ejected by them, and that these crippled persons migrate toward the lower socioeconomic areas by virtue of their impaired capacity to get along in our complex society. There is evidence to support both points of view.[30]

The development of community mental health centers under the National Mental Health Acts of 1963 and 1965 will provide increased resources for public education and sensitization in regard to mental illnesses. Programs for parent education and surveys of mental health needs are underway as a part of their first work, but there is a long history of projects for parent education.[26,41,47,51]

Basing their efforts on the assumption that effective intervention during periods of life crisis may set the course for more healthy adaptation and prevent a regressive development leading to a schizophrenic breakdown, Caplan has formulated a program for mental health consultation in schools, industry, obstetrical and other medical clinics.[41] The hope that increasing sophistication about the importance of stress in the precipitation of emotional breakdowns, and belief in the prophylactic value of effective counseling, has led to various studies and programs to recruit clergy and others in the task of primary prevention.[50]

Child Guidance

What can be said about the effectiveness of child guidance clinics in the prevention of schizophrenia? These centers were extensively developed after the second world war, and follow-up studies are now becoming increasingly possible. There is regrettably little data on which to draw any conclusions as yet. There is one report to the effect that among patients referred to a child guidance clinic thirty years previously, the prevalence of psychiatric disease was the same as that in a group of matched controls.[53]

Psychologic and Family Investigations

As early as 1894 Freud challenged the fatalistic view of psychoses which was so characteristic of French psychiatry—the view that these illnesses were deteriorations predetermined by an inferior heredity.[22] He described paranoia as a defense, necessary to maintain psychic equilibrium in the face of overwhelmingly distressing memories. He subsequently developed a patient centered point of view which has largely dominated the psychologic studies of schizophrenia until recent years, when analysis of the interaction in selected families wherein schizophrenia occurs has begun to occupy the attention of a variety of workers.

Freud took the view that there are two sorts of pathogenic determinants in the production of mental ills—constitutional and environmental. Of the former he wrote that full understanding could only come about from further biologic research.[24] Although he placed more weight on the physical factors than some later psychoanalytic writers, he did not attribute the capacity for developing a neurosis to these alone, but described their cooperation with experiences in infancy in the development of a libidinal fixation which established later vulnerability to illness.

He separated dementia praecox from obsessional and hysterical disorders by noting that the psychotic patients had a certain capacity in libidinal economy which the others did not, namely capacity for massive decathexis of other persons, and the turning of the libido back on to the ego. He viewed this operation as a regression to the early narcissistic period of infancy, and ascribed it to a weak spot in development, i.e., a fixation.[25] He again referred to this early fixation when writing about Schreber's psychosis, and suggested that in dementia praecox, the fixation lay even further back in the developmental continuum than in paranoia.[23]

In outlining the peculiarities of narcissism in these patients, and in directing attention to the earliest weeks of life, Freud implied certain questions which have continued to occupy students of schizophrenia. What from the environment can be said to contribute to fixation at the infantile level? What experience in early life promotes narcissism of this degree?

Abraham took the view that from earliest life those persons destined to develop dementia praecox were limited in their capacity to transfer their libido to others, and thereby anticipated certain later American studies in the psychoses of childhood.[1]

It is certainly a mistake to equate schizophrenia as it occurs in adults with the so-called schizophrenia of childhood; these disorders may have little more in common than a name and certain manifest characteristics in behavior. There is one group of children, however, that display to a degree of extreme exaggeration the diminished capacity to invest libido in others, namely those suffering from autism of early childhood as described by Kanner.[37] Confused as the nosologic problem may be in the description of psychoses in childhood, psychosis in a child probably cannot be properly diagnosed unless there is a severe impairment in capacity to relate to others. Although adequate follow-up studies of psychotic children are few, there is evidence that upon maturation, many of the children which fit Kanner's diagnostic criteria are not distinguishable from chronic simple schizophrenics.[18]

Although one could suggest the hypothesis that such children are limited in the capacity to advance beyond the point of primitive narcissism, whereas adult schizophrenics regress to the same point when breaking out into the psychosis, there is little evidence in support of the idea. Students of these disorders of childhood are divided between those who concentrate their attention on the early relationships between mother and child, and those who pursue a physiologic explanation. The research in both directions is still very much an on-going affair.

For some years those workers who concentrated their attention on the environment of the infant tended to emphasize the pathologic effect of certain patterns in mothering. The concept of a "schizophrenogenic mother" emerged, the near witch who unconsciously exploited and mistreated her little child for selfish satisfactions of her own. This work has been reviewed by Reichard and Tillman.[56] In contrast, Mahler professes her incapacity to properly weigh the relative importance of constitution and the mother's psychopathology in the genesis of a childhood psychosis, noting that in many instances the mother does not appear to lack warmth, love, or acceptance for her child, nor does she appear to be exceptionally possessive, infantilizing, or restrictive.[48]

Other workers, notably Bender, take the view that schizophrenia is a life long disorder of the whole organism, manifesting itself by disturbances in central nervous system function at every level, and manifesting itself in different ways at different periods in life. She places considerable emphasis on hereditary factors.[6]

Among the most enlightening studies is that of Goldfarb,[28] which suggests that "schizophrenia" in childhood should be divided into two general classes.

He presents convincing data for the establishment of this division. In one class he would place those children with nonintact central nervous systems. The ego deficits and primary behavioral incapacities observed clinically are the result of central nervous system pathology. In the other group he would place those children with unimpaired central nervous system functioning, whose ego deficits and behavioral difficulties are the functional reflections of the psychosocial inadequacy of the families in which they are reared. This study stands out above many others in that it is carefully controlled and statistically well analyzed.

Goldfarb's work emphasizes the importance of the interplay between the child's basic neurologic endowment and the environment in which he grows up; neurophysiologic studies are now becoming available which establish without doubt that at least in cats, functional connections in the visual cortex present at birth pass through a susceptible stage during maturation, when they are dependent on a normal visual imput. Newborn kittens which have one eye covered, whether to exclude all light or to permit only patterned input (i.e., form vision), will be blind in the deprived eye after several months. When these animals are examined with single cell recording methods, it is found that the deprived eye retains practically no functional connections to cortical neurons.[73,34,72,27] Further research may reveal a similar interplay between the early emotional environment of children and their neuronal organization as maturation proceeds.

British workers continue to emphasize the importance of the mother-child interaction in the genesis of schizophrenia. Winnicott takes the view that the environment is so vitally important during early infancy that schizophrenia may be viewed as a "sort of environmental deficiency disease," since a perfect environment at the start can "at least theoretically" be expected to enable an infant to make the initial emotional or mental development which predisposes to mental health in later life.[74] Rosenfeld concluded on the basis of his analytic experience that psychogenic trauma in infancy plays an important part, although he seems to make some room for constitutional factors.[60]

Departing somewhat from earlier workers who emphasized the hostility and anxiety in the relationship between mother and child is Searles who has had extensive experience in psychoanalytically oriented psychotherapy with schizophrenic patients. In his view it is the ambivalence in which the two are bound which leads to schizophrenic development in later life. He emphasizes the intensity of love which the little child feels for its mother, a love which drives him to collaborate with her in his own psychologic destruction rather than resisting her unconsciously determined ravages. He further emphasizes the excitement and pleasure which the patient may experience in himself perpetuating and inviting the pathologic interaction. Searles states that "the initiating of any kind of interpersonal interaction which tends to foster emotional conflict in the other person—which tends to activate various areas of his personality in opposition to one another—tends to drive him crazy (i.e. schizophrenic)."[64] He shares a point of view with other workers who have concentrated on total family studies rather than on the treatment of individual patients, namely that not the mother alone, but other family members as well, have their parts to play in the generation of schizophrenia. The agreement between Searles and these other workers, who have approached the problem with a different research method, is stimulating and suggestive.

The workers who have concentrated on the total interaction of the family include Bowen,[8,9] Lidz,[46] Bateson,[5] Jackson,[35] Wynne[75] and others. Their clinical findings are in close agreement, although terminologically they tend to differ.

Theodore Lidz[46] and his co-workers have concentrated on the detailed, long-term study of schizophrenic patients and their families and have concluded that these patients almost always come from strife-ridden or markedly eccentric home environments. They stress the importance of the family as the agency through which certain "cultural instrumentalities," essential for successful adult social integration, are transmitted. These instrumentalities include language, ways of thinking and reasoning, mores, sentiments, and particular ways of perceiving that "tint" the inborn sense organs. Inasmuch as the acquisition of these instrumentalities depends on interaction and identification with adults who are relatively "expert" in their use, it follows that disturbed family relations may lead to disturbed ways of relating to the outside world in the child who acquires the peculiar modes of his exceptional parents. The fact that some families impose mutually exclusive demands, provide "inconsistent" emotional experiences, and teach paralogical ways of thinking establishes the basic ground for later schizophrenic development. Lidz refers to the *folie a famille,* reminiscent of the phenomenon observable in certain cases of *folie a deux,* in which one partner in the psychosis, and sometimes more than one, participates in a common delusional system, the renunciation of which by any one member would be disruptive to the family relations. These cases clearly demonstrate how relationships may be more important than reality perception to certain individuals with the requisite narcissistic constitution.[15]

Lidz is similar to other students of family interaction, but more explicit, when he suggests that the importance of the very early mother-child interaction seems less important than the late Oedipal and pre-Oedipal years in the genesis of schizophrenia. The instrumentalities of culture are being acquired during this latter developmental stage. Particular attention is paid to the extreme and peculiar adaptations which can be observed in families as an effort is made to accommodate to the psychopathology of one or another, and sometimes both, of the parents—adaptations which frequently involve a greater or lesser degree of reality repudiation.[46]

Bateson, Jackson, and their associates[5,35] emphasize the importance of a certain kind of communication in the upbringing of schizophrenia-prone individuals which they have named the "double bind." This kind of interaction takes place when verbal communication and nonverbal communication denote opposite meanings. A mother may verbalize love and warmth to her child but reject him when he responds to her words. These writers suggest that a certain inner conflict results in the child in which various alternative choices may be mutually contradictory, but he cannot recognize this fact. The conflict evident in the mother becomes a part of the child himself and can be observed in the thinking of the adult schizophrenic.[5]

From the Wynne group comes the term "pseudomutuality," that manifest family relationship which is engineered to prevent and conceal the conflict and divergence which is always ready to break out. Indiscriminate approval, contradictory and mutually obscuring levels of communication (reminiscent of Bateson's "double bind"), and projection are some of the devices employed to keep up the precarious family balance. The phenomenon of introjection of such strained parental attitudes, with all the contradictions and difficulties implied, these workers are continuing to study. They point out that the anxieties transmitted to the children in such families need not come primarily out of the mother-child relationship itself, but that anxieties and difficulties between the parents may be played out by both mother and father on the child.[75]

Bowen[8,9] and co-workers report similar findings. They take the view that a final schizophrenic development in a family member is the expression of the peculiarities of family relationships, sometimes reaching through three generations. The "symbiotic" relation between mother and child is emphasized, the pair living and acting and being exclusively for each other. This kind of development is dependent upon and takes place within the context of certain kinds of family pressures that make the mother and child turn to each other exclusively. This relationship is suffused with hostility or anxiety, which the mother typically denies, manifesting only loving outward behavior.

The parents are said to cope with their difficulties in closeness by a combination of covert, highly emotional disagreement and formal, overly controlled overt agreement. Frequently they cooperate to maintain an impersonal distance in order to keep their disagreements to a minimum.[8,9]

If we turn our attention away from the damaging effects that some home environments may have on the children who are growing up in them and address ourselves to certain other gross stresses, such as the effect of institutional rearing and early parental loss, we still find little actual proof that such traumata lead to adult mental disorders.[66,67] Spitz and Bowlby[10] have made valuable contributions to our understanding of devastating deprivations and losses in childhood, but their work is not immediately relevant when we inquire if such experiences predispose to later schizophrenic developments. The research is not yet complete.

Some authors argue that such early childhood catastrophies have lasting effects on development, and others argue to the contrary. Skeels has presented evidence from his comparative study of children raised in an orphanage and children removed from the same orphanage after a period of care to suggest that the environment is of great importance, and invites the conclusion that the changes reported by Spitz have long lasting effects.[65]

A recent British report presents evidence that the early loss of a parent has a lasting psychonoxious effect; bereavement in childhood was found to be associated with a higher incidence of schizophrenia and depression than might be expected under normal circumstances.[14]

Completely at variance are other studies. Another British report finds that individuals who had a two year period of childhood institutional care do not differ from a control group in psychiatric disability, psychosocial adjustment, or intelligence.[33]

It is very clear that further careful inquiry into the effects of early parental loss, institutional rearing, and emotional deprivation is indicated. Research of somewhat greater refinement will be necessary before any final conclusions can be drawn, since any pathologic effects of such difficulties are likely to vary with the age of the child and the kind of substitute caring he receives.

It may be that at some point in the future definitive evidence will appear to show that psychologic factors are critically important in the genesis of schizophrenia. Many workers are convinced of this on the basis of their clinical experience, but the matter remains uncertain. What kind of primary preventive program could be devised in the event of some lucid demonstration of this sort?

The belief that psychologic stresses give rise to mental illness has prompted innumerable educational efforts to inform parents, teachers, and others who impinge on growing children. Since 1914 there has been a proliferation in mental health education. Pamphlets, newspaper and magazine articles, television series, motion pictures, university courses, and seminars of considerable sophistication have all played their part. The movement has revolutionized the practice of pediatrics in the United States. This massive educational effort will now be examined with one narrow question in mind, namely, what has it contributed to the primary prevention of schizophrenia?

Education of the public toward the needs of the mentally ill and the mentally retarded has without any doubt been helpful in improving facilities, treatment, and rehabilitation resources. This kind of benefit, however, is more pertinent to questions of secondary and tertiary prevention.

The value of educational efforts to change the ways in which people behave toward each other, and toward developing children, is much more open to question. Television programs, motion picture films and the like have been produced and directed at large, heterogeneous groups of uncertain composition. The evidence is that although such programs inform, they do little to alter deeper attitudes, motivations, and behavior. This will not surprise experienced workers who have an appreciation for the force of the unconscious, and who know that neurotic patterns are given up with the greatest of reluctance, even after prolonged psychotherapy.[69,52]

An example of such an effort is provided by a pamphlet disseminated by the Louisiana State Association for Mental Health. This pamphlet, depicting moments in the life of a pelican named Pierre, was distributed to expectant mothers. Although the follow-up report indicated that the information was helpful to those who responded, only half of the sample did indeed respond, and the utility of the effort is at best doubtful.

Balser in New York[3,4] and Gildea[26] subjected small groups to a seminar on mental health principles. Tests of participating individuals, before and after the seminars, suggested that some positive gains in the mental health of the persons involved did take place, but the usefulness of educational technics most certainly remains in doubt when the intent is to improve mental functioning and to prevent disorders. This is demonstrated by an excellent review from Pennsylvania.[54] Mental health educators, public relations consultants, science writers, and representatives of the mental health professions participated in a conference, the published report of which leaves one with the distinct impression that there is no evidence that any known form of mental health education is effective in the prevention of any kind of mental illness.

"Even if we could be sure, for instance, that changes in attitude and action were related education-wise, which is better to start with? Using what media? The honest answer appears to be that we do not know. In planning we have not been able to relate specific techniques with specific target groups—far less to describe how these might be related to each other. Such issues are made vivid across the country in both the wide range of educative programs and the intensity with which program extremes are defended. Nevertheless, among planners and practitioners alike, there goes a predilection for hypotheses to test as contrasted with conviction to be demonstrated. . . . Such education for mental health may be likened to public health educational activities designed to build sound bodies. For sound bodies the requisite nutriments, minerals and vitamins are identified while the comparable ingredients with which to build sound minds are not known. Specific research evidence of the validity and effectiveness of present mental health educational programs is almost non-existent." (*Ibid.*, pp. 113-114)

Inspection of the views, theories, and findings of those who tend to emphasize the importance of the childhood environment in the generation of schizophrenia, from Freud and Abraham through the most modern studies, raises awesome questions when one considers what steps might be taken in the primary prevention of this disorder if one or another of them is correct.

What can be done to prevent psychologic fixation at the early, narcissistic-phase? How can one best promote the capacity of a little child to invest love and trust in others, and discourage his tendency to keep all his libido turned in upon himself? What can be done to reduce the tendency of some mothers to treat their babies like dolls, and to use them only for their own narcissistic gratification, forgetting the needs of the child in the process? What can be done to change the attitudes of invasive, infantilizing, overindulgent, or otherwise destructive mothers and fathers? How can we promote the correct transmission of cultural instrumentalities in families where they are likely to become distorted? The reduction of "double-bind" communications and the diminution of "pseudomutual" marital relationships would all be desirable.

The present means at hand are not adequate to the task. Presently available educational, psychiatric and social work technics make the psychologic reeducation of one family alone a formidable task, and the personnel required to carry out such projects on a large scale would far exceed what is presently available. It seems appropriate to note that some individuals are clearly not reeducable, and that our present technics often prove sorry weapons indeed when they are turned against the tremendously strong narcissistic defenses erected by some individuals. An additional problem is encountered when one considers the difficulty in selecting in advance those families in which schizophrenic illnesses are destined to occur, so that the preventive efforts can be directed to the proper breeding grounds of schizophrenia, and in sufficient time.

Clearly any effective primary preventive program would have to await the development of revolutionary new technics, effective for changing human nature on a large scale.

SECONDARY PREVENTION

Secondary prevention refers to the early detection and prompt treatment of new cases of a disorder. There is abundant evidence that prompt diagnosis and vigorous treatment of schizophrenia alters the clinical course in a favorable direction.[7]

Present practice in the United States reflects this point of view. Typically each case of schizophrenia is considered treatable, and some combination of psychotherapy, drugs, and milieu will be brought to bear, according to the resources available and the requirements of a given patient. This eclectic approach is in general not modified by the physician's basic orientation, whether his interest lies in psychoanalytic-psychologic understanding, the biology of psychosis, or the sociology of mental disease; the treatment is largely empirical in its design and nonspecific in its attack.

Obviously this kind of treatment program is not selective, and little effort is made to differentiate between the different kinds of schizophrenic states. Whether early detection and treatment are really valuable for all cases we do not know. If an aggressive approach of this sort is useful for those cases which might be described as schizoid or schizophreniform, is it equally useful for "process schizophrenia" or "reactive psychosis"?[43,44,71]

More precise studies might well lead to refinements in our use of treatment resources. It might emerge, for instance, that schizoid forms respond well to psychotherapy, while the process schizophrenics continue to deteriorate in spite of treatment by depth psychology. It might also appear that the process schizophrenic can benefit to some extent from the judicious use of drugs, milieu, and environmental manipulation, while the schizoid, though influenced by such measures, can recover with less intensive efforts of that sort. Such a discovery would lead to more efficient and effective deployment of the available personnel; psychotherapy would be reserved for those who could best benefit from it, and intensive nursing activity and social work would not be wasted on those who did not really require it for recovery.[2,16,17,31,40]

It is obvious from this discussion that some refinement in diagnosis is required for any such replanning of therapeutic activities. There is no great interest or effort directed into careful diagnosis in most United States centers, and skills would have to be developed for the correct subdivision of the various schizophrenic states in order to make such a reorganization of treatment possible.

It is the new cases of psychotic breakdown which should receive the greater share of the available therapeutic attention. This is particularly true in terms of the distribution of available psychotherapy. If a schizophrenic illness persists in a form so severe that institutional care is needed for a period of more than one year, the chances for significant recession of the symptoms are small.

Since the details of intensive treatment of schizophrenic illness will be elaborated elsewhere in this volume, suffice it to say that therapy should be begun early, that it should be energetic, and that all therapeutic approaches that give promise of help in a given case should be brought to bear. Psychotherapy has its place as one of these therapeutic approaches, but special modifications are indicated when schizophrenia is the diagnosis. This technic has been described elsewhere.[19]

TERTIARY PREVENTION

In spite of the best efforts, and sometimes because of the lack of them, a large number of patients who suffer from a schizophrenic disorder remain in the hospital for a prolonged period. To confine their impairments and disabilities to those inherent in the illness and to avoid those which follow from institutional mismanagement, family crisis, and social rejection is the work of tertiary prevention.

All too commonly deterioration and the development of irreversible withdrawal follows upon prolonged institutional care. The management of chronic schizophrenic patients follows the custodial model of the 19th century in most of our hospitals.[64] Further investigation into the management of chronic mental illness is very much in order; special procedures appropriate to this group need to be devised. Perhaps our concepts about the correct management of long term mental illness will be radically revised in the near future.[57,58,59]

THE SCHIZOPHRENIC SYNDROME

IN SUMMARY

Interest in primary prevention continues to occupy an important sector of the efforts to eradicate the schizophrenias from our population.

Extensive efforts to detect some specific disorder of genetic origin are under way, but to date no consensus has been reached. We believe that these efforts will continue, and how a hypothetical metabolic error might form the basis of a program of prevention is discussed, as well as the problems such a program might entail, depending on the nature of the abnormality, if one does exist.

It is obvious from our survey that interest in depth psychology as a basis for a program of primary prevention is presently focused on social application, via parental education, of the insights obtained from a study of growth and development and of parent-child relationships by psychoanalysts and other dynamically oriented mental health professionals.

BIBLIOGRAPHY

1. Abraham, Karl: Selected Papers on Psychoanalysis. New York, Basic Books 64-79, 1953.

2. Appleton, William S.: The snow phenomenon: Tranquilizing the assaultive. Psychiatry 28: 88-93, 1965.

3. Balser, Benjamin H., Brown, Fred, Brown, Minerva L., Laski, Leon, and Phillips, Donald K.: Further report on experimental evaluation of mental hygiene techniques in school and community. Am. J. Psychiat. 113: 733-739, 1957.

4. Balser, Benjamin H., Brown, Fred, Brown, Minerva L., Joseph, Edward D., and Phillips, Donald K.: Preliminary report of a controlled mental health workshop in a public school system. Sept. 1953-Feb., 1954. Am. J. Psychiat. 112: 199-205, 1955.

5. Bateson, Gregory, Jackson, Don D., Haley, Jay, and Weakland, John: Toward a theory of schizophrenia. Behav. Sci. 1: 251-264, 1956.

6. Bender, Lauretta: Schizophrenia in childhood. Its recognition, description and treatment. Am. J. Orthopsychiat. 26: 499-506, 1956.

7. Bond, Earl D.: Results of psychiatric treatment with a control series; A 25 year study. Am. J. Psychiat. 110: 561-566, 1954.

8. Bowen, Murray, Dystinger, Robert H., and Basamania, Betty: The role of the father in families with a schizophrenic patient. Am. J. Psychiat. 115: 1017-1020, 1959.

9. Bowen, Murray: A family concept of schizophrenia. In Don D. Jackson (Ed.) The Etiology of Schizophrenia. New York, Basic Books 346-372, 1960.

10. Bowlby, John: Grief and mourning in infancy and early childhood. The Psychoanalytic Study of the Child 15: 9-52, 1960.

11. Caplan, Gerald: Principles of Preventive Psychiatry. New York, Basic Books 1964.

12. Caplan, Gerald: Mental hygiene work with expectant mothers. Ment. Hyg. 35: 41-50.

13. Caplan, Gerald: Patterns of parental response to the crisis of premature birth: A preliminary approach to modifying the mental health outcome Psychiatry 23: 365-374.

14. Dennehy, Constance, M.: Childhood bereavement and psychiatric illness. Brit. J. Psychiat. 112: 1049-1069, 1966.

15. Deutsch, Helene: Folie a deux. Psychoan. Quart. 7: 307-318, 1938.

16. DiMascio, Alberto: Paradoxical drug effects: The role of personality. Paper presented at 4th World Congress of Psychiatry, Madrid, Spain, Sept. 8-11, 1966.

17. DiMascio, Alberto: Personality factors and variability of response to chlorpromazine. Paper presented at 35th An-

nual Meeting of the Eastern Psychological Assoc., Philadelphia, Penna., April 16-18, 1964.

18. Eisenberg, Leon: The course of childhood schizophrenia. A.M.A. Arch. Neurol. & Psychiat. 78: 69-83, 1957.

19. Ewalt, Jack R.: Psychotherapy of schizophrenic reactions. In Jules Masserman (Ed.) Current Psychiatric Therapies. New York, Grune & Stratton, Vol. 3, 150-170, 1963.

20. Ewalt, Jack R., Zaslow, Stephen, and Stevenson, Patricia: How non-psychiatric physicians can deal with psychiatric emergencies. Ment. Hosp. 15: 194-196, 1964.

21. Faris, R. E. L., and Dunham, H. W.: Mental Disorders in Urban Areas. Chicago, University of Chicago Press, 1939.

22. Freud, Sigmund: Further remarks on the neuropsychoses of defense (1896). Standard Edition 3: 174-185. London, Hogarth Press, 1962.

23. Freud, Sigmund: Psychoanalytic notes on an autobiographical account of a case of paranoia (Dementia Paranoides). (1911). Standard Edition, 12: 9-82. London, Hogarth Press, 1958.

24. Freud, Sigmund: The disposition to obsessional neurosis (1913). Standard Edition 12: 313-326. London, Hogarth Press, 1958.

25. Freud, Sigmund: Introductory Lectures on Psychoanalysis (Part III) (1916-1917). Standard Edition 16: 412-430. London, Hogarth Press, 1963.

26. Gildea, Margaret C. L., Domke, Herbert R., Mensh, Ivan N., Buchmueller, A. D., Glidewell, John C., and Kantor, Mildred B.: Community Mental Health Research: Findings After Three years. Am. J. Psychiat. 114: 970-976, 1958.

27. Goldfarb, William: Receptor preferences in schizophrenic children. A.M.A. Arch. Neurol. and Psychiat. 76: 643-652, 1956.

28. Goldfarb, William: Childhood Schizophrenia. Cambridge, Mass. Harvard University Press, 1961.

28a. Gottlieb, Jacques, Frohman, Charles E., and Beckett, Peter G. S.:

Characteristics of a serum factor in schizophrenia. In Max Rinkel (Ed.) Biological Treatment of Mental Illness. New York, L. C. Page & Co., 334-354, 1966.

29. Gurin, Gerald, Veroff, Joseph, and Feld, Sheila: Americans View Their Mental Health. (The Joint Commission on Mental Illness and Health Monograph Series, No. 4) New York, Basic Books, 1960.

30. Hare, E. H.: Family setting and the urban distribution of schizophrenia. J. Ment. Sci. 102: 753-760, 1956.

30a. Heath, Robert G., Marten, Sten, Leach, Byron E., Cohen, Matthew, and Angel, Charles: Effect on behavior in humans with the administration of taraxein. Am. J. Psychiat. 114 14-24, 1957.

30b. Heath, Robert G. (Ed.) Serological Fractions in Schizophrenia. New York, Harper & Row, 1963.

30c. Heath, Robert G., and Krupp, Iris M.: Schizophrenia as an immunologic disorder: I. Demonstration of antibrain globulins by fluorescent antibody techniques. Arch. Gen. Psychiat. 16: 1-9, 1967.

30d. Heath, Robert G., Krupp, Iris M:, Byers, Lawrence, W., and Liljekvist, Jan I.: Schizophrenia as an immunologic disorder: II. Effects of serum protein fractions on brain function. Arch. Gen. Psychiat. 16: 10-23, 1967.

30e. Heath, Robert G., Krupp, Iris M., Byers, Lawrence, W., and Liljekvist, Jan L.: Schizophrenia as an immunologic disorder: III. Effects of anti-monkey and anti-human brain antibody on brain function. Arch. Gen. Psychiat. 16: 24-33, 1967.

31. Heninger, George, DiMascio, Alberto, and Klerman, Gerald L.: Personality factors in variability of response to phenothiazines. Am. J. Psychiat. 121: 1091-1094, 1965.

32. Heston, Leonard, L.: Psychiatric disorders in foster home reared children of schizophrenic mothers. Brit. J. Psychiat. 112: 819-825, 1966.

33. Heston, L. L., Denney, D. D., and Pauly, I. B.: The adult adjustment of per-

sons institutionalized as children. Brit. J. Psychiat. 112: 1103-1110, 1966.

33a. Hoagland, Hudson: Introduction, Chapter 17. *In* Biological Treatment of Mental Illness. Max Rinkel (Ed.) New York, L. C. Page & Co., 317-322, 1966.

33b. Hoffer, Abram, and Osmond, Humphrey: The adrenochrome model and schizophrenia. J. Nerv. Ment. Dis. 128: 18-35, 1959.

33c. Hoffer, Abram, Osmond, Humphrey, Smythies, John: Schizophrenia: A new approach. J. Ment. Sci. 100: 29-45, 1954.

34. Hubel, David H., and Wiesel, Torsten, N.: Receptive fields of cells in striate cortex of very young, visually inexperienced kittens. J. Neurophysiol. 26: 994-1002, 1963.

35. Jackson, Don D.: A critique of the literature on the genetics of schizophrenia. *In* The Etiology of Schizophrenia (Ed.) Don D. Jackson, New York, Basic Books, 37-87, 1960.

36. Kallman, Franz J.: The genetics of mental illness. *In* American Handbook of Psychiatry (Ed.) Silvano Arieti. New York, Basic Books, 1959, Vol. 1, 175-196.

37. Kanner, Leo: Autistic disturbances of affective content. Nerv. Child, 2: 217-250, 1943.

38. Karlsson, Jon L.: The Biologic Basis of Schizophrenia. Springfield, Illinois, Charles C. Thomas, 1966.

39. Kety, Seymour S.: Recent biochemical theories of schizophrenia. Int. J. Psychiat. 1: 409-446, 1965.

40. Klerman, Gerald L., DiMascio, Alberto, Rinkel, Max, and Greenblatt, Milton: The influence of specific personality patterns on the reactions to phrenotropic agents. *In* Biological Psychiatry, (Ed.) Jules Masserman, New York, Grune & Stratton, 1959, Vol. 1, 224-242.

41. Kotinsky, Ruth, and Witner, Helen L. (Eds.): Community Programs for Mental Health: Theory, Practice, Evaluation. Cambridge, Mass., Harvard University Press, 1955.

42. Kringlen, Einar: Schizophrenia in twins: An epidemiological-clinical study. Psychiatry 29: 172-184, 1966.

43. Langfeldt, Gabriel: The Schizophreniform States. Copenhagen, E. Munksgaard, 1939.

44. Langfeldt, Gabriel: The prognosis in schizophrenia and factors influencing the course of the disease. Acta Psychiat. Neurol. Suppl. 13, 1937.

45. Leighton, Alexander H.: My Name Is Legion: Foundations for a Theory of Man in Relation to Culture. (Stirling County Study of Psychiatric Disorder and Sociocultural Environment, Vol. I) New York, Basic Books, 1959.

46. Lidz, Theodore, Fleck, Stephen, and Cornelison, Alice: Schizophrenia and the Family. New York, International Universities Press, 1965.

47. MacLeod, A. W., Silverman, B., and Poland, Phyllis: The well-being clinic. Am. J. Psychiat. 113: 795-800, 1957.

48. Mahler, Margaret S.: On child psychosis and schizophrenia: Autistic and symbiotic infantile psychoses. The Psychoanalytic Study of the Child 7: 286-305. New York, International Universities Press, 1952.

49. Marks, Paul A.: Thalassemia syndromes: Biochemical, genetic and clinical aspects. New Eng. J. Med. 275: 1363-1369, 1966.

50. McCann, Richard V.: The Churches and Mental Health. (The Joint Commission on Mental Illness and Health, Monograph Series No. 8). New York, Basic Books, 1962.

51. Miles, Harold C., and Gardner, Elmer A.: A psychiatric case register. Arch. Gen. Psychiat. 14: 571-580, 1966.

52. Nunnally, J. C., and Osgood, C. E.: The development and change of popular conceptions of mental health phenomena. Final Report, Mental Health Project. Institute of Communications Research, University of Illinois, 1960, (mimeographed).

53. O'Neal, Patricia, and Robins, Lee N.: The relation of childhood behavior problems to adult psychiatric status: A 30 year follow-up study of 150 subjects. Am. J. Psychiat. 114: 961-969, 1958.

54. Pennsylvania Mental Health, Inc.

(The Cornell Conference). Mental Health Education — A Critique. Pennsylvania Mental Health Inc., 1960.

55. Planansky, Karel: Heredity in schizophrenia. J. Nerv. Ment. Dis. 122: 121-142, 1955.

56. Reichard, Suzanne, and Tillman, Carl: Patterns of parent-child relationships in schizophrenia. Psychiatry, 13: 247-257, 1950.

57. Reiss, David: Individual thinking and family interaction: I. Introduction to an experimental study of problem solving in families of normals, character disorders, and schizophrenics. Arch. Gen. Psychiat. 16: 80-93, 1967.

58. Reiss, David: Individual thinking and family interaction: II. A study of pattern recognition and hypothesis testing in families of normals, character disorders, and schizophrenics. 1966. (Unpublished paper).

59. Reiss, David: Individual thinking and family interaction. III. An experimental study of categorization performance in families of normals, character disorders, and schizophrenics. 1966. (unpublished paper).

60. Rosenfeld, Herbert A.: Psychotic States. New York, International Universities Press, 166-168, 1965.

61. Rosenthal, David: Some factors associated with concordance and discordance with respect to schizophrenia in monozygotic twins. J. Nerv. Ment. Dis. 129: 1-10, 1959.

62. Sachar, Edward J., Cobb, Jeremy C., and Shor, Ronald E.: Plasma cortisol changes during hypnotic trance. Arch. Gen. Psychiat. 14: 482-490, 1966.

63. Sachar, Edward J., Mason, John W., Fishman, Jacob R., Hamburg, David A., and Handlon, Joseph H.: Corticosteroid excretion in normal young adults living under basal conditions. Psychosm. Med. 27: 435-445, 1965.

64. Searles, Harold F.: Collected Papers on Schizophrenia and Related Subjects. New York, International Universities Press, 1965.

64a. Schwartz, M. S., and Schwartz, C.

G.: Social Approaches to Mental Patient Care. New York, Columbia University Press, 1964.

65. Skeels, Harold M.: Adult status of children with contrasting early life experiences. Monogr. Soc. Res. Child Develop., Vol. 31, No. 3, 1966.

66. Spitz, Rene A.: Anaclitic Depression. The Psychoanalytic Study of the Child 2:313-342, 1946.

67. Spitz, Rene A.: Hospitalism. An Inquiry into the Genesis of Psychiatric Conditions in Early Childhood. The Psychoanalytic Study of the Child 1: 53-74, 1945.

68. Srole, Leo, Lang, Thomas S., Michael, Stanley T., Opler, Marvin K., and Rennie, Thomas A. C.: Mental Health in the Metropolis. (Mid-town Manhattan Study, Vol. II). New York, McGraw Hill, 1962.

69. Star, Shirley A.: National opinion research center study. In Psychiatry, the Press and the Public: Problems in Communication. Am. Psychiat. Assoc., Washington, D. C. American Psychiatric Association, 1-5, 1956.

70. Tienari, Pekka: Psychiatric illnesses in identical twins. Acta Psychiat. Scand. 39: Suppl. 171, 1963.

71. Vaillant, George E.: The natural history of the remitting schizophrenics. Am. J. Psychiat. 120: 367-376, 1963.

72. Wiesel, Torsten, N., and Hubel, David H.: Single cell responses in striate cortex of kittens deprived of vision in one eye. J. Neurophysiol. 26: 1003-1017, 1963.

73. Wiesel, Torsten, N., and Hubel, David H.: Effects of visual deprivation on morphology and physiology of cells in the cat's lateral geniculate body. J. Neurophysiol. 26: 978-993, 1963.

74. Winnicott, Donald W.: Collected Papers. New York, Basic Books, 162, 1958.

75. Wynne, Lyman C., Ryckoff, Irving M., Day, Juliana, and Hirsch, Stanley I.: Pseudomutuality in the family relations of schizophrenics. Psychiatry 21: 205-220, 1958.

EPILOGUE

LEOPOLD BELLAK

It is extremely unlikely that many a reader will have read through this volume from beginning to end. Even browsing or selective reading will have impressed on him the complexity of the schizophrenic syndrome as portrayed in the broad panorama of the contributions to this volume.

The epidemiological importance of schizophrenia is made abundantly clear. This is one area in which some progress has been made. The development of some uniformity in case recording, the use of model reporting institutions gives some more definitive shape to the important statistical aspects. A decrease of length of hospitalization and a decrease of ten per cent of hospital resident schizophrenics between 1955 and 1967 is encouraging. It does not invite complacency as data derived from incident studies lead to an estimate of at least two per cent of people born in 1960 having a schizophrenic disorder sometime in their lifetime; and under certain conditions as many as six per cent of them may be so afflicted.

One must also keep in mind that at the end of 1964 schizophrenics accounted for one half of the resident patients in the state and county psychiatric hospitals (and those of the Veterans and the psychiatric ones among the Veterans Administration Hospitals), or for about 250,000 patients on any given day of the year. This is one quarter of all bedpatients (medical, surgical, etc.) in the United States.

A report from NIMH just available as this book goes to press* mentions that mental illness cost the United States 20 billion dollars in 1966 alone. The most modest part of this financial appraisal is the 2.5 billion dollars spent on inpatient care alone, not mentioning outpatient care or home care or the measureable loss of productivity. On the basis of the other statistical figures one must then conclude that about a billion and a quarter dollars were spent on the inpatient care of schizophrenia during 1966,—just a fractional part of what this disorder really cost in dollars and cents alone in one year.

Further progress is obviously urgent. Even better epidemiological appraisal will depend on the development of better diagnostic formulations; these in turn are predicated upon further clarification of etiology and pathogenesis of the syndrome: or, if one agrees with me, on the many different types of etiological and pathogenic factors which may play a primary role, or a role in combination with many other factors in producing the schizophrenic syn-

*Yolles, S., NIMH Report, Medical Tribune, March 11, 1968.

drome. Certainly, no data are presented in the exhaustive reviews in the relevant chapters which could claim definitive support for any etiological or pathogenic notion. Progress over the previous ten years is notable only in the much greater methodological sophistication of current studies in genetic biological, and psychological research. It is my firm belief that no substantive progress has been made because investigators continue to look for one factor to hold true for all schizophrenics instead of examining the large sample for subsamples of differing nature.

This same basic problem still reflects itself of course in the discussion of symptomatology and prognosis. For clarification of the sociocultural aspects, an international research organization is suggested to facilitate at least the kind of standardization of data collection which has made some headway in the United States.

This same need for better classification (and differential diagnosis and prognosis) is also the main conclusion from the review of childhood schizophrenia. Adolescent schizophrenia is reviewed here for the first time as a separate unit, possibly as an outgrowth of the general development of adolescent psychiatry as a subspecialty.

Among the treatment considerations, the growth of the use of psychotropic drugs is the outstanding event. A more systematic appraisal than ever conducted before in controlled and coordinated studies, makes it possible to arrive at more definitive conclusions about their value than has been possible for other therapeutic modalities heretofore. One can conclude that the phenothiazine group has a definite contribution to make to the symptom improvement, length of hospitalization and modification of hospital care, and care outside the hospital of schizophrenic patients.

With the growth of the use of the psychotropic drugs, the employment of other physical treatment modalities has greatly declined, and some of them have for practical purposes disappeared. A point can be made for the possibly excessive decline of electro-convulsive therapy, which might still have appropriate, limited indication under certain circumstances. As there are distinct cycles in therapeutic modes, from overenthusiasm to disappointment to selective rational use, it is quite feasible that there be some increase in the use of ECT again. In fact, at the point of writing, its complete disappearance from some hospitals has already been reversed.

The psychotherapeutic modalities, individual and in groups, have shown the development of some new techniques. An increase in interest in group approaches is consistent with the flourishing of community mental health, the attempt to offer as much help as possible to as many as possible. Parallel to this significant development of the past decade is the emphasis on care of schizophrenics in general hospitals, and in the community itself—in the patient's home and in rehabilitation centers of various kinds.

Increasing attention to attempts at primary, secondary, and tertiary prevention of schizophrenia is bound to be of growing concern in the next decade. It is of course likely to be tied to developments in etiology and pathogenesis (as well as therapeutics). Yet, there are very few-if any-who would deny that a poor social and psychological environment is likely to increase the liability of the manifestation of the schizophrenic syndrome even if genogenic, chemogenic, or histogenic factors should play an important primary role in some. What is more, it is very unlikely that there be much ideological disagreement on what constitutes undesirable sociopsychological circumstances, if one stays for a start at least with the major, gross conditions.

I have not run across anyone who would claim that crowded living conditions, with six or eight people sleeping in one room, are conducive to any kind of mental health, or not likely to precipitate or aggravate whatever liability there might be. I have not heard of anyone who thinks that upbringing by a grossly mentally disturbed parent is beneficial; nor have I heard that death of a parent or other catastrophes are not likely to aggravate whatever liability for mental disturbance there might be, including schizophrenic disorders.

The likelihood then is that community mental health methods designed to minimize the general factors related to mental illness are likely to increase in the coming years, and likely to have an increasing effect on the prevalence of schizophrenic disorders. The economics of psychiatric care alone will be an increasing force for greater attempts of prevention on all levels.

If I should be in a position to edit and write for another volume on schizophrenia ten years hence, as I would like to do, what else might one predict?

In the field of prediction, there are some relatively easy feats and some more difficult ones: a consistency prediction is relatively easy—namely that there will be more of the same: more of a role of community mental health (as discussed for prevention and therapeutic care), more and better psychotropic drugs, and better epidemiological data.

It is more difficult to make predictions of a relative change of trends, and of course the wish is likely to be the father of many expectations. I will not even attempt to deny that my bias enters in, hoping that it will serve as an heuristic bias.

I do not believe that a biochemical or other biological etiology will be found to be basic for *all* forms of the schizophrenic syndrome. On the other hand, I expect that some biological factors will be established for *some* schizophrenics, if there will be central integration and control of studies as I have been recommending for twenty years—especially in the form of a potent schizophrenia research center. I believe that genogenic factors will be found to play a marked role in about 25 per cent of the schizophrenic population, fluctuating in both directions with the degree of sociopsychological disturbance interacting with the genetic liability. I believe that neurological disorders, both of histogenic and chemogenic nature, will be found to contribute a percentage of primary etiological factors to the manifestation of schizophrenic symptoms. Many undiagnosed febrile disorders of infancy and childhood probably will account for some of the morphological changes. Severe lack of neurological maturation in the perceptual and affective and motor field are certainly likely to lead to marked secondary psychopathology. Metabolic biochemical factors will turn out to play a role especially in those psychoses precipitated in adolescence and the climacterium and senescence. I am fairly certain that purely psychogenic factors will be demonstrated to play the primary role in the etiology and pathogenesis of about 50 per cent of all schizophrenic pathology. These psychogenic factors may vary from those primarily due to gross socioeconomic factors and their impact on the deprived and minorities to gross overstimulation and the subtler disturbances of development in interaction with the parents. Much of schizophrenic pathology may be simply ascribed to a failure of psychogenic ego development or its interference by unfavorable drive development and poor superego structure.

From this set of facts would have to follow attempts at prevention and treatment related to these etiological factors.

No prediction is complete without some hedging: psychiatry does not live within a social vacuum. A social, financial, military upheaval would definitely affect psychiatric progress, mostly negatively. Even minor political trends are likely to reflect themselves in other spheres, including psychiatry. If there should be a marked trend towards political conservatism or reaction, increasingly heavy emphasis on genetic and biological research can be expected. A liberal trend would bring more interest in environmental psychological approaches to etiology and therapy.

Understandably, I have some interest in seeing whether I will be around in a decade to comment on my rashness. Meanwhile, I am willing to take some bets.

Appendix I

Editor's note: In order to decrease the usual publication lag—the writing of a manuscript and its appearance in print—we invited all contributors to send us material which they had overlooked or which had appeared since they wrote their chapters. The material below is published in response to this request. No effort is being made here for uniformity.

—June, 1968

APPENDIX TO CHAPTER 2 BY LEOPOLD BELLAK

At the time of going to press, the plans for further work interrelating ego function patterns to etiology and pathogenesis have taken on some more form.*

Strictly empirical data, including a preliminary analysis of ego psychological profiles, suggest that it might be useful to keep five groups in mind: a) with primary neurological etiology (due to encephalitis-like illness or other inherent disorganization), b) with primary psychogenic factors, c) with primary genetic implication, d) with primary biochemical factors, and e) a residual group of various biological factors.

If it is likely that some schizophrenics might have a primarily neurological involvement, one might pick them up by virtue of their having low stimulus barrier, maybe coexisting with a low score for regulation and control of drives (especially if due to encephalitis-like disorder in infancy) and a low synthetic function and/or low autonomous functions due to perceptual-motor problems like the minimal brain syndrome.

If the ego function profile reveals such a pattern in some schizophrenics, it should then be especially useful to study them by EEG, etc. and see if they cannot be shown to be significantly different neurologically from other schizophrenics not showing such an ego function pattern, or even from a random sample of schizophrenics.

Using groups already known for an apparently marked *genetic* involvement (twin studies), one might be able to compare their ego function patterns to one known to have low genetic involvement or to a random group: it might be possible then in the future to identify other schizophrenics by ego function patterns as primarily genetically caused if one excludes the ones characterized by the neurological pattern and a group identified—by a parallel study—as having a primarily psychogenic etiology and pathogenesis.

I would expect the *psychogenic* group to be significantly lower in object

---

*At the occasion of presenting the current research to the staff of the Division of Extramural Research at the National Institute of Mental Health, June 27, 1968.

relations and sense of reality than others. A cluster of low stimulus barrier, poor regulation and poor control, and low synthetic functioning could be related to psychogenic *or* biological factors.

In order to increase the yield of clues, I would also want to study carefully the individual history of each patient. The presence of an unexplained, severe febrile episode in infancy would suggest neurological involvement and follow-up by EEG. On the other hand, part of the sample with that cluster might reveal a history of early continuous and marked overstimulation by aggressive and sexual impact. (If this latter subgroup of the ego function cluster should then also appear to have a normal EEG in distinction to the first subgroup, we would be further along in identifying some of the subgroups of the schizophrenics by etiology and pathogenesis.) It is conceivable that the psychogenic group might have associated with the triangle of low stimulus barrier, low synthetic functioning and low regulation and control, a low score on defensive functioning, while the neurological subgroup might have a great deal of rigid defensiveness associated with it. If that is so, ego function study alone might permit future identification of etiology and pathogenesis.

This should leave us with the residual group which might indeed have a high percentage of *various other biological components,* including biochemical ones further to be "sieved."

For instance, one might see if this residual group gives a much higher incidence of catecholamine, or other metabolic disturbances, than a random group, or shows a significant difference in terms of serum globulin or erythropoesis or any number of other factors occasionally claimed to be implicated.

A detailed research plan for our own future work and suggestions for an interlocking research scheme along these lines (using centers which have already elaborated sophisticated methods in one given area, neurophysiologic, genetic, biochemical, or psychological) was presented on June 27, 1968, before the Extramural Research Division of the National Institute of Mental Health.

Addendum to bibliographic review:

The Origins of Schizophrenia, John Romano, Ed. Proceedings of the first Rochester International Conference on Schizophrenia, March 29-31, 1967, Amsterdam: Excerpta Medica Foundation, 1967, p. 288.

This is an excellent review of the genetic problems of schizophrenia research with original work reported by E. Kringlen, D. Rosenthal, and S. Mednick, and a review of biochemical and physiological aspects by Kety and others, and a variety of other useful background papers, including family dynamics by Wynn, Thaler, and other psychological studies.

APPENDIX TO CHAPTER 9 BY THOMAS FREEMAN

F. W. Graham has reported that an early sign of motor disorganization in schizophrenia is a disturbance of eye movement. He observed that the eyeball is frequently motionless in relationship to the head for a period of five seconds or longer. This contrasts with the eye of the normal individual which moves several times within four seconds.

Few publications on the signs, symptoms, diagnosis and course of schizophrenia have appeared in 1967 in the American, British or Scandinavian literature. The Royal Medico-Psychological Association of Great Britain published the proceedings of a symposium held in London entitled "Recent Developments in Schizophrenia." Only one contribution (Stengel, 1967) is relevant here even although it deals with the problems of classification. The author specially refers to the classifications of Langfeldt and Leonhard which have been mentioned in this review. He expresses a doubt about the value of constructing classifications when knowledge of etiology is so inadequate. On balance he considers such attempts are necessary if psychiatry is to progress. A short paper by Stierlin (1967) deals with Bleuler's concept of schizophrenia. In this paper an account is given of the changes which Bleuler made in his conception of schizophrenia over the years from 1911 to 1939 and how these changes widened and blurred the boundaries of the concept.

An interesting paper by Chapman (1967) describes the relationship between visual imagery and abnormal motor behavior. This paper is an extension of his earlier paper published in 1966. Lukianowitz (1967) provides a full account of the literature of body image disturbances in the schizophrenias and a statement of those he has personally found in a paper entitled "Body Image Disturbances in Psychiatric Disorders." Finally, a paper by Searles (1967) offers a description of the way in which the schizophrenic patient fragments and de-differentiates perception thus providing a unique mode of experiencing the world.

REFERENCES

Chapman, J.: Visual Imagery and Motor Phenomena in Acute Schizophrenia. Brit. J. Psychiat. 113: 771-778, 1967.

Graham, F. W.: The Clinical Diagnosis of Early Schizophrenia. Med. J. of Aust. 725, 1958.

Lukianowitz, N.: Body Image Disturbances in Psychiatric Disorders. Brit. J. Psychiat. 113: 31-47, 1967.

Scott, R. D. and Ashworth, P. L.: The 'axis value' and the Transfer of Psychosis.

Brit. J. Med. Psychol. 38: 97-116, 1965.

Searles, H. F.: The Schizophrenic Individual's Experience of his World. Psychiatry 30: 119-131, 1967.

Stengel, E.: Recent Developments in Classification. In: Copper, A. and Walk, A. Headley, (Ed.) Recent Developments in Schizophrenia. London, 1967.

Stierlin, H.: Bleuler's Concept of Schizophrenia. Amer. J. Psychiat. 123: 996-1001, 1967.

APPENDIX TO CHAPTER 10 BY LEOPOLD BELLAK AND LAURENCE LOEB

Philip R. A. May, M.D.: Treatment of Schizophrenia. Science House: 1968; p. 352.

This volume by May, with contributions by Aronson, Cole, Distler, Dixon, Feldman, Fine, and Leavitt, offers a brief review of the treatment of schizophrenia by Tuma, but, primarily, gives an account of a large-scale research project concerned with a comparison of the results of different commonly used methods of treatment of schizophrenic patients in a good hospital. 228 schizophrenic patients at Camarillo State Hospital were assigned to 1) individual psychotherapy alone, 2) ataraxic drugs alone, 3) individual psychotherapy plus ataraxic drugs, 4) electroshock, and 5) milieu, a control group which received none of these specific treatments. A great number of methodological precautions were used in order not to contaminate the results.

Basically, it was found that drugs alone and psychotherapy plus drugs were the most effective treatments and the least costly in time and money. Except for greater insight by psychotherapy plus drugs, the differences were insignificant. By cost, "drugs" alone was superior. Psychotherapy alone and milieu were the least effective and the most expensive forms of treatment. ECT occupied an intermediate position. The volume abounds with thoughtful considerations of many aspects of this study, including the suggestion that characteristics of those who do and those who do not respond to a particular treatment need to be identified, among other things, to possibly help identify different types of schizophrenia. Cole, in his discussion, suggests that this excellent study may never be repeated because the weight of its own evidence would make anyone reluctant to treat acutely ill schizophrenics again without drugs, though there may be a number of patients who might indeed do better on milieu therapy or psychotherapy alone.

APPENDIX TO CHAPTER 11 BY MAURICE W. LAUFER AND DONALD S. GAIR

Bettelheim, B.: The Empty Fortress: Infantile Autism and the Birth of the Self. New York: Free Press, 1967, 484 pp., illus.

In this, Bettleheim reiterates his view of autistic behavior as resulting from the interaction of pathogenic parents with a susceptible infant during early, critical phases of development and a therapeutic program geared to reverse this.

Bonnard, A.: Primary Process Phenomena in the Case of a Borderline Psychotic Child. Int. J. of Psychoanal. 48: 221-236, 1967.

A most detailed and thoughtful discussion based upon careful work with such a child.

Call, J. D.: Interlocking Affective Freeze Between an Autistic Child and his "As If" Mother. J. Amer. Acad. Child Psychiat. 2: 319-343, April, 1963.

A failure of appropriate affective communication of mother with child and resultant failure of the child to develop an appropriate affective life and object relations is regarded as the significant etiologic factor, and treatment of child and mother is described.

Des Lauriers, A.: The Schizophrenic Child. Arch. Gen. Psychiat. 16: 194-201, February, 1967.

The author feels that the core defect in a schizophrenic child is a capacity to separate and differentiate himself from his environment or to establish stable relationships to a mother, experienced as being separate and differentiated. He describes a therapeutic approach meant to overcome this.

Eaton, L. and Menolascino, F. J.: Psychotic Reactions of Childhood: A Follow-up Study. Am. J. Orthopsych. XXXVII, 521-529, April, 1967.

Authors present a five-year follow-up study of thirty-two psychotic children. Authors question validity of different diagnostic categories previously proposed. Clinical picture of psychosis results from something which reduces integrative capacities or interferes with a previous level of integration, and clinical subgroups depend on age and stage of development of child at onset of psychosis, underlying protoplasmic endowment and nature of his interpersonal environment.

Fenichel, C.: Mama or M.A.? J. of Spec. Ed. 1: 45-51, 1967.

The author criticizes proposals for using untrained mothers as teacher-aides in dealing with disturbed children in a public school system.

Fish, B.: Maturation of Arousal and Attention in the First Months of Life: A study of Variations in Ego Development J. Amer. Acad. Child Psychiat. 2: 253-270, April, 1963.

The author presents methods for studying these phenomena, depicts the normal course of their development and indicates how their study may offer much of significance in regard to the evolution of childhood schizophrenia, as well as other conditions.

Frommer, E.: A Day Hospital for Disturbed Children under Five. Lancet 377-379, February, 1967.

The author describes such a day hospital unit, which included psychotic children among its patients and involved the parents with encouraging results.

Gittelman, M., and Birch, H.: Childhood Schizophrenia. Arch. Gen. Psychiat. 17: 16-25, July, 1967.

Central nervous system factors were felt to be most significant etiologically, rather than those stemming from parental psychopathology.

Green, A.: Self-Mutilation in Schizophrenic Children. Arch. Gen. Psychiat. 17: 234-243, August, 1967.

Psychodynamic hypotheses are offered to explain the occurrence of such behavior.

Griffith, R. and Ritvo, E.: Echolalia: Concerning the Dynamics of the Syndrome. J. Amer. Acad. Child Psychiat. 6: 184-193, January, 1967.

Winnicott's conception of "transitional objects" and their role between inner and outer representations help to explain this phenomenon.

Harrison, S., Hess, J., Zrull, J.: Paranoid Reactions in Children, J. Amer. Acad. Child Psychiat. 2: 677-692, October, 1963.

Five cases of paranoid delusions in children are presented in detail, and it is felt that such phenomena are more common than recognized, especially at the end of the latency phase in boys with problems with sexual identification and conflicts between impulses toward passive submission and a more aggressively dominating masculine role.

Hewett, F., Mayhew, D. and Rabb, E.: An Experimental Reading Program for Neurologically Impaired, Mentally Retarded and Severely Emotionally Disturbed Children. Amer. J. Orthopsych. XXXVII: 35-48, January, 1967.

This enabled several autistic children to acquire reading skills previously thought impossible.

Hingtsen, J., Coulter, S., and Churchill, D.: Intensive Reinforcement of Imitative Behavior in Mute Autistic Children. Arch. Gen. Psychiat. 17: 36-43, July, 1967.

An operant conditioning approach was used to reinforce imitative responses. This allowed later progression to a possibly more significant, spontaneous behavioral repertoire.

Jenkins, R., and Shoji, T.: Charting Disturbed Children's Behavior. Hosp. Community Psychiat. 230-233, August, 1967.

A diagnostic and evaluative format is presented.

Jensen, G. and Womack, M.: Operant Conditioning Techniques Applied in the Treatment of an Autistic Child. Amer. J. Orthopsych. XXXVII: 30-34, January, 1967.

Authors observed that such techniques not only resulted in gratifying clinical improvement, but also improved morale of therapeutic team.

Kaufman, I.: Crimes of Violence and Delinquency in Schizophrenic Children. J. Amer. Acad. Child Psychiat. 1: 269-283, 1962.

Author discusses the personality structure of such children; the transformation of the fear of being passive and overwhelmed by massive anxiety into the active process of destroying their object relations being at the oral dependent level; and family history.

Kaufman, I. et al.: Delineation of Two Diagnostic Groups Among Juvenile Delinquents: The Schizophrenic and the Impulse-Ridden Character Disorder. J. Amer. Acad. Child Psychiat. 2: 292-318, April, 1963.

The schizophrenic delinquent, whose object relations are at the primary level, is overwhelmed by primary anxiety, wishes to be close to people, fears destruction in the process, and reacts with delinquent phenomena.

Kurtis, L.: Clinical Study of the Response to Nortriptyline on Autistic Children. Int. J. Neuropsychiat. 2: 298-301, August, 1966.

This uncontrolled pilot study suggested that nortriptyline is useful in the symptomatic treatment of autistic children.

Langdell, J.: Family Treatment of Childhood Schizophrenia. Ment. Hyg. 51: 387-392, July, 1967.

The author describes the efficacy of conjoint psychotherapeutic treatment of psychotic child and parents illustrated by the fact that in the course of fourteen years of weekly interviews, a boy between the ages of 16 and 17 was able to take over the task of wiping himself after going to the toilet.

Lebovici, S., and McGougall, J.: Un Cas de Psychose Infantile, Étude Psychanalytique. Paris: Presses Universitaires de France, 1960, 487 pp.

Reviewed by René A. Spitz, J. Amer. Acad. Child Psychiat. 2: 199-204, January, 1963.

The reviewer summarizes the authors' contributions and offers his own concepts as to psychopathology and psychodynamics.

Mahler, M. and Furer, M.: Development of Symbiosis, Psychotic Psychoses, and the Nature of Separation Anxiety. Int. J. Psychoanal. 47: 554-560, 1966.

Authors stress that their concept deals not with physical separation but for normal intrapsychic processes. The "symbiotic" psychotic picture represents a *defense* formation in which the child clings to a representation of the part-object, a concrete symbol substituted for the mother.

Menolascino, F. and Easton, L.: Psychoses of Childhood: A Five Year Follow-Up Study of Experiences in a Mental Retardation Clinic. Amer. J. Ment. Defic. 72: 370-379, November, 1967.

Literature on follow-up studies is reviewed. Their study suggests multiplicity of factors making clear initial diagnosis difficult. "Soft neurological signs" may indicate an ongoing process rather than residuals of "old" central nervous system dysfunction or damage. Speech development does seem significant in prognosis. "Islands of intact functioning" in psychological testing may be misleading. They found no correlation between treatment and prognosis.

McDermott, J., Jr. et al.: Social Class and Mental Illness in Children: The Question of Childhood Psychosis. Amer.

J. Orthopsychiat. XXXVII: 548-557, April, 1967.

This study showed no significant difference in incidence of psychosis according to social class group, unlike other forms of emotional and mental illness.

Meyer, R. and Karon, B.: The Schizophrenogenic Mother Concept and the TAT. Psychiatry 30: 173-179, May, 1967.

The findings are felt to substantiate the belief that when there are conflicting needs between mother and child, mothers of schizophrenics satisfy their own needs.

Nurcombe, B. and Parker, N.: The Idiot Savant. J. Amer. Acad. Child Psychiat. 3: 469-487, 1964.

The "idiot savant" should be regarded as part of a continuum within the autistic and mental defective groups.

O'Gorman, G.: The Nature of Childhood Autism. London: Butterworth's, New York: Appleton-Century-Crofts, 1967.

The author draws on a wealth of experience with severely disturbed youngsters which he presents in 14 case histories to illustrate points made in his eight chapters (125 pages) entitled: 1. What is Childhood Autism? 2. Childhood Schizophrenia. 3. Defense Mechanisms against Intolerable Reality. 4. The Aetiology of Autism. 5. The Symptoms of Autism. 6. The Nature of Autism. 7. The Pseudoschizophrenic Syndromes. 8. Treatment, Education and Training.

However, the book does not live up to the promise of its title. Doctor O'Gorman cites the confusion in definition and labelling of "autism" but uses autism, psychosis, schizophrenia interchangeably. He skillfully criticizes the nine points of Creak et al., rather polemically dismisses Rutter's delimitation of a syndrome of early childhood psychosis while failing to justify his own broadening of the term autism from Kanner's original usage although he credits Kanner with its contribution. His literature references are limited and inadequate to support his bold, but often incomplete, assertions.

His general approach is eclectic and will not mislead the reader clinically in his discussion of diagnostic and management principles which is wise and thorough for the study and care of a large number of very sick children for whom precise understanding and classification are no clearer for this book.

Oliver, B. and O'Gorman, G.: Pica and Blood Lead in Psychotic Children. Devel. Med. Child Neurol. 8: 704-707, 1966.

Such children in long term care frequently display pica and above-normal blood-lead levels, suggesting an area of concern.

Ornitz, E. and Ritvo E.: Perceptual Inconstancy in Early Infantile Autism. Arch. Gen. Psychiat. 18: 76-98, January, 1968.

The authors postulate that early infantile autism, atypical development, symbiotic psychosis and some cases of childhood schizophrenia are based upon faulty homeostatic regulation of perceptual input, and are therefore essentially variants of the same disease.

Pollack, M. and Woerner, M.: Pre- and Peri-natal Complication and "Childhood Schizophrenia." J. Child Psychol.-Psychiat. 7: 235-242, 1966.

Five studies are reviewed and reported to show a significant association between complications of pregnancy and childhood psychosis. Previous reproductive loss, severe postnatal illness and birth complications may also be significant variables. There was no relationship between low birth weight per se and childhood psychosis.

Ritvo, E., Ornitz, E. and Walter, R.: Clinical Application of the Auditory Averaged Evoked Response at Sleep Onset in the Diagnosis of Deafness. Pediatrics 40: 1003-1008, December, 1967.

This technique may help to clarify the presence or absence of deafness in children with emotional disturbance, including infantile autism.

Sachs, L.: Emotional Acrescentism. J. Amer. Acad. Child Psychiat. 1: 636-655, October, 1962.

A condition which reflects emotional deprivation in children who are outgoing, charming, evoking affection from others, but with stunted, corrupt superegos, marked by lacunae, with fleeting hallucinations and immature ego structures, all of which are contrasted with and differentiated from childhood schizophrenics.

Salkin, J. and May, P.: Body Ego Technique: An Educational Approach to Body Image and Self Identity. J. of Spec. Educ. 1: 375-386, Summer, 1967.
A technique which may prove of use with psychotic children.

Schaffer, H. and Emerson, P.: Patterns of Response to Physical Contact in Early Human Development. J. Child Psychol.-Psychiat. 5: 1-13, 1964.

Thirty-seven infants' patterns of and responses to cuddling are reported on. The data is largely derived from careful questioning of mothers in a well-baby clinic population not selected for any presenting problem. On the basis of reports at the children's ages of 12 and 18 months, "cuddlers," "non-cuddlers," and "intermediates" were selected. Only the cuddlers and non-cuddlers were studied and compared. There were 19 cuddlers and 9 non-cuddlers. The well-drawn conclusions of the study strongly indicate that cuddling tendencies are innate and do not correlate significantly with handling preferences of the mothers. Non-cuddler children whose mothers liked to cuddle caused the mothers some initial distress, but all in this group adjusted and accepted this as the child's way without feeling rejected. The factor in the non-cuddler seemed to be a high level of motor restlessness and resistance to being restrained. These children sought human contact and proximity in other ways.

This reference is included because of its relevance to the frequent reports quoting mothers of autistic children as perceiving the child as rejecting and resisting cuddling. From this study, this characteristic appears to be rather widespread among the normal population of infants.

Schowalter, J.: States in Infantile Psychosis. J. Amer. Acad. Child Psychiat. 6: 539-550, July, 1967.

The author concludes that childhood psychoses regardless of etiology can be viewed as developmental disorders of the ego and that the descriptive diagnosis of any psychotic child depends on his position on the spectrum of ego development, determined by the severity of impairment and the age at which it becomes manifest.

Shodell, M.: A Day Center for Severely Disturbed. J. of Rehab. 22-25, July-August, 1967.

The mode of functioning of such a center is described.

Sperling, M.: Some Criteria on the Evaluation of the Treatment Potential of Schizophrenic Children. J. Amer. Acad. Child Psychiat. 2: 593-604, October, 1963.
Ways of evaluating the accessibility of the child for forming some object relationship with the therapist and workability of the parents are presented, and the resulting potential for treatment evaluated.

Stabenau, J. and Pollin, W.: Early Characteristics of Monosygotic Twins Discordant for Schizophrenia. Arch. Gen. Psychiat. 17: 723-733, December, 1967.
Though this study deals with adult patients, it may be significant for the childhood condition. Study suggests that differences in early biologic maturity relate to difference in competence and in turn to the development of schizophrenic symtomatology. The interplay between innate capacities of the child and environmental, familial, and social forces may best explain the development of schizophrenia in one child and not another.

Szurek, S.: The Psychoses of Very Early Life. Int. J. of Psychiat. 3: 380-382, May, 1967.

The author, while maintaining his basic psychoanalytic orientation, calls attention to the significance of Sullivanian theory as to the role of conflictful attitudes of adults in child conflict and the importance of work with the parents to reduce these. He also stressed the need to consider genetic and pathophysiological components as well.

Tessman, L. and Kaufman, I.: Treatment Techniques, the Primary Process and Ego Development in Schizophrenic Children. J. of Amer. Acad. of Child Psychiat. 6: 98-115, January, 1967.

The schizophrenic child confronts the therapist with primary process phenomena, and the authors discuss how the therapist may help the child to deal with this.

Weiss, H. and Born, B.: Speech Training or Language Acquisition, Amer. J. Orthopsych. XXXVII: 49-55, January, 1967.

Authors stress need to differentiate between the overcoming of speech deficits and the actual acquisition of language when operant conditioning methods are used. They also suggest there is a group of children who could better be labelled "linguistically retarded" than "autistic."

Wenar, W. et al.: Changing Autistic Behavior. Arch. Gen. Psychiat. 17: 26-35, July, 1967.

A scale for evaluating autism was presented. With this as a tool, it was found that a small, psychoanalytically oriented day care unit brought about the most improvement in areas of relationship, mastery, and psychosexual development, while no milieu produced changes in communication and vocalization. Progress in general seemed to be area-specified rather than generalizing to other aspects.

Williams, F.: Family Therapy: A Critical Assessment. Amer. J. Orthopsychiat. XXXVII: 912-919, October, 1967.

The utility of this approach is described.

Wolff, P.: The Role of Biological Rhythms in Early Psychological Development. Bull. of Menninger Clin. 31: 197-218, July, 1967.

Speculates that "recognizing the biological substrata of motor mannerisms and devising methods for converting stereotypic mannerisms from global ends into motor means" may be the way to deal with apparently aimless self-sufficient stereotypics in psychotic children and young adults.

Zruss, J.: The Psychotherapy of a Pair of Psychotic Identical Twins in a Residential Setting. J. Amer. Acad. Child Psychiat. 6: 116-136, January, 1967.

The intense interidentification between the twins both contributed to their illness and was used as a focus of treatment.

Appendix II

RATING SCALES FOR SCORING EGO FUNCTIONS FROM CLINICAL INTERVIEW MATERIAL*

GENERAL GUIDE FOR USE OF THE MANUAL

Preceding the specific scales of ego functions, we wish to offer the rater a few suggestions for maximizing reliability and validity of ratings.

First, the way the *ordinal* scales have been constructed is summarized to aid all raters in using them in a uniform manner.

Secondly, there are pointers on how to use the scales for making the most effective *global* ratings.

Finally, a step-by-step *procedure* for using the scales and the interview material in co-ordination, is outlined in detail.

Each scale is preceded by an *Instructions to Raters* section, where the particular ego function is defined; component factors are explicitly delineated; and suggestions are offered as to how to interpret and apply that particular scale as a unique measuring instrument.

Ordinal Scales

Each of the eleven scales is an ordinal scale. The variables being dimensionalized are rank-ordered along a 13-point continuum which are numbered 1, 1.5, 2, 2.5, etc. Scale points 1, 2, 3-7 (called modal stops) are defined in the manual, while points 1.5, 2.5, 3.5, etc. are not defined. Modal stop 1) represents the most maladaptive manifestation of the function being rated, while modal stop 7) represents the most adaptive. While maladaptation-adaptation is the general dimension common to all scales, each scale is also ordered along a specific dimension or set of dimensions (components).

The scales are not equal-interval scales. That is, stop 2) reflects more adaptation than stop 1); stop 3) shows more adaptation than stop 2); and so forth. But stop 2) is not necessarily more adaptive than stop 1) to the same degree that stop 3) is more adaptive than stop 2), (i.e., the scale stops are not equi-distant from one another).

However, an attempt has been made to peg all stops across scales so that

---

they reflect about the same degree of adaptation at any given stop. That is, stop 2) on any given scale is *approximately* equal in maladaptiveness to stop 2) on any given scale. Similarly, stop 6) reflects an approximately equal degree of adaptation from one scale to the next. Thus, strictly speaking, the scales cannot be considered precisely ordinal, but somewhere imprecisely between ordinal and interval scales.

Another point to bear in mind with respect to ordinality is that stops 1) and 7) serve primarily as anchorage points to orient the rater with respect to the two extremes of the dimension(s) he is rating for each function. Rarely will a person's functioning actually correspond to the modal descriptions of each extreme point, so that stops 1) and 7) may infrequently apply to any of the subjects of this study. An exception might be a backward patient of many years standing, who may truly represent a 1) rating on some functions.

A final point about the rank-ordering of modal stops involves the scale placement of "average" functioning. It was decided to consider stop 6), as average. Thus, the meaning of average, as used here, has less to do with the statistical norm of functioning of some known population group but more with a meaning denoting average in the sense of absence of any notable maladaptation, yet just short of optimal. In fact, according to the study by Srole et al. (1963), over 80 per cent of New York City's population suffered from a measurable degree of psychopathology.

Making Global Ratings

The rater's major task is to make an accurate global rating on a 13-point scale for each of 11 ego functions for all subjects interviewed. The following points will serve as guidelines for making the best possible ratings.

1. Each scale is dimensionalized *generally* in terms of least to greatest adaptation. Each individual ego function, however, contributes uniquely to general adaptiveness (overall ego strength). The uniqueness is reflected qualitatively in the modal stops of each individual scale. Keeping in mind the aim of the most accurate global rating, the rater is urged to use whatever information is available (whether systematically or more loosely organized) according to his best overall clinical judgment when he makes his rating.

2. Each scale is based also upon *specific component factors* pertinent to the ego function being rated. These specific dimensions are listed and defined for the rater in the section of the manual just preceding each scale. For some functions, the scale-stops are specifically written out with descriptive statements explicitly representing each component factor. For other functions, the component factors are included implicitly in each stop-description.

3. For each scale an attempt has been made to describe the function it represents both abstractly, (as in accordance with the component-factor definitions) and concretely, (with illustrative clinical material for each stop).

4. Degree, intensity, frequency, pervasiveness and extensity of the phenomena being rated for any scale are always to be kept in mind. They may supersede, in importance, the specific modal description in determining the rating. E.g., a specific illustrative example may appear at just one modal stop on a scale, but the rater must understand that the phenomenon being illustrated may occur as well at other levels or modal stops (implicit when not spelled out as such in the manual). This is where expert clinical judgment is particularly essential in making good global ratings.

With respect to pervasiveness, especially, the rater is directed to consider, for any scale, whether the evidence for some given item of pathology is observed only during the present, for a given subject, or whether it has been noted throughout his life history. That is, the distinctions between *acute,* in remission, and *chronic* should influence the rating assigned. In general, the more pervasive with respect to long-range time spans, the more maladaptation would be reflected in the behavior, and thus in the assigned rating. Adaptive resiliency and rate of recovery after temporary lapses in functioning would also be considered here.

5. With respect to the type of data gleaned from interviews, some scales lend themselves best to global ratings from the subject's responses to the questions *designed specifically* to tap information pertinent to the function being rated (e.g., *Stimulus Barrier*). Other scales are applied most effectively to the person's *general style* of answering *all* interview questions (e.g., Defensive Functioning).

6. Another factor for the rater to keep in mind in making his final assessment is the congruence between degree of actual disruption in behavior at any level of ego functioning and the degree of disturbance reported as such. Thus, a person may report no difficulty in certain areas, but the sensitive clinician can infer from other interview data that there is in fact a disturbance in functioning that the subject either does not experience or does not report. Such a disturbance would be rated lower (as less adaptive) than a mere acceptance of the person's report would superficially suggest.

7. A final point to bear in mind in making the ratings is that the problem of specifying adequacy of adaptation must include some concept of the efficacy of any ego function in transaction with environmental conditions. Here we must consider whether the behavior reflecting any given function which we are rating occurs in an *"average expectable environment"* or if it occurs following some precipitating, potentially traumatic *stress.* Thus, a person who suffers a disruption in autonomous functioning, or who hallucinates following a life threatening surgical experience would not be viewed as responding as pathologically as a person who experiences identical difficulties when there is no such extreme precipitating factor.

Rating Procedure

The following sequential approach has been found useful by raters in general, and tends to maximize reliability.

1. Familiarize yourself with all scales, the component factors, and the implied psychological dimensions upon which the modal stops of each have been ordered.

2. Familiarize yourself with the interview questions. This will be of greatest help in identifying what function any particular interview segment provides information about.

3. Read through the complete interview, making *marginal notes* as you go along, indicating what ego function and what component factor of that function (not necessarily what stop) is reflected whenever such a judgment is possible from the material.

4. On the *Rating Sheets,* sections are provided for recording evidence for each ego function rating. The rater then transfers to the Rating Sheets each bit of evidence he has jotted in the margins which represents the function being rated. For each function, the component factors are designated on the rating sheet, so the rater can immediately record his evidence under the component factor to which it pertains. The rater then picks that scale point which most closely reflects the subject's level for the given ego function, basing the rating on the specific evidence he has recorded on the Rating Sheet, qualified by the rater's overall impression based on the entire interview. When the subject falls between two defined (modal) scale points, then the rating would be made at the non-defined stop falling between the two (i.e., 1.5, 2.5, 3.5, etc.).

I A. REALITY TESTING

Instruction to Raters:

COMPONENT FACTORS

a) the distinction between ideas and perceptions

b) accuracy of perception (includes orientation to time and place, and accuracy of perception and interpretation of external events

c) accuracy of inner reality testing (i.e., psychological mindedness and awareness of inner states)

The ability to differentiate between percepts and ideas refers to veridicality of perception of outer and inner reality. It involves continuous selective scanning, and a matching of contemporary percepts against past percepts and ideas. Reality testing here also involves the checking of data from one sense against data from other senses: i.e., consensual validation, both intra- and interpersonally.

Inner reality testing is included in this scale insofar as it refers to a person's subjective sense of the accuracy of his perceptions. Another way of stating this is the relation between the observing and the participating aspects of ego-functioning or the extent to which the ego is free to perceive itself. Inner reality testing here would also be reflected in the degree to which the person is in touch with his inner self. Stated another way, this implies "psychological-mindedness".

At the most maladaptive end of the scale would be included those disturbances of reality testing involving alloplastic defenses in the extreme (delusion and hallucinations); severe disturbances in orientation with regard to time, place, and person, and, in general, the encroachment of drives and regressive ego states upon perceptual functioning. These disturbances become less severe, less pervasive and less frequent at stops 2) and 3). At stops 4) and 5) are included excessive reality testing and perceptual vigilance, as well as less pathological forms of the sorts of inadequate reality testing described in stops 1)-3). Optimal reality testing is defined along these dimensions as sharp and *flexible,* including some lowering of vigilance in the service of overall adaptation.

SCALE

1. Person is primarily deluded and hallucinated; extremely disoriented with respect to time, place and person; no awareness that his perceptions are in any way inaccurate. No psychological mindedness.

2. Delusions and hallucinations are restricted to somewhat narrower area than in 1). Subject may be unsure whether an event really occurred, or happened only in his mind or in a dream. Disorientations are also less pervasive and frequent. Maybe déjà vu and déjà reconnu consistent with fairly high degree of disorganization. Drives still determine perceptions such that subjective awareness of inaccuracies is largely absent.

3. Less extreme than 1) and 2) especially in that distortions and misinterpretations are likely to occur under unusual circumstances, such as under influence of drugs, alcohol, and fatigue. Beginning emergence of some subjective sense of one's misperceptions, if only after the fact. Some little psychological mindedness.

4. Same as 1)-3) but to lesser degree and with greater subjective sense or objectivity about one's perceptual errors and relative out-of-touchness. That is, there may be occasional coarse misinterpretations of inner and outer reality but with self-recovery. In addition, there might be excessive reality testing, as in "perceptual vigilance" or special sensitivities predisposing to projection. A stimulus-bound sort of reality testing might occur at the cost of libidinal investments and gratifications.

5. Like 4), with relatively minor perceptual inaccuracies, and relatively quick recovery due to fairly good subjective sense of accuracy of one's perceptions. There may also be hyper-alert reality testing here, but not as excessive as in 4).

6. Average reality testing. This includes occasional use of rationalization

and denial in the service of adaptation, as in difficult or stressful circumstances. Usually, however, accurate perception prevails with the person's subjective awareness of the accuracy as gleaned from appropriate use of consensual validation.

7. Optimal. Sharp and flexible (as opposed to hyper-vigilant) reality testing; even in stressful or emotionally burdensome circumstances. Person is well-oriented, and perception resists social contagion, such as suggestion and group effect. Distinction between percept and idea holds up even under many drug states and other physiological alterations. Inner reality testing and psychologicalmindedness are optimal.

I B. REALITY TESTING

(Soundness of Judgment)

Instructions to Raters:

COMPONENT FACTORS

a) awareness of likely consequences of intended behavior (e.g., anticipating probable dangers, legal culpabilities and social censure, disapproval or inappropriateness)

b) extent to which manifest behavior reflects the awareness of these likely consequences

Sometimes it is possible to assess only behavior or activity. Awareness of consequences, independent of whether activity is congruent with such awareness, may be harder to evaluate. It is also important to know whether behavior, when there *is* awareness of consequences, takes that knowledge into account, or whether the subject disregards what he knows. Rating would be affected in the following way:

The judgment of a man consistently reporting late for a job he consciously desires and where he knows punctuality is valued, is better than that of the man who wouldn't know he could be fired. We would also be less inclined to rate a pregnant 14 year old who had no access to valid birth control information as low as we would rate an older more informed girl who finds herself with an unwanted pregnancy. While the incidence of pure ignorance will probably be rare, the rater should be guided by whether or not the person has had an opportunity to learn the consequences of the specific action. It should also be kept in mind that most "ignorance" and/or "stupidity" can sometimes be thought of as one factor associated with defective judgment.

We base ratings for judgment on interview data revealing verbal reports of overt behavior, and on verbal responses indicating comprehension and appraisals of hypothetical and real situations; and the person's evaluations of the consequences of action related to those situations.

Contemplated future judgmental activity and answers to questions about hypothetical "what would you do if"-type situations should be taken into account, noting especially any discrepancies between what a person says he will do in the future (or in a hypothetical situation) and what he, in fact, does or would do.

A guideline to rating here might be that *activity* based on poor judgment will get a more maladaptive rating than either poor evaluations made *short* of action, or poorly contemplated future activity. e.g., the college student who cheats on an exam in full view of the proctor, convinced that he will not be caught, would be rated lower than one who either announces that he plans to cheat in the future or one who makes the statement that if he were to cheat in this situation, he would not be caught.

Some elaboration of the Component Factors:

a. The extent to which the person *is aware* or believes he and/or others are vulnerable in truly dangerous situations (extent to which the person is aware of *knowable consequences* of his behavior with respect to the danger to himself and/or others it may bring). At the maladaptive end of the scale, there is no cognizance of actual dangers inherent in *extremely* dangerous situations as well as distortions of garden-variety threats. Toward the middle of the scale, the person may be aware of extreme dangers but not of more moderate and mild ones. Toward the adaptive end, there is awareness of a whole range of true dangers, as well as repudiation of false ones. This last notion implies that the reverse situation must be evaluated on the same scale; where all degrees of danger are *overestimated*.

b) Extent to which behavior is congruent with dangers inherent in situations. Here, we have to consider how behavior is related to perception of dangers as well as to its own consequences. Ratings would tend toward the maladaptive end when behavior is congruent with extreme distortions of perceptions, and would tend to be somewhat more adaptive if behavior were appropriate despite perceptual distortions, (i.e., faulty awareness). Similarly, ratings would be somewhere toward the middle if the converse held; when awareness of dangers is fairly accurate, yet behavior tended to be inappropriate. At the most adaptive end, there would be appropriate behavior corresponding to accurate perception of situations and behavioral consequences.

SCALE

1. Judgment is so defective as to frequently involve potentially high danger to life and limb. Person fully believes, however, that he is invulnerable to dangers (which the average person can realistically assess), and acts in accordance with his false belief, either totally indifferent to the consequences or with the positive belief that the consequences are not ever destructive. For the reverse situation, mild or nonthreatening situations are perceived as extremely dangerous.

a) Person indicates no awareness of *severe* dangers (e.g., those inherent in jumping from the top of a 20 story building). When dangers are overestimated, the most benign situations are seen as a threat to life.

b) Person actually acts on the belief that he is invulnerable. He may behave or attempt to behave in ways which would be lethal under ordinary circumstances (e.g., could actually have made happy-go-lucky attempts to "fly" out of window).

c) The person might claim that he and/or others could survive a jump because of being blessed with certain powers, such as the ability to fly, extra layers of padding in the skin, or the benefits of an amulet around the neck.

2. Judgment as defective as 1), but less chronically so, *or* judgment only slightly less defective than 1) so that only the most extremely dangerous situations would be judged as such.

a) Person might know that knifing a person in the heart would kill him, yet not know that neglecting to feed a child could also result in a death. In overestimating dangers, person might feel a plot was being hatched to hurt him (delusions of persecution) and

b) Would act so as to stay the harm. Maybe a history of behavior just short of the most dangerous, congruent with the perception that the situations were not inherently dangerous. (E.g., may have subjected self to five weeks of serious starvation). In the case of overestimation, person might be involved in chronic litigation against imagined offenders to life and limb.

c) Person would know that jumping from window could cause death, but fully believe that prolonged starvation is good for the figure, with no detrimental consequences.

3. Judgment defective, but behavioral consequences not so severe as to cause serious danger to life, but could endanger health, work, and interpersonal relationships.

a) Person thinks he can pass a Calculus or German examination without studying. This reasoning applies to any work or task involving the mastery of complex skills or specific information. He might rationalize his lack of good judgment by saying, "I can get by without studying or ever expending effort because I have a high I.Q."

b) Behavior involving defective judgment tends to be repeated; e.g., if exam is failed, person might take it again without studying, convinced that his high native intelligence will bring him an A. Repetition of unsatisfactory patterns in relationships also included here (e.g., divorces and remarriages to same type of "unsuitable" partner, such as alcoholic, without attempting to take stock).

c) Poor evaluation of consequences of activity inferred also from tendency to repeatedly seek out destructive situations short of total or sub-total damage to life and limb.

4. Awareness of dangers fluctuates from situation to situation. At this stop,

we begin to see fairly *encapsulated* areas of non-awareness of danger. Where dangers are overestimated, it is as in the more specific phobic-like reactions.

a) Person who has been a relative failure in his chosen field of work believes that it is all fate, and he hasn't received the breaks, which he trusts are coming. In overestimating, person may feel a symptom is inevitably a dangerous sign, despite reassurances to the contrary (moderate hypochondriasis).

b) Although person may continue to look for jobs in field where he has not succeeded, and does not prepare to work in a more suitable area, he still responds with relatively good judgment in other areas of life.

c) Consequences are evaluated poorly only in encapsulated or conflict-related areas.

5. Errors in judgment are minor and infrequent, whether they span a range of activity or are related to limited but crucial areas of functioning.

a) Behavior relating to the more garden variety of situations. E.g., person is fully aware he has had no medical checkup in a few years, knows it is advisable to have one, yet puts it off for one inconsequential reason or another. Or smokes a pack a day despite knowing of recent findings; or drives without seatbelt, although he, himself, had them installed.

b) Consequences of actions are pretty much appreciated, but this knowledge is not carried over so that behavior is congruent with the knowledge.

6. No gross defects in judgment. Errors are even less consequential than (5) and even more of the garden variety; E.g., putting off a dentist's appointment a few months; only occasionally forgetting seat belt.

7. Optimal. Very sound judgment in all spheres: Social, physical, work, etc. Behavior congruent with sound awareness of consequences. May even include excessively fine judgments.

II. SENSE OF REALITY OF THE WORLD AND OF THE SELF

Instructions to Raters:

COMPONENT FACTORS

a) the extent to which external events are experienced as real and as being embedded in a similar context (e.g., degree of realization, deja vu, trance-like states)

b) the extent to which the body (or parts of it) and its functioning, and one's behavior are experienced as familiar and unobtrusive and as belonging to (or emanating from) the individual (e.g., degree of depersonalization)

c) the status of self identity (including self-esteem)

d) the feeling of separateness from the external world and from other individuals (from fusion-merging phenomena up through full separation-individuation)

This scale measures the extent to which one's sense of self, as it relates to the outside world, is realistic. It refers, optimally to a subjective experience, usually preconscious, of one's unique, dynamic wholeness, mentally and physically, as defined by clearly delimited self boundaries from other people and the general physical and social environment.

SCALE

1. Oceanic feeling or feeling of nothingness. Feeling dead, inanimate, selfless, as with no continuity from past to present, moment to moment. Identity grossly distorted: e.g., feeling of being a wild animal, werewolf, or ghost. Person may perceive himself with extreme changes of body size, feeling he is Atlas or a Lilliputian, or perceive the world around him as much smaller, as in micropsia. May harbor grossly inflated (omnipotent) or deflated (depressive) feelings of self-worth. Prominent might be phenomena of fusion, merging, and other states indicating loss of boundaries between self and outer world.

2. Dream-like states, trances, fugues, major disassociations, delusion of identity. Projections of inner disorganization and disintegration of ego-boundaries may produce the feeling of the world being in chaos (e.g., world-destruction fantasies). Emergence of poorly repressed ego states; unrealistic feelings of unworthiness. Fusion and splitting phenomena slightly less extreme than 1).

3. Severe depersonalization or derealization. Parts of body experienced as separate entities or distorted; e.g., tongue too large, head too small. Self esteem still poor, and few signs of stable identity or self image.

4. Self-esteem and quasi-stable sense of identity can begin to be seen, but only with continuous feedback from outside sources. When external signals and cues are absent, identity can falter and be poorly integrated, but with related phenomena less severe than in 3). That is, may be partial and occasional depersonalization; feelings of being in a fog or at sea; "as-if" personality; some unrealistic feelings about the body (e.g., too bloated, too fat or thin).

5. Stable identity and self image are more prominent here than in 4), dependent, but not as totally dependent on environmental feedback. There are signs of independent sense of self, with a moderately good sense of inner reality, continuity and internalized self-representations. Adverse circumstances and stress may interfere with these representations, as well as with individuation.

6. Stable identity, distinct sense of self and self-esteem are well internalized, requiring only occasional feedback to maintain themselves, as under conditions of unusual stress.

7. Identity, sense of self, and self-esteem are so well established and solid that they remain intact even under conditions of unusual stress. Feedback is essentially not required, so that there might even be a heightened sense of self

in situations of extreme danger, stress, or of minimal external cues ordinarily required for self-anchorage points.

III. REGULATION AND CONTROL OF DRIVES, AFFECTS AND IMPULSES

Instructions to Raters:

COMPONENT FACTORS

a) the strength (prominence-absence) of drive, affect, and impulse indicators. Evidence here is from dreams, fantasies and conscious experience (independent of overt motor behavior)

b) the degree to which these elements are overtly manifest in behavior

c) the effectiveness of delay and control mechanisms (degree of over-or under-control)

Note: "Frustration tolerance" would span components b) and c).

Regulation and control might very well be regarded as one aspect of defensive functioning, but since our concerns here are limited to behavorial and ideational indices of impulse expression, and since drives and impulses may be controlled and channeled by ego structures other than defenses, *Regulation and Control* would appear to merit a scale of its own.

Among the drives under consideration are the libidinal and aggressive, in both their developmentally earlier and more advanced forms. Included also are impulse expressions deriving from superego pressures such as guilt and self-destructive urges, ranging from suicidal tendencies to less extreme manifestations of depression, or moral and instinctual masochism. Where relevant, we would also include pressures from the ego-ideal, e.g., in the regulation of self esteem, such as "driving ambition" when it reflects varying degrees of impulse control.

SCALE

1. a) Aggression, and/or depression and/or sexual manifestations at their most extreme. E.g., evidence of intensely strong impulses toward murder or suicide, or sexual urges experienced most intensely and chronically.

1. b) Person has committed or attempted murder, suicide or rape. Behaves with wild abandon.

1. c) Primarily extreme lack of control. Over-control would not appear at this stop.

2. a) Impulse-ridden personality, but not as extreme as 1).

2. b) Impulse-ridden behavior prominent. May engage in assaultive-type acts short of homicide. Chronic fits of irritability and rage. Sadistic superego pressure against the self could include serious self-inflicted injury short of suicide.

2. c) Undercontrol is central. Thus, has great difficulty holding back sexual, aggressive, or other urges because of drive pressure and weak controls.

3. a) Strong urges experienced frequently. Sometimes, although present, they are not experienced at all, and knowledge of them can only be deduced.

3. b) Low frustration tolerance, so that person flies off the handle easily. Maybe sporadic rages or temper tantrums. Patient engages in periodic binges, either with alcohol, sex or food—as patterned responses to frustration or from pressure of urges. May exhibit hypomanic behavior. Self-destructive behavior might be along the lines of severe masochism, such as surgery addiction, getting oneself beat up or otherwise seriously abused.

3. c) Urges are controlled either very poorly or excessively. Excessive controls would be of the extremely rigid or brittle sort so that periods of overcontrol alternate with impulsive breakthroughs or psychosomatic spill-over.

4. a) Experience of drive may be less intense than in previous stops, or may be as intense but less frequent.

4. b) Drive-dominated behavior is less severe, less pervasive and less frequent than in stops 1)-3). Person generally regards displays of such behavior as ego-alien, but often after the fact. Aggressive behavior is more verbal than physical. Self-destructive behavior is of the moral masochistic type.

4. c) Controls may appear reasonably good, but more likely of the "grit-your-teeth" or "count-to-ten" variety than of the smooth, automatic sort. Attempts to keep a rein on drive expression leads to a somewhat rigid picture, at times.

5. a) Drives, etc., are experienced somewhat more or somewhat less than average. The more-or-less than average experience may be limited to a specific drive, affect or impulse, rather than as characterizing all such factors. (Person may feel hyper-or hypo sexual, but other urges are felt with average intensity).

5. b) Any breakthroughs of irritability or impulsivity in behavior are responses to specific or conflict-ridden areas or to situational stress rather than a function of a characterological disposition. Sometimes he over-responds, sometimes he under-responds to moderate affect-arousing events. Although the person is more easily upset or irritated than the average, he experiences any lapse as ego-alien, even as it is occurring. Self-destructive behavior takes the form of mild moral masochism.

5. c) Controls are less than fully automatic, but may be automatic in conflict-free areas. In certain circumscribed areas where they are not automatic, they can be mustered on the spot with only moderate effort.

6. Average: Average experiencing of urges, with reasonably smooth expression in behavior with the aid of fairly flexible control devices. Degree of tightening or loosening of controls, and thus impulse expression is appropriate to the situation.

7. Optimal: A minimum of subjective and objective difficulties with

automatic regulation and control of drive expression such that the person functions extremely smoothly in work, sex, play and object relations, generally. Automatic drive, affect and impulse regulation permits optimal adaptation to varying conditions.

IV. OBJECT RELATIONS

Instructions to Raters:

COMPONENT FACTORS

a) the degree and kind of relatedness to others (taking account of withdrawal trends, narcissistic self concern, narcissistic object choice)

b) the extent to which present relationships are adaptively or unadaptively influenced by or patterned upon older ones; from being patterned on the earliest mother-infant relationship, through those of later childhood to those which are relatively less limited to earlier developmental experiences (e.g., fixations on and repetitions of old experiences)

Object Relations contribute to adaptation insofar as one's relations with all others, particularly significant others, is based on an accurate understanding of and response to the other person for what he is today. Optimal relationships would then be relatively free of maladaptive elements, suggesting patterns of interaction which were more appropriate to old situations than to the present. The most pathological extreme would be essentially an absence of object relations; next would be present relations based on early fixations and unresolved conflicts. Optimal relations would be the most mature: Free of transference distortions, and gratifying to adult libidinal and ego needs.

Intensity, diversity, pervasiveness and so forth are not always essential components to span the entire scale, but to make global ratings, the rater is instructed to keep in mind the *quality* of the person's relationships to significant people as having more weight than relationships to peripheral people. For more pathological adaptations the disturbances in object relations will be assumed to extend to a broader range of contacts than they would in the moderately maladaptive categories, where pathology might be limited to one or two significant relationships.

SCALE

1. Essential lack of any object-relatedness. Withdrawal, as into stupor or muteness; or living like a hermit or recluse; "relationships" are pre-symbiotic, mostly autistic.

2. Withdrawal, but not as extreme or pervasive as 1): e.g., schizoid detachment rather than total withdrawal. Or else severely narcissistic or symbiotic relationships: e.g., folie à deux, vicarious objects, intensely sadomasochistic binds. In general, either under-attachment, or over-attachment of an infantile nature. Relationships characterized by such childish traits as oral envy, destructive clinging, intense unresolved ambivalence, anal sadism. Present

relationships characterized by transference based on very early fixations, and may reflect other disturbances in early mother-child relationship. Separation anxiety may be prominent, as well as maladaptive reactions to object loss, loss of love or narcissistic injury.

3. Same as 2, but less pathological, pervasive and frequent.

4. Relations with significant people are characterized by neurotic-type interactions. Can be withdrawn, or of narcissistic (as in object choice) or symbiotic type, but not as regressed as levels 2) and 3). Examples would be Don Juanism, varietism, less infantile forms of sadomasochism, dependency, and where only some (usually significant) relationships are of this sort. Relationships might tend toward either the tenuous or the over-attached type. Would also, then, include the fringe, hanger-on person, most of whose relationships are tangential, yet degree of detachment less than in 1) to 3). Transference from early fixations usually involving strong oedipal elements are found in current relationships. Castration anxiety would be superimposed upon separation anxiety, determining the quality of relationships.

5. Like 4) but less severe. E.g., disturbed interactions with fewer people, or with one or more people but less of the time than 4). Variability and fluctuations are seen, from stable "average" relationships to the more disturbed.

6. Tending toward mature, object relations with "genital" goals. Occasional difficulties occur, but are resolved reasonably well.

7. Optimal relationships. No substantial evidence of fixations or distortions from early relationships. Gratifications are appropriate to current adult needs. Relationships are characterized by mutuality and reciprocity, and are so smooth as to permit optimal functioning in other areas, as well.

V. THOUGHT PROCESSES

Instructions to Raters:

COMPONENT FACTORS

a) the adequacy of processes which adaptively guide and sustain thought (e.g., attention, concentration, anticipation, concept formation, memory, languge)

b) the degree to which thinking is organized and oriented in accordance with reality consideration, as reflected in the relative primary-secondary process influences on thought (e.g., extent to which thinking is delusional, or autistic; degree of looseness of or intrusions upon associational processes)

In sum, Component a) refers to controlling processes, and Component b) to orientation to reality. Most likely, when one is rating pathology which falls at the extremes of this scale, it may be difficult to distinguish Component a) from Component b) as they are empirically interdependent. However, when rating pathology at the middle stops of this scale, raters may find that only one of the dimensions will be represented in the interview material. In such a case, ratings should be based upon the dimension represented.

Ratings will be based to a great extent on formal questioning, but person's overall style of language response and other communication to interview in general will also be determining factors in evaluating this function.

SCALE

1. a) *Extreme Disruption of Control Processes*: Attention totally distracted by irrelevancies. Minimal capacity to respond to questions due to complete loss of sustained concentration. Severe impairment of both recent and remote memory. Total loss of abstracting ability—can think only in most concrete or absurdly syncretistic (over-inclusive) modes. Minimal ability to communicate verbally due either to mutism, "word salad", flood of barely related sounds, words, and phrases; word play including neologisms; and clang associations.

1. b) *Extreme Breakdown of Reality Orientation and Organization*: Thought predominantly bizarre and delusional with loose and fluid associations, autistic logic, fragmentation, symbolization, condensation, and contradictions.

2. a) *Prominent Failures of Control Processes*: Person attempts to focus and sustain attention and concentration, but is unable to stick to trend of thought because of interference from intruding associations. Memory impairment seen in inability to supply once readily available information such as number and names of family members. Overly concrete, with no ability to see relationships between discrete events. Frequent blocking of verbal expression.

2. b) *Prominent Failure of Reality Orientation*: Well organized and unquestioned delusional system encompassing significant areas of functioning. Overly symbolic thinking in terms of interpretation of events as having more meaning than is ordinarily attributed to them so that such interpretations border on the fantastic. Some autistic and many peculiar ideas. Thinking often extremely fragmented and illogical (but not always). Rigidity of thought prevents practically any meaningful exchange of information.

3. a) *Episodic Failures of Control Processes*: Frequent but circumscribed disruption in communication because of diverted attention and difficulty sustaining trend of thought. Considerable impairment in remote memory seen either in inability to supply information on such events as job history and schooling, or in gross inaccuracies and inconsistencies. Relies heavily on concrete mode, but some ability to see relationships between events. Categorization may be over-inclusive, hence crucial differences between events are missed. Thus, difficulty in discriminating between degrees leads to "all-or-none"-type thinking. Unable to entertain more than one possibility. Rigidity of thought.

3. b) *Limited Failure of Reality Orientation and Organization*: May be very circumscribed delusions accompanied by some doubt, indicating rudimentary-forms of an adaptive self-critical function in thinking. Other areas of functioning are free of distortion. At times thoughts are disorganized and difficult to follow. Questionable logic. Some peculiar or queer ideas. Intolerance for ambiguity.

4. a) *Failure of Control Processes under Stress*: Some distractibility or intruding thoughts resulting in disruptive communication, particularly under stress. General vagueness and lack of specificity in memory for remote events or occasional failure of memory. Some limited ability for flexibility in conceptualization, but under stress resorts to either concrete or syncretistic modes. Rigid, meticulous forms of communication: severe doubting, some blocking. Use of automatic phrases.

4. b) *Failure of Reality Orientation and Organization under Stress*: Thinking occasionally disordered or illogical under stress. While there are no gross breaks in reality testing, there could be a questionable reality basis to some notions. Some peculiar ideas expressed, typical of schizoid-like disorders. Imprecise substitutions and some peculiar expressions. Rigidity interferes with free exchange and exploration.

5. a) *Minor Failures of Control Processes Under Stress*: Some distractibility under stress but is able to recover and respond appropriately. Occasional inability to stick to trend of thought because of pressure from intruding associations (i.e., tangentially related but irrelevant thoughts or events). Some evidence of vagueness in remote memory or occasional and minor inconsistencies which are then corrected. Tendency toward concreteness or over-generality but can correct when asked to expand or delimit concepts. Occasional vagueness, unclarity, or obsessionally over-precise thinking under stress.

5. b) *Minor Failures of Reality Orientation and Organization under Stress*: Possible reality distortion recognized and left either questioned or corrected. Occasional peculiar thought or expression. Occasional vagueness or unclarity in some areas under stress. Some rigidity, or inability to go beyond the objective facts.

6. a) *Satisfactory Functioning of Control Processes*: Ability to attend and to carry on uninterrupted conversation. If thought process is interrupted, shows recognition of irrelevancy and is able to continue meaningful exchange. No evidence of memory impairment. Conceptualization rarely breaks down even under stress. More often than not, communication is clear, precise and flexible. Rare imprecision or vagueness, even under stress.

6. b) *Satisfactory Reality Orientation and Organization*: Thinking for the most part logical and ordered—consistent with estimated level of intelligence. Possible egocentric notions, minor distortions, or vagueness under stress, but

no gross peculiarities. Evidence of flexibility seen, e.g., in willingness to entertain and explore new ideas.

7. a) *Optimal Functioning of Control Process*: Acute attention and unimpaired ability to concentrate (should be differentiated from paranoid and obsessional vigilance with respect to detail and error). No disruption from pressure of internal associations. Associations meaningfully integrated into communication. Memory acute and accurate. Flexible and appropriate use of functional, abstract, concrete, or symbolic frames of reference. Unusual clarity, coherence, and flexibility of expression, with no signs of disruption in the verbal flow.

7. b) *Optimal Reality Orientation and Organization*: Thinking unusually well organized and logical-consistent with above-average level of intellectual functioning. No peculiarities of expression. Flexibility expressed in ability to entertain contradictory thoughts and to shift levels of discourse.

VI. ADAPTIVE REGRESSION IN THE SERVICE OF THE EGO

Instructions to Raters:

COMPONENT FACTORS

a) first phase of the oscillating process: relaxation of perceptual and conceptual acuity (and other ego controls) with a concomitant increase in awareness of previously preconscious and unconscious contents

b) second phase of the oscillating process: the induction of new configurations which increase adaptive potentials as a result of creative integrations.

ARISE refers to the ability of the ego to initiate a partial, temporary and controlled lowering of its own functions (keep in mind here the component factors of the other ten ego functions) in the furtherance of its interests (i.e., promoting adaptation). Such regressions result in a relatively free but controlled play of the primary process and are called regressions in the service of the ego.

In this scale, the oscillating function has been dimensionalized in the following way. At stop 1), there is no oscillating function, but only the prototypical anchoring point of total regression. Stop 2) includes both aspects of the oscillating function, but one aspect predominates over, or more or less excludes the other. Stops 3) through 5) include both aspects of the oscillating function, progressing from less to more stability and smoothness in the alternation between partial regression and its use in adaptive functioning. Stops 6) and 7) approach and then reach the optimal oscillation.

The rater is instructed to consider the *final product* (e.g., the work of art, the solved problem, the creative act), only insofar as it reflects the *process* of regression in the service of the ego. It is conceivable that a lesser work of art could involve more adaptive use of controlled regression than a greater work of art, such as a later Van Gogh.

Concrete illustrations have been deliberately avoided in this scale because they encourage a stimulus-bound use of the manual at the expense of good global ratings. This difficulty appeared to be a major source of poor reliability in using previous scale-drafts of this function.

Scale

1. When regressions occur, they are in their most pathological form and so maladaptive that they cannot be used as detours in the service of any ego function. There is primitivization of functions without recovery. (Only the regression part of the oscillating function is present).

2. Phenomena in this category are similar to 1) but are slightly less extreme in that they are transitory and/or a shade less primitive.

or

Absence of any regressions. This is due to extreme rigidity in character formation, thinking and behavior: e.g., a highly over-ideational or obsessional person who cannot engage in any fantasy or play because all energy is rigidly bound in primitively constricted defensive functioning.

In sum, there is still no oscillating function as such, but there is either very primitive regression, or else absence of regression and presence of the most rigid, stimulus-bound defensive functioning.

3. At this point, the oscillating function can be observed, but it is very "rocky". E.g., the person may be obsessively preoccupied, yet also able to regress. The *transition* from regression to adaptation is hampered by difficulties in smoothly emerging from the regressed state. There might also be a relative inability to loosen or relinquish the more constricted types of controls. Unevenness in shifting, (e.g., from passivity to activity) or in using regression as a detour towards adaptation prevents creative, humorous, fanciful activities in general. The regression of all ego functions here are experienced as ego-alien and are likely to produce anxiety, symptoms and disruptions in adaptations.

4. The oscillating function is smoother than in 3); regression of ego functions is a bit more ego-syntonic, permitting more enjoyment of primitive thoughts, feelings and fantasies. The person, however, has difficulty channeling the outcomes of such regressively based enjoyments productively or adaptively. Or else, the person could be productive and adaptive at the expense of enjoyment.

5. Similar to 4) but where enjoyment of regressions is greater (possibly due to greater acceptance of temporary passivity), and where regressions are employed more adaptively. The oscillating function, however, lacks the stabili-

ty, sustaining power and smooth operation under stress that would ensure the creative-adaptive uses of regression which characterize a 6) or a 7) rating.

6. Like 7), but falls somewhat short of that ideal anchorage type. Differs from 5) in that the oscillating function has good stability and sustaining power, but the adaptive-creative uses of regressive content are not as highly developed as in 7).

7. A flexible, automatically controlled oscillation between employment of more primitive modes of functioning and the concomitant channeling of such regressions to permit the optimal use of all ego functions in the service of adaptation. Such controlled regressions (e.g., playful fantasies, primary process thinking, etc.) are essential to enjoyment of and active participation in art, humor, play, sexual performance and gratifications, imaginative and creative activity in general. Achievement of adaptive ego functioning is arrived at by a regressive detour.

VII. DEFENSIVE FUNCTIONING

Instructions to Raters:

COMPONENT FACTORS

a) degree to which defensive components adaptively or maladaptively affect ideation and behavior.

b) extent to which these defenses have succeeded or failed (e.g., degree of emergence of anxiety, depression and/or other dysphoric affects, indicating inefficiency of defensive operation).

Defensive functioning contributed to adaptation by controlling the emergence of anxiety-arousing or other dysphoric psychic content, such as ego-alien instinctual wishes, (including depression) affects, thought, and perception, which conflict with super ego and reality demands.

This scale differs from the *Regulation and Control of Drives* scale in that the latter measures the degree of impulse expression and motor discharge in behavior. *Defensive Functioning* is not a scale of impulsivity but of measures employed to deal with disturbing elements of mental content and intrapsychic conflict.

Formation of a hierarchical ordering of the specific, classic, ten or twelve defenses with respect to pathology is an issue which has yet to be resolved in psychoanalytic theory, so the basis for ordering the scale will be a dimensionalization of the efficacy of defensive functioning. While certain stops explicitly list certain defenses and not others, the rater is not to be stimulus bound to the defense names, but is to rate according to the overall rationale of the scale. The rater should consider that defensive functioning and organization may be recognized not only by the frequency, intensity, and pervasiveness of the usual defense mechanisms, but that almost any personality function may at times be operative defensively against any others. That is, id processes may defend against ego processes; one drive (e.g., aggression) may defend against another (e.g., passivity); or early regressive drives may substitute for later ones, etc.

At the most pathological end is massive failure of all defensive functioning. At stop 2), in addition to relative failure of defenses is added excessive use of defenses. Stops 4) and 5) illustrate defenses as they are used in symptoms or compromises, and stops 6) and 7) delineate circumstances where the ego defenses operate optimally to accomplish the most adaptive aims of the ego, and not as intrusions. Thus, at its most adaptive level, the ego disposes of unwelcome instinctual demands by some process of judgmental repudiation or other more mature countercathectic means.

In making his ratings, the rater is instructed to rely not so much on the specific questions designed to tap defensive functionings as on the person's *style* of responding to all questions throughout the interview. For example, pedantry in verbal behavior, generally, would tell more about how excessive the person's defensive functioning is than would a direct answer to a specific question about defenses.

SCALE

1. Massive *failure* of all defensive functioning so that there is emergence of id derivatives and unconscious contests. The person's waking state may resemble the dream state of most people, with respect to mental contests. Degree of anxiety and panic are extreme.

2. Failure of defenses is slightly less extreme or pervasive than in 1). Anxiety is acute, free-floating and unbound so as to interfere with adaptive functions to a significant degree.

or

Massive, extensive and inflexible use of the most primitive character defenses pervading *total functioning* and not limited to specific conflict situations. Might be massive repression and blocking where affect substitutes for any reflective thinking. Or could be all pervasive obsessional systems where extreme intellectualization and isolation choke off all affect. Or projection in its most extreme, all encompassing form, manifest in broad delusional systems. Extreme forms of denial of inner and outer reality are included here, as is nearly total withdrawal from reality. Primitive splitting, the defensive use of archaic introjects, and pathological forms of identification with the aggressor are also included.

3. Like 2, but less extreme. Frequent breakthroughs of drive-related material, ego-alien thoughts, parapraxes. Free-floating anxiety, but not as pervasive as in 2): more like the sort seen in agoraphobia or claustrophobia. Affect may predominate over reflective thought.

or

Obsessional systems not as pervasive as 2); projections and delusions or quasi-delusions are more encapsulated than in 2); may be extreme perceptual vigilance, avoidance, evasions, severe inhibitions and ego-restrictions; overideational defenses such as intellectualization and isolation, where thought predominates disproportionately over affect.

4. Defenses here have the status of an aspect of symptom formation. They represent one half of a compromise between drive expression and defense against drive derivatives in *specific conflict situations*. Examples would be rationalization, reaction-formations, transient projections as in transference reactions, occasional parapraxes, malaproprisms and limited repressive devices. Also, symptomatic acting out (i.e., where action is a substitute for a repressed thought—not to be confused with impulsive "acting up" as in the *Regulation and Control scale*.).

5. Like 4, but less severe, pervasive and frequent, with some ability to recover and relinquish defensive operations.

6. Defensive functioning is employed only under extreme stress or in the service of adaptation (e.g., denial) with good resiliency and recovery to non-defensive modes. Otherwise, an absence of excessive or insufficient uses of defenses.

7. Optimal: Balance between id, ego, superego and external reality so that the executive (synthetic, adaptive, etc.) ego functions pre-empt the defensive function. Access to unconscious contents and id derivatives do not produce disruption or anxiety; thus, there is no need for defensive operations. The warding off of painful or dysphoric material is accomplished by recognizing, considering, making judgments and taking appropriate action about it.

VIII. *STIMULUS BARRIER*

Instructions to Raters:

COMPONENT FACTORS

a) threshold for, sensitivity to, or awareness of stimuli impinging upon various sensory modalities (externally, primarily, but including pain).

b) nature of response to various levels of sensory stimulation in terms of the extent of disorganization, avoidance, withdrawal or active coping mechanisms employed to deal with them.

Both thresholds and response to stimuli contribute to adaptation by the organism's potential for responding to high, average or low sensory input so that optimal homeostasis (as well as adaptation) is maintained: a) in the average expectable environment; and b) under conditions of unusual stress. *Stimulus Barrier* determines, in part, how resilient a person is, or how he re-adapts after the stress and impingements are no longer present.

Thresholds, as described for component a) refer not only to reaction to external stimuli, but also to internal stimuli which provide proprioceptive cues, or those originating within the body but eventually impinging on sensory organs. Light, sound, temperature, pain, pressure, drugs and intoxicants are the stimuli to be considered relevant to assessing thresholds.

Responses, other than threshold variables, referred to in Component b), include motor responses, coping mechanisms, effects on sleep, and certain aspects of psychosomatic illness.

Together, the two components represent a way of scaling the degree to which the ego effectively and adaptively organizes and integrates sensory experience.

At first, it seemed a simple thing to define Low Stimulus Barrier (LSN) as maladaptive, and High Stimulus Barrier (HSB) as adaptive. This polarity proved invalid theoretically and clinically, so the scale was designed to include *three* qualitatively different types of classification to be considered at *each* quantitative or modal stop. They are delineated most specifically as modal stop 1), and then vary in degree through the seven stops appropriate to their place in the scale.

Thus, a 1) rating may include: a) *LSB* with chaotic motor discharge; b) *LSB* with catatonic prototypes of defense; and c) contain some clinical or behavioral similarities. So if the rater has a difficult time judging whether the person has a *HSB* or a well-defended *LSB,* he will still rate the person the same way. And so on through all the stops up to 5), where one or more of the types merge. For each stop, some variant of both low (*LSB*) and high (*HSB*) stimulus barrier.

SCALE

1. a) *LSB*: extremely low thresholds; awareness of stimuli may be hyperacute. Coping modes reflect vulnerability through hyperkinetic, or chaotic type of motor discharge pattern, such as aimless flailing about. Experience of overstimulation may lead to sleep disturbances, psychosomatic spillover or severe, maybe chronic migraine. Excessive response to drugs and intoxicants. Sensitivity to prodromal and sub-clinical cues of illness. Slow recovery rate. Possibly "photophobic". Extreme sensitivity to subliminal, peripheral, and incidental stimuli which could disrupt adaptational tasks and inner homeostasis.

1. b) *LSB*: extremely low thresholds where person makes attempts to keep the level of stimulation low by massive defensive maneuvers, such as defensive raising of thresholds; catatonic prototypes of withdrawal, avoidance, massive repression and denial. These defensive operations serve to avoid incipient chaotic motor discharge. Motor response is, thus, instead, more like a catatonic stupor.

or

1. c) *HSB*: may appear behaviorally similar to the LSB Catatonic *prototype* 1b)

Extremely high congenital thresholds; little or no awareness and experience of stimuli which are more intense than average, or of subliminal stimuli. Unusually high levels of stimulation are tolerated with the aid of "zombie"-like defenses; modes of coping are defective, by way of being under-responsive or overly rigid or overly contained. Headaches rare or non-existent. Can't predict illness; e.g., with lights on following overstimulation because neither bother him. Effects are ego impoverishment, stunted growth of ego structures.

2. a) and b) *LSB*: Same as 1.a) and 1.b) but not as extreme.

or

2. c) *HSB*: Characterologically rigid defenses against awareness of extraordinary, ordinary, and potentially even minimal levels of stimulation: e.g., lives through "5 o'clock mayhem" without apparently hearing or seeing or batting an eyelash. High sensory thresholds lead to rigid defenses and controls, rigidly contained motor discharge patterns, poor discrimination and impoverished aesthetic judgments.

3. a) *LSB*: low thresholds but not as low as 1) or 2). Less chaotic motor discharge, and more likely a general irritability: "ants in the pants", or "jumping out of the skin" type reactions. Women may experience high degree of premenstrual tension. Sensitive to moderate changes in temperature, etc., but responds with less extreme disorganization that in 1) or 2): e.g., sweater coming on and off. Defensive efforts at keeping stimulation low are relatively poor, as opposed to utterly ineffective; wakes up and falls asleep many times a night.

or

3. b) *LSB*: along the catatonic-prototype dimension, person, despite relatively low threshold, may be behaviorally habituated to high sensory input, possibly due to high sensory stimulation during childhood. Continues to need excess of stimuli, as in frenetic quests for aesthetic experiences as seen in some drug-users or seekers of psychodelic experiences. May be defensive falling asleep with overstimulation.

or

3. c) *HSB*: high thresholds lead to "thin-skinned" responses, but not so much as in 1) and 2). Relatively oblivious to high levels of sensory input; high pain threshold; might make, e.g., good construction worker out-doors in Times Square area. Little or no awareness of subliminal stimulation.

4. a) *LSB*: moderately well defended against excessive stimulation despite low threshold. With high sensory input, motor expression is contained—grins

THE SCHIZOPHRENIC SYNDROME

and bears it despite inner irritability. This leads to fatigue with relatively poor recovery and adaptive resiliency. Adaptive behavior is less disrupted by peripheral or subliminal stimuli than in 1)-3).

4. b) *LSB*: sometimes a high level of sensory input is sought, but not as frenetically as in 3b). This may be for defensive purposes or because of basic stimulus hunger; e.g., prolonged silences, quiet places, make patient restless or "itchy".

4. c) *HSB*: threshold sometimes too high. Person is relatively oblivious to high levels of sensory input, and also overly constricted and under-responsive to environmental stimuli within average intensity range. At times, too, he may even appear lethargic, responding to high input calmly, if not with distinction. Not too aware of subliminal stimuli.

5. a) LSB: At this point, distinctions between a) and b) would disappear, due to some balance between discharge and control patterns, rather than one or the other predominating. Relatively low thresholds, but patient can grin and bear it, but with aids of relatively mature ego-controls rather than defenses. As in 4), this may lead to some fatigue, but resiliency and recovery may be fairly good. Motor discharge patterns are fairly even, so long as person has opportunity to compose himself after each potential assault upon his sensitivity.

HSB: difference from previous stops is mainly quantitative. Person relatively oblivious to high levels of sensory input, and somewhat constricted and underresponsive to stimuli within average intensity range. May comport self like proverbial "solid citizen" e.g., Rotarian, who appears to ride the waves comfortably and with dignity, as when attending a rousing roisterous convention.

6. Here, the distinction between *LSB* and *HSB* as distinctive types tends to disappear. Instead, there are reasonably flexible and automatic fluctuations in thresholds from *LSB* to *HSB*. Hard to determine whether thresholds are congenitally high or low, but there is a good screening mechanism to permit adequate input and screening out of overload. (There is a relatively smooth operation of both the protective and receptive function.) Awareness and experience of stimuli vary with the situation; defenses and controls are flexible. Coping modes (including motor discharge patterns) are reasonably flexible, but not as refined as would be optimal: e.g., rarely ill, receptive to mild noises, unruffled by loud ones; sleeps well without recourse to defensive withdrawal. Sensitivity to subliminal stimuli varies adaptively with the situation.

7. An extension of 6) to the optimal degree. Exquisitely flexible and automatic fluctuations in threshold from *LSB* to *HSB* in all their degrees. Defenses and controls employed only in the service of optimal adaptations, not so much for the purposes of resolving intra-psychic conflict.

Unusually sensitive and receptive in the experiencing phases (*LSB*); flexible, non-defensive coping modes, due to optimal screening out (looks like *HSB*) in executing tasks in the service of adaptation. Other ego functions are not disturbed by high input or periods of sensory deprivation. Like astronauts or model leaders of state.

IX. AUTONOMOUS FUNCTIONING

Instructions to Raters:

COMPONENT FACTORS

a) degree of freedom from or lack of freedom from impairment of apparatuses of primary autonomy (e.g., functional disturbances of sight, hearing, intention, language, memory, learning or motor function.)

b) degree of, or freedom from impairment of secondary autonomy (e.g., disturbances in habit patterns, learned complex skills, work routines, hobbies and interests)

The degree of resistance of both primary and secondary autonomous structures to deneutralization is a major focus in determining impairment of either the primary or the secondary apparatuses and functions. Neutralization is defined by Hartmann as a change of both libidinal and aggressive energy away from the instinctual and toward a non-instinctual mode.

The apparatuses and functions of primary autonomy as specified by Hartmann are:

Perception	Language
Intention	Recall
Object Comprehension	Productivity
Thinking	Motor development

SCALE

1. a) Severe (total or sub-total) interference with the functioning of one or more of the apparatuses of primary autonomy by conflict. Examples would be abulia (crippled intentionality), functional blindness or deafness, mutism, catatonic postures, delusions and/or hallucinations which seriously interfere with perceiving or thinking in a wide range of situations.

1. b) Habit patterns, work habits and/or learned skills of any kind are massively hampered, so that the person is unable to utilize most of these at all. Examples would be a skilled worker who cannot carry out his job (because the component activities have taken on sexual and aggressive meanings to a marked extent.) A person who can no longer feed, dress and care for himself because of massive shifts in the impulse-defense-adaptation balance toward the impulse-end.

The person's primary and secondary autonomous functions show minimal resistance to deneutralization, and thus, minimal autonomy from either the instinctual drives or from the environment (an example of the latter might be proneness to social contagion and "brain-washing").

2. a) Interference with primary autonomous functions is significant, but not as overwhelming as in 1). Delusions, hallucination, and will disturbances may score at this level when the degree of disturbance is less than sub-total. Visual disturbances involve, e.g., selective scotoma (but not blindness); serious interference with intentionality (but not total).

2. b) Utilization of skills and habits is interfered with to a serious degree, rather than totally or subtotally as in stop 1). Thus, a housewife's ability to carry out her previously routine tasks is so interfered with that even when she expends the maximal effort she can muster, her performance falls short of what is minimally adequate. Writer's cramp would be another relevant example here, if it is severe without being totally disabling, but does not allow a performance to carry out one's job adequately.

Resistance to deneutralization is quite low but not minimal. Thus, ongoing behavior is easily disrupted when drive-related stimuli intrude, and may be interfered with when one broaches sexual or aggressive topics. Reading, e.g., may become easily associated with voyeuristic components, and as a result be seriously impaired.

3. a) Interference (by conflict) with primary autonomous functions is present to a moderately high degree. In the areas of thinking and perception disturbances may include illusory experience and fleeting hallucinatory phenomena, but not persistent or organized hallucinations or delusions. Visual disturbances (blurring of vision while reading school assignments), writer's cramp to a moderate degree on numerous occasions also score here.

3. b) Skills, habits and automatized behaviors are interfered with to a moderately high degree, so that much effort must be expended to perform tasks previously automatic and routine, and the level of functioning in these areas nevertheless is only minimally adequate. Hobbies are rarely actively pursued by persons scoring at this level.

Resistance to deneutralization is low in many instances.

4. a) Disturbances of primary functions to a moderate degree. Vision, motor behavior, language, intention, etc., could be interfered with, less frequently and/or less severely than under 3).

4. b) Secondary autonomous habit patterns, skills, etc., are interfered with to moderately low degree. Greater effort must be expended to carry out routine tasks of the time in one area.

Resistance to deneutralization is moderately low in many situations.

5. a) and b) Some extra effort is required to perform previously done with little strain. Primary autonomous structures may be interfered with by conflict derivatives to a mild but noticeable degree.

Moderate resistance to sexualization and aggressivization of secondary autonomous habits and skills is found.

6. a) Structures of primary autonomy are interfered with rarely or only to a minor degree.

6. b) Habit patterns and skills are utilized with a relative ease or with relatively minor interference most of the time.
Moderately high resistance to sexualization and aggressivization of aspects of skills and habit patterns when these would tend to interfere with the requirements of ongoing behavior.

7. a) and b) Optimal. The utilization of primary and secondary autonomous functioning with ease, adaptive success and without drive interference.
There is a high resistance to sexualization and aggressivization of habit patterns and perception, thinking, etc., when the task requirements preclude drive interference.

X. SYNTHETIC INTEGRATIVE FUNCTIONING

Instructions to Raters:

COMPONENT FACTORS

a) degree of reconciliation or integration of *discrepant* or potentially incongruent (contradictory) attitudes, values, affects, behavior, and self-representations (e.g., role conflicts)

b) degree of *active* relating together (i.e., integrating) of psychic and behavioral events, whether contradictory or not

c) degree of organization and stability maintained under varying levels of stress
The synthetic-integrative function is most likely the ego function with the largest G factor of ego strength and overall adaptiveness of the organism.

SCALE

1. a) Integration of affect, thinking, behavior and self-image is very low. This could be reflected in discrepancy between affect display and behavior or with expressed thoughts (such as laughing while telling bad news). Or, serial behavior may reflect extreme lability, incongruity and inconsistency, such as being alternately loving one minute and violently hostile the next. The person has virtually no feeling of continuity between events in his life. This may be expressed in a major dissociative symptom, such as multiple personality, amnesia and/or fugue states.

1. b) Active connection-making among different aspects of experience in the service of adaptation is nil. For example, the person does not adequately utilize relevant past experience toward the solution of current problems. The ability to carry out planned activities is minimal.

1. c) Ability to remain organized and stable under changing or stressful external conditions is nil.

2. a) Some degree of synthesis and integration in experience, behavior and self-representations, although major areas of experience show serious contradiction and fragmentation. Thus, person's behavior frequently is at odds with his view of himself; e.g., person claims he hates violence, but regularly manifests violent behavior.

Dissociative symptoms may be found, but not as severe as multiple personality. (Depersonalization feelings, complaints of the unreality of external environment would be examples here).

2. b) Small degree of effort expended in relating different aspects of experience. Person rarely utilizes past experience in the solution of current problems.

Poor continuity is reflected in disorganization in daily life regarding time commitments, planning and carrying out of purposeful activities is low.

2. c) Changing external conditions, and even minor environmental stress adversely affect the limited degree of organization and stability most of the time.

3. a) Significant indications of unintegrated aspects of ego-functioning. No consistent life goals, very divergent career notions; serious psychosomatic illnesses may be present (ulcerative colitis). Major dissociation, is not found at this level, but identity conflicts may be significant.

3. b) Only moderate efforts to relate different aspects of experience are seen, alternating with periods of little or no effort expended in this direction. Not adequately organized in daily life, but simple activities can be carried out, though not reliably. Difficulty in finding things, important deadlines are missed because patient failed to remind himself in an effective manner.

3. c) Some decrease in his usual level of organization under conditions of mild stress involving relatively small changes in the external environment.

4. a) Some major areas are integrated, while others show contradictions in various aspects of ego functioning, such as discrepancies in different goals or attitudes, or self-images (self-representations). Such an individual is inconsistent as well as contradictory.

4. b) Active efforts to relate different areas of experience together are only moderately successful, and are expended by the person only about half the time.

Purposeful, planned activities can be carried out, but considerable trouble results in the patient's attempts to keep up with the schedule demands of everyday life. He always is a step or two behind in meeting obligations and in carrying out what he has agreed to do.

4. c) Small changes in external conditions and the presence of mild stress result in maintenance of the individual's ongoing level of organization as often as not.

5. a) Major areas of the personality show a fair degree of consistency, such

that affects and behavior tend to be consistent, but with some exceptions that result in periodic difficulty. The self-representations are integrated enough to rule out major identity problems. But examples of inconsistent attitudes, values, affects and behavior periodically occur.

5. b) Active efforts to relate different areas of experience in the service of adaptation show periodic lapses. Carrying out of purposeful activities, meeting demands and commitments show periodic lapses.

5. c) When external conditions rapidly change, and/or stress is introduced, ongoing activity and organizational levels are maintained for the most part, if changes and stresses are mild.

6. a) Consistency and a fair degree of integration in the major sectors of the personality is found, with no major areas of experience left out, although minor inconsistencies in behavior, affect and thinking can be seen. Social, sexual and vocational areas are satisfactorily integrated.

6. b) The person scoring here shows effort to make causal connections among different areas of experience, and succeeds to a moderate degree in this endeavor. Behavior is generally well organized, and the person can deal with demands and external requirements with relatively little stress and strain.

6. c) With external conditions changing quickly and/or stressfully, (potentially traumatic to a less integrated person), this individual maintains relative stability and organization.

7. a) Person shows high consistency and integration in thinking, feeling and behavior. His attitudes and values are consistent, his self identity is solidly established.

7. b) Such an individual actively makes connections among different aspects of his experience in the service of adaptation, and in this respect responds creatively to problems.

7. c) Persons scoring at this level reveal an unusually high ability to remain relatively stable, organized and in balance when external conditions change suddenly or stressfully.

ID SCALE
(Drive Strength)

Below you will find 7 point scales for rating strength of libidinal and of aggressive drive manifestations. We are attempting to rate instinctual drive derivatives, and have utilized behavioral and sometimes ideational reactions as criteria for drive strength. One problem with the scale is that, for example, high masturbation rate may primarily be based on attempts to reduce tension and anxiety, rather than upon high sexual drive. We shall attempt to take account of this source of unclarity indirectly. While only 7 points are spelled out, you are to utilize the intermediate scores (1.5, 2.5, etc.) as in rating *Sublimation and Neutralization*.

Please rate here the extent to which you judge libidinal and aggressive drives to be sublimated and neutralized.

Libidinal	Somewhat		Well
Negligible	Low	Moderate	Neutralized
Aggressive	Somewhat	Moderate	Well
Negligible	Low		Neutralized

SCALE

A. Indications of Libidinal Drive

1) Masturbation extremely frequent with no attempt to hide it (due to pressure of urges as opposed to poor social judgment), even in public places, sometimes with intent to arouse others, often leading to arrest.

Sexual fantasies present, but not as prominent or overt as the most extreme sort of sexual behavior.

Intercourse is very frequent with no discriminative selection of partners, (again, due to pressure of urges, as opposed to a primary defect in object relations). Polymorphous perverse patterns predominate to the total exclusions of object-related modes.

Might see public disrobing; acting on irresistible urges to rape; making aggressive, exhibitionistic advances on subway. Homosexual activity, if present, takes form of cruising, with repeated encounters with the vice squad due to urges being so powerful they interfere with self-preserving judgment.

Frequency of sexual content in dreams is variable, and is itself an unreliable indicator of this scale stop. Type of content here would be the most bizarre, uncensored primitive sort, producing little or no anxiety.

Behavior is sex-oriented to the extent of extreme sexualization of all activities. Incest, rape, and other forms are prominent and frequent.

2. Masturbation extremely frequent, but pressure of urges makes it difficult to channel appropriately (i.e., privacy).

Sexual fantasies and daydreams slightly more prominent than (1) but still relatively lacking.

Frequency of intercourse similar to (1) but slightly less so than (1).

3. Masturbation very frequent, but pressure of urges, while great, is not so great as to interfere with rudimentary controls on selection of time and place. Occurs frequently even when the whole range of other sexual outlets are available.

Sexual fantasies may be even more prominent than in stops (1) and (2), especially when there is rigidity in overt behavior.

Intercourse either very frequent or very rare. There may be total impotence or frigidity. When frequent, controls are adequate to channel urges into reasonably appropriate directions. When rare, derivatives of direct sexual impulses are prominent.

Symptom-formation sometimes replaces overt sexual behavior. In case of over-control of direct impulse-expression (first seen at this stop), sexual preoccupations receive outlets in areas other than behavior. Where sexual urges are unusually low, as in chronic depression, few manifest or disguised outlets or expressions are available. In cases of strong urges and undercontrol, outlets are likely to be voyeurism, limited exhibitionism, promiscuity, "addiction" to pornographic material, visual or verbal.

Homosexuality, when present, causes much distress, either because of inability to integrate the urges into a productive life, or because of extreme defensiveness, where latent homosexuality pushes the person into difficult interpersonal situations.

Likely to be much sexual content in manifest dream, or else much symbolism representing sexual content in latent dream thoughts, especially in those cases where actual sexual behavior is overcontrolled and waking sexual thoughts are subject to censorship.

Behavior is very sex-oriented. When this is directly expressed, it is likely to take the form of chronic, indiscriminate flirting, inappropriate sexualization, as in work contexts. When not so directly felt, it may easily be noticed by the observer, but not by the subject—as in very frequent parapraxes, unconscious sexual mannerisms and sexualization of the usual autonomous functions so that there is notable interference with task-performance. We also observe the other extreme, where low sexual urge produces a paucity of sexual expressiveness.

4. Masturbation is either moderately frequent or totally absent. When it occurs, the accompanying fantasies are crucial determinants of scaling it at this stop. Fantasies are likely to be derivatives of early conflicts: e.g., direct or disguised "beating" fantasies.

Other sexual fantasies might begin to predominate over any terribly unusual behavior at this point. Sometimes they reflect the sexual urges directly (as in type of activity desired), and so at times symbolization is prominent as in object choice. For the overcontrolled or very conflict-ridden person, fantasies are less likely to occur in daydreams than at night, where the latent content rather than the manifest is more likely to contain the expression of sexual wishes.

Homosexuality could be present, often ego-alien and anxiety-arousing.

Intercourse is either more or less frequent than usual. May be sub-total impotence or frigidity at this stop.

5. Masturbation, when there are other opportunities for sexual expression (intercourse) will occur with mild frequency.

Sexual fantasies occasionally intrude upon thought, but primarily when there has been no opportunity for direct discharge of sexual urges, or in unusual circumstances causing lack of opportunity.

Intercourse occurs a bit more or less than average, sometimes with irregularly spaced periods of impotence, frigidity, decreased or increased desire. Fluctuations are limited either to extreme conflict-laden situations, or to life circumstances (e.g., temporary loss of libido due to sudden object loss, or hypertrophy of sexuality due to longish periods of enforced privations).

Homosexuality could be present, but would not interfere with general adaptation too much.

6. Average: Masturbation usually limited to time when there is no opportunity for intercourse.

Sexual fantasies rarely intrude during day, and when they do, they are reasonably well integrated with routine activities.

Intercourse is the preferred outlet for sexual urges, and impotence and frigidity are rare except under extreme or prolonged stress, or with temporary revival of old conflict-situations.

Sexual behavior other than intercourse is rare, and homosexuality would drop out from the picture at this stop. Any partial-impulses, if present, are reasonably well sublimated. Unusual sexual behavior will be seen only under the most extreme situations bringing undue pressure to bear upon the individual.

7. Optimal: Masturbation occurring only when there is no opportunity over prolonged period for heterosexual behavior. Intercourse reasonably frequent, and any necessary privations are borne with ease. With impulse-frustration, even fantasies and dreams are likely to reflect a smooth-functioning sexual apparatus. Any "sexualization" of behavior is extremely appropriate and enriching.

B. Indications of Aggressive Drive

1. Physical assaultiveness so frequent and extreme as to occur under little or no apparent provocations. Results in extreme damage to life and limb, even murder.

Verbal abuse frequent, accompanying extreme acts of violence, (above), rather than occurring instead of them.

Hostile fantasies, when present, accompany violent behavior. Aggressive content in dreams is of most primitive, uncensored sort, similar to fantasies of waking life. Both may be sufficient stimuli to violent behavior.

Self-diverted aggression in the extreme: suicide resulting from aggression turned inward; or bizarre, self-inflicted injury, such as actual self-castration.

Indirect aggression not observed at this stop, as impulses achieve full discharge through acts of extreme violence.

"Interests" and general behavior are aggressively oriented, not through "choice" but from severe pressure of urges so as to render any attempts at control utterly ineffective.

2. Physical assaultiveness is extreme, falling short of murder, stemming

solely from person's urges (can be set off by minor or imaginary provocations, inflicting serious injury on others.

Verbal abuse frequent, accompanying violent behavior, and substituting only for murder.

Hostile fantasies may include undisguised death wishes. Other fantasies vary little from actual violence perpetuated in behavior.

Self-diverted aggression falls short of suicide but may include extreme gestures and attempts. Self-inflicted injury causes serious damage to body parts and functioning; e.g., chronic cutting of wrists.

Indirect aggression still rare to non-existent here.

Interests may be aggressively oriented: e.g., to extent that person enjoys employment in organizations like Murder, Inc.

Aggressive content in manifest dreams similar to that in waking fantasy and behavior, occurring with variable frequency.

3. Physical assaultiveness frequent, due to pressure of urges producing loss of control. Or else, it is very rare (in those with low drive, or where aggressive drive is over-controlled). Such cases, first observed at this stop, exhibit drive-derivatives, at times. e.g., convulsive disorders with psycho-motor rage equivalents. Rigid, obsessional personalities with excessive reaction formation might display flurries of assaultiveness in contrast to their otherwise over-controlled aggression. Low-drive types appear bland even with provocation.

Verbal abuse may be very frequent. In undercontrolled types it is undisguised as a direct drive expression, substituting for the most extreme physical violence, accompanying somewhat less extreme expression of physical behavior. In over-controlled types, takes form of self-righteous preaching or sadistic, moralistic punishment. Low-drive types remain blandly silent even when very provoked.

Self-directed aggression may take form of suicide gestures, or it may be inferrable from proclivity to form intense sadomasochistic relationships, where person vicariously identifies with the one who inflicts harm upon himself.

Indirect aggression may be seen, here, as in severe reaction-formation, violent protests against aggression, or the prototypical "insisting the people accept democracy or I'll ram it down their throats" attitude, etc. Stubbornness in the form of pain-inflicting withholding, teasing to the point of torture would be more prominent than the more sublimated sort of hostile joking.

General behavior and interests would be aggressively oriented in such ways as enlisting as a career Marine with the expressed aim of obtaining satisfaction from hand-to-hand combat; or being a professional hangman within the boundaries of law; or enjoying hunting animals for the thrill of satisfying "bloodlust".

Aggressive content in manifest dreams either very prominent or not present at all, but is to be found rather, in the latent dream thoughts with great fre-

THE SCHIZOPHRENIC SYNDROME

quency. Hostile fantasies, similarly, are prominent either in direct or symbolically disguised forms.

4. Physical assaultiveness is either present after moderate provocation in circumscribed areas with specific people, or else it is hardly ever seen, but with its derivatives very strong.

Verbal abuse may be quite strong at this stop, directed either to the original targets or displaced into scapegoat people, groups or issues.

Hostile fantasies sometimes include undisguised wishes to kill and harm, but more often are of the type involving insulting, mortifying and humiliating others in return for real or imagined narcissistic hurts.

Self-diverted aggression may be intense and pervasive moral masochism.

Indirect aggression could include many displacements, reaction-formations and stubbornness, limited to specific people and situations; teasing which gets out of hand and tending toward torment, and excessive joking with thin disguises for the hostile undertones.

General behavior and interests are aggressively oriented, sometimes in career choices, such as prosecuting attorney, judge, correction officer, butcher; and sometimes in choice of hobby, such as deep interest in Judo, Karate or boxing.

Extreme aggressive content in manifest dreams occurs with breakthroughs of anxiety. Less extreme aggressive content is similar to behavior.

5. Physical assaultiveness occurs only under actual extreme provocation in ordinary circumstances, or in self-defense in the interest of survival.

Verbal abuse may be quite marked and "raw" under stress, but usually contained under "civilized" modes of expression. Or else, may be held back and expressed in "one fell swoop" after much stewing.

Hostile fantasies have mainly to do with retaliation in kind for really received wrongs. Aggressive content in manifest dreams may be proportional to the degree that "legitimate" aggressive expression has been withheld or controlled.

Self-diverted aggression may correspond to degree of guilt feelings, and take form of moderate moral masochism or self-denigration.

General behavior and interests may be aggressively oriented in the form of enjoying gossip. Mainly it would be indirect expression, such as mild teasing, or a somewhat exaggerated interest in hostile joking, or "sparring" repartee with others.

6. Average: Physical assaultiveness occurs only in the interest of survival of self or others when there is no other alternative.

Verbal abuse is virtually absent, but verbal aggression may occur under sufficient provocation, as in effective polemics when some injustice has, in reality, occurred to self or loved ones.

Hostile fantasies are also infrequent, occurring only in response to extreme provocation, and they serve an adaptive discharge function, rarely used for "wallowing" or "stewing".

Self-directed aggression is limited to "legitimate" guilt over avoidable errors, but is short-lived and corrected by effective, responsible behavior.

When general behavior and interests are aggressively oriented it is with effective sublimation and neutralization.

7. Optimal: Aggressive behavior or derivatives are seen only when there is no other alternative, as in the interest of survival, and the regulation of esteem along effective, adaptive lines. Indirect expression is not seen, nor are urges to its expression felt. Effective action in mastering tasks and achieving life goals makes unnecessary any sort of aggressive behavior short of that mentioned above.

INTERFERENCE OF SUPEREGO FACTORS WITH EGO FUNCTIONS

Below you will find some ways in which superego factors may interfere with each ego function. These are a supplement to the 7 point scales for each ego function above, and may help clarify some maladaptive factors not focused on in the ego function scales. Following the superego scale proper, you will be asked to rate overall interference of superego factors with adaptive ego functioning:

Negligible	Mild	Moderate	Severe
1	2	3	4

Reality Testing:

Strong underlying hostility in conjunction with a superego which "prevent" direct awareness of the hostility can result in projection of the hostility and thereby interfere with reality testing.

Judgment:

Judgment can be interfered with by a mechanism similar to that described above for reality testing.

Sense of Reality:

1) Feelings of depersonalization (an important disturbance in the sense of self) can result from underlying guilt over strong hostility.

2) Both guilt and shame can affect the person's sense of self.

Object Relations:

1) Projection of superego attitudes (blaming, fault-finding, etc.) can vitally affect object relations.

2) A weak superego (being associated with irresponsibility, unfairness,

cheating, taking advantage of, etc.) also can be seen to vitally affect an individual's interpersonal relations.

3. A superego response (prohibition) to felt aggression can result in withdrawal from another person.

Thought Processes:

1) Obsessive thought mechanisms may be a result of superego prohibition of aggressive and /or sexual drive derivatives.

2) Indecisiveness can result from the unconscious idea that decisiveness constitutes destructive aggressive behavior.

ARISE:

This function requires the becoming aware of more primitive (sexual, aggressive and forbidden) contents and the utilization of more primitive psychic mechanisms. Individuals with a strong superego will show relative difficulty in the exercise of this function (people with strong authoritarian trends, low tolerance for ambiguity, etc.).

Defensive Functioning:

A severe superego will tend to be associated with excessive defensive strength. Some defensive maneuvers are directed primarily against superego contents.

Stimulus Barrier:

1) Strong voyeuristic trends, when "disapproved" by a superego, can result in disturbances in vision and headaches (sée paper by Greenacre on "Vision, Headache and Halo"). The same appears to be true in the auditory sphere.

2) High hostility in conjunction with superego blocking can result in projection of the hostility and a consequent vigilance and sensitization (depressives often manifest high sensitivity to noise, which may reflect the above mechanism). Insomniacs may also illustrate the above mechanism: Fear of aggression and of being attacked at night is often found.

Autonomous Functioning:

Reading disabilities may involve an invasion of voyeuristic trends. Writing cramp can occur when phallic or hostile trends intrude. The general formulation here is: 1) The autonomous functioning becomes libidinized. 2) Superego disapproves. 3) Ego functioning is interfered with by the ensuing inhibition.

Synthetic Function:

If deneutralization interferes with synthetic function, then the superego will not approve of the hostility and synthesis will be defensively decreased.

SUPEREGO SCALE

At the low, or maladaptive end of the scale, either a *weak* or a severe superego may score (weak superego is added to strong at stop 2). A *strong* (or mature, or autonomous) superego characterizes the adaptive end.

COMPONENT FACTORS

a) Guilt and blame: includes
  1) degree of self-directed punishment
  2) transformations and displacements of unconscious guilt
  3) degree of blame avoidance
  4) degree to which talion principle operates strict demands/self-indulgence vs. flexible, lenient attitude toward behavior and impulses
  5) unrealistically high guilt/no guilt vs. realistically based guilt feelings
b) Ego ideal status: includes
  1) extent of realistic evaluation of ego's strivings in terms of current consequences
  2) sense of worth: severe self-criticism or overinflated sense of worth vs. realistically critical self-observations. Archaic, strict standards vs. lax, indulgent standards
  3) self-esteem regulation: archaic, external and lax vs. internal and not based on current opinion of others.

SCALE

1. *Extremely Severe Superego*

  a) Self-directed punishment in the extreme, such as suicidal behavior, related to "goodness" or "badness" impulse expression and wishes. May be associated with extreme depression.

  b) Extreme, self-criticism, where person rigidly regards his actions as bad and unworthy.

2. *Very Severe or Extremely Weak Superego*

  a) For *severe* superego; self-directed punishment short of suicidal behavior such as self-mutilation, or ardent wishes to have (or fear of having, or connection that he has) an incurable disease. If guilt is less conscious, may be delusional guilt, as if chronic undeserved persecution by others. Delusions about committing unpardonable sins.

or

For *weak* superego, no conscience, or guilt feelings, whether realistic or not. Psychopathic personality or impulse-ridden character in the extreme.

  b) For *severe* superego: archaic, strict standards of good and bad goal-achievements for self and others. Extreme self-abnegation and denial

or

For *weak* superego, lax, indulgent standards; "immorality" (acting with little regard for consequences to others)

3.

a) For *severe* superego: transformations of guilt into such experiences as fear and hate: Guilt defended against by extreme projection; tendencies to characteristically attribute blame; high blame avoidance. Rigid, authoritarian, moral attitudes; acting according to "talion" principle.

or

For *weak* superego, lax with respect to impulses and urges, which are expressed directly, but with a bit more concern for realistic consequences to self, if not for others' needs.

b) Unrealistically critical self-observations most of the time. Severe self-criticism could alternate with overinflated sense of worth. Also, hypercritical of others; very demanding of others in achievement area or in area of ideals. Self-indulgence; careless self-evaluations independent of outside validations. Overconcern with minutiae in assuming obligations in order to avoid blame and criticism.

4.

a) Sizeable puritan streak in moral judgment. May be "do-gooder" type person as reaction-formation against opposite wishes. Over-conscientiousness, seeks "fitting" punishment for moderate infractions. Tendency to protest innocence too usual,

or

"happy-go-lucky type"; overly glib when can't meet responsibilities. Casual underinvolvement or oversubscription.

b) Perfectionism about self, work, etc. Often interferes with task performance. That is, may be delays, blocks, inhibitions of activity when inordinate strivings are difficult to realize,

or

loose, lax, opposed to flexible standards and values.

5.

a) Person overcautiously anticipates criticism for limited range of "infractions". Some guilt feelings can be tolerated or lived with, with rudimentary forms of constructive alteration of behavior and environment to eliminate true source of guilt feelings. When guilt is not acceptable, or is unconscious, there are likely to be sporadic displacements, projections, etc. Occasional limited compulsive behavior to deal with guilt over impulses, wishes, deeds, etc.,

or

is concerned with acceptable behavior, can role play what is right, but no internal pressure to do so.

6. *Average*:

Reasonably *strong superego* despite occasional evidence of strictness or weakness.

a) Realistically based guilt feelings, but guilt serves primarily as a signal to reinforce fair-minded behavior.

b) Reasonably realistic approval of ego's actions in terms of current consequences. Realistically critical self-observations. Moral values independent of external pressures. Self-esteem regulation internal—not dependent on current opinions of others.

7. *Optimal*:

Like 6, but more so, with no lapses. In addition, superego is optimally integrated, consistent and unified.

The rater is also to rate the subject on a 4-point scale for Integration and Consistency of superego. Stops 1) and 4) shall be illustrated to provide anchorage points.

1) Most maladaptive: extreme inconsistencies between behavior and standards, among standards, or among segments of behavior. "Swiss cheese" or extremely corrupt, lacunae-ridden superego.

2) Most adaptive lax in optimal 7), above): Optimally unified superego. Absence of contradictions between standards and behavior among standards, or among different segments of behavior.

MASTERY-COMPETENCE SCALE

Component Factors

a) *Competence*: the person's performance in relation to his existing capacity to interact with and master his environment (how he actually does).

b) *Sense of Competence*: the person's expectation of success, or the subjective side of actual performance (how he feels about how he does and what he can do). This sense of competence is scored to coincide with the subject's conscious belief or estimate, even though we recognize this to be a defensive exaggeration of an underlying low expectation of success and sense of competence or a spuriously low conscious sense of competence based on underlying guilt and/or other factors.

You are asked to score Competence and Sense of Competence separately, since a number of different relationships between the two are possible: 1) they may be congruent; 2) actual performance may exceed the sense of competence; 3) sense of competence may exceed master-competence.

The specific environment and the limitations it imposes on the *form* of a person's competence should be carefully considered. That is, a highly intelligent minority group person, for example, from a truly restrictive environment who performs a menial task skillfully would receive a higher score than his counterpart from an "advantaged" majority group performing the same work. Similarly, a well-educated housewife, realistically restricted to the rearing of four young children would be rated in the context of competency within that role.

SCALE

1. a) The person does almost nothing with respect to altering or interacting with his environment because he is largely unable to utilize abilities and capacities in relation to reality.

1. b) The sense of competence is almost nil, and the person feels powerless to act effectively in most ways.

2. a) The person is able to utilize only minimal efforts in interacting with the environment. What little effective action might be seen results merely from passive reactivity rather than from active coping.

2. b) A sense of competence is only minimally or sporadically present, so that any realistic effectuality is experienced as "luck" or "fate." At this stop, we might also observe an exaggerated sense of competence, as in grandiose beliefs of what might be accomplished, though in flagrant violation of realistic standards of what is expectable or likely.

3. a) Successful interactions with the environment come primarily from passive mastery, or passive manipulation of people. Typical might be the "underachiever" college student with very high aptitudes, who has "coasted" by and then falls progressively lower in his achievements as more active efforts than he can muster are actually required. Tools and skills have been poorly mastered. Also, the person may be employed at a level considerably below his ability, training and aptitudes.

3. b) An unrealistically low sense of competence, as among severely masochistic people who suffer ego restrictions and the concomitantly low sense of effectuality. Or, sense of competence is often inflated because of illusory or passively-come-by successes.

4. a) Mastery is partial—sometimes passive, sometimes active. Active efforts, however, may be more likely directed toward getting others to achieve the desired outcomes rather than direct coping and altering. Other stumbling blocks to complete mastery might be a restricting of activity due to inordinate fear of failure, rejection, risk-taking, etc. Or it may be inhibited because the sense of competence is lower than actual competence.

4. b) Sense of competence may be low because the person devaluates his own efforts, no matter how effective they actually are (due to guilt, masochism, fear of envy or rejection, etc.). Overvalued sense of competence is observed, too, as in somewhat less grandiose states than in stops 2) and 3).

5. a) Performance level is high a good part of the time, but in limited areas there may be some underachievement and lapses in competence. Such an area might be seen in the person in psychotherapy who has achieved maximal in-

sight about conflict areas but who delays exerting his own energy to actually resolve the conflicts. In extreme cases, such a person scores at a 4 or a 3 level (as in the "negative therapeutic reaction"). At this level would also be the exaggerated "do-it-yourself" person whose needs for active mastery are inordinate, and who fears relinquishing them even for temporary passive adjustments.

5. b) Sense of competence is high a good part of the time. In the case of limited failure to exert effort, it is probably congruent with actual performance.

6. Average

6. a) Actual competence is quite high with occasional but not chronic inhibitions or lapses in efforts to actively master the environment.

7. Optimal

7. a) The prototype here is the "do-it-yourself" person who is unusually resourceful at coping with, mastering, and altering the environment in the service of adaptation. His performance level is characteristically in his environmental context. Accomplishments are often considered "high." Though exceptionally self-reliant, he also is appropriately receptive to others, alternating with optimal exertion of effort in the direction of the most gratifying forms of work, love and play. His efforts would include enlisting help, when necessary.

7. b) Subjective awareness of competence is usually congruent with maximal performance. The sense of competence develops and sustains itself mostly from appropriate interpretations of feedback from actual effective capacities and performance.

SCORE SHEET FOR RATING EGO FUNCTIONS FROM CLINICAL INTERVIEWS*

Please record your rating for each Ego Function and then enter the basis for that rating, including specific content and the relevant page numbers. (Use back where necessary) Also, please indicate your confidence rating.

I. Reality Testing A:
          1 1.5 2 2.5 3 3.5 4 4.5 5 5.5 6 6.5 7 (circle one)
Confidence:
Highly Confident___Rather Confident___Somewhat Lacking___Minimally Confident___
                    Basis for Ratings (use back when necessary)
a) distinction
   bet. ideas &
   perceptions
b) accuracy of
   perception
c) accuracy of
   inner reality
   testing

_____

I. Reality Testing B:

1 1.5 2 2.5 3 3.5 4 4.5 5 5.5 6 6.5 7

Confidence:

Highly Confident___Rather Confident___Somewhat Lacking___Minimally Confident___

a) awareness of
  consequences

b) manifest in
  behavior

II. Sense of Reality:

1 1.5 2 2.5 3 3.5 4 4.5 5 5.5 6 6.5 7

Confidence:

Highly Confident___Rather Confident___Somewhat Lacking___Minimally Confident___

a) events exper-
  ienced as real

b) body experienced
  as familiar

c) self identity

d) feeling of
  separativeness

III. Regulation and Control of Impulses and Affects:

1 1.5 2 2.5 3 3.5 4 4.5 5 5.5 6 6.5 7 (circle one)

Confidence:

Highly Confident___Rather Confident___Somewhat Lacking___Minimally Confident___

a) strength of
  drive

b) manifest in
  behavior

c) degree of
  control

IV. Object Relations:

1 1.5 2 2.5 3 3.5 4 4.5 5 5.5 6 6.5 7

Confidence:

Highly Confident___Rather Confident___Somewhat Lacking___Minimally Confident___

a) degree & kind
  of relativeness

b) based on
  earlier relations

V. Thought Processes:

1 1.5 2 2.5 3 3.5 4 4.5 5 5.5 6 6.5 7

Confidence:

Highly Confident___Rather Confident___Somewhat Lacking___Minimally Confident___

a) attention,
  concentration,
  memory, etc.

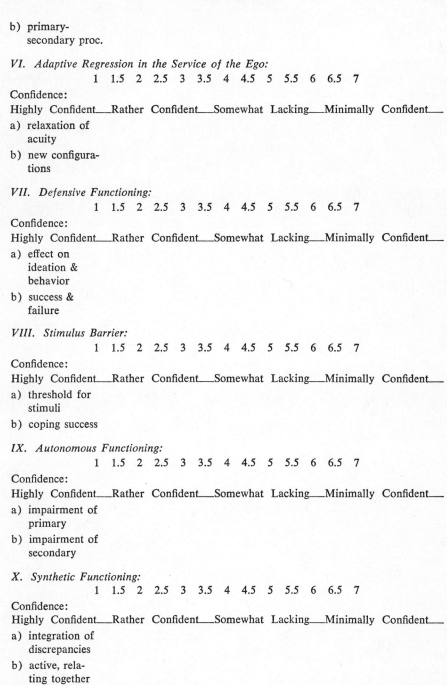

b) primary-
   secondary proc.

VI. *Adaptive Regression in the Service of the Ego:*
    1 1.5 2 2.5 3 3.5 4 4.5 5 5.5 6 6.5 7
Confidence:
Highly Confident___Rather Confident___Somewhat Lacking___Minimally Confident___
a) relaxation of
   acuity
b) new configura-
   tions

VII. *Defensive Functioning:*
     1 1.5 2 2.5 3 3.5 4 4.5 5 5.5 6 6.5 7
Confidence:
Highly Confident___Rather Confident___Somewhat Lacking___Minimally Confident___
a) effect on
   ideation &
   behavior
b) success &
   failure

VIII. *Stimulus Barrier:*
      1 1.5 2 2.5 3 3.5 4 4.5 5 5.5 6 6.5 7
Confidence:
Highly Confident___Rather Confident___Somewhat Lacking___Minimally Confident___
a) threshold for
   stimuli
b) coping success

IX. *Autonomous Functioning:*
    1 1.5 2 2.5 3 3.5 4 4.5 5 5.5 6 6.5 7
Confidence:
Highly Confident___Rather Confident___Somewhat Lacking___Minimally Confident___
a) impairment of
   primary
b) impairment of
   secondary

X. *Synthetic Functioning:*
   1 1.5 2 2.5 3 3.5 4 4.5 5 5.5 6 6.5 7
Confidence:
Highly Confident___Rather Confident___Somewhat Lacking___Minimally Confident___
a) integration of
   discrepancies
b) active, rela-
   ting together
c) stability
   under stress

ID SCALE (Drive Strength)

Indications of Libidinal Drive (circle one)

1   1.5   2   2.5   3   3.5   4   4.5   5   5.5   6   6.5   7

Basis for Ratings:

Indications of Aggressive Drive

1   1.5   2   2.5   3   3.5   4   4.5   5   5.5   6   6.5   7

Basis for Ratings:

Extent to which you judge Libidinal and Aggressive Drives to be sublimated and/or neutralized.

Libidinal

Negligible	Somewhat Low	Moderate	Well Neutralized
1	2	3	4

Basis for Ratings:

Aggressive

Negligible	Somewhat Low	Moderate	Well Neutralized
1	2	3	4

Basis for Ratings:

SUPEREGO FACTORS

Interference of Superego Factors with Ego Functions

Severe	Moderate	Mild	Negligible
1	2	3	4

Basis for Ratings:

Superego Scale

1   1.5   2   2.5   3   3.5   4   4.5   5   5.5   6   6.5   7

a) Guilt:

   self diverted punishment
   unconscious or conscious guilt
   blame avoidance
   talion
   unrealistic vs. realistic

b) Ego Ideal:

   realistic self evaluation
   sense of worth
   self esteem regulation

Integration and Consistency of Superego

Very Poorly Integrated	Poorly Integrated	Moderately Well Integrated	Very Well Integrated
1	2	3	4

Basis for Ratings:

Actual Competence:

Mastery-Competence

       1 1.5 2 2.5 3 3.5 4 4.5 5 5.5 6 6.5 7

Basis for Ratings:

Sense of Competence

       1 1.5 2 2.5 3 3.5 4 4.5 5 5.5 6 6.5 7

a) sense of mastery-competence
b) extent of actual mastery-competence

RATING SHEET FOR CLINICAL PSYCHOLOGICAL TESTS (SAMPLE PAGE)

I *Reality Testing* (A. Distinction between 1) ideas and perception and 2) perceptual accuracy).

I.D.

Bender	1	1.5	2	2.5	3	3.5	4	4.5	5	5.5	6	6.5	7_____
Figure-Drawings	1	1.5	2	2.5	3	3.5	4	4.5	5	5.5	6	6.5	7_____
WAIS	1	1.5	2	2.5	3	3.5	4	4.5	5	5.5	6	6.5	7_____
Rorschach	1	1.5	2	2.5	3	3.5	4	4.5	5	5.5	6	6.5	7_____
TAT	1	1.5	2	2.5	3	3.5	4	4.5	5	5.5	6	6.5	7_____
Overall Rating	1	1.5	2	2.5	3	3.5	4	4.5	5	5.5	6	6.5	7_____

Confidence in   Highly   Rather   Somewhat   Minimally
Overall Rating   Confident_____ Confident_____ Lacking_____   Confident_____

I *Reality Testing* (B. Soundness of Judgment)

Bender	1	1.5	2	2.5	3	3.5	4	4.5	5	5.5	6	6.5	7_____
Figure-Drawings	1	1.5	2	2.5	3	3.5	4	4.5	5	5.5	6	6.5	7_____
WAIS	1	1.5	2	2.5	3	3.5	4	4.5	5	5.5	6	6.5	7_____
Rorschach	1	1.5	2	2.5	3	3.5	4	4.5	5	5.5	6	6.5	7_____
TAT	1	1.5	2	2.5	3	3.5	4	4.5	5	5.5	6	6.5	7_____
Overall Rating	1	1.5	2	2.5	3	3.5	4	4.5	5	5.5	6	6.5	7_____

Confidence in   Highly   Rather   Somewhat   Minimally
Overall Rating   Confident_____ Confident_____ Lacking_____   Confident_____

II *Sense of Reality*

Bender	1	1.5	2	2.5	3	3.5	4	4.5	5	5.5	6	6.5	7_____
Figure-Drawings	1	1.5	2	2.5	3	3.5	4	4.5	5	5.5	6	6.5	7_____
WAIS	1	1.5	2	2.5	3	3.5	4	4.5	5	5.5	6	6.5	7_____
Rorschach	1	1.5	2	2.5	3	3.5	4	4.5	5	5.5	6	6.5	7_____

AUTHOR INDEX

Page numbers in *italics* indicate illustrations. Page numbers followed by the letter "t" indicate tabular information.

836   THE SCHIZOPHRENIC SYNDROME

Bacon, H. M., 542
Bacsik, E. J., 542
Bae, Kae Kioon, 304
Baer, P. E., 400, 440
Bahn, Anita K., 106, 108,
  109, 111, 112, 270, 293,
  294, 309, 698, 702, 710,
  713
Baill, N. Q., 704
Bakan, P., 255
Baker, A. A., 542, 566
Baker, H., 568
Baker, R. A., 552
Baker, W., 306
Bakwin, H., 440
Bakwin, R. M., 440
Balazs, R., 169
Baldessarini, R. J., 162,
  166, 170
Balducci, M., 542
Baldwin, I. T., 112, 308
Baldwin, J. A., 694, 698,
  707, 711 713
Balian, L., 249, 457
Ball, H. V., 271, 298
Ball, M., 170
Balogh, J. K., 248
Balser, Benjamin H., 769,
  772
Bambaren, V. C., 232
Ban, T. A., 542
Bandfield, C., 690, 701
Bandler, B., 698
Bannister, D., 231, 232,
  233, 254
Baraff, A. S., 249
Barber, J. E., 560
Barclay, W. A., 698
Barker, J. C., 542
Barnes, G. J., 526t, 542
Barnes, R. H., 701
Barnum, M. C., 621, 640,
  660
Baroff, A., 648, 662
Barrès, P., 729, 731
Barrett, W. W., 542
Barrios, S. F., 542
Barron, A., 542
Barry, H., 131, 145, 560
Barry, H., Jr., 141, 142,
  145
Barry, H., III, 141, 142,
  145, 237
Barsa, J. A., 524t, 542
Barte, H., 200
Bartholomew, A. A., 542
Bartholomew, L. G., 542
Barton, R., 677, 698
Barton, W. E., 673, 698
Barucci, M., 698
Basamania, Betty, 772
Baschina, W. M., 729
Basham, J., 607, 651

Bashina, V. M., 433, 440,
  472, 474, 754
Bastide, R., 276, 293
Batchelor, I. R. C., 338
Bateson, Gregory, 353,
  374, 619, 651, 766, 767,
  772
Bateman, J. F., 118, 151
Battegay, R., 601, 630,
  637, 646, 652
Batusch, A., 145
Bauman, G., 661
Baumé, S., 695, 711
Baumer, H., 118, 145
Bautsch, 140
Baxter, J. C., 233, 235,
  290, 295
Bay, A. P., 702
Bazzaoui, W., 286, 293
Beach, W. B., Jr., 440
Beamish, P., 134, 145
Bean, Lee L., 264, 293
Beard, A. W., 342
Beard, J., 614, 652, 754
Beaujard, M., 426, 440
Beck, G., 476
Beck, R. A., 198, 201
Beck, Robert, 11f
Beck, S. J., 225, 229, 233,
  382, 389, 412, 440
Beckenstein, L., 635, 663
Becker, A., 693, 698
Becker, E., 258, 259, 293,
  654
Becker, J., 233, 237
Becker, W. C., 233, 251
Beckerman, A., 698
Beckett, Peter G. S., 168,
  201, 233, 471, 475, 773
Beckman, W. G., 554
Beecher, H. K., 542
Beerstecker, E., 171
Beerstecker, E., Jr., 154
Behrens, M. L., 440
Behymer, A., 605, 652
Belenkaya, N. Y., 196, 729
Belinkoff, J., 647, 652
Bell, C. E., 166
Bell, D. S., 134, 145, 338
Bell, N. W., 258, 293
Bell, S. C., 555
Bellak, Leopold, 1, 11, 12f,
  14, 34, 46, 62, 63, 131,
  143, 145, 247, 297, 343,
  368, 374, 380f, 381,
  386, 389, 398, 402, 403,
  475, 477, 542, 595, 652,
  667, 690, 693, 698, 699,
  729, 754, 776, 780, 783,
  789f, 829f
Bellville, T. P., 542
Beloff, H., 250
Benady, D. R., 687, 699
Benda, C., 440

Bender, L., 233, 382, 385,
  388, 392, 393, 394, 397,
  399, 402, 406, 410, 411,
  414, 426, 434, 446, 465,
  470, 474, 475, 764, 772
Bene, E., 441
Benedetti, G., 362, 374,
  597, 652, 726, 729
Benedict, 291
Benedict, P. K., 380f, 595,
  652
Benjamin, J. D., 137, 146,
  419, 441
Benjamin, L. A., 338
Bennett, A. E., 699
Bennett, D. H., 233, 339,
  756
Bennett, I. F., 543, 571,
  591
Bennett, J. L., 543
Bennett, S., 233, 432, 441
Benney, Celia, 735, 754
Benoist, A., 296
Benson, W. M., 543
Bental, E., 441
Benton, A. L., 233, 398,
  441
Beran, M., 600, 652
Bercel, N. A., 130, 146
Beres, D., 11, 14, 62, 388,
  389, 417, 441, 463, 475
Berg, I. S., 441
Berg, P. S. D., 246, 250
Berg, S., 543
Bergen, B. J., 238
Bergen, J. F., 166
Bergen, J. R., 192, 196,
  199
Berger, A., 233
Berger, F. M., 543
Berger, Hans, 173, 174,
  196
Berger, M., 248, 414, 455
Berghorst, J., 733
Bergman, 403, 406
Berkowitz, A., 618, 657
Berkowitz, H., 233
Berkowitz, P. H., 413, 441
Berlet, H. H., 166, 543
Berlin, I. N., 406, 425,
  429, 440, 442, 446, 459
Berliner, O. A., 422, 441
Berman, H. H., 639, 652
Berman, S., 285, 293
Bernard, J., 541
Bernard, V. W., 691, 699
Bernardi, G., 197
Bernardino, M. C., 276,
  294
Berne, 283, 293
Bernstein, S., 699
Berrent, I., 638, 655
Berry, H. K., 171
Berry, J. S., 171

SUBJECT INDEX

Page numbers in *italics* indicate illustrations. Page numbers followed by the letter "t" indicate tabular information.

Abstract thinking, 215, 220
Acetophenazine, 504; effectiveness, 488
Acetylcholine, 132
Acidosis, 130
Acromegaly, 579
ACTH, 580
Acting-out behavior, in adolescent schizophrenia, 466
Adaptability, environment and, 18
Adaptive regression in the service of ego, assessment of, psychological tests in, 28; component factors, 16; disturbances of, 47-48; functions of, 47t; interference of superego factors with, 824; rating of, 805-807
Adipose dysplasia, 579
Admissions, first. *See* First admissions
Adolescence, definition, 463; ego in, 463-465; group psychotherapy in, 362, 618; sexual drive in, 464
Adolescent schizophrenia, 462-477; acting-out behavior in, 466; age at onset, 462; course of, 471-472; diagnosis, 468-471; early infantile autism and, 465; electroencephalographic responses in, 471; physical characteristics in, 466; physical growth in, 466; prognosis, 726; pseudo-psychopathic forms, 470; psychological testing in, 469; recent literature on, 465-467; school characteristics and, 466; treatment, 472-473
Adoption, of children of schizophrenics, 6
Adrenal steroids, 580
Adrenalin cycle, natural error in, 133
Adrenalin metabolism, 132, 134
Adrenochrome, 132, 164; blood levels of, 129
Adrenocortical activity, 124
Adrenolutin, 132
Affective reactions, 327
Africa, sociocultural studies in, 284-286
Age, at onset of schizophrenia, 462, 467
Aggressive drive, indications of, 820-823
Aggressive overstimulation, ego functions and, 33

Agranulocytosis, from phenothiazines, 529, 530t
Alcoholism, psychotic symptoms from, 329
Algeria, sociocultural studies in, 287
Allergy, schizophrenia as, 194
Alpahabetic free association, in assessment of ARISE, 28
Ambi-tendency, 325
Ambivalence, motor, 325
Amine metabolism, 160-161
Amino acid metabolism, 160-161
Amobarbital, electroencephalographic reactivity to, 182, 184
Amphetamine psychosis, 134, 329
Anemia, 129
Anger, 327
Anthropometric studies, 130-132
Antiparkinsonian drugs, 516; withdrawal of, 496
Antipsychotic drugs, 478-568; clinical effectiveness, 481-492; historical introduction, 478-480; methodologic problems of evaluation, 480-481; nonphenothiazine, 531-539; patient improvement from, 490, *489-491;* placebo versus, 481, 482t; sedation versus, 508; studies of relative effectiveness, 483, 484t-485t. *See also* Pharmacotherapy and Phenothiazines
Anxiety, 364; core of, in childhood schizophrenia, 394; object, 365
Aphasia, 319; in children, 399
Apraxia, 325
Arabian countries, sociocultural studies in, 286
Archimedes spiral afterimage duration, 183
Architecture, of psychiatric institutions, 697
Argentina, sociocultural studies in, 275
ARISE. *See* Adaptive regression in the service of ego
Asiatic countries, sociocultural studies in, 279-283
Aspiration, level of, 220
Atabrine, psychosis from, 129
Athletics, in group therapy, 596
Attention, disturbances of, 317-319

863